A Companion Guide to Architecture in Ireland, 1837-1921

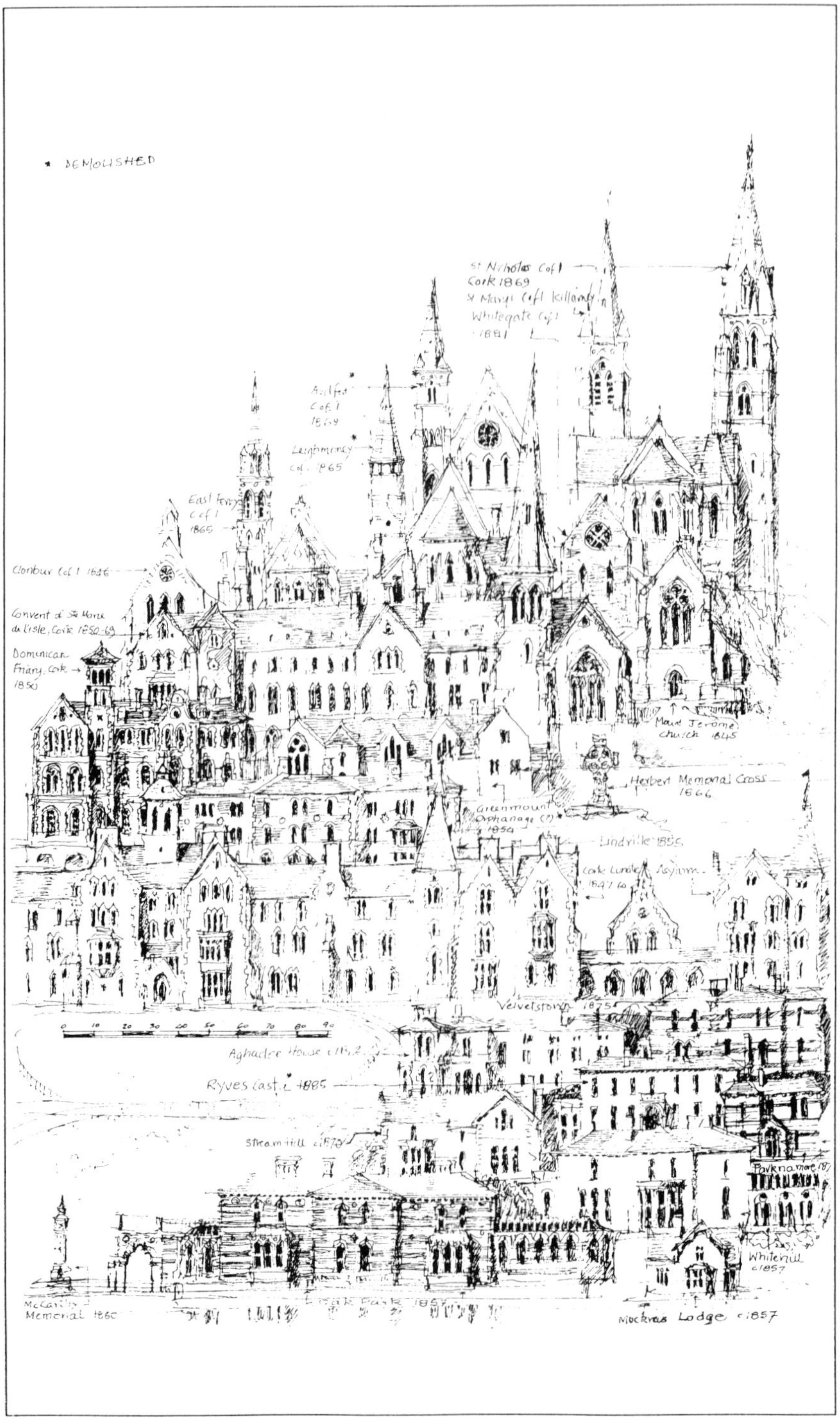

Composite view of William Atkins' buildings by Jeremy Williams

JEREMY WILLIAMS

A companion guide to

ARCHITECTURE IN IRELAND, 1837-1921

with a foreword by MARK GIROUARD

IRISH ACADEMIC PRESS

This book was typeset by
Gilbert Gough Typesetting, Dublin, in
9.5 on 10 point Ehrhardt and
first published in 1994 in Ireland by
IRISH ACADEMIC PRESS LTD
Kill Lane, Blackrock, Co. Dublin,
and in North America
IRISH ACADEMIC PRESS LTD
c/o International Specialized Book Services,
5804 NE Hassalo Street, Portland, OR 97213.

A catalogue record for this book
is available from the British Library.

ISBN 0-7165-2513-5

Printed in Ireland by
Colour Books Ltd, Dublin

FOREWORD

As a small English schoolboy on holidays in Ireland I discovered that the broad straight balustrade of the staircase in my great-aunt's neo-Greek Whitfield Court, near Waterford, was easier and more comfortable to slide down than the thinner, steeper and more curvaceous banisters of the 18th-century houses belonging to other Irish relatives. I did perhaps absorb a certain feeling for Irish Classicism of the 1840s through my trousers. But like many of my generation and background I was brought up to believe that Irish architecture reached its peak in the 18th century, and then entered on a steady and often disastrous decline.

It was only gradually, by travelling and using my eyes, that I realized how wrong I was, and how much enjoyment and quality (not always joined together) was to be found in the rich orchestration of Irish buildings from the 1840s onwards. I travelled, I looked at and sometimes wrote about Irish 19th-century architecture, but Jeremy Williams has shown me how much more there is to see—and also made me want to see it, for he has the gift of the best gazetteers of both providing compulsive browsing, and also making the buildings which he describes seem desirable.

'Never accept a commission in Ireland' was the advice of the English architect Edward Godwin, mortified by the failure of his buildings to keep out the Irish climate. Fortunately many of the best English or Scottish architects of the period acquired fine examples of the work of stars such as the two Pugins, Burges, Butterfield, Street, White, Hardwick, Lutyens, Lorimer, Blore, Playfair, Goldie, Burton, Slater and Salvin. But Ireland's native stable of architects—Ashlin, McCarthy, Lanyon, Lynn, Turner, Hague, Scott, Atkins, Woodward, Deane, Barre and Mulvany, to name only a few—combined to produce a body of work of which Ireland has every reason to be proud, and gave an Irish inflexion to anything which they took from overseas.

Jeremy Williams understands the resulting stylistic complexities, and can illuminate them with a few deft phrases. I am amazed by how much he has seen, how much he has discovered and how seldom he is compelled to admit 'architect unknown'. Moreover, he enjoys finding out about people as well as buildings. 'Pulled down by a great-nephew, whose wife lost her life in the resulting explosions; 'planted a park in the shape of a heart, and all for the love of a woman who never responded'; 'the second baronet insisted on being buried with his horse'—plums like these are scattered freely, as he pursues his way, savouring everything from pubs to palaces in this illuminating and enjoyable work.

MARK GIROUARD

PREFACE

This is the first gazetteer covering architecture in Ireland from the start of the Victorian period up to the partitioning of the country in 1921. Its beginning coincides with the death of William Vitruvius Morrison, the retirement of his father and the death of their rival, George Pain. The year 1921 coincides ironically with the death ofthe architect who could have given the new Irish State aesthetic self-confidence—William Scott and the demise of two survivors of the previous generation, George Ashlin and Arthur Hill. Not all the architects considered can be categorized so neatly but I have used the chronology of the majority of their buildings as the basis of their inclusion, hence the appearance of some earlier works by Charles Lanyon, Daniel Robertson and James Sheil.

Inevitably there are omissions due to ignorance, prejudice or myopia. Indeed many of my opinions have been revised in the course of writing, some too late to be included. It is very easy to underestimate the Victorians: having written derisively of John McCurdy's Physics laboratory in Trinity I recently passed it and realized how wittily he treated the north-east corner; I was on my way at the time to a book launch in the Deanes' National Library where a recent redecoration revealed tiny owls nesting in its Ionic capitals. I have tried throughout to stress this allusiveness of Victorian building at the expense of its respectability.

Inevitably also, one's opinions of contemporary architecture colour one's assessment of the past, especially when faced with so much mutilation of 19th-century Catholic churches. I suspect that the reason that there has been a comprehensive study of every period of Irish architecture except the Victorian has been the strain engendered by continuous discrimination. It is more difficult to exclude than to include.

So much has been demolished due to a lack of knowledge that a comprehensive history could be based on obituaries for what has been destroyed. In exploring an unknown territory my researches have often ended abruptly. The granddaughter of 'Townie' Trench was unaware that he had designed Glenveagh. But I hope this publication will disinter the reputations of other architects, artists and sculptors, now as anonymous as their mediaval peers, but remembered only by their as yet untraced descendants.

Much information comes from the *Dublin Builder*; although renamed after a few years the *Irish Builder*, its prejudice against Belfast and Cork led to practitioners in those cities contributing directly to English publications, particularly the *Architect*. There also appeared from 1911 to 1914 the *Irish Architect and Craftsman*. Most of the five hundred illustrations came from these journals to be supplemented by the work of outstanding contemporary illustrators—Maureen Shaffrey, Sean Rothery, Michael Lunt, Kieran Doyle O'Brien and Michael Craig, to whom a special word of thanks is due. Where necessary I have provided my own drawings. At all times I have tried to show the original concept for comparison with the executed building.

This book would not have been written without the assistance of Michael Adams and his staff. But I have also been immeasurably helped by David Griffin and his staff in the Irish Architectural Archive. I have also received much encouragement from Mark Girouard, who has written the forword; from Nicola Gordon Bowe with her knowledge of Irish stained glass; from her husband Patrick and his knowledge of Irish gardens; from John Gilmartin, as an expert on Victorian painters in Ireland: and from Homan Potterton with his pioneering study of Irish funereal monuments. I am especially grateful to Frederick O'Dwyer for showing me the results of his illuminating researches into the great architectural dynasties ofthe last century—the Owens, the Mulvanys, the Pugins, the Deanes and most notably Benjamin Woodward. What is so valuable is his discrimination, the same discrimination discernable in the published work of Paul Larmour on Belfast.

In additition to those mentioned above I should also like to thank the following: Colonel Julian Aylmer, Myrtle Allen, Mark Bence-Jones, Bolton Street College Library, Patrick Bowe, Hon. Garech de Brún, Dominic Berridge, the late Howard Cooke, Charles Cooper, Peter Cormack, Catherine de Courcy, Maurice and Agnes Craig, Professor Anne Crookshank, John Cunningham, the Marchioness of Dufferin and Ava, Lord Dunboyne, the Earl and Countess of Dunraven, David Durdin-Robertson, Olivia Durdin-Robertson, Fergus Flynn-Rogers, Lady Georgina Forbes, the late Mary Fuller, William Garner, Gilbert Library Dublin, Daniel Gillman, Knight of Glin, Bernie Goggin, George Gossip, David Griffin, the late Mariga Guinness, Brian Hannon, Richard Haughton, Lord Headley, Anne Henderson, Derek Hill, Renagh Holohan, Brian Joyce, Susan Kellett, Lord Killanin, Colonel King-Harman, Peter Lamb, Jeffery Lefroy, Tessa Lefroy, Desmond Leslie, the Earl of Limerick, Simon Lincoln, Linenhall Library Belfast, Magda Loeber, Rolf Loeber, Diana Luxmore, Charles Lysaght, John Madden, John Maher, Annesley Malley, the late Lady Mander, Geoffrey Mandeville, the late Daphne du Maurier, Reverend Robert McCarthy, Tony McNamara, Zita Mulhern, Peter Murray, National College of Art and Design Library, National Library of Ireland, Professor Kevin Nowlan, Emmet O'Brien, Ciaran O'Carroll, Sean O'Criadain, Gerard O'Flaherty, Peter O'Keefe, Sean O'Reilly, John O'Sullivan, Michael O'Sullivan, William O'Sullivan, James O'Toole, Thomas Pakenham, Richard Pierce, Homan Potterton, the late Henry Puxley, Lord Rathdonnell, Alison Reid, the late Lord Revelstoke, Leslie Roberts, the Earl and Countess of Rosse, Alistair and Anne Martha Rowan, Daniel Ryan, William Semple, Maura Shaffrey, Nicholas Sheaff, Jeanne Sheehy, Anne Simmonds, the late Anthony Symondson, Redmond Smyth, John Cole Talbot, Dom Mark Tierney OSB, David Tomkin, Robert Travers, Trinity College Library, the late Arlan Ussher, Jane Waller, Peter Walsh, Julian Watson, Mrs Peter Welsh, the Countess of Wicklow, David Willis, Miss Willis, John Wilson-Wright and Richard Wood.

CONTENTS

A NOTE ON MAPS, INDEXES AND THE ORDER OF ENTRIES

The entries are arranged alphabetically by county and, within the county, by town or nearest town. Some entries for larger towns are arranged by street and then by building, but the general practice has been to list buildings within a town by their names, on the grounds that they are easy for a visitor to find.

There are special 'chapters' for three cities—Belfast, Cork, and Dublin. Dublin City and County are divided in the following way: Dublin City, North (from the Liffey to approximately the Royal Canal); Dublin City, South (from the Liffey to approximately the Grand Canal); Dublin: North Suburbs and North County; and Dublin: South Suburbs and South County. Many of the entries in the North and South Suburbs are politically parts of Dublin City or are within the Dublin Postal District.

THE MAPS

The maps indicate the location of most of the towns and villages (or, in the case of cities, streets) under which entries appear. For the location of a country house, the Index of Buildings should be consulted to discover the town or village under which the entry appears.

INDEXES

The Chapter Contents shows at a glance the buildings listed.

The Index of Buildings covers country houses and other buildings better known by name than by location.

The General Index covers architects, builders, decorators and artists; it also notices some literary and other figures mentioned in the text.

CHAPTER CONTENTS

AIB	Allied Irish Bank
BoI	Bank of Ireland
CC	Catholic Church
Ch	Church
CoI	Church of Ireland
Pres.	Presbyterian

ILLUSTRATION CREDITS

Numbers refer to pages, letters to the order in which the illustration appears on the page. Drawings not listed are period illustrations.

Liddy, Pat: 114, 119b, 120a, 122, 132b, 138b, 144a, 144b, 152a, 163a, 165a, 169, 191
Lunt, Michael: 134, 223
O'Brien, Kieran Doyle, and Appletree Press, Belfast: 34, 39b, 106, 119a, 142, 184, 189b, 238, 281a, 297a, 391c
Rothery, Sean: 35b, 44, 53, 126a, 162b, 163b, 192a, 292, 387a
Shaffrey, Maura: 2, 40a, 59b, 90b, 110b, 128, 154, 243a, 269, 283b, 287, 288a, 294, 310b, 316, 325b, 342c, 347, 349
Williams, Jeremy: 1, 3, 5a, 7, 8, 11b, 13a, 13b, 14a, 27, 28a, 36, 37, 38, 40b, 41, 42a, 50, 51, 52, 55, 58b, 59a, 61, 62, 65a, 65b, 68, 71, 73, 74, 77a, 80a, 82, 83, 84, 91, 97b, 98, 101, 102, 105, 108, 110a, 111a, 111b, 117, 120b, 130, 132a, 137a, 141, 150, 158, 173a, 175, 180a, 180b, 180c, 182a, 185, 193, 195, 196, 199b, 200, 201a, 202, 205a, 206b, 208, 210a, 212, 214, 219b, 222a, 222b, 222c, 224, 225, 226b, 227, 229, 231, 234, 235a, 235b, 240, 241, 243b, 244b, 245, 249b, 251, 253a, 255, 256, 259a, 259b, 260a, 261a, 275a, 276, 277b, 281b, 284, 288b, 288c, 289b, 298, 300, 301a, 301b, 302a, 302b, 303b, 305a, 306, 307a, 308a, 308b, 310a, 312, 315a, 317a, 317b, 317c, 318b, 321, 322a, 326c, 327, 330, 331, 332a, 332b, 332c, 333, 334, 335a, 335b, 336a, 336b, 336c, 337, 341, 342a, 342b, 344, 346, 348b, 351, 352, 356a, 359, 360, 361b, 363, 365, 366, 367, 370b, 373, 374, 375, 376b, 377, 379a, 379b, 382, 385, 386, 389a, 389b, 391b, 393, 394, 395. The frontispiece was first published in Jeremy Williams, 'William Atkins 1812-1887', in *Decantations. A Tribute to Maurice Craig*, edited by Agnes Bernelle (Dublin 1992) and is reproduced by courtesy of Lilliput Press.

The following illustrations also appear by courtesy of those named: The Irish Architectural Archive 157; John Baird 97a; Michael Byrne 328a; Jackie Connolley and Armagh Tourist Information 12a; Pamela Drew 43; the Directors of the Gaiety Theatre 140; William Garner 254; N. Kelleher and Cork/Kerry Tourism 79; Dermot Mulligan 273a; Derry O'Connell 256b; An Post 87b; Ian Sherrif 372; Paul Sweeney 160; An Taisce and Derry O'Connell 104; An Taisce 237

ANTRIM

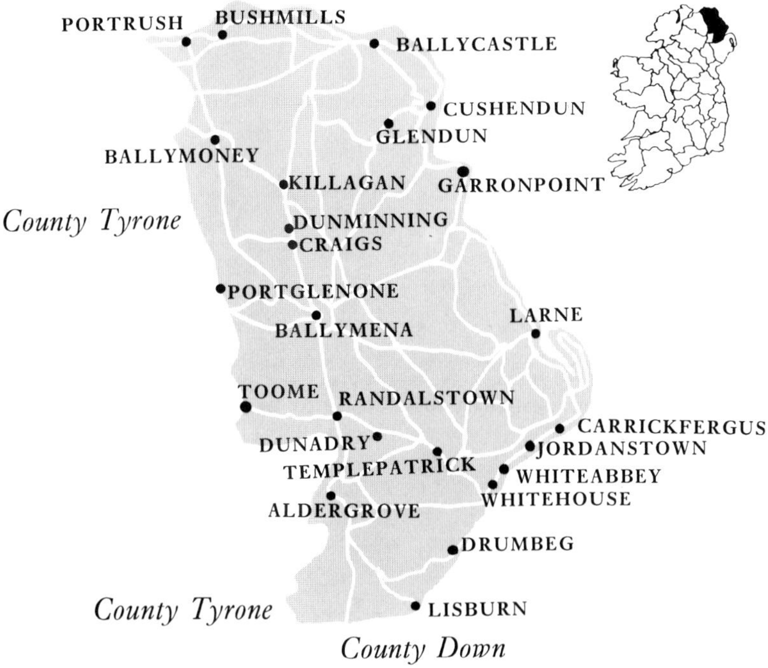

ALDERGROVE: **Dunore**
Rare if decidedly amateur example of the Egyptian Revival—an obelisk rises from a pediment upheld by four pharaohs' heads resting on inverted tapering pilasters. The hieroglyphic decoration that once linked them has disappeared.

ANTRIM: **The Castle**
A Victorian corner tower (1887) survives of the celebrated castle set in what is now a public park. But the only architecture that remains intact is the stables, *c.*1840, a neo-Jacobean composition with central gateway between twin ogee towers linked by screen walls to scroll-gabled stable blocks. Gatelodge by W.J. Fennell (1885).

ANTRIM: **Church of Ireland**
The church contains memorials to the Viscounts Massarene and Ferrard, the most elaborate by J.R. Kirk (1865), a recumbent effigy behind a Gothic screen, to the Lord Massarene who died after a fall from his terrace on to a shrub that gave way under him (*c.*1840). Tomb of Lord Massarene with a fiddle (1905). Stained glass dating from 1890 to 1895.

ANTRIM: **First Presbyterian Church**
One of the most striking neo-Classical churches in Ulster, designed by an unrecorded architect and built in 1834-7. Temple front with seg-

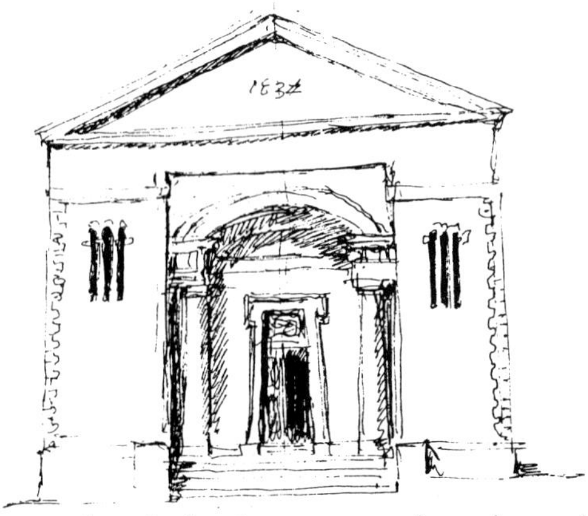

mental arch framing a recessed portico and resting on two columns modelled on the Greek temple of Thoricus. Side doors open into vestibules but the central doorway opens into a ceremonial staircase with twin flights rising directly to the gallery; this encloses three sides of the central nave resting on cast-iron columns. After the originality of the entrance, the interior seems conventional and demure. Remodelled (1903) by W.D. Taggert.

BALLYCASTLE: **Catholic Church of St Brigid and St Patrick**
A competent design by O'Neill and Byrne with their characteristic asymmetrical steeple dominating the façade; started in 1874.

BALLYCASTLE: **Magherintemple**
The family seat of the Casements, one of whom was Sir Roger Casement. Built *c.*1875 in a subdued Scottish Baronial idiom. The architect remains unknown.

BALLYCASTLE: **O'Connor Memorial**
Gothic Revival memorial designed in 1899 by S. Kelway Pope and carved by Darragh and Verdon.

BALLYMENA: **Adair Arms**
Symmetrical five-gabled façade in local basalt with sandstone trimmings; attributed to Charles Lanyon. Date of 1846 in the spandrel of the central oriel masked by modern porch. Bland neo-Georgian decor and suspended ceilings within.

BALLYMENA: **Church of Ireland**
Gothic Revival church with asymmetrical tower built in 1855; ascribed to the elder Welland in his obituary. Remodelled *c.*1885 after a fire. Glass by Heaton, Butler and Bayne. Furnishings influenced by the Arts and Crafts movement, especially two Art Nouveau windows.

BALLYMENA: **The Courthouse**
Unusual adaptation of the Gothic vocabulary to a small functional courthouse. By linking the main door and window overhead in one double-height recessed archway flush with single-height paired arches on either side (thereby deflecting attention from the conventional neo-Elizabethan elevations), the architect (thought to be Charles Lanyon) has devised a façade full of light and shade. Built in 1846.

BALLYMENA: **Crebilly**
Italianate house by either Charles Lanyon or one of his followers. Symmetrical seven-bay façade, centred on triple-arched loggia framed by piers of rock-faced rustication that reoccurs on the reveals of the adjoining windows. Service wing by Timothy Hevey (1870).

BALLYMENA: **Kintullagh Castle**
Jacobean Revival house with ogee-roofed tower and curvilinear gables that repetitively loom above a series of single-storied bay windows. Dating from 1863. Attributed to Thomas Turner while he was working for Lanyon, Lynn and Lanyon. Now the Convent of the St Louis Sisters; little altered.

BALLYMONEY: **Ballynachree**
An earlier house remodelled by Fitzgibbon Louch in 1861. A single-storied portico with a central window in a recessed panel above gives a sense of tension to the five-bayed façade. Ground-floor windows with segmental pediments, camber-headed windows above, and bracketed eaves all show evidence of an opulent Italianate interior. Hall with columns from the Tower of the Wind and bifurcating staircase with wrought-iron balusters.

BALLYMONEY: **Catholic Church**
An early church of John O'Neill, built in 1878. Lofty tower and spire, nave of six bays, chancel with high altar and side chapel furnished and decorated by Earley and Powell. In the graveyard, a Mr Kirgan had the gratifying experience of outlasting by thirty years the tomb he commissioned from J.J. McDonnell in 1911, an ogee-domed shrine graced by kneeling angels.

BALLYMONEY: **Church of Ireland**
Earlier church with spire, apse and aisle added by Welland & Gillespie in 1868. The aisle is treated by them characteristically as a series of transverse gables. Stained glass of the same period by Heaton, Butler and Bayne.

BALLYMONEY: **The Courthouse**
Subtle neo-Classical design with central double-height pavilion between single-storied wings. These are articulated by very wide piers rhythmically linked by the central projecting tapering doorcase. Design of 1838 attributed to Charles Lanyon.

BALLYWHAT: **Presbyterian Church**
A low-slung church entered through a stubby octagon tower designed in 1895 by Vincent Craig. Nave with double-braced collar-beam roof.

BUSHMILLS: **Dundarave**
This is Charles Lanyon's stateliest palazzo, the culmination of a sequence that starts with Drenagh (q.v., 1837) and Ballywalter (q.v., 1845). Dundarave (1847) is a distillation of the grandest features of its two predecessors. The double-storied elevation is derived from Drenagh; also as in Drenagh the principal staircase defers to the central hall instead of

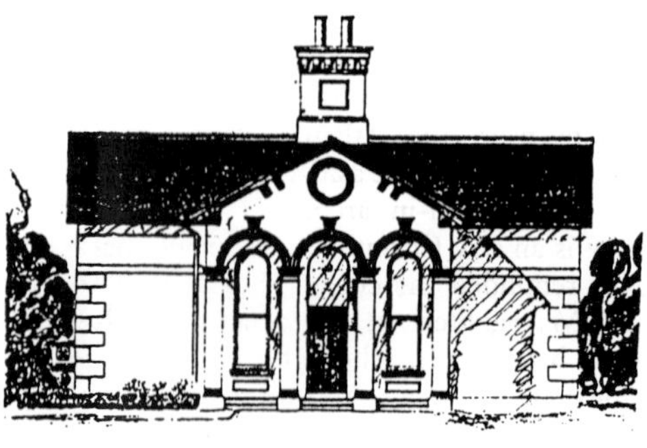

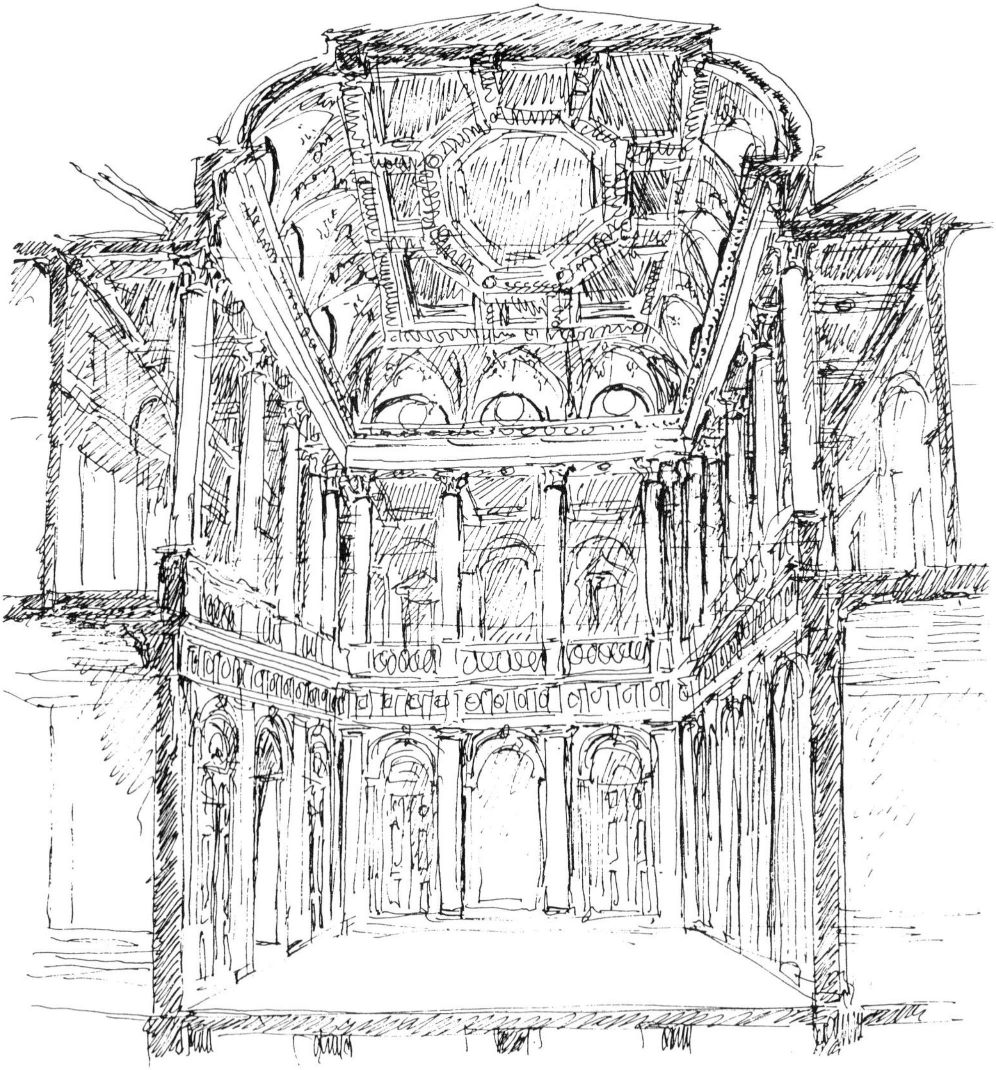

maintaining the equilibrium achieved albeit uneasily at Ballywater; but from Ballywater comes a greater spatial complexity. To enter one descends before a porch—the intended *porte-cochère* extension was never built—articulated by Ionic columns that reoccur round the central bow of the garden front. The vestibule is an austere tunnel vault with classical reliefs on either side. This makes even more overwhelming the triple-storied hall beyond. Inspired by Barry's Reform Club of 1840, it still achieves its own individuality by developing a sense of enclosure at ground level—an oasis of calm remote from the Atlantic storms. Walls of painted Siena marble ashlar articulated by pilasters and walled-in arches. The intermediate story is an airy Corinthian colonnade that must have reminded the client, Sir Edmund Workman-Macnaghten, of Calcutta, where he had made his fortune. The lightness of the colonnades allows the space to expand into the continuous landing, and the bedroom walls are carried transversely across the reception rooms. The topmost level is an arcaded lantern that Lanyon was to develop in his Northern Bank head office in Belfast, roofed with a highly-corbelled octagon. Dundarave is one of the few great Victorian houses to preserve the sequence intact between the diningroom and the kitchen, an impressive double-height room (overlooking a service courtyard on a lower level) with its original range gleaming. During the regulatory five-minute walk between the two rooms the mother of the present owner expressed her disagreement with the modern trend of bringing kitchens upstairs.

BUSHMILLS: **Market Tower**

Circular clock tower built by John Hall in 1874 for Sir Francis Macnaghten of Dundarave (q.v.). Now a forlorn survivor after the destruction of a symmetrical architectural layout.

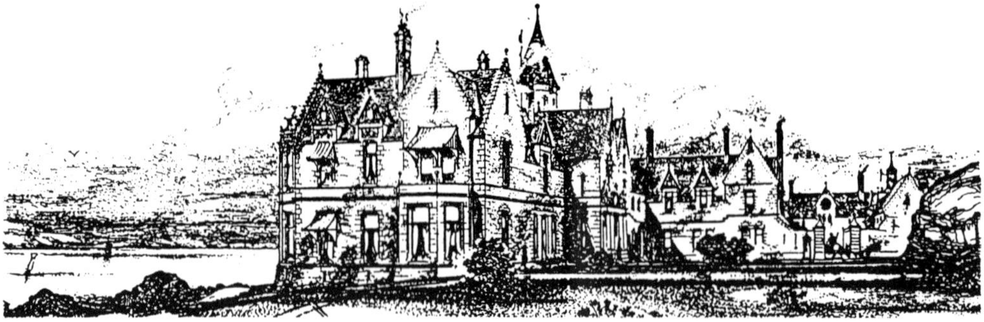

BUSHMILLS: Runkerry
It is curious that while the elder Macnaghten brother built Dundarave, the finest Italianate room in Ulster, the younger brother Edward, a successful barrister who ultimately inherited Dundarave, built this bleak baronial affair, as ungiving as the rocky coast and the Giant's Causeway beyond. Designed in 1883 by S.P. Close, whose perspective survives showing the house framed by what could be either rocks or trees. Now an institution for the elderly.

CARRICKFERGUS: Sheil Almshouses
Characteristic example of the series of almhouses designed by Lanyon, Lynn and Lanyon and built in 1868-70. Polychromatic stonework, shoulder gabling and focal clock tower.

CRAIGS: Parochial Schools
A formal neo-Elizabethan composition designed by Charles Lanyon dating from 1841.

CUSHENDUN: The Square
Formal village housing with dormers set into mansard rooves. Designed in 1912 by Clough Williams Ellis for Ronald McNeill and his wife, later Lord and Lady Cushendun.

DRUMBEG: Ballydrain
Neo-Elizabethan manor house built for Hugh Montgomery to the designs of Edward Blore. Asymmetrical façades, picturesque grouping of chimney stacks, mullioned windows with an oriel above the entrance door. The house was enlarged but not improved in 1876 by W.H. Lynn, who made a new entrance porch and added a bay window to a garden front. A billiard room was added in 1880 when a conservatory was erected by James Boyd & Sons of Paisley. Derelict for twenty years until acquired as a clubhouse by the Malone Golf Club and restored—but at the expense of its original character.

DUNADRY: Loughanmore
Georgian house extended by two towers at either end, the highest with five floors and a spire marking the entrance. Castellations and a chapel also added.

DUNMINNING: Craigdun
Serious Scottish Baronial castle built *c.*1870 for Edmund McNeill. At the side, a five-storey keep enlivened by pepperpot bartizans and crow-stepped gables. Attributed to Lanyon, Lynn and Lanyon.

DUNMURRY: Conway
Symmetrical villa *c.*1870 with central belvedere. Façade extended by verandahs to single storied wings, one of them a conservatory. Now a hotel.

FINAGHY: Rathmore
Italianate country house built in 1870 for the ironfounder Victor Coates; as Paul Larmour states, probably by Lanyon, Lynn and Lanyon. Externally similar to their Newtownabbey (q.v.) in Co. Wexford. Internal similarities with Stradbally Hall (q.v.). Tuscan porch and Corinthian coffer-vaulted hall lit by a coloured rooflight. Now a school and convent, a use far more appropriate to its style.

GALGORM: National School
Perpendicular Revival church complex, designed in 1878, possibly by the office of Charles Lanyon. Picturesquely composed boys' school with intersecting gables meeting at a vented lantern. Gothic windows, like a small church.

GARRONPOINT: Drumnasole
This Georgian house built by Francis Turnley of the East India Company was completed *c.*1840, reputedly by Charles Lanyon while he was working on the Antrim coast road. Central hall with circular lighting-well wreathed with frothy ironwork beneath a glazed dome. Early Victorian reception rooms on either side overlooking the sea. Behind the house cliffs rise between hidden glens. Inherited by John Turnley, whose politics were inspired by his cousin, Sir Roger Casement, and who headed a party proclaiming Irish unity until he was murdered on his avenue.

GARRONPOINT: **Garron Tower**
Designed by Lewis Vulliamy for Frances, marchioness of Londonderry, in 1848; intended as a replica of Burg Rheinstein on the Rhine, to take advantage of a spectacular site. An austere design made even more so by the choice of stone—the local black basalt. Apart from a polygonal tower and a few Gothic machicolations, grimly rectangular. Chapel and banqueting hall added later. Interior destroyed between the wars after conversion into a hotel. Restored as a school by Padraic Gregory, who added the chapel *c.*1950.

GLENDUN: **The Viaduct**
Impressive viaduct built by Charles Lanyon in 1839.

JORDANSTOWN: **Church of Ireland**
One of the finest Celtic Revival churches in Ireland, designed by W.H. Lynn and built in 1865-8. Modelled on the church of St Finghin at Clonmacnoise but enriched with High Victorian complexity. A convincing Irish round

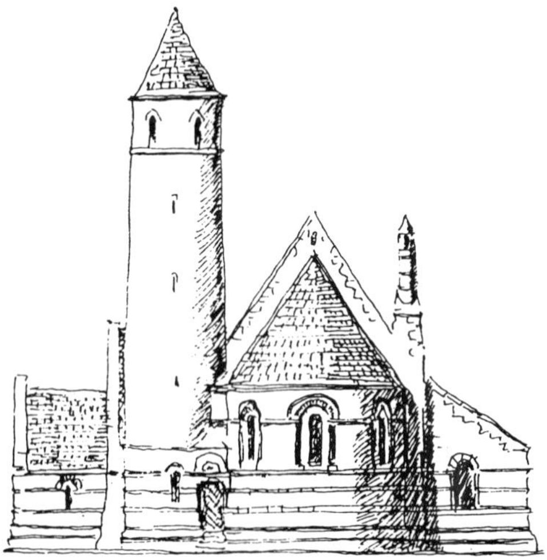

tower, ingeniously adapted to serve as vestry, is bonded by polychromatic stonework to an effective if un-Irish round apse. Interior in red and black brick with Celtic Revival stained glass by Clayton and Bell contemporary with the church. Glass by Cox and Buckley in the nave. Note the ingenious treatment of the transept roofspace. Marble reredos set into stone arcading added in 1894.

KILBRIDE: **Stephenson Tomb**
Miniature Taj Mahal built in the graveyard; dating from 1837, it records for posterity one family's obsession with India.

KILLAGAN: **Lissanoure Castle**
The house of the diplomat Lord Macartney, an Ulster version of Luggala, was pulled down by his great-nephew, whose wife lost her life in the resulting explosion. All that had been built of the new house was a battlemented gateway beneath an octagonal belfry. This has been attributed to J.B. Keane (presumably responsible for the cottage ornée beside the lake to which the bereaved family retired).

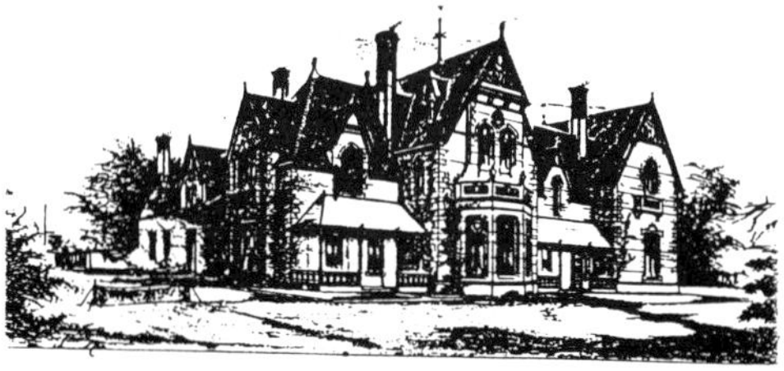

LARNE: **Cairndhu**
Rambling multi-gabled seaside villa partially built onto a simple Georgian cottage, now unrecognizable. A continuous verandah haplessly attempts to tie together a series of disparate gables overhung with bargeboarding. Designed by S.F. Close in 1882.

LARNE: **Chaine Memorial Tower**
Only when the Victorians had satisfied their consciences by doing something useful, could they then fantasize with conviction. This round tower, designed by S.F. Close in 1887 to commemorate a son who had died young, looks Celtic at first sight until one realizes that the top floor has been fitted with navigation lights to guide boats into Larne Harbour.

LARNE: **Drumalis**
Late-Victorian country house resembling two villas pivotting out from a central turreted viewing tower. Conglomerate of single- and double-storied bays, porches and verandahs. Designed by S.F. Close in 1872 for the Smylie family.

LARNE: **Magheramorne House Hotel**
A restrained Tudor Revival country house with an almost symmetrical gabled main block linked

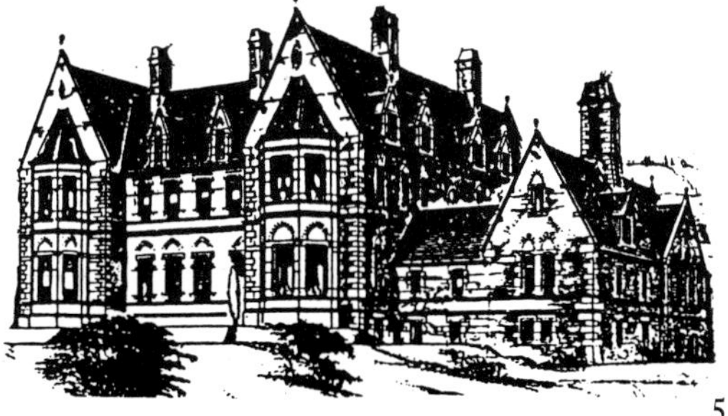

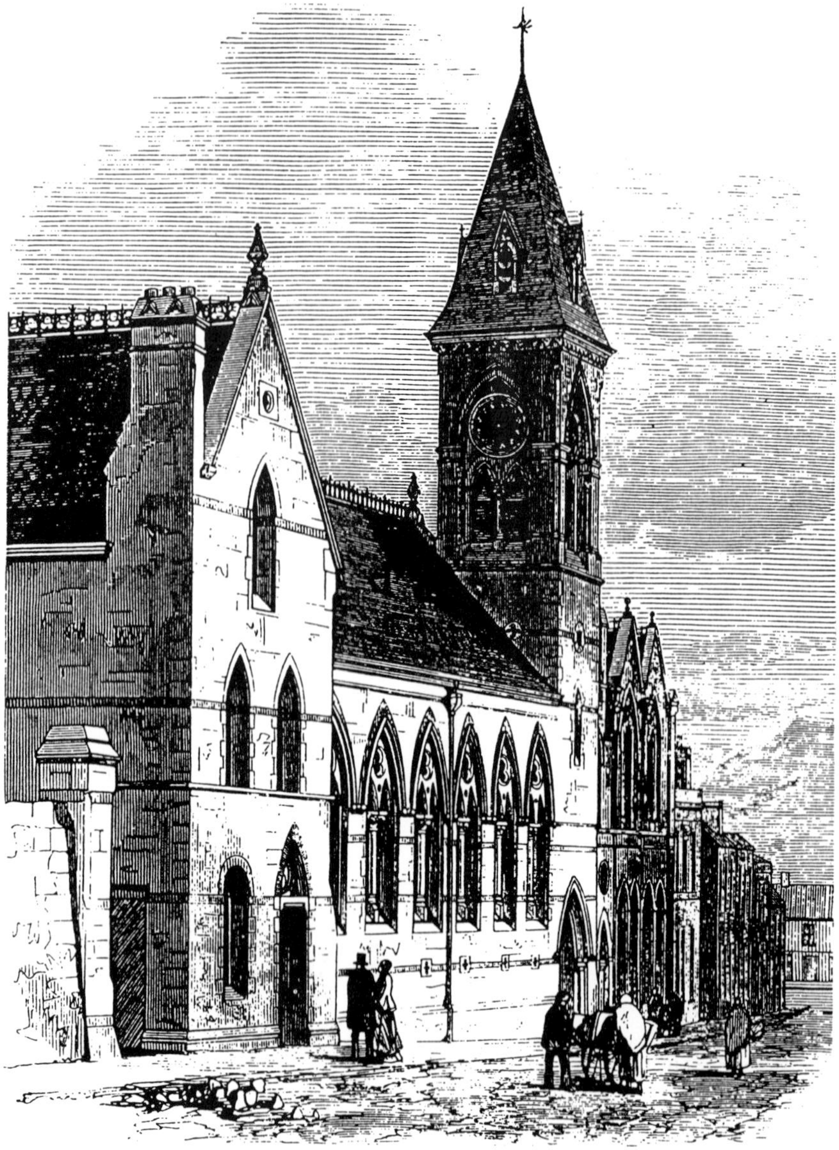

to gabled annexe. Pillared porch. Bay windows on garden façade overlooking impeccably maintained formal terraced gardens. The seat of Mr M'Greel and then of the Hogg family. Now an hotel. Designed in 1880 by S.F. Close.

LARNE: **McGarvel Buildings**
Housing complex (built for a local philanthropist) influenced by the Sheil Homes. Double-storey gabled terrace dominated by off-centre clocktower. Architect possibly Alexander Tate.

LARNE: **Moyle Hospital**
Typical symmetrical neo-Elizabethan workhouse by George Wilkinson *c.*1840. In this case very much altered and renewed with unfeeling fenestration.

LARNE: **The Townhall**
Picturesque complex, admirably adopted to the existing streetscape with its Venetian Gothic polychromatic fenestration reflecting its varied functions—council offices, museum, library, clock tower, assembly hall and curatorial accommodation. The hall still retains a pair of forceful fireplaces. Date over doorway: 1870. The architect was Alexander Tate assisted by S. Close.

LISBURN: **Catholic Church**
A disjointed exterior by an unknown architect *c.*1890; striped stone tower and spire. More assured interior in the Romanesque idiom with well carved capitals and imposing reredos. Adjoining church hall of the same period, in vernacular Baroque.

LISBURN: Church of Ireland
Designed in 1842 by Charles Lanyon using dark forbidding local stone, more effective externally than internally. Dominated by a pinnacled tower; the transepts were added in 1859. Nicolson memorial sculpted by Foley. Glass by Heaton, Butler and Bayne.

LISBURN: Nicholson Memorial
Life-size statue by F.W. Pomeroy dated 1920. One plaque on the pedestal portrays his death, another the surrender of the rebels.

LISBURN: Wallace Fountain, Public Park
The prototype was modelled by C.A. Lebourg. Three nymphs rotate in their dance of the blessed spirits, far from Paris, even further from their casting foundry, the Val d'Osne, where they were produced to provide water to the devastated city. A more apt memorial to Sir Richard Wallace than the conventional Gothic shrine (1882) by Robinson and Son.

LISBURN: Wallace House
Red brick and mansard roofs in an uninspired transplantation of French design as in Sir Richard Wallace's London seat, Manchester House, and stylistically equally remote from his Parisian home, the Bagatelle.

PORTGLENONE: Catholic Church
Designed in 1870 by O'Neill and Byrne. Well sited with sacristy, belfry and parochial house making a picturesque composition in the landscape. Glass by Heaton, Butler and Bayne.

PORTGLENONE: Portglenone House
Georgian house remodelled and extended for Nathaniel Alexander MP, from 1850 onwards by FitzGibbon Louch. The entrance front was given an overscaled porch and Ionic *porte-cochère*. Then a wing was added to contain a new staircase rising beneath a glass dome. Finally the reception rooms had their woodwork and plasterwork enriched in a frothy Italianate. Now a convent.

PORTRUSH: Northern Bank
Designed by Vincent Craig and built in 1901. Freely treated Tudor with distinctive circular corner turrets.

PORTRUSH: Railway Station
A stockbroker Tudor station here is an incongruous afterthought to the sober Italianate original started by Charles Lanyon (and continued by his son John) that distinguishes the line from Belfast to Londonderry. However, they have all suffered equally from illiterate renovation. The chief casuality here is the cafeteria. Fortunately, the drawings of Barclay Wise dated 1893 have been preserved.

PORTRUSH: The Townhall
Designed by W.H. Lynn when he was working with the Lanyons. One of his formidable Gothic

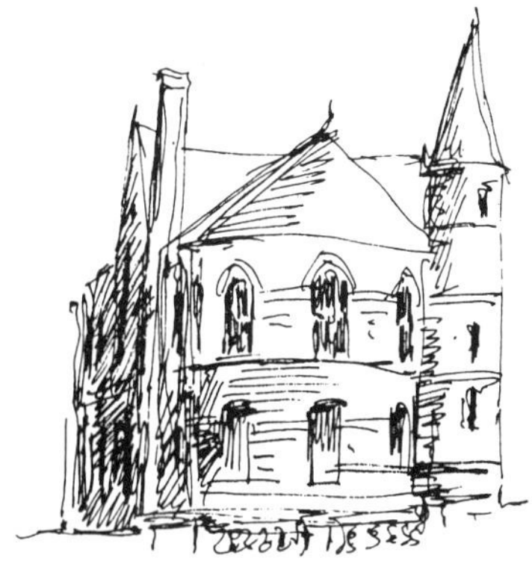

Revival designs, now partially altered with what the UAHS terms a 'repulsive' addition. The original building with its bow and circular turret dated from 1872.

RANDALSTOWN: Shane's Castle
Felix Kelly was commissioned recently to recreate in one of his paintings the fantastical castle intended by John Nash in 1815, but not the sensible and severe High Victorian castle built fifty years later in the mid-1860s to the designs of Lanyon, Lynn and Lanyon as the third castle on the site. This was burnt out in 1922 and subsequently removed. Apart from Nash's camelia house, the only Gothic Revival structure to survive is the castellated Randalstown gateway. This is boldly polychromatic with portcullis, coats of arms and octagonal look-out tower, its architecture too serious for Nash but too frivolous for Lynn.

RANDALSTOWN: The Viaduct
Seven tapering piers of local basalt support a majestic series of brick-lined arches; in disuse since 1959. Built by William Dargan in 1855 to the design of Charles Lanyon.

TEMPLEPATRICK: Castle Upton
In 1837 Edward Blore was commissioned to remodel the Plantation castle (*c.*1600) already remodelled and extended by Robert Adam for the 1st Lord Templeton. Blore made minimal external alterations, replacing the windows with neo-Elizabethan glazing, but casually destroyed most of Adam's internal decoration, replacing it with panelling and fretted ceilings. Sold, unhappily reroofed and then abandoned this cen-

tury. Rescued by the present owners, whose restoration shows more concern for the original than either Blore or Adam did.

TOOME: Carey's Monument

Eccentric tomb in the graveyard of Duneane Presbyterian church erected *c.*1860. Sealed off by barley-sugar railings held in place by life-size hands and arms dissected at the elbow, all in wrought iron, though that would not be easy to discover in the semi-darkness. The body-snatching theme is taken up in the memorial that rises to an immense finger pointing heavenwards. Underneath an inscription refers the reader to Burke's *Landed Gentry* for further information; one suspects that genealogy was the livelong *raison d'être* of the departed.

WHITEABBEY: Abbeylands

Comfortable mid-nineteenth century Italianate villa built by the McCalmont family with symmetrical three-storied façade and an Ionic porch set between two bay windows. Now extended as an old people's home. The ornamental grounds descend to Belfast Lough.

WHITEHOUSE: Catholic Church

If Hevey's spire to the Catholic church dominates the eastern shore of Belfast Lough, here is its counterpart on the western shore. The church is an early work of John O'Neill built in 1865-7. There is a trefoiled door beneath a slender triple-lancet, but the apex of the gable is merely a third of the height of the adjoining steeple. Even by the competitive standards of Belfast, the belfry stage is immensely tall, rising to pinnacles, lucarnes and an octagonal spire. The interior is unexpectedly snug. Stained glass includes some by Mayer. The pulpit has been removed, but fortunately the high altar and the reredos (carved out of Caen stone with red marble colonettes by Thomas Earp of London) have been spared.

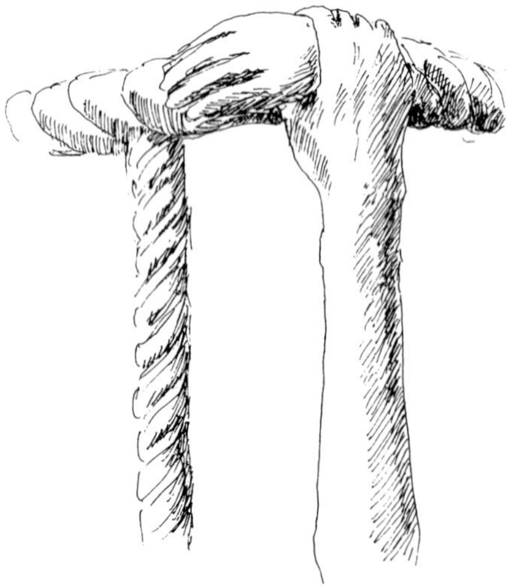

CAREY'S MONUMENT

ARMAGH

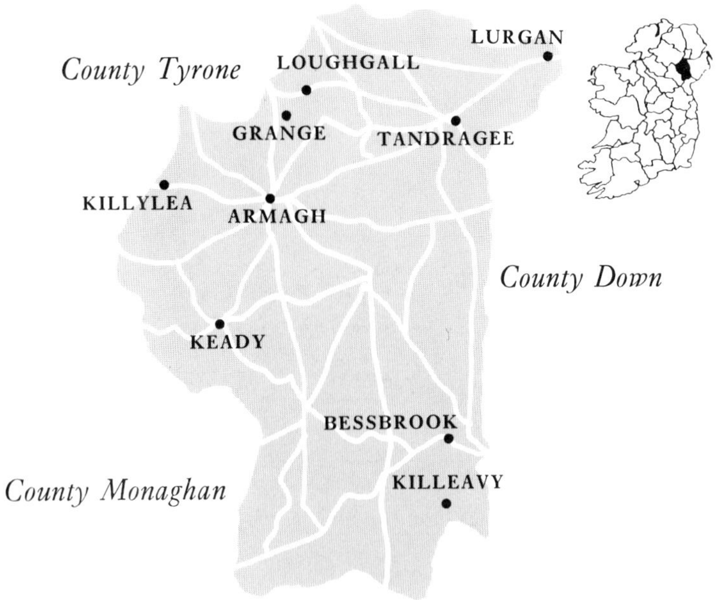

ARMAGH: **Boer War Memorial**
Unpretentious bronze soldier blows his bugle towards the cricket pitch before dying on the distant veld. By Kathleen Shaw, 1905.

ARMAGH: **Catholic Cathedral**
Sited on a rival hill to its Church of Ireland counterpart, despite the initial impression of one building campaign successfully terminated by the twin spires of the west front, there are four cathedrals superimposed one upon the other. The first, intended by its architect, Thomas Duff of Newry, to recall 16th-century Gothic, was started in 1840 but halted by the Famine. The second cathedral is that resumed in 1840 to the designs of J.J. McCarthy that changed the idiom to the 14th century. This was completed some twenty years later. The third cathedral is the shrine by George Ashlin, conceived in marble, mosaic, stained glass and fresco within the existing shell. This was partially destroyed by the fourth cathedral as conceived by Liam McCormack (1977-82) in an attempt to express the liturgical trends of twenty years before; it appears, however, to revive the worship of the Druids whom St Patrick had supplanted. This dramatic reversal of history eclipses what Maurice Craig terms the absurdity of McCarthy's decorated Gothic walls built on Duff's neo-Perpendicular. The ruthless destruction of the high altars, pulpit (by Beakey's of Dublin) and Puginian rood screen is only explicable by the resurgent Irish nationalism due to the Northern Troubles. Certainly it is embarrassing that the country's national saint should have been honoured by Duff's abbreviated version of York Minster, superimposed by McCarthy's version of a French cathedral as interpreted by Pugin, glazed then entirely by the German stained-glass firm of Mayer (though not the eastern window: by J. Clarke) and then fitted out under Ashlin's direction by what the 1962 *Shell Guide* refers to as Italian 'artists'. These included Oreste Amici who painted the ribbed panels using the hammerbeam roof structure articulated by sculptures of flying angels. He also painted (assisted by Joshua Clarke) the Coronation of the Virgin serenaded by Irish harps above the arch before the crossing. This blends with the mosaics by Early throughout the chancel. The reredos carved by Cesare Aureli still survives in the cathedral along with two side altars. The remainder of his work was either cast on the scrapheap or else sold off to two of Dublin's most luxurious hotels. The doorways carved by M. Dorey of Dundalk survive, but not his choir stalls; the high altar was removed to the nearby Gothic church of Kilmore. Another casualty of this iconoclasm was the 1875 Telford organ. While this took place during the episcopacy of Cardinal Ó Fiaich, it had been planned by his predecessor.

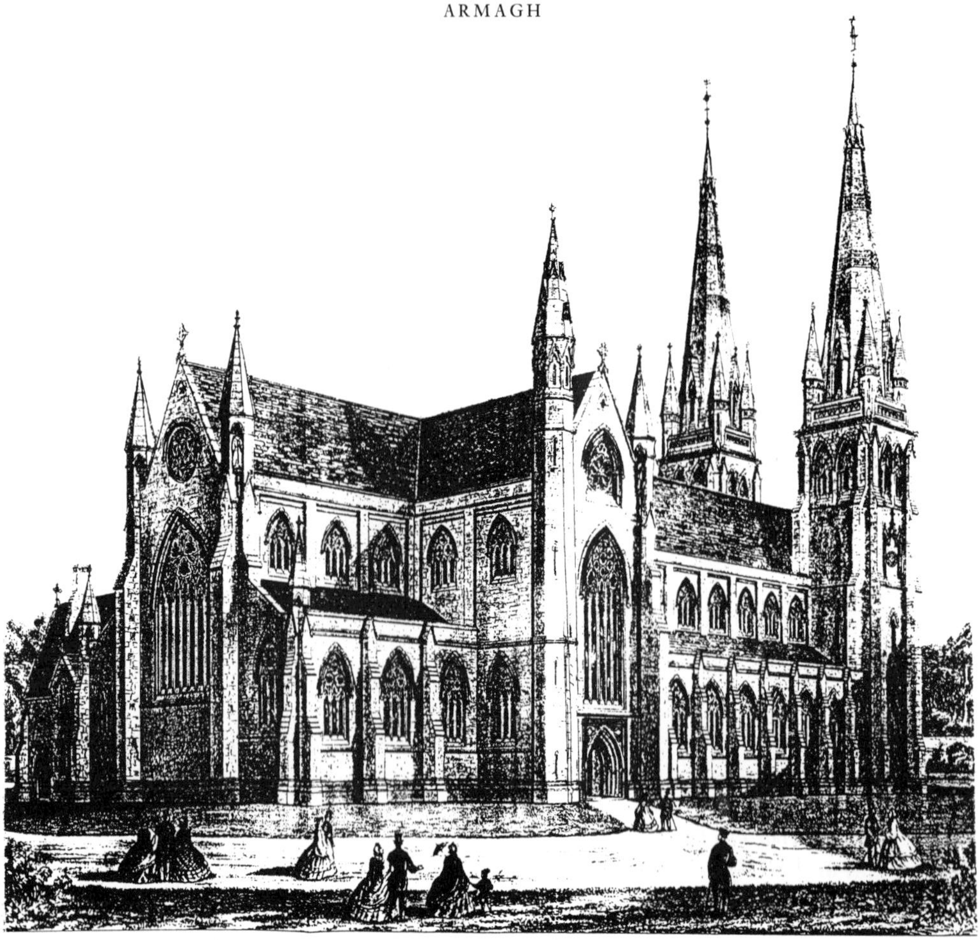

CATHOLIC CATHEDRAL

And the book that Cardinal Ó Fiaich wrote on the cathedral is as schizophrenic as the interior today that retains its rotting cardinals' hats.

ARMAGH: **Church of Ireland Cathedral**
The rebuilding of the cathedral, commissioned by Archbishop Lord John Beresford in 1834 from the English architect Lewis Cottingham, has been ever since much criticized for its replacement of so much that was medieval without the conviction of the full-blooded Gothic Revival. Thackeray claimed that it had less religious feeling than a drawingroom. In 1903 efforts were made by Thomas Drew to improve the interior, when the crossing and the chancel were heightened and their flat ceilings replaced with oak-sheathed Gothic vaulting. Ironically Cottingham's contribution with the most semblance of authenticity (his stone screen between the nave and crossing) had been already been removed to a less prominent position in the south transept. In 1910 his reredos and high altar on the eastern wall, painstakingly derived from St Alban's Abbey, were relegated to a newly created lady chapel and hidden from view by another reredos and high altar a bay in front of it. This was designed by Fellows Prynne. Its centrepiece, a Last Supper in opus sectile, was executed by Percy Bacon Bros, also from London. Prynne's contribution is certainly successful in giving the interior a much needed focal point, but it is still extraordinary that there is so little Irish in the Victorian embellishments of both Armagh's cathedrals dedicated to the island's patron saint. In the 18th century the procedure was to commission the best sculptors working in Europe, hence the presence here of the Rysbrack and the Roubilliac. In the Victorian era, when decency was all that was required, there should have been no need to go as far as London. There are several unremarkable recumbent effigies of archbishops laid out between the nave and aisles, including those of Lord John Beresford and Marcus Beresford (1862-85) by John Taylor. Tomb of Lt. Thomas Kidd by Thomas Farrell. Windows by Warrington (aisle of west front), Clayton & Bell (south aisle and the Evangelist south-east window of chancel), and Heaton, Butler and Bayne (east window) are all overshadowed by

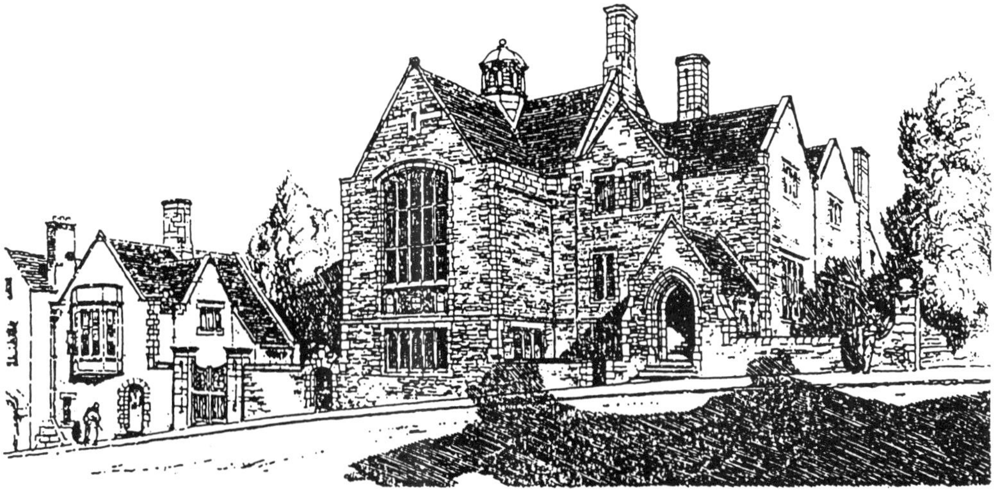

the Beresford memorial window in the south transept by Lavers & Beraud. The cathedral has not been improved by more recent changes. The sense of space at the crossing has been irredeemably spoilt by sealing off the north transept and turning it into the chapter house, while the uncertain Gothic of the new chapel in the south transept contributes little to the memory of the Royal Irish Fusiliers.

The Diocesan Hall (*above*) is a Neo-Elizabethan building, dated 1912, with intersecting plaster barrel vaults. Architects, W. Jervais and Richard Orpen.

ARMAGH: **No. 12, Melbourne Terrace**
Exuberantly carved shopfront, with Baroque entablature (partly upheld by clustered columns since recent bomb damage), sheltering the entrance to solicitors' offices.

ARMAGH: **Plymouth Brethren Meeting House**

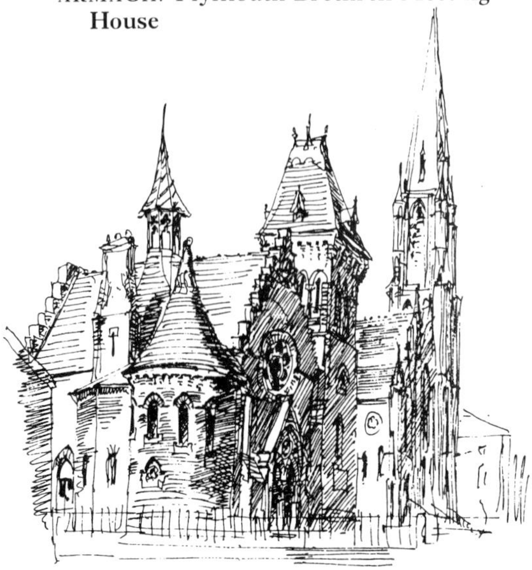

Built in 1884 as a Masonic hall flaunting its red and yellow brick and lively silhouette against the sober grandeur of its Presbyterian neighbour. Wedge-shaped belfry, turreted staircase, rooftop *flèche* and even boiler chimney jostle for dominance on its corner site that cuts a piquant angle off its chancel. Trefoil-shaped timber-vaulted chapel on the upper floor. Architect, J.H. Fullerton.

ARMAGH: **Precentors' houses**
Four houses designed in a restrained manner by John Boyd for Archbishop Lord John Beresford. Austerely Elizabethan, but Boyd reveals his individuality in his treatment of the front doors and their side lights, enclosing them in a single hooded moulding. Dated 1854.

ARMAGH: **Presbyterian Church**
A faded photograph in the vestry of a bearded patriarch commemorates the architect, Robert Young, who was responsible for the best churches of his firm (Young and Mackenzie). Armagh (1878) is more conventional than his earliest Presbyterian church in University Street, Belfast (1874) but also relies for its impact on richly sculpted portals juxtaposed to a soaring spire, an external drama that an earlier generation of worshippers would have approached with deep foreboding. Twin apsidal staircases with elegant ironwork give access to the galleries that are wrapped round three sides of the interior, the side galleries contained in aisles roofed separately from the nave. Stained glass includes the McCrum window by Heaton, Butler and Bayne.

ARMAGH: **St Luke's Hospital**
Standard lunatic asylum of Francis Johnston extended by wings and a single water tower (1875) by John Boyd. Additions by J.J. Phillips

(1891). Then more than duplicated in size by a new institution on the hill above for 250 patients (*c.*1910), Jacobean in style with compact mansarded centrepiece and galleried wings linked to single-storied wings projecting forward with polygonal bays, their form replicated on a minor scale by twin octogonal lanterns that flank the overall layout. As in the earlier building in the valley the only asymmetrical feature is the water tower.

ARMAGH: **St Mark's Church of Ireland**
Apsidal chancel added by William Slater in 1872 to the Gothic church designed by Francis Johnston in 1811 but rebuilt by William Farrell in the 1830s. Glass by Ethel Rhind. Pulpit designed by J.J. Phillips.

ARMAGH: **Scotch Church**
Simple Palladian façade of 1837 that does not quite live up to the monumentality of its gate piers. Austere interior apart from the unexpected Baroque of its balcony carved in curving timber fretwork.

ARMAGH: **Sheil Almshouses**
Designed in 1863 by Lanyon, Lynn and Lanyon as a charitable housing trust and still being maintained as such over a century later. Armagh is one of their simplest designs but with splayed layout to follow the contours of the hill.

ARMAGH: **Sunnymeade**
Suburban villa in the style of William Barre but built in 1890, as recorded on a plaque in a vine-laden Gothic conservatory through which one enters. Painted glass in the staircase hall. Now an old people's home. Probable architect, J.H. Fullerton.

ARMAGH: **Tourist Board Office**
Formerly the Northern Bank. Just a door surmounted by a coat of arms, and a window each side of it, but magnificently scaled and exuberantly detailed. The door and windows are set into strongly rusticated arches. Sculptured keystones break into the frieze below a bracketed cornice; balustrading conceals the roof. One spacious room inside with decorative, lightly moulded, plaster ceiling. Architect, Sir Charles Lanyon, who is recorded as rebuilding the premises in 1867.

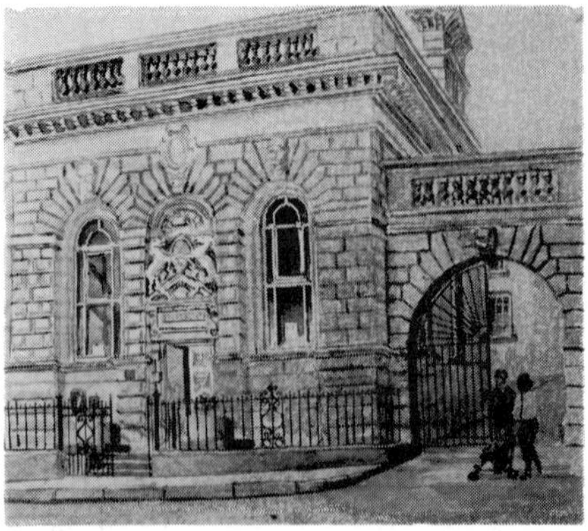

ARMAGH: **Towerhill Hospital**
The standard workhouse design by George Wilkinson preserved and converted into a general hospital. Completed in 1846.

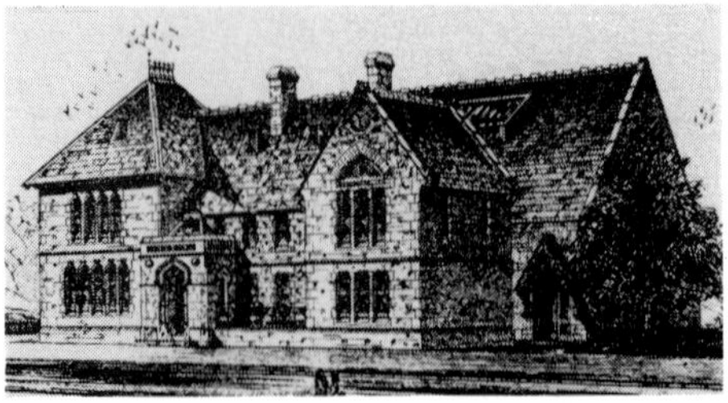

BESSBROOK: **The Townhall**
The model village was founded by the Richardson family *c.*1845 and developed as a self-sufficient entity. It remains so to this day. The most prominent building in the village is not a church but the town hall, now known as the community centre. Designed by the local Gothic Revival architect William Watson, it was built in 1886. Two parallel ranges, the front containing the meeting rooms, the rear the hall. The architectural idiom is that of William Barre but without his brio.

GRANGE: **Church of Ireland**
There is little evidence here of Philip Hardwick (commissioned to adapt this Regency Gothic church of the Molyneux family to the requirements of the Ecclesiologists) apart from the chancel and the pulpit. Interior now dominated by a goods Arts and Crafts window by Beatrice Elvery above the altar (1910).

KEADY: **Catholic Church**
Old-fashioned T-shaped structure, with impressive open timber roof; built in 1860. Recently transformed in a valiant attempt to unite Victorian and modern architecture, ultimately let down by the low standard of its stained glass so reverently retained and its depressing surroundings now mercilessly exposed to the view of the worshippers.

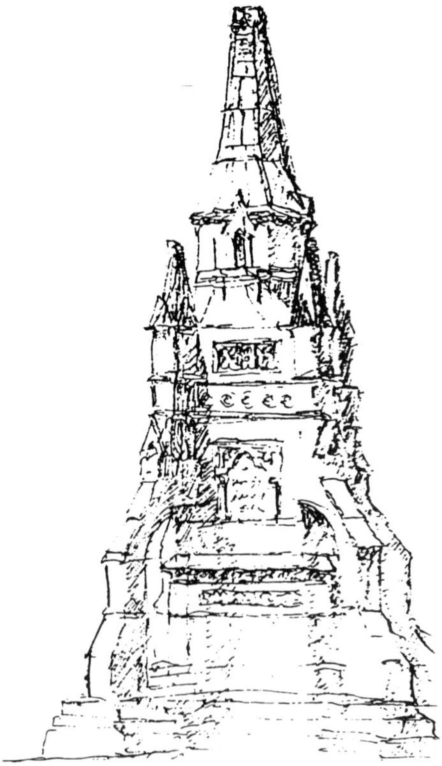

KEADY: **William Kirby Memorial**
Forceful Gothic octagonal spire ascending from a massive drinking fountain to commemorate the 1872 philanthropic exertions of the local MP. Designed in 1871 by Fitzgibbon Louch, who had his signature carved in reverse. He also designed a lively High Victorian courthouse, but this has been destroyed.

KILLEAVY: **Catholic Church**
An Ashlin church in his late so un-Irish Romanesque. Tower with curvilinear cupola. Mosaics and stained glass try to compensate for lack of Celtic feeling by interlacing scrolls and beasts that adorn the chancel.

KILLEAVY: **Killeavy Castle**
Sugar-plum Gothick castle built for the Foxall family by George Papworth (design exhibited, RHA 1836) on the lower slopes of Slieve Gullion. Touchingly rendered with its now vanished conservatory, garden pavilions and fountain protected by an immense battlemented and turreted terrace from the valley below as depicted in an anonymous watercolour in the Armagh Museum. The façade to the mountain reveals that this is a small geometric Georgian villa since here the drawingroom bow window projects unaltered. Its opposite number on the entry front has been gothicized and heightened, four varied corner towers tacked on and the chimneys castellated. All this deception would be believable were it not for the irrepressible fantasy of the architect. Papworth also designed the derelict church of Ireland in the valley—his signature being the cast-iron Gothic trusses.

KILLYLEA: **Elm Park**
Georgian house belonging to a branch of the Maxwells, remodelled and extended *c.*1880 by Rawson Carroll. Double-storied glazed loggia added to existing house; rear wing of two floors that reaches to the same height as the three floors of the original. Drawingroom with curved corners and sumptuous plasterwork (now allocated to white turkeys) once opened into double-apsed cast-iron conservatory (recently dismantled). Drawing in Armagh Museum.

LOUGHGALL: **Loughgall House**
The seat of the Cope family, rebuilt by them in an innocuous rambling Tudor that in no way can measure up to the fantastic Jacobean entrance gates at the start of a long, straight avenue leading up from the village to the house—four piers crowned with heraldic hounds, between curving arcaded screens through which are seen oriels and curvilinear gables of twin lodges. Wrought-iron gates signed 'R. Marshall 1842, Caledon'. Now an agricultural research centre.

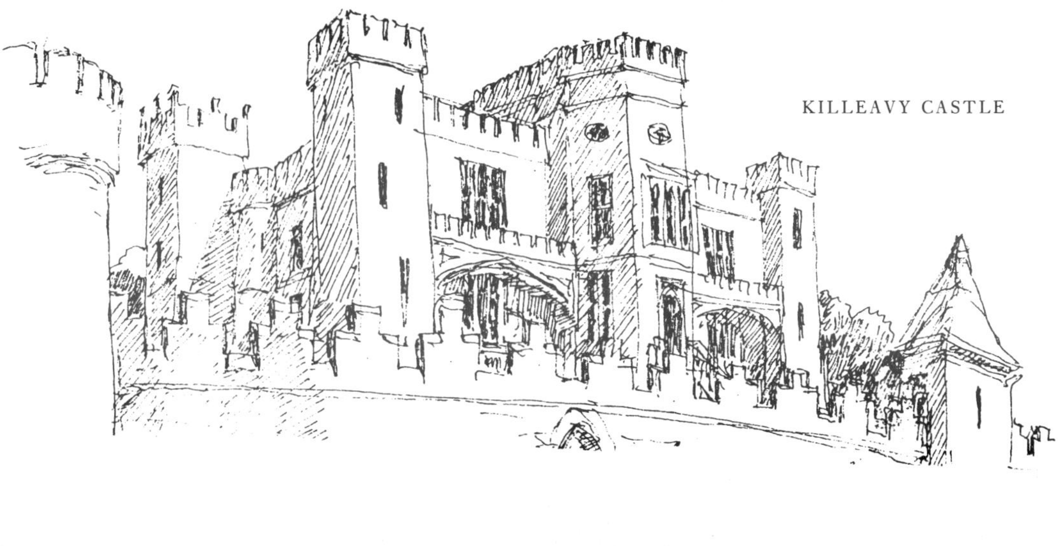

KILLEAVY CASTLE

LURGAN: **Church of Ireland**
Large church built out of local calp, with a brutish spire which dominates the town square, beside a small commemorative domed rotunda built after the First World War. Raw-boned interior made spatially more interesting by the insertion of a narrow gallery round three sides but kept well away from the triple arches that divide the side aisles from the nave. The nave dates back to 1725, its transformation and enlargement (1863) presumably the work of Welland and Gillespie. Window in north transept by Heaton, Butler and Bayne. Earlier heraldic glass of 1853 commemorates the Brownlows of Lurgan Castle.

LURGAN: **The Courthouse**
In a broadly composed Romanesque, and built out of contrasting red and yellow brick dating from 1865. Horizontality is assured by arcades resting on chubby columns. A forerunner by Williamson and Turner for their Magherafelt courthouse (q.v.) in 1874, in what has also been called their 'frontier' manner.

LURGAN: **No. 16, High Street**
Handsome commercial premises, disfigured now at ground level. The centrepiece of the floor above is an arcaded loggia with bulging columns. These uphold a central gable flanked by dormers. All symmetrically composed but aware of Art Nouveau. Possibly by Vincent Craig.

LURGAN: **The Institute and Townhall**
Neo-Classical with bell tower. An unusual stylistic choice for the Gothic Revivalist architect, Raffles Brown (1858).

LURGAN: **The Library**
Restrained neo-Tudor with a twinge of the Arts and Crafts. Built out of red brick, and entered through scrolled tower flanked by contrasting gables of different heights.

LURGAN: **Lurgan Castle (Brownlow House)**
The most important country house of the Edinburgh architect William Playfair to survive in Ireland after the demolition of his nearby neo-Classical Drumbanagher. The client was the 1st Lord Lurgan who selected Tudor, and the result was a large pile of honey-coloured stone enlivened by innumerable gables, finials, chimney-pots and a domed lantern tower. Off-loaded by the Brownlow family in 1903 to the Orange Order, who have maintained the house ever since, preserving the heraldic stained glass in the windows and the painted decoration of the principal rooms—walls panelled with painted marble, and their ceilings grained to resemble exotic woods. The stableyard is contracted out and would make a suitable backdrop for filming a John Buchan thriller.

TANDRAGEE: **Tandragee Castle**
The medieval fortress of the O'Hanlons was rebuilt (1830-8) by Viscount Mandeville, later 6th duke of Manchester in a restrained neo-Elizabethan. Its smooth ashlar is treated with such austerity as to verge on neo-Classicism, especially in two minor ranges of an imposing courtyard. The principal livingrooms were gathered in one corner into a T-shaped gabled keep with one angle filled in by a tower: this overlooks the river far below with a double storied canted oriel. Star-shaped fortifications along the crest of the hill shield a more conventionally treated entrance front. Turreted gate house attached to a slender octagonal lantern crowned with a castellated cupola. The medieval ruins were presumably left untouched, since these were rebuilt a generation later in a grim Baronial that looms above the approach with canted machicolations, crow-stepped gables and narrow windows. Its only concession to easefulness was a balustraded conservatory in the cente of the garden front linked to both keeps. The third era of architectural transformation occurred when the father of the present owners acquired the castle as an improbable potato crisp factory, filling in half the courtyard and building on his own copper roofed reception turret. The interior of the castle, partly gutted by fire in 1983, is now inaccessible. There is a Gothic Revival gatelodge on the avenue to Markethill, dated 1862.

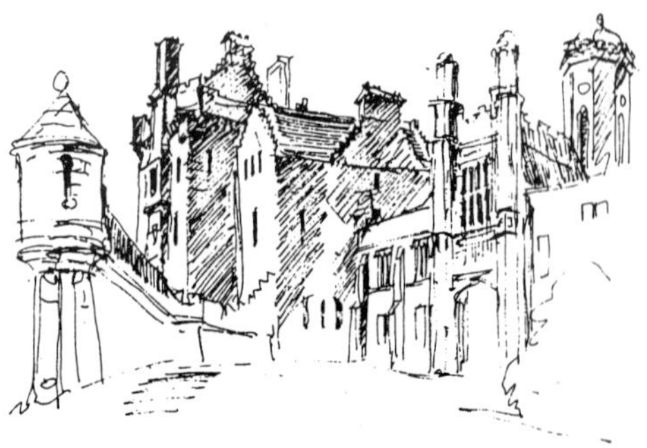

BELFAST

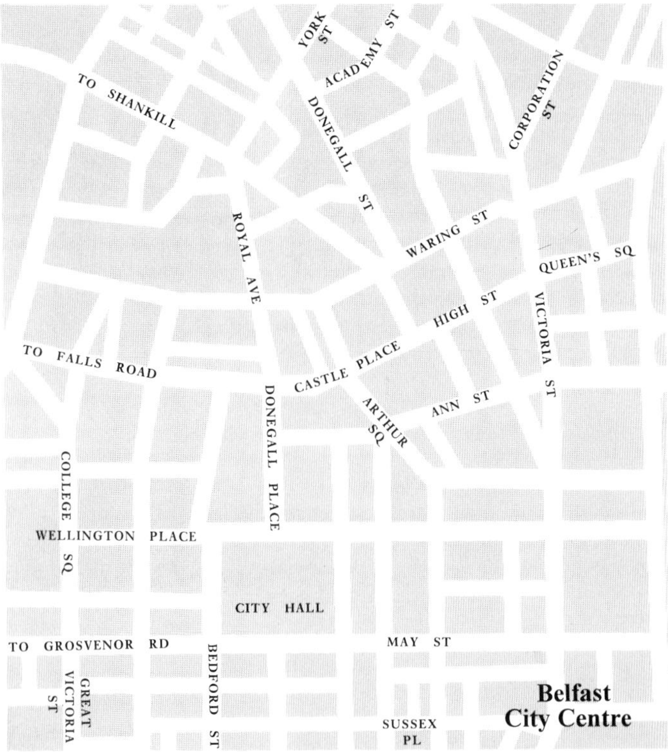

ACADEMY STREET: **Kirker, Greer & Co.**
Designed by Samuel Stevenson and built in 1899-1901, a late Gothic Revival warehouse in the Flemish style in red brick with a long façade broken up by two turreted pavilions either side of an orieled centrepiece.

ALFRED STREET: **St Malachy's Catholic Church**
The winning entry submitted by Thomas Jackson to a competition held in 1840. His solution was inspired by the rural galleried Catholic churches of his time with their unequalled ability to shelter the most people in the least space. The result is T-shaped with the three altars laid out in front of the longest wall. The height of the interior spanned by a spectacularly frothy fan vault, a plaster version of Henry VII's chapel in Westminster, with the high altar set into a later lacy triumphal arch—all this celebrates the return to a pre-Reformation Gothic before a new generation found such a style too frolicsome and irreverent. Internal fittings were replaced *c.*1930, when the interior was further embellished. The altar was recently set back into a top-lit recess beneath Piccione's reredos as a reaction against post-Vatican II excesses.

ALFRED STREET: **Nos. 19 & 20, Warehouse**
Five-storied warehouse by Dennis Hanna; built in 1911-12 in a severe neo-Elizabethan anticipating the functionalism of the post-war generation but with a saving sense of humour vented in zoomorphic carvings on stumpy columns.

ALBERT BRIDGE ROAD: **Mount Pottinger YMCA**
An inventive building by the English architect W.J.W. Roome, who had settled in Belfast at the start of the century. Double-storied oriels set into segmental arcades change their style to Gothic in the double-arched centrepiece.

ANN STREET: **Riddel's Warehouse**
Designed by Thomas Jackson and son; built in 1865-7. Four-storied arcaded palazzo in polychromatic brick and stone. As they rise the floors diminish in height with a subtly defined centrepiece at each level. Inner courtyard with glazed roof. Now disused.

ANTRIM ROAD: **Barnageehy**
Difficult now to discover in the grounds of St Patrick's School, this is Belfast's most striking example of the Greek Revival introduced into Glasgow by Alexander Thomson. However, this house of *c.*1866 lacked Thomson's refinement even before unsympathetic alterations replaced the first floor windows and removed the top of the lantern as well as the staircase. But the essentials remain of an asymmetrically massed neo-Classical villa with spreading eaves and distinctive chimneys; the colonnaded drawing-room bow is echoed by the circular tempietto on the roof.

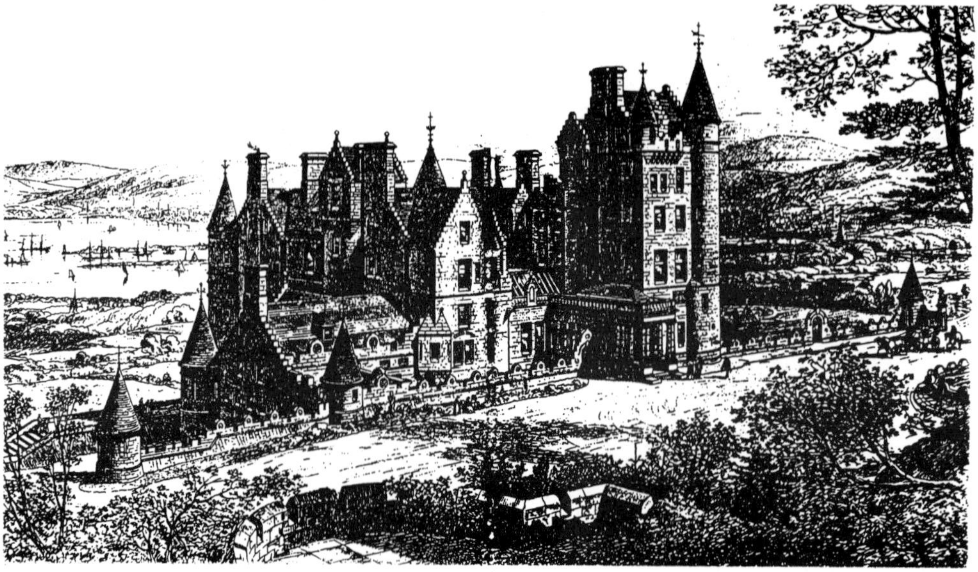

ANTRIM ROAD: **Belfast Castle**
This Scottish Baronial pile makes an effective silhouette against the mountainside when seen from afar, but from nearby pettiness of scale militates against a sense of grandeur, and the deployment of turrets and oriels appears merely gratuitous. Designed in 1865 by Lanyon, Lynn and Lanyon and built in 1868-70, the architect is said to be the young John Lanyon but so influenced by W.H. Lynn that their styles are indistinguishable. To prove that John Lanyon in his own right developed into an able if underestimated architect, one need look no further than his Jennymount mill extension in the valley that has so much more of a castle air than the self-consciously imposing seat of the marquises of Donegall. Thus it is tempting to ascribe the most spectacular feature of the castle, the twirling spiral staircase (added in 1894, to link the *piano nobile* to the garden terrace), to a more mature John Lanyon freed from the influence of Lynn. Since the castle was presented to Belfast City by the earl of Shaftesbury in 1937, the interiors have been trivialized into a series of function rooms, the grounds built over, the chapel vandalized and the turreted Strathmore Park gatelodge disconnected from the original demesne.

ANTRIM ROAD: **Belfast Castle Chapel**
Designed by Lanyon, Lynn and Lanyon; built in 1865-9 to enclose the finest Victorian memorial in Ireland (a white marble earl of Belfast who died in 1853, being mourned by his mother), carved by Patrick McDowell which has now found sanctuary in the City Hall. The fittings have been removed to St Peter's Church, Antrim Road. Four-bay apsidal interior now deconsecrated and vandalized.

ANTRIM ROAD: **Duncairn Presbyterian Church**
Designed by William Barre, who had the most varied church practice of his generation, this 1860 building was modelled on his church in Newry, the first Presbyterian church to have a tower and spire. Duncairn hung the first Presbyterian bell. Aisles, staircase tower, and organ chamber added by Young and McKenzie, 1871, 1884 and 1906 respectively. Galleried interior with hammerbeam roof. Barre's forceful manse survives with rear additions by Young and McKenzie, who pulled down his hall and replaced it with one of theirs in 1914.

ANTRIM ROAD: **St Malachy's College**
A Gothic Revival complex with central monastic range and adjoining classroom wing, part of the rebuilding to the designs of John O'Neill carried out in 1866-8. Adjoining spire and church not carried out as O'Neill intended when Mortimer Thompson got the commission in 1881.

ANTRIM ROAD: **St Peter's Church of Ireland**
Designed by S.P. Close and built in 1881. Exterior, conventional Gothic Revival. Richly decorated interior with traceried windows based on Irish medieval precedents. Altar of unglazed ceramic: 'The Women at the Open Sepulchre' by George Tinworth, who worked for Doultons. Fittings salvaged from Belfast Castle chapel. East window by Heaton, Butler and Bayne.

ARTHUR SQUARE: **Mayfair Building**
Designed by Blackwood and Jury and built in 1906. A lively corner block freely interpreting the Flemish Renaissance with Art Nouveau detailing. A delicate octagonal turret is nicely played off against a heavy pedimented gable.

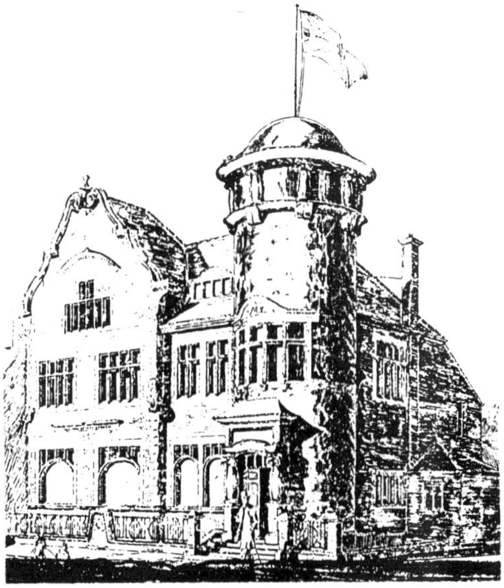

BALLYMACGARRET: **Public Library**
Designed by Blackwood and Jury and built in 1903 with a curious flat-topped corner tower that achieves individuality. Style described by contemporaries as 'a *mélange* of Tudor and Queen Anne'.

BEDFORD STREET: **Ulster Hall**
The first major success of William Barre was to win the competition with a more elaborate design than what was built (1859-62). While Barre was happier in Gothic, this hall shows his mastery of the classical language as exemplified by the Non-Conformist churches of the time. Corinthian pilasters articulate arched windows transformed into arched recesses at the rounded corners. Beneath them, galleries rest on cast-iron columns. Pride of place goes to the immense organ donated by Andrew Mulholland and restored by the 4th Lord Dunleath, his descendant, to take advantage of the superlative acoustics.

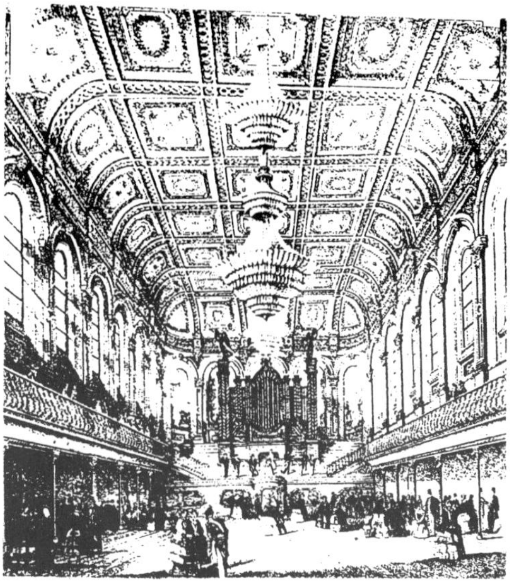

BEDFORD STREET: **Bryson House**
Designed by William Barre, built in 1867, a three-storied Italianate Gothic palazzo, in red brick with stone enrichments. Flush façades disrupted by sculptural doorways and corbelled chimneys.

BEDFORD STREET: **Ewart's Warehouse**
Designed in a rich Glasgow Venetian style by the Glasgow architect James Hamilton and built in 1869. Corner entrance into circular hall marked at roof level four floors above by domed tempietto clasped by twin belvederes on either side.

BELMONT ROAD: **Belmont School**
Designed by Vincent Craig and built in 1890-2. Craig gives proof of his individuality by his belfry, a pyramidial spire raised on an open timber lantern. Adjoining double-storied gabled block extended in 1910 by Thomas Houston.

BELMONT ROAD: **Campbell College**
The most famous public school in the Belfast region, designed in a freely treated Tudor Revival by W.H. Lynn late in his career and built in 1892-4. The epicentre is a five-storied tower with dormered spire. The adjoining ranges are of varied heights. The grandest interior is a galleried assembly hall roofed with hammer-beamed trusses. Here is the First World War Memorial by James Reid Young with sculptures by Rosamond Praeger.

BELMONT ROAD: **Presbyterian Church**
Church designed originally by William Barre and built in 1860-1; south aisle and transept by Anthony Jackson, 1873; north aisle and transept by Young and Mackenzie, 1887. Nave extended and roof timbers enriched by Vincent Craig, who added the pinnacled tower in 1898-1900.

BOTANIC AVENUE: **Union Theological College**
Competition won by Charles Lanyon and built in 1852-3 in his characteristically uninhibited improvization based secondhand on Italian Manneristic architecture, given strength and

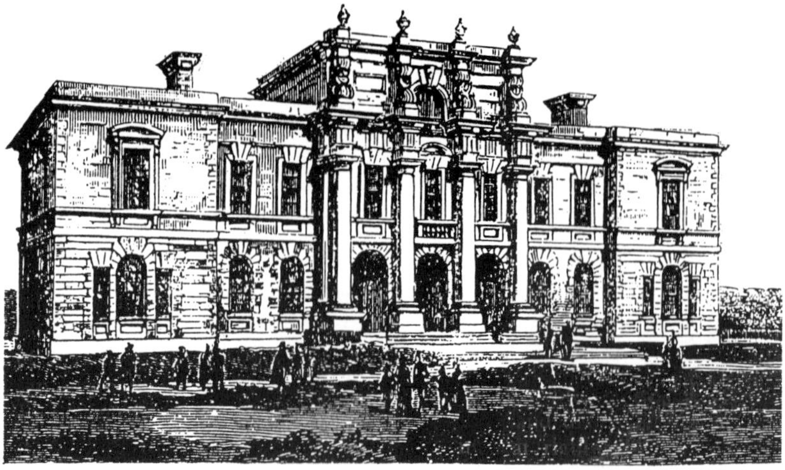

variety by his surface manipulation of Scrabo sandstone. Triple-bay centrepiece articulated by attached giant Tuscan columns upholding scrolls and urns. Vaulted porch, twin-columned entrance hall and imperial staircase leading to first-floor library subdivided by Corinthian colonnades. Enclosed courtyard at rear, with southern wing by Young and Mackenzie (1868-9) and northern wing enclosing a quirkily detailed chapel by John Lanyon (1878).

BOTANIC GARDENS: **Palm House**
Designed by Charles Lanyon and constructed in 1839-40 by Richard Turner of Dublin, predating his other public conservatories (Glasnevin dates from 1842). Lanyon intended that the twin curvilinear ranges constructed first should link three tentatively designed pavilions; but of these only the central one was built (in 1852) and to a more assured design: curvilinear to the extreme of bulbousness and constructed by an Edinburgh firm called Young, who have not been entirely successful in linking their work to Turner's wings. Renovated in 1983 using mild steel to replace decayed wrought iron. The reaction in botanical circles against curvilinears is demonstrated by the nearby pitch-roofed Tropical Ravine House (built in 1886, extended in 1900, saved at the eleventh hour in 1980).

CARLISLE CIRCUS: **Methodist Church**
Named after both Lord Carlisle (the amiable viceroy who showered the populace with teacakes and was recalled insane) and the hard-headed Belfast builder, James Carlisle, who lost his son and who built this church in his memory. His architect was W.H. Lynn, who appears to have chosen a funereal red sandstone—a grim, vast, Gothic Revival church dominated by a restless, cluttered spire, called by Charles Brett the ugliest church in Belfast. Adjoining cloister and schools by J.H. Philips dated 1980. Complex now disused like St Enoch's across the street, making what had been the most impressive approach to the inner city now the most melancholy.

CARLISLE CIRCUS: **St Enoch's Presbyterian Church**
Ironically the only double-galleried churches in Ireland were both built and both destroyed within years of each other. St Enoch's was designed by Anthony Jackson, built in 1870-2 and burnt out in 1985, five years before its

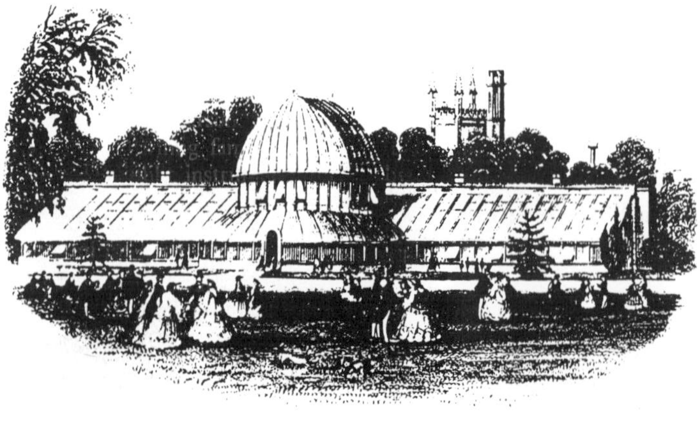

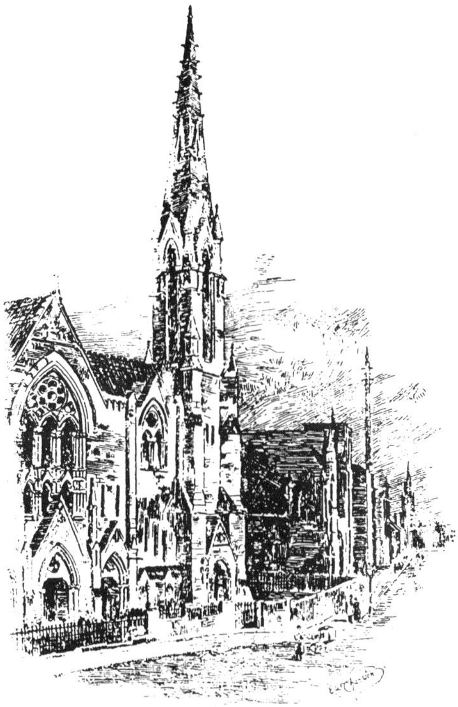

Dublin counterpart, Merrion Hall. The only external evidence of its gutted state is the loss of its pinnacled spire, but the four great portals opening on to the Circus remain firmly shut.

CASTLE PLACE: **Bank Buildings**
A late design by W.H. Lynn, uneasily adapting his Classicism to current American trends—a cast-iron structure clad in red Dumfries stone with granite Corinthian double-height columns, the one above the entrance being arbitrarily omitted. The pedimented electric clock by Sharman Neill appears added as an afterthought.

CASTLE PLACE: **Castle Buildings**
Designed by one of the most adventurous architectural firms of Belfast, Blackwood and Jury. Built in 1904-5 and extended asymmetrically with a tower two years later. Executed in a composite stone made by Doultons of Lambeth to the detailed specification of Percy Jury with swirling fruits and foliage in spandrels, freizes and serpentine pediments. Glazing and internal fittings, once equally Art Nouveau, but since replaced unmourned. Contemporary critics even found the term Art Nouveau detestable.

CLIFTONVILLE ROAD: **Belfast Royal Academy**
Designed by Young and Mackenzie and built in 1878-80. Symmetrical Gothic Revival façade of Scrabo sandstone with entrance in central orieled tower, buttressed ranges on either side with gabled pavilions enlivened by circular corner staircase turrets that give the complex a Scottish Baronial air—more appropriate to studying the reason for the Fall than to painting Adam and Eve before they ate the forbidden fruit.

CLONARD GARDENS: **Redemptorist Church and Monastery**
Dramatically sited above the present Peace Line, the church takes up one wing of a three-sided courtyard, linked by a tower to the residential quarters of the monastery extension which is built out of red brick with sandstone dressings—four floors, topped by an attic in the dormered mansard. The church of 1908-11 was originally intended to be Romanesque but was built in a lavish if regressive Gothic. Surviving high altar and side altars designed by Henry Bergman CSSR and carved by Davis of Cork (the present author counselled their retention in 1977). The windows were to have been replaced by Gabriel Loire of Chartres, but since the earlier stained glass was not removed he devised symbolic mosaic wall decorations (1960-61). Architect, J.J. McDonnell (1898).

COLLEGE SQUARE EAST: **College of Technology**
The unfortunate decision was made in 1900 to commission a new quadrangle rather than complete Sir John Soane's ambitious Doric designs of 1809 (realized only in part due to financial stringencies), with the result that Samuel Stevenson's design (built in 1900-7) is a palatial affair half-concealing Soane's façade. Stevenson completely overshadows it with a triumphant display of the Ionic order deployed double-height and wrapped round reduced versions of the City Hall corner towers. Equally pompous interiors.

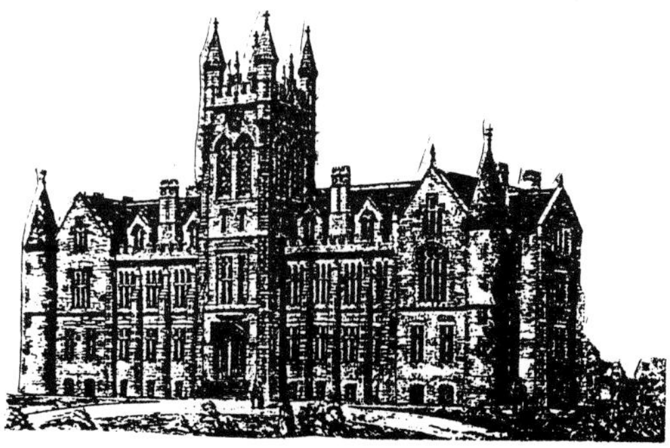

BELFAST ROYAL ACADEMY

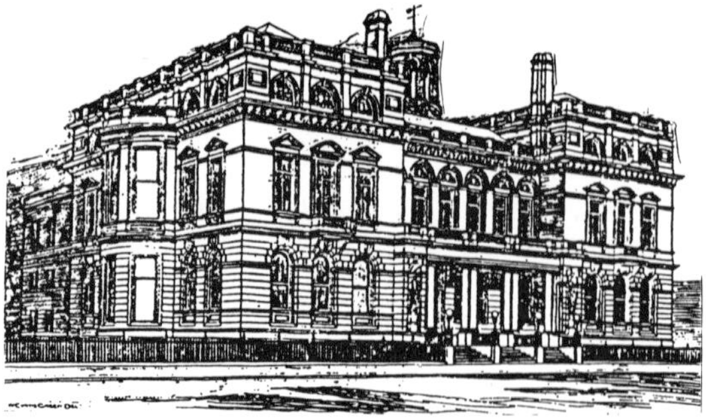

CORPORATION SQUARE: **Harbour Office**
Built in 1852-4 originally as a freestanding Renaissance palazzo to the designs of the engineer to the harbour commissioners, George Smith. Symmetrically enfolded by W.H. Lynn in 1891-5 using a more opulent idiom, with Ionic rather than the original Doric for his portico and an attic of arched lunettes to the *piano nobile*. Ceremonial sequence of interiors of both periods—vestibule with Coalbrokedale lamps, Corinthian columned staircase, leading up to the public hall; one of Lynn's most impressive spaces This is modelled on Sir Robert Taylor's Assembly Room, which Lynn was at that moment gutting, for the Northern Bank.

CORPORATION SQUARE: **Sinclair Seamen's Presbyterian Church**
Designed by Lanyon and Lynn; built in 1856-7. An L-shaped church brilliantly adapted to its corner site. On the corner itself a free-standing campanile linked dramatically by a flying staircase to the organ gallery of the church itself. The idiom is North Italian Romanesque, particularly effective in the campanile, where the unbroken shaft rises to a richly treated belfry. If Lynn had died at the same age as Woodward, their standing would be equal. The interior is celebrated for its furnishings added by the Revd Stanley Cochrane from 1902, starting with the pulpit projecting with a prow like a ship, to a binnacle installed in 1927 as a font. Port and starboard lanterns enliven the corner organ. Ship's bells and model anchors verge perilously close to the Stygian depths of superstition.

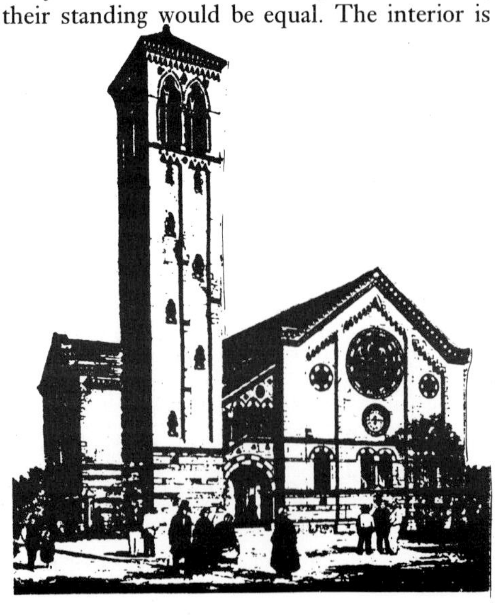

CRUMLIN ROAD: **County Courthouse**
Designed in 1848 also by Charles Lanyon to dramatically confront his earlier prison; now both are almost invisible due to temporary precautions. The courthouse has submitted to further indignities—a thoughtless extension programme in 1905 that filled in the original recesses on either side of the central portico and coated everything with stucco, subsequently garishly repainted. Least altered is the boldly projecting Corinthian hexastyle portico above impressive steps, its pediment surmounted by Joseph Kirk's statue of Justice.

CRUMLIN ROAD: **Former Edenderry Mill**
Designed by William Barre and built in 1865 as the largest linen mill of its time. Five floors of regular cambered fenestration set into load-bearing brick panels between boldly exposed floor slabs; their brutal simplicity anticipates 20th-century functionalism.

CRUMLIN ROAD: **Holycross Church and Monastery**
The monastic buildings here pre-date the adjoining church by twenty years. They were designed by O'Neill and Byrne and built in 1877-81 in an austere Romanesque Revival, its severity relieved only by an arcaded porch. The church, externally even more militantly Romanesque, was designed by Doolin, Butler and Donnelly but built by Butler in 1900-2 after Doolin's early death. Twin towered façade on the crest of the hill. Tympanum, 'The Descent from the Cross', carved by James Owens. Lavish interior where the exposed wall surfaces are covered with frescoes by a member of the order, Brother Mark, or with mosaics by J.F. Ebner of London, or with ceramics by Dunnill & Co. of Jackfield. Capitals carved by Thompson and Copeland. Neo-Renaissance pulpit and lady chapel to R.M. Butler's own designs.

CRUMLIN ROAD: **Mater Hospital**
A conventional design with administrative block leading to galleried chapel and flanked by twin blocks of wards which are unusual since their intended pitched roofs were replaced by Vulcanite and then developed into roof-top gardens with grass lawns (now gone) and gravelled walks for convalescents. Designed by William Fennell and executed in 1895-1900.

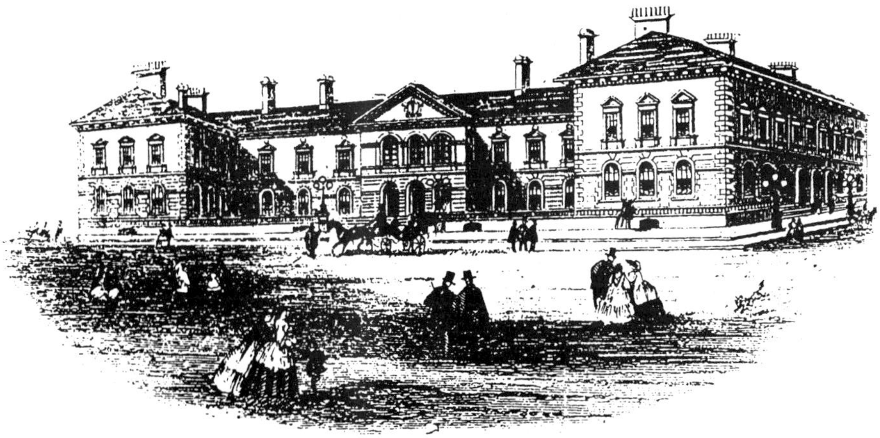

CRUMLIN ROAD: St Mary's Church of Ireland

This church, built in 1865-8, shares with Kilmore Cathedral (q.v.), the earlier Irish commisison of William Slater, a cruciform shape and a tower above the crossing; but otherwise they have little in common: the cathedral was built for a landlord on the perimeter of his demesne; this was built for a poor sector of Belfast. But constraints were a challenge to Slater, whose dream was to construct a series of cheap churches throughout the British Empire. Here his stonework has been gaily painted red and white like a barber pole. His most experimental feature, the iron roof trusses, were destroyed in the blitz. Their steel replacements are conventionally disguised.

CRUMLIN ROAD: St Paul's Convent of Mercy

Designed by J.J. McCarthy and built in 1855-9, his only Belfast commission. Four ranges round a central cloister. Three-storied façade with projecting gables giving a pronounced vertical feeling. Built of red brick with blue brick relieving arches and sandstone dressings. A later chapel by T.J. O'Neill (1909) has been recently demolished.

CRUMLIN ROAD: The Prison

Designed by Charles Lanyon, built in 1843-4 and 1849-50. Modelled on the Pentonville Road prototype. Four long ranges radiate from a central hall with the governor's house (now sandbagged against explosions) projecting out beyond the walls like the fortress of a North Italian Renaissance princeling; rusticated Scottish sandstone window surrounds contrast with walls of local basalt. A recessed semi-Tuscan portico imparts a forbidding air to all who enter there.

CUSTOM HOUSE QUAY: Customs House

Charles Lanyon's quayside palazzo is the first of his public buildings to express Belfast's new-found assurance and prosperity. Unlike Dublin, the interiors are still intact, serving their original purpose and still linked directly to the port. It was built in 1854-7 out of Glasgow freestone round three sides of a raised forecourt facing inland and reached by a shallow flight of steps. The two wings are treated asymmetrically, the office wing accommodating three floors over basement, the stateroom wing a storey less to fit a lofty *piano nobile* that extends the full length of the central link. Triple arches on coupled Corinthian columns mark the centrepieces of both fronts, but that to the river is the more richly carved (by Thomas Fitzpatrick to the designs of S.F. Lynn—angels in the spandrels of the arches, Britannia between two sportive sea gods, Nepture and Mercury, within the pediment). Riverine heads following a hallowed tradition are the keystones in the lower floor.

Nearby, the elegant neo-Classical Calder fountain was erected in 1854-7 by George Smith to the memory of Commander Caldwell, the founder of the Belfast RSPCA—an elliptical stone drum diagonally articulated by elongated scrolls.

DERBY STREET NORTH: Jennymount Mill

The earliest industrial building here dates from 1856, extended in 1864 by a two-storied office block with busts of writers and scientists forming the keystones of each arched window. Then in 1891 John Lanyon built his massive seven-storied extension, with sharply battered base and strongly articulated upper floors sprouting corner flues and a spiral staircase tower. One of a select group of industrial buildings that rival in fantasy the fortresses of feudal times.

DONEGALL PLACE: Queen's Arcade
Glazed shopping arcade designed by James McKinnon in 1880, linking Donegall Place to Fountain Street. Galleries giving access to arched windows at mezzanine level. Now much altered.

DONEGALL SQUARE: Belfast City Hall
The most imposing example of imperial architecture in Ireland, a secular version of St Paul's complete with dome and in this case four corner towers, pedimented centrepiece on each façade, the grandest with a temple-like *porte-cochère*, a backdrop to a voluminous Victoria, Queen and Empress, sculpted by Sir Thomas Brock. Started five years before she died with a competition held in 1896, finished five years after her death in 1906 and paid for by a tax on the urban gas supply. The successful architect was Alfred Bromwell Thomas from London, suitably knighted on its completion. He was the town hall architect par excellence in an age when town halls had replaced both houses and churches as symbols of a self-confidence that failed to survive the carnage of the First World War.

Each façade is treated differently. The dome dominates the entrance front to the north of two floors. The adjoining front to the east, also two-storied with the great hall stretching along the *piano nobile*, has its ceremonial entrance sheltered by a tempietto borrowed from Gibb's St Mary le Strand. The southern façade robustly expresses three floors of offices with a five-bay, colonnaded, pedimented centrepiece above an archway to the courtyard. The west façade is identical to the south but for the centrepiece of three bays, not five. The Ionic order is used throughout, indeed to the point of satiation in the north façade where it is deployed on six different scales. Amid all the opulence the colossal sculptural set-piece framed by the pediment ('Hibernia bearing the torch of knowledge, encouraging and promoting the commerce and arts of the city' by F.W. Pomeroy of London assisted by J.E. Winter) strikes a note of impending doom, a line-up to the launch of the *Titanic*.

Inside, Thomas grapples with the age-old problem of making the dome as impressive within as without. His precedent is St Paul's with its double dome and whispering gallery but here balanced on four rather than eight arches. Thomas also provides a preview of his dome at the expense of the *piano nobile* by inserting an open well, lighting the ground-floor vestibule. Beyond, an imperial marble staircase. The staterooms are entered through Ionic screens of Greek Cippalino marble; Italian marbles elsewhere, sculpted by Farmer and Brindley of London; plasterwork by Rome of Glasgow. The excellent stained glass is by Ward; leadwork by Campbell; and joinery by Purdy and Millard—all local firms. Grinling Gibbons is the inevitable model for the embellishment of the lord mayor's throne. There is only one major fresco, that by John Luke (1951) below the dome. But the finest work of art is still Patrick McDowell's memorial to the earl of Belfast, moved to a vestibule off the entrance hall from the chapel of Belfast Castle.

The finest of the numerous memorials in the grounds is that raised to the 1st marquis of Dufferin and Ava, sheltering in an Ionic pavilion to the designs of Thomas, and sculpted in bronze by F.W. Pomeroy in 1906 along with bronzes of Canada and India that weep on either side. Brock was responsible for Queen Victoria between Spinning and Shipbuilding and also the Titanic Memorial. The Boer War memorial was modelled by Sidney March and cast by Elkington in 1905. Thomas himself designed the First War Memorial in 1925, a crescent forming a fake ruin that one feels it would be sacrilegious to describe as witty. Indeed the real reason that this is the only significant commission of his last forty years, may well be that, unlike Wren, Hawksmoor or Lutyens, he had not one shred of humour. He died in 1948, long after his generation had decided to stop building great civic monuments and pay less rates. Today, rare occasions do it justice, like a recent ball graced by the queen of Romania designated to stand in for an absent film star.

DONEGALL SQUARE NORTH: Linen Hall Library
Originally designed by Lanyon, Lynn and Lanyon in 1864 for linen manufacturers Moore and Weinbert in a restrained Classical manner, carefully adapted for its present use as a library by Young and Mackenzie in 1896, so carefully that it has needed minimum alterations ever since. Has played a pivotal role in the intellectual life of the city.

DONEGALL SQUARE EAST: Methodist Church
Designed by Isaac Farrell in 1846; interior gutted by fire four years later and subsequently rebuilt. Imposing six-columned Corinthian portico with steps leading up through rusticated arcade and vaulted lobby.

DONEGALL SQUARE EAST: Ocean Buildings
The last of the commercial headquarters designed by Young and Mackenzie; built in 1899–1902, where they reverted to their earlier Gothic

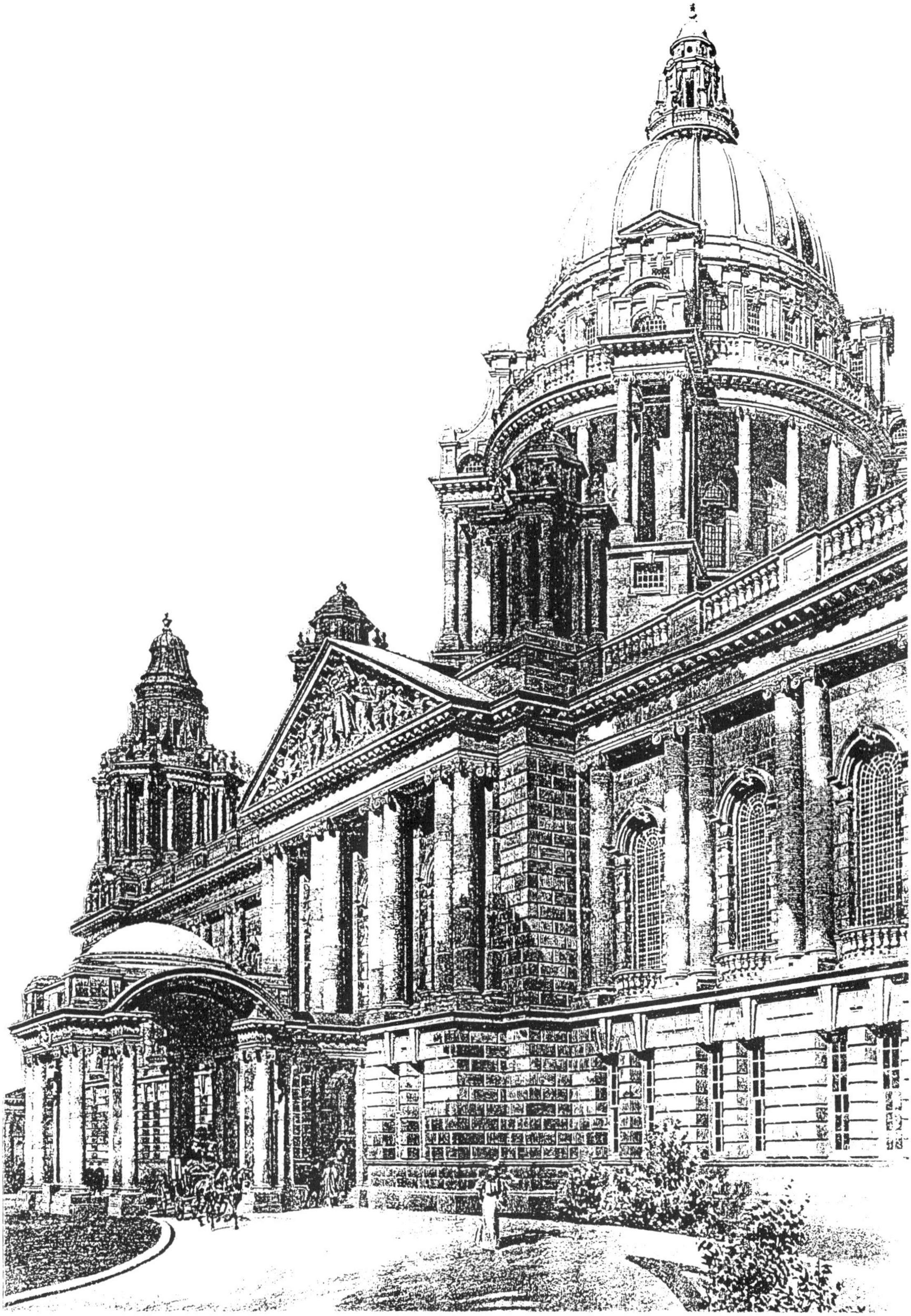

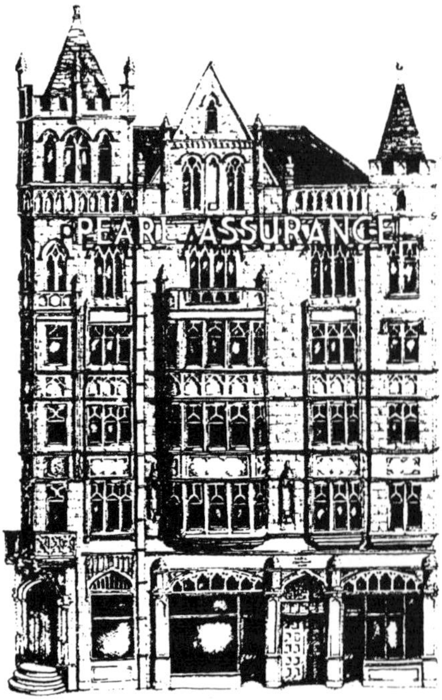

Revival manner. Asymmetrical elevations in red sandstone treated with a certain nerveless refinement. Pinnacled corner tower with a suspended triple-tiered corner oriel. Good animal sculpture by James Edgar Winter.

DONEGALL SQUARE NORTH: **Richardson's**

An impressive Gothic Revival warehouse designed by W.H. Lynn and built in 1867-9. Four floors high with a once-dormered roof broken up by massive chimneys now destroyed. Fenestration gathered over the central doorway in the Venetian manner. Roundels in the spandrels enlivened by lions. Interiors were gutted in the blitz of 1941 and recently internally remodelled yet again by Scott, Tallon, Walker.

DONEGALL SQUARE NORTH: **Former Robinson and Cleaver Store**

One of the most prominently sited buildings in the city; six stories high with curved corners rising to free-standing tempiettos crowned with ogee domes. Designed by Young and Mackenzie and built in 1884-5 with a flurry of decorative carving by Harry Hems of Exeter, for once liberated from Gothic replication, balconies borne by infants, fruit imported across the world, symbolic continents and busts of Queen Victoria between her late husband and her empire's most distinguished rebel, General George Washington and other celebrities. Palatial internal marble staircase removed to Ballyedmond, Co. Down (q.v.) when the building was revamped by its new owners.

DONEGALL SQUARE NORTH: **Scottish Provident**

An equally spectacular response to Robinson and Cleaver's (built by the same architects, Young and Mackenzie, a decade earlier across the square). There are differences with the introduction of the neo-Baroque, here expressed by the three upper floors tied together by a gigantic composite order raised on enriched pedestals and projecting forward in a curved centrepiece emphasized by coupled columns; this is crowned by a pedimented pavilion played off against the domed corner octagonal towers. Stone-carvings by Purdy and Millard of personalized colonies and plaques depicting the city's staple economic activities. Built in two stages, the Wellington Place block in 1897, the remainder in 1899.

DONEGALL STREET: **Church of Ireland Cathedral**

Belfast commisioned two civic monuments in the same year (1896). While the city hall was completed within a decade the cathedral remains unfinished, beset by financial delays and architectural revisions made easier by the choice of Romanesque. Thomas Drew, who received the commission, had designed a Gothic scheme but was talked into the Romanesque by his consultant and successor, W.H. Lynn. Lynn kept to Drew's intentions, but since his death in 1915 subsequent architects have tried to diverge

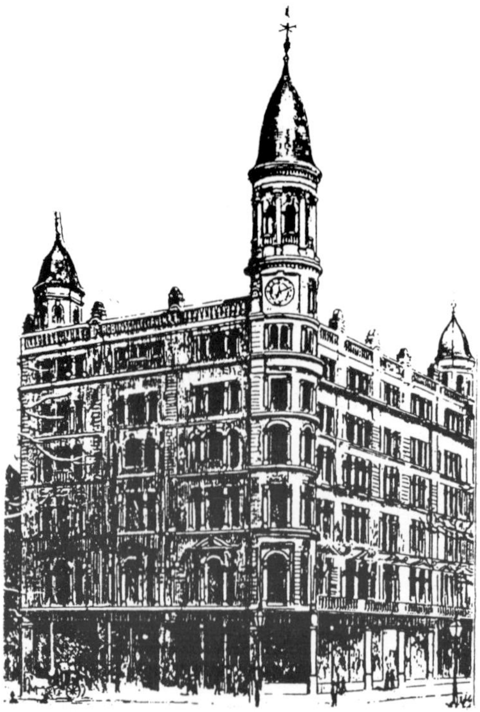

ROBINSON & CLEAVER

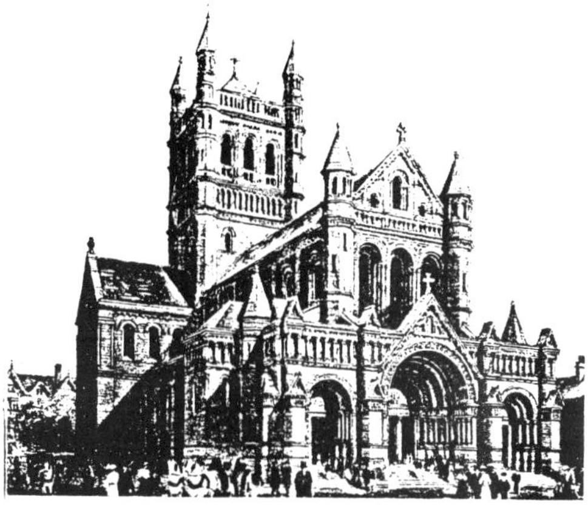

(fortunately beyond the scope of this volume). The pulpit designed by Gilbert Scott for Westminster Abbey was gratefully received by one architect to be dispatched to the United States by his successor, sinking in the sea en route. Today the finest portions are Drew's majestic nave (consecrated in 1904) and Lynn's apsidal baptistery with its posthumous decoration. Drew's façade, central tower and square chancel have all been set aside—ironically, since Drew himself had scant respect for the masterpieces of other architects, being quite happy to mutilate Gandon at the Coolbanagher Church of Ireland (q.v.).

DONEGALL STREET: *Newsletter* **Offices**

Three-storied beneath a central turret flanked by double dormers. Below two rows of Gothic arcading articulated by granite colonettes that reoccur as columns to subdivide the large trabeated bays opening directly on to the street. Medallions of celebrities in the spandrels of the *piano nobile*. Built in 1872-4 to the designs of William Hastings.

DONEGALL STREET: **St Patrick's Catholic Church**

Designed by Timothy Hevey and built in 1874-7 with the assistance of Mortimer Thompson. Façade inspired by Edward Pugin's Augustinian Church in Dublin (q.v.), boldly expressing the inner volume of the nave by a deeply recessed arch (here enclosing portal, arcades and plate traceried rose). Astride this arch he positions a pinnacled steeple ingeniously given lateral strength by paired pinnacles on either side at a lower level. The statue of St Patrick above the door was carved by Neill and Pearse, who also carved the high altar that still dominates the cavernous interior. St Patrick reappears in an altarpiece by Sir John Lavery originally inset in an altar designed in 1919 by Sir Edward Lutyens, now vanished.

EGLANTINE AVENUE: **St Thomas' Church of Ireland**

Impressive High Victorian Gothic Revival church designed by John Lanyon in 1845. Bold external polychromy with red and white sandstone, with red marble introduced into the belfry colonnettes and red marble disks inserted into the spire. Glass by Heaton, Butler and Bayne. Rectory added in polychromatic brickwork.

ELMWOOD AVENUE: **All Saints**

Designed by a London architect, Walter Planck, and built in 1895-6 out of Scrabo stone with Doulton dressings. Tower short and with finely worked detail. Arts and Crafts interior with continuous vaulting lit by large windows at either end. Memorial board by Charles Braithwaite, 1908, the year W.J. Gilliland designed the adjoining hall.

FALLS ROAD: **No. 193, The Beehive**

The lower floor and the pub itself have been badly mutilated, but the boldly modelled upper floors survive, sporting the beehive that gave this pub its name. Architect unknown. Date *c.*1890.

FALLS ROAD: **Belfast Cemetery**

Laid out in 1866-9 by William Gay of Bradford, who imported cast-iron fountains from George Smith of Glasgow. Tombs include two rarities —the Egyptian Revival Herdman memorial dating from the 1870s and the Art Nouveau Carson memorial dating from 1905. Several

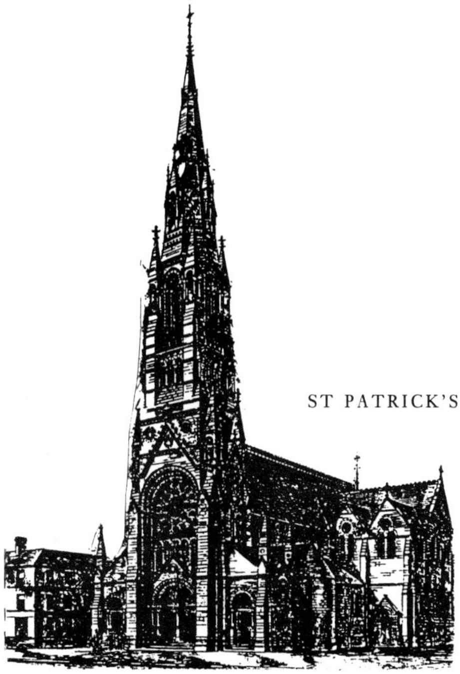

ST PATRICK'S

architects are also buried here, most having chosen Gothic Revival. W.H. Lynn designed his own tomb *c.*1876, forty years before his death. The Phillips family erected a memorial cross to themselves in 1882. The best tomb of the early part of this century is the Inglis memorial with delicate allegorial bas reliefs contrasting with Art Nouveau corner colonettes of uprooted trees; attributed by Larmour to Rosamond Praeger.

FALLS ROAD: **Carnegie Library**

In 1905 a competition was held for three Carnegie libraries donated to the city; limited to thirty local practices it was won by Watt and Tulloch, who here adapted the neo-Georgian. There are details that are Art Nouveau, including the scroll-bearing angels in the entry arches by Rosamond Praeger, who also cast the bronze figurative doors, now replaced by fibreglass replicas. Here Helen Mirren was employed in the firm *Cal* as a librarian, daughter of an Italian ice-cream maker and married to a murdered member of the UDR.

FALLS ROAD: **Dunville Fountain**

The centrepiece of a park commissioned by distiller Robert Dunville in 1892 and then presented to the public, who have subsequently treated his munificence with indifference, so that this immense ceramic fountain has been partly vandalized and disused for many years. Attributed by Larmour to A.E. Pearse, the chief designer of Doultons in Lambeth.

FALLS ROAD: **Milltown Cemetery Entrance Gates**

Designed by Timothy Hevey in a chunky Romanesque and erected in 1869-70. Central triumphal arch with arcaded and pinnacled sweeps. Varied repertoire of different coloured stonework. Hevey designed the inaugural memorial in the cemetery itself, a cross aligned to the entrance arch. The most imposing memorial is the pinnacled, traceried Matthew Bowen tomb dated 1876.

FALLS ROAD: **St Mary's Dominican Convent**

Symmetrical façade with three floors of round-arched fenestration on a raised basement in polychromatic brick work; steps up to a Romanesque porch. Designed by John O'Neill and built in 1868-70. Interior contains stained glass by Evie Hone. The neo-Gothic chapel of 1926 by Padraic Gregory falls outside the scope of this book.

FISHERWICK PLACE: **Presbyterian Assembly Buildings**

Robert Young was given this commission after he had been asked to organize a competition with an unrealistic budget which he had set himself but with which no competitor could comply. He then went on to exceed the estimate by more than double. The Presbyterians got a grimly impressive complex, gabled, turreted and pinnacled, dominated by a corner tower (appropriately inspired by St Giles' in Edinburgh) with one of Sharman Neil's ingenious clocks. External sculpture by Purdy and Millard with door surrounds by J.E. Winter, who also carved John Knox within. Art Nouveau makes an unexpected appearance. An external hint is the Celtic Revival decoration in the spandrels, but the coloured glass rooflight above the double-tiered, double-apsed assembly hall with floral patterns executed by Ward and Partners comes as a shock to those sedated by traditionalism. Built 1900-5.

FORTWILLIAM PARK: **Gateways**

Two triumphal approaches (on Antrim Road and Shore Road) to a select residential park—the earliest on the Antrim Road, to the design of William Barre and erected in 1864. Today the gates on the Antrim Road have been removed as has their central cast-iron pier, but the paired stone arcaded piers and small gate-lodge survive. The other approach from Shore Road dates from 1870, a pair of triumphal arches again deprived of their ironwork. The most likely architect is James Hamilton, who built a house within the park (now demolished) and who reveals in his Ulster Bank (q.v.) the same top-heavy Classicism.

FORTWILLIAM PARK: **Presbyterian Church**

Designed by Henry Chappell of Newtownards and built in 1880-5. The church itself is raised up on the parochial hall so that imposing steps lead up to the triple porch, arcaded above and surmounted by a rose window. Façade flanked by polygonal staircase to gallery on one side and spiky steeple on the other. After all this external drama, one finds a restrained galleried interior abruptly focussed on the organ built across the chancel arch.

FORTWILLIAM PARK: **No. 38, Walton**

Built as a select private villa, now effortlessly transformed into a Dominican convent. Central tower over an arcaded porch flanked by symmetrical pavilions from which extend asymmetrically treated bay windows. Larmour attributes the house to James Hamilton and dates it to *c.*1865.

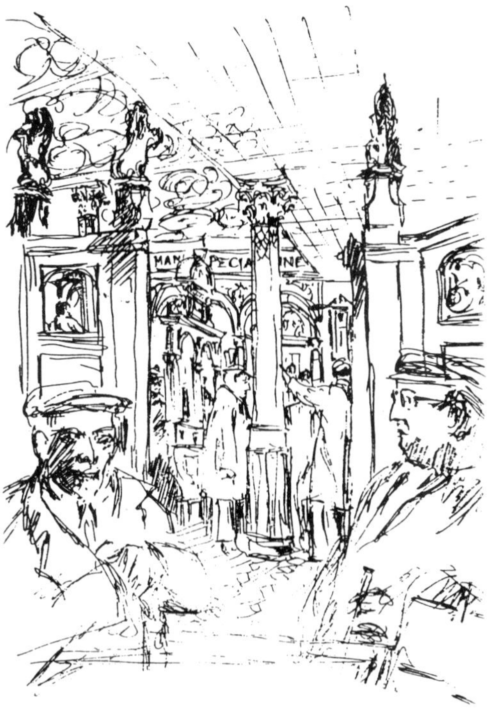

GREAT VICTORIA STREET: **Crown Bar**
Much-loved public house, proving that even in Belfast, royalty is acceptable if united to alcohol. The first licensed premises to be acquired by the National Trust, which is currently restoring the stained glass after damage from a blast nearby. The upper part, once an hotel, dates from 1839; the interior was remodelled by a local firm, E. and J. Byrne, in 1885, who thirteen years later re-cased the exterior in faience for the same proprietor, Patrick Flanagan. All the decorative arts are brought together—wood-carving, brass, ceramic and mosaic—to create an earthly paradise that closes nightly after final orders when heraldic beasts survey mere mortals cast into external darkness.

GREAT VICTORIA STREET: **Grand Opera House**
One of Belfast's best-loved buildings, designed by the veteran London theatre architect Frank Matcham and built in 1894-5. Eclectic exterior enlivened by onion-domed ventilators set into richly scrolled pediments. Interior celebrated for its elephant-head brackets that give an atmosphere of invincible jollity, even after bomb damage which led to a second restoration by Robert McKinstrey. Tiepoloesque ceiling paintings by his wife Cherith date from his first restoration. More bomb damage, May 1993.

GROSVENOR ROAD: **Former Mulhouse Works**
Thirty-one bays long and three floors high, the façade has carved keystones over each arched first-floor window—industrial architecture at its most eloquent, the design of an otherwise unknown William Waters and built in 1894-5.

GROSVENOR ROAD: **Royal Victoria Hospital**
Designed in 1900 by Henmam and Cooper, the Birmingham architects who were specialists in hospital design and innovators in air conditioning. The one-storied wards, set above a basement used for air ducts and opening on to balconies articulated by ventilation towers, had an international impact. Two much more conventional four-storied administrative blocks frame the entrance court supervised by a bronze Queen Victoria—the work of J.W. Rollins—once above the arch but now safer on the ground. Stained glass by W.J. Douglas working for Ward and Partners. Later additions by Young and Mackenzie.

HIGH STREET: **St George's Church of Ireland**
The portico John Bowden salvaged from the earl bishop's house at Ballyscullion and added to this church of 1811 does not prepare us for the richly trussed roof added by William Barre in 1867, one of his last works. He is commemorated by a stained-glass window. The pulpit is by him also. Pre-Raphaelite decoration to chancel added by Edward Braddell in 1882.

KNOCKBREDA CHURCHYARD: **Fitzpatrick Memorial**
Designed by William Barre *c.*1865 for the Ferguson family at the Balmoral Cemetery but moved here and re-erected to the Fitzpatrick family. Barre later adapted the design for his father's tomb in St Patrick's, Newry (q.v.).

LIGONIEL ROAD: **St Mark's Church of Ireland**
Gothic Revival parish church built in three different phases: firstly a small church of 1854 with adjoining steeple; designed by the office of Charles Lanyon. This church was remodelled as a transept when a new nave and chancel was built (1877-9) to the designs of W.H. Lynn. The nave was lengthened by J.J. Philips (1885-6) along with the northern transept. Philips was responsible for the furnishing and the now largely vanished internal decoration, but his stencilled dado, chancel rails, organ and font cover still survive.

LINFIELD STREET: **Murray's Tobacco Factory**
Designed by Watt and Tulloch, then built in 1900. The unusual oriental features with its corner pagoda towers and forceful eaves held up by corbelled brackets were added to Robert Watt's repertoire by his younger London partner, Frederick Tulloch, whose contribution anticipates Art Deco.

MALONE ROAD: **No. 149, Dallas**
The only Irish commission of Charles Voysey, built in 1911-12 for a linen merchant, Robert Hetherington. A sensible unassuming block with dormered third floor reached by attached staircase tower. The exterior depends simply on its informal fenestration setting up a delicate balance between void and solid. White walls without and within where they are played off against arched brick fireplaces.

MALONE ROAD: **Fisherwick Presbyterian Church**
Late Gothic Revival complex designed by S.P. Close and built in 1898-1901, in local sandstone. Slender western spire contrasting with chubby twin turrets serving as porches at the rear. The stained glass in the apse is by the Belfast firms of Ward and Douglas; elaborate two-light window by Swaine, Burne and Son of Birmingham.

MALONE ROAD: **Danesfort (NIE)**
After the loss of Roxborough Castle, this is now William Barre's most ambitious extant private house, built in 1864 for a linen tycoon, Samuel Barbour. A chateau-like arcaded tower is boldly sited over the corner bay of a *porte cochère* and linked back to the main house by a dramatically expressed service staircase and double-height

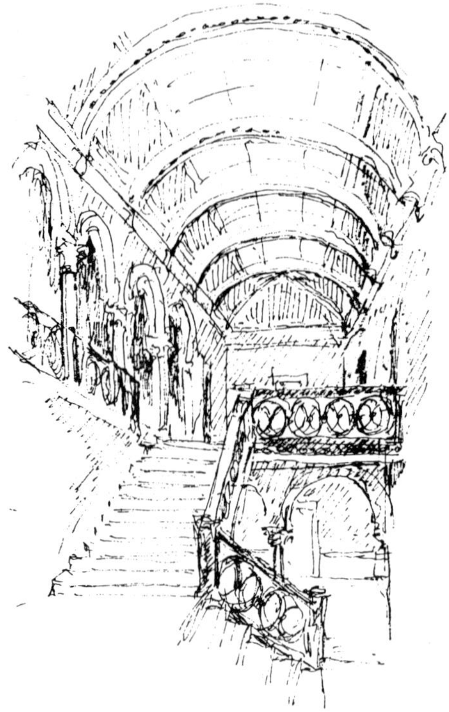

entrance hall. In contrast to this clotted dissonance, the principal reception rooms are simply expressed, with the drawingroom marked by an assertive colonnaded bow. Coupled colonettes articulate the curved bow of the master bedroom overhead. Well-defined foliated capitals and interlaced balustrading to the corbelled balconies. Now headquarters of Northern Ireland Electricity Board.

MALONE ROAD: **Methodist College**
Limited competition won by William Fogerty

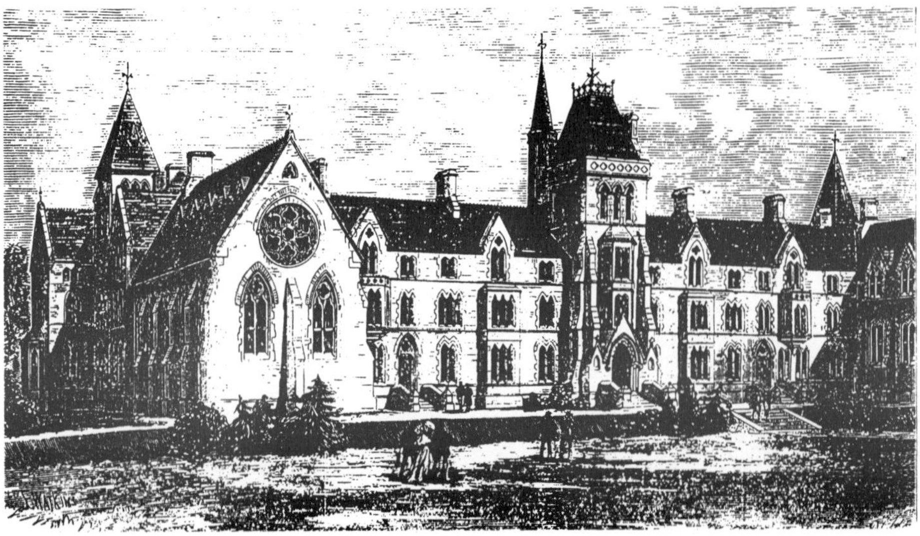

of Limerick which resulted in his largest commission, larger than his now demolished Methodist College in Dublin. Work started in 1865 and continued until 1871. Institutional Gothic Revival forming a reduced, slated, dormered version of Queen's University across the road but with two extra wings extending outwards to embrace a public forecourt. Interior with beamed dininghall, arched corridors and stone staircases. Gatelodge added in 1879 by John Lanyon.

MALONE ROAD: **St John's Church of Ireland**
Designed by Henry Seaver and built in two phases, chancel and transepts in 1893-5 and nave in 1905. Undemanding exterior with incomplete tower. Interior celebrated for its stained glass—five windows by Ward and Partners, three by Evie Hone (including the western rose), several windows by William McBride, some by Heaton, Butler and Bayne, a Catherine O'Brien of St Patrick, and the extraordinary early masterpiece of Wilhelmina Geddes, 'The Leaves of the Tree . . .'.

MAY STREET: **Clarence Place Hall**
Belfast never commissioned Deane and Woodward, but this is one of the few buildings that could have been designed by that firm. The architect was W.H. Lynn, who had personally been influenced by the writings of John Ruskin the decade before, as proved by his banks in Dungannon and Newtownards (q.v.). Larmour believes that the main influence is Street's *Brick and Marble Architecture in Italy*. Polychromatic banded and diapered brickwork creates strongly patterned voussoirs over the Gothic arches of the windows with their plate tracery and French casements opening behind slender colonettes; fretted cornice and shallow roof. Built in 1865. Recent award-winning conversion into auctioneering premises.

MAY STREET: **St George's Market**
See Oxford Street Fishmarket.

MYRTLEFIELD PARK: **No. 46, Haslemere**
Designed and built in 1905 by the London architect Frederick Tulloch as his own residence with a diagonally braced half-timbered bay clasped by two rough-cast gabled projections. Unusual chimneys with vertical strips of brickwork. Painted glass set into leaded lights in the ground floor windows.

OLD HOLYWOOD ROAD: **The Moat**
Red-brick villa enlivened with polychromatic stonework, designed by William Barre for Thomas Valentine, a Belfast linen tycoon. Double-storied with arcaded fenestration on both floors. Asymmetrical façades, garden front with double-height bow, adjoining entrance front with sumptuously sculpted stone loggia. Carving of birds, nests and snakes attributed by Larmour to the Fitzpatricks. Built in 1863-4.

ORMEAU AVENUE: **Thompson Memorial**
Erected in 1884-5 by an unknown designer. Crocketted and pinnacled octagonal shrine inspired by the Cross of Eleanor.

ORMEAU ROAD: **Ballynafeigh Methodist Church**
Alfred Forman's masterpiece, built in 1897-9. Despite the loss of pinnacles, a fleche and an extraordinary spire more appropriate to the suburbs of Moscow than to those of Belfast, one can still relish his melange of style and geometry, shoe-horning an oblong nave into a radiating octagon. One of the last quasi-religious, quasi-communal complexes built by the Non-Conformists in Belfast; but whereas an earlier generation would have achieved coherence and given to the secular appendages an ecclesiastical treatment, Forman reverses that trend. He domesticates the architecture of his church to match the adjoining hall. The squat

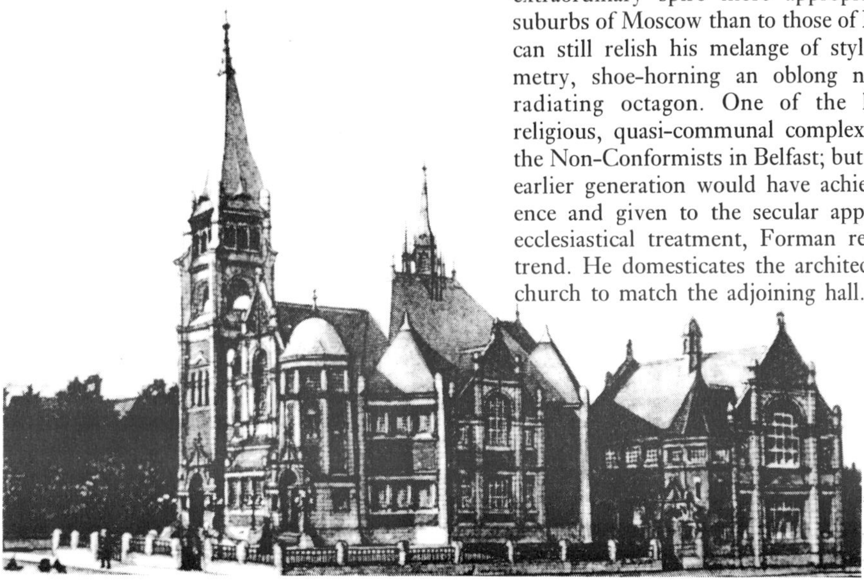

tempietto over the stairs to the organ gallery reappears in his own office block on the Londonderry Diamond (q.v.). His interior has survived unspoilt, full of 'Sweetness and Light' with an open roof structure resting on slender columns and a theatrical gallery wrapped round three sides of the central space, termed by his bemused contemporaries as an adaption of American Romanesque.

ORMEAU ROAD: **Gas Works Offices**
Long, red-brick range with decorative unglazed terracotta panels dominated by a punchy circular clocktower with a now altered lantern. Designed by Robert Watt in 1887-8. Lavish internal staircase ascending to boardroom with decoratively compartmented ceiling upheld by Corinthian ceramic pilasters. Ceramic also introduced to the friezes, pediments, dadoes and balusters of the landing. Staircase of carved oak. Declared by Sir John Betjeman to be his favourite interior in the city.

ORMEAU ROAD: **St Jude's Church of Ireland**
Designed by Thomas Drew in 1869, built in 1871-3 and then twice extended by him, in 1889 and 1898. The contractors were the Fitzpatrick brothers, who donated the site and paid for its most distinctive feature, a round tower with an Italianate belvedere surmounting a Celtic Revival shaft.

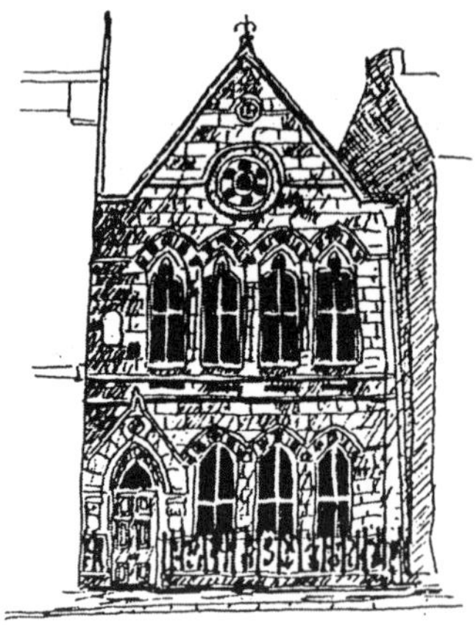

OXFORD STREET: **St Malachy's School**
A bouncy Gothic Revival school designed by Alexander McAlister, an architect converted to Catholicism. Built by the Christian Brothers in 1896. Two floors of glazed arcades with striped voussoirs; off-centre hexafoil in the gable above.

OXFORD STREET: **Fish Market**
This and St George's Market, May Street, are adjoining market complexes, both designed by J.C. Bretland and both completed in 1896. Triumphal arched entrances inset into Classical screens that protect light, functional interiors upheld on cast-iron columns made by Ritchie, Hart & Co., a local firm.

PRINCE'S DOCK STREET: **St Joseph's Catholic Church**
Again designed by Timothy Hevey and built with the assistance of Mortimer Thompson in 1878-80, although here Hevey died before work could start. As in his St Patrick's, Donegall Street, he balanced a symmetrical steeple on wider façade below with a daring absence of connecting vertical elements. Here his lateral support is provided by coupled flying buttresses. Timber barrel-vaulted interior framing a rose window above the altar. Corbelled saints by John Loughlin. Parochial house by Mortimer Thompson, 1879.

QUEEN'S SQUARE: **Albert Memorial**
The last of the major competitions won by William Barre, beating his rivals Lanyon, Lynn and Lanyon in 1865. He died prematurely in 1867, two years before its completion. Incorrect foundations has caused its present inclination and led to a discreet lightening of the load: part of the topmost shrine was removed in 1879, and the Prince Consort as sculpted by S.F. Lynn has since lost the protection of a heavy stone canopy later deemed too dangerous. However, the clock modelled on Big Ben still attests to the skill of its maker, Francis Moore of High Street.

RAVENHILL AVENUE: **Co-Op Bakery**
Four-storied warehouse with ground floor and top floor arcaded. Porch of banded brick and stone counterbalanced by canted tower at the further end of the façade. Designed by W.J. Gilliland in 1904 and extended twice in the 1920s.

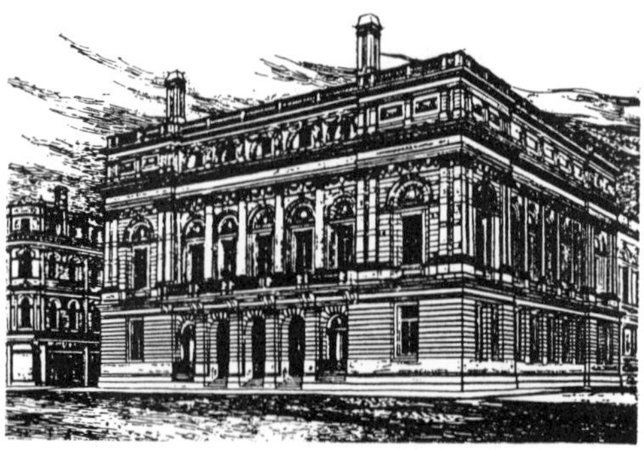

ROYAL AVENUE: **Central Library**
Designed by W.H. Lynn after winning a competition in 1883, and completed in 1888. Inspired by the Louis XVI style, if a trifle self-

consciously. Horizontally rusticated ground floor, Corinthian *piano nobile* and garlanded attic. Inside, ceremonial stairs ascend to central domed and columned reading room. Staircase balustrade by Brown & Co. of Birmingham.

ROYAL AVENUE: **First Trust Bank**
One of William Barre's last buildings (1864-9), a Provincial Bank completed posthumously by Turner and Williamson, and one of his more successful attempts to spice Classicism with Gothic. Here the seven-bay front follows Palladian prototypes accented by lively sculpture that should have filled the pediment if the full programme had been carried out. Internally the same sculptor (Barnes) carved emblematic dwarfs upholding the pendentives of a central circular dome. This hovers between robust arcades following Byzantine precedents, but with Barre asserting his individuality by resting the drum on stubby corbelled columns (a favourite device of his). These support an unexpectedly delicate Gothic gallery interpenetrating the dome that rises to an oculus framing a horizontally positioned stained-glass rose window. No one else in Ireland took such stylistic liberties.

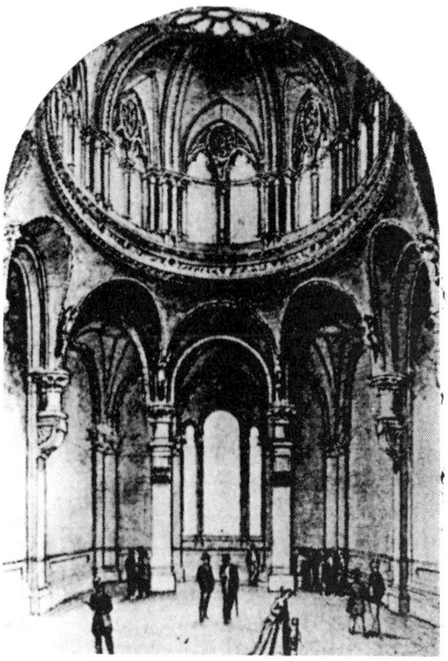

ROYAL AVENUE: **Former Gresham Life Office**
Rich, red terracotta façade with barley-sugar colonettes; windows arched with quatrefoils in the *piano nobile*; shallow segmental arches span the windows of the three floors above. The original firm's name immortalized in the frieze. Built to the designs of William Gilliland in 1887.

ROYAL AVENUE: **Reform Club**
Designed by the Manchester architects Maxwell and Tuke and built in 1883-5. Three storeys with entrance into rounded corner, marked at roof level by circular tempietto. The building survives but no longer as a political club.

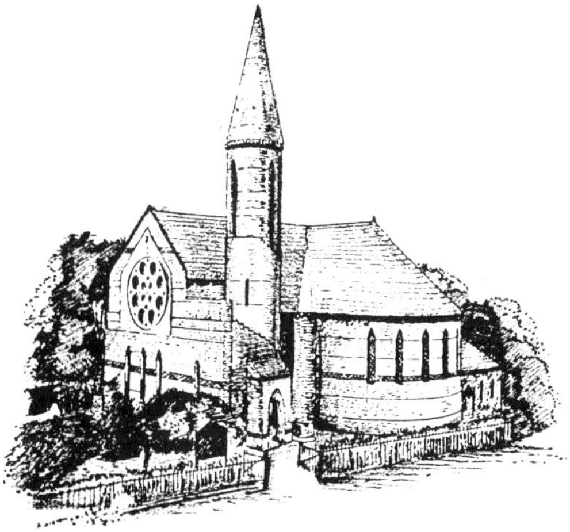

SHANKILL ROAD: **St Matthew's Church of Ireland**
No other Irish Victorian church anticipates with more conviction the values of current religious architecture. Nor is there any counterpart in the considerable output of its architects, Welland and Gillespie. However, St Matthew's (1870-2) comes at the end of a series of rural Gothic churches protesting against Disestablishment with heroic grandeur on a tiny scale. This is an urban church that looks to a classless future, not to a hieratic past. There are echoes in the exterior of Ballyeglish (q.v.) with the round tower expressing its inner staircase by spiralling brickwork, but here polychromatic brickwork is used throughout. The symbolic plan shape is a shamrock, the stem taken up with an organ gallery illuminated by a plate traceried rose. The transepts and chancel make up the leaves. That this does not suit the seating focussed on one altar (with reredos by Sir T.G. Jackson) is of minor importance. The four ribs resting on slender colonettes that define the intersecting apses with no distinction between wall and vault (both rendered with white plaster) sweep us up into the immaterial.

ST PETER'S SQUARE: **St Peter's Catholic Cathedral**
Designed in 1860 by an architect turned priest, Jeremiah MacAuley, and his only church. The twin towers and spires that dominate the Falls were added by Mortimer Thompson in 1886 and effectively screen the absence of transepts. Long nave with hammerbeam vault, painted

with angels in the terminating apse. Murals and stained glass crudely but effectively interpretate Paradise. A Gothic baldachino by Padraic Gregory from 1946 has survived recent unhappy alterations to the sanctuary.

STRANDTOWN: **Craigavon**
High-Victorian villa with asymmetrical façades—arched windows on the lower floor, chamber-headed windows above. Two-storied bow on garden front and Venetian-arched *porte-cochère* on the adjoining entrance front. Designed by Thomas Jackson in 1870. A neo-Palladian billiard room, added *c.*1880 and linked by an arcade, is attributed by Larmour to W.H. Lynn. The house was inherited by James Craig, later Lord Craigavon, first prime minister of Northern Ireland, brother of the architect Vincent Craig. Given to the nation and now a hospital.

STRANMILLIS ROAD: **Stranmillis House**
Designed for the financier Thomas Batt by Lanyon, Lynn and Lanyon and built in 1857-8, this is the first of a series of distinctive neo-Jacobean mansions with curvilinear gables and ogee-roofed corner tower that Lanyon's assistant Thomas Turner would subsequently adopt for all his major country-house commissions. Extended in a simpler manner when taken over as a college of education in the 1920s.

SUSSEX PLACE: **St Malachy's School & St Joseph's Convent**
Four-storied convent built in 1879-80 by Alexander McAlister; linked to earlier school block with attached belfry by Timothy Hevey; the complex in brick throughout with banded stonework, well suited to its urban context.

TOWNSEND STREET: **Presbyterian Church**
Designed by Young and Mackenzie, built in 1876-8 in a muted Romanesque Revival. Incomplete, twin-towered façade with three recessed doorways. Galleried interior with stained glass by Geddes ('Faith, Hope and Charity') and two further windows attributed to Rhind.

UNIVERSITY ROAD: **Crescent Presbyterian Church**
Accomplished Gothic Revival church by the Glasgow architect John Bennie Wilson; built in 1885-7. The exposed use of iron and the dominance of rose windows in the fenestration characterize the interior. Exterior made memorable by prominently sited off-centre steeple with paired lancets soaring upwards to a discreetly pinnacled pyramidal spire.

UNIVERSITY ROAD: **Elmwood Hall**
Previously Elmwood Presbyterian church. Designed by the builder of Lanyon's Presbyterian College, John Corry, this is his only church, an accomplished essay in the North Italian Romanesque as reinterpreted by John Ruskin: note the framed circles of coloured marble on the spandrels of the richly sculpted arcaded entry loggia. Built in pink Scrabo sandstone dating from 1859. Tower (not completed until 1872) also Ruskinian but showing as well the influence of Hawksmoor, who would have approved of the way that the octagonal spire rests on a belvedere of twelve columns rather than the expected eight. Carvings attributed by Larmour to the Fitzpatrick brothers. The interior has been preserved for graduation ceremonies at the expense of its stained glass and original fittings.

UNIVERSITY ROAD: **Methodist Church**
Built in 1864-5. William Barre, having at first given his non-Conformist clients churches that were indistinguishable from those of the Church of Ireland, in his last designs forged for the Methodists a separate and radical identity. That the interior is galleried is expressed by stressing the stepped-up fenestration of the staircase rising from the nave, while the first-floor arcading is carried across into an otherwise windowless tower that rises abruptly to a machicolated cornice. The forceful vertical composition is counteracted not merely by the fenestration but also by the horizontal brick and sandstone banding carried round on to the double-storied side elevations. Bomb damage destroyed the façade's rose window but spared Barre's interior (since restored).

UNIVERSITY ROAD: **Upper and Lower Crescents**
Built by James Corry between 1846 and 1852, two imposing neo-Classical terraces, the earlier curved and more highly finished. Both terraces have centrepieces articulated by double-height Corinthian columns, boldly designed as six bays wide so there is no need to rely on a fake central bay. Side pavilions with similar colonnades three bays wide. Above, an attic storey of paired arched windows with interlacing balustrades. The simpler interlinking houses step up with the rising ground.

UNIVERSITY ROAD: **Queen's University**
One of the three so-called godless non-denominational Irish universities set up by Westminster in 1852. Between the post-Georgian Gothick of Galway and the revived Medievalism of Cork, in Belfast Charles Lanyon steers a middle course, the assured and casual Gothic

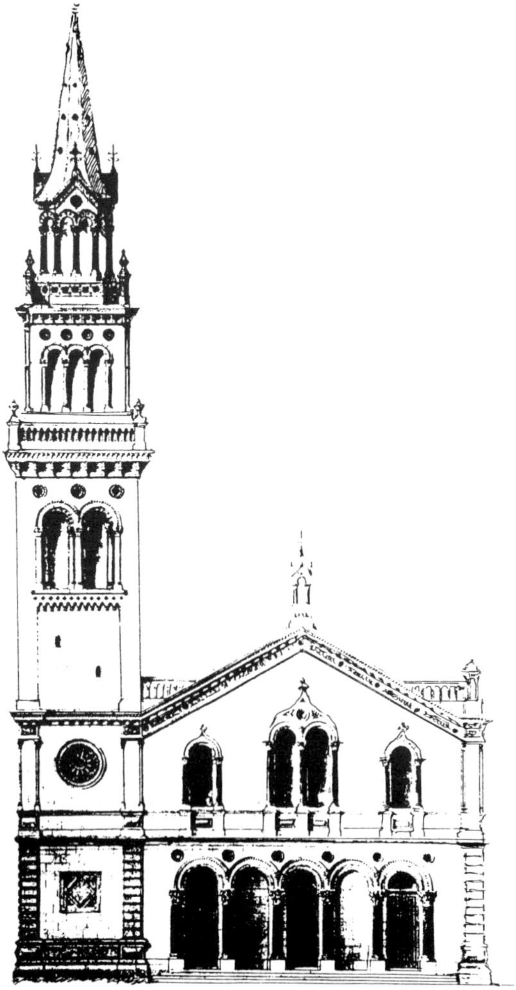

ELMWOOD HALL

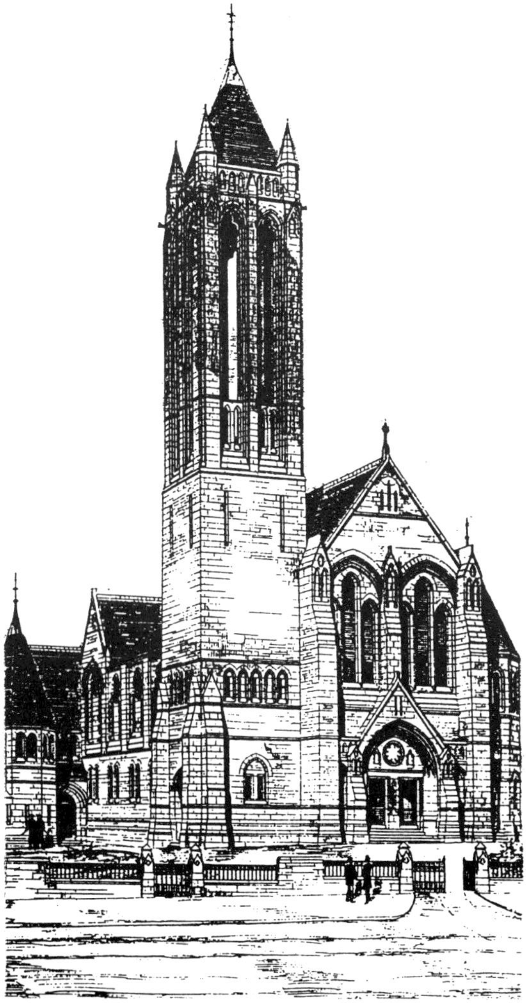

CRESCENT PRESBYTERIAN CHURCH

QUEEN'S UNIVERSITY

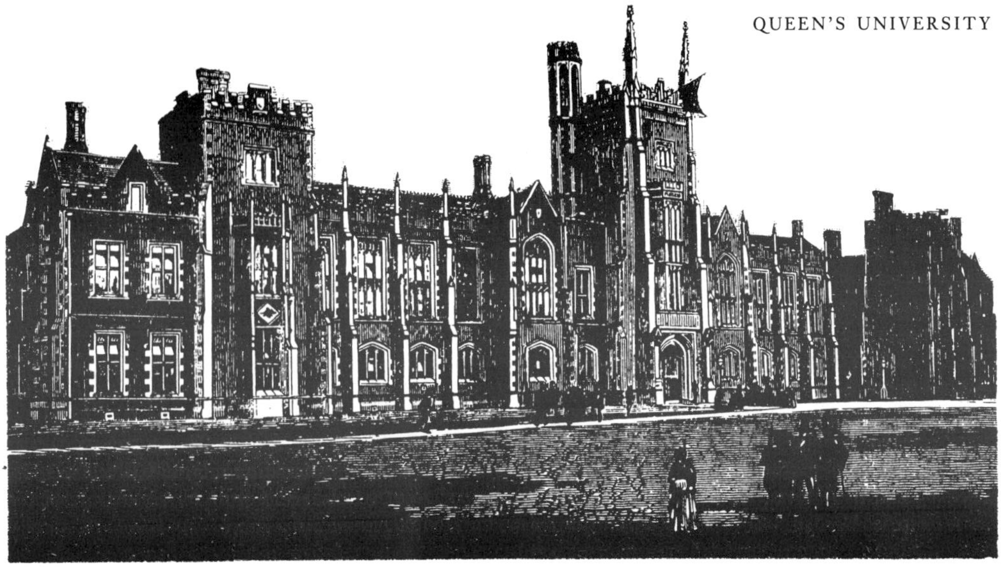

Revival that Pugin despised. Despite the cutbacks, the executed building is more mature than the original scheme, introducing Gothic arches and gables to vary the regularity of the long façades (further enlivened by their cheerful polychromy with dark blue diapering introduced into the rosy brickwork). Its central feature is the entry tower, a slimmed-down version of Magdalen's tower in Oxford with a functional front door (rather than an arch to canter through on horseback, as realized by Deane and Woodward in Cork). Lanyon's great hall was intended to take up a wing that extended behind the tower. Due to economies it had to be concealed in one of the front ranges, with an improvised approach substituted for his proposed ceremonial sequence. At each end gently asymmetrical ranges extend backwards to form a three-sided court.

The first major addition was the library by Lanyon's partner, W.H. Lynn, which was built out of matching materials in 1865-8; this gave the university what appears to be a collegiate chapel, especially after its recent modernization (an interesting idea crassly executed) that reinforces the impression that this was once a church inspired by the Church of Ireland architects Welland and Gillespie. Central nave and aisles of counter gables lit by sexafoil rose windows articulated by buttresses, gargoyles and over-scaled chimneys positioned on a raised crypt that forms the lower reading room; the upper reading room is open to the roof. Seamlessly extended by Lynn in 1911 after he had won a competition for enlarging the university when he was aged eighty. As a result of his victory, he lengthened the arms of Lanyon's court, adding a new gatehouse and tower to the south. Subsequent unsympathetic extensions have at last given way to a more conservation-minded attitude, even to the extent of retaining the diamond panes.

UNIVERSITY STREET: **Fitzroy Presbyterian Church**

This is by Robert Young of Young and Mackenzie and was built in 1872-4. Church with detached corner belfry, hall and school with its own staircase tower, massed together in a heavyweight interplay of Gothic forms, all in craggy Scrabo sandstone unintentionally dramatized by weathering. The tower (with brutal but effectively treated spire rising between four conical tourelles) is connected to the gallery by a flying stair, derived from Lynn's Seamen's Church of 1856 (q.v.). Glass by Heaton, Butler and Bayne.

VICTORIA STREET: **First Trust Bank**

Formerly the Northern Bank head office. Built in Portland stone on a granite base, this is

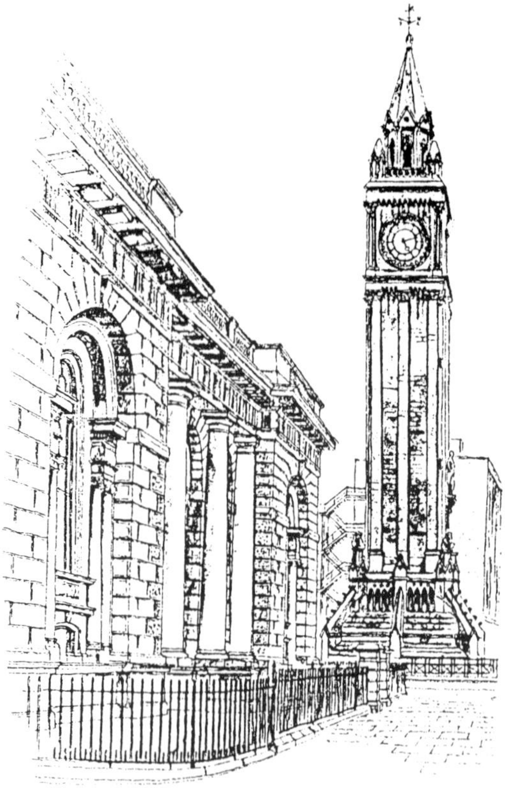

Charles Lanyon at his most masterly—a single-storied palazzo on a raised basement deploying Palladian conventions instilled with a new energy. His dominant motif is an Ionic Venetian window inset into the upper half of a rusticated archway. The entrance is set into a recessed triple arcade articulated by giant Doric columns upholding a Roman frieze and generous cornice. The internal banking hall has parallels with Lanyon's central saloon in Dunderave, Bushmills (q.v.). Later acquired and restored by the Trustee Savings Bank.

VICTORIA STREET: **Lytle's and McCausland's Warehouses**

Two adjoining warehouses, both four stories high. Lytle's is arcaded on the two floors with square-headed windows above; in McCausland's the process is reversed, with arcades at the upper level. Both were designed by William Hastings and built in 1866-7. Sculpture designed by Michael Fitzpatrick. Lytle's is enlivened by a bestiary, McCausland's by allegories of the five continents. Both disused.

VICTORIA STREET: **No. 10, Heyn Offices**

Designed by Thomas Jackson and son; built in 1863 as an opulent Italianate palazzo with curved rusticated corner bays and complicated three-storied centrepiece containing a focal diminutive Venetian window above the sculptural doorcase.

VICTORIA STREET: **Former Townhall**
Designed by Anthony Jackson and built in 1869–71 in a provincial version of Napoleon III; three interlinked pavilions with mansard roofs, and round-arched windows throughout. Individuality expressed only by the stubby half-columns (derived from Barre) that flank the doors. Totally eclipsed by the splendour of its successor a generation later.

WARING STREET: **Ulster Bank**
Even if this bank in purely architectural terms does not measure up to the best of Barre and Lanyon, this is the most sumptuous of Belfast, winning a competition that attracted sixty-seven entries in 1857. James Hamilton was a young Glasgow architect overwhelmed by Venice, in particular St Mark's Library. Compared with the original, this is top-heavy and weighed down with allegorical sculpture and constricted fenestration; but these defects are hardly noticeable in the façade's exuberant triumphalism. Double-storied portico, Doric below, Corinthian above, surmounted by Britannia between Justice and Commerce. The stonework is carved by Thomas Fitzpatrick; the ironwork cast by Laidlaws of Glasgow. Interior almost Indian in its opulence, centred on a multi-tiered stained-glass dome, partly balanced on the side walls, partly on

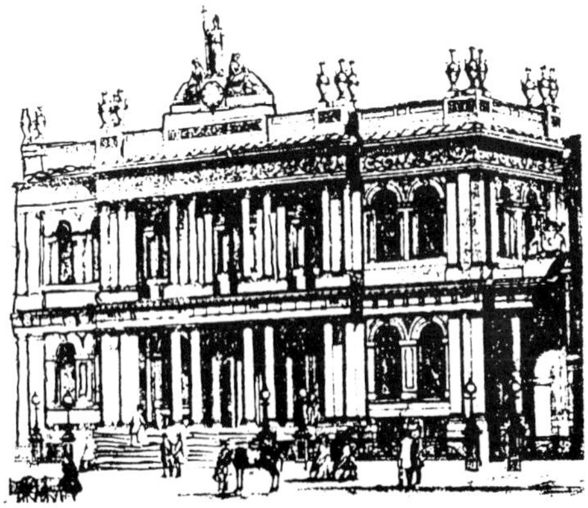

screens of columns enlivened by allegorical plasterwork. This is by George Crowe. But decorative murals by Sibthorpe have been removed and recent repainting lacks subtlety.

WARING STREET: **Northern Bank**
From 1776, when Sir Robert Taylor superimposed his Assembly Rooms on to a single-storied market house, until 1895, when W.H. Lynn destroyed Taylor's interiors, the most interesting Palladian monument in the city. In between, Charles Lanyon had remodelled the exterior into a fruity, stucco-coated palazzo but had retained Taylor's interiors. Lynn's contribution demonstrates that the best architects can make the worst conservationists.

WELLINGTON PARK/LISBURN ROAD: **Housing**
Speculative corner residential scheme in red brick with stone enrichments overhung by half-timbered upper floors. An expansive design by Forman and Aston built in 1897.

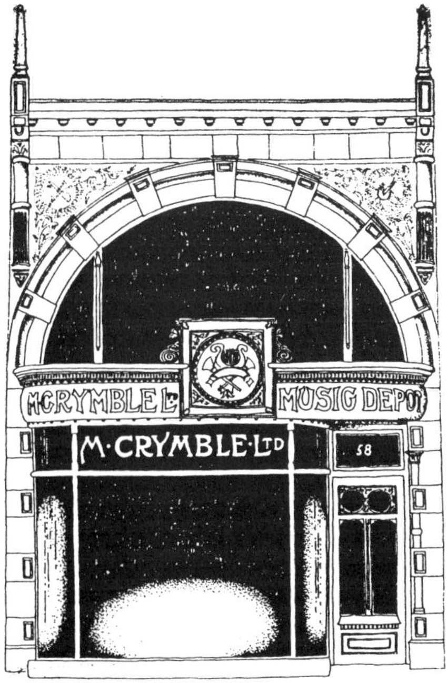

WELLINGTON PLACE: **No. 58**
Designed by W.J.W. Roome and built in 1903 as a music shop. One of the few Irish examples of Art Nouveau. A curved shop window set into a double-height terracotta rusticated arch with coloured mosaic spandrels framed by corbelled obelisks. Further decoration on the curved metal fascia with musical instruments set into central copper medallion. Now a tea shop.

WOODSTOCK ROAD: **Willowfield Church of Ireland**
One of John Lanyon's finest churches, built in 1871–2, heavily indebted to the radical Gothic introduced by Welland and Gillespie—its aisles roofed by transverse gables framing plate traceried rose windows set into polychromatic brickwork; at the eastern end, the polygonal apse, octagonal belfry and semi-circular staircase turret all interconnect. The belfry has since been truncated. Lanyon's façade was replaced when the nave was extended by W.J. Fennell in 1900. Glass by Heaton, Butler and Payne.

YORK STREET: **St Paul's Church of Ireland**
Small Gothic Revival church by Sir Charles Lanyon (1850), possibly assisted by W.H. Lynn. Octagonal spire set on tower at junction between nave and chancel. Later north aisle (1872).

CARLOW

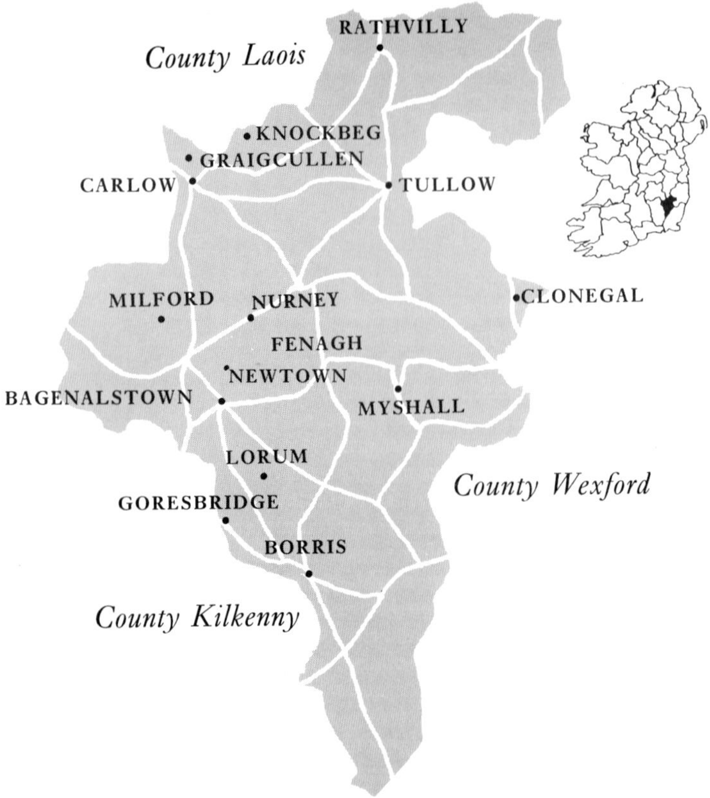

BAGENALSTOWN: **Catholic Church**
Church attributed to Thomas Cobden with façade delicately carved from local granite. Entrance set between saints in niches at the base of a tower with tapering spire. Modified interior.

BAGENALSTOWN: **Church of Ireland**
Church attributed to Frederick Darley *c.*1835, with a curiously asymmetrical interior. Early neo-medieval stained glass donated by the Newtons of Dunleckney.

BAGENALSTOWN: **The Courthouse**
Small Ionic temple overlooking the Barrow, attributed to Daniel Robertson as one of his commissions for the Newton family.

BAGENALSTOWN: **Dunleckney Manor**
Dunleckney, designed *c.*1840 by Daniel Robertson as the most sumptuous of his Tudor Revival houses. Built of ashlar limestone, the façade is dominated by three gables, the smallest joined to a corner turret decorated with panels of miniature tracery, repeated in the bow of the adjoining garden front. Lavishly carved chimney-stacks and oriels, but all treated somewhat casually as would have happened in medieval times. At the back, some traces of the 17th-century house remodelled as a servants' wing. The client, Walter Newton, who inherited the estate from his mother (a Bagenal), loved building, and added towers to many of his outlying farms, extending as far as Mount Leinster, ostensibly as protection against the Fenians. He was also an enthusiastic salvager, and rescued much of the woodwork that was being thrown out of St Canice's Cathedral in

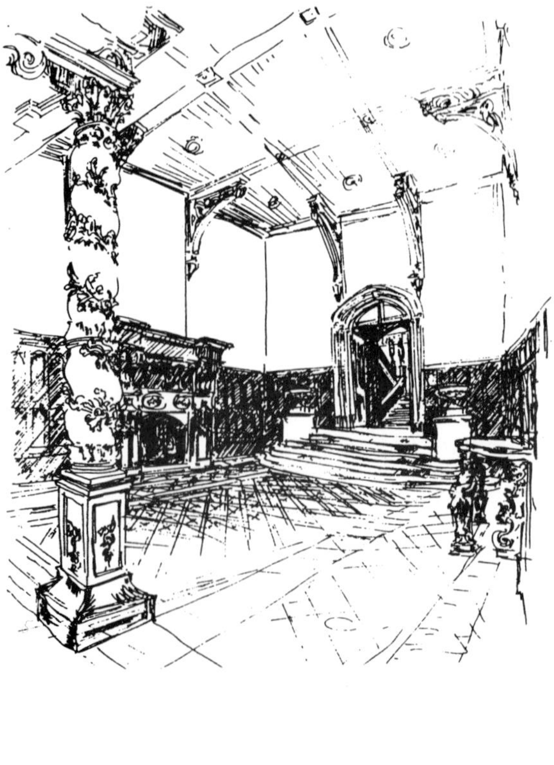

Kilkenny during one of its ill-judged restorations. Thus one enters the hall through a carved porch derived from Bernini's baldachino in St Peter's. Angels support a sidetable and reappear as candelabra holders on the newels of the imperial staircase in the galleried hall beyond. This leads up to the main bedroom lined with discarded choir stalls. Below, well laid-out reception rooms with double drawingrooms opening south on to the garden terrace, lead into a bow-windowed billiard room. The billiard table was the only piece of furniture to survive when the house went through several changes of owner. Once owned by Mr and Mrs Thomas Donnelly (see Parkanaur, Co. Tyrone), whose son threw the centrepiece of Dublin's 1950 celebrations, the controversial Bowl of Light, into the River Liffey. Then the property of a bankrupt steel firm; almost acquired by an American who wanted to envelop it in a plastic bubble and gas the dry rot out of the woodwork. Rescued eventually from dereliction by Mr and Mrs Colloton who sold their Wexford farm to save it, take in guests and open it to the public; but having received no support, apart from Hidden Ireland, they had to resell. Now the European headquarters of Helen Sheen.

reroofed with pantiles in a simpler manner.

CARLOW: **Castletown**
Castellated manor house (attributed to Daniel Robertson) incorporating a porch, and off-centre tower flanked by the dormers of gabled wings, the longer ending with a turret. The tower is a truncated tower house, so this may be Robertson's earliest use of a formula that worked out so well that he continued to build many variants. Built *c.*1835.

CARLOW: **The Cathedral**
Thomas Colden was born in England; he settled in Carlow, and in 1829, the year of Catholic Emancipation, he supplanted the obscure Joseph Lynch as architect of the cathedral started by Bishop Doyle three years before. Despite Carlow being one of the poorest Catholic dioceses in Ireland, £18,000 was raised, much of which must have been absorbed by the elegant octagonal entrance tower, in silvery granite, inspired by the Boston Stump. Simple spacious interior approached beneath a columned organ gallery raised on clustered columns which in a larger version divide the shallow transepts from the nave. The result is a clearest

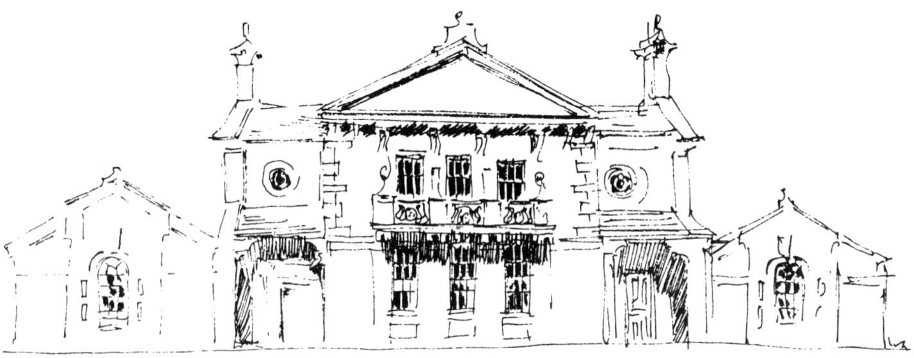

BAGENALSTOWN: **The Station**
A delightful Palladian composition, its centrepiece a pedimented stationmaster's quarters, with his apartment spanning twin corbelled entrances to the platform. At each end gabled pavilions with arched windows. Possibly by W.D. Butler, but its very liveliness makes this attribution uncertain; *c.*1850.

BAGENALSTOWN: **Wykeham**
An austere neo-Elizabethan of local granite with gables and polygonal chimney-stacks *c.*1840.

BORRIS: **Mount Leinster Lodge**
Built for the Bagenal family in the 1840s with all the characteristics of Daniel Robertson, who would have been at the time working on Dunleckney (q.v.) for the same client. Recently

view of the high altar in any Irish cathedral. Cobden's altars and communion rails were replaced *c.*1900. The elaborate wooden pulpit designed by M.J.C. Buckley was carved in Bruges in 1898. The stained glass is German, inevitably Mayer of Munich. The only fittings of Cobden to survive are the gasoliers and the choir stalls, optimistically heated by a single hot-water pipe. Organ made by Berington. One of the most memorable masterpieces of John Hogan is his statue of Bishop Doyle consoling a weeping orphan (Erin?) by gesturing towards the spacious vaulting of the cathedral to which he had devoted the last years of his life. That the neo-Classicism of Hogan's sculpture is not out of place in its Gothic setting reflects the ability of the architect to master the two rival styles.

CARLOW: Chapel of St Laserian
Simple cruciform Gothic Church serving the mental hospital. Interior redecorated in 1926, with the installation of stained glass by Bockhann of Munich. German medieval carved Entombment of Christ.

CARLOW: Duckett's Grove
Mid-Georgian farmhouse remodelled as a neo-Classical mansion by John Gandon for William Duckett. Transformed into an improbable Gothick fantasy by Thomas Cobden for William's son, John Dawson Duckett, during the 1820s. Extended in the 1840s by John McDuff Derick, who added little extra space, a basement kitchen, with a billiard-room above and an adjoining circular flag tower; but superbly built out of local granite prefiguring the neo-Medieval improvizations of White and Godwin. He screened the farm buildings at the rear with fortifications rising from a dummy moat crossed by a bridge to a machiolated gateway. This severity makes a telling contrast to Cobden's stucco-clad towers enriched with statuary. Ironically, the noblest interior is the double-height neo-Norman kitchen; this might authenticate to visitors the Ducketts' descent from the lords of the manor of Graywigg during the reign of King John. Rumours (in the local press) of ghosts have been strongly denied.

To underscore his family's feudal origins John Dawson Duckett commissioned from

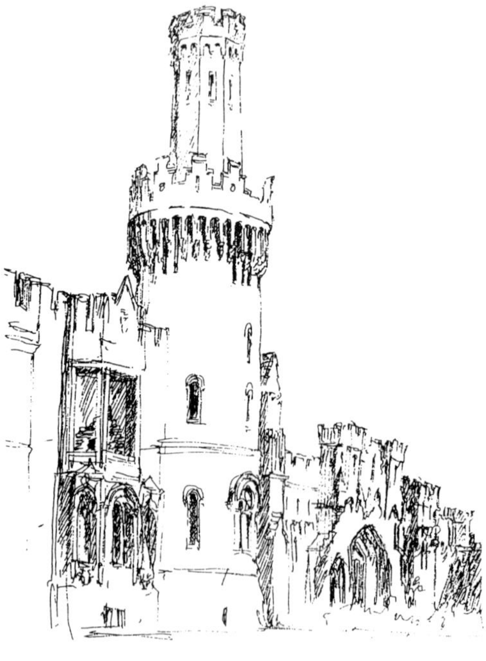

McDuff Derick the grandest neo-Gothic entrance gates in Ireland. Built also in local granite, a single fortress incorporates entrances to two avenues. One, reserved for the tenants, has become a public road. The entrance reserved for the family has been blocked up and remodelled as a country pub which retains an immense coat of arms (once coloured and gilded) carved by Kelly and Kinsella, completed in 1855. So daring is Derick's use of granite that his turrets outcorbel the pub signs.

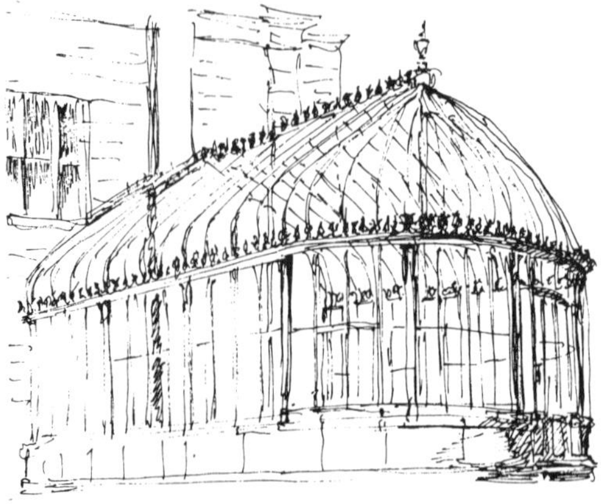

CARLOW: Kelvin Grove
Regency villa, now a home for the elderly who can enjoy the sun in one of Richard Turner's most flower-like conservatories, an apsed curvilinear. Wrought-iron ribs springing from behind a corona of neo-Classical acroteriae curve upwards to make a Gothic semidome.

CARLOW: Little Moyle
Farmhouse remodelled and extended in the mid-1860s for the Kane-Smith family by John McCurdy when he was working on the Shelbourne Hotel. Atmospheric drawingroom that retained its original decoration until 1993.

CARLOW: Mount Hanover
House demolished and replaced by supermarket, approached through the magnificent Italianate entrance gates *c.*1840, commendably retained.

CARLOW: Oak Park
Sir Richard Morrison's concentrated classicism was diluted and institutionalized eighty years before the house became an agricultural college. The wings were built by McCurdy and Mitchell (1876-9). William Mitchell lived long enough to rebuild the house after a fire in 1902, and inserted a new staircase. He was responsible for the deadening plate glass. Of Morrison's interiors, only the hall, the library and diningroom, both bow-fronted, survive with his characteristic plasterwork. The Shinkelesque bow windows, elegant in themselves, are now over-

whelmed by the increased length of the garden front. However, the park conceals two unspoilt architectural treasures—the cast-iron bridge by George Papworth, with serpent-infested balustrading spanning between two lakes, and the mausoleum. This was commissioned in 1841, eleven years before his death, by Col. Henry Bruen, but never completed, it now resembles a Roman temple pillaged during the Dark Ages. The architect was J.B. Keane at his most cubistic and austere. There is no external hint of the internal layout, a nave articulated by pilasters leading to a semi-domed apse, a space that should have rivalled the music room at Lisadell. Here is buried the last of the Bruens, Col. Arthur Bruen, who lived on alone in considerable grandeur after his wife had eloped during the Second World War with the uncle of the last sovereign of Montenegro, Prince Milo: he had been brought to Ireland by her and then billeted out on an unsuspecting neighbour, the author's grandmother.

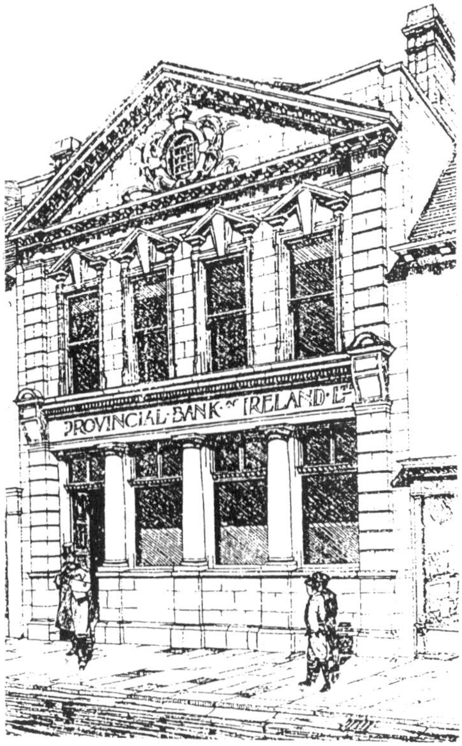

CARLOW: **Former Provincial Bank**
A forceful neo-Palladian façade, four ways wide but with its duality resolved by a generous pediment. The solemnity of its *piano nobile* is upheld by three chubby columns that articulate the fenestration of the banking hall. Designed in 1902 by Carroll and Batchelor.

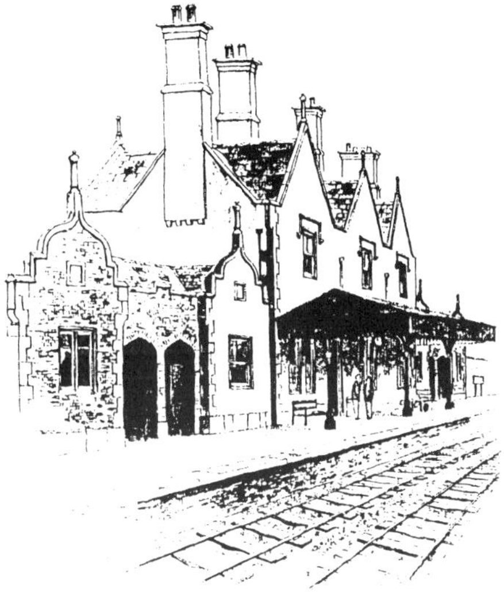

CARLOW: **The Station**
Neo-Elizabethan on a domestic scale. Designed by Sir John McNeill himself for the South-Eastern Railway and built *c.*1845 out of stock brick and stone trimmings, now rendered.

CARLOW: **Prumplestown**
Comfortable mid-Victorian gabled house with drawingroom leading to flower-filled conservatory.

CLONEGAL: **Church of Ireland**
Eighteenth-century church rebuilt in First Fruits Gothic. Stained glass Durdin Robertson window over the altar by C.E. Kempe (1904). Also, window by Joshua Clarke.

CLONEGAL: **Huntington Castle**
A plantation castle (*c.*1620) continuously inhabited by the same family, Huntington has been remodelled and extended over the centuries. From Victorian times dates the present entrance range in castellated brick *c.*1880, terminating in a later chapel *c.*1910 built by Herbert Robertson for his wife, designed either by himself or by his son Manning Robertson, the architect. Recently deconsecrated, the chapel is now devoted to the cult of Isis and repositioned in the basement of the original keep. Red-brick farm buildings in similar Breughelesque idiom by Manning Robertson but on his father's instructions. Castellated conservatory overlooking pleasure grounds laid out (1884-94) with rare trees; currently being restored following an account preserved in the library. All this is possible to visit, along with recent minimalist steel pavilion designed by Ulrich Ruckheim to house his own sculptures; but as yet it has proved too fascinating to be accepted by any official body devoted to opening Ireland's historic houses to the public.

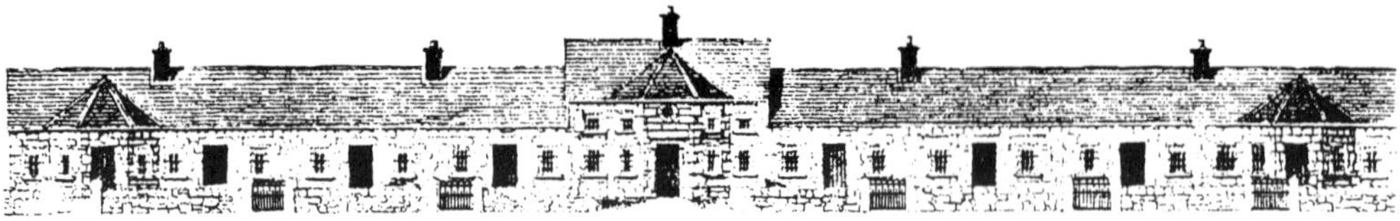

FENAGH: The Village
An elegant row of wayside cottages built out of local granite to a Palladian concept with three polygonal pavilions, the central one double-storied and adorned with the Pack-Beresford coat of arms (as a contemporary noted, the 'antidote to the pig sty'). The cost of each house was £62. The date is inscribed (1859). By William Butler, who rebuilt Fenagh House for the Pack-Beresfords four years later.

FENAGH: Ballydarton
One of Daniel Robertson's miniature castles that only he was able to design as the perfect solution for the Irish squirarchy who preferred horses to houses—in this case the Watsons, who were for several generations the most celebrated masters of hounds in Ireland. Central battlemented tower with gabled wings and polygonal turret built out of local granite. Spacious stableyard and kennels. In her memoirs, Lady Fingal recounts that an English solicitor arrived here to inform Robert Watson that he had the best legal claim to the earldom and castle of Rockingham in Northamptonshire, and was asked to leave as it would have meant giving up the best hounds in the land. Robert Watson is buried as a fox in Larch Hill, Co. Kildare.

FENAGH: Fenagh House
An austere, neo-Classical country house built out of local granite in 1863 to the designs of a tenant called William Butler, who did not master the art of proportioning (so necessary with such severity). The portico of baseless columns, even before being filled, must have been painfully constricted, and the plate glass windows add to its bleakness. The family tradition is that the house was really designed by its builder, Capt. Pack-Beresford and it certainly has a defensive air, accented by the steel shutters inserted by a general, his grandson. The exuberant internal plasterwork comes as a surprise, although its realism is High Victorian. Top-lit granite cantilevered staircase. Double drawing-room remodelled later to give 'Sweetness and Light' with views across the arboretum to the mountains. It had a hidden rear access down to a now-vanished conservatory propped up against the earlier Georgian house. Fine Classical stableyard.

FENAGH: Upton
Classical house built *c.*1840. A small version of Ballinkeele, Balllymurn, Co. Wexford (q.v.) by Daniel Robertson. The same emphasized corner piers and emphatically projecting portico.

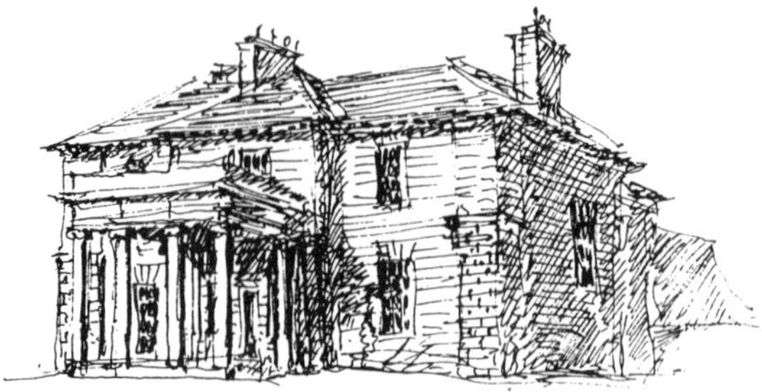

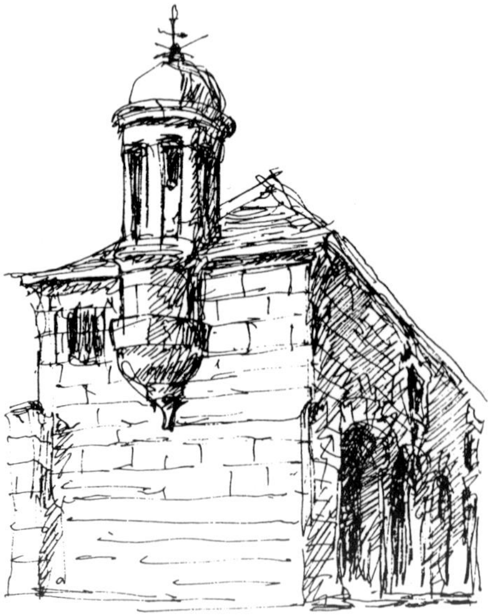

Subtly asymmetrical ground plan. Elegant, corbelled domed bell-tower in the yard.

GRAIGCULLEN: Catholic Chuch
No other Irish Victorian church has submitted to such a radical metamorphosis: a Protestant church (St Anne's) on the east bank of the Barrow with a central steeple for its first eighty years, and then a sixty-year stint as a Catholic church (St Clare's) on the west bank of the Barrow, with the tower moved to the corner of

the façade, transplanted in 1920 by a charismatic parish priest at the prompting by the mother superior of the Poor Clares' Convent. The church was a gift by the supporters of Henry Bruen, who had just managed to defeat the son of Daniel O'Connell in the parliamentary elections of 1841. The architect appointed was J. McDuff Derick, so that this church is the earliest of his Irish commissions. Derick was so proud of his roofing system (a series of granite trusses) that he sent drawings of it over to the *Builder*. This system has been retained in the rebuilding, especially effective in the porch, where the inclined soffits are exposed slabs of stone. Granite vault at the crossing. Elaborate Gothic window tracery throughout and many sculpted heads, the liveliest not saints but gargoyles.

GRAIGCULLEN: **The Constabulary**
Granite and crenellated with corner tower, enlivened by grotesque heads, carved presumably by the sculptor of the Bruen Memorial Church and Duckett's Grove. A plaque of Hercules is inscribed 'Erected AD 1867 by Rowan McCombe'.

KNOCKBEG: **Knockbeg College**
Three-storied late-Georgian institution transformed into a naive palazzo enlivened by pediments, pilasters and Venetian windows without the slightest concern for rules. Evidently not a consideration of the judges who awarded the 1901 competition to Moore and Aylward.

LORUM: **Church of Ireland**
Set high up in the hills between the Barrow and the Slayney, with a spire that is visible for miles around; built by the Pack-Beresfords of Fenagh as a reprimand to their neighbours, the Rudkins of Corris, for not doing enough for the religious life of their tenants. The steeple is typical of Welland's Gothic. The earlier church (pre-1840) is in an unusually forceful Tudor, presumably Frederick Darley rivalling the originality of Semple, his predecessor, and contemporary with Coolbawn. Interior also unusual with timber-sheeted trefoil-shaped Gothic vaulting (*c.* 1890 by J.F. Fuller. Glass by Heaton, Butler and Bayne. In the valley below is a school and rectory, now a guesthouse and part of Hidden Ireland, likewise Tudor, likewise granite.

MILFORD: **The Mill**
Twenty years ago, Milford had the most remarkable industrial complex of the Barrow valley. The vast scale of its abandonment was screened from the outside world by magnificent trees, so there was no public outcry when the derelict buildings were swept away. A swing bridge was spared across the canal and upstream, one mill remains, being restored by the local squire to generate electricity for the government.

MYSHALL: **Adelaide Memorial Church**
Clinging to the western foothills of Mount Leinster, the village of Myshall is dominated by the last of George Ashlin's memorial churches. Its inception was due to the inability of the Sicilian marble, used in an outdoor statue of Innocence to withstand the rigours of the Irish winter. The statue commemorated Constance Duguid. In 1888, on a visit from Dover, Cornwall she became engaged to a Brady, the heir to Myshall Lodge but she lost her life in a hunting accident. Her parents, John and Adelaide Duguid decided to bury her in Myshall and commissioned the statue from Sir Thomas Farrell. Ten years later, Adelaide died and wished to be buried beside her daughter. The bereaved husband decided to devote the remainder of his life to building a church in her memory that would serve as his own tomb. He

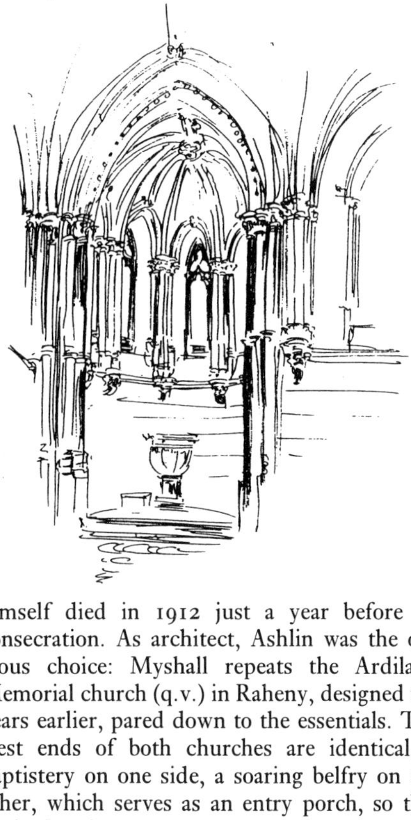

himself died in 1912 just a year before its consecration. As architect, Ashlin was the obvious choice: Myshall repeats the Ardilaun Memorial church (q.v.) in Raheny, designed ten years earlier, pared down to the essentials. The west ends of both churches are identical, a baptistery on one side, a soaring belfry on the other, which serves as an entry porch, so that one's first internal vista is of the apsidal baptistery revolving round the font. But the east ends are different. The mortuary chapel and matching vestry that fill the angles between the chancel and transepts in Raheny are here contrived within the transepts, to create a miniature cathedral, while the congregation fits snugly into the nave with their view into the chancel unimpaired. There is no crossing as such, but the fifth and final bay of the nave is widened, raised a step and furnished as a choir. Stone carved archways open off this choir into the smaller chancel and into transepts that repeat the chancel on a smaller scale. The carving is varied round each archway. That of the mortuary chapel alternates roses with thistles: Adelaide was English, her husband Scottish. They frame a delicate wrought-iron grille veiling the marble statue of Innocence. On the other side, pulpit and organ are built into a low partition screening the vestry beyond. Note the way Ashlin adjusts the fenestration of the south transept's gable end to this unusual plan—a rose window above two lancets, a motif repeated in the fenestration of the tower. No Church of Ireland architect was able to match Ashlin's subtlety in housing its rituals. But what gives the interior a sense of eternity is that the creamy Bath stone (confined to the walls in Raheny), is here carried up into continuous vaulting, acting as a foil to a few deft polychromatic touches: Aberdeen granite columns flank the arches to baptistery and mortuary, and recur coupled each side of the richer arch into the chancel. Here the geometrical mosaic work of the floor changes from black and white to a Venetian serpentine and amethyst. The stained glass, by Powell of Whitefriars, is conceived on a symphonic scale. Colour is reserved for the most important windows—gold in the east, red in the four-light to the west, where a saint is depicted with a model of the church. But the glass is at its most original in the nave, in virtually black and white illustrating the forces of creation, a rare apparition in Ireland of Art Nouveau. Ashlin did the best and the worst churches of his era. This is his best. And what of the Bradys, or rather the Beauchamp Cornwall Bradys? They have departed; their house has vanished. If Constance had been able to live out her natural lifespan, she would have experienced the destruction of her home by the Republicans in the civil war. All that remains is a Celtic cross on the hillside above where the house once stood, the tomb of her would-be mother-in-law, who refused to be buried with the family. She was a Watson of Fenagh who had strong ideas on these subjects: Robert Watson MFH insisted on being buried as a fox.

NEWTOWN: **Catholic Church**
High-spirited church, a reduced rural version of Cobden's Carlow Cathedral (q.v.), lovingly preserved even to its fretwork confessionals.

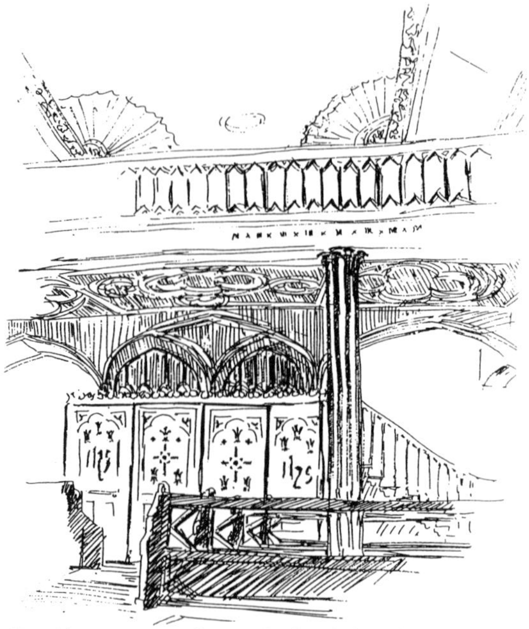

Cruciform externally, articulated by diagonal pinnacles. Sophisticated planning gives direct access to three galleries; the main gallery, extending more than half-way down the nave, is supported by two rows of clustered columns—a church within a church. Exemplary adaption to 1960s' liturgical requirements. Several windows by Joshua Clarke. Here even the external Marian mosaic (1954) has charm.

NURNEY: **Rathwade**
Delightful, neo-Gothic house by Daniel Robertson at the end of a lime avenue leading to an earlier house. Of two floors, the upper gabled with an asymmetrical tower. A more elaborate scheme by Robertson was recently discovered

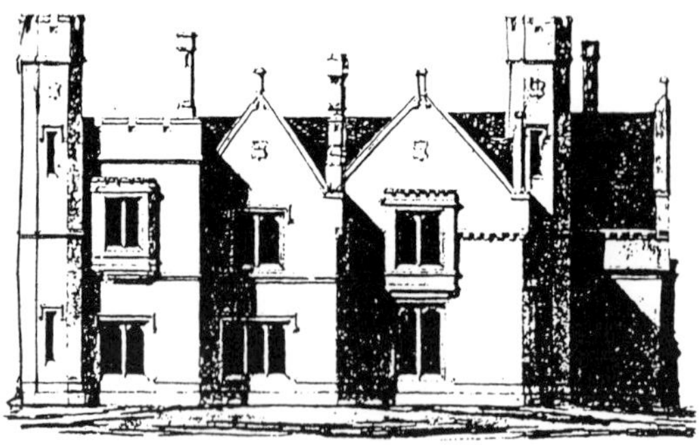

in Shankill Castle and presented to the Architectural Archive by Moira Toler-Alyward.

RATHVILLY: **Lisnavagh**
The house that we see today is a third of what Evelyn Waugh almost acquired in 1950; Mrs Waugh liked it also. But by the standards of its architect, Daniel Robertson, it was curiously

unimpressive—rambling collegiate Tudor with prefunctory Louis XV interiors, built by the 1st Lord Rathdonnell (post-1840) and completed by John McCurdy. When the Waughs failed to buy it, the trustees pulled down the three main ranges. This left a self-contained staff wing (even that had been thoughtfully provided with its own *porte-cochère*). Within, the more intimate scale and the simpler finishes create a more authentic Tudor than what was there before. But there was no great room until the late Lady Rathdonnell, the war artist Pamela Drew, knocked three rooms together and made a library out of salvaged bookcases, lit by a great salvaged oriel that successfully conceals the amputation. The fireplace is made out of a granite Gothic arch more dramatic than the reproduction Lous XV (by then all discarded into the shrubbery to acquire patina and to await discovery from jungle-clearing grandchildren). Member of Hidden Ireland.

TULLOW: **Ballykealey**
Tudor Revival house as rebuilt in the 1830s for John James Lecky by Thomas Cobden with a triple-arched loggia linking twin double-storied bay windows, all this surmounted by a gabled attic floor. Service yard at the side behind Gothic screen and rear wing both now remodelled as hotel extensions. The round-arched double-height hall, carefully designed to underplay the asmmetry occasioned by incorporating the earlier house, was filled in during later use as a novitiate. The last of the Leckys to live here sold the house and disappeared without trace off the Sussex coast. Now a hotel.

TULLOW: **Mount Wolseley**
Tediously Italianate commission by Lanyon, Lynn and Lanyon built *c.*1866 as the seat of the Wolseley family and acquired by the Patrician Brothers, who engaged a local primitive named Tom Lonergan to marbleize the hallway *c.*1930 and paint murals of India with ever increasing skill.

TULLOW: **St Austin's Abbey**
Pitiful traces of the country house built for the Doynes in 1856 by Benjamin Woodward. Yet, while the main house has been whittled down with the occasional bash by a combine harvester, enough of the service wing and the adjoining stables survives to reveal Woodward's obsession with geometry. Kitchen block (separately hipped) and pyramidal outhouse dominate the ruined remainder with its columned windows opening on to traceried balconies at first-floor level in local granite. Burnt out, in 1922. Stables built out of red brick with bands of granite. A granite gatelodge, a miniature chateau in its own right, now houses the owner.

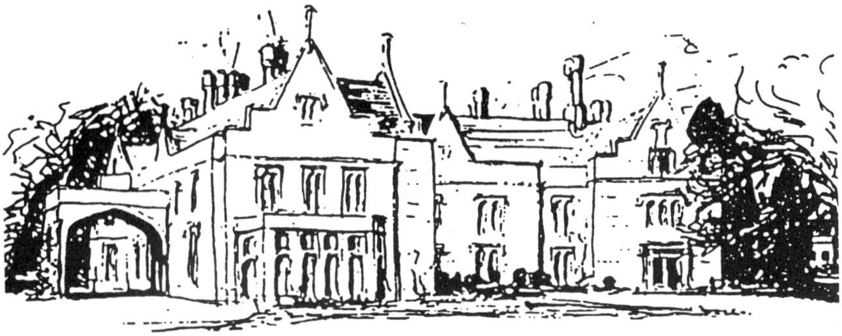

LISNAVAGH

CAVAN

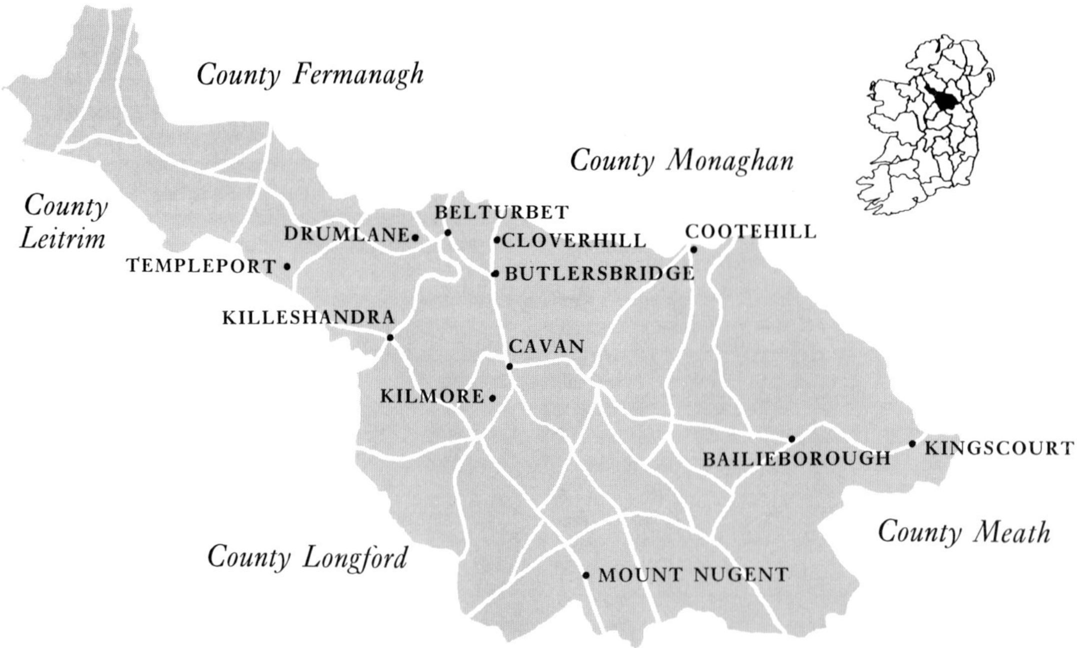

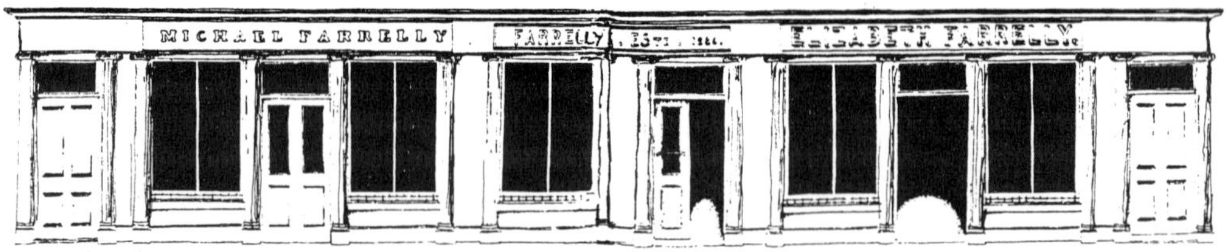

BAILIEBOROUGH: **Farrelly's**
Long façade to a shop, pub and residence, articulated by delicately fluted attached Ionic columns.

BELTURBET: **Castle Saunderson**
Seat of the Saunderson family remodelled (pre-1840) to rival nearby Crom, by an unknown architect, possibly collaborating with Blore, who, if he was involved, could have played little part in the supervision. A baronial gatehouse and corner towers were symmetrically inserted into the original stucco façade that still retained its Georgian glazing bars. The adjoining garden front also mixes stonework and stucco, extended by a series of turrets into a Gothic conservatory. When the partition of Ireland left their estate surrounded on three sides by another country, the Saundersons departed for Canada. Their castle was rescued and restored by the Maguires, a local business family, in the early 1980s, who sold it (along with a border concessionary petrol station at the gates) to a London Pakistani. Interior half destroyed by fire in 1990. Grim little church halfway up the avenue, *c.*1850.

BELTURBET: **Post Office**
In a remote town, architectural liberties can be taken and not criticized: hence the extraordinary doorcase with banded bulbous half-columns set beside a mullioned window beneath a Flemish gable, all in sandstone trim against bright red brick. By Robert Cochrane; dated 1904.

BUTLERSBRIDGE: **Catholic Church**
Early work by William Hague built in 1863 out of local limestone with relieving arches of polychromatic brickwork. Low porches flank the façade that rises symmetrically until the gable is raised on one side to support a delicately columned octagonal belfry. The interior is even more refined and unusual, due to its cast-iron arcades complete with foliated capitals. This

gives a rare sense of oneness to the congregation. The transepts are not expressed on the ground plan but by their roofing, which is pitched to give more illumination through rose windows set into their gables—a trick also used by Welland and Gillespie. Apsidal choir. Stained glass by Earley.

CAVAN: **Farnham Hall**
Red brick Venetian Gothic, symmetrical, double-storied. Architect unknown, winner of limited competition held in 1874.

CAVAN: **Poor Clares' Convent**
Designed in 1864 by an obscure Dublin architect called John Ryan, whose crude but effective Gothic dominates the main street of the town with its corner belfry of brick and stone. Adjoining chapel with ornate interior. Stencilled choir and marble fittings still intact.

CAVAN: **St Patrick's College**
Designed in 1869 by William Hague, but not started until two years later, it is one of the finest late Gothic seminaries in Ireland. Three floors, with centrepiece and end pavilions projecting further forwards. Built from local sandstone with red brick dressings; and red brick chimneys surmount the high pitched roof. The overall austerity is lightened by modulating the rhythm of the fenestration—running two floors together to make a double-height central Gothic window—and by the insertion of delicate Gothic staircase towers nestling into the angles formed by the projection of the wings. The windows of these towers increase in height as they rise; elsewhere they decrease. Timber-boarded ceil-

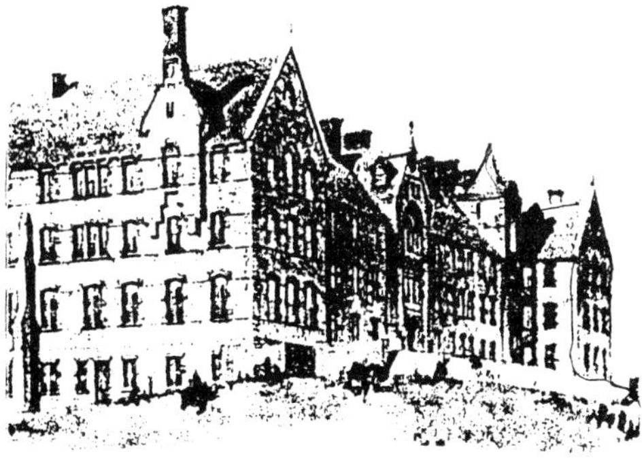

ings inside and red tiled floors except for the chapel (unhappily altered, *c.*1950).

CAVAN: **Church of Ireland**
The Gothic Church of Ireland (1820) by John Bowden with its chantry memorial to Lord Farnham predates our period, but its sanctuary was remodelled in 1860, when the church was given a new pulpit and altar carved by Charles Harrison.

CAVAN: **Dromkeen**
The seats of the Saundersons, remodelled by William Hague in 1868, consisting of two floors with seven bays, the central three projecting forward in a bay crowned with battlements and finials. Now a convent.

CAVAN: **The Townhall**
Designed by William Scott in 1908 and completed in 1910, this is the only Irish contribution to a series of provincial townhalls that sprang up in the remoter parts of Europe, directly challenging the officialdom of the metropolis

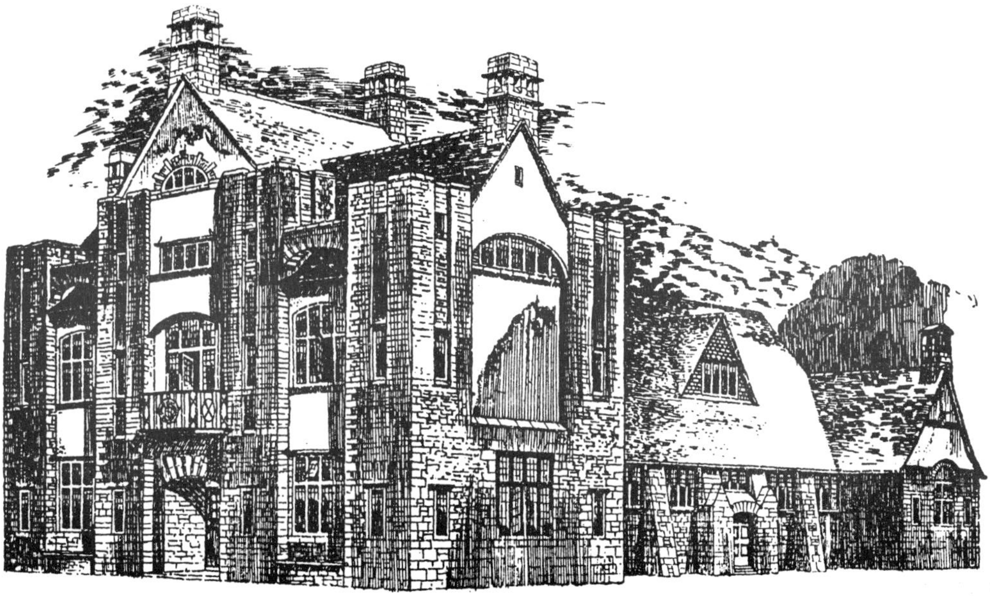

and rejecting the tired stylistic conventions of their day.

Their architects were both traditionalist and progressive—searching for their roots and yet organizing a new world of fresh air and sunlight, health and literacy, not for the cause of church or state, or for individual advancement, but for the family and the community. Hence the significance of their houses, and their townhalls, set up to discuss public drainage schemes and destroy empires. Scott's work expresses this efficiency and subversion. His quest for roots led him to the partly Scottish, partly Ulster vernacular, just then emerging as a separate identity. Not that his contemporaries recognized it as such: they called the style Norman; a later generation would term it Art Nouveau; today we would say post-Modern. The result is both tower house and office block, two symbols of administrative power, but here their formal elements are used to counteract each other and create a sense of tension and uncertainty. Thus two different systems of fenestration: small and defensive for the ancillary accommodation alternate with lofty indefensible windows for the offices.

Massive chimney-stacks set on central gables, dominate three of the elevations, but then the dominance of each is undermined—on the sides by attic windows immediately below them set into relieving arches; on the front by projecting the whole gable slightly forward over the entrance. The gables appear to balance on coupled pilasters, but these vanish into the rustication of the ground floor. Local sandstone is used, exposed throughout apart from the sparing use of brick in the relieving arches. The assembly hall at the rear is treated as a contrasting volume with a large room lit by triangular dormers. This hall harks back to Scott's romantic period that did not survive into a harsher age, but neither then did his eloquent ambiguities: they had to wait until our day for rediscovery. As for the political undercurrents they reveal, they still disturb this island.

CLOVERHILL: Church of Ireland

Built for the Sanderson family presumably by the Wellands (*c.*1855), remarkable for its diagonally positioned belfry that serves also as vestibule so that one enters through a canted doorway. Tiered buttresses rise to an octagonal belfry and spire, anticipating the geometrical experiments by Welland and Gillespie during the next decade. Interior of five bays articulated by trusses, the last truss springing from between coupled lancets that are introduced to light the altar.

COOTEHILL: Ashfield

All that survives of this Clements estate is a pretty gatelodge on the Drum road, by John McCurdy.

DRUMLANE: Catholic Church

Unorthodox Tudor Revival façade with castellated porch, and the gable enlivened by a cross-shaped window between niches enshrining saints and a Madonna set in a pinnacled recess on its apex. Dated 1846. Entered beneath an exuberantly carved organ gallery. Spandrels still articulate a much modernized nave. Chancel added in the style of William Hague (1863).

KILLESHANDRA: Catholic Church

One of the earliest churches of William Hague, revealing a roguery that did not survive into middle age. Like many of his advanced contemporaries he welcomed the chance to design the church in reverse, with the back facing the road to ensure correct orientation. The projecting gable of the chancel is assured dominance over the minor gables of the aisles and the sacristy; this is balanced at the other end by an unfinished tower. The interior is disjointed and abrupt. The open roof has trusses of wrought iron. The timber arcades are squat and menacing; they open into aisles where the lean-to roofs are broken up by interpenetrating gables. The central lancet of the eastern window is blocked in to take a crucifix above the altar. The other lights are filled with discordant glass (by Maumejean of Paris and Hendaye).

KILLESHANDRA: Martin Mausoleum

The 17th-century Protestant church of Ireland was replaced in the early 19th century, but the ruins remain, screening from public view this precisely detailed Gothic memorial (*c.*1860) with its austerity relieved by the spirited carving of its coat of arms.

KILMORE: Church of Ireland Cathedral

The most arcadian of Irish cathedrals set in a wooded park with views across a pastoral valley. This gives an air of monastic seclusion, if now undisturbed by monks, their only memorial being an Hiberno-Romanesque doorway to the vestry, transplanted from the ruin on Lough Oughter. The cathedral owes its existence to the generosity of the earls of Farnham, who commissioned William Slater in 1857; it was built over three years. Cruciform with central tower. Its interior is only 100ft long, but such is Slater's mastery of proportion that he has transformed a small parish church into apparently a large cathedral. This is achieved at the expense of the nave, a mere three bays in length with all

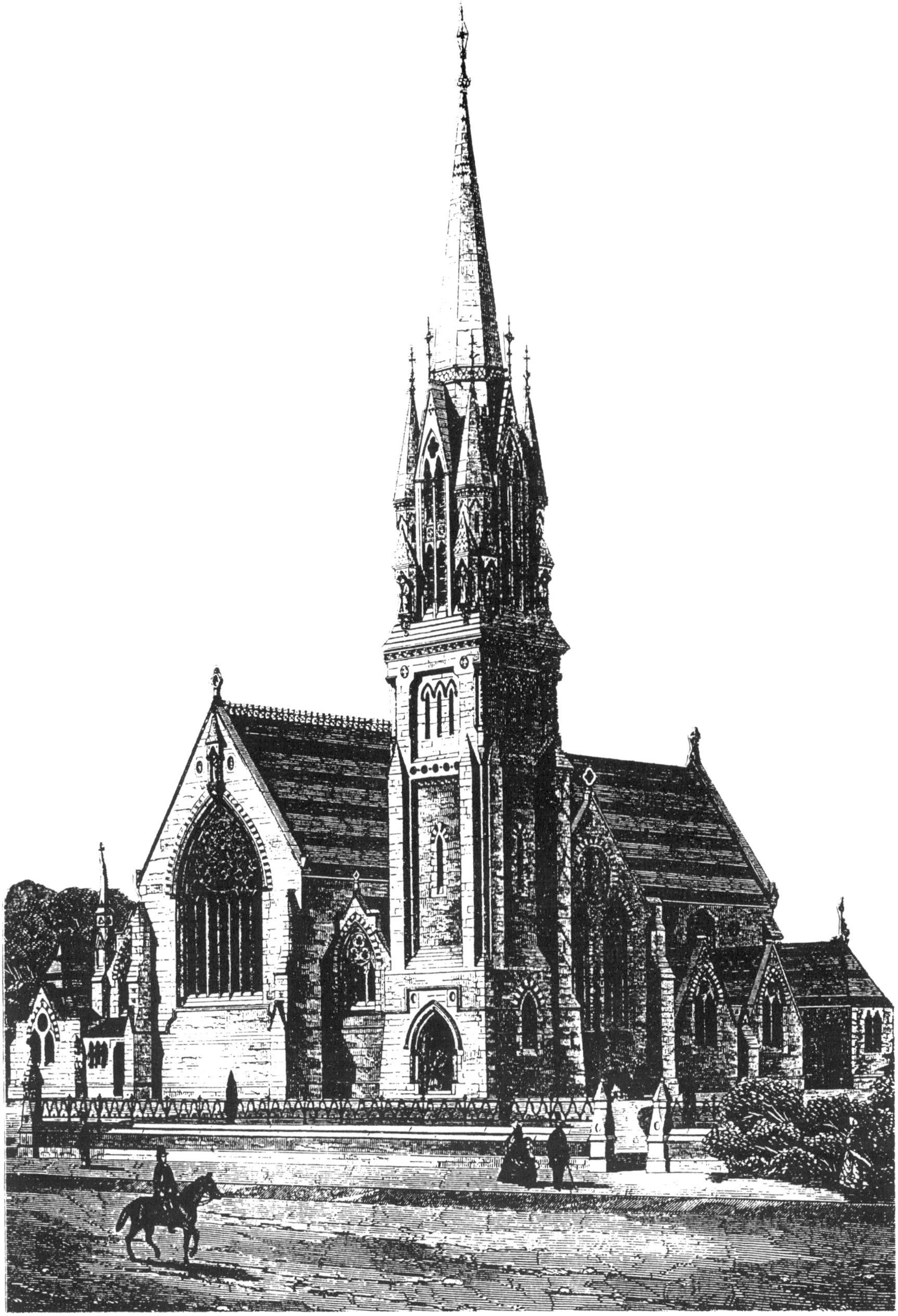

KILLESHANDRA CATHOLIC CHURCH

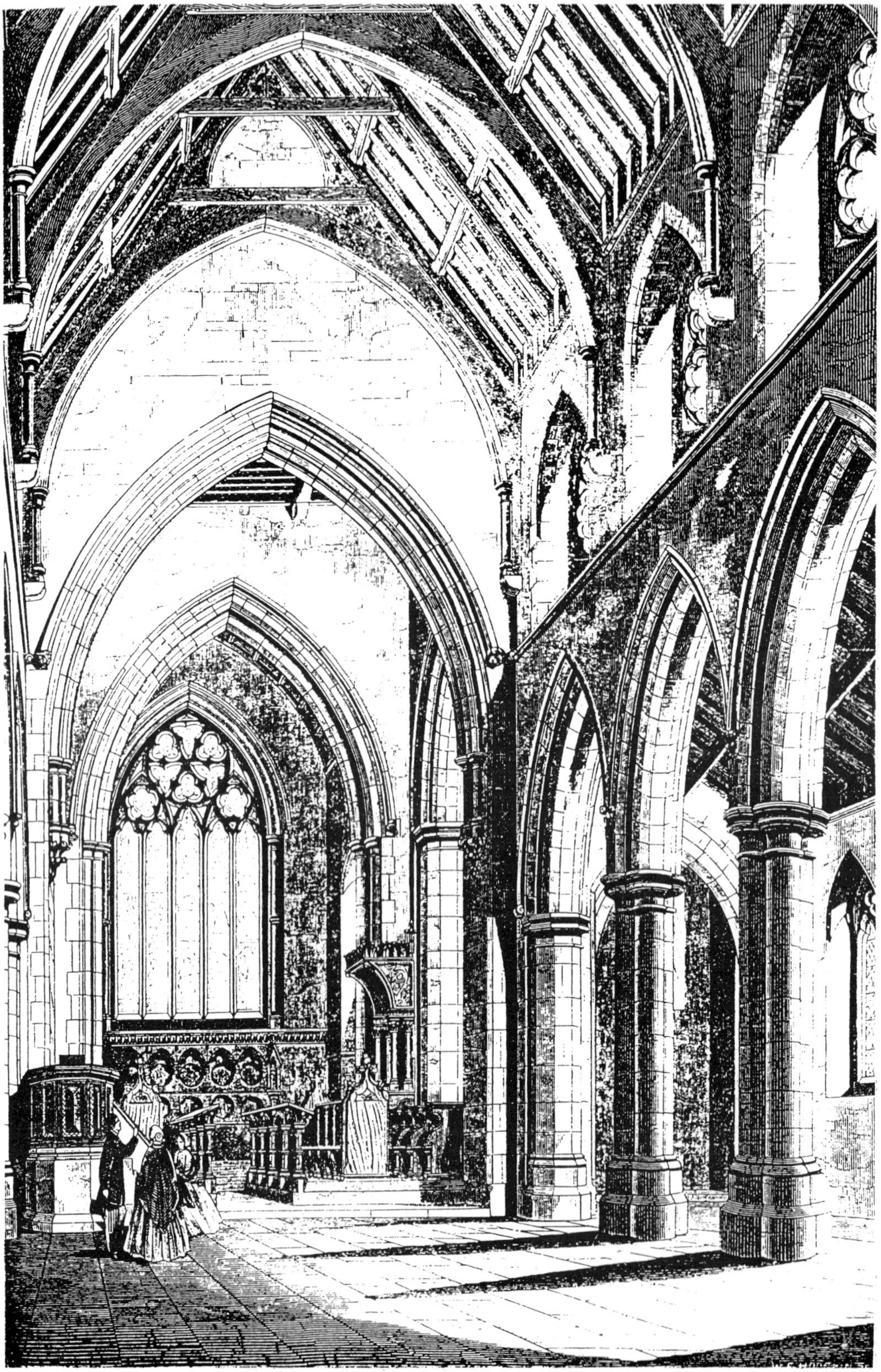

KILMORE CATHEDRAL

attention concentrated on the crossing that appears as a further bay articulated only by a corbelled archway. Beyond, a chancel arch conceals the shortness of the choir. Consistent furnishings to Slater's design with woodwork carved by Forsyths of London who did the later figurative retable in sgraffito. Furnishings now rearranged in the crossing—a pity. Stone carving by Purdy and Outhwaite. The contractor was the father of the architect William Hague. The Victorian glass is of the same quality as the architecture, the three earliest windows being installed before the consecration—two by Muller in the south transept, and one in the south aisle by Clayton and Bell. Glass in the double lancet of the west façade by Mayer. The most richly coloured window is the five-light above the altar, by Wailes of Newcastle (1868). Further windows by Heaton, Butler and Bayne. Good war memorial window to the sons of Lord Farnham by Catherine O'Brien, who executed two further smaller windows. Slater also designed the Gothic entrance arch (and adjoining lodge) to an avenue vanishing into the parkland towards a neo-Classical bishop's palace.

KINGSCOURT: Cabra Castle

Once known as Cormey Castle it was acquired, enlarged and castellated by Col. Joseph Pratt in the 1830s. He kept the modest scale of the original, merely extending it through a chain of towers into castellated outbuildings higher up the hillside, all coated with white painted stucco. The result was intended to be Norman, and may have looked more venerable when it was covered with ivy and surrounded with trees, and before plate glass was introduced into the windows—but feudal it never was. Inside, the only large room is the drawingroom set in the entrance tower over the front door, approached by a triple-height galleried staircase; it no longer retains its original gilt wallpaper. Now a hotel.

KINGSCOURT: Catholic Church

Designed by William Hague and built in 1869-78, to overlook the town, its polygonal east end rising above the remnants of the earlier church. Unfinished tower. Lavishly detailed interior, if more conventional than Hague's earlier commissions. The three large windows of the apse are filled with richly coloured stained glass by Evie Hone (1947-8).

MOUNT NUGENT: Kilnacrott

Early 19th-century Tudor revival. Elegant asymmetrical façade with *porte-cochère*, mullioned windows and tall chimneys. Inventive internal vaulting. Attributable to James Sheil. Inherited by William Hague. Now a Norbertine abbey.

MOUNT NUGENT: Kilnahard Castle

House remodelled as small Gothic castle (*c.*1860) sited on the edge of Lough Sheelin, which provided the stones for the grotto-like entrance arch. Saved from dry rot by the late Sir Cecil Boyd-Rochfort, on his retirement as trainer to the racehorses of Queen Elizabeth II.

TEMPLEPORT: Catholic Church

Sited on the summit of a hill on the road between Ballyconnell and Ballinamore, the ascendant character of this church has to stand in for a belfry that was never built. William Hague's perspective shows an elaborate spire rising from a shaft boldly unadorned. Though this church is small and simple, here in 1866 Hague is revealed at the height of his powers, when he had freed himself from the awkwardness of youth, but had still retained his brio. The fenestration is made up mainly of rose windows, coupled trefoils in the nave, single quatrefoils in the chancel. The outsize rose window on the western gable is answered by a lesser rose balanced over lancets above the altar. Red marble columns add an unexpected rich articulation to the interior. Chubby cylinders between the nave and aisles are wittily reduced to divide the coupled roses in the celestory above and are corbelled out in a more delicate version to define the chancel from the nave. The foliate sculpture of the capitals is an advanced Ruskinian, but the corbelled heads of saints beneath the trusses hark back to the naivety of rural Gothick.

KILNACROTT

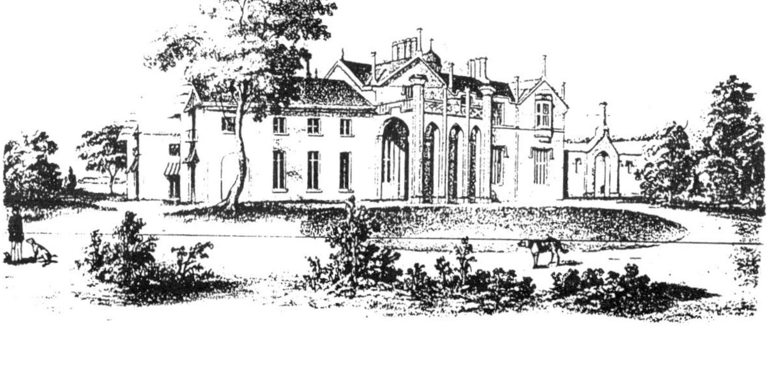

CLARE

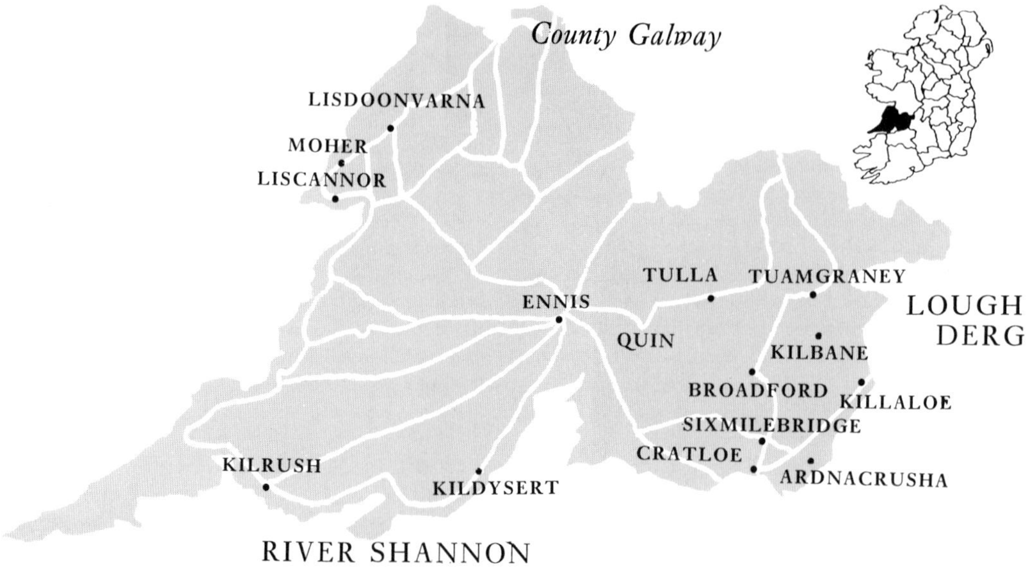

ARDNACRUSHA: **Parteen-a-Lax**
A rare example of an Irish Edwardian architect in 1901 building his own house untrammelled by conventions, and as a result pre-empting the Modern Movement. He was Robert Donough O'Brien, son of the Young Ireland leader, William Smith O'Brien. He came up with the idea of a large, cut-stone, single-storey rectangle spanned with a shallow segmental vault perforated by the occasional skylight to give top-lighting to the circulation spaces and service rooms that take up the centre of the house. A glazed dome in the centre of the drawingroom. Four circular chimneys at the corners like cotton reels. The modernity of this today is counterbalanced by its surroundings, a flower garden sloping to the river, made by the artist Geraldine O'Brien.

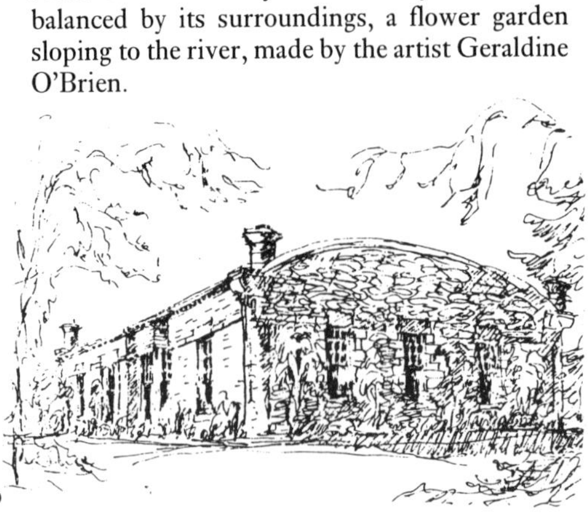

BROADFORD: **Hurdlestown House**
Compact stone-built shooting lodge with gables and steeply pitched roof. Designed by William Fogerty in 1871 for a Colonel White. Now a guesthouse.

CRATLOE: **Cratloe Wood**
One of the longest-inhabited houses in Ireland to survive without change of ownership; now open to the public. Built originally by the Stafford O'Briens as a 'long house' with room after room. The unrecorded 19th-century architect, possibly James Pain, behaved with great tact adding a corridor and a staircase wing to the entrance front, and a central gabled projection to the garden front, so that its distinctive atmosphere remains undisturbed. Victorian parterres are being recreated by the present owners, Mr and Mrs Robin Brickendon.

ENNIS: **Bank of Ireland**
Previously the Northern Bank. Architecturally the most distinguished of the town's four banks, a small symmetrical palazzo in a kind of Hiberno-Romanesque. The undercutting of its capitals is contrastingly frothy. Architect, William Caldbeck (1864).

ENNIS: **Catholic Pro-Cathedral**
One of the few attributed works of the mysterious Dominic Madden, architect of Tuam

Cathedral. The exterior has nave and aisles of equal height with galleries at the entrance and in the transepts. The piers are diagonally positioned. From them intersecting Gothic arches with traceried spandrels rise to support a flat panelled ceiling painted by Early and Powell a generation later. The result is Gothic on the cheap, but refreshingly unconventional. The spatial interplay of the raked galleries to the unexpected double height of the aisles has survived the ministrations of subsequent architects since its completion in 1842: J.J. McCarthy designed in the 1860s the high altar, chapels to the Sacred Heart and the Blessed Virgin, the tower and spire; O'Malley and O'Rourke did further work in 1911; finally, in 1973, a new altar and lectern were inserted in the organic boulder style harking back to the druids. The original reredos inset with paintings is now partly hidden by a lamentable baldachino.

ENNIS: Church of Ireland

The most westerly of W.H. Lynn's churches, built when he was at his most hard-pressed by commissions and borrowing much from Castlemacadam, Co. Wicklow (q.v.), a church he had designed a year before on the other side of Ireland. Both churches had the same problem. To be correctly orientated, the back had to face the road, and in the case of Ennis the rear view is at the end of a fashionable street. The composition rises from an overlying porch through two adjoining aisles to a massive corner tower. Tension is generated by giving the tower a saddle roof aligned to the aisles below and by deploying a prominent boiler flue as a rival upright. Even the most prominent component of Lynn's design, the polyglonal chancel, has to beat off the challenge of an adjoining vestry. With so much happening at the back, the unseen front is of small account, and the main door is discreetly hidden on the side. An opus sectile by Catherine O'Brien is set into an elaborate reredos with miniature saints sculpted by James Leech. Further windows by Jones and Wills (1909). Stained glass by Catherine O'Brien in the porch. Murals by Brigid Ganly.

ENNIS: The Courthouse

The Keanes were one of the principal families in Ennis and one of them is recorded as a brilliant architect. However, it is doubtful that J.B. Keane was a relation as he made no impact here and his courthouse has always been credited locally to Henry Whitestone, presumably the executant architect, since while the drawings date from 1838, the building was not erected till 1850, when Keane was languishing in a debtor's prison. The limestone exterior with its hexastyle Ionic portico is handsome and self-assured, but some of the interiors are of uncertain proportions, and the seated statue of Sir Michael O'Loughlen, Master of the Rolls, by Joseph Kirk is sited only too evidently as an afterthought. The elegantly galleried district courtroom still retains its original woodgraining finish.

ENNIS: The Mausoleum, Ruan

Impressive Egyptian Revival tomb of Sir

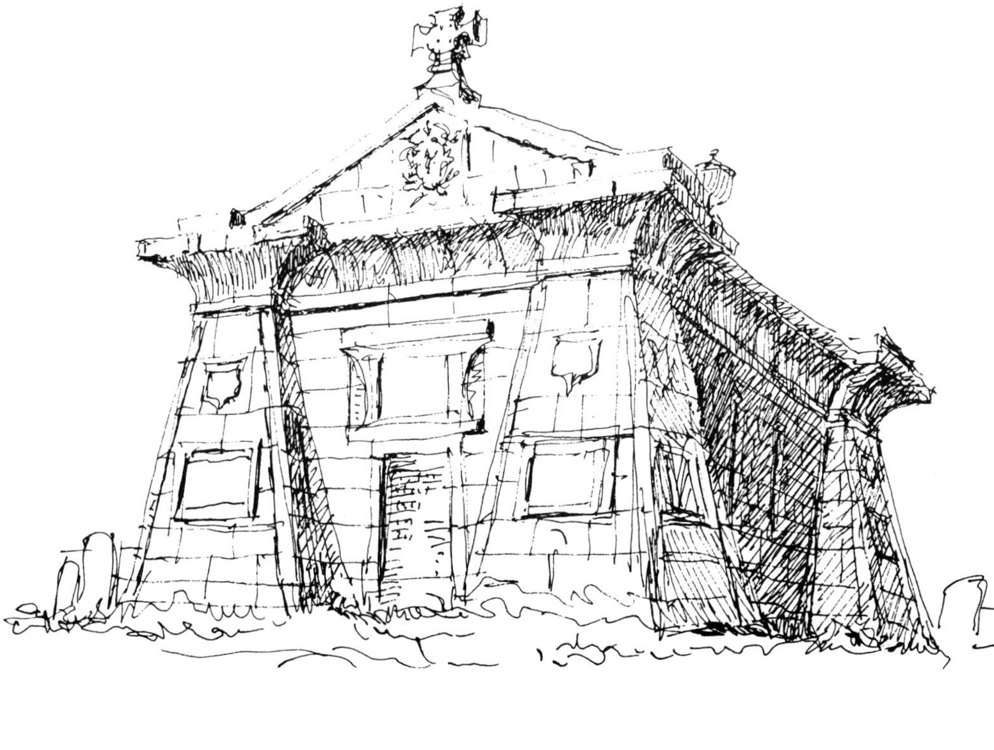

Michael O'Loghlen, the first Catholic to be appointed Master of the Rolls, who died in 1850, and who is also commemorated by a statue in the courthouse of Ennis. Blithely medieval stone shields enliven the massively tapered corner piers.

ENNIS: **O'Connell Memorial**
A lofty Doric column erected in 1850 in memory of the Liberator to the design of the Dundalk architect John Neville and carved by James Cahill of Dublin; the contractor was the architect of the nearby Franciscan church, William Carroll. The design is not quite strong enough for its massive base. The statue is too highly perched to be assessed as a portrait, but would appear to represent him at the time he was first elected to parliament for Clare in 1828, with a billowing cloak concealing the corpulence that has inspired his Dublin memorial.

ENNIS: **Our Lady's Hospital**
Designed in the third phase of providing the provincial towns of Ireland with an adequate system of mental institutions it is a reaction against the grimly Tudor complexes of the 1840s, being somewhat more relaxing and humane. This asylum is the one that owes most to the Georgian in concept, following a symmetrical layout but with round-arched windows, occasionally grouped in twos and threes. Entry under the central Italianate tower balanced on what appears to be a Georgian house. Further Italianate towers contain staircases to the wings. Cut stone throughout. The architects were William Fogerty of Limerick and his obscure collaborator named Adair, who were commissioned in 1863 and completed their work in 1868.

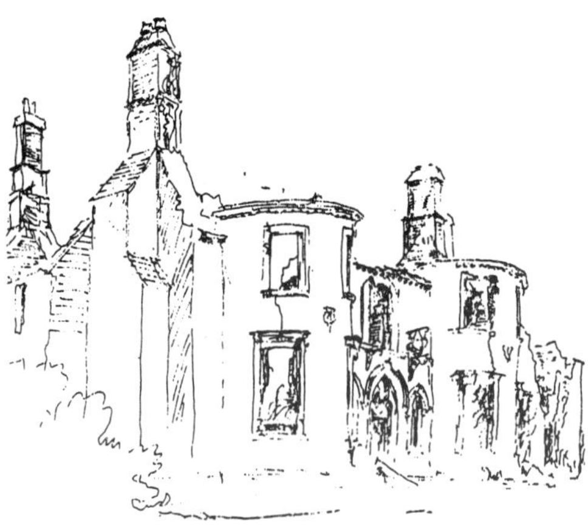

ENNIS: **Paradise**
A Georgian house built by the Henns of Paradise and remodelled (*c.*1870) for them by John McCurdy as a small French chateau complete with candle-snuffer spirelets flanking with a doorcase of Batty Longley Gothick. The house is set on a wooded hill with views up the Shannon, above acres of farmland reclaimed from the river by generations of Henns but now abandoned. The house itself was sold and subsequently destroyed by fire.

ENNIS: **Presbyterian Church**
Built in 1853 as a simple high-pitched cell, by William Fogerty. Imaginatively altered and extended in 1975 by Anthony O'Neill to serve as the de Valera museum and library.

ENNIS: **St Flannan's College**
The principal seminary of the diocese of Killaloe, vaguely Gothic but indisputably institutional, sited on the Limerick road but at a discreet distance from the distractions of the town. Entrance beneath a tower with a slated roof. Designed by a local architect, Frank O'Connor, and built in 1889.

ENNIS: **Westbourne House**
Italianate villa in the idiom of J.S. Mulvany with pillared porch bay windows and eaved roof. Built for the Bannatynes; now the residence of the Catholic bishop of Killaloe.

KILBANE: **Catholic Church**
Simple Gothic Revival barn church in a small village south-east of Broadford (*c.*1840).

KILDYSERT: **Cahercon**
Georgian house remodelled and extended for Colonel White *c.*1873 by a local architect, W.S. Cox (his only important country house commission). He retained the earlier house as his centrepiece and added wings, to give his client every modern convenience—a billiard room to the north and a conservatory to the south, with bay-windowed pavilions inserted between them and the main house. One of these contains an immense drawingroom converted into a chapel by the present owners, the Salesian nuns, who have made their sacristy out of the detached smokingroom reached only through the conservatory.

Cox was not a country-house architect and his interiors reflect the uncertainty of his client's predelictions (Byzantine in the diningroom, Adamesque in the drawingroom), but he made a genuine effort to preserve the finest features of the original house, including its superb Regency plasterwork. The most decorative of his contributions is the conservatory. This has an arched structure to give the impression of being a curvilinear from within; traceried windows and decorative grilles, with a polyglonal apse to give the best view of the river.

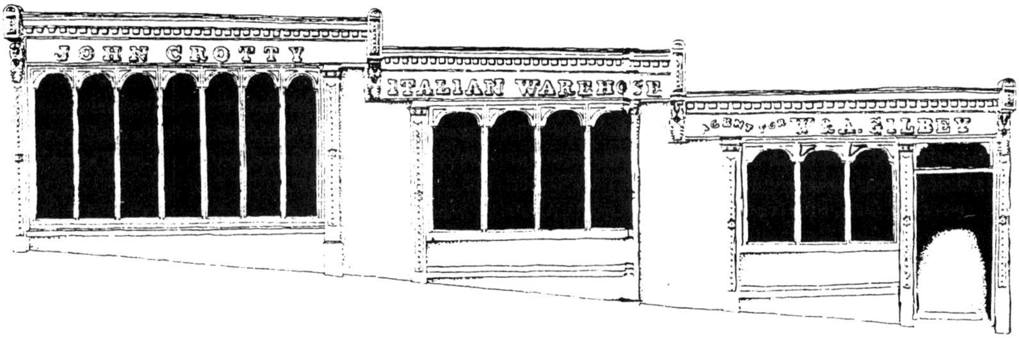

KILLALOE: **John Crotty's**
Three shopfronts with decorative signboards staggered so that they adapt to the level of the street that descends towards the Shannon.

KILLALOE: **Ballina Catholic Church**
Cruciform church in simple vernacular Gothic now modernized. Characterful incised slate tombs in the adjoining graveyard. Glass by Harry Clarke (1927).

KILLALOE: **Tinerana**
Late Victorian country house incorporating an earlier structure sited on a wooded promontory extending into Lough Derg. The home of the Purdon family, who also built a small square-towered church for the Church of Ireland halfway up their avenue. When the estate was sold to the Gleesons, who were Catholics, the church was abandoned until it was sold for a record sum as a weekend retreat. In recent years the house itself has been sold, and its atmospheric collection of big game trophies and oriental baubles, accumulated by the Gleesons during their years of service to the British Empire, has been dispersed.

KILRUSH: **Catholic Church**
Commissioned in 1840 for his tenantry by Col. Vandeleur, who presumably chose the architect as there is no evidence that William Owen (who got the job) ever designed another church. He was one of the seventeen children of Jacob Owen, who ran the Board of Works for thirty years to further the careers of his sons and pupils. Interior distinguished by its sense of spaciousness. Otherwise this church has had a typical history—completed by J.J. McCarthy who added the lofty belfry in 1861; remodelled by George Ashlin at the turn of the century; and recently modernized. Stained glass by Barff in 1859 and the Clarke Studios in 1932.

What makes the Catholic church of Kilrush so unusual is Owen's choice of Norman, made at the moment that Pugin had chosen the same style for the Catholic church in Gorey, but more influenced by his father's church at Arbour Hill in Dublin (q.v.). Outside he terminated his walls with Irish battlements. Internally there is a forceful contrast between the unbroken void of the nave and the columned galleries of the transept. McCarthy's painted decoration of the ceiling survives, as do all the liturgical fittings. Elegant Lombardesque tomb in coloured marbles (1868), presumably by McCarthy, on the south wall of the nave.

KILRUSH: **Convent of Mercy**
One of the most concentrated designs of J.J. McCarthy, impressively sited on the edge of valley, with the chapel on the first floor approached by elaborate twin doors of an arched landing. Massive chimneys and steep roofs reveal the influence of Pugin's Maynooth, as also the paned, sashed and trefoil-headed windows. Designed in 1854 and built in 1860.

KILRUSH: **Glynn's Mills**
Two castellated mills at the harbour edge with differing façades due to one serving as a warehouse.

KILRUSH: **Martyrs' Memorial**
This brutalistic Hiberno-Romanesque monument dominates the marketplace but the architecture is negated by the insipidity of the sculpture (Erin and her wolfhound). Dated 1903.

KILRUSH: **Vandeleur Tomb**
A Norman Revival mausoleum with triple arches at the gable ends and five arches along the sides concealed from casual view by the ruins of the medieval parish church. Built for his family by Col. C.M. Vandeleur in 1873, possibly to the design of William Fogerty, who designed the Smith O'Brien mausoleum in Ardagh (q.v.).

LISCANNOR: **Birchfield**
Cornelius O'Brien MP is remembered today for the compulsory contributions written into the leases of his tenants towards a memorial that would immortalize his 'liberality' and his exertions on their behalf. As a result, the nobility

of the triumphal column has been overlooked and its architect ignored. Judge O'Loghlen is recorded as being head of the committee and, as he was responsible for commissioning Ennis Courthouse from J.B. Keane: he may have commissioned this from Keane as well. When completed in 1853, Cornelius had four more years to contemplate the panorama of his estate, his four-towered castle and two far-flung castellated barns), so that to the present viewer the complex has the semblance of a ruined city.

Cornelius O'Brien had also four years left to ensure a mausoleum of appropriate grandeur in the adjoining graveyard. The tomb is set into the hill inspired by the royal tombs of Mycenae, but here surmounted by Gothic cast-iron railings round a limestone pinnacle. One face of the pinnacle commemorates Edward O'Brien, the eldest son, who had escaped from such an appalling father only to predecease him by losing his life on the battlefields of India.

LISCANNOR: **Catholic Church**
Tower added to the existing church by William Scott in 1917.

LISCANNOR: **St Bridget's Well**
Annual pilgrimage centre for the Aran islanders with the central shrine, a grotto, post-Lourdes, encircled by a stream that has been channelled through walls of local stone, so the noise of the water deafens the worshippers.

LISDOONVARNA: **The Spa**
A modest bungalow surrounded with a verandah like a rural tennis club is still the centre of this celebrated spa. On the spur above a handsome Gothic villa (*c.*1870), built by a rich doctor.

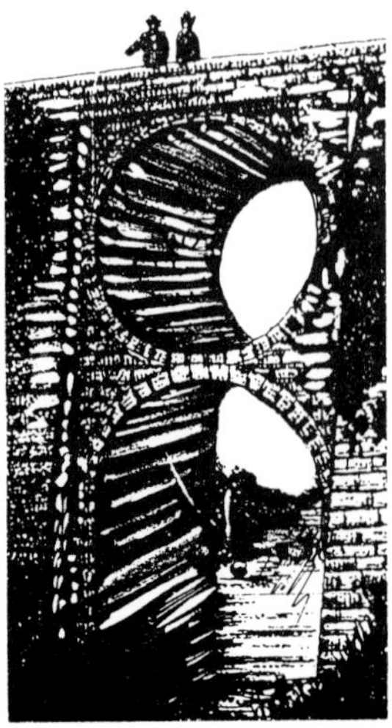

LISDOONVARNA: **Spectacle Bridge**
The most extraordinary Victorian bridge in Ireland, an outsize version of a Chinese moon gate balanced over a conventional arch spanning a gorge with the river Aille far below. Built *c.*1850. Architect, the engineer of the Corkscrew Road, Michael O'Loghlin.

MOHER: **O'Brien's Folly**
Gothic Revival look-out tower built *c.*1850 by Cornelius O'Brien MP on the highest point of the Cliffs of Moher, its tininess a dramatic contrast to the vertiginous cliffs taking the full onslaught of the Atlantic.

QUIN: **Ballykilty Manor**
Georgian house remodelled after a fire and given a new Italianate front range with a pillared porch. Home of the Blood family, including the collector of books and coins, Bindon Blood (known locally as 'The Vampire'). Now a hotel.

QUIN: **Knappogue Castle**
A medieval castle of the McNamaras that had lapsed into dereliction at the start of the 19th century, when it was acquired by a family called Scott. Their cheerful Norman Revival additions were remodelled by James Pain in a less obtrusive manner *c.*1850 for the new owner, Lord Dunboyne. Pain raised the corner towers of the stable block, and linked them by a windowless curtain wall as medieval as the tower house that looms behind it. Staff quarters built on (1900-6) by Albert Murray. The castle was sold for the timber of its parkland in 1938 and dismantled. Seen as a ruin from the air by a treasurer of the American Navy, the late Mark Edwin Andrews, and acquired by him and restored by his architect wife, Lavone Dickensheets Andrews, with Alan Hope. Lent by the Andrews to Shannon Development, who run banquets there while seven savage centuries are recounted in declamation and song.

SIXMILEBRIDGE: **Belvoir Castle**
Small Gothic Revival chapel added in 1862 to a Regency Gothic castle now in ruins.

TULLA: **Clooney**
Built in 1863, the most sumptuous of E.H. Carson's Italianate houses, as can be still discerned today. A half-century of total dereliction has done little to age the crispness of Carson's classicism chillingly cut in local limestone. At first sight the architecture is pure Regency until one notices the curious three-quarter columns embedded into rustications at the corners and the compressed Venetian window above the porch with its machine-age detailed balustrading. One then realizes how much more beautiful this house is as a ruin. Originally the seat of the Georgian architect Francis Bindon, and acquired by the O'Carrolls, the patrons of

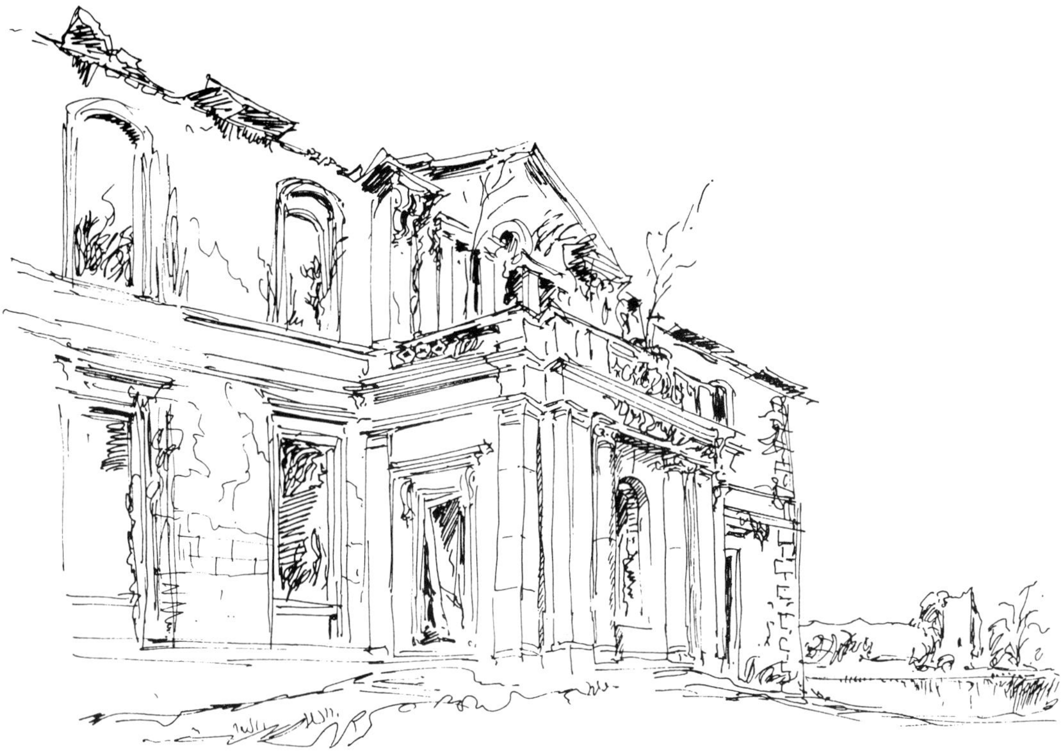

Carson, from the last of the Bindons. Carson surrounded the earlier house on two sides with an entrance range to the south and an adjoining range facing east to the garden. This is centered on the polygonal bay window of the drawingroom (since collapsed). The hall is T-shaped with the door of the drawingroom at the end of one arm—the principal staircase at the end of the other. At the rear Carson built an austere neo-Classical stable block in marked contrast to the house.

All this was in perfect condition when it was bought back by a Bindon daughter who had married a rich husband in Australia, to where her father had emigrated. Her husband spent all his money keeping his wife in grandeur and gambling on the side. He was given a pauper's funeral, and the house was abandoned to the elements by his widow, like the medieval tower-house in what was once the park, reflected in a reed-fringed lake against a backdrop of the Clare hills.

TUAMGRANEY: **Raheen Manor**
Earlier house remodelled 1898 by Clifford Smith into an Arts and Crafts version of an Irish castle for the poet, novelist and industrialist Sidney Royse Lysaght, who, much to the embarrassment of his son, Edward MacLysaght, the authority on Irish families, claimed in his memoirs to be the last Englishman to see R.L. Stevenson alive. House destroyed by an accidental fire and almost entirely demolished. The gatelodge by Clifford Smith survives, with bay windows at the champferred corners and central chimneystack—delightful.

CORK CITY

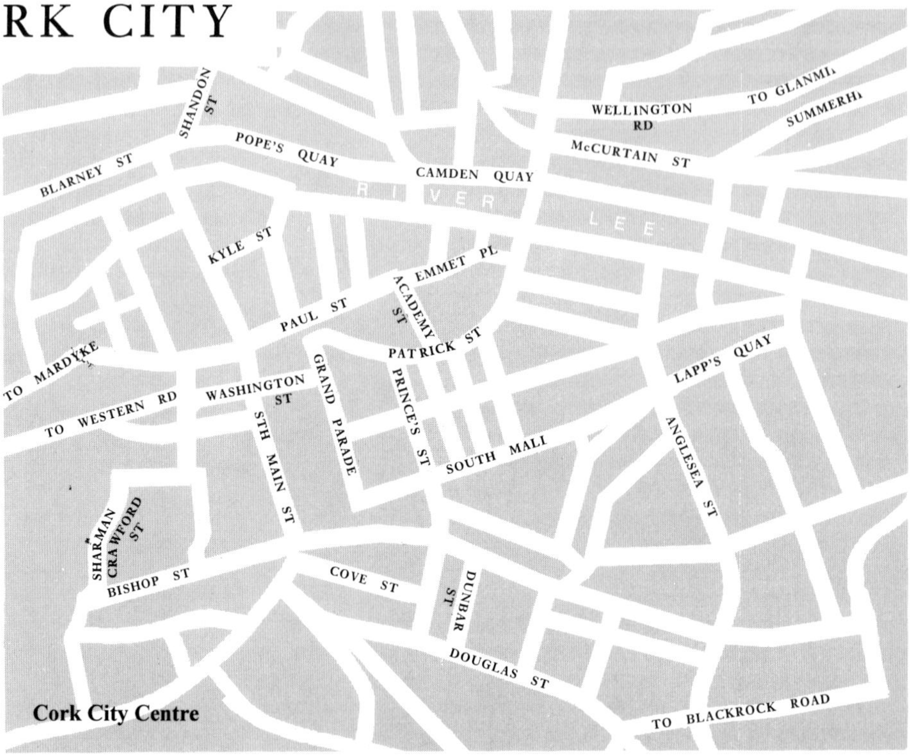

Cork City Centre

ACADEMY STREET: **Dillinger's Restaurant**

Manneristic urban warehouse built in red brick for Baker and Wright, dated 1852; windows inset into segmental arches. Extended and remodelled.

ALEXANDRA ROAD: **St Luke's**

Designed by W.H. Hill in 1881 as a 'Home for Protestant Incurables'. A rigidly symmetrical red-brick institution enlivened by Gothic fenestration in the central pavilion; spacious semicircular bay window jutting out from the pavilion at either end joined by double-storied cast-iron verandahs that open off the linking ranges. This gives a sense of colonial nostalgia.

ANGLESEA STREET: **Model Schools**

One of the finest of the Irish model schools built to the designs of E.T. Owen and R.A. Gibbons *c.*1862. A far-flung complex given focus by an asymmetrically sited campanile, executed throughout in polychromatic brickwork with zig-zag ornament round the voussoirs of the windows. Additions by James McMullen.

ANGLESEA STREET: **SS Joachim and Anne**

Commissioned by a Protestant benefactor to accommodate fourteen Catholic orphaned girls. A constricted Gothic design executed in red brick with limestone trimmings. Henry Hill's drawing (*c.*1850) survives in the Hill collection.

BISHOP STREET: **St Finn Barre's Cathedral**

Sited above the river Lee on the foundations of St Finbar's monastery, this cathedral is the architectural answer to Disestablishment, when the Church of Ireland sought refuge from contemporary reverses and retreated into a dim medieval past. A generation of Cork merchants and landowners built and embellished this improbable realization of a crusader's vision, closer perhaps to an illustration in the margin of an illuminated manuscript than to the ideal cathedral as engraved by Viollet-le-Duc.

As in the 13th century, all aspects of the design were controlled by the master architect, here William Burges, who supplied designs to his specialist craftsmen both on and off the site. For example, all the designs for the external sculpture were modelled and cast by Thomas Nicholls in London, and then brought to Cork to be copied by a team of masons directed by a master carver, R. McLeod. Some casts are to seen in the ambulatory.

The international architectural competition of 1862 for the cathedral of St Fin Barre attracted sixty-eight competitors. The design of Burges was unanimously chosen, but the defeated competitors complained that his cathedral

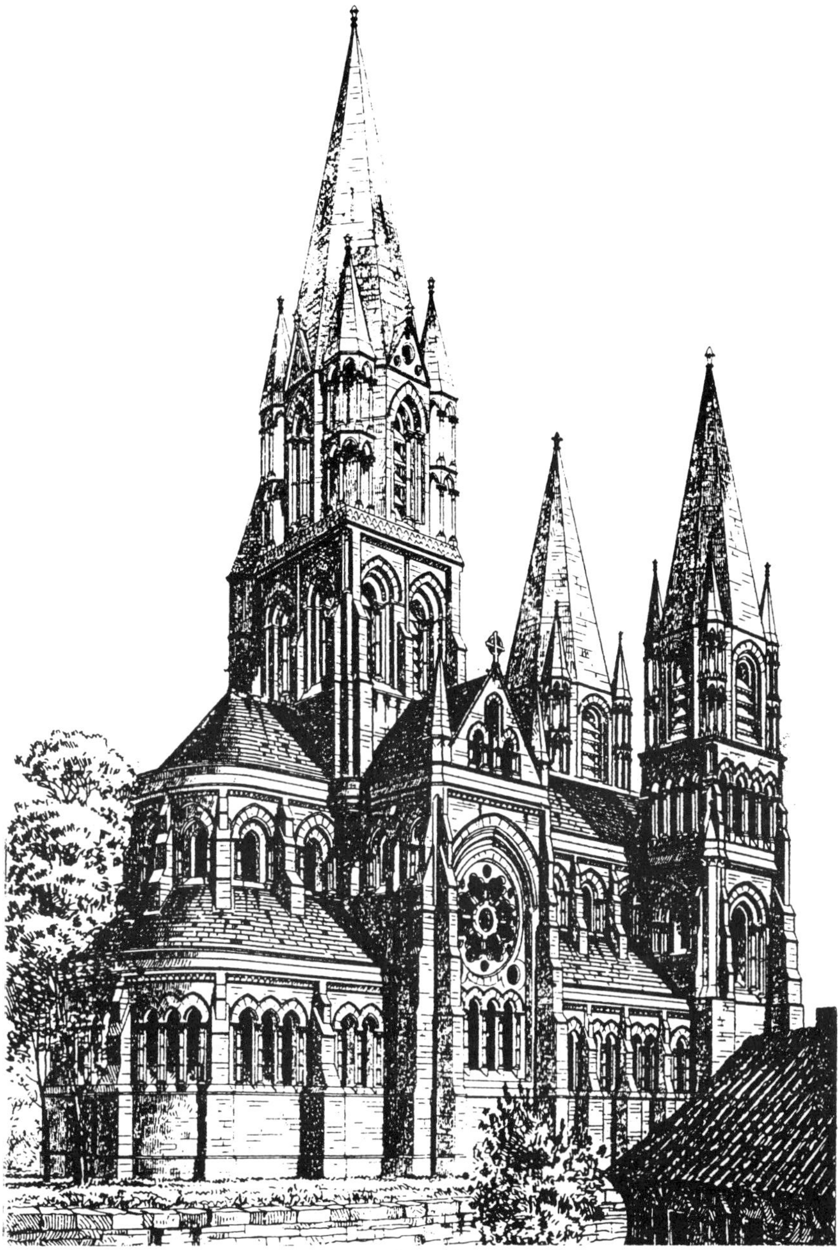

could not be built for the stated budget of £15,000. Burges replied that the triple towers and spires, the decoration and the stained glass would be the work of future generations, and this serene optimism permeates every nook and cranny of what he lived to complete himself over the next twenty years, the most consistent 19th-century interpretation of a medieval cathedral but at the same time an intensely personal vision. Burges was immersed in the 13th century, but not out of a sense of misery or guilt; rather by his determination to hold on to the imaginative life of his childhood. So, while there is lot of Chartres, Noyon and Laon in St Fin Barre's, there is also of a lot of that gingerbread hut discovered by Hansel and Gretel when they were lost in the forest. But here the children are diverted from gobbling up the house by pranks and puns. When we penetrate into the sanctuary we discover that the mosaic floor is designed as a fishing-net full of fish and people kept afloat by a series of bobbing corks.

Inevitably there are sacrifices. In St Fin Barre's the tension of the interior is generated by the conflict between scale and size. The accommodation even for a mere seven hundred, as the brief required, still gives under half a clear view of the altar. For many their vision would be blocked off by the pulpit and the lofty

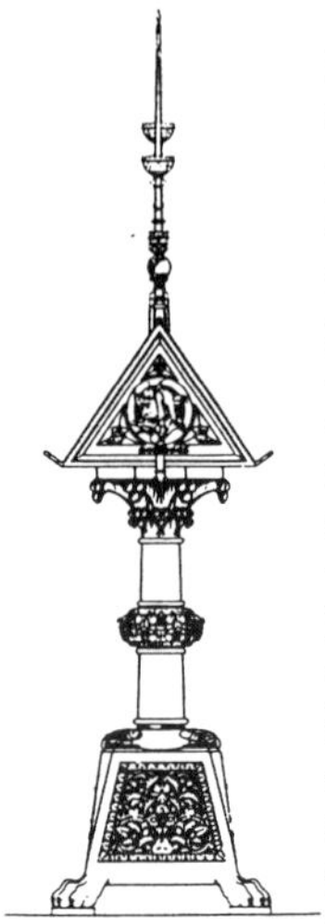

bishop's throne (an afterthought). Not that these fittings would be thought of as large in a conventional cathedral, but here they seem gargantuan: between them they halve the aperture into the chancel. The capitals are of normal cathedral dimensions, and their shafts would be also, were they only double their height. Not all the life-size statutes of the apostles can fit into one portal; they have to be split into two. The positioning of the three belfries, so magical from a distance, from nearby only emphasizes the shortness of the nave. And such are the limitations of the site that the cathedral balances precariously on its ledge. The single bay of the northern transept plunges precipitously towards the street, but ingeniously accommodates the sunken organ, one of the finest Victorian instruments in Ireland. The south transept is embarrassingly embedded in the hillside. Detached cathedral library with earlier interior reinforced by star-perforated trusses (*c.*1870).

BISHOP STREET: **Stabling, Beamish and Crawford**

The most accomplished industrial building in the city, erected in 1900-2 by Houston and Houston of London. Corner office built like a cottage ornée; gatelodge with overhanging upper floor and diagonally positioned chimney-stacks.

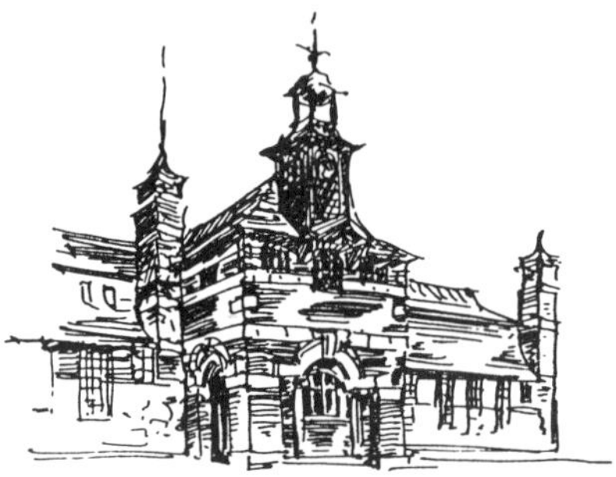

Pairs of ventilation towers also built out of brick with coursed banded stonework. Horizontal roofs and dormers play against these vertical foils. Concave cowls to the ventilation towers give a final whimsical flourish in contrast to Burges' cathedral that looms beyond. Elegant gatehouse with clock tower faces the courtyard at the rear. Now an enterprise centre.

BLACKROCK: **Diamond Hill**

Earlier house extended and remodelled under the influence of the Arts and Crafts movement. Entered through arched porch. Adjoining drawingroom with fireplace centred in a polygonal bay lit by tiny windows. Leaded lights and fretted ceilings.

BLACKROCK: **Diamond Hill Memorial**

If William Atkins was unsuccessful in major competitions of the 1860s, in what he was able to build his materials became more varied, his detail more delicate, his polychromy more daring. In Cork this phase is best seen in the Diamond Hill memorial put up by Alexander McCarthy in honour of his Milesian ancestors. Local vandals of long ago have made off with the bronze commemorative plaques at the base, before they won unanimous acceptance from rival claimants to the lost title of the McCarthy Mor. The bronze medallions above have also lost their names but are still inset in contrasting coloured marbles.

BLACKROCK: **Linden Convalescent Home**

A grimly designed neo-Romanesque private lunatic asylum designed for a Dr Osborne in 1855 and built with the proceeds from his ingenious invention to force-feed patients. Osborne had been a significant force in the selection of William Atkins as the architect for Cork Lunatic Asylum; Atkins is the architect here, apart from a later half-timbered additions by Arthur Hill, who must have felt that to complete the symmetry of the original design would have been too depressing.

BLARNEY STREET: **Presentation Novitiate**

Triumphalist composition in harshly detailed Gothic to overlook the valley of the Lee, executed in an undimmed polychromy of red and yellow brickwork. Two wings at the rear, one of them terminating in an apsidal chapel with glass by Mayer. Designed by S.F. Hynes and dated 1891.

CAMDEN QUAY: **McKenzie's**

A lively, stucco-coated Lombardesque commercial building *c.*1880 distinguished by a closely spaced glazed arcade running the full length of the first floor and repeated in a later extension. Architect unrecorded.

CATHEDRAL ROAD: **St Mary's Catholic Pro-Cathedral**

Known traditionally as the North Chapel, built in 1802, interior remodelled after a fire by George Pain in 1828, extended by John Benson in 1862-7, chancel rebuilt *c.*1964 in Art Deco Gothic by Boyd Barrett, who removed Pain's galleries, the high altar and the Strawberry Hill Gothick decoration (including twenty-seven saints, the earliest known sculptures of John Hogan carved for Bishop Murphy in 1818-9, spared from the fire of 1820 and now lost). A large perspective survives to indicate that Benson would have been equally contemptuous of Pain's lightheartedness. Benson's major contribution was the massive tower built in local sandstone with limestone dressings. This has never received its intended spire. Benson's chevet, fleche and transepts also remained unbuilt. Instead a baptistery and sacristy were added by Samuel Hynes, whose patron Bishop Delaney is commemorated in front of the church by J. Lawlor's statue of 1889. Inside, stained glass by the local Eugene Daly and memorials to Bishop Moylan; a bust by Turnerelli (1818). A mural monument to Bishop Murphy (1853), one of John Hogan's last works, disappeared also in 1964, presumably destroyed.

CAREY'S LANE: **SS Peter and Paul's**
A competition to replace a penal chapel here was won by John Hurley, but the commission went to the unplaced Edward Welby Pugin, causing so much discontent that the chief grumbler among the participants (J.P. Jones) was paid off. Pugin's original Irish partner, James Murray of Armagh, was replaced by George Ashlin. This is Ashlin's earliest commission (1859) and stylistically a decisive influence on every other church he designed. Firstly, the materials (red sandstone and limestone dressings); secondly, the plan (a wide nave and aisles that take up the entire cramped site; contrastingly shallow transepts; but no crossing). Instead, the clerestory windows are carried across the transepts as screens, an idea that reaches its apotheosis in Cobh Cathedral. A polygonal apse, a superabundance of stained glass and sculpture. The most striking external feature, a belfry soaring to over 230 feet, remains incomplete. Altar entirely to the design of Ashlin. Glass by Barnetts of Leith (1870) and Earley. Lavish confessionals guarded by angels. Other angels act as lampholders.

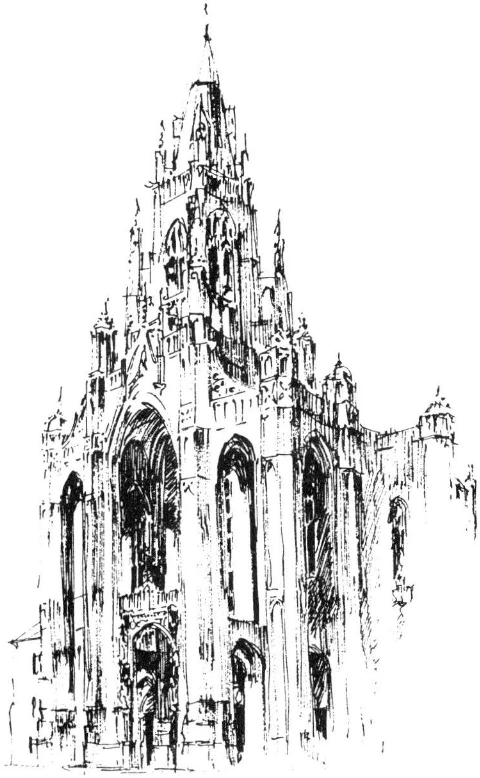

FR MATHEW QUAY: **Holy Trinity and Capuchin Monastery**
Commissioned by Father Mathew, the apostle of temperance, from George Pain in 1825 and then completed (at least the interiors) ten years after Pain's death by William Atkins. Pain's airy Gothic portico, one of his happiest inventions, was not implemented until 1889, and only then after a competition. Fortunately this was won by Dominic Coakely, who, apart from reducing the tower and spire, realized Pain's intentions. Today Atkins' interior is barely recognizable, firstly due to the refurnishing by George Ashlin (1906-8), who lengthened the chancel, and then due to a drastic modernization of recent years that has replaced the original arcades with

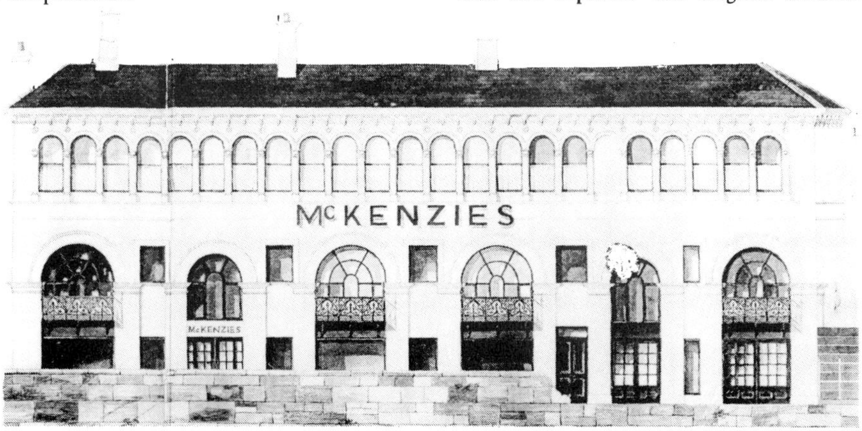

slender steel supports to improve the sight lines from the aisles. This sets a precedent that has never been imitated and here one can see quite well why. Stained glass: the O'Connell memorial window by Hemmings of Newcastle; and the Clarke Studios have made windows for the aisles. Exquisite Gothick carving on Pain's façade resembling Coolclough (q.v.) church. The adjoining monastery, a robust but crude design in Ballintemple limestone banded with red brick, was jammed up against the church by Robert Walker in 1888.

COVE STREET: **St Nicholas' Church of Ireland**

The exterior of this church rebuilt by Joseph Welland in the 1850s is dominated by the handsome tower and steeple added by William Atkins predating the triple spires of nearby St Fin Barre's Cathedral. Atkins must have found building this steeple some compensation for losing the cathedral competition to Burges. The interior reveals Welland at his most historical and austere, stung no doubt by the criticisms of the Ecclesiologists, since the plan conforms to all their requirements—nave and aisles of equal height and long narrow chancel, all with open roof structure and white washed walls. Apart from the south transept window to Dr Webster by Hemmings, the only colour comes from crude heraldic glass. Just when the interior has aged to be indistinguishable from its medieval models there are plans for closure.

CRAWFORD STREET: **Convent of St Marie de l'Isle**

William Atkins was one of the rare Church of Ireland architects to cross the religious divide and work also for the Catholic Church, as in this commission, a convent, designed in 1850. The chapel (completed 1869) is here linked to the main structure by a tower with unbuilt spire, balanced at the further end by another tower with a projecting oriel, its corner bays not windows but unexpected niches enshrining statues. Niches and statues snuggle also into the splayed buttresses of the chapel. The neighbouring orphanage (*c.*1855) is also freely treated and reveals a deepening understanding of Gothic architecture and Pugin. Extended by S.F. Hynes in 1892.

DOUGLAS STREET: **South Presentation Convent**

A labyrinth of convents, schools and chapels enclosing a secret Italianate garden with its tomb of the foundress, Nano Nagle. The Gothic ranges are in Cork's characteristic polychromy of limestone and sandstone, in one case precariously balanced on a retained Georgian ground floor. Architect unknown.

DUNBAR STREET: **South Chapel**

The oldest Catholic Gothic Revival church in Cork, but a victim of insensitive restoration. However, when the altar was moved forward, John Hogan's marble life-size effigy of Christ was carefully retained.

EMMET PLACE: **Crawford Art Gallery**

Designed by Arthur Hill, at first in collaboration with his father Henry, who died in 1887. The earliest designs show a Late Gothic Revival Arts and Crafts, but this was toned down into a restrained Anglo-Dutch to blend with the adjoining 18th-century custom house in the same red brick and limestone dressings. This forms the northern range, though few interior features survive. A corner entrance leads diagonally past the double-height sculpture galleries designed to house the earliest known casts of the Elgin

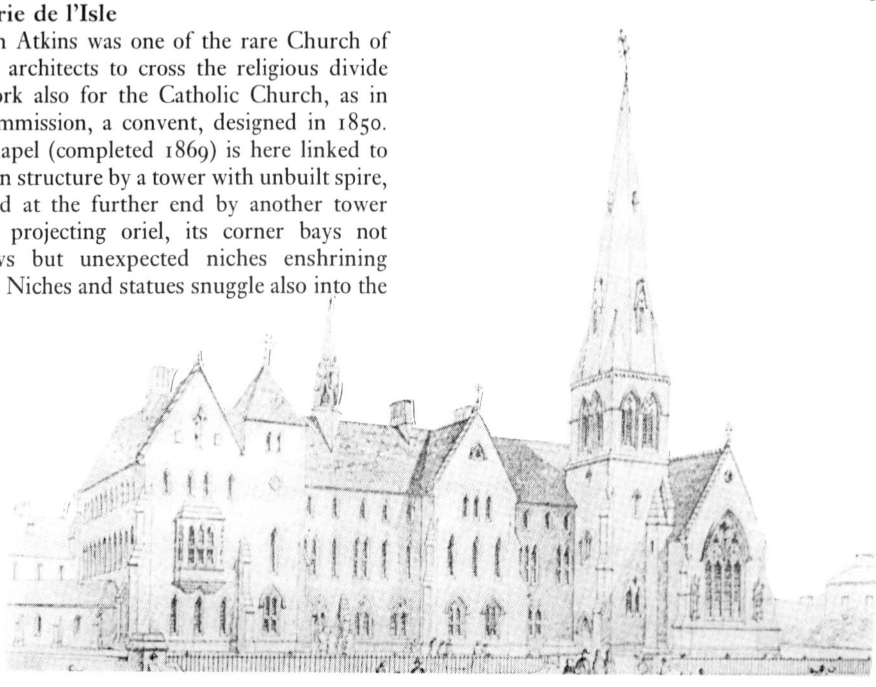

marbles (presented to Cork by George IV but dispersed in the 1970s). An imperial staircase ascends to an axial sequence of first-floor galleries. A wing contains a panelled boardroom and library with studios above. The atmosphere is not that of an institution but of an intimate, leisurely country house that has survived a period of long neglect. Impeccably restored under the supervision of its present curator, Peter Murray.

FERNHURST AVENUE: **Berkeley College**
Designed *c.*1860 as a residential college for the Church of Ireland attached to University College, Cork. Commissioned by William Bence-Jones from James St Aubyn, the architect for his family church at Kilmalooda. Its completion was delayed by labour problems, and imposed economies reduced its architectural qualities. Ironically, acquired as a Catholic student hostel attached to the Honan Chapel.

GLANMIRE ROAD: **St Patrick's Catholic Church**
Designed by George Pain in 1836. Up to ten years ago renderings by Pain of more elaborate schemes survived in the presbytery (they have been sold out of the country). As built, a Corinthian portico projects beneath his most neo-Classical campanile—a cruciform tempietto upholding a rotunda encircled by saints (as the parish church of Marylebone). The dark interior was made even more ungainly by Sir John Benson's extension of 1873 and George Ashlin's of 1894, both showing scant respect for Pain's design. Baptistry contains stained glass by McGoldrick (1924); opus sectile Resurrection by Rhind (1908).

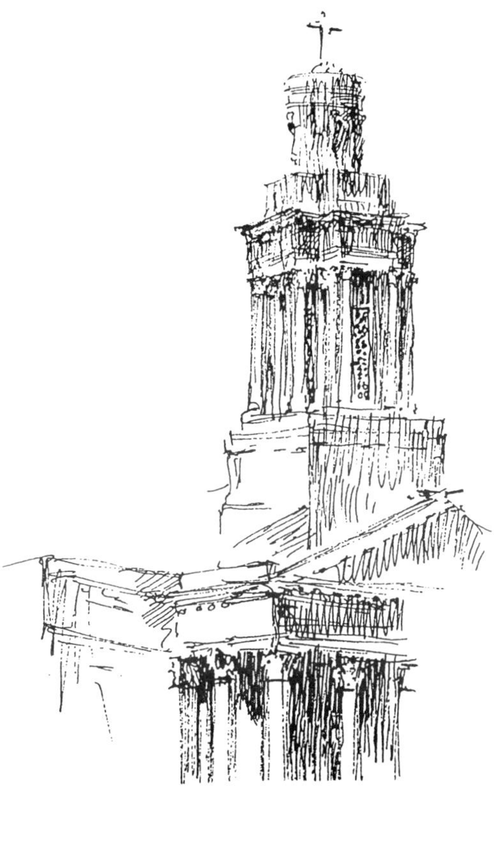

GLANMIRE ROAD LOWER: **Kent Railway Station**
A noble Tuscan portico intended by Sir John Benson is recorded by his perspective (now in the Hunt collection)—nine-bay central projection, five bays either side terminating in triumphal arches modelled on Pearce's Dublin Parliament Building. This was the proposal illustrated in the *Dublin Builder* of 1860. What was built was half the shed without the columns, now relegated to a service entrance when a new station was built in 1893 by Bayley and Gordon. They used a harsh red brick that has refused to mellow; the design is redeemed, however, by the gently curving railway shed behind. This curves due to the pioneering decision to abolish the existing terminus and link together the Cobh and Dublin lines for functional, not aesthetic reasons—Ireland's answer to York Station.

GLASHEEN, BOTANIC AVENUE: **St Patrick's Cemetery**
This cemetery took over from the earlier St Joseph's as Cork's most fashionable burial ground, but the commemorative sculpture is less inspired. The architecture is more ambitious. The most striking evidence of this is the pair of almost identical churches designed by Sir John Benson and built in 1867-9. They are proof of Benson's adaptability since they have the miniature scale and precision of detail more associated with the Gothic Revival churches of William Atkins. Benson's historicism is more fanciful and he grafts an Hiberno-Romanesque round tower on to the nave of one church and on to the chancel of the other. The interiors are of exposed brickwork. Chamfered arches rest on corbelled columns that support the open roof structure. Each vista terminates in an elaborately vaulted apsidal chancel lit by five stained glass lancets. Small oratory to Honan family in the style of Ashlin *c.*1875.

GRAND PARADE: **Queen's Arcade**
A bland Classical façade screens the earliest surviving shopping arcade in Cork and the one whose restoration twenty years ago heralded a revitalization of the inner city. The original design is credited to Henry Hill by his obituarist writing in 1887. Further remodelling by Samuel Hynes *c.*1890.

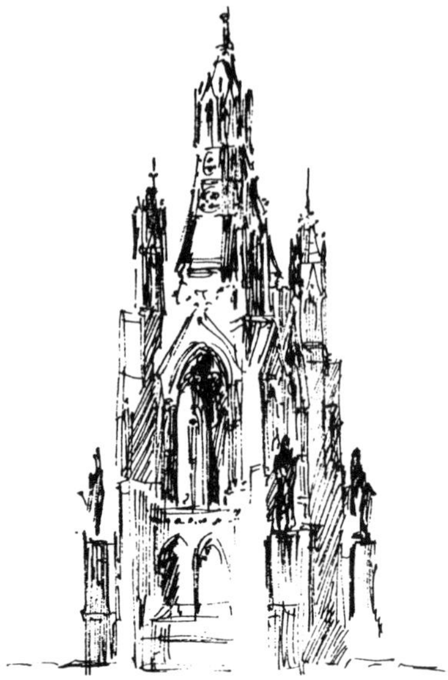

GRAND PARADE: **Martyrs' Memorial**
Designed by Dominic Coakley as a Gothic shrine and erected in honour of the centenary cele- brations for the 1798 rebellion.

GREENMOUNT: **Greenmount Schools**
The finest building in this complex (the Orphanage, 1858-60, attributable to William Atkins) was needlessly demolished ten years ago. This leaves a more pedestrian classroom block built out of sandstone rubble in 1854-6 to the design of Brother Paul Townsend, a Christian Brother turned amateur architect. His work has a certain humanity totally absent from the far more accomplished Gothic Revival institution designed by S.F. Hynes in 1890 and executed in red-brick and limestone dressings, unassailably symmetrical and now impervious to change.

KYLE STREET: **Woodford Bourne's Spirit Store**
Simplified Gothic Revival structure crisply detailed by an unknown architect *c.*1875 (most probably H. Hill, who was employed by Woodford Bourne as their architect). This was built as their spirit store—three parallel gabled sheds joined by lower two-storied links. A triple lancet above the central archway.

LADYSWELL: **Murphy's Brewery**
Large industrial complex of many periods dominated by a massive chimney-stack. Offices beneath it added by Samuel Hynes in 1893. Recently remodelled by Burke, Kennedy and Doyle.

LAPPS' QUAY: **Cork Savings Bank**
Competition won in 1839 and completed three years later by Thomas Deane and his brother Kearns. Thomas Deane had designed the original premises and had been made a trustee of the bank, a position he resigned when he won the competition. The neo-Classical design attributed to Kearns alone deserves its success on its own merits, with the horizontal coursing of the ground floor masterfully balanced by the vertical pilasters and Ionic columns that articulate the *piano nobile*. Executed throughout in silvery Ballintemple limestone. Internal banking hall no longer dominated by a sculpture of the philanthropist William Crawford carved in 1840 by John Hogan (the statue is now to be found in the Crawford Art Gallery). Heavily plastered ceiling, more appropriate to the Allied Irish Bank across the street (q.v.).

LOVER'S WALK: **St Finbarre's Seminary**
Substantial Gothic Revival institution, three stories beneath a steeply raked roof. Symmetrical façade with entrance flanked by polygonal bays. Asymmetrical side elevation enlivened by chimney-stacks and hip-roofed belfry. Pointed arched windows on the third floor, elsewhere polychromatic relieving arches, trefoiled on the middle floor. Designed in 1885 by S.F. Hynes, strongly influenced by Goldie's monastery for the Vincentians at Sunday's Well (q.v.).

LOUGH ROAD: **St Finbar's West**
A conventional Romanesque design of 1881; George Ashlin at his most predictable; extended in 1929 by James F. McMullen. Its best feature is the decorative mosaic and stained glass in the chancel.

MacCURTAIN STREET: **Thompson's Bakery**
The most freely designed of the Victorian commercial buildings that line up along the north side of MacCurtain Street. Incorporates a later low tower and linking block set flush alongside its gabled centrepiece inspired by William Atkins' convent of St Marie de l'Isle (q.v.). Built in red brick and limestone dressings with round arches introduced to accent the fenes- tration. Designed in 1889 by Robert Walker, who had already built the Hamburg branch. Extended by Walker in 1914.

MacCURTAIN STREET: **Victoria Buildings**
Designed by Arthur Hill *c.*1880 and ultimately incorporated into the Hibernian complex, since everything was built for £30,000 by his relative Samuel Hill, who submitted the successful tender. In the prevailing red-brick and stone idiom of the street. Octagonal spire has been removed.

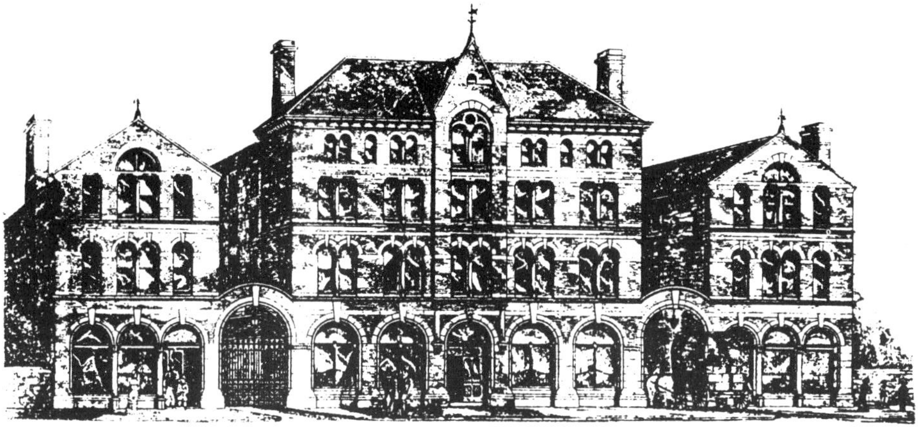

MACCURTAIN STREET: **Hibernia Buildings**
One of the finest commercial buildings in the city but with a complex history. In 1879 the *Architect* illustrated the proposals of Robert Walker for three separate structures linked by arched gateways to make a symmetrical composition. While the triple-bayed, gabled side-buildings reveal Walker's verve when faced with a constricted site, in the central building of five bays, where he had the space, the result is ungainly and monotonous. Before the tendering stage Walker was replaced by Arthur Hill, who joined the separate structures together by double-storied oriels resting on single columns corbelled above the linking archways. This bold device deflects attention from Walker's central block, where Hill toned down and varied the fenestration. After languishing for many years, thoughtfully restored by Stewart and White.

MAIN STREET, SOUTH: **Oval Bar**
Accomplished corner public house built for Beamish and Crawford in a Scottish vernacular idiom with traces of Art Nouveau *c.*1905. Rendered with stone-mullioned windows, relieving arches and framing to the scrolled gable. Amusing oval interior. Architects presumably the Beamish and Crawford architects, Houston and Houston.

THE MARDYKE: **Maltings**
Built as a grainstore in the mid-19th century. Saved from demolition by an enlightened decision of University College, Cork and developed as a student hostel.

MODEL FARM ROAD: **Agricultural Institute**
Symmetrical complex designed in 1853-6 for the Board of Works by Frederick Darley in his customary neo-Elizabethan idiom apart from a central Italianate belvedere, above an incongruously Palladian portal. Now empty.

OLIVER PLUNKET STREET: **Clancarty Buildings**
Stucco-coated, multi-storied office block lit entirely by round arched windows on a reduced scale. The design is by W.H. Hill and the building was erected in 1895.

OLIVER PLUNKETT STREET: **Post Office**
A large but unassertive building with a glazed arcade set on a curving bend and incorporating an earlier theatre on the site. Designed by J.H. Owen in 1879. Extended *c.*1905 by T.J. Mellon, another architect of the Board of Public Works.

PATRICK'S STREET: **St Patrick's Buildings**
Quirky corner building in total command of its strategic site, where Patrick Street curves acutely into Grand Parade. In brick and limestone with Art Nouveau detailing to the doors and windows. Above, corbelled dragons uphold a half-timber gable with the date of 1914. Now known as a Mortgage Store. Architect: D. O'Connor.

PATRICK STREET: **Woodford Bourne**
Characteristic Victorian store devoted to selling food and drink; designed by W.H. Hill and built *c.*1890; carefully adjusted to its curved frontage that transforms the street's otherwise pedestrian architecture.

PATRICK STREET, OFF: **Oyster Restaurant**
Atmospheric eating-house opening on to a pedestrian alleyway strategically sited to get the best cuts of meats and the freshest fruit and vegetables from the Princes' Street Market. Tudor half-timbered bar gives access to the reality of polished mahogany panelling in the main diningroom offset by the fantasy of mirrors.

PAUL STREET: **SS Peter and Paul School**
Designed by Robert Walker and built in 1879. Asymmetrical façade with hip-roofed tower in-

terposed between triple-storied classroom block and four-storied residence enlivened by a multi-storied corner oriel resting on a single column, detailed in Cork's characteristic polychromy. For many years neglected but now the focus of an urban piazza, a rare example of Irish urbanism.

POPE'S QUAY: **St Mary's Catholic Church**

The most important religious commission of the Deanes. Designed originally by Kearns Deane free of charge, built in 1832-8, façade completed

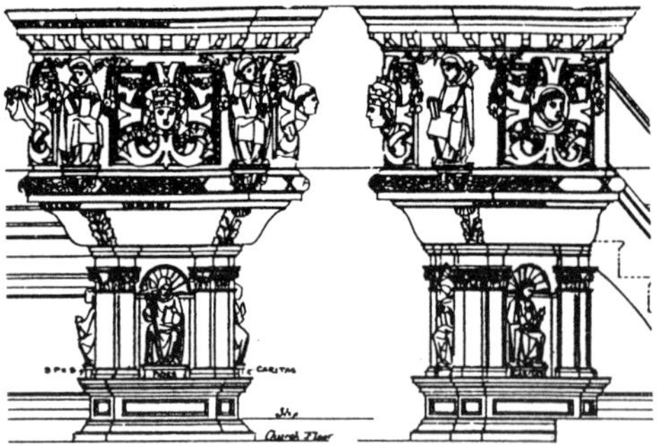

by Deane and Woodward, who erected the portico in 1861 but without the intended flanking towers or the dome above the crossing. The external order is Ionic, the internal Corinthian. Fluted shafts and plaster vaults with decorative plasterwork. Apse hollowed into rock by George Goldie in 1861, when he designed the altar, baldachino and pulpit. The rotund figurative pulpit owes much to Burges, but here perfectly adapted to the *gravitas* of neo-Classicism. Indeed Goldie was far more successful in preserving the original characteristics of the church than George Ashlin in St Patrick's downriver. Side altars executed by Daly's of Cork in 1895 to the designs of S.F. Hynes. The adjoining priory is by William Atkins, possibly a re-

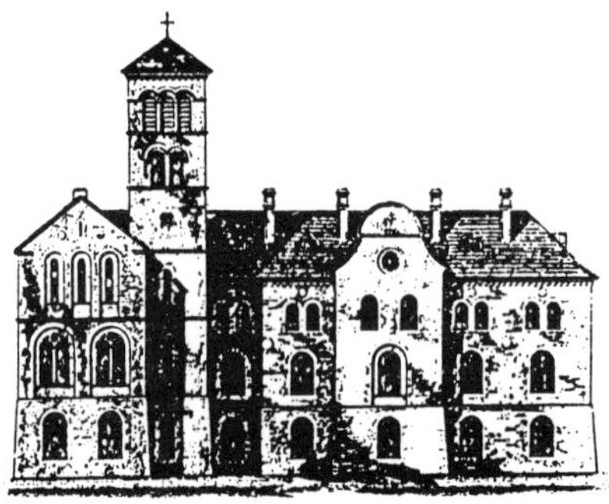

modelling of an existing Georgian house in an ingenious Romanesque compromise between Classical and his preferred Gothic with round-arched fenestration and curvilinear pediment, linked to a new wing by a six-storied Italianate campanile (1850), all executed in that characteristic Cork mixture of red sandstone and silvery limestone dressings.

PRINCES' STREET: **Central Markets**

Designed by John Benson in 1840 and completed in 1860. Still unsurpassed in its use of urban space, a network of pedestrian passageways linking streets and alley ways. The most ceremonious approach is from Princes' Street with a symmetrical Byzantine façade built out of polychromatic brickwork containing a central double-height archway beneath a pedimented Diocletian window. Within, a galleried hall with a central decorative cast-iron fountain. Well restored after a fire some years ago.

REDEMPTION ROAD: **Bishop's House**

Yet another Gothic Revival structure by the diocesan architect S.F. Hynes; built *c.*1885.

SHANAKEIL ROAD: **St Mary's Church of Ireland**

Built in a conventional decorated Gothic, cruciform with off-centre western tower and spire, designed by W.H. Hill and consecrated in 1879. Carefully detailed interior with mosaics designed by Lonsdale and stained glass facing uncertain future since the church has now been closed and put up for sale.

SHANDON: **Butter Market**

The epicentre of Cork's 19th-century prosperity; entered by a grandly scaled triumphal arch (flanked by coupled columns); designed by John Benson and erected in 1849 it dominates John Redmond Street. The circular market at the rear was rebuilt twenty years later, again by Benson. Restored to be the headquarters of the Irish Ballet Company but since seriously damaged by fire.

SHARMAN CRAWFORD STREET: **Crawford Institute**

Commissioned in 1909 by the noted philanthropist after whom the street is named. His architect was Arthur Hill, whose design reveals a temperate Classicism that could have been built anywhere in the British Empire. Completed in 1915.

SOUTH MALL: **Allied Irish Bank**

Opulent Italianate palazzo built for the Provincial Bank in 1840 to the designs of William G. Murray adopted from his unsuccessful entry in the competition for Cork's City Hall. In striking contrast to the cool neo-Classicism of the Deane's Savings Bank across the street. Arched windows set in a rusticated ground floor; *piano nobile* articulated by Corinthian

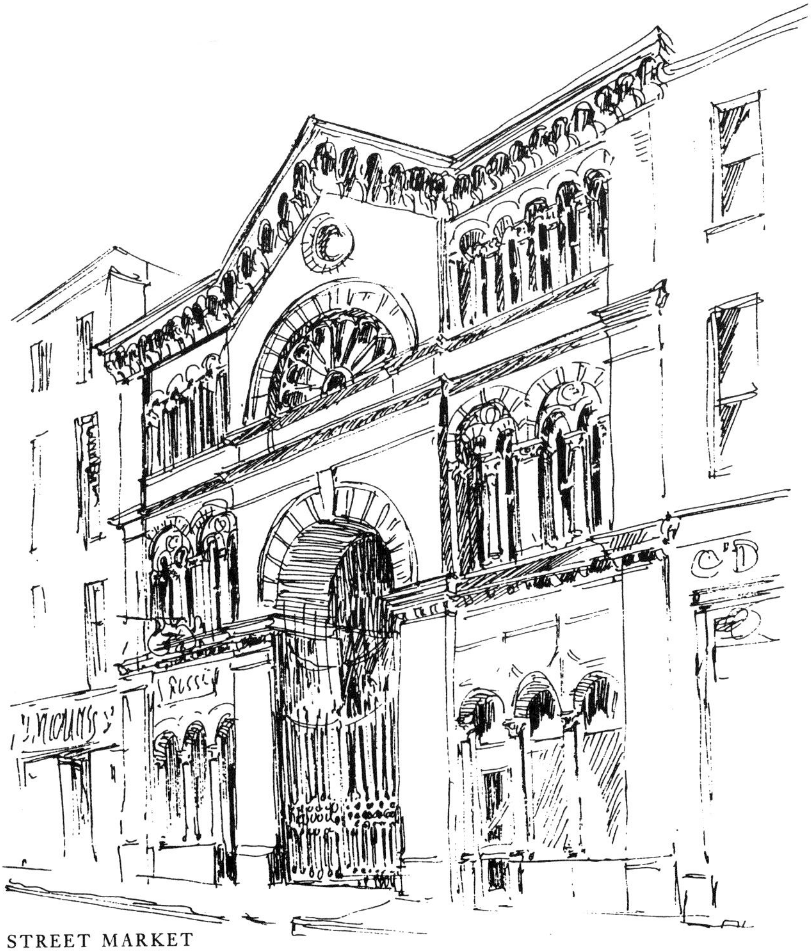

PRINCES' STREET MARKET

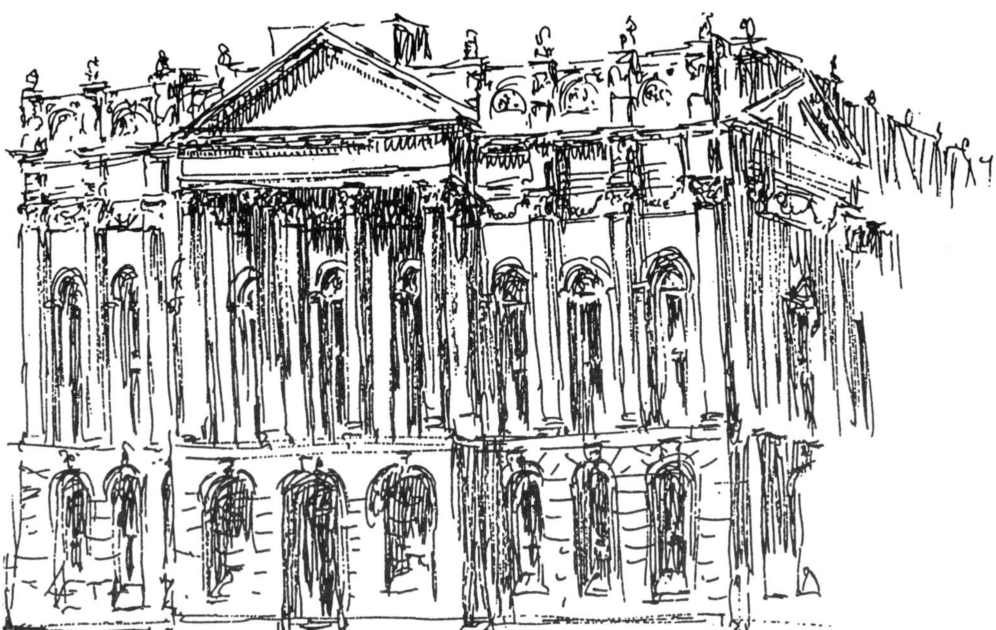

ALLIED IRISH BANK

columns interwoven with garlands upholding a blind attic; the centre of the *piano nobile* projects with triple-bay pedimented portico. Characteristic of Murray's palazzo style is the carved shell inscribed into an arch above each of the principal windows. Galleried interior. Coved ceiling rising to raised lantern.

SOUTH MALL: **Assembly Rooms**
Designed in 1860 by Robert Brash (1817-76), the architect and antiquarian, whose pedantic approach to restoration led him to organize the opposition to Street's rebuilding of Kildare Cathedral. He is remembered today for that opposition rather than for his buildings. This is his most important, with its double arched and decorated façade.

SOUTH MALL: **Gas Company**
Elaborately treated Italianate Romanesque with the principal level like its Georgian predecessor set half a floor above the street; built in 1871. Architect unknown, but there are parallels with R. Brash's Church Assembly Hall further down the street.

SOUTH MALL: **No. 5, Gresham's**
A narrow street frontage compresses this commercial headquarters into a ground-floor arcade that is repeated with ever bolder variation in brick and stone on every floor above, culminating in a corbelled bay of coupled arches. In total defiance originally of Georgian urbanity and now of contemporary conformism, it has been spared not because it is listed but due to its concentrated use of space. Designed by Robert Walker, 1889.

SUMMERHILL: **St Luke's Church of Ireland**
Gothic Revival church by George Pain (1837) rebuilt first by John Benson in 1873 and in an ungainly Romanesque by W.H. Hill with off-centre belfry, apse and double transepts. Consecrated in 1889. Glass by Eugene Daly.

SUMMERHILL: **Presbyterian Church**
Attached to the southern transept is an entry tower terminating in a soaring slender spire. Gothic Revival; remarkable for the delicacy of

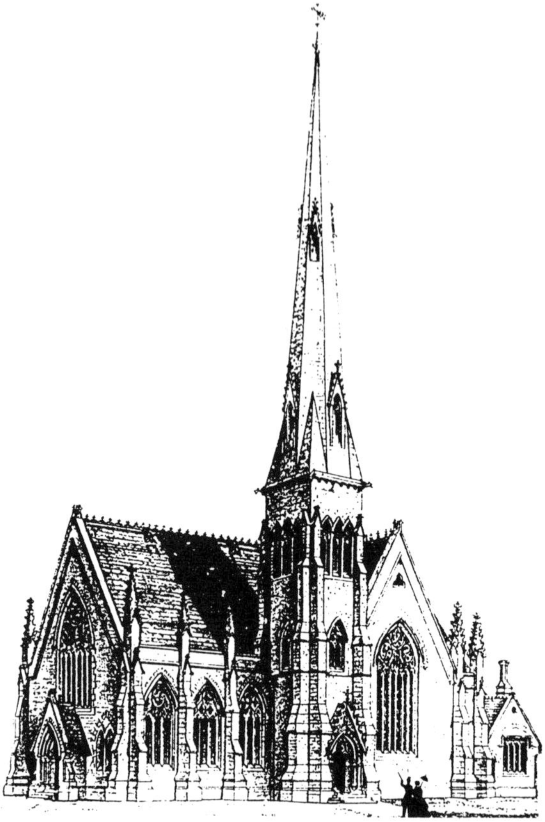

its window tracery; a luminous interior. Thoughtfully designed by the London architect John Tarring in 1861 to be appreciated from its main approach, which is from below, so that the leaded spire of the octagonal belfry attached to the nestling gatelodge is silhouetted against the silvery limestone vision that rises up beyond.

SUNDAY'S WELL: **Good Shepherd Convent, Convent Avenue**
Gothic Revival complex sited among a cluster of institutions that give to this steeply rising hill a semblance of Lhasa. Centre block of five bays screening chapel at the rear. Far-flung symmetrical wings in Lombardic Gothic. Built during the 1880s to the design of George Ashlin.

SUNDAY'S WELL: **Our Lady's Hospital**
Designed by William Atkins in 1846 and built from 1847 to 1852, this is his largest work, and

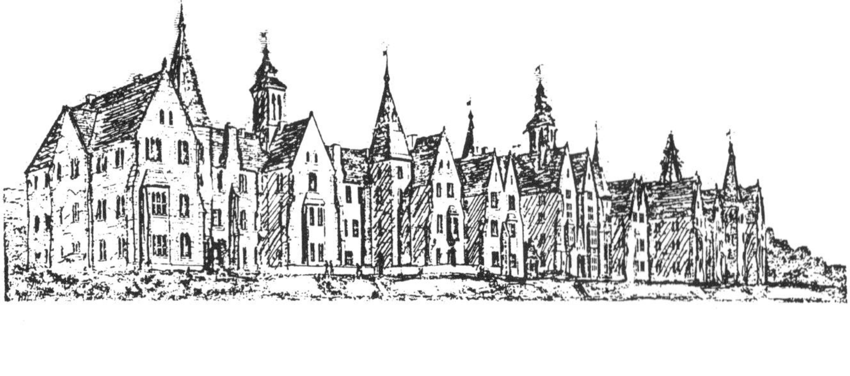

his most prominent—too prominent for a society concerned to house its victims with more discretion; an interminable façade and panopy of spires spectacularly sited to dominate the valley to the Lee. The endlessness at least is not in the original scheme. As first built, it consisted of three separate blocks linked by low arcades, which serve also as entries to a chapel and refectory (sited further back but on an upper level), so that the gable end of the refectory and the spire of the chapel would have been clearly visible from below. At each end of the façade the ground falls away to reveal a battered basement. The composition is further enlivened by six staircase towers, lit by double-height windows that set up a counter-rhythm to the horizontal emphasis of the fenestration elsewhere. The weakest feature of the design is the centre, where a heavy brick and stone steeple straddles a conventionally pitched and slated roof. The same steeple, more securely positioned, marks the centre of each wing. In contrast, his deployment of chimneys as vertical features in their own right, and the irregular spacing of the windows as indicated by the internal layout, are evidence of his receptivity to Pugin and a more reflective reaction to the monotonous and soulless workhouse architecture of the previous decade. The desire of the Board to update its image must have the reason why they appointed a relatively young and inexperienced radical, whose name they misspelt. Also crucial was the intervention of the Cork expert on mental health, Dr Osborne. There would have been two further reasons for their choice: Atkins was a local man, secondly he was not Sir Thomas Deane. Deane had built up the largest architectural practice in Cork against the competition from the Pains and the Hills through his talent-spotting in the arts and well-judged political interference. But the Deanes were involved in the construction of Cork's newly-founded university college across the river, and to receive another vast com mission from the Government would have led to charges of corruption. Compared with their Killarney Lunatic Asylum, Cork's three separate blocks with their changes of material and their plethora of spires,were extravagant and impractical. Indeed the cost of Cork (£85,000) was double that of Killarney, and in 1861 Atkins was forced to increase the accommodation by joining his three blocks together. By then also the architecture of the asylum would have compared with Sir John Benson's masterful Lombardic waterworks on the river bank below, to its detriment. The *National Gazetteer* (1860) called it 'a hideous structure like an overgrown cruet stand'. Its quasi religiousness, as detected by that hostile critic, has since been emphasized by the public lighting of its approaches, designed as an illuminated rosary beads, a device that must have shocked many Cork Protestants back into sanity. This has been removed, the institution emptied and put up for sale. The finely detailed Puginian interiors have been altered and subdivided, but the spandrelled refectory still tolerably survives. Later additions by Samuel Hynes, who also built the Catholic chapel. Atkins built the Church of Ireland chapel at the gates.

SUNDAY'S WELL: **The Vincentians**

Having decided that there was no Catholic architect with the necessary experience to cope with anchoring an ambitious church on to a precipitous site, Father Michael O'Sullivan awarded the commission to the self-taught architect and engineer, Sir John Benson in 1851. But even Benson's abilities did not prevent disaster. The incomplete walls were blown down in 1853 and had to be rebuilt. The massive tower and spire that would have dominated the city were never attempted. The substitute pinnacles, by S.F. Hynes, are a generation later, and to Hynes also is due the surgary internal decoration. The end wall to the east with five lancets flanked by roses in the aisles are now set into a reredos of carved scenes that have withstood so far all assaults by liturgical reformers. The glass, mainly by Mayer of Munich, awaits the Last Judgment with equal assurance.

But what makes the Vincentians the most successful architecturally of the innumerable Lhasa-like religious institutions of Cork, is the retreat house added to the west front of the church by George Goldie in 1873. Like Butterfield, Goldie enjoyed a difficult site. He prolonged the southern aisle with a residential range, three floors high, that turns a right angle before abruptly halting at the street, making up two sides of a little piazza in front of the church. This should have been dominated by the tower moved by Goldie to the corner but never built. A floor below the level of the piazza a vaulted hall opens directly on a garden terrace to the south. Above, a pivotal corner turret is corbelled out on a stunted column. Similar stunted columns hold up the arches that divide the flights of the principal staircase.

TORY TOP ROAD: **St Joseph's Cemetery**

A marble angel by John Hogan (under a cast-iron canopy, since removed), more faun than angel, with a challenging stare commemorates Patrick Murphy, who died in 1837. This the first evidence that the cemetery embedded in council housing contains carving of extra-

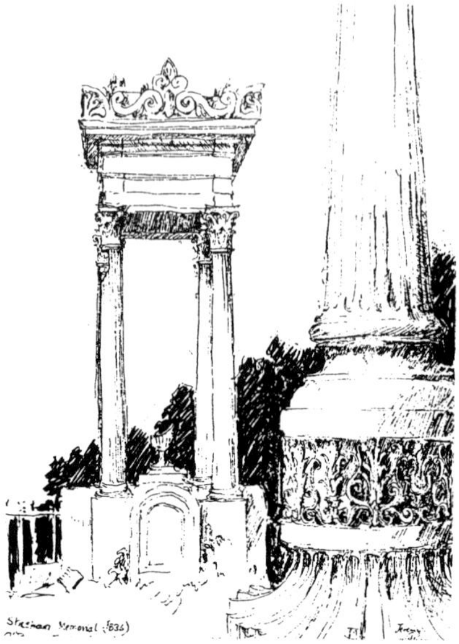

ordinarily high quality. A stylistic encyclopaedia—Egyptian, Greek, Roman, Hiberno-Romanesque, Gothic and at least one example of the Charles O'Connell school, a chubby hand clutching a fluttering scroll. The most elaborate tomb is a small Corinthian temple with a dramatic contrast between a heavy entablature and excessively slender columns, such as one seen in the contemporary caprichios painted by George Mulvany. The most striking is a circular fluted Egyptian Revival tomb revealing the influence of Soane. The contrast between this early inventiveness and the deadening conformity that gradually absorbed Irish memorial sculpture is to be seen here at its most poignant.

WASHINGTON STREET: **The Courthouse**

Designed by the Pains in 1835 and built by the Deanes, who subsequently claimed sole credit as designers for its spectacular octostyle Corinthian portico surmounted by a sculptured group of Justice (removed). The interior was destroyed by fire and a competition held in 1891 gave first prize to W.H. Hill of Cork's third great architectural dynasty. He replaced the original neo-Classical austerity with a chubby Early Renaissance Revival that is fortunately contained within. Its only outward expression is a series of heavily corbelled stone balconies.

WASHINGTON STREET: **Dwyer's**

Handsome brick and stone commercial headquarters sited opposite the courthouse. Its forceful verticality and its judicious deployment of arched windows to accent the design have parallels with the Hibernia Buildings in MacCurtain Street; by Robert Walker. Date: 1888.

WATERWORKS

Sir John Benson not only supervised the Cork railway system tunnelling into his Glanmire railway station; he also took charge of the water supplying the city from the river Lee, and housed his steam pump in a plant to his own design (*c.*1858). Having mastered both Gothic and Classical, this, his masterpiece, is Lombardic. The origins of western civilization are here adapted to industrial efficiency. Two groups of sheds are joined by a central chimney, with a further shed built out into the river twenty years later (this is by Barry McMullen). Continuous arcading set into bands of limestone and sandstone work emphasize the horizontal in contrast to the forceful chimney, also in tiered panels of polychromatic stonework. Set into wooded hills above the weir; would that all our industrial development was housed as beautifully as this.

WELLINGTON ROAD: **St Vincent's Orphanage**

Designed by George Goldie in 1889; modelled on the robust Gothic Revival that he had earlier devised for the Vincentians in Sunday's Well. Characteristic of Goldie is its deceptive symmetry, its picturesque massing of the chimneys and the elaboration of the central bays focused on a canopied saint above the doorway. Executed in Cork's traditional polychromy—local red sandstone rubble walling and limestone dressings. Gothic fenestration of *piano nobile* recently mutilated in a modernization that spared the windows of the polygonal chapel above the hallway. Second chapel added by S.F. Hynes to the east, a cruciform structure in a more conventional Gothic Revival idiom; beyond it, St Patrick's hospice (also by S.F. Hynes).

WESTERN ROAD: **Honan Chapel, University College**

The Hiberno-Romanesque architecture of this church has never aroused the enthusiasm reserved for its contents. The architect, James McMullen, based his façade on St Cronan's in Roscrea and his round tower on St Finghin's in Clonmacnoise; the stonework is impeccable but impersonal. The even more conventional interior, however, due to the efforts of Sir John O'Connell, the trustee of the Honan family, superseded Loughrea Cathedral as a shrine of the Celtic Revival, even if the most Celtic contribution, the mosaic floor of the chancel, is by a German firm, Oppenheimer, working in Manchester. The tabernacle is by Oswald Reeves, the embroideries by Dun Emer. The sculpture of St Fin Barre is by Olive Sheppard; the ironwork by William Scott.

The eight main windows were given to An Túr Gloine under Sarah Purser and were executed by Child. But the five windows commissioned from the young Harry Clarke were so extraordinary that Sir John O'Connell rewarded him with the commission for the remainder of the glass; he produced an unequalled series of saints—St Finbarr, St Ita, St Albert, St Gobnait, St Brendan, St Joseph, Our Lady of Sorrows, and the triple light of St Patrick. For the Túr Gloine O'Brien did the windows of St Flannan and St Munchin; Rhind the St Carthage; Child the Resurrection above the Altar, St Ailbe, St Colman, St Fachtna and scenes from the life of Christ.

WESTERN ROAD: The Hospital

Neo-Romanesque with central door beneath an archway resting on corbelled columns. Designed by James McMullen in 1895.

WESTERN ROAD: University College

The Government introduced the necessary legislation to found their three colleges in Belfast, Galway and Cork in 1845 mainly to benefit Catholics precluded from Trinity. But since they were non-denominational, they were spurned by the Catholic Hierarchy. Cork is the most Puginian of the three. The commission went to Thomas Deane, but most of the design was due to Kearns Deane, who died (aged 42) in 1847, two days after the working drawings had been signed. Alexander Sharpe Deane, a second brother, died a year later. The void that they left was filled by Benjamin Woodward, who was probably responsible for the medievalizing alterations sketched on to the working drawings and for additional features like the porter's stairs, inspired by medieval Irish monasteries. The library fireplace is borrowed directly from Holy Cross.

What distinguishes Cork from the other Queen's Colleges is its organic composition based on the medieval Magdalen in Oxford. This allows a three-sided quad to face southwards loosely attached to a rear right-angled range. This, containing the library and the aula maxima, extends northwards to the edge of a wooded precipice descending to the Lee. The complex is entered from the river front through a turreted gatehouse asymmetrically positioned in the quad's central range. The east arm of the quad houses the president and vice-president. The first president, Robert Kane, was a distinguished chemist. The western range was devoted to laboratories. This range was crowned with lanterns, which were not replaced when it was burnt out (in 1862) by a suspected prisoner to destroy incriminating evidence. The most impressive interior is the aula maxima, its fenestration to the river expressing the dais by a double-height bay window. The first surviving perspective of T.N. Deane shows an impressive hammer-beam roof, as built, and a gallery supported on screens, simplified by Woodward in execution with his characteristic ivy-leaf ironwork. A stone staircase leads up to the first floor library with its open scissor trusses but now much altered. External changes have included the removal of the statute of Queen Victoria from the gable end of the aula maxima, the queen having witnessed its installation by Sir Thomas Deane himself on her visit to Cork in 1849. The best additions have been by Arthur Hill and his son Henry. The science block is a masterly asymmetrical composition with top-lighting coming from long horizontal dormers that interpenetrate low pitched roofs. Gatelodges on the western road by E. Fitzgerald (1879), as is the observatory, where he was assisted by Howard Grubb.

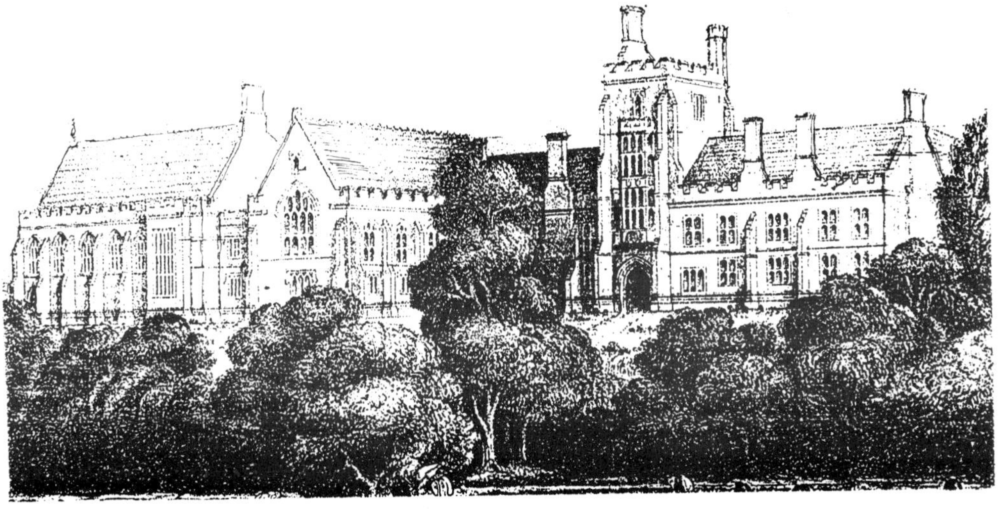

CORK COUNTY, NORTH

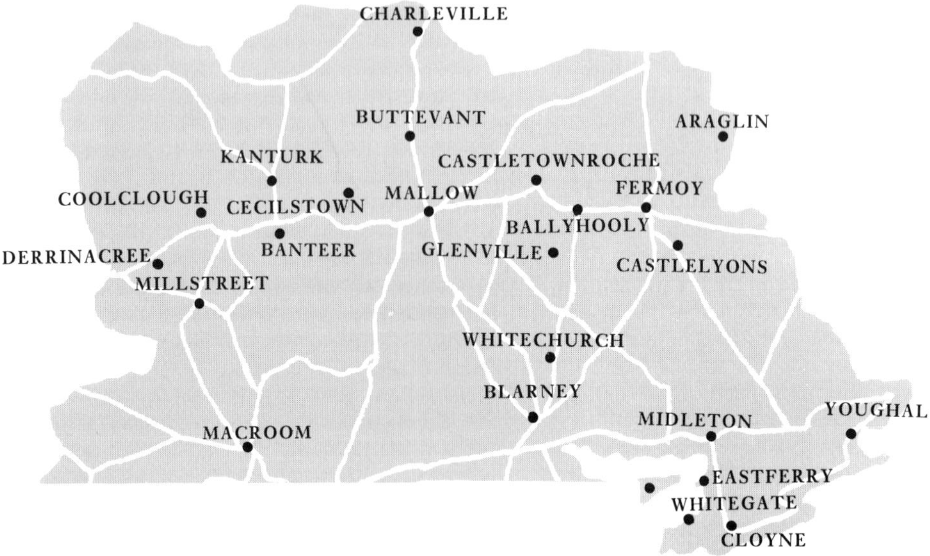

ARAGLIN: **Araglin House**
Tudor cottage ornée attached to small fortified farm hidden in a remote river valley, designed by Charles Frederick Anderson for Edward Viscount Kingsborough, heir to the largest estate in Ireland. Here he could live uninterrupted by creditors and finish his magnum opus, a nine-volume compilation of Aztec

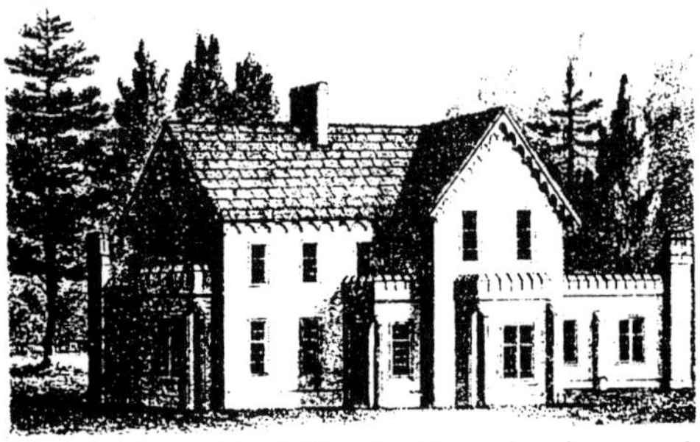

manuscripts pillaged by the Conquistadores and scattered throughout Europe. The footnotes increase with each volume eventually to outstrip the text, corresponding to the progress of his obsession, that the Aztecs were the lost tribe of Israel.

The date 1838 is inscribed over the door. A year later Lord Kingsborough was arrested for not paying his paper manufacturer, and succumbed to typhoid in a debtors' prison; his father, the 2nd earl of Kingston, who had been insane for nine years, died a few months later.

BALLYHOOLY: **Catholic Church**
Minor example of the prolific George Ashlin, *c.*1870. Nave with low lean-to aisles leading to square chancel. Polychromatic stonework but no evidence of Woodward's favourite sculptors, the O'Sheas, who came from this village.

BANTEER: **Clonmeen**
A spacious villa-style country house built for Stephen Grehan to the designs of George Ashlin and completed in 1893. Almost symmetrical façade with columned porch between bay windows of different widths. Gabled and dormered attic floor. Extended service wing. Interior planned round a double-height inner hall surrounded by galleries and illuminated from above by a glazed dome.

BLARNEY: **The Hydro**
Private hospital set facing south across a hidden wooden valley; built to his own designs, *c.*1866, by Dr Richard Barter (1802-70), who set up a series of Turkish baths across Ireland while masquerading as a Turk (and architect). The baths have all been demolished and his hospital has almost vanished into the undergrowth—apart from a clock tower, which has lost its upper tier but which would no doubt once have served as a minaret. An adjoining gymnasium is still decorated with faded Turkish frescoes. The last to live here were a group of elderly

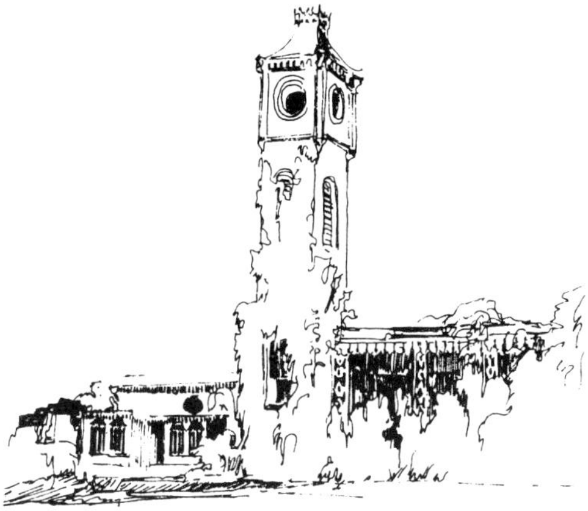

who refused to be treated by the doctor who had bought the property as a going concern *c.* 1950.

BLARNEY: **New Castle**
Built in 1874 for the St John Jefferyes family, whose earlier house had been attached to the medieval castle. Erected on a separate site deeper into the demesne, a decision probably taken due to the increasing popularity of the Blarney stone. The architect was John Lanyon, the style an uncomprising Scottish Baronial. Completed just in time before the agrarian agitation that was to lead to the Wyndham Land Acts that saved Ireland from Marxism at the expense of the country house. Elevated basement with front hall enclosing flight of stairs up to a top-lit inner hall very much in the Lanyon tradition. Staircase rising to arcaded gallery resembling its counterpart in Belfast Castle built by Lanyon at the same time. Adamesque decoration in the principal reception rooms give no hint of their external grimness. The castle, originally built to avoid the public, is now open during the summer months.

BLARNEY: **The Mills and Housing**
In the last century the Blarney Woollen Mills were developed into the largest of their kind by the Mahoneys, who extended the village with rows of repetitive cottages. Many were built on a felt-roof system as first developed by the Malcolmsons at Portlaw, Co. Waterford (q.v.). After a hiatus twenty years ago, the textile industry has been revived and many old buildings readapted, including one mill as an hotel and conference centre.

BUTTEVANT: **Flour Mills**
Castellated mill with corner turrets designed *c.* 1840 to complement remains of a medieval castle and abbey.

BUTTEVANT: **Velvetstown**
The last house designed by William Atkins (in 1875) for his cousin and his co-heiress to Fountainville, Sarah Crofts née Lysaght. Built out of red and yellow brick set in strong horizontal bands harshly interrupted by seg-

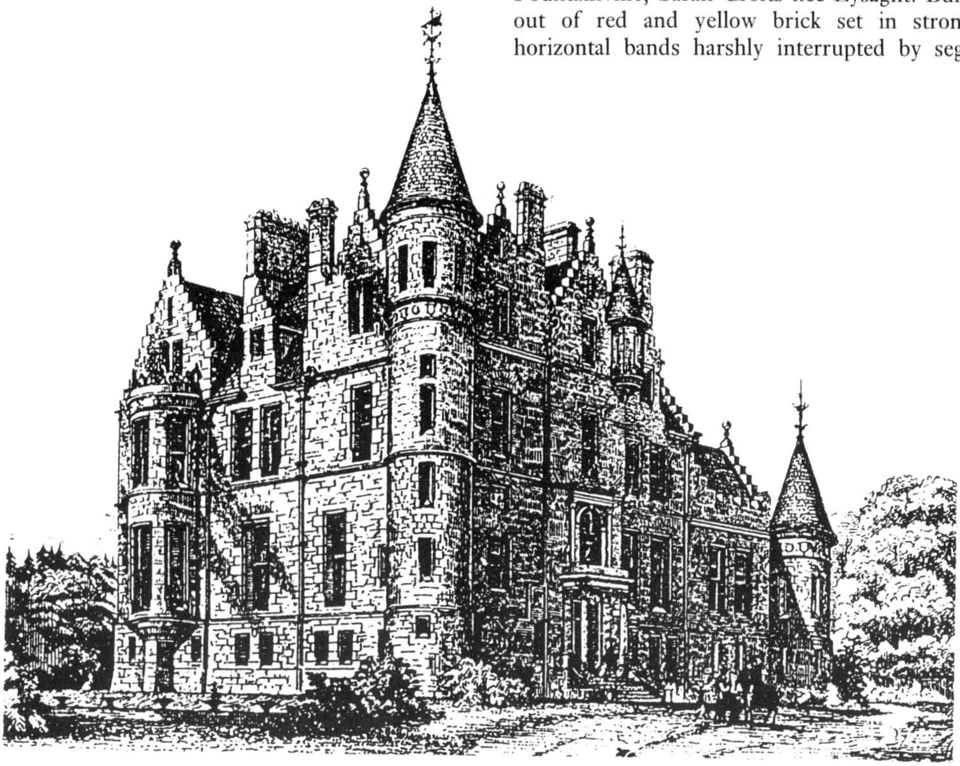

mental headed windows, the exterior makes no concession to its pastoral setting. Burnt out after twenty years, it was not rebuilt. Its shell remains with its discordant polychromy, undimmed by time, used as a silo pit by Sarah's descendants.

CASTLE HYDE: **Church of Ireland**
Georgian church built by the Hydes of Castle Hyde. Remodelled in Gothick by George Pain for John Hyde, the last of the Hydes to live here, before he sold up, bankrupted by the Famine. Traceried roof, bow-fronted organ gallery. Derelict at the time of writing.

CASTLE LYONS: **Ballyvolane**
Victorian Italianate country house *c.*1870. Impressive hall seen first through a screen of slender Corinthian marbleized columns. Interiors well restored. Member of Hidden Ireland.

CASTLETOWNROCHE: **Annsgrove**
Benjamin Woodward was a friend of the Annesleys of Annsgrove, so it is not surprising to find a variant of his 1847 gatehouse for University College Cork, adapted to make the entrance gates to a country house, with sham portcullis and battlements. The lodge is built upwards into a small keep, with a staircase turret counter-balanced by a massive chimney. The avenue, lined by azaleas and rhododendrons, divides the Victorian walled garden from the wilder oriental river garden created later (1907) by Richard Annesley along the river valley of the Awbeg. Gardens open to public.

CASTLETOWNROCHE: **Catholic Church**
Designed and built from 1848 onwards by the parish priest, the Revd James Fitzpatrick, inspired by Pugin. Burnt accidentally in 1896, it was rebuilt by Samuel Hynes to the original design. External stonework sadly rendered. Glass by Watson of Youghal.

CECILSTOWN: **Lohort Castle**
Medieval keep of the MacCarthys restored first by the earl of Egmont *c.*1750 and by his descendants in 1876, when the stepped gables and the chimneys were rebuilt along with the outer bawn. The unknown restorer brilliantly solved the problem of guest accommodation by refusing to add to the keep itself but by building a separate double-towered gatehouse with an elaborate coat of arms surmounting the central archway. This gives a dramatic silhouette to the castle when first seen at the end of a long vista, unforgettable against the sunset. Keep and gatehouse burnt out in 1921. Keep partially restored The ground-floor kitchen clad with blue and white Delft tiles has survived the fire.

CHARLEVILLE: **Catholic Church**
Late Gothic Revival church with orientation reversed so that the façade with its off-centre tower and spire faces eastwards. Chancel still retains elaborate mosaics and frescoes. Walter Doolin exhibited designs in the RHA, 1898.

CLOYNE: **Ardnavilling**
Long, low-gabled Tudor-style house centred on a polygonal bay window as the focal feature of the façade. Built for the Litton family *c.*1860.

COBH: **Admiralty House**
built as a private house *c.*1870 and rebuilt as a seminary after it was destroyed by fire during the Troubles. Its most striking feature is its double-tiered verandah facing the sea.

COBH: **Catholic Cathedral**
Edward Pugin and George Ashlin's most important commission, won in 1867, the year that Ashlin married Pugin's sister Mary. They were given the job after a controversial competition. They were the only entrants to agree with the

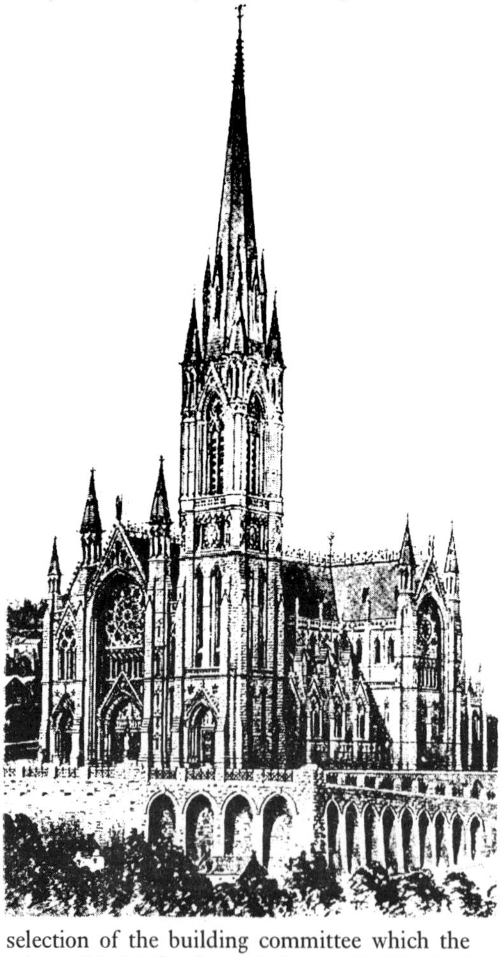

selection of the building committee which the others, J.J. McCarthy and George Goldie, had refused to accept. There were good reasons to doubt the committee's impartiality, since the Ashlins and Bishop Keane were old family friends and an Ashlin brother was a priest in the diocese. The budget fixed at £25,000 was also queried—again with good reason, since the final cost came to £235,000, but that was over fifty years later. Though the partnership broke up in 1868, Pugin and Ashlin continued to collaborate on the cathedral, so it could be said that the commission took up the rest of both their lives. Pugin's concept; Ashlin's supervision and decoration.

The earliest designs have the tower in the centre of the west front as in their Dublin Augustinian church (q.v.), but a less forceful design since the wedge-shaped tower of the Augustinians is replaced by the more conventional square shape rising to a pointed spire. The revised design moves the tower to the southern bay, its most dominant position above the town, and deploys a reduced wedge-shaped tower to terminate the northern aisle. External carving by the Harrisons. The addition of transepts gave the interior its moment of greatest drama since the arcades, triforia and clerestories of the nave are carried across them, a device first used by the partnership in 1859—in Cork's SS Peter and Paul. A third and even more elaborate version to satisfy Bishop Keane adds further height, traceried transepts and flying buttresses, and it was this that was ultimately built. Dalkey granite brought by sea was used with Mallow limestone dressings. Elaborate foundations were built and an impressive arcaded embankment (due to the steeply sloping site). All this caused costs to rise, but by then the tradition of emigration from Cobh had endowed the cathedral with pilgrimage status, so that the 300ft-high spire, completed in 1915, might prove for many to be the last glimpse of Ireland.

The interior was usable by 1879, five years after Dr McCarthy succeeded Bishop Keane, but it was not until 1893 that the cladding of the walls with Bath stone started. This permitted the extraordinary wealth of figurative sculpture (recalling Rheims Cathedral) so that the altars merge into an overall decorative scheme, perceived like apparitions through dimly illuminated vistas. Earley and Powell carved the high altar and lady chapel altar. Altars of Pieta and the Sacred Heart are by J.A. O'Connell of Cork. The transept altars are by G. Smith. The lighting is reduced through the profusion of stained glass (mostly by Mayer apart from that of the baptistery and lady chapel by Earley and Powell). Further windows by Hardman and also Cox and Buckley which are reflected in the polished floor mosaics and the varnished pine that sheaths the vaulting overhead. Pulpit, throne and screens by Beakey. Cobh is the only Irish Catholic Victorian cathedral to remain unchanged by liturgical agitation of the last thirty years, so there is still hope that the interior may survive to be listed by Cork County Council.

COBH: Church of Ireland

Small Gothic Revival church *c.*1850. Now a museum.

COBH: Leemount

Characteristic of Cobh is the semi-detached palazzo, each block set into a spacious garden and looking southwards towards the open sea. The most striking example is Leemount, four storeys, including attics, with the corner bays brought forward to make pavilion-like towers enlivened by varied fenestration that successfully counteracts the monumentality of the composition.

COBH: Robin Hill

Built *c.*1860 as the rectory to a simpler design than that originally proposed by Henry Hill. Nearby, the semi-detached villas, the Benmore and Silverdale, again a simplified version of Henry Hill's designs.

COBH: Sirius Centre

Built in 1854 for the Royal Cork Yacht Club (said to be the oldest yacht club in existence), which abandoned it in 1969 when it moved to Crosshaven. Rescued from dereliction and restored in 1989 by the Sirius Project headed by Peter and Sarah Murray. Due to the patronage of J.H. Smith-Barry, the original commission

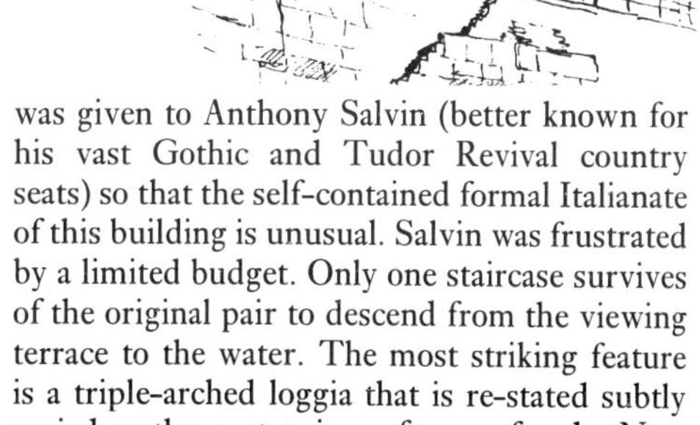

was given to Anthony Salvin (better known for his vast Gothic and Tudor Revival country seats) so that the self-contained formal Italianate of this building is unusual. Salvin was frustrated by a limited budget. Only one staircase survives of the original pair to descend from the viewing terrace to the water. The most striking feature is a triple-arched loggia that is re-stated subtly varied as the centrepiece of every façade. Now a restaurant and maritime exhibition centre; a showpiece for the Heritage Council.

COBH: **The Townhall**
Classical, two-storey, thirteen-bay structure with projecting triple-bay centrepiece to form, unusually in Ireland, a triumphal arch for the public street, in this case West View, that rises to the cathedral. Attributed to Alexander Deane, *c.*1840.

COBH: **Urban District Council Offices**
Built as the offices of the Harbour Commissioners, a round-arched, well-proportioned, single-storied pavilion with asymmetrically attached three-storey tower; the eastern counterpart of the Yacht club; *c.*1860.

COBH: **The Waterfront**
Speculative neo-Classical residential scheme by Decimus Burton in 1849 which if only partly carried out was still the principal influence on the town's development. Two terraces curving into the main square lead up to a crescent of villas above. The most complete range starts with the Methodist church with its Corinthian portico and pepperpot cupola. Now a nightclub called 'Desmond's Bar'. As no architect has been recorded, it is possible that the architect was Burton himself. The early neo-Classical details gave way to Gothic, no doubt due to the pervasive influence of the cathedral on the hill above.

Proceeding eastwards from the Methodist church we pass three ranges of speculative housing, the central range appropriately framing the city's largest hotel, the Commodore, built as the Queen's Hotel. This is Cobh's urban Italianate at its most impressive, as long as we do not penetrate indoors. Then the first Gothic intrusion, the Bank of Ireland on the curve. Beyond Casement Square, West Beach still has some original shopfronts. The Admiral with its frosted glass; no. 17, a butcher's shop, and no. 19 with a mosaic threshold advertizing billiards. Then Pearse Square with a robust arcaded pub, the Rob Roy.

COOLCLOUGH: **Catholic Church**
The flowering of religious art in Ireland received impetus from Catholic Emancipation, to be cut short by the Famine. This is nowhere more clearly demonstrated than in this rural church. Built due to the exertions of two men, the parish priest Father Barry and the sculptor architect Charles O'Connell. Father Barry's triple-tiered tomb, a blend of Classical and Gothic, guards the entrance. The topmost tier houses a statue of the priest himself rising from the dead with a sense of awe that permeates a six-winged angel inhabiting a niche in the church beyond. Beside the angel and carved from a cornerstone, St Peter with his keys. Symmetrical west façade

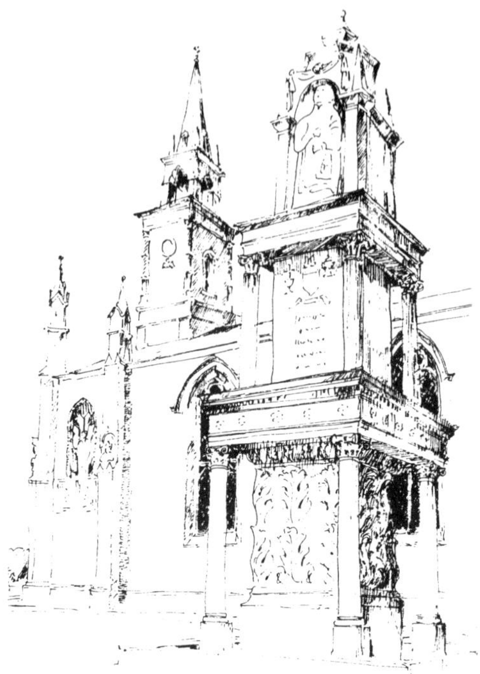

enlivened by further thoughtful carvings to include a realistic clock face rising to a steeple, partly Classical, partly Gothic, like the tomb. Interior of slight consequence terminating with a polygonal apse added, according to local tradition, by O'Connell's son, and later remodelled by his grandson. Glass by Eugene Daly.

DERRINACREE: **Catholic Church**
Gothic Revival village church evidently started by Charles O'Connell; note the exquisite carving round the west door. Work interrupted by the Famine and then restarted but without his fantasy. Interior stripped after the Second Vatican Council.

EASTFERRY: **Church of Ireland**
Since the destruction of Leighmoney and Ardfert, the finest church of William Atkins to survive the Church of Ireland rationalization of the 1960s. Superbly sited guarding a wooded inlet off the estuary of the Lee, its polychromatic spire beside a polygonal apse is like a beacon precariously balanced on a rock above the tide. From the distance a cathedral rivalling Cobh or Cork; from nearby a tiny wayside chapel, a triumph of scale over size. Its building was spurred on by a double challenge—the disestablishment of the Church of Ireland, and the construction of St Fin Barre's Cathedral (Cork) by Burges, who had won the competition that Atkins himself had also entered. The interior is influenced by Burges and Street, especially the semicircular chancel, an Irish response

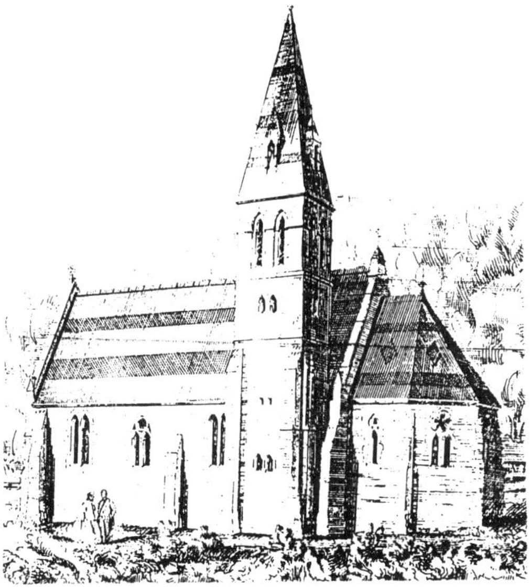

to Street's Ardamine (q.v.). All the materials that it is built from are exposed throughout. By introducing combinations of black, red and yellow brickwork matched by the colours of the patterned floor tiles, we are enfolded into a polychromy, that serves also to define the chancel from the nave—black and yellow voussoirs in the chancel, red and yellow in the nave. The open timber roofs are also contrasted—braced, arched and rising from tiny colonettes over the nave; delicately ribbed to hover weightlessly above the apse. Between them the chancel arch abuts against the unseen belfry. Glass of varying quality, the best behind the altar in the style of Saunders and Holliday. Closure rumoured.

FERMOY: Catholic Church

Outward appearance largely due to George Ashlin and Edward Pugin, who were called in to add the asymmetrical tower and spire in 1867, and supplied buttresses to stress the verticality of the façade. Therefore, that they left the interior intact comes as a surprise: the Pain brothers with their most light-hearted Gothick *c.*1825. Wide nave and aisles of equal height, divided by clustered columns. Galleried transepts and shallow choir enlivened by canopied niches. Plaster Gothic vaulting throughout, with ribs meeting in perforated bosses. An inlaid marble tomb shipped back from India commemorating a Dennehy who had died there, is almost unnoticeable in this ambiance. Painted angels, rails and altar, still surviving, added by Samuel Hynes in 1901.

FERMOY: Glandalane

House built in a late Tudor Revival manner *c.*1902 for the Hallanan family. Attached turret with ogee-roofed tower. Architect: W.H. Hill.

FERMOY: Loreto and Presentation Convents

The Loreto Convent was founded in 1853, subsequently extended by George Ashlin with a Gothic residential block, tower and chapel, 1869. Interiors preserve their original ambiance with Gothic fireplaces and painted ceilings by Hodgkinsons. The adjoining Presentation Convent is the last of a series of religious institutions (precipitously sited to dominate the commercial town centre in the river valley below them) bonded together by the uniformity of their materials—purply sandstone for the walls, silvery limestone for the dressings.

FERMOY: Main Square

One of the best of its kind in Ireland due to its layout by its Regency developer, John Anderson, and its rebuilding *c.*1908 by W.H. Hill in an attentuated Anglo-Dutch verging on Art Nouveau.

FERMOY: St Colman's College

Built in the Lombardic manner. Round-arched windows clustered in symmetrical rhythm as designed in 1856. Sympathetically extended in 1884. Further entrance added under arcaded campanile with corner niche for patron saint. Architect unknown.

GLENVILLE: Church of Ireland

Board of First Fruit church containing good stained glass by Ward and Hughes and by E. Rhind commemorating the Hudson-Kinahans.

GLENVILLE: Glenville Park

Spacious Italianate house built in front of an earlier three-storied Georgian house for the Hudson-Kinahans in 1887 to the design of Sandham Symes; of two stories but the same height as the original. Projecting Venetian porch. Two double-height bay windows flanked on either side by recessed bays. Interiors retain their original decoration and wallpapers. At the rear Turkish style billiard room opening into the garden and first-floor chapel made in 1949 out of three housemaid's bedrooms by the father of the present owner, the novelist and historian, Mark Bence-Jones. His wife is the poetess, Gillian Bence-Jones.

GLOUNTHANE: Catholic Church

Based on George Ashlin's Ballyhooly church (q.v.) but built a decade later to the design of S.F. Hynes deploying the local red sandstone with contrasting Ballintemple limestone dressings.

GLOUNTHANE: Father Mathew Tower

Circular Gothic Revival tower with attached

circular staircase turret overlooking the estuary of the Lee. Originally designed in honour of Father Mathew, the apostle of temperance, by George Pain but not erected until 1843, five years after Pain's death. The supervising architect was Murphy O'Connor. The client was William O'Connell, who commissioned the statue of Father Mathew—an early experiment in concrete and as such of enormous interest to inquisitive vandals. Tower recently modernized rather than restored as a private house.

KANTURK: **Catholic Church**
Lofty Gothic Revival church by J. Hurley built in 1867 retaining the tower and entrance gates attributed to Charles O'Connell *c.*1835 that belong to the earlier church Hurley replaced.

KANTURK: **Church of Ireland**
Characteristic Gothic Revival church by Welland cruciform with western bellcote, *c.*1860.

KILLAVULLEN: **Castle Kevin**
The seat of the Badham Thornhills, hereditary agents of the earls of Kingston, who got rid of the economist Arthur Young before he declared them redundant. Earlier house transformed into the present castle for Edward Badham Thornhill some years before 1837 by a Cork architect called Flood. He added a turreted porch and two circular corner towers to the front; to the rear an octagonal tower with a staircase illuminated by heraldic glass. So successful that, half a century later, an importunate genealogist was silenced by the last of the family, another Edward, with 'My castle is my pedigree.'

LITTLE ISLAND: **Church of Ireland**
No drawings survive for this small church but the geometrical precision of its diagonally positioned spire (rising above the adjoining entry porch flush with the western façade) and the delicate contrast of texture and colour in its external stonework indicate Welland and Gillespie at their most radical in the early 1860s.

MACROOM: **Catholic Church**
Early Gothic Revival church by an unrecorded architect; enlarged and remodelled by Dominic Coakley in 1893.

MACROOM: **Church of Ireland**
Board of First Fruits Gothic refitted by Welland and Gillespie, who added a polygonal chancel in 1869. Glass by Heaton, Butler and Bayne.

MACROOM: **Macroom Castle**
Only the fake Gothic gatehouse survives crudely repointed to dominate the market square. At the rear the castle was restored by Richard Hedges Eyre, an amateur architect. Burnt out in 1922 while in the possession of his great-granddaughter Lady Ardilaun as recounted by Katherine Everett, it has crumbled into the river.

MALLOW: **Annakisha Catholic Church**
This austere mid-Victorian Gothic Revival rural church at Torpey's Cross contains a surprise: the interior was carefully designed to enclose the reredos of its predecessor. This is in a richly fruity Gothick if less spectacular than its counterpart in Holycross, Co. Tipperary (abandoned and destroyed since the restoration of the abbey); this at least survives.

MALLOW: **Catholic Church**
To enter this church is to be charmed by the unexpected, since the graceful unpretentious Florentine Renaissance of 1822 has been retained eloquently expressing the hopefulness that preceded Emancipation. The two bays added to the nave and the façade of 1900 are also expressive, but this time of the triumphalism that instituted the *Ne Temere* decree.

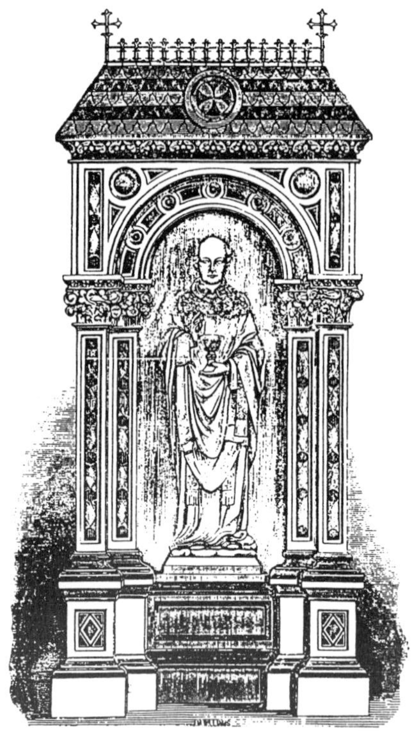

George Ashlin was the architect, and his design is modelled on his polychromatic Romanesque of thirty years before, but on a grander scale —raising the nave to double the original height, and inserting a rose window. Detached campanile built over open archway. In one of the aisles a marble wall memorial to a parish priest by J.J. McCarthy. In the graveyard a tomb by Charles O'Connell of Coolclough (q.v.).

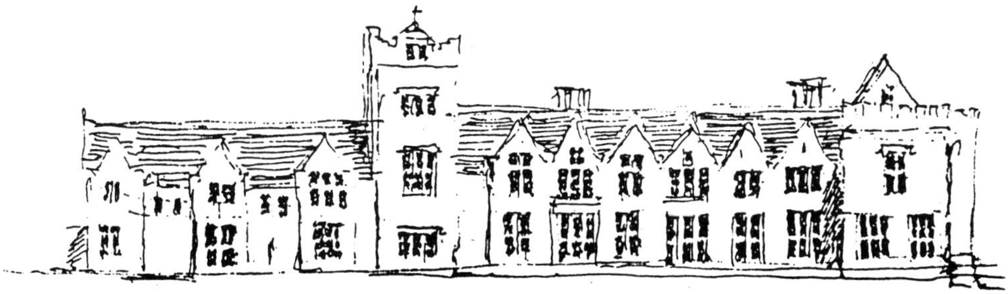

MALLOW: **County Council Offices**
Italianate palazzo now cheerfully rendered but peeling and woe-begone when acquired as a run-down railway hotel. Designed by an obscure architect called Ward in 1864.

MALLOW: **Presentation Convent**
Late Gothic Revival complex with main range dominated by slated spire. Built out of red sandstone and limestone dressings (*c.*1860). S.F. Hynes added the later dormered wing (1909).

MALLOW: **Mallow Castle**
A convincing transformation of the original stable block to which the Jephson-Norreys family would retreat after the periodic burning of their Elizabethan castle (now a ruin in their deerpark). The final transformation of the stables was effected by Sir Denham Norreys-Jephson with the assistance of Edward Blore *c.*1835—long gabled ranges either side of what had once been the gatehouse tower. At one end a low entry-tower linked by the staircase to a further tower, started by Sir Denham but not completed till 1954 by Brigadier Maurice Jephson. The interior is as convincing as the exterior. Scholarly neo-Elizabethan staircase designed by Sir Denham and carved by his estate carpenters, who also executed the more fantastical chimneypieces in the elm-panelled reception rooms. These have interesting parallels to the church of Coolclough (q.v.). Sold by the Jephsons *c.*1975 with some of its original contents to the present owner.

MALLOW: **Shortcastle Presbyterian Church**
Gothic Revival church and manse, both constructed out of random polygonal blocks of local limestone with darker trim. Architect unknown. Church now a furniture emporium.

MALLOW: **The Clockhouse**
Sir Denham Orlando Jephson, who inherited the castle and thereby the town of Mallow in the early 19th century, was an amateur architect who is said to have designed or rather remodelled this house (that closes the vista of the main street) after he had returned from an Alpine holiday. A double-storied oriel is framed by decorative bargeboards. The adjoining clock-tower was once double-tiered, but the timber lantern became dangerous *c.*1970, was dismantled and not replaced. Yet the overall picturesqueness survives, unlike the nearby Spa cottage, where the decorative half-timbering has been stripped away. The Spa promoted by Sir Denham was never a success. The leading medicinal water expert of the day, attacked by Sir Denham for his failure to write anything after a visit during which he had been lavishly entertained, eventually replied that if the water was boiled twice, it was no longer dangerous.

MIDLETON: **Allied Irish Bank**
Formerly the Munster and Leinster Bank. Anglo-Dutch red terracotta composition with scrolled gables and corner ogee-roofed turret designed by George Ashlin and built in 1901.

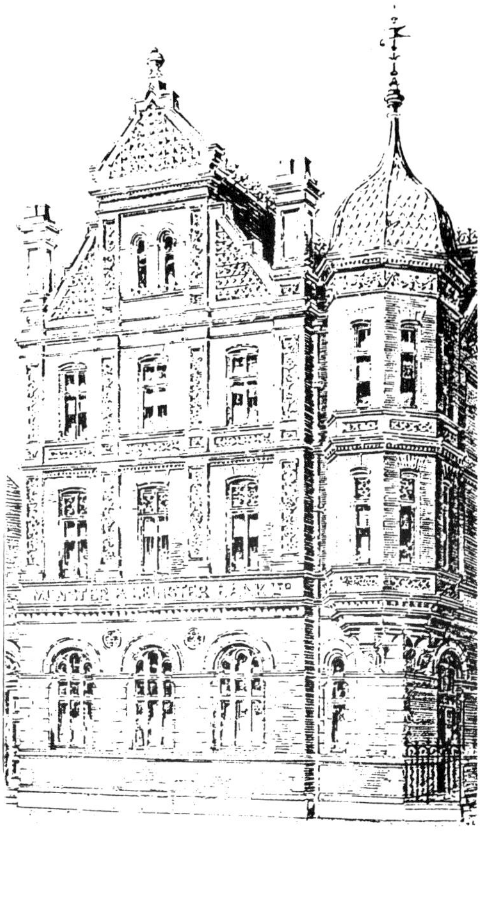

MIDLETON: **Midleton Arms**
Although these adjoining houses, one a shop, the other a pub, are dated 1861, they could be

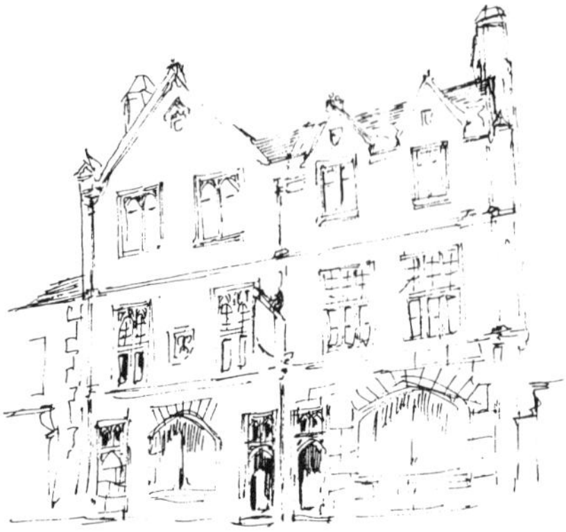

the commission that A.W.N. Pugin is recorded as having received. Possibly completed posthumously by his son Edward Pugin, who had just commenced partnership with George Ashlin. In any case they are a textbook illustration from Pugin's *Contrasts*, providing cheer as in olden times. Built out of local limestone ashlar. Powerful rear façade of rubble stone with lofty stacks penetrating into hipped roofs. Renamed 'Pugin's'.

MIDLETON: **Catholic Church**
Late Gothic Revival church designed by George Ashlin, whose Coppinger mother came from Midleton. Ashlin's favourite form of spire rising between octagonal corner pinnacles. Continuous nave and choir. A scaled-down version of Clonakilty. Exhibited by Ashlin in the RHA in 1894.

MIDLETON: **Cloonmullin**
Picturesque, red-brick Queen Anne-style villa with its façade enlivened by a boldly expressed staircase window. Designed by an unrecorded architect, *c.*1900.

MILLSTREET: **Drishane Castle**
The Georgian house built beside a medieval MacCarthy keep was insubstantially Gothicized by the Wallis family between 1845 and 1860, who retained the low ceilings and the multiple fenestration of the three-storied original house. The gingerbread battlements on the house and the outlying wing walls contrast with the austere restoration of the tower house carried out in 1879. A convent since 1909, the interiors retain pre-First World War furnishings that include Anglo-Chinese curiosities. Now being developed as a hotel and conference centre.

MILLSTREET: **Dromagh**
The house of the Leader family was demolished many years ago, but the stableyard survives as one of the most convincing Irish Victorian evocations of a medieval fortress—castellated cylindrical towers at each corner, turreted entrance gates leading to just a grassy space, but still offering protection from cattle rustlers.

MILLSTREET: **Duarrigle Castle**
Picturesque miniature Gothic Revival castle with two blocks of different heights linked by an octagonal staircase tower; sited on the crest of a wooded ravine. It is difficult today to think of this ivy-clad ruin as the birthplace of Lord St John Stevas' grandmother.

MILLSTREET: **Allied Irish Bank**
Compact double-storied hip-roofed block designed by Brett & Sons in 1878 for the National

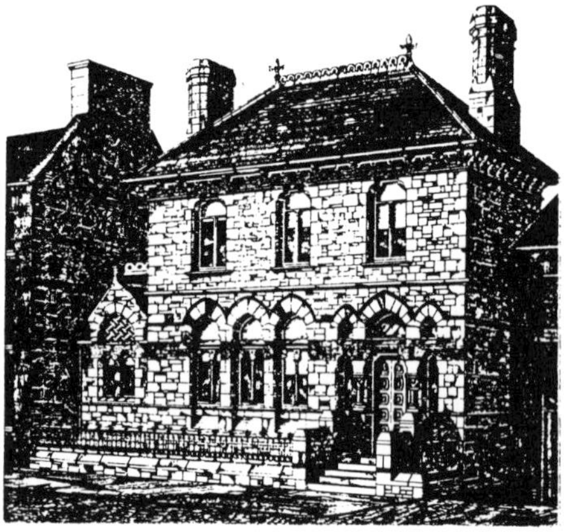

Bank. Arcaded ground floor, the entrance door restating the Georgian formula with side lights but in muscular High Victorian Gothic, the avant garde of twenty years before.

RUSHBROOKE: **Church of Ireland**
Board of First Fruits Gothic, rebuilt by Joseph Welland *c.*1850. Transepts by Welland and Gillespie in 1862. Retains its original light fittings. Glass by Heaton, Butler and Bayne, 1874.

RUSHBROOKE: **Rinn Ronain**
Asymmetrical Tudor Revival villa in red-brick; polygonal bay windows with decoratively carved bargeboards; set directly on the seashore; now mutilated. Said to have been built for himself in the 1860s by the nationalist politician, Joseph Philip Ronayne MP, who was also an artist and engineer. Adjoining it, three similar villas—Homeville, Riverview and Ballynoe, the last being the residence of Abraham Hardgrave, a member of the Cork architectural dynasty (raising the possibility that a Hargrave may have been responsible for the design of the series).

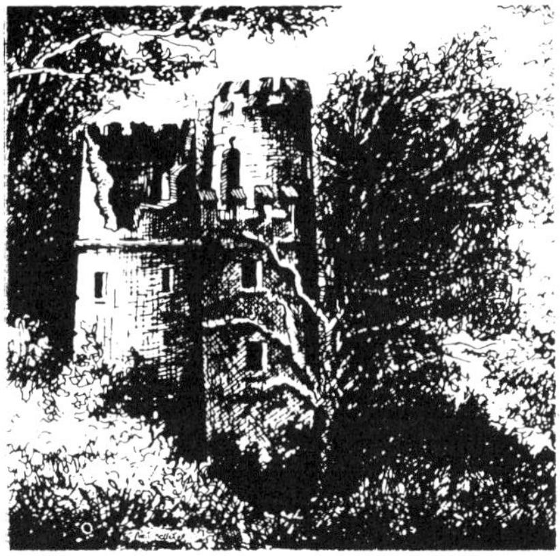

SHANBALLYMORE: **Wallstown Castle**
Also known as Castle Curious, this was built by Johnny Roche, an itinerant scuptor, inventor and musician, in order to win a wager. Three circular towers bonded together and three to four stories high. Now that it has lost its stairs and floors, there is no way of checking the truth of his claim that he built seventy rooms. By the stream are the ruins of the mill he built to supply his castle with water; but apparently, like his contemporary Ludwig II of Bavaria, he hardly spent a night there.

WHITECHURCH: **Carrignavar**
Medieval keep with subsequent extension remodelled in 1903 by James McMullen to blend with the earlier tower adding a dormered roof and battlemented bow. Seat of the M'Cartys; now a religious institution.

WHITEGATE: **Church of Ireland**
The last commission of William Atkins, faithful till death to the ideals of the Ecclesiologists of forty years before. While the leading Irish church architects such as Drew, Fuller, Hague and Ashlin were moving towards serenity, even complacency, this church of 1881 at Whitegate is challenging and discordant. Tautly composed as first glimpsed across the ruins of a medieval predecessor. A saddle-roofed tower (completed in 1892) above the entrance porch counterbalances a single asymmetrical transept which supports a lean-to vestry. Nave and chancel are linked by an unbroken roof, the internal dividing arch serving as support for the boiler chimney. There is no door at the west end; instead a pair of lancets between two massive buttresses incised with stone rosettes, contrasting with slender corner colonettes. This duality is resolved above by a geometrical rose window set high into the gable. The verticality of the architecture is offset by bands of red brick, a foretaste of the interior, which is entirely lined with that material, predominantly red but banded with black and white. The polychromatic brick frames sumptuous stained glass by Heaton, Butler and Baynes, so what little light filters through is dispelled and the open roof is lost in darkness. But this sombre mood is lightened by the white marble altar added ten years later in curvilinear Gothic flanked by arcades with richly coloured mosaics of singing angels.

YOUGHAL: **Collegiate Church of St Mary's**
Medieval church restored *c.* 1850 by its eccentric antiquarian rector, the Revd. Pierce Drew, who found a partial ruin on his appointment. His architect was one of his neighbours, Edward Fitzgerald, but one assumes their work to be a collaboration.

YOUGHAL: **Clay Castle Villas**
A row of Gothic Revival seaside villas rendered in cement with cambered windows and arcaded porches, built during the 1860s. They were not a success and caused the bankruptcy of D.L. Lewis, their builder. Their most remarkable features are the beasts crawling along their string courses: but was the sculptor paid?

YOUGHAL: **The College**
Elizabethan house bought by a London speculator, D.L. Lewis, in 1860 and rebuilt retaining an elaborate original fireplace. A heavy collegiate Gothic composition with lancet windows, tapering buttresses and steep roofs broken by massive chimneys. Lewis lived here till his bankruptcy in 1868 and had commissioned a sculptor to carve mythological beasts, but only a few were executed. Now a convent.

YOUGHAL: **Heathfield Towers**
Elegant Georgian rectory, the home of the Revd Pierce Drew, whose first addition *c.* 1840 was an adjoining library designed like a church with windows of painted glass. His second addition was even more extraordinary, a veritable castle with seven towers, the highest (of rombhoid shape) seven floors high built as a granary during the Famine and embellished with carved heads of his unappreciative bishop and flock. A service yard is successfully disguised as a ruined abbey church complete with stained glass. This aesthetic ruin is now imperceptibly merged with the original rectory which was burnt out thirty years ago and not rebuilt. In the grounds an obsolete brickworks.

CORK COUNTY, SOUTH

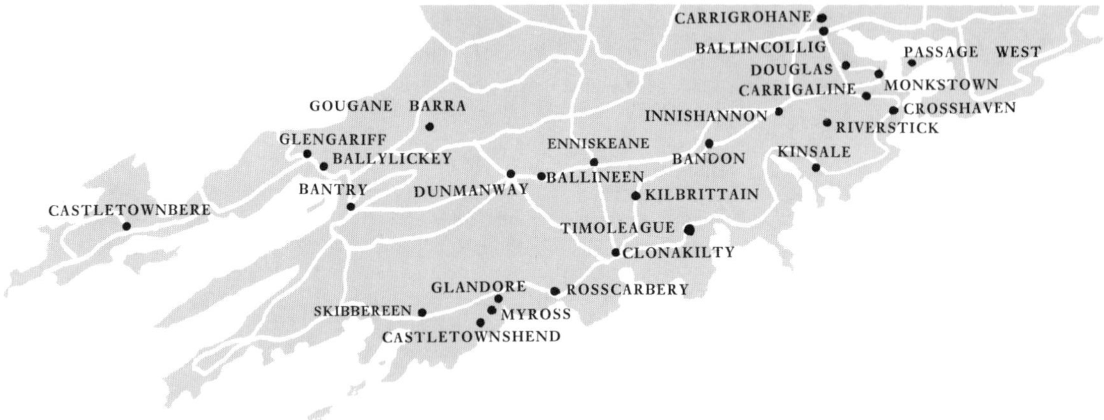

BALLINCOLLIG: **Catholic Church**
Cruciform Gothic Revival built *c.*1870. Impressive symmetrical façade rising to the bellcote at the apex of the gable. Architect unknown.

BALLINCOLLIG: **Hodder Villas**
Engaging Arts and Crafts housing with double-storied bay windows tucked into mansard roofs and linked by verandahs. Built *c.* 1900. Architect unknown.

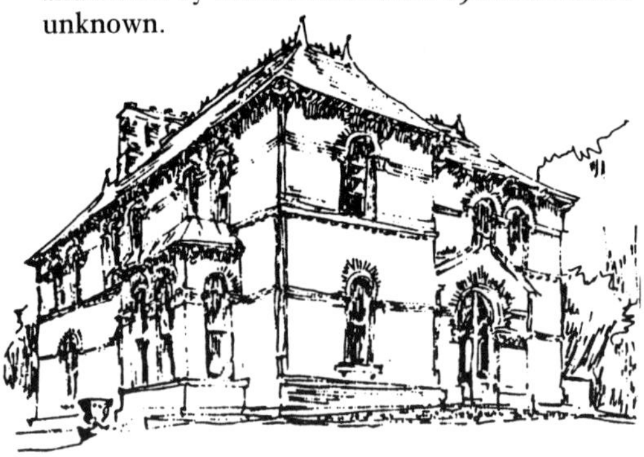

BALLINCOLLIG: **Parknamore**
High Victorian Romanesque villa. Built of brickwork (now rendered), stone string courses and voussoirs to the round, arched windows mainly grouped in pairs. Asymmetrical elevations with steep, crested roofs resting on continuous corbels. On stylistic grounds attributable to William Atkins, *c.*1870.

BALLINEEN: **Church of Ireland**
Set in the countryside close to its medieval predecessor and designed by Joseph Welland in an archaeologically inspired Romanesque. Executed, however, in a more conventional Gothic.

BALLYLICKEY: **Snave**
Arts and Crafts house built to overlook Bantry Bay *c.*1910. By Henry Hill.

BANDON: **Allied Irish Bank**
Formerly the Provincial Bank. Forcefully detailed Gothic Revival designed by T.N. Deane and measured up by Patterson and Kempster in 1877.

BANDON: **Ballymodan Church of Ireland**
The impressive scale and siting of this Church, designed by Joseph Welland and completed in 1847, did not preserve it from the castigation of an anonymous critic in the *Ecclesiologist*, who objected to the 'Cockney' Gothic of its tower with pinnacles placed in every position and its unchurch-like embattled parapets with gables topped by cabbages rather than by crosses. The interior was found also objectionable, with its galleries at the west end and in the transepts. After this savage review, Welland started to change to a more serious Gothic. Memorials to the earls of Bandon, the finest being to an

18th-century ancestor by Scheemakers (1731), moved here from an earlier church. Reclining effigy of the 2nd earl of Bandon (1859) by Edward Richardson. Boyle Bernard tomb (1850) by Saunders of London.

BANDON: Castle Bernard

While many Irish ruins have been sacrificed to add a few more square feet to the holdings of land-hungry farmers, others like Castle Bernard have been allowed to linger on as an ivy-clad backdrop to the herbacious borders of descendants. Here the indoor staff are now a couple of goats, with an interlocutory stare acquired by butlers after a lifetime of service. They have munched the weeds in many roofless rooms, since the 1st earl of Bandon built his new house in 1798 a long way from the adjoining medieval Mahoney keep.

His house was Classical, but he surrounded the keep with Gothic appendages, including a stable block masquerading as a chapel. At several times throughout the century efforts were made to transform the whole house into a castellated pile with mullioned windows, but they were never completed. No architect is recorded.

By then the 3rd earl did up the tower as a family suite. He was kidnapped from there in 1921 by revolutionaries who left his wife behind to watch her home go up in flames.

BANDON: Catholic Church

Built on a rival hill to Welland's church, both with uncompleted spires; designed by George Goldie in 1861 and completed in 1865, this church must be approached not by a sloping car-park of formless asphalt but by a sequence of steps that rises from the narrow streets below; these were added by the builder Philip McAuliffe and considered more impressive by the editor of the *Skibbereen Eagle* (writing in 1884) than the Spanish Steps in Rome. Cruciform with asymmetrical tower. A snug northern porch gives access to a well-proportioned interior more dimly lit than intended due to the later stained glass and the stripping of its internal plaster to reveal the stonework.

BANDON: The Townhall

Designed by Robert Brash and dating from 1862.

BANTRY: Bantry House

The 2nd earl of Bantry was an indefatigable traveller, collector, amateur artist and architect. He was not able to transform the family home into the setting for his treasures until his father died in 1845. He then turned a sensible Georgian house into the lair of a pirate king, the so-called Wallace collection of Ireland, salvaged from a disintegrating Europe of thirty years before.

His father had already extended the house, a typical three-storied Irish cube, by adding a range to overlook the sea, bow-fronted at either end. The 2nd earl built a range on the opposite side of the cube and then an immensely long range beyond, also bow-fronted at each end, articulated by giant Corinthian pilasters, but built in two phases, the extremities first and secondly the centrepiece, a library subdivided by two screens of columns and insulated from the garden by an exotic conservatory. This conservatory, probably by Turner, has vanished, leaving the upper half of the pilasters floating in mid air; vanished also the pergolas in the upper garden that linked two stable blocks enlivened by cupolas. However, the Victorian parterres have recently been meticulously recreated and missing statuary replaced by a tenant sculptor in the mews.

What makes Bantry such an architectural triumph, when so many of the 2nd earl's rival collectors ended up building for their treasures second-rate town halls? The main reason was the ability of the 2nd earl to think in three dimensions and to grasp the potential of the site. This led him to throw rooms together and create unexpected vistas between indoors and out. No professional would have dared to set the front door off-centre in the entry portico masked by a column; nor would he have juxtaposed two- and three-storied fenestration underneath a continuous parapet with such levity—placed the service staircase in the corner of the diningroom, so that the room expands as one proceeds, climaxing in the sideboard. (This looks as if it was retrieved from a ruined South American Baroque monastery but was in fact carved on the estate.) The most theatrical gesture is the entry to the library through a glazed screen at the end of the half-landing of the original staircase. This transforms the Georgian staircase when viewed from the hall into the first flight of another staircase seen vanishing up the terraced hillside on the other side of the formal garden.

But did the 2nd earl design everything himself or did he collaborate with a professional who has so far eluded identification? In the list of buildings that he had designed drawn up by Charles Frederick Anderson before his emigration to the United States, Bantry House is included. Anderson spent his last years living off a pension voted to him by Congress after he had claimed that he was responsible for the extensions to the Capitol in Washington, even though the history of that edifice records his name only in connection with the central heat-

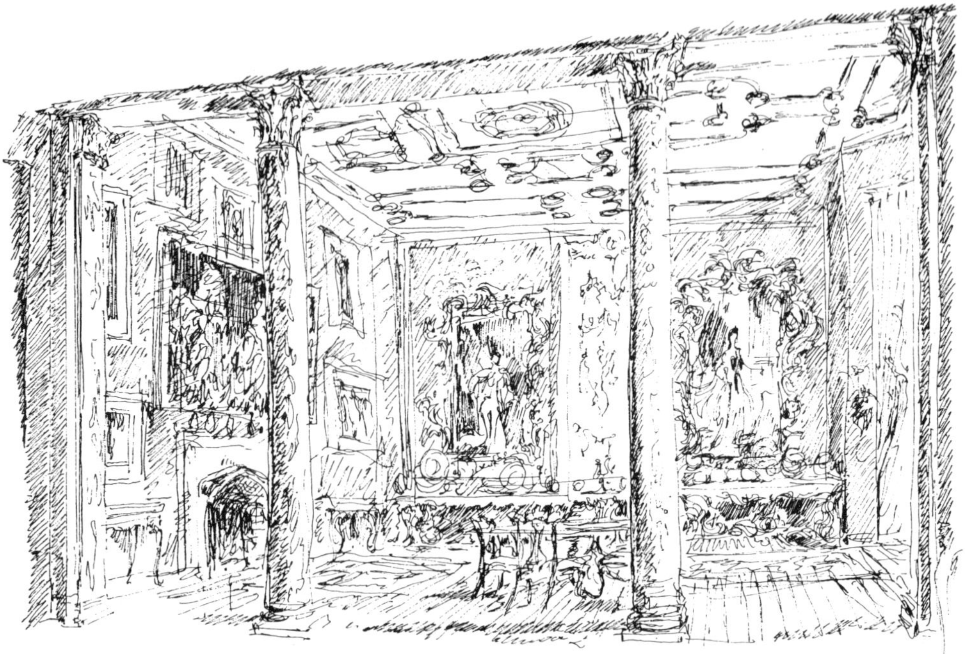

ing. The parallels between the Capitol and Bantry are so intriguing that it is tempting to take Anderson's claims seriously—that he was both architect and technician, playing Hawksmoor to the 2nd earl's Vanbrugh.

BANTRY: **Presentation Convent**
Chapel added by S.F. Hynes (1877) to Romanesque Revival complex constructed twenty years before. The elegantly arcaded organ gallery has survived internal alterations. Glass by Eugene Daly.

BLACKROCK: **Besborough**
Georgian seat of the Pike family, now a convent. Elegant well-maintained curvilinear with conservatory glazed pilasters and a segmental fanlight set into the gable—devices characteristic of Richard Turner's art. Cast-iron gutter lengths linked wittily by fluttering ribbons.

BLACKROCK: **Church of Ireland**
The church designed in 1819 and completed ten years later is by George Pain. The interior contains John Hogan's most ambitious funerary monument—to William Beamish, a marble relief completed in 1844 but started three years before—an emaciated nude woken from his tomb by three angels, one sounding the last trumpet. Graveyard contains the tomb of Sir Thomas Deane, his wife and his mother.

BLACKROCK: **Dundanion Castle**
Purchased in 1823 by Thomas Deane, later Sir Thomas, and rebuilt by him as a neo-Classical villa. He put new battlements on the ruined tower which gave his property its name and designed a private Puginesque Gothic bridge (1847) across the new railway after it had bisected his grounds. The other bridges and stations along the Cork-Passage West line were Italianate and designed by Joshua Hargrave. House burnt out but rebuilt *c.*1860.

BLACKROCK: **Lichfield**
Tudor cottage ornée built *c.*1840 for a Deane cousin, most probably by Kearns Deane. Symmetrical façade with front door set a gable with an elaborate bargeboard. Adjoining coach house added later with triangular dormer as deployed by Benjamin Woodward.

BRINNY: **Church of Ireland**
Board of First Fruits Gothic refitted by Henry Hill *c.*1870, when he added the saddle-roofed tower above the entry porch. Late Gothic Revival carved wooden reredos.

CARRIGALINE: **Coolmore**
Late Georgian cube with a drawingroom (overlooking the estuary) redecorated by Sibthorpe in neo-Adamesque—tempera medallions on a blue ground with red and green borders articulated by gilded pilasters, decoration comparable to the ceilings of Fota. The setting for the film of Mollie Keane's *Good Behaviour*. The room lost its specially commissioned gilded furniture and its fireplace at the auction that dispersed the contents of the house. The murals also were sold off, but their purchaser was unable to detach them. The seat of the Newenhams.

CARRIGROHANE: **Carrigrohane Castle**
Medieval castle on the edge of a precipice above the valley of the Lee rebuilt in Elizabethan times by the Barretts, and then burnt out by Cromwell. Leased from the Hoares by the McSwineys, soon to be created marquises of Mashanaglass by Pius VII. Reroofed in the 1840s. The reception rooms on the lower two floors have magnificent carved-stone fireplaces, one with a freize of wheat sheaves subtly alluding to the source of the family wealth. Tudor windows and ceilings with ornamented joists left exposed as in University College, Cork. The architect was presumably Benjamin Woodward working for Sir Thomas Deane, but so much under the influence of Pugin at the time that his work is indistinguishable from the master. The McSwineys ran out of money and had to hand back the castle to the Hoares fully restored. They are not mentioned in the memoirs, *The Road to Glenanore* by Jessie Hoare, who recalls her home only as the setting for her enchanted childhood.

CARRIGROHANE: **Church of Ireland**
Medieval church rebuilt by Joseph Welland in 1854 as a long low nave and chancel dominated by a north-western tower and spire, quietly extended by Burges in 1867 with a lean-to side-aisle to the south accessible through a new arcade. As he had to nestle under the existing roof, and still allow as much daylight into the nave as possible, Burges was reduced to using square-headed windows. These are placed in triplets subdivided internally by free-standing colonettes. The result anticipates the Arts and Crafts by a generation (cf. Letherby's Brockhampton Church). He also added the vestry and inserted stained glass by Saunders and Holliday into Welland's eastern window.

CASTLETOWNBERE: **Catholic Church**
Designed by R.M. Butler in his ponderous Gothic; approached from the street by one of his characteristic flights of steps. Dates from 1907. Stained glass chancel window (1909) by Child. Other windows by O'Brien and Rhind.

CASTLETOWNBERE: **Dunboy Castle**
Commissioned in 1866 by Henry Puxley three years after his copper mines had reached the peak of their productivity. Said to be built by him to distract his wife from her ill-health due to continuous childbearing. An extension of an earlier Georgian house attached to a strange Gothick tower.

His London architect, John Christopher, sited the new castle directly in front of the old, maintaining the existing axis. The staircase has a half-landing communicating with the original bedrooms. Its informal grouping relied on chimneys rather than pinnacles or towers for vertical emphasis. Its mullioned windows (more glass than wall) show the influence of Nesfield's Cloverly Hall, Shropshire (1864). A library and diningroom are built over an arcaded 'fernery' that gives the castle a Venetian character when seen from the water. Only at roof level was there a loss of scale, a clutter of gabled dormers, closer to a grand hotel than to a feudal castle.

Cockburn, the Dublin builder, started work under the supervision of Edward Carson (father of Sir Edward). However, a new plan for the hall dated January 1867 was drawn up by Christopher. He superimposed (on his earlier scheme) a nave, aisles and galleries—a typical Gothic ecclesiastical interior of five bays. The four transverse arches, braced by aisles, galleries and two series of clerestories, support open triforiums which subdivide the lantern-like

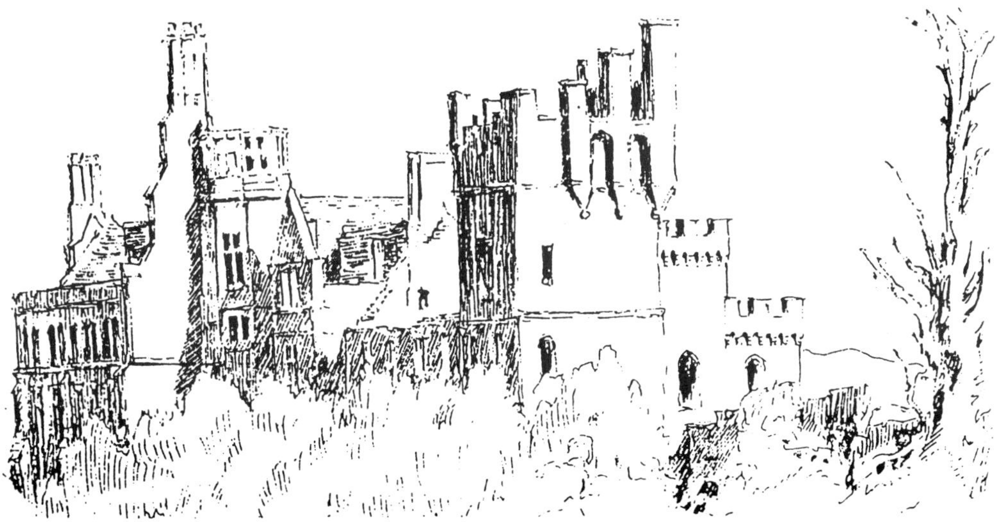

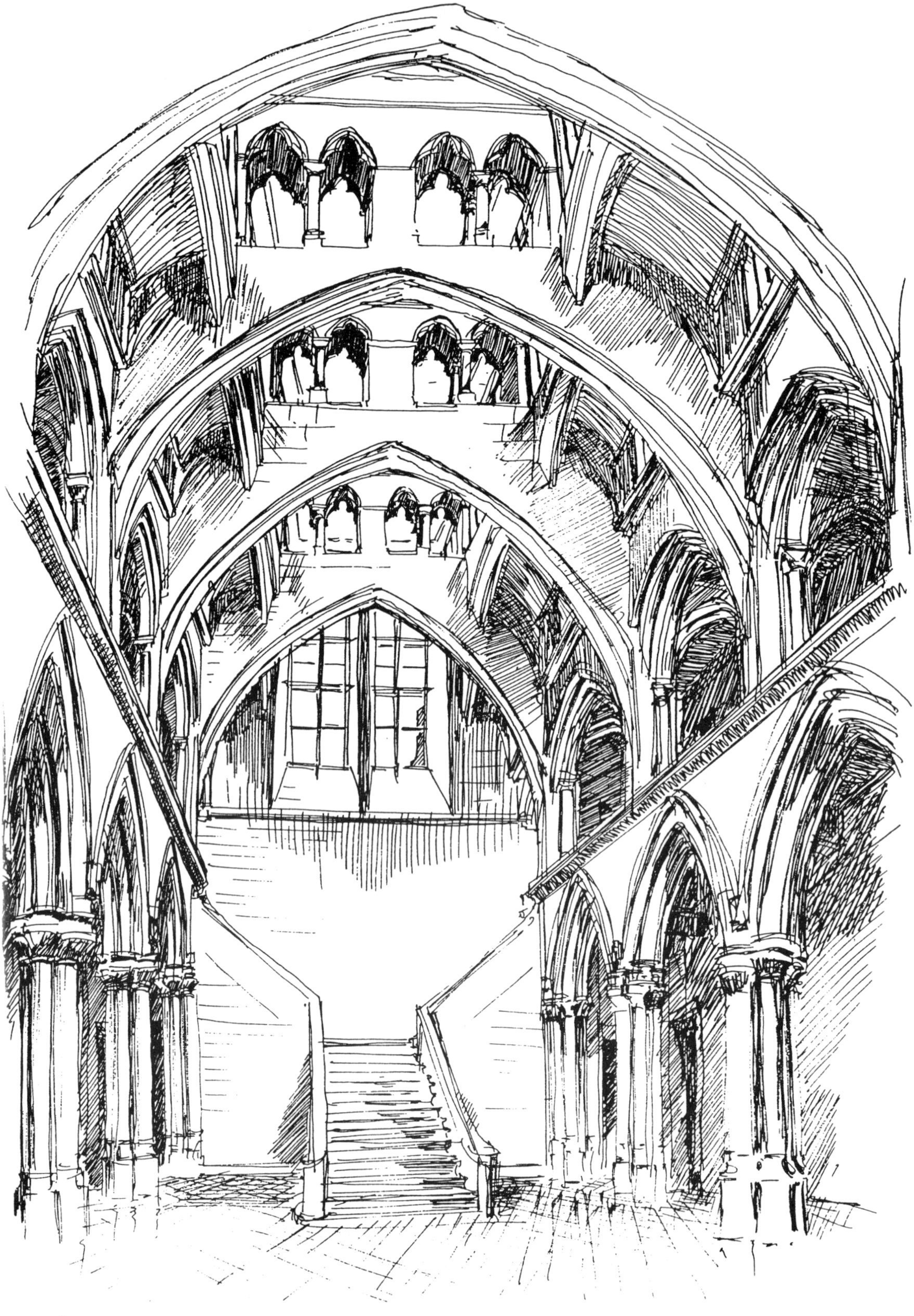

DUNBOY: THE GREAT HALL (AS INTENDED)

volume overhead into five inter-penetrating spaces. The heavy stone piers of the earlier design are, in reality, four detached shafts of red marble. Metal girders take the lateral thrust of the arches to the side walls that in turn distribute it throughout the structure. Christopher plays with arcade, clerestory, triforium, the traditional elements of a Gothic cathedral to create an interior that has no medieval counterpart. The nearest is Mayfield Palace (Kent). The only contemporary architect who could have designed such a hall, Norman Shaw, never built anything as dramatic as Dunboy, but his unexecuted plans for Bradford Exchange of 1864 have many parallels, raising the question of a collaborator as he and Christopher had gone to Italy together as students.

After the builders successfully sued him for variations to the original contract, Henry Puxley lost his wife in childbirth. He departed for London, remarried and never returned, though he lived for nearly forty years more.

Burnt out by the local IRA. The setting of Daphne de Maurier's *Hungry Hill* written while she was billeted with the Puxleys in Hertfordshire during the Second World War.

CASTLETOWNSHEND: **Castle Townshend**

Battlemented tower joined to a castellated house by a dormered range; set on the shore of Castle Haven, seat of the Townshends (George Bernard Shaw's mother-in-law changed her name from Townsend to Townshend so that she might appear to be related to them). Today what was the Townsend house is a level field, while the outlying towers and stables of the Townshends have been resourcefully transformed by the current Mrs Salter-Townshend into self-catering accommodation.

CASTLETOWNSHEND: **Church of Ireland**

Church built by James Pain in 1826 but associated above all with Edith Somerville, who not only played the organ here for seventy years, but who was also responsible for commissioning from Harry Clarke three windows which between them span his working career. The Nativity window above the altar with its Irish shepherds dressed as Russian ballet dancers was the first commission after he completed the Honan Chapel, Cork (q.v.) in 1915. The window in the nave dedicated to St Louis and St Martin was made after he had taken over the firm on his father's death, his most prolific period of major commissions. The tiny St Luke window in the chancel is thought to be the last window that was entirely his own work, since ill-health had forced him to rely on his assistants for his larger windows. His windows sparkle with captured light and render the three earlier commemorative windows by Powell of London even more dimly funereal. Edith Somerville herself designed the mosaic floor before the medieval altar in the chancel; executed by Rust & Co. of London, it incorporates a Maltese cross, much to the horror of the vicar when he discovered he had been standing on it for over four years.

CASTLETOWNSHEND: **View Holloa**

The only architectural commission of Edith Somerville, built for her huntsman in 1915, a quarter of a mile from the village of the Bawnalahan road. Unassuming double-storied cottage.

CLONAKILTY: **Catholic Church**

Ambitious church by George Ashlin designed in 1869 as a scaled-down version of Cobh Cathedral, complete with an elaborate corner tower and spire. The nave arcade screens the transepts so that there is no visible crossing. The vaulting throughout is sheathed with dark varnished timber, at its simplest in the Gothic tunnel of the transepts, repeated over the aisles on a reduced scale where it is enriched with ribbing; more elaborate still above the nave, due to the interpenetration of the clerestory; and at its most complex in the apse above the high altar. This, the satisfying culmination of the interior, is accented by stained glass, mosaics and painted panels of singing angels. The later high altar of 1897, still protected by its communion rails, is by G. O'Connor. Most of the glass is of the same period, inevitably by Mayer, and at its most effective in the rose windows of the transepts.

CLONAKILTY: **Convent of Mercy**

Designed by Pugin and Ashlin in the Romanesque style, an unusual choice for the architects but chosen to match the buildings already built on the best part of the site. The new work of 1867 is not visible from the town below; asymmetrical massing of the chapel, the campanile and the adjoining wings is withheld until the moment of arrival.

CLONAKILTY: **Lisselane**

An underplayed French chateau built above the River Arigadeen with adjoining three-storied turret and later smoking-room wing. Designed by Lewis Vulliamy for William Bence-Jones. T.N. Deane designed the wing and two gate-lodges *c.*1870. Robinsonian gardens laid out on both sides of the river by Mr and Mrs Reginald Bence-Jones, who also added a conservatory that they bought from the Cork Exhibition of 1902.

CLONAKILTY: **Methodist Church**
Modest Gothic Revival town church of 1860 with adjoining hall. Rose window above the altar. Architect unrecorded.

CLONAKILTY: **Post Office**
Ingenious adaptation of a Gothic Revival Presbyterian church of 1861 without any obvious external deformation, so that its adjoining belfry with a stone steeple springing from corner gargoyles still dominates the surrounding streetscape. Architect unrecorded.

CLONAKILTY: **West Cork Craft Centre**
Derelict distillery across the river from the Catholic church with three chimneys enlivening the townscape. Warehouse fronting the street recently taken over as a craft centre open to shoppers.

CROSSHAVEN: **Catholic Church**
Not to be outdone by the Church of Ireland, the formidable parish priest, Canon Denis McSwiney, commissioned his church from another leading English architect, Edward Welby Pugin. Work started in 1869 but was halted by litigation the following year when the builder, Richard Evans (see Enniskeane), was sued by the canon for not using the random masonry that Pugin intended but did not clearly specify. The contractor lost and Pugin failed to get his fee. 'I can only say that Canon McSwiney is the most extraordinary client I have ever come across in my life. . . .' The church was Pugin's last Irish commission. Chancel modernized. The lacy belfry is by another architect, possibly Coakley, and has been rebuilt.

CROSSHAVEN: **Church of Ireland**
Also known as Templebrady, this compact parish church was designed by William Burges after he had won the competition for St Fin Barre's Cathedral (q.v.); built in 1864-6. Nave entered through projecting porch. The spacing of the windows in the smaller chancel is subtly diffentiated from those in the nave. Interior of stark simplicity revealing the love of Burges for the rural Gothic of France. Wagon vault braced by inverted T-bars. Plate traceried rose above triple window behind the altar. Robust cylindrical pulpit. Glass by Heaton, Butler and Bayne. A round tower, more appropriate to Poitou, was never built.

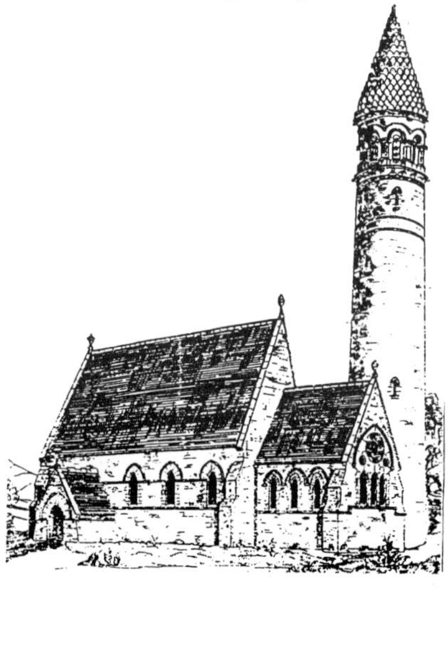

CROSSHAVEN: **The Hotel**
Comfortable but undistinguished; now the HQ of Quest Biocon Ltd. Designed by James McMullen in 1887.

DOUGLAS: **Church of Ireland**
Gothic Revival church built in 1875 by an engineer, Osborne Edwards. Ten years later the nave was extended and a tower with spire added by W.H. Hill built out of a local limestone. Henry Hill, his uncle, had designed the medieval-style Reeves tomb.

DOUGLAS: **Redgarth**
The house built for himself by Arthur Hill inspired by the Arts and Crafts style of Norman Shaw. Double-gabled façade with varied fenestration. Tile-clad upper floors. Decorative tiled floors and plasterwork, also to be found in his Metropole Hotel.

DUNMANWAY: **Coolkelure House and Church**
Low rambling house with many bay windows and gables with their timberwork exposed. Attached pyramidial tower. Designed by Henry Hill for the Shuldham family, who also commissioned from him the small Gothic Revival church in 1865.

DUNMANWAY: **Model National School**
Built in 1848 to the standard Tudor design of Frederick Darley. Gabled and dormer asymmetrical central block, between adjoining one-storied assembly to the south, and to the north a detached master's residence, now a guesthouse, rendered and brightly painted, whereas before it had been exposed limestone like the remainder. Semi-derelict, but the gardens are well cared for, always in Ireland a sign of faith in the future.

ENNISKEANE: **Catholic Church**
An impressive church on a tight budget designed by a builder to expose, one senses, architects as superfluous. He was Richard Evans, the unfortunate builder, who lost the case taken against him by Canon McSwiney of

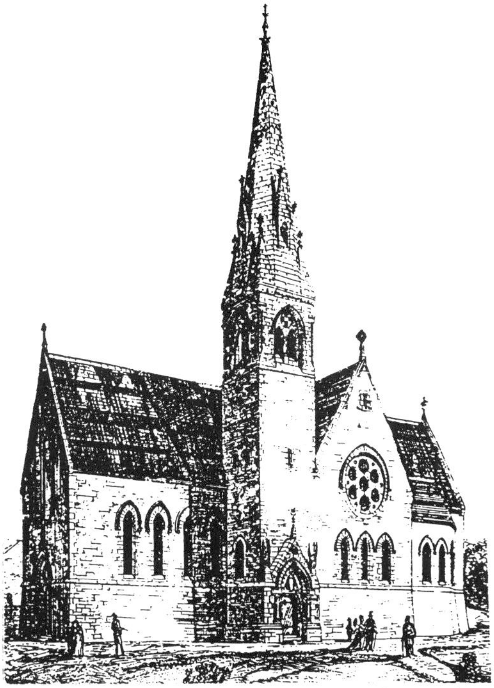

Crosshaven due to the ambiguous instructions of E.W. Pugin. Here he was working directly for the parish priest. A simple cruciform without aisles. Single belfry set flush with the southern transept; square chancel flanked by polygonal chapels. Austere interior that could well be an Irish medieval monastic church with open roof and asymmetrical fenestration due to the siting of the tower. Dated 1871.

GLANDORE: **Church of Ireland**
Tiny Gothic Revival church fitting snugly into a wooded grove above Glandore and the sea. Simple cruciform interior with open trusses intercrossing. Will those who make decisions on the future of such churches in distant cities taken into account its dramatic approach, an arch cut through the natural rock?

GLENGARIFF: **Eccles Hotel**
The exterior of this Victorian hotel with its bedrooms opening on to a double-storied cast-iron verandah survives reasonably intact, but the interior suffered an unsympathetic restoration ten years ago. The owner's collection of oil paintings has vanished with replacable engravings taking their place.

GLENGARIFF: **Garinish Garden, Illnacullin**
Paradise garden hidden in a wooded islet off the shore of Bantry Bay, acquired as a bare windswept rock by a Belfast industrialist, John Annan Bryce, in 1910. The first architects that he commissioned were Young and McKenzie, but for the garden he went to the most gifted of the Edwardian garden architects, Harold Peto, and Peto not only designed the garden but also the architectural elements that frame the vistas which are hidden to the outsider and then suddenly revealed, as in the gardens of the Italianate Renaissance. Peto had already worked in the South of France, but Garinish is his *tour de force*, started just before the death of Edward

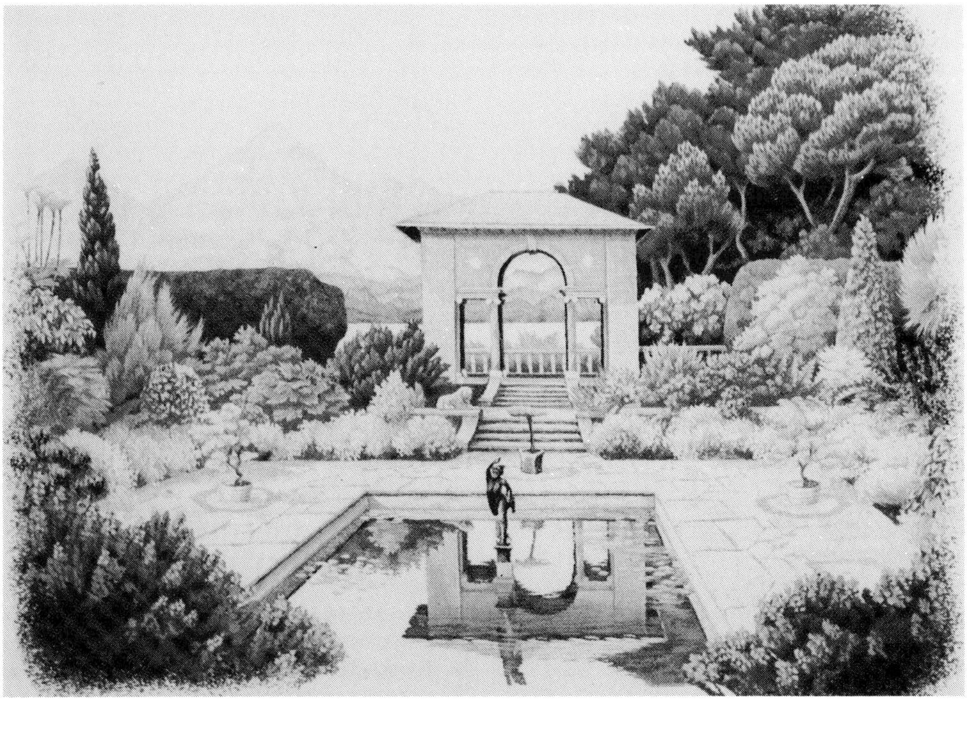

VII, to whom Peto was to raise an obelisk in his own garden during the First World War, inscribed 'Edward the Peacemaker'. Garinish survived a hostile climate, the change of regime and the death of its founder in 1924. It also survived another danger, the temptation to build a house. Peto's unexecuted scheme to convert the ruined fort on the highest point of the island into a brash Italianate castello would have dominated all the vistas and absorbed all the funds; the drawings can be seen in his exquisite *casita*. Its inlaid floors and coloured marble columns, their wide spacing revealing their Edwardian origins. Bequeathed to An Taisce by Rowland Bryce in 1953, it has been since then under the provisional care of the Board of Works, and is one of the most visited gardens in Ireland.

GOUGANE BARRA: **Oratory of St Finbarre**

Small Celtic Revival church set on island hermitage of St Finbarre. Designed with stone roof, stained glass and mosaic floor. By S.F. Hynes (*c.*1900). Stained glass, altar and fittings designed by M.J.C. Buckley in a Celtic idiom and made by his workshop (1903).

INNISHANNON: **Church of Ireland**

Joseph Welland built countless churches, but in none is he so gratefully acknowledged. A scroll carved in stone records him as architect, James Hunter as builder, a group of donors and the date, 1856. The early church across the road was abandoned as too low-flying. Perhaps a new church was preferred to be more imposing than the Gothick Catholic church designed by George Pain in 1828 (and still reasonably intact, with an elegant spire). Welland's spire is not as high, but his church is more prominently sited, influenced by the muscular Gothic of his younger contemporaries. Only the internal trusses springing from corbelled heads of the apostles indicate his birth in the 18th century. Interior embellished by Late Gothic Revival fittings; stained glass by Holiday (over the altar), Watson, and Heaton Butler and Baynes (their great west window only recently eclipsed by the installation of a new organ).

KILBRITTAIN: **Kilbrittain Castle**

Impressively sited 16th-century keep of the McCarthys extended to make a house two hundred years later, that was convincingly transformed into a castle by an unknown Victorian architect. Burned out in the Troubles, and partly demolished. The remainder was acquired by the inventor and aviator Russell Winn, who rebuilt the castle in a simpler and more medieval idiom. Sold by his widow after his death in a flying accident before he could complete the interior.

KILMALOODA: **Church of Ireland**

Commissioned by William Bence-Jones and built at his own expense. The architect he chose was English, James St Aubyn, who gave his patron a seigneurial church appropriate for Anglican ritual, full of Victorian self-confidence. Executed precisely in accord with the drawings (apart from the tower) of 1856. As a result, the architect was awarded the commission, through Bence-Jones, of the ill-fated Berkeley Hall in University College, Cork.

KINSALE: **Perryville**

Two Georgian town houses remodelled in the 1890s by Capt. Adam Warren-Perry, their junction masked by adding a three-storied bay. On the ground floor a new front door arched by Moorish plasterwork overhung by a cast-iron verandah opening off the *piano nobile* above. Inside once, a French-style drawingroom and a ballroom that remained unused. All this fantasy must have aroused grim suspicions among neighbouring dowagers of a potential nightclub in their midst, which surprisingly it never has become. In more recent times, a sedate bed and breakfast.

MONKSTOWN: **Catholic Church**

Designed in 1866 by the partnership of E.W. Pugin and George Ashlin, and built on a difficult terraced site above the estuary of the Lee. Cruciform plan with double transepts screened by the nave arcades as in SS Peter and Paul in Cork (q.v.). The roof structure is also derived from the same prototype. Apse with inset gabled central window. Built out of local red sandstone

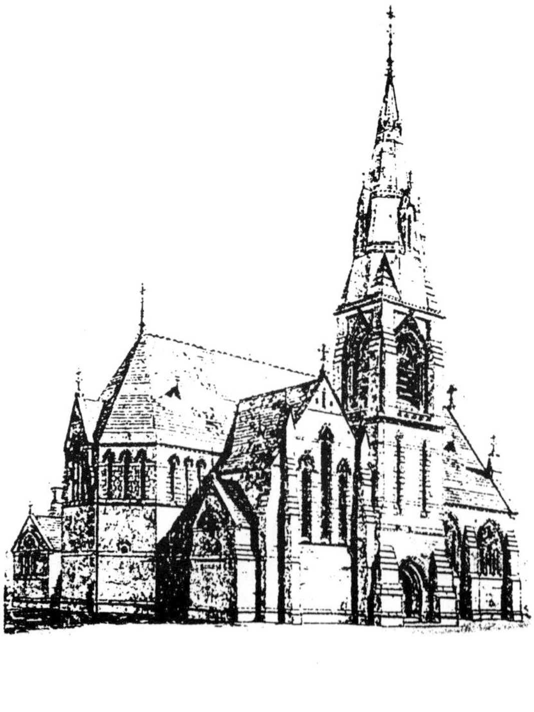

with Ballintemple and Bath stone dressings. Adjoining belfry with more elaborate spire completed in 1881. The red-brick presbytery below the church dates from 1868 and reveals the predominant influence of Pugin.

MONKSTOWN: **Summerland Buildings**
The property of Henry Hill designed (before 1841) to look like separate blocks of semi-detached villas—a continuous terrace enlivened by bays projecting in pairs. Traceried Gothick windows derived from Dromore Castle, Co. Kerry (q.v.) (just completed by the Deanes). The terrace was not a commercial success, and work dragged on until the mid-1850s.

MONKSTOWN: **Thorncliffe**
Gothic Revival villa commissioned by Cork's leading ironmaster, John Perrot, in polychromatic stonework with a three-storied entry gable of pink granite flanked by walls of purple limestone. Staircase window on half-landing above ponderously corbelled entry porch. Adjoining full-height chimney shaft. Four floors to the rear overlooking the sea treated with equal brutalism. Attributable on stylistic grounds to Thomas Newenham Deane. Dated 1865.

MYROSS: **Church of Ireland**
Designed by Henry Hill in 1869. Small cruciform Gothic Revival church of slight architectural importance but well sited above the village of Union Hall overlooking Castle Haven.

PASSAGE WEST: **Church of Ireland**
Small Gothic Revival church with perky buttressed western turret. Roofed with bands of polychromatically treated slates.

PASSAGE WEST: **Horsehead**
Tudor Revival villa built in 1836 for John Craig, the Bank of Ireland's Cork agent. Drawings in the National Library signed 'Thomas and Kearns Deane'. Their most accomplished villa, showing a grasp of asymmetrical composition that was to distinguish the domestic output of Deane and Woodward in the 1850s. All windows have Gothick fanlights set in square frames modelled on Dromore Castle, Co. Kerry (q.v.). Lofty chimney-stacks.

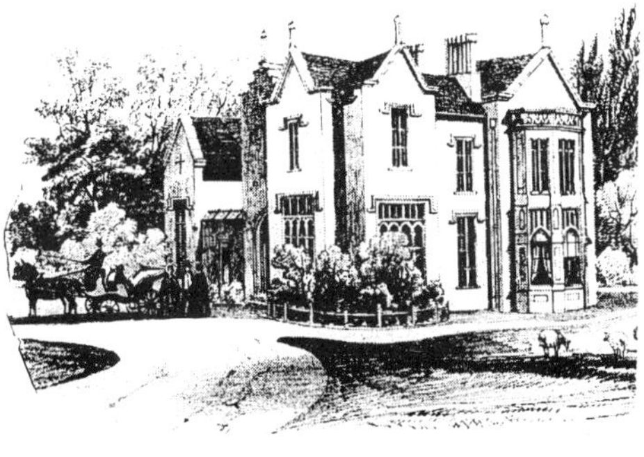

PASSAGE WEST: **Leacarrow**
Gothic Revival villa built *c.*1860 with fussy asymmetrically treated double-storied bays underneath heavy bargeboards. Architect unknown.

PASSAGE WEST: **Marmullane**
One of the first few Irish Greek Revival villas comparable to the Glasgow commissions of Alexander Thompson; built between 1850 and 1861 for a local shipbuilder, Henry Brown, whose daughter married the son of John Craig of Horsehead (q.v.), so presumably he went to Deane and Woodward. The quality of the design is such as to suggest that Woodward himself responded to the challenge of an unfamiliar idiom. A pinwheel plan like Clontra (q.v.) in Shankhill, Co. Dublin, radiates out from a central roof light above the landing. French windows open from the main rooms into the garden; they were once protected by verandahs with colonnades of drainpipes sheathed with slatted timber, now removed.

PASSAGE WEST: **Mount Prospect**
Gothic Revival villa built round the same period as Marmullane (q.v.) for William Browne, a brother of Henry. The design with Tudor features modelled on Horsehead (q.v.) built twenty years before. Possibly by Sir Thomas Deane himself.

RIVERSTICK: **Heathburn Hall**
Insubstantial castellated folly tower added in 1905 to a sedate Georgian country house by Lt-Col. F.G. Shaw, a cousin of George Bernard Shaw, said to have been his own architect.

ROCHESTOWN: **Bloomfield**
Three-storied villa in a severe Tudor Revival idiom with mullioned windows and steeply pitched roofs. Built in 1896 by an unrecorded architect on the site of an earlier house.

ROSSCARBERY: **Castle Freke**
Georgian house built *c.*1780 by the 6th Lord Carbery, castellated and extended by him forty years later to the designs of Richard Morrison (as more appropriate to its dramatic siting above Rosscarbery Bay). Additions included varied towers and a far-flung courtyard but the house remained incomplete until the 1830s. The family home of the 3rd countess of Bandon, who had to watch the destruction of Castle Bernard, Castle Freke survived the Troubles. Perhaps

this was due to its accidental destruction by fire in 1910 so that it was impregnably rebuilt in reinforced concrete by Kaye, Parry and Ross (executant architect James McMullen), which has permitted its intended reclamation as a management training centre despite a demolition sale. Traces of its lavish neo-Jacobean interior remain.

SKIBBEREEN: **Bank of Ireland**
Red-brick palazzo with limestone trimmings, by Millar and Symes *c.*1880. The birthplace of the novelist William Trevor.

SKIBBEREEN: **Catholic Cathedral**
Lombardesque choir with apse and side chapels added by George Ashlin to the Classical church of 1826. Later work tied to earlier by heavy arcading that also frames the vista up into the apse with paintings, mosaics and stained glass enclosing the marble rotunda of the high altar. Marble memorial now painted white of 'Religion' gazing at a cameo of Bishop Collins (+1832) by John Hogan.

SKIBBEREEN: **Church of Ireland**
Rebuilt on a limited budget by W.H. Hill in 1890. The new church retains the old as its transept complete with entry tower. Arcades of red marble and trefoiled clerestory show Catholic influence reinforced by Mayer's glass. Other glass by Heaton, Butler and Bayne. Adjoining church hall designed also by Hill in 1907 reveals the influence of William Scott.

SKIBBEREEN: **Convent of Mercy**
French Gothic chapel added by George Ashlin and E.W. Pugin in 1867 to overlook the cathedral, linked to the earlier chapel transformed into a transept for the nuns. Rose window set above a row of lancets blocked with red marble. Gallery staircase contained in chateau-like

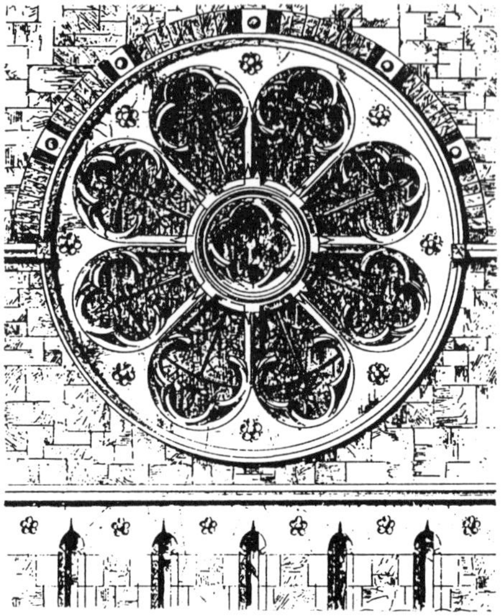

corner turret. Controlled polychromy throughout. Neo-medieval glass in window above the altar.

SKIBBEREEN: **Hollybrook**
A delightful octagonal gatelodge anticipates the neo-colonial Classicism of the house itself (a Diocletian window is set into the pediment of its portico and dormers peep behind the chimney stacks). The architect was Scottish—R.S. Balfour—and this is his largest domestic commission. Built 1903-4 for Lt-Col. A.H. Morgan incorporating carved heraldic marquetry panels made by an aunt, Jane Morgan, for her house on Staten Island, New York. These now decorate the ceiling and freestanding chimney in the double drawingroom. More conventional neo-Caroline decoration in the diningroom and the double-height hall entered beneath the half landing. The reception rooms open through a colonnade into a formal garden. An octagonal tower beneath the main

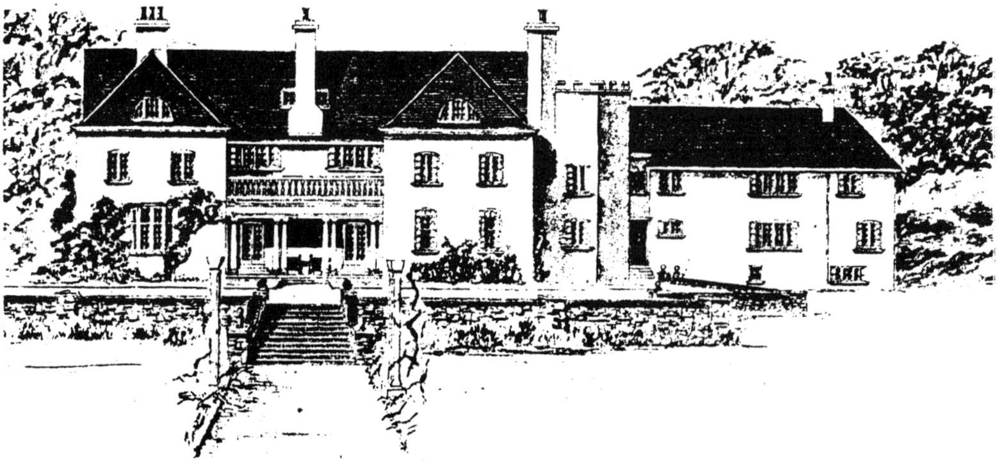

block and the service wing contains a circular oak-lined study.

The loss of Spiddal (q.v.) and Kilteragh (q.v.) in 1921 leaves Hollybrook as the most important Irish new-built house exemplifying 'Sweetness and Light'.

TIMOLEAGUE: **Catholic Church**

A competent essay in the Hiberno-Romanesque revival designed in 1880 by the Cork architect Michael Hennessy (otherwise known for his spire to the Catholic cathedral of Limerick: q.v.). Here there is no intimacy of the original Celtic Churches due the congregation required by the brief. The different elements, like the rectangular chancel, while kept within the Irish canon are amalgamated in a new way: thus a gabled porch interpenetrates the base of the round tower. Observe the nice touch of linking the tower to the side aisle by a tiny apsed chapel. Spacious well-proportioned interior with flooring and communion rail still undisturbed. Cylindrical columns between the nave and aisles, square piers elsewhere at the organ loft above the entry, and at the crossing. Celtic Revival high altar with mosaic flooring to the chancel. The stained glass is unfortunate in its timing. The east window was put into too soon and is therefore decadently English Gothic; the west window was put in too late—Harry Clarke Studios but long after his death and with no trace of his subtlety.

TIMOLEAGUE: **Church of Ireland**

The exterior hidden by the trees of the encircling graveyard is of slight consequence: a typical First Fruits church of 1811 refitted by Welland and Gillespie in 1862. But the porch beneath the tower contains a faded photograph of the mararajah of Gwalior gazing up at his very tall doctor, Surgeon-General Aylmer Crofts. Their twenty years of friendship are immortalized by a gift of the mararajah, the mosaic decoration of the interior started in 1894 to commemorate the dead members of the Travers family. Completed in 1925 ten years after the doctor's death. The workmen were Italian and they laid out each panel on the lawn of the family's home nearby. The designer is unrecorded but was most likely W.H. Hill, the Church of Ireland architect of the region, who used mosaics in many of his documented commissions and whose nephew Henry was chosen by the family to design their new house in 1924 after the old one had been destroyed in the Troubles. Apart from a continuous frieze recording the lifespan of relations, and the inevitable loss of sons in the First World War, there is little that is funereal: it is a living friendship that is being recorded in an extraordinary blend of the European and the Islamic—a hidden masterpiece of the Arts and Crafts movement in Ireland. Most of the decoration is composed of stylized plants and leaves, framed in geometrical patterns, boldly overscaled and simplified to set off the delicacy of the earlier Gothic Revival—the elaborate hammerbeam roof of the nave, the panels of gilded angels in the ceiling of the chancel, and a series of stained glass windows, a Warrington above the altar, glass by Lavers, Westlake and also Mayer elsewhere. The mosaics only lapse into the sentimental when they depict the faces of Christ and his apostles on the western wall, who pose in a group correctly garmented beneath a topographical Jerusalem. The purely Italian contribution is the font held by a marble angel, a sister to the pair in the Catholic church of Tralee (q.v.). The British Empire momentarily transcended the sectarian divide between the Irish Catholic and Protestant, the Indian Muslin and Hindu, personal friendship breaking up, hereditary distinctions of caste and colour. In the guest book, comments are asked for. While foreigners, dazzled by this unanticipated splendour, are unanimous in their praise ('beautiful', 'belle' and 'schön'), interspersed by the occasional Irish put down, such as 'spooky'.

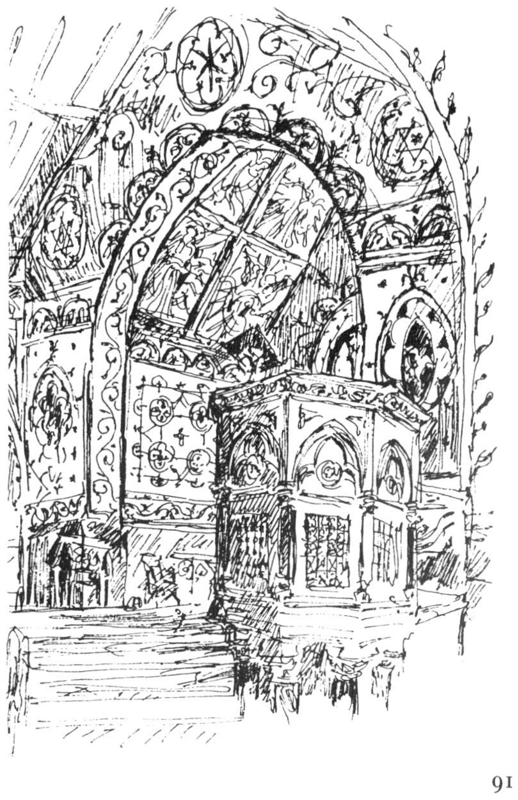

DONEGAL

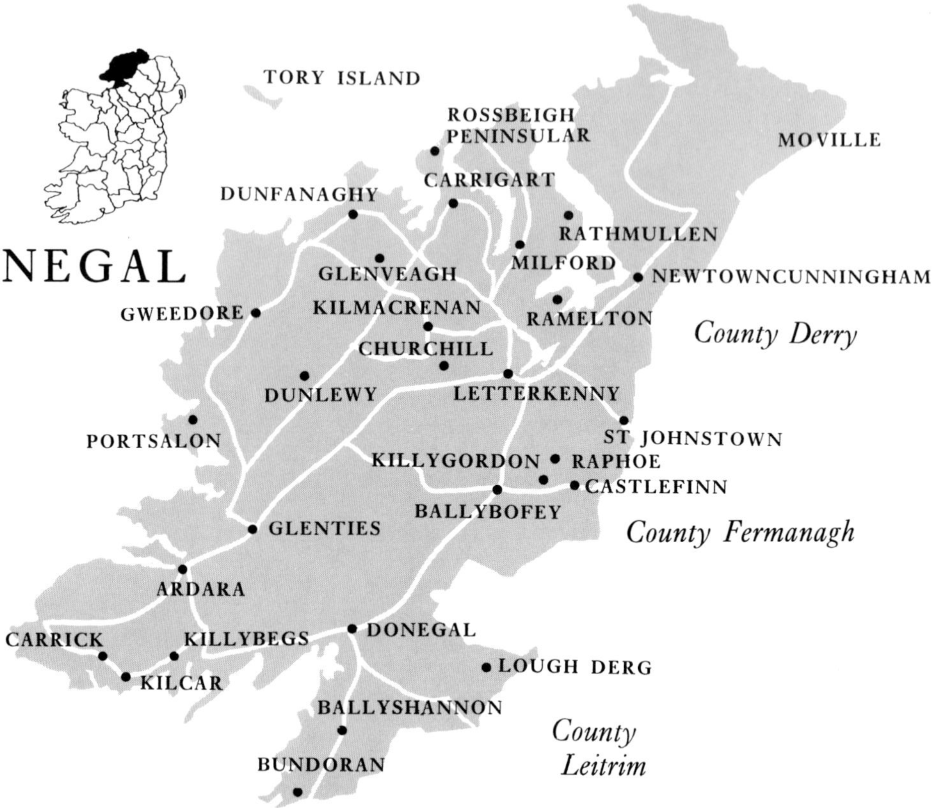

ARDARA: **Catholic Church**
Designed by the Derry architect E.J. Toye in 1900 in the Romanesque idiom. A wide nave leading into an apsidal chancel with arcades to transepts leading into side chapels with wheel windows. Larger wheel window over the western entrance porch filled with glass by Evie Hone (1954).

BALLYBOFEY: **Catholic Church**
Gothic Revival church built by a Manchester architect, William Nicholson, and designed in 1859. Tower added, 1893. Open roof. Austere interior divested of its original fittings apart from an entombed Christ beneath a pinnacled reredos and a chancel window of Mayer glass.

BALLYSHANNON: **Allied Irish Bank**
Formerly the Provincial Bank; entirely upstaged by the ostentation of its neighbour, the former Royal Bank (now Gallogly's), with whom it refuses to compete. Instead, a single-storied arcade dating from 1885. It is curious to find T.N. Deane for once providing such an exemplary model of bankerly discretion, but this is no doubt due to the influence of his son, Thomas Manley.

BALLYSHANNON: **Bank of Ireland**
Formerly the Royal Bank built in 1885 by an unknown architect. The commission appears to have gone to his head, since the result with its multi-tiered clock tower dominates the town centre as if it were the townhall.

BALLYSHANNON: **Camlin Gates**
The only evidence of a toy castle spared by the Erne drainage scheme but demolished nevertheless. A flag tower with an arch set into a curved screen wall, crowned with battlements throughout. Designed by J.B. Keane.

BALLYSHANNON: **Catholic Church**
The tower alongside this church is inscribed with the date (1842) and the name of the otherwise unknown builder, Daniel Conroy. Gothic Revival without, vaguely Classical within. Open, richly trussed roof decorated by Barff and Co. Polygonal chancel added by J.J. McCarthy in 1860. High altar by Messrs Farrell.

BALLYSHANNON: **Church of Ireland**
Designed by 1839 by William Hagerty of Derry, whose drawings are preserved by the Representative Church Body, Dublin. The earlier tower is retained and rebuilt, while the new nave is crisply detailed with lancet windows set into five recessed panels similar to Rossory Church, Enniskillen (q.v.) (also designed by Hagerty at the same time) and repeated over the next two decades in the Catholic churches of John Bourke. This pared-down military Romanesque is echoed in the interior with its galleries supported on cast-iron Norman columns. Exe-

cutant architect, William Farrell (1841), who appears to have taken all the credit for the design. Stained glass in east window by Percy Bacon (1900).

BALLYSHANNON: **Old Workhouse**
Built in 1842 by George Wilkinson following the usual formula. Now the core of the local hospital.

BUNDORAN: **Church of Ireland**
Designed in 1839 by William Hagerty but in a conventional Gothic Revival rather than his idiomatic Romanesque. Airy interior with scissors trusses alternating with kingposts over nave and lean-to roofs over aisles. Arch opening into chancel. Triple lancet with trefoil above altar.

BUNDORAN: **Great Southern Hotel**
It is paradoxical that one of the most northerly hotels is known by such a name, but presumably this is a matter of marketing. It is still possible to discern the design of Thomas Drew who was commissioned in 1894 by the Irish Highlands Hotel Company. They built his second scheme after they had rejected his first, better architecture but too cottagey.

CARRICK: **Catholic Church**
Remote rural Gothic Revival church built *c.* 1850 and still containing an elaborate pinnacled reredos designed by George Ashlin in 1883. The tower was raised an extra storey this century and crowned with Irish battlements.

CARRIGART: **Mulroy House**
The seat of the Leitrim family near where the 3rd earl was murdered just after he had disinherited his nephew and left all his estates to his cousin, Col. H.T. Clements, who handed over Mulroy to the 4th earl. The house is a two-storied, gabled, unassuming neo-Tudor extended by an architecturally more interesting service wing with small gabled dormers alternating with hipped half dormers. Architect possibly William Murray, who may also have designed for the family Lough Rynn, Co. Leitrim (q.v.). Delightful timber bungalow built nearby as winter retreat. Vast azalea and rhododendron garden created by the widow of the 5th and last Lord Leitim and then recreated after Hurricane Debbie (1958).

CASTLEFINN: **Doneyloop Catholic Church**
Designed in 1867 by John O'Neill. Tower and broached spire added in 1891. Cruciform with aspidal chancel.

CHURCHILL: **St Columb's**
Georgian rectory acquired and restored 1953 by the artist Derek Hill, using tiles by De Morgan and William Morris fabrics, carpets and wallpapers—Golden Lily, Blackthorn and Apple. William Morris dragon fabric is used in the curtains. De Morgan tiles round the fireplaces in the diningroom and the upstairs study. The wrought-iron verandah on the garden front was salvaged from a derelict house in Clontribret, halfway to Dublin. House and collection now open to the public.

DONEGAL: **Catholic Church of St Agatha**
Situated two miles to the north of the town at the foot of the mountains. Large, spare, Gothic Revival church by O'Neill and Byrne, built 1869-71. Cruciform with apsidal east end, entered through porches tucked into the angles of the nave and transepts. Well restored by Bernard Rhatigan in 1967.

DONEGAL: **Lough Eske Castle**
A neo-Jacobean castle built by the Brooke family as a reconstruction of their original Plantation fortress, of which nothing survives apart from intermediate Georgian additions, (ironically the only part that survives intact today after a fire in 1939 that also destroyed a ballroom wing built in 1914). The architect, Fitzgibbon Louch of Derry, is contrastingly forceful and casual—a turreted porch enclosing steps to a *piano nobile.*

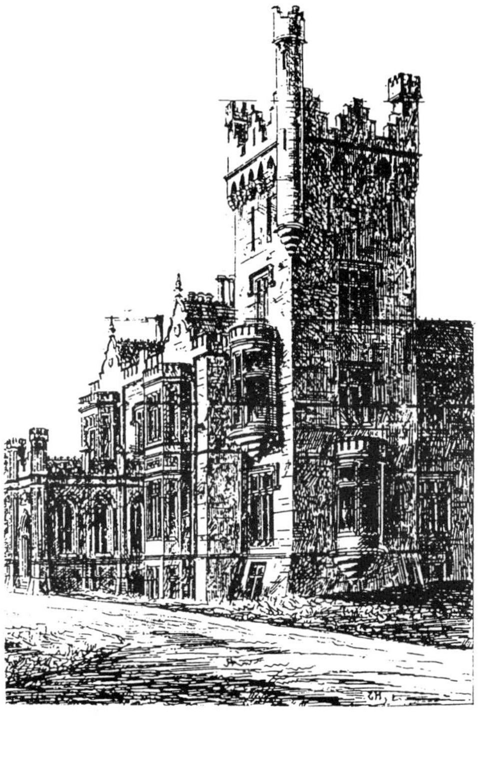

Reception rooms on each side with spacious bay windows rising up to light the bedrooms above, and crowned by curvilinear gables breaking the line of the castellated battlements that are corbelled out on sculpted heads. Adjoining four-storied orieled flag tower to view the lake.

DONEGAL: **Methodist Church**
Replica of Cookstown and Newtownards (q.v.). Double-storied hall with quirky neo-Norman façade topped by a machicolated bellcote.

DONEGAL: **Old Workhouse**
The standard 1842 design of George Wilkinson with a five-bay administration block set in front of a nine-bay block for accommodation. Now pebbledashed.

DUNFANAGHY: **Methodist Church**
Designed by Robert Young for a minister who preferred Hiberno-Romanesque to the Gothic in which Young excelled. The result is a high-pitched, gabled hall with a rose window recessed into a semi-circular arch. Entered through adjoining tower rising to an octagonal belfry and spire. Built 1875-8.

DUNLEWEY: **Catholic Church**
The last church designed by Timothy Hevey a year before his premature death in 1878, and dramatically sited beneath the quartzite peak of Mount Errigal. Its desolate setting emphasizes its volumetric simplicity with an apsed cell of five bays sheltering beside a robust version of a traditional round tower, its topmost floor a multi-arched belvedere, more Italianate than Irish. For once the rock-faced rubble finish so much cherished by the later Victorians is successful, since it matches its mountain setting and is boldly contrasted to bands of pale limestone, punctuated by being polished up to become white marble. Paired colonettes articulate the internal junction between the nave and apse. As so often in the Celtic Revival, the patron was an outsider, in this case from Mayfair, William Ross, who had just acquired the Dunlewey estate.

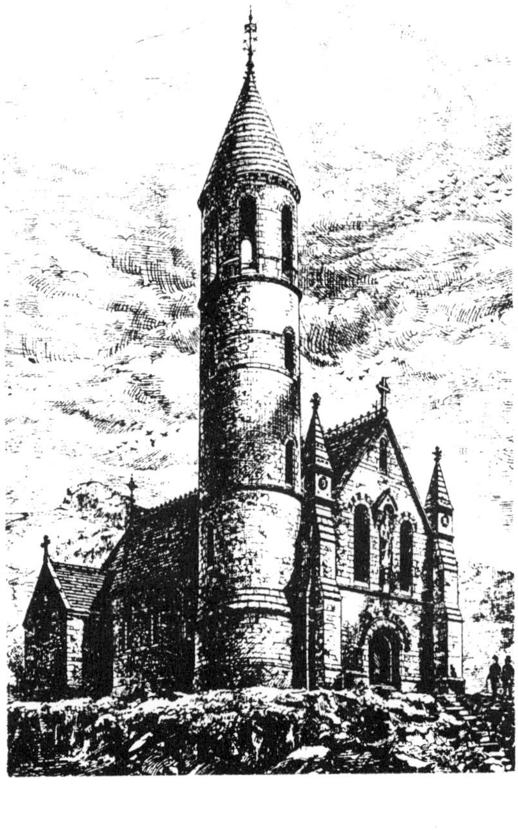

DUNLEWEY: **Church of Ireland**
Delicate Gothic Revival, built in 1844, and now a roofless ruin, but memorable due to the contrast of its white limestone tower with the green of the Poisoned Glen beyond.

GLENTIES: **Catholic Church**
Built in 1852. A vigorous porch was added by Timothy Hevey in 1866.

GLENVEAGH: **Glenveagh Castle**
The square keep and the south wing were built in 1870 by John Townsend Trench for his cousin J.G. Adair who had married an American heiress and acquired 25,000 acres of Donegal mountainside from which he evicted his tenants to replace them with Scottish sheep. The east wing was added in 1900 after Adair's death by another architect, since it is not in Trench's perspective (preserved within). One of the most successful of Irish Victorian castles, even thought it is the only castle Trench designed and his grandchildren were unaware that he was an architect. Superbly sited on a promontory in Lough Veagh, its Irish battlements silhouetted against the mountains, they distract attention from the un-medieval windows and the grimness of the local granite. Unlike the other scenic castles of the West of Ireland, it is designed to be defendable and to ensure a sybaritic existence to inmates holding out against the vagaries of Irish politics or climate. The interiors, apart from the shellwork in the hall put in by a previous owner, are entirely the work of the late Henry McIlhenny, whose reign here commenced in 1938, but who started its restoration after the war. One of the few of his generation to appreciate the High Victorian paintings, his interiors reflected his enthusiasm, even today after his replacement of all this Landseers and Ansdells by engravings before handing over the castle to the Board of Works—a fateful decision,

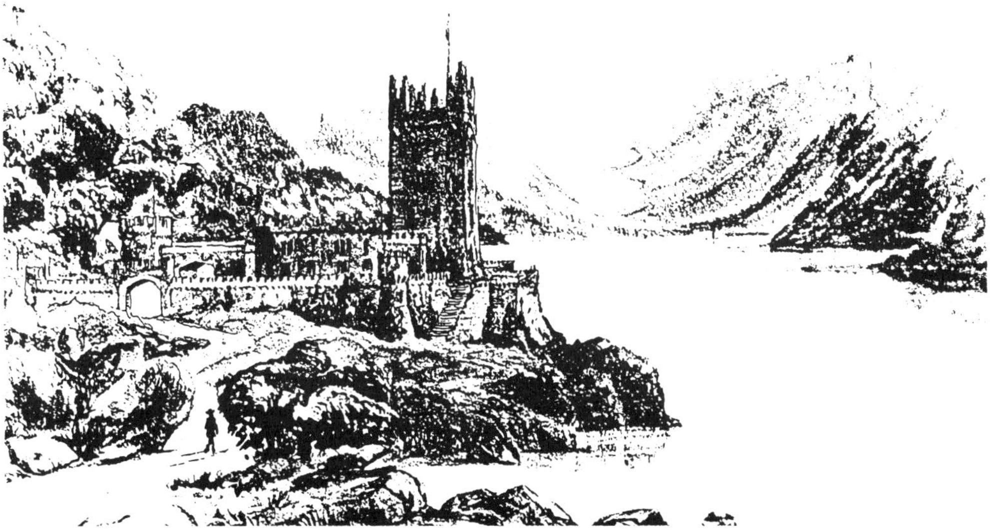

since it has led to building the prototypical interpretative centre. A chair designed by Queen Victoria is suitably enshrined in a circular music room lined with Balmoral tartan.

The gardens were started by Cornelia Adair, who planted the earlier rhododendrons. The basic shape of the walled garden is also hers, though the Gothick conservatory is a post-war collaboration of Michael Scott and Philippe Jullian in a blissfully naive alliance against the rain. The remainder of the garden is a creation of Henry McIlhenny assisted by Russell and Roper. Berenson remarked that, having made that garden, there was no need for Mr McIlhenny ever to do anything else.

GWEEDORE: **Dunbeg Catholic Church**

The church here is T-shaped, lit by lancets and consecrated just before 1860. Sanctuary extended by Timothy Hevey with rose window in the gable and circular sacristy.

KILCAR: **Catholic Church**

Designed by Doolin, Butler and Donnelly, then built 1903-4 in a lucid simplified Romanesque that Butler was to continue himself in a series that culminated in Newport (q.v.) six years later. Nave with arcade of four bays, arched and braced cedar barrel vault cantilevered from the walls, leading to high altar of marble and stone with domed tabernacle.

KILLYBEGS: **Catholic Church**

Cruciform church with arcaded transepts and substantial tower, designed by J.B. Papworth for the Scottish landlord of the village, Alexander Murray, it was built from 1838 onwards. The unusual centralized plan has allowed this church to survive. Papworth's more traditionally-designed Gothic church in Rush, Co. Dublin (q.v.) has been replaced by an autocratic parish priest and left to moulder.

KILLYBEGS: **Church of Ireland**

Polygonal chancel added by Welland and Gillespie (1856-62) to Gothick church of 1829. Stained glass by Heaton, Butler and Bayne (1910).

KILLYGORDON: **Catholic Church**

Late Gothic Revival designed by O'Neill and Byrne and built in 1893-5. Impressive stone exterior with slender steeple bonded to the west façade by semi-circular staircase turret. Sculptural interior with arcades of polished pink granite columns rising to heavily undercut capitals between the nave and aisles. Open roofs panelled with three different timbers. Chancel arch upheld by corbels of singing angels. High altar with multi-pinnacled reredos. Now part of an abstract liturgical set-up just a little too large for the existing dimensions. Stained glass by Mayer.

KILMACRENAN: **Church of Ireland**

Built in 1840-6; though the working drawings survive unsigned, this church has always been attributed to Joseph Welland. Tower above the porch linked to octagonal bell turret. Recently interior decorated by Professor Anne Crookshank.

LETTERKENNY: **Bank of Ireland**

Designed in 1874 by Timothy Hevey as the Hibernian Bank, who at that time were exploiting the potential of architecture to gain new business and more discreetly introducing a quasi-religious note to appeal to new Catholic wealth. On these terms Hevey's bank is entirely successful. Six bays, symmetrical façade with the banking hall flanked by corbelled porches, upheld by columns of polished granite. The columns reoccur between the coupled windows

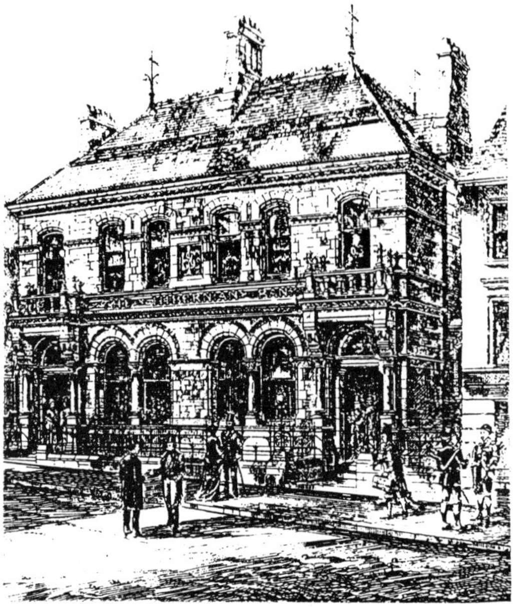

of the banking hall. The duality of the ground floor is resolved above by a central monogram carved between the first floor windows. This has been left intact as the only record of the founding institution, now that the lettering on the frieze below has been replaced.

LETTERKENNY: **Catholic Cathedral**
The last of the major Gothic Revival cathedrals to be built in Ireland, begun in 1891 to the design of William Hague. He died in 1899 two years before its completion by his junior partner, T.F. McNamara, and is depicted as St William in a stained glass memorial window close to the crossing. His patron was Bishop, later Cardinal O'Donnell. The cathedral is architecturally orthodox as all Hague's later churches, but architecture is merely one of the ingredients: stained glass, sculpture, frescoes and mosaics are orchestrated into triumphant unison. But there are several departures from the norm: the orientation is reversed, and the single steeple is attached to the southern transept rather than the façade to effectively counterbalance the steeply rising site. This allows the twin-pinnacled flying buttresses that articulate the façade to rise into four belfries in their own right. When aligned with the spire springing from four further spirelets, at one point to the worshippers wending upwards from the town below, they gave an uplifting vision of the city of God. They also deflect attention from the absence of flying buttresses elsewhere.

The external sculpture is distributed throughout the façade by Purdy and Millard of Belfast. They were the firm responsible for making the most unusual feature of the interior—the sculpted arch inserted at the crossing unravelling legends of St Eunan and Columcille intertwined with Manuelline ropework (attributed by Larmour to Gilliland). Nave of five bays, transept of two, choir with ambulatory and encircling chapels. Timber and plaster lierne vaulting throughout, with pendant star vaulting at the crossing. The decoration started too early for the Celtic Revival to dominate: one has to search for it in the sculpture of the transepts (by Purdy) and in the mosaic tiling of the choir (by Willicroft Ltd of Hanley). More Celtic still are gilded and painted vaults of the choir, the ambulatory and apsidal chapels, including the top-lit lady chapel (by Amici of Rome). The high altar, the throne, the pulpit and the communion rail, all happily retained during the remodelling of 1985, despite the resolute use of native Irish materials, reveal the English origins of their sculptors—the Pearse brothers. Only in the stained glass is there Celtic work by Irish artists, and even then that was after Mayer had filled all the major windows. However, in the transepts Michael Healy comes into his own—the five-light window depicting the Convention of Druceatt, the St Helena window, and the SS Dallan and Conan Maol window, dating from 1910-11. Further windows by Child (St Finan and St Moibhi), Elvery (St Columbanus and St Gall), O'Brien (St Columba), Rhind (St Charles Borromeo), dating from 1911-12. The understated clerestory abstract stained glass windows (1928) were the ultimate embellishment, designed by Harry Clarke and one of his last commissions.

LETTERKENNY: **County Museum**
Standard Tudor design of George Wilkinson dating from 1843; a workhouse converted in 1987.

LETTERKENNY: **Loreto Convent**
Modest Gothic Revival complex with adjoining chapel and belfry built out of local rubble stone. The earlier part dating from 1860 is by Hadfield and Goldie.

LETTERKENNY: **Mental Hospital**
Designed by George Wilkinson in 1862 towards the end of his career when he was turning away from Tudor and reverting to Georgian. Additions in 1872 and 1886 by John Boyd, and in 1893 by William McElwee.

LETTERKENNY: **Presbyterian Church**
Built in 1907 starting with Perpendicular Gothic and rising to Art Nouveau, with a curvilinear parapet as the termination of the stunted tower and the traceried windows curtailed by segmental arches. The galleried church is at an

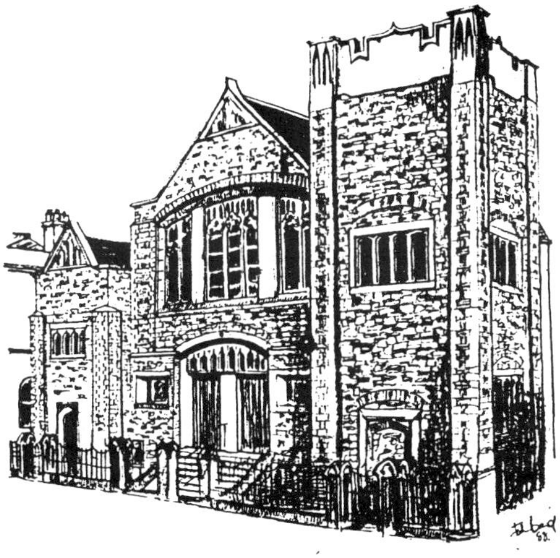

upper level approached by a flight of steps recessed between the tower and a porch that serves the crypt. Architects, Blackwood and Jury.

LETTERKENNY: **St Eunan's College**
Since no private patron commissioned a Celtic Revival castle, this seminary has no secular counterpart—a fortified monastery set high above the cathedral which T.F. McNamara had just completed when he was given this commission in 1904. Guarded by four circular corner towers, alternatively conical and battlemented; a further corbelled tower, bonded together at ground floor level by Hiberno-Romanesque arcading that is developed into a cloister around the central courtyard. Columned vestibule and staircase hall—now that Dublin's Capitol music hall has been destroyed, McNamara's most impressive surviving interior. The original contractors were Messrs Laverty of Belfast, the cost, £22,000. Additional

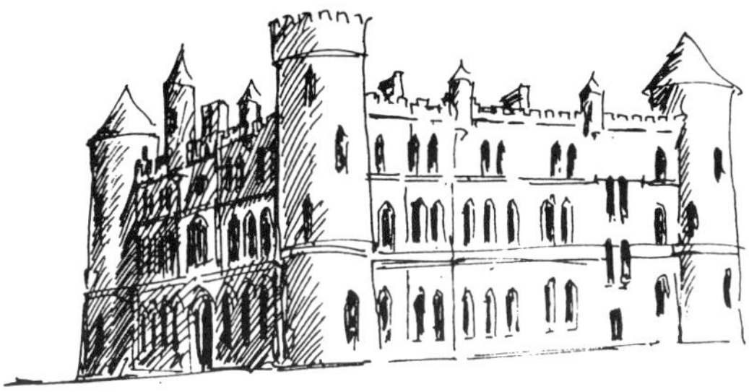

wing of 1930 by Ralph Byrne. New buildings unfortunate.

LOUGH DERG: **Basilica**
The earliest surviving church is the modest Gothic Revival cell of four bays, chancel and tower (St Mary's), built in 1870. This is now overshadowed by William Scott's ultimate monument, started the year of his death (1921) and completed much later by T.J. Cullen with the result that the concept is admirable but its realization lacks the subtle unexpected tensions that reveal the more wayward aspects of Scott's personality. Yet this is no place for individual criticism, rather its abnegation. Scott had earlier expressed the spirit of this island in his New Hostel of 1912, a brutal, castellated, concrete penitentiary containing 220 cubicles. The vast centralized church is the logical outcome for a religion that levels, however briefly, social distinction. Contemporary communism had the same aims but on a full-time basis—hence its abandonment by an exhausted humanity. To return to Scott's church: it is a massive pyramidal octagon with short cruciform arms, the entry arm flanked by low circular towers. A continuous external ambulatory gives shelter from the rain. Inside, the effect of a more

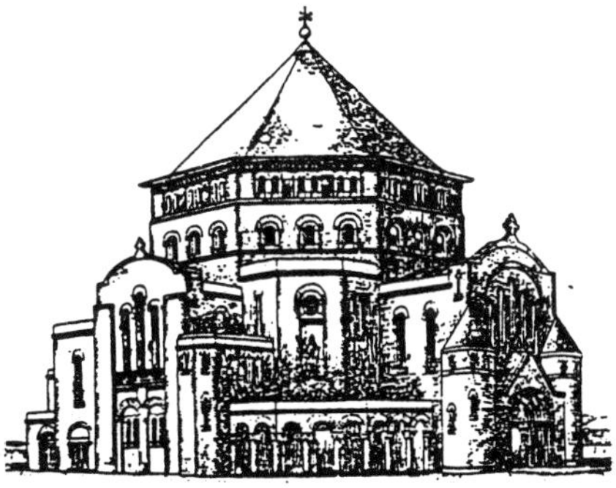

Ottoman than Byzantine. Its most remarkable feature is the set of stained-glass stations of the cross by Harry Clarke, carefully devised so that he could make the small-scale medallions himself, but which like Scott, he never lived to see in place.

MILFORD: **Old Workhouse**
Tudor Revival complex set in open countryside, designed *c.*1845 by George Wilkinson; now derelict with an uncertain future.

MOVILLE: **Church of Ireland**
Designed in 1858 for a rector of the Montgomery family commemorated within. Fit- tings including a chubby pulpit added in 1882. Octagonal belfry clasped by corner buttresses rising to trefoils that alternate with lancets.

MOVILLE: **Dring Catholic Church**
A simple Gothic Revival cell set on a terraced hillside looking southwards across Lough Foyle. West façade dominated by wedge-roofed bellcote rising from the apex of the gable. A steeply rising roof intersects pinnacled buttresses, a

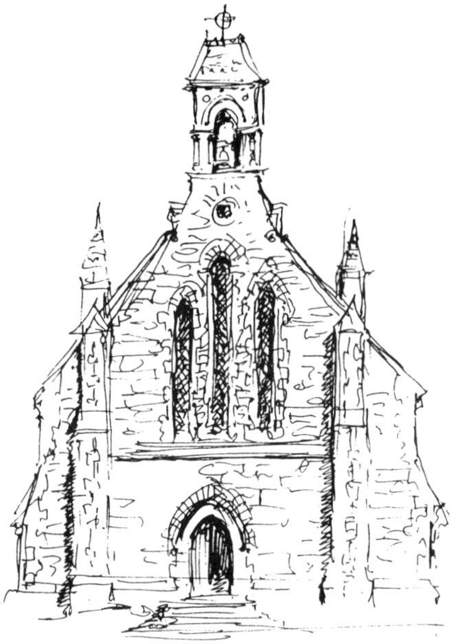

device often deployed by Timothy Hevey, but the architect was John O'Neill. Interior spanned by alternating trusses, braced and scissors. These survive drastic modernization. A plaque commemorates the date: 1871.

NEWTOWNCUNNINGHAM: **Catholic Church**
A village church now much altered but, even when built, so unassuming that it would have been difficult to identify the architect as Edwin Godwin. Built in 1861 as a long low church with two southern porches. The gallery was inserted by Daniel Conroy in 1902. Godwin's apse was removed in 1971.

PORTSALON: **Portsalon Hotel**
Late Victorian country house built to overlook Ballymastocker Strand with battlemented tower and crowstepped gables. Now that the all-timber Rosapenna Hotel has been destroyed by fire, this is the only evidence left to the entrepreneurial 4th earl of Leitrim, who converted the earlier house into a hotel.

RAMELTON: **First Presbyterian Church**
A late Gothic Revival church in a conventional Perpendicular idiom that dominates the village, with a heavy tower and spire. Built of rubble stone trimmed with red sandstone by Young and McKenzie in 1906.

RAMELTON: **Former Northern Bank**
Italianate design of G.W. Ferguson, less interesting than his Art Nouveau but still attractive. Built in 1903.

RAMELTON: **Warehousing**
The finest grouping of warehousing is at the eastern end of the curving river quay facing upriver, their seried rows of windows contrasting with the continuous verticality of their central access. One of them is dated 1864.

RAPHOE: **Catholic Church**
Perhaps no other Irish church so anticipates our own century with its intimate scale, informal composition and geometrical concision. Designed (1874) by Timothy Hevey, who restated the same formula of apsidal cell and Irish round tower in his last church, Dunlewey (q.v.), 1877, but with more High Victorian elaboration. The tower encloses a staircase to the western organ gallery. Timber tunnel vault with braced trusses, those articulating the apse resting on corbelled colonnettes. The original sacristy is now a chapel, and the new sacristy is a geometrical pavilion in front of the west façade, resembling a baptistery that it is not allowed to exist by current liturgical regulations.

RAPHOE: **Church of Ireland Cathedral**
Conjectural rebuilding of a medieval choir by Sir Thomas Drew in 1892 after he had removed the Georgian transepts. He also reroofed the slightly lower nave; its kingpost trusses fix the height of his chancel arch and contrast with the continuous braced timber vault of the choir. Here we can see the medieval sedilia and piscina that Drew excavated and then surmounted with his own deeply-splayed fenestration, carefully modelled on Irish prototypes. Stained-glass Evangelist windows by O'Brien and Rhind (1906). St Eunan designed by S. Purser, executed by Rhind.

RATHMULLEN: **Church of Ireland**
Board of First Fruits Gothic (1814), only once altered when the interior was refitted in 1887 by Hume Babington and R.E. Buchanan, who tactfully retained its original character.

RATHMULLEN: **Coastguard Station**
Designed in the simplified Baronial as developed by Board of Works during the 1870s.

ROSSBEIGH PENINSULAR: **Tirnarossa**
Holiday home built by Sir Edwin Lutyens to overlook two of Donegal's contrasting inlets, deceptively sheltered Mulroy to the east, and Sheephaven exposed to the full force of the Atlantic. Lutyens retained and remodelled an existing cottage while he built a new cottage alongside with a livingroom opening into a verandah supported by stone piers and sheltering an open staircase to the upper floor—romance evoked by the simplest means.

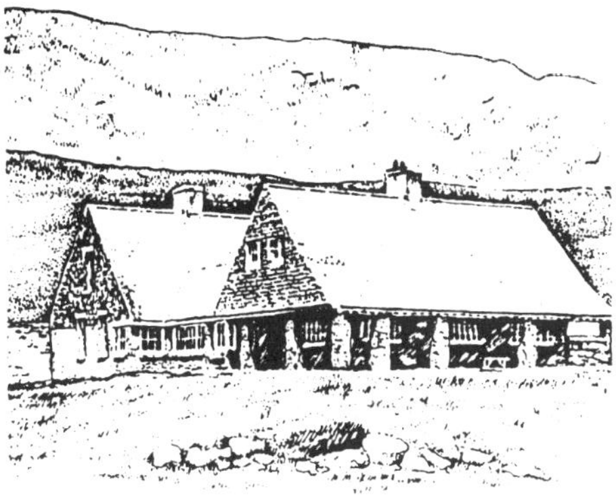

Donated by the Hon. Mrs Phillimore to An Oige, as recorded in a faded photograph.

ST JOHNSTOWN: **Catholic Church**
Although this, one of the earliest commissions of Edwin Godwin, was successfully built (1856-61) despite a tight budget and supervision, he was never given an opportunity to build major churches. As such, he joins the small rank of Victorian Arts and Crafts architects who were too adventurous or dangerous to be patronized by organized religion. A century later, his church fell yet another a victim to the liturgical hari-kari occasioned after the Second Vatican Council when the interiors of all Catholic churches were placed under interdict, regardless of their architectural quality.

The first view of this church, overwhelmed by a vast asphalt carpark, and its west front extended into a new utility block, is depressing; but at least Godwin's massing at the eastern end on its rocky outcrop has remained undisturbed, with the chancel boldly projecting forward, the cill of the eastern window aligned to the roof of the adjoining vestry, and a stone-roofed lean-to against the only visible transept. The composition builds up, not to an expensive central tower, but to an economical if no less eloquent double bellcote on the eastern gable of the nave. The tracery of the windows is equally individualistic, if also gawkily pre-Raphaelite, each with triple arches, the centre one carried up to the window's apex, apart from the eastern window dominated by three hexafoils (the shamrock and the Trinity). The interior relies on contrasting the transept arches (low, segmental, unadorned) with the chancel arch, soaring up and corbelled out on colonettes, framing what was once the altar but is now an empty choir, redeemed only by Godwin's crude heraldic glass.

TORY ISLAND: **Catholic Church**
Small Gothic Revival church built in 1857-61 to the design of Edwin Godwin, his most remote commission but one which must have given him much satisfaction working in the traditions of early Irish Christianity. Stained glass Crucifixion window (1910) by Beatrice Elvery.

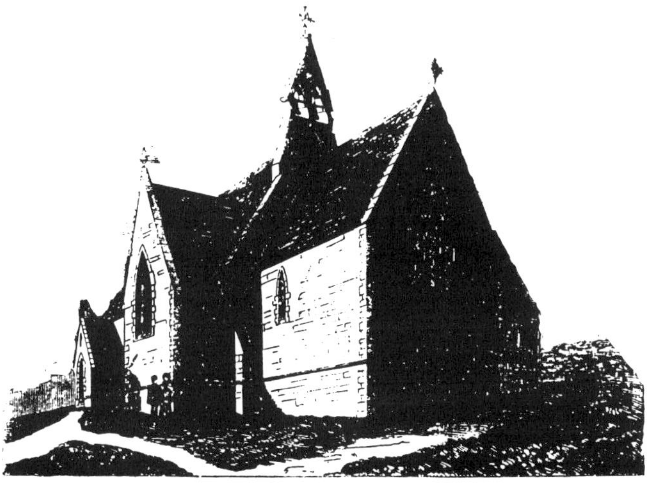

ST JOHNSTOWN CATHOLIC CHURCH

DOWN

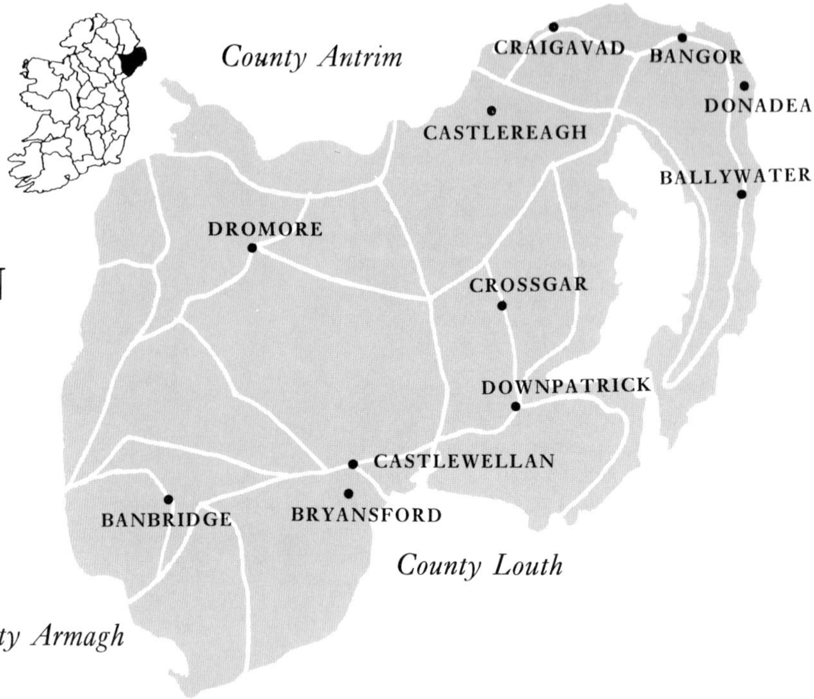

BALLYWATER: **Ballywater Park**

The most extensive and sumptuous country-house of Charles Lanyon, designed for a personal friend, Andrew Mulholland, mill owner and lord mayor of Belfast; one senses that need for civic splendour which found its realization half a century later with the building of the City Hall. But Ballywater is a palazzo built on a remote coastal site for private relaxation and hospitality so lavish that Lanyon's house, despite its size, was successively extended (the last time by Andrew Mulholland's grandson, the 2nd Lord Dunleath) to accommodate a visiting cricket team. The parkland is contemporary with the house, sealing it off from the outside world. However, from the moment of entry one can experience Lanyon's ability to combine grandeur with convenience—the generous width of the *porte-cochère* leading into the three-storied central block (originally built in 1810) flanked by temple-like single-storied Corinthian pavilions. The austere entrance hall panelled with mahogany, housing a collection of organs, acts as a foil to the splendour of the double-height inner hall, Doric at ground level, Corinthian above. The space is divided by a double-tiered colonnade into which we enter, with an imperial staircase to one side that ascends beneath a glazed dome. The staircase well is surveyed by niches for sculpture and by arcades into the bedroom corridors. On the other side this central colonnade opens into a double-height picture gallery with cantilevered balconies and coves rising to a glazed ceiling. This communicates with the principal ground-floor rooms. The result lacks the sublimity of its equivalent in Dundarave (q.v.) but compensates by its complexity, all the more remarkable since Lanyon achieved his spatial effects within the walls of the Regency house. The library, in one of the pavilions that flank the façade, with its bookcases added by the 1st Lord Dunleath, leads through double doors into the drawingroom. At the far end, screened by Corinthian columns, a bow window curves out into the garden terrace. The diningroom is set alongside also overlooking the garden, while a breakfastroom takes up a bow window matching the drawingroom. Beyond this Lanyon added (1863) lavatories and a billiard room and then set at right angles to the garden front an enchanting conservatory, with Corinthian colonnades wrapped round a central glazed dome, a reduced classicized version of his Botanic Gardens conservatory (q.v.) in Belfast. Three years after its erection, Andrew Mulholland died. Ballywater has been vigorously maintained ever since by his descendants with an increasing sense of hopelessness since the First World War until the late Lord Dunleath who, when he inherited the house in 1956, invited Sir John Betjeman to tea. This led to an enthusiastic restoration including the original heating system. A serious fire in 1975 was treated as only another opportunity to restore the interior to its initial resplendence.

BANBRIDGE: Seapatrick Church of Ireland

Complex Gothic Revival structure since of the early church (1834-7) only the belfry and part of the transept survive. The remainder was rebuilt and extended first by William Barre (1864) and by Thomas Drew (1882) with unexpectedly homogenous results. Barre's work in the spacious north transept is distinguishable only by the more forceful quality of the foliated capitals. Pulpit by Sharp (1883). Further furnishings by Hems. Alabaster reredos carved by Earp from portions of Street's original reredos of Christchurch Cathedral, Dublin. Memorial to Capt. Crozier of his doomed ship embedded in ice, carved by Joseph Kirk (1856). Glass in east window by Heaton, Butler and Bayne.

BANBRIDGE: Crozier Memorial

The Crozier family of Banbridge commissioned Joseph Kirk to carve a plaque commemorating Capt. Francis Crozier in the Church of Ireland ten years after his disappearance in search of the North West Passage. When it was discovered that he had been the first explorer to reach the Pacific, the town commissioned from Kirk a larger than life-size statue and held in 1861 a competition to find an architect to design the pedestal. William Barre won the competition with his distinctive brand of allusive Gothic. Four snarling polar bears gingerly back up diametrical buttresses to protect an arched tempietto with its arches curving outwards to uphold a truncated spire. This is wreathed with ropes, anchors and military crosses. Above, the captain reposes on his sword; beneath him, niches enshrine inscriptions and triple-masted boats embedded in the ice. The depiction of nature's revenge is intensified by the subsequent decay of the stonework.

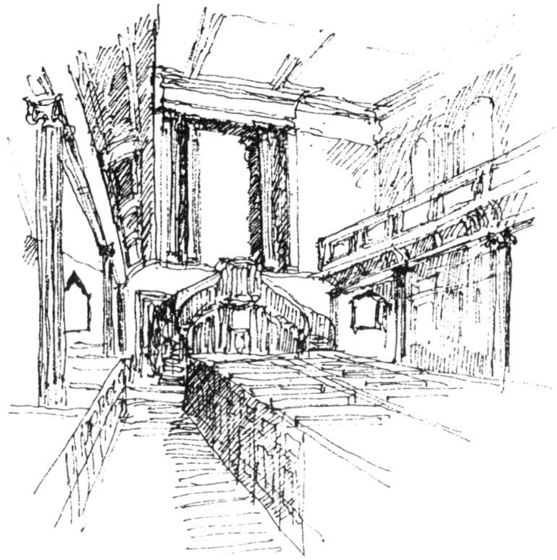

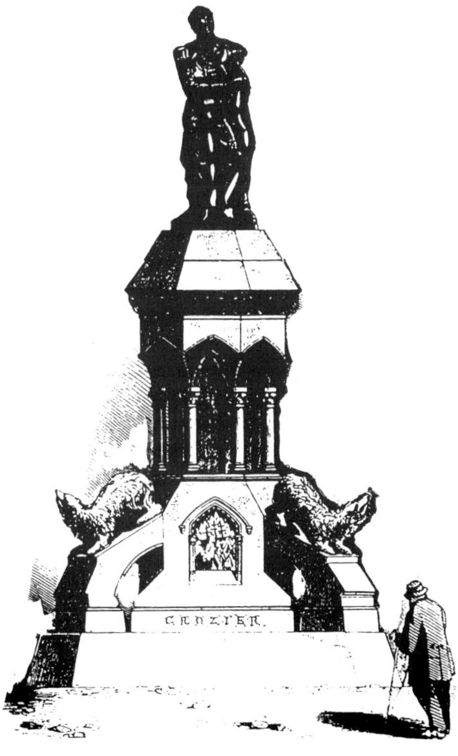

BANBRIDGE: Unitarian Church

Built for the Presbyterians in 1846 and barely altered since then. Architect unknown. Five-bay front preceded by a stucco tetrastyle Ionic portico. Vestibule between twin curving staircases. Superb interior with a delicate coved U-shaped gallery upheld by delicate cast-iron Ionic columns contrasting in scale with the monumental Ionic-columned recess articulating the east end, behind a pulpit which is reached by twin staircases, eloquently carved to embrace the congregation seated in pews that retain their original upholstery.

BANGOR: The Castle

A characteristic gesture of a younger brother in the Romantic era to fabricate an ancestral home that appears to predate by several hundred years the family seat. This was the reason for Robert Ward, a grandson of the 1st Viscountess Bangor, who was responsible for the avant-garde Gothick of Castle Ward, commissioning a neo-Elizabethan manor house from William Burn in 1847, calling it a castle. There is one corner castellated tower, but the remainder is gabled with wide mullioned windows and bays opening sedately on to a spacious garden terrace. The slightly more militant stable block is attributed to Anthony Salvin, who worked here, possibly carrying out Burn's designs. Interior with its heraldic glass maintained by the municipality but not easily accessible. Museum in the stables; gardens a public park.

BANGOR: **Church of Ireland**
Prominently positioned on its island site, this is W.H. Lynn at his most perfunctory, giving everything that his clients had asked for, but no more than that. Part of his problem was the size of the brief, too large to concentrate his mind on the exquisite, too small to reach towards the sublime. In this Lynn resembles his contemporary, George Ashlin. Sombre interior made even more so by the stained glass (Heaton, Butler and Bayne). Exterior of dark reddish stone, lighter dressings, lancet windows, and off-centre steeple competing with a much earlier and wittier Presbyterian neighbour.

BANGOR: **Carnalea**
A villa built in the Dutch style that never quite manages to ramble into Art Nouveau. Designed *c.* 1900 by Vincent Craig for the Bradford family.

BANGOR: **Clandeboye**
Georgian house inherited by the 5th Lord Dufferin, afterwards 1st marquis of Dufferin and Ava, governor-general of Canada and then viceroy of India, who attempted several times to pull it down and replace it with something else. His favoured scheme was an immense fantasy (described by Harold Nicolson, his grandson, as part François premier, part Prince Consort) by W.H. Lynn, who was rewarded instead with a commission in Ottawa and a few alterations to the existing house. These included switching the front entrance to a former service yard at a lower level and contriving new outer and inner halls, while the former hall became the enlargement of the library. More windows were opened up, disrupting the external Palladian symmetry, and the interior was crammed with trophies from the Empire awaiting a more ceremonial distribution in his unbuilt palace. The architectural ambitions of the 1st marquis were more successfully realized in his demesne —firstly the private railway station designed for him by Benjamin Ferrey (approached by a monumental turret gateway set beneath his coat of arms); then the Scottish Baronial tower by William Burn (built in 1848-62) to contain poems written on bronze tablets to commemorate his devotion to his mother Helen,

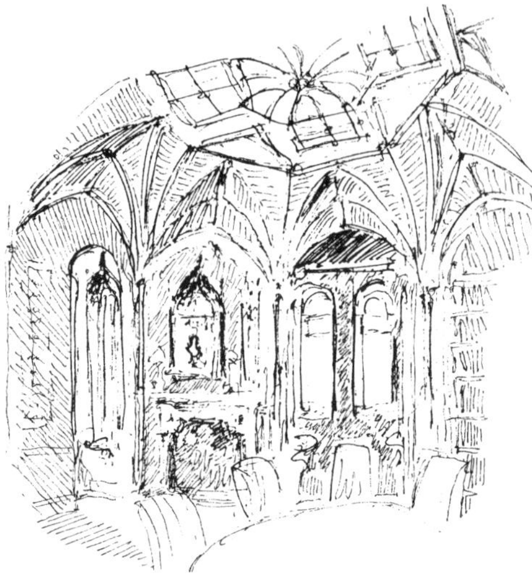

HELEN'S TOWER: OCTAGONAL LIBRARY

granddaughter of Richard Brinsley Sheridan. One poem is by the Laureate, Tennyson.

BANGOR: **Clandeboye Schoolhouse**
When J. Rawson Carroll came within the ambit of the Arts and Crafts he could be a very good architect; here, doubtlessly spurred on by the rivalry with Lynn, he built a picturesque complex lit by lofty gable windows but tied securely down to earth by low lean-to porches.

BANGOR: **Crawfordstown**
Georgian seat of the Sharman-Crawfords, rebuilt for them in 1896 by the usually witty Vincent Craig in a grim Baronial style that fails to live up to the elegant lodge by John Nash or do justice to its spectacular setting on the shore of Belfast Lough. Till recently an old people's home but now empty and awaiting sale.

BANGOR: **Royal Ulster Yacht Club**
The most affluent of the Irish yacht clubs, a half-timbered red-brick neo-Tudor manor house but vigorously detailed with corbelled balconies and gables to give what could have so easily been pompous a festive air. Built in 1895-7. Makes an interesting comparison to Clifford Smith's Shannon Yacht Club in Limerick. Architect, Vincent Craig.

BRYANSFORD: **Estate Cottages**
A couple of estate cottages set on a cul-de-sac that joins the main road in front of the post office. An unexpected example, showing the influence of W.E. Nesfield's cottage architecture. Following his invention, lead pies are cast into the targetted spandrels of the lean-to open porches and into the gable apexes at either end. Dormered windows set into a shingled roof.

CASTLEREAGH: **Presbyterian Church**
Inventive Greek Revival church designed by John Miller and built in 1834-5. Ionic portico *in antis* adapted from the internal colonnade of the temple of Bassae, surmounted by an elongated version of the monument to Lysicrates. Galleried interior.

CASTLEWELLAN: **Castlewellan Castle**
Austere granite castle built in 1852-8 for the 4th Earl Annesley. His architect was William Burn, who produced a Scottish Baronial design but shorn of any identifying Scottish features, doubtlessly in deference to its Irish setting, so that the result is merely nondescript with its serried ranks of plate-glass windows rising to a dormered roof between corner towers. One of these is circular in a vain attempt to introduce the picturesque. An Italianate garden is the centrepiece of a lavish arboretum planted by successive generations of the family. Inherited by the artist Mabel Annesley, the castle was abandoned by her son because of dry rot. He later sold the demesne to the Government as a forest park. The castle is now a Christian conference centre never open to the public.

CASTLEWELLAN: **Catholic Church**
Characteristic late Gothic Revival church, probably by H. O'Neill; begun in 1884 and completed *c.*1900. Showy west façade flanked by incisive tower and spire. Caen carving set into typanum. Cruciform interior dimly lit through Mayer's glass.

CASTLEWELLAN: **Church of Ireland**
Cruciform Gothic Revival church designed in 1847 by Charles Lanyon with separately roofed organ chamber and vestry each side of the chancel. Entered through a porch beneath a tower and spire treated with polychromatic stonework. Crossing emphatically articulated with multiple piers. Austere reredos built across the base of the eastern window. Equally austere are the memorials to the earls of Annesley.

CRAIGAVAD: **Craigavad House**
Italianate house designed for John Mulholland, later 1st Lord Dunleath, whose father had already commissioned Charles Lanyon to design Ballywalter (q.v.). In Craigavad the architect was Thomas Turner, brother of Richard, who worked for a few years in Lanyon's office. Double-height central hall with galleries round a circular well beneath a glazed dome.

CRAIGAVAD: **Culloden House Hotel**
A determinedly Scottish Baronial country house built in 1876-9 by Young and McKenzie for W.A. Robinson MP to overlook Belfast Lough

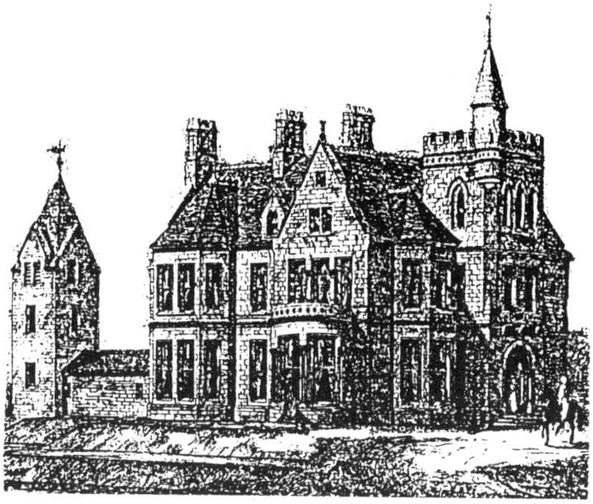

and called after the family of his wife. Entry tower at one end. Adjoining garden front with asymmetrically treated bay windows, lively decorative stone carving; the stone itself came from Scotland. The finest interior is the staircase hall, especially suitable when the house was a residence for the Church of Ireland bishops (1898-1919), lit through an impressive Gothic window. Stained glass by Heaton, Butler and Bayne. Now a luxury hotel. The garden front currently being filled in between the bays—a pity, since all the other extensions are added to the rear.

CROSSGAR: **Lissara Presbyterian Church**
William Barre, who designed this modest church with limited resources *c.*1860, went further than any other architect in evolving a separate identity for Ulster Presbyterians: a master of confrontation, he pitted a rigorously conventional hall of worship against a wilfully individualistic narthex, dramatizing the conflict between the private search for biblical truth and the conformity to communal worship. The belfry appears hunched challengingly close to the apex of the western gable of the façade, its fenestration expressing its staircase, and higher up its small rose window is remorselessly linked by a mutual hood moulding to a strong plate, tranceried rose window set above the double doorway. Asymmetrical buttressing imparts a sense of movement to the corners. All these tensions are resolved by an orthodox interior.

CROSSGAR: **Rademon, Sharman-Crawford Obelisk**
An obelisk (set on a hill in the demesne) erected in *c.*1864 by the tenants of the radical politician, William Sharman-Crawford MP. Carved by Arthur Hammond of Sheephouse (1863). Sculptural medallion by S.F. Lynn set into the shaft.

DONADEA: **Church of Ireland**
Remodelled and extended by Timothy Hevey, 1870.

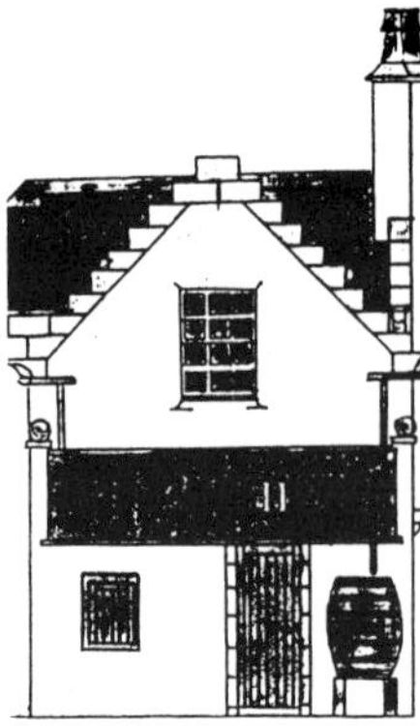

DONADEA: Dunsky
Edwardian Baronial country house. The main house dates from 1750 and was originally remodelled in 1837; the wings were added in 1898. By James Kennedy Hunter of Ayr.

DOWNPATRICK: Catholic Church
Gothic Revival with prominent spire, double transepts and polygonal apse. Lavishly decorated within, designed by O'Neill and Byrne in 1870. Sumptuous altar, illuminated by Mayer's stained glass. Organ by Telford. Currently being extended by a vast apsidal transept in 20th-century Gothic Revival.

DOWNPATRICK: Assembly Rooms
Prominently sited in Ruskinian Gothic with a corner tower set at the junction of two wings (one containing the first-floor hall, the other offices for the patron, John Mulholland) expressed by different fenestration to conform with the 'Lamp of Truth' above a continuous arcade. Designed by William Batt in 1882.

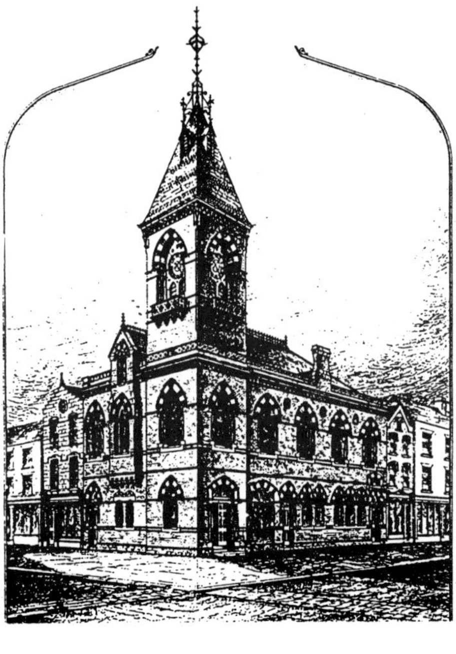

DOWNPATRICK: District Mental Hospital
Far-flung red-brick idiosyncratic complex designed in 1883 by Henry Smith. Central dining-hall block between symmetrical wings demanding an exact equilibrium between the sexes even in lunacy, extending to isolation wards in the corner pavilions. Contrasting vertical features—a central sprocketted clock tower and two polychromatic twin factory flues set at each side contrasting with the Georgian country-house imagery of the long façades.

DROMORE: Church of Ireland Cathedral
Extended by Thomas Drew, who added (in 1869) the apsidal chancel and the northern aisle as large as the original church. The windows are fitted with adequate neo-medieval stained glass by Heaton, Butler and Bayne. Memorial to Bishop Percy by Sir Richard Westmacott.

DRUMBEG: Church of Ireland
A rebuilding by Drew of an earlier church of which only the west wall and the tower survive. Cruciform with banded masonry dating from 1868; approached through a lychgate that Drew added ten years later. Celtic cross to Walter Henry Wilson by O'Dwyer of Kilkenny (1904).

DRUMBO: Church of Ireland
Harsh but strait-laced example of Welland and Gillespie dating from 1863-4, inhibited by the incorporation of an earlier tower and by the surburban requirements of the congregation: their most exciting work is rural. However, the bold plate rose windows could only be their work. Classical mausoleum to the Batt family *c.*1845 in the churchyard.

DUNDELA: Church of Ireland
Apart from the chapel of St Columba's in Dublin (q.v), the only Irish commission of William Butterfield. Nave and tower built in 1876-8, chancel in 1889-91. The exterior suffers from his lack of empathy for suburbia, all attention concentrated on the massive wedge-roofed tower raised above the continuous roof of nave and chancel, its vertical thrust counter-balanced by the horizontal banding of different coloured sandstones. The interior is more characteristic of the master; baptistery beneath the tower is developed as a rival attraction to the chancel; it is seen from the nave through an arch inscribed with tracery resting on an excessively slender colonette, so that the opening relates to the two windows on the western wall beyond. This is contrasted with the heavy chancel arch, chopping off from the view of those entering the tracery of the eastern window. This chancel arch is a mere screen rising between two perforated hexafoils only to the springing of the

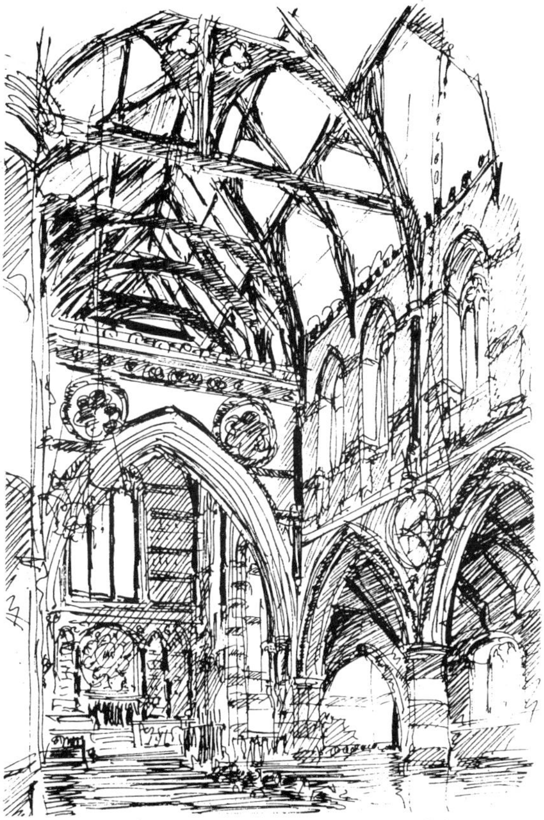

vault. Above, a void opens to a vista of the open roof of the nave, continued above the chancel with its alternating kingpost trusses. So typical of Butterfield's love of ambiguity is his treatment of the colonettes that take the kingposts. Instead of being the strongest structural element, they are the most delicate, in blue-grey stone in contrast to the red sandstone that is deployed throughout as a patterned framework to contrast with the white plaster infill. These colonettes rest on corbels that clasp perforated roundels within the spandrels of the nave arcade in conflict with the laws of gravity. It is this determination to create the miraculous in materialistic terms that distinguishes Butterfield from his church-building contemporaries. Fortunately for his clients he was too absorbed by questioning the dogmas of architecture to interrupt the platitudes of their sermons. But in this case his client was evidently happier to retreat to the security of a rectory designed by somebody else, S.P. Close (built in 1887 between the completion of the nave and the start of the chancel). Stained glass by Michael Healy (1932), Ward and Partners, and Shrigley and Hunt; windows terminating chancel and south transept by Powell. The church has been recently restored by J. Dykes Bower.

DUNDELA: **Ormiston House**
An assertive Scottish tower house built in 1865-7 by a Scottish architect, David Bryce, for a Scottish tycoon, James Coombe, who had come from Edinburgh. Tension generated by massive walls punctuated with commonsensical rectilinear fenestration and didactic inscriptions on one hand, and on the other romantic touches of ornamentation—the porch, oriels, gargoyles, crests.

DUNDONALD: **Cleland Mausoleum**
One of the most spectacular neo-Classical memorials in Ulster, erected in 1842 to the design of an unknown architect in memory of Samuel Cleland, one-time owner of Stormont Castle (q.v.). Two separate temples grafted together, a circular Ionic tempietto above a coursed ashlar cube topped with corner urns, with pedimented friezes on each façade upheld by three-quarter Doric columns.

DUNDRUM: **Murlough House**
Austere Italianate house designed by William Haywood of London for the 4th Marquis of Downshire. Monotonous façade of seven bays prolonged by a service wing of five bays. The only architectural evidence of its date (1860) is the cambered heads of the windows on the upper floor and their closeness to the eaves. Leased currently to the Church of Ireland as a conference centre.

EGLANTINE: **Church of Ireland**
Although Thomas Drew designed many churches he was at his happiest when designing them for devout private patrons where he could revert to the hand-made qualities of rural Gothic. Picturesque composition made out of separately articulated elements like a collection of cottages. Open timber porch leading to single-cell nave and apsidal chancel.

GILFORD: **Elmfield**
Country house built in the 1860s by William Spence, the Glasgow architect who had been commissioned to design the neighbouring Gilford Castle. Here the client was a younger brother, Dickson. The result was smaller but more castle-like. Interior partially destroyed, but now restored after many years of abandon. Asymmetrical sequence of reception rooms set out to overlook the garden and the lake beyond.

GILFORD: **Gilford Castle**
William Spence (1806-83) had a long career as a Glasgow neo-Classicist, so he was a surprising choice of the wool magnate Benjamin Dickson for his baronial country seat on the edge of a wooded gorge. Spence came up with a half-castle, half-manor house inspired by Burn and Bryce—not unexpected since he had started off in Bryce's office. A large-boned austere design

with a multiplicity of bay windows. The front suffers from the *porte-cochère* having been reduced in execution to a porch. His inexperience as a country-house architect is revealed by the way that its most castle-like feature, the chauffeur's tower, is hidden by the main bulk of the house until one rounds the corner on the way into the service yard. Despite a change of ownership at the turn of the century, the interiors are remarkably intact—square hall with walls marbleized in Connemara marble adjoining a central passage lit through the stained glass of the half-landing window. Columned drawingroom retaining original decoration stencilled, it is said, by Italians. Domed billiard room overlooking the private garden. The loft in the stable has been recently converted into a theatre and concert hall: this would have pleased Spence, as the many theatres that he designed in Glasgow have all been destroyed.

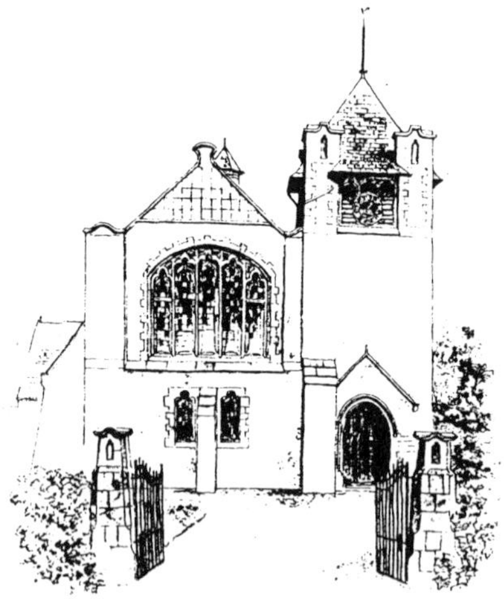

HILLHALL: **Presbyterian Church**
The church was designed in 1900 by Blackwood and Jury at their most experimental, juxtaposing Gothic Revival and Art Nouveau. The belfry has a pyramidal roof interpenetrated by four corner piers that wittily repeat the piers of the entrance gates. The main stylistic influence is Charles Harrison Townsend. Stained glass by Ward and Partners

HILLTOWN: **Catholic Church**
Restrained Classical architecture designed by P.J. Byrne *c.*1840. Campanile dates from fifty years later.

HOLYWOOD: **Church of Ireland**
Discreetly sited in a wooded park beside a suburban avenue is an earlier and more modest church built in 1844; the later nave dates from 1869. Both were designed by Charles Lanyon, the second with the assistance of W.H. Lynn, so it is more wholeheartedly Gothic focused on the altar in its raised apse. What unifies the interior is the exposed red brickwork that complements the unrecorded stained glass. There is a marble relief by Rosamond Praeger, who lived nearby.

HOLYWOOD: **The Library**
Cheerful red and yellow brick schoolhouse with hall and clocktower added in 1877. Called 'old Sullivan Schoolhouse', it has been carefully converted into a prominently sited library and cultural centre in 1984.

HOLYWOOD: **Presbyterian Church**
A good Classical edifice of 1849. With recessed portice. Architect: Charles Lanyon.

HOLYWOOD: **Catholic Church**
The impressive steeple still dominates the approach from Belfast, and it is not until nearby that the remainder of the church looms up as a burnt-out ruin behind locked gates. The stonework survives of the nave and smaller chancel, including the tribune that once upheld the organ above the entrance. The inscription carved halfway up the tower still proudly proclaims '1874', the year of its completion (after the competition of 1869). Now purged of accumulated pious trivia and changing liturgical regulations, the first success of Timothy Hevey has been received into the half-world of Coventry Cathedral, the Dresden Frauenkirche and the blitzed churches of Croatia. Nave demolished, 1994.

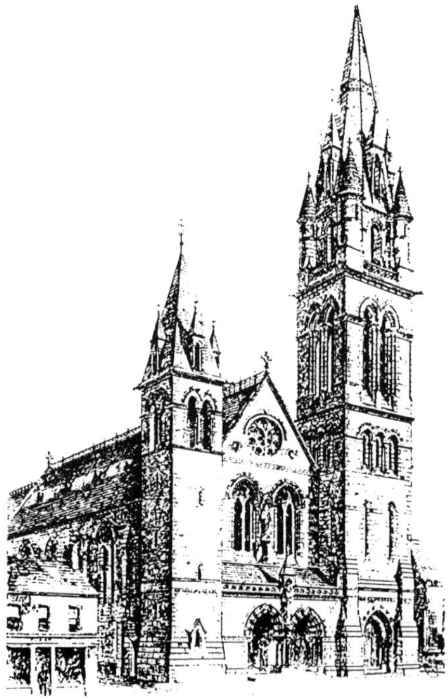

KILLOUGH: **Sheil Almshouses**

The most rural of the series of almhouses designed in 1866 by Lanyon, Lynn and Lanyon to comply with the charitable bequest of Charles Sheil, articulated by a series of gables and a single tower.

KILLOUGH: **Tyrella House**

An example of Charles Lanyon's Georgian manner incorporating an earlier house. Bow-fronted diningroom to view the sea as recorded in a contemporary watercolour now in Belfast City Art Gallery. Member of Friendly Ireland.

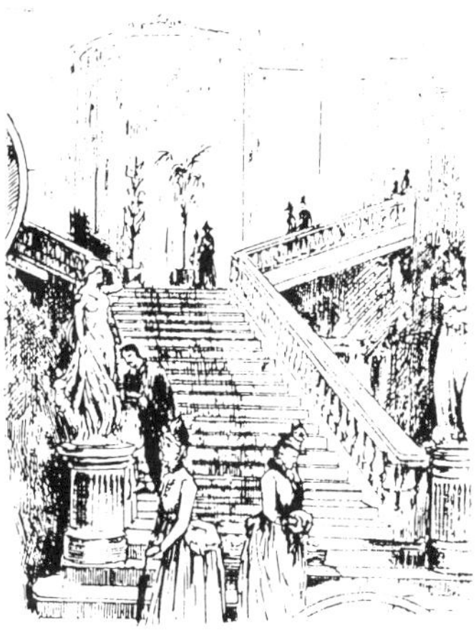

KILLOWEN: **Ballyedmond**

Baronial red-brick house with castellated turreted tower, mullioned and traceried windows and many gables. For a long time an atmospheric if somewhat run-down hotel. Now restored as a private house. A palatial setting for the white marble imperial staircase salvaged from Robinson and Cleaver in Donegall Square, Belfast (q.v.).

KILMORE: **Church of Ireland**

Accomplished Gothic Revival church of 1870 by Thomas Drew with the horizontal thrust of the nave and chancel balanced by the vertical uplift of the adjoining steeple; this has an unbroken shaft rising to a louvered belfry and a terminating spire.

KILLYLEAGH: **Killyleagh Castle**

Archibald Rowan-Hamilton, grandson of the United Irishman, commissioned Charles Lanyon to restore his ancestral castle. He had married an heiress and resolved with the 1st marquis of Dufferin and Ava to end a family feud that had led to the subdivision of the estate leaving the Rowan-Hamiltons in the castle and their Blackwood cousins in the bawn with the gatehouse rebuilt as their Georgian residence. This was the dwelling inherited by the 1st marquis, who pulled it down and commissioned Benjamin Ferrey to recreate a baronial gatehouse to match the two surviving corner towers, which were enlivened by further candle snuffers enclosing spiral staircases. Before its completion in 1860, Lord Dufferin had handed it over to Archibald Rowan-Hamilton, in return for a quit-rent of silver spurs and golden roses on alternate years. He then married Rowan-Hamilton's daughter. This allowed the Rowan-

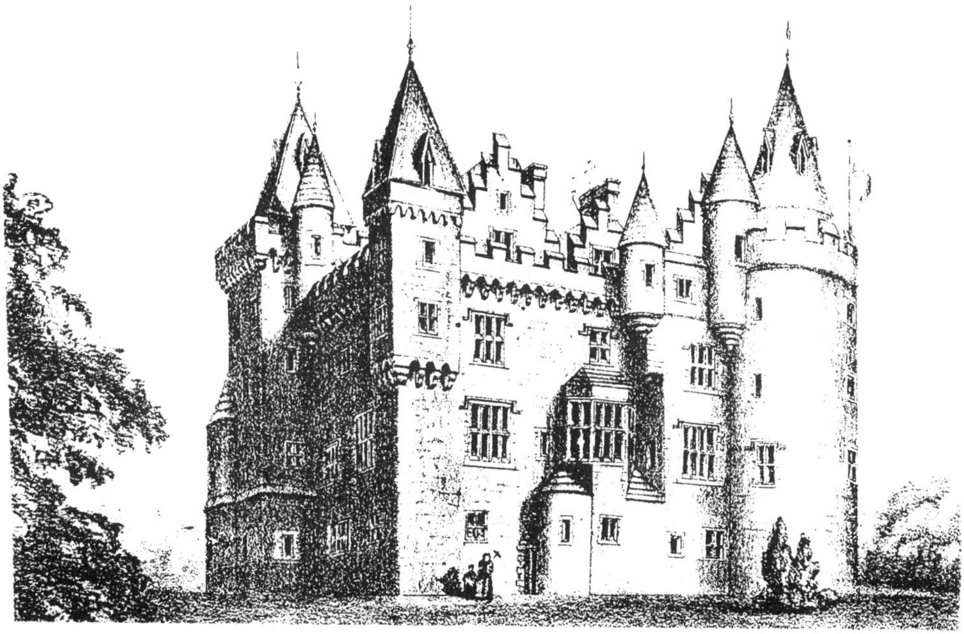

Hamiltons access through their front door for the first time in almost two hundred years, a circumstance celebrated by Lanyon, first by inserting an imposing doorcase, and then by devising a staircase up to the *piano nobile* that makes up for limited dimensions by grandeur of scale. Lanyon's first thought as shewn in plans preserved in the castle was to make one staircase giving access to all the floors. But by displacing the upper flights to an adjoining gallery visible through a richly columned arcade, he creates monumentality and suspense. The woodwork (apart from the cupids on the diningroom) is a convincing mixture of sophisticated Manneristic orders and crude figurative sculptures. The heavy plasterwork is by a Mr Fulton. Drawingroom, library and diningroom interconnect, and all look south into the garden, so that Lanyon was able to unite habitability with splendour. He also retained the vaulted rooms in the northern circular tower and the pentagonal rooms in its Georgian counterpart. He re-cased the entire exterior, while respecting the original fenestration. He raised the roof, inserting lofty dormers screened by machicolations. With a final gesture he crowned his towers with a flurry of *flèches* and extra candle-snuffers, a tribute to medieval France of the duke of Berry, to please a client whose grandfather in his passion for France had befriended Robespierre—such are the effects of the counter-revolution.

KILLYLEAGH: **Martin Memorial, Shrigley**
The Martin family founded the cotton mills here, and built a self-contained village for their workers at the gates of their family seat. All that remains of their enterprise today is one immense factory chimney and the memorial clocktower designed by Timothy Hevey and erected in 1860 to the memory of John Martin. A set-piece of High Victorian ebullience interconnecting the utilitarian with the fantastical. The central octagonal core is a spiral staircase to give easy access to the maintenance man and (ultimately) the looter of the clock itself. The other function was to provide drinking water to the village round it. The monument is a masterly superimposition of overlapping forms with eight flying buttresses rising from an arcaded octagon to prop up a square clock tower roofed with a diagonally orientated spire, so that while not one curve is used, the entire structure appears to rotate. The village was replaced *c.*1970 with a now forlorn housing estate, and the memorial was left to deteriorate. Today it has been at least repaired, if not restored.

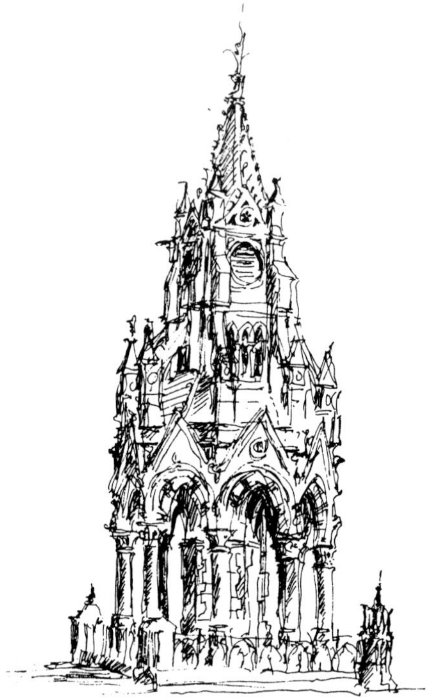

MARTIN MEMORIAL

MILLISLE: **Woburn House**
Large asymmetrical Italianate palazzo entered through a *porte cochère* set beneath a projecting pilastered tower. Adjoining garden front containing double drawingrooms. Built for the Dunbar family by John McCurdy (1867). Now let out as an institution by the family, who remain in the dower house. Important Late Victorian arboretum.

NEWCASTLE: **Enniskean Hotel**
Victorian country house with drawingroom linked to an oriel turret carried up three floors to take advantage of the spectacular views across the valley to the Mournes.

NEWCASTLE: **Old Lifeboat Station**
A winning combination of half-timbering superimposed onto walls of local granite. Built in 1880 and now admirably little altered by its present users, the Pentecostal Church, who have made it the only centre of religious worship of outstanding architectural merit in this seaside town.

NEWCASTLE: **Slieve Donard Hotel**
The epitome of a lavish Victorian hotel where afternoon tea would be served among the palms to orchestral accompaniment. Designed by Young and McKenzie and built in 1896 to embrace the view with a gentle sweep of multistoried bays, burgeoning balconies and dormers, climaxing in a viewing tower that rises up seven floors. Constructed throughout in a red-brick

with stone desssings; it has a triumphal *porte-cochère* with a serpentine pediment enclosing an elaborate double coat-of-arms carved in a ruddy sandstone. Interiors recorded by Lawrence in all their turn-of-the-century splendour lingered on until their recent modernization by the Hastings Hotel group which spared only the diningroom. This occurred just before it could be used as the set for J.G. Farrell's film, which had to be made instead in Markree Castle (q.v.)—better architecture but not as appropriate, since the film appeared to portray the resourcefulness of a landed family opening up to guests, rather than a professional hotelier who refuses to accept that the outside world has disintegrated.

NEWCASTLE: The Station

Cheery, red-brick Gothic Revival station built as late as 1905. Forceful clock tower with spire set between four corbelled corner turrets.

NEWRY: Allied Irish Bank

Designed for the Belfast Bank by Barre and rebuilt in 1890 by W.J. Watson to dominate the central intersection of the town on its corner site. Three floors of glazed arcades below, enlivened by a buttressed oriel and corbelled balconies. A fourth floor of massive dormers that interpenetrate the roof. The ground floor was recently mutilated, but the main doorway is still intact, sheltered by a gabled arch upheld on tiny corbelled columns.

NEWRY: Barre Tomb, St Patrick's Churchyard

William Barre designed this tomb for his father. When he died himself at the age of thirty-seven, his mother erected it to his memory also. An open archway bristling with crockets, rising from a splayed base and terminating in a colonetted pinnacle and topmost wrought-iron cross is set on a hillside with panoramic views of the town he did so much for. Today the cross, struck by lightning, lies twisted on a heap of shattered stonework.

NEWRY: Catholic Cathedral

Most worshippers would consider this cathedral sumptuously Victorian. They could not be further from the truth. The nave and the chancel date from 1826 and were designed by Thomas Duff in the Perpendicular style. All that should be termed Victorian are the 1891 transepts, the high altar, pulpit and the detached belfry (added by George Ashlin); but proposals for a complete decorative scheme were drawn up by Ashlin's pupil, Timothy Hevey, and these were fully implemented twenty years later by Ashlin himself when he extended the nave and chancel in 1904 (the chancel by a polygonal apse). Today it would appear that Dr O'Neill, the Edwardian bishop, was such an advanced liturgist that he had made provision for all the dictates of the Second Vatican Council. Then one perceives that the plinths of the altar and pulpit have been engulfed by the dais, while the reredos has been split into three by a celestial thunderbolt. The alterations that bring the cathedral into alignment with the Second Vatican Council were completed in 1990, but with marble and mosaic are indistiguishable from what had been inserted in 1904-9. The existing mosaics were ceramics by Oppenheimer of Manchester to the design of Ashlin. The new mosaics are marble by the Centro Domus Dei (working on the designs of amateurs as in medieval times). The existing sanctuary was extended one bay further at the expense of the nave, and the existing altar table repositioned at the crossing—all standard procedure—but not the spectacular coloured marble throne sited against one of the piers of the crossing, for the bishop to preside, his coat-of-arms depicted in mosaic overlooking the most triumphant upsurge on this island of the Victorian Revival.

NEWRY, Basin Walk: Cash and Carry

Two-storey warehouse in the Gothic idiom, built out of rubble stone with brick dressings. Symmetrical façade with three gables to define the access.

NEWRY: Dominican Church

After the death of Duff and Barre, all Catholic commissions in Newry went to George Ashlin, whose first job here was the Dominican priory, grim and charmless (1871) but attached to one of his sumptuously decorated churches, completed as illustrated in the *Irish Builder* of 1875. A foretaste of the interior is given by the lavish stone-carving above the principal door. Nave and aisles of five bays with two clerestory windows to each bay. Choir of one bay subdivided into two. Apsidal chancel with later fittings, the side chapels discreetly lit by concealed glass semi-domes and still intact with their plethora of gilding and mosaics. Main altar by Pearse; side altar by Leonardi of Rome.

NEWRY: Egyptian Arch

The main Dublin-Belfast railway was built by William Dargan in 1851 and this is its greatest bridge, making a triumphal arch at the entry to Newry from the direction of Camlough. What makes this bridge so exceptional is the choice of Egyptian for its style, especially since the Egyptians ignored the arch. Here the outer rectangular lintels merge gradually into an inner arch with such assurance as to suggest the

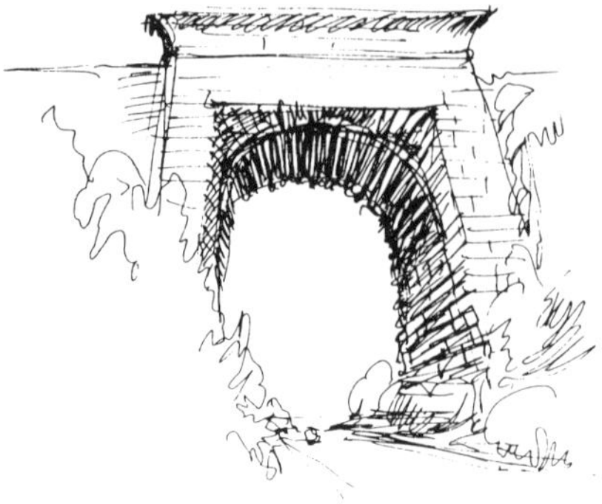

possible intervention of J.S. Mulvany, who would at that moment been building for Dargan the neo-Egyptian Broadstone terminus in Dublin (q.v.).

NEWRY: **Riverside Reformed Presbyterian Church**

Newry preserves not only Barre's first Non-Conformist church but also his last. They have little in common. Whereas the early church is impeccably built in granite, this is built out of cheap red and yellow brick. And whereas the earlier church is correctly Decorated Gothic, this church of 1866 is an amalgam of many styles, but welded together with such conviction that one cannot question why is a French Flamboyant rose window the centrepiece of a Lombardesque façade attached to a Rhenish belfry. If the earlier church expresses a sublimation of materialism, here we are confronted by a rejection of such an easy compromise. Everything is ruthlessly exposed as the upward winding of the belfry staircase reveals the inner workings of the tower. The visionary earlier church has been maintained, while the realism of the later church has proved more difficult to live with. It was sold by its original congregation after twenty years. Ten years ago a false ceiling was inserted and the rose window blocked up to save heating bills. But the interior still preserves Barre's individualistic pulpit and organ loft with their seried arches and perforated spandrels.

NEWRY: **St Colman's Hall**

Once a bank with a curved Romanesque façde between two entrance archways, elegant and symmetrical, now successfully screening a modern bingo hall from the public street.

NEWRY: **St Mary's Church of Ireland**

Galleried Regency Gothic church but with chancel remodelled and raised by Sir Thomas Drew to concur with High Victorian ideals. Immense east window (1884) commemorating the Revd Beddell Swanzy. Later glass by Abbott and a richly coloured Clokey of Belfast. Pulpit of 1881.

NEWRY: **Sands Mill, New Street**

Posthumous tribute to the architecture of William Barre, since it overlooks his last church and is built of the same materials. The architect was W.J. Watson; a roundel frames the date of 1873, six years after Barre's death. Seven floors of neo-Romanesque with arcades resting on projecting stone string courses that alternate with flush hands of blue brick. A further subtlety is that the openings are grouped in pairs (except on the first floor), expressed most forcefully by the semi-detached dormers of the top floor. Rounded in corners. The ultimate accolade for Victorian industrial architecture: it is still in use.

NEWRY: **Toner's Television Headquarters**

Tucked away behind the dreary townhall of 1890, another superb example of industrial

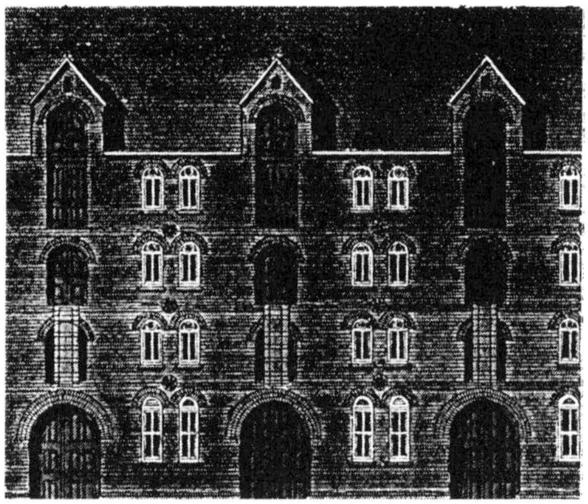

architecture overlooks the canal. Designed by W.J. Watson in 1879 for Messrs Martin Nesbit and Irwin. Built out of the same materials as Sands Mill; five floors high, with three double-height arched doorways rising up into dormers that support the hoists. The floors are strutted together by steel tie bars decoratively expressed by plates like cast-iron flowers. The design still strong enough to survive a ground floor modernized in the 1960s.

NEWRY: **The Townhall**

Large and pompous Italianate structure dating from 1890, its architect William Batt, who won the second round of a hard-fought competition.

NEWRY: **Unitarian Church**

One of the earliest independent commissions of William Barre, who was born here. Up until then, all Unitarian churches had been neo-Classical, so there was considerable alarm when Barre won a competition in 1853 with a Gothic Revival scheme which sceptics said could not be built for the budget. By working in local granite detailed with studied concision, Barre disproved his critics, inaugurating according to his biographer Durham Dunlop, a new era of Non-Conformist architecture. Barre's ability to handle scale means that we never sense the modest dimensions. The nave façade is given over to a single, richly traceried window, while a deeply recessed doorway is set into a tower alongside, that rises upwards into an incisive spire. Exterior cruciform, but not the interior, since Barre fills in the chancel with an organ loft. Richly varnished, exposed timber roof throughout articulated by traceried trusses, intersecting at the crossing. Beneath them a pinnacled pulpit like a hollowed-out altar.

NEWTOWNARDS: **Catholic Church**
One of the most delightful churches of its time in Ireland designed by J.A. Hansom and built in 1877. Cruciform with central lantern tower, transepts of one bay each flush with the aisles,

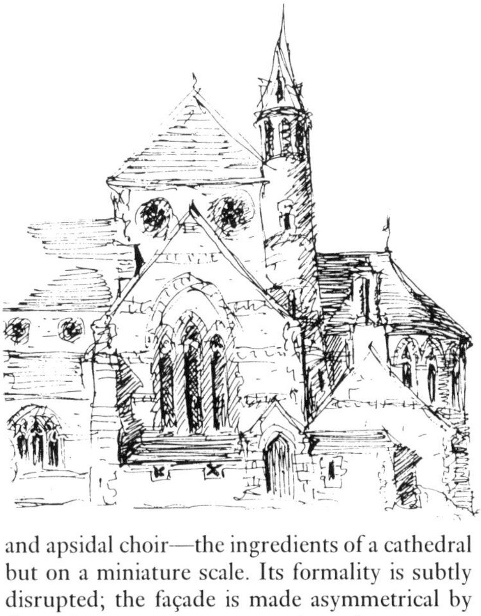

and apsidal choir—the ingredients of a cathedral but on a miniature scale. Its formality is subtly disrupted; the façade is made asymmetrical by the staircase to the organ and southern porch, while one Irish round tower is diagonally attached to the central lantern, leavings its fenestration undisturbed—eight rose windows inserted into the spandrels to give a mysterious illumination to the crossing.

NEWTOWNARDS: **Killynether House**
Earlier house remodelled and enlarged in 1875-6 for the 5th marquis of Londonderry by a local architect, Henry Chappell; rambling old-fashioned neo-Tudor; sited below the memorial tower of Scrabo (q.v.).

NEWTOWNARDS: **Northern Bank**
One of the earliest commissions of W.H. Lynn, designed in 1854, in which he was influenced by Ruskin's *Stones of Venice*; a compact Venetian palazzo, ogee Gothic façade with adjoining entrance front in unexpected round-arched style. But this is proof of Lynn's precocious eclecticism: the roof rises to a single, massive chimney-stack like an Irish Georgian rectory. Resembles his Dungannon bank (q.v.).

NEWTOWNARDS: **Model School**
Neo-Elizabethan complex designed by Frederick Darley and built in 1863.

PORTAFERRY: **Presbyterian Church**
Greek Doric temple designed by an unknown architect to take the advantage of a steeply sloping site. Porticos at both ends, one directly on the ground giving access to the galleries; the other (matching) portico is raised a storey up with the access to the main church beneath. Subsequently alterations due to the refusal of the congregation to treat neo-Classicism as sacrosanct have unwittingly resulted in a shrine to Post-Modernism: tiny windows have been introduced to light the stairs to the pulpit and the porticos have been partially glazed.

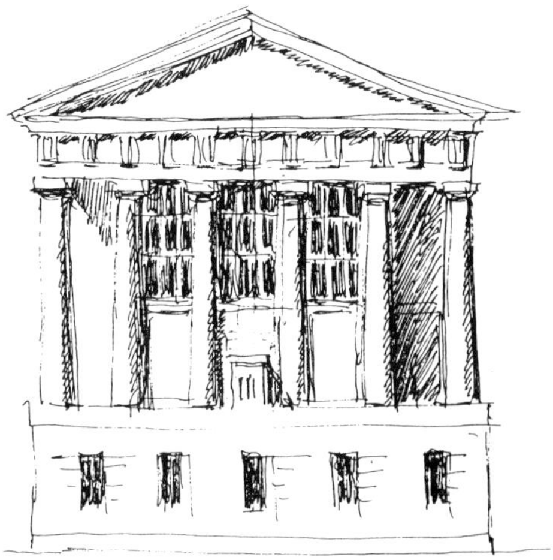

PORTAFERRY: **Quintin Castle**
Dramatically sited cliff-top castle protected from the spray of the sea by long, castellated curtain-walls leading to flanking towers. The core of the castle is 17th-century, but most of the rebuilding was carried out in 1830-40 by one of the Ancketills, a long-forgotten playwright and novelist. No architect is recorded, so he may have acted as his own. There is certainly a Byronic air of menace and exoticism. Formality is surrendered to the freedom of an organic composition where the major tower with its machicolations and Irish battlements are replicated on an increasingly reduced scale. The

ranges in between are underplayed but are designed with wide windows set in regular fenestration to enjoy the view. Earlier this century Quintin was an appropriate setting for seances and pentagons chalked upon the floorboards. Now it has settled down to a more mundane existence as a residence for the elderly.

ROSTREVOR: **Catholic Church**
Perpendicular Gothic Revival church built *c.*1854 by Patrick Byrne. Later tower and spire. Sanctuary reorganized at the expense of the lower half of the stained glass behind the altar.

ROSTREVOR: **Clermont**
Large seaside villa built out of red brick with polygonal tower, circular tower and much decorative boarding. Architect unknown.

ROSTREVOR: **Rostrevor House**
Long, low Tudor Revival house with many gables and chimneys; apparently an early Georgian house extended on either side. Staircase expressed by oriel on the half landing to save the façade from monotony. The seat of the Ross family, known as Ross of Bladensberg, a victory won by Major-General Robert Ross over the Americans and commemorated in the nearby obelisk. A once-celebrated arboretum is now lost in undergrowth.

SCRABO: **The Tower**
Memorial tower to the 3rd marquis of Londonderry, erected to the designs of W.H. Lynn working for Sir Charles Lanyon after a competition (1858) that generated much ill-feeling since supporters of William Barre claimed that the conditions had been transgressed. Certainly Barre and Lynn as the two best Gothic Revivalists in Ulster never collaborated, and in several later competitions Barre got his revenge. The Scrabo memorial is a multi-storied Scottish Baronial tower with four corner-turrets, three corbelled, and a spiral stairs; more curious than beautiful.

STRANGFORD: **Myra Castle**
Restrained castle designed *c.*1850 by an unknown architect for Rowland Craig-Laurie. Asymmetrically composed with façade linking circular tower to higher, square, entry tower. The rectangular headed windows and rendered walls are frankly expressed throughout. In this, the castle anticipates the architecture of the 1920s.

WARRENPOINT: **Northern Bank**
Three-storied corner block pivoting on an octagonal turret. Designed in 1914 by S.P. Close. Sited to overlook the People's Park, a Victorian period piece complete with a bandstand from Glasgow's Saracenic Ironworks.

WARRENPOINT: **Catholic Church**
Cruciform Perpendicular Revival church in the manner of Thomas Duff; dated 1841. The western tower and spire, built out of local granite and inspired by 13th-century France, were added by Hevey in 1875. Chancel decorated with jolly mosaics and Michael Healy's triple-light stained-glass window above the altar.

WARRENPOINT: **Convent of Mercy**
Two adjoining seaside hotels built *c.*1890 converted into a convent in 1922. The southern hotel, built by the Great Southern Railway Company, has an octagonal tower ringed by wrought iron, a reduced version of the Slieve Donard (q.v.). Presumably by W.J. Watson.

WARRENPOINT: **Methodist Church**
Snugly proportioned nave with lean-to aisles topped by a louvered pyramidal *flèche* dated 1880. Panelled interior. Designed by W.J. Watson.

WARRENPOINT: **Narrow Water Castle**
The most impressive domestic commission of Thomas Duff, designed in 1830 for Roger Hall, incorporating an earlier house set above the medieval castle sited on the shore of Carlingford Lough. Duff's favourite style was Tudor Gothic, and the façades here are resplendent with pinnacles, bays and oriels. Corner entrance tower with ogee cupolas crowning its four turrets so that one enters the first-floor staircase hall through what is now the billiard room. Furnishings by Curran of Lisburn include the castellated bookshelves and heraldic fireplace in the library and at the further end of the state rooms an atmospheric diningroom. Chinese wallpaper decorates an intervening drawing-room.

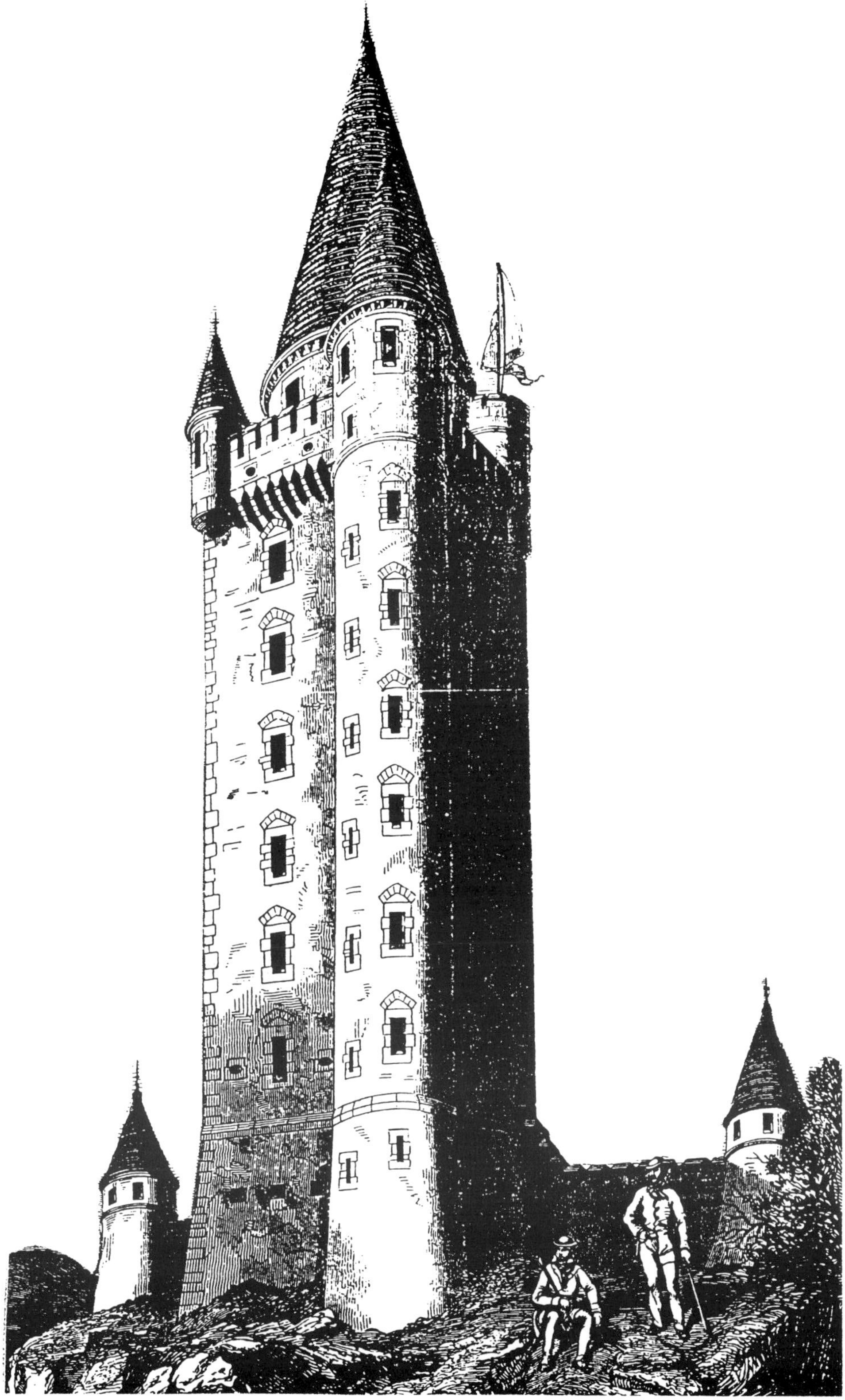

LONDONDERRY MEMORIAL, SCRABO

DUBLIN CITY, NORTH

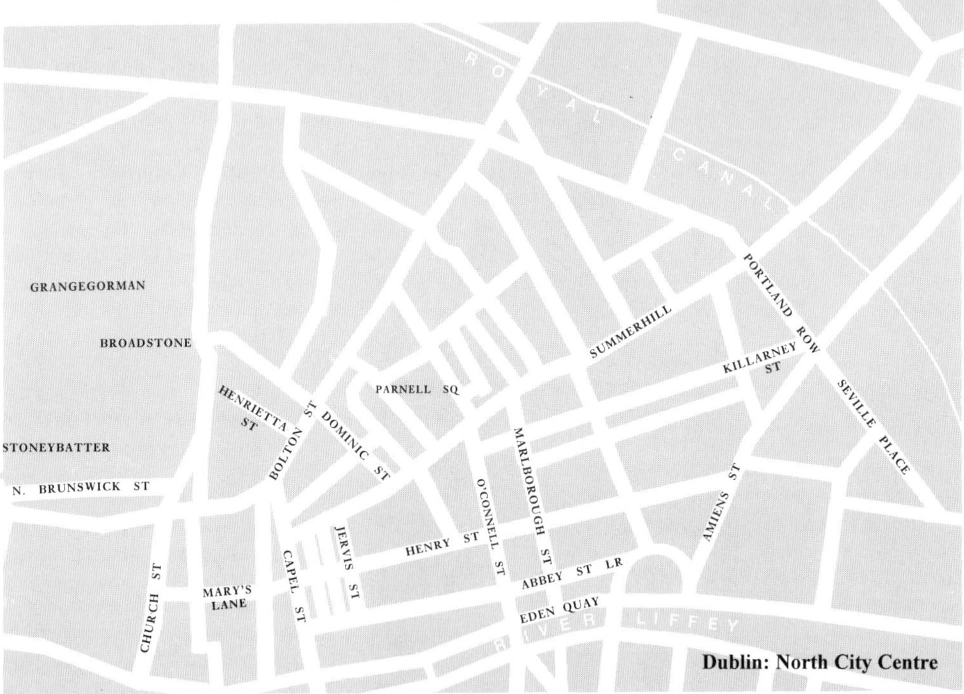

Dublin: North City Centre

ABBEY STREET, LOWER: **Mooney's Public House**

Rebuilt by Lawrence McDonnell on a grand scale with plasterwork in the Dublin tradition that flourished unfettered only in public houses —succulent fruit interwoven with flowers and painted up to rival what was being sold out of street barrows at the door. Completed in 1917. Now remodelled as part of a banking hall with a replica of the ceiling concealing extra office space.

ABBEY STREET, LOWER: **Scots Church**

After the destruction of Wesley College in 1972, this is the only Dublin building by the Limerick architect, William Fogerty. A conventional Gothic Revival church made less memorable by the failure to build an intended tower. Interior completed in 1867.

ABBEY STREET, LOWER: **Trustee Savings Bank**

Urbane neo-Classical bank, designed by Isaac Farrell in 1839. Little evidence remains of his interior.

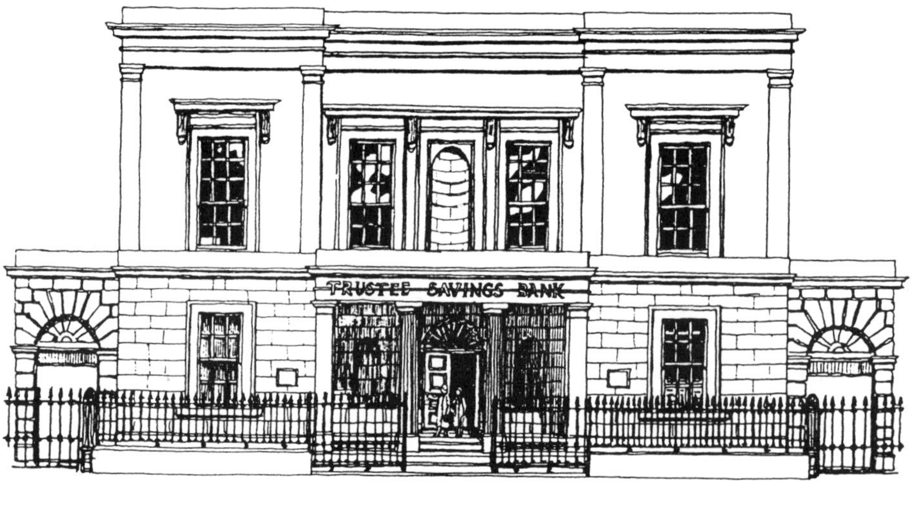

ABBEY STREET, MIDDLE: **The Oval**
If Anthony Blunt was intrigued by the cupola of L. McDonnell's O'Connell Street bank (see page 119), he would have been amused by the nearby public house McDonnell was reconstructing at the same time as another offshoot of Borromini's Baroque, expressed in its name, 'The Oval'. Blunt would have distanced himself from the clientèle, the leading Irish political journalists of their era. Interior remodelled.

AMIENS STREET: **CIE Offices**
Designed to serve William Deane Butler's station by John Lanyon in 1879. He appropriately uses brick in deference to the station's granite and introduces an Italianate tower which groups picturesquely with the station's three but is discreetly kept at a lower height.

AMIENS STREET: **Connolly Station**
Earliest of the monumental Dublin stations, designed by William Deane Butler for the Dublin and Drogheda Railway Company and built in 1844-6. Symmetrical three-towered façade, the central belvedere set on the axis of Talbot Street. Devastatingly observed by Craig to be 'coarse in detail and poorish in conception'. He exempted the cab ramp added thirty years later and the cast-iron Doric double

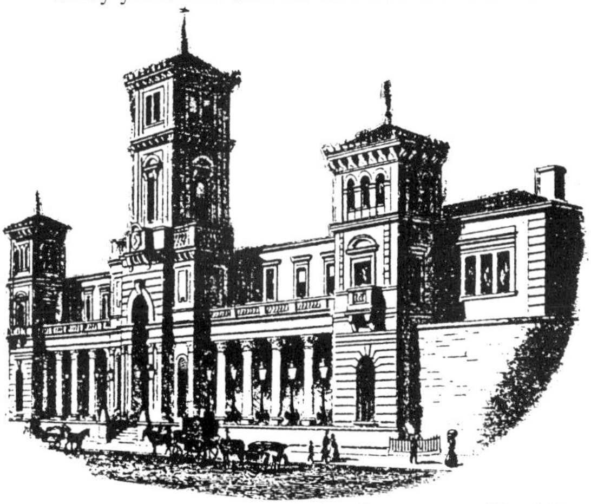

colonnade that carried the line across Sheriff Street (by Courtney, Stephens and Bailey, *c.*1884) that comes nearer than the Pro-Cathedral to recreating the interior of a Greek temple. The same firm also built the much-maligned loopline bridge.

AMIENS STREET: **Parcels Office**
Designed by Howard Pentland in 1892 shortly after he had taken over the architectural department of the OPW from J.H. Owen; he uses a robust Flemish Revival style, which he adopted also for his post offices. In red brick and stone dressings.

ARBOUR HILL: **Arbour Hill Prison**
The smallest but most successful of the Dublin prisons designed by Jacob Owen *c.*1835 to present an embattled neo-Norman façade to the outside world; rebuilt in 1845 by Sir Joshua Jebb (executive architect, Frederick Clarendon). The central gatehouse to the gaol is linked by screen walls to the governor's house on one side and to the chapel on the other. The chapel is a large cruciform structure spanned by an elaborate open roof. A triple window with stained glass (possibly by Harry Clarke Studios) is set behind the altar. Galleries for visitors in the nave and transept are reached by an open arcaded staircase reminiscent of India but copied from the National Scotch Church, Bow Street, London by Robert Wallace. An adjoining Celtic round tower reminds us that this was an Irish outpost of the British Empire—entirely appropriate for its inmates, long-term political prisoners.

AUGHRIM STREET: **Holy Family Church**
The last commission of J.S. Butler; built in 1876, two years before his abrupt resignation from his post as city architect and his flight after the police were called in to investigate unspecified irregularities. There is no evidence of impending disaster in the complacency of its mid-Gothic Revival idiom. The aisles, richly decorated with many Irish marbles and murals, are later, to the designs of R.M. Butler (no relation). Sanctuary predictably altered after the Second Vatican Council, but the altar of our Lady by John Valentine Hogan remains.

BOLTON STREET: **College of Technology**
Designed by C.J. McCarthy. The crisp scholarly neo-Georgian entry block built in 1907-12 and executed in red brick and Mount Charles sandstone is in reality an early Victorian hotel (by an unknown architect) that McCarthy remodelled and doubled in length while retaining its palatial proportions, ignored to their cost by architects responsible for later extensions.

BROADSTONE: **Broadstone Station**
The most dramatically sited of Dublin's stations, especially when approached by the elevated canal that once lapped against its colonnaded cab shelter (added in 1861 by George Wilkinson). This is neo-Grecian at its most austere but lighter in mood than the station, John Skipton Mulvany's neo-Egyptian masterpiece in mountain granite—pairs of pedimented bays project, but well behind a central tapered double-height pylon porch. This leads to a top-lit hall with a compressed apsidal staircase seen beyond, acutely rising to a continuously cantilevered gallery round the central well. Its lonely grandeur hardly tallies with the affable

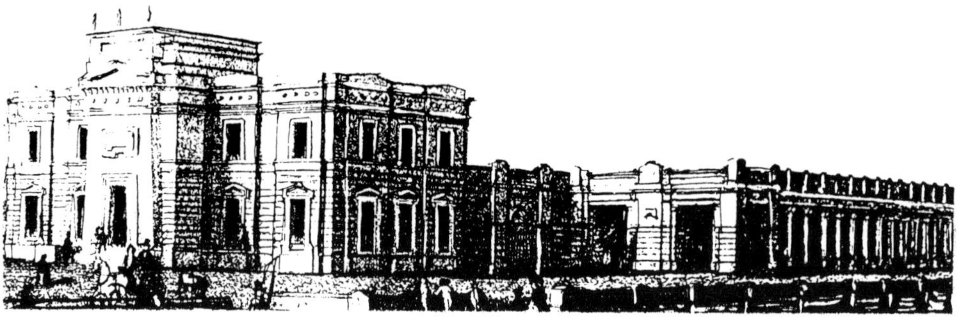

impression Mulvany gave his contemporaries—'a prodigious smoker of cigars and fond of fox hunting'. Broadstone is called by Craig the last monument worthy of Gandon, in its present desolation we sense impending catastrophe, the first spattering raindrops of the Deluge. At the rear, a station shed originally roofed by Richard Turner. This proved too daring for the span and had to be replaced (after 1851) by a more conventional structure, the work of G.W. Hemans.

BRUNSWICK STREET NORTH: **Former Carmichael School of Medicine**
Compact Lombardesque Revival designed in

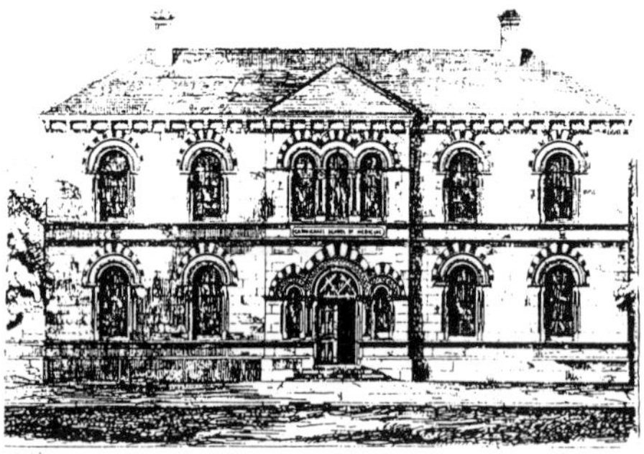

1864 by Benjamin Woodward's favourite pupil, J.E. Rogers. Symmetrical façade with improvized sculpture as in Woodward's Trinity Museum. The top-lit staircase hall inside reveals the paucity of funds.

BUCKINGHAM STREET: **Fire Station**
The earliest of the fire stations designed (in 1899) by C.J. McCarthy for Dublin—all in a North Italian Romanesque idiom built out of red brick with an attached bell-tower to sound the alarm. Now a series of artists' studios partly directed by the local community.

CAPEL STREET: **No. 134-6**
One of the Boland's Bakery premises designed by Charles Geoghegan. In 1867 he rebuilt three Georgian houses along Capel Street with enriched fenestration and mansard roofs. At the rear a glazed gallery with a boldly cross-braced roof leads to the former Presbyterian church: the congregation had moved to Findlater's church in Parnell Square). Later a bakery; now sheltering a congregation of cars.

CAPEL STREET: **Slattery's Public House**
An exuberant stucco-clad Dublin corner pub, an architectural mesalliance between Regency and Lombardesque. A memorable setting for folk balladry, even if no original interior has survived. Architect unknown.

CHURCH STREET: **Housing**
Unobtrusive housing renewal scheme *c.*1900 carefully linked into the urban fabric. Designed by C.J. McCarthy with double- and single-storey housing to climax in the vista towards the façade of his father's Capuchin church, which becomes cathedral-like in contrast.

CHURCH STREET: **St Mary of the Angels**
Designed by J.J. McCarthy and built from 1868 to 1881 for the Capuchin Order. The best view of the façade is through the formal vista of the corporation housing designed by his son, C.J. McCarthy. The architecture of the façade reverts to the austerity of his early rural churches. At the rear the walls of unrelieved black scalp that sweep round a high-pitched apse are equalled in the eloquence of their asceticism only by St Audoen's across the river. The interior was originally a simple timber-sheathed barrel-vault springing from coving through which the arches of the clerestory windows interpenetrate. Natural light enters the church mainly from the south, giving a sense of theatre to the later enrichments. Altars by James Pearse; façade statues by Leo Broe. The overscaled tower that should have stood alongside the nave was never built; instead, the money went into the rebuilding of the monastery. As McCarthy had died, the Capuchins chose George Ashlin to add the side aisle and the organ gallery (1910) and J.J. O'Callaghan to design the adjoining hall. His assertive façade to the hall, the Father Mathew Hall, was toned down twenty years ago out of recognition for its present use—Bingo.

DOMINIC STREET: St Saviour's Church
The finest of J.J. McCarthy's Dublin churches, at least until its internal reorganization after the Second Vatican Council. The foundation stone was laid in 1852 and the dedication took place in 1861, but the projected tower was never started. Instead, money was more sensibly spent on the adjoining monastery designed in a complementary Gothic Revival by J.L. Robinson in 1885. A new aisle was added in 1895 by George Ashlin. The façade is modelled on French rather than English 13th-century prototypes with its rose window above a gallery of blank arcades (carved by H. Lane). An unbroken nave flanked by aisles and continuous side chapels terminates with a polygonal apse which once contained a high altar (now dismantled) and an elaborate tabernacle designed *c.*1900 by William Scott (now lost). However, the 1857 *pietà* by John Hogan, completed posthumously by an assistant, J. Cahill, survives beneath the Holy Name altar. Successive alterations have made the Telford organ unplayable. Stained glass by O'Connor & Son.

DORSET STREET: Fire Station
Designed by C.J. McCarthy in 1901 as a variant of his Buckingham Street station (q.v.) built two years before.

EDEN QUAY: Horse and Tram Bar
The least ambitious of Mooney's Dublin pubs, but one that survives more or less intact. Pretty painted glass throughout. Architects, O'Callaghan and Webb (1917).

ECCLES STREET: Mater Hospital
Until quite recently an immense Ionic capital lay at the entrance to Ballyknockan quarry in the Wicklow mountains, intended for the central portico of this façade but left behind, bearing witness to the perfectionism of the architect, John Bourke. The last monumental Palladian complex in the city survives through laisser-faire rather than appreciation. Built in 1855-61 as both convent and hospital round a central courtyard surrounded by a vaulted corridor so that all the wards have an outward aspect. It must be admitted that the façade, which never received its intended dome, exposes faults of logic and proportion: the terminal pavilions are insufficiently articulated and the Palladian windows in the centre block are too compressed; but the simpler courtyard is free from these faults. Here a bow-fronted boardroom with Corinthian columns behind the hall faces across to a cruciform chapel. This was not started until 1886, designed by J.L. Robinson, whose Classicism is dutiful but lacks Bourke's conviction. Since extended.

GRANGEGORMAN: All Saints Church of Ireland
Double-aisled Gothic Revival of which only the entry aisle to the south is original. That to the north was destroyed by arson and rebuilt not unsuccessfully fifteen years ago. Designed by Thomas Drew *c.*1863 with capitals of stylized ferns. Stained glass by O'Brien (Ruth and Naomi, 1914) and external First World War memorial in opus sectile by Rhind, 1921.

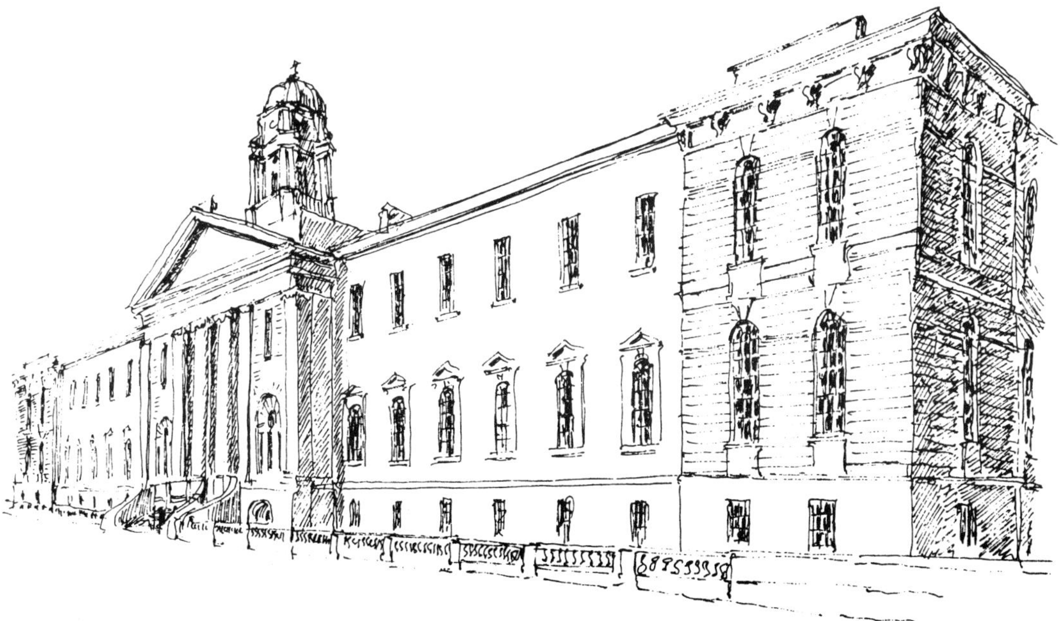

MATER HOSPITAL

GRANGEGORMAN: **Grangegorman Hospital**

Designed by William Murray in collaboration with his son W.G. Muray and A. Denny and built in 1847-9 in an insistent neo-Elizabethan. The largest of Dublin's lunatic asylums, the asymmetry of the central block and the canting of the far-flung wings attempt to domesticate its grimness. William Murray, who had spent so much of his life designing asylums and penitentiaries that he was evidently unable to forget them when designing country houses, died the year of its completion. Later additions include the laundries and stores of 1851 by J.S. Mulvany, the Church of Ireland chapel by George Wilkinson (1860), and further infirmaries and a chapel added in 1863 by W.G. Murray. A further block was added by Edward Carson in 1866. Though threatened with demolition by distraught psychiatrists, apart from its fenestration it has improbably survived.

HENRIETTA STREET: **King's Inns Library**

Annex tacked on in 1892 to the rear of Frederick Darley's neo-Classical library to accommodate extra books. Multi-level, grilled, stack structure as in Deane's National Library, but here expressed in Sullivanesque elevation. The spiral staircase is expressed with equal boldness. Architect unknown. The library itself still contains the fascinating cast-iron furniture made by Robert Mallett.

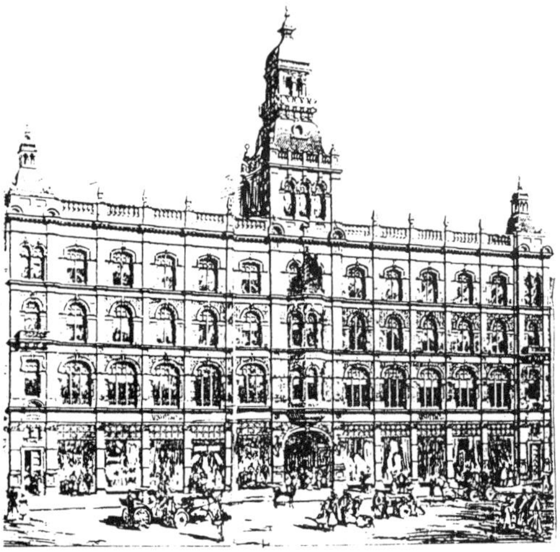

HENRY STREET: **Arnotts**

Top-lit galleried department store with a steel structure sheathed in Classical colonnades. Designed by G.P. Beater in 1894; extended in 1904. His ebullient clock tower, which dominated the street, was removed in 1949.

HENRY STREET: **Nos. 6 and 7**

The only intact mid-Victorian street architecture *c.* 1870 to survive redevelopment in this street. Architect: A.G. Jones.

JERVIS STREET: **Former Hospital**

Impressive if harshly detailed mid-city hospital built by Charles Geoghegan in 1884-7. The façade in banded stone and red machine-made brick monumentalizes the theory that infection cannot survive in double-height wards. Entrance doorway of matching double-height scale. Dizzy cast-iron verandahs at rear allowed patients to sit out and enjoy the morning sun or escape in the event of fire. Due to be absorbed in a shopping complex.

KILLARNEY STREET: **Presbyterian Church**

A remarkable survivor, although for many years a cornstore, its authoritative Doric portico confers distinction on an otherwise desolate streetscape. Designed by D.C. Ferguson, whose major known work is Glenmaroon, Chapelizod (q.v.). Drawing exhibited by him in the RHA exhibition of 1848. Now bricked up.

MARLBOROUGH STREET: **Department of Education**

The Talbot Street block, a restrained Italianate palazzo, was designed by Jacob Owen, the OPW architect in 1842 and extended by J.H. Owen in 1859. A severe Grecian entrance hall with fluted Doric columns. At its rear the gardens of Tyrone House were developed with a central vista, flanked on one side by the original house with its centrepiece remodelled. An almost identical twin mansion was added in 1835 and a rather insignificant model school placed between them. A much-needed focal point was provided by Luppi's marble *pietà* given by the Italians. At the end, F. Darley's neo-Byzantine schoolroom block-cum-gatehouse (1859), burnt out some years ago by vandals.

MARY'S LANE: **Fruit and Vegetable Markets**

Dublin's version of Les Halles but which has so far eluded demolition and still invigorates the surrounding city. Elegant functional sheds screened by characterful façades that unite the monumental with the lighthearted; entered through limestone triumphal arches surmounted by sculptural groups (the work of Charles Harrison). These in turn are linked by arcades filled with variegated brickwork and wrought-iron grilles. The façades are adorned with decorative terracotta tiling and pendants depicting the wares being sold inside, the last echo of Woodward's sculptural programme for

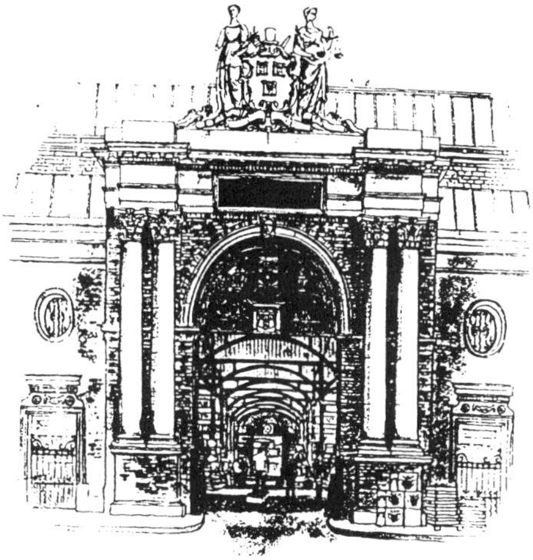

the TCD Museum building of thirty years before. Simpler fish market across the street. Executed in 1889-92 by Spencer Harty following the 1884 designs of Paul Merrill, who had died in 1886.

MARY STREET: **Primark**
A green copper dome floats resplendently above a terracotta confection, itself serenely unaware of the frantic ground-floor alterations to attract the masses by keeping up with the latest trends after abandoning the security of the original design. Architect, W. Mitchell; the date, 1902-5. The original clients were Todd Burns.

MARY STREET: **Former Todd Burns**
Terracotta façade with scrolled skyline survives above the ground floor now divided into three different shops. Designed by C.B. Powell in 1911.

O'CONNELL STREET, LOWER: **Allied Irish Bank**
Delightful post-Edwardian Italianate as rebuilt for the Munster and Leinster Bank in 1917 by McDonnell and Reid. The corner cupola was glimpsed by the late Anthony Blunt on his way to lecture on Borromini and gave him his opening cue.

O'CONNELL STREET, LOWER: **Clery's**
The most palatial of the Dublin stores, commissioned from Ashlin and Coleman after the destruction of 1916. The real designer was Robert Atkinson, who had worked for Root in Chicago and had just designed Selfridges in London. Clery's is smaller than Selfridges but more monumental: a giant Classical order levitates above a continuous theatre for shop window designers. The columned interiors have survived alterations better than its Grafton Street counterparts (q.v.): note the bifurcating staircase that still leads to the first floor (unlike its rival in Switzers, sacrificed to retail space).

O'CONNELL STREET, LOWER: **O'Connell Monument**
Few of the committee appointed to erect a fitting monument to Daniel O'Connell—who had died in 1847, fifteen years before—could have realized they would have to sit 214 times over thirty years, offend all the leading architects of Ireland by rejecting their designs in two abortive competitions (followed by one despairing ballot) and break the health of the country's most celebrated sculptor, John Henry Foley, after he had not only won the commission for the statue but also had been compelled to design the pedestal as well. The unsuccessful entries no longer survive to illustrate mid-Victorian bathos—O'Connell depicted 'under a Gothic canopy apparently in the act of making love to a young lady' (No. 41), 'seated on a stove' (No. 37). So appropriate to us today is the massive drum rising behind four corner angels, girdled with twenty figures rotating in sympathy to the rotundity of the Liberator that it is difficult to understand the continuous controversy. The cloak (to our eyes so tactful) Foley would most probably have had to remove, had he not died the year before. The monument was at last completed by Foley's assistant, Sir Thomas Brock, in 1883.

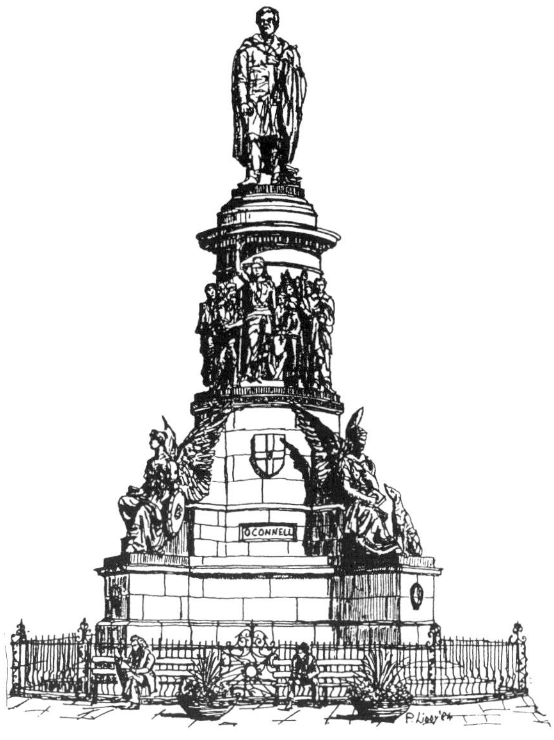

O'CONNELL STREET, UPPER: National Irish Bank

An imposing neo-Classical design of David Bryce built for Standard Life from 1853 onwards amid criticism from Dublin architects that Bryce had poached in their demesne. The ground floor has been more or less removed, but the double-height fluted Corinthian columns articulate the upper floors and uphold a pediment sculpted by Sir John Steel assisted by Miss Redmond; it has an apt theme for a bank to commission from a man assisted by a woman—the Wise and Foolish Virgins.

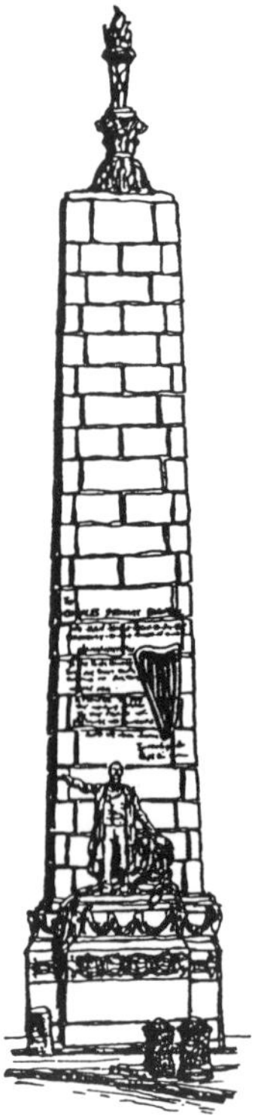

O'CONNELL STREET, UPPER: Parnell Monument

In eloquent contrast to the triumphalism of the O'Connell monument at the other end of the street, the taut triangular obelisk crowned by a bronze tripod and eternal flame suggests continuous sacrifice. At its base Parnell's outstretched arm indicates the nation's invincible march. The commission was awarded to the Dublin-born American sculptor, Augustus Saint Gaudens (chosen in 1900). The monument took over ten years of dissension to complete, with the assistance of two architects, the American Henry Bacon from the office of McKim, Meade and White, and the Irish executant architect, George Sheridan.

PARKGATE STREET: Ryan's Public House

The doyen of the Dublin public houses, although the identity of the architect has been lost. He was evidently influenced by church design, since the central display unit is the secular counterpart of a Gothic Revival reredos that looms over the polished counter, lit by converted gaslamps. The snugs are set close to the window—and the exit. The most ingenious compartments at the rear are controlled by catches positioned behind the counter. Impeccably maintained. Red brick externally with

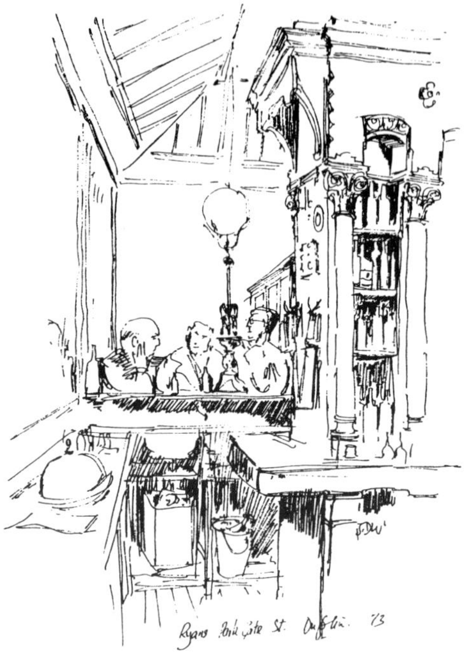

upper floors resting on chubby columns of polished Aberdeen granite (1905).

PARNELL SQUARE: Findlater's Church

Started in 1862 and completed two years later. The architect Andrew Heaton of Perth had aroused local hostility as a Scottish outsider although he received his Irish commissions through his family connections. His hallmark is his reliance on a graceful 14th-century French Gothic—at its most effective in his soaring corner spire strategically sited at the intersection of several vistas. The façade is counterbalanced by an octagonal staircase turret, but it vertically reverberates along a series of gabled windows on the Frederick Street elevation. Richly panelled galleried interior with comfortable pews and excellent acoustics. Fine stained glass in the west window. Architect's perspective on display. Now Abbey Presentation Church.

PARNELL SQUARE: Writers' Museum

Georgian town house acquired by the Jameson family and remodelled for them by Sibthorpes *c.*1890. Few architectural changes were made apart from linking the two first-floor drawing-rooms through a screen of chubby Ionic columns. Heavy fibrous gilded friezes complement the original plasterwork; doors were painted in the style of Angelica Kauffman; and pre-Raphaelite stained glass was inserted in the windows of the staircase hall. For many years the College of Marketing and Design and subsequently pillaged by vandals, it now is one of the city's principal attractions. Unfortunately the restoration has given the house neither its appearance of 1890 nor that of 1790, but has tried to a adopt a tasteful compromise which robs the Victorian alterations of all their boisterousness.

PORTLAND ROW: **Convent School**
Externally red-brick Gothic Revival educational institution; built round two sides of an enclosed garden, chapel built into the two lower floors in a diluted Romanesque. Well lit classrooms recently taken over by the College of Marketing and Design. Architect, George Ashlin. The date *c.* 1900.

PORTLAND ROW: **Five Lamps**
The five lamps, marking the intersection of five streets, are set on a pentagonal pedestal with five taps and scalloped basins. Once lit by gas, now electrified.

RUTLAND STREET, LOWER: **Schools**
Bleakly impressive multi-storied Gothic Revival school block, built into an urban context but now isolated since the destruction of Stapleton's Summerhill and Drew's adjoining tenements. The gradient of the site is adapted to the assumption that more boys went to school than girls. Designed by George O'Connor and built in 1904. Currently empty.

SEVILLE PLACE: **St Laurence O'Toole's**
Gothic Revival church designed by J.B. Keane and completed in 1850 by his pupil John Bourke after Keane had been consigned to the debtors' prison. Bourke himself modelled the tower and broached spire as a counterpart of his St Mary's, Athlone (q.v.). Simple vaulted interior with crude but effective stained glass. Part of the high altar donated by the clergy in Dublin in 1850 has been permitted to remain.

STONEYBATTER: **Kavanagh's Public House**
Chirpy turret balanced out about the front of a corner pub. Designed by George O'Connor in 1905.

SUMMERHILL: **Whelan's Public House**
As so often, only a public house survives the devastation of still-born redevelopment. A sprightly façade dated 1908 has been renamed 'The Millennium Inn'.

WILLIAM STREET NORTH: **Convent and Orphanage**
Austere but forceful street elevation in polychromatic brickwork with Gothic arches linking the fenestration on adjoining floors to achieve a more monumental scale. Designed by Pugin and Ashlin in 1865. Later block at the rear.

WILLIAM STREET NORTH: **St Agatha's**
A rare example of a Classical church by O'Neill and Byrne tucked away in a quiet street; unexpectedly damaged in the Second World War. Construction took from 1880 until 1908. The austere Corinthian façade is pervaded with a sense of the counter-Reformation and makes a telling contrast to the fortress-like side elevations that sweep round an unbroken apse. This is decorated internally with arches framing paintings. Stations of the Cross by Goodland Bradshaw.

WOLFE TONE STREET: **New PMPA**
A vigorous round-arched composition (1865) by W.G. Murray, who could be very straitlaced when working with high quality stonework for important institutions, but obviously enjoyed the chance to unbend, working in stucco on a corner warehouse for a client (Patrick Beakey) who must have run out of money, since the Mary Street façade breaks off abruptly.

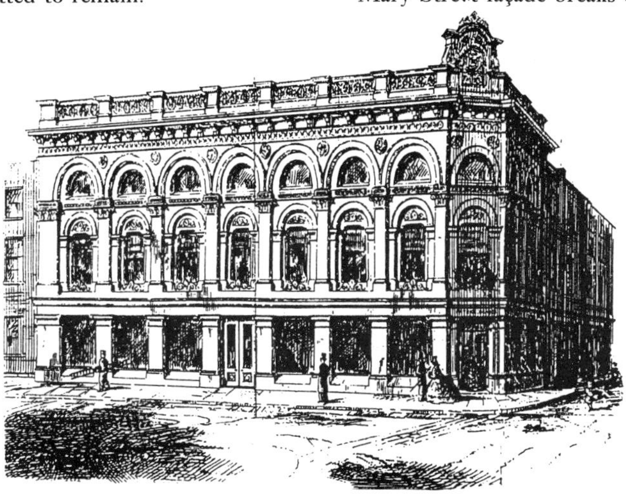

NEW PMPA

DUBLIN CITY, SOUTH

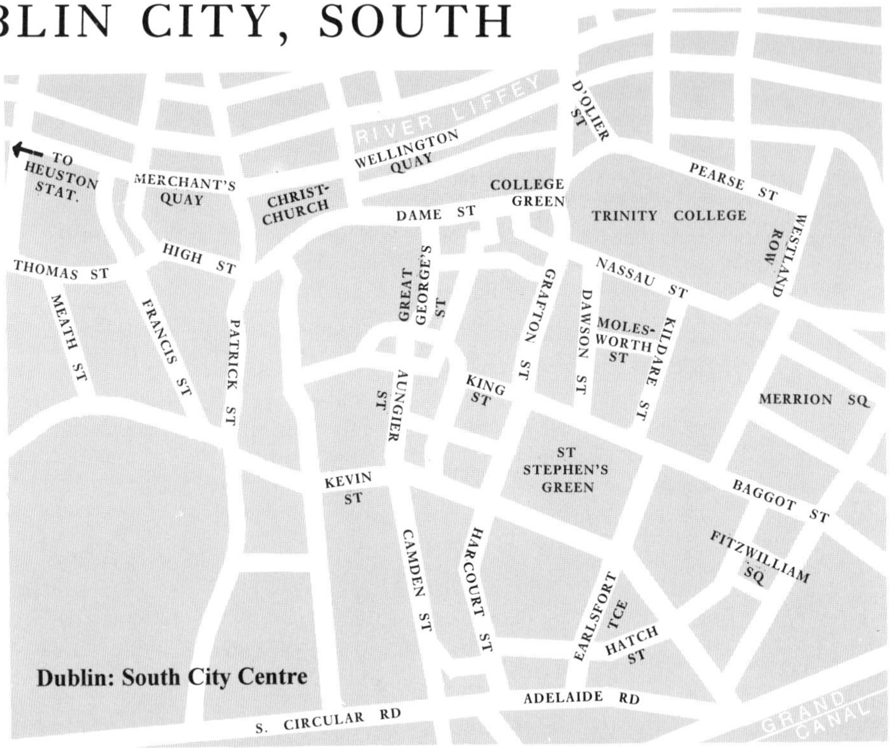

ADELAIDE ROAD: **Eye and Ear Hospital**
Symmetrical Queen Anne Revival with skimped circulatory spaces but well-lit wards. Designed by Carroll and Batchelor in 1901.

ADELAIDE ROAD: **Jewish Synagogue**
The last pathetic echo of Benjamin Woodward's Byzantine Revival, aptly designed by his longest-living pupil, J.J. O'Callaghan, who nursed a unbroken attachment to Gothic. Here, due to being commissioned in 1892 to house Dublin's rapidly expanding Jewish community (mainly expelled from Eastern Europe), he reverted to the Byzantine; two floors of polychromatic brick arcading, more office-block than church. Extended in 1915 by W.R. Jacobs.

ADELAIDE ROAD: **Lutheran Church**
A small, radical Gothic Revival cell built in 1863 by E.T. Owen for the Dublin Irvingites and later used by the Church of Ireland for their services in Gaelic; hence its dedication to St Finian.

ADELAIDE ROAD: **Presbyterian Church**
Neo-Palladian church built *c.*1840 by an unknown architect. Façade by H.J. Lundy. Surly external Ionic portico inspired by the Villa Malcontenta, so that the principal entrance is to the organ gallery. Delightfully intact interior focussed on a decorative organ case placed behind the pulpit. Subjected to recurring schemes for closure.

ANGLESEA STREET: **No. 10**
A more conventual exercise of the Queen Anne Revival than No. 28 across the street. First-floor

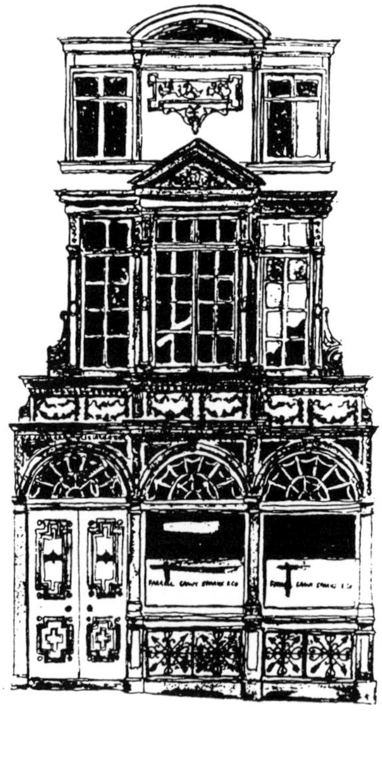

bay window cantilevered above a triple-arched ground-floor loggia. Dated 1898. The architect remains unknown.

ANGLESEA STREET: **No. 28**
Queen Anne Revival façade, the prettiest of its kind in Dublin treating the Classical orders with an unanswerable irreverence. The doorway, ingeniously integrated into the shopfront, is upheld by miniature herms. Dated 1895; the architect has been considered too flippant to be recorded.

ANGLESEA STREET: **Stock Exchange**
Tucked into a narrow street. A sedate façade screens a relatively intact Italianate interior. Designed in 1878 by Millar & Symes.

ASDILL ROW: **Crampton Buildings**
Still the most sophisticated urban renewal development in Dublin although it was completed in 1891, just over a hundred years ago. The architect, Charles Ashworth, was born in Liverpool but had been a pupil in Dublin of W.M. Mitchell. The clients were the Dublin Artisan Dwelling Company, whose contribution to the regeneration of Victorian Dublin has never received due recognition. This complex, known as Crampton Buildings, remains their most ambitious project: two stories of housing above ground-floor shops are grouped round three sides of a private courtyard. Each unit is a rural cottage with access by lively cast-iron stairs and open galleries. The shops give life to the surrounding streets. Of those that face south at least four are restaurants. Considering that Crampton Buildings exemplifies every heresy known to 20th-century planning dogmas, its survival has been miraculous. Due to be destroyed by a comprehensive development of CIE and their architects, Owing, Skidmore and Merrill, it (along with the rest of Temple Bar) was reprieved by Charles Haughey to become the centre of Dublin's nocturnal street life.

AUNGIER STREET: **Avalon House**
Built as the Carmichael School of Medicine in two phases—the earlier (1879) by C.G. Henderson, who successfully restated Dublin's urban brick tradition without falling back on Georgian imitation. He died young, and his partner Albert Murray added the Aungier Street block with its copper roof and corner entrance ebulliently framed by terracotta barley-sugar columns (1905).

AUNGIER STREET: **Carmelite Church**
The church designed in 1827 survives as the southern aisle with its segmental vault and continuous arcaded fenestration along the outer wall. The present Romanesque nave with its reversed orientation is by an unknown architect. Restrained to the point of characterlessness, it was remodelled last in 1955 by W.H. Byrne. Not so the chapel added by George Ashlin in 1867 to house the miraculous Madonna claimed to have been carved by Durer and enthroned in an excessively devotional setting. Papworth's Ionic high altar has been replaced with a free-standing neo-Byzantine baldachino through which one sees a late McGoldrick chancel window. Friary extended by C.B. Powell in 1915. At the rear an excellent school by J.L. Robinson (1890)

BAGGOT STREET: **Mercy Convent**
Neo-Georgian complex by John Bourke (c.1865) which includes an elegant vaulted chapel. In the garden a neo-Gothic shrine in memory of the foundress, Mother Catherine McAuley, with stained glass. Kneeling angels instead of corner pinnacles.

BRIDE STREET: **Iveagh Baths**
The centrepiece of the largest urban renewal scheme of Edwardian Dublin, commissioned at his own expense by the earl of Iveagh, partly to remove the slums that then surrounded St

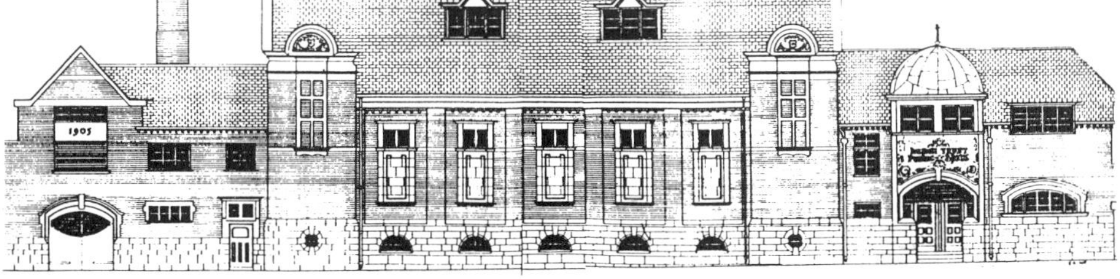

Patrick's Cathedral. Lord Iveagh brought over his London architects, Joseph, Smitherm and Joseph, and their designs were carried out by Kaye, Parry and Ross. Set on a granite plinth, in red brick and sandstone dressings, the façade's most striking feature are the floreated terracotta panels set above the doorways. The baths were built parallel to the street to the highest technical standard. Entered through a squat tower crowned with a cupola once sheathed with copper (since removed by knackers). It is a scandal that Dublin Corporation should have abandoned Dublin's only important example of Art Nouveau, not merely in its architectural idiom but also in its enlightened social programme.

BULL ALLEY: **Corporation Housing**
Designed as a pendant scheme to the Iveagh housing but without its liveliness. The architect, C.J. McCarthy, kept to the existing street lines and building heights and (unusually) rehoused the existing population. Completed in 1904.

BULL ALLEY: **Iveagh Play Centre**
Commissioned from L.A. McDonnell in 1915 by the 1st Lord Iveagh to take advantage of the best site in the Iveagh Trust development looking south across the new park to St Patrick's Cathedral. A finely proportioned Flemish Renaissance symmetrical double-storied structure in brick and stone decorated with generous swags of flowers and fruit. Its carved cupids have been censored by a more suspicious generation and have been removed.

BULL ALLEY STREET: **Iveagh Trust Housing**
The largest private rehousing of Dublin financed personally by the 1st Lord Iveagh and based on the schemes that he had already started in London. Hence Iveagh's choice of London architects, N.J. Joseph, his son Delissa Joseph and Smitherm, who were familiar with the Queen Anne and Dutch Revivals which had as yet made little impact in Ireland. The earliest and the most Georgian are the three blocks parallel to Heytesbury Street dating from 1894, 1896 and 1901; the executant architect was R.J. Stirling. They suffer from the lack of integration into the existing street pattern, a defect remedied when the Trust collaborated with the Corporation in Bull Alley, its most ambitious scheme—to pull down the slums and rehouse the existing population. The layout reveals the quiet ability of C.J. McCarthy to relate to existing monuments and vistas. The two large five-storied complexes (dated 1901 and 1904) frame the baths, the Hostel (1905) and the Play Centre. The ground floor of Patrick Street is devoted to shopping. Here Art Nouveau is tentatively introduced until it asserts itself in the gable ends and the copper domes crowning the staircase towers, before its final triumph in the masterly composition of the Iveagh Baths.

CAMDEN STREET: **No. 25, Bleeding Horse**
Despite being surrounded on three sides by streets, Dublin's most memorably named pub has miraculously survived road widening. Cast-iron colonnettes set in front of the windows support the load of the wall above. This reflects the engineering ability of R.J. Stirling, who rebuilt the pub in 1871.

CAMDEN STREET: **No. 39, Carvill's**
Edwardian wine shop with interior intact including manager's curvilinear cubicle to ensure continuous supervision of the counter. Dated 1906.

CASTLE STREET: **Rates Office**
Original the Newcomen Bank. The side elevation of Ivory's exquisite palazzo was impeccably duplicated for the Hibernian Bank in 1862 by William Caldbeck, the joint being masked by a curved columned porch. Rear elevation remodelled with a wall fountain and dated 1881, when Lord Edward Street was built.

CHRISTCHURCH PLACE: **Christchurch Cathedral**
After the controversial restoration of St Patrick's Cathedral (q.v.) by Sir Benjamin Lee Guinness without the assistance of an architect, in 1871 the distiller Henry Roe commissioned George Edmund Street, the leading expert on the repair of English medieval churches, to restore Christchurch. This decision cost Roe his personal fortune before the completion of the job in 1878 and aroused bitter controversy. Street demolished the 14th-century choir, replacing it with a chevet as suggested by the crypt—an irregular polygon sprouting three parallel chapels. He also pulled down the chapel of Great St Mary, which he replaced by a chapter house and library, completed by Thomas Drew. As such he exposed the dilemma of all restorers—to repair the real or to rebuild the dream. Street had all the unquestioning self-confidence of his generation to follow unswervingly the second course. Fortunately he died before his selected stone from the original quarry in Caen weathered so disastrously that it had to be replaced by Drew. The hapless Roe had long since been declared a bankrupt. But if one does not know what was there before, Street's east end has childlike consistency like the visionary basilicas painted by Van Eyck. The Norman transepts and the

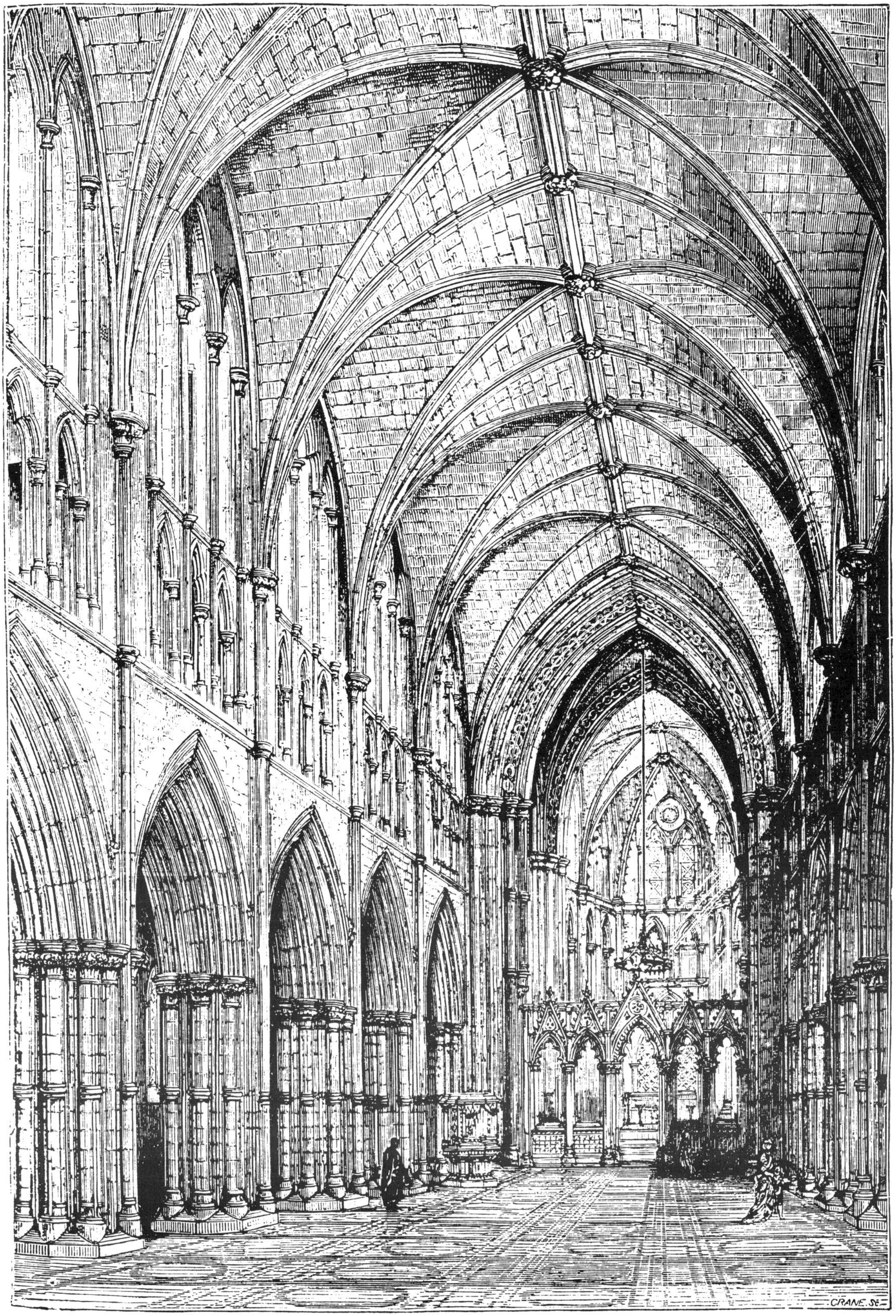

CHRISTCHURCH: INTERIOR AS RESTORED

Gothic north wall of the nave by 'the Christchurch Master' were retained. The remainder is Street, punctilious in his reconstruction but at his happiest when inventing—the tiny baptismal chapel and the flying bridge to the synod hall have no precedents. Street commanded anonymous obedience from his craftsmen—tiled floor (by Minton) based on 67 medieval prototypes discovered during excavations, stone carving by Thomas Earp and his assistants, stained glass throughout by Clayton and Bell. But in his furnishings he came full tilt against the Islamic dislike of religious imagery which still permeates the Church of Ireland and is the real reason for the continuous campaign to remove his rood screen. By depicting Christ as a lamb beneath a cross he caused an uproar. Today pressure comes from a group who believe that by getting rid of it, they will optically lengthen the interior. That the reverse is true Street knew full well—witness the stately pile up of its chevet against the central tower, that makes up in grandeur for what it lacks in size. The baptistery he added is a tiny rectangular space; into this he fits six vaults resting on two slender columns, thus defeating our experience in the assessment of dimensions: we regain the innocence of childhood in the thrall of a conjuror.

CHURCH STREET: **O'Neill's Pub**
This popular Old English half-timbered pub with corbelled gabled oriel at topmost level still survives as rebuilt by G.P. Sheridan in 1908.

CITY QUAY: **St Mary's Catholic Church**
Designed by John Bourke (after work had already started on a neo-Classical design by a Dublin builder) and completed in 1863, this church is the only Dublin example of his Gothic style. Bell tower and forecourt completed in 1900. Interior comparatively unaltered, having survived the threat of closure.

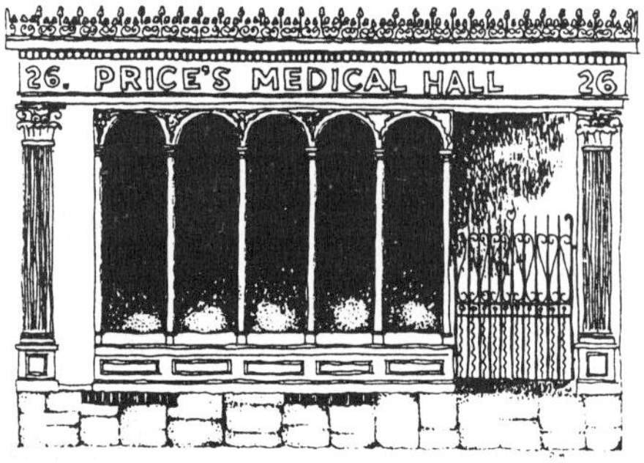

CLARE STREET: **No. 26, Price's Chemist**
Elegant shop front *c.*1840 with presumably at one time an interior of equal merit. However, the façade with its gently curving bow framed by Corinthian pilasters survives.

CLARENDON STREET: **St Teresa's Church**
Earliest surviving Catholic church in Dublin built in 1793 but twice extended during the 19th-century. Firstly by John Bourke in 1863, who added a transept and campanile to the east in his characteristic Italianate; secondly by O'Neill and Byrne, who added the western transept with its Lombardesque Revival façade to Clarendon Street and its adjoining monastery in a matching idiom. The interior contains a John Hogan's Dead Christ beneath the altar, having survived alterations after the Second Vatican Council. Stained glass in the chancel, pioneer windows by Earley and Powell.

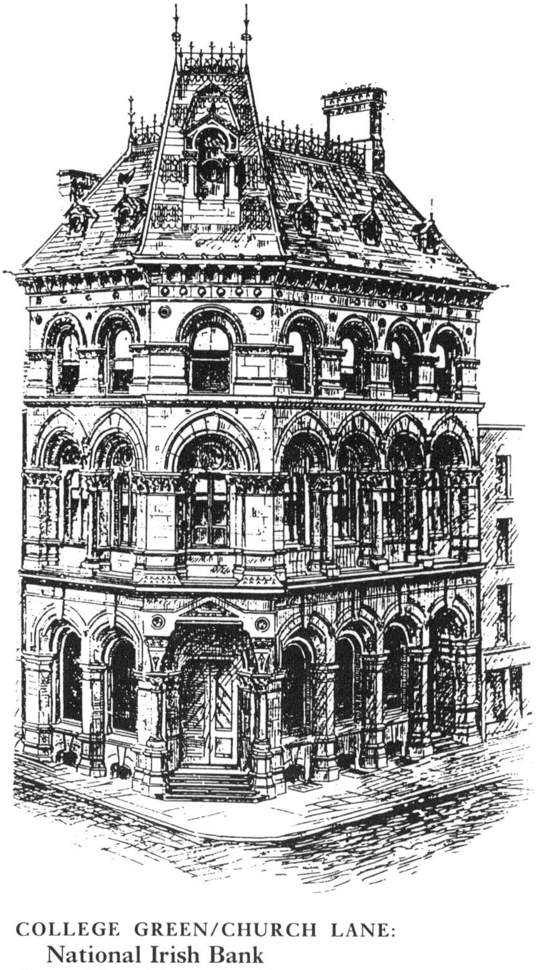

COLLEGE GREEN/CHURCH LANE: **National Irish Bank**
Opened in 1867 as the Union Bank with four bays on College Green and two bays on Church Lane; designed by William G. Murray and his assistant Thomas Drew. After six months the bank failed and their headquarters was bought by the Hibernian Bank, who employed Drew in 1873 to add further bays on either side

differentiated only by the change of initials above the windows. The prevailing idiom is Italian Gothic, with the French chateau taking over the roof level, notably the corner tower. Carving of stylized foliage and grotesque heads by Charles Harrison. Decoratively vaulted interior restored with panache by the present owners after a period of uncertainty. The only disruption is a recent goods entrance inserted into a rear range added by W.H. Byrne in 1925.

COLLEGE GREEN: No. 9

Built as the Sun Patriotic Insurance Company, as a fragment of Palladian urban palace with attached double-height Ionic colonnade articulating the upper floors. Architect: Horace Porter (1909).

COLLEGE GREEN: No. 12

The only Irish commission of A. Bloomfield Jackson; designed in 1899. A free Classical design that adds little to his reputation, though Jackson must have been happy enough with it to illustrate it in the *Building News*. This had been forgotten in 1905 by the *Irish Builder*: 'an insurance office in Dame Street which somehow does not appear to most architects to be designed by any architect at all'.

COLLEGE GREEN: No. 20, Allied Irish Bank

A Franco-Scottish design by W.H. Lynn dating from 1893 and built as the Royal Bank. A lively juxtaposition of a pedimented banking hall block and a circular office turret; executed in Caledonian sandstone. Neo-Adamesque interior with screens of widely spaced Corinthian columns upholding segmental vaults of painted glass.

COLLEGE GREEN: Allied Irish Bank

Formerly Provincial Bank. Designed by William Murray in 1863, who died while his fees were in dispute after the cost had almost doubled the estimate. Conventional, even pompous, Palladian seven-bay three-storey façade with the upper floors articulated by a double-height Corinthian order. Central pediment carved by S.F. Lynn mythologizing colonialism with a hard-working negro relegated to a corner. Murray's abilities were tested by the irregularity of the site so that the spectacular banking hall is unexpectedly two bays off-centre and approached up a half-flight in a vestibule ingeniously axised parallel to the façade. The awkward corners of the site are filled with staircases (one circular), so that no space is wasted. At the rear a robustly detailed round-arched office-block overlooks Fleet Street. Money had run out before the directors could house themselves on the *piano nobile* overlooking College Green in a splendour commensurate with that enjoyed by their customers below.

COLLEGE GREEN: No. 34, Bank of Ireland

Formerly the National Bank, founded by Daniel O'Connell, hence his statue by Andrew O'Connor. The architects of the early building (pre-1850) were Farrell and Barnes. After Geoghegan's success in the Royal Bank across the square, he was asked in 1863 to redesign the interior, and his top-lit circulation spaces with their slender columns gradually ascend to the new Suffolk Street rear entrance. The sculpture (surmounting the façade) by Pearse and Sharpe dates from a later remodelling (1889) trying to assert itself against its neighbour, Drew's overbearing Ulster Bank. It depicts Erin go Brá (between round tower and wolfhound) with a concessionary resemblance to Queen Victoria.

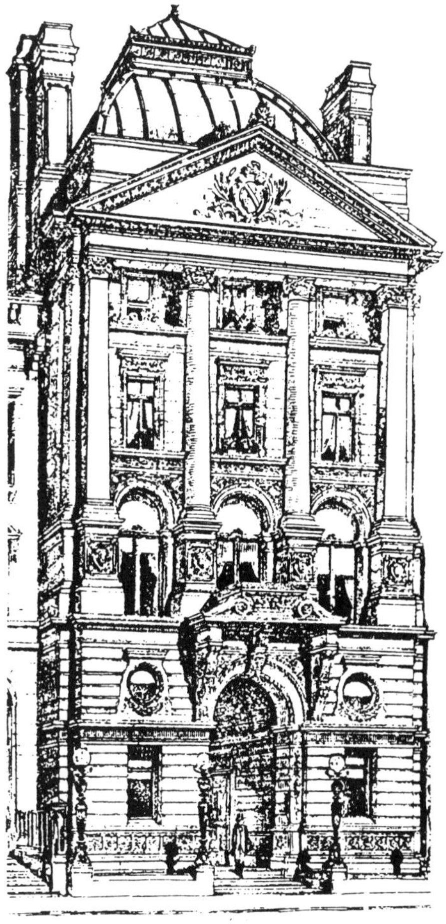

COLLEGE GREEN: Ulster Bank

Designed by Sir Thomas Drew and completed in 1891. Drew at his most confident—inflating Palladian monumentality with overweening self-importance in a constricted site. Its finest feature, the banking hall, with its richly stuccoed vault was inexcusably destroyed in 1976 'to improve the working conditions of the staff'.

COLLEGE GREEN: **Statues**
The eloquence of these statues by John Henry Foley—Henry Gratttan, Edmund Bourke and Oliver Goldsmith—has never been surpassed. His ability to capture the individuality of his subjects by their stance is still memorable, even if Grattan's eloquence is inaudible amid the noise of the city traffic, and it is the lugubrious Davis behind him who means far more to us, at least in the southern part of this island. Burke and Goldsmith were commissioned in 1862 and 1866, Grattan in 1876, but there are no traces of mid-Victorian pomposity.

CORK STREET: **Nurses' Home**
Heavily detailed, bay-windowed, and gabled red-brick nurses' home, set at right angles to the street and overlooking an unloved garden. Designed by W.F. Mitchell and built in the mid-1890s.

CROWN ALLEY: **Telephone Exchange**
Masterly use of load-bearing brick coursed with stone; asymmetrical façades at right angles to each other. Designed by T.M. Deane in 1897.

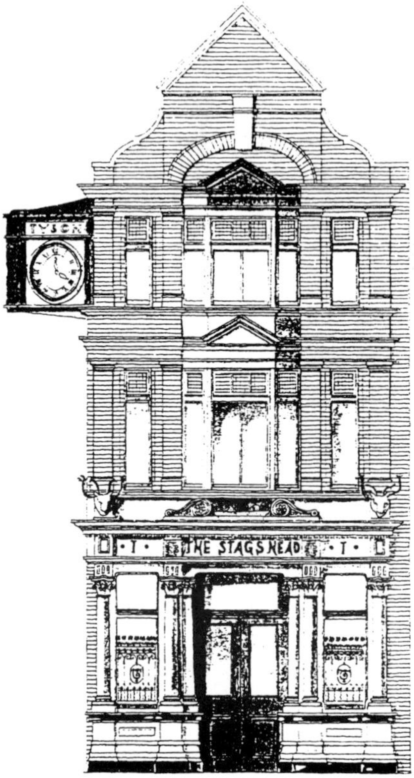

DAME COURT: **Stag's Head**
The most lavish of Dublin's late Victorian pubs (1895) and with its panelling, arcading and stained glass the secular counterpart to the religious architecture of its time. This is not surprising, since its designer, A.J. McLoughlin, was employed by George Ashlin to draw perspectives of his churches (and supervise Portrane). One of the few Dublin pubs to have been sympathetically maintained by subsequent owners.

DAME STREET: **Allied Irish Bank**
Formerly the Munster and Leinster Bank. The most monumental commercial commission designed by T.N. Deane (1872) based on the Museum in TCD built almost twenty years before. Both structures are two storeys in the Lombardesque-Romanesque manner with decorative marble insets modelled on the Palazzo Dario in Venice. Its resemblance to the Trinity Museum was reinforced by the bank's decision to extend in 1956 and to screen their new offices by lengthening the façade (architects, McDonnell and Dixon). The double-height banking hall has been treated with less sensitivity.

DAME STREET: **No. 31**
The finest commercial work by J.E. Rogers, opened in 1866. Built for the Caledonian Insurance Company on a narrow street frontage as ordained by the Wide Streets Commissioners but in utter defiance of their neo-Classical uniformity while keeping flush to the existing buildings. Built out of red brick horizontally articulated from the limestone ground-floor arcade by a band of red marble. Colonettes of polished pink granite frame the entrance and adjoining windows. Above, grey limestone string courses and voussoirs incised with stylized decoration verging on the Celtic Revival. Interior altered out of all recognition.

DAME STREET: **Nos. 13-16**
Gothic Revival shop. Designed by J.J. O'Callaghan (1879).

DAME STREET: **No. 46**
Designed by T.N. Deane in 1868; directly inspired by the London head office of Crown Life designed ten years before by Benjamin Woodward (at that moment being demolished to make room for Blackfriars Bridge; Deane also built a London replacement in Fleet Street, which has also been demolished). This building survived an effort by its owners, Hibernian Insurance, to demolish it *c.*1975—due to Skidmore Owings and Merrill recommending

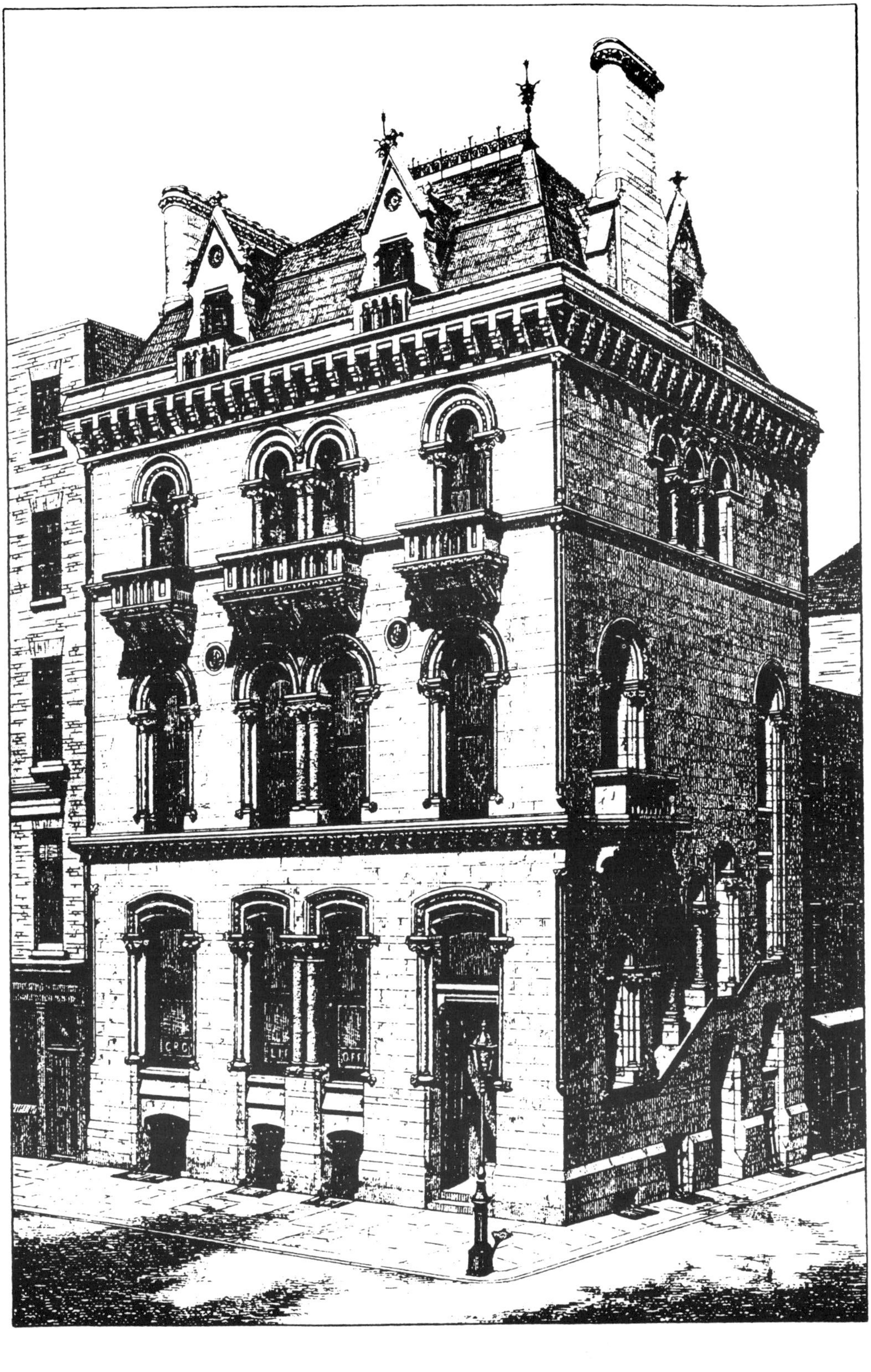

to their clients, CIE, that it was one of only two buildings worth preserving in Temple Bar.

Built in the Lombardesque idiom with polychromatic voussoirs above segemental windows to Dame Street; a semi-circular-headed stepped arcade enlivens the Fownes Street elevation and lights the principal staircase. Its great defect is that the main entrance appears to be a service door. Despite its corbelled balconies, strongly modelled roofscape and carving by Charles Harrison, the design lacks the subtlety of the Caledonian across the street.

DAME STREET: **No. 40**

Designed by the Edinburgh architect David Bryce and built in 1863. A small robust palazzo in serene occupation of its corner site. The vertical pilasters that articulate to the upper floors are balanced by the horizontal stonework of the two lower floors.

DAME STREET: **Olympia Theatre**

Remodelled in 1897 by R.N. Bruton from what was known at that time as Dan Lowry's music hall (designed by J.J. O'Callaghan in 1879) after a fire that claimed the life of the manager, identifiable by the keys as observed by the six-year-old Winston Churchill. Porch by Saracen Ironworks when remodelled by James Farrell *c.*1900. Superb interior, the only Victorian theatre in Ireland to retain its Gods. Almost redeveloped during the 1970s, it survived due to an enthusiastic restoration committee set up to repair the interior after the proscenium arch had collapsed during the rehearsal of *Joseph and his Amazing Technicolour Dream Coat.*

DAWSON STREET: **Nos. 26-8, Dawson Chambers**

A Georgian terrace rebuilt by G.P. Sheridan (1911) in a discreet Arts and Crafts idiom, with curved bay windows set above decorative spandrels. Admired by Richard Neutra during a walk round Dublin.

DAWSON STREET: **No. 36**

Polish granite columns uphold an arcaded shopfront with polychromatic marble spheres set into the granite spandrels. Designed by William Caldbeck for a clothier called Sexton in 1860.

DAWSON STREET: **Nos. 57-8, Hodges Figgis**

Formerly Drummonds. The most extrovert of Albert Murray's Dutch Revival carried out in 1903—his favourite blend of red brick and golden terracotta, called 'Murray's Mellow Mixture' after a popular tobacco of the day. Multi-scrolled many-tiered gable still holds its own against the adjoining grids of recent office blocks.

DAWSON STREET: **Mansion House**

An extra hall was added to Semple's Round Room beside the Mansion House by an obscure Dublin architect called D.J. Freeman in 1895. He also added the elaborate cast-iron canopy over the steps leading up to the front door.

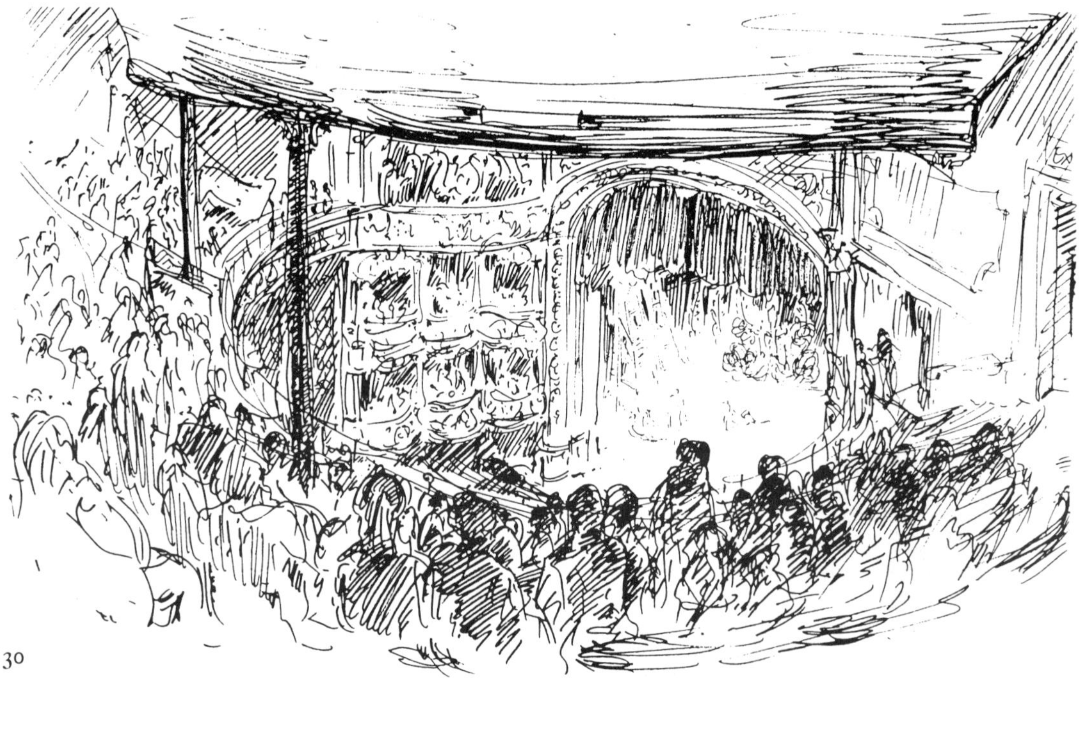

DAWSON STREET: Royal Irish Academy

No planning regulations hindered the RIA *c.*1850 from filling in their back garden with a top-lit library and a museum, impeccably maintaining the Georgian house as a buffer against the outside world. These quiet luminous high-ceiling rooms fuse an austere neo-Classicism with a technology that has never been surpassed. This is due to the collaboration of the architect Frederick Clarendon with the inventor Robert Mallet. Mallet fabricated the ironwork of the balconies with work-tops cantilevered off the balustrades; he also provided the heating, lighting and ventilation. In the reading room he glazed the four sides of a trapezoidal lantern, which he then subdivided by a series of floating partitions perforated underneath so that they act as ducts to extract the air. The resulting luminosity parallels the recent Houston Art Gallery by a latter-day Mallet, Peter Rice.

DAWSON STREET: St Ann's

The superb Roman Baroque façade of St Ann's, designed by Isaac Willis in 1720, remained pitifully incomplete until its demolition by T.N. Deane in 1868. Deane's own Lombardo-Romanesque façade in its turn has never been finished. The highest tower to the north has a simple conical cap instead of a planned massive belfry, so that the intended diagonal gesture sweeping up from Deane's adjoining rectory has been cut short. But the central doorway, the arcade and rose windows above look impressive from Anne Street, despite being exposed as a mere screen when one enters. No Dublin Georgian church has more stained glass concealing from the worshippers the intrusions of surrounding office development; offices come so close that they reduce the impact of the three windows on the southern aisle by Wilhelmina Geddes—her only Dublin City commission. On the opposite side, a window by Rhind. In the chancel, a resurrection by Mayer has replaced the so-called Knox window by Warrington, now re-sited in the north-west corner. A contributor to the *Dublin Builder* suggested that Knox, who spent his life smashing up stained-glass windows, would have been appalled by being depicted in stained glass himself. Also in the chancel is a Warrington window commemorating the poetess Felicia Hemans. The gallery windows, all from the mid-1860s (apart from one replacement) are the most remarkable achievement in Dublin of the O'Connor family, whose contribution to Irish stained glass has been so overshadowed by the next generation. Further glass by Heaton, Butler and Bayne.

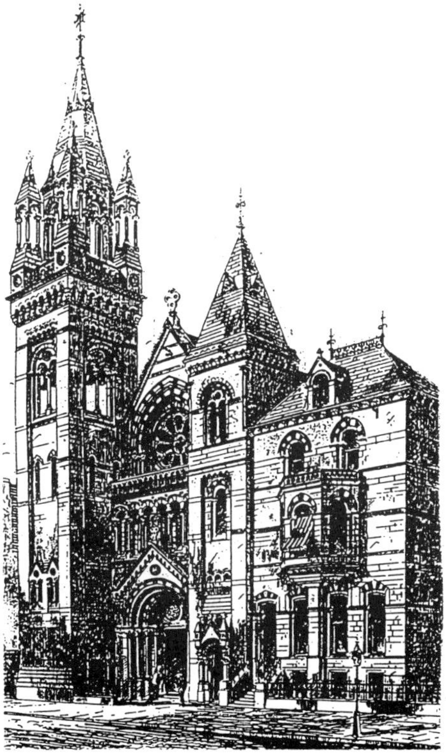

D'OLIER STREET: D'Olier Chambers

J.F. Fuller was the architect chosen by Gallagher's Tobacco Company. Built in 1891 out of yellow brick and terracotta on yet another prominent corner site. Crowned by arcaded chimneys surmounting scrolled gables on adjoining elevations.

DOLPHIN'S BARN: Methodist Church

Most of George Beckett's Methodist churches were crisply Gothic. Dolphin's Barn (completed in 1902) has a trim neo-Byzantine exterior built out of red brick to match the neighbourhood. Rational interior devoid of historicist detailing: a central octagon surrounded by an arcaded aisle (now disused as a church and made into a youth centre).

DONORE AVENUE: St Catherine's Church

One of the last Gothic Church of Ireland to be built in Dublin using simple red brick and a modest scale, but it still took fifteen years to build (1897-1912); architect, Robert Stirling. Interior made memorable by its stained glass. Three windows by M. Healy (Hope, St Catherine, St Victor) and one by O'Brien (St Columba).

EARLSFORT TERRACE: National Concert Hall

Originally designed by Alfred Gresham Jones as an assembly hall for the 1863 Dublin Exhibition to remain after his adjoining crystal palace had been dismantled. Contemporary with William Barre's Ulster Assembly Hall that it now even more resembles since its conversion into the National Concert Hall which has toned down its Corinthian fruitiness. The ground floor sculpture gallery was linked to the upper picture gallery by a monumental staircase; these spaces were cunningly converted into foyers in 1981 by the OPW architects Noel DeChenu, Michael O'Doherty, Allen Smith. Extended first as a Royal College by an obscure architect, Edward Kavanagh (1884), retaining the Italianate idiom with a campanile disguising its ventilation shaft; and then by R.M. Butler with a neo-Classical entry block won in competition (1912). Constructed entirely in solid limestone to give a doleful air to this last tribute to Gandon: the composition restates the river façade of the Custom House. Refined Grecian joinery. One doorway was shattered by a student riot, others replaced by glass doors during the conversion. The final indignity is the refusal of the modern development across the street to honour the axis. The entrance gates designed by Jones survive grasped by powerful cast-iron hands that serve as hinges. Stained glass in the Kevin Barry room by the Clarke Studios.

ESSEX STREET: **The Granary**
Formerly Nugents. Red-brick and stone Gothic Revival pub built to outlast all competition in 1879, the date inscribed on the façade. Carefully adapted to an acutely angled site by deploying a canted recess in an outer archway. Architect, J.J. O'Callaghan. Completed in 1891.

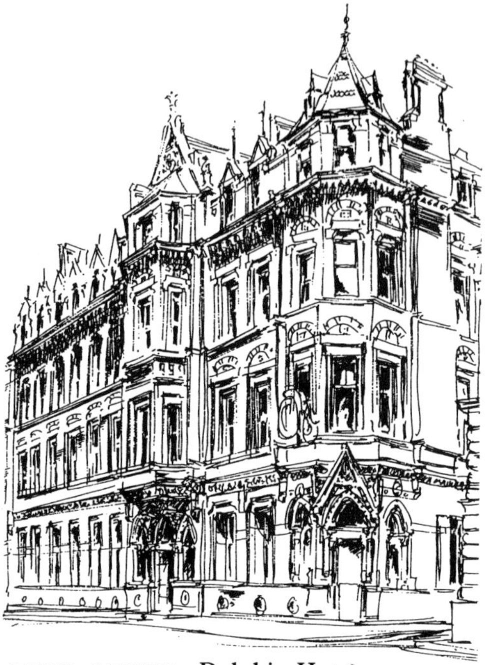

ESSEX STREET: **Dolphin Hotel**
Gothic Revival, in red brick with stone trimming, livened up by a diagonal corner entrance surmounted by carved dolphins. Designed by J.J. O'Callaghan in 1898. Closed and due for demolition, the exterior was reprieved. O'Callaghan's interiors were destroyed along with the early Art Deco cocktail bar. But the exterior has been retained as memories of Dublin's most famous steakhouse merge into myths.

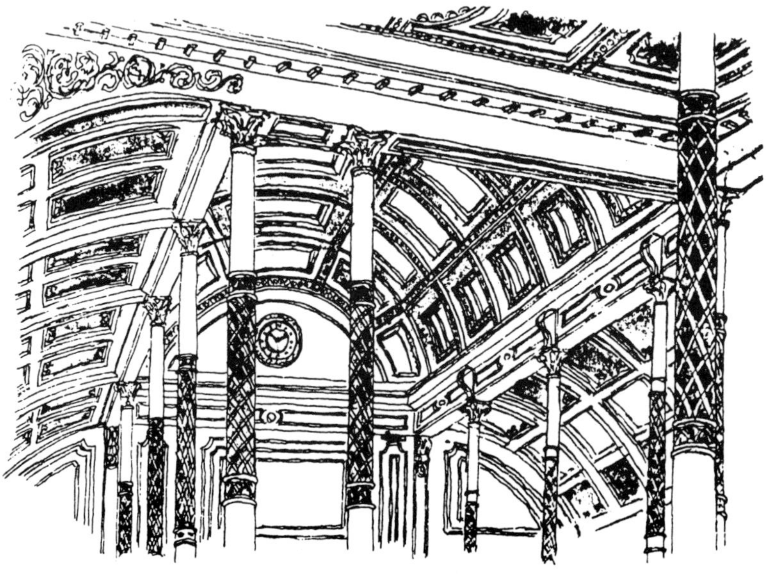

AIB, FOSTER PLACE

FITZWILLIAM PLACE: **No. 28**
One of the few Victorian Gothic townhouses; free-standing when built but later linked by a standard Georgian infill to the existing terrace. Its exposed side wall sports a triple H in polychromatic brickwork standing for Hans Henry Hamilton, who had commissioned his house from Deane and Woodward in 1855. The corner site permits a rear wing with balconies and French windows overlooking a garden with stables at the rear. Internally the house follows Georgian precedents but with Gothic detailing. The most medieval interior is the chapel added by George Ashlin for Christopher Palles, the subsequent owner.

FOSTER PLACE: **Allied Irish Bank**
Formerly the Royal Bank. An uneventful exterior (apart from an incised neo-Classical porch added by George Papworth *c.*1850) does not prepare us for Dublin's finest Victorian banking hall added at the rear by Charles Geoghegan in 1859. Geoghegan removed the first floor, so that one enters a double-height hall that leads directly into a transitional arched bay before the luminous banking hall: a delicately glazed and coffered barrel vault rises from scrolled freizes upheld by rows of slim cast-iron diapered Corinthian columns that screen quarter-circle vaulted side aisles. An arcaded mezzantine to ensure constant supervision was never executed. The opulently scrolled 120ft curving counter maintains a generous but impenetrable barrier between cashiers and customers.

FRANCIS STREET: **Iveagh Markets**
Designed by Frederick Hicks, who reveals his Banbury origins with a robust Wrennish façade of red brick and stone dressings screening a functional cast-iron galleried market hall and dependencies. Dated 1902.

FRANCIS STREET: **St Nicholas in Myra**
One of the finest of Dublin's Classical churches, built in 1829-34 by John Leeson. Patrick Byrne also worked here in 1858. He blocked up the windows to provide a more temple-like setting for John Hogan's *pietà* above a neo-Classical Italian altar flanked by angels. Hogan also is thought to have modelled the tableaux above the side altars; further statuary by John Smith. Portico and campanile completed by John Bourke in 1860. The baptistery contains stained glass windows in the style of Joshua Clarke. In the nuptial chapel a tiny scene by Harry Clarke's studios (1928). Saucer dome above the crossing with neo-Byzantine painting by Charles O'Byrne; segmental ceiling recently stencilled by Patrick Gorton. The only church in the city to preserve intact two sets of communion rails.

GRAFTON STREET: **No. 2**
Corner site comfortably occupied by a red sandstone and matching brick neo-Tudor redevelopment by L. McDonnell (1902). Shops below, mullioned offices above.

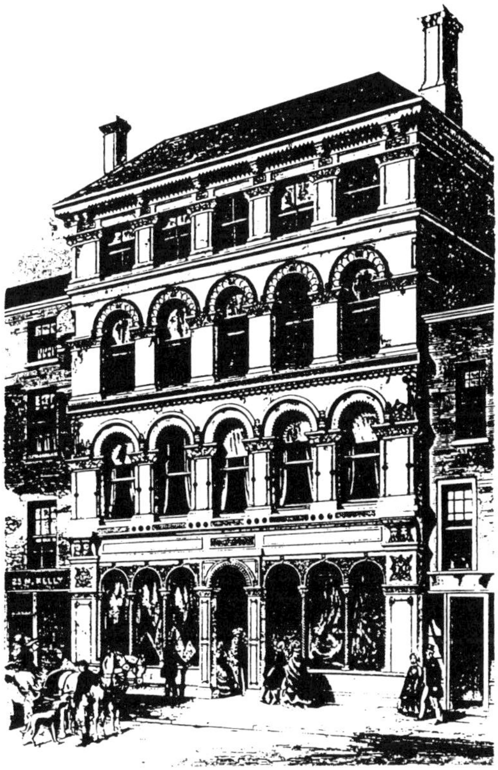

GRAFTON STREET: **No. 26**
It is paradoxical that the first attempt to introduce the Celtic Revival onto the streets of Dublin should have been made by an English authority on historical ornament, Matthew Digby Wyatt, who lectured at the V. and A. He rebuilt a three-storied Georgian house to have four floors, each arcaded differently as they diminish in height—a lively concept but grimly executed in grey cement. Politely admired as an example of the National Style, there have been no imitators.

GRAFTON STREET: **Allied Irish Bank**
A late work by W.H. Lynn (1903) built for the Royal Bank. The Classical façade is an abbreviated version of his Bank Buildings in Castle Place, Belfast (q.v.). Charles Geoghegan installed here Dublin's first hydraulic lift. In the 1960s an extra floor was inserted which ruined the proportions of Lynn's banking hall.

GRAFTON STREET: **Bewley's**
Famous Dublin cafe meeting-place of artists, students, bankers, housewives and coffee-

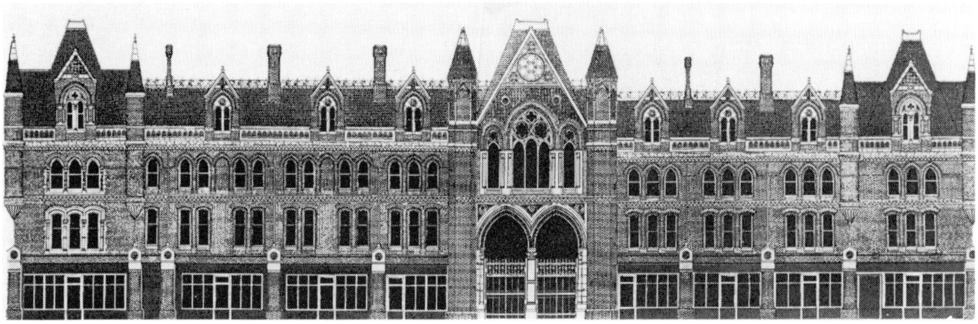

sipping observers of their fellow humans who were once attended by lace-aproned waitresses but now have to serve themselves. Designed in 1911 by A.G.C. Millar with panelled Tudor Revival walls and plasterwork that reverts to rococo but with side-long glances to Art Nouveau. That style is also suggested by the attenuated red velvet couchettes that line the walls. All this occurs in the South George's Street and the Westmoreland Street branches, designed also by Millar the year before. However, here the neo-Egyptian entrance from Johnson's Lane is unique, as are the six stained-glass windows designed by Harry Clarke in 1928 in the rear room during its remodelling by McDonnell and Dixon. All branches have been adjusted to contemporary trends, at first disastrously but now with more sympathy and success.

GRAFTON STREET: **Fox's Cigars**
Formerly the Commercial Union Assurance Co. The Gothic Revival here in full spate turns an awkward corner with consummate ease, juxtaposing varied gables to an octagonal lantern. Designed in 1881 by Thomas Newenham, but the main input came from his son, Thomas Manly Deane, who had just returned from the office of William Burges. Completed in 1885.

GREAT GEORGE'S STREET, SOUTH: **No. 51, Long Hall Pub**
Jolly exterior with standard Georgian street elevation decked out with red and gold as if for a coronation. Interior still atmospheric, though short of many of its treasures such as Jack B. Yeatses and Dresden vases dizzily perched on top of its wooden screens. But a bewildering array of chandeliers survives to spangle the interior with light, while the adjoining hall is kept discreetly dim. This is connected to the pub by sliding panels so that women can drink unobserved as if protected by confessionals. Designer unknown.

GREAT GEORGE'S STREET, SOUTH: **South City Markets**
The exuberance of Gothic Revival when adapted to commercial urban development is epitomized by this entire street block rebuilt round a glass-covered market using imperishable red brick and terracotta; by the Bradford architects Lockwood and Mawson after winning a competition in 1878, the year of Lockwood's death. What we see today is a much more muted restoration by W.H. Byrne after a serious fire destroyed the glass-roofed market in 1892. Byrne was responsible for introducing the present intercepting arcades; he also built at the same time many of the shops in the surrounding streets; but he removed the central tower and the corner spires from the Georges Street frontage. The complex was due to be demolished twenty-five years ago but was reprieved and revived to float serenely above the strident fascias of supermarkets, nesting like rival cuckoos oblivious to the turrets and pinnacles they disfigure. Note the pentagonal pavilion at the corner of Drury Street and Exchequer Street modelled on Manchester Townhall.

HARCOURT STREET: **The Station**
After a long career building identical workhouses throughout the country, George Wilkinson came up in 1859 with a successful adaptation of monumental Roman Baroque. Craig praises its blend of brick, rubble calp and dressed granite. The station is entered through a triumphal arch flanked by colonnades; the offices, so prominent in the other Dublin stations, are relegated to the rear. The platform is on the first floor because the rail-line came in across the existing streets. The shed was built as an apsidally ended terminus, although on one memorable occasion a train treated it as a transit station, and the engine was photographed emerging from the apse to hang like a caterpillar over the street. Its hidden architectural treasures are the awe-inspiring vaults beneath the platform; these the practically-minded Victorians had built as a bonded spirit store. Recently

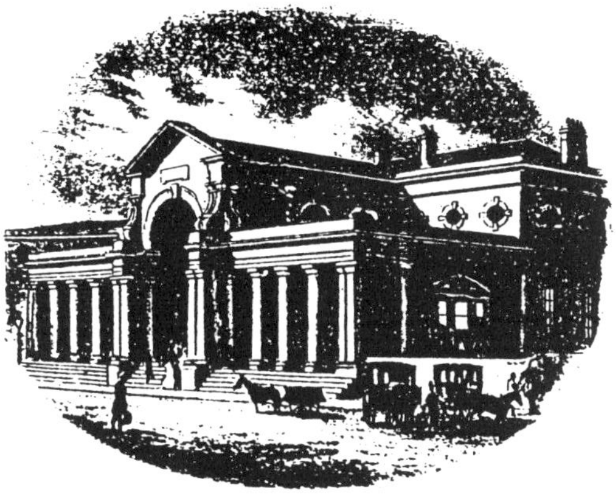

restored to its original use and also to house an exhibition on the firm of Findlaters.

HARCOURT TERRACE: **No. 6**
Centrepiece of an urban terrace created by tacking on a neo-Classical façade to a series of existing Georgian houses *c.* 1840. Attributable to Daniel Robertson, who was engaged on the nearby church of St Matthias (now demolished).

HARCOURT TERRACE: **Housing for Clergyman's Widows**
Built as the Asylum for Aged Governesses. Red brick; Gothic Revival. Designed by J.H. Bridgford, who exhibited his scheme in the RHA of 1879.

HARRINGTON STREET: **Catholic Church**
One of the last group of Gothic Revival churches designed by the partnership of E.W. Pugin and George Ashlin, begun in 1867 and completed in 1872. Ashlin later added the charmless presbytery. The church is also harsh but is lightened by the spacious chancel. Altar designed by W.H. Byrne in 1884. Cast-iron Gothic pews.

HARRY STREET: **Bruxelles, No. 7**
Brick and stone Flemish Gothic pub (originally Mooney's) enlivened by a perky corbelled staircase turret that overhangs the street like a signboard. Lavishly decorated interior with painting and mosaics framed by arcading *c.* 1890. The finest of the many Dublin pubs designed by J.J. O'Callaghan.

HATCH STREET: **University Hall**
The last Gothic Revival public building to be erected in Dublin; designed in 1913 by C.B. Powell for the Jesuits to serve as a student residence with accommodation grouped round a central quad sealed off from the corruption of the outside world. Incisively detailed; in red brick with stone trimmings revealing Powell's proverbial crankiness (cycling round Dublin with a long white beard he was known as 'God-on-a-bike'). Stained glass in the chapel by Evie Hone. Note the oriel that appears to rest on a slender column excavated from the surrounding brickwork.

HEUSTON STATION:
Formerly Kingsbridge Station. Commissioned in 1846 from Sancton Wood, the English architect, by the great Western Railway who had already built the station shed to the designs of Sir John McNeill. McNeill's light and functional architecture is so apt that it has never been altered. The decision to block the rail-lines with a robust fruity palazzo was so retrogressive that Dublin's transport system has never recovered. However, judged as architecture, Sancton Wood's station is an effortless success, at least externally. *Piano nobile* articulated by projecting Corinthian columns nicely balanced against twin flanking domed campanile. There were no funds left when it came to the decoration of the interior, and hideous redevelopment has removed from public view the embarrassment of its rear façade.

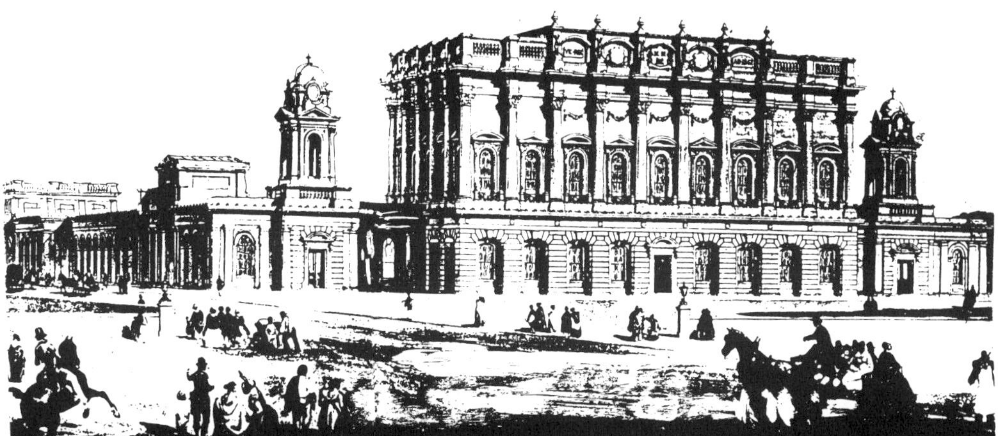

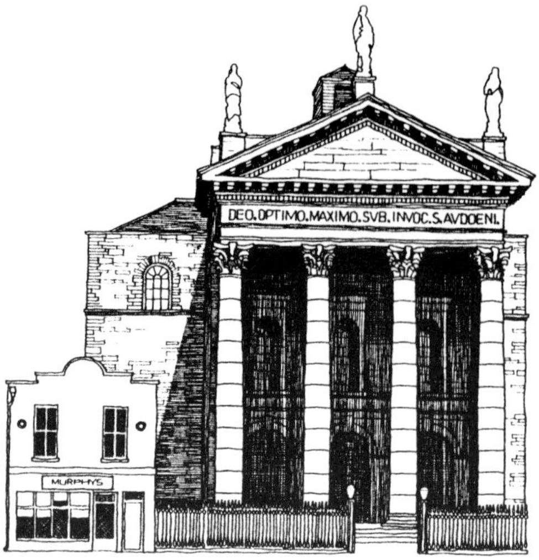

HIGH STREET: **St Audoen's Church**
The masterpiece of Patrick Byrne built in 1841-6 except for the granite portico, added in 1893 by George Ashlin to relieve Byrne's external austerity, today only appreciable from the rear where it dominates Dublin's reconstructed walls—a fortress of the Faith prefiguring in its starkness the post-war German churches of Rudolf Schwarz. The rear exposes the double-storied crypt converted (until recently), into a Viking adventure centre. The church has less happily been partitioned off so that Byrne's sumptuously Italianate nave (with its bays articulated by fluted Corinthian pilasters illuminated by lunettes cut into the barrel-vaulting) is impossible to see. The crossing which is visible suffers from the loss of the central dome which collapsed in 1880. What we see today is a flat-ceilinged substitute. Stained glass lunette by Earley (1903). Madonna sculpted by Bonanni (1849).

JAMES STREET: **Arthur Guinness & Co.**
Although Sir Benjamin Lee Guinness was an amateur architect himself, and his three sons privately commissioned the leading architects of their day, they never attached any aesthetic importance to the brewery, leaving everything that had to be built in charge of the resident engineer. This post was held by Samuel Geoghegan (1845-1928) throughout a long career. George Wilkinson was responsible for the rebuilding of the main offices that front on to James Street, externally respectable but uninspired. The interiors retain atmospheric, mahogany-panelled offices and boardrooms due to the late Lord Moyne's hostility to change. But one can attribute also to Geoghegan other Guinness buildings such as the superb stone warehouse curved round the terminus of the Guinness canal, made obsolete when the canal was filled in and sold off to store furniture. One can also attribute to him the Hop Store (1876-82), built in two phases, now restored as an art gallery and exhibition centre with the Guinness visitors' centre on the ground floor. This has been well restored by Scott Tallon Walker, but the adjoining Belview housing which Geoghegan designed for the Guinness employees has been demolished by Dublin Corporation; likewise his impressive kiln house that overlooked the Liffey.

In 1875, the engineering firm of Ross and Baily were called in to build the Brew House behind the office and then the Robert Street Store (1884) designed by Robert Worthington, a massive vaulted, multi-storied structure clad with the tallest load-bearing brick walls of its time. Cast-iron fluted Doric columns at ground level make a striking setting for the locomotive designed by Geoghegan himself. He also built the double revolving ramp under James Street. But as a structure this was to be surpassed by the Market Street Store House built in 1900-2 on a widely spaced steel frame following the most advanced technology of the time, not

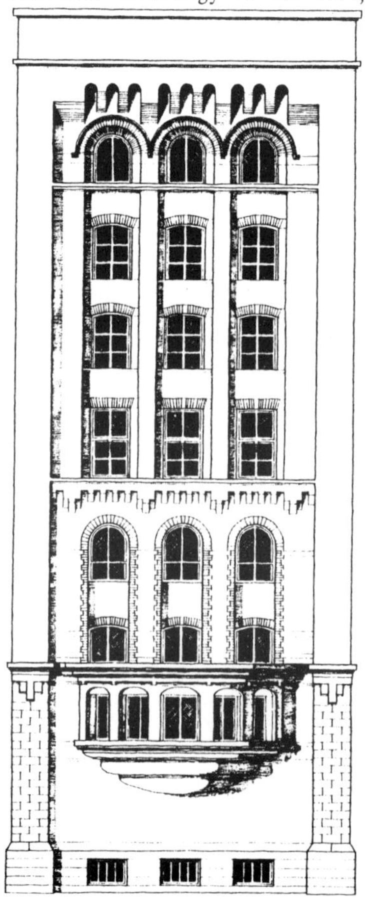

MARKET STREET STOREHOUSE

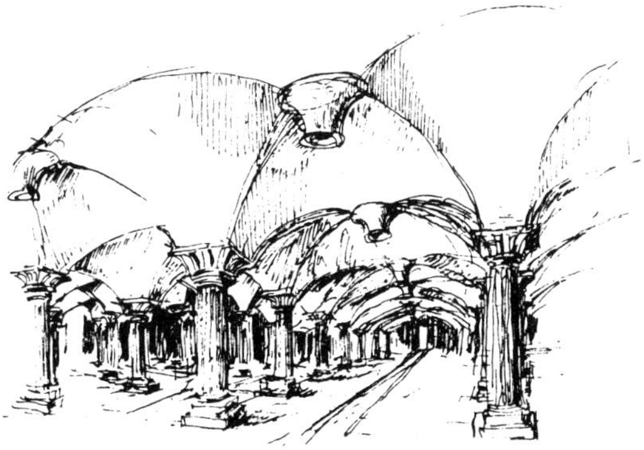

ROBERT STREET STOREHOUSE

merely in the structure but in the outward expression of that structure. The arcaded elevations soar upwards clad with granite and polychromatic brick, held in place by triple-bay corner bastions crowned with machicolated parapets. At first-floor level there are giant oriels corbelled out along one of the elevations like glasses of stout, brimful of froth. The steel structure tapers at every floor level, allowing more natural light to penetrate down nine floors from the glazed roof. The designer of this would have remained conjectural were it not for an inspection by the Institute. They were taken round by A.H. Hignett, the Guinness engineer, and they commented on how today an engineer like Hignett could design like an architect as he had absorbed the architectural innovations of Chicago. The steelwork was by Sir William Arnott; the builders M'Laughlin & Harvey. At the present time Hignett's masterpiece is obsolete and empty, reprieved a few years ago due to the sheer cost of its demolition.

JAMES STREET: **St James' Church**
Built by Patrick Byrne in his pedantic version of the Gothic Revival carefully adapted to an irregular site so that the off-centre axis is never perceived. Foundation stone laid by Daniel O'Connell in 1844; completed 1854. The best stained-glass window in Dublin by Michael O'Connor *c.*1860 is above the high altar. Wooden screen by Boyle exhibited in the Dublin Exhibition of 1861.

JOHN DILLON STREET: **Housing**
A Dublin Artisan Dwelling Company project (less ambitious than Crampton Buildings: q.v.). Charles Ashworth here combines one- and two-storey brick housing, skilfully turning corners by giving projecting gables to the terminal houses. This gives a sense of medieval urban scale to the streetscape dominated by St Patrick's Cathedral, which rises above the huddled roofs from the valley below.

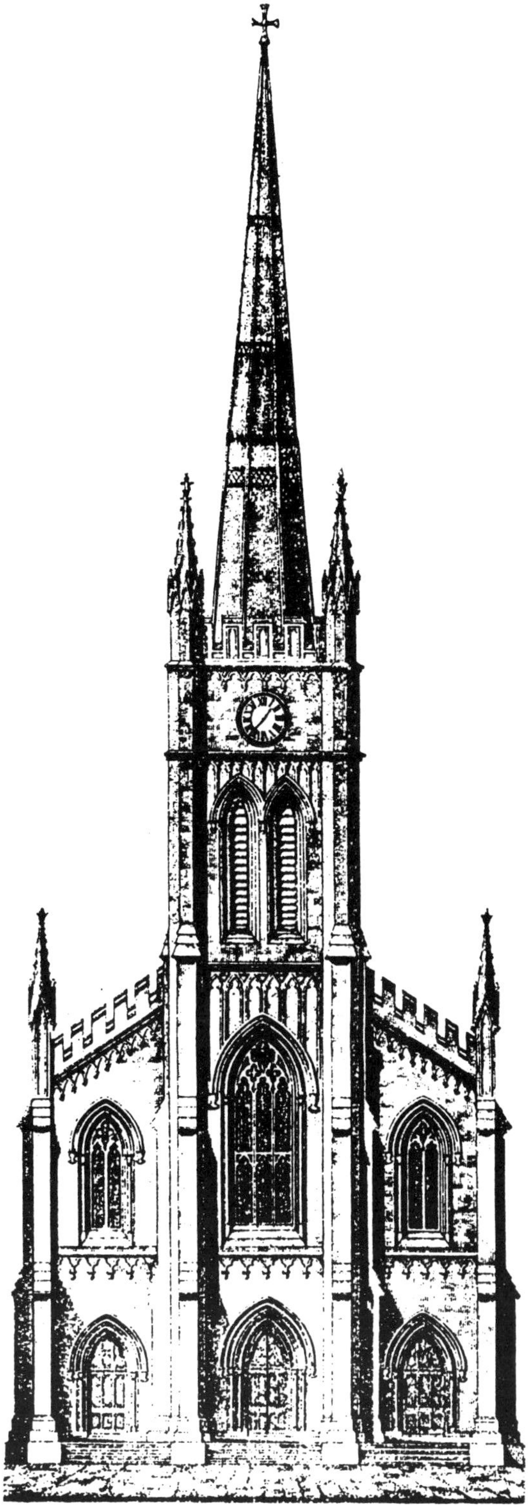

KEVIN STREET: **Moravian Church**
This two-storied pedimented façade (its religious imagery pasted over after its transformation into a commercial concern in 1980) still downfaces would-be demolitioners from the city's road widening department. Architect, O'Callaghan and Webb, *c*.1905.

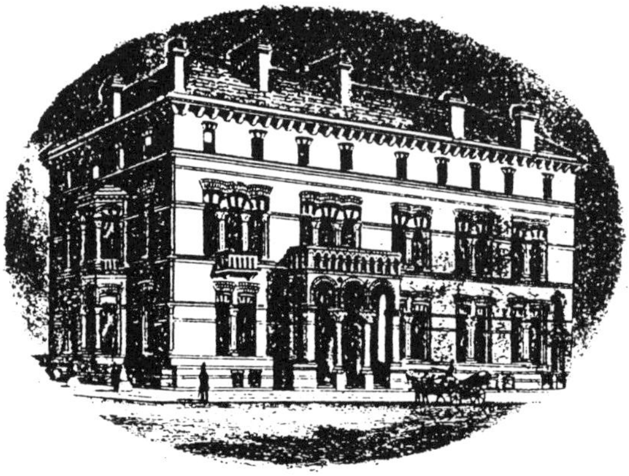

KILDARE STREET: **Alliance Française and Genealogical Museum**
Until 1971 this was the Kildare Street Club, the intact summation of Deane and Woodward's architecture, begun in 1859 and completed in November 1861 after Woodward's death. The realization of their Government Offices (competition entry), except that here the inspiration was not Gothic but Byzantine in deference to its Georgian neighbours. In order to catch as much light as possible, the plate-glass windows are inserted behind delicate stone limestone columnar screens contrasting with the polychromatic voussoirs, the massive arcaded porch, the corbelled cornice and sculptural chimneystacks (the latter now removed). The central bay window of the side elevation rests not on the expected corner piers but on detached columns. The façades are horizontally articulated by carved Portland stone string courses that in Girouard's words are the frothy cream through which one savours the rich coffee of the red brick. The carved menagerie clustered round the pedestals at eye level including the celebrated monkeys playing billiards (doubtlessly with a skill inherited by the club members entitled by Darwin to claim them as forebears) has been attributed by Harbison to Charles Harrison on the basis of sketchbooks preserved by the family. The firm that got the credit was Purdy and Outhwaite, who went bankrupt before the completion of the job.

Harrison's internal carving of the staircase hall that included snakes, snails and butterflies was destroyed (apart from a few fragments now in Tullynally) when the staircase hall was replaced in 1971 by lavatories and lifts. Victorian Dublin lost its most spectacular interior, a double-tiered cortile through which coiled the staircase: this started within the lower arcade to emerge and vault across the central void, permitting a continuous gallery at first-floor level. The circulation problems that remained unsolved in the Trinity Museum had been triumphantly overcome with a double use of concentrated space. The major rooms as fitted out by Sibthorpes with their plaster friezes and corbelled beams unexpectedly survive, although subdivided by mezzanines to double the office space. Only the diningroom retains its original dimensions, a conscientious replication rather than a restoration by the OPW. The top-lit rooms at the rear that included a smoking room modelled on the Glastonbury Kitchen and a racquet court once said to have been the best in Europe have been destroyed over the last fifty years (victims of aesthetic prejudice): the architect who recommended the removal of the staircase hall told his client that it was the ugliest in Dublin.

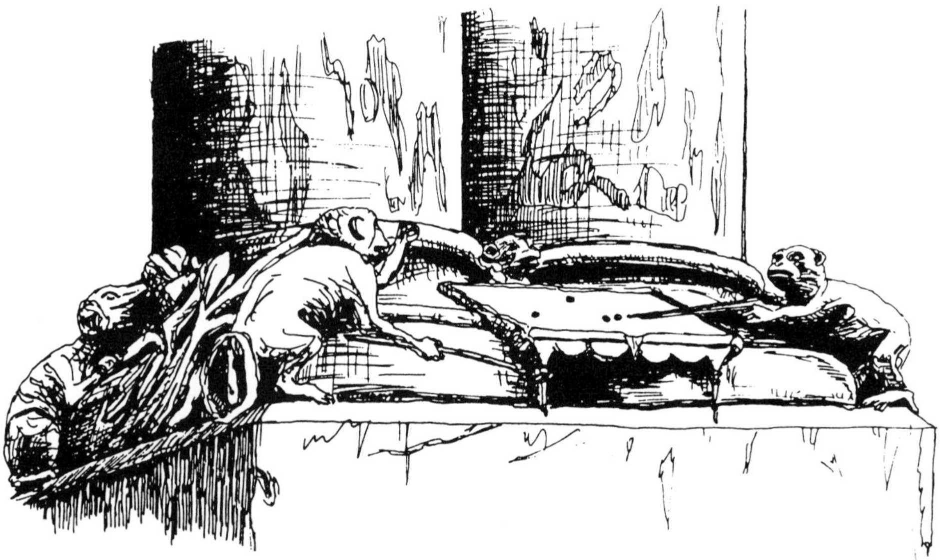

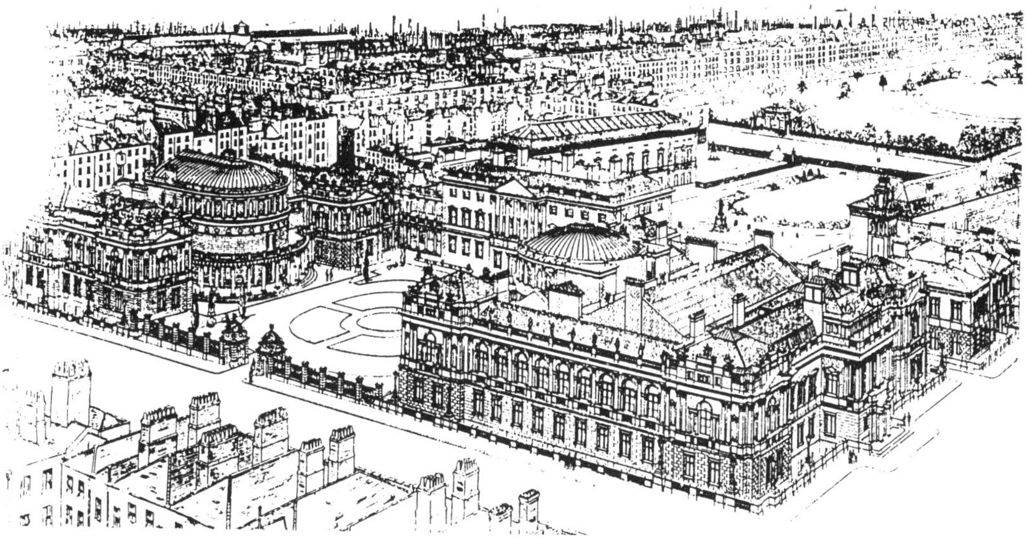

THE DEANES' FIRST SCHEME FOR THE LIBRARY AND MUSEUM

KILDARE STREET: **National Library and Museum**

The competition held in 1885 was won by Thomas Newenham Deane, assisted by his son Thomas Manley Deane. They deserved to win, since their concept of twin rotundas facing each other across the forecourt of Leinster House, which they intended to dramatize with a projecting portico, ensured enough geometrical variety to counterbalance the bulk of building necessary to accommodate the brief. A further clever device was to develop the rotunda of the library into the apse of the barrel-vaulted reading room so that while the library is the smaller building it looks the more monumental. However, stylistic lapses intrude: the junction of the corner pavilions is especially awkward, and the Corinthian order is used throughout with such profusion as to be ultimately devalued. The Mountcharles sandstone has deteriorated so badly that it has been replaced in the Library. Subsequent development has not been helpful to the ambitions of the south façade of the Museum, designed on the basis that Kildare Place would be made longer. The obstructive Georgian houses have been demolished but the square was never extended. In the library, site limitations cramp the imperial staircase into suburban dimensions and would-be expansionists are faced with an impossible scenario. In the Museum only a shortage of funds and a miraculous recovery from what had been branded incurable dry rot saved it from being rebuilt as government offices. Instead there is now a gradual realization of its internal grandeur. The entry rotunda modelled on Schinkel's Alte Museum in Berlin is now cleared of plaster replicas of Celtic crosses. The majolica in the adjoining rooms has been cleaned during a stylish renovation to provide a surreal setting to de Valera's boots. The gallery's central hall with its decorated ironwork upholding a glazed roof is recovering its original elegance although not as yet its potted palms.

So why are these two palaces of culture only celebrated for their contents and for those who once frequented them. The answer lies in the Oxford Museum built thirty years before by T.N. Deane and Woodward to be one of the most innovative of its time. The equivalents of Dublin's National Library and Museum were being built throughout Europe in the 1880 to display the origins of each nation's past. The work of T.N. Deane had in the intervening years lost its radicalism, to become provincial yet imperialistic, devoid of Irish interest. Having exported Irish craftsmen to Oxford, Deane now imported the Cambi from Siena into Dublin to carve his neo-Renaissance woodwork.

KILDARE STREET: **College of Physicians**

One of the least altered of Dublin's High Victorian interiors concealed behind a Palladian façade where the choice of a defective Scottish sandstone led to its complete replacement *c.*1960. Designed by William Murray, who won a competition held in 1861. As in his Allied Irish Bank, College Green (q.v.), the conventionality of the façade conceals a resourceful use of a difficult site. Tiled vestibule presided over by marble worthies; imperial staircase rising to the library directly overhead, but giving access at the half-landing to the coved reception hall. From this a link between two light-wells leads to the Convocation Hall, completed in 1874 by McCurdy and Mitchell.

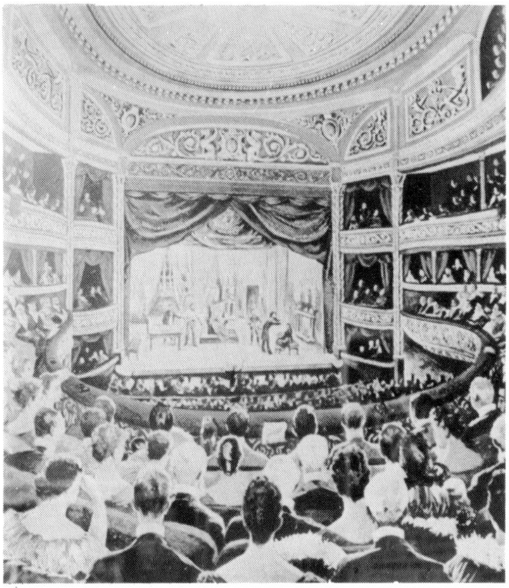

KING STREET, SOUTH: **Gaiety Theatre**
The stated reason for the *Irish Builder* of 1871 criticizing the new theatre was that, with the Theatre Royal already in use, there was no future for another of its size in Dublin. The unstated reason was that the architect, C.J. Phipps, had been imported by Michael Gunn from England. Phipps had ten years of experience in building London theatres. His London Gaiety (demolished *c.*1900) was the immediate prototype. The Dublin Gaiety came close to demolition in the early 1970s, partly due to the cavalier attitude in that period to listing interiors. The neo-Byzantine exterior of far lesser importance (by Charles Ashworth, 1913) has also been preserved to inspire the shopping centre across the street. The foyers and bars are intimate in scale, warm and mahogany panelled, in contrast to the white and gold rococco fantasy of the horseshoe-shaped auditorium. Despite the loss of its Gods and the substitution of synthetic textiles when the lights dim, this is still the theatre that Phipps intended.

LINCOLN GATE: **Dental Hospital**
Built in a freely composed red-brick and terracotta Flemish idiom by Richard Caulfield Orpen, half-brother to the painter William Orpen; his most important public building to survive (if with some uncertainty). Admirable top-floor laboratories with the windows carried up into north-facing roof-lights. Built in 1894-6.

MALPAS STREET: **Former Distillery**
While the large breweries and distilleries have replaced their kiln-houses due to technological development as at Guinnesses, here they survive as two corner towers of a compact complex opening off a central courtyard. The vent stacks were removed when the distillery was closed, but the extraordinarily sinister brick labyrinths survive within. Currently being restored as an enterprise centre.

MEATH STREET: **St Catherine's Church**
Gothic Revival church designed in 1852 by J.J. McCarthy. The side elevations with their perforated buttresses and trefoiled aisle windows above stone-roofed aisles are more indicative of the interior than the dessicated façade with its unfinished tower. Excellent glass in the style of O'Connor. William McBride's painting above the chancel depicts St Catherine's martyrdom.

MERCHANT'S QUAY: **Adam and Eve's**
Neo-Classical church originally designed by Patrick Byrne in 1834 but subsequently much altered—by Ralph Byrne in 1923, who added the campanile, and by Simon Leonard, who added the dome (1959). Byrne's west façade survives intact, but the church is screened from the river by Georgian housing, rebuilt *c.*1860 in a coarse grained Italianate for the Franciscans by John Bourke, who spared the corner house (now derelict) with its exquisite Stapletonesque plasterwork. The monastery was further remodelled by Walter Doolin *c.*1900.

MERCER STREET: **College of Surgeons**
Only the façades and tower survive of a recent rebuilding that has devalued the original Palladian Mercers' Hospital but has been kinder to the Victorian wing with its vigorously textured vermiculite ground floor, its lively paired fenestration and its tower with a spiked cupola set at the end of one of Dublin's longest vistas. Won in competition by J.H. Brett in 1884.

MERRION ROW: **No. 89, Finnegan Menton**
Elegant turn-of-the-century remodelling of an earlier house with first-floor oriel cantilevered over the pavement. Architect unknown.

MERRION SQUARE: **No. 88**
House built by J.J. McCarthy in 1859 in his Romanesque idiom with bay windows on the side façade to take advantage of the lawn in front of the National Gallery.

MERRION SQUARE: **National Gallery of Ireland**
The robust assurance of this Italianate palazzo conceals a complex and protracted evolution. The earliest designs were by the surveyor Sir Richard Griffith (1856), who had never designed a building before but who had the good

sense to copy the excellent elevations of its counterpart across Leinster Lawn, Clarendon's National History Museum. Difficulties with the board led to his replacement by Charles Lanyon, who devised the dramatic imperial staircase that links the sculpture galleries on the ground floor and the painting galleries above. Further difficulties with the board led to Lanyon's replacement by Francis Fowke, whose superb working drawings survive to reveal his technological abilities that made the gallery when completed one of the most advanced in Europe in heating, ventilating and above all lighting the collection. Opened to the public in 1864, the year before Fowke's premature death, the gallery was almost doubled in size by Sir Thomas Manly Deane (1903). He reveals an uncharacteristic lack of self-confidence (not shared by subsequent OPW architects in 1969 and 1989) in the nervous rustication of the portico and the attenuated Baroque of his galleries (not improved by the loss of their dado in the most recent restoration). However, this recent restoration has been far more sympathetic to the interiors of Fowke, and the restoration of the mezzanine gallery for the Carravaggio exhibition by Sergio Bendetto in 1992 was a model of how to revive a Victorian interior and give it a new meaning.

MERRION SQUARE: Natural History Museum

Designed by Frederick Clarendon and built in 1856-7. An austere, well-proportioned granite palazzo gives little hint of its internal excitement—its exhibits crammed together or swinging across voids in startling juxtapositions to provide a lucid demonstration of the survival of the fittest as postulated by Darwin. No other Dublin gallery contrives to display so much—a cataloguer's nightmare. This is partially due to Clarendon's ingenious cast-iron detailing of the cantilevered galleries and display shelves he had devised two years before for the Royal Irish Academy (q.v.). Today its survival seems as extraordinary as that of the dinosaurial skeletons exhibited within. Threatened by three decades of imminent conversion into overflow office space for the Government departments that surround it. Despite public indifference, at the last moment it was reprieved—some steely-

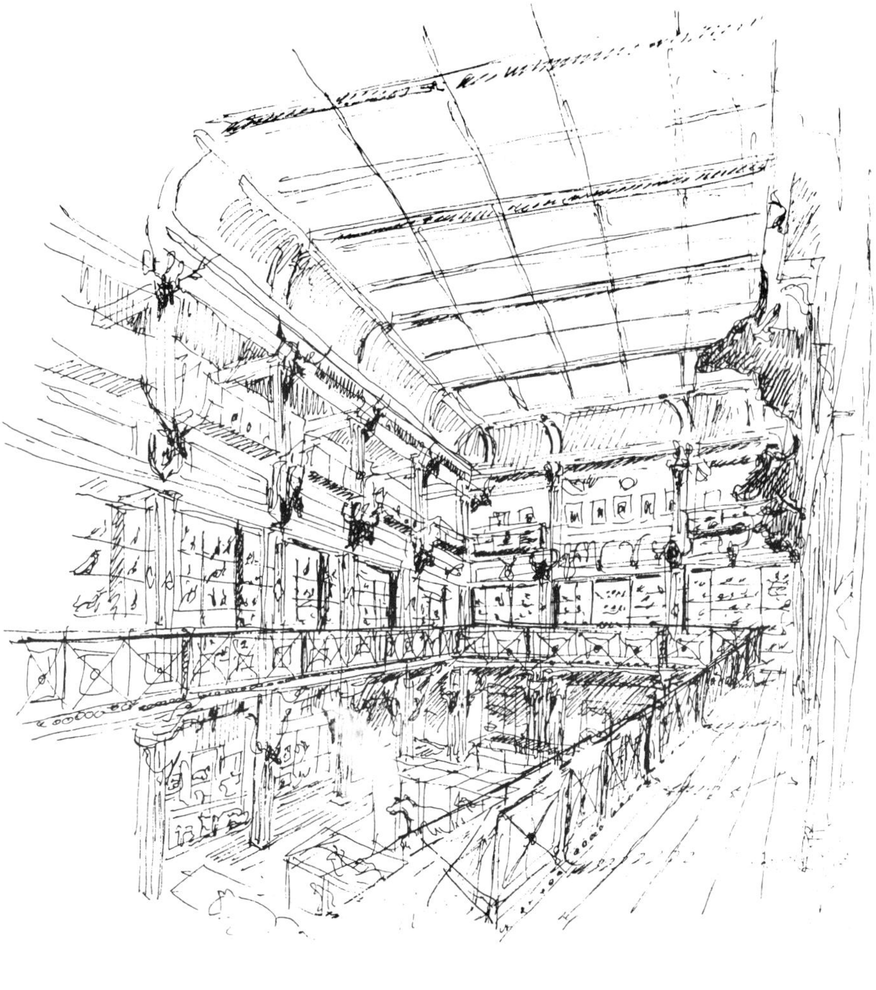

hearted bureaucrat must have realized that he was going to deprive his children of so much pleasure. Beside it in Leinster Lawn is the statue commemorating Prince Albert by John Henny Foley, the finest official statue to survive the change of regime.

MERRION STREET: Davenport Hotel

Only the façade survives here after a fire (in 1990) that destroyed an triple-galleried cast-iron interior built by the Congregationalists in 1862 to accommodate hundreds of worshippers who never materialized, so that the Plymouth Brethren who took over the church in recent years confined their services to the crypt. The architect was Alfred Gresham Jones, who a year before had designed the Dublin Exhibition Crystal Palace, long since destroyed, like the prototype for this church, the Metropolitan Tabernacle in Stoke Newington. Its most remarkable feature was the conoid vaulting upholding the galleries that swirled round the central elliptical void illuminated by a skylight of amber glass 'to suggest to the worshippers the continuous radiance of heaven'. The retention of the attenuated Italianate façade cannot compensate for our loss of this celestial intimation. However, the building's recent re-emergence as a Grand Hotel with walls of Austrian yellow has restored theatricality to the exterior.

MERRION STREET: Government Buildings

The most imperial of Dublin's monuments, built at the expense of a fine row of Georgian houses pulled down in 1913, nine years after Edward VII had laid the foundation stone. The complex was not completed until 1922 after British rule had ended. Sir Aston Webb was chosen by the Government, but due to political pressure he had to take on Thomas Manly Deane, whose offices were in one of the houses due to be demolished. Deane received a knighthood but played little part of the design. The interiors were floored with concrete and lifts were installed. The centre block with its shrunken dome and cramped entrance hall was given over to a College of Science, the wings to the Board of Technical Instruction and Agriculture. Originally the centre block was set beside the street, but this arrangement was altered in execution to the present columnar screen between flanking wings taking their cue from Hawksmoor, although the figures sculptured at roof-top level by C.W. Harrison reveal their era from their girth. Lavishly restored by the last Haughey administration.

MOLESWORTH STREET: Masonic Hall

Edward Holmes won the competition in 1860, shortly after he was awarded its counterpart in Birmingham. A triple-storied façade correctly articulated at ground level by the Doric order, an Ionic *piano nobile* and a Corinthian upper floor surmounted by a giant pediment inset with masonic designs. This outer consistency conceals an extraordinary stylistic diversity within. The principal assembly hall follows the decorous Classicism of the façade, but during 1877 a Knight's Hall was added by John Gibson in full-blown Gothic Revival, like a set for the Mass Wagner was writing at the time for *Parsifal*. Each knight has his own niche beneath a suspended sword. This chapel was demolished by the Setanta development *c.*1877, but the fittings were reassembled on the top floor; the spectacular neo-Egyptian room coloured and gilded to re-enact another opera, *The Magic Flute*, survives *in situ*.

PARLIAMENT STREET: Sunlight Chambers

Designed by the Liverpool architect Edward Ould, who worked on Port Sunlight for Lord Lever and who usually worked in the 'ye olde' English style. But here he turned to a romanticized Italianate—wide eaves, arcaded upper floors and two multi-coloured terracotta continuous freizes illustrating the powers of soap (and

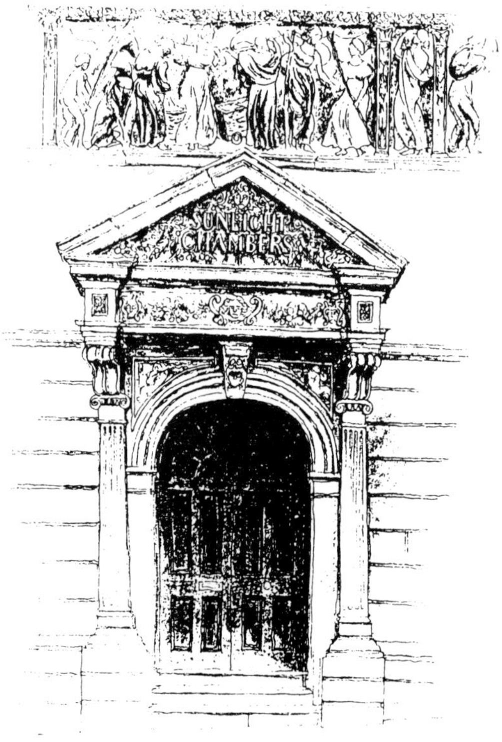

currently in need of a wash). At the time of its completion (1901) the *Irish Builder* remarked on a consensus that the ugliest building in Dublin was not a hundred miles from Grattan Bridge. In 1905 there was a more direct attack—'pretentious and mean'. It has always been controversial. Dublin Corporation used it as an example that deserved European conservation funds (unaware that the traffic engineers had listed it for demolition). Now reprieved but empty.

PATRICK STREET: St Patrick's Cathedral

The largest medieval cathedral in Ireland had been reduced to such a delapidated state that its architect in 1805, Theodore Park, recommended its demolition. That it has survived is due to three building campaigns—at the start, in the middle and at the end of Queen Victoria's reign. These neatly illustrate the divergent views of each generation and even still incite controversy. The early Victorian restoration (1844-52) was romantic and fanciful; Richard Carpenter was a gifted architect, but he was up against failing health and working to a miniscule budget, a tenth of that intended. His most serious defect was his lack of building experience, which led to the choice of Caen stone, replaced by the architect in charge of the last campaign, Sir Thomas Drew, with Somersetshire Oolite. Drew's restoration appears to be more scholarly but in reality quite different from the original—renewing the choir, and lady chapel with concrete vaulting (1899-1904). His most striking addition, the stone staircase, modelled on one in Mayence Cathedral, leads to an organ loft successfully concealed in the roof space. But the bitterest criticism has been directed at the mid-Victorian restoration of the nave and transepts, by Sir Benjamin Lee Guinness (in 1860-5), whose main crime was to act as his own architect. He may have good reasons: J.J. McCarthy refused to believe that the extraordinary trefoiled vaulting of the nave was original. Nothing that Sir Benjamin did in St Patrick's can compare with the arrogance of Street destroying the 14th-century choir of Christchurch. Carpenter would have destroyed the Irish battlements of the belfry which Sir Benjamin retained. He obeyed Carpenter in removing the reredos and in clustering the nave arcades with columns. The nave triforium is an invention, but comprehensible in its attempt to do what the medieval architect would have intended. The north and south porches are also new but structurally justifiable. The north transept is entirely new but duplicates the south, repeating its wider central bay, the only visible medieval optical subtlety.

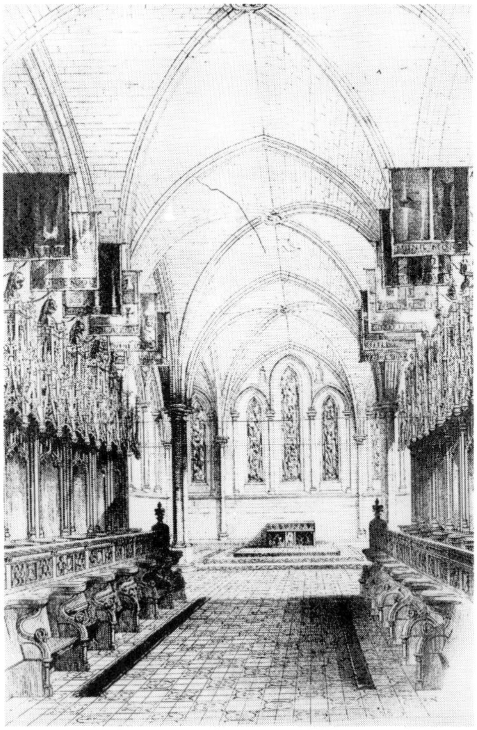

The cathedral contains the finest collection of English Victorian stained glass in Ireland, notably the triple neo-medieval end windows to the nave and south transept (by Wailes) and the Kempe windows in the north choir aisle, surrounding one by Tower. The only Irish windows are in the north transept—the Cormac window by Child and the French window by McBride. The neighbouring Law window by Davis is of high quality. Sadly, the commission of the great Iveagh window did not go to Michael Healy but to Sir Frank Brangwyn. Further windows by Barff (in transept) and by Heaton, Butler and Bayne. The frontals of the high altar and the lady chapel altar are masterpieces of the Royal Irish Art School of Needlework by Ninian Comper, 1899-1900. Also, diverse collection of Victorian sculpture. In the north aisle: bust of John Curran by C. Moore of London (1841); monument to Carolan by J.V. Hogan (1879); statue of Dean Dawson by E.H. Bailey of London (1843); statue of Judge Whiteside by Albert Bruce Joy (*c.*1880); memorials commemorating the wars in China (1842), Burma (1852), both by Sir Thomas Farrell; bust of James Culwick designed by Sir Thomas Drew executed by Oliver Sheppard (1907); William Brooke designed by Sir T.N. Deane (1861); effigy of Archibishop Whately and statue of Capt. John Boyd (1861) by Sir Thomas Farrell. Outside the cathedral, statue of its restorer, Sir Benjamin Guinness by John Henry Foley (1875).

PEARSE STREET: Enterprise Centre
Handsome multi-storied warehouse with attached staircase tower. Traditional masonry walls support an early rolled-steel joist structure, one of the earliest in these islands, devised by the Manchester architect Alfred Darbyshire in the 1860s. Reprieved from demolition to become the showpiece of a new enterprise centre, at the expense of the original structure (now sheathed to comply with present day fire regulations).

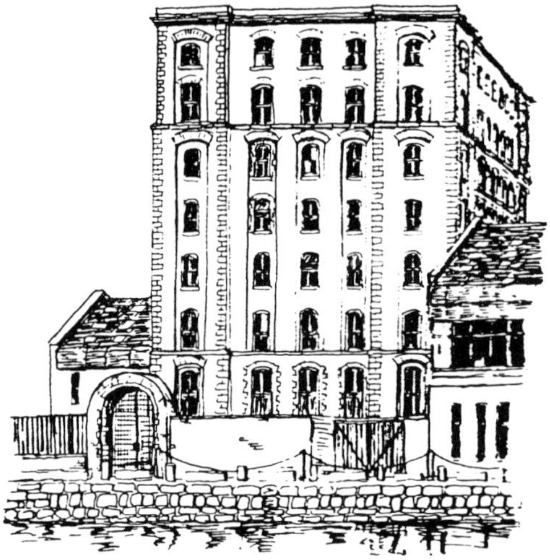

PEARSE STREET: Garda Station
Accomplished Scottish Baronial that takes the maximum advantage of its awkward corner site while still imposing a symmetrical central layout. Designed by A. Robinson, M.J. Burke and H.G. Leask in 1915. Corbelled heads of the Royal Constabulary uphold segmental arches in a valedictory appearance on the streets of Dublin.

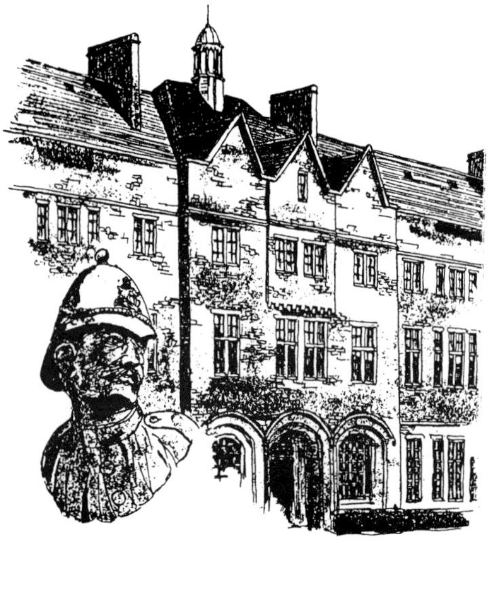

RIALTO STREET: Housing
One of the earliest tenement schemes in the city with simple well proportioned apartments each side of a shared staircase. Merits preservation.

ST ANDREW'S STREET: St Andrew's Church
Again a hard-fought competition won by W.H. Lynn of Lanyon, Lynn and Lanyon due to his ability to turn the disadvantages of an awkward site into assets. Built in 1860-2. Lynn was a controversial choice since his scheme was more elaborate than the budget permitted, but his eventful combination of steeple, staircase turret and fragmentary cloister gave his church continuous interest when seen at the end of every vista, almost compensating us for the loss of Francis Johnston's oval Gothick Church. So much effort has gone into the architecture that the contribution of the glass and sculpture is comparatively negligible; nor have the spatial qualities of the interior been improved by sealing off the north aisle to make a separate chapel of healing.

ST MICHAEL'S HILL: Synod Hall
The first idea of George Street was historically correct—to rebuild Dublin's original courthouse that once had been the chapter house of the medieval abbey—but his perspective shows that his reconstruction would have dwarfed the cathedral. So it was a brilliant improvization (in 1874) to place the synod hall on the other side of St Michael's Hill, linked to the cathedral by a Gothicized version of the Bridge of Sighs spanning the public thoroughfare. He retained only the 13th-century tower of St Michael's church and utilized it as an escape staircase for the hall, which he placed on the first floor, reached also by a leisurely stone staircase with an apsidal half-landing. Note his clever way of setting the synod hall roof at the back so it does not appear to be the same height as the cathedral. Further stairs reach the arcaded tribunes at each end below gable windows. But the wide span of the roof, is secured at the cost of obtrusive tie bars. Sold off by the Church of Ireland at the time that there were proposals to demolish it for road widening, it has since housed varied ventures, the best being a conference set up by 500 outraged citizens to save Dublin from its bureaucrats. Now contains an interpretative centre on the history of the city of Dublin.

ST STEPHEN'S GREEN
The bronze Lord Ardilaun is serenely seated at the western entrance to St Stephen's Green, which he acquired and remodelled at his own

THE SYNOD HALL

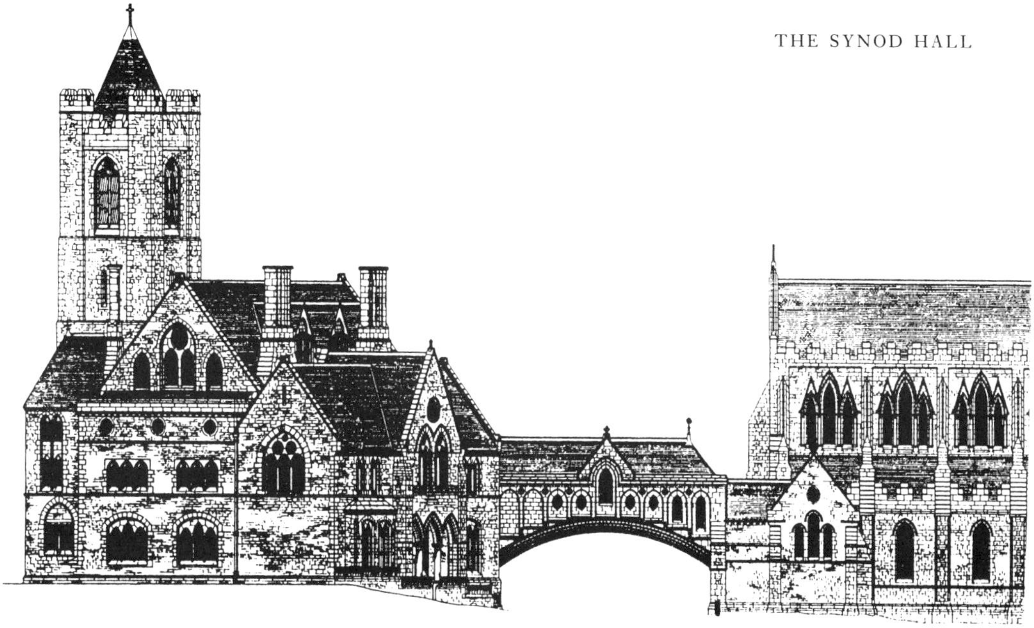

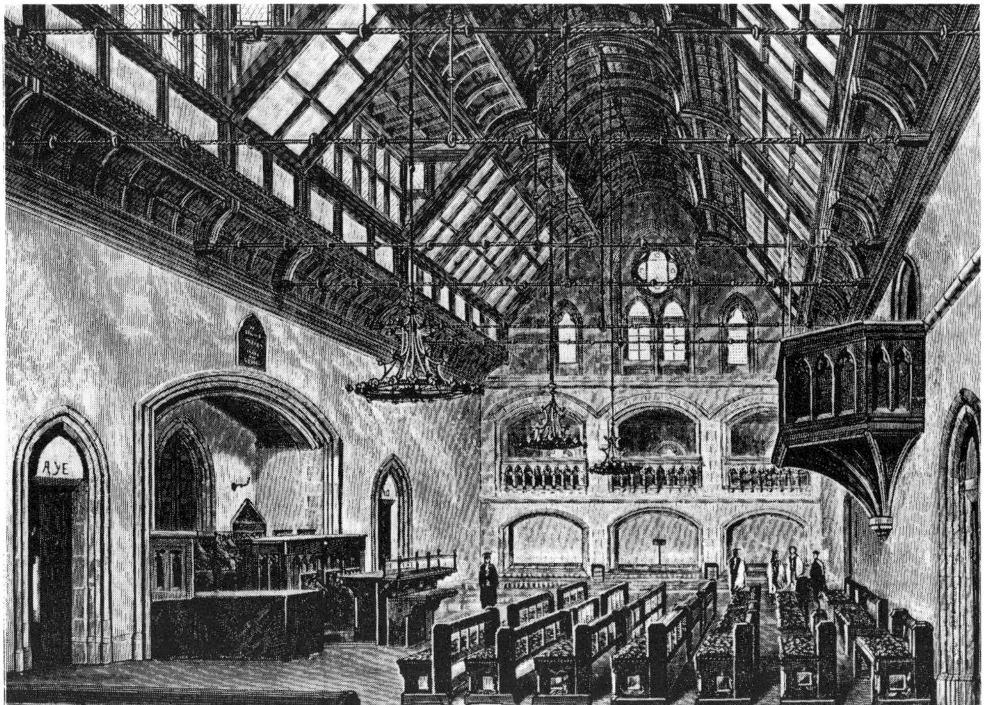

expense. His serenity recalls the memorial of his father, Sir Benjamin Lee Guinness, also by Henry Foley, seated imperturbably in front of St Patrick's Cathedral, whose restoration was another act of philanthropy that aroused controversy and ingratitude. The correspondence during the late 1870s of the *Irish Builder* is taken up with complaints against Lord Ardilaun and his team—J.F. Fuller, the architect, William Shepherd, the landscaper, and the firm of Pulham and Sons, who designed the immense dripping cliff that blocks the view of a long irregular pond from the College of Surgeons. When just completed this must have looked very depressing on a wet day. Now it is magical with reflections along the lake receding into distant forests disturbed by skimming waterfowl. A focal bridge spans a rocky gorge. The lake

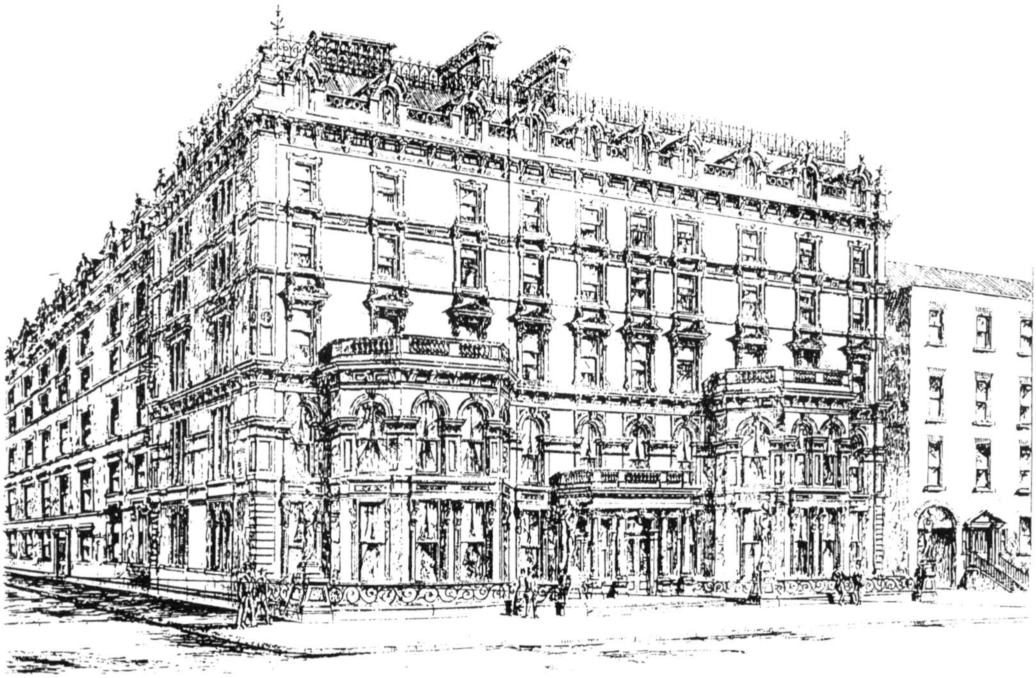

reflects a vista of a triumphal arch added by H. Pentland at the north-west entrance to commemorate the Boer War. A waterside pavilion and a cast-iron bandstand still surpass in delicacy and ease later structures. Even the perennial bedding and the curious cacti-like fountains have a period charm in the formal gardens centred on the now dismantled George II by Van Nost. The keeper's lodge with its overhanging eaves has been attributed to Fuller's assistant, L. McDonnell.

ST STEPHEN'S GREEN: **The Galleria**
A High Victorian façade with French chateau touches still survives above a much-altered shop, once a famous delicatessen, then part of a bankrupt shopping arcade, currently awaiting another metamorphosis. Designed by Thomas Drew in 1867.

ST STEPHEN'S GREEN: **United Services Club**
Remodelled by W.G. Murray, assisted by his son Albert, in 1852. A good example of how the Victorians were able to subvert Georgian architecture to their own values: two bays of the façade were removed to make a spacious bow window beside twin curving flights of steps leading to the front door. Internally the original plasterwork is replicated in the additions. The staircase is made into a Victorian interior by glazing the windows with stained glass and covering the floor with enamel tiles. Recently redecorated to match the swagger of Murray rather than the delicacy of Stapleton.

ST STEPHEN'S GREEN: **Shelbourne Hotel**
Designed in 1865 by John McCurdy, the most fashionable hotel architect of his day. The original clients, the Jury family, remained the proprietors until they sold out (*c.* 1970) to the present owners, Trusthouse Forte, who have been continuously redecorating the interiors ever since while never quite succeeding in returning to the easeful assurance of the original. However, recent restorations have been more successful than one in the 1960s that prompted Elizabeth Bowen to try to withdraw her book commissioned by the management to celebrate the centenary.

ST STEPHEN'S GREEN: **Iveagh House**
Town house of the bishop of Killala designed by Richard Castle, remodelled and extended as an Italianate palace of Sir Benjamin Lee Guinness, who acted as his own architect. Inherited by Lord Iveagh, who in 1881 inserted the marble staircase (designed by J.F. Fuller) and the opulent ballroom entered from its half-landing (added in 1897). While Sir Thomas Drew was the executant architect, this was one of the last works of the Scottish architect William Young, who was unequalled in his ability to invigorate an ailing Italianate with a new sense of glamour (here achieved by the use of onyx and alabaster), fulfilling the desires of aspiring municipal councillors or hospitable grandees. Now that the house has become the Department of Foreign Affairs, it must give many British delegations a shock, since it is so like Young's last commission, the War Office in

Whitehall. Lord Iveagh's bequest included the collection of sculpture, although Hogan's Italian Shepherd Boy (1846) came from his uncle's collection at St Anne's, Clontarf (q.v.), via another donor. The spacious gardens at the rear (designed by Niven) were presented to University College Dublin after Wesley College had rejected them due to their dependence on stout. They contain a Celtic-cum-Saracenic temple (probably by Sir Benjamin Guinness) overlooking an archery lawn and an Italianate grotto guarded by crumbling river gods.

ST STEPHEN'S GREEN: University Church

A discreet exterior slotted in between two unsuspecting Georgian houses that support a belfry held aloft above the doorway. Effectively entered down steps through a darkened tribune. Commissioned in 1856 by the then Dr Newman from his friend and fellow Oxford Movement convert to Catholicism, John Hungerford Pollen. Newman disliked Gothic as not being Christian enough (despite Pugin) and chose instead that Cinderella of the historical styles, the Byzantine. But the most impressive architectural feature of the interior, the baldachino above the altar, is pure Muslim—rivalled only by St Bartholomew's in Oxford, now that Pollen's only other Catholic church (at Rhyll) has been ruthlessly destoyed. This orientalism is reinforced by the bottle glass windows, by the arcaded tribune on one side of the altar with a lattice to screen the choir (possibly female) from the congregation, and by the foliate designs of the open roof painted by Pollen himself (he modelled it on his own Merton College Chapel vault in Oxford a decade before). Pollen also painted our Lady as Seat of Wisdom celebrated in a series of medallions linked in a stylized tree that fills the semidome above the altar. Unfortunately the decoration of the end wall and that of the side walls with their indigestible marble patterning, clash. The thoughtless replication of Raphael's cartoons (now darkened by damp) effectively dispels any sense of a shrine to Pre-Raphaelite sensibility. For that we have to go to Benjamin Woodward's contemporary Museum staircase hall in Trinity, the rival university. Posthumous bust of Newman (1892) by Terence Farrell.

Newman did not live to see what should have been the materialization of his ideas—Cardinal Vaughan's Westminster Cathedral. Ironically fellow Oratorians in London and Birmingham were waylaid by the Baroque.

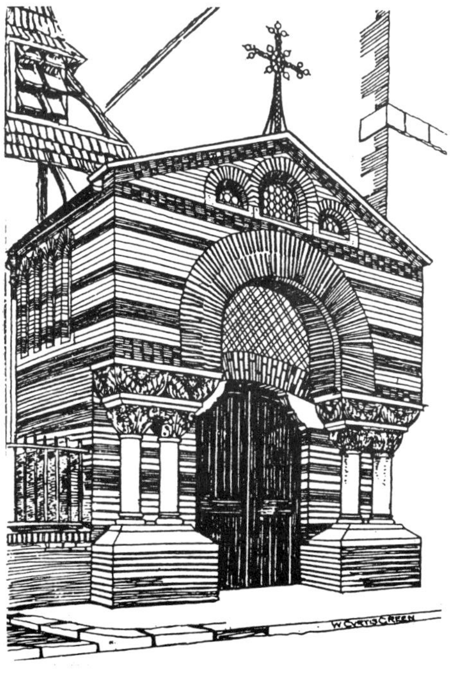

ST STEPHEN'S GREEN: Methodist Church

Only the Ionic portico projecting from a five-bay façade survives the sale of this church and the adjoining school to commercial interests after a fire that destroyed the interior of the church, designed in 1843 by Isaac Farrell to commemorate the centenary of the founding of the first Methodist church in Ireland. Adaptation to its present use does not repay scrutiny.

ST STEPHEN'S GREEN: College of Surgeons

Most of the interior predates the Victorian era, but T.N. Deane could not resist the opportunity of making Ruskinian alterations to the intrusions into the staircase hall. He was more tactful in his refitting of the library. Millar and Symes were called in subsequently (1878). They are responsible for the fibrous Classicism of the banqueting hall.

ST STEPHEN'S GREEN: Unitarian Church

Won (*c.* 1863) in competition by W.H. Lynn of Lanyon, Lynn and Lanyon shortly after his success in the competition for St Andrew's, and built also in a complex version of Decorated Gothic to get as much natural light as possible into a constricted site, hemmed in by Georgian houses (now replaced by egg-crate office blocks). Lynn departed further than his fellow competitors from the norm by taking up the area with nave, a single aisle and transept raised up above the street level on the church hall underneath. Glass by O'Brien, Rhind and Child. The Child window depicts Christ between Columbus, Luther, Caxton and Florence Nightingale.

SOUTH CIRCULAR ROAD: **Mosque**
Designed by William Sterling in 1884 as a Presbyterian church. Spire never completed. Commendably converted into a mosque by Dublin's Muslims after they had acquired the church in preference to the Jewish synagogue across the street.

SOUTH CIRCULAR ROAD: **St Kevin's Church of Ireland**
Known appropriately as the 'Red Church' due to the use of red sandstone, this Gothic Revival structure reflects the Ulster origins of its architect, Thomas Drew, who won the competition here in 1863. Carroll and Batchelor designed the adjoining church hall, since sold for commercial development along with the church itself.

TARA STREET: **Central Fire Station**
C.J. McCarthy was the city architect of Dublin from 1893 to 1922, and this (completed in 1900) is his most prominent building. On a corner site, arcaded on the ground floor to allow access for fire engines. The most striking feature is the lofty red-brick tower modelled on an Italian belvedere; a look-out on the top floor, with the shaft beneath used for drying hoses. Seriously threatened for ten years by road widening, but now fortunately reprieved.

THOMAS COURT: **Belview Buildings**
The survivor of two parallel four-storied blocks that should itself have been sacrificed to road widening, but was reprieved at the last moment. Entered through communal staircases decorated with terracotta plaques. Lively multi-storied cast-iron verandahs at the rear have been destroyed. Attributed to R.J. Stirling, the Guinness housing architect, *c.*1895.

THOMAS STREET: **No. 10**
Robustly designed offices with warehousing at the rear. An impressive glazed arcade at street level lights the principal room. Designed for his family by A.G.C. Millar in 1908.

THOMAS STREET: **National College of Art & Design**
The 18th-century distillery of the Power family was extended throughout the succeeding century. Many of these buildings survive, converted into the National College of Art (in some cases only after demonstrations by students). The huge vats (by Spence of Cork Street) that now adorn the piazza were to have been removed when the building that housed them was demolished. The office block that William Caroe built in 1880 also survives although it reveals little evidence of Caroe's experimentalism as expressed in Kilteragh (q.v.). Only the circular entrance hall and office above have a *frisson* of Art Nouveau.

THOMAS STREET: **No. 120, Spice of Life**
Late Gothic Revival brick offices on arcaded shops c.1880. Trapezoidal plan cleverly concealed by an ingeniously hipped roof.

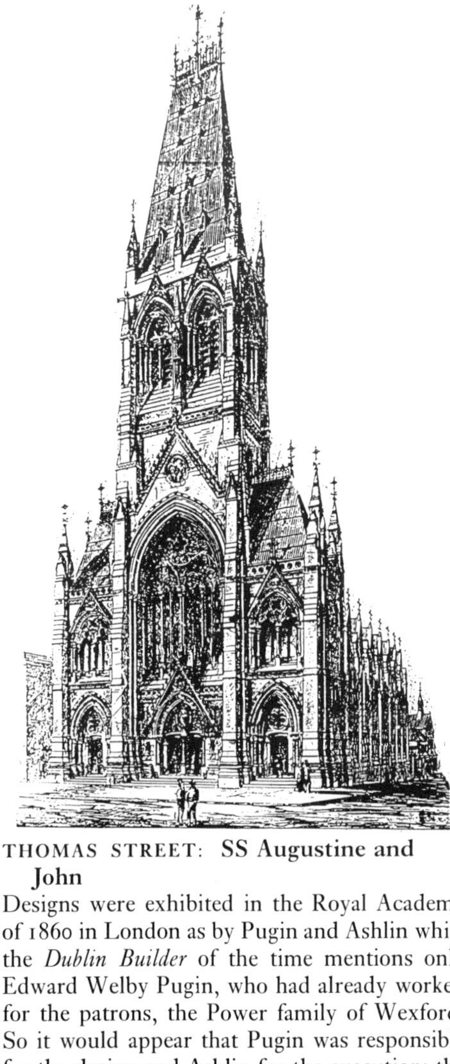

THOMAS STREET: **SS Augustine and John**
Designs were exhibited in the Royal Academy of 1860 in London as by Pugin and Ashlin while the *Dublin Builder* of the time mentions only Edward Welby Pugin, who had already worked for the patrons, the Power family of Wexford. So it would appear that Pugin was responsible for the design and Ashlin for the execution; the spire was completed twenty-four years later. Nothing by George Ashlin alone rivals this façade for dramatic impact: a massive rectangular tower rising to a wedge-shaped spire is held aloft above a cavernous nave window between two hipped-roof abutments that mask the aisles. Recent cleaning has revealed the original abrasive polychromy—red sandstone with limestone and granite dressings contrasting to the white Caen statuary. The scale of this sculpture extends from the just larger-than-life Christ at ground level via St Augustine by

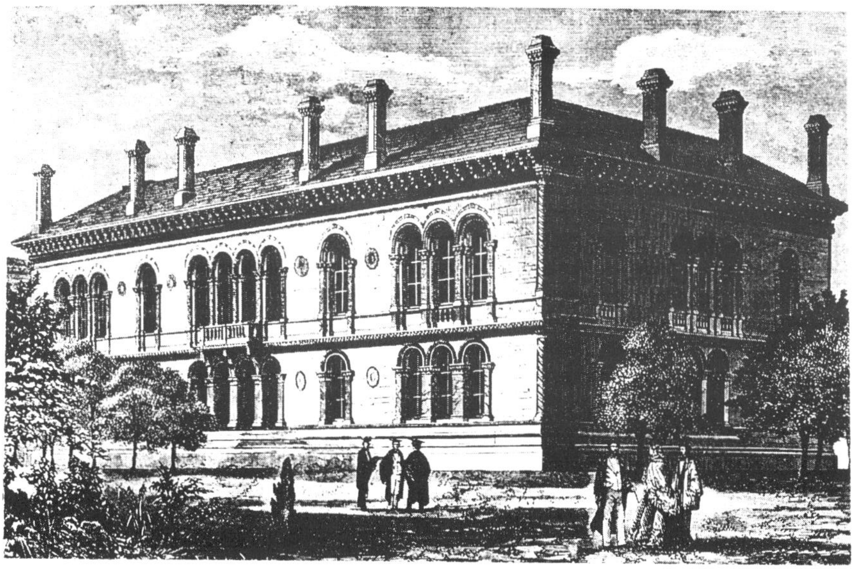

Earley and Powell (1869) to the colossal twelve apostles who hold their vigil on pinnacles round the spire. These are carved by James Pearse to overlook a city that his son Patrick was prepared to sacrifice in 1916. The church is sited on the crest that falls steeply to the Liffey so that it dominates the river valley. This permitted Ashlin to slot in his grim multi-storied conventual buildings at a lower level jammed up against the apse, the site being too confined to accommodate the usual cloister.

The interior restates the dominant motif of the façade—but in a different way: each archway that divides the nave from the aisles upholds a double bay lit by a pair of hexafoil clerestory windows, vaulted separately by the timber-sheathed roof. An intended transept was omitted. Instead, the nave terminates in a gorgeous apse, curiously completed by William Hague in 1895; Ashlin managed to retrieve the commission after Hague's death in 1899 to design the lavish decoration of the side chapels. Ironwork by McGloughlin, sculpture by Pearse, mosaics by Oppenheimer. The stained glass sadly charts the decline of the Harry Clarke Studios but includes one window with some of Dublin's most beautiful stained glass, though partially blocked by a hideous light fitting—St Augustine meeting his mother, St Monica, by Michael Healy; note the magical trireme in the tracery above.

Since the church is in Dublin, it has done little to advance recognition of the younger Pugin's reputation: his other religious masterpiece, St Francis', Gorton, is to be made into an apartment block. Of his contemporaries only Timothy Hevey (in his two Belfast churches) was inspired by the originality of the façade.

TRINITY COLLEGE

The original competition for a block of lecture halls that would include a museum was held in 1834 and won by George Darley. His scheme was never executed, but he built instead student rooms on the two remaining sides of the intended square, deploying a chilly neo-Classical idiom indistinguishable from that of thirty years before. The first structure to reveal the values of the new reign was Charles Lanyon's forceful Italianate campanile, evoking its predecessor by Castle but shorn of its flanking wings. Lanyon was the loser in a run-off against Deane and Woodward in a second competition held in 1852 to design the Museum Buildings. Work started in 1854 and took three years. Only a small group of aesthetes grasped its significance as the first statement in architecture of the pre-Raphaelite ideal. Benjamin Woodward reinterpreted Charles Barry's palazzo style in a Byzantine Revival vocabulary, following the example of the Lombardo dynasty (*c.*1480-1502), whose Venetian palaces had just been rediscovered by Ruskin. The Ca Visetti inspired the entrance-door composition; the interlacing polychromatic marble disks of their Palazzo Dario were re-used here by Woodward on a more monumental scale. The personal influence of Ruskin has been exaggerated—the incised voussoirs with pointed arches introduced above the first floor windows, and even that's conjectural. But *The Stone of Venice* inspired the organization of the sculptors headed by 'Mr Roe of Lambeth' and the O'Shea brothers of Ballyhooly, all encouraged to develop their own fantasy. However, this improvization is kept within bounds by the repetitive carving of the plinths, balconies and chimneys. At least some of the designs of the 180 varied

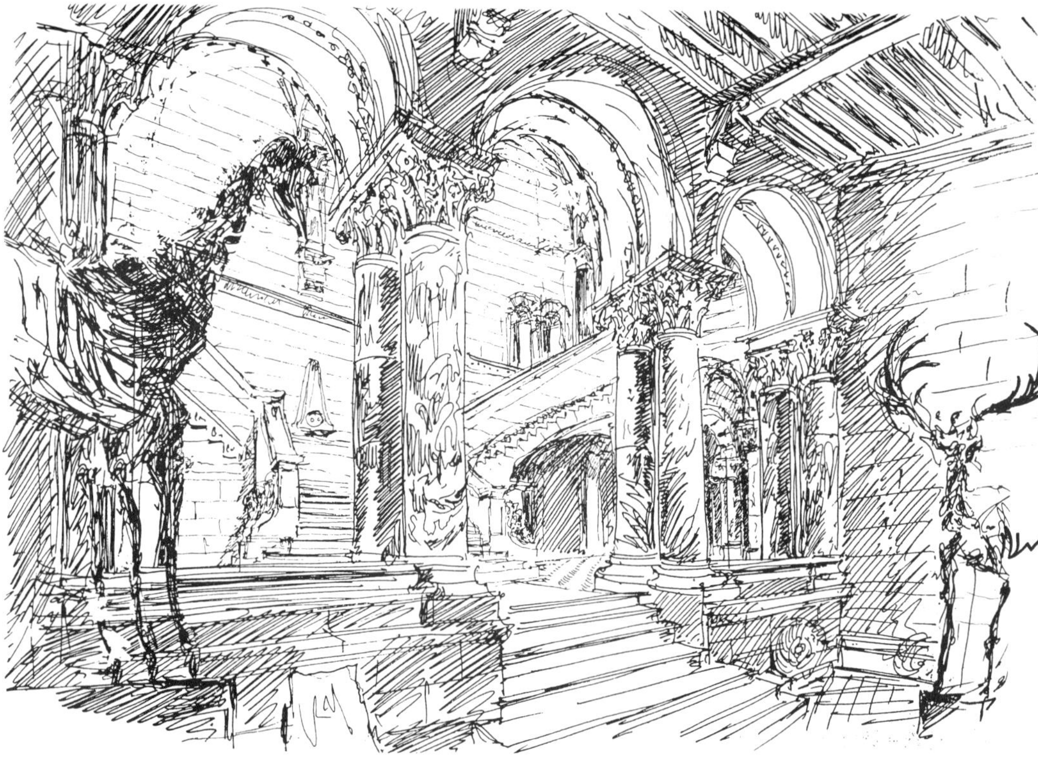

capitals were supplied by others (the 'Mice eating Corn' by Millais), but an 'Angel and Children' by Lizzie Siddal was deemed by Ruskin too beautiful to be carved.

Attempts to replace the specified enamelled brick of the interior with frescoes (possibly by Rossetti) did not get beyond a perspective, a watercolour by Henry Hill. The columned vestibule leads into the double-domed staircase hall axised on its traverse archway. The stairs bifurcate into arcaded tribunes on either side, a Byzantine version of Victor Louis's Grand Theatre in Bordeaux, except that here one ascends to a series of botched lecture halls with inherent access problems at first-floor level. These failings were blamed on the college architect, John McCurdy, who had got his plans selected by one board meeting in preference to the Deanes and was appointed executant architect.

McCurdy's independent college buildings are of minimal importance (the warden's house, the medical school), so his attempts to claim responsibility for the design of the Museum must be viewed with scepticism. The finest interior is the ground-floor library, recently well restored.

The grand Deane and Woodward interior that one should have reached by that impressive staircase, does exist—but next door, in Burgh's Library built in 1712 and then in need of drastic restoration. Again the board was caught between two rival proposals. McCurdy proposed retaining the appearance of the interior while inserting a hidden cast-iron frame designed by Robert Mallet. Deane and Woodward's solution was to remove the cause of the problem—the flat ceiling with its 40 ft span (not the original) and replace it with a central sheathed timber barrel vault resting on a new inner structure that absorbs the original Corinthian gallery with new vertical supports carried up to their vaulting and extended downward by ground-floor columns. Each library bay becomes structural and is vaulted segmentally along its upper level at right angles to the central tunnel. The result is a Romanesque cathedral inserted to give structural stability to a great Georgian interior, with the new detailing paraphrasing rather than replicating Burgh's. A contemporary noted that what had been superb they had made sublime. Accusations of vandalism from the McCurdy camp (mainly due to the new mansard roof) have been forgotten.

There were no protests when Burgh's ground-floor arcading was made into book storage in the 1890s by Drew, with glazed arcades that have at last been painted in discreet dark colours.

Drew's great opportunity to add another showpiece came with the Graduates Tercentenary Building in 1892. This meant pulling down an Early Georgian range. The result (in Scottish Jacobean), while recalling the origins of the college on a grand scale, is extraordinarily lacking in assurance, as if haunted by the Banquo's ghost of its predecessor. The adjoining Rubrics, despite its dormered upper floor added cheerily by G.P. Beater in 1892, is far more interesting. Beater's philistinism is also more stimulating than the bland neo-Georgian additions to the medical school by William Marshall (pathology school, 1895-8; school of physics and botany, 1907) that would make a charming country house but no more than that. Far better to end this account with the valedictory Classicism of the First World War memorial pavilion by T.N. Deane (who had lost his only son in combat) turned by Richard Orpen into the vestibule of his library.

The sculpture within the college contrasts with Burke and Goldsmith at the entrance from College Green (q.v.). Both Lecky (1906) by Sir W.C. John and Salmon (1911) by John Hughes are set each side of the campanile as rivals in sedentary wisdom.

WELLINGTON QUAY: Nos. 2-5, Dollard House

Late Victorian office block built in 1886. The architect remains unknown. Neo-Elizabethan river façade, but the rear to Essex Street is as austere as any in the Chicago School.

WESTLAND ROW: St Andrew's Church

Designed by James Bolger in 1832 and when completed in 1837 the largest Catholic church in Dublin—which must have satisfied Daniel O'Connell, the principal motivator of the building campaign. It was also the most fashionable, with the transepts reserved for Dublin's leading residential families protected from the rabble in the nave by an elegant balustrade. This division between pharisee and publican was quietly removed when the present interlocking granite altar was installed after the Second Vatican Council—alterations that worsen what Craig calls 'the uneasy wall-spaces and unresolved duality' of the interior. The present redecoration has only emphasized the insubstantiality of the pilasters at the upper level. However, even William Scott, commissioned to redress the faults of the interior in 1910, failed to do so. All that survives of his designs are the light fittings and the painted heads of the apostles by W. Nairn. The monumental neo-Palladian altarpiece, designed by Patrick Byrne in 1860, at long last frames its original painting, a Descent from the Cross by G.F. Beghley (supplanting a crucifix by Oisin Kelly, which had been intruded). Other sculpture include a Madonna by William Pearse, the brother of Padraig, in the mortuary chapel (itself added in 1910 in an assured Italianate by Ralph Byrne along with a nuptial chapel) and the Farrell memorial by Hogan at the crossing. The exterior is masterly in the way its monumental Doric portico is tied into the streetscape by its flanking presbyteries. Impressive rear façade to Cumberland Street.

WESTLAND ROW: Pearse Station

The earliest of the Dublin stations built by Charles Vignoles, extended in 1861 and then transformed from a terminus into a virtual non-building by extending the elevated rail link across the city with a decorative cast-iron bridge over Westland Row by Courtney, Stephens and Bailey (*c.*1884).

WESTMORELAND STREET: No. 5

Vigorous Lombardesque Revival built in 1867-70 by W.G. Murray as Cramer's music store and fitted by James Gibson. In polychromatic brickwork with stone trimmings, tension is generated between the overall verticality and the separate horizontal articulation of each floor, multiplying and thereby compressing its arcades as the façade rises upwards. Door altered by R.G. Hopcraft *c.*1940.

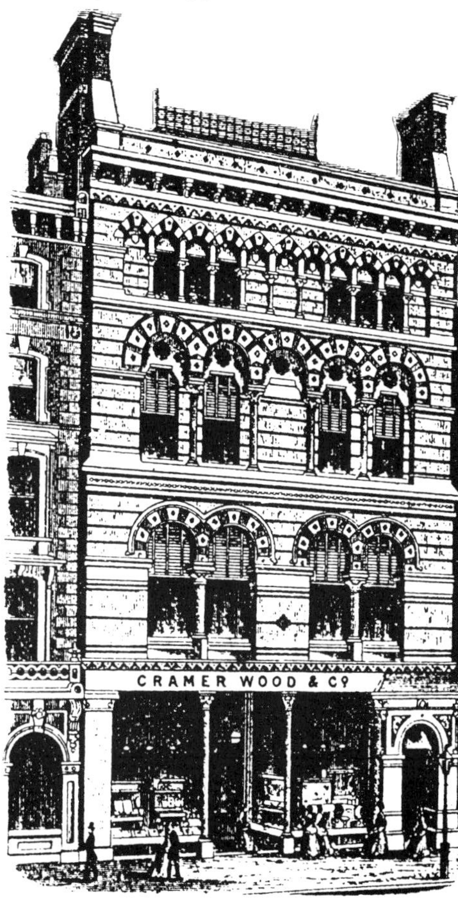

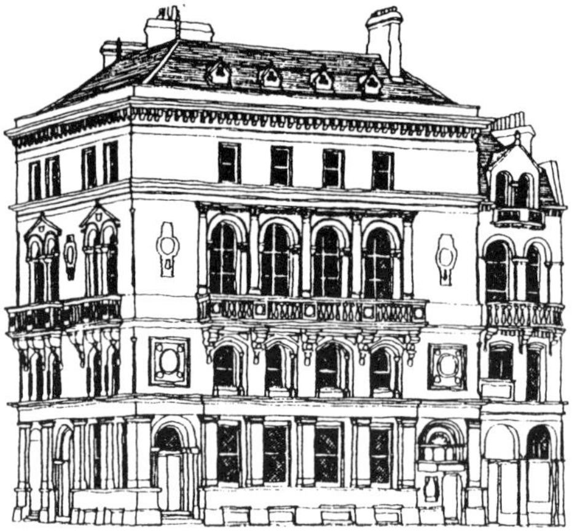

WESTMORELAND STREET: **No. 41, Allied Irish Bank**
Formerly Scottish Widows Insurance. An unexpectedly delicate design for T.N. Deane (1875) using an Italianate Romanesque vocabulary with its balconies corbelled out on gryphons. Cool grey marble shafts articulate the windows in delicious contrast to the warm red ochre of the Scottish sandstone. Elegant internal stone staircase leading to second floor *piano nobile*.

WESTMORELAND STREET: **No. 14, Beshoff's**
Designed in 1866 for the Scottish Equitable Insurance Company, hence W.G. Murray's appropriately Baronial style with a crow-stepped gable. Now successfully converted at ground level into a restaurant.

WESTMORELAND STREET: **No. 7**
George Ashlin was the winner in the competition held in 1886 for the Northern Insurance Company. An uneasily proportioned French Renaissance corner pavilion that cruelly exposes Ashlin's incomprehension of Classicism.

WESTMORELAND STREET: **No. 22, ICS**
Having been defeated by George Ashlin in the competition to build an insurance HQ on the corner of Westmoreland Street and Fleet Street, J.J. O'Callaghan adapted his unsuccessful entry in a competition for the most prominent site in the city—the apex of Westmoreland Street and D'Olier Street. He exploited the acute angle to dramatize his full-blooded Gothic Revival chateau that appears to ignore the neo-Classicism of its setting. On closer view it is subtly tied into the fenestration of its neighbours and like them links the second and third floors, achieved in his case by recessing their windows in double-height arches. Built for the Liverpool and Lancashire but called by his friends O'Callaghan's Chance (1894).

WESTMORELAND STREET: **No. 32, EBS**
Designed in 1914 by Frederick Jermyn, the young partner of J.F. Fuller, for the most fashionable photographic studio of the day, Lafayette's. The semi-circular pediment expresses the glazed tunnel vault of the roof-top studio that must have stunned its contemporaries. This has been rebuilt as a canteen for the EBS, who were going to demolish everything including the façade with its triple storied recessed archway inset between Art Nouveau terracotta spandrels enclosing a chubby oriel half-way up. This oriel acted as the focal point of the Paradiso Restaurant. In 1976 the façade was spared due to a change of heart by Stephenson and Gibney the architects and integrated with the new Minimalist façades on either side.

WICKLOW STREET: **International Bar**
Public house that has survived reasonably intact since its completion in 1911. Designed by George O'Connor.

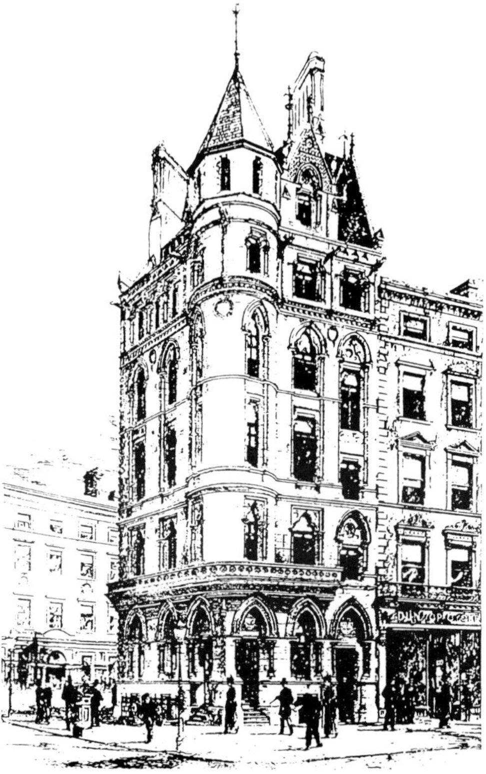

DUBLIN: NORTH SUBURBS AND NORTH COUNTY

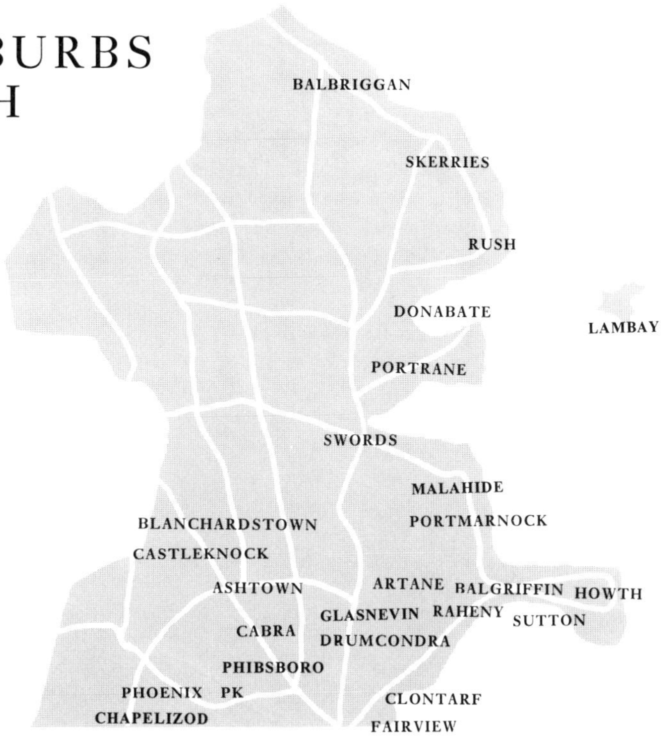

ARTANE: **Industrial School**
Italianate institution designed by Charles Geoghegan and built in 1879.

ASHTOWN: **Ashton House**
Victorian Italianate restatement of a Palladian cube with the central pavilion three stories high and double-storied wings, parapeted and balustraded and bedecked with urns throughout. Segmental pediment surmounting the principal block, over triple-arched window. In the style of John McCurdy. Now an equestrian centre.

ASHTOWN: **Ashtown Lodge and Phoenix Park Racecourse**
Half-timbered Tudor Revival house built in 1906 for the Arnott family by Edwin Bradbury when they were developing on their estate the Phoenix Park racecourse in the same idiom, so presumably they employed Bradbury here as well. Charming neo-Tudor turnstiles, stables and grandstands.

BALBRIGGAN: **Catholic Church**
Large, single cell Gothic Revival church (1838-47) by Patrick Byrne. Internally remodelled by George Ashlin in the 1890s, who subdivided it into nave and aisles. The church contains two of Harry Clarke's finest windows, dating from 1924.

BALBRIGGAN: **Carnegie Library**
Built in 1905 to the design of George O'Connor, whose attraction to bright red brick and corbelled circular turrets makes it the most assertive building in the town.

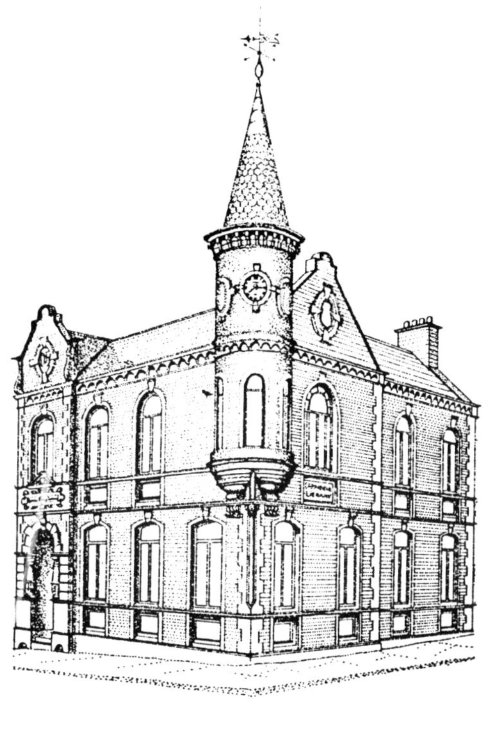

BALBRIGGAN: **Railway Station**
Crisp Palladian pavilion; nicely contrasting rustication against brick work. Designed by George Papworth in 1853.

BALGRIFFIN: **Belcamp Hall**
Georgian house acquired in 1893 by the Oblate Fathers and extended for them by George Ashlin in a red-brick neo-Romanesque range which terminates in the chapel (1903), almost entirely lit by the stained glass by Harry Clarke and his studio (1925)—too dimly for his clients, who have since lightened the borders.

BLACKHORSE AVENUE: **McKee Barracks**
The most grandiose barracks built in Victorian Ireland, named at first the Marlborough Barracks after the viceroy, the duke of Marlborough. Completed in 1893, when cavalry had lost its military significance, and a mere thirty years before the collapse of the regime which led to its change of name. Such was the sublimation of the individual in the British army of that time, that if the architect, Captain J.T. Marsh of the Royal Engineers Department, had not taken the precaution of inscribing his name on the entrance gates he would be unknown. A contemporary account credits only the executant architect, Major R.M. Barklie. The same account describes the officers' block as a mixture of Elizabethan and Queen Anne, and the two men's blocks (facing west so as allow the officers to face south) were thought to be part Tudor and part Swiss. Today the architecture is so redolent of imperialism that it is generally believed that the drawings were misplaced on their way to India. What is certain is that Marsh had a masterly grasp of the 'Sweetness and Light' style introduced by Nesfield and Shaw. Note the great chimney-stack above the central arch of the first block of the men's accommodation that echoes Nesfield's Kimmel Park. However, the profusion of tourelles that assert themselves against the red tiled mass of the roof are Marsh's own contribution. By building the sleeping accommodation of the men directly above arcaded stables, the piazzas are made more palatial. The officers' block, on the other hand, has its reception rooms on the ground floor with French windows opening out on the terraces as if it were a country house. The recreation block with its crisp geometry reverts to another ancient empire for inspiration—the Byzantine—while the riding school looks forward to 20th-century functionalism. This school has maintained the equestrian tradition as demonstrated in jumping competitions throughout the world.

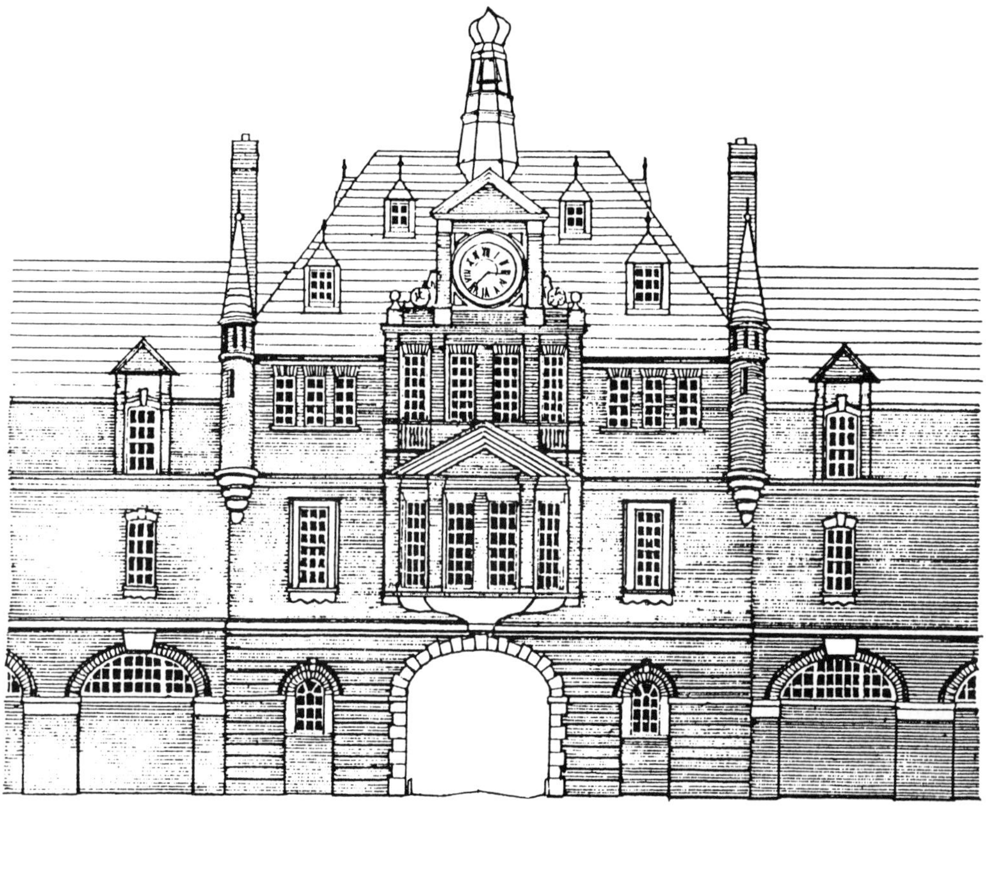

BLANCHARDSTOWN: **Catholic Church**
Modest Gothic Revival church designed pre-1860 by Charles Geoghegan, who added the distinctive shingled spire. One of the few Dublin churches to be successfully extended in radical contemporary terms (by Randal McDonnell *c.*1965).

CABRA: **Dominican Convent**
Early Georgian house of the Segrave family given curved arcades and symmetrical wings along with Italianate towers by John Bourke in 1848-53. Later embellishments and extensions of less distinguished architecture. O'Neill and Byrne added an austerely treated wing in 1879. The chapel was designed by Bourke to accommodate nuns in a long choir set at right angles to the nave. Domed crossing with curved apse, decorated with frescoes and mosaics that date from a more recent remodelling by George Ashlin, who added arcades and aisles to the nave and the new façade between twin towers. Stations of the Cross painted by Bayeart of Bruges.

CABRA: **St Joseph's, Navan Road**
Gothic Revival institution designed by Charles Geoghegan in 1864, as recorded in an impressive bird's eye view of the three storey complex. Built in rubble stone with red-brick reveals.

CASTLEKNOCK: **Castleknock College**
Georgian house extended into a monastery and, subsequently a school. Chapel built *c.*1840 and modelled on P. Byrne's St Paul's, Arran Quay. Walter Doolin was the architect here in 1901, but on his death he was succeeded by Ashlin, who remodelled the chapel in 1912, retaining but enriching the classical idiom of the original.

CASTLEKNOCK: **Church of Ireland**
Board of First Fruits church extended symmetrically by Welland and Gillespie, who added aisles and transepts in the 1860s. Chancel enriched by Sir Thomas Drew. Interior with its painted inscriptions recently restored at the expense of most of its Victorian radiators. Stained-glass window dedicated to St Hubert by Harry Clarke (1928), commissioned by Raymond Brooke.

CASTLEKNOCK: **Farmleigh**
Georgian residence of the Coote family, then of the Trenches, acquired by the 1st earl of Iveagh in 1870 and extended for him twice—firstly in 1870 by James Franklyn Fuller and then in 1893 to the designs of William Young, who was simultaneously employed on Elveden in Suffolk. Both houses are externally underplayed apart from their size, all too evident, to conceal their internal sumptuousness. Whereas the spectacular interiors of Elveden are Indian, Farmleigh is far more conventional. The earlier interiors are a cheerful Baroque with much exposed honey-coloured panelling. The later interiors are a chilly neo-Adamesque, an appropriate idiom for an ambitious London Scot—a drawingroom, ballroom and conservatory beyond. Young's *coup de théâtre* is to unite the four elements by contriving a window over a fireplace that looks into a fountain court.

In 1880 the *Irish Builder* reported that J.F. Fuller was the architect of additions to Farmleigh, but did not state what they were. That was the year of the most prominent architectural embellishment to the demesne, the clocktower in the garden. It is like an isolated tower of Ashford Castle (being built at the time by Fuller for his client's brother), but capped with a Rhenish spire, 200 ft high. Primarily a water tower, it houses one of the great clocks of its era, designed by Sir Howard Grubb, the inventor.

CASTLEKNOCK: **Knockmaroon**
Georgian house extended in identical idiom for the 1st Lord Moyne in 1905. Queen Anne style ballroom added to the rear—probably by L.M. McDonnell, who is the most likely architect for the gatelodges and stables in his more characteristic half-timbered neo-Tudor. Compartmental garden in the style of Norah Lindsay laid out along the crest of the hill. Swimming pool filled through a pitcher held aloft by a marble nymph.

CASTLEKNOCK: **Somerton**
A Georgian villa attributed to Michael Stapleton is embedded in extensions by Orpen and Dickenson, who used the existing plasterwork as the starting-point of their own internal decoration. Their client, T.K. Laidlaw, was a discriminating collector of 18th-century furniture who also demanded the most up-to-date comforts. As a result Somerton is still the epitome of a great Edwardian country house with its tiled bathrooms and fitted dressing rooms. Original contents dispersed when the house was sold by the family *c.*1987.

CHAPELIZOD: **Catholic Church**
Built (1845) in the austere militant Gothic that the architect John Bourke was to develop further in Baltinglass—recessing each bay between shallow piers beneath continuous machicolations and castellated parapets. This was an effective economy, since it reduced the materials, and the church cost only £2,500. Raised above the Liffey valley on a lofty crypt. Hence

there have been no extensions to disrupt the simple vaulted interior (intact apart from the usual loss of fittings and the addition of an ugly organ gallery).

CHAPELIZOD: Glenmaroon

There are two houses that make Glenmaroon today, back-to-back, with the public road between them. The earliest, to the west, was originally called Liffeyside, and was built *c.*1860 for Gilbert Burns, the proprietor of Todd Burns, a Dublin department store. His architect was D.C. Ferguson. Elaborate gardens were laid out in the Dutch and the Italian manner. The Dutch water garden has mainly vanished, unlike the Italian garden, robustly terraced to the river. Acquired by Ernest Guinness, who then bought the property across the road and commissioned L.M. McDonnell, who had already remodelled and extended Liffeyside, to build an idealized version of an Elizabethan Sussex manor house, to palliate his wife's homesickness for England. Eclectic as ever, McDonnell obliged. Deprived of the original contents during a week-long sale in 1950 and sold to a convent, the best interior today is the double-storey flying staircase.

CLONTARF: Blackheath

An earlier house, replaced in 1870 by Sir Thomas Drew and then lavishly extended nine years later in an overloaded version of Queen Anne. Panelled and stencilled drawingrooms with bay windows articulated by marble pilasters overlooking vanished vistas of Dublin Bay. Good neo-rococo plasterwork. The house survives today as the centrepiece of an old folks' home recalling to its present inmates the lost grandeur of their childhood, real or imagined, if they ignore the intrusion of innumerable fire precautions.

CLONTARF: Seafield Road Church of Ireland

Gothic Revival church designed by Welland and Gillespie in 1864 and consecrated two years later. Chancel remodelled by Fuller in 1899. The site was given by the Vernon family, who then commissioned the twelve-light chancel window depicting the apostles (from Michael O'Connor of London, 1866). 'Christ Blessing Little Children' by Catherine O'Brien (1950); robust Celtic cross war memorial.

CLONTARF: Mount Temple

Gothic Revival manor house designed in 1862 by Lanyon, Lynn and Lanyon with juxtaposed curvilinear gables. Red brick coursed with stone, most noticeably in the clustered octagonal

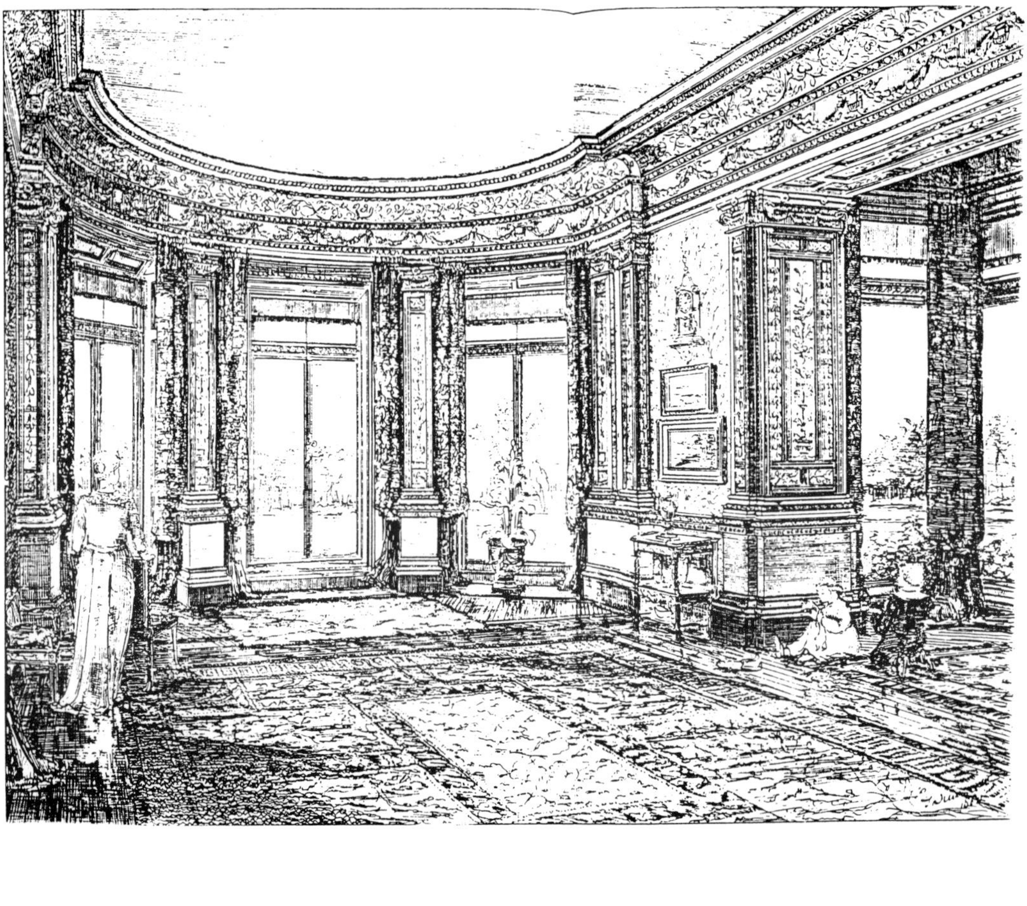

chimney-stacks. Service tower with diagonal spire echoed in the diagonal position of the gatelodge's bay window. Lived in by the maternal grandparents of Elizabeth Bowen, but their interiors have not survived transformation into a boarding school.

CLONTARF: **Presbyterian Church**
Drew's northern origins gave him the ability to adjust his religious architecture to the austerity required by the non-Conformists, and this church of 1889 illustrates the point: its most picturesque feature is the tower dressed in red sandstone with Irish battlements. Interior with timber-sheathed roof. War memorial west window designed by Harry Clarke in 1919 and made by his father's studio.

CLONTARF: **St John the Baptist's Church**
An Early Gothic church by Patrick Byrne; built in 1835. Chancel, sacristy and belfry added in 1896 by W.H. Byrne.

CLONTARF: **The Stables, St Anne's**
The only surviving structure of Lord Ardilaun's demesne apart from a few overgrown and vandalized garden temples. No trace remains of the silvery palazzo at the end of a long vista of ilexes that Fuller raised here *c.*1875 (totally engulfing the original Georgian house) with its

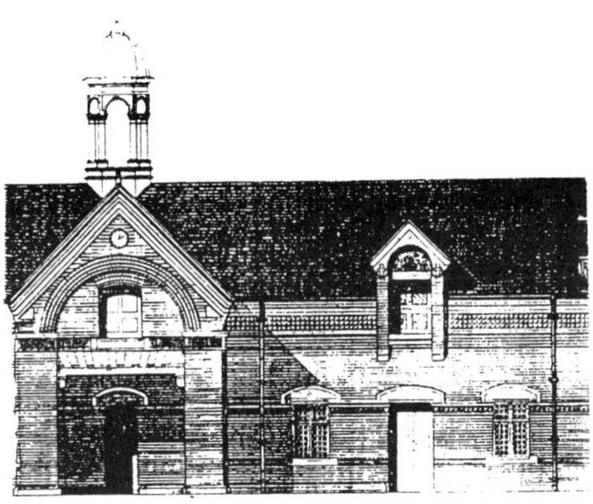

Italianate drawingroom by Millard and curvilinear added by Turner for Sir Benjamin Lee Guinness. Fuller salvaged the roof-top observatory designed by Sir Benjamin himself based on the Roman tomb of the Julii at St Remi, and mounted it on a wooded hill above the lake where it still survives. Katherine Everitt, whose own home had been rebuilt by Fuller, is cutting about the chill and damp: she came as a companion to her cousin Lady Ardilaun after the First World War and noted that the house was built round the depressing failure of a winter garden that had always leaked. Is that the reason why the Ardilauns turned in 1886 to George Ashlin for a Moorish boudoir, a jolly Sussex-style stable block as well as for their memorial church in Raheny? Acquired by Dublin Corporation in 1939, the house was burned out in 1943 to pre-empt an enquiry into missing fire-fighting equipment stored there for the city. More beautiful as a ruin until its demolition in 1968. Even today the gardens are pillaged by Dublin Corporation—the most recent loss a circular pool transported to make the Garden of Peace beside Christ Church Cathedral.

DONABATE: **Catholic Church**
Designed by George O'Connor in a *retardaire* Gothic Revival apart from its execution in a perennial harsh red brick; unchanged since its completion in 1906. Described by Belacqua in Beckett's *More Pricks than Kicks* as 'the horrible red chapel of Donabate' and carefully avoided on his walk with Winnie along the coast of Fingal. Harry Clarke window, 'Suffer Little Children' (1926).

HOWTH: **Carrickbrack**
The seaside retreat of Dr William Stokes, acquired in 1856. An exquisite late watercolour by Benjamin Woodward shows an intended Gothicization never executed apart from a verandah (since removed), but Woodward's gatelodge with its strutted timber porch was constructed. Dr Stokes revealed that Woodward recommended copying it since he could do no better. For many years the home of Mungo Park, the explorer, and his descendants.

HOWTH: **Catholic Church**
Diluted Romanesque Revival church over-prominently sited in the centre of the main street of the village with attached tower that never received its spire. Built out of Wicklow granite to the designs of W.H. Byrne in 1899. Windows by Messrs Mattin.

HOWTH: **Church of Ireland**
Built in 1866 to the designs of J.E. Rogers incorporating the base of an earlier tower which he refaced and capped with a new broached spire. Stone columns, brick arches, trefoiled clerestory and plastered walls create an interior that almost lives up to the ideals of his master, Benjamin Woodward. Organ by Telford. Fine window behind the altar by an unknown artist to the last of the St Lawrences (1910). Glass in south aisle by Child (1905), Rhind (1910 and 1920), Hone (1943) and O'Brien (1961).

HOWTH: **Drumleck**
An earlier house with views across Dublin bay, remodelled and extended as an Italian villa by

Hugh Carmichael in 1852 for a solicitor, William McDougall, who was later to employ Woodward to design Brownsbarn in Co. Kilkenny (q.v.). Inherited by a daughter, Frances, who married J.P. Mahaffy. More recently the home of the collectors Mr and Mrs John Hunt, who complemented the house by creating an Italian garden descending to the sea.

HOWTH: Glenaveena

Simplified Venetian Gothic villa designed by Benjamin Woodward in 1859 for Sir Edward Borough; built on a terrace hillside overlooking Dublin bay. Reception rooms on the upper level with splayed ceilings rising into the roof space and loggias opening southwards to the sea. Underneath the ground falls away to expose the service floor. Now owned by the Sisters of Charity.

HOWTH: Howth Castle

Different architects were called during the 1830s to medievalize and extend the irregular pile of buildings that already had served the St Lawrences as the family home for eight centuries. The architect eventually chosen was Sir Richard Morrison. At the death of the last Lord Howth (*c.*1910) Edwin Lutyens was commissioned to house the library of the Gaisford who had married the eldest daughter. Lutyens added a new tower with a square room spanned by intersecting beams lined with books. He carried up the corners of his tower to three stories, paraphrasing the existing battlements. He linked his new turret bedrooms to the main stairs by a corridor wittily corbelled out on tiny oriels but only appreciable from the kitchen yard. Elsewhere he dallies with Italian Renaissance—the garden loggia, the domed Catholic chapel, the hall fireplace framed by a salvaged Venetian window, the Ionic pilastered diningroom with the earliest example of using of Chinese Chippendale to conceal a central heating system. Against the south-eastern wing Lutyens designed a formal herb garden in 1910.

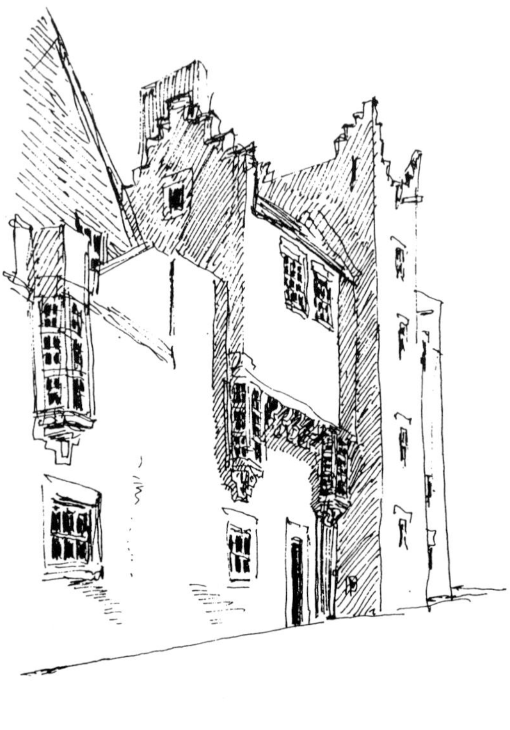

HOWTH: Presbyterian Church

Church, hall and manse make up an indivisible cluster, so unusual in Ireland. Designed by A. Young, an otherwise unknown London architect, in 1900. His idiom, Perpendicular Gothic invigorated by the influence of the Arts and Crafts. Classical entrance gates, neo-Elizabethan manse. Interior has suffered later alterations.

HOWTH: Methodist Church

Crisply designed Romanesque Revival church with witty diagonal spire (the architect's signature). Designed by George Beckett in 1902.

HOWTH: Seaside

Said to have been built to his own designs by a retired sea captain in 1860 but in any case an extraordinary example (in banded brick and stone) of an amateur inspired by the Gothic of his contemporary Benjamin Woodward and mixing it with borrowings from Ireland's Celtic past (then being rediscovered by his neighbours, the Stokes). The articulated corner piers, the corbelled upper floors, and the occasional arched window crazily mixed with the conventional sash are Celtic; the steep roofs, the chimneys, dormers and rows of tiny trefoils are Woodward. The massing from the rear with the attached kitchen block (a miniature of the house itself) could have started off as the proverbial sketch by Woodward on the back of an envelope. Surprisingly convenient if compressed interior with many zig-zag mouldings.

DRUMCONDRA: All Hallows

The Early Georgian house was extended to the rear in 1853 by J.J. McCarthy with his characteristic institutional Gothic that ultimately advances forward again to terminate in an almost free-standing collegiate chapel, designed by George Ashlin, his rival, in 1876. Façade dominated by large rose window now filled with stained glass of Evie Hone (1953). Fittings by Ashlin, adapted during the 1960s. Architects subsequent to McCarthy have taken more notice of the Georgian house and have tried to blend in their own additions with little success. J.J.

O'Callaghan was the earliest, with his large symmetrical Italianate novitiate of 1884.

DRUMCONDRA: **Archbishop's House**
Red-brick villa with stone trimmings built as a typical Ailesbury Road villa by an unidentified architect for the Dublin archdiocese *c.*1875.

DRUMCONDRA: **Garden Farm**
Italianate villa designed by Albert Murray. Restless exterior but with spacious south-facing reception rooms that were or should have been effortlessly converted to its present use as the Airport Regency Hotel. Fortunately there are signs today that these rooms are being appreciated in their own right.

DRUMCONDRA: **High Court Convent**
By O'Neill and Byrne, 1878. Neo-Romanesque in red brick.

DRUMCONDRA: **Holy Cross Church and College**
The church was commissioned by Cardinal Cullen, who commanded J.J. McCarthy to build in the Roman idiom. All long-living Gothic Revivalists who worked for Roman Catholicism had to at some point of their career sublimate their personal beliefs. In Ireland McCarthy was the most successful because his sublimation was so wholehearted: his Roman precedents for the church were St Agata dei Goti and St Francesca Romana in the Forum. The restraint of the flat, coffered ceiling recreates Rome's early Christian architecture, if less so since the removal of some of Gagliardi wall paintings, victims of the Irish damp. Sculptures of Pius IX (by Matteini) and Cardinal Cullen (after Farrell) guard the arcaded porch against doubters of infallibility. Austere neo-Georgian college designed by John Bourke in 1861.

DRUMCONDRA, **Iona Road: Redemptoristine Convent and Chapel**
An external grimness effectively insulates this 1873 commission of George Ashlin from the outside world. His clients were an enclosed order of nuns whose only external contact was in the daily celebration of Mass heard from a grilled tribune. Ashlin juggles with so many styles to create in restricted dimensions one of his most memorable interiors. Called at its consecration Late Norman, the chapel is in reality a compendium of religious architecture over the last millennium—a five-bay nave with the first two bays double-storied, the public on ground level, the nuns above, their presence sensed only as a disembodied choir. The nave ends with a Palladian triumphant arch that frames a domed crossing flanked by barrel-vaulted transepts and an arcaded apse beyond. The increasing complexity of the architecture is mirrored by the richness of the inlaid marble decoration. The only external evidence of all this is a skylight in the roof fixed above the dome.

DRUMCONDRA: **St Patrick's Training College**
Early Georgian house extended by the Vincentians in 1885. Their architect was J.L. Robinson, who worked here for six years but died before he could build the chapel. Hence George Ashlin got the job (in 1899). However, Robinson's aggressive Italianate belvedere still dominates all distant views despite many later extensions.

FAIRVIEW, **Jones Road: Dublin Whiskey Distillery**
A distillery started in 1873, long since made redundant but still occupied as an industrial enterprise centre. The original machinery was provided by Lagan Foundry of Belfast, who also

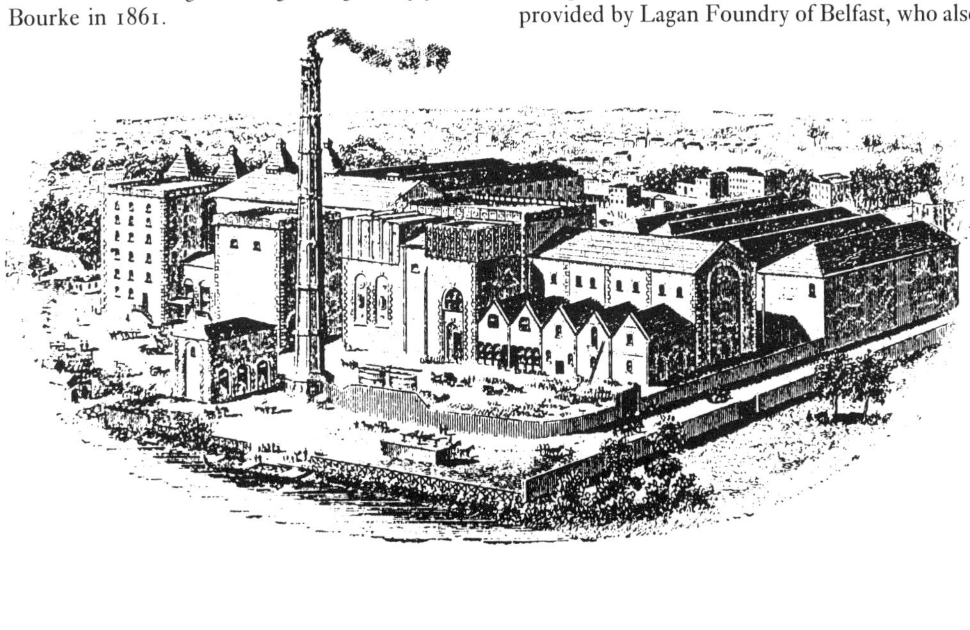

made the roof trusses, but there is no record of the architect with his fondness for semi-circular arches. The most impressive interiors are in the house with steel columns and concrete umbrella vaults. Compare with Guinness' Robert Street Malt Store (q.v.).

FAIRVIEW: **O'Brien Institute, Marino**

J.J. O'Callaghan was totally unembarrassed when asked in 1881 to build this charitable orphanage so close to the Casino, the masterpiece of Sir William Chambers. His banded red-brick and stone façade, symmetrical apart from the adjoining chapel, proclaims the superiority of Gothic to all manifestations of Classicism based on pagan antiquity. Alas, he had not reckoned with the new science of psychology. Closed down like all orphanages and acquired by Dublin Corporation as a trainee centre for the fire brigade; it is still empty. The Casino beside it has been restored and is filled to overflowing with visitors. Will the next century see the Casino too fragile to be visited, and to be viewed instead from the O'Brien Institute set up as an Irish Georgian interpretative centre?

GLASNEVIN: **Agricultural College**

The only major Government commission awarded in 1908 to J.F. Fuller throughout his long career despite his loyalism. Built in a grim neo-Elizabethan institutional idiom of half a century earlier.

GLASNEVIN: **Botanic Gardens**

The celebrated curvilinear conservatory that on first sight appears to have been erected as fast as the Crystal Palace is in reality a series of interlinked pavilions built by Richard Turner throughout his long career as a Dublin ironmaster. Such was the consistency of his style that he was able in his last commission of 1871 and 1876 to match the eastern wing he had built thirty years before. In 1871 he was erroneously described as 'the late Mr Turner'. The loftier centre block of 1876 is braced by a network of arches springing from colonnettes like stylized palms. The earliest (1843) range had been designed by William Clancy, the 1845-6 central pavilion by Frederick Darley, the last wing by his son William after his father had retired from the ironworks (having lost the commission of the nearby palmhouse that the RDS awarded to James Owen of the OPW in 1862). Ironically this gabled structure collapsed a few years later and had to be rebuilt by Boyd of Glasgow (in 1884), who, though they could not make their curvilinear structure graceful, at least made it safe. Boyd subsequently built the cactus and the succulent house in 1895.

Indeed Turner went closer than any of his contemporaries in parallelling the structure of the plants he had been asked to house. He had started as a maker of Dublin fanlights and his conservatories are Dublin fanlights turned into three dimensions. His formal vocabulary is neo-Grecian but mobilized to resist the continuous wind and rain of northwestern Europe. The cornices are in reality gutters, the columns drainpipes; the acroteriae and palmettes are wind deflectors; the glazed pilasters have capitals that mask ventilators. All this anticipates present trends of post-modern minimalism: fantasy and technology are interlinked.

The gardens themselves were redesigned to suit Victorian taste by Ninian Niven from 1834 onwards.

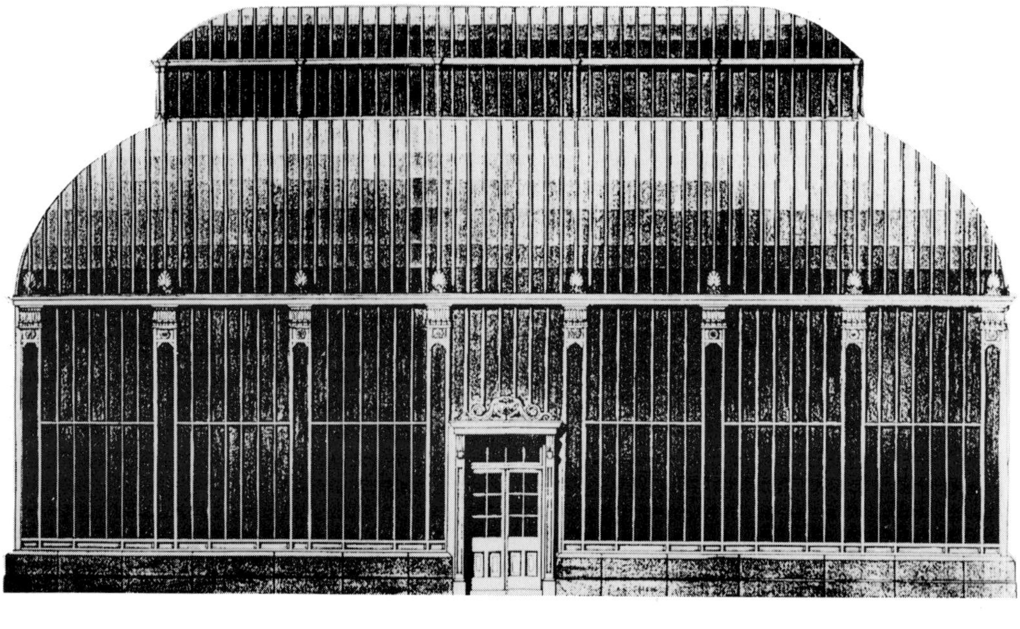

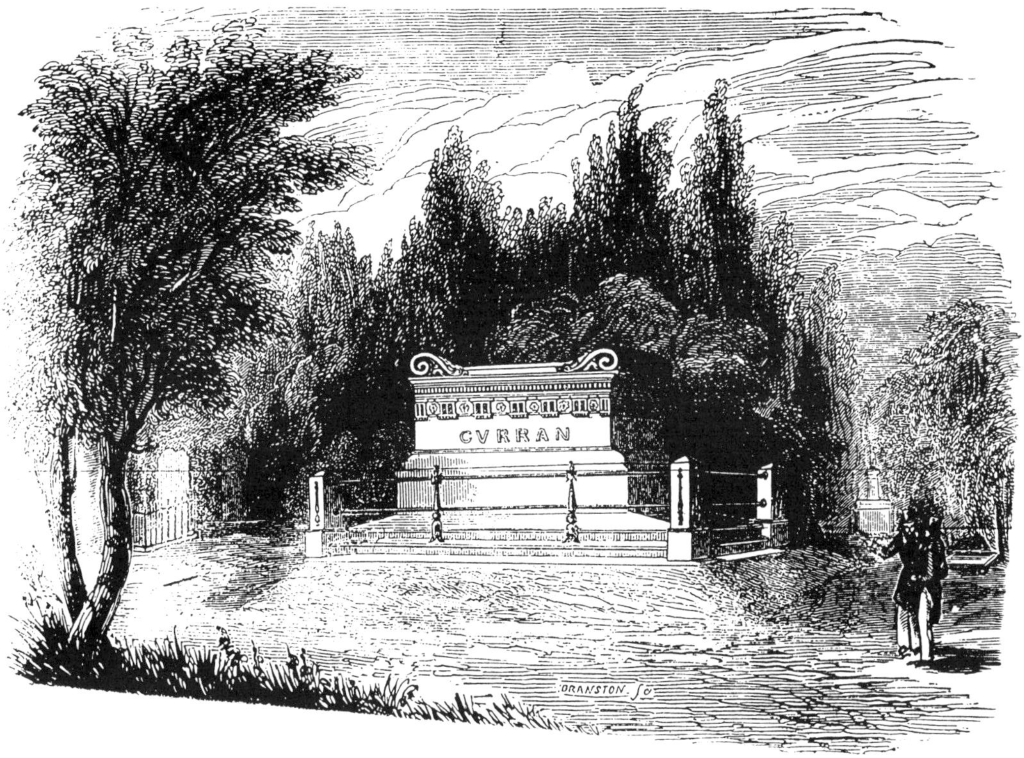

GLASNEVIN: **The Cemetery**

The national necropolis, its focal point the round tower erected above O'Connell's tomb, the highest in Ireland, completed in 1861. When originally designed by George Petrie it was intended to be part of an Early Christian complex but on a smaller scale. The over-sized tower used up all the funds. The crypt beneath houses the Hiberno-Romanesque tomb carved by Earley and Powell and supervised by the Liberator's grandson, Daniel O'Connell (1869). The circular moat gives access to the vaults of the most favoured tombs. The Celtic Revival predominates, the best high cross being the Ellen Burke memorial, carved by Pearse and Sharp to the design of W.H. Byrne (1879) and the less correct Yore memorial to the design of Cally and Farrell (1862). The Devitt Cross of 1872 by Fitzpatrick and Molloy. The highest cross is the Emmet memorial by Earley. Disrupting this sequence is a weak St Michael by C. Smyth for the Meades (1866) and the Gothic fantasy of the Boland chapel (1859) carved by Pettigrue: the probable architect, Charles Geoghegan, sets up a star-shaped chevet that integrates his triangular transepts into a continuous rhythm. Beside it the Campbell mortuary chapel (1869) follows the conventional pattern repeated in the Keogh and the Lawlor oratories. The Farrell firm responsible for the Lawlor tomb (1865) was headed by Sir Thomas Farrell, whose most noted statue is of Barry Sullivan (1891), the actor. He also sculpted the effigy of Cardinal McCabe in the Celtic shrine carved by Charles Harrison and designed in 1888 by George Ashlin to upstage the church of his recently deceased rival, J.J. McCarthy. This church (1870-8) marks the closest McCarthy ever came to the Celtic Revival, but it was built too late in his career to reveal the challenging Brutalism of his Kerry Romanesque. An eastern apse, a transept, an attached campanile and stained glass by Clayton and Bell militate against its Gaelicism. One of the few monuments to express the primitive force of Irish nationalism is the 1916 memorial by Dora Shorter. The 1914 Cadic memorial is designed by William Scott and sculpted by Michael Shortall. The Celticism of the political establishment on the other hand is expressed by Sir Thomas Drew in his memorial to Thomas Burke murdered by the Invincibles (1882).

The most atmospheric grouping is that of the chapel circle where immense beech trees shelter the monuments—the Ionic tempietto raised to Sir Timothy O'Brien (1862); the Grecian Merriman tomb by H. Carmichael (1850); the Gothic Sullivan tomb (1860); and the eclectic Thunder tomb with its curtained campanile (1840). Beyond, near the original gates to Prospect Square designed by Patrick Byrne, is the Curran tomb based by George

Papworth on that of Scipio Barbatus in Rome. Beside it is the elegant Grecian tomb sculpted by Michael Kirwan for Edward Southwell Ruthven, who laid the foundation stone of O'Connell's tower. In contrast, the Gothic

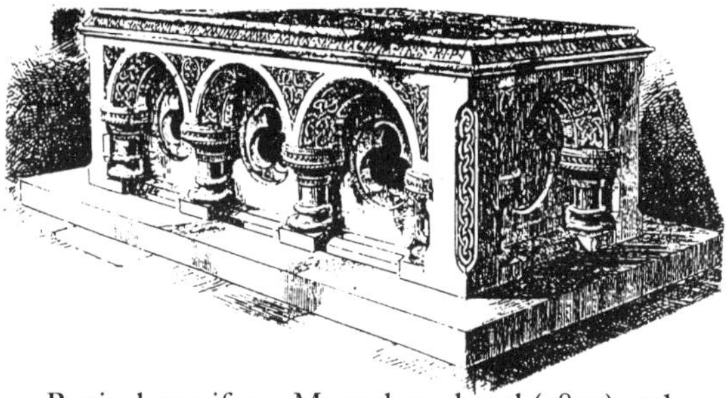

Revival cruciform Monaghan chapel (1855) and the pinnacled Connolly tomb of 1860. The latter is in the style of William Deane Butler, the best of its kind here, better than the octagonal polychromatic marbled Cassidy shrine (carved by Fitzpatrick and Molloy), one of the few to be signed by an architect—Charles Geoghegan (1870). A decade later a replica lapses into kitsch—the Anne McCabe tomb. The most notable Celtic Revival kitsch is the John Keegan Casey tomb with a wolfhound guarding the manuscript of his most famous song; of the neo-Classical kitsch, the Coppinger tomb (1847), a voluminously draped urn on the perimeter of the O'Connell circle. The formidable Revd Daniel Cahill by James Cahill express the full authority of rural Ireland. The cemetery's memorials chart the rise and fall of self-aggrandisement in the face of death.

LAMBAY

An Elizabethan fortress built by the Talbots to protect the northern approach to their port of Malahide and sold to Cecil Baring, later 3rd Baron Revelstoke, as a retreat from social ostracism after he had eloped with the wife of his American partner, having managed to lock up her psychotic husband in the vault of the family bank. Their exile from London society came to an end when her father became the first American to win the Derby, but in the meantime they had enlisted Edwin Lutyens to create their private paradise. He began in 1905 and continued till the 1930s, when he designed the neo-Classical memorial for the Revelstokes. Since then the house and grounds have been scrupulously preserved by their son as an indissoluble work of art. The contents are still placed where Lutyens and his clients decided, supplemented by the furniture designed by the architect and made by Heals (thereby inventing Habitat).

But more extraordinary than Lutyens' inventiveness at Lambay was his ability to absorb what already existed and by a few deft touches imprint his personality. Lambay illustrates the aphorism of Borges that the true original invents

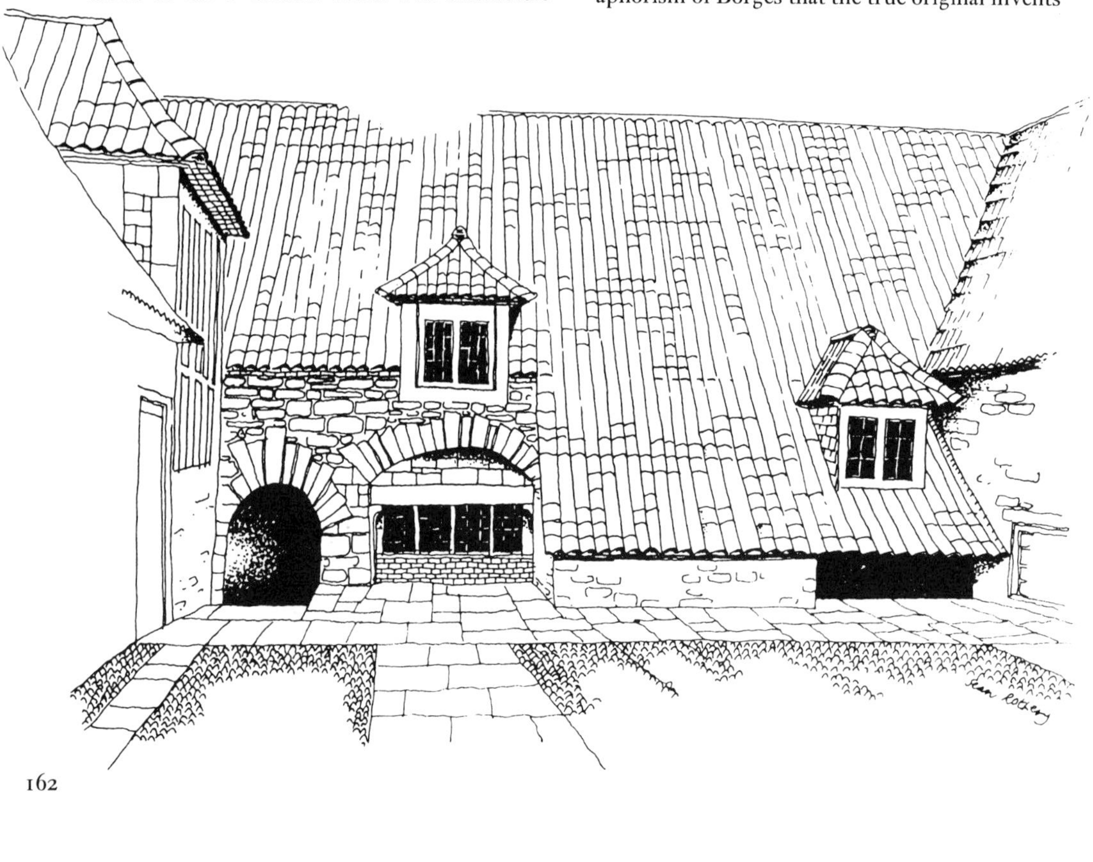

not our future but our past. The ordnance map of the 1840s reveals that much that we assume today to be designed by Lutyens was already in place, including part of the circular *enceinte* centred on the castle and the service courtyard rebuilt to accommodate Edwardian house parties. The link between the castle and this courtyard was regarded by Lutyens himself as one of his most brilliant coups. The castle that appears only one-storied at that point due to the contours of the site still dominates its dependencies, since they appear to be just great pantiled roofs leisurely disrupted by the occasional dormer and brought almost to ground level in the court itself. The same pantiles were used to reroof the castle. The new walls, like the old, are of unpolished porphyry—'coppery green and coppery brown with purple streaks, like a stormy sea, shot through with feldspar crystals'. Unlike the woodworkers, the masons were local, and every fireplace gave Lutyens an opportunity to improvize unexpected variants. All walls were whitewashed, all floors of scrubbed oak in revulsion to the gilding and alabaster of the Style Rothschild.

The gardens originally planted by Gertrude Jeykell emphasize the splayed vistas and the gently rising gradient of the site that subtly and often wickedly disrupts the apparent formality. This play is discerned only by the initiated.

In contrast to this are the existing coastguard cottages remodelled by Lutyens, each with a tiny back garden; beside them lies the White House built later for the Baring children. Above, the chapel perpetuates the only difference of opinion between the Revelstokes: one believed and the other did not: hence a Greek temple lit from above the altar by a glazed Maltese cross now filled with the stained glass of their grandson Patrick Pollen.

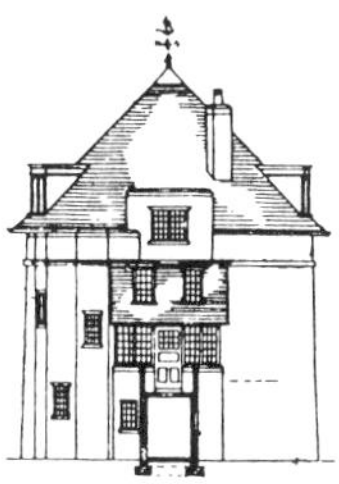

MALAHIDE: **Hicks Tower**
Martello tower converted by Frederick Hicks into his own residence; disguised by dormers and a conical tower to resemble a converted oast house in rural Sussex. Built in 1911 to rank as one of the few Arts and Crafts houses in the country.

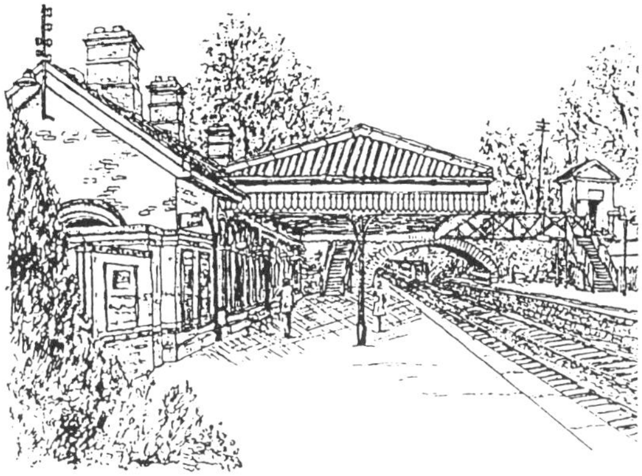

MALAHIDE: **Railway Station**
Picturesque Italianate single-storey complex built with polychromatic brickwork. Designed with an enviable user-friendliness by George Papworth (1851).

MALAHIDE: **St Dolough's Church**
Medieval fortified church restored by the antiquarian Lord Talbot and interconnected with a new church set beside it in 1863. His architect W.H. Lynn tied the old and new churches together by copying the steeply pitched roof (repeated on a smaller scale in his projecting chancel). He wisely refrained from adding a tower, relying instead on that of its predecessor. Cool, correct interior.

MALAHIDE: **Seamount**
The home of the Jameson family, who are still remembered as the epitome of impeccable Edwardian hospitality. Restrained neo-Elizabethan house set on a hill with a terraced garden. Rebuilt by Frederick Batchelor after a fire in 1904. Delightful timber gatelodge, now derelict.

PHIBSBOROUGH, **North Circular Road: Mountjoy Gaol**
Designed by Lt-Col. later Sir Joshua Jebb (in 1847-50) immediately after he had designed the Pentonville Gaol in London on the double-loaded corridor principle, thereby radically transforming prison design and causing most of the Irish prisons to be rebuilt over the next two decades. The assistant architect was Jacob Owen of the OPW. Jebb was brought in by the Government after Owen had complained of overwork. Impressively forbidding triumphal arch flanked by towers; military architecture reduced to essentials. Adjoining women's gaol, 1855-8.

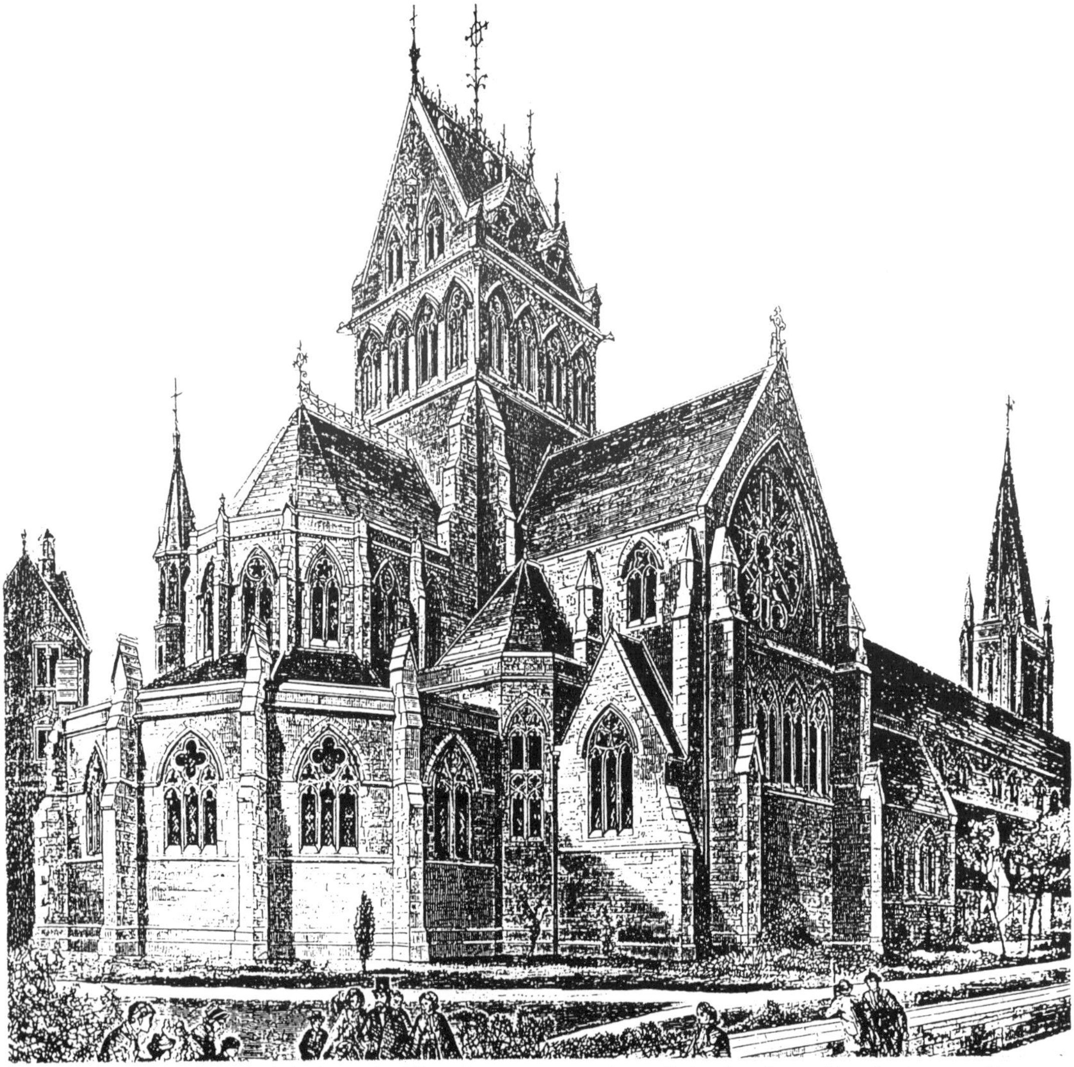

PHIBSBOROUGH: St Peter's Church

Since Ashlin and Coleman in 1902 rebuilt the nave of 1831 (already remodelled in 1850), the earliest part of the church that survives is the full-blown chevet at what should have been the east but is here the west end. This was commissioned in 1862 for the Vincentian Order, by the superior, Father McNamara, from George Goldie, who had also been commissioned to extend the sister house in Cork. In Cork Goldie could rely on the engineering expertise of Sir John Benson, but in Dublin he got into serious trouble: his saddle-backed crossing tower, the satisfying climax to the original design, had to be taken down just after its completion (its stone was reused in a local pub). A protracted court case followed during the next decade which certainly affected Goldie's Irish practice. But what survives is one of the most remarkable adaptions of Early French Gothic in Ireland, as logical as its prototype but inventive in its own right: note his treatment of the transept chapels that adjoin the chevet (inspired, according to a contemporary, by Linz Cathedral). They are built up against the earlier monastery (of Strawberry Hill Gothic), less delightful now that the original timber traceried windows have been replaced with aluminium. Recent alteration has also disimproved the proportions of the altar and damaged the church's greatest treasure, the triple window by Harry Clarke in the mortuary chapel which has lost its upper lights. Further stained glass in the chevet and transept by Lobin of Tours. The Mayer windows of the nave were installed just after the remodelling of the nave, which George Ashlin extended with a tower and spire above the entrance. In contrast with the Augustinian church, where Ashlin had collaborated with E.W. Pugin forty years before, St Peter's belfry relies not on its originality of design but merely on its height—over 200 ft; its spire is a counterpart to Killarney Cathedral's (which Ashlin was completing at the same time).

PHIBSBOROUGH, Berkeley Road: St Joseph's Church

The largest Dublin church by O'Neill and Byrne, designed in 1880 and characteristic of their output. Built out of granite treated in rock-faced ashlar. Polychromatic slated roof with alternate horizontal bands. Tower added to the façade in 1893. The mid-Gothic Revival interior is spacious, with a lofty nave leading directly into a polygonal chancel. Stained glass by Hardman (west window of the Blessed Virgin aisle). The reredos carved by Mary Redmond to the designs of George Ashlin was removed when the church was adapted to the liturgical trends of the early 1960s, but side altars and shrines were spared.

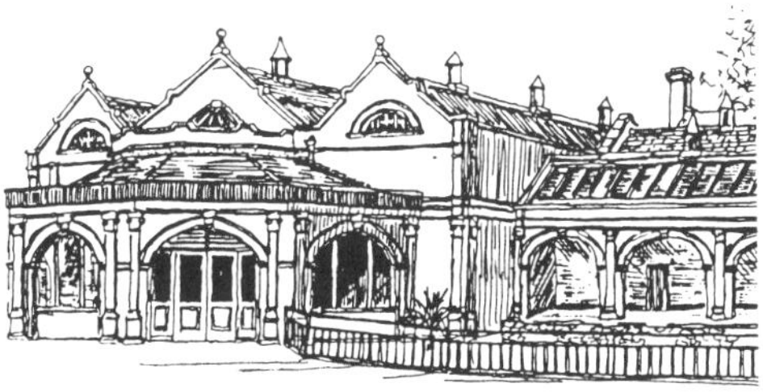

PHOENIX PARK: The Zoo

The best of the Victorian buildings here is the Haughton memorial restaurant by L.M. McDonnell, characteristic of his half-timbered neo-Tudor style; completed in 1900. McDonnell also designed the functional Lion House four years later.

PORTMARNOCK: Country Club

A Georgian house known originally as St Marnock's was remodelled and extended in 1893 by the *bon viveur* and yachtsman Willie Jameson to provide an appropriate setting for his legendary hospitality, at least on land. He also owned one of the great yachts of his generation where he entertained Edward VII. Due to the family's Scottish origins, the commission was given to Sir Robert Lorimer, his only work in Ireland. The exterior, like the gatelodge, is restrained; the staff wing is treated as an austere Scottish tower house; and the unorthodox stone carving of the entrance is hardly a foretaste of the exuberance within. A vaulted corridor leads into a living hall with luxuriant coffered plasterwork and pannelled marquetry paraphrasing the 17th century. Beyond, a staircase hall with scrolled balusters and arcades of wreathed columns leads to the upper floor. Throughout polychromatic marble bolection fireplaces with blazing fires still dispel all damp and chill.

Lorimer's garden was designed to shelter its planting from the sea by curvilinear parapets to red-brick walls which at one point turn into a series of concave screens. Garden access from the house axised on a viewing platform inscribed with the date, 1907.

PORTRANE: Mental Hospital

The largest secular commission of George Ashlin won in a limited competition. It subsequently turned out to be the most expensive job ever executed by the British government in Ireland. Part of the problem was the inaccessibility of the selected site. Another was the choice of so many imported materials, including a particularly harsh red brick. Thirdly, there was the complexity of the plan due to a valiant attempt by Ashlin to counterbalance institutionalism by giving a domestic scale to the kernel of the scheme that then branches out to absorb the larger buildings; but the rigidly symmetrical segregation of the sexes is everywhere only too evident.

The most highly organized of the Late Victorian asylums accommodating four cate-

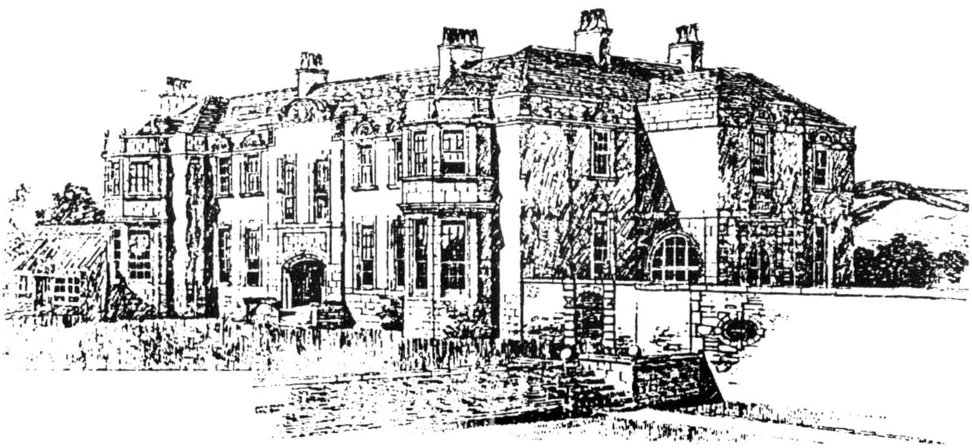

gories of the insane—the chronic in three-storied units; the melancholic or suicidal in two-storied units; the recent or acute likewise housed on two floors; the epileptic or infirm kept in twin bungalow blocks the furtherest from the entrance. Each sex was kept apart and assumed to be of equal numbers in the four categories. Symmetry was broken down only in the two chapels, the Catholic chapel being inevitably larger. Pyromaniacs were frustrated by consistently fireproof construction.

PORTRANE: Round Tower

Replica of Celtic round tower built by Sophia Evans née Parnell, a grand-aunt of the statesman, as a memorial to her husband George, who died in 1844. Said to have acted as her own architect. Noted by Belacqua in Beckett's *More Pricks than Kicks*.

RAHENY: Bettyglen

One of the country-house commissions given in 1910 by the Jamesons to the partnership of Batchelor and Hicks. This is designed like all Jameson houses to overlook a terraced garden and the sea. Rendered in pebbledash with granite dressings, the most prominent feature of the entrance front is a sweeping roof broken by a double tier of dormers (the influence of Lambay: q.v.). The reception rooms extend asymmetrically far into the garden, seeking both sun and view of the sea (now visible through chinks of a recent housing estate).

RAHENY: St Assam's Church

A Late Gothic Revival church designed by Patrick Byrne and posthumously erected in 1864. A single cell of modest dimensions but organically composed following the principles of Pugin. Now a community hall.

RAHENY: Church of Ireland

Commissioned by Lord and Lady Ardilaun from George Ashlin as their final resting place, and only excelled by Myshall (Co. Carlow) as his most elaborate and thoughtful memorial church, completed in 1891. His favourite ritualistic sequence—the entry through an asymmetrical southwestern belfry focused on an apsidal baptistery, projecting to the north. The major axis of the interior is at right angles, focused on the chancel. The funeral chapel is discreetly inserted between chancel and transept counterbalanced by the vestry. It is the only interior to be vaulted with stone, the remainder of the church being roofed in Riga oak. Pulpit and altar carved by A.P. Sharp. Mosaic floor by Oppenheimers. Stained glass by Heaton, Butler and Bayne, apart from a pair of trumpeting angels by Rhind (1917). The ilex avenue planted by Lord Ardilaun survives but leads only to a levelled site that was once his home. The lodge commissioned from Ashlin for the verger is still intact and appreciated.

RUSH: Catholic Church

Early Gothic Revival church by George Papworth, *c.*1835, extended but not improved by George Ashlin, who built the inconsequential tower with a belfry (since removed), the transepts and the chancel. The church was the victim of a dispute between a parish priest and his dissident flock, who, appalled at his decision to replace it with a new church, called a mass protest which ended with the election of a committee secretly supportive of him. Thus did Communism control Eastern Europe. The compromise retained the old church beside the new as a poignant reminder despite its condemnation as a dangerous structure. Now being restored by a FÁS scheme.

RUSH: Church of Ireland

Built by J.E. Rogers *c.*1865 for the Fenwick Palmers of Kenure Park. Simple cell, polychromatic stone without and lined with brick within. Rose window beneath the western bellcote filled with heraldic glass by J.H. Powell. Fine neo-medieval glass in the eastern window contemporary with the church. Stylized stone-carving at its finest in the off-centre font and the chubby pulpit. School and rectory also by Rogers (attempting the idiom of his late master, Benjamin Woodward, 1842, but without his concision).

RUSH: Kenure Park

The two wrought-iron gates and Italianate gate-lodges give an illusion of entering into a demesne surrounding a great countryhouse. But only a determined campaign by local residents of Kenure Park has preserved George Papworth's immense granite portico, while the remainder of the house has been demolished. Gone is the sequence of outer and inner marbled halls, with a leisurely imperial staircase leading to Robert West's first-floor salon erected a century earlier. The Fenwick-Palmers had survived 18th-century penal legislation despite the dangers posed to the established church by the beauty of Miss Palmer as noted by Lord Chesterfield—but would have sold their house to Eton College in the 1960s if the Labour government had implemented its policy against English public schools. Acquired instead by Dublin County Council as a housing site and left to its dry rot.

SKERRIES: **Carnegie Library**
Designed in 1905 by Anthony Scott and his son William. Witty enough to be by William alone—a square entry tower with scrolled side bays, one of which accommodates the staircase to the upper floor. The scrolls crown a stepped parapet, and are repeated at the top of the tower in a reduced version. The primitive Romanesque entrance reacts against this flurry of Baroque.

SKERRIES: **Church of Ireland**
Designed by J.E. Rogers for Lord Holmpatrick and built in 1869 with nave, chancel and off-centre tower and spire. After the grimness of the exterior with its bush-hammered ashlar, the repose of the neo-medieval interior comes as a relief. Timber-sheeted wagon vault held in place by crossbars and uprights inspired by Burges that make the rose window of the western gable impossible to see from the chancel. A forceful arcade upholds the gallery for the choir. Stylized stone-carving characteristic of Harrison.

SUTTON: **Sutton House**
The principal seat of the Jameson family, designed by the Manchester architect Alfred Darbyshire, who had worked many years before on their distilleries. The house is built on several terraces to take advantage of its spectacular views south across Dublin bay, and Darbyshire mixed a formidable neo-Tudor with a gracious neo-Adamesque. One dismounts in front of an immense red-brick pile attached to a four-storied tower; enters a ground floor with only one major room, the diningroom; ascends a Baronial staircase to reach the rest of the reception rooms (in what appears to be a Late Georgian addition). These have lacy plasterwork and salvaged fireplaces; they open southwards into a secret hanging garden. However, the internal decoration, although accomplished, cannot compare with the *joie de vivre* of the contemporary Portmarnock House (now Country Club: q.v.), created by Lorimer for an extravagant younger brother. Now an hotel and conference centre.

SWORDS: **Brackenstown**
Only the porch of the house attributed to Galilei (*c.*1720) survives as a summer house in the Italianate garden. The present house is a neo-Geogian replacement by Orpen and Dickenson, completed just before the First World War was to destroy that world of continuous house parties for which it was so thoughtfully designed—with its generous *porte-cochère* and endless subsidiary wing to accommodate the overflow of guests.

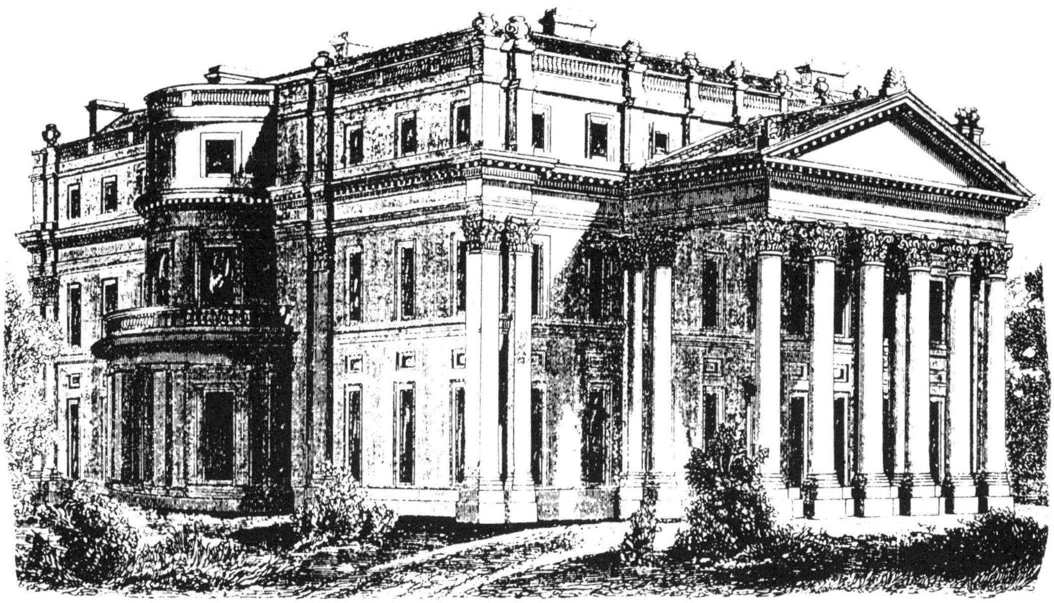

KENURE PARK

DUBLIN: SOUTH SUBURBS AND SOUTH COUNTY

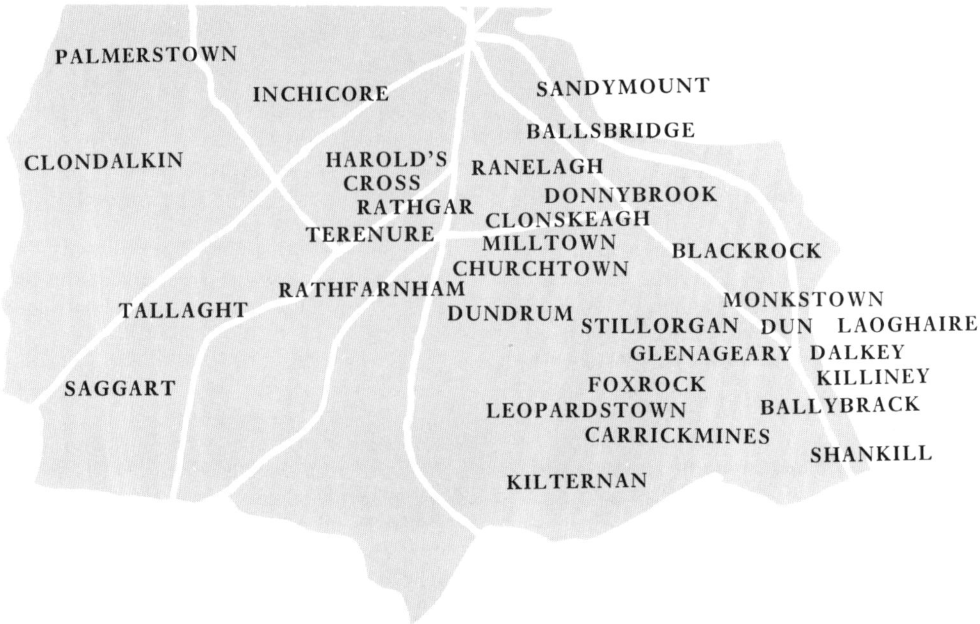

BALLSBRIDGE, **Ailesbury Road: Correen**
Capacious Tudor Revival with touches of Art Nouveau, a combination that Richard Orpen made so acceptable to his clients—here R. Manifold, who acquired this prominent corner site in 1898. Acquired by Edmund Williams of the Tullamore brewing family. Recently painlessly divided into three houses by de Blacam and Meagher.

BALLSBRIDGE, **Ailesbury Road: Rockville**
Sedate red-brick Victorian villa (by an unknown architect), given a touch of fantasy by a tower crowned for four corner lions.

BALLSBRIDGE, **Ailesbury Road: St Michael's**
Sumptuous Italian Romanesque villa complete with tower, conservatory and stable block (the two last-mentioned now demolished). Commissioned by Alderman Meade and named after his patron saint. Attributed by Frederick O'Dwyer to J.J. McCarthy. Extended by F.G. Hicks with a half-timbered billiard room for Sir Ernest Cochrane. Now a school.

BALLSBRIDGE, **Ailesbury Road: French Embassy**
Elegant yellow-brick Franco-Italianate villa with imposing stone rising to a semicircular columned porch. Built by an Irish emigrant, George Bustard, who became a millionaire in Australia and who employed his unmarried sisters to supervise the construction of his Dublin dream house. His architect, recently identified by the discovery of a stylish perspective *c.*1870, was Alfred Gresham Jones, who, after his retirement, himself emigrated to Melbourne, where he died aged ninety-three. Interiors were remodelled in the Avant Garde of the 1960s but have now reverted to Second Empire.

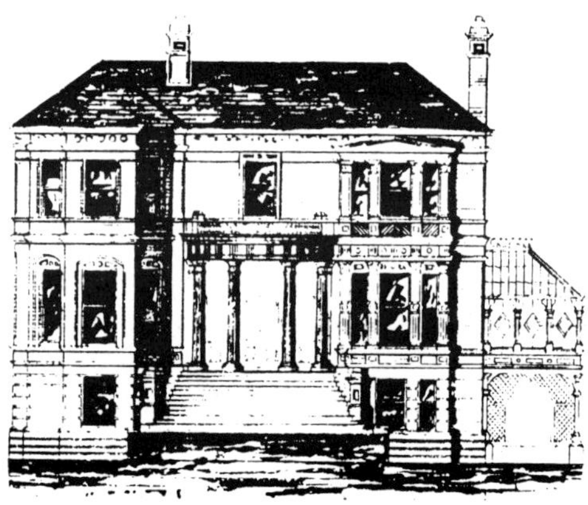

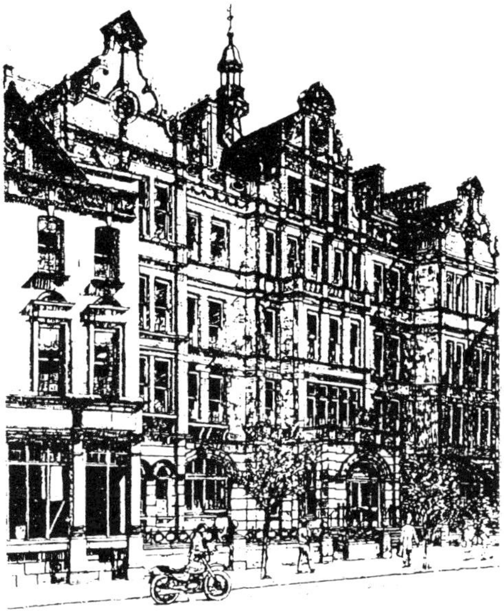

BALLSBRIDGE, **Baggot Street Upper: The Hospital**

Red brick and yellow terracotta triple-gabled façade tacked on to earlier institution has transformed this streetscape into a homage to Vermeer. Architect: Albert Murray; date: 1892. Other architects who worked on the adjoining shops, restaurants and pubs included James Farrell, Robert Stirling and J.J. O'Callaghan, whose Gothic detailing can always be singled out as the most incisive.

BALLSBRIDGE, **Clyde Road: St Bartholomew's**

T.H. Wyatt was the architect of the parish church of Wilton for the earls of Pembroke—hence his choice as the architect of the new Gothic Revival parish church built as the centrepiece of the Pembroke residential development throughout the inner southern suburbs as masterminded by Sidney Herbert. Work started on the selected corner site in 1864, but the central octagonal tower here incorporated into the chancel still remains incomplete. Instead, all attention has been lavished on the interior, with decorative murals executed by Sibthorpe to the designs of Thomas Newenham Deane. Victorian stained glass by Heaton Butler and Bayne apart from the fine glass in the chancel and at the west end by O'Connor (1869). The later stained glass in the church is by Catherine O'Brien, who also executed opus sectile along with McGoldrick. Deane found his inspiration during his Italian rambles, notably the Sicilian cathedral of Monreale with its suggestion of Arabian exoticism, a suitable backdrop to the High Anglican ritual as practised in the remote recesses of the British Empire and today a remarkable survival even if Deane's parish hall of *c.*1880 has been sold off along with the adjoining rectory of 1872 by J.E. Rogers. These have been acquired and scrupulously preserved by the Knights of Malta as the only Victorian private residence to survive intact on Clyde Road.

BALLSBRIDGE, **Eastmoreland Place: Hibernian Hotel**

Built as the nurses' home of the nearby Baggot Street hospital, and designed in 1900 by the same architect, Albert Murray—also in his favourite mixture, red brick and yellow terracotta trim. Successfully converted into a discreetly luxurious hotel.

BALLSBRIDGE, **Haddington Road: Catholic Church**

Gothic Revival church designed by an unidentified architect. When built, the church had an earthen floor, but since then Charles Geoghegan added the polygonal chancel, flanking side aisles and turret by J.J. O'Callaghan *c.*1888 and W.G. Doolin raised the tower in 1894. Harry Clarke, who decorated the interior with a series of angels in tempera (1924), made this church one of the most opulent in Dublin until the late 1960s when his angels were relegated to the rubbish tip; retrieved by James White, they are now in the National Gallery. Stained glass: St Cecilia (1904) by Child; Baptism of Christ by Elvery (1910). The adjoining schools of 1870 are by yet another architect involved here, J.J. McCarthy.

BALLSBRIDGE, **Merrion Road: former Masonic Girls' School**

A bluff brick and terracotta structure with the red and yellow polychromy of its walls contrasting with the green copper of its cupola. Set in front of it is an expensive cream-coloured ornamental fountain. Designed in 1882 by John McCurdy and W.F. Mitchell as their first incursion into the Queen Anne Revival, although here still weighed down by neo-Tudor, notably in the interior of the adjoining assembly hall. Acquired by the RDS but sold on by them.

BALLSBRIDGE, **Merrion Road: Pembroke Town Hall**

Ruskinian Gothic townhall with adjoining fire station designed by E.H. Carson in 1879 with the assistance of his pupil J.L. Robinson, who afterwards went on to win the competition for the townhall of Dun Laoghaire (q.v.). This was Carson's most important commission but not important enough to dispel a sense of failure discernable in the memories of Edward Carson, his more famous son, who invented an Italian

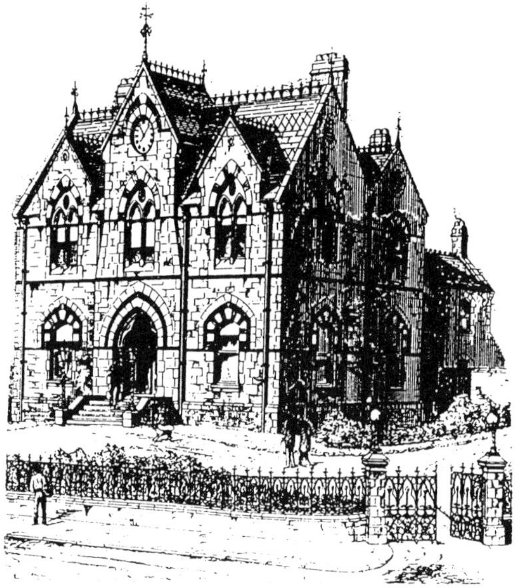

ancestry, from stuccodores in Dumfriesshire called Carsoni.

BALLSBRIDGE, Merrion Road: The Moorings and Cliveden
Accomplished double villa that verges on the American stick style. Designed by R.C. Millar *c.*1910.

BALLSBRIDGE, Merrion Road: Pembroke Housing
Compact gabled housing complex built for hardworking artisans but sought after to turn into luxury lovenests. Designed for the Pembroke Estate by H.E. Fitzgerald of Lismore, who won a competition in 1884. Other versions exist off Northumberland Road and Shelbourne Road, and in Donnybrook and Dundrum.

BALLSBRIDGE, Northumberland Road: St Stephen's Schools
With the loss of St Anne's schools to office development, the survival of these Deane and Woodward schools on an even more lucrative site is miraculous, since they are one-storied: three separately-roofed classrooms make up an H-shaped composition. The banded glazing and steep roofs are like their Dundum schools (q.v.), but here a dramatic note is introduced by accommodating the masters' private staircase into a circular turret as a vertical foil along with an adjoining chimney-stack to counteract the horizontality of the composition. Designed in 1856 for Sidney Herbert, but as half the money had to be raised by public subscription not started until 1859. The open scissors-truss structure is carried by piers to ground level, framing the casement windows and hooded chateau-style fireplaces. These features were badly copied by J.F. Fuller in his 1886 addition. More recently the roofs were felted at an immense loss to its original texture.

BALLSBRIDGE, Shelbourne Road: Post Office
Powerfully modelled red-brick horizontally treated composition topped by indented parapets. Designed by Howard Pentland in 1891 for the OPW.

BALLSBRIDGE, Shrewsbury Road: Hawthorn
Picturesque composition by Richard Orpen livened up by combining red-brick and half timber protected by a red-tiled roof held in place by asymmetrical chimney-stacks. The house epitomizes the security so sought after by stockbrokers.

BALLSBRIDGE, Shrewsbury Road: Runnymede
Name commemorates a marriage between the families of Rooney and Meade. A partly brick and partly half-timbered house of asymmetrical design by an architect called Dunlop *c.*1900. One of the rare houses of its kind to have a distinguished Arts and Crafts interior—accommodation grouped round a free-ranging double-height hall lit through a southern oriel. The first-floor balcony frames a set of later wall paintings commissioned from Sean Keating. Intimate inglenooks, that in the drawingroom lit by tiny windows.

BALLSBRIDGE, Shrewsbury Road: Woodside
A grimly serious 14th-century French Gothic-style house in red brick and Bath stone dressings. Now the appropriately institutional if eccentric headquarters of the Pharmaceutical Society of Ireland. Commissioned by J.C. Parkes in 1903 from the English architect Sylvanus Trevail, who a few months later jumped off the Taunton Express to his death.

BALLYBRACK: Ashurst
Red-brick Gothic Revival villa asymmetrically linked to a square viewing tower. Designed by W.H. Lynn for the Dobbs family and built in 1861-3. Acquired by the Catholic archdiocese of Dublin. Here died Archbishop J.C. McQuaid. Interior recently dismantled.

BALLYBRACK: Avonmore
W.G. Murray was the architect most influenced by the private houses of Benjamin Woodward, and this house of 1863 could have been by

Woodward were it not for a certain lack of finesse in the proportions. Also the combination of local granite and plate-glass windows gives a certain Ulster dourness in the interpretation of Ruskin's Lamp of Truth.

BALLYBRACK: Catholic Church

Gothic Revival church, one of the last designs of Patrick Byrne, built *c.*1860. Tower and spire added by a parishioner, George Ashlin, *c.*1880.

BALLYBRACK: Montebello

Elegant neo-Classical house probably by J.S. Mulvany, built for the Goodbody family, *c.*1840. Alterations by McCurdy and Mitchell in 1918.

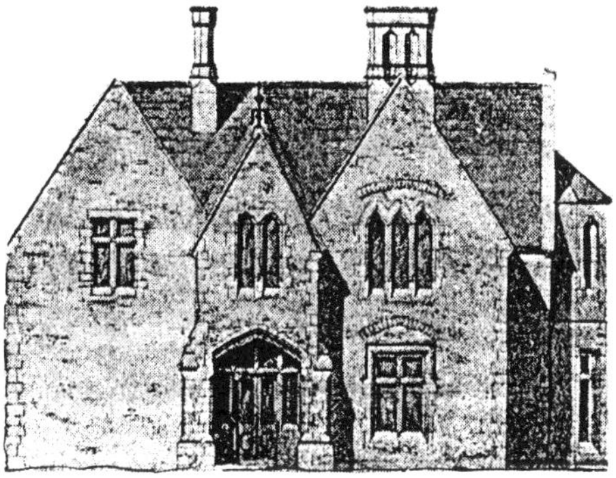

BALLYBRACK: Stonehurst

A villa built in 1861 that might appear to be a late work of Benjamin Woodward. In fact the house is the work of one of Woodward's most prolific contemporaries, William Murray, who indulged the public taste of his contemporaries by designing in a sumptuous Palladian, but here in his private house expressed his admiration for the Gothic Revival villas of his more gifted contemporary, though with a certain dourness, appropriate for an Ulsterman who had also assisted his father on the interminable neo-Tudor of Grangegorman Mental Hospital (q.v.).

BLACKROCK, Avoca Avenue: Church of Ireland

Commissioned in 1864 by Lord Carysfort from John McCurdy. The result is indistinguishable from the radical Gothic Revival of Welland and Gillespie—steeply roofed lean-to aisles glazed with trefoils; transepts glazed with quatrefoils. Built with adjoining rectory in bush-hammered granite Glass by Heaton, Butler and Bayne..

BLACKROCK, Avoca Avenue: Priory Lodge

Italianate villa with just a bay-windowed *piano nobile* set on an elevated basement. Designed by William Fogerty in 1864.

BLACKROCK, Avoca Road: Nos. 14 and 16

A pair of semi-detached Greek Revival villas with their division masked by a pedimented recess but with decoration round their doorcases, which led the *Dublin Builder* to term their architecture 'Byzantine'. Designed by A.G. Jones in 1862.

BLACKROCK: Blackrock College

Far-flung education complex built by the Holy Ghost Fathers after they had purchased Williamstown Castle, an example of Strawberry Hill Gothic. Upstairs drawingroom, now a private chapel with stained glass by Evie Hone. The driving force behind their expansion was their Alsatian prior, Father Martin Ebernecht. He designed the college chapel in 1867 and with the help of an in-house woodcarver, Father Eugene Devena, he recreated the late medieval churches of his childhood. Assembly hall by George Ashlin.

BLACKROCK: Catholic Church

Commissioned in 1842 by Lord Cloncurry from Patrick Byrne and the architect's most important attempt at Puginian Gothic modelled on the master's Staunton Harold church. The most impressive quality of the interior is the height of the chancel, preceded by an even loftier nave. But this leads to certain stilted Gothickry in the detailing, especially discernable in the reredos. Church twice extended by Byrne, in 1850 and 1856. Stained glass by Earley and more recently by Evie Hone and the Clarke Studios.

BLACKROCK, Cross Avenue: Church of Ireland

The Gothic Revival church by John Bowden of 1824 and twice extended by Rawson Carroll—in 1867, a polygonal apse enriched by pinnacles and the southern tran- sept; in 1876, the organ chamber and northern transept. Two windows of archangels by Geddes. A third window by her in the porch was destroyed by fire.

BLACKROCK, Cross Avenue: Glenvar

Villa designed by J.S. Mulvany in the RHA exhibition of 1867. Asymmetrical design with Grecian elevations but with Japanese concave roofs (originally sheeted with Malcolmson's patented felt and neo-Tudor chimneys). The closest Mulvany came to creating his own style. Extended by Alfred Cochrane.

BLACKROCK, Grove Avenue: Ardnaglaise

Red-brick and half-timbered villa still protected by its original ornamental grounds.

BLACKROCK, **Grove Avenue: St Heliers**
This imposing three-storied Queen Anne Revival house with symmetrical bow-windowed façade and more intriguing split-level rear bravely ignores the irrelevant intrusion of new houses into its garden.

BLACKROCK, **Mount Merrion Avenue: Presbyterian Church**
The most unusual of Dublin's Non-Conformist churches—a galleried octagon. Entered beneath a square tapering tower flanked by circular staircase turrets boldly built out from the angles of the octagon. Scottish Baronial vocabulary adapted by a London partnership, Murray and Forrester, who interpret the Gothic Revival of their own terms. Date 1898.

BLACKROCK: **Newtown House**
Spacious neo-Classical villa in the style of George Papworth. Lavish internal decoration—cloud-encircled stucco eagle grips the lantern in the hall. Frothy cornices in the double drawingroom beyond. The Corinthian pilasters frame sliding doors with inserted mirrors that divide the rooms. The larger is frescoed with Alpine scenes in the style of Edwin Hayes. Series restored and completed by Peter Pearson in 1983.

BLACKROCK: **Oriel House**
Charming polychromatic brick Tudor Revival cottage ornée, the home of the Orpen family where Richard the architect and William the artist were both brought up. Symmetrical gabled façade. Architect unknown.

BLACKROCK, **Temple Road: Council Flats**
Three-storied red-brick blocks of flats with open cast-iron balconies approached by enclosed staircases. Designed by A.G.C. Millar in 1896.

CARRICKMINES, **Brennanstown Road: Coologue**
The tile-capped conical gatepiers give a foretaste of this comfortable suburban retreat Richard Orpen built for himself in the early 1900s. More concise than his houses built for others, with a single pitched roof sweeping down to shelter sunny verandahs overlooking well tended terraced gardens. Interior has been altered since Richard Orpen died here in 1938.

CARRICKMINES, **Brennanstown Road: Glenacarraig**
Spacious Edwardian villa built for Joseph Mitchell Symes (1901). Attributed by Daniel Gillman to Millar and Symes.

CARRICKMINES, **Brennanstown Road: Lisheen**
Built for his brother Charles, this is one of the largest of Orpen's villas, but, despite its size, genial and informal. This is due to his pitched roof, sweeping down on the garden front to cover a low verandah. Its descent is broken by massive chimneys and varied dormers. At one end what appears to be a belvedere is only another first-floor bedroom, *c.*1905.

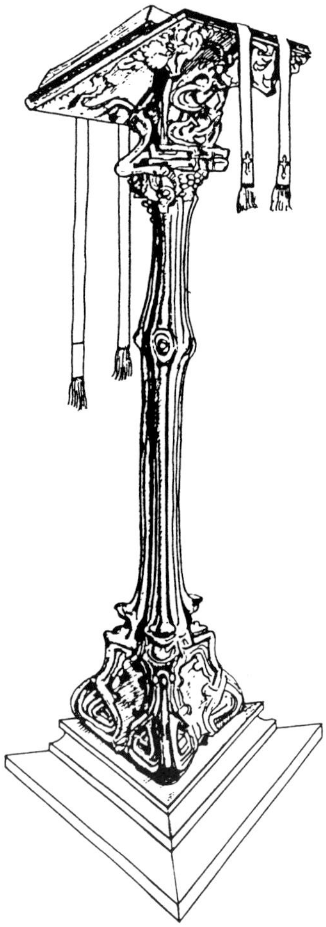

CARRICKMINES: **Tullow Church of Ireland**
The elegant octagonal Gothic spirelet is part of the original church (designed in 1864 by Welland and Gillespie) that has been continuously extended, so rare in the case of the Church of Ireland as to be remarkable and proclaimed in a kind of space-age Gothic porch added on to the façade. Its internal counterpart is the extraordinary bronze lectern of Beatrice Elvery, cast in Paris and the purest Irish example of Art Nouveau (1905). The architect in charge was Richard Orpen. He replaced J.F. Fuller, who had just added the nave. Orpen

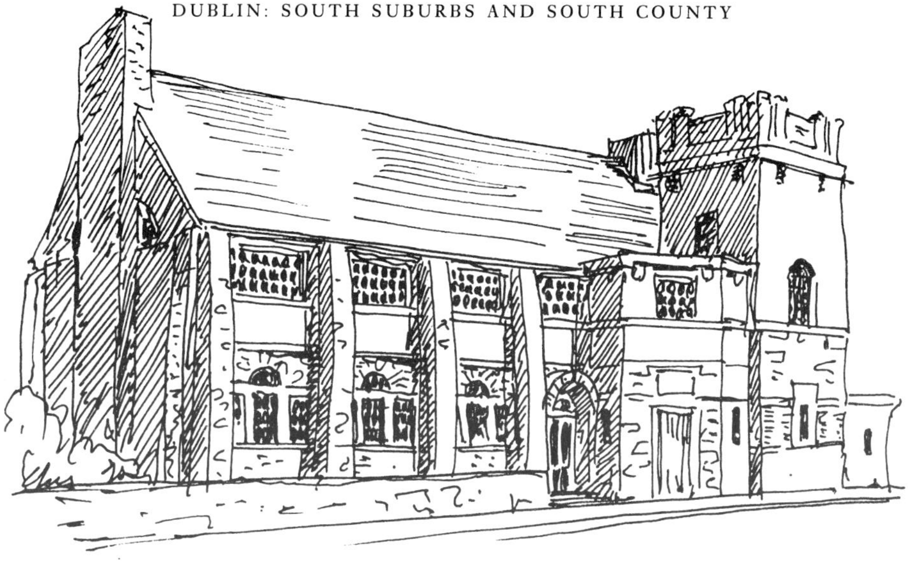

designed the reredos. Beatrice Elvery, more predictably, was involved with the stained glass —Prodigal Son (1908), War Memorial (1919). Further windows by C. O'Brien.

CHURCHTOWN, Braemor Road: Representative Church Body

A cheery red- and yellow-brick and terracotta Flemish-style institution designed by G.P. Beater in 1894 as a convalescent home for the Adelaide Hospital. Now painlessly converted into a training college for the Church of Ireland.

CLONDALKIN: Catholic Church

Designed in 1856 (along with an adjoining convent) by William Caldbeck in a Puginesque Gothic Revival idiom—his largest religious commission. Well preserved interiors.

Stained glass windows by Thomas Earley, who committed suicide while installing them. His mistress commissioned a further window to mark the spot.

CLONDALKIN: Public Library

A powerful Arts and Crafts double-storey structure built to be the focal centre of rural life but now it dominates unending suburbs. Like the contemporary Cavan Townhall (q.v.) by William Scott—façades of horizontal fenestration contrasting to vertical buttressing. The architect here was T.J. Byrne, Scott's brother-in-law. L-shaped façade with splayed porch tucked against the angle tower. The interior preserves much of its original furnishing.

CLONSKEAGH: Ardilea

The robust gatelodge on Mount Anville Road in brick and stone with lofty chimney-stacks *c.*1870 was spared when the house was demolished to make way for a luxurious housing estate. Architect, A.G. Jones.

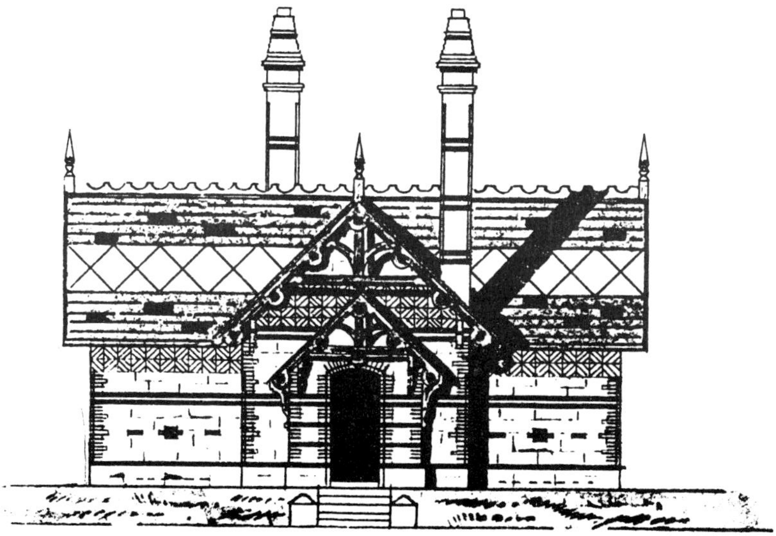

CLONSKEAGH: Mount Anville

The home of the celebrated railway entrepreneur, William Dargan. An earlier house rebuilt by him as an Italianate villa with asymmetrical garden front adjoining a lofty viewing tower (1849), which Queen Victoria climbed when she visited him in 1853. No doubt she approved, since his tower was inspired by the pair that Prince Albert had designed for her at Osborne. Additions by George Ashlin for the Nuns of the Sacred Heart after they acquired the property from Dargan, who died bankrupt a year later. Lodge in the cyclopean style of J.S. Mulvany.

CLONSKEAGH: Richview

Designed by Sir Thomas Drew as the Male Masonic School in 1884 in a free version of Tudor and later extended by Drew in the same style. Now converted by Professor Cathal O'Neill into a homely faculty of architecture in UCD). This is at its most successful in the assembly hall and the library, which have retained their inspiration from the Arts and Crafts movement.

CLONSKEAGH: Roebuck Castle

The ruined castle of the Trimlestowns was rebuilt by them in 1790 as a Georgian house but was then remodelled in an unconvincing suburban Gothic by E.P. Westby in 1874, who employed an unrecorded architect. Stepped gabling and arched plate-glass windows are not sufficient to evoke its embattled past. The overweight chateau-style marble chimney-piece is at variance with the entrance hall. Now a convent marooned in new housing estates. The gatehouse, where the architect was not inhibited by an existing structure, is more effective—polychromatic stone dominated by an asymmetrical spire.

DALKEY, Barnhill Road: Moytura

Although J.L. Robinson designed the most pretentious speculative Gothic Revival villa in Dublin, this wisely remained unbuilt. The house he designed for himself was sensible and undistinguished. In red brick with heavy chimneys and half-timbered gables.

DALKEY, Castle Road: Catholic Church

Rural Gothic church *c.*1840; architect unknown. Cruciform with later western tower. Fan-vaulted interior recently restored.

DALKEY, Castle Road: Tudor Lodge

Symmetrical three-storied Tudor Revival villa built *c.*1840 by an unknown architect (possibly George Papworth). Ceilings with geometrical Gothick plasterwork and heraldic stained glass in the window tracrery.

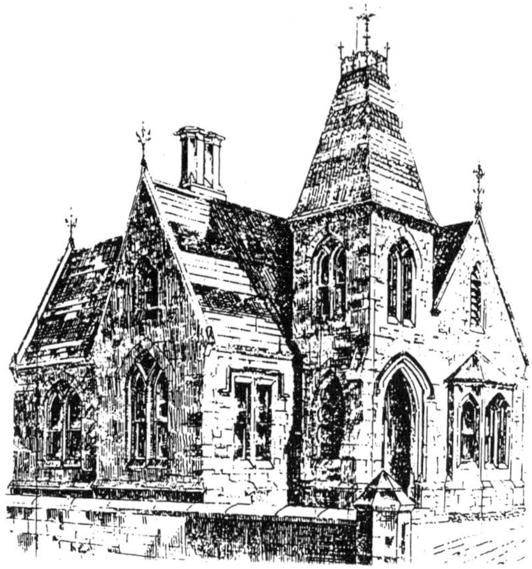

DALKEY, Church Road: Church of Ireland

Gothic Revival church designed in 1840 as an independent commission by Jacob Owen, who before his Irish appointment had built several churches in England. Built out of local granite and inspired by the incisiveness of Semple but which he diluted to conform to the conventionality of his parishioners as did Semple's successor, Frederick Darley. But the strongly articulated Star of David set into the tracery of the window above the altar must have raised many eyebrows. Gothic Revival granite gate-lodge built in 1868 by E.H. Carson.

DALKEY, Coliemore Road: Loreto Abbey

Austere symmetrical pseudo-castle set on the edge of the cliffs, built by Revd Mother Ball of Rathfarnham Abbey in 1842, presumably to the designs of Patrick Byrne, as a summer home for her community. She commissioned a marble Nativity from John Hogan in 1843 as the centrepiece of the convent chapel.

DALKEY, Coliemore Road: Carrigrehane

Granite Tudor Revival villa built on the rocks above the sea, *c.*1840. Slightly asymmetrical composition. Architect unknown.

DALKEY: Elsinore

Comfortable villa built for himself by the architect John McCurdy. Well designed to take advantage of its site. Hence the record price the last time it changed hands.

DALKEY, Vico Road: Monte Alverno

Regency villa remodelled *c.*1905 as a Baronial castle complete with flag tower by its owner, Alexander Conan, reputedly to his design. Conservatory added against the cliff face. Richly panelled interiors.

DALKEY: The Station
The most unassuming of the stations designed by J.S. Mulvany (*c.* 1850), adapting the idiom of the Regency bungalow to shelter the public and provide humane working conditions for the staff. Mulvany evokes Classicism here more subtly than by the columns and pilasters of his Dun Laoghaire station (q.v.), using his distinctive granite piers and corbels while projecting a symmetrically a bow window off one of the side gables.

DONNYBROOK, Auburn Avenue: Housing
High density red-brick council housing designed by E. Bradbury and built in 1912. Competent but unrelieved by variation.

DONNYBROOK: Catholic Church
Originally designed by Patrick Byrne, who resigned in 1863 at the age of eighty and was replaced by the fledgling partnership of E.W. Pugin and George Ashlin. Built out of hammer-dressed granite with Bath stone dressings, notably the geometrical rose window in the west façade. Tympanum carved by Earley and Powell, who also sculpted the high altar and stencilled the open-truss timber roof (painted over in 1963). After Pugin's departure all the money was spent on diffuse extensions at the eastern end rather than on the completion of the intended spire: the present pinnacles date from 1910. Stained glass of varying quality, mainly by Mayer and Earley. The finest windows are the St Patrick window by Healy (1914) and the SS Rita and Bernard window by Harry Clarke with its central light by William McBride. A Child window (St Christopher) and a Healy (SS Philip, Peter, Paul and Andrew).

DONNYBROOK, Eglinton Road: Lisateer
Heavyweight red-brick villa designed *c.* 1875 for his own occupation by James Franklyn Fuller, relieved only by the cliché of putting plate glass in the lower sashes and small panes in the upper ones. Adjoining houses in a similar idiom. Here the elderly architect wrote his memoirs *Ad Omniana* (garrulous on all subjects except his own buildings), looked after by his unmarried daughter. Her only outlet was revolutionary politics, which led her to put up revolutionaries on the run without her father ever knowing.

DUNDRUM: Ardglass
Neo-Elizabethan villa for Arthur Crookshank with sweeping roofs held in place by a mixture of dormers and chimney-stacks jammed against lower entry block. Completed before 1908. Has survived the intrusion of recent housing estates. Architect: Richard Orpen.

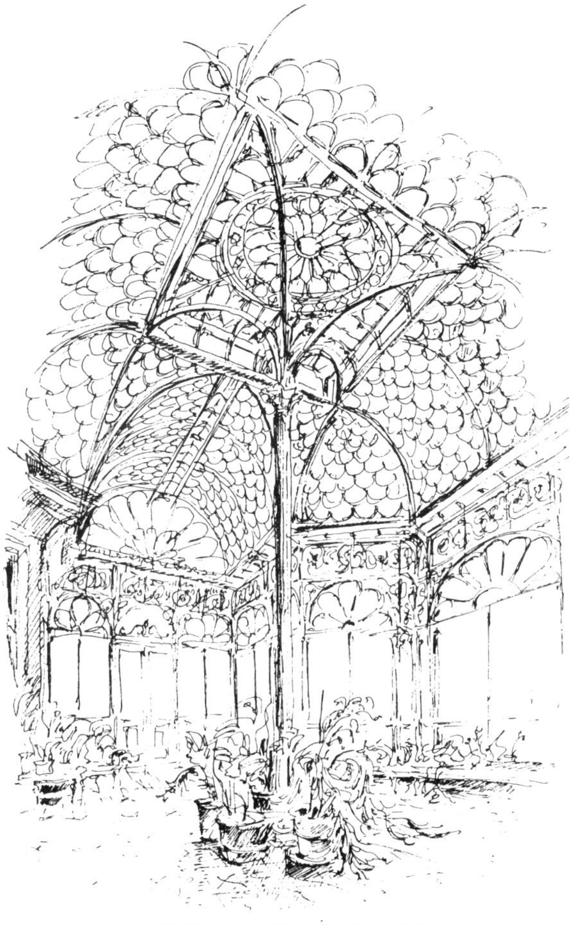

DUNDRUM, Ballinteer Road: Gort Mhuire
Formerly Gortmore; built by the Atkinsons, poplin manufacturers, in the 1850s, as a typical suburban neo-Classical villa, in the manner of J.S. Mulvany. From this time dates the well-proportioned granite portico and an imposing flight of steps. In the 1880s it was bought by Edward Burke, a wine merchant who had the sole agency for exporting Guinness. He remodelled the interior, adding a billiard room and music room with a conservatory contrived between them. These overlook an elaborate garden with rockeries, a grotto, an artificial lake and fountains. To provide the necessary water pressure, he housed the tank in an unusually convincing replica of a medieval Irish tower house, the most practical of follies since today it contains the boiler for the monastery added by the Carmelites, who own the house today and run it as a residential conference centre.

They have carefully maintained the principal interiors. First, the oak-panelled entrance and staircase hall, with a fireplace and inglenook beneath the half-landing. Stained-glass staircase window depicts a white cat enthroned above a flowery brook. The reception rooms along the garden front are remodelled with a certain Classical restraint, though there is no stint in the use of rich materials: an arcade of onyx divides the double drawingrooms. But the new rooms are more ebullient, with central lanterns upheld by arcaded trusses. The music room is hung with embossed leather between an oak-panelled dado and a plaster frieze of dancing putti. An oriel projects into the magical conservatory. This has fish-scaled vaulting of tinted glass interpenetrated by a domed lantern upheld by arches converging onto a single flower-sprouting column. On the outside a corona of cast-iron scrolls intersect in the open air.

The architect of all these fantasies remains unknown, although the conservatory is identifiable as coming from Walter McFarlane of the Saracens Ironworks in Glasgow. The loss of other 'Saracen' embellishments to Dublin such as the Queen Victoria fountain in Dun Laoghaire, blown up by the IRA, the Coombe fountain, done in by a lorry, and the dismantling of the staircase of Switzers, makes the survival of the conservatory all the more remarkable).

DUNDRUM: Catholic Church

Designed by George Ashlin. Unpromising exterior hides simple but effective interior, where there are no aisles to the nave, only to the choir, and they screen off the transept, so that the treasure of the church, a Michael Healy window in the north transept, appears as a sudden apparition.

DUNDRUM: The Courthouse

Only the courthouse survives the removal of the adjoining police barracks (demolished in 1970 and unsympathetically replaced). The architect was Benjamin Woodward, who designed it in 1855 for Sidney Herbert (1810-61), who was in charge of the Pembroke estates in Dublin. If Herbert had lived longer, he would not only have succeeded to the earldom of Pembroke, but might well have become prime minister. The courthouse is small, squat and forceful, entered from the side through a doorway recessed into an extended buttress.

DUNDRUM, Eglington Terrace: The Schoolhouse

Designed, like the courthouse, by Benjamin Woodward for Sidney Herbert, and built in 1857-61. Consists of a school entered by a tautly designed timber porch. At the other end it is linked to a master's house of rubble stone and brick relieving arches. The front wall and verandah of the master's house was moved forward in 1910 when the school was extended. Acquired recently by developers who would have mutilated it, were it not for the intervention of the Board of Works. Sold on, and now sensitively converted into offices.

DUNDRUM: Taney Church of Ireland

There are two churches here that intersect. The first is an remodelling in 1842 of an earlier church entered dramatically through a Gothic rotunda beneath the tower, with staircase curving up to the gallery. Light and spacious interior with pretty Gothick plasterwork. But twenty years later this church proved to be too small. More worrying, it was incorrectly orientated. Joseph Welland boldly solved both problems by building a new nave to the west and a new chancel to the east. The result resembles Pugin's church at Tagoat, Co. Wexford (q.v.), except that Welland's internal arrangements have remained unaltered (these include not one but two pulpits and a lectern). Neo-medieval glass in the chancel, pre-Raphaelite glass elsewhere. Goulding window by Eugene Daly of Cork.

DUN LAOGHAIRE: Catholic Church

Late Gothic Revival church by C.J. McCarthy, who took over from J.L. Robinson; destroyed by fire and replaced by a new church that failed to live up to the promise of the temporary church by the same architects (but they at least retained the steeple).

DUN LAOGHAIRE: Dominican Convent

A Regency villa retained as the centrepiece of a Palladian composition by John Bourke with curved wings raised to the same height as the

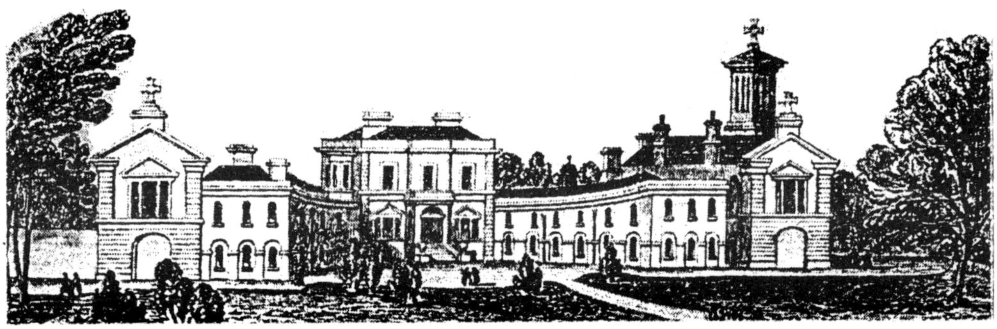

original *piano nobile*. Linked to pedimented pavilions containing classrooms and chapel, the latter distinguished by an Italianate campanile. Engulfed in later extensions of little merit, but now threatened with mass demolition apart from the tiny Celtic Revival oratory. This was frescoed by Sr Cecilia Lynch, whose father was an expert on the Celtic script. For three years his daughter, in failing health, lay on her back decorating the ceiling like Michaelangelo in the Sistine chapel (as documented in the minutes of the convent) but died before she could complete the interior with her tribute to the Book of Kells.

DUN LAOGHAIRE: **Mariners Church**
Built originally as the principal church of Ireland of what is now Dun Laoghaire—in two phases, 1837 and 1865—and now adapted to contain the Maritime Museum. The austerity of Joseph Welland's 1837 structure was counterbalanced by the eastern window added by Raffles Brown along with a striking steeple that unites Gothic verve to Romanesque robustness with a perforated stone spire revealing a pronounced entasis (1865). Brown was assisted by Thomas Turner. Refitted by T. Drew in 1884. Glass by Heaton, Butler and Bayne

DUN LAOGHAIRE, **Park Road: Church of Ireland**
Gothic Revival church of 1836 reversed and extended in 1879 and then remodelled in 1887. Of slight architectural consequence but illuminated by atmospheric stained glass naively commemorating soldier martyrs of the British Empire in Africa. Other glass by Mayer and Child.

DUN LAOGHAIRE: **The Piers**
Built by John Rennie in 1821 to enclose the harbour. The southern pier was transformed into a promenade. Cast-iron bandstand by Walter McFarlane.

DUN LAOGHAIRE: **Royal Marine Hotel**
Self-confident High Victorian hotel built to overlook the berthing of the mailboat (1863-6) by John McCurdy. Its cost sent the company into receivership in 1869. A century later it lost its central lantern and its northern wing was erected in a bland international idiom. Recently redecorated more in sympathy with McCurdy.

DUN LAOGHAIRE: **Royal St George Yacht Club**
J.S. Mulvany designed this yacht club in a less formal manner than the Royal Irish with a façade of pedimented pavilions that could be a trio of private villas. At the rear, symmetry is sacrificed to a long diningroom that projects out into the harbour and terminates with a curved bay, presumably the 1885 addition of Edmund O'Kelly, the architect of the (destroyed) International Hotel in Bray. Redecorated by the late Sir Basil Goulding; at its re-opening the specially commissioned contemporary Irish sculptures where flung out onto the rocks below.

DUN LAOGHAIRE: **Royal Irish Yacht Club**
Designed by J.S. Mulvany and built in 1850 as the most elegant of Dublin's yacht clubs; entered through a single-storied Ionic colonnade linking terminal pavilions kept flush with the façade. The rear façade terminates with curved bays to float serenely on a rusticated lower floor reserved for boats with wide arches spanned by cyclopean stonework. Symmetrical ground plan with pilastered central hall lit by a glazed dome from above, its serenity a foil to a set of seascapes by Edwin Hayes, painted as overdoors.

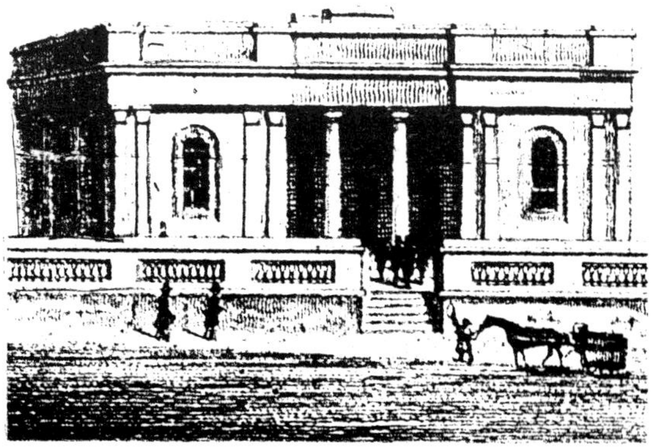

DUN LAOGHAIRE: **The Station**
The third of the neo-Classical pavilions J.S. Mulvany built along the Dun Loaghaire seafront—a granite palazzetto floating on a neo-Primitive raised basement that contains the functions of the station. Although the last of the three to be completed (1854), it was the earliest to be designed (1834), and reveals traces of an old-fashioned Palladianism along with some uncertainty in the proportions. Now converted into a luxury restaurant at the expense of its original severity. At the lower level the parcels office, top-lit by an apsidally-ended arched roof-light resting on cantilevered scrolls, has been unaccountably destroyed *c.* 1970.

DUN LAOGHAIRE, **Silchester Road: Church of Ireland**
Gothic Revival church designed in 1865 by A.G. Jones in bush-hammered granite. Chancel extended in 1913 and decorated by Sibthorpes, whose murals have since been painted over.

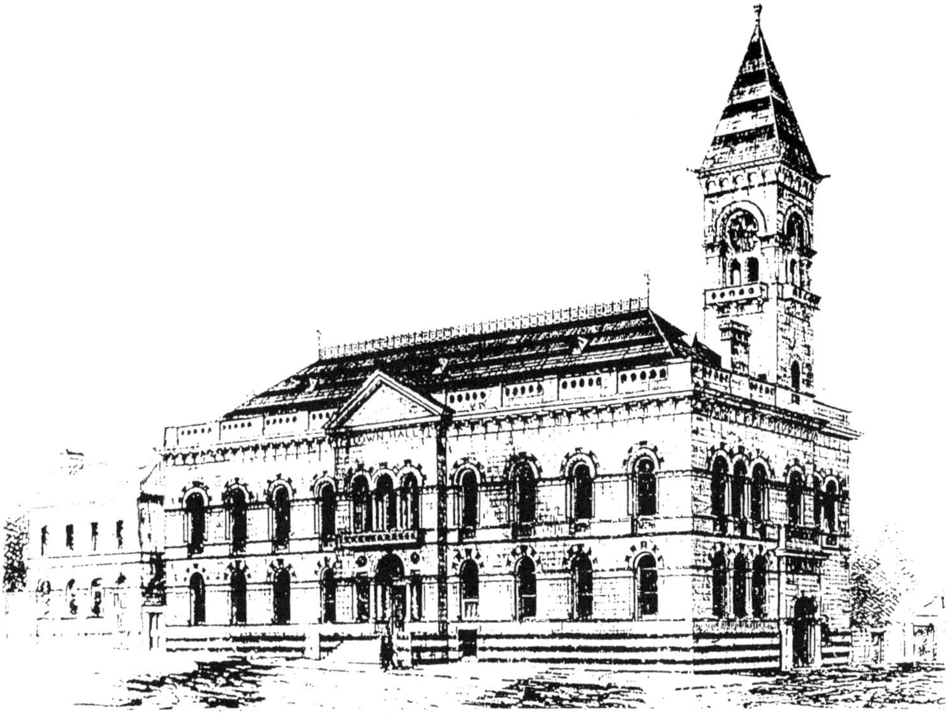

DUN LAOGHAIRE, **The Townhall**
Designed (after winning a competition in 1877) by J.L. Robinson in a muted chromatic Romanesque recalling the architecture of Deane and Woodward. Symmetrical palazzo apart from the belltower surmounting the side facing the harbour. A building that reflects the self-confidence of its era and the wealth of the borough. Recently restored, with some of the original painted ceilings of the interior brought back to their former splendour.

DUN LAOGHAIRE, **York Road: Presbyterian Church**
The third of Andrew Heaton's Dublin churches in his characteristic version of French 14th-century Gothic; the sloping site is adjusted to an upper and lower church, the latter doubling as a community hall. Executant architect, G. Cockburn. Erected in 1863.

FOXROCK, **Brighton Road: Avalon**
If Richard Orpen when interviewed in 1923 by the *Irish Builder* was credited with the invention of the bungalow, perhaps he designed this delightful retreat—a generous roof enclosing the upstairs accommodation with windows artfully taking advantage of a chimney's substructure and recessed into a decorative brick arch. Below, elegant verandahs wrap round the garden front, carefully hidden from the road. Built in 1906 for W. Garland.

FOXROCK, **Brighton Road: Carrickbyrne**
Long asymmetrical Tudor façade with nice balance between half-timbering and local granite, shaded by surrounding cedars. The domestic masterpiece of Fredrick Batchelor, who built the house for the Good family (*c.*1901).

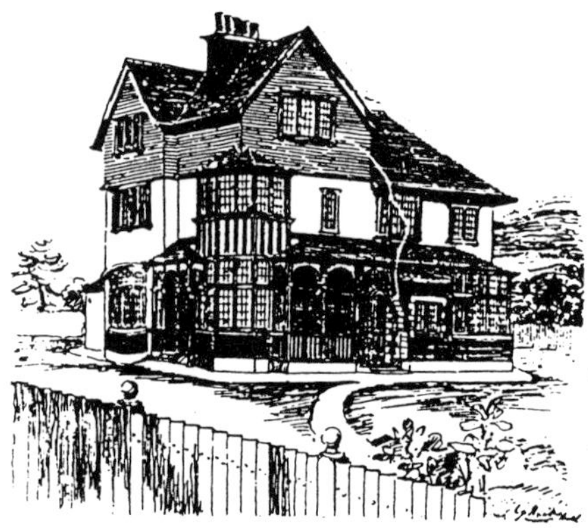

FOXROCK, **Brighton Road: Coolnadrinagh**
Half-timbered and tile-hung stockbroker's villa built in 1903 by W.F. Beckett, father of Samuel Beckett (born here in 1906). Designed by F.G. Hicks with a double-storied octagonal corner bay to get the sun and the view of the mountains and also of a racecourse (Leopardstown), like the mansion of Mr Knott in *Watt*. A verbena-clad verandah gives access to a croquet lawn shaded by a grove of larch that Samuel Beckett continuously recalled. But he never returned here.

A visit was once arranged, but he did not arrive. Later the then owners were told that an elderly man had been sighted motionless at their gates.

FOXROCK, Brighton Road: Kerrymount
Freely treated neo-Tudor villa designed by Albert Murray for The O'Morchoe and built *c.*1905.

FOXROCK, Brighton Road: Wroxton
Built 1910 for the Rainsford family. Powerful asymmetrical composition with intersecting pyramidal roofs. Architect unknown.

FOXROCK, Leopardstown Road: Rock House
Three-storied villa with overhanging pitched roof broken by dormers and gabled bay windows. Tile-hung at first-floor level. Designed by Richard Orpen before 1910. Originally known as Chaddesley House.

FOXROCK, Westminster Road: Kilteragh
Commissioned in 1904 by Sir Horace Plunkett so that he could entertain his friends and bring together both sides of the political divide in rooms that were so designed to catch the sun all the day long, hence the butterfly plan. Sir Horace himself slept in a pavilion on the roof in a bed that he rotated with the sun, following the example of Cecil Rhodes in Groote Schuur. His architect, W.D. Caroe, was engaged on the marbled columned ballroom of nearby St Helen's (q.v.) so that the directness and simplicity of Sir Horace's ideals brought out Caroe's Scandinavian origins with an austerity tempered by shifting vistas linking house and garden, and a few deft touches of Art Nouveau—the canopy of the porch that still survives. Lady Fingal dismissed Caroe's furniture designs as cold and modern and bought Plunkett old furniture (cheaper and, in her view, more beautiful), but she praised the acoustics of Caroe's music hall, and the warm brickwork of the drawingroom fireplace. Interior entirely destroyed (along with the ethereal frescoes of A.E.) by Republicans in 1923 led by a Plunket with one 't' (i.e., a Church of Ireland Plunket). Rebuilt as a terrrace of five houses by Richard Orpen and George Beckett in the late 1920s. The garden has been preserved by all the current owners. The gatelodges with their pyramidal roofs and central chimney-stacks still give a sense of mystery even if their avenues are now converted into public roadways.

GLENAGEARY: Altidore
The finest of the neo-Classical villas designed by Sandham Symes and exhibited by him in the RHA of 1844. For his client John Aylmer he expanded the formula of a one-storied cube above an elevated basement by adding terminating pavilions, one square and the other circular. The house is entered symmetrically on both levels with twin curving flights of stairs leading to a delicate verandah on the upper level. This is supported by metal columns that arch outwards to support the curvilinear lead-canopied roof structure. Even Mulvany never reduced his Classicism to such geometric minimalism. Recently altered after its acquisition as a nursing home.

GOLDENBRIDGE: Mortuary Chapel
Well-proportioned Ionic temple built by an

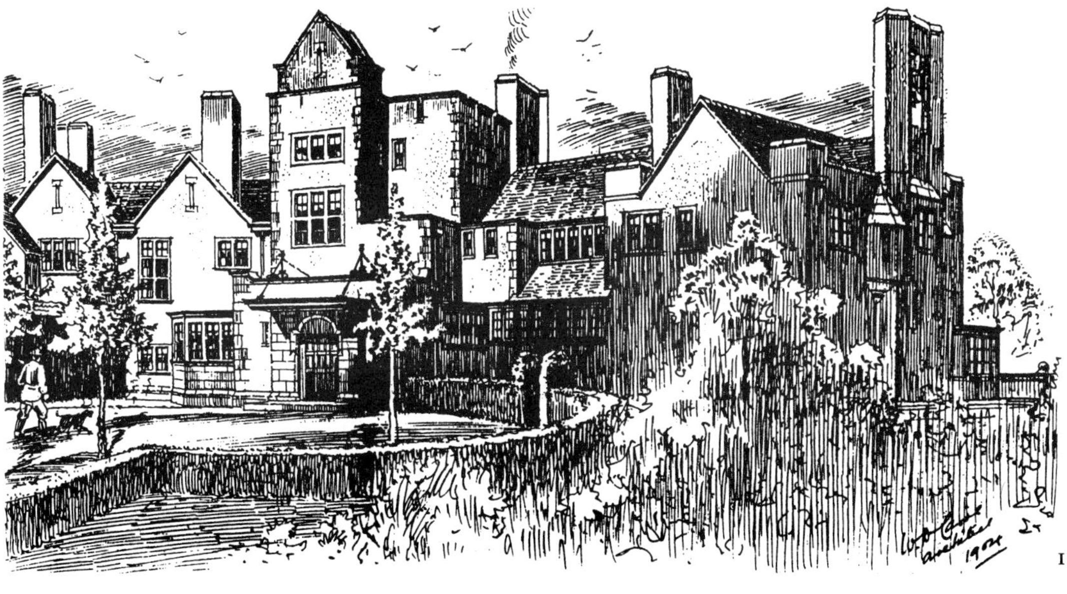

unknown architect in the 1830s as the centrepiece of the first Catholic graveyard permitted in the confines of Dublin, laid out in 1823. The temples and tombs are lost among undergrowth. Gates locked against latterday body-snatchers.

HAROLD'S CROSS: **Church of Ireland**
Spiky Gothic Revival church designed in 1836 by John Louch; remodelled by his son Fitzgibbon Louch, and now in danger of closure. Glass by Heaton, Butler and Bayne.

HAROLD'S CROSS: **The Green**
A charming example of an ornamental park laid out in 1894 by William Shepherd.

HAROLD'S CROSS: **The Hospice**
One of the largest Gothic Revival commissions by Charles Geoghegan where he uses asymmetry and picturesqueness to counteract institutionalism, *c.*1860. Now engulfed in later additions.

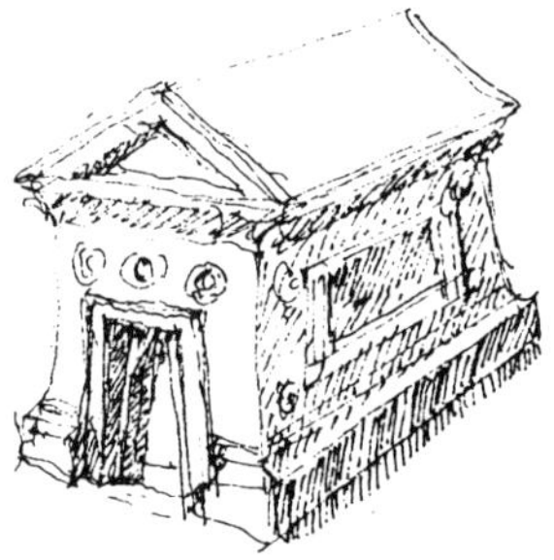

PERRY VAULT, 1844

HAROLD'S CROSS: **Mount Jerome Cemetery**
The most Keatsian of Dublin's cemeteries, with its predominantly neo-Classical tombs standing out against the dark cedars and cypresses. In this setting one of the earliest and purest of Dublin's Gothic Revival churches has no precedence, and little progeny. The result of a competition won in 1845 by the Cork architect, William Atkins, imbued with the ideals of Pugin, it earned him the post of Irish representative of the Ecclesiologists. But the tombs around follow the precedent set by the impressively Grecian Drummond tomb (1840) of George Papworth, unequalled in this genre. Papworth had earlier designed the gatelodge in his Tudor idiom. The most ambitious memorial is the miniature temple on a lofty plinth, the Cusack memorial of 1861, designed by Sandham Symes, evidence of his southern travels. Beside it an inconsolable hound wails noiselessly for its master. An appropriate resting place for many of Dublin's leading architectural families—the Morrisons (beneath a tomb of their own design), the Owens, the Mulvanys, the Turners.

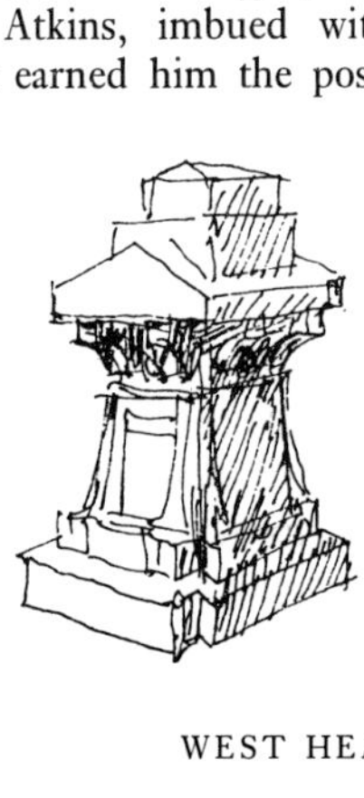

WEST HEADSTONE, 1850

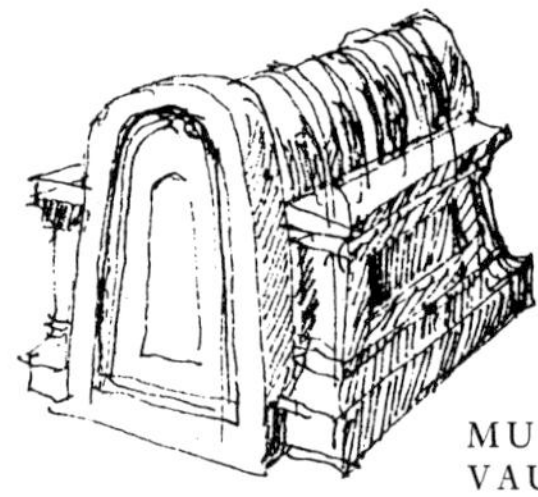

MULVANY VAULT, 1853

Three memorials are attributed by Frederick O'Dwyer to J.S. Mulvany—the Perry vault (1844), a miniature centrepiece of Broadstone Station (q.v.); the West headstone of 1850, a monumentalized gate pier; and the brilliantly original Mahony vault, *c.*1853, a ribbed parabolic cell clasped between two tapering plinths.

HAROLD'S CROSS: **Passionist Monastery**
An austere monastic block with adjoining tower. Round-headed window within set into Gothic relieving arches; designed in 1862 by J.J. McCarthy. There is no evidence today of the problems that he had with his builder and his clients, but all was forgiven when he was called back in 1874 to add the church, admittedly using a dictated Italian Romanesque, in deference to the origins of the Passionist order. Externally the church with its twin towers and profusion of sculpture by James Pearse rises with gathering triumphalism, but the interior is curiously vacuous. It is not improved by subsequent enlargement and alterations that appear to have done away with the original vaulting. Pearse's pulpit has also been removed.

INCHICORE: **Catholic Church**
Designed in the 1870s by George Ashlin in his habitual prickly French Gothic idiom with a façade flanked by twin octagonal spirelets and a polygonal apse. Interior remarkably intact, with high communion rails and pulpit by James Pearse. Mosaics by Oppenheimer. Painted ceiling. New altar donated by ex-parishioner on

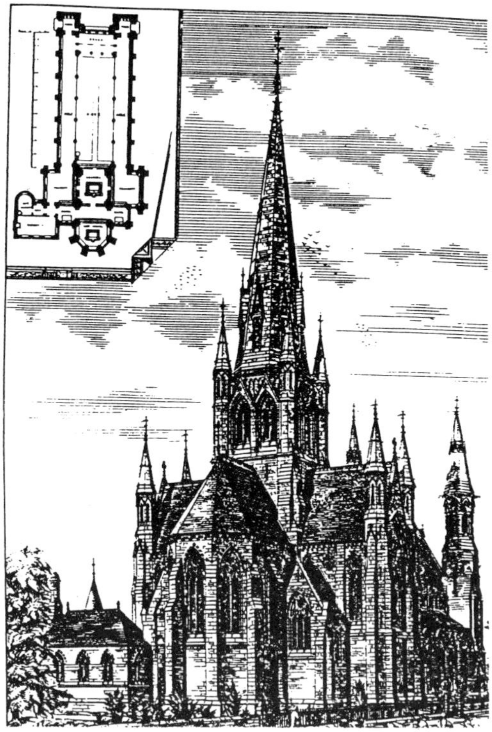

condition that the old high altar would be left intact. A decade later an ambitious scheme by Ashlin would have added a central belfry and transepts and extended the choir. This never went ahead: instead Ashlin used his design in the completion of Killarney Cathedral (q.v.). The façade of Inchicore was not completed until the 1920s. The adjoining home of the Oblate Fathers was designed by John Bourke in the 1860s, symmetrical, austere, Italianate.

INCHICORE: CIE Depot

An unusual stylistic choice for the stores of Dublin's largest station, Heuston. Designed with castellated towers and diamond-paned windows by the same architect, Sancton Wood, his curiously cranky Gothic, *c.*1850.

KILL O' THE GRANGE: Church of Ireland

The most remarkable Welland and Gillespie church in the Dublin region, consecrated in 1864—small but pugnacious with its saddle-roofed belfry and hip-roofed transept contained within the rectangular ground plan where the only concession at ground level to the picturesque is the polygonal chancel. Built out of local granite, the interior is warm and welcoming, illuminated by stained-glass lancets grouped in ones, two and threes beneath a vault sheathed with varnished timber. Windows by McGoldrick (the Good Shepherd, 1931) and O'Brien (1947).

KILLINEY: Church of Ireland

A rare incursion into the Gothic style by the architect Sandham Symes, who in 1858 received this commission from his Warren uncles. They had developed Killiney round a tiny hillside fishing hamlet. Symes slotted his church onto a terrace set precipitously into Killiney Hill. Entry through a corner belfry with later copper spire. Cruciform interior articulated by the trusswork of the open roof. Stained glass by Heaton, Butler and Bayne; a memorial window by Harry Clarke (1919); and a two-light by McGoldrick depicting an Annunciation and a Crucifixion (1944). Reredos by Richard Orpen.

KILLINEY: Eirene

An early example of stockbrokers' Tudor designed by T.N. Deane and his son T.M. Deane for Henry Palmer in 1883 to overlook the bay. Red-brick ground floor, half-timbered above; inglenook within.

KILLINEY: Gaileen

The most delightful of the half-timbered villas designed by T.M. Deane at the turn of the century with a symmetrical gabled façade incorporating an airy verandah—formal and yet intimate. More elaborate neighbouring houses also designed by T.M. Deane in the same idiom include 'Aileen' and 'Namur'.

KILLINEY: Killiney Court Hotel

Previously Court-na-Farraga. Designed in 1865, most probably by T.N. Deane, for William Exham as one of the largest villas on the coast in Deane's neo-Jacobean idiom with scrolled gable strapwork and adjoining turret, replicated when the house was extended as a hotel in 1973. Small curvilinear plant house against a garden terrace.

KILLINEY, Killiney Hill Road: Fernside, Green Hill and Illerton (now called Alloa)

Three further villas designed by Benjamin Woodward on adjoining sites overlooking Killiney Bay. All are rendered, with stone and brick confined to details. This allowed them to be quite large and geometrically complex. Illerton was the last to be built (1863) with neo-Jacobean features never found in Woodward's work, only in T.N. Deane's.

KILLINEY: Mount Druid

Half-timbered gabled neo-Elizabethan villa (*c.*1863) corbelled out from an existing house built half a century before as an extension to a Georgian cottage. The architect of the Edwardian remodelling for William Shannon was Richard Orpen.

KILLINEY, St George's Road: St George's
Designed for himself by George Ashlin (1872) on a sheltered terrace overlooking the sea. A spacious family villa with a few Baronial features such as battlemented tower, elegantly detailed staircase and an oratory on the half landing with heraldic stained glass by Frampton portraying the architect and his wife in prayer. Originally rooms papered by William Morris. Here Mrs Ashlin would have felt at home since she had been raised in a similar neo-medieval ambiance also overlooking the sea, the house at Ramsgate built for his growing family by her father, Augustus Welby Pugin. Next door, a coarser Queen Anne-style house (called Carrigrenane after the original Ashlin house in Cork) was built by his nephew Stephen 'Sporty' Ashlin in 1903 but to his uncle's designs. Lodge used as studio by Mia Cranwell.

KILLINEY, Strathmore Road: Undercliffe
Designed in 1860 by Benjamin Woodward for Francis Robinson, a promoter of the Antient Concert Hall, and thereby one of the last of Woodward's Irish commissions, probably under construction when he left Ireland for the last time. Built on a demanding site with a tight budget, the house is L-shaped with the front door set diagonally between the two arms. Two turrets—one beside the entrance to contain the staff staircase, the other a viewing turret to the

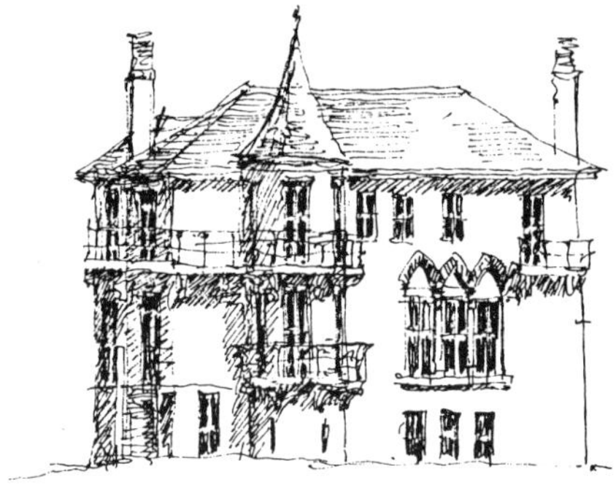

sea. Balustraded balconies and external staircase, since renewed with concrete. Chimneys also rebuilt.

KILLINEY: The Townhall
Not very municipal but rather a picturesque cottage ornée designed by T.M. Deane in 1891. Harmoniously blending with council cottages, also designed by Deane and carefully adjusted to the contours of the site.

KILLINEY, Vico Road: Ayesha Castle
Norman Revival granite castle built at the same time as Mount Eagle (q.v.) and therefore attributable to Sandham Symes, here revealed as a master of the picturesque. The castle revolves round a circular corner tower. The external treatment is assured (note the corbelled arches

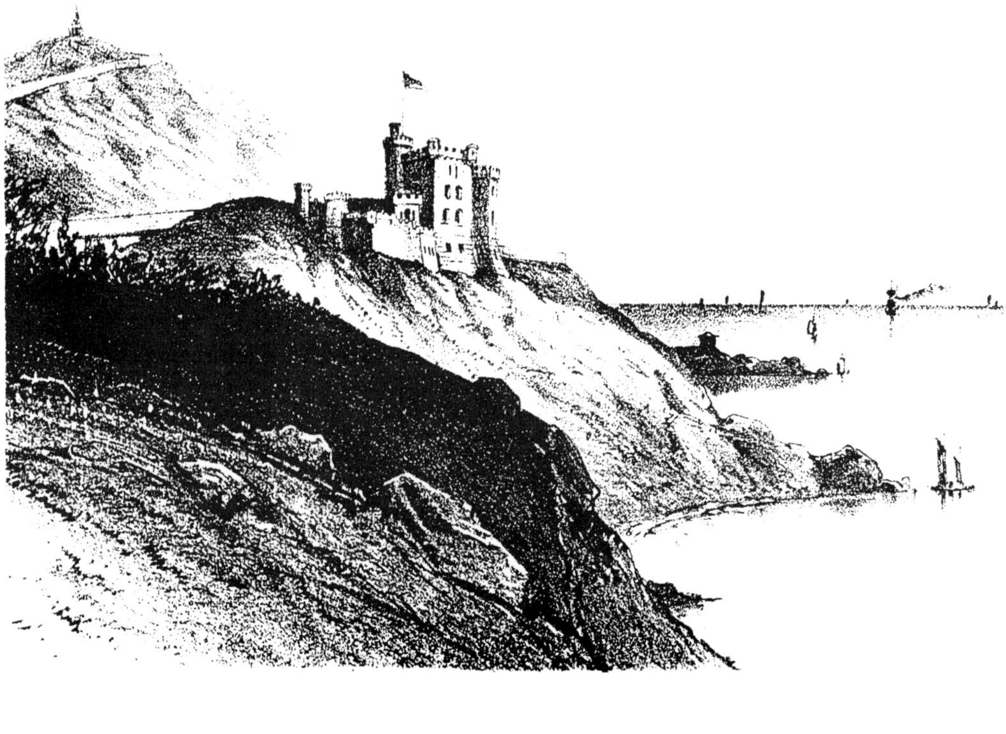

of the stableblock). The client, Robert Warren, named his castle after Queen Victoria. After the interior was destroyed by fire in 1924, the new owner, Sir Thomas Power, who restored it four years later, christened the castle 'Ayesha' (inspired by Rider Haggard). The interiors are the work of Edwin Bradbury. They are open to the public. Two gatelodges survive as separate residences the more remarkable being a fortified entrance gateway over what is now a public roadway; this is known as Camelot. The *Irish Penny Journal* commented that, while having towers and crenallated battlements and large windows in abundance, it is unlike a real old castle as such structures usually are.

KILLINEY, Vico Road: Mount Eagle

Known originally as Kent Lodge. Geometrical butterfly-shaped neo-Classical villa built out of local granite set on an immense curved terrace with vertiginous views across Killiney Bay. Symmetrical plan with bifurcating staircase based on a speculative villa published a few years before by William Bardwell. However, the architect was not Bardwell but the young Sandham Symes given this speculative commission by his Warren uncles in 1837. It is probable that William Warren, the architect of Spur Royal (q.v.) in County Tyrone with its canted wings, was one of his uncles and that he may have assisted his nephew. In any case a model that despite varied owners has always remained in the house is signed 'Sandham Symes'.

KILTERNAN: Church of Ireland

John Semple's church of 1826 was embellished during the incumbency of the O'Morchoe (1894-1921), The chancel reredos was inserted in 1899, possibly by Fuller. Interesting stained glass: window above the altar by Heaton Butler and Bayne (1908); chancel windows by H.W. Bryans (1990); Trouton window by Sir Ninian Comper (1920); two windows commemorating the Murphys (1922) by A.K. Nicholson; and a small panel 'Searcher after Wisdom' attributed by Nicola Gordon Bowe to Austin Molloy (1915).

KILTERNAN: The Grange

Restrained neo-Tudor pavilion built out of local granite. Drawingroom nicely housed in attached pavilion.

LEOPARDSTOWN: Glencairn (British Embassy)

Built in 1859 for a solicitor, George Gresson, to the designs of Benjamin Woodward. For Woodward, an old-fashioned neo-Tudor in contrast with the most geometrical of his gatelodges and the simplified treatment of the service yard. The latter survived unchanged when the main house was transformed for the returned Irish-American Boss Croker, whose shocking behaviour has passed into local legend. His involuntary architect was J.F. Fuller, who bitterly regretted what he was forced to do—add lavish interiors, a Baronial tower and colonial colonnade. Heraldic stained glass by Frampton. Has served as the residence of the British ambassador for many years. The origin of Mr Knott's mansion in *Watt*. Sympathetically restored by Sir Nicholas and Lady Fenn, who uncovered a ceiling painted with every known type of bird.

LEOPARDSTOWN: The Hospital

Georgian house rebuilt in a Victorian Italianate manner by Lanyon, Lynn and Lanyon (*c.*1850). Symmetrical layout centred on imperial staircase with richly scrolled ironwork. Their clients were the Talbot Powers, of Power's distillery.

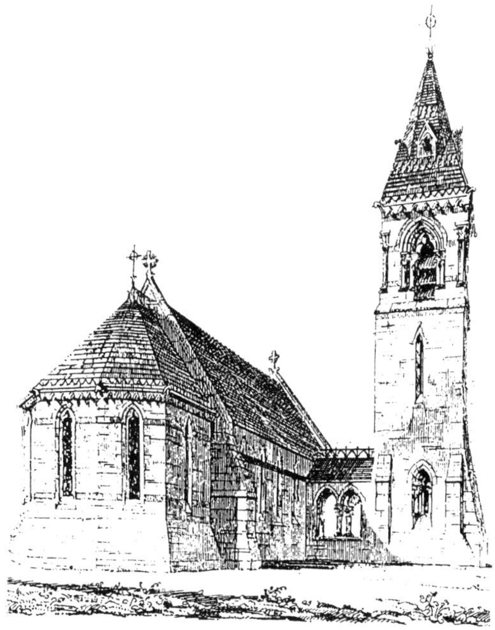

MILLTOWN: Church of Ireland

An early commission (1857) of Thomas Drew dedicated to St Philip and donated to serve the well planted suburb south of Palmerstown Park. Entry through an open porch beneath an intended belfry and arcaded link to shelter a slow-leaving congregation in inclement weather. Sensible restrained interior, still with original heating system, suffers from being widened by an extra aisle. Stained glass includes 'Sacrifice, Peace, Victory' by Child (1920): parish hall (*c.*1900) with open roof and large windows.

MILLTOWN, **Temple Road: No. 28**
Partly Grecian, partly Swiss villa built by an unknown architect (*c.*1860) for the Temple family, who developed Milltown as a garden suburb.

MILLTOWN: **The Convent**
Georgian house extended for the Sisters of Charity by W.H. Byrne in polychromatic brick with stone trimmings; linked to a neo-Romanesque chapel with attached round tower. Dated 1888.

MONKSTOWN, **Alma Road: Gortnadrew**
Baronial red-brick residence built for himself by Thomas, later Sir Thomas, Drew. Eclectic interior dating from the 1880s. Now divided into two. The curious resemblance to the tenements he designed at around the same time in North Buckingham Street can no longer be savoured, due to their demolition.

MONKSTOWN, **Alma Road: Balnootra**
Designed in the 1850s for a lawyer named Sweeny by Deane and Woodward, and so carefully integrated into the existing streetscape that the house remained unidentified until discovered by Frederick O'Dwyer. Woodward deploys the decorative Tudor Revival of his youth with its perforated bargeboards and half-timbered bay window. The more geometrical rear elevation clearly expresses the split-level layout. Ivy leaves are perforated into the balustrading of the staircase and are woven into the plaster cornice. Annexe added *c.*1890 in Arts and Crafts Tudor style to house Sweeny's executrix, Frances Redmond; attributable to Richard Orpen; now a separate house.

MONKSTOWN: **Belgrave Square**
Massed along the south side of this residential square are some of the finest of Dublin's neo-Classical suburban houses. In the style of George Papworth with emphatically panelled double doors and shutters. Grecian freizes and frothy plasterwork. John Bourke was reported to be working here in 1850, but by then a gauche Gothic Revival was being introduced on the west side by McCurdy and Mitchell; even this had petered out by the time the innocuous housing had been built along the remaining sides.

MONKSTOWN: **Catholic Church**
Designed by Edward Welby Pugin and George Ashlin in 1865, midway through their partnership, as one of the four Dublin church commissions they received due to the success of their Thomas Street church. Like the others, built in granite with an open-scissors roof. But only here was the intended tower and spire completed. While its conventionality is overshadowed by the flamboyance of the Church of Ireland across the street, the interior survives reasonably intact. Stained glass by Mayer.

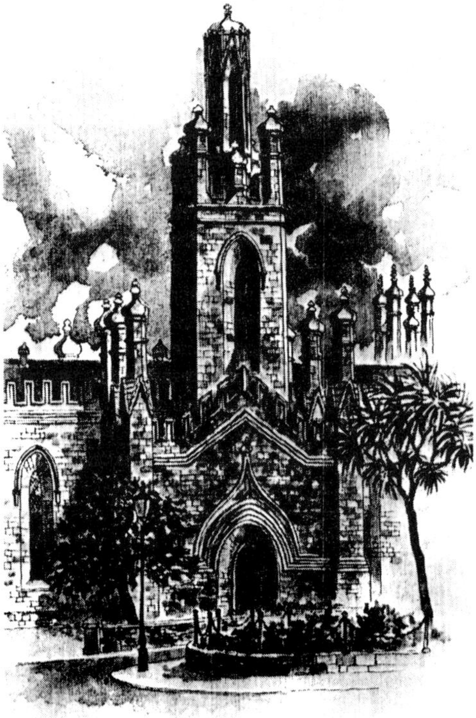

MONKSTOWN: **Church of Ireland**
The last record of John Semple, who remodelled the church of 1789 in 1830, was an unsuccessful entry in the competition for St Andrew's Church in 1860 (although he had been assumed dead by the *Building News* in 1857). In any case it was John McCurdy who got the job of adding a chancel in 1868. His work shows such reverence for Semple's controversial masterpiece that today few would guess the church was extended. The only evidence is the demure reredos of 1884, but this is the work of Thomas Drew (a parishioner), unable to compete with the high jinks of the organ gallery, which prefigures Art Deco. Betjeman's favourite church, preferred by him to the Palace of Westminster. Glass by Heaton, Butler and Bayne.

MONKSTOWN: **Longford Terrace**
The most urban of Monkstown's terraces, protected from the mainstream of coastal traffic by a battered retaining wall. Attributed to Papworth and Murray and built from *c.*1850 onwards. Double-drawingrooms take up the *piano nobile*, occasionally subdivided by Venetian arches.

MONKSTOWN: **Monkstown Castle House**
Italianate castle in a diluted Romanesque idiom appropriated by the partnership of Carmichael and Jones. Built for James Pim in 1859. Slender viewing tower designed to overlook once-celebrated formal gardens. These have now been replaced by playing fields while the house has been converted into a community centre. Corinthian columned hall leading to imperial staircase with richly scrolled balustrading.

MONKSTOWN, **Monkstown Road: Dalhousie**
Gatelodge designed by W.M. Mitchell in 1881 with gables crammed with fretwork. Compensates for its small size by its assertiveness.

MONKSTOWN, **Mountown: St John's Church**
Built for the Church of Ireland *c.*1860 by the Wellands in a Gothic Revival that reveals no evidence of their radicalism. Chancel refitted by Richard Orpen. Conveniently adapted to Tridentine use by the Irish followers of Archbishop Lebfevre, who celebrated Tridentine mass on an altar salvaged from R.M. Butler's Dominican Convent chapel in Eccles Street before its demolition.

MONKSTOWN, **Mountown: Glandore**
Designed in 1858 by Benjamin Woodward for W.J. Vesey, younger son of the 2nd Viscount de Vesci. Drawings survive to show that the house was modified in its execution but retains the contrast between the complex entrance front and the serenity of the garden front. Simple interiors. Diningroom spanned with corbelled beams. The smaller stable block coils out of the main house like a tail. The garden front carefully integrates its columnar Venetian Gothic staircase into the more restrained fenestration of the adjoining rooms. Now a private nursing home jostled by a surrounding housing estate.

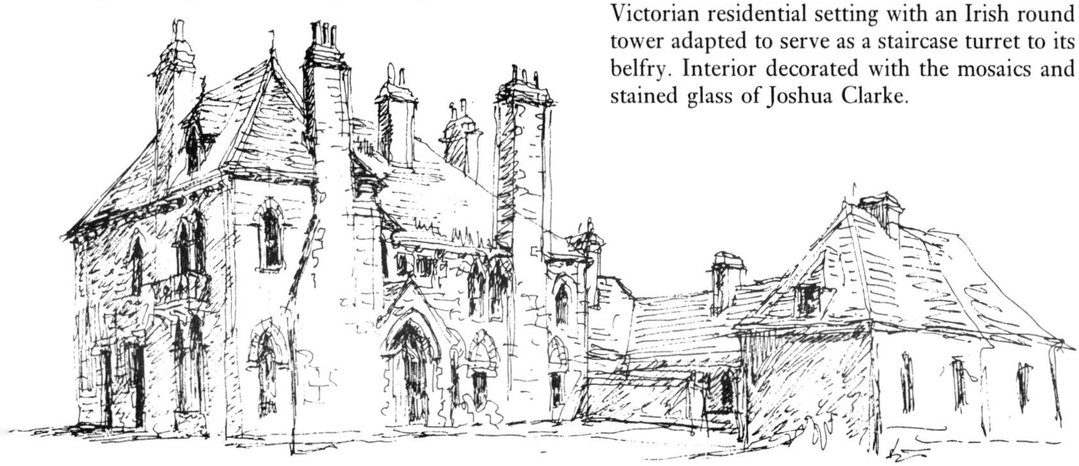

MONKSTOWN: **The Priory**
Attractive Gothic Revival villa in the style of George Papworth. Interiors decorated with traceried plasterwork of the late 1830s.

MONKSTOWN, **Queen's Park: Riversdale**
Only surviving, neo-Gothic villa built by A.G. Jones for his Queen's Park estate. A symmetrical red brick composition dominated by assertive tower. Impeccably maintained in its own grounds.

MONKSTOWN: **Queen's Park Villa**
Built by A.G. Jones for himself as the centre-piece of a speculative suburban development now replaced by modern apartment blocks.

MONKSTOWN, **Richmond Hill: No. 2**
Minimal curvilinear conservatory added *c.*1850 to a one-storey over-basement neo-Classical villa. Elegant apse curving out from the corner of the façade in the style of Richard Turner.

MONKSTOWN: **Rockbrook**
The largest domestic commission given to T.N. Deane after his completion of Portumna Castle twenty years before. Built for William Robert Bruce in 1881 out of Dalkey granite, incorporating an earlier house. A rambling Tudor Revival complex of competing ranges with an entry tower attempting to dominate the mêlée.

PALMERSTOWN: **Stewart's Hospital**
Hospital for handicapped named after its founder, who commissioned Lanyon, Lynn and Lanyon to add to an existing Georgian house dramatically sited above the River Liffey. Further wings added in 1894 by G.P. Beater.

RANELAGH, **Beechwood Avenue: Catholic Church**
Neo-Romanesque church by W.H. Byrne; commissioned in 1907, it still dominates its sedate Victorian residential setting with an Irish round tower adapted to serve as a staircase turret to its belfry. Interior decorated with the mosaics and stained glass of Joshua Clarke.

RANELAGH, Leeson Park: Church of Ireland

An early commission by Rawson Carroll, who was at the same time involved in designing speculative housing in the adjoining Leeson Park. Conventional Gothic Revival, cruciform with attached tower and spire. The masonry is unrelieved by polychromy, and its general greyness is compounded by the adjoining Molyneux Home for the Blind (designed also in 1862 in an obligatory Gothic institutional idiom). However, it does have one feature of great charm, a cast-iron south-facing verandah that links it to the church hall designed in a lighter Gothic manner with its diagonally positioned central spirelet by Albert Murray (1877). Due to be demolished in 1975, a successful appeal forced Michael Scott, Architects, to integrate the hall into their new Methodist centre.

The church is now used in alternation by the Church of Ireland and the Methodists. The internal decoration by Sibthorpes is sufficiently restrained to complement both rituals. Two late windows by Child (1936)—the Nativity and the Supper at Emmaus. Glass by Heaton, Butler and Bayne.

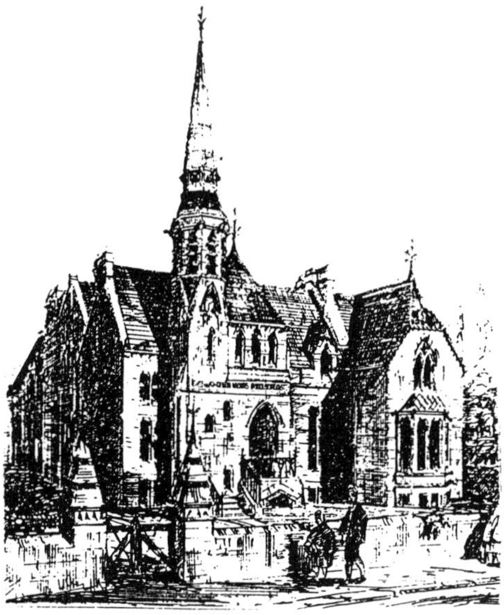

RANELAGH, Northbrook Road: Asylum

Gothic Revival part villa, part institution, designed by W.G. Murray in 1864 for inmates who had seen better times. Asymmetrical composition entered through porch beside a corner tower.

RANELAGH: Park Drive

Terrace of speculative villas, each one differently designed, adding up to a complex of great exuberance accented by oriels and turrets served up with half-timbering and pebble dash. The overall impression is now toned down by discreet planting. Designed by an obscure architect called Pickering after he had won a competition organized by a speculative builder in 1907.

RANELAGH, Sandford Road: Church of Ireland

Earlier church built in 1826 and given a new façade and open roof by Lanyon, Lynn and Lanyon in 1860, their first Dublin commission. Inspired by the Italian Romanesque with unusual roof trusses; a symmetrical façade apart from a jaunty bellcote. Galleries removed and aisles added in 1880. The interior has recently lost its original decoration round the chancel arch. Stained-glass window of St Peter and St Paul by Harry Clarke (1921).

RATHFARNHAM: Catholic Church

Gothic Revival church designed in 1875 on a corner site. West façade crowned by corbelled spirelet. Interior shows George Ashlin at his spikiest. The Stations of the Cross incorporated into the stained glass were made by Eugene Denis of Nantes.

RATHFARNHAM: St Columba's College

The original concept of St Columba's was the vision of the 3rd earl of Dunraven; an Irish Eton set on a rebuilt Rock of Cashel. As such the school was founded in Stackallen, Co. Meath, to be moved here a few years later; the acquisition of the Georgian residence of Lundy Foot was regarded as a temporary measure. Despite his conversion to Catholicism, Lord Dunraven still continued his subsidy and no doubt due to his influence the architect chosen for the residential additions was Philip Hardwick the Younger. In his overbearing Puginian scheme Hardwick intended to demolish the original house as he had destroyed Adare Manor. In the end he did very little, adding a cloister and another floor in 1858 to the earlier hall by William Atkins. (This hall and an austere dormitory block making two sides of a quad are all that was built of a far more accomplished 1852 scheme as recorded by Atkins in exquisite watercolours).

In 1875 further additions were made by McCurdy and Mitchell, but the trustees had more ambitious plans for the new chapel. William Butterfield was asked to provide a design, and surprisingly agreed. He chose to build his chapel as an isolated unit, for once modest and reassuring, its only entrance on the side crowned resourcefully by a single bellcote. The collegiate interior, entered through a porch beneath a saddle-roofed tower, is unexpectedly quiescent. Recent minimal alterations by John O'Connell to increase capacity. Richard Orpen, an old boy, also built merely a fragment in his attempt to complete the quad, superimposing a narrow dormitory on Hardwick's cloister. This was the last attempt to achieve architectural cohesion. Subsequent additions are separate buildings starting off with Orpen's own study hall (1899).

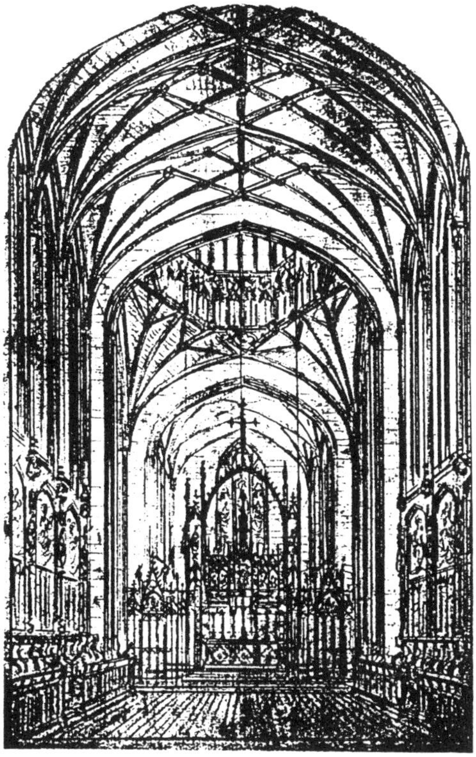

RATHFARNHAM: **Loreto Abbey**

A.N.W. Pugin was consulted by Patrick Byrne, the nuns' architect, in 1839, a year after Byrne had been commissioned to design a military-style Gothic Revival church. This was linked to the 1730 house that Mother Mary Ball had acquired and which still forms the nucleus of the present complex. Pugin's proposals of an octagonal lantern and an elaborate reredos screening the nuns' choir were executed in simplified form by Byrne and J.B. Keane. The reredos is less fanciful, and the vaulting of the lantern is simplified, but Pugin's idea of a glazed triforium allowing sick nuns to view the altar below them and to gaze up into the sunlit uppermost tier above, translates the rococo architecture of Vittone into the language of the Gothic Revival. The high altar frames a marble *pietà* by Hogan (1843) and is flanked by his kneeling angels (1848) modelled on his daughters, who were subsequently pupils. Another Hogan daughter became the reverend mother and donated several of her father's sculptures. The altar of the chapel dates now from 1894, designed by J.L. Robinson. Additions were made to house the school—firstly a chateau-like structure by W.H. Byrne *c.*1870. The interesting Gothic Revival extensions by C.B. Powell (1921) fall outside the scope of this book. Despite recent alteration and demolition there must be few places in Ireland where the history of its architecture can be followed as an interplay of the Gothic and the Classical styles.

RATHFARNHAM: **Tibradden**

Symmetrical Italianate country house built for Thomas Hosea Guinness on his wife's estate. Richly Corinthian hall with scagliola columns. Designed in 1861 by Joseph Maguire—and his grandest commission, since generally his practice was confined to suburban villas.

RATHFARNHAM: **Whitestown Library**

One of the most delightful buildings of T.J. Byrne (1910) even if it lacks the force of his Clondalkin library (q.v.). A blend of Arts and Crafts and Queen Anne Revival with the duality of a double-gabled façade challenged by a central porch below, the strength of Wicklow granite exploited against brick and half-timbering. Unconventional fenestration treated with a levity never repeated after he became head of the OPW.

RATHGAR: **Catholic Church**

One of the last designs of Patrick Byrne, but evidence of his failing powers, even though he is usually at his best when inspired by the counter-Reformation of Rome (1860). The black calp exterior with its fortress of an apse has a certain rugged power, but the façade never received its intended portico. The stripped Classicism of what was built instead reveals a loss of scale that is only too evident in the three-storied internal elevation of the nave. The use of giant Corinthian pilasters throughout only increases the monotony. Again as in the exterior, it is redeemed by the apse and ambulatory, with tiny curved chapels decorated by O'Neill and Byrne, who also designed the high altar carved by J. Farrell.

RATHGAR: **Methodist Church**

Gothic Revival church designed by Thomas Holbrook and built in 1874. Cast-iron arcades dividing nave from aisles. Open timber roof. Transepts added in 1924. Stained glass of the same period by Heaton Butler and Baynes in a latter-day pre-Raphaelite style. One window by Catherine O'Brien.

RATHGAR, Orwell Park: No. 58, Lisnoe
Detached asymmetrical villa (1886) enlivened by triangular oriel. The architect is unknown.

RATHGAR, Orwell Park: Ingleside
Villa by W.M. Mitchell with half-timbered gables, bay windows and a corner verandah (*c.*1900).

RATHGAR, Orwell Park: No. 14
Quintessential Victorian Gothic Revival forming a carefully composed asymmetrical composition with its adjoining conservatory, surrounded by gardens. Architect unknown.

RATHGAR, Orwell Road: St John of God's
Sedate villa ('Drumfillan') designed by Charles Geoghegan for the Drummond family in 1865. Not attached to the house but to the heated wall of the adjoining garden is an elegant Turneresque conservatory with a door at the centre of its projecting bow front set beneath Grecian scrolls. Recently restored at the expense of its original fittings.

RATHGAR, Orwell Road: Carrickbrack
Three villas, two of them semi-detached, built in 1886 for the Drummond family, possibly by Charles Geoghegan. The architect exploited a varied range of decorative devices—terracotta panels infilling brick arches and spandrels, banded stone columns free-standing in front of arcaded fenestration, inset enamelled tiles and chimneys springing from bewilderingly staggered corbels. The separate villa is now an hotel.

RATHGAR: Presbyterian Church
The earliest Irish church to be designed by Andrew Heiton, who received his commission through his coal merchant relations despite xenophobic opposition in the Dublin architectural press. His work is consistently inspired by the 14th-century 'Style Rayonnant'. In each case the church itself takes advantage of a sloping site to incorporate a parish hall at a lower level entered from the side, while impressive steps ascend to the main doorway flanked by a silvery spire. Aisleless interior with double transepts. Completed in one year—1864-5. Stained glass depicting St Peter preaching to the Jews (1914-15) by Geddes and an adjoining 1882 window by Cottier.

RATHGAR, Terenure Road: No. 33, Hopeton
Well-proportioned eclectic villa with adjoining mews both crowned with Jacobean style gables. Neo-Classical *piano nobile* with pillars linked by low wrought-iron balustrading. Dated 1862. In the style of T.N. Deane.

RATHGAR, Terenure Road: Nos. 52 and 54
Avondale (later Trieste), the most elaborate suburban tribute to Woodward's Trinity Museum, semi-detached, two floors and elevated basement, and built out of polychromatic brickwork contrasting with the blue enamel tiled panels below the side lights of the drawingroom French window opening on to a wrought-iron balcony. Contrasting with the round-arches fenestration, a Gothic-style doorcase with sculpted Bathstone infill. Prominently bracketed eaves copied with strange results by a Georgian neighbour. Date 1890. Architect possibly J.L. Robinson, who was an ardent Parnellite and therefore may have called it after his hero's home.

RATHGAR: Winton Avenue
The most elegant Greek Revival residential development in the southern suburbs—five detached villas with a central Ionic portico *in antis* the focus of the *piano nobile* raised on a semi-basement and approached by a flight of steps. Drawings for the fifth house survive, dated 1860; builder Robert McCleane, architect Edmund Figgis. Two other villas of the same design were built on Annaville Road in Ranelagh.

RATHGAR, Winton Avenue: Infant Schools
Small but forcefully composed terracotta set-piece with central hall flanked by symmetrical classrooms for boys and girls *c.*1890.

RATHGAR: Zion Church of Ireland
A large but extremely conservative Gothic Revival church by Joseph Welland, who died before its construction. Executed by his son with Gillespie. There is no indication here that when they completed construction in 1861 they were building in rural Ireland the most radical churches of their generation. Exterior dominated by a heavy slated spire set alongside the chancel. Attached circular tower. Interior improved by a pervasive gloom due to open roofs of varnished woodwork and stained glass inserted later. Gilbert Cockburn was the builder. Windows by Child: 'St Luke' (1914); 'Of such is the kingdom of heaven' (1932). Further windows by Heaton, Butler and Bayne.

RATHMINES: Bank of Ireland
Well-bred French Renaissance banking hall built in red sandstone, designed for the National Bank in 1899 by Walter Butler. His internal cheerful Corinthian decoration survives above head height.

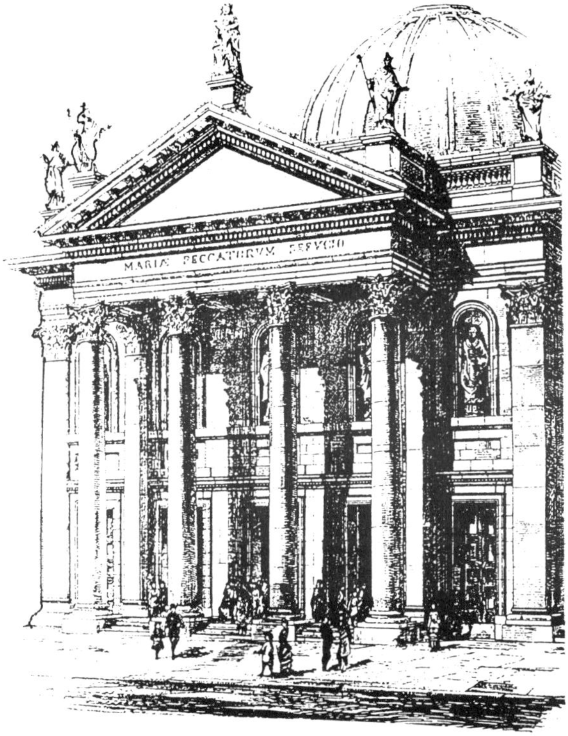

RATHMINES: **Catholic Church**
The final masterwork of Patrick Byrne dates from 1854. Subsequent generations were incapable of appreciating his abrupt transition from an austere almost windowless but extraordinarily eloquent exterior to a refined and sumptuous Palladian within. His design has been executed by others, firstly by W.H. Byrne, who added the portico with sculptures by Patrick Farrell, and then by Ralph Byrne, who restored the church after the interior had been destroyed by fire in 1920. The most successful addition is the soaring cupola that floats serenely above Patrick Byrne's massive walls. Fabricated from cast-iron in England and intended for a church in St Petersburg but never collected due to the Russian Revolution, Ralph Byrne saved it from the scrap heap but unfortunately placed beneath it an insensitive baldachino in an uneasy blend of Baroque and Hiberno-Romanesque. To appreciate Patrick Byrne's grandeur one must turn round and look up to the western gallery, vaulted by a geometrically coffered semi-dome to reverberate with triumphant chords of an organ by William Bourke of Camden Street.

RATHMINES, **Charlestown Road: Methodist Church**
Two Gothic Revival churches recently carefully converted into offices by Lavin and Chandler. Set side by side, since the earlier church by Isaac Farrell (1843) was retained as the parochial hall when the Belfast architect J.J. Phillips built the larger church in a combination of calp and red sandstone redolent of Ulster. Timber-sheathed Gothic barrel vault.

RATHMINES: **Church of Ireland**
In 1863, A.G. Jones was asked to enlarge the Semple church of 1833. He did this by building aisles and transepts in a similar idiom, removing the most striking feature of the interior—the stone vault—for structural reasons. This was replaced by an open roof articulated by cross bracing and lit by dormer windows. Stained glass by Heaton, Butler, Bayne and by Child (St Christopher). Recently these additions have been partitioned off into offices and church hall, so all the work of Jones has been rendered superfluous.

RATHMINES, **Cowper Road: McGeogh House**
Polychromatic brick instutional Gothic Revival complex built 'for elderly ladies of good character' round three sides of a garden, its centrepiece a chapel with an asymmetrical belfry rising above the towers that articulate the wings. Completed 1878; architect, Rawson Carroll.

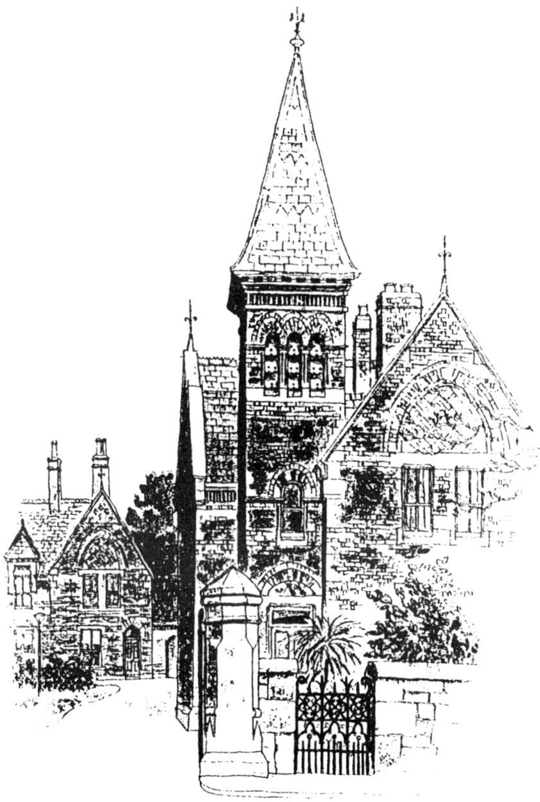

RATHMINES, Grosvenor Road: Baptist Church

Built in 1859, the architects being Carmichael and Jones. Pinnacled façade fitting into residential street. Plain interior, especially since it has lost its original vaulting (now replaced with a flat ceiling).

RATHMINES, Grosvenor Road: No. 17, Gosford

Built in 1862 for William Acheson, who named it after the ancestral family seat at Gosford. His architect was E.H. Carson, who came up with a concoction of Gothic, Swiss and Byzantine styles. Now appropriately housing an academy for ballet.

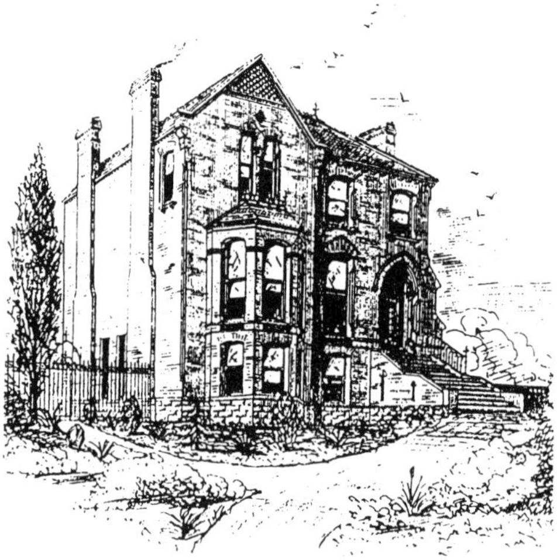

RATHMINES, Grosvenor Road: No. 20, Ashbrook

Elegant Gothic Revival detached villa (1879) on an elevated basement. Hall approached up steps and lit by floor to ceiling lancets. Architect G.P. Beater.

RATHMINES, Grosvenor Road: Nos. 53-60

The most ambitious Gothic Revival speculative terrace built in the Dublin suburbs; designed in the rather spikey Gothic idiom employed by both A.G. Jones and E.H. Carson. Four stories with three-storey prominent semicircular bow windows. Adjoining pairs of houses share a mutual flight of steps below and dormer above.

RATHMINES, Kenilworth Square: No. 3

Elegant symmetrical Greek Revival villa in the style of Carmichael and Jones (*c.*1860).

RATHMINES, Kenilworth Square: Nos. 83 and 84

A curious example of a pair of semi-detached houses treated to look like an asymmetrical Gothic Revival villa. The execution does not match up to the concept.

RATHMINES: Kensington Lodge

The only Dublin commission given to the curious Irish 19th-century namesake of William Chambers. As always, a modest budget and a compressed location has not deterred him from cramming every decorative device into his design. Here everything is in terracotta, climaxing with a pair of female herms that uphold the central scrolled gable (1881).

RATHMINES: Library and Technical College

Neo-Georgian complex of brick and stone hightened by curving bay window. Designed by F.G. Hicks and completed in 1913.

RATHMINES: Palmerston Park

The best preserved of the Victorian suburban developments built on the Temple estate *c.*1870. A segmental park divides straight terraces that face south across it towards a crescent of detached villas. Park laid out by William Shepherd and carefully maintained by Dublin Corporation.

RATHMINES: Palmerston Park, Balnagowan

Three-storey Scottish Baronial villa *c.*1870 named after the Perthshire home of the Ross family who built it while they were also building Dublin's three Presbyterian churches by the Perth architect, Andrew Heaton. Therefore he is the most likely archiect.

RATHMINES: Sunbury Gardens

Speculative three-storied villas grouped symmetrically round a private park. Carefully composed so that the two corner villas most visible from the main road are the largest, with lavish conservatories attached to them, while the furtherest from view are simplified, even omitting the curvilinear gables of the earliest; *c.*1890; architect unknown.

RATHMINES: Trustee Savings Bank

Scottish Baronial with corner turret, built for the Belfast Banking Company in 1901 by their architect, Vincent Craig.

RATHMINES: The Townhall

The most ambitious of Dublin's suburban townhalls, designed by Sir Thomas Drew and built during the 1890s. Its prominent siting is achieved at the expense of town planning since it destroyed the chance of a wide avenue approaching the capital city from the south. Instead, the vista is blocked by a formidable red sandstone neo-Elizabethan structure attached to a top-heavy domed tower. The assembly hall

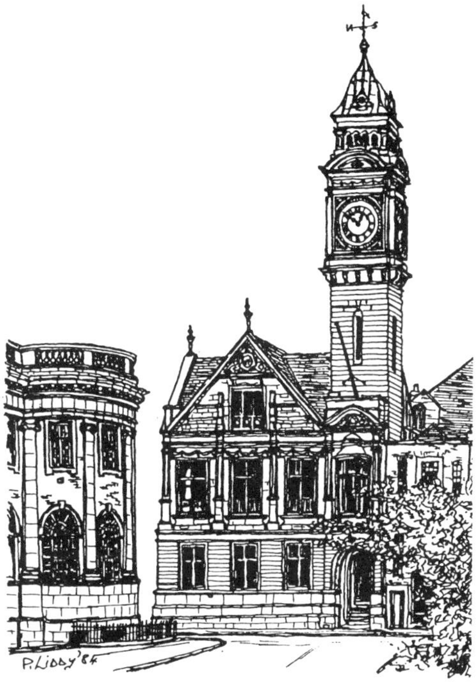

has been gutted, but the council chamber on the first floor has retained its overmantle and its painted glass.

SAGGART: **Catholic Church**
Cruciform Gothic Revival church *c.*1840 entered through western tower. The exterior conceals the delicacy and spatial inventiveness of the interior. This is due to the unknown architect's ability to use the unvarying, slim, clustered quatrefoils that uphold the plaster rib-vaulting throughout this hall church to create a forest of columns. But, instead of a uniform grid, the spacing alternates between wide and narrow bays in the transepts and chancel, with an intermediate dimension regulating the module of the nave.

SANDYFORD, **Fernhill**
Regency house remodelled in 1893 by Judge William Darley as the centrepiece of his gardens, cascade, lake and ornamental grounds which he had been embellishing since 1860. A rambling composition successfully tied together by a central pyramidal tower. The architect was unknown so the house was not accepted as being of historic merit in its own right by the Government. In fact no other Dublin Victorian villa can rival its integrity of house and garden. Carefully maintained by the Walker family—gardens open to the public.

SANDYMOUNT: **Catholic Church**
The triple-gabled façade expresses the internal layout of a nave and aisles all of equal width; an example of Pugin's influence on the early work of J.J. McCarthy (1851-8). Further elaboration by W.H. Beardwood (1889-91) restricted to additional sacristy, so that the initial simplicity survives. Dark atmospheric interior with stained glass by Earley. Church bell ringing across the strand heard by Gertie McDonnell in *Ulysses.*

SANDYMOUNT: **Church of Ireland**
Neo-Norman church (1850) in St John's Road donated by Sidney Herbert, whose favourite style was the Early Romanesque as expressed by the church he had built at Wilton. His architect here was Pugin's biographer, Benjamin Ferrey. The exterior, currently being restored, contrasts rubble masonry with Bath stone dressings. It was enlivened by sculpted beasts, but were removed on the instructions of a horrified archbishop before its consecration; one dragon, by being entwined round the vestry chimney, outwitted the purge. The appropriately High Anglican interior retains Ferrey's fittings. Glass by Joshua Clarke.

SANDYMOUNT, **Gilford Road: Old People's Home**
Snugly sheltered by surrounding birch trees contrasting with the red of the brick walls and pantiled roof broken by half-timbered gabling—an asymmetrical composition by Richard Orpen dating from 1901. Now much extended.

SANDYMOUNT: **Methodist Church**
A simple Gothic Revival cell built out of granite rubble by A.G. Jones in 1864. West façade enlivened by a diminutive rose window and later timber porch added as a First World War memorial by G. Beckett. Stained glass by Evie Hone, Child ('St Paul') and Rhind ('Dorcas').

SANDYMOUNT: **Pembroke Corporation Housing**
An intact housing development commissioned from G. O'Connor in 1912. Terrace of two-storey housing approached between rows of cottages with projecting porches. Resourceful deployment of polychromatic brick, tiles and slating.

SANDYMOUNT: **Presbyterian Church**
Gothic Revival church in Tritonville Road and adjoining hall with attached belfry that has recently lost its spire. However, picturesqueness is maintained by the granite rubble of the walls and the thoughtfully planted trees. Stark interiors. Designed by J.W. Hay and Son, imported from Liverpool at unnecessary expense,

according to the xenephobic *Dublin Builder*. The complex is currently threatened with demolition to enlarge an old people's home.

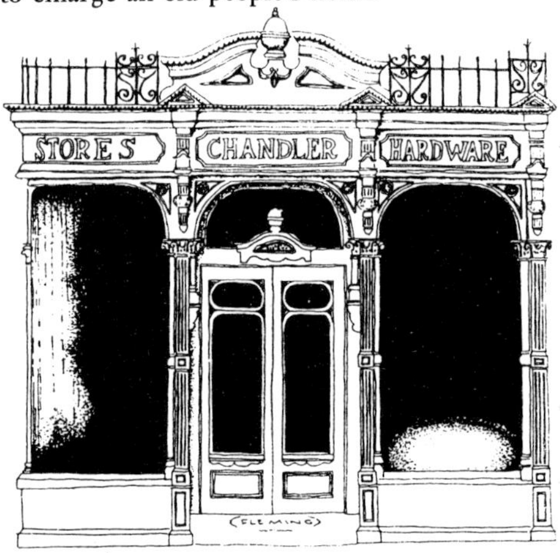

SANDYMOUNT, **The Green: Former Chandler's Shop**

An expected flowering of Art Nouveau. Curvilinear shopfront added *c.*1900 by an unknown designer to give light to an old lady who sold everything in a setting she refused to alter. Sold to become a self-conscious restaurant. Sold again.

SHANKHILL: **Church Hall**

Terracotta church hall designed *c.*1895. Close parallels to R.J. Sterling's Winstanley Hall in Dublin (now demolished).

SHANKHILL, **Quinns Road: Clontra**

To James Lawson QC, later Attorney General for Ireland and a now forgotten philosophical poet whom the Invincibles attempted to assassinate in 1882, is due the credit of having commissioned the most aesthetic house of his generation. His architects were Deane and Woodward, who started the job in 1856; his decorator, J. Hungerford Pollen, who in 1862 completed his frescoes, Spring and Autumn in the diningroom, and the Seven Ages of Woman dominating the drawingroom. Here coalesce the Gothic Revival (as radicalized by Webb in the Red House), the Dublin suburban Regency villa tradition of a single floor above an elevated basement, and Woodward's private obsession with geometry. Four pitched roofs are grouped in a pinwheel plan round the glazed pyramidal roof of the upper hall. This is reached by an internal stairs, frescoed with swallows, that rises from the hall door (discreetly sheltered by a long lean-to verandah). The bedrooms are on the ground level; above, the livingrooms rise to the collar height of the steeply pitched roofs to display what an anonymous critic called 'the naked timbers'. Likewise exposed is the half-timbered construction of the first-floor oriels contrasting with the rough granite of the outside walls, the red brick of the relieving arches, the Caen stone Venetian balconies, and the slating of the massive roofs.

The geometrical kitchen was added to the rear by T.N. Deane in 1863, linking the house to the stable court built a few years before (at the same time as the gatelodge). The last structure to be erected was the decorative cast-iron Gothic conservatory. A private house, not open to public.

SHANKHILL: **Rathmichael Church of Ireland**

The only Irish church designed by Benjamin Woodward, commissioned by the Domville family in 1860; the nearest that Woodward ever

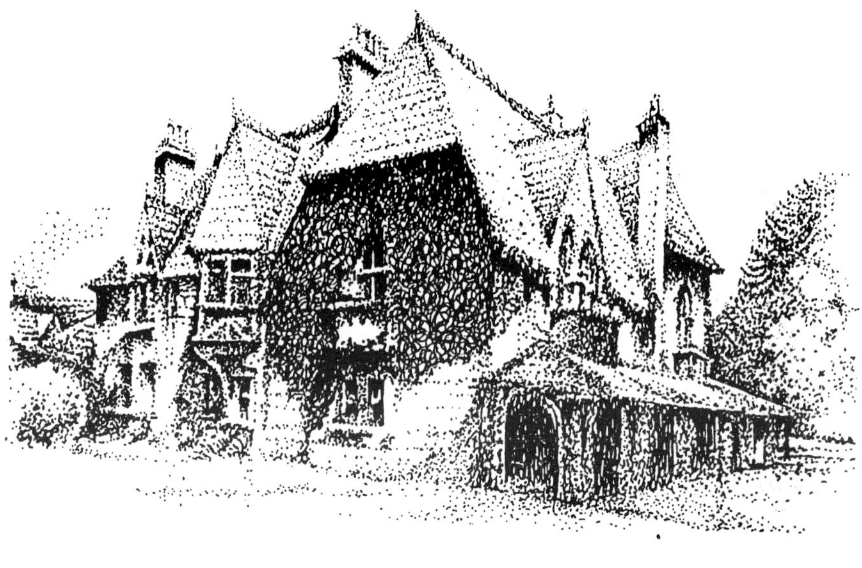

came to the Celtic Revival. West façade with rose window modelled on Rahan Church, Co. Offaly (q.v.). Simple cell internally with scissors-truss roof and semi-circular apse. Later additions, although more determinedly Celtic in detail, have inevitably developed a High Victorian complexity—adding an apsidal vestry and porch to the south and a lean-to aisle on the north. These extensions were tactfully designed by T.N. Deane, who dismantled Woodward's façade and rebuilt it two bays further west. Pulpit designed by Fuller. Windows by Heaton, Butler and Bayne. Good Samaritan window by Purser (1903). Later glass by O'Brien and Child. Celtic memorial in the grounds.

STILLORGAN: Convalescent Home

Victorian charitable housing institution now a centre for the deaf. Neo-Elizabethan complex in a cherry-red brick with limestone dressings; 1883. Architect, Rawson Carroll.

STILLORGAN, Foster Avenue: Church of Ireland

Tiny Gothic Revival church built in the mid-1860s. Subsequently the nave was extended in the same idiom and an Arts and Crafts hall and rectory built to the designs of R.G. Hopcraft in 1941, the last example of its style in Ireland. The rector of the time was the father of the poet Monk Gibbon. Stained glass includes two windows by Child of 1920 and a Hone of 1941.

STILLORGAN, Leopardstown Road: Sheils' Homes

The most elaborate of the charitable housing complexes commissioned by Charles Sheils in 1869, because, after the premature death of his wife, he had no close relations. His architects were Lanyon, Lynn and Lanyon; this is Lynn's most playful design, effortlessly adapting to its corner site and revolving round a dragon-infested clock tower. Hipped gables alternate with corbelled dormers. It is remarkable how Lynn, so often competent but unfeeling when working for the very rich, has here struck just the right note for widows of very modest means. A measure of its success is its survival as the centrepiece of a new speculative housing scheme which incorporated modern apartments that were made over to the original residents.

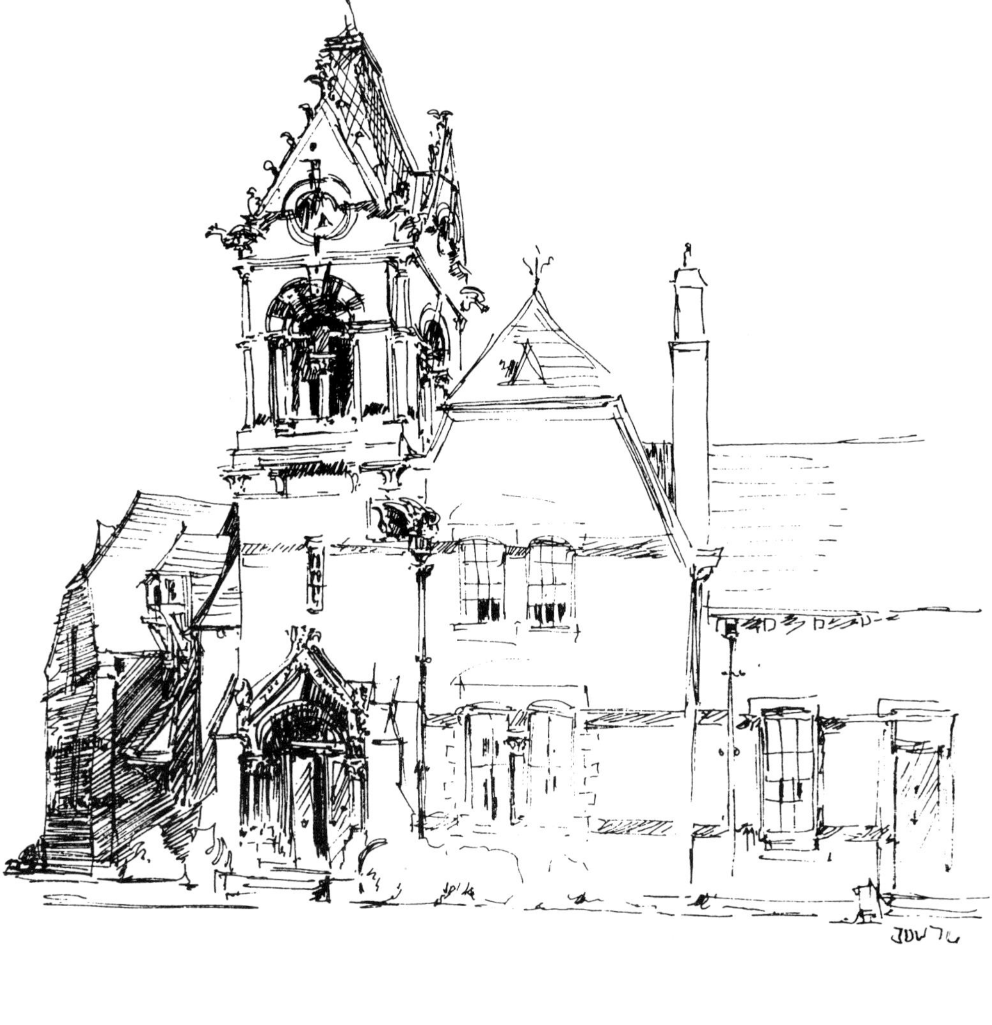

STILLORGAN: **Obelisk Park**
Georgian house rebuilt by a Quaker, James Perry, in 1874 and then presented to his son-in-law Marcus Goodbody, who made a Japanese garden and lake centred on the obelisk designed by Edward Lovett Pearce inspired by Bernini's on the Piazza Navona. Perry's architect was Thomas Drew, here working in a ponderous Italianate manner. In 1923 acquired by a religious order and extended by them as a home for the handicapped at the expense of the garden.

STILLORGAN: **Park House**
Sedate Victorian villa still retaining its ornamental grounds, walled-in gardens and crested curvilinears against to once-heated walls. Only comparatively recently sold by the Proby family, who had been responsible last century for the residential development in this part of Co. Dublin.

STILLORGAN: **The Reservoir**
Robust octagonal pavilion with rusticated quoins built as the pumphouse in 1884. Architect presumably Parke Neville.

STILLORGAN: **St Helen's**
Georgian country house remodelled and extended *c.*1863 by John McCurdy in a formidable Italianate for Field-Marshal Gough, who laid out formal gardens terraced towards the sea with parterres based on his military decorations and who hung his curvilinear conservatory with momentoes of the Afghan War. Subsequently acquired by the grandfather of Sir Anthony Nutting (the Conservative politician who resigned after Suez). W.D. Caröe was chosen to make the interior even more opulent—with mixed results: the Art Nouveau fireplace and repoussé copper freize he introduced into the diningroom does little to lighten the mood of the room. He had more success in his remodelling of the ballroom with a resourcefully inserted minstrel's gallery upheld by well-fed songsters and a spectacular Portuguese rose marble chimneypiece transformed by the last owners, the Christian Brothers, into the reredos of their altar. A casualty was the adjoining conservatory, regarded as too epicurean to remain when the ballroom became their chapel.

The most attractive room is still Lady Nutting's boudoir above the entrance hall, painted throughout with garlanded arcades retained as the unlikely study of the head of Ireland's austerest teaching order. The elegant minimal neo-Georgian timber extensions of the Christian Brothers are due to be demolished when the house is developed as the centrepiece of an office park. The developers have already converted the stables into housing with the consequent loss of Caröe's well-appointed interiors. His client was a keen horseman who left Ireland to become MFH of one of the grandest hunts in England, after the Meath Hunt had spurned him due to his connections with trade.

STILLORGAN: **St John of God's**
Originally known as Stillorgan Castle but to all intents a three-storied Regency country house when acquired by the Brothers of St John of God to look after the alcoholic and insane. Their ever greater numbers have led to continuous extensions, the earliest a formidable three-storied institution in rock-faced masonry. This links into a chapel of diluted Romanesque. Architect, W.H. Byrne, who had to rebuild after a fire. The twin gatelodges and terraced gardens are a source of pleasure to MacMann in Beckett's *Malone Dies*. Here he and his insane warder are collected by the local do-gooder Lady Petal on their ill-fated excursion to Dalkey Island.

TALLAGHT: **Dominican Monastery**
Gothic Revival monastery designed by J.J. McCarthy in 1863. Chapel added in 1886 after his death by George Ashlin, his rival. Ashlin returned in 1908 to enrich the interior with murals, mosaics and altars, but these were mostly removed when a neo-Gothic aisle was added by Edward Brady in 1969.

TERENURE: **Catholic Church**
Vacuous essay in neo-Romanesque by W.H. Byrne in 1904. Tower never completed, hence the retention at its foot of a more interesting delicate cast-iron bellcage. The church was doubled in length *c.*1950 so that the apocalyptic Crucifixion window by Harry Clarke (1920) has been repositioned. A see-through altar containing a replica of John Hogan's Dead Christ gives a further shock to the sedate architecture. More delicate Clarke windows in the lady chapel, which still remains in its original position.

FERMANAGH

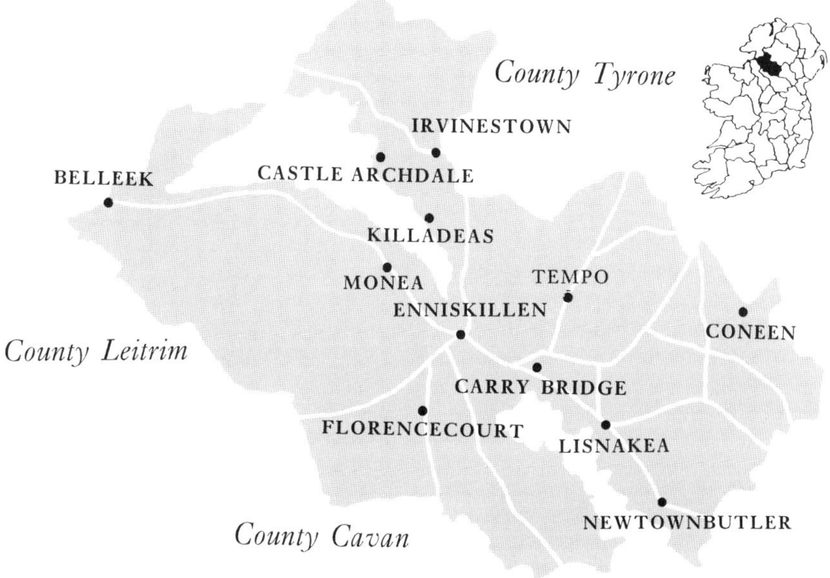

BELLEEK: **Magheramena Castle**
Of the three Tudor Revival castles built by J.B. Keane during the 1830s in the valley of Lower Lough Erne. Camlin has been swept away, and Necarne has been left roofed if derelict. Magheramena is in an intermediate site. Abandoned and dismantled in the 1950s, only its outer walls remain intact. These are boldly asymmetrical and articulated by lofty octagonal turrets. The five principal rooms are strung along the garden front so that today through gaping apertures one can enjoy the view southwards across the lake as Keane's client James Johnston must have done when his walls were starting to rise, and he was about to marry.

BELLEEK: **The Pottery**
The village is dominated by the three-storied Italianate porcelain factory that has made its name throughout the world. Built in 1865, its design is attributed to its founder William Armstrong.

CARRY BRIDGE: **Belle Isle**
The destruction by fire of Spiddal, Kilteragh and Kenmare, make Belle Isle a rare example of an Irish Arts and Crafts country house. The rebuilding of 1885 encases an 18th century seven-bay house extended by a Regency wing, reusing its woodwork but leaving no external trace of it on approach. Instead, the composition rambles from a five-storied viewing tower, a canted entrance arch, a gabled range (broken by adjoining oriels), to a self-contained Georgian agent's house and a service yard. All this is in imitation of Devey, but the architect was Morley Horder. His client was John Grey Vesey Porter, who, on inheriting the estate, had added the stable court in 1856. An arcaded entrance hall, beamed and panelled, leads to the principal reception rooms of the early house facing south across Lough Erne with a bay window added to the drawingroom to take more advantage of the view. Galleried staircase lit by roof lantern leading to charming bedrooms, each with their

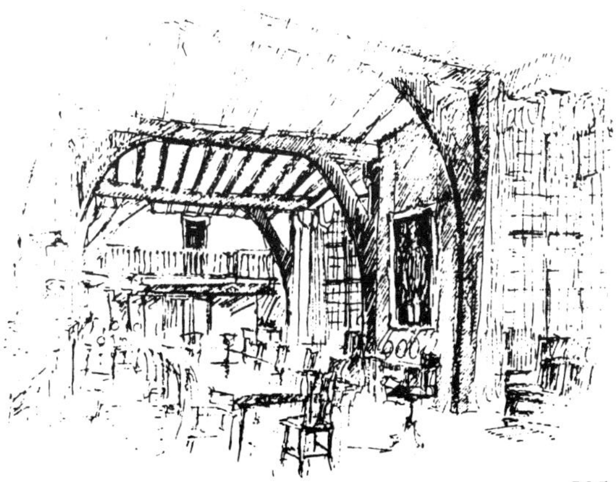

tiny dressing closet. Bathroom wing clad in old blue and white Delft tiles. The principal interior dating from 1907 is a baronial hall at a lower level to the rest, so that one enters and descends into the room opposite a minstrel's gallery at the further end. On one side a jutting chimneypiece, on the other the twin oriels. Beamed roof braced with prominent spandrels. Late Victorian profusion of portraits and furnishings now dispersed after the recent sale of the estate by the last of the Porter family to live here. Now being restored for the new owner by Richard Pierce and David Hicks.

CASTLE ARCHDALE: **Church of Ireland**
One of the last churches of Sir Thomas Drew, begun in 1905, when he had been in architectural practice for fifty years, and completed in 1908, two years before his death. Comparable to Monea (q.v.), as both represent the last 'Arts and Crafts' phase of the Gothic Revival. Built in dark sandstone and limestone trim. Tower above north transept guarded by spouting gryphons. Varied fenestration throughout. Large windows at east and the west ends illuminate the oak wagon vaults of nave and chancel opening into lesser transepts Internal ashlar-lined walls with heraldic carving inset above the entrance. Two stained glass windows by Child—Te Deum (1908) above the altar and St George and St Patrick (1910).

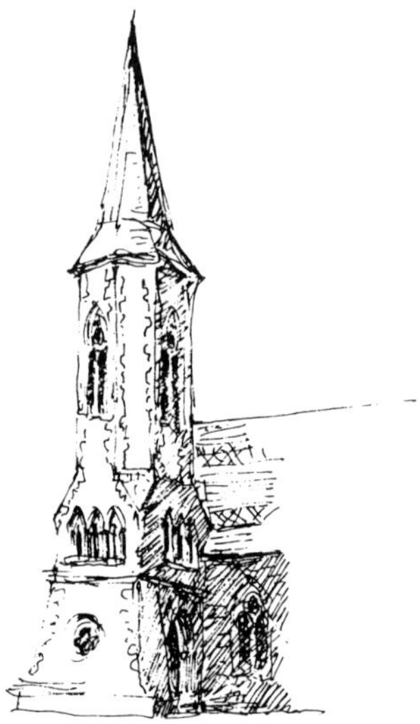

CONEEN: **Church of Ireland**
Gothic Revival church (1871-3) enlivened by its piquant octagonal belfry which rises from a battered plinth interpenetrated by a quatrefoil window and jamming a doorway of clustered columns against the adjoining nave. Interior conventional except for curiously braced apse. Architects, presumably Welland and Gillespie.

ENNISKILLEN: **Blake's Public House**
Discreet, substantial and unchanged Victorian pub set into the main street. Snugs lined with pine.

ENNISKILLEN: **Boer War Memorial**
Statue of 1904 now resited on new bronze plinth designed by Richard Pierce to commemorate the victims of the 1987 atrocity.

ENNISKILLEN: **Butter Market**
Built in 1835 by William Frith and recently well restored by Richard Pierce: a once-open, free-standing shed has been thoughtfully glazed while retaining the cast-iron columns and the open-timber trusses of the original structure (now an exhibition centre). Enclosed by two long, low ranges today accommodating craftsmen.

ENNISKILLEN: **Main Gatelodge, Castle Coole**
Built in smooth ashlar of Lombardic inspiration. Arcaded doubled windows. Architect unknown.

ENNISKILLEN: **Catholic Church**
Designed by O'Neill and Byrne and built in 1870-5 except for the belfry level of the tower (the spire recently added, to a different design). Up till now the best view is from the Castle, where the church appears to borrow the belfry of the Church of Ireland cathedral and its apse projects beyond the crest of the hill. In the interior everything has been sacrificed to height so that the boldly scaled arcades reminiscent of Florentine Gothic reveal too much wall space, partly frescoed but not with masterpieces (by Charles Russell)—better left unrestored—that correspond to stained glass windows mainly by Mayer in the opposite aisle. The altar of 1882 fails to give a sense of uplift to the apse. The two Michael Healy Nativity windows need seeking out among the preponderance of Mayer's glass. Their sculptural counterpart, the 1908 Byzantine pulpit by William Scott also needs time to emerge from Gothic gloom. The fresco of the Nativity is also the work of Michael Healy.

ENNISKILLEN: **Church of Ireland Cathedral**
Rebuilt by William Farrell retaining the tower of the Plantation church, now sited off-centre to the new, much wider nave. Unusual triple-tiered elevation, since it includes both gallery and clerestory, the latter penetrating the plaster Gothic vault. Chancel extended in 1889 when the remarkable east window by Warrington of 1856 was retained—for its subject the Garden of Getsemane, not for its exciting use of acid.

Unhappy changes this century included removing one bay from the north gallery and roofing the two adjoining aisles bays with a suspended ceiling to make a chapel for the Inniskillings. A martial air had already been imparted by two lifesize marble generals facing each other across the chancel—the 2nd earl of Enniskillen (*d.* 1840) and General Sir Galbraith Lowry Cole (also commemorated by the column in the public park).

ENNISKILLEN: **Convent of Mercy**

The original scheme was drawn up by J.J. McCarthy but what was built in a comfortable but outdated Georgian has never been attributed to him. Half-a-century later, in 1904, William Scott added the neo-Byzantine chapel rising with impressive buttresses above the river

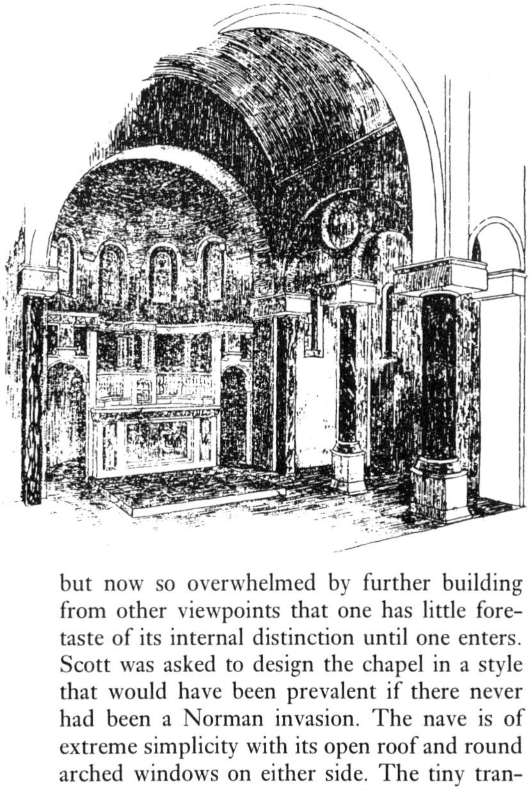

but now so overwhelmed by further building from other viewpoints that one has little foretaste of its internal distinction until one enters. Scott was asked to design the chapel in a style that would have been prevalent if there never had been a Norman invasion. The nave is of extreme simplicity with its open roof and round arched windows on either side. The tiny transepts occur between two arcaded screens with their still uncarved capitals in eloquent contrast to the exquisite marble reredos beyond by William Malone of Dublin that screens the apse and gives the interior a Greek Orthodox reserve. The altar is set into a central curved recess. The hidden space behind is illuminated by five stained-glass windows (Michael Healy). Healy is also responsible for the remainder of the glass apart from two windows by Sarah Purser painted by O'Brien—St Michael and St Elizabeth—and six by Lady Glenavy—the Sacred Heart, the Immaculate Conception and four saints, St Macartan, St Margaret, St Joseph and St Mary and St Joseph (bearded like D.H. Lawrence, the artist's future friend).

ENNISKILLEN: **Fort Hill Public Park**

Well-preserved public park focused on a lively cast-iron bandstand, with a pagoda roof, a clock forming the upper tier. Above it, Sir Terence Farrell's statue to General Sir Galbraith Lowry Cole (1845-57) surmounts a lofty Doric fluted column.

ENNISKILLEN: **Methodist Church**

Built in 1863-7 to the design of William Barre in a surprisingly Palladian idiom—a façade five bays wide and a slightly projecting Corinthian tetrastyle portico. After all this gravity, the interior is without classical orders, luminous and delicately lit from both sides with a horseshoe-shaped gallery. Cast-iron balusters swell outwards (it is said) to facilitate the crinolines of the congregation. The church was refitted by Thomas Elliot, who was presumably responsible for the neo-Tudor two-storied hall behind, with its first floor on the same level as the congregation. Plasterwork recently restored.

ENNISKILLEN: **Model School**

Only the master's house survives demolition and rebuilding in 1973. Round-arched fenestration sedately paned but set in walls of polychromatic brick work. By J.H. Owen, 1865-7.

ENNISKILLEN: **Olde Paint Shop**

Cottage ornée estate offices of the Collum family who once owned Bellevue. A polygonal corner building with windows set beneath a series of lacy gables.

ENNISKILLEN: **Presbyterian Church**

Gothic Revival church of 1897. Hipped timber roof articulated by elaborate hammer-beam trusses. Stained glass First World War memorial window by Wm. Morris and Co. after a G.H. Swinstead painting of Christ appearing to two soldiers.

ENNISKILLEN: **Killyhevlin**

The transformation of Killadeas (q.v.) into an hotel is admirable compared to the fate of Killyhevlin, originally designed by William Scott in 1904 with views over Lough Erne. What makes the destruction of Scott's interior even more unforgivable is that the architect in charge of the conversion appreciated William Scott's architecture enough to re-use it in the exterior of his own extensions, even replicating several times in reduced versions Scott's service

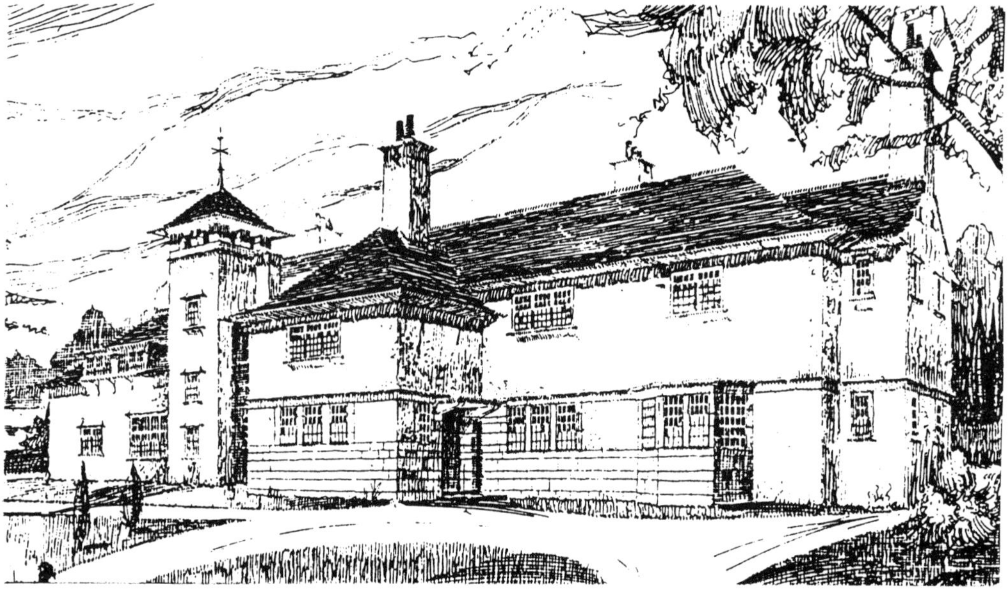

tower, so one enters in anticipation. One's reward is one staircase on the way to the lavatories, its tulip balustrading the sole evidence of what must once have been.

ENNISKILLEN: **Rossory Church of Ireland**
Sited on a wooded hill, this church was built in 1839-43 by the Derry architect, William Hagerty in his distinctive blend of Norman and neo-Classicism. Thus the narrow arched windows are set into wide, shallow, recessed bays. The chancel with its triple window barely projects beyond the transepts. At the other end a tower with rather self-consciously Irish battlements was added in 1915. The flat ceiling is broken by central tunnel vaults in nave and transepts that intersect above the crossing. Two remarkable stained glass windows; that over the altar is by an Ascension by Child and O'Brien (1910); that in the south transept is a Te Deum by O'Brien (1921).

ENNISKILLEN: **The Scotch Store**
The Scottish Co-operative Wholesale Society set up a series of creameries and commissioned Thomas Elliot in 1893 to design their headquarters and their adjoining manager's house. Long road frontages with the offices stretching between the factory and (at the apex) the formidably Baronial residence for the manager known as Thistle House. Serpentine gables rising to corbelled chimneys.

ENNISKILLEN, **Tamlaght: Bellevue**
Georgian house on a peninsular in Upper Lough Erne, remodelled *c.*1875 and extended to contain a galleried top-lit inner hall leading to a bay-windowed drawingroom opening to a conservatory. This has now vanished, but an earlier curvilinear survives in the garden. Undocumented but with all the characteristics of Richard Turner. The doorway shows Turner's origin as a manufacturer of Dublin fanlights. In this case the fanlight fits into a glazed vault that interpenetrates the lean-to curvilinear topped with characteristic cresting linking elegant urns. The gutters reveal similar finesse, carried at dado level and articulated by breakfronts sporting scrolls and sunflowers. Decay has not lessened its jollity.

ENNISKILLEN: **The Townhall**
Won in a competition by Anthony Scott assisted by his son William (1897). Completed four yeras later for almost double its original estimate. Assembly hall takes up the *piano nobile* approached by a generous coloured-marble staircase. The idiom is generally Italianate and reveals none of the tensions that mark William Scott's Cavan townhall (q.v.). The exterior is dominated by a corner clocktower rising up via sculpted niches to a belfry and a circular domed tempietto flanked by four octagonal tourelles. Assembly hall reduced after bomb damage in the 1970s. Adjoining reception room retains the fireplace of its 17th-century predecessor.

FLORENCECOURT: **Druminiskill Church of Ireland**
Small red-brick cell with stone trimmings of four bays entered through a side porch attached to a corner belfry. This rises from a strongly battered base cut into by a rectangular window

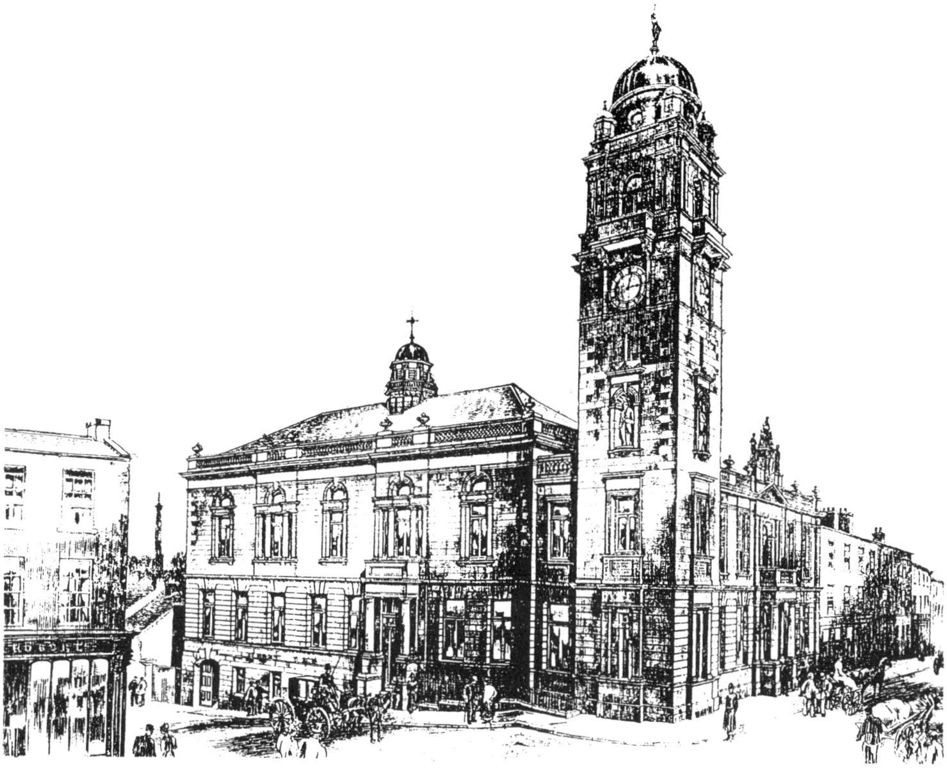

with a zig-zag frame (evidence of an unusual mind). The only work in Ulster of J. McDuff Derick, the architect of Duckett's Grove (q.v.). Built during the same period (1855-60)

IRVINESTOWN: **Castle Irvine or Necarne Castle**

Two castles, the later built across its predecessor, which appears to have been a geometrical plantation castle: four-storied with two circular five-storey corner towers. Inherited by Judge d'Arcy, who in 1833 commissioned J.B. Keane to add a precise, symmetrical, axially-sided neo-Tudor entrance block, of two stories with a projecting single-storied arcaded porch. Behind all this Keane extended the original castle, eastwards to a new diningroom, westwards to make a towered gabled servants' wing screening the stableyard. Now that the castle is inaccessible, the startling contrast of the neo-Classical interiors can no longer be savoured, especially the entrance hall with double doors behind Corinthian columns that open into reception rooms on either side to create one

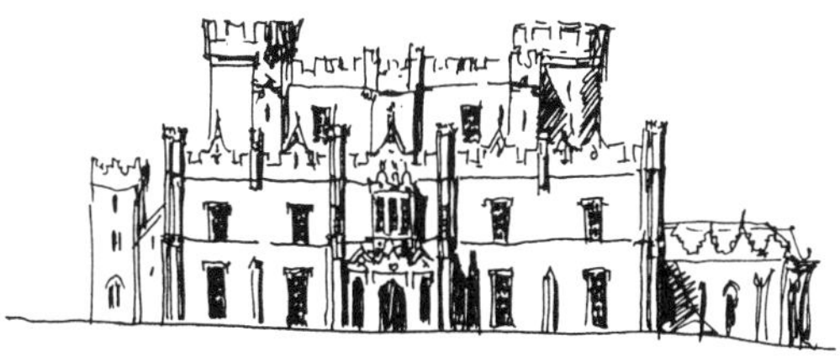

flowing space. Writhing gilded plasterwork culminating in the serpents twisting round the drawingroom ceiling centre. Staircase inserted into the original castle lit by heraldic stained glass. Current plans are to sacrifice the interior and construct a new adventure centre in the existing shell, an idea that has so far inspired such apathy that it may never come to pass. However, the neo-Elizabethan gatelodge is well maintained beside neo-Egyptian gates, the only evidence of Keane's stylistic schizophrenia.

KILLADEAS: **Church of Ireland**

J.F. Fuller in his memoirs when recalling his architectural commissions omits most of them but includes the churches of Castlemacadam and Killadeas. The former, the *Dublin Builder* reports as being by Lanyon, Lynn and Lanyon, the latter by William Armstrong. Surviving drawings are signed Welland and Gillespie. William Armstrong as an amateur could have got professional assistance from Fuller as the church was being built, since Killadeas has many features that Fuller was to use over the next three decades—the steep pitches, the grim external stonework, the plate tracery, the timber ribbed arches articulating the plaster curved vaults and the ceremonial treatment of the baptismal font at the west end. Church built in 1864, tower added in 1881.

KILLADEAS: **Manor House**

Georgian house transformed into Italianate

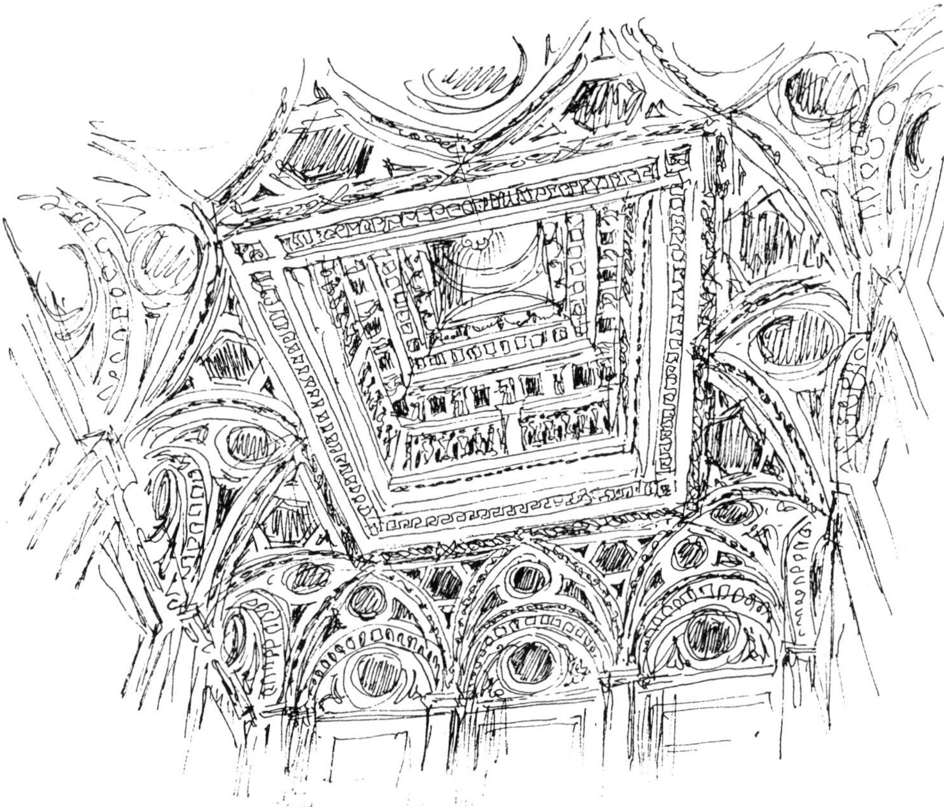

palazzo for J.G. Irvine by William Armstrong in 1861–8. A new front was added dominated by a tower with an arcaded belvedere. Matching arcades reappear above an arched and columned porch. Sensational inner hall with central light well cut into its groined vaulting and rising via corbels at first-floor level up into a spandrelled dome. The staircase rises to a columned apse. All this is more appropriate to a grand hotel. The house has alas become a modernized hotel instead.

LISNAKEA: **Colebrooke**
The walled garden of the Classical mansion by William Farrell (1820) contains an early curvilinear by Richard Turner *c.*1840. Now derelict. A recent estimate for its repair exceeded that necessary to restore the house itself.

MONEA: **Catholic Church**
Although the architect here was William Scott and the date 1908 (his best period), there was evidently too little money to compete with Drew's church in the valley below. Scott's church is a simple cell with a pitched roof overhanging the buttresses that articulate every bay. Bellcote at the apex of the western gable corbelled out on splayed planes; otherwise puritanically conventional. Perhaps all this austerity was intended as a contrast to a rich altar. If that ever existed, it has now been replaced.

MONEA: **Church of Ireland**
A minor masterpiece by Thomas Drew built in 1890, but deploying the tower of its Georgian predecessor and a 15th-century window from Devenish that takes seeking out due to the attention Drew gave to his own windows. One approaches from the rear where a lean-to vestry roof descends almost to the level of the gravestones, so that one has to go round the church to gain the shelter of its spacious porch. The interior has a medieval quality due to the irregular fenestration of the nave and the siting of the chancel arch before the transepts. These are screened by double arcades with their central columns marking off the corners of the raised choir. Timber wagon roofs, simplest in the transepts and most elaborate in the nave. Only the stained glass lets down the quality of the interior (exceptions being a Geddes of 1908 and the recent memorial window to the dowager duchess of Westminster by Alan Younger that perfectly matches this ecclesiastical counterpart of 'Sweetness and Light'.

NEWTOWNBUTLER: **Armagh Manor**
Miniature, Scottish-French chateau built in 1865 by a Scottish architect (according to the family), for a barrister, James Haire, who planted a park in the shape of a heart, all for the love of a woman who never responded. Ingenious plan recalling Benjamin Woodward.

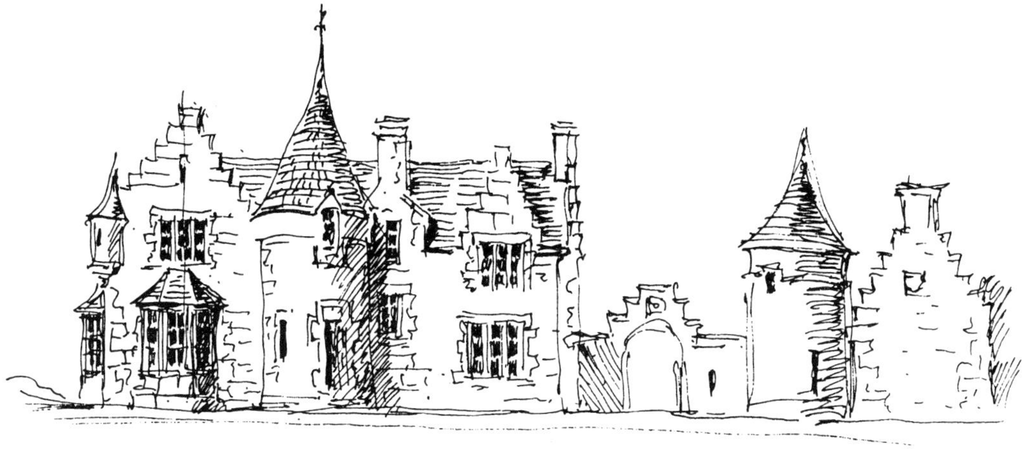

Entered through circular tower in an angle of the façade. Adjoining reception rooms aligned to bay windows set at right angles to each other open off a staircase hall lit from a hidden window on the half landing. Separate turret adjoining stable range, counterbalanced by turret corbelled off the principal bedroom. Neo-medieval fireplaces, the one in the diningroom inscribed in Old English to the effect that one sits down to eat like an ox and rises like an ass. Further inscriptions over front door, punning 'herein' with Haire, and over archway to yard. He never married, but today his house is still cared for by his brother's descendants.

Also several cottages in the valley below, the most elaborate earlier than the manor (1856), with a verandah round a double-storied bay. Regency Gothick but with touches of humour: the doorway to his coachhouse is shaped like a horseshoe.

NEWTOWNBUTLER: **Crom Castle**
The largest Irish commission of Edward Blore. Built in 1834-6, extended by a conservatory wing in 1838, destroyed by fire in 1841 and then rebuilt under the supervision of an obscure Dublin architect, George Sudden. In 1890 William Hague, in one of his rare secular commissions, added a billiard room and altered some adjoining interiors. Built from a dark local limestone, first impressions are forbidding especially as the entrance front is raised up on an exposed basement, so that the first internal flight of stairs reaches the level of the entrance hall at garden level. Beyond, an imperial staircase screened by an arcade of Perpendicular

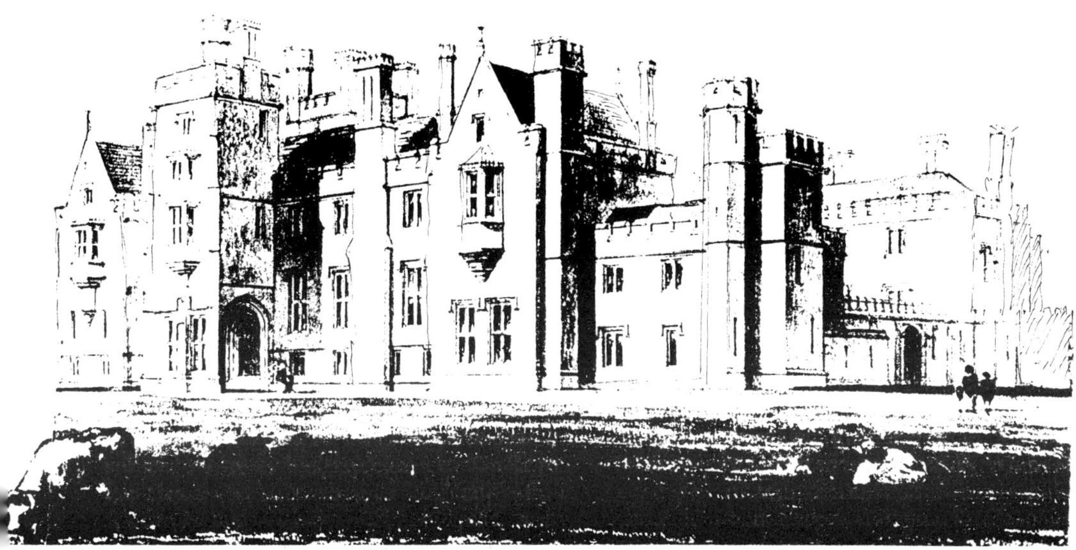

Gothic is lit from above through an octagonal lantern. The furnishings were commissioned from William Trotter of Edinburgh. Externally the most successful structure is the Gothic conservatory that reveals a lightness of touch missing from the symmetrical garden front. The most delightful interiors are those of William Hague, redolent of Italy. The castle overlooks upper Lough Erne, with its woods and islands rendered even more picturesque by a series of follies—an observatory in a neo-Tudor tower (1847), an ornamental cottage (1840). This has an elegantly tented interior above the open Gothic arches from which boats themselves are suspended and a barge-boarded boathouse by George Sudden (1850). The demesne, landscaped by W.S. Gilpin (1838), is now the property of the National Trust.

NEWTOWNBUTLER: **Crom Church**
Built 1840-4, and tentatively attributed by Alistair Rowan to J.S. Mulvaney. Entered through a more elaborate tower designed by William Fullerton in 1885. Georgian pews in the nave. Gothic Revival in the chancel. Stained glass east windows by Capronnier (1869). Access from the castle by boat across the lake.

TEMPO: **The Manor**
Designed by Sir Charles Lanyon and his assistant Thomas Turner in 1862 for Sir James Emerson. Campanile and billiard room wing added five years later. A Jacobean Revival interpretation of a Gothick cottage ornée with bedrooms lit either through dormers or lofty arched windows set into ogee gables. The reception rooms have bay windows with parapets of delicate interlacing strapwork. Sited above terraced towns that descend to a chain of lakes planted with rare shrubs and trees. The companile that rather primly dominates the entrance front, when seen from the garden appears to be a playful belvedere with inverted squinches rising to a convex spire. Interiors with neo-Elizabethan fireplaces and panelling. The library still preserves its original William Morris paper. Member of Hidden Ireland.

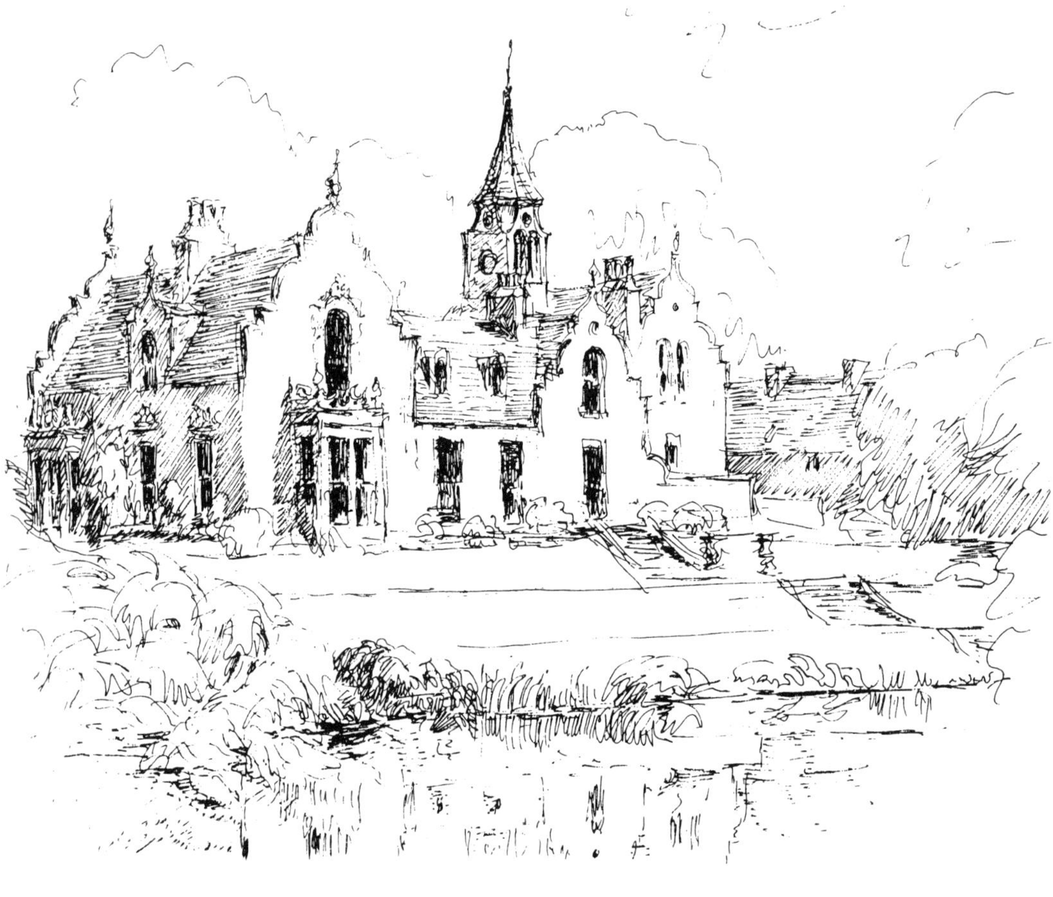

GALWAY

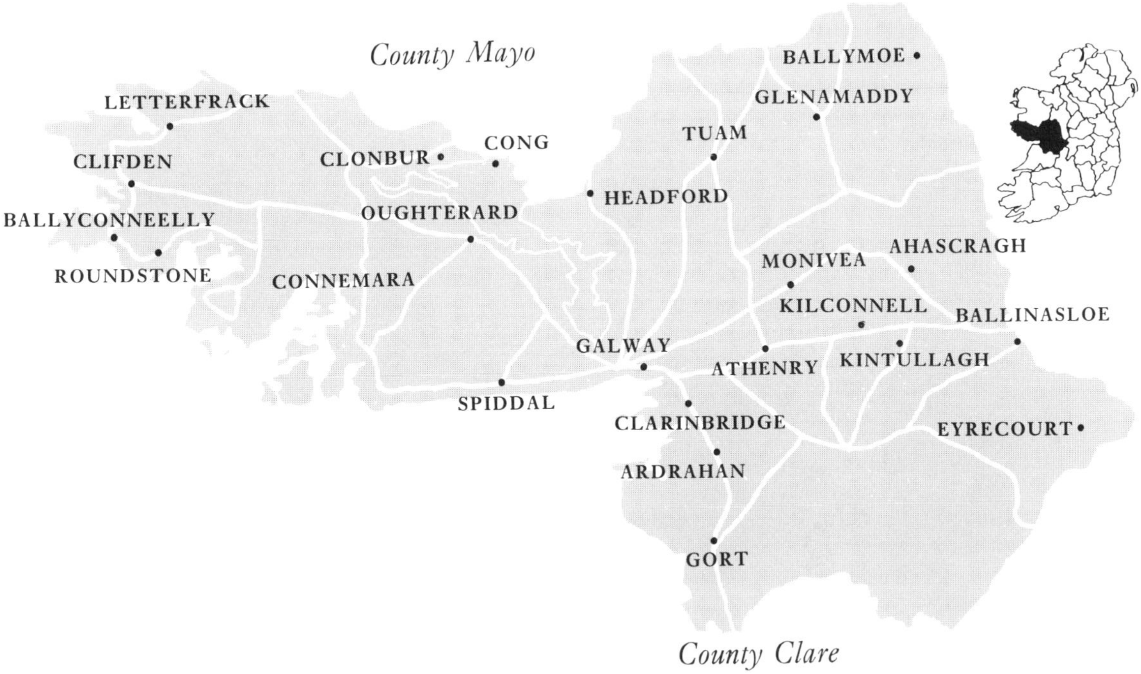

AHASCRAGH: **Church of Ireland**
Board of First Fruits church, *c.*1815, unassumingly extended by Rawson Carroll in 1865 who added transepts, chancel and vestry. Burned out in the Troubles of 1920. Subsequently rebuilt by Richard Orpen. Undisturbed since then.

ARDRAHAN: **Laban Catholic Church**
Parish church of Edward Martyn, who commissioned William Scott to design the baldachino in 1915 inspired by the Early Gothic of Italy in reaction to the pedantry of the Celtic Revival: sculptor Michael Shortall. This has been tough enough to withstand a rebuilding campaign that shattered the fragile Gothick of the original vernacular. Martyn's stained glass commissions also survive, if partly repositioned. They reflect his determination to commemorate his family while raising the aesthetic standards of Irish religious art. The windows of St Robert and St Anna (1901) by Selwyn Image are therefore of crucial significance in the history of Irish stained glass. Later windows by Child executed by Healy assisted by O'Brien and Townshend; the windows of St Peter and St Elizabeth designed by Whall and executed by Rhind. All these contrast to the Mayer windows commissioned by his mother. Nearby village hall also designed by William Scott.

ARDRAHAN: **Tulira Castle**
It is sad that the commission given by Ireland's most formative aesthete, Edward Martyn, to the most distinguished Gothic Revivalist of his contemporaries, George Ashlin, should be so disappointing. Ashlin rebuilt an earlier house linked to a medieval keep of the Clanrickarde

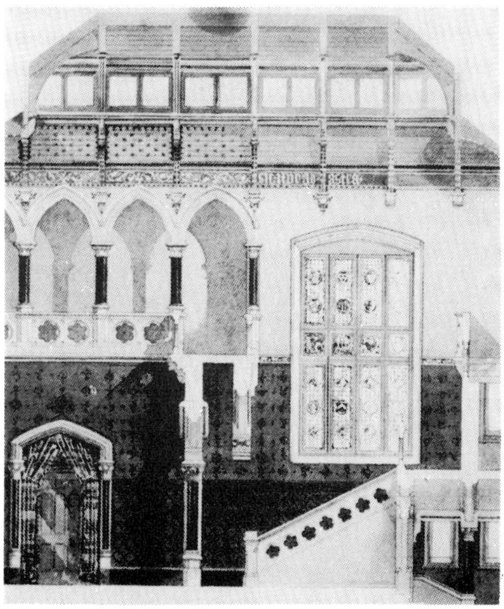

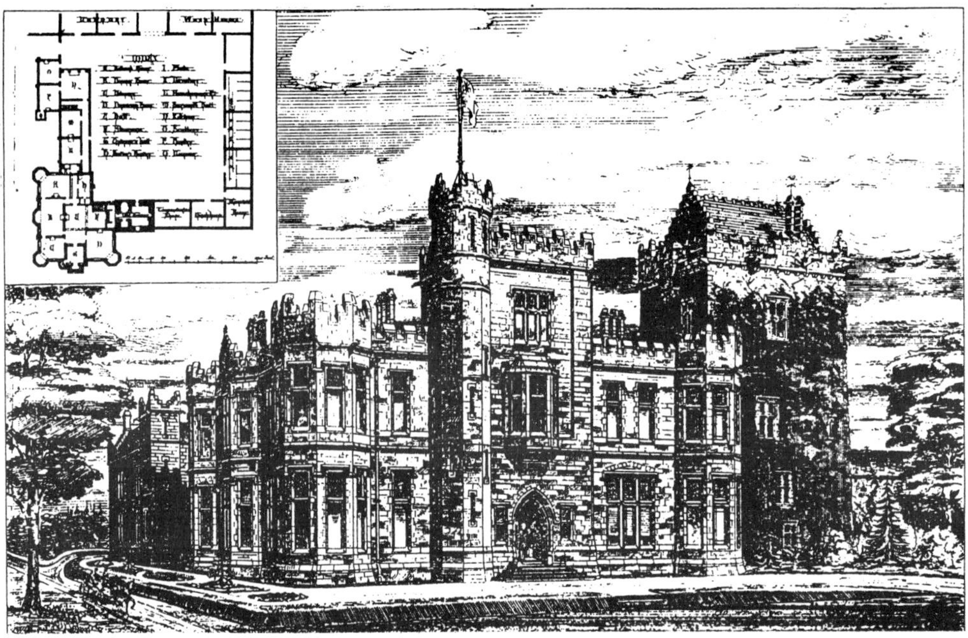

Burkes as a rival castle which, despite its Irish battlements, polygonal bays and heraldic devices, remains incurably suburban. Martyn grew to dislike it, blamed his mother, never completed Crace's decorative schemes and withdrew into the tower house, which he remodelled with the help of William Scott, although he retained Ashlin's panelling and stained glass (executed by Frampton). Every evening he would slip through a secret door to the staircase hall and play the organ. This is Ashlin's most successful interior, given greater height by the subtle handling of the upper flights that link the new castle to the tower house. The quatrefoil balustrading reveals a debt to Burges. The reception rooms are dominated by polychromatic marble fireplaces. But they are denuded of their original contents, when sold by the 5th Lord Hemphill *c.*1980, dispersing also a Connemara pony stud that aroused more attention at that time. Acquired and restored by an American Shakespearean actress who died before she could open the castle to the public.

ATHENRY: Agricultural College

One of the most ambitious schemes of William Scott was his projected agricultural college at Athenry, revealing the influence of Art Nouveau. Only a fragment was built. The director's house is formal but ungainly (as are many of his presbyteries). The farm buildings are far more interesting—a central archway between two long ranges of cowsheds, one terminating with a small gabled dwellinghouse, the other with a small office complex, also gabled. Porch ingeniously fitted in under the half-landing of the staircase. Behind it more buildings by Scott, including a neglected hall for recreation—tantalizing evidence of unfulfilled promise. Who had heard of William Scott in the 1960s? Not the architects of the adjoining extensions.

ATHENRY: Church of Ireland

Set into the ruins of a small medieval friary and entered through a roofless nave, it is dominated by a central tower and spire, attributable to Joseph Welland. Transepts and choir incisively rebuilt. Now unexpectedly accommodating the local youth club.

BALLINASLOE: Catholic Church

Commissioned from J.J. McCarthy in 1846 and built in 1852-8 (showing little evidence of A.W.N. Pugin, who was called in by the parish priest). The church as built was repudiated by McCarthy—a harsh design in local limestone with asymmetrical steeple of 1852-8. Interior of more interest for its mural decoration by Joshua Clarke, its stained glass (St Rose and St Patrick) by Harry Clarke, who also designed a now restored canvas of the Trinity above the chancel arch (1924). The altar sculpted by Albert Power contains an extraordinary Celtic Revival tabernacle by Mia Cranwell.

BALLINASLOE: Church of Ireland

The town green is dominated by this characteristic example of Joseph Welland of 1840, cruciform with a western tower ruthlessly exploiting the Norman motte on which it is set to give it added height. Fine interior with soaring open roof.

BALLINASLOE: **Church of Ireland College**
Gothic Revival complex constructed by Bishop Trench in the 1860s using an unknown architect as part of his campaign to convert local Catholics to Protestantism through the medium of Irish. Ironically acquired by the Catholic Church as a seminary. This also closed. Now converted into housing as 'The Pines'.

BALLINASLOE: **Convent of Mercy**
Institutional Gothic double-storied block, chapel above, refectory and classrooms below and adjoining tower with octagonal spire cleverly sited to dominate every view of Society Street. A Gothic porch is misguidedly tacked on to the neighbouring Georgian house in attempted consistency. Designed in 1864 by a local architect, J.F. Kempster.

BALLINASLOE: **Garbally Court**
The central courtyard of the Regency house built by Thomas Cundy in 1819 for the earls of Clancarty was filled in *c.*1850 to make a picture gallery, probably by George Papworth, with sky lights set into barrelled vault, supported by columns (now a chapel with altar carved by Albert Power). Remnants of an elegant neo-Classical conservatory. Two Italianate gate-lodges.

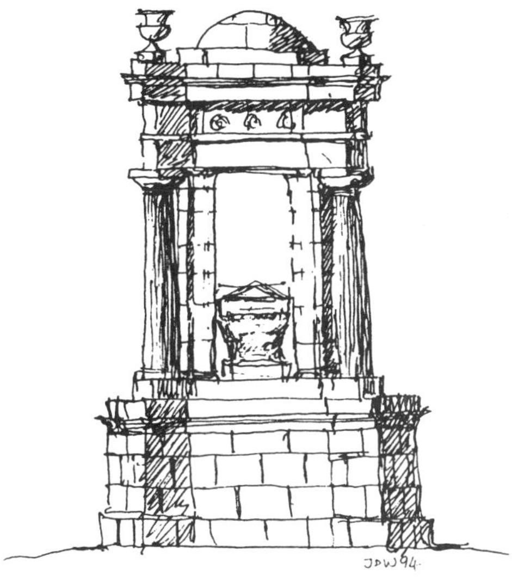

BALLINASLOE: **Le Poer Trench Monument**
Fine Greek Revival memorial disconnected from the Market Green by the main road to Galway and ignored. Drawings exhibited in the RHA of 1840 by George Papworth.

BALLINASLOE: **Presbyterian Church**
A simple Gothic façade dated 1846. Stained-glass window of St Michael by E. Rhind (1911).

BALLINASLOE: **The Station**
Designed for the Great Western Railway Company in 1851, by George Wilkinson, a successful foray in the Tudor style—a picturesque massing of steep roofs hipped and gabled against a variety of chimney-stacks. A pair of diagonal flues are braced against each other by a flying arch; next stack along, they are held between two further cylindrical flues. Delicate window tracery (where surviving). Slating renewed recently, with asbestos, but artfully scalloped. School and residence nearby attributed to a Mr Maxwell.

BALLYCONNEELLY: **Bunowen Castle**
An early 18th century house built for the Geoghegans after their expulsion by Cromwell from the rich pastures of Co. Westmeath. The saying 'To Hell or Connaught' must have been repeated many times on this desolate peninsular. Bunowen was inherited in 1838 by a branch of the Blake family who remodelled and extended the house as an insubstantial castle linked to a series of castellated courtyards to give some protection from the wind. The castle was abandoned by 1900 and is currently appreciable only from the barbed wire along the perimeter of the demesne.

BALLYMOE: **Bagot Tomb**
The church of Ireland (now derelict), with spiky but rusty railing wards off the unadventurous from exploring this archaeological make-believe, a tumulus modelled like a truncated pyramid. Irish yews at each corner have sadly disappeared. In the centre the raised tombstone serves as plinth for a stone-carved crusader lying full length on his back with his favourite dog crouching at his feet. Yet this is not a listed medieval monument; rather, as the inscription records, the burial ground from 1863 onwards of the Lloyd Neville Bagots of Ballymoe, and now the only evidence of their existence.

CLARINBRIDGE: **Mercy Convent**
Georgian house quietly extended with symmetrical wings, one concealing a Gothic Revival chapel, presumably designed by George Papworth while he was building Kilcornan for the Redingtons across the road—an unexpected setting for the superb 1844 neo-Classical altar with its carefully selected marbles. A Lamb of God set into lapis lazuli, kneeling angels, and a tempietto surmounted by John Hogan's Transfiguration of 1849.

CLARINBRIDGE: Kilcornan
With the demolition of Kenure Park, this is George Papworth's largest surviving country house, built for Sir Thomas Redington in 1838. An understandably rare excursion into the Tudor style, since this three-storied pile is entirely devoid of the sense of scale that marks his neo-Classicism. The façades have suffered from alterations. Were it not for its pretty pinnacled entry tower and chapel it would be indistinguishable from many of the workhouses built in the next decade. Now run by a religious order for the handicapped. Some of the principal interiors survive with their heraldic carvings and stained glass. Music room treated as an organ loft above the chapel which has excellent glass. Puginesque drawingroom possibly by Crace.

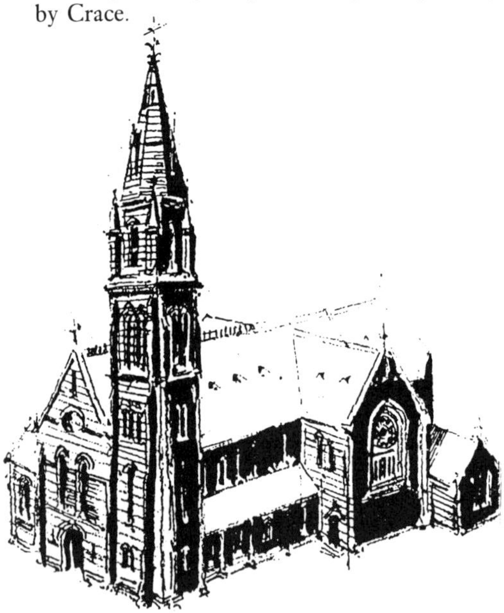

CLIFDEN: Catholic Church
Designed in his habitually forceful version of the Gothic Revival by J.J. O'Callaghan and built in 1875-91. Its western steeple is seen in counterpoint to its Church of Ireland counterpart from all distant viewpoints of the town. The high altar by Earley dates from 1907. The mural decorations, added a year later, are by the firm of Joshua Clarke. Adjoining convent by J.S. Butler dating from 1855.

CLIFDEN: Church of Ireland
Conventional Gothic Revival church built in 1850 to the designs of Joseph Welland. Tower and spire added by Welland's son in 1864.

CLIFDEN: Coastguard Station
A large and dramatically sited complex built by the Board of Works (*c.*1880) and then abandoned by them roofless to the elements.

CLIFDEN: Errislannan Church of Ireland
The Heather family who owned this remote headland (momentarily made famous by the aviators Alcock and Brown) privately commissioned this hilltop church from Joseph Welland in 1859. Since Welland died a year later it was presumably carried out by Welland and Gillespie. In toughly detailed local stone. An austere interior still shelters a small congregation from the Atlantic winds.

CLONBUR: Church of Ireland
Tiny church of 1846 sited to look across a wooded valley towards the mountains, and there is just enough of its interior left to see the reason why. The architect was William Atkins of Cork, who at that time had completed one building, the chapel of Mount Jerome cemetery in Dublin (q.v.). Although he had just been appointed to design the largest lunatic asylum in Ireland for his native city, one suspects he could have lavished greater care on this more congenial commission, adapting the ideals of Pugin to the needs of the Church of Ireland. Looking upwards from the altar to a rose window above a triple lancet with just enough stained glass surviving to decipher a triumphant Resurrection, it is difficult to grasp that one is not in a cathedral, and yet one would be crowded out by a congregation of forty. The church is just a single cell of five bays with a lean-to vestry to the north dominated by a monumental boiler chimney that challenges the pre-eminence of the western bellcote. On the south side the base of the trefoiled windows is progressively raised to reflect the floor within rising to the altar.

Inside, immense timber transverse arches corbelled out on colonettes brace the open roof.

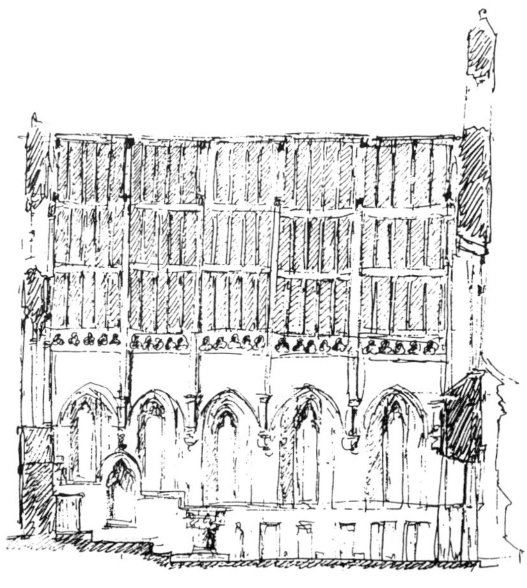

The corbel under the last colonette squirms into a twisted root above a recessed credence niche: Atkins knew his Irish medieval friaries well. Like the English Catholic churches of Pugin, this is also the architecture of a minority searching their justification in the past.

Still inset among the Minton tiles, the dedicatory slab lies before the altar: 'in memory of H.R.S. whose example encouraged the building of this church and who died before it was completed' and deconsecrated and abandoned. As in the mausoleum of Drunacoo immortalized by Betjeman, among shattered fittings, broken glass, slipping slates with roof and windows open to the sky, 'another distinguished family waits a Church of Ireland resurrection'.

CONG: **Ashford Castle**

A small 18th-century Baroque shooting lodge was built by the earls of Oranmore and Browne, who still retain the woodcock shooting rights. Their stable block incorporated a medieval keep of the Burkes. To link the lodge and this somewhat distant castle became the overriding ambition of Sir Arthur Guinness, later Lord Ardilaun. Sir Arthur's father, Sir Benjamin Lee Guinness, who had acquired Ashford as an encumbered estate in 1855, had contented himself with asymmetrical French chateau-like pavilions. These his son decided to retain, with the result that the immense baronial additions by J.F. Fuller built from 1870 onwards are edged off the centre of the stage and engulf the two genuine medieval towers so overwhelmingly that few would recognize them as such today. £41,000 had been spent on the castle by 1875 and £1 million by 1915. Fuller had started off on excellent terms with his client, since as a genealogist he had proved that Sir Arthur was descended seven times from Alfred the Great, and as such Ashford was designed as an appropriate retreat, but their relationship deteriorated. Fuller ruefully admitted in his memoirs that he saw no reason to treat the ultra-rich with awe. He was replaced by George Ashlin, re-enacting his own takeover of the Kylemore commission from S.U. Roberts. Ashlin's contribution is stylistically distinguishable only by a smoother finish and sharper detailing as in the six-arched, battlemented bridge leading to a gatehouse dominated by a coroneted 'A' commemorating Sir Arthur's elevation to the peerage as Lord Ardilaun—the name of an island on the Corrib, but chosen for its euphony. He is commemorated by an obelisk and thousands of trees. Two knights in armour kitted with what appears to be Chinese restaurant red and gold wallpaper prefigure the improbable interiors where both Fuller and Ashlin failed dismally to live up to their external grandeur. An unfortunate decision was made to gut the original house and create a double-height galleried hall surrounded by too much off the peg balustrading. The reception rooms rely for their impact on over-monumental chimney-pieces and exude the sense of an incredibly grand hotel which indeed it has now become. More recent changes include increasing the height of the stable yard to make further bedrooms thereby creating one of the few successful 20th-century castles. Less happy have been various attempts to medievalize the entrance front of the Brownes' shooting box and the needless removal of one of Sir Benjamin's pavilions on the garden front.

The architectural pretensions of Ashford have attracted continuous witticisms. Douglas Richardson speaks of 'threatening little gestures'. Even during Lord Ardilaun's lifetime, a precocious critic, Oscar Wilde, whose father owned nearby Moytura, when asked to admire the gardens by Lady Ardilaun refused to do so, but suggested instead his own parterre based on Lord Ardilaun's heraldic device—a pig.

CONNEMARA: **Ballynahinch Castle**

A Georgian house remodelled desultorily as a castle at various times by its most celebrated owner, Richard Martin, founder of the RSPCA and known as Humanity Dick. Victorian alternations were made to the interior by the Berridges when they acquired the estate from Martin's granddaughter (ruined by the Famine). Battlemented gatelodge by S.U. Roberts. Owned between the wars by the cricket playing Maharaja Ranjitsinhji. Now a comfortable hotel of the pre-country house hotel era.

CONNEMARA: **Lisnabrucka**

Unconventional shooting lodge designed in 1910 with the reception rooms on the upper floor opening on to a continuous terrace built out on the bedrooms beneath. Intact Edwardian interiors.

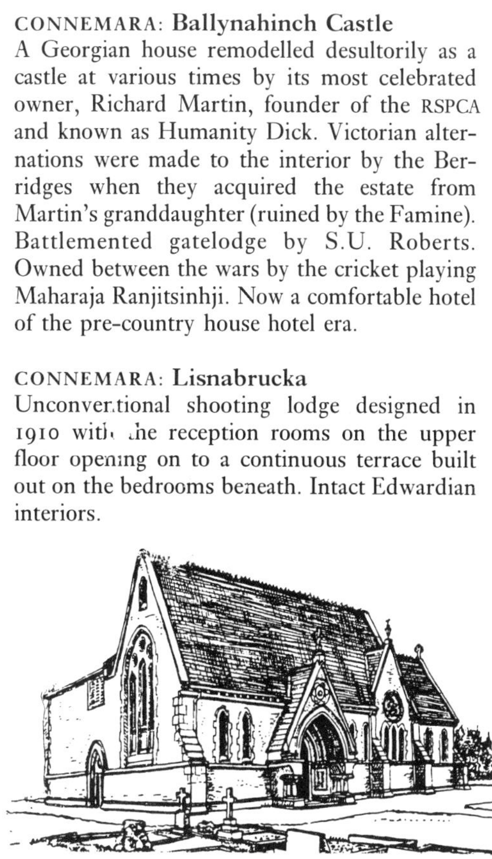

EYRECOURT: **Church of Ireland**

A dinner given in Dublin by a group of friends to honour his retirement from his surveyorship

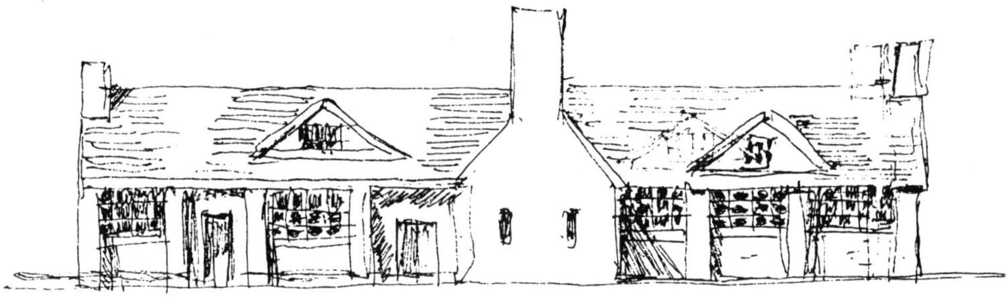

in Co. Galway is the only contemporary record of William Martin. The radical Gothic Revival church of Eyrecourt (1867) is his only documented building. An equally abrasive design to replace Roundstone Church of Ireland remained unexecuted. The tower that would have dominated Eyrecourt also proceeded no further than the drawing-board, as did much of the carving; but the entrance still impresses with its deeply recessed arches springing from stunted columns. Warm brick-lined interior testifies to the influence of William Butterfield in this western outpost of the Ecclesiologists.

GALWAY: **Former Catholic Cathedral and St Patrick's**
Only the early Gothic Revival façades of these churches survive, with just enough delicate limestone carving to attest to the skills of Galway's masons and to cause regret for their lost interiors. Both have been dispiritingly rebuilt, St Patrick's as a church hall, the cathedral as a shopping centre.

GALWAY: **Claddagh Shopping School**
Simple classical three-storied school, with commemorative plaque appropriately inscribed as 'Piscatory School, 1846'.

GALWAY: **Franciscan Church**
Neo-Classical church by James Cusack, started in 1835 and completed in 1849. Reduced version of Dublin's pro-cathedral; columned basilica lit by central dome, here further christianized by the insertion of stained glass windows.

GALWAY: **Moon's Department Store**
Designed in 1863 by E.H. Carson. He had married into a local landowning family called Lambert, who were no doubt instrumental in getting him the commission, just as they were to prove of use to the son of that marriage, Edward, at the start of his legal career. In both cases their string-pulling was rewarded: Moon's is still the most elegant shop in Galway, its curving colonnade taking full advantage of its prominent site where William Street turns in Eglington Street.

GALWAY: **Rovers Sports and Social Club**
Built as a fishing cooperative beside the harbour to the Claddagh. Massive buttresses support a long, low-pitched roof broken by triangular gables and divided asymmetrically by a short range at right angles ending with a forceful chimney. Built sometime before 1920 by William Scott. Now a social club, open only at night.

GALWAY: **Mellowes Barracks**
Well designed Victorian barracks strategically sited in Renmore. Architect, Col. Ewart, 1877.

GALWAY: **Methodist Church**
Small, punchy rogue Gothic by Raffles Browne in brick and stone (1863). Now deconsecrated and appropriately housing an experimental theatre.

GALWAY: **St Anne's, Taylor's Hill**
Baronial mansion built in 1860, as stated in an elaborate circular plague. Asymmetrical adjoined façades, the entry front with a tower and turret, the less defensive garden front with double drawingrooms overlooking the sea. Matching gatelodge. Attributable to S.U. Roberts.

GALWAY: **St Augustine's Church**
Town church still surrounded by four narrow streets, thereby unique in Ireland. Interior fails to live up to its urban setting nor has it been improved by a new roof which has left its corbelled apostles redundant. However, restorers have spared the elegant communion rail. Architect: B. Moran, completion date: 1869.

GALWAY: **St Ignatius' Church**
The Jesuit church of the city, designed in 1863 by S.U. Roberts, in collaboration with his contractor, John Semple Jnr (1812/3-80), son of the more celebrated Early Gothic Revivalist, They were probably executing the 1860 designs of J.J. McCarthy. Façade made asymmetrical by off-centre spire. Cruciform interior with open roof. Redecorated by William Hague in 1878. Corner chapel with early Louis le Brocquy mosaic (1957).

GALWAY: St Mary's College

This diocesan seminary was designed by William Scott in 1910, six years after the church at Spiddal (q.v.), but it belongs to a different world, that of Catholic triumphalism. The dark and secretive mysteries of Spiddal have no place in this hilltop citadel, facing south with spectacular views over the city and the bay. A concrete structure with two contrasting stone claddings, one for the spandrel panels and the other for their framing. The composition builds up to a central entry with an arch filled by rich mosaic at its topmost level, now partly merged in an additional upper floor. Large plaques added to each side of entrance commemorate two more recent extensions, by the formidable Bishop Browne in 1950s and 1970s, the earlier in the same style as the original, a style abandoned by the time of the second. Interior much altered. Oratory replaced by new church at rear and converted into dormitories. Scott's buildings reveal the state of mind of his clients, and no more so than here. The same triumphalism spawned the new cathedral in the valley below.

GALWAY: Station and Great Southern Hotel

The station was built as the terminus of the Midland Great Western Railway that started out from the Broadstone (q.v.) in Dublin. Both stations were designed by J.S. Mulvany in 1850, and roofed with elegant wrought-iron trusses by Richard Turner (both since replaced). The main façade is one-storey, but raised above ground and approached by a long ramp. Regular bays, subdivided by attached pilasters and Mulvany's characteristic corbels. The adjoining hotel also by Mulvany and much altered, is dull but distinguished, the only structure fronting the square that gives the feeling of a great city. When completed, a replica was commanded in California but never built.

GALWAY: St Mary's Catholic Church

Built by William Hague, working in the Romanesque idiom. A simple nave of five bays and lean-to aisles leading to a resplendent vision of Paradise in marble, mosaic and stained glass celebrating Mary as Queen of Heaven. St Mary's served the Claddagh, the fishing village of thatched cottages torn down for sanitary reasons in the 1950s; but there is nothing vernacular in the chancel of the church. The glass of the east windows is Mayer of Münich, the mosaics with their commingling of saints and donors are Salviati of Venice, and it is Venice that one thinks of here, with its churches rich with treasures from the east, unloaded on its quays. Windows also by Healy, St Dominic receiving the Rosary (1935); and McGoldrick, St Dominic and nuns of St Sisto (1939).

GALWAY: University College

The original structure designed by J.B. Keane and built in 1846-50 has remained remarkably unaltered despite a recent fire that gutted the interior of the great hall. This intactness is due to the enclosure of the quad and its unremitting symmetry, Gothick rather than Gothic Revival. Entry front with central archway under reduced version of Wren's Tom Tower in Oxford rising above diagonally positioned pinnacles. The lecture halls were planned to have windows on both sides, reached by adjoining staircases. The entrance to the great hall is on the other side of the quad flanked by ground-floor arcades. Half way up the original interior a new floor was inserted to make two halls where there had been one before; unhappy interior below but an unexpectedly successful chamber music hall above, due to the restoration of Keane's elegant Gothick vault. The college overlooks a tree-lined playing field and atmospheric clubhouse.

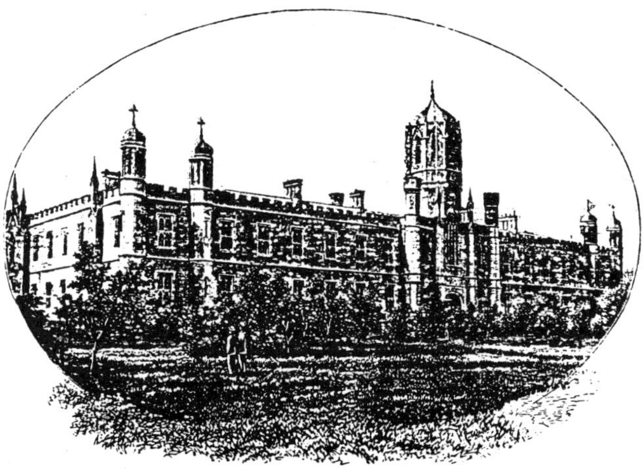

GLENAMADDY: **Clonbern Graveyard**
Cast-iron cylindrical tomb crisply detailed with Greek Revival enrichments. Commissioned by the Dennis family *c.*1865. Dr Maurice Craig suggests a Scottish origin.

GORT: **Convent of Mercy Chapel**
The only interior in the town that bears witness to its seminal role in the Celtic Revival due to the redecoration of the chancel by Joshua Clarke. The framework is a conventional Gothic church (*c.*1870), matched by the marble reredos and the earlier stained glass. But each window is bordered by mosaics inspired by the Book of Kells, and each segment of the vault overhead frames a dreamy archangel, evidence of the mixed origins of the Celtic Revival—Gaelic Nationalism, the adored mother; Welsh pre-Raphaelism, the unacknowledged father. Stained glass by Elvery (1904) and others.

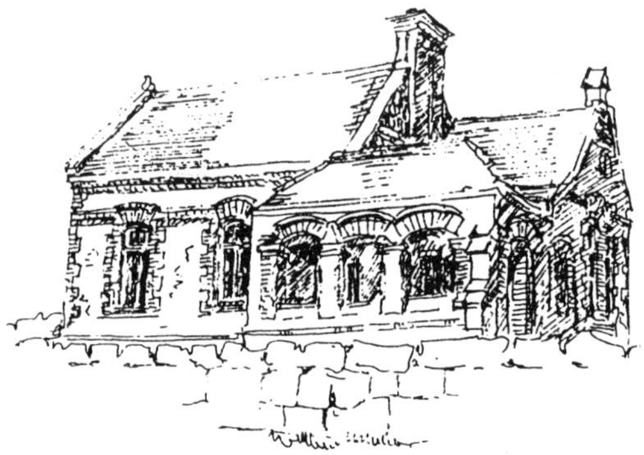

GORT: **Kiltartan School**
Commissioned by Sir William Gregory in 1900 reputedly inspired by his memories of Ceylon. The architect he chose was his wife's younger brother, F.H. Persse, who had just started to practise. The result is a small Arts and Crafts structure crammed with brilliant ideas to the point of indigestion. Instead of following the regimented government prototype, the school is treated as a fairy-tale cottage ornée entered asymmetrically by an arcaded loggia. Persse built out of local limestone, red brick and terracotta, a combination that due to his inexperience slips out of his control: the arcade changes from stone to brick propped up at one corner by a single stone Gothic buttress. Derelict for many years when a new standardized school was built. Just acquired by a local group, many of whom were taught there, the Kiltartan Gregory Cultural Society. They intend to set up a museum to the Gregorys that will placate an increasing number of foreign illiterates blissfully ignorant of Coole's destruction as they have not read all their Yeats.

HEADFORD: **Catholic Church**
One underestimated characteristic of Irish Victorian architects was their ability to travel and build throughout the island. An example of this is the Connacht churches of the Wexford-based Richard Pierce. Headford dates from 1863. Cruciform, without aisles, open timber roof strongly braced at the crossing. Three altars across the east end, the central altar recessed into a separate chancel beneath Mayer's glass. Completed after Pierce's death by W.G. Murray in 1866.

KILCONNELL: **Woodlawn**
A grandiose palazzo in the style of Charles Barry impassively surveys the gradual disintegration of its demesne, with the now almost mythical intrusions of the Land Commission supplanting its parkland. Of its many avenues, only one gives today a sense of what must once have been: a bend reveals the façade reflected in the waters of a wood-fringed lake to be crossed by an immense balustraded bridge. One of the seats of the Trenches. Remodelled and extended by the 2nd Lord Ashtown *c.*1860, who did not have to go further than Ballinasloe to find an architect with the necessary bravura to adopt the grand manner, James Kempster. The austere, three-storied Georgian cube was enlivened by a portico; its roof was masked by balustrades and finials. The new wings are a story lower and end in pedimented pavilions. The interior was remodelled by Kempster, who inserted a central

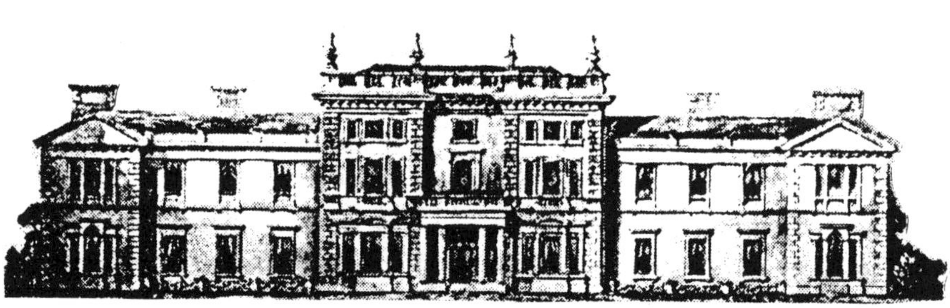

stone cantilevered imperial staircase. John Huston in his memoirs recalls the le Poer Trenches, the last owners of Woodlawn to live there. Instead of bringing the kitchen up from the basement to beside the diningroom, they constructed a timber link between both rooms to keep their dishes warm. To avoid making a new door into the diningroom, they built this link across one end of the double apsed mirrored and columned drawingroom. Eventually they put in a kitchen beside their bedroom, but this caused a fire that burned out half that wing.

Although the Trenches were a family of amateur architects, Kempster is the most likely designer of the steward's house, gatelodges (including a credible replica of a tower house at the entrance towards Athenry), a schoolhouse, a private railway station, a rec- tory and a pretty Gothic church. This appears from the house to be private also, but there is a public road in between sunk into a ha-ha—a single cell with flanking spire, built in 1875 by Lord Ashtown to the memory of his son. The tomb is marked by a decorative stone cross that recurs on the gable end of the church positioned directly above it. Glass by Heaton, Butler and Bayne.

Lord Ashtown had evidently decided that the family mausoleum was too pagan as a burial ground for his son. This is an enormous concentric circular structure, described by Maurice Craig as 'in many ways the most impressive in Ireland' and seen by him 'only in heavy rain, which suited it well'.

KINTULLAGH: Catholic Church

This simple T-shaped barn is enlivened by corner pinnacles and corbelled bellcote (1840). The interior is enlivened by cheerful plasterwork more appropriate to a Regency diningroom. This levity is counterbalanced by the stained glass of Mayer and the stations of the cross, a set of oils by Evie Hone.

LETTERFRACK: Kylemore Abbey

In his rambling autobiography, James Fuller devotes a mere paragraph to his architectural output, in order to concentrate instead on his now unread plays and novels. More illustrations are devoted to his collection of handwriting by now forgotten celebrities than to his own buildings. Kylemore is accorded one photograph, and a brief mention. A footnote acknowledges the collaboration of Samuel Ussher Roberts, district engineer for Galway. The truth was that the castle was designed in 1864, presumably by Roberts, since this was six years before Fuller started his country-house practice. The client was Mitchell Henry MP, a rich Merseyside industrialist who had fallen in love with Connemara. Roberts was not only the county surveyor; he was also a castle builder—notably Gurteen, Co. Waterford (q.v.), which he had just begun, and which has much in common with Kylemore. Indeed all the castles of Roberts are the same—severe and incurably old-fashioned, but composed with a certain flair for the picturesque and executed with a military precision, as one would expect from such a remarkable dynasty of architects, artists and soldiers.

What makes Kylemore such a show-stopper today is not merely its spectacular scenery, but its skilful siting on a series of terraces rising up Mount Doughruagh from Lake Pollacappul, so that its full extent is impossible to grasp from a single viewpoint and the choice of Dalkey granite. This ruinously expensive decision, much criticized at the time by Puginians with their belief in vernacular materials, transforms Kylemore into a fairytale, emerging from the rain to glisten in the sunlight. The lushness of Mitchell Henry's planting of rare trees and shrubberies has long since engulfed the occasion for Fuller's involvement, the private church built further along the lake shore. He was commissioned by Henry to design this while he was working for the Church of Ireland, *c.*1866, so it is his first major work. It is a spirited recreation of an English 14th-century church complete with stone vaulting throughout in both church and crypt (the vaulting once stained dark green with damp is now being restored with European funds). Conceived as a setting for weekly worship at a brisk walking distance for the family, the Benedictine nuns from Ypres who acquired Kylemore after the First World War had replaced it with a more convenient chapel within the castle. It is hard to disentangle the work of Fuller from Roberts in the principal rooms which were much more splendid, especially as Fuller was called in again *c.*1905 after its sale to the duke of Manchester, and made alterations that he subsequently regretted. The new owner seems to have been an unsatisfactory client. He must have been the only English duke to be regarded as an unsuitable son-in-law by an American millionaire. He had eloped with the daugher, who, on becoming his duchess, was disinherited by her father. Many of the interiors were destroyed in a serious fire twenty years ago. Although now repaired and open to the public, it is only the exterior that is memorable.

And what of Mitchell Henry himself, this industrialist who broke his wife's health and ultimately bankrupted himself on the maintenance of his dream to die only five years after he had to sell up. Until then he was building:

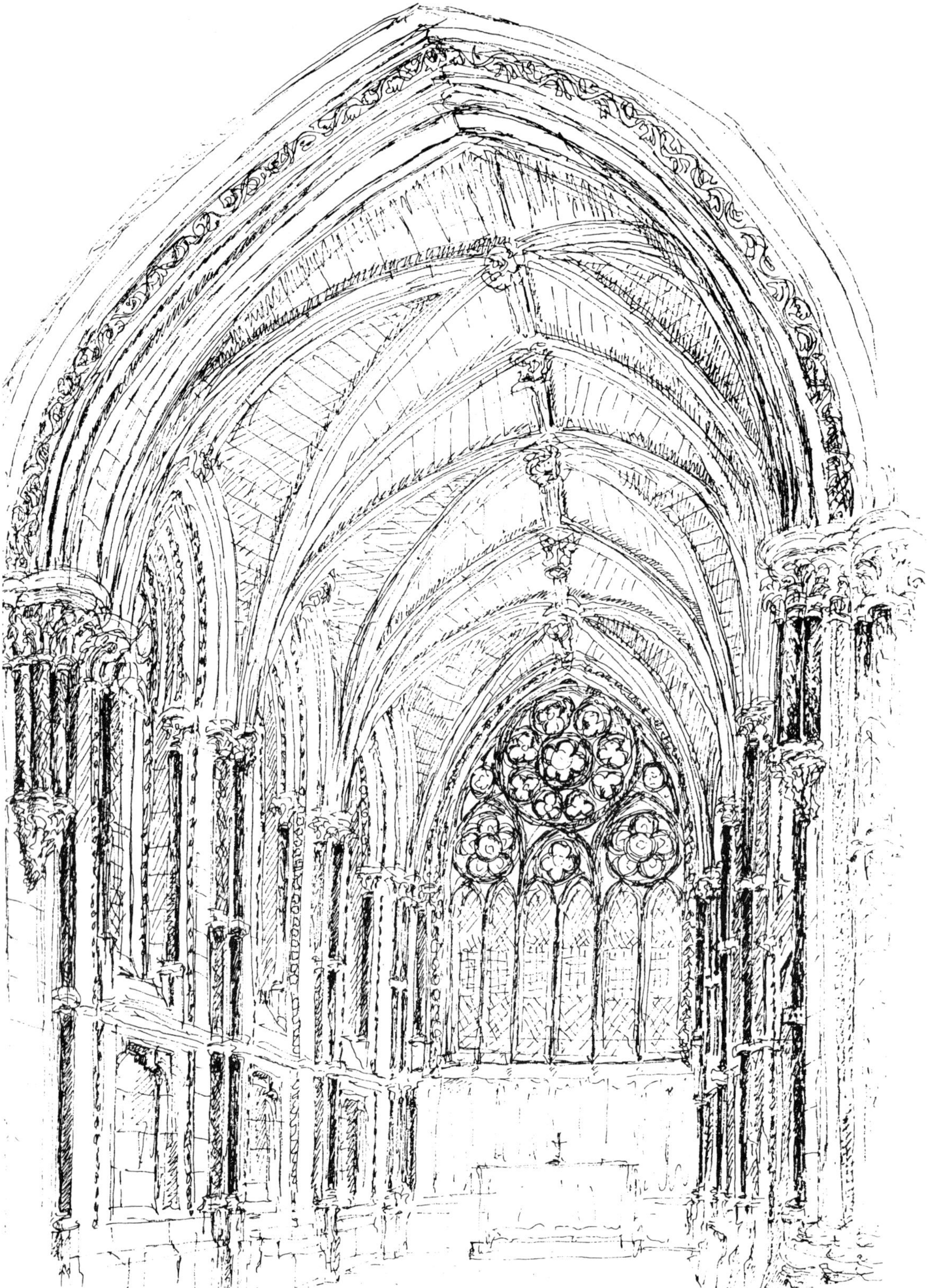

KYLEMORE CHAPEL, CO. GALWAY

in the 1890s he constructed five curvilinear conservatories, and a formal parterre (now barely traceable). But even in its heyday Kylemore resembled an industrial estate offering no place to linger pleasurably. He seems to have lacked charm and humour. But there is still a single-mindedness about him that affects us all. Recently an embezzler was given a particularly heavy sentence since he had angered the London judge with the fictitious claim that he was Mitchell Henry's grandson and Kylemore's rightful heir.

LOUGHREA: **Convent and Chapel**
Gothic Revival. Built by J.J. O'Callaghan in 1880. Chapel now a basketball court.

LOUGHREA: **The Cathedral**
William Byrne was commissioned in 1897 to build a cathedral which was completed five years later. Being on a modest scale there is little to differentiate it from the numerous churches he was building at the same time throughout Ireland, all in bush-hammered ashlar. The most interesting feature of Byrne's architecture is the screened double transepts that withhold from those entering the initial view of the cathedral's greatest treasures, Michael Healy's Ascension and Last Judgment windows. With the completion of the fabric, both William and Ralph Byrne were thenceforward ignored by the building committee under the guidance of Edward Martyn, who succeeded by 1904 in bringing in his own architect, William Scott, but (as in his own home Tulira) too late: the monumental entrance gates give a tantalizing indication of what might have been if Scott had been given the original commission. As it is, the first impression of visiting this shrine of Irish Art is always baffling: Where is the Celtic Revival? Its only overt expression is to be found in the communion rails designed by Scott in collaboration with the sculptor Michael Shortall (spared by post-Vatican II radicals, although their rearrangement of the sanctuary has left no space for Scott's candelabra). But it has to be admitted that both Scott and Shortall were too reverential to the existing idiom to express their own individuality, and that, while Shortall's tactile qualities ensure that his modelling repays close inspection, his reredos shows up only too clearly his architectural deficiencies despite the strength of its bronze Man of Sorrows by John Hughes. More successful are Scott's side altars, especially that with the Madonna (also by Hughes), though this is set against a background of polychromatic marbling that Scott himself unhappily extended to the walls of the chancel. But all these uncertainties are redeemed by the

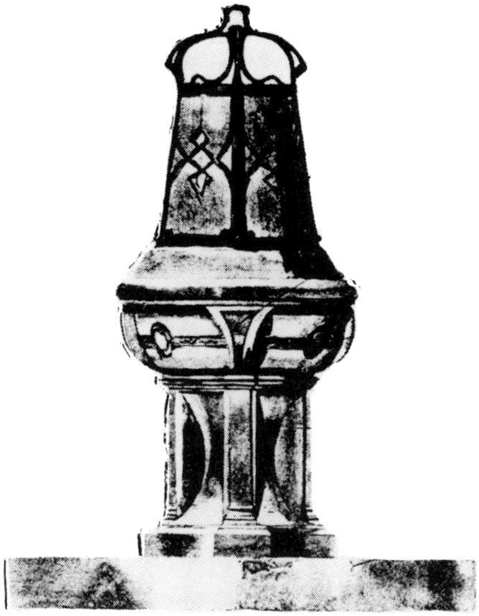

stained glass of An Túr Gloine from its inception by Whall and Child through Purser, Elvery, O'Brien, McGoldrick, Hone and Pye with the earliest and the last windows of Michael Healy. So, despite the absence of Geddes and Clarke (Sarah Purser could not risk a direct confrontation after Clarke's takeover of the Honan Chapel), as an ensemble of Irish glass, Loughrea remains unrivalled.

MONIVEA: **The Mausoleum**
Francis Persse, younger brother of Lady Gregory, started his practice in 1890 with a flurry of commissions which unsuspecting readers of the *Irish Builder* could not have known were all for his relations, including the National school of Kiltartan for his sister (q.v.). Two of his commissions were for the diplomat Robert ffrench of Monivea. No evidence of either survives. The church of Ireland in the village that he altered has been swept away, leaving just a tower. Only the medieval keep and yard remain of the castle. There is no trace of his dormered wings, which should now house Ireland's most distinguished writers and indigent writers and artists if the family and the government had agreed to honour the bequest made in 1938 by Robert's only child, daughter of a Russian heiress. Kathleen de Kindiard ffrench died after twenty years of penury in Manchuria following her escape from the Bolsheviks who had seized all her lands along the Volga.

Kathleen had also decreed in her will that the indigenous oak forest of Monivea should never be felled. The coniferous plantations that replace it today at least safeguard the battlements that conceals the memorial chapel she

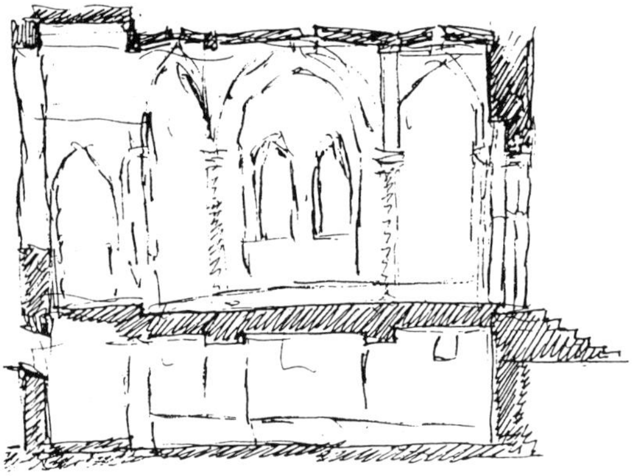

commissioned for her father in 1897 and which took four years to build. He had parted from his wife for health reasons and had gone to live in Italy. He had died in Naples and his body lay embalmed in Milan until the vault was ready to receive it. The upper floor houses his recumbent effigy in Carrara marble by Jerace guarded by four black marble columns that hold up a network of Wicklow granite Gothic vaulting. Two further granite columns guard the entrance to the tiny barrel-vaulted chancel. The altar of black and white marble boldly patterned with intersecting circles nestles in the embrasure of a triple-lancet window. This (by Mayer) depicts the Resurrection and is so orientated that every morning the rays of the rising sun shine through it on to the memorial below.

Why is this masterpiece (so carefully maintained by the local village for monthly masses) unattributed? Perhaps Francis Persse as the family architect received the commission but relied on a more experienced architect to ghost his design. If so, the most likely possibility is George Ashlin, who would have been engaged on the two most lavish memorials of the time (the Ardilaun church in Raheny and the Adelaide church in Myshall: q.v.). They are very beautiful, but they lack the tension of Monivea, the contrast between the prophetic grimness of the exterior and the repose within. Here Kathleen herself is also buried beside her father. Photographs of her are not flattering but as one of the richest women in Russia she must have turned down countless proposals. Did her rejected suitors realize that they had been judged against a marble effigy hidden in the oak forest at the other end of Europe, and been found wanting?

OUGHTERARD: **Currarevagh House**

A Victorian country-house hotel still owned by the family who built it. The date was after 1846 and the architect commissioned by the Hodgsons remains unknown (possibly S.U. Roberts). The house superseded an earlier one on a different site, demolished in 1950. Built in a sub-Italianate idiom to take advantage of its setting above Lough Corrib. Passages are cluttered with fishing paraphernalia and the occasional tiger skin. Carravagioesque paintings as dark as the varnished woodwork survey high-ceilinged rooms that resonate at the appointed hour of eight to an immense Burmese gong.

ROUNDSTONE: **Costello House**

Small country house built by Sir Edwin Lutyens in 1913 as a retreat for Bruce Ismay, the chairman of the White Star Line who escaped from the *Titanic*, wearing, it was said, women's clothing. Hence this remote retreat. Burnt in 1921 but then rebuilt.

SPIDDAL: **Catholic Church**

The least satisfying way to approach the masterpiece of William Scott is by road, past a succession of souvenir shops and craft centres, so that his church appears as yet another manifestation of their Celtic Revival. The better way would be to come by sea and put into land at a little harbour dominated by a stone-roofed oratory, echoed by Scott in the stone-roofed side chapels of his church beyond. And when we decipher from an inscription that this oratory was rebuilt by a Martin Gentleman in 1776, we realize that we are in the presence, not of a revival, but of a tradition. The dedicatory stone of the church is beneath the tower, commemorating the patron, the 2nd Lord Killanin, a friend of Edward Martyn, and the date (1904).

The exterior depends on the tension generated by a long, low-slung nave against an asymmetrically-sited, saddle-roofed belfry. All this is not unusual but verticality is further reinforced by curious pinnacles at each corner of the nave, like the ears of a donkey. The façade is down-played, the main entry being from the side past an external monumental freestanding font. The nave is kept deliberately low, so low that the organ gallery is relegated to the upper level of the south transept, subtly disrupting the symmetry of the interior. In true Irish Late neo-Gothic style, the nave arcades are carried across double transepts. The stone piers are admirably strengthened to take the bracing of the roof. There is no crossing as such, just a suspended corona of bronze, so that the movement of the nave is halted only by the chancel. If Scott's altar appears today as too abrupt and too domineering, this is due to the loss of his communion rails that would have given the choir a greater sense of distance, but these were destroyed in 1984 to kowtow to the liturgical trends of the 1960s.

The stone carving is by Michael Shortall, the

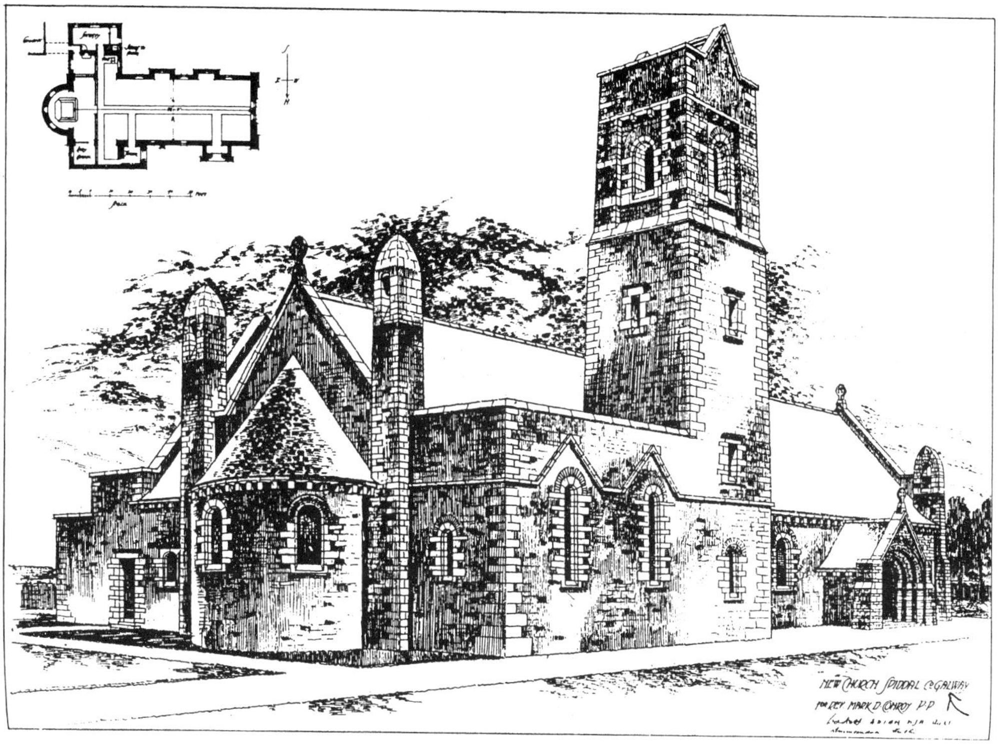

stained glass by Catherine O'Brien, the stations of the cross in opus sectile by Ethel Rhind.

It is a sad comment on the architectural aims of the Celtic Revival and Irish Catholicism, here so tightly interwoven, that this church, despite its rapturous critical reception at the time, should in the end have so little influence on creating a national style. No new cathedral commissions followed, only the decoration of what had been built by others (such as the cathedral of Loughrea: q.v.). And when commissions for new churches did come, Scott himself had changed. He was no longer a medium able to translate into everyday architecture a cryptic language of a secretive people. He had lost his closeness to the earth and its hiding places.

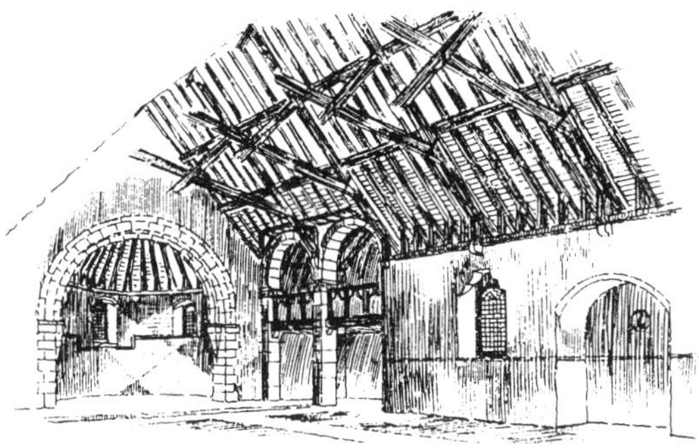

SPIDDAL: **Spiddal House**

While William Scott was building the Catholic church at Spiddal the 2nd Lord Killanin asked him to expand Spiddal House. The commission included a new avenue from the village. This meant a triple-arched entrance that still survives, and a castellated lodge that has lost its upper floor. It also meant a delightful bridge across the Owenboliska River, with seats for weary travellers recessed into miniature turrets corbelled out over the waterfalls below. This meant that one approached the house from the side, and the entry was marked by a three-storied tower with an open belvedere and beside it a double-storied loggia.

The adjoining garden front which had been once the entrance, was extended by a colonnade and a further arcaded loggia, all with views of the sea withheld from the approach. Yet more arcades at the rear provide a hidden bridge to the stable block. The carving was the work of Michael Shortall taking time off between ecclesiastical commissions. This attempts to make a country house out of Hiberno-Romanesque recalls McCarthy's Cahirmoyle for the O'Briens a generation earlier, but here the Edwardian art of fusing house and garden with the surrounding landscape is exploited to the utmost.

There is no record of Scott's interiors, all destroyed when the house was burned down in 1923. In 1927, and again in 1945, the house was partially rebuilt by the present Lord Killanin,

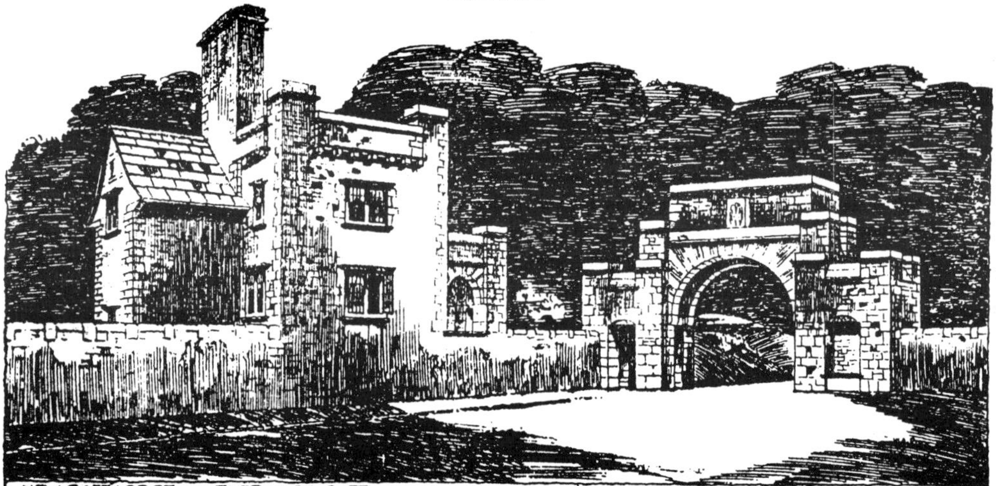
NEW GATE LODGE AND ENTRANCE GATEWAY AT SPIDDAL Co GALWAY FOR THE RT: HON: LORD KILLANIN, D.L.

but with a more Georgian manner. The architect was Ralph Byrne. It was ironic that Byrne should get the commission, since William Scott had taken over the interior of Loughrea Cathedral from William Byrne, his father.

TUAM: Catholic Cathedral

Founded two years before Emancipation by Archbishop Kelly, and consecrated by his successor, Archbishop McHale, in 1837, this is one of the finest examples of Ireland of Early Gothic Revival, designed by the mysterious Dominic Madden and his major work. The distinctive tower, dominates all distant views. Stained glass by Joshua Clarke and the Harry Clarke Studios. The finest window is that by Michael O'Connor (1860) immediately behind the high altar, which is sculpted by Leonardi of Rome. Outside the cathedral statue to Archbishop McHale by Farrell (1874). In 1979 the baldachino, transept altars, pulpit and altar rails were removed. A recent screen inserted in the chancel blocks out the lower section of O'Connor's window.

TUAM: Church of Ireland Cathedral

St Mary's Cathedral is a Victorian building defeated by its own success. Few of its visitors today realize that they are in a 19th-century building. It looks like a restoration so insensitive that all evidence of authenticity has been suppressed. The intentions of the architect, Thomas Newenham Deane, were admirable—to give permanent protection to the chancel arch, one of the treasures of the Hiberno-Romanesque, and restore it to its original purpose. This arch, the widest Hiberno-Romanesque arch in Ireland, and the barrel-vaulted choir beyond were all that survived collapse in 1184. The second cathedral, two centuries later, turned it into an entry porch and built behind it. Deane's solution was to build a third cathedral on the site of the first, and turn the second cathedral into a library, registry and synod hall. For his new cathedral of 1863, he wisely chose contrasting Gothic rather than matching Romanesque. He supervised the installation of the fittings and the stained glass, commemorating himself in the seven-lancet window under the western rose. Glass by Heaton, Butler and Bayne.

Tuam makes an instructive comparison with another cruciform cathedral, also with a central spire, Pugin's Killarney (q.v.), slightly larger but seemingly so much more so due to Pugin's mastery of scale. Deane compounded his problems by having to adapt to the low vaulting of the original choir. The arch, battered by its exposure to the elements, is not easy to see in the dimness of the chancel with its now internal windows opening into the 14th-century cathedral beyond. Our attention is distracted by the extraordinary Post-Modern Gothic choir stalls made up out of shafts of Connemara marble. These replaced the stalls presented by the Coopers of Markree, and sold off to an Italian dealer, who recognized that, while seemingly Rococo, they were in reality masterpieces of Renaissance marquetry in Rococo framing.

Tuam lacks something else more indefinable than scale—humility. The stained glass depicts a civilization that perceived Paradise as the ultimate colony of the Empire. In one window Christ interrupts a young man (sporting dundrearies) fishing, not on Galilee but on the Corrib, who will put away his rod and go to die in defence of some remote Indian outpost.

TUAM: The Townhall

Although prominently sited in the centre of the town, its corner clocktower is too weak to become a focal point. Limestone façade detailed in a spindly Anglo-Italianate idiom. Architect unknown, *c.*1880.

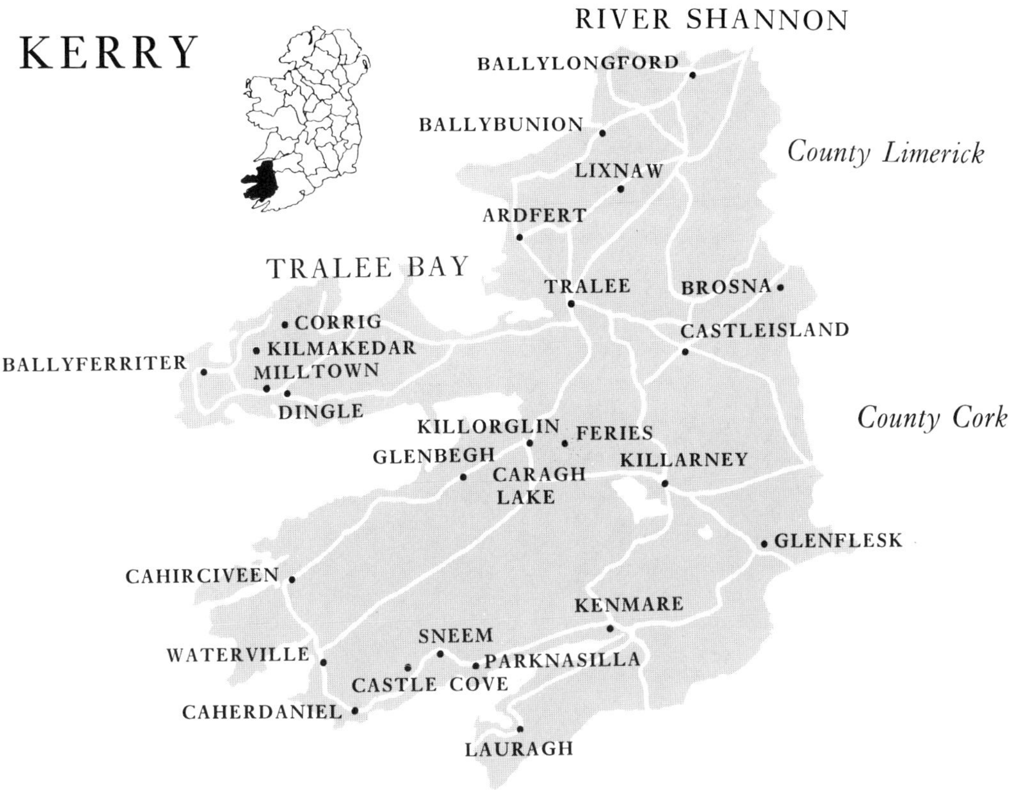

ARDFERT: **Catholic Church**
Both parents of J.J. McCarthy came from Kerry, hence the abundance of commissions. This church, built in 1853-5, is not to be confused with the nearby Catholic church of Kilmoyle of 1871 designed by Ashlin. Puginian Gothic with nave and smaller chancel propped up by their respective aisles. Corner tower and spire beside the entry porch. Interior stripped of plaster *c.* 1970, when the altar that had replaced the original by Hardman in 1917 was in its turn superseded.

ARDFERT: **Entrance Gates and Fountain**
The medieval ruins remain, but not the 17th-century house of the earls of Glandore, or the church that William Atkins built for their heirs, the Talbot-Crosbies, in 1868. However, the Gothic entrance with its wrought-iron gates survives (transferred to this site in 1880 by Patrick Dineen and his son) and in front of it the small Hiberno-Romanesque memorial fountain. Commissioned by Lindsey Talbot-Crosbie to commemorate his father William so that he would be remembered for the village water supply even if in his lifetime he was called by his tenants, 'Billy the Leveller'.

ARDFERT: **Meeting Hall**
Disconsolate fledgling of Pont Street Dutch, built in 1914 as the last absurdly optimistic gesture of an enlightened landlord, Lindsey Talbot, who was to die on the eve of the First World War. His first venture had been the Hiberno-Romanesque water supply. In red brick with stone trimmings. Now derelict.

BALLYBUNION: **Church of Ireland**
Tiny Gothic Revival Church of Ireland built (1877) in Ratoo (q.v.), a few miles inland, to the design of J.F. Fuller as an oratory of the Guns. After the last Protestant in that village had died, it was moved here by a Dean Griffin, who could not contemplate either its demolition or its sale. Tiny nave of four bays entered through projecting porch. Chancel of one bay between vestry and organ chamber, both externally expressed. Now a library.

BALLYFERRITER: **Catholic Church**
Designed by J.J. McCarthy *c.* 1865 and built out of local freestone with nave and lean-to aisles. Interior modernized.

BALLYLONGFORD: **Catholic Church**
The façade is a literal transcription of J.J. McCarthy's Foynes (q.v.), with a single rose window in the gable made to appear vaster by a half-height turret housing the staircase to the organ gallery. Otherwise the exterior, if Romanesque, is conventional. Not so the interior, an unexpected tribute to the architecture of

William Burges. But even Burges might have recoiled from the nave arcades, the sheer size of their pedestals and the squatness of their columns. This bravado perversely ends before the crossing, where totally undecorated transept arches cut through the walls that extend round to enclose the apse. Similar arches define the first bay on entry to give the nave a discreet symmetry. There is no internal evidence of the tower built over the northern transept. The date (1865) is recorded but not the architect—either J.J. McCarthy or an assistant out of control.

BROSNA: **Catholic Church**
Gothic Revival church by George Ashlin dating from 1863, typical of his output. Three-light windows by S. Purser (1909).

CAHERDANIEL: **Derrynane**
One of the few Gaelic Catholic 'big houses' to survive in Ireland. On a remote inlet sealed off by mountains from the outside world. Inherited by Daniel O'Connell, the Liberator. He acted as his own architect; he extended the existing back wing to contain the principal reception rooms, diningroom below, drawingroom above to overlook the sea, in the Queen Anne idiom of the original house. He intended to flank his wing with two pavilions, slated and surmounted by Irish battlements to make an imposing forecourt, but only one pavilion was ever built. Instead his son John added in 1844 the Gothic chapel to celebrate his release from prison.

The house remained in the family for a further century until acquired by the Board of Works, unfortunately in a period when interest in historic interiors was at its lowest ebb. The earliest house was pulled down, and O'Connell's additions were smartened up to look like a London gaming club apart from the Dun Emer carpets (a solecism), but at least they still contain his portraits, trophies and relics. The only interior that has survived ill-considered restoration is the chapel with its rustic Gothic fittings. However, the most miraculous survival of all is the Gothic viewing tower built by O'Connell to his own design in the woods above the house, a shell grotto below and a now rooflesss writing room, almost hidden by the foliage and holly. Here he escaped from the chores of domesticity and the fatuousness of callers.

CAHIRCIVEEN: **Catholic Church**
A massive memorial to Daniel O'Connell, designed by George Ashlin in 1885 for Canon Brosnan. Almost a cathedral with its stone vaulting, apsidal east end strongly pronounced transept attached to a single tower. Intended spire never completed. Despits its cost and size, the church cannot compare with Ashlin's small-

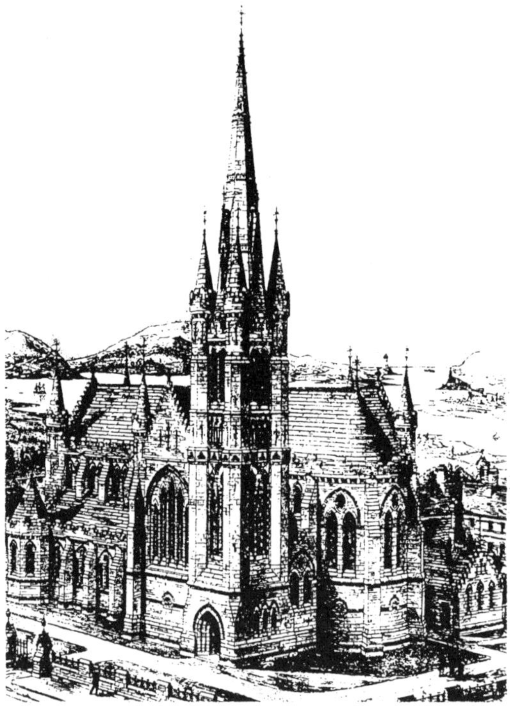

er funeral churches. Where they are exquisite, this is vapid and tendentious. The exterior is an uneasy compromise between Irish and Continental Gothic with its French-inspired apse buttressed and battlemented in the Irish manner. A main entrance (through a castellated porch beneath a group of Early English lancets) demonstrates only too clearly the failure of medieval Ireland to evolve a national style. Bush-hammered stone finish adds to the coarseness of the design.

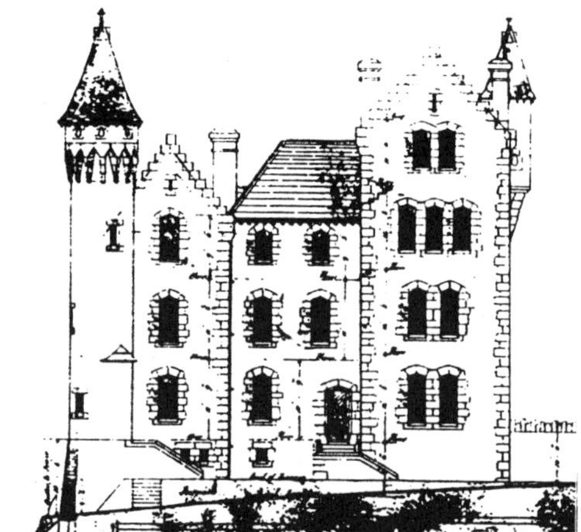

CAHIRCIVEEN: **The Barracks**
Scottish Baronial structure built in 1871 by the British government. A simplified version of the

Dungannon Barracks (q.v.) also by E.T Owen. Destroyed during the Troubles, but its restoration has been mooted.

CAHIRCIVEEN: **Church of Ireland**
Modest hard Gothic single cell by Welland and Gillespie, *c.*1865, and now a deconsecrated enterprise centre.

CARAGH LAKE: **Ard na Side**
Edith Lady Gordon in her memoirs, *The Winds of Change*, describes herself as the ninth demented member of her family to build in Kerry. She had already described her childhood home, Callinafercy (q.v.), near Killorglin (still lived in by her family), as needlessly built by her father without any redeeming feature. But her own house was so conscientiously designed to rebut the charge of being a pseudo-castle, that the result is tastefully Home Counties, despite all the materials being Irish. Her architect was Morley Horder, the date 1871. More remarkable is the garden made by Lady Gordon to overlook

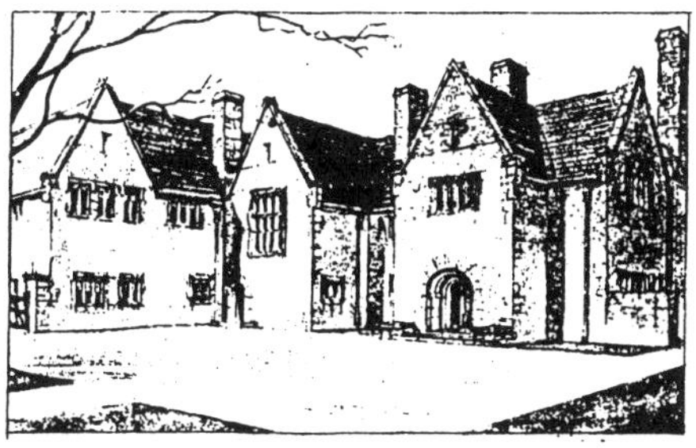

Caragh Lake, inspired by Jeykell and Lutyens. Now a country-house hotel.

CARAGH LAKE: **Caragh Lodge**
Modest Victorian villa with bay windows and verandahs designed to overlook the lake and range over range of the Reeks. Garden mainly from the 1930s. Now a country house hotel.

CASTLE COVE: **Coastguard Station**
Coastguard station built *c.*1885 by the Board of Works, then acquired and extended as a sanitorium by the sister of Lord Midleton, Albinia Brodrick, who championed Sinn Féin and the suffragettes. Never completed due to her financial difficulties and her disagreements with local authorities. Hubert Butler speaks of this half-finished hospital on a desolate stretch of the Dunkerron peninsular as a fitting memorial to her.

CASTLEISLAND: **Catholic Church**
Late Gothic Revival, by Doolin (1896-1900) in local limestone; later spire.

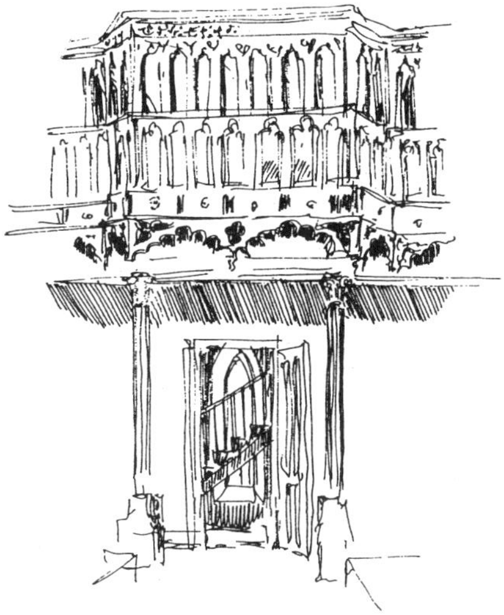

CASTLEISLAND: **Church of Ireland**
Early Gothic Revival in the style of Welland. Pretty organ gallery corbelled out on cusped arches. Now an enterprise centre.

CORRIG: **Ardamore Catholic Church**
Hiberno-Romanesque Revival church inspired by nearby Kilmachedar, *c.*1865. Design attributed to J.J. McCarthy. Square-headed door set into recessed arch with inclined reveals. Projecting corner piers and narrow windows result in the most convincing Celtic Revival façade of the 19th century. All illusions are dissipated by a later copper-sheeted roof.

DINGLE: **Burnham House**
Three-storied Georgian house with symmetrical two-storied wings. Seat of the Mullins family, subsequently De Moleyns, Lords Ventry. Rebuilt after a fire *c.*1890 by J.F. Fuller, who added the ungainly pediment and porch to the front and the bay windows to the garden front. The exterior was then rendered. As rebuilt the house lacks the dignity of the estate cottages, very attractive where they remain unaltered, built from local stone with large sash windows. The main house is now an Irish-speaking college.

DINGLE: **Lispoole Catholic Church**
Well-sited Gothic Revival church, designed by J.J. McCarthy, *c.*1860, a twin to Feries (q.v.). Built from local limestone with central nave held between low-roofed aisles. Diagonally placed bellcote corbelled out on buttresses from the corner of the façade. Interior altered by the insertion of skylights and the removal of the high altar designed by H. O'Neill and carved by Scannell in 1870.

DINGLE: **Presentation Convent**
The chapel is by C.J. McCarthy, the son of J.J. McCarthy who as the architect of the adjoining parochial Catholic church had also received the commission of the convent. Whereas the upper portions of the church have been demolished to make way for a single, depressing copper roof with the loss of all its fittings, the chapel has not only survived this century but has received its greatest treasure, twelve windows by Harry Clarke. They were commissioned from Clarke in 1922, and installed two years later under the supervision of R.M. Butler. The glass itself was mainly executed by Clarke's asssistant, Philip Deegan, but not the comatose disciples engulfed in the flowers of Gethsemane, or a celestial pinnacled city. These are by Harry Clarke himself.

FERIES: **Catholic Church**
A twin church of Lispoole (q.v.), with a similar geometrical bellcote diagonally corbelled out on buttresses from the corner of the façade, is proof that J.J. McCarthy had the ability to be as harsh and incisive as his contemporary Church of Ireland architects.

GLENBEGH: **Glenbegh Towers**
Fuller's first Irish professional success was to destroy Edwin Godwin's architectural career in Ireland that ended in a courtcase like the careers of some of Godwin's clients (Whistler and Wilde). In his memoirs, Fuller reveals that his concern was not to create a work of art but to keep the damp out. And this he did with money given him by Roland Winn, who had commissioned a castle from Godwin in 1867. When the rain poured in, Winn withheld the balance of his fees. Godwin sued and lost. 'Never build in Ireland,' he advised his students. His castle was one of the most remarkable in Ireland—a tower house fortified against the Fenians, raised on a battered basement, defended by an entry bawn that acted at the same time as a horizontal foil to the verticality of the keep. Further tension was generated by horizontal string-coursing at each level. The topmost conflict between a massive roof against a slender lookout tower never materialized: the tower was never completed.

One feels that Glenbegh must have made a congenial setting for the lifestyle of Roland Winn's son, the 5th Lord Headley, who became a convert to Mohammed, and went on a pilgrimage to Mecca, where he was given permission to be addressed as Al'Haz. He was then made president of the British Muslim Society. All this did not prevent him being burnt out of Ireland by the IRA. Indeed Glenbegh was set on fire as early as 1915.

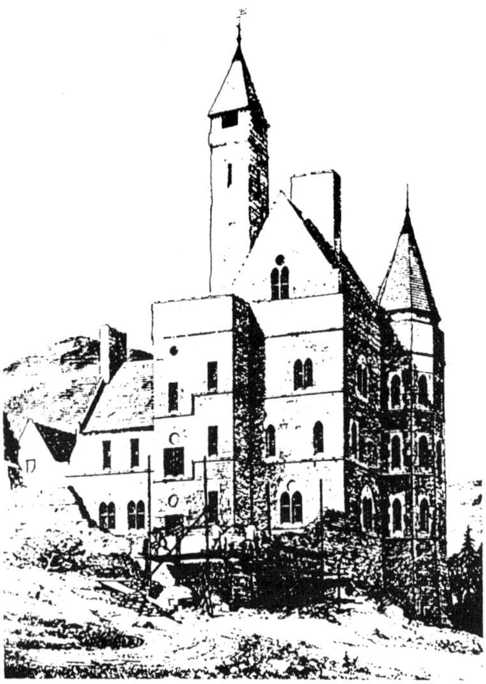

GLENFLESK: **Catholic Church**
Small Gothic Revival Church, built out of local stone by J.J. McCarthy, sited at the start of a mountain pass from Kerry to Cork. Tower never completed.

KENMARE: **Ardtully Castle**
Once a stronghold of the MacCarthys. A modest house designed by L. Cotter existed here in 1840, but this was pulled down *c.*1860 by Sir Richard Orpen and replaced by a Baronial castle with large plate-glass windows, stepped gables and a turreted corner tower. His architect is unknown, but the idiom is that of Lynn and Lanyon. Its destruction during the Troubles has left a ruin that no longer competes for domination with the river and the mountains. Now it is a fantasy as insubstantial as those invented by the 18th century Irish landscape painters in their search for the sublime.

KENMARE: **Catholic Church and Convent**
Gothic Revival complex, lauded on completion in 1863 by a critic in the *Tralee Chronicle* who informed his readers that he had sojourned in Italy and travelled in other lands, but that this to the eye of the connoisseur was decidedly the chastest even in Kerry, and that it was fully worthy of the genius of its creator, Mr Hansom. But which Mr Hansom? Was it the cab inventor, John Aloysius, or his obscure brother Charles. The commission was a collaboration until a dispute which left Charles in charge (apart from

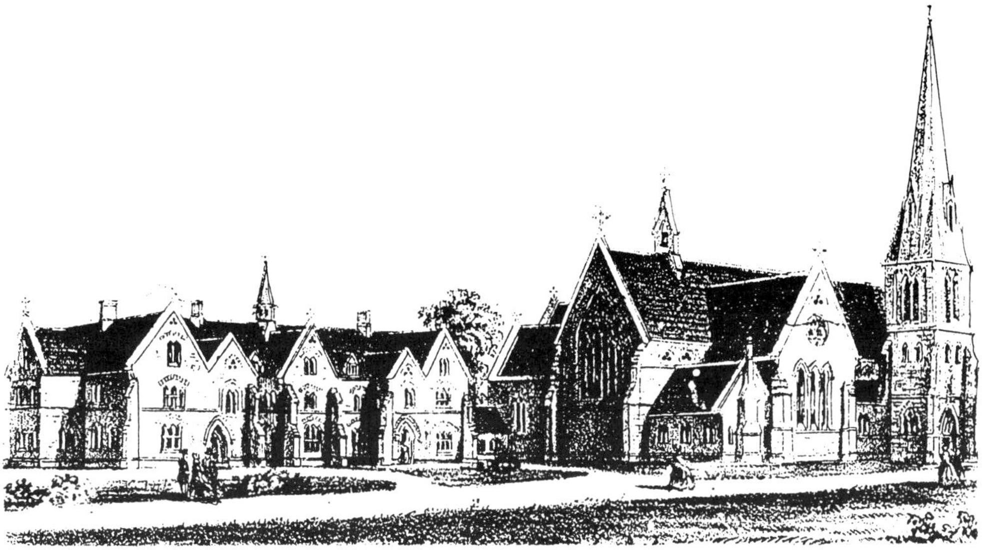

an interfering parish priest). This was recalled many years later by a pupil of John Aloysius, Daniel O'Connell, son of the Liberator, who also remembered that the carved Bath stone spire (according to the *Chronicle* the first in Ireland) had to be replaced with concrete. Interior dominated by the Mayer stained glass of the eastern window, a storm-laden crucifixion.

KENMARE: **Dromore Castle**

The only major country-house commission of Sir Thomas Deane, although the real designer was his brother Kearns. The client was the Revd. Denis Mahony, who lived too far from Cork to be affected by Deane's political career, which so aroused the hostility of the great landowners that they gave their patronage to his rivals, the Pains. Dromore is very indebted to the castles of the Pains, but is even more geometrical in plan, with its circular tower slipped in between to polygonally-ended rooms. Yet the exterior lacks the lightness of touch that the Pains were able to give the grimmest of their designs. The Roman cement imitating ashlar now contrasts too strongly with the limestone dressings, and its machiolations, carried round three sides of two non-existent towers, are comparatively fussy in scale. However, the fenestration, still painted red with the rust of barons' wars, adds an enlivening note; its tracery is suitably dramatic for the Perpendicular Revival window lighting the half-landing of the imperial staircase and then delicate in the main rooms with fanlights inspired by Sezingcote framing views across the sea to the Caha Mountains. Dromore was completed in 1838, but ten years later, the Revd Mahony recalled the Deanes to provide the main entrance with a gatehouse. The designer was Benjamin Woodward (one of his earliest works), and this time the fortifications were real, so that the keeper could leap out of his bed, up a stone spiral staircase and pour down boiling oil on to the heads of the Fenians. The gatehouse is now derelict but the castle has survived. Until re-

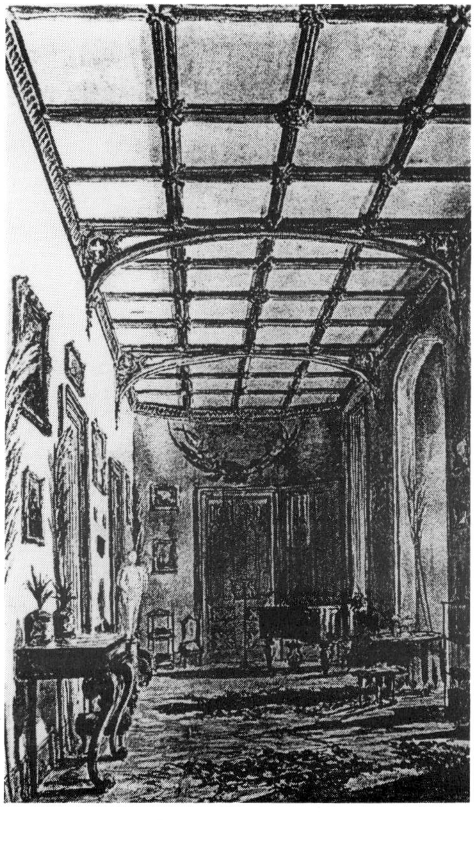

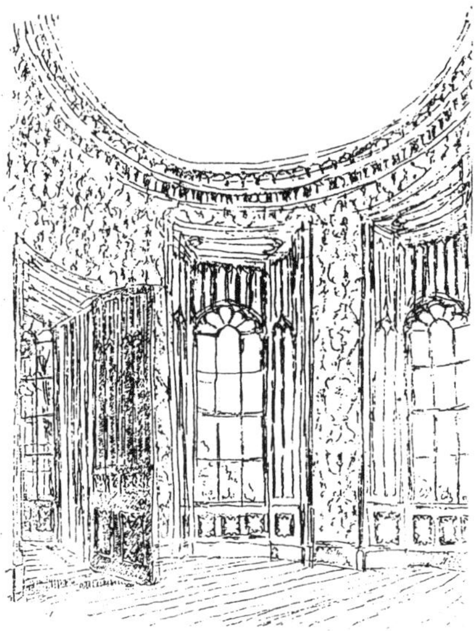

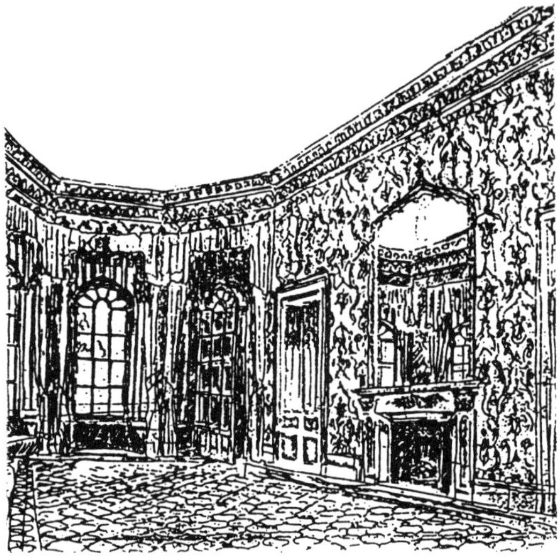

cently still lived in by descendants of the original patron who dine by gaslight in the diningroom that retains its original scarlet wallpaper (of Tudor roses alternating with fleur-de-lis) and its pelmets and embroidered curtains.

KENMARE: **Drumquinnan**
House built in a leisurely Queen Anne Revival *c.* 1890 for Sir John Columb. Now more successful as a hotel. Architect, J.F. Fuller.

KENMARE: **Park Hotel**
Designed by J.F. Fuller *c.*1890 as the last stop before Parknasilla (q.v.), the ultimate goal. The Park has now supplanted all rivals as the most luxurious hotel in the South of Ireland. Although the bluff no-nonsense approach of Fuller's institutional manner is at first sight forbidding, this acts as a foil to the comfort, even intimacy, of the interiors. Much of Fuller's detailing survives even to his mannered treatment of the fenestration, which he deployed also in his own house—little panes above increasing in size to end up as plate glass at the bottom.

KILLARNEY: **Aghadoe**
The 3rd Lord Headley was an English visitor so enchanted with Killarney that he built a house nearby, while his younger brother employed E.M. Godwin at Glenbegh (q.v.). The architect of the elder brother was William Atkins, who based his plan on the Venetian Gothic house he had just completed near Tralee (Oak Park: q.v.). But the idiom that he chose here was a curious Lombardesque with mannered proportions and abrupt changes of sale. Inherited by the eccentric 5th Lord Headley and destroyed by the IRA five years after the destruction of Glenbegh. Rebuilt with simplified roof. Now a youth hostel.

KILLARNEY: **Bishop's Palace and Diocesan College**
Imposing Gothic Revival complex built behind Pugin's cathedral. The architecture (with possible contributions by McCarthy and Ashlin) has still to be unravelled.

KILLARNEY: **Cahernane**
Katherine Everett in her memoirs *Bricks and Flowers*, laments the loss of the early 18th-century family home, pulled down in 1877 by her father, Henry Hubert, to please his neurotic wife, and replaced by a grim Baronial mansion of J.F. Fuller, which cost so much that his client could not afford furnishing or heating. Katherine had harsh words to say about St Anne's, built by Fuller for her cousin, Lady Ardilaun ('more a mausoleum than a home') and she was equally critical of Cahernane—its dark cement going black with constant rain and the Bathstone dressings turning green with Kerry damp. She failed to mention the lively carvings that decor-

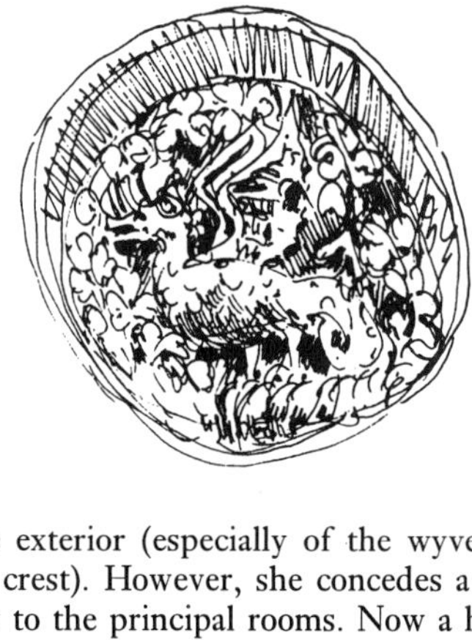

ate the exterior (especially of the wyvern, the family crest). However, she concedes a certain dignity to the principal rooms. Now a hotel.

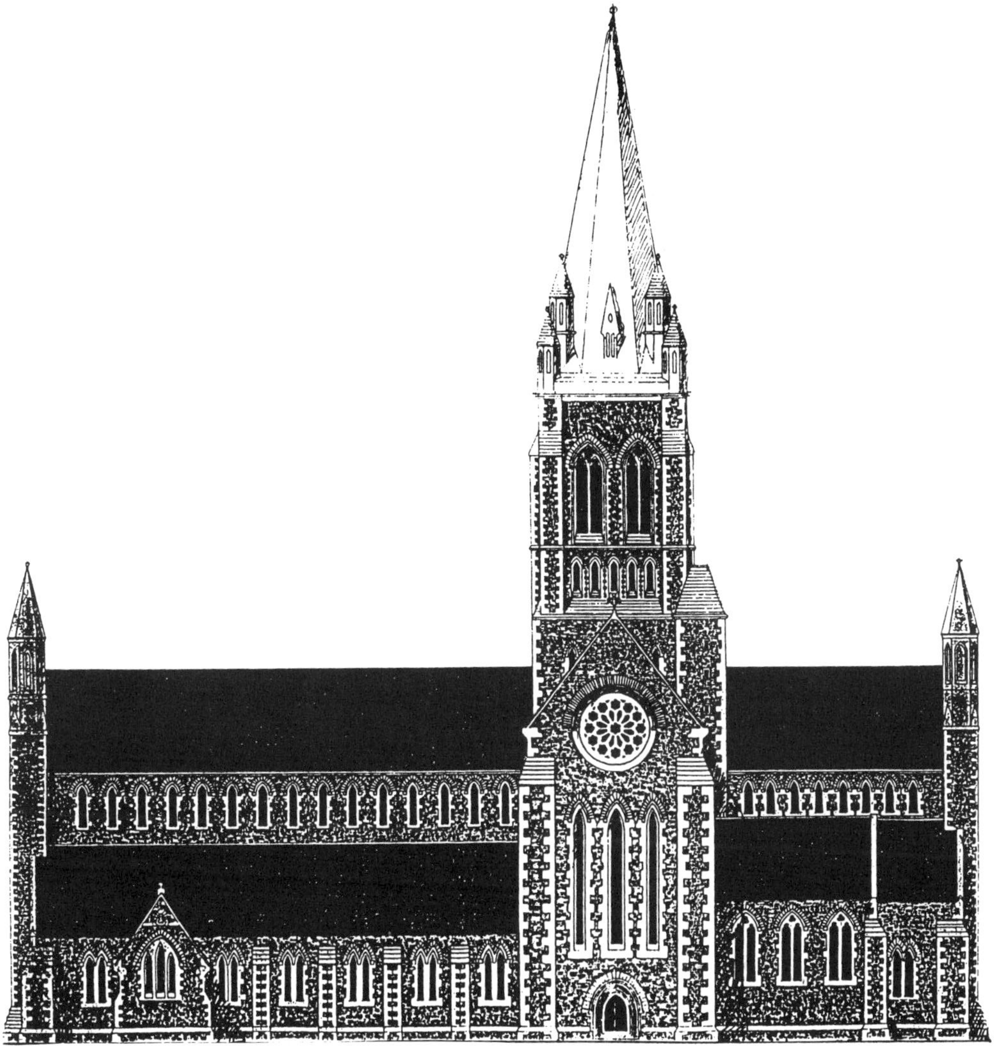

KILLARNEY: Catholic Cathedral

The Irish masterpiece of A.W.N. Pugin, standing in for all the unbuilt cathedrals which would have brought the English back into the Catholic faith. Killarney should have exceeded the cathedrals of England in the wooded grandeur of its setting, as Lord Kenmare, the Catholic landlord of Killarney, had promised a site on his estate. But Lady Kenmare objected and was not pleased when one of their tenants offered a site without permission opposite her front gates. History does not record if she was mollified by this vision of Salisbury, for Killarney was Pugin's personal homage to his favourite cathedral. In any csae, she is buried beside her husband in the south eastern chapel.

Work started in 1842 under the direction of Bishop Moriarty and continued throughout the Famine until completed in 1850. Due to its masterly simplification of Early English Gothic, it appears more immense than Pugin's larger cathedral at Enniscorthy built over the same period. After Pugin's death the nave was extended from five to seven bays and the west façade rebuilt while the piers of the crossing were thickened to take a more elaborate 300ft high spire to the design of George Ashlin. This can be compared with the more austere spire in Pugin's wooden presentation model adapted as a cover for the baptismal font and as such almost discarded. 'I'll see Eamon,' the author was told by a builder when he offered to buy it from the top of a rubbish heap, 'Eamon' being Bishop Eamon Casey, who was responsible for the restoration in the early 1970s.

The font model was saved but this proved to be a controversial restoration. Not only was the new high altar placed under the tower, but the Victorian high altar and choir stalls were swept away and at first replaced by a cross suspended in the chancel arch and stabilized by a mesh of illuminated cables. The stone of the floor was covered by a monotonous yellow tiling while the stone of the wall was revealed by the removal of all plaster. However, the interior of the cathedral has survived these alterations. Indeed the high altar and the stalls had been overbearingly designed not by Pugin but his son Edward Welby. The internal plaster that Pugin would have been decorated with richly coloured patterns, was discoloured with dampness, and its removal has parallels with the romantic High Victorian restorations of the medieval cathedrals of Tuam and Kilkenny (q.v.). Even the rough stones round the arches (never intended to be exposed) add a certain poignancy, a reminder of Pugin's plea to the Irish clergy to desist from building new churches and reroof instead their ruined abbeys. The suspended cross, despite its irresistible parallel with the flying trapeze act in a circus (and therefore now partially dismantled) gave the choir a sense of mystery that Pugin himself would have achieved by a rood screen.

The restoration of the exterior involved no further alteration. It is extraordinary that such a sense of Irishness should be achieved by a Huguenot convert to the Church of Rome, obsessed with the cathedrals of England. But here his inspiration was the ruined medieval predecessor of his cathedral, Ardfert, three massive corner buttresses contrasting with long slender lancets a theme that he takes up and subtly modulates with and without rose windows at the end of each transept, nave and choir.

Killarney Cathedral is best visited in winter to be viewed from the once forbidden demesne, through a flooded leafless forest. The town, with its tourists, jarveys and souvenirs, recedes into insignificance.

KILLARNEY: **Church of Ireland**

In 1871, a visiting critic called Edis deplored that in this church William Atkins had deserted the native Irish school to become yet another victim of the French style emanating from William Burges of Cork Cathedral. Atkins had been an unsuccessful competitor, and it is regrettable that this tribute to his rival was gutted by a malicious fire in 1888 and subsequently rebuilt by J.F. Fuller in what was possibly a more faithful manner than was admitted at the time. The boarded roof with its notched arches is more characteristic of Atkins than Fuller. As for the stained glass (by Heaton, Butler and Bayne), commemorating the Herbert family, most of it appears to predate the fire, even to the rendering of Holman Hunt's 'Light of the World'. Organ by Telford (1887).

KILLARNEY: **Coolclogher**

The first country house of William Atkins to reveal his personal style, dating from the early 1850s. The client was a local landowner, John Leahy. His site had a spectacular view that Atkins exploited to the full, with a sequence of reception rooms dominated by the semi-circular bow of the principal drawingroom, and ending with a conservatory leading to the garden. The architecture is Italianate, partly Romanesque, partly neo-Classsical.

KILLARNEY: **Flesk Castle**

One of the most successful of the amateur-Gothic Revival castles in Ireland, built by its owner, John Coltsman, an English visitor who became enraptured with the scenery and decided to remain. The plan of his castle reflects his enthusiasm, dictated by the contours of his site and his view across the lakes to the Reeks. Thus he escapes the tryanny of the right angle. However, his design is held together by a series of pivotal towers, square, circular and polygonal. The entrance hall is canted forward so that it

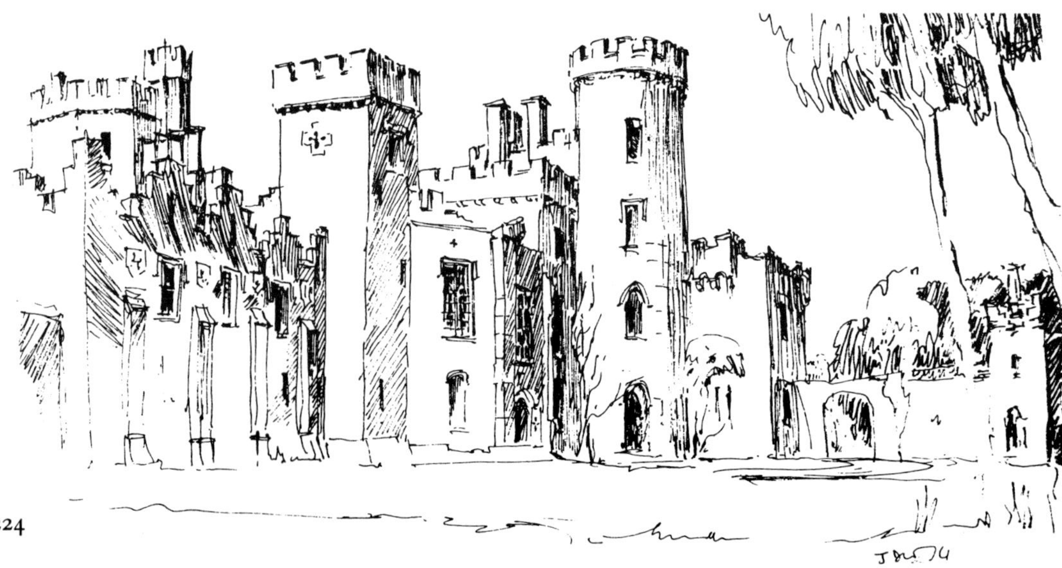

becomes in effect a shallow double-height bay window with a groined vault. This leads through a sequence of five reception rooms climaxing with an octagonal drawingroom in the polygonal tower. The last to live here was a younger brother of the McGillycuddy of the Reeks, who bought it from a Coltsman descendant, but he had to abandon it eventually and it is now a total ruin. One looks up into a staircase tower amazed by its whorl-like vault and then one realizes that this is the last surviving flight of the staircase that had spiralled to the summit.

KILLARNEY: **Franciscan Abbey**
Monastic complex built in 1868 by J.J. McCarthy round central cloister, prominently sited at the southern approach to the town. Asymmetrical façade flush with the west front of the church, all built from a greenish rubble stone and contrasting dressings, inspired by Pugin's treatment of Enniscorthy Cathedral. Continuous nave and chancel with light lattice vault. Chancel remodelled in 1917 with frescoes and mosaics. Neo-Gothic high altars and side altars on rear wall still survive, carved in wood, coloured and delicately gilded in the Flemish manner. Western stained-glass window in total contrast in its forceful brilliance, by Philip Deegan for the Harry Clarke Studios in the 1920s.

KILLARNEY: **Great Southern Hotel**
William Atkins won the limited competition for the hotel beside Killarney station, but the unsuccessful entry by Frederick Darley was built instead, for what reasons we do not know. Perhaps Darley's design looked more comfortable and undemanding. The exterior is a quiet neo-Georgian. The architectural gestures are reserved for the interior, where they do not have to contend with Kerry's climate. The progression from the hall through foyers and reception rooms to the Corinthian-columned grandeur of the diningroom focused on a generously curved south facing bay is still the most impressive of its kind in Ireland. Additions made in 1906. Desperate attempts by earlier managements to speed up its stately tempo have been singularly unsuccessful, and indeed there are signs today of a desire to recreate its leisurely reassurance as an interlude between the long train journey across Ireland and the vertiginous jaunts in the jarvey cars.

KILLARNEY: **Killarney House**
The great red-brick mansion built by the earls of Kenmare on a hilltop site (said to have been chosen by Queen Victoria) overlooking elaborate formal gardens with vistas of lakes and mountains, was burnt out twice—once on completion in 1879, the next time thirty years later. Its ruins were dismantled *c.*1920. Its loss, unlike the 17th-century house that it replaced, is not regrettable, despite being designed by George Devey. That feeling of being built up over the centuries that distinguished Devey's work was entirely lacking, partly due to the job being supervised by W.H. Lynn at his most relentless. What still remain are the stables made into the house (*c.*1912), the dairy, a Queen Anne-style retreat in the park, and the western-most gate-lodge, gabled and galleried, Devey at his most delightful.

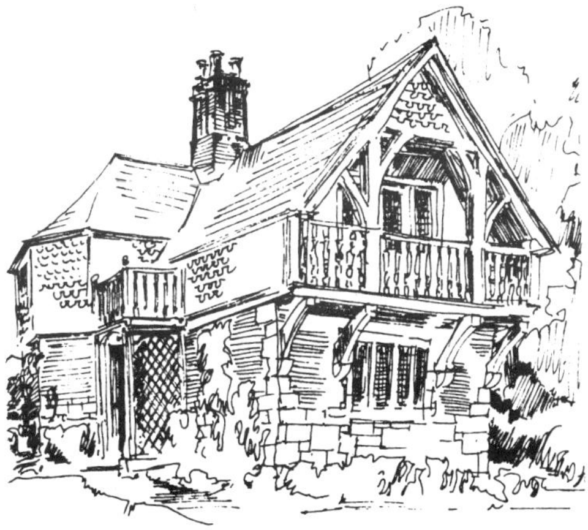

KILLARNEY: **Methodist Church**
Small, precise, late Gothic Revival church distinguished by miniature diagonally placed belfry. Architect, G.F. Beckett (1912).

KILLARNEY: **Lakeview**
Italianate house built beside Lough Leane *c.*1870 by Sir Morgan O'Connell. Ionic *porte-cochère* on the entrance front, polygonal bow window to loverlook the lake. Unaltered interiors.

KILLARNEY: **Muckross House**
Elizabethan Revival House designed by William Burn and built in 1839-43 for Col. H.A. Herbert, who received Queen Victoria in 1861, a visit from which the family finances never recovered. Col. Herbert had married a Scottish heiress and imported all his stewards also from Scotland. Hence the choice of Burn, who got the commission that had been given to Lewis Vulliamy in 1836. The formula of an asymmetrical entrance front and adjoining symmetrical garden front on a higher level with the reception rooms ensuite opening off an inner staircase hall is handled with competence but without fantasy despite its magical setting. After the Herberts had to sell up the demesne was

saved from speculators by their cousin's husband, Lord Ardilaun. Presented to the nation by the next owners, the Bourne-Vincents in memory of Mrs Arthur Vincent; hence its survival. The house is shewn to the public on Marxist principles, with the reception rooms entered from the basement by the pantry staircase. As a child exploring those on rooms empty once due to their dry rot treatment I felt like the chimneysweep Tom in *The Water Babies*. Note the diningroom curtains woven in Brussels for the Queen's visit and the heraldic sideboard, carved in Italy.

Col. Herbert became ever more Irish, employing William Atkins to design the front gates and lodge, with its ironwork by Perrot, as also a *porte-cochère* for the main house, farm buildings, and a church in the village. The basement has been successfully converted into a folk museum and craft centre giving sanctuary to the carved timber pulpit designed by Ashlin for Dublin's Thomas Street church (q.v.). The gardens have always been celebrated. W.E. Nesfield advised the Herberts in the 1840s but what we see today are mainly the alterations by Arthur Bourne Vincent, including formal parterres of cottage flowers laid out in 1906 by R. Wallace (later employed by Lutyens).

The church is a simple Gothic Revival structure now happily converted into a youth hostel, overlooked by an outsized Celtic cross which Atkins placed on the summit of a hill with a panoramic view of the estate lands which

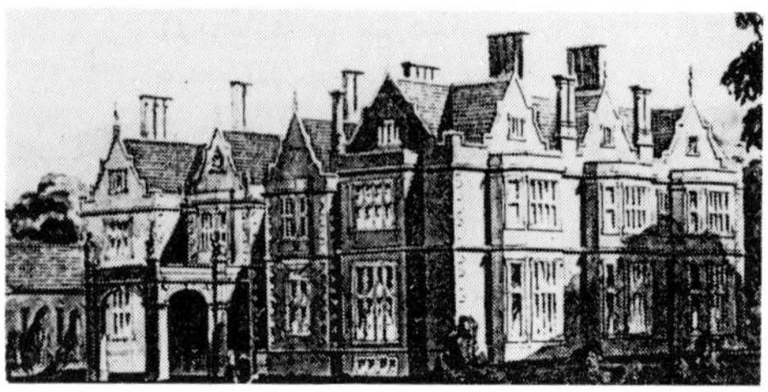

within twenty years Herbert's son was to lose after a fruitless search for copper and an unsuccessful attempt to corner the world market for cotton reels. A small lake cut into the limestone rock is still known as 'the Copper Folly'.

KILLARNEY: **Presentation Convent**
Monastic complex in the shadow of Pugin's cathedral, now being remodelled as a rehabilitation centre. Built in 1855. The most likely architects are the Hansoms, who were building nearby the private chapel of the Kenmares (especially as the elaborate high altar was designed by G. Hansom in 1872).

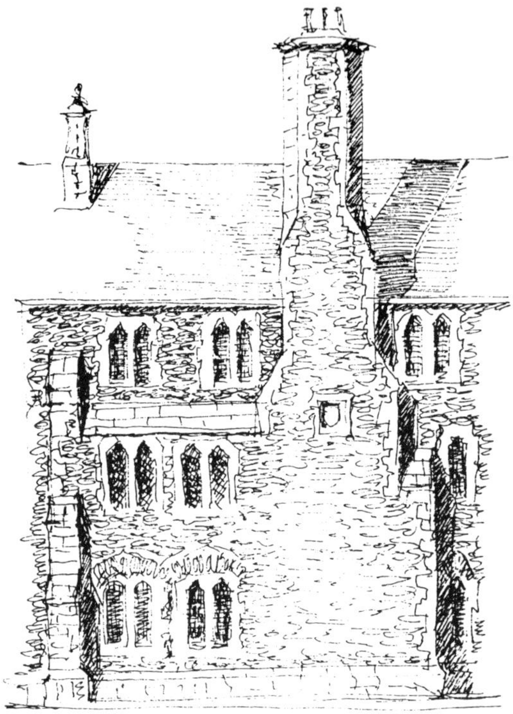

KILLARNEY: **St Finian's Hospital**
Formerly the lunatic asylum, the first major building to be conceived and built by Benjamin Woodward for Sir Thomas Deane, having been employed on Cork University after the design stage. His sketch proposals survive, inspired by Pugin's *Contrasts*. In the much simplified executed building, the influence of Pugin is still paramount, notably the chimneys and dormers that appear to be lifted wholesale from Pugin's Maynooth. The work force employed had been engaged on Killarney Cathedral (q.v.) but laid off due to the Famine. The front is of three floors, with projecting central block and end pavilions joined by recessed links and staircases housed in saddle-roofed towers in a slightly asymmetrical composition. First-floor chapel at the rear built on an undercroft of offices. Shortly after its completion in 1852 a critic praised it: 'With nothing adventitious, or introduced merely for the sake of ornament, the building is very picturesque and effective.' These qualities have since been diluted by subsequent additions each executed with decreasing concern. The first (probably by J.H. Owen) in 1874 retains the original polychromy, but this was discarded by Fuller in his 1890 extension, which still preserves Woodward's idiom. Not so the extensions of this century. Windows recently replaced with aluminium.

KILLORGLIN: **Callinafercy**
Built in 1861 by the Leeson-Marshall family who should have inherited the contents of

Russborough from the last earl of Milltown, had he not donated them to the nation. Undemanding gabled Tudor Revival. Well-proportioned almost Georgian interiors. Additions by J.F. Fuller *c.*1909.

KILLORGLIN: **Catholic Church**
Elaborate Late Gothic Revival church by W.G. Doolin in his characteristic manner, with ponderous rose windows and screened transepts, built in 1887-90, after he had won a hard-fought competition to replace an earlier church by McCarthy. Spire remains unexecuted.

KILLORGLIN: **Laune Viaduct**
Impressive bow-stringed girder viaduct bring the Valentia railway across the River Laune. Designed by S.G. Frazer in 1885.

KILMAKEDAR: **Church of Ireland**
Kilmakedar has always been a sacred place and this church was built *c.*1840 at the end of a remarkable attempt of a few Church of Ireland missionaries to convert the native Irish speakers to temperance and Protestantism as the religion of St Patrick. So successful was the architect, Joseph Welland, in recreating a Celtic oratory, that a replica was built by David Lean, as a Catholic church, for his film *Ryan's Daughter*. Now an artist's studio.

LAURAGH: **Derreen**
The seat of Petty-FitzMaurices, and the favourite home of the 5th marquis of Landsdowne, who spent all his summers there, landscaping the grounds and planting rare trees, following the principles of William Robinson, so that his work merges into the primeval forest and the indented coastline. The house he built makes no attempt to rival the grandeur of its setting, appearing at first sight to be modest cottage ornée. However, most of it is three stories high, and commodious enough to fit large house-parties of eminent Victorians, including the historian J.F. Froude, who stayed on for three years. The marquis' architect was J.F. Fuller at his most understated. The interiors were looted and burnt in 1922, but rebuilt in 1924. The gardens, restored by the grand-daughter of the 5th marquis, Lady Mersey, are open to the public.

LIXNAW: **Catholic Church**
One of the Celtic Revival experiments of J.J. McCarthy, but predictably more Norman than Celtic, due to having to flank the nave with aisles that open off it through robust round arched arcades. Modernized interior.

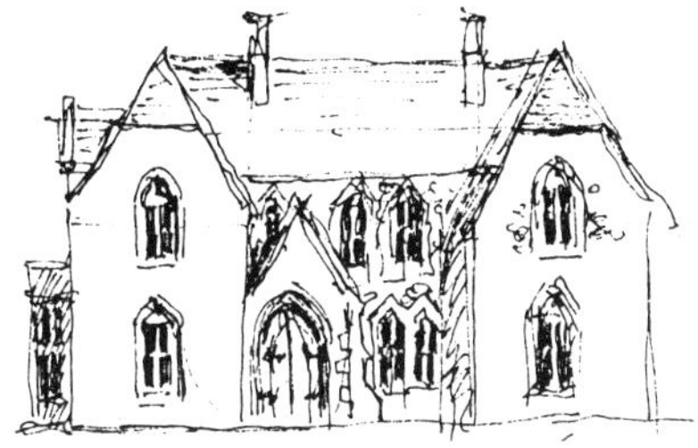

LIXNAW: **Rattoo House**
An unusual Gothic Revival house built in the idiom of Benjamin Woodward but without his grasp of proportion and geometrical precision. Built by the Gun family *c.*1860 in front of a much earlier house. The symmetry of the façade is disrupted by an over-large gabled porch attached to one of the flanking semi-hipped pavilions and rises up into the Gothic fenestration of the upper floor. Central hall bounded dog-leg staircase with barley sugar balustrading.

MILLTOWN: **Catholic Church**
Gothic Revival church designed by Daniel O'Connell, architect son of the Liberator. Interior deprived of most of its original furnishings. Adjoining school designed by Brother Townsend.

PARKNASILLA: **Great Southern Hotel**
The most ambitious of the chain of Great Southern Railway hotels, since it is sited so far from the nearest railway. Originally a shooting lodge of the Graves family adjoining Derryquin Castle, home of the Blands, the in-laws of J.F. Fuller. Fuller was chosen as the architect, and he came up with a dependable simplified Scottish Baronial, built out of local stone. Its institutionalism was relieved by its asymmetry and redeemed by its natural setting. Built *c.*1890. Characterless additions, and much mutilated interiors, although there have been recent efforts to recreate its original atmosphere, even if musak has replaced a small palm court orchestra that played a generation ago at teatime. Threatened with destruction during the Troubles, the IRA were persuaded to burn out Fuller's in-laws who lived next door instead.

SNEEM: **Rossdohan**
The curious house was built here by J.P. Seddon *c.*1875 for Dr Samuel Heard. Its double-height, frescoed music room leading to glazed verandahs with lunettes of coloured glass, was destroyed during the Troubles. The ruins were demolished in 1941, and a new house was built in the Dutch Colonial style designed by Michael Scott. Burned down, on this occasion accidentally, it is now a romantic ruin. Only Seddon's retaining walls remain. His stable block on the

other side of the island is now the house. Heard's subtropical garden inspired by William Robinson with its exotic transplants from the southern hemisphere has survived through the dedication of the Walker family, as one of the great paradise gardens of Ireland. Sold in 1992.

SNEEM: **Catholic Church**
Commissioned by the 3rd earl of Dunraven, and designed by his architect, the younger Philip Hardwicke. According to Daniel O'Connell, they were both up against a parish priest who wanted to design the church himself—with unhappy results. Whatever merit survived has been diluted through modernization.

SNEEM: **Garinish Island**
Not to be confused with the more famous Garinish in Glengariff, this is another island garden, but created a generation earlier by the 3rd earl of Dunraven round a cottage ornée, built for him by J.F. Fuller on a rocky plateau with its eaves almost descending to the ground appropriately developed as an Alpine garden. The subtropical wild garden was made by his son, the 4th earl, in a series of hidden valleys that run up through miniature mountain ranges from the sea to the uplands of the island exposed to the full force of the Atlantic, along paths once strewn with cowerie shells. Put up for sale at a nominal price in order to maintain the garden, it has just been sold twice again. No other Irish garden is as deceptive in its use of scale.

SNEEM: **Glashnacree**
The country house built for himself by J.F. Fuller, and therefore understated and sensible, the rooms snug and the windows few. As there are ceilings of dark varnished timber throughout the ground floor, coupled with dark evergreen planting for protection against the sunlight, all this led to certain cluttered gloom, against which the next generation rebelled. Fuller's daughter became a Sinn Féiner, his son a spendthrift. The house he built to embody his family's ancestral link was sold. But it is well maintained by subsequent owners.

TRALEE: **Ballyseedy Castle**
A three-storied Georgian house with an extended stable wing, screened by Gothick fortifications. Interior destroyed by fire in the late 1880s and rebuilt as an unconvincing castle by J.F. Fuller for the Blennerhassets (curved plate-glass windows with hood mouldings). The towers received shallow battlements. Fuller detailed the interior with a heavy hand, but installed a 17th-century fireplace in the library. Converted into a country-house hotel by a Sheraton descendant of the chairmaker. His wife designed all the costumes for medieval banquets at which their son, transformed into a medieval minstrel, presented a rose to the most beautiful woman in the room until he eloped with a harpist. Subsequently acquired by an American consortium marketing the 'Aloe Vera' water as a cure to Irish ills. Now a country-house hotel once again.

TRALEE: **Catholic Church**
One of the most attractive of J.J. McCarthy churches; built 1854-61. It gives an impressive vista on entering of continuous nave and choir. This impressiveness was redoubled by a decision to strip the plaster twenty years ago and reveal the polychromatic local rubble stone. So successful was it here that it inspired a similar policy in Pugin's Killarney Cathedral (q.v.) with less fortunate results. Exterior dominated by George Ashlin's western tower and spire (1868-70) built from local sandstone with silver limestone dressings. Immense stained glass sanctuary window (and windows north and south adjoining the high altar) by Michael O'Connor (1861). Art Deco Gothic balchadino by J.J. Robinson. Fonts held by kneeling marble angels. High reliefs sculpted by Sibthorpes. Alabaster pulpit by Earley (1904).

TRALEE: **Dominican Church**
This is George Ashlin at his most opulent. Strategically sited at the end of Tralee's smartest square, ready for donations. However, not enough money came in to complete the western tower and spire. Lavish interior dated 1866.

TRALEE: **Oakpark**
William Atkins' most important country house, built in 1856-61. His client, Maurice Fitzgerald Sandes (1805-79), had been Registrar General of Calcutta and had amassed a fortune in indigo before returning to Ireland to settle near Tralee, marry Ellen Dennis from Fort Granite in Co. Wicklow and decided to build a completely new house on a more elevated site. The house faces south across the vale of Tralee towards the Dingle mountains. As in Coolclogher (q.v.) Atkins devises two parallel sequences, that to the rear with the entry and the stairs, that to the front with the principal reception rooms opening on to a terrace and taking full advantage of the sun and view. But here the scale is more imposing, and there are far more surprises, within rather than without. Instead of an entry porch, there is a far-flung *porte-cochère* and the front door is framed by a series of trefoiled arches, with the arms of Sandes impaling Dennis. A flight of steps leads to the vestibule with front hall and staircase hall beyond. The stairs themselves, balustraded with sheaves of

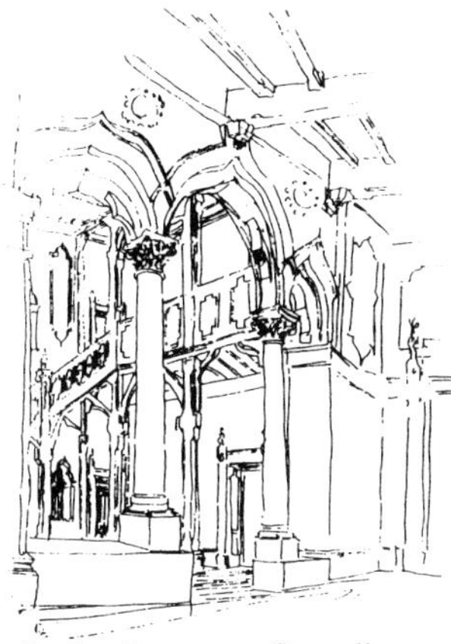

corn in glinting brass, are first glimpsed through a columned screen of purple marble. The walls are treated marbleized with a sombre olive, and ceilings are lined with darkly varnished timber as a foil to their pattering in luminous red, green and gold. The staircase hall is the architect's most spectacular interior. It is double-height with the stairs ascending to a timber galleried structure braced tautly to the walls. The far wall is perforated with arcades lighting service corridors off hall and landing. This allows the staff to supervise new arrivals, and to be sighted in return. 'That is not Juliet waiting on the balcony, but the assistant housekeeper wondering if there are enough hot water bottles.'

The sequence of reception rooms is arranged symmetrically along the garden front but terminates with two contrasting conservatories. The craftsmen involved in the interior decoration were Thomas Dixon and Frederick Taylor. Dixon (late of Dublin) advertised in Laing's *Cork Mercantile Directory* (1863) 'Imitations of woods, marbles and painting will be executed in the best manner and at Prices that will be found to suit the prevailing economy of the day'. Interiors similar to Oakpark survive at Dunkathel and Ballinatray in Co. Cork. Taylor is registered as a painter in the same directory. To him must go the credit for the painted ceilings. They are inspired by the French Renaissance and are without Irish counterpart. On the other hand, the doorcases with their poppy head terminations are copied from the *Ecclesiologist* and resemble Pugin's interiors at Adare Manor executed ten years earlier. The brasswork hinges, locks, bolts, bell pulls and fingerplates are also Puginesque.

However, the dominant influence on the design of Oakpark is not Pugin but Ruskin of *The Stones of Venice* and *The Seven Lamps of Architecture*, who had not yet lost faith in the regenerative powers of art, best nurtured by domestic architecture in medieval Venice. How to adapt that style to the requirements of the day was not his concern. He showed little interest in the architects who tried to put his ideas into practice. He made only one exception —Benjamin Woodward. Woodward's Curator's House in Oxford dates from the same year as Oakpark, and ogee arches, quatrefoils, columns without pedestals, polychromatic banding, and windows underplayed behind delicate arcades of stone occur in both commissions, or rather did occur since the Curator's House was demolished between the Wars. It is a curious reflection on the values of Academia that the Oxford Museum authorities destroyed Woodward's masterpiece, while its obscure Kerry counterpart survived the struggle for independence and civil war to be lovingly cared for by a novitiate of Presentation nuns, most of whom were unaware (until they were instructed by their order to sell up) that their convent had ever been a country house. The new owners are the County Committee for Agriculture, who have barricaded the main door and filled the hall with filing cabinets. For sale in 1993.

TRALEE: Presentation Convent

Built round two courtyards with polychromatic stonework to match the adjoining Catholic church. The architect was J.J. McCarthy. Later extended by S.F. Hynes (1911-4), who rebuilt the chapel to house the Mayer windows of its predecessor. Mosaic floor by Oppenheimer (1915). Stalls by Bayaert.

TRALEE: YMCA

The earliest recorded commission by J.F. Fuller, designed in 1861, in an asymmetrical urban Gothic with large, square-headed windows to let in the maximum of daylight. Reveals the influence of his mentor, Alfred Waterhouse. The original (unexecuted) scheme was more elaborate.

WATERVILLE: Butler Memorial Fountain

Replica of Irish high cross balanced on a substantial pedestal which contains the fountains and drinking trough, dated 1889. Attributed to J.F. Fuller.

WATERVILLE: Church of Ireland

Designed by Welland and Gillespie and consecrated in 1866. Single cell with western bellcote corbelled out on central buttress. Chancel remodelled in 1906 with details inspired by a ruined Hiberno-Romanesque church on an island in Lough Curane.

WATERVILLE: Hogs Head Coastguard Station

One of a series of stations built along the coast in the 1880s to control the widespread smuggling. They were not successful and the new government abandoned them. Beyond, an abandoned vernacular village.

KILDARE

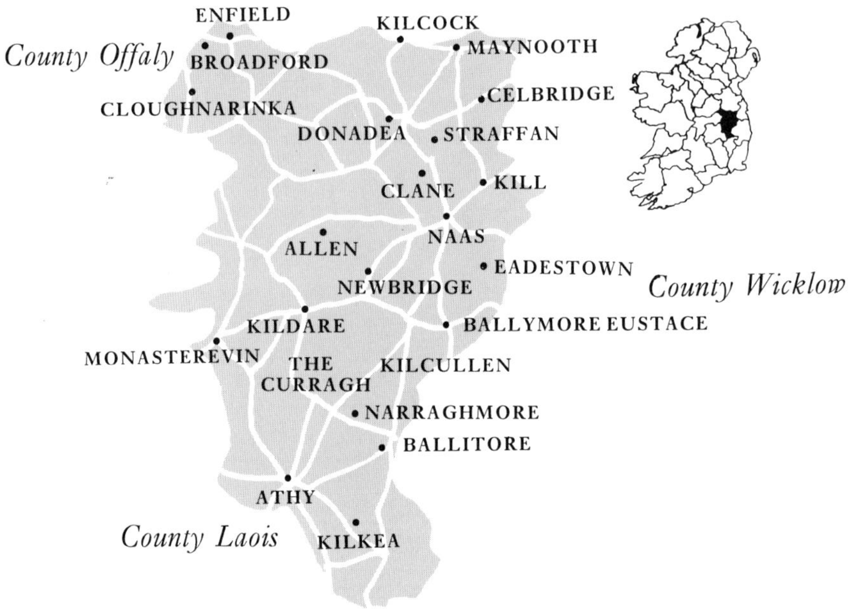

ALLEN: **Catholic Church**
Cut-stone Gothic Revival church built in 1866 to the designs of J.S. Butler. Plate tracery in the façade and the adjoining belfry. Detached colonettes articulate the fenestration of the side elevations. Sculptural capitals remain incomplete. Simple interior apart from the painting and mosaics of the polygonal apse. Stained glass by Earley.

ATHY: **Church of Ireland**
Designed in 1839 by Frederick Darley for his patron, the 3rd duke of Leinster. Exterior austere articulated by emaciated buttresses. Entry through western tower and steeple (added in 1859). Interior with extended transepts and shallow chancel framed by a delicate Gothic screen that would have matched the original furnishings. These are replaced in abruptly carved stone articulated by marble of contrasting colours, probably by Fuller.

ATHY: **Levitstown**
A roofless mill still in working order with power coming from a mill stream, sited between the river and canal. Architecturally the finest to survive along the Barrow Valley, with battered walls rising up through many floors to rooftop castellations. Approached by swing bridge in perfect repair.

ATHY: **The Library**
Formerly the Market Hall. Jolly, neo-Elizabethan building, arcaded to the square with curvilinear gables topped by finials, one of the improvements of the dukes of Leinster, dating from the mid 1850s. Possibly by Frederick Darley.

ATHY: **Methodist Church**
Simple, Gothic structure, the work of the long-living Frederick Darley, then a partner of Thomas Holbrook (1875). Adjoining manse and school. Across the road the Model School built by Darley thirty years before.

ATHY: **Model School**
The principal improvement in Athy of the 3rd duke of Leinster, the agriculturalist, to teach farming and nutrition after the horrors of the Famine. His architect was Frederick Darley, the date 1850. School complex with strict segregation of boys and girls, adjoining headmaster's house, and chapel across the road. All built in a direct, large-boned Elizabethan, of initial grimness, but relaxing into snugness at the rear, now a small office park. Remainder being restored by the Government at the eleventh hour.

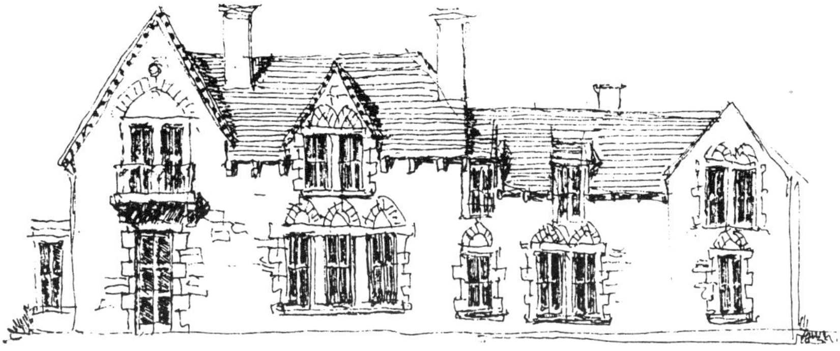

ATHY: **The Rectory**

Built by the Revd Frederick Trench, the owner of a neighbouring estate, Kilmoroney, who died in what was described as a riding accident: he fell out of his carriage in 1860. The rectory is by Deane and Woodward. The asymmetrical pyramidal composition, the façades kept flush, Gothic relieving arches expressed in the stonework above the clustered windows, the French fenestration, the naturalistic ironwork and inside the notched woodwork of the staircase, are all characteristic of Benjamin Woodward, but not the timid brick corbelling at the level of the eaves. The most likely executant architect is J.E. Rogers, Woodward's favourite pulpit, who became the diocesan architect before abandoning his profession to become an itinerant watercolourist.

BALLITORE: **Catholic Church**

Rare attempt by J.J. McCarthy to create a national style by building a rural church in Hiberno-Romanesque, started *c.*1860. Many features comparable to St Patrick's, Kilcullen (q.v.)—heavy arcading, apse subdivided into four, metal strutting from the roof—without the compensatory *élan*. Resulting Germanic grimness unconvincingly relieved by painted medallions of saints in the chancel vault, and more recently central heating and entrance lobbies of Swedish wood.

BALLYMORE EUSTACE: **Barretstown Castle**

Gothic Revival castle built in 1853 incorporating an old tower house for the Revd Sir Erasmus Burrowes. Subsequently altered by McCurdy and Mitchell in the 1880s, and then more drastically by Michael Scott for Elizabeth Arden. Bequeathed by the late Galen Weston to the Irish government who use it for weekend cabinet meetings, but so rarely one can only assume they have not been a success. Recently leased by the Paul Newman Foundation that gives educational holidays to disabled children.

BROADFORD: **Catholic Church**

While J.S. Butler built conventional enough churches in Dublin, here in a rural parish in Co. Kildare he reveals the rarest gift to be found in Irish Victorian churches—wit. The façade expresses the simple layout with a doorway below a gable window and lean-to aisles. The gable window is made up of five lights, the entry is set in an arcade that should also be five bays, were it not for the outer bay being interrupted by projecting buttresses the same height as the aisle. The arches each side of the door frame fonts. Simple, well-proportioned interior, with plaque to Canon Farrell, who started the church in 1862. Sadly Butler ended his Irish career in 1872 with a hurried departure for the mail boat to forestall an unspecified scandal.

CELBRIDGE: **Castletown**

The billiard room contrived by T.N. Deane in the north pavilion (a reduced secular version of St Canice's Cathedral, Kilkenny: q.v.), was destroyed by fire *c.*1970. But what improbably survives is Deane's garden house with its barley sugar columns, although shorn of its adjoining arcades due to the intrusion of a housing estate. A pyramidally roofed octagonal summer house has likewise been spared.

CELBRIDGE: **Catholic Church**

Characteristic example of J.J. McCarthy's Gothic Revival dating from 1857. Central high-pitched nave held in place by steeply-raked aisle roofs, internally visible through arches whose loftiness contrasts with the stubby piers and compressed clerestory. Glass by Hardman and Wailes above the altar. Painted chancel. Original pulpit.

CELBRIDGE: **Church of Ireland**

A suave example of Sir Thomas Drew's scholarly Gothic Revival. Exterior random ashlar with sandstone trim, fenestration spaced widely in the nave, closely in the chancel. Entered through porch added in 1882. Interior made asymmetrical by north aisle added a year later. Chancel embellished with an Arts and Crafts stone and alabaster reredos by M.J.C. Buckley; stone stalls of the 1940s commemorate the Conollys of Castletown, who built the church within their demesne. Appropriate stained glass *c.*1890 behind the altar and in the south wall of the nave, also by Buckley.

CELBRIDGE: **Old Workhouse**
The standard formula of G. Wilkinson's workhouse is discernable if much altered by its conversion into a modern industrial complex.

CLANE: **Clongowes Wood**
The original Jesuit church that conceals its galleried Italianate interior from the outside world by its outward Georgian domesticity no longer satisfied later 19th-century Catholic triumphalism. Hence the construction of another church for the school attached to the castle, ostentatiously Gothic Revival without, collegiate within. George Ashlin was the obvious choice as architect and his designs date from 1907. Altar sculpted in Carrara but Ashlin had died by the time the decoration had been completed: the stations of the cross painted autobiographically by Sean Keating and the memorable stained glass by Michael Healy outshining Mayer in the chancel (1916). Healy's windows were continued by Evie Hone after 1940.

CLANE: **Church of Ireland**
In 1940, a local landlord, Thomas Cooke-Trench, sold his hunters, deprived himself of his holidays in Italy, reduced his staff and halved, with her consent, his wife's allowance, to build a new church away from the village on the highest hill of his estate, dedicated to St

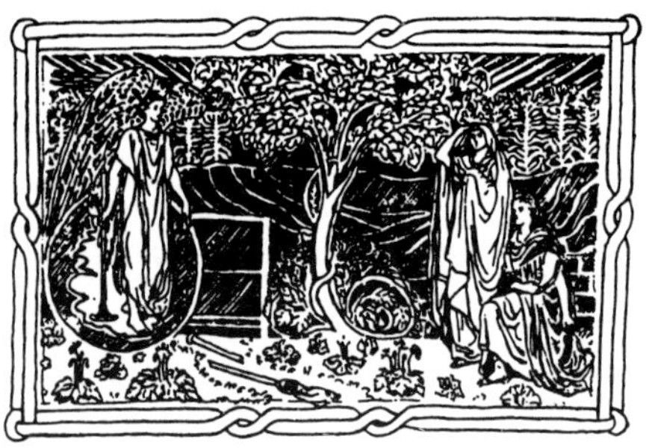

Michael and All Angels. He had been deeply affected by Disestablishment and had devoted the remainder of his life to, as he put it, 'setting up again the pillars that had fallen down'. The church was consecrated in 1883, but the decoration was not completed till 1894, paid for by unsolicited donations. As he wrote: '. . . two main ideas prevail: the first is the glorification of our Lord's Humanity, and the second, the office and ministration of angels'. With such ideas in mind, one can see why he took the precaution, in his original offer to his fellow parishioners, of allowing them to accept or reject, but not to amend. Hence the mass apparition of angels unparalleled in Ireland, disingenuously ascribed by Cooke-Trench to its dedication, a dedication that he had himself devised.

His architect was J.F. Fuller who was evidently inspired by the singlemindness of his client to adapt the Hiberno-Romanesque to the rebirth of the Church of Ireland. His source was Cormac's Chapel, except here there are two chancel arches instead of one, the second arch added in front of the crossing. But the architectural impact is the same—a central constriction that conceals on entry the limits of the chancel. However, the tunnel vault is not of stone but of timber, based on the non-Irish precedent of Romsey Abbey. For the timber fittings he had to improvise, since no prototype survived. Yet his continuous inventiveness, spurred on by Margaret Stokes, resulted in a continuous variation of over a hundred and fifty capitals and corbels. The stained glass is more discreetly Celtic, entirely by Heaton, Butler and Bayne, and very conventional compared to the wall decoration. The cross walls are *cloisonné* by Clement Heaton, whose dramatic archangels flank the western rose window above the recess for the medieval baptismal font. The side walls are incised with sgraffito murals by Heywood Sumner. Mosaic floors in the chancel by Burke; mosaic murals by Powell of Whitefriars. Capello of Venice executed the angels on the spandrels of the eastern arches to the designs of Heaton, Butler and Bayne. Everyone is meticulously credited and their work illustrated in Cooke-Trench's booklet of 1894, which ensured an exemplary restoration half a century later after vandals had set fire to the church and partially destroyed the chancel.

CLOUGHNARINKA: **Catholic Church**
Built in 1894 by Canon Farrell at the same time as Broadford (q.v.), a few miles away and also by J.S. Butler. Door set into massive relieving arches and with unbroken movement tapers upward to remarkable broached spire of local limestone. Completed differently to Butler's original design.

THE CURRAGH
The earliest structure here is the boiler plant and the most prominent is the 1894 water tower, the only structure here of architectural significance. The rest of the complex retains an

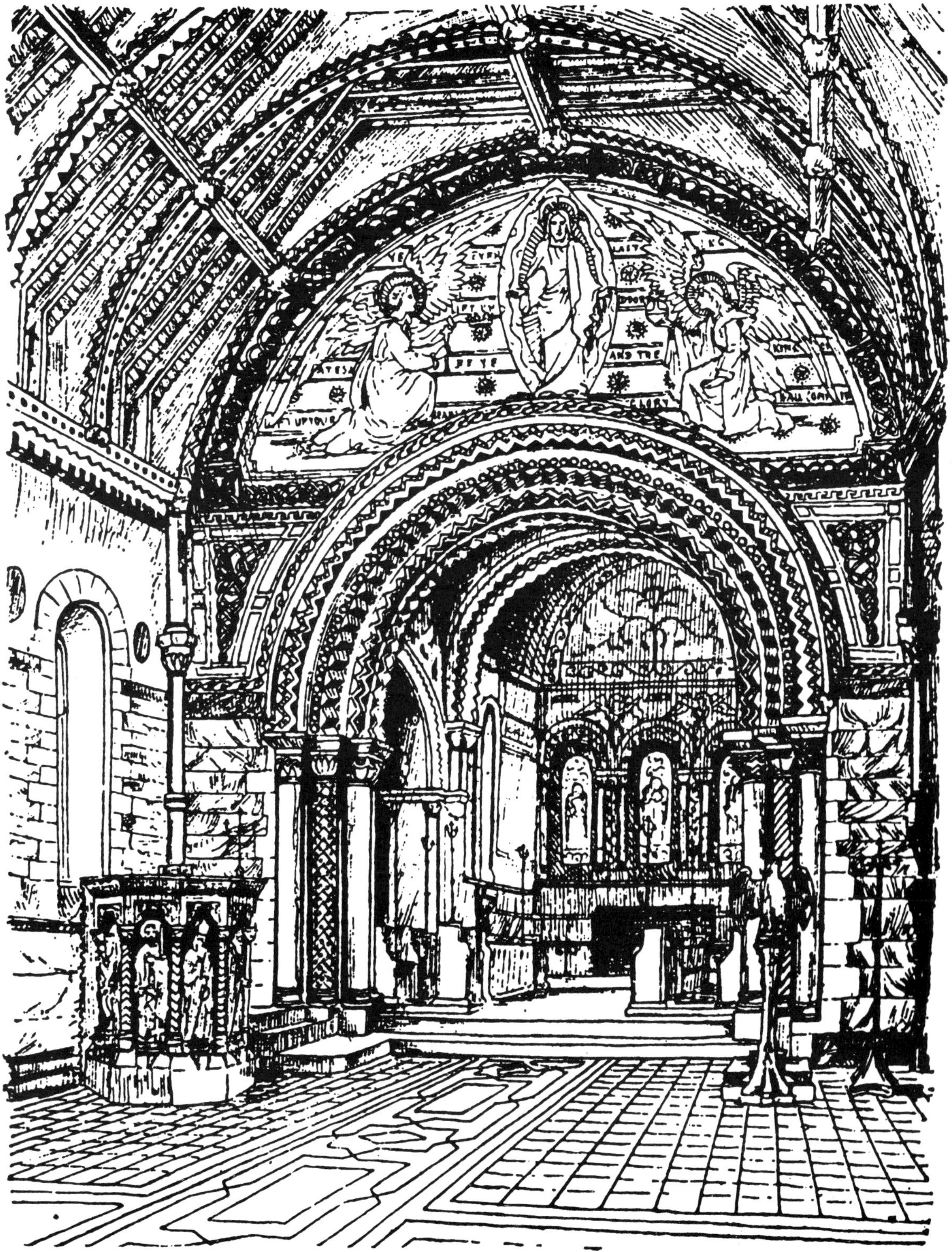

CLANE CHURCH OF IRELAND

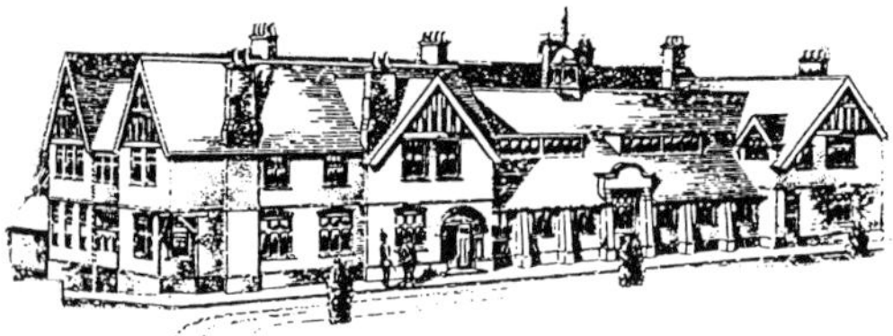

ambiance unaffected by the change of regime, with accommodation strictly reflecting military rank. Designed by the military themselves apart from Miss Sandes' Soldier's Home (Edwin Bradbury, 1912) and the recreation centre (1917) by Frederick Batchelor.

DONADEA: **Knockanelly**
Georgian house rebuilt *c.*1850 and attributed to W.D. Butler: almost a cube if its height is assessed on the three-storied central bay. Single-storied Ionic portico flanked by Venetian windows with a third Venetian window above it between windows that open on to heavy corbelled balconies. These balconies are repeated on the side elevation. The rooms open off a dramatic double-height toplit hall with the staircase confined to a long apsidal recess rising to a cantilevered gallery, a reduced version of the hall in Dublin's Broadstone station (q.v.) by J.S. Mulvany which raises the question of his possible collaboration with Butler on this unusual neo-Classical villa. Now a golf club.

EADESTOWN: **Drinking Fountain**
Small but aggressive wayside fountain erected to designs of J.J. O'Callaghan in 1899 by the grateful tenants of a Capt. Tinkell.

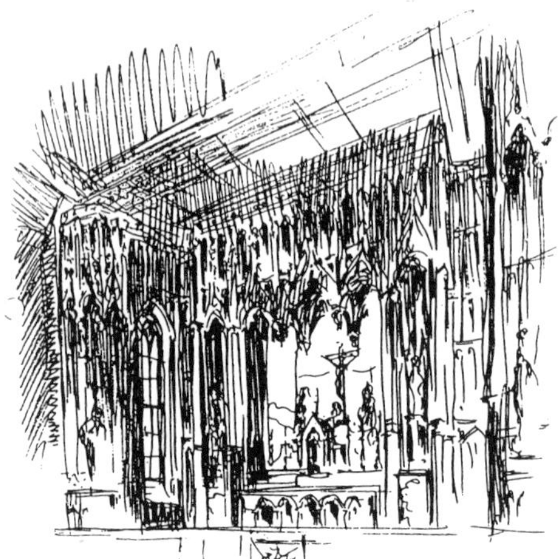

ENFIELD: **Johnstown Bridge Catholic Church**
Early Gothic Revival church set facing a forecourt that is flanked by twin neo-Tudor schoolhouses, now unhappily restored. The interior has also suffered: the reredos is a spectacular triumphal arch that takes up the entire end wall, but this no longer frames a frescoed Crucifixion.

KILCOCK: **Catholic Church**
Designed by J.J. McCarthy and built in 1868 in his Puginian manner—quatrefoil clerestory with steeply raked roofs over the aisles. The vertical uplift of the façade is abruptly cut short by the failure to build the intended spire.

KILCOCK: **Church of Ireland**
Designed in the Hiberno-Romanesque by J.E. Rogers and completed in 1870 with a belfry based on an Irish round tower, complemented by an unIrish chancel apse. Recently sold off as a private house so the stained glass, contemporary with the church and possibly designed by Rogers himself, has been removed.

KILCOCK: **Courtown**
Regency house given new entry front in 1906 by Richard Orpen for J.A. Alymer. New entrance hall and oak staircase given an Edwardian swagger. In the garden, a curvilinear large conservatory in the style of Richard Turner backed against a heated wall.

KILCOCK: **St Joseph's Hall**
Small Gothic Revival village hall with a symmetrical façade but with subtly asymmetrical fenestration. Built in 1860-8 and attributed to J.J. McCarthy.

KILCULLEN: **Baptist Church, Giltown**
A small Gothic Revival church and adjoining manse designed in 1881 by W. Mitchell (beside a bus transformed into a Gothic mobile chapel) are the surviving evidence of a late conversion of John Latouche of Harristown to the Baptist faith under the influence of Charles Spurgeon. He was the father of Rose Latouche, the young girl who died insane after she had rejected Ruskin's marriage proposal. His wife had mistakenly believed that she herself was the object of Ruskin's adoration, unaware that the writer had fallen hopelessly in love with her twelve-year-old daughter. This austere, white interior must have been a refuge for this sporting squire from the fevered aesthetism of his home and a total contrast to the Celtic Revival family church of Carnalway (q.v.).

KILCULLEN: **Catholic Church**
Characteristic Puginian Gothic of J.J. McCarthy designed in 1869 for Canon Langan. The

stained glass of the lady chapel depicts a model of the church with the steeple that was never built. The interior has open timber roof with restless metal struts, supported on arcades of red marble columns with over-sculpted capitals. The chancel apse is challengingly subdivided into four bays, with neo-medieval glass, but at a lower level the impact of this is dissolved by a painted semi-cyclorama of adoring angels.

KILCULLEN: Carnalway Church of Ireland

One of the more appropriately named churches of Ireland, built on the edge of the demesne of Harristown, home of the Latouches.

Originally a Board of First Fruits church, with work by Welland in 1856. J.F. Fuller, in 1889, added a new porch, chancel and an extension to the remodelled nave, all in the elaborate Hiberno-Romanesque manner he had evolved for Clane. He was also rebuilding Harristown after a fire. Stained glass by Harry Clarke commemorates the last Latouche to die in Harristown. Chancel screen pews, reredos and stained glass above the altar by Ninian Comper, *c.*1900.

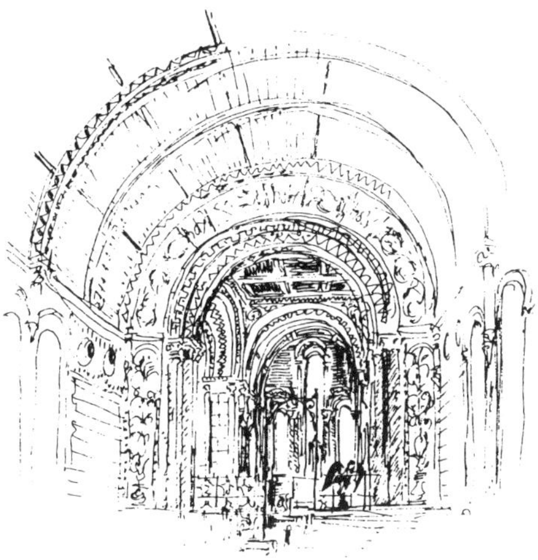

KILCULLEN: Giltown Gatelodge

Scottish Baronial gatelodge with steeped gables, one corbelled from diagonal ground floor projection. Designed *c.*1860 by David Bryce.

KILCULLEN: Harristown House

When the Georgian house was destroyed by fire, J.F. Fuller, who had already remodelled the church of Carnalway for John and Maria Latouche, was chosen by them as their architect for the reconstruction. Fuller's lack of sympathy with the refined Georgian of Whitmore Davis is only apparent in the interiors: chubby columns subdivide the hall and the failure to reinstate the proper cornices gives a cavernous quality to the rooms. His ebullient fireplaces were discreetly replaced by the grandfather of the present owner. But apart from removing the top floor Fuller make little external change. All work was completed by 1893. The Brannocks-

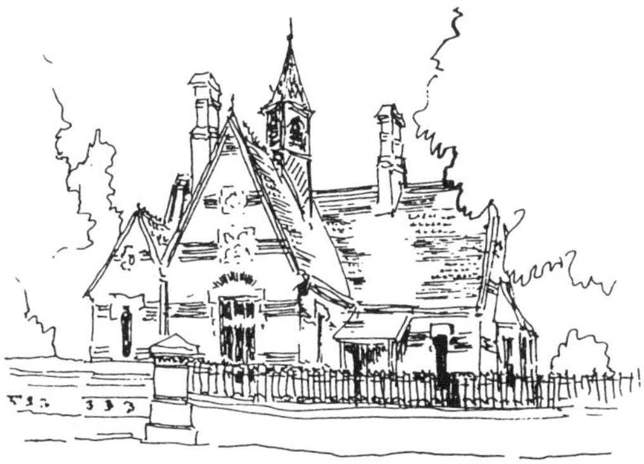

town Lodge (1866) has been erroneously attributed to Ruskin, who had fallen in love with the twelve-year-old Rose Latouche with tragic consequences. She died insane as he was to do himself many years later. In reality the lodge is not even by Ruskin's favourite architect, Benjamin Woodward, but by Woodward's arch-rival, John McCurdy, who never ceased to claim credit for Deane and Woodward's Trinity Museum. The lodge is Ruskinian Gothic but uninspired.

KILCULLEN: Martinstown House

Gothic cottage ornée built originally for the Burrowes family in the 1830s, replacing a love nest of the 3rd duke of Leinster. Attributed by Frederick O'Dwyer to Decimus Burton. Approached by avenues of Irish yews. Entered from the side so that the main façade with its Gothic verandah opens southwards into the garden. Unexpected changes of scale within. Miniature arcaded staircase hall. Spacious double-height drawingroom. Member of Hidden Ireland.

KILDARE: Carmelite Friary Church

Gothic Revival work of William Hague, started in 1884, dominated by a lofty spire. Interior with transepts veiled by arcades in the Irish manner. Recently remodelled to conform with liturgical trends of the 1960s.

KILDARE: Church of Ireland Cathedral

The only Irish cathedral ruin to have been restored; its cost slightly exceeded the original estimate of £5,000 given by George Edmund Street when asked to report on the feasibility of its reconstruction. Street found only the south transept and the rebuilt choir of the 1243 cathedral still intact. His proposals were bitterly rejected by the *Irish Builder* on the grounds that these remnants were not worth retaining and a new cathedral should be built instead—a familiar story in Ireland. Fortunately his scheme was accepted and executed, with variations; the harshly detailed choir was carried out ten years after his death by J.F. Fuller. But in general, his understated approach has been vindicated, even if it has aroused little controversy and less gratitude. He reverted to the original concept in all its simplicity—a cruciform structure with a central fortified tower to which he added a new roof linked to a nave with battlements carried along both sides over relieving arches, an unusual feature repeated as an afterthought round the transepts. That this is a romantic restoration is revealed by the internal dark rubble stone left unplastered. But the resulting gloom increased by the stained glass is counterbalanced by a flood of natural light from the lantern of the central tower. Medieval floor tiles discovered during excavating were copied, and then set in formal compositions as at Christchurch, Dublin (q.v.). The scultural details were all re-used and what was missing re-made. Less successful is the glass, figures of saints against a backdrop of self-conscious Celtic Revival ornament by Heaton, Butler and Bayne. Superb altar fontal by Ninan Comper woven by the Royal Irish School of Art Needlework. The south transept has become a fitting sanctuary for medieval sculpture, including the effigy of Walter de Wellesley, moved here recently at the expense of the duke of Wellington.

KILDARE: **Japanese Gardens**

Commissioned by Col. Hill-Walker later Viscount Wavertree, from Tassa Eida, a Japanese

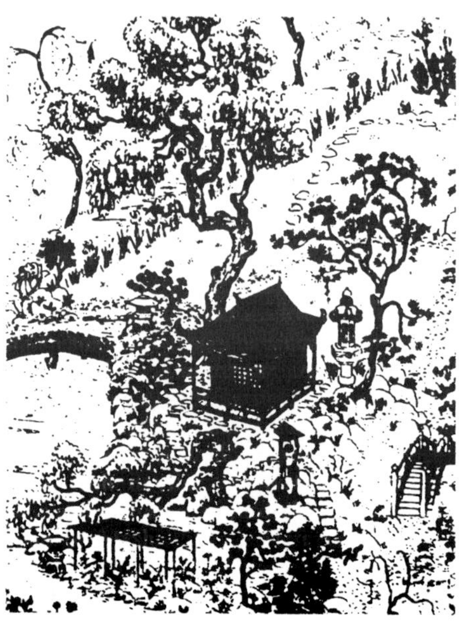

gardener already working in England. Work began in 1906 and a workforce of forty spent four years moving rocks, trees and shrubs creating streams and lakes as a setting for a traditional timber house (fabricated in Japan, symbolizing old age), that has sadly lost its thatch. The imagery throughout this garden is popularized so that it can be instantly accesible to European intelligence following the pilgrimage through life, now repeated by thousands of visitors. Recently the son of the original gardener with an anglicised name turned up as a visitor to rescue his father's reputation from oblivion.

KILDARE: **Kildangan**

Large country house built in 1882-6 to the designs by W.J. Hopkins for D.M.J. More O'Ferrall. Originally in red brick with rectilinear fenestration enlivened by curvilinear gables and dormers. Subsequently Georgianized by the late Roderic More O'Ferrall *c.*1950, who created an important arboretum. At the time that the house was built, the More O'Ferralls were criticized as descendants from Gaelic chieftains in the press, not for pulling down their medieval castle to get building materials, but for employing an English architect, albeit an obscure provincial from Worcester.

KILKEA: **Church of Ireland**

As one of the leading Catholic church architects J.J. McCarthy was an unexpected choice by the 4th duke of Leinster for the little church in the model village at his gates in 1863. McCarthy himself never publicized his appointment, and if the drawings had not survived, there would be no evidence that he was the architect. His church is reserved and sober, with no outward evidence that this is a ducal chapel. Entry gained by Puginian key under western tower to a simple cell with whitewashed walls in contrast to the grey limestone tracery of the windows. Open roof braced with timber Gothic arches. Triple lancet over altar, later filled with stained glass by Child commemorating the FitzGeralds. In contrast to the devastated demesne of the castle, the wooded grounds are well cared for, as is the church, quietly used for services by both denominations.

KILKEA: **Kilkea Castle**

Castle built in 1180 by Hugh de Lacy. Like Malahide, extended by a great hall (1535). Seat of the Wizard earl of Kildare. Neglected by the dukes of Leinster, who preferred Carton, until the restoration by the 3rd duke after a fire in 1849. His architect is unknown but may have been Frederick Darley, engaged at the same time by the 3rd duke on the Church of Ireland and the model schools in nearby Athy. These are also in a somewhat harsh unromantic Gothic as revealed in the new gabled stable courtyard and adjoining farmyard.

An anonymous artist recorded three views of the castle before and three views afterwards, and they show how much of the essential character of a medieval castle is destroyed by even the most sympathetic Victorian restoration. The worst loss was the great hall, rebuilt as a dining room on the lower level with bedrooms above. The defensive fenestration of the original is replaced by regular rows of trefoil-headed windows. The Irish battlements confined to the great hall were extended throughout, not for their ability to repel invaders, but for their romantic silhouette. In the interior, the spiral staircase and the principal rooms are all rebuilt. The formal gardens with their parterres and trellises record the FitzGerald family's obsession with France.

The recent past of Kilkea has not been happy. Sold by the present duke of Leinster in 1960 with 100 acres for £8,000 to make an unsuccessful hotel. Reopened as an uneconomic health farm. Acquired by Mr Tatton and his partner, Mr Shanley, the owners of Coolattin. Sold by them to the present hoteliers in a transaction that did not include a medieval stone table, which was broken during its surreptitious removal and abandoned after the village manned a gate block. The castle has since been refurnished at great expense with silver trophies to Napoleon III.

KILKEA: The Rectory

Having completed the church, McCarthy was asked to design the rectory in 1865. Restrained Victorian, with minimal use of Gothic detail, now a comfortable private house.

KILL: Church of Ireland

Board of First Fruits church with chancel added by William Mitchell, *c.*1880. Stained glass by Heaton, Butler and Bayne. Ascension window by Cox of London. Organ by Telford.

MAYNOOTH: Carton

The 4th duke of Leinster was a great builder and improver, but while he wrote accounts of his restorations at Carton and Kilkea, he does not name his architects. Plans for cottages exist by Edward McAlister and Frederick Trench. The only Victorian embellishment of Carton that is not anonymous is the neo-Baroque organ and wall decoration inserted into the saloon, designed by his brother, Lord Gerald FitzGerald, in 1857 with such conviction that few today realize they are a century later than the Franchini ceiling. On this evidence Lord Gerald

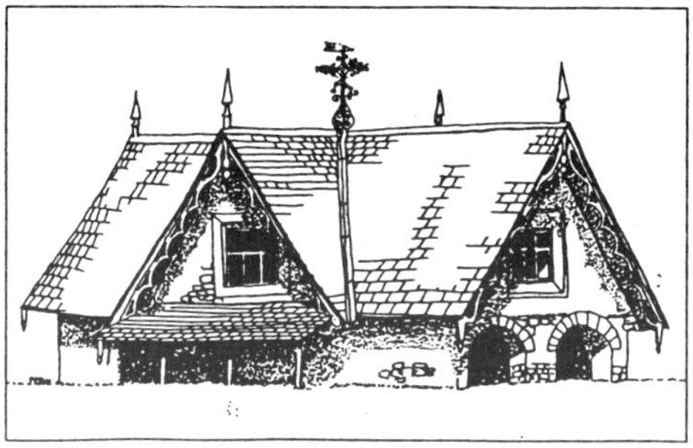

becomes yet another candidate for the design of the picturesque boathouse and the dream cottage ornée built for the visit of Queen Victoria onto the shell house of the duchess Emily. It has incredibly tall chimney-stacks, carved barge boards, and verandahs upheld by cast-iron tree trunks sheltering ceramic seats beneath diamond-paned windows, to view the lake, cascade and Chinese bridge. To discover this retreat at the end of avenue of limes is to risk the imprudence of Hansel and Gretel.

The most mysterious of the Victorian family graveyards is the FitzGerald burial enclosure on a hill to the west of the house. Here are their tombs of utmost simplicity, encircled by trees regaining oneness with nature. Here lies the beautiful duchess Hermione and her mad son the 6th duke, who was hidden in a lunatic asylum in Scotland and buried under the cover of darkness.

MAYNOOTH: Moyglare Church of Ireland

Small Gothic Revival church *c.*1860 by Edward McAlister and enclosed by graves and yews with the rich pastures of Kildare beyond.

MAYNOOTH: St Patrick's College

After Sir Robert Peel's government decided on three 'Godless' colleges, they attempted to placate the Irish Catholics bishops by extending Maynooth. Sir Robert himself selected A.N.W. Pugin whose original scheme came in priced at double the budget; Pugin resigned, but after a bid by W.D. Butler and Jacob Owen of the OPW he was reinstated and told to build two-thirds of his original scheme, without his chapel. Work started in 1847 supervised by Richard Pierce and was completed in 1851, the year of Pugin's breakdown. It was to give the Irish Gothic Revival a new seriousness even if the architecture of his disciples never matched their master's intensity. This can be seen here in the College Chapel as started by J.J. McCarthy in 1875; by adding the chevet he departed from Pugin's more austere design to avoid confrontation with the litigious Edward Welby Pugin. McCarthy also designed the Senior Infirmary, but his scheme for completing Pugin's quad with a great hall was set aside. The present hall of 1895 was the first ugly building to be built by the College authorities. Fortunately it is overshadowed by their last great gesture, proclaiming the triumph of the Irish Catholic Church to the boglands of Kildare, William Hague's tower and spire designed in 1895 and built posthumously (1902-5).

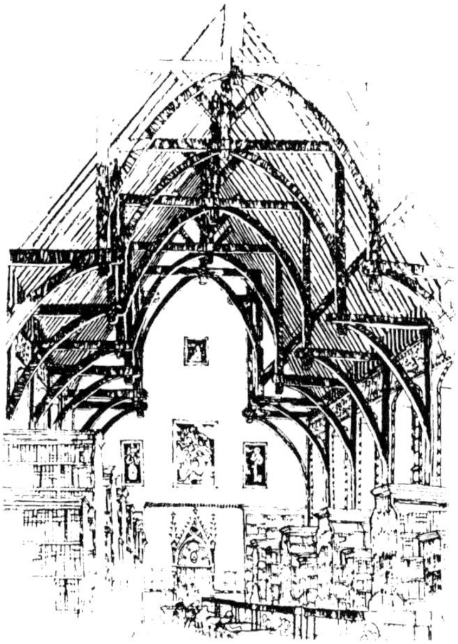

In the interiors there is a striking contrast between the austerity of Pugin's sparing but effective use of ornamentation and the profusiveness of the chapel. Pugin's most intact interior (the library) is built on relieving arches over an undercroft of book storage; it is lightly spanned by the hammer-beam roof with its spandrels springing from the base level of its clerestory and ornamented by a stencilled freize with painted panels at either end. In the recently restored refectory a statue of the Madonna presides over a great hall made loftier again by delicate spandrels and sensational brass chandeliers. This is linked to Pugin's kitchen, once a pyramidal volume braced by a pair of massive chimney-stacks, but now emasculated by suspended ceilings. Pugin's cloisters have also suffered, stripped of a stone floor that should have lasted centuries. This cloister is extended by McCarthy alongside his chapel and provides hanging space for cartoons by Cox and Buckley of Youghal.

To climb a flight of steps from this cloister, and enter the stalls of the Collegiate Chapel is the Irish counterpart of climbing the spiral stairs and emerging in the upper chapel of the Sainte Chapelle. Woodcarving, painting, gilding and stained glass, unmemorable themselves, are anonymously fused to anticipate Paradise. Archbishop Healy's centenary volume of 1895 omits the identification of all the artists who worked under William Hague in the completion of J.J. McCarthy's interior after a limited competition. But the Monan Brothers of Louth carved the 416 stalls. The paintings were executed by Cox and Buckley of Youghal, the stained glass by Mayer, the mosaics by Oppenheimer. Hague's vast white marble altar, insufficient in 1908 and replaced in alabaster by Ashlin, has so far survived liturgical alteration.

MONASTEREVIN: **Cassidy's Distillery**
Large industrial complex once the thriving distillery of the Cassidy family who built Togher House as their private residence. Now due to be reprieved from dereliction and converted into an hotel.

MONASTEREVIN: **Catholic Church**
Designed *c.*1845 by William Deane Butler; his only church façade to have twin towers. They never received their spires, but were built high enough to screen the economy of the design—a continuous nave and choir between lean-to aisles. Sanctuary completed by William Hague (1880); painted ceiling by Robert Mannix; and French stained glass by Lobin of Tours. Western organ gallery approached from vestibules in the towers with a rival Mayer window even more resplendent. Remarkable Italian Baroque communion rails have so far survived liturgical trends of the 1960s.

MONASTEREVIN: **Drogheda Agent's House and Rectory**
These two small suburban villas are the most sensible of the zany and mostly unbuilt designs that enlivened architectural periodicals of the 1880s sent in by William I. Chambers, one of a rare breed, an Irish Queen Anne Revivalist. His attempt to house the head groom of the marquis of Drogheda as an arcadian Chelsea aesthete did not materialize.

MONASTEREVIN: **Togher**
Sedate Italianate villa built for local distillers, the Cassidys, who had donated part of their land for W.D. Butler's Catholic church, so it is possible that he might have also been their architect. Clever use of internal vistas culminating in a drawingroom with glazed doors set between twin bay windows overlooking a sheltered lawn. House and garden being carefully restored.

McCARTHY'S PROPOSAL FOR MAYNOOTH COLLEGE (above); PUGIN'S PROPOSAL (below)

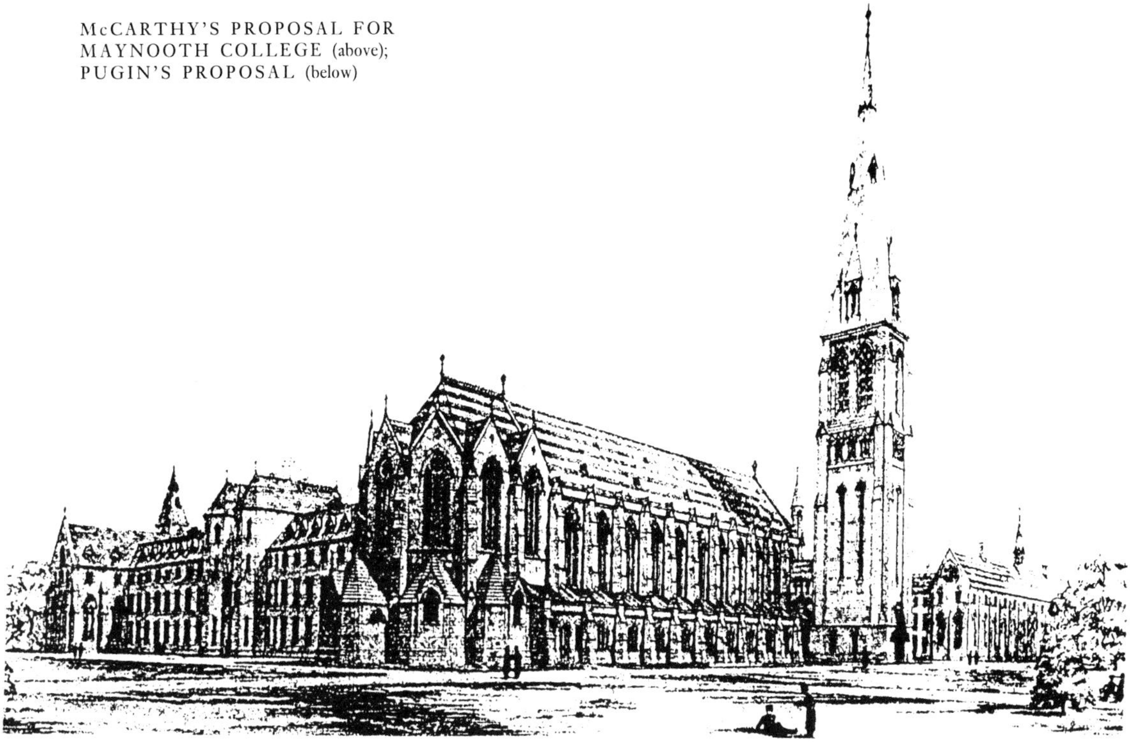

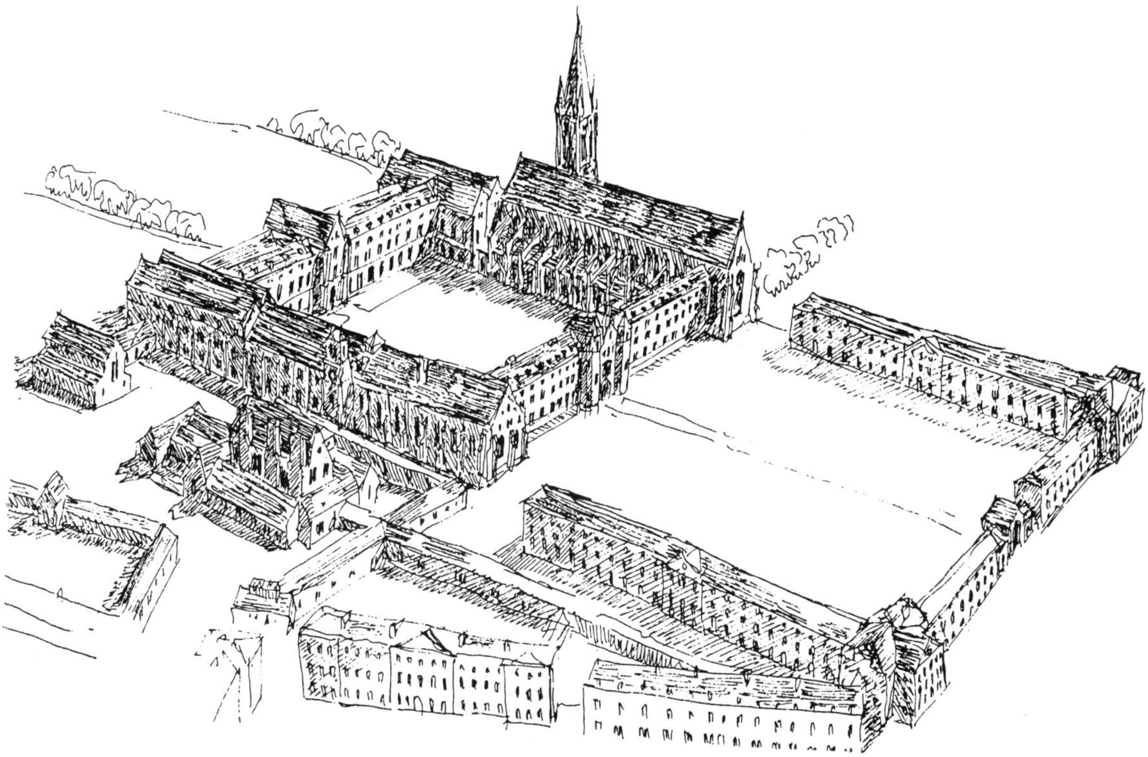

MOYVALLEY: **Balyna**
The ancestral seat of the O'More family, the present house is built on the vaulted basement of its Regency predecessor destroyed by fire in 1878. By then J.S. Butler, whom the More O'Ferralls had employed to build their surrounding churches, had fled disgraced to England, so they turned to another Catholic architect, W.H. Byrne, and everything was completed by 1892. It is Byrne's largest country house; Georgian in concept, but with a Frenchified mansard attic. Its inspiration is T.H. Wyatt's Palmerstown (q.v.). The interior has an impressive staircase with balustrading of decorative ironwork beneath a stained glass window with arcade of red marble on the top floor. Celtic Revival cross in the park and exquisite Turneresque conservatory unexpectedly attached to neo-Classical chapel in the garden (now removed to Drogheda: see Belchebourne). Acquired by Bewleys Ltd *c.* 1960. Sold on to the current owners, who have been responsible for the spectacular restoration at the last moment.

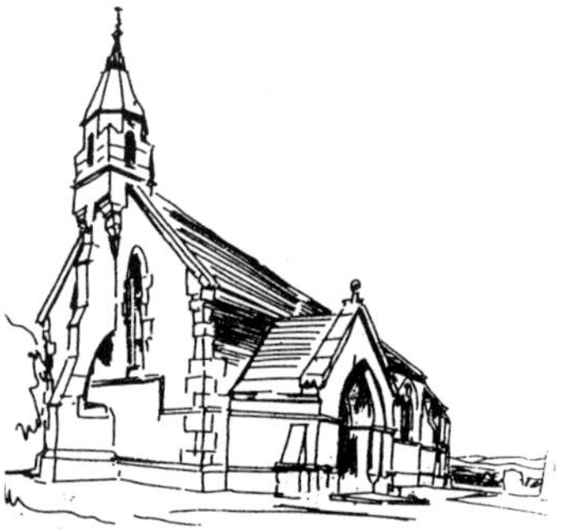

NARRAGHMORE: **Church of Ireland**
A tiny church approached through fields of rich farmland that suddenly fall away to reveal a valley and the distant Wicklow mountains. Porch counterbalancing vestry. Western bellcote precariously balanced on single buttress. Built in 1862 by the London architect R.J. Withers.

NAAS: **Allied Irish Bank**
Comfortable neo-Tudor in brick and stone; previously the Munster and Leinster Bank. Designed by T.M. Deane in 1875.

NAAS: **Catholic Church**
Triple-aisled, divided by clustered columns, tentatively attributed to Thomas Cobden. The plaster was never replaced (so exposing the timber roof structure); then a rustic, double-tiered organ gallery was inserted at the west end. J.J. McCarthy was called in 1875 to add the majestic tower and spire. Polychromatic tomb to Father Doyle (1867). A successor, Father Morrin, embellished the interior with lavish marble fittings and a complete set of stained glass windows, including Lobin and Mayer. These were installed over a period of 30 years and gave the semblance of unity in a dim religious light. This was dispelled in the 1984 restoration by Hurley and Hogan, who were prevented by local feeling from carrying out a more radical transformation. Instead, skylights were inserted into the roof ruthlessly to expose all the inconsistencies of the interior. The only compensation for the loss of the original furnishings is the elegant tabernacle by Benedict Tutty. A fascist mortuary chapel, *c.* 1950, was too sinister to be disturbed.

NAAS: **Church of Ireland**
Ruined medieval tower dramatically adapted to make a roofless narthex with a decorative cast-iron spiral staircase. Anticlimatic interior—by Welland and then Drew at their blandest *c.* 1860. Glass by Heaton, Butler and Bayne.

NAAS: **Gowran Grange**
Substantial Gothic Revival manor house built in two phases, 1857 and 1872, for the 4th Baron de Robeck by John McCurdy with the collaboration of W.H. Lynn, who was called in to improve the Gothic detailing of the interior. Monumental oak chimney-piece in the hall.

NAAS: **Killashee**
'Unless the Lord buildeth this house, the labour is vain': this inscription is more appropriate to the preparatory school that Killashee has now become than to a private residence. The seat of the Moores, large, serious and uninspired; one can imagine a later generation afflicted by staff troubles, disposing of it without regret. Built in 1860, by Lanyon and Lynn, but strongly resembling the work of Thomas Turner as pointed out by Bence-Jones. So, as Turner worked in the Lanyon's office he could well have been the architect. Certainly what strikes the lightest note, the corner tower with an arched belvedere beneath a curvilinear copper turret, is repeated in two of Turner's contemporary houses, Kintullagh (q.v.) and Knocknamoe.

NAAS: **Palmerstown House**
Earlier house reconstructed by public subscription for the son of the 6th earl of Mayo, Viceroy of India until his assassination during his state visit to the Andaman Islands in 1872. The style was a sensible and even enlightened 'Queen Anne', a new departure for the elderly architect, T.H. Wyatt. Symmetrical façades, porch of coupled columns and a dormered mansard roof which was not replaced when the

house was reconstructed after its destruction by the IRA in 1923.

NAAS: **Roseboro**
Regency house extended for Lady Aelfrida Bourke by Richard Orpen in 1906. Large living hall added to look south over the compartmental garden made at the same time by her cousin Norah Lindsay, now also viewed from the access ramp to the dual carriageway.

NEWBRIDGE: **Sundai International College**
Formerly Curragh Chase. Luxurious, Queen Anne style red-brick and pebble-dashed country house with adjoining half timbered stud farm—what one would expect to see beside Newmarket rather than the Curragh. Previously owned by the McGrath family. Built in 1904 by Richard Orpen. Bifurcating staircase. Neo-Adamesque reception rooms. Comparable Ballymany nearby that Orpen designed for the duke of Westminster is now owned by the Aga Khan.

STRAFFAN: **The Barracks**
Picturesque asymmetrical composition. Polygonal bays sculpted with pistolets designed to repel the Fenians still supervise the street.

STRAFFAN: **Church of Ireland**
Family church of the Bartons built in 1833 by an unrecorded architect but furnished, embellished and now preserved so that the general impression of the interior today is High Victorian. The most interesting stained glass are the three by Child on the south side of the nave which strike a balance between the etiolated Edwardian windows opposite them and the ebullience of the High Victorian floral windows (designed by the Mrs Barton of the time to depict her garden produce) lighting the transept. An assertive window by O'Brien (1948) contrasts with the delicacy of the Gothic Revival woodwork (1903). Encaustic tiled floor. Finely carved pulpit (1875), designed by McCurdy and Mitchell. Organ by Telford.

STRAFFAN: **Straffan House**
The Late Regency house built by the Bartons from the profits of their Bordeaux vineyards to the designs of Frederick Darley was transformed into a French chateau twenty years later by adding an attic in a mansard roof, that meant raising and embellishing the stacks in the French manner. At the same time a water tower was added to the service wing with a double-tiered open belvedere topped by a gilded vane. This has been attributed to Sir Charles Lanyon on the basis of a Lanyonesque gatelodge to the gates beside the Liffey and a drawing of a conservatory designed by Lanyon but never built. The formal parterre was laid out by the alcoholic James Howe in 1863, originally in brick and stone, to link the house to the river. Here two suspension bridges, one by Courtney and Stephens, the other by Baily and Ross in contrasting styles, lead to a wooded island with traces of an ambitious Robinsonian garden planted in 1893 as a reaction to the formality of the previous generation. After many vicissitudes, partial demolition, reconstruction and now duplication, the house has become a luxury hotel and country club hopefully reviving the opulence of its heyday.

TAGHADOE: **Catholic Church**
Austere Gothic Revival church designed by J.J. McCarthy in 1859-63. Asymmetrical steeple set flush with west façade. Altar carved by Purdy.

TIMAHOE: **Coolcarrigan**
The most perfect example of the Celtic Revival in Ireland is the private church in the park immortalizing a student friendship between the son of the house, who died young, and the Gaelic Revivalist Douglas Hyde, first president of Ireland. The architect's identity remains problematical. Although the church is mentioned in the Church of Ireland *Gazette* of 1884, no one is credited with its design. However, the obituary of Sir Thomas Drew in 1910 mentions additions to Coolcarrigan. Like the Wilsons, Drew came from Ulster, but in this most Irish of church complexes with its round tower, high cross and pre-existing motte, there are some

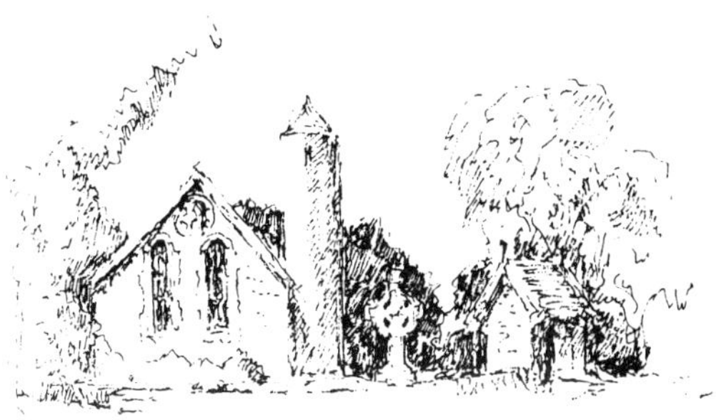

very English features: the lych gate and red-tiled roof would not be inappropriate in Sussex but were proposed by Drew for his unexecuted church in Crumlin, Co. Antim. The tiny, perfectly proportioned interior is frescoed by Douglas Hyde himself with Latin inscriptions in Celtic script. The stained glass is a more literal transcription of Irish manuscripts. Commissioned from Catherine O'Brien, the earliest window is 1911, the last 1927. Impeccably maintained by the Wilson-Wrights ever since. Open by appointment.

KILKENNY

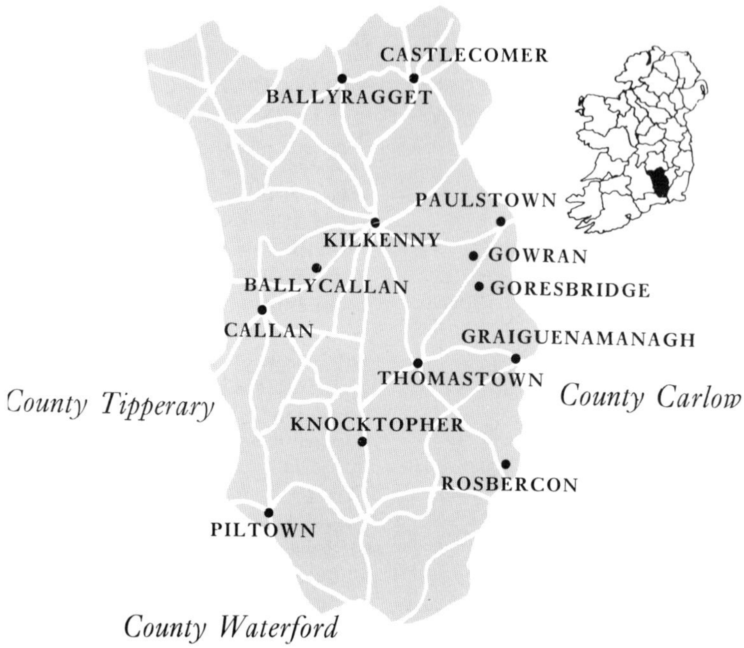

BALLYCALLAN: **Catholic Church**
Large cruciform rural church in 1840s Gothic, school of Thomas Cobden; façade articulated by pinnacles. Interior decoratively painted *c.*1870. To have been replaced by a new church, but reprieved due to the protests of its parishioners.

BALLYRAGGET: **Catholic Church**
One of the many W.D. Butler churches built in the diocese of Ossory. Each church has its own individuality. Ballyragget is distinguished by severe stone arcades dividing the nave from the aisles and curiously contrasting with the frivolity of the Gothick plaster vaults. Seven bays leading to short square-ended chancel. Fine mid-Victorian high and side altars. Gothick memorial to the builder (Revd Foran), who died a year after the date inscribed on the façade—1842.

BALLYRAGGET: **Jenkinstown Castle**
Of the pasteboard Gothic castle built by William Robertson for the Bellews *c.*1820, only the chapel survives with its pretty chancel window of painted glass, although it is now disused since its inexplicable replacement by a modern church nearby. The castle it was attached to had already started to give trouble in the 1830s; the far end of it was rebuilt more substantially by Charles Frederick Anderson *c.*1840 with mullioned windows and corbelled bartizans. He evidently intended to rebuild the centre block, since this was pulled down, but only a makeshift passage was ever erected to link Lord Bellew to his servants in the other wing. This also collapsed and today only Anderson's outer walls survive as part of the stable, now the centre of a forest park. Possibly the castle that collapsed and led to Anderson's emigration to the United States as remembered by the wife of the Revd Nicholas Mandeville who had to keep up Castle Anner (q.v.).

CALLAN: **Bank of Ireland**
Small but impressive Italianate palazzo with an almost symmetrical façade. Such grandeur is rarely achieved without sacrifice, here at the expense of the sleeping accommodation of the manager (in the roof), and of the banking hall itself (banished to a side pavilion).

CALLAN: **Catholic Church**
Built 1836-43. Attributed to J.B. Keane simply on the basis of its sophisticated neo-Classicism, with the dangerous combination of portico and steeple for once successful. The portico is held firmly *in antis* and one feels that it is able to take the full weight of the tower. There is a pediment, but not as expected above the portico; instead at the upper level of the tower rising up to the base of the spire-cum-obelisk. Rarely have the pagan inventions of the Greeks been

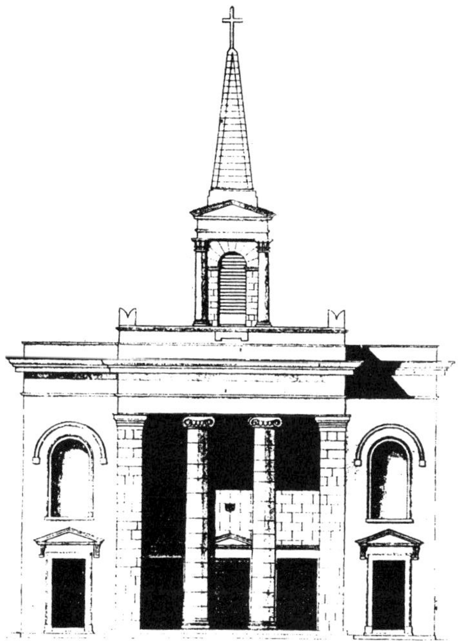

christianized with such concision. The church, entered through a vestibule beneath the tower, has a galleried interior with good plasterwork not improved by the insertion of stained glass in the style of Mayer. Architectural reredos. Altars date from 1925.

CALLAN: **Old Workhouse**
Standard design by George Wilkinson, one of the hundred and sixty that he built for the Poor Law Commission. Like so many, partly mutilated by posterity and partly preserved by neglect.

CASTLECOMER: **Catholic Church**
Designed by William Deane Butler, whose drawings have survived (dated 1836-43). Impressive double-tiered façade with corner turrets enclosing access to the organ gallery. The interior is one vast, simple space with a plaster vaulted richly painted ceiling. The artist here, and builder, was George Hetherington, succeeded *c.*1836-43 by his son Edward (information from the latter's grandson). Chandeliers of the same period, as also the fittings and the stained glass.

CASTLECOMER: **Housing, Kilkenny Road**
Two contrasting group of employees' housing commissioned by the Wandesford family, who developed the mines. They embody the differing aims of Victorian and Edwardian philanthropy. The earlier is a row of terraced cottages with lofty chimneys articulating their separateness. Built out of a local bright-red brick that distinguishes them from the remainder of the village. The Edwardian housing (possibly by William Scott) is integrated into its surroundings, built round three sides of small courts open to the street with the individual units impossible to identify.

GORESBRIDGE: **Mount Loftus**
The Georgian house was demolished *c.*1906 by Major J.E.B. Loftus to please his wife and was replaced by a large rambling sub-Italianate structure designed by an obscure local architect called Morrisey. Alterations planned in 1917 by Douglas Lyons were never executed, so the destruction of most of it by fire in 1934 was not an architectural disaster. The two surviving wings still give accommodation and they are now linked by a new front hall made out of the service archway, screened by the original porch repositioned for a second time and opening through a conservatory into the garden.

GOWRAN: **Blanchville**
Tower built in a naive blend of Classical and Gothic and Classical modelled on Wren's St Mary's, Aldermanbury, by Capt. James Kearney in 1834 to house his collection of clocks and bells. The clocks have disappeared; the bells, having woken up his complaining neighbours at all hours of the night, have been (since 1930) respectably contained in the tower of the Augustinian Church in Limerick, so no longer disturb his sedate neo-Classical residence, now a comfortable guesthouse. Member of Hidden Ireland.

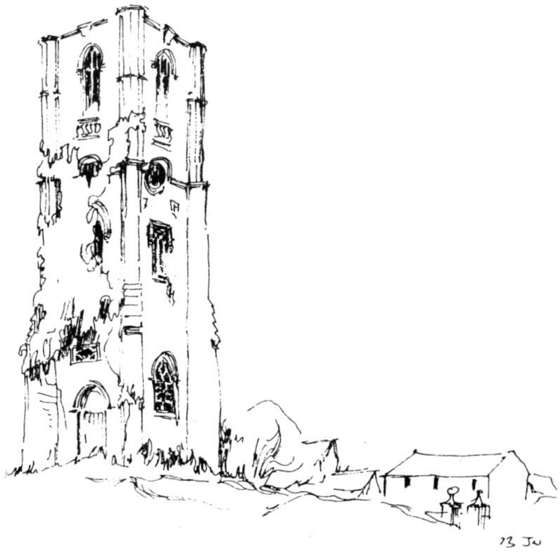

GOWRAN: **Church of Ireland**
The ruined medieval nave served as a forecourt to the church in First Fruits Gothic, which in 1871 was deemed unworthy of its setting and T.H. Wyatt was commissioned to reconstruct the original chancel, which he did with his usual

thoroughness and with a harshness that time and now disuse have refused to mellow, leaving its current owners (the Board of Works) undecided whether to restore it or pull it down and start again. Tragically its interior was once far more rewarding than external appearances would suggest due to the splendour of its earlier furnishings (which Wyatt carefully retained, from the medieval font to the Palladian Kearney tombs). These were complemented by the stained glass including an exquisitely decadent early McGoldrick: all now lost, sacrificed to the pursuit of a chimaerical authenticity.

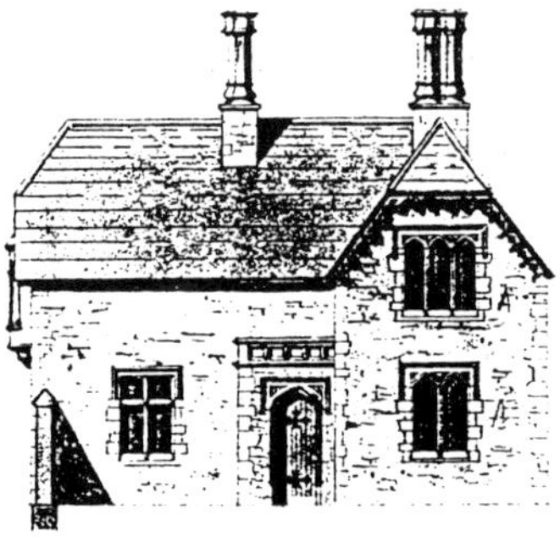

GOWRAN: **Forester's Lodge**
Set into the wall of the demesne that has been preserved as the racecourse. Designed by W.G. Murray for Lord Annally in 1855 with an upper window corbelled out over the road. Murray's dourish Gothic is also detectable in the gate lodge in the village. He may well be responsible for the more rustic, and more charming, housing along the main street.

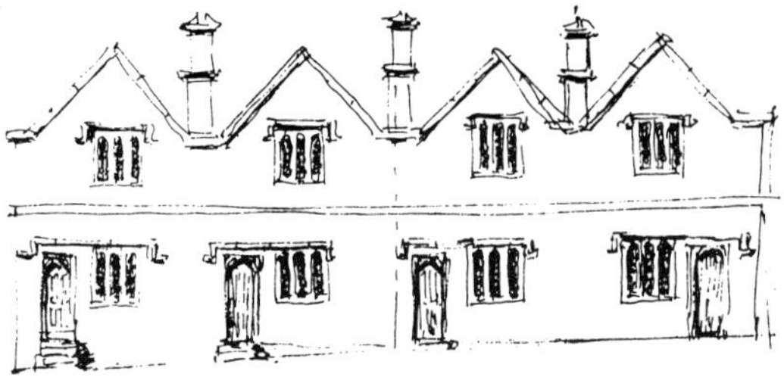

GRAIGUENAMANAGH: **Widows' Houses**
Built to overlook the abbey church by the estate architect of Lord Annally *c.*1840. Delightful group of four in the Tudor style with a hood moulding over the door of each extended to enclose the adjoining window. Chimney-stacks flush with the façade separate the gables of each upper floor.

KILKENNY: **Aut Even**
Designed by William Scott for Ellen, dowager countess of Desart, née Bisscofheim, and completed in 1907, when she made a triumphal procession through Kilkenny from the home of her brother-in-law, Otway Cuffe; as reported in a local newspaper, 'she entered into possession of her picturesque bijou residence'. All the furniture except the grandfather clock had been provided by the Kilkenny Woodworkers, the industry founded by her brother-in-law and housed in the model village of Talbot's Inch (q.v.) at her gates. Entry front with long, low façade broken asymmetrically by chimney-stacks, two more being added to the original design. Many windowed garden front, ending

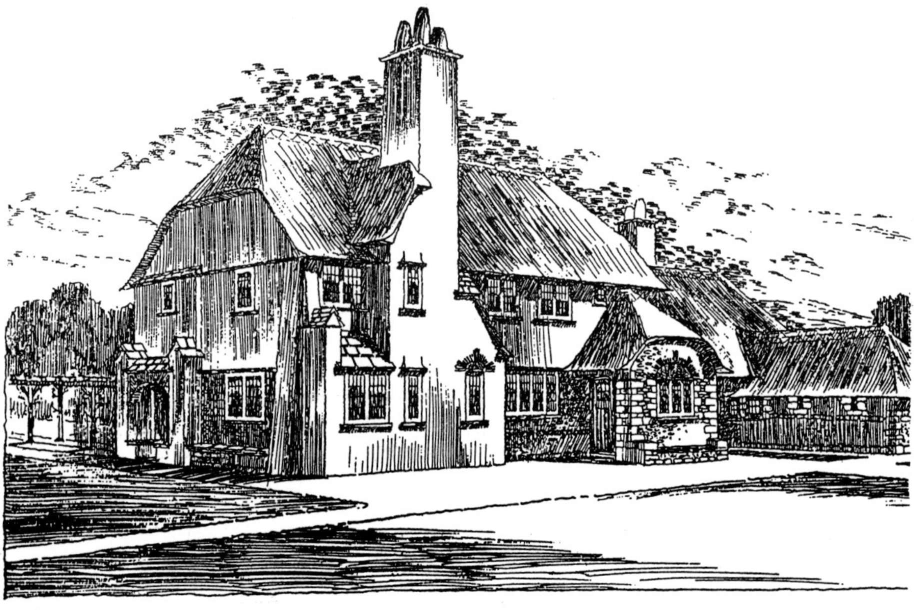

in half-timbered cottage ornée. All windows have leaded lights and medallions of stained glass. Serpentine ironmongery. Panelled Arts and Crafts interior mainly one room deep to allow natural lighting from both sides. Carefully maintained today as Scott's most distinguished private house.

KILKENNY: Aut Even Hospital

The most enduring of the philantrophic enterprises of Ellen, dowager countess of Desart, even if its very success has led to her original building being quite overshadowed by modern additions. This is not too disastrous, since her architect was Albert Murray, working in a conventional Edwardian idiom *c.* 1908. Why the job did not go to the architect of her own house, William Scott, is unrecorded. Perhaps Lady Desart had enough of what William Yeats called his 'drunken genius'.

KILKENNY: Avonmore Creameries, Patrick Street

Designed as the Hibernian Bank by J.S. Butler in 1865. A 17th-century-style façade with a centrepiece two bays wide flanked by a pilastered bay on either side.

KILKENNY: Bank of Ireland

Three-storied limestone Italianate palazzo. Symmetrical façade of seven bays shoe-horned into a corner site by curving each bay at either end: this involved introducing curved plate glass into the fenestration. Designed by Sandham Symes in 1870.

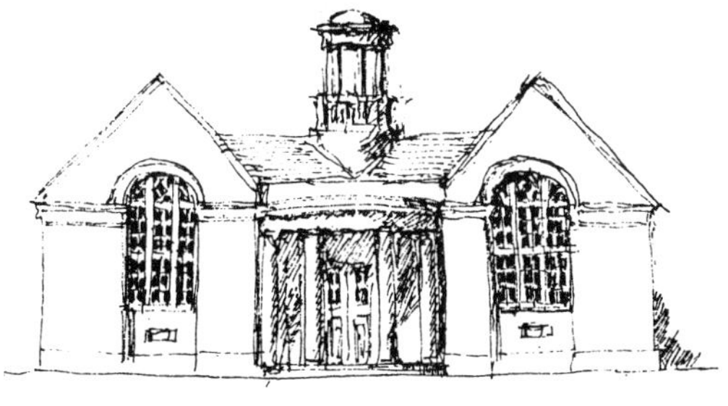

KILKENNY: Carnegie Library

Partly neo-Georgian, partly Arts and Crafts with a trim symmetrical façade facing the river, an hexagonal portico nestling between two gabled returns. Airy interior subdivided by columns with coved ceilings broken into by half-exposed trusses. A real Arts and Crafts building such as William Scott might have designed would have fused the classical and the medieval traditions; here they are juxtaposed by an obscure Dublin architect, E. Stewart-Lowrey in 1910. The fittings were commissioned by Lady Desart, who gave the site to the Kilkenny Woodworkers, the firm started by her brother-in-law, Otway Cuffe; these have now been replaced, but what survives is preserved next door in the headquarters.

KILKENNY: The Castle

In 1797 a young London architect, William Robertson, exhibited a drawing: 'Kilkenny Castle, seat of the Earl of Ormonde'. In 1812, two years after the Butlers had received £216,000 compensation on giving up their right to tax all wine imported into Ireland, Robertson (by now settled in Kilkenny) wrote of the castle: 'This extensive pile of building is much injured by the injudicious mixture of styles.' In 1825, while walking round the courtyard with the wife of the 1st marquis, he noted that the main wall was out of plumb. This was followed by his ruthless rebuilding that after fifteen years left only the outer walls intact. This was a serious loss to Irish architecture. The only gain was an external consistency of castellated Baronial, and a different external consistency of a diluted Louis XV, that has now disappeared after the Board of Works gutted the interior in the 1970s when it came to their turn to get rid of the residual dry rot. Its two most distinguished rooms had their Chinese wallpaper half torn off by the participants of a CIE ghost tour in the 1960s.

Certainly an outbreak of dry rot (occasioned by Robertson's reliance on barely sloping lead), is the most likely explanation for Deane and Woodward reroofing the entire castle for the widow of the 2nd marquis in 1858-62. Their architectural remodelling, apart from the questionable Venetian apertures to the north front, was confined to the eastern range. Here they transformed Roberston's picture gallery and adjoining stairs. Drawings by Woodward survive of a more radical transformation into a fairytale chateau. But a more conservative scheme was carried out, blocking out Robertson's east windows to gain extra wall space, now toplit from a partly glazed hammerbeam roof. The remaining windows were transformed into oriels and the triple lancet was made at the far end from the entrance to overlook the park. That this is not unquestionably the finest High Victorian interior in Ireland is due firstly to the technical deficiencies of Hungerford Pollen who was chosen by Woodward to paint the open roof with strange birds, beasts and goddesses—a brilliant idea but unevenly executed, and now faded. Pollen also designed the double fireplace with its seven dynastic episodes drily carved for him by Charles Harrison, so different from the lively animals carved by Harrison on his own in the adjoining arcaded stairs. These enclose a

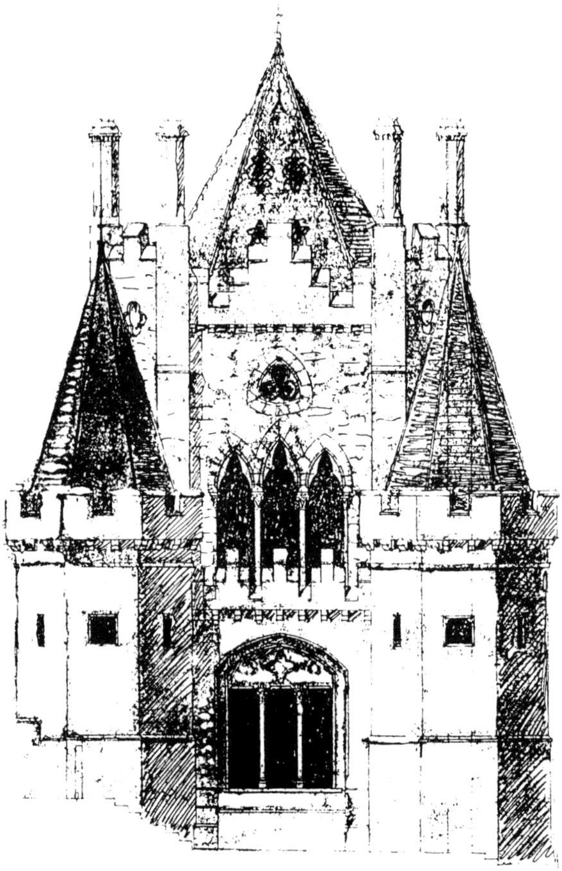

fernery sensibly not replaced. But the second and more serious problem is the persistent refusal of Board of Works to return the room to its High Victorian splendour by restoring its plethora of contents, and repainting the walls their original magenta. To experience today what it must once have been, one has to travel across the Irish Sea to the restored City Art Gallery in Manchester.

KILKENNY: Catholic Cathedral

Designed by William Deane Butler and dedicated to St Mary, it overshadows its more venerable Church of Ireland counterpart in every prospect of the city. While both cathedrals are cruciform with naves of five bays, aisleless transepts and towers above their crossings, the tower of St Mary's is carried up a further floor into a triumphant lantern articulated by spiky pinnacles. Early critics mischievously stressed its English origins. In fact, as proved by the apsidal chancel, its inspiration is more Norman than English, as befits a Butler city. Today the cathedral gives the impression of a structure that sprung into instant being. However, work started in 1843 under Bishop Kinsella and its completion under Bishop Walsh in 1857 coincided with the death of the architect. The decoration of the interior was given to the firm of Earley and Powell and not completed until 1865. That firm were responsible for most of the stained glass and painted decoration, most notably in the ceiling of the chancel apse (inspired by St Finbarre's, Cork: q.v.), and the liturgical fittings, including the elegant lights. Murals in the chancel by Westlake; mosaic flooring by Bourke of London. The presbytery dates from 1864. The chapter house (1899) is by William Hague, completed after his death by W.H. Byrne.

All this created a High Victorian ensemble that remained remarkably intact until *c.*1975 when the late Bishop Birch instigated a campaign to conform to the liturgical fashions of the 1960s. While many of his churches suffered horribly, his cathedral escaped comparatively lightly. This was partly due to retaining so many fittings and also due to the sensitivity of the sculptor chosen to design the new central altar, Edward Delaney, whose animalism struck a note in sympathy with the Early Gothic aims of the design. The cathedral is Butler's master work; he had already built so many churches in the diocese, all distinctive, and expressing a sense of freedom after Catholic Emancipation, particularly noticeable here at the crossing with the upper gallery lit by quatrefoils of stained glass.

KILKENNY: Church of Ireland Cathedral

Sir Thomas Newenham Deane was an obvious choice as the restorer in 1863 as he had been working on his designs for Tuam Cathedral (q.v.) since 1861, had been engaged on the restoration of Kilkenny Castle since 1858, and had been put in charge of the National Monuments due in some measure to Benjamin Woodward's superb survey of Holy Cross, which, twenty years after his partner's death, he claimed that he had done himself. Nevertheless the initial enthusiasm of the chapter at the start of the work soon evaporated, and in 1870 Deane resigned having far exceeded the budget. The programme was completed by a local architect, Richard Langrishe. As Drew later wrote, 'In 1860 the Irish clergy and insular archaeologists following by some years the English example, had but arrived at the study of Rickman and Parker's Glossary. . . . The pedantry of this land was not congenital to the original genius of Deane.' In general Deane's treatment of the medieval stonework was exemplary, but he did take several liberties, the 'Irish' crenellation of the walls of the aisles and the 'non-Irish' sculpted hammer-beam roof that replaced the Georgian plaster ceiling. However, bearing in mind that the decisions had already been taken to throw out Bishop Pococke's Gothick fittings, expose the internal stonework and widen the vista between the nave and choir, inserting contemporary stained glass throughout, all these standard if dubious procedures of the period would have taken place in any case, so we should be grateful for Deane's improvisatory powers; his roof certainly contributes much to the dim solemnity of the interior.

The trusses, each with a dragon's head, were carved by Charles Harrison, who was also responsible for the pulpit. The tomb of the 1st marquis of Ormonde is by T. Denham (1838). The finest Victorian sculptures are the recumbent effigies of the 2nd marquis and his wife (1854) by Edward Richardson. Choir stalls by M.J.C. Buckley. The altar in the chancel was redesigned in 1922 by Sir Reginald Bloomfield, and sculpted by Gabriel Leward. While the best glass in the cathedral is post-Victorian, the Connellan window by Purser and Rhind (1918) and the Loftus window by A.E. Child (1931), both on the south side, the earlier glass has received less than due recognition. West window over door by Holland and Holt (1873). Later glass by Mayer.

The most interesting window is at the west end of the north aisle, the Bainbridge window of 1877, designed by William Burgess and made by Saunders and Londsdale. The most tragic window is the Woodward memorial put by Deane into the north choir aisle with the date of death incorrect.

KILKENNY: **The Hospital**
Built in a competent neo-Elizabethan idiom, well orientated to get the sun and views of the River Nore. Designed originally as the lunatic asylum in 184_ by George Papworth. Later extensions include two hip-roofed water towers that give the feeling of a far-flung chateau, probably by Drew who with Langrishe added the Catholic chapel in 1893.

KILKENNY: **Kilcrene**
Earlier house remodelled and extended by Charles Geoghegan in 1865 for the Smithwick family, and barely altered since, so that there are few parallels to its sumptuous drawingroom with its generously curving bow window festooned with faded chintz built out to overlook an ornamental canal, and opening into the garden through a conservatory. Billiards and smoking separately housed at the rear.

KILKENNY: **Kilkenny Theatre**
Founded by Lady Desart and her brother-in-law, Otway Cuffe, at No. 26 Patrick Street; finally closed in 1962. However, the theatre remains substantially intact with its stage and proscenium arch behind Wray's Lighting Emporium. Beside the theatre opening on to New Street, Lady Desart built the Desart Hall for community use, a lively Flemish gable masking its triangular steel roof. Subsequently acquired by the Catholic diocese of Ossory.

KILKENNY: **Lyrath**
The most important surviving country house of John McCurdy, built by Sir Charles Wheeler-Cuffe to appease his prospective father-in-law, Lord Stuart de Decies, who permitted his daughter's marriage if the house was made grand enough. The reconstruction sent Sir Charles into debt in which he ultimately died. His wife never recovered from an earlier love affair with a Scottish railway engineer who had committed suicide.

Only now have McCurdy's interiors mellowed into perpetual serenity. Architecturally there are moments of over-reaching and of compromise. The immense hall contains an imperial staircase of startling steepness that rises perilously close to the cornice upheld by attenuated Corinthian columns, so steep that Lady Wheeler-Cuffe, who had traversed Burma as a watercolourist on horseback, had to cut the back legs off a chair and fix it on to the stairs as a resting point half way up. The upper flights are asymmetrical, linking the earlier Georgian house to a detached military barracks, both now make up wings at the rear. To the north a study, and to the south a sequence of three reception rooms overlooking the garden. All rooms preserve their wallpaper, white and gold in the drawingroom and anteroom, magenta and gold in the diningroom. Both drawingroom and diningroom project with arched windows set into curved bays to overlook the formal gardens with their now grassed-over parterres designed by W.E. Nesfield. Sold in 1993.

KILKENNY: **Model Farm Institute**
Tudor style institution built in the open country to the south of the city. Architect unknown.

KILKENNY: **Newpark**
Originally a geometrical Gothic villa *c.* 1830. Remodelled and extended by a billiard-room wing in 1901; architects, Carroll and Batchelor. Now engulfed in a modern hotel.

KILKENNY: **O'Connell's Pharmacy**
Good Victorian shopfront with brass aprons wrapped round the semi-columns holding up well-painted signboards.

KILKENNY: **Ormonde Almshouses**
Conventional E-shaped neo-Tudor façade with

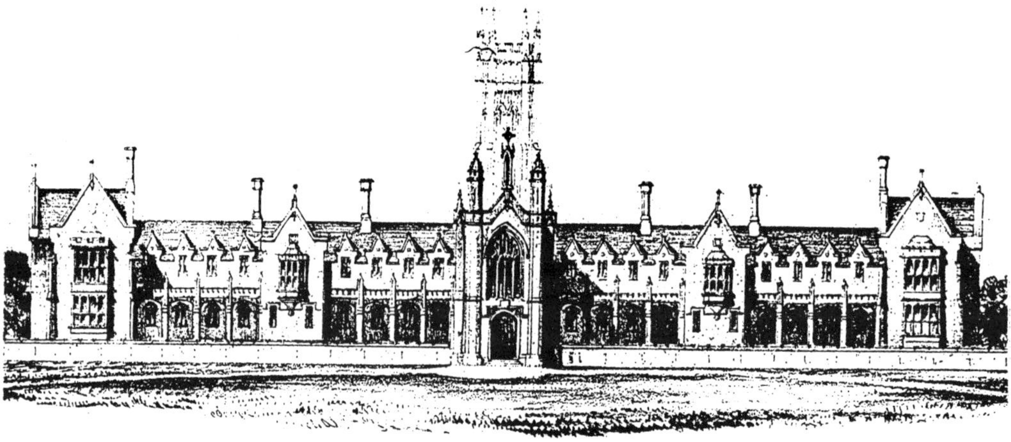

central castellated porch. Built in 1839. Architect unknown.

KILKENNY: **Presbyterian Church**
Built in 1839 by Charles Anderson. Simple interior, pulpit set under a small rose window of painted glass.

KILKENNY: **Rosehill**
The private house of William Robertson, the architect who rebuilt Kilkenny Castle in the 1830s. Rosehill dates from about that time, a typical architect's house, ingenious but constricted with a nod to every style. The approach is beneath a Tudor oriel, through a Renaissance arcade containing an asymmetrical porch reached up a curving stair. Tiny circular lobby, in Robertson's neo-Classical manner leading to top-lit central hall. This leads into a drawing-room with an axial vista through doors of painted glass into a conservatory of Hindu Gothick. Despite being turned into a hotel for many years, Rosehill remained unchanged. Guests could go to Robertson's timber summer house, and sit like him in coloured sunbeams coming through the painted glass. But today mass tourism has swept away these individual pleasures. The summerhouse has disappeared. A vast new curvilinear replaces the bijou Hindu Gothick predecessor, that was dismantled, left on one side and, despite the blandishments of folly fanciers, relegated to the rubbish tip.

KILKENNY: **St John's Bridge**
Built in 1910 as the longest single span ferro-concrete bridge in the British Isles by Alexander Burden during the mayorality of Otway Cuffe.

KILKENNY: **The Station**
Designed in 1846 by Captain Moorsom and built on a plan modified a year later by Sancton Wood. Originally a terminus with its main façade onto the Castlecomer road, but this was destroyed when the line was taken through and carried up to Mountmellick in 1868, so that the arcaded return façade has been adapted as the principal entry.

KILKENNY: **St Kieran's College**
After Maynooth, architecturally the most distinguished Catholic seminary in Ireland where the original design of 1836 by W.D. Butler has been implemented with just enough variation to reveal its evolution over one hundred and twenty years. Butler's concept was a central hall beneath a first-floor chapel symmetrically linked by lower ranges to gabled residential wings. The north wing was designed by George Ashlin (1875) in a more elaborate Gothic. Ashlin added arcades to the links which give such light and shade to the ensemble. In contrast, the south wing by Simon Leonard built in 1955 with stone salvaged from the original Catholic church of St John is satisfyingly austere. However, the entrance gates are a forgivable extravagance, transplanted from Jenkinston Castle in 1941. The only serious deficiency has been the failure to build Butler's lantern over the crossing of the chapel, which instead was reorientated (1929) and then modernized, gaining a window by Harry Clarke Studios. Painted ceiling; altar by Harry Stafflesser of South Tyrol.

KILKENNY: **St John's Catholic Church**
A sumptuous church built by the O'Loughlin family from 1903 to 1908 in a over-ripe and somewhat exhausted Late Gothic Revival. Tower never received its intended spire; polygonal apse. With sculptural panels beneath stained glass windows. Celtic mosaic floor. Altar tactfully adapted to recent liturgical trends. One of the last designs of William Hague, executed after his death by W.H. Byrne.

KILKENNY: **St Patrick's Catholic Church**
Late Gothic Revival church in rock-faced ashlar, attached to earlier convent with transept reserved for nuns. Varnished timber vault. Built in 1896-9. Architect S.F. Hynes of Cork.

KILKENNY: **Talbot's Inch**
Model village commissioned in 1896-9 by the dowager countess of Desart at the gates of her new house, Aut Evan, to put into practice the

Utopian theories of her brother-in-law, Otway Cuffe. While Cuffe's attempts to set up a self-sufficient community able to build their own houses, till their own land, and derive their income from the factories that he had set up for them (woodworking and tobacco) was to founder in sabotage as chronicled by Hubert Butler, the village remains to this day overlooking its green, spoilt only by the intrusion of aluminium to which no preservation society has ever bothered to object. But the general ensemble is preserved by the way the architect William Scott varied with different forms and materials the formula of four cottages gathered under one roof. Village hall and detached houses for the management sited informally. No sign of gates, lodge or church. Otway Cuffe was to die as a

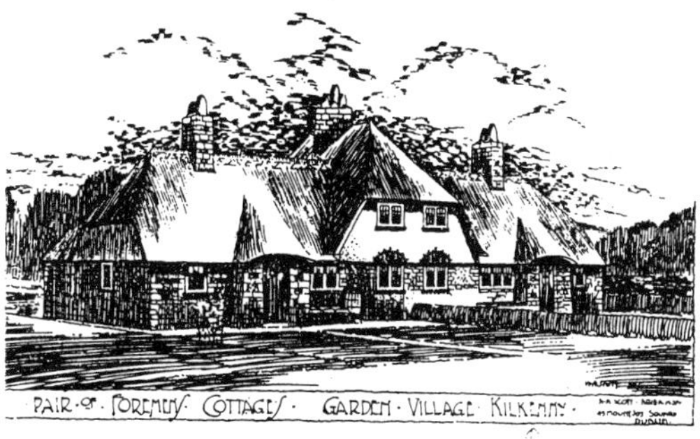

voluntary exile in Western Australia. Desart Court, his family home, was to be destroyed in the Troubles. Rebuilt by Orpen it was later sold and demolished, its only trace a wrought-iron gate into what was once a garden.

KILKENNY: **Tynan's Pub, Horseleap Slip**
Good Victorian pub overlooking the river, well maintained by continuous family ownership. Sympathetic modern stained glass by Patrick Muldowney.

KILKENNY: **Ulster Bank**
Lively design dating from 1915 in brick and limestone, with porch upheld by black Kilkenny marble, polished, it is said, by continuous dossing. Architects: Blackwood and Jury.

KILKENNY: **Old Workhouse**
Standard workhouse designed by George Wilkinson and built to his formula in the 1840s. Now an engineering firm and partially disused.

KNOCKTOPHER: **Knocktopher Abbey**
John McCurdy was commissioned by the Langrishes to rebuild their 17th-century house incorporating the remains of a medieval abbey after a fire *c.* 1866. The result was the closest he ever reached to the French chateau idiom of his dead rival, Benjamin Woodward, but without Woodward's distinction. The result is not dissimilar to Killoskehane Castle, Co. Tipperary (q.v.) by T.N. Deane, where the same High Victorian Gothic deadens the retention of earlier features which, however fascinating in themselves, here inhibit rather than inspire. Now a country house hotel with time-sharing in its dependencies.

PAULSTOWN: **Shankill Castle**
Medieval tower house remodelled and extended by the Aylward family to make a Georgian house with no trace of the medieval keep. William Robertson was called in the 1820s to a make a pretty Gothick villa out of it. But by then castles were fashionable and a second scheme was carried out. The keep re-emerged with a dining-room wing beyond and a Gothick glazed porch shielded the Classical door. The next generation called in William Deane Butler to make a new diningroom and kitchen wing at the rear. His Elizabethan-style proposals of 1856 were partially carried out. The drawingroom was made out of William Robertson's diningroom. It opened into an elegant conservatory, attributable to Turner (since dismantled). A further rural Gothick conservatory on a half-landing at the rear that Butler intended to remove, has survived. Castellated entrance gates attributed to Daniel Robertson.

PILTOWN: **Church of Ireland**
The 5th earl of Bessborough commissioned George Edmund Street to design what is today the finest Irish example of a High Victorian seigneurial church, outwardly robust, rarified

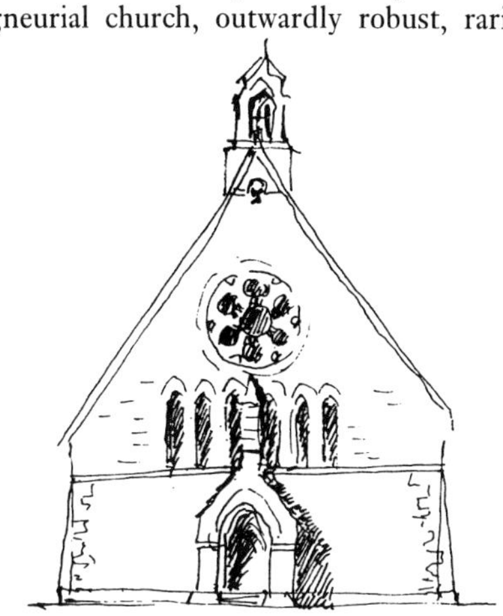

within. Just a simple nave in plan leading to a smaller chancel, but Street expresses his individuality by his treatment of the entrance porch with its stone roof capped by buttress which bisects a row of six lancets to strengthen the base of a rose window, all this without any internal evidence. Dark interior; windows filled with stained glass (except for one beside the pulpit), so that the open roof rises into obscurity. The church dates from 1859-62, glass by Curtis, Ward and Hughes.

ROSBERCON: Annagh Castle
Georgian house overlooking the estuary of the Nore, burnt and rebuilt with a mansard roof by Charles Geoghegan in 1867.

THOMASTOWN: Brownsbarn
Shooting lodge of a Howth solicitor, William McDougas JP (*d.*1875), who commissioned Benjamin Woodward in 1856 and then built the house by direct labour so that it was not completed until 1863, two years after Woodward's death. Brownsbarn has survived as one of Woodward's least altered houses, even to its entrance gates with their irregular polychromatic stonework. The entry façade is Woodward at his most original—two adjoining gable ends of different sizes, sliced off into one plane, and built up out of horizontal bands of polychromatic stonework, extended on one side into a mini-gable and a low service wing. From this plane of strong horizontals, he projects a trefoiled balcony and a delicate varied marble columned porch. The other elevations are more conventional, with large windows like glazed loggias to look down into the wooded valley of the Nore. The side elevation to the service court is quite different—architecture pared to its essentials, with all four floors revealed and contrasted with low buildings round the courtyard. Here is the nearest one comes to discovering the unremarkable Georgian house which Woodward transformed retaining the basement including kitchen unaltered. This has now been brought upstairs. Unusual fireplace of stone alternating with enamel tiles in hall. Fretted cornices in reception rooms. Carved timber staircase characteristic of Woodward, bannister rail terminating with a bewhiskered head—said to be Mr McDougal himself.

THOMASTOWN: Catholic Church
Built *c.*1859-62 to replace an earlier church of which the tower survives, competing with McCarthy's own belfry, a round tower embedded into the transept of the church. McCarthy achieved real rather than fictional authenticity by reusing the altar of Jerpoint, but this has now vanished.

THOMASTOWN: Kilmurray
Birthplace of the artist Mildred Butler, who made one of the most remarkable studios of her time simply by removing a wall between a late Georgian drawingroom and the garden without injury to the Adamesque plasterwork. Arts and Crafts fireplace in the study carved by E. Holohan dating from 1896. House now open to the public as an art gallery and guesthouse.

THOMASTOWN: The Viaduct
One of Ireland's most ambitious bridges of its time (1850) with a timber lattice girden construction spanning the Nore, approached by viaducts of stone. Designed by Robert Mallet. Central span was replaced in 1877 by wrought-iron bowspring girders to the design of C.B. Galwey.

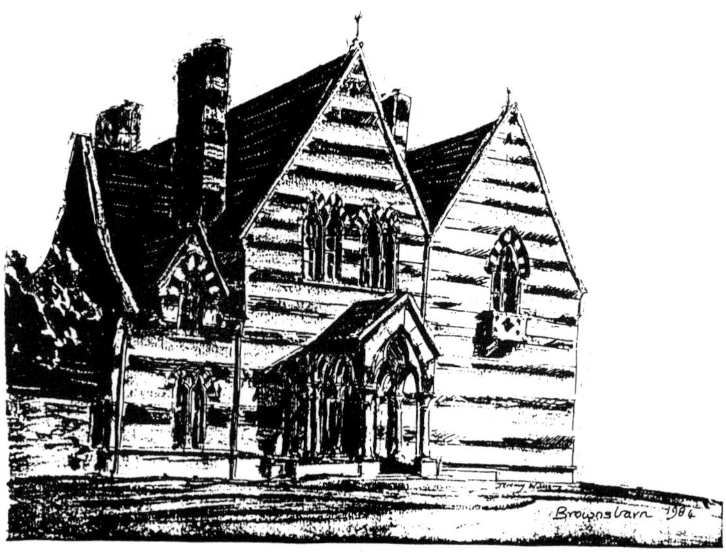

BROWNSBARN

LAOIS

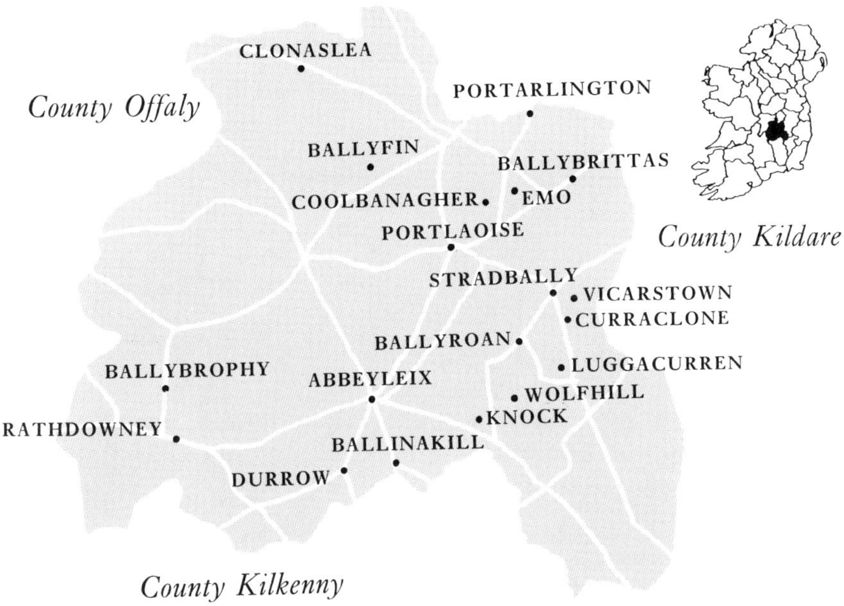

ABBEYLEIX: **Abbey Leix**
The house built by James Wyatt in 1773 for the 1st Viscount de Vesci was remodelled twice during the Victorian era by two quite different English architects. Firstly T.H. Wyatt (born in

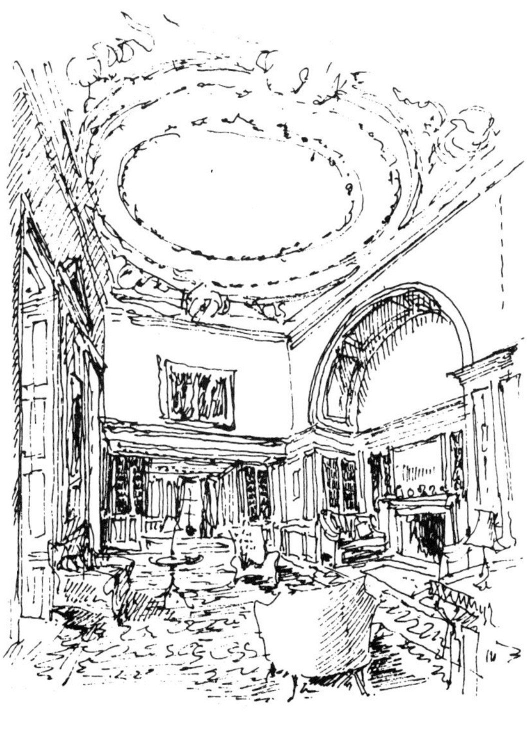

Co. Roscommon) was commissioned by the 3rd viscount, who had married the daughter of the 11th earl of Pembroke (commemorated by T.H. Wyatt's sumptuous parish church of Wilton). In Abbey Leix, T.H. Wyatt re-cased the house to give it the appearance of an Italianate palazzo and added a columned library, now subdivided, that led to a conservatory swept away by the 'Great Wind' of 1902. The terraced gardens were inspired by those of Aloupka in the Crimea, the house of Lady de Vesci's grandfather, Prince Woronzov. All this early Victorian work is bluff and self-confident. The 4th viscount married a 'Soul', a daughter of the 10th earl of Weymss, and the drawingroom was redecorated with a superb blue Morris wallpaper. Then the study was remodelled by Gilbert's architect, Howard Ince, in a thoughtful Arts and Crafts manner, inspired by the Philip Webb interiors of Clouds, the countryhouse of her sister-in-law and the gathering place of the Souls. Further work by Detmar Blow (1920). Many of the rooms have carpets woven in a factory founded by Lady de Vesci in the village. In the demesne is the private church. This served the parish until Semple's church was built and it is still the funeral chapel of the de Vescis. Their recumbent marble effigies do not prepare one for the tomb of Eustace Vesey by Alfred Gilbert; he lost his life fighting abroad and Gilbert's bronze tomb of 1889 suggest a

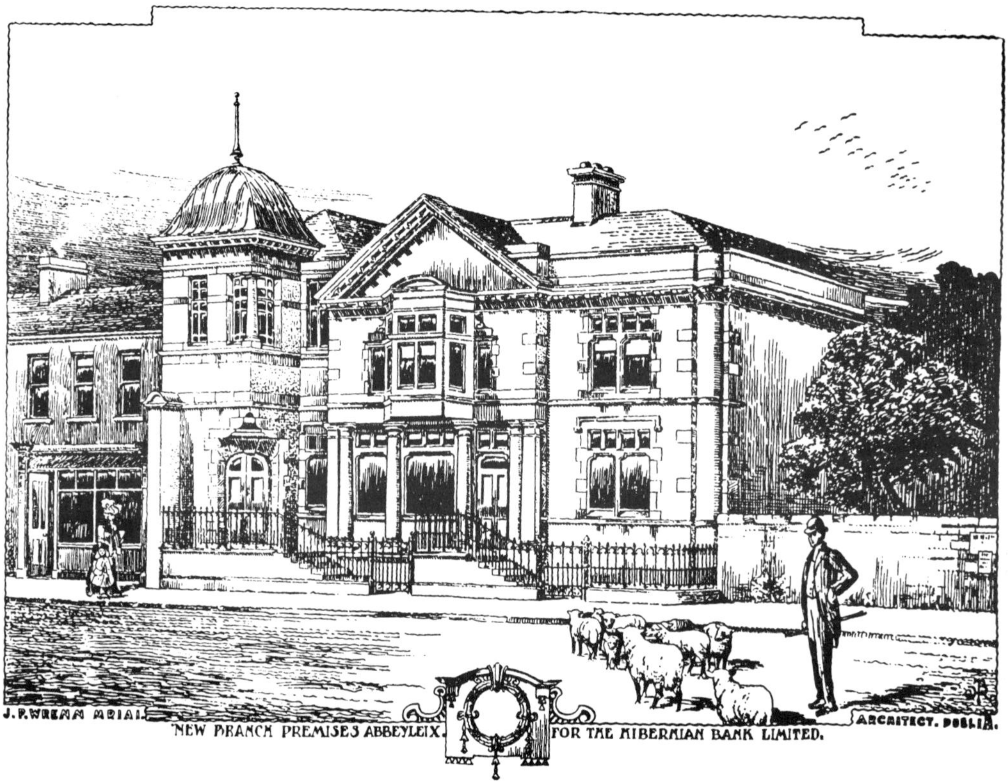

military great coat, while the whorls and spirals suggest a stylized flowing river, harking back to Celtic art and anticipating the Art Nouveau of Klimt and the Secessionists. Exhibited in the Royal Academy Gilbert retrospective.

ABBEYLEIX: **Catholic Church**
A muted Hiberno-Romanesque design attached to an earlier convent. Designed by William Hague in 1895. Cruciform with belfry detached from the southern transept. Top-lit apse illuminated sugary frescoes; marble altar still undisturbed.

ABBEYLEIX: **Church of Ireland**
In the circumstances we must be grateful to T.H. Wyatt that he did not entirely replace the church already built by John Semple (*c.*1825) but retained the western spire with side lobbies reinforced by gabled buttresses. Wyatt's church (1865) is competent but does not compensate us for the loss of Semple's church, which was entirely vaulted with stone. Stained glass by Child (1825): the Good Samaritan.

ABBEYLEIX: **Bank of Ireland**
Formerly the Hibernian Bank. A lively composition, irreverently mixing classical columns and mullioned windows. The door of the residence is set on a splay and sheltered by a corbel that supports a column set before a corner oriel above. A copper dome is fitted on the cube of the tower. Sadly its architect J.P. Wren, after he had built this in 1909, practised a dreary classicism until his death in 1955.

ABBEYLEIX: **Hibernian Hotel**
An Irish example of the kind of posting inn one would find in the Cotswolds. Built *c.*1839, possibly by the Pains.

ABBEYLEIX: **Mortells**
The exterior of this pub and shop is impeccably discreet. So indeed is the interior, enfolded by an immense counter with its timber partitions thoughtfully placed to screen drinkers from the shoppers and surround a free-standing cast-iron stove. Above the Edwardian delivery bicycle of the firm, now honourably retired, is displayed. To those who are accustomed to experience this ambiance as the backdrop to the kitchen comedies of our national theatre, this is a precious survival, but so carefully tended by generations of the same family that one feels that to list it for preservation would be impertinent.

ABBEYLEIX: **Memorial of the 2nd Viscount**
An obelisk set on a robust rusticated plinth in the centre of the market square. Designed in 1860 by J.S. Butler (not usually known for his Classicism.

ABBEYLEIX: Memorial of the 3rd Viscount

A Gothic octagonal shrine built after a competition in 1877 to the design of Rawson Carroll, who beat an almost identical design by S. Hynes into second place.

ABBEYLEIX: The Schools

The two school complexes were built by the 3rd Viscountess de Vesci. The southern schools are an extended cottage ornée, an idiom abandoned for the northern schools, which are in a grimmer, more institutional Gothic. Architects unknown.

ABBEYLEIX: The Townhall

An existing market house remodelled in vernacular Italianate by Howard Ince in 1896 while he was working on Lord de Vesci's house. Ince committed suicide in 1920.

BALLINAKILL: Heywood

The most admired demesne of Co. Leix at the end of the 18th century with its house built by the owner, M.F. Trench, an amateur architect who enlisted Gandon to assist him in the interior, and who adorned his demesne with still extant ruins he salvaged from medieval abbeys. This elysium was called after his mother-in-law. Inherited by his son, Sir Frederick Trench, who published a visionary scheme for the Thames Embankment. The gardens which Sir Edwin Lutyens created for Sir Frederick's grandniece, Mrs Hutchinson Poe, in 1906 are a realization of a fragment of that scheme with their colonnades, pergolas, and terraces raised on immense retaining walls, their immensity said to be due to a miscalculated dimension. Lutyens told the family that their house needed massive shoring up to preserve it, but the final account was double the estimate. Ten years before, the house had been engulfed in ungainly mansarded additions with a pompous *porte-cochère* flanked by a pair of rumbustious towers by Thomas Drew, who tried to create a series of interlinked reception rooms climaxing in an elaborate library with strong resemblances to the Dublin National Library (q.v.). Certainly the woodwork appears to be by Cambi of Siena; as Hutchinson Poe was one of the government appointees to the building committee of the library, this is understandable. This was the house destroyed by fire in 1960 after its acquisition by a religious order; the ruins were demolished, so that the gardens designed by Lutyens to upstage the house now exist in a curious vacuum at its upper levels. The great surprise of the garden, the elliptical fountain pool encircled by squatting stone toads in a sunken amphitheatre, is now revealed too suddenly. But the planting has been

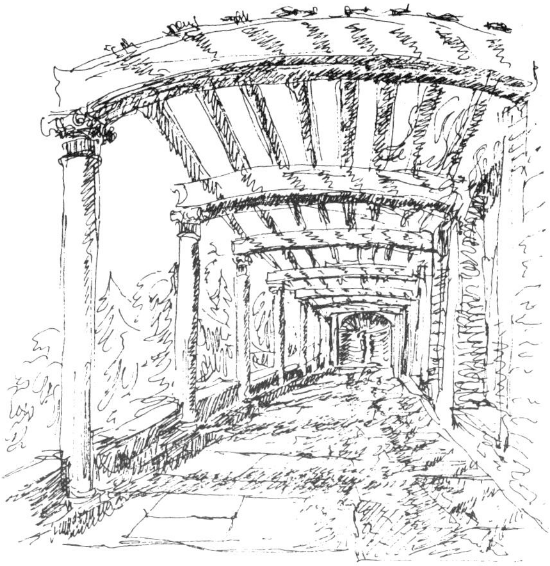

scruplously restored by G.S. Thomas in accordance with Jeykell's drawings and are maintained by the OPW. Do not overlook the rear of the Italianate loggia articulated by massive pilasters half-buried in its stonework.

BALLYBRITTAS: Rath House

Richard Turner added one of his most delicate conservatories to this Regency house joined by a glass link to the drawingroom and opening on to a formal garden. The interior is still vented by an ingenious device of revolving perforated double discs. Commissioned by the Deases *c.*1850, who also added a balancing wing to the north to contain their private chapel.

BALLYBRITTAS: Rathdaire Church of Ireland

Yet another case where the only remaining evidence of a great estate is a ivy-clad ruin of a house and nearby a scrupulously maintained memorial church, recording here a widow's devotion to a husband so execrated by his tenants that it took her three days to bury him: every time his grave was dug, it was defiled by dead dogs and cats. She was an American

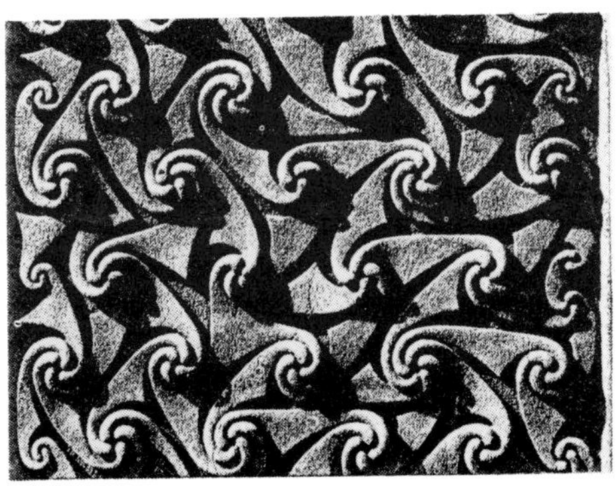

heiress, Cornelia Wadsworth, who had married a minor Irish landowner, John Adair. Together they had built Glenveagh Castle, Co. Donegal (q.v.), creating its demesne by driving out hundreds of tenants in a notorious expulsion. The tenants of his ancestral estates in Co. Leix were equally alienated. How ironic that he should be recorded by such an Irish church (a phantom parish, set up by Mrs Adair herself) in the national style of Hiberno-Romanesque that even Daniel O'Connell was not allowed in his Cahirciveen memorial church of the same time. But so it must have been in pre-Norman Ireland, whose abbots are remembered for the remnants of their exquisite churches that survived the atrocities they committed against each other. Glass by Heaton, Butler and Bayne.

The architect of Cornelia Adair was James Fuller, engaged also at that time on the churches of Clane and Carnalway (q.v.), but this is his most Hiberno-Romanesque church. Although the façade is based on Roscrea, its real inspiration are on the high crosses of Ahenny. So often richly carved façades of that time are betrayed by their vacuous figure sculpture. Here the abstract spiralling and stylized beasts lend themselves to High Victorian repetitive precision: carving by Sharp; rose window over doorway and flanking tower. Nave of the five bays, transepts with one containing a vestry slotted beneath a gallery; altar in semi-circular apse. The interior, however, was never properly completed. Three years after work started, Bellegrove, the Adair home was burned down, apparently accidentally, in 1887. The lectern and pulpit were put in by the Trench heirs to the Adair estate, and up until his recent death, Mr Trench of Trench Acres, a self-built bungalow, would supervise the religious services of the current rector. The Italianate ruins of Bellegrove, built round three sides of what was once a winter garden remain, but not the spectacular terracotta Romanesque conservatory added by Thomas Newenham Deane in 1887, modelled on the cloister of St John Lateran in Rome. Its elaborate columns were dismantled some years ago to make a folly at nearby Rath House that has never materialized.

BALLYBROPHY: **The Station**
Muscular Gothic railway station, possibly by Sancton Wood. Built *c.*1850.

BALLYFIN: **Ballyfin House**
The most palatial country-house commission of the Morrisons, extending a house already started by Dominic Madden, dates from 1822. But the superb curvilinear conservatory (attributed to Richard Turner), perhaps the most graceful in Ireland, was added in 1850, replacing a re-

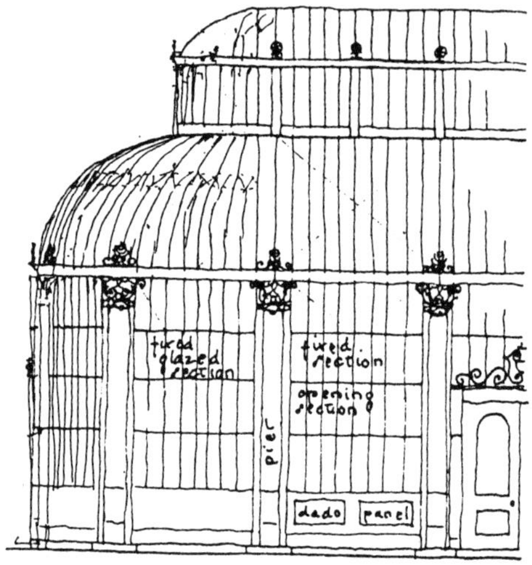

strained lean-to. Almost free-standing, with nave apsed at each end and aisles that become ambulatories. The fenestration is articulated by perforated pilasters. The minimalist structure still astonishes, rivalling the webbed leaves of the palms to defy the laws of gravity. The doors at the centre of each façade are surmounted by lacy pediments and cast-iron coots, the heraldic device of Sir Charles Coote. Two doors are curved with the apses, while the mirrored door to the house is approached over a glazed bridge. Sir Charles would have no doubt have approached his conservatory by opening up a dummy bookcase, reserved for the study of botany, concealing not videos or gin bottles, as one would expect today, but his rarest plants. Even more miraculous than the conservatory is its survival. A few years ago, the Patrician Brothers, depressed by its deteriorating condition, arranged for the Irish army to blow it up over Easter. But directions were misinterpreted and no one came. Now the first phase of restoration has been set in motion relying on proceeds from the National Lottery.

BALLYFIN: **The Folly**
Circular medieval tower, rebuilt, castellated and then surrounded by a moat crossed by the remnants of a drawbridge. Curious earthworks in the bawn are said to have been improvised by Lutyens.

BALLYROAN: **Catholic Church**
Elegant Gothick in the style of Cobden, retaining its original arcaded reredos. Witty tower reversing the roles of pinnacles and crosses. Built for the Revd Thomas Nolan in 1840.

CLONASLEA: **Brittas Castle**
Castle built by Major-General Dunne MP on the foothills of the Slieve Bloom mountains, de-

signed in 1869 by John McCurdy, extended and 'improved' by Millar and Symes in 1879. Glimpsed *c.*1950 as a ruin with an oriel against the sunset, but now mostly demolished apart from an insubstantial flag tower holding out against an uncontrollable upsurge of rhododendrons as observed by Hubert Butler.

COOLBANAGHER: **Church of Ireland**
Gandon's exquisite church for his patron, Lord Portarlington, did not measure up to the religiosity required by its Victorian congregation. By then the church was attributed to an unknown Italian. Thomas Drew satisfied them by removing the ceiling to expose the roof structure, pushing out a new apse, and inserting a tubby pulpit. The recent restoration serves only to emphasize Drew's determination not to be polite.

CURRACLONE: **Church of Ireland**
Celtic Revival wooden reredos carved by members of the Stradbally school of woodworkers in 1913.

DURROW: **Moyne**
Mid-Georgian house remodelled and extended *c.*1880, so that one enters a formal neo-Adamesque drawingroom in the new wing through a fluid Baronial living hall made out of the original house. Architect, Rawson Carroll.

DURROW: **Knocknatree**
Elegant Tudor Revival, by an unknown architect, for the Flower family of Castle Durrow but abandoned by them *c.*1940. Now a ruin dominated by its clusters of chimneystacks. Drawing-room with semi-circular window to view the meanders of the Nore.

EMO: **Catholic Church**
Gothic Revival church by J.S. Butler, who exhibited his scheme in the RHA of 1868. At the rear a marble effigy of the 2nd countess of Portarlington, a convert to Catholicism, sculpted by Sir Richard Boehm (1874).

EMO: **Emo Court**
Gandon's great house for the 1st earl of Portarlington was not completed until 1874; the 2nd earl called in Lewis Vulliamy to complete the garden front portico in 1860; the 3rd earl commissioned William Caldbeck to complete the double-height rotunda with marble pilasters rising to a coffered dome. A marquetry floor partially removed by the Jesuits but now replaced during the restoration by the present owner, Mr C.D. Cholmeley Harrison.

KNOCK: **Catholic Church**
Rural Gothic, rendered with limestone dressings, cruciform in shape. The modernized interior retains some panelling and glass by

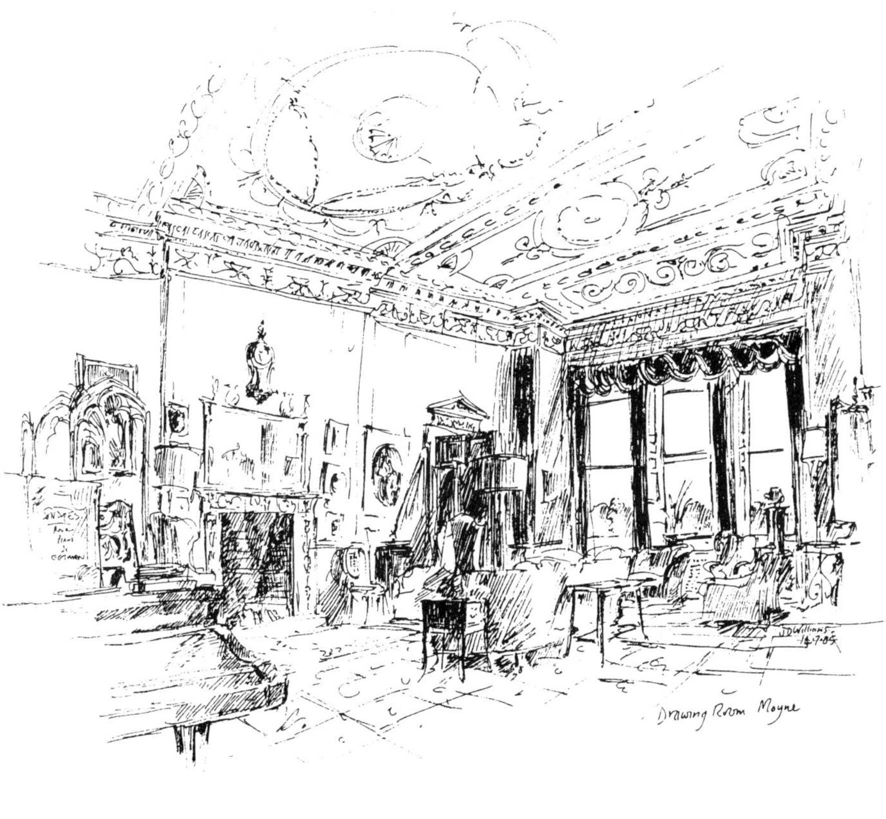

Mayer. Elegant façade with doorway flanked by cusped niches. A plaque above proclaims its dedication to St Laserian, the parish priest (James Delaney) who built it, and the year, 'Anno Fatuus et Pestis'—1847.

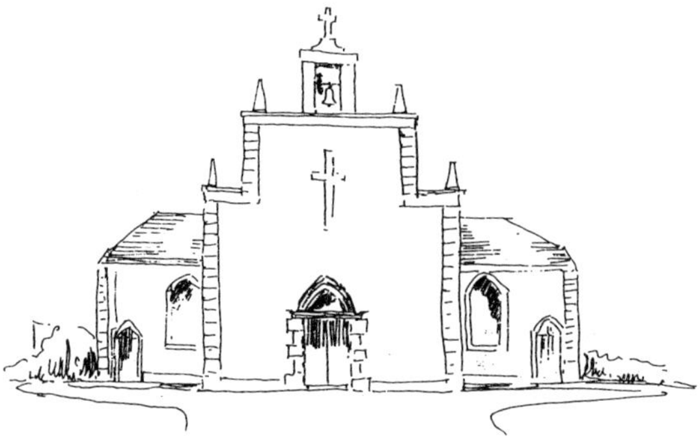

LUGGACURREN: **Catholic Church**
The Cubistic façade of this vernacular Gothick chapel has survived 'improvement' *c.*1980 that gutted the interior.

PORTARLINGTON: **Catholic Church**
Said to have been built from a sketch by A.W.N. Pugin while he was staying at nearby Emo Court, *c.*1845.

PORTARLINGTON: **Church of Ireland**
Imposing but charmless Gothic church by Joseph Welland, built in 1851 and prominently sited between the market square and the river.

PORTARLINGTON: **The Station**
One of the more elaborate of Sancton Wood's mainline stations, built in his characteristically restless Gothic *c.*1851 while he was engaged on what is now Heuston Station, Dublin (q.v.). Grimly detailed in local limestone to give temporary respite from the wind and rain of the Irish midlands.

PORTARLINGTON: **Woodbrook**
Georgian home of the late Victorian artist Chetwode Aitken. Drawingroom decorated with murals inspired by the French Rococo, painted by Edwin Hayes, the Edinburgh artist responsible for the redecoration of Holyrood Palace.

PORTLAOISE: **Allied Irish Bank**
Formerly the Munster and Leinster Bank. Designed by J.J. O'Callaghan in 1891 and built out of red-brick and limestone dressings, with yellow brickwork filling in the spandrels of the Gothic arches.

PORTLAOISE: **Methodist Church**
Gothic church designed in 1883 by Frederick Morley; concise and cantankerous.

PORTLAOISE: **Minch Norton's**
Modest maltings designed in brick and stone by an unknown architect and built alongside an adjoining manager's house with its drawing-room shielded by a conservatory from the sun and the glances of the entering workforce.

PORTLAOISE: **New Gaol**
Designed by William Deane Butler *c.*1830. The clarity of its plan has been obscured by a later wing (1900) and by present-day precautions to contain its inmates. Butler's frowning machicolations over the entrance have been out-corbelled by concrete observation posts.

PORTLAOISE: **Shaen**
Castellated gateway to a late Georgian house, now a home for the elderly. The architect, W.D. Butler, exhibited a design for the main house in 1831.

PORTLAOISE: **The Station**
Designed *c.*1851 by Sancton Wood in his characteristically strenuous Gothic, harshly built out of local limestone.

RATHDOWNEY: **Allied Irish Bank**
Tudor Revival bank designed as the Munster and Leinster Bank by T.N. Deane in 1875. Now much modernized.

RATHDOWNEY: **Easton Lodge**
This aggressive Late Victorian brick-and-stone gatelodge with diagonally positioned chimneys serves as a backdrop to a fountain commemorating a wife of one of the Perry family who owned the local brewery. The brewery has been transformed into a modern factory, while their house was demolished in the 1950s. All that survives is their stables, sensitively converted into a private house entered through a cast-iron, curvilinear conservatory salvaged from the convent of Abbeyleix. Architect, possibly Joseph Maguire, who built a farm and cottage residence near Rathdowney in 1870.

RATHDOWNEY: **FitzPatrick Tomb, Clough**
One of A.N.W. Pugin's elusive Irish commissions was a chantrey chapel for the FitzPatrick's, *ci-devant* earls of Ossory. It is not clear if it was ever built. Only the gravestone exists, with an incised cross. An elaborate Catholic church for a small village, *c.*1890.

STRADBALLY: **Arles Catholic Church**
Designed by Pugin and Ashlin (1865) in their typical manner. More memorable is the stone-roofed Gothic Grace mausoleum of 1818 covered with inscriptions that record the family's past glory.

STRADBALLY: Catholic Church
Designed by William Hague and built in 1893-6, the church is characteristic of his later, blander manner. Triple window by Earley.

STRADBALLY: Estate Cottages
In 1876, Col. Cosby won second prize for the estate cottages submitted to a national competition which failed to name the architect (T.W. Webber). The cottages were solidly built each side of the road to Carlow.

STRADBALLY: Market Hall
Elegant market hall, with corrugated iron concave roof resting on arcades of ironwork with decorative spandrels; *c.*1890. A suitable setting for the annual Stradbally Steam Rally.

STRADBALLY: Stradbally Hall
The Georgian seat of the Cosby family remodelled and extended (1866-9) by Charles Lanyon in a heavy Italianate that leaves little external trace of the earlier house. Lanyon added an arcaded loggia to the garden front, and an entrance block with a new parallel range of rooms. A pillared porch leads into a vestibule enclosing a flight of stairs rising to the principal level. The original entrance hall was made double-height and lit through a curved glass dome, its walls reserved for the family's collection of old masters. Judged simply as architecture Lanyon's alterations were disastrous, but as a setting for paintings, they were magisterial. While the 18th-century portraits remained in the reception rooms (which Lanyon left untouched) along the garden front, the 'prayer room' in the new range beside the vestibule was reserved for Victorian religious art (show stoppers of their era). Lanyon built his new study around a painting—an anonymous bird's eye view of the house, its gardens and demesne, with the conquered O'More castle of Dunamase on the skyline.

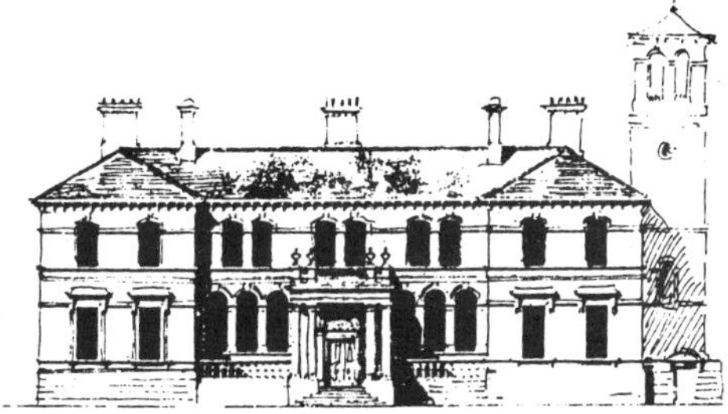

The ballroom, the largest room that Lanyon added, has a ceiling decorated not by ornate plasterwork, but by a series of French neo-Classical wallpaper panels in demure grisaille (nothing in an Irish house is predictable). Today, the death duties have dispersed the most valuable of the original paintings, but the atmosphere of a great Victorian art collection remains. In the 1960s there was a brief possibility of exposure to the twentieth century. Edward Heath accepted an invitation to address a conference of Young Conservatives, but then cancelled at the last moment, possibly having heard that the family cook had fallen through the ceiling on to the diningroom table—not that the ceiling collapsed, merely that the ceiling centre had been removed for repair and that cook had failed to notice the hole in the floor. Recently the setting for a conference on Bosnia.

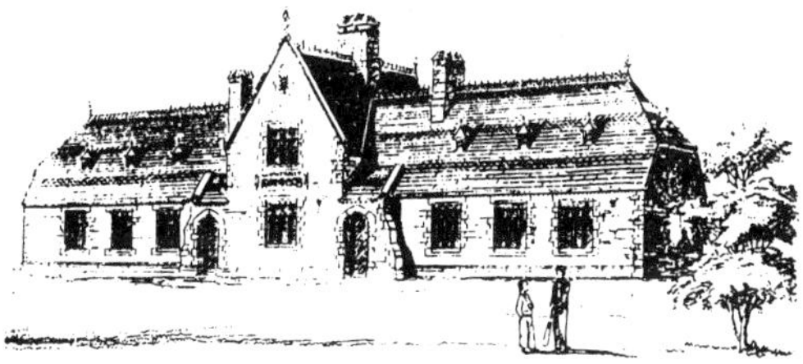

VICARSTOWN: The Rectory
Asymmetrical composition by J.F. Kempster (1877). A central hall with oval skylight.

VICARSTOWN: The School
The village of Vicarstown was given to the statesman Henry Grattan and today is still the property of his descendants. One of the Grattans rebuilt the school and the rectory as part of a programme of improvements to his estate in 1868. His architect, for the schools, was Charles Geoghegan, who built them in a low-keyed Gothic.

WOLFHILL: Catholic Church
For the Irish midlands an unexpected mountain setting gives this church a sense of pilgrimage to a place apart. Nor has a ruthless restoration damaged the essential simplicity of its airy, luminous interior with windows once transparent to the sky. Entered through tiny twin porches flanking the façade in separate pavilions, so that no doorway disturbs the serenity of the west end to the nave, with its triple lancet, a trefoil above and then a statue of the Virgin hollowed into the topmost pinnacle. Massive limestone buttresses, splayed at the corners articulate the five bays of the nave and contribute to the uplift. Projecting chancel between tiny twin sacristies. What liberties of scale were taken by unknown provincials before the urban professionals did them out of business?

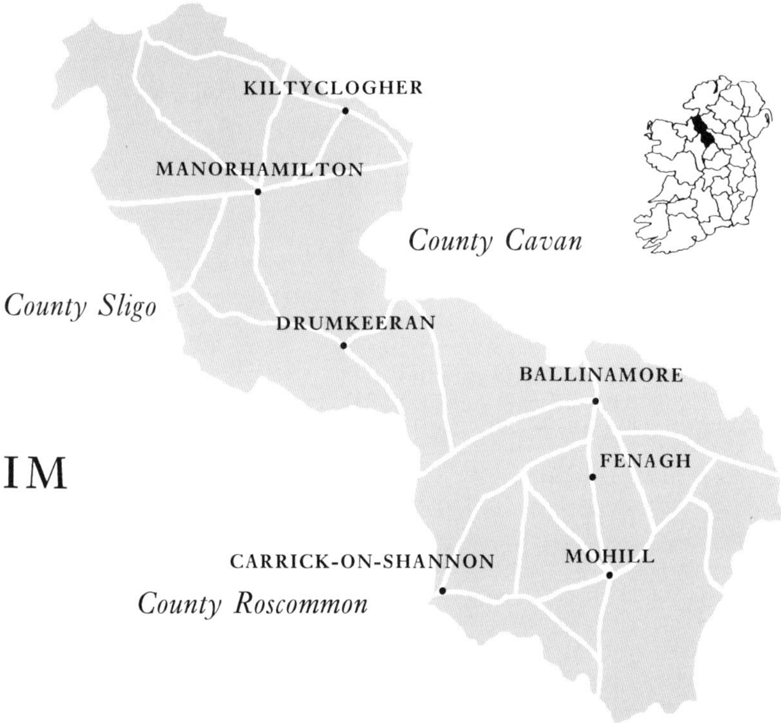

LEITRIM

BALLINAMORE: **Builders' Providers Store**
Although deconsecrated as a Catholic church in the 1960s, this delightful example of the Gothic Revival (remodelled *c.* 1910 by William Scott) survives as a store of a builder's provider, its internal decoration—down to its stencilled friezes—far more intact than if it had remained in ecclesiastical care. Originally an harmonious blend of scholarly Perpendicular and rural tradition; T-shaped with the high altar set into a shallow triple-niched recess, and the side altars in polygonal apses that still retain their stained glass. Currently being reslated.

CARRICK-ON-SHANNON: **Catholic Church**
Designed by William Hague in 1879 and completed 50 years later by his pupil T.F. McNamara, who added the tower and installed the stained glass over the high altar, a curious composition—three lancets below and a rose above set into the vaulting of the timber trefoiled roof. Trusses rest on spindly marble columns corbelled out on sculpted angels. The original high altar was dismantled in 1979, parts of it distributed to a new tablernacle in the chapel on the right and to a new baptismal font in the chapel on the left, its place taken by a zany singing gallery of boarded wood enfolding a colossal oil of the Last Judgment with Christ looming behind fleeing figures: artist, Ray Carroll. Victorian church decorators believed that they were already in Paradise. This nightmare is a sinister reminder that their optimism was premature.

CARRICK-ON-SHANNON: **Church of Ireland**
Earlier church remodelled by Welland. Stained glass by Watson of Youghal. Organ with its pretty Gothic Revival case intact by Telford.

CARRICK-ON-SHANNON: **Costello Chapel**
A leaflet in this tiny stone-roofed oratory squeezed between two main-street shops claims that this is the second smallest church in the world. Where is the smallest? Commissioned by a local shopkeeper, Edward Costello, who lost his wife in 1877. He acquired a Methodist chapel, and replaced it with this memorial to conjugal love. Completed in 1879. No architect is recorded; however, the Gothic tunnel vault, the creamy Bathstone ribs contrasting with black Kilkenny unpolished marble, the small square-headed windows filled with trefoiled tracery, and the altar with its enamelled tabernacle are all to be found in the churches of George Ashlin, and this would fit into the series of his stone-roofed funeral chapels—Ballymurn, Fore, Myshall (q.v.). A dais of Mintern tiles separates two glass top vaults, so husband and wife can lie side by side, separated only by the celebrant as in their marriage ceremony.

CARRICK-ON-SHANNON: **Hatley Manor**
A rarity in Ireland, a town palazzo entered by a forecourt off the main street, which makes all the more surprising the vista from the rear, across the garden lawns down to the Shannon meandering through a wooded valley. Built by a branch of the St George family in the 1830s. Designed in the Italianate manner but garden front altered to Gothic during execution—the windows given hooded mouldings, the parapet castellated, and the central staircase extended into a battlemented tower and lit by a tall Gothic window off the half landing. In 1865 the last St George reverted to Classicism for the design of his mausoleum in the garden, a robust cube with vermiculated quoins entered by a Doric porch. Wrought-iron gates guard the approach, the piers sumounted by shrouded urns. William Caldbeck's account book records a payment from a job in Hatley Manor—presumably this mausoleum.

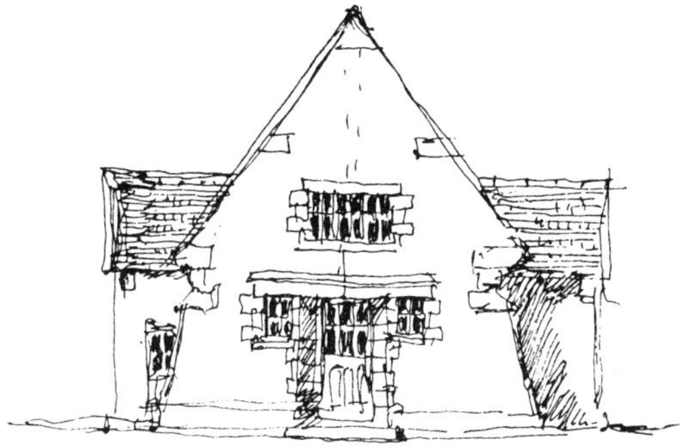

DRUMKEERAN: **Village hall**
Small Arts and Crafts hall with symmetrical façade and battered walls.

FENAGH: **Church of Ireland**
Chancel added in 1859 to an earlier church by Welland for the Pack-Beresford family, remarkable for the east window, a careful copy of one in the ruined medieval abbey church nearby, and filled with richly coloured heraldic glass. After years of dereliction, recently restored by the local community.

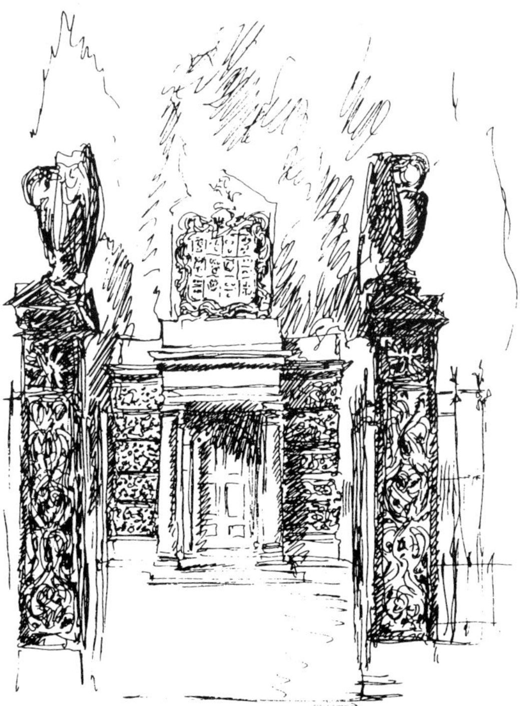

CARRICK-ON-SHANNON: **Post Office**
A minor but scholarly example of the Baroque Revival dating from the first decade of the 20th century, possibly by Howard Pentland.

KILTYCLOGHER: **Market House**
Well designed classical structure of *c.*1850, the focal point of this remote border town.

MANORHAMILTON: **Catholic Church**
A late church by William Hague and one that must have been a cause of much worry since the nave collapsed in the great storm of 1884 before completion and had to be reconstructed. Six bays leading to a chancel of two bays; the altar (now replaced) is beneath a slender four-light window. Rock-faced masonry gives the exterior a deceptive grimness, which is emphasized by the mechanical quality of the later tower, but the interior reveals Hague's love of polished marbles and sculptural enrichments that outlived his architectural inventiveness.

MANORHAMILTON: **Lurganboy Church of Ireland**
This tiny corrugated cast-iron church overlooks the mountains of Sligo and Fermanagh from its hilltop outpost, as in a distant colony of the British Empire.

MOHILL: **Bank of Ireland**
Formerly National Bank. One of the rare Irish examples of Art Nouveau, an asymmetrical composition focused on two almost circular windows. Possibly by W.H. Byrne, who was

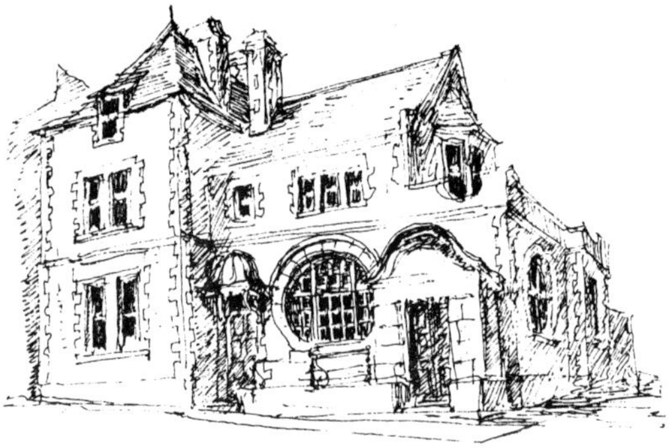

commissioned to design an Hibernian Bank here in 1904. Roof altered after a fire in the 1930s.

MOHILL: Franaught Church of Ireland
Estate church built for the Clements family by Welland (1853) with gargoyled tower; local limestone rubble walls. Elaborate Late Gothic tracery in the windows of the tower. Interior

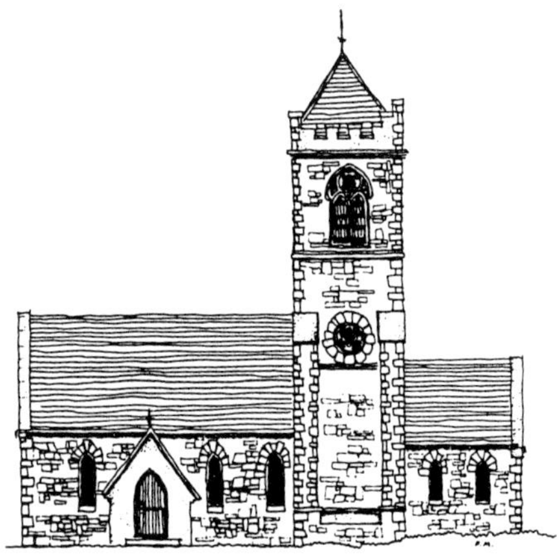

altered by Welland and Gillespie with stained timber open roofs. Fine pre-Raphaelite glass in east window; three windows by Ethel Rhind memorial bust (1839) by C. Moore to Viscount Clements.

MOHILL: Lough Rynn
The seats of the earls of Leitrim. House presumably by William Murray, who exhibited a house for a nobleman in Co. Leitrim in the RHA of 1832; built for Robert, Viscount Clements, in 1833. Most of the estate buildings date from the time of the 3rd earl, who was assassinated in 1878 along with two of his staff on his other estate, Mulroy (q.v.) in Donegal (he had been a notoriously unpopular landlord, and his death precipitated the Irish Land War). As he had quarrelled with his heir, he left all his estates to his cousin Col. H.T. Clements, who handed Mulroy back to the 4th earl but retained Lough Rynn. Sir Thomas Drew was commissioned to extend the house, and the immense saloon is his finest secular interior. Drew took as his point of reference the undemanding neo-Tudor of the earlier house using a porch to the front, and an oriel to the garden to graft the new work on to the old. The porch, hall, boudoir, and saloon are all panelled with English oak by Harry Hems of Exeter with stained glass in the upper windows and fretted plaster ceilings prompting, in the words of the *Irish Builder*, the 'travelled mind' to think of ancient houses such as Haddon Hall. But today the most remarkable characteristic of the saloon is not the ornate inglenook, the largest in Ireland, but its lofty mullioned windows, more glass than wall, to view the farther reaches of the lake.

The gardens, laid out for the 3rd earl, are terraced towards Lough Rynn, with an octagonal viewing turret by J.E. Rogers. The steward's house is by M.D. Wyatt. The outer stableyard is by the master of Rogers, Benjamin Woodward—designed in 1858 like a French Late Gothic chateau, with dormers interpenetrating steeply rising roofs. This is being restored as *gites* by the present owner, an Irish businessman living in the Philippines, who has reopened the house and gardens to public, and converted the outbuildings into craftshops and restaurants. The estate was first opened to the public by Marcus Clements, last of his family to live there. Despite an inauguration which ensured that the hospitality of the Clements would be remembered forever in the annals of Mohill, his tenure coincided with the greatest public apathy to remote stately homes, and during his last season he received four visitors.

Delightful entrance lodge at the Mohill gates presumably also by Drew.

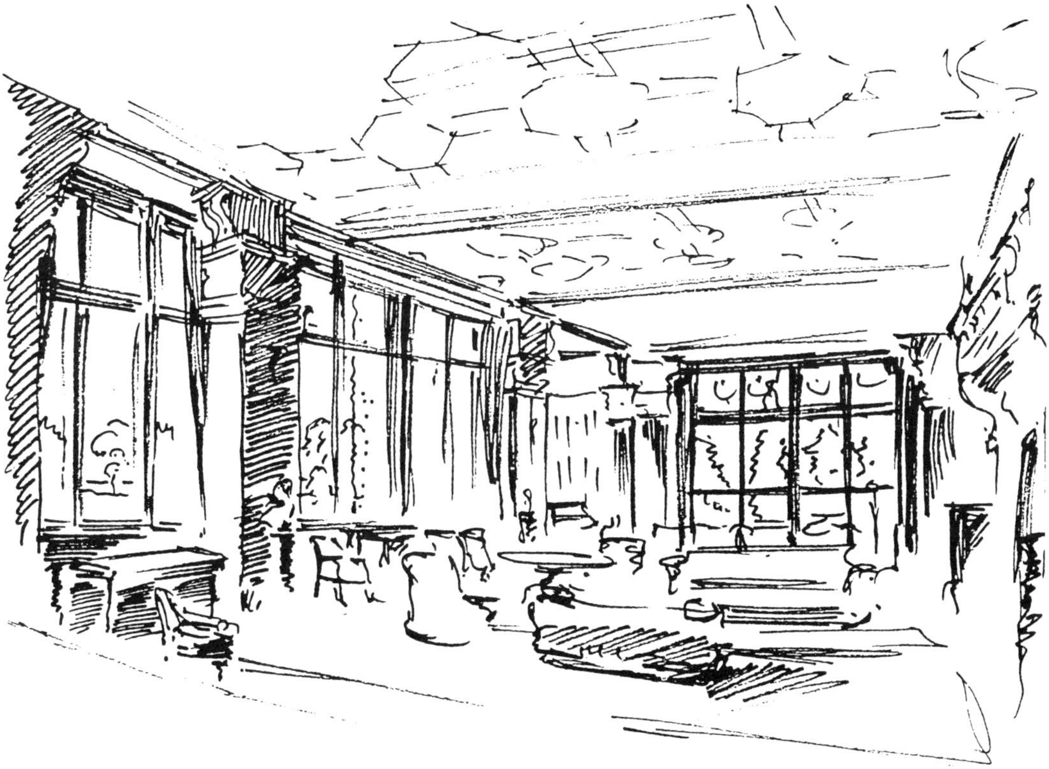

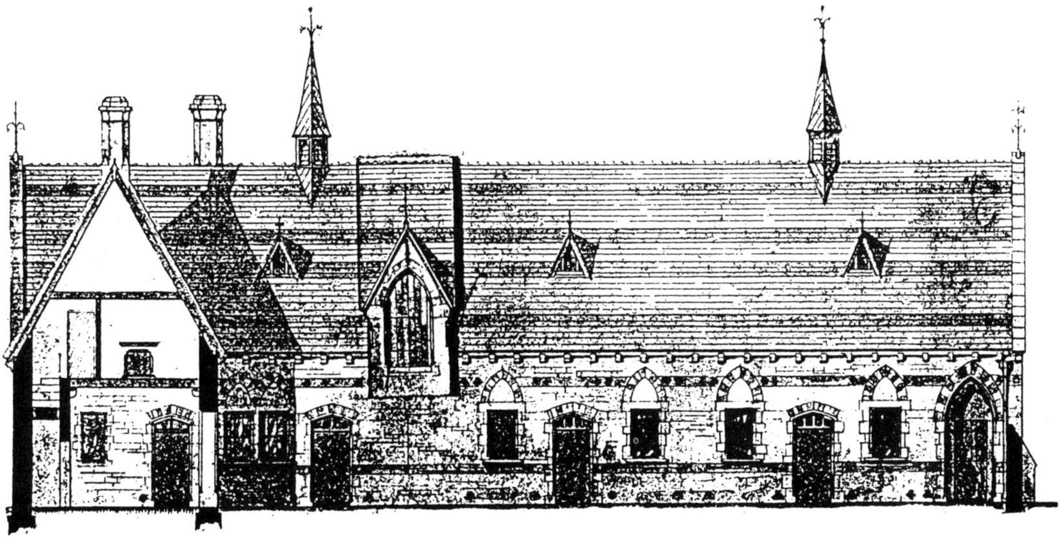

LOUGH RYAN: SALOON AND STABLEYARD

LIMERICK

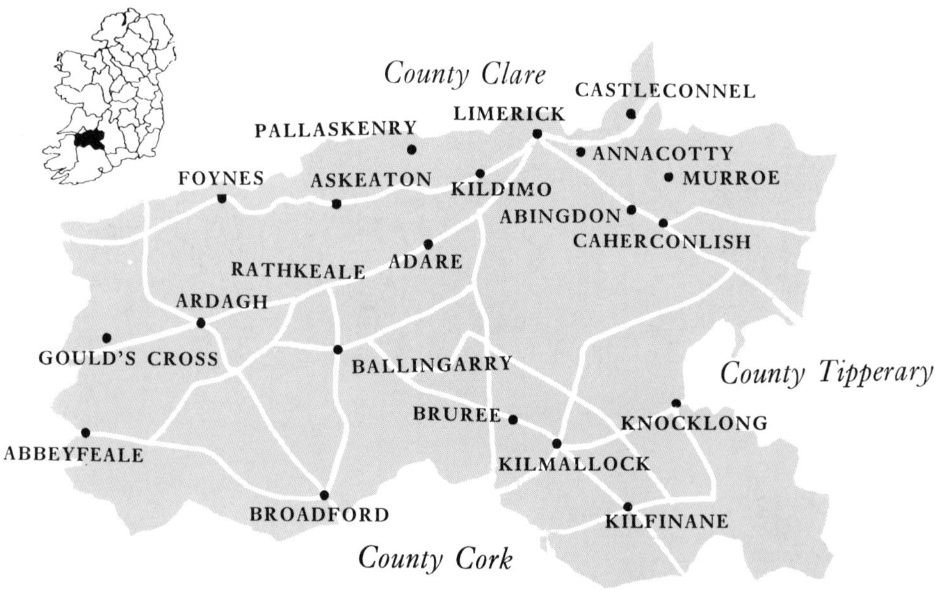

ABBEYFEALE: **No. 2, Main Street**
O'Connor's shop and pub with residence above. An outlying example of the Celtic Revival stuccowork that enlivens Listowel and by the same craftsman, Pat McAuliffe.

ABINGDON: **Church of Ireland**
The best church designed by J. Rawson Carroll (1870). External stonework now subtly polychromatic. Entered through an open porch behind an offset tower, that ascends to decoratively sculpted octagonal spire. Internal decoration is still intact, impeccably maintained by a tiny congregation who fit snugly into the nave. Four bays lead to a short trefoil-vaulted chancel. Triumphant composition above the altar with a triple lancet beneath four quatrefoils. At the western end, a pentagonal rose. Lively interplay of white and red stone in the coursing of the walls and the voussoires of the windows. Painted inscriptions at dado height and gilded stars against a ground of midnight blue at the springing of the open roof. Resplendent glass by Mayer and one window by Child (1908).

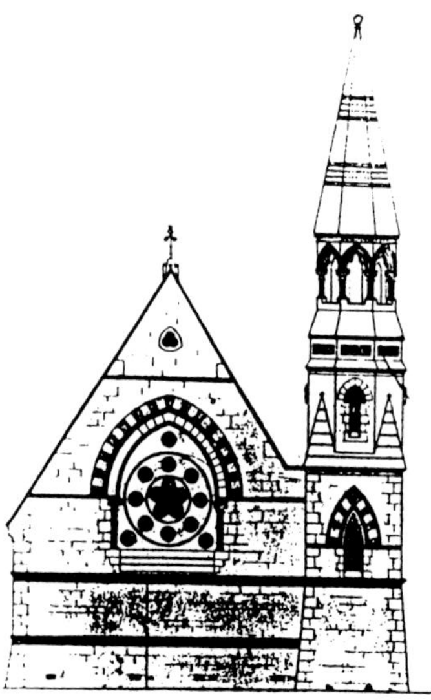

ADARE: **Adare Manor**
From tower house to early Georgian country seat to an immense feudal fantasy now stripped of its ancestral treasures to be yet another luxury hotel, the history of Adare mirrors that of Dromoland, the seat of the O'Briens, who had long ago driven the O'Quins from Clare to a less warlike part of Ireland. But while Dromoland was rebuilt by the Pains as a castle, Adare was rebuilt, with the unacknowledged assistance of the Pains, as an Irish medieval manor house, almost a myth, but this idealized vision gives the house a curious sense of the unreal that oddly accords with its present use. There are three phases of its long building history from

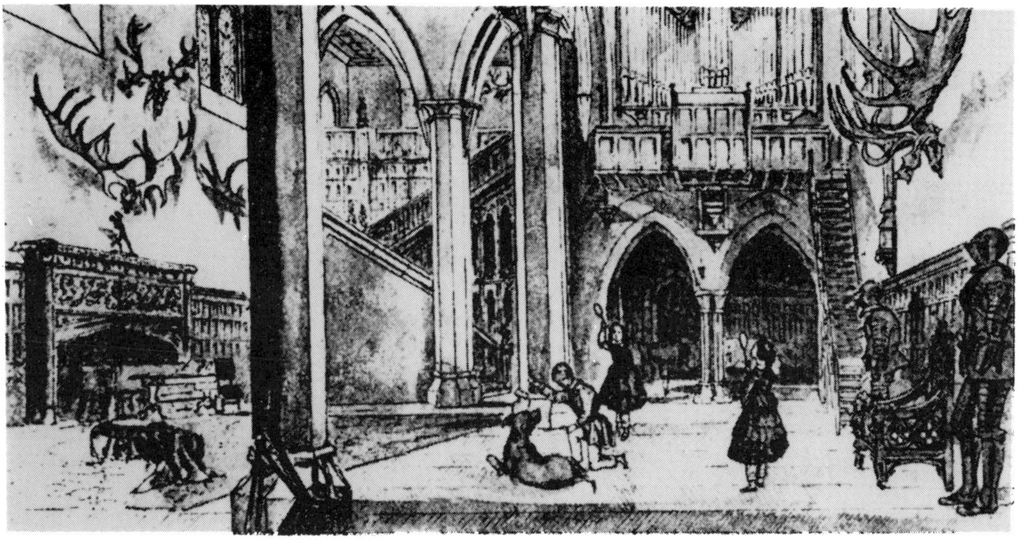

1832 to 1870, the first two phases under the control of the master mason, James Connolly. The 2nd earl of Dunraven and his heiress wife were inveterate travellers and incorporated into their designs their favourite buildings—the gatehouse from Eton College, a service tower from Haddon Hall, the winding approach to the long gallery from an old castle near Stuttgart. The long gallery takes up the first floor of the northern range, 130ft long, lit by double-height oriels with stained glass by Willement and a hammer-truss roof; when crammed with its original contents, the only Irish interior to recreate Beckford's vanished Fonthill. The German doors, and the Flemish choirstalls extended by Irish copies, survive the sale as fixtures. On the ground floor there is a Celtic Revival vestibule and a succession of rooms terminating in Lady Dunraven's boudoir with a vault uplifted by angels framing an oriel that overlooks the weir.

The second phase was the great hall linking the gallery range to the original house. A plan of 1834 by James Pain shows a predictable imperial staircase. By relegating this staircase to a side gallery and making a fireplace in its stead, the Dunravens transformed the space, making it mysterious and unpredictable. They also called in A.N.W. Pugin as their designer: he was responsible for the fireplace, the new stairs and an organ loft (removed by Detmar Blow). He also prepared designs for the main rooms in the southern range due to replace the early house.

This, the third phase, neither Pugin, nor Connolly nor their patron (the 2nd earl) lived to see. In the succeeding vacuum, the 3rd earl and his mother called in Philip Hardwick the younger to complete the three-storey southern range overlooking the formal gardens with parterres. Hardwick's contribution commands respect but not affection.

A strained pedantry replaces the effortless enthusiasm. The interlinking of the oriels on the garden front and the overloaded wedge-roofed tower lack assurance. His reception rooms are overwhelmed by his chimneypieces. The even vaster diningroom chimneypiece by Pugin is delicate and fanciful. This is the finest later interior, but it has never received the gallery that Pugin intended. Stable block by Hardwick assisted by William Corbett (1864). Garden houses by Clifford Smith. Parkland improved by James Frazer, but the demesne was devastated by the dredging of the River Maigue. Tactful additions were made to the river front when the house was converted into an hotel; but the recent neo-Tudor bedroom wing looks like a half-built Victorian orphanage. Hardwick's present-day successor also found adding to such a guileless fantasy inhibiting.

ADARE: **Catholic Church**

It is ironic that, despite the archaeological learning of the client, the 3rd earl of Dunraven (a convert to Catholicism) and the competence of his architect, the younger Hardwick (a convert to Pugin), this restoration conveys so little sense of Irish medieval monastic architecture, unlike the nearby Augustinian church restored by the unknown and the unscholarly a generation before. Of course the changes this century have not helped—stripping the plaster and remodelling the high altar. But the ultimate responsibility is Hardwick's. Although he added very little to the groundspace (a porch, a lady chapel, a side chapel and twelve feet to the nave), he left the imprint everywhere of his complex restless personality, without evolving a distinctive language of his own. This means we can only surmise what is his and what is medieval. It would appear that the double font is authentic, but it is now dominated by his massive marble-columned canopy. He is much better when he is designing without an Irish precedent—the brass screen between the chancel and the lady chapel. The glass is of varying quality, the best being the east window in the south aisle by Willement. The adjoining Trinitarian monastery was rebuilt as a hall, school for the Convent of Mercy, and presbytery, the last with its fenestration recently replaced with aluminium. But everything is still in use, as is Hardwick's hexafoil memorial fountain of 1855 at the gates.

ADARE: **Church of Ireland**

Two plaques record the restoration of this medieval Augustinian church by the 2nd earl of Dunraven, and by the 5th earl a century later. That to the 2nd earl was put up by his formidable widow Caroline, who used income from her Welsh estates to subsidise the recreation of Adare's feudal splendour; her architect was Joseph Welland (1860). Her daughter-in-law's memorial of 1865 by Harrison dominates the nave with High Victorian assurance. The choir contains stalls carved by the woodworkers who worked on the manor house in the 1830s. The stone-carving team of the manor sculpted the gargoyles of the south aisle. Robert Thompson of York carved the rail and lectern in the crossing, leaving his signature—a tiny mouse. The stained-glass windows commemorate generations of the Wyndham-Quins, from the earliest, in the chancel (by Willement), via the more neo-medieval glass by Hardman, to the autumnal variations of the later pre-Raphaelites (Heaton, Butler and Baynes). The adjoining Dunraven mausoleum inserted with pre-Victorian insouciance into the western range of the cloister in 1826 is a minor masterpiece, its external stonework formal, precise and delicate, its brick interior austere and chillingly unsentimental.

ADARE: **Village Hall; Adjoining Cottages**

The original scheme for the hall survives as a drawing, a brilliant adaptation of Voysey's idiom to a communal building by the English architect, Clifford Smith, working in Limerick. What was built in 1911 is much more conventional, but still informal and domestic, with a dormered bungalow concealing from the main approach the galleried hall behind. Two terraces of dormered and gabled cottages radiate from the hall, their porches upheld by rustic posts. These were designed by Detmar Blow. Similar groups of housing occur on outlying portions of the Dunraven estate, a formula that looks back into the past unlike William Scott's contemporary Talbot's Inch (q.v.). There are further village houses in the same rustic idiom, such as the present Mustard Seed Restaurant that blends with its thatched neighbours so well that it is difficult to think of Smith as an architect in his own right, indeed one of the most successful Arts and Crafts designers to work in Ireland.

ANNACOTTY: **Woodstown House**

Comfortable country retreat sited to overlook the Mulchair river; designed in 1879 for the Bannatyne family who were employing William Cox to erect their chateau-like mill (q.v.) on Limerick docks. Here their architects were

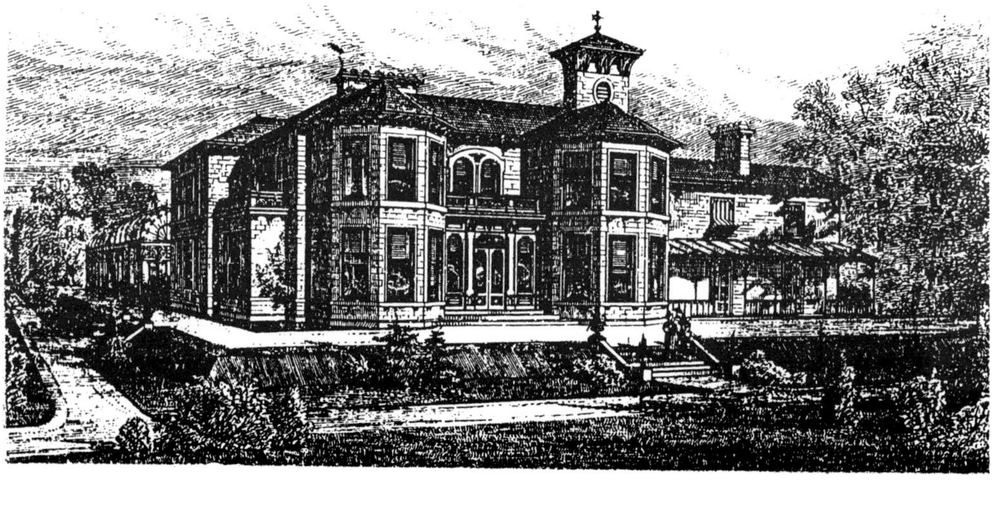

Joseph Fogerty and son. Leisurely bay windows flank an arcaded porch. Façade asymmetrically extended by a verandah set against a family wing beneath Italianate water tower. Formal gardens arranged in front of vanished curvilinear. Now extended as a religious institution helping handicapped children.

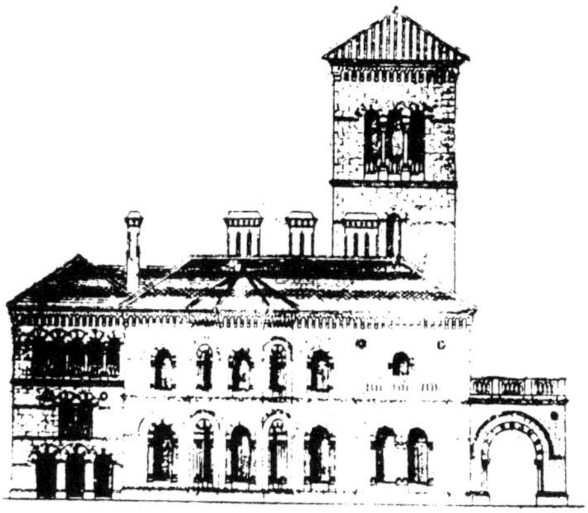

ARDAGH: **Cahirmoyle**
J.J. McCarthy's most important country-house commission, even if today it appears to have been built for its present use, a home for the elderly, or a religious institution, which it was before. The house is constructed round a double-arcaded staircase hall, upheld by McCarthy's characteristically over-scaled arcades with marble shafts and richly sculpted capitals, a muted variant of Woodward's destroyed staircase hall in the Kildare Street Club. The principal rooms have polychromatic marble fireplaces and delicately painted ceilings. Ponderous *porte cochère* on entrance front and bay windows on adjoining garden front that polychromatic shafts and voussoirs fail to enliven (McCarthy had built too many churches) and the loss of the loggia on the adjoining tower has added to its external sultriness. The client, a son of the patriot William Smith O'Brien and a descendant of the high kings, dictated Hiberno-Romanesque as his choice of style.

ARDAGH: **Rathronan Mausoleum**
The burial ground of the Smith O'Briens of nearby Cahirmoyle with an Hiberno-Romanesque arcaded mausoleum designed for them by William Fogerty in 1865. The choice of style prefigures that of Cahirmoyle (started six years later but by another architect, J.J. McCarthy). The Celtic Revival is an appropriate sepulchre for William Smith O'Brien, who led the Young Irelanders into revolt against the British government in 1848.

ASKEATON: **Catholic Church**
A carved inscription records the building of this church in Latin along with the first part of the Ave Maria in gratitude. Another inscription records its restoration or rather mutilation in 1977. Where there was before a delicate balance between the vernacular and the High Victorian Gothic, now there is compromise between puritanical modernity and the ecclesiastical counterpart of bungalow bliss. Trussed roof concealed by plaster ribbing; galleries replaced; reredos removed; clear glass now frosted to prevent distraction from the beauty of God's creation.

BALLINGARRY: **Catholic Church**
Hard French Gothic parish church, built in 1876 by an unrecorded follower of J.J. McCarthy, designer presumably of Ballylongford. Cruciform; western tower and spire; single lean-to side aisle; arcades carried across transepts; compressed chancel; chubby columns of red marble; glass by Mayer; altar designed in 1893 by George Ashlin.

BROADFORD: **Glanduff Castle (also known as Castle Ievers)**
Seat of seat of the Ievers family and remodelled for them in the mid-1830s by C.F. Anderson, who added battlemented towers at either end and a double-storied turreted porch.

BRUREE: **Bruree House**
Simplified Gothic Revival country house with pointed windows and steeply rising roofs. The Irish home of the second duke of Westminster; lived in by his daughter, the wife of the poet Stephen Vernon.

CAHERCONLISH: **Church of Ireland**
Small, single-cell church (designed by E.H. Carson in 1866) terminating in three-sided apse with coupled lancets rising into adjoining gables. Stonework polychromatically treated. These are parallel with nearby Abington, except that here the more ambitious belfry was never attempted.

CASTLECONNEL: **Catholic Church**
Cruciform Gothic Revival church showing the influence of Philip Hardwick, whom its architect (William Corbett) had been assisting for the previous decade. Dated 1865.

FOYNES: **Catholic Church**
Although only a simple cell of four bays, this is one of J.J. McCarthy's most incisive designs, with a projecting cavernous porch resting on tiny coupled red marble columns. The west façade has the same contrast of scale—an immense rose window and a tiny corner turret enclosing a staircase to the organ loft. McCarthy's transepts, chancel and central tower were never built. Instead, a modern fan-shaped nave was

added alongside the south wall of the church, which was then removed, so that the original nave has now become a reorientated chancel. This makes nonsense of the exterior but works surprisingly well within.

GOULD'S CROSS: **Athea**
A textbook version of an Irish high cross, raised (as grimly recorded on every face) in 1863 by his grateful tenantry to Thomas Gould, great-grandfather of Countess Marcievitz, prophetic evidence of her family's involvement in the Celtic Revival.

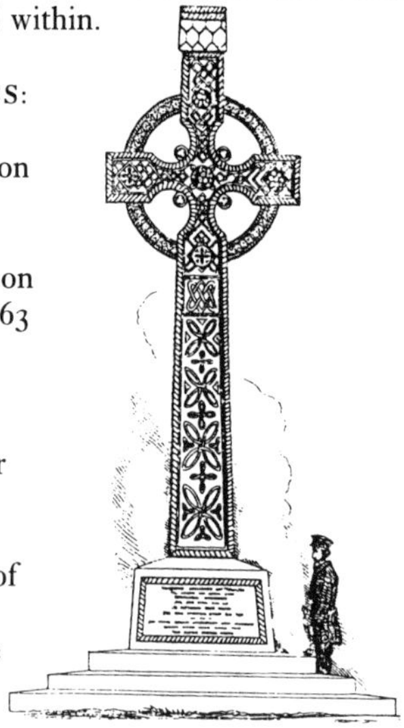

FOYNES: **Spring-Rice Memorial**
Harshly carved Celtic Revival cross built to overlook the harbour. Now surrounded by coniferous plantations, so no longer a dramatic silhouette against the setting sun.

FOYNES: **The Station**
Built in cut stone and designed as the focal point of the model village commissioned from Sir Reginald Bloomfield by Lord Monteagle *c.* 1910. Now used merely as offices and a bus shelter since trains no longer run. Adjoining Arts and Crafts post office with bands of rock-faced ashlar alternating with rendered walls. Matching housing which was continued between the wars by a local builder, Denis Powers.

KILDIMO: **Elm Park**
Just two gatelodges survive, the principal one designed to match the castle built in the 1830s by C.F. Anderson for the Massey family in the same cubistic Gothick style, but which was burnt out in 1922 and the ruin demolished.

KILDIMO: **Vermont**
Wayside Gothic memorial cross commemorates a forgotten landlord.

KILFINANE: **Castle Oliver**
Designed in Scottish Barnonial in 1865 by G. Fowler Jones, an architect from Yorkshire, assisted by Sir Thomas Deane. Entered from the side with double-storied *porte-cochère* projecting from battlemented keep at the corner of adjoining garden front. Protected by raised terrace with balustrade and now vanished gryphons cast in Portland cement, its first recorded use in Ireland. The high pitched slate roofs conceal another innovation—wrought-iron and cast-iron trusses. Commissioned by two sisters, Mary and Elizabeth Oliver, to replace the house where their unacknowledged cousin, Lola Montez, mistress of Ludwig I, was born. The two sisters were accomplished artists and decorated the castle by painting on glass their heraldic devices and scenes from the life of St Patrick. Both sisters married Trenches and the estate was sold by the widow of the last Trench heir fifteen years ago. Since then the castle has been vandalised, their stained glass broken, the fireplaces painted by the sisters removed. Restoration has been started by the present owner.

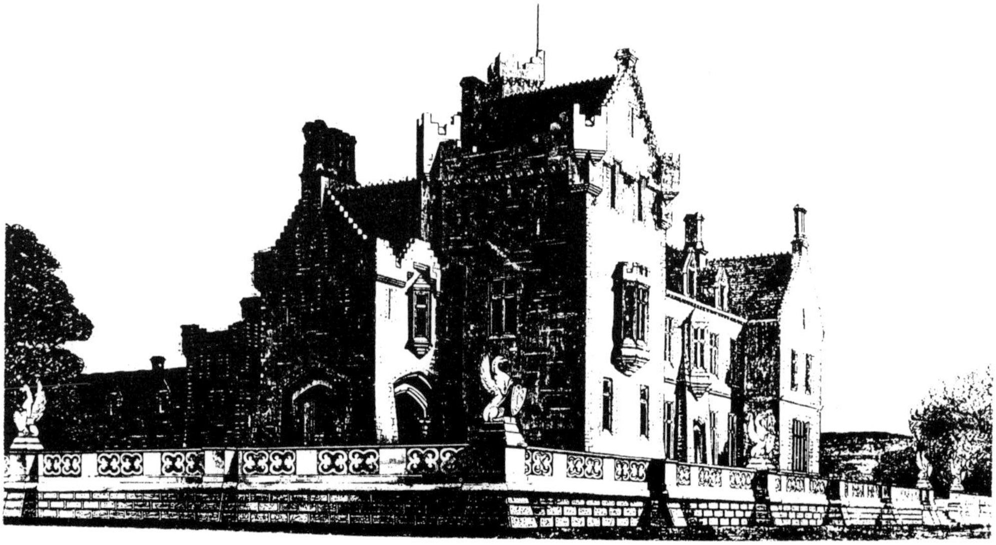

KILFINANE: **Catholic Church**
Gothic Revival church designed by George Ashlin in 1878.

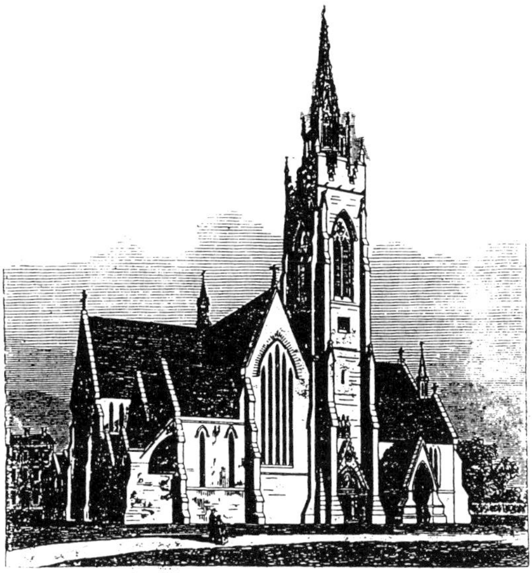

KILMALLOCK: **Allied Irish Bank**
Built as the Munster and Leinster Bank in 1877 by Henry and Arthur Hill in the Elizabethan style to match Kilmallock's medieval architecture (now all swept away). The Hills re-cased two earlier adjoining houses with stone mullions screening the original windows, and made new Gothic doors and ground-floor windows.

KILMALLOCK: **Ash Hill Towers**
Picturesque array of Gothick towers and defences built on to the rear of a Georgian house in 1837; hence the change of name. A few towers have survived the demolition this century of most of these embellishments, which were designed by C.F. Anderson for the Evans family. Currently under restoration.

KILMALLOCK: **Catholic Church**
One of the later churches of J.J. McCarthy, built in 1878 simplified in plan with organ loft, nave and chancel beneath one continuous roof contasting with off-centre tower and spire. The second-last bay of the aisles is carried upwards to make small transepts screened from the nave. There is sumptuous internal carving and decoration, despite the present altar's being made up out of its predecessor's debris. Here the central pinnacle has been retained as a freestanding tabernacle and a pair of dislodged marble angels stand guard on either side, above a window inspired by the ruined Dominican church of the town. Venetian mosaics in the chancel, under direction of George Ashlin; glass by Mayer and Earley.

KNOCKLONG: **Kilfrush House**
Large sub-Classical country house of the Gubbins family designed *c.*1835 by C.F. Anderson, who also built the Doric gatelodge with a sense of the monumental so lacking in the elevations of the house.

LIMERICK, **Baker Place: Clock Tower Testimonial**
The largest Victorian store, Cannocks, has been so rebuilt as be unidentifiable, including its clock tower that once dominated O'Connell Street. However, this memorial to one of Cannock's founders, a self-made Scots entrepreneur, Peter Tait, survives—another clock tower. An international competition was held and the first three prizes were won by Limerick architects. But at least the winning prize was built. The architect, William Corbett, was at that time a committed Gothic Revivalist, in this case influenced by Barre's Albert Memorial in Belfast (q.v.) of the same period, but only 65ft high. Completed 1867.

LIMERICK, **Bishop Street: Convent of Mercy**
Designed by John Neville of Dundalk, whose two daughters became nuns—hence the commissions for convents. This is his most distant and largest. The convent is linked to the school block with a long return façade via an unexpected companile. On the other side there is a cruciform chapel with its own tower and spire in the angle between the nave and transept. Elaborately tranceried windows but simple interior to the chapel. Dated 1852. Behind the chapel, twelve houses for widows, also by Neville.

LIMERICK: **Catholic Cathedral**
The most effective Puginian cathedral in Ireland not built by the master himself. The architect, Philip Charles Hardwick, had been brought over from London to complete Adare Manor (q.v.) by the 3rd earl of Dunraven. But while his work at Adare is dry and self-conscious, his cathedral interior is inventive and moving, the individual response of a sensitive outsider to a religion of the masses. What makes Hardwick's cathedral of 1856-61 so memorable is his mastery of light. His nave and aisles are roofed separately, usually an excuse for a large clerestory. Instead, Hardwick keeps his windows at the upper level small and sets them into reveals that send shafts of daylight downwards so that the roof above is

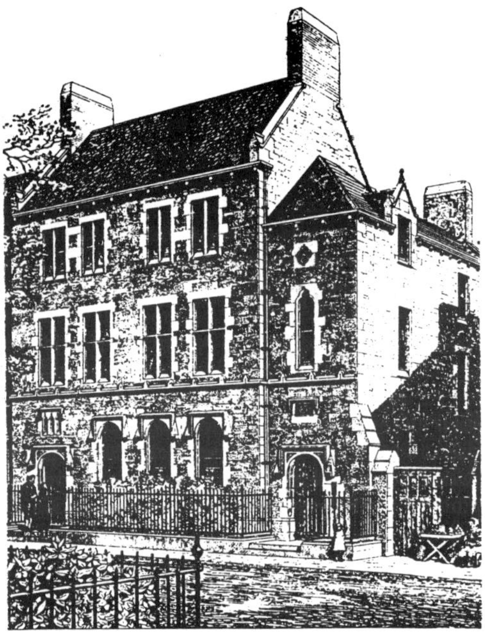

lost in darkness. After the darkness of the nave with its columns alternating as cylinders and octagons, the simple device of projecting the chancel a bay beyond four side-chapels (grouped in pairs on either side of it) allows the illumination of the high altar by unseen windows. Against this light-filled paradise, a rood screen spans the springing of the framing arch with Christ crucified between the Virgin and St John seen in darkened silhouette, immune from liturgists. If Pugin had raised his own roods to such a height, they too might have survived destruction. While the diocese of Limerick has an horrific record in the removal of Victorian fittings, the cathedral has survived this ordeal comparatively unscathed. The main casualty is the bishop's throne, carved (like the rood) by the Belgian firm of Phyffers, which has been remade into the Blessed Sacrament altar. Pulpit and communion rail remain intact, as does the reredos of the high altar, again by Phyffers, but re-sited and raised in a redecoration programme of J.J. O'Callaghan in 1894, which also has been spared. The stained glass is in the style of Mayer of the 1880s (apart from the eastern window of 1867). The exterior is dominated, as Hardwick intended, by a tower and spire, but not to his more economical design. The spire was built to the design of a local architect, M.A. Hennessy, at 280ft high it is said to have been the highest in Ireland when it was completed in 1883. In living memory the cathedral served admirably as the setting for two of the treasures of medieval Ireland, the crozier and mitre of Conor O'Dea. It is hoped that some day that they will be returned to their rightful context.

LIMERICK: Church of Ireland Cathedral
The Victorian restoration of St Mary's cathedral was a continuous process that goes on today inspired by the same dangerous purism—to disengage the original medieval Cistercian structure from the accumulation of centuries. Thus the triple lancets above the altar are purely Victorian, inserted by William Slater to replace a Perpendicular-style window erected by James Pain twenty years before and now in the chancel of St Michael's Church of Ireland church. Slater spared Pain's crocketted bishop's throne, which is due to be removed today as the impact of the Second Vatican Council percolates into the remote recesses of Irish Anglicanism. It could be argued that Pain, by using a later debased Gothic for his restoration, was more ethical than Slater, who by replicating the original deceives us all. Indeed the more successful the Victorian restoration of a cathedral, the more we are deluded. For the Victorians, who worshipped truth, this paradox was acutely disturbing.

The chapter of the cathedral approached a bewildering number of architects—James Pain in the 1820s, William Bardwell in 1839, William Slater, who in 1850 did the principal restoration, including the new structure; then, inevitably, Welland for fittings. Next Joseph Fogerty, followed by another local, William Cox. They called in G.E. Street, but his scheme was rejected on the grounds of cost, and an alternative was commissioned from J.F. Fuller, who was responsible for the hilarious heating system of double-towered radiators; these (having subsumed enough funds to pay for the solution of Street several times over) are to be given away to whomever will remove them. Restoration of south aisle by Robert Fogerty in 1891. Memorials include the Westropp tomb in the south transept carved by James Redfern; the Pery chapel with its recumbent effigy, by Richard Westmacott (1845), visible through a flamboyant traceried screen. The east chancel window, the west window to the nave and the south transept window are all by Clayton and Bell. The later north transept window is by Heaton, Butler and Baynes. The O'Brien chapel has small Arts and Crafts windows by Catherine O'Brien, the best 20th-century glass in the cathedral. The reredos carved by James Pearse in 1907 is to be retained in situ, but a new chapel partitioned by the rood screen will be repositioned. This was designed in a kind of Gothic art deco in 1921 by Conor O'Brien, but it was originally incorrectly positioned while he was sailing his yacht round the world.

LIMERICK, Cork Road: Model Schools
Characteristically mullioned and gabled Tudor Revival institution, one of the series designed

by Frederick Darley and built in the early 1840s. Neglected and then burnt out, its blackened ruins imparted an unexpected frisson to its select neighbourhood. Now restored with aluminium fenestration matching the harshness of the original stonework.

LIMERICK, The Crescent: Jesuit Church
Design attributed to Charles Geoghegan but in any case executed by William Corbett, who completed the interior in 1869, added the transepts in 1874, and rebuilt the façade in 1900 as a neo-Classical centrepiece to the west side of the Crescent. An unfortunate choice of red, machine-made brick has caused an irreparable breakdown of relations with its Georgian neighbours. The interior is much better, unusual for that date for its Palladian inspiration with marbleized pilasters articulating apse and transepts. High altar of many marbles designed by Corbett to upstage the earlier altar to the Virgin commissioned privately from George Goldie when he was working for the nearby Redeptorists.

LIMERICK, The Crescent: O'Connell Monument
One of the last commissions of John Hogan, unveiled in 1857, a year before his death. The Liberator is depicted swathed in a great cloak. Compared with the Dublin memorial (q.v.), the pedestal is extremely simple, but the architectural setting of the Crescent with its long vistas north and south is more imposing.

LIMERICK, Dock Road: Bannatyne's
The masterpiece of the Limerick architect and engineer William Cox that is both functional mill and dream chateau. From a technological viewpoint it was built as the most advanced cornmill in Ireland when completed in 1874 using a system that dropped the corn from the ground floor to the basement and then raised it by elevators to the topmost floor. From then on gravity was used to process it on its descent. Each floor has its own cooling system and storage. Dormers and gables interpenetrate the roof to house the hoisting equipment. The adjoining tower, entered through a massive chiselled doorway, houses the engine room on the first floor and a clock below the roof. The walls are built of rubble-and-limestone dressing with the arches of white Scotch firebrick that adds a lighter note to its forbidding grandeur.

The foundations in some places go down for twenty-five feet. The two lower floors are vaulted; the two upper have their timber planks connected by iron tonguing. Cast iron is also used for the internal columns. While our best industrial architecture is demountable, the best industrial architecture of the Victorians was built to last for ever.

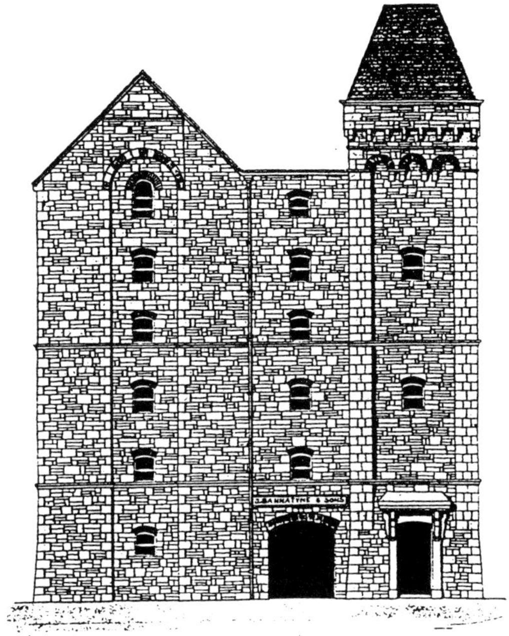

LIMERICK, Dock Road: Dock Clock
Italianate tower erected in 1880 to the designs of the harbour engineer, William Hall.

LIMERICK: Franciscan Church
The most successful of the three Classical churches designed by the Limerick architect, William Corbett at the end of the century. This was started in 1876. The portico projects boldly over the pavement and looks especially impressive from a distance. A nearer view reveals only four columns grouped too close together. The interior is inspired by Santa Maria Maggiore in Rome, with the nave divided from the aisles by Corinthian columns and a straight entablature. Polished Aberdeen granite, used in the shafts, recurs in the much smaller columns that subdivide the clerestory into groups of three. The terminating windowless apse was not built until 1931, but the architects, Jones and Kelly, followed Corbett's intentions. Their altar lost its culminating pillared rotunda to the liturgical trends of the 1960s.

LIMERICK, Glentworth Street: Cork and Limerick Savings Bank
One of the purest examples of Irish neo-Classicism—and one of the last, since it was commissioned in 1839 from W.H. Owen and built by Sir Thomas Deane, who may have

collaborated with the design. A Doric temple entered through a portico of four baseless columns with fluted shafts.

LIMERICK, Glentworth Street: Dominican Church

The Regency Gothic church designed by the Pains in 1815 was remodelled to accord with High Victorian taste by George Goldie, the chancel in 1868 (now altered after the 2nd Vatican Council), the nave in 1870 (which has remained reasonably intact). The high altar was carved originally by P. Scannell of Cork to incorporate three bas-reliefs by a Mr Bolton of Worcester. The stained-glass window above by Wailes of Newcastle has survived but not the decoration by Hodkinson of Cork replaced by the religious pop art of Father Buckley. The open roof, clerestory, organ gallery and the arcades of red Aberdeen granite are all due to Goldie, but supervised by Michael Hennessy, who added the Sacred Heart chapel in 1898.

LIMERICK, Hartsonge Street: Leamy School

Delightful Tudor Revival college in mellow brick with stone trimmings. Oriels and niches decorate the multistoried gatehouse. Sensitivitely converted into a factory by Crescent Clothes Ltd. Date 1841; architect:, Joseph Fogerty.

LIMERICK, Henry Street: Presbyterian Church

As the leading Catholic church architect in Ireland, George Ashlin was a surprising choice for the Presbyterians of Limerick in 1899. Ashlin himself used brick—for him an unusual decision. It is a harsh red brick from Ruabon that has refused to age, unlike the now crumbling Portland stone that he reserved for the trimmings and the plate tracery, notably the rose at the end of the nave. The result is the architectural counterpart of a Salvation Army hymn, difficult to adapt to the secular context. Unexpectedly successful conversion into offices by Murray and O'Laoghaire (1992), far more sympathetic to its innate sanctity than so many adaptations of Ashlin's Catholic churches to current liturgical trends.

LIMERICK, Henry Street: Redemptorist Church

Gothic Revival church and adjoining monastery designed by P.C. Hardwick and built in 1858-62 (supervised by William Corbett). Belfry attached to one side of the façade and treated with a subtle polychromy of pink and grey. Spire completed by Michael Hennessy; George Goldie designed the present high altar in 1865. Monastery extended by George Ashlin in 1901, who remodelled the side chapels of the nave, two of them sensationally top-lit through vaults of stained glass. Goldie's high altar is contained inside a windowless apse. A Gothic arch rests on marble columns overscaled to match the towering high altar enshrining six colossal saints, carved by Phyffers. Above, a painted vault gathers saints beneath the Coronation of the Virgin. The mosaic by Oppenheimers of Manchester dates from 1927

LIMERICK: Mungret College

Monastery made into an architectural college and grimly extended in the Gothic Revival idiom—*c.*1880. Now closed due to cutbacks in the Government's education policies.

LIMERICK, North Circular Road: Lansdowne House development

A good example of Clifford Smith's speculative style with his favourite combination of pebble dash and limestone dressings built *c.*1910 in what is still Limerick's most fashionable suburb. Symmetrical composition of central detached residence with two pairs of semi-detached houses on either side.

LIMERICK, O'Connell Avenue: Housing

This consists of a speculative housing scheme, Verona Terrace, and a series of adjoining residences. The housing scheme is disciplined and uniform; the individual three-storied residences are extraordinarily varied to the verge of Art Nouveau, with the mixture of arches and bay windows introduced to Limerick by Clifford Smith in his Shannon Boat Club. Despite their formal freedom, the complex is held together by a controlled urbanism not found in the Dublin of that period.

LIMERICK, O'Connell Road: Technical Institute

A government competition held in 1909 was won by an elderly London architect, W.P. Ryan, who had been born in Limerick. The result is an isolated instance of the Queen Anne Revival, with its hipped roof and vertically treated façades inspired by the earliest Irish country houses such as Mount Ievers. Spacious interiors still preserving their 'Sweetness and Light'.

LIMERICK, O'Connell Street: Bell Table

Terraced Georgian house extended as the Gaiety Cinema in 1919 by Clifford Smith. Ground floor replaced by shallow arch on bulging columns. Interior remodelled by Murray and O'Laoghaire as theatre and art centre juxtaposed to the headquarters of Limerick's religious confraternities.

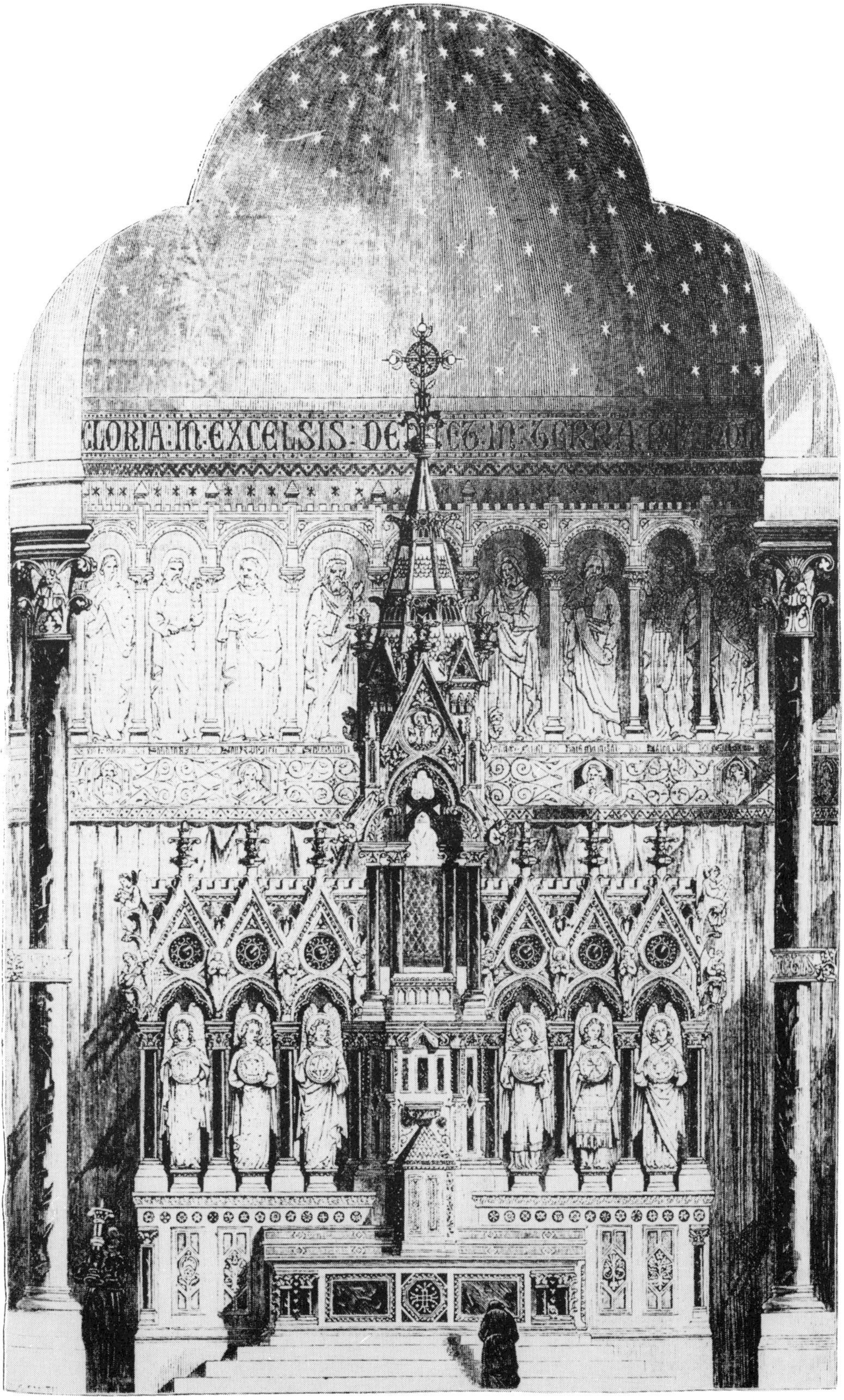

REDEMPTORIST CHURCH: HIGH ALTAR

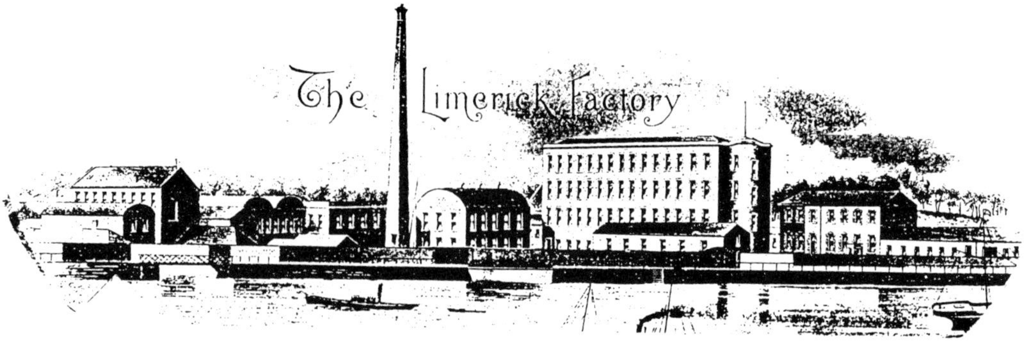

LIMERICK: O'Mara's bacon factory
Built during the 1860s to make agricultural equipment; later transformed into a condensed milk plant, and now part of O'Mara's bacon factory, this multi-storied warehouse with attached circular tower for vertical access still dominates the west bank of the River Shannon.

LIMERICK: Old Workhouse
Gothic Revival structure, now part of St Camillus' Hospital. Designed by Thomas and Kearns Deane and also built by them, 1839-41. Aluminium glazing. Chapel drastically remodelled.

LIMERICK, Pery Square: Carnegie Library
This was built in 1906 in Pery Square (which had been transformed into the People's Park in 1874). The architect was G.P. Sheridan, who had won the second prize in the competition, G. Beckett having won the first. Sheridan tried here to adapt the Celtic Revival to what it was never meant for, a spacious well-lit open plan. The result is that after the front door, which is Celtic, the interior reverts to diluted Arts and Crafts, the expected norm for philanthropic educational establishments of the time. Still functioning, but only as an art gallery, now that the library has been removed elsewhere by an administration that had not sensed its primary aim—to unite the arts to learning. Beside it, a triumphal arch of 1874 by Richard Russell.

LIMERICK, Pery Square: St Michael's Church of Ireland
The Georgian church was replaced when Pery Square was being redeveloped by the Pains in the 1840s. The idiom of the church is Gothic, but the adjoining terraces are neo-Classical and give to this quiet corner of the city a sense of Edinburgh. Its view terminates with the opposition, the Dominican Church by Pain from the same time. Both were improved in the 1870s, when William Fogerty and his cousin Robert heightened the tower of St Michael's, laid out a new forecourt and added a chancel replacing the arcades with marble columns, inserting new flooring and roof of varnished timber. Glass by Heaton, Butler and Bayne.

LIMERICK: Plassey House
Italianate villa with columned porch and imposing interiors. Asymmetrical service wing with hidden third floor lit at the roof bracket level. The original estate was acquired by Robert Clive, who renamed it Plassey after his Indian victory in order to become Lord Clive of Plassey in the peerage of Ireland. The house was rebuilt for the Russell family (*c.*1875) and attributed to Joseph Fogerty and son. Now carefully preserved as the centrepiece of the new University of Limerick.

LIMERICK: Protestant Orphan Society Hall
Although William Fogerty was Limerick's leading Gothic Revivalist with a nationwide practice, he was never given the commission of a new church here. The nearest he got to one was erecting this double-storied assembly rooms in a collegiate Gothic dating from 1865.

LIMERICK: St John's Church of Ireland
A 1843 experiment by Welland in the Norman style. There are stylistic parallels with Glenstal Abbey (q.v.) by William Bardwell, except that Bardwell, as an English outsider, incorporated the Hiberno-Romanesque. Welland, who as an insider built more churches than any other Irish architect (partly due to being first cousin to the bishop of Down and Connor), had no reason to take up the Celtic Revival, and St John's is grimly, and since its closure forlornly, conventional. Turned into a heritage centre, but too late to save from vandalism the stained glass windows in the south aisle by J. Gibson of Newcastle-on-Tyne, exhibited in the Great Exhibition of 1851. It is hoped that at least Welland's internal decoration of purple and golden stars will be retained.

LIMERICK: Shannon Boat Club
International competition won by an English architect, Clifford Smith, in 1902, on condition that he came to live in Limerick. This was the start of a long prolific career as an Arts and

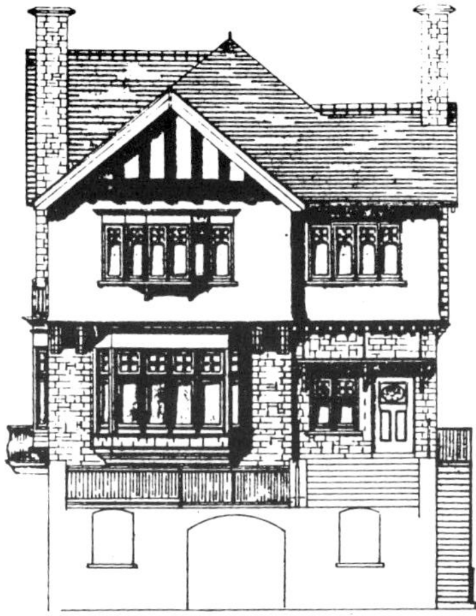

Crafts architect, and the firm he founded still flourishes in the city and preserves all his drawings. Dublin architectural journalism accords him only a fleeting mention. This boat club, despite its prominent siting on Nimmo's great bridge, is not recorded. All Clifford Smith's abilities are clearly demonstrated—his grasp of asymmetrical massing, his interplay of arches and corbelled bay windows, his exploitation of contrasting textures with rusticated limestone against pebbly roughcast and half-timbered gables. Spatially flowing interiors with panoramic viewing of the Shannon.

LIMERICK, **Tipperary Road: Boru House**

More like a minor convent than the dream house of a successful builder, the father of the novelist Kate O'Brien. She was brought up here and not allowed, one suspects, to play with the children of her neighbours, still less to consort with the inmates of the gaol across the road.

LIMERICK, **William Street: Nos. 11-12, Boyd's**

Vigorous terracotta composition of four bays, articulated by pilasters rising from a now mulitated ground floor to the skyline. Arcaded topmost floor. Designed by William Fogerty *c.*1865.

LIMERICK, **William Street: Nos. 7-9, Todd's**

The glamour of the smartest shop in the city, as recalled by Kate O'Brien, is today just discernible now that it is split into three. But a terracotta palazzo rises pompously above the modernized shops, ignoring their competitive unneighbourliness. Designed in 1887 by Robert Fogerty as a prelude to Revington's, his great store in Tralee. Interesting architectural comparison with the less pompous Boyd's just up the street, designed by his cousin twenty years before.

MURROE: **Glenstal Castle**

After Gosford, the grandest Norman Revival castle to be built in Ireland. The client was a Limerick lawyer and railway engineer, Sir Matthew Barrington, who in five years (1833-8) commissioned five schemes from different architects—the Pains, Decimus Burton, two versions from an obscure Dublin architect, John Kelly, and the English William Bardwell. The last was ultimately built, at least partially, in the 1850s, supervised by a John Kelly of Dublin, an unnamed employee of Dargan, and Joshua Hargrave, of Cork. Despite this complex history, the castle is remarkably consistent, with two embattled ranges converging on a circular keep inspired by Windsor. The focal point of the entry range is the gatehouse modelled on Rockingham Castle; that of the adjoining garden range an immense square keep derived from Rochester. This became the terminating feature when economies were made by Hargrave in 1850 to cut short Bardwell's design. The keep lost its defensive character due to the ground floor

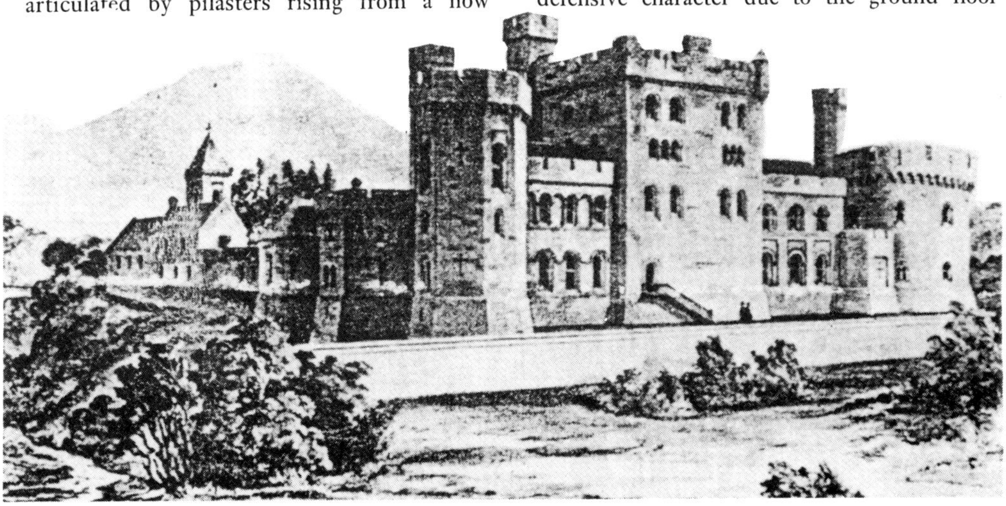

being adapted to contain the diningroom. However, plausibility had already been sacrificed to give the adjoining drawingroom and the picture gallery spacious arched windows with views south across the Golden Vale. A real medieval castle has to withstand assault from the army of a rival baron; that of its Victorian counterpart is set up by the contradictory requirements of habitability and archaeological exactitude. In the library beyond the picture gallery that takes up the ground floor of the circular keep, it is not possible to see out of the windows. Instead, all attention is concentrated on the central octagonal core: eight massive columns are linked by mirrors above two fireplaces set back to back. From them spring a massive rib-vault to columns around the perimeter, the ribs in stone, the vaults painted blue with gilded stars.

Although Bardwell supplied the Barringtons with appropriate furnishings, armour and stained glass, none of these survive. What remains today is two painted rooms and the stone sculpture. This was originally by Kelsey of London (working for Bardwell), but he was replaced by local carvers inspired by Celtic models. Thus, while the pierglass above the drawingroom fireplace is framed by an adaptation of Iffley, the room is entered through a replica of the Hiberno-Romanesque doorway in Killaloe Cathedral, carved by a sculptor called White. The castle itself is entered between sculptures of Edward I and Eleanor of Aquitaine. This naive evocation of the relationship between Ireland and England was to have a tragic sequel. In 1921 the daughter of the 5th baronet accepted a picnic invitation from the local Black and Tans and was killed in an ambush by the IRA. The castle, rejected as a presidential residence, was acquired by Monsignor Edward Ryan and donated to the Belgian Benedictines. With the exception of one wing that ruined forever the chance of completing Bardwell's design, their additions have been thoughtful and discreet. The monks have maintained the Barrington's shrubberies and arboretum. The encircling oak forest is the original setting of Le Fanu's *Uncle Silas*.

PALLASKENRY: **Dromore Castle**

Commissioned in 1866 by the 3rd earl of Limerick, president of the Architectural Society in London. His vice-president was Edwin Godwin, who had just recreated the pageantry of medieval times with his townhalls for Northampton and Congleton; but Dromore was his first large commission from an enthusiastic private patron. Godwin studied Irish castles, and his surveys of them have never been excelled. Unfortunately his travels coincided with

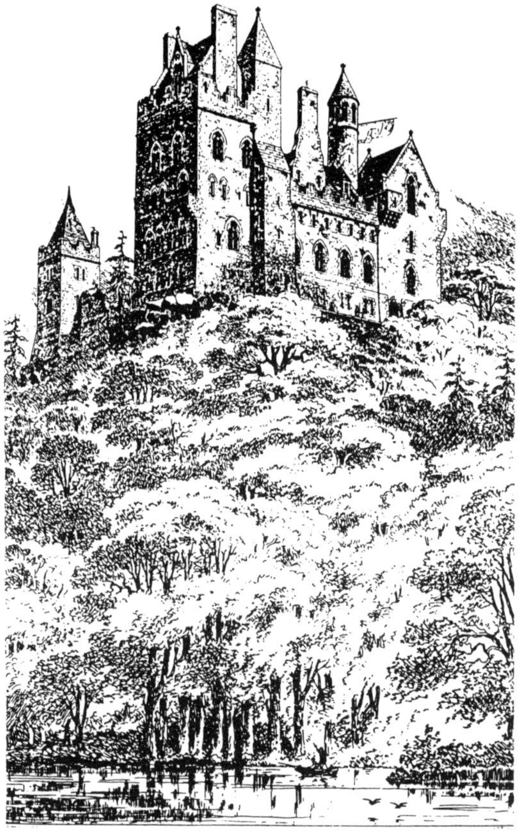

rumours of Fenian uprisings—hence his decision to site the principal rooms facing into an enclosed courtyard and keeping the corridors along the outside walls, with the result that sunlight rarely entered. All this was to ensure that the 'inmates of Dromore Castle might not only feel secure themselves but give shelter to others'. In fact the sculpted entrance arch was built too narrow to take the family coach. This restricted entrance occurs within a lower range containing the great hall and chapel.

From this *porte-cochère* a staircase vaulted with stepped transverse arches rises to the *piano nobile* of the adjoining range. A long corridor leads past the principal rooms, with their claustrophic outlook, to the drawingroom (the only room that overlooks the lake) set in a keep that projects forward on three sides. The courtyard is defended on its two open sides by curtain walls with a walk-way linking the first floor to a minor gatehouse and a corner tower. Now that the castle is a roofless shell with only one function that survives (it is still defendable), we can more easily admire the way Godwin sets up a pin-wheel motion by alternating the orientation of the chimney-stacks and gabled roofs that straddle the varied towers. This motion revolves around his most daring improvization, a replica of a round tower inspired by Cashel. If this was introduced to suggest an ancient

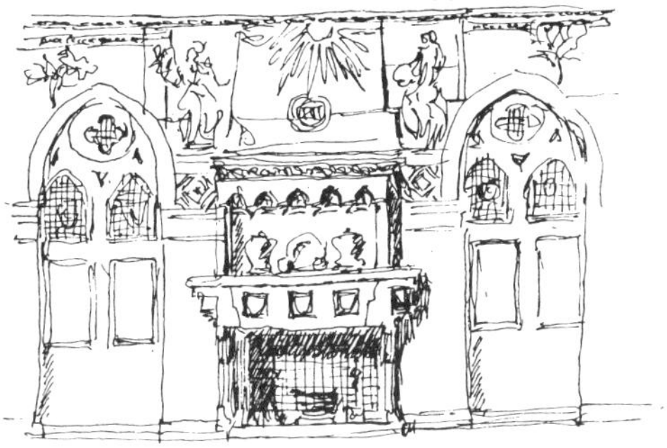

monastic site too venerable to be violated, one can only say today that this ploy, as in Cashel, has not succeeded. Thirty years after the death of the 3rd earl, the Limerick family, on the verge of bankruptcy, sold the estate (*c.* 1925) to the McMahons, who in due course gave a last ball, at which the guests played musical chairs to Wagner. The castle was ultimately offered free to anyone who wanted to live there. By then the frescoes painted by Henry Stacey Marks, never completed due to the damp, had faded beyond recognition, and the Anglo-Japanese furniture that Godwin had especially designed for here (which if discovered and sold off today would pay for the restoration: a table and a sideboard were sold by Christie's for over £250,000 in 1993, having languished in a local garage from which they had been acquired for £600) had been broken up and lost. At the time of its dismantling nobody was interested even in the carved-stone fireplaces, so they still remain, inaccessible in the ruins.

There have been several recent schemes to restore Dromore. The current scheme does not, one hopes, follow the precedent of the rebuilding of the stable block. Godwin himself sketched the castle as a ruin silhouetted against the moonlight, a scene that prefigures the work of his son by Ellen Terry, Gordon Craig. His vantage point was the ruined church of Killulta. This alone is mentioned in the 1962 *Shell Guide*, so visitors following directions to the smallest Celtic church in Ireland must have been overwhelmed by this nameless apparition looming above them, rivalling King Ludwig's Neuschwanstein and King Arthur's Camelot.

RATHKEALE: Catholic Church

In the porch beneath the tower a large plaque records the donors. They include the architect, J.J. McCarthy, who donated the stained glass of the last window of the south aisle embellished by his heraldic devices. Carefully sited to allow carriages and cars access from the rear, the masses ascend an imposing staircase to the western front, reminiscent of Armagh (q.v.). The church was started in 1876 and the spire completed by 1881. The interior ranks as one of McCarthy's most impressive, where he achieves a sense of spaciousness by carrying the nave arcades across the transepts so we are unaware of their limited dimensions. He uses the same device between the transepts and the loftier side chapels that flank the chancel; these are treated asymmetrically. Red marble columns and good neo-medieval glass. Altar dismantled to conform with liturgical thinking of the 1960s but regurgitated as table, lectern and seat.

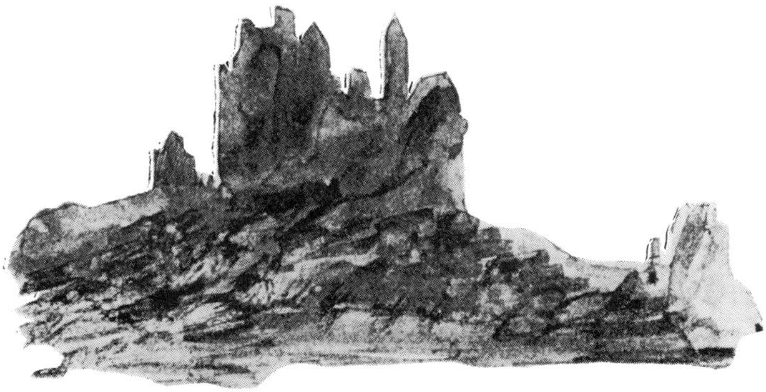

LONDONDERRY

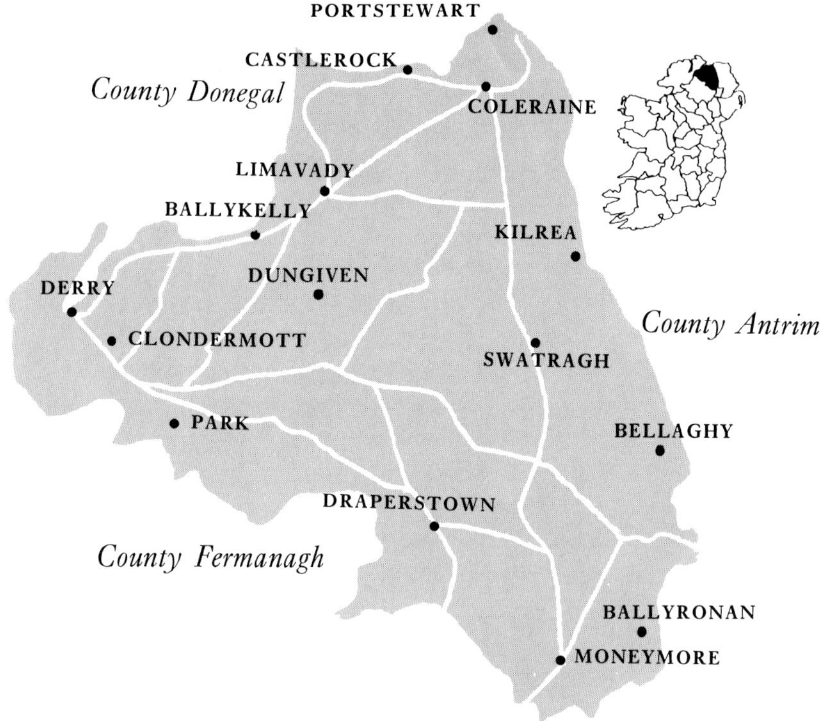

BALLYKELLY: **Cather Mausoleum**
A massive neo-Classical cube built into the medieval church ruin in 1849, but never completed. The acroteria at each corner remain uncarved on the sides that face the rear.

BALLYKELLY: **Sampson's Tower**
Folly tower built in 1849 to the north of the main road to Limavady and now almost hidden by a belt of woodland. A square tower with a circular stair turret dedicated to the memory of Arthur Sampson JP.

BALLYRONAN: **Ballyeglish Church of Ireland**
Built in 1866-9 by Welland and Gillespie, with all the concentrated monumentality unequalled by their Irish contemporaries. One feels that Woodward might have designed a church like this if he had lived. Just a simple cell with an apse nudging against a square vestry projecting perversely forward to compensate for a transept articulated only by the structure of the roof. The asymmetry of the church is emphasized by the off-centre wedge-headed bellcote attached to the western gable and echoed on the eastern gable by the chimney of the boiler. Polychromatic construction in polygonal limestone rubble banded with red sandstone. Whitewashed internally apart from painted inscription over the chancel arch.

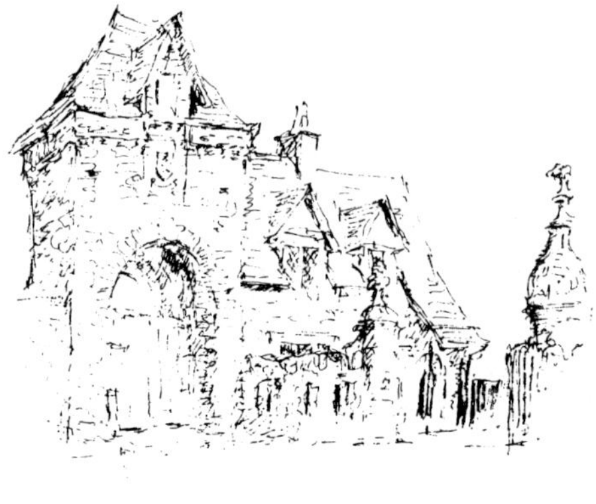

BELLAGHY: **Ballyscunnion House**
The oval palace of the Earl Bishop Harvey that predated Ickworth has vanished. Instead there is a freestanding Italianate villa of 1850 built by the Bruces, presumably to the designs of Charles Lanyon with five-bayed entrance front and a four-columned Doric porch re-using some of the stone of the vanished palace. Spacious double-drawingroom with a Wyatt window to the garden.

CASTLEROCK: **Twelve Apostles**
A row of twelve cottages with dormers set into a steeply pitched roof. Commissioned in 1882 by the Bruces from a local architect, F.H.

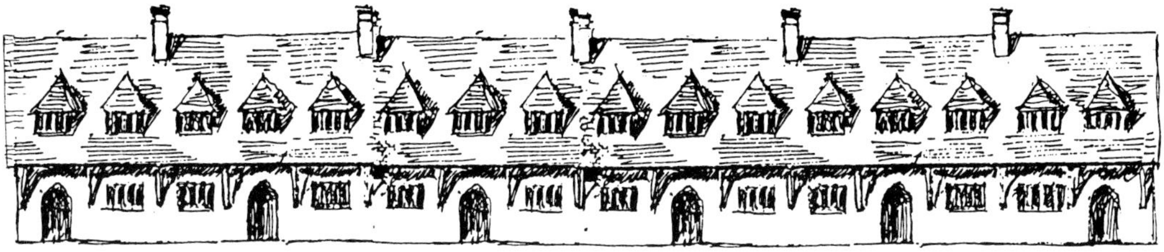

Goodwin. Simple but original with rows of spandrels supporting the eaves creating a semi-arcade.

CASTLEROCK: **Church of Ireland**
Built by the Bruces in 1850 to the designs of F.W. Porter, architect to the Clothworkers Company. The church is cruciform with an asymmetrically-sited broached steeple. As it is built of the local black basalt, the exposed red-brick of the interior comes as a surprise, especially cheerful when illuminated by the ten brass candelabra that line the nave. Contrastingly, blue stencil decoration still intact in the south transept. West window with stained glass by Wailes and Strang. Stained glass windows (St Patrick and St Columba) both by Michael Healy (1918) and (1932).

CLONDERMOTT: **Beech Hill**
A jumble of every period with a private Catholic chapel set unexpectedly above a Lombardesque *porte-cochère*, lit by a multiple oriel and a trefoiled lantern. The Skipton family had already extended their Georgian home by adding a wing with a neo-Classical library (now a bar) that anticipates Post-Modernism in its naivety. They sold the estate to the Nicholsons in 1875 who called in R.E. Buchanan for their chapel, and who romanticized the grounds with lakes and ornamental bridges, converting the existing gatelodge into a ruined castle—one of the finest of its kind in Ulster. Now a hotel.

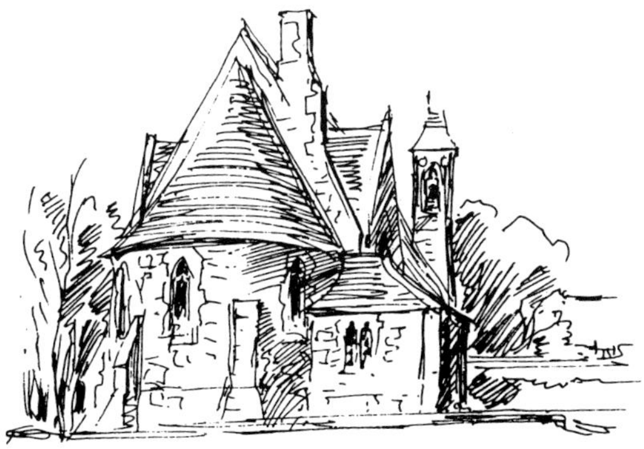

COLERAINE: **Academical Institution**
Neo-Georgian central block by Isaac Farrell extended with an unhappily remodelled palazzo by Young and Mackenzie in 1935. Memorial arch of 1906 by Vincent Craig.

COLERAINE: **Catholic Church**
Sited far from the town centre on the opposite hill above the River Bann, the church designed by an otherwise unknown architect, J. Kirkpatrick, dated 1834 is still effective from a distance—five large Gothick windows, the central window opposite the altar, slightly projecting and flanked by octagonal turrets, slender as minarets. Alas, the church no longer repays closer attention after insensitive restoration in the 1960s which has not prevented yet another (current) restoration.

COLERAINE: **Church of Ireland**
The 17th-century church was extended by Welland and others until rebuilt in 1884 by Thomas Drew, who gave the congregation an ambience of late medieval opulence, modelled on the wool-rich shires of England. Drew's most striking addition is a massive western tower carefully poised beside an elaborate southern porch, both bristling with the sculpture of a local carver, Charles Magowan. A churchyard that sets the church back from the main street. Spacious interior heightened by Drew, who raised the roof of the nave and the arch leading into Welland's chancel. Pulpit by Richard Orpen. First World War memorial stained glass by J. Clarke (1919). Further glass by Heaton, Butler and Bayne (west window)

COLERAINE: **Irish Society Schools**
A memorial window in the townhall depicts the Irish Society schools (1869), designed also by Thomas Turner and Richard Williamson, who was probably the only partner responsible, in a chuncky vigorous Gothic that today livens up a series of dreary car parks. Juxtaposed gable ends, asymmetrical bay windows, repeated (apart from the dominating octagonal clock tower) when enlarged by M. McQuigg in 1935 but with a certain loss of the original concision.

COLERAINE: **Laurel Hill**
Seat of the Kyle family, just to the south of the

Killowen Catholic church. Charles Lanyon added a new five-bayed block in his Italianate manner (1841-3) at right angles to the original house. Corinthian porch beneath a first-floor triple lancet. Columned screen in the hall, inaccessible for security reasons.

COLERAINE: **Methodist Church**
Designed by the leading Dublin Methodist church architect of his time, Isaac Farrell, with a portico of five bays, the central three recessed to shelter the entrance. Curved walls on each side, one linked to the house of the minister.

COLERAINE: **St John's Church of Ireland**
Church of 1830, remodelled and extended by J.G. Ferguson in 1875. Interior later disfigured by baleful glass.

COLERAINE: **The Station**
An austere arcaded portico. Charles Lanyon (at his most Italianate in 1855) screens the cast-iron columns, scrolled brackets and frilly eaves of the platforms.

COLERAINE: **The Townhall**
Designed by Thomas Turner and erected in 1859, this is one of the best provincial Irish townhalls although its construction entailed the loss of its predecessor by George Dance. But there is still a link with 18th-century London, since the design and massing recall St Mary-le-Strand in its free-standing site and its idiom of restrained Baroque, most highly modelled in the clock tower with its chamfered concavities. The entrance hall is a concealed rotunda beneath the first-floor public assembly hall. This is now approached by a staircase added by W.S. Given in 1902, which is presided over by W. Merret's busts of Edward VII and Queen Alexandra.

DERRY: **Austin's Department Store**
The most prominent shop in the city designed by M.A. Robinson (1906) with a tower to punctuate one entry to the Diamond. Uninhibited Edwardian Baroque (especially the ogee cupola that crowns the corner tower), but verging on Art Nouveau (the curvilinear oriel of the *piano nobile*). The ground floor has fallen victim to transient fashions and intransigent politics. Currently inoffensive. The original triple-height internal space was filled in long ago by a space-hungry proprietor.

DERRY: **Apprentice Boys' Hall**
Only the tower and the altered adjoining bay survive of J.G. Ferguson's 1873 structure. The remainder is by Robinson and Davidson and dates incredibly from 1937, to pre-date rather

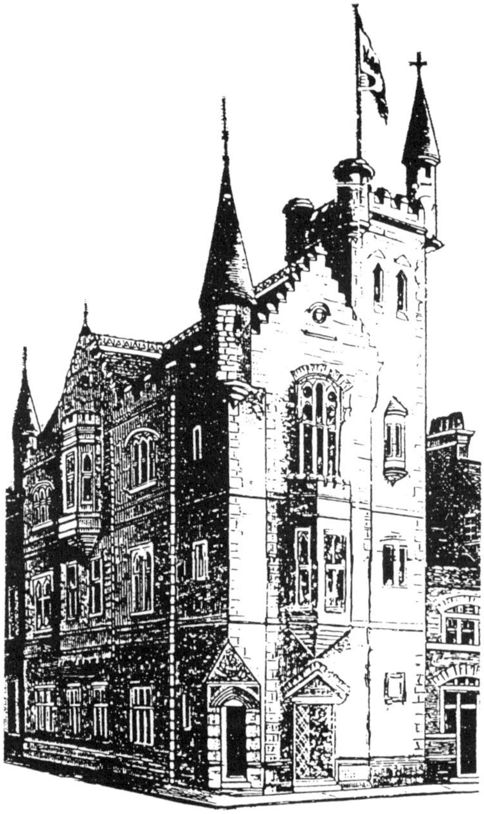

than post-date the siege by a quarter of a millennium. Sadly they removed all Ferguson's quirky Gothic features that paralleled Altnachree Castle (q.v.) and its original forcefulness is now diffused. Prematurely aged as result of recent disturbances.

DERRY, **Bishop Street: Northern Club**
A remodelling by Alfred Forman in 1866, with giant pilasters rising to support pedimented windows on the top floor. Most of the public rooms are unaltered, but they are disappointingly subdued. All the money was spent on the exterior.

DERRY, **Bishop Street Without: St Columb's College**
Scholastic institution with the earliest block dated 1877. This was the model for a later block, the Senior House, by Croom and Toye, dating from 1892. The third block of Victorian interest is the Museum, which transplants the portico of Bishop Harvey's casino onto the first floor above the entrance.

DERRY, **Bond's Hill: Waterside Station**
Designed by John Lanyon in 1873 and blown up a hundred years later. Rebuilt as a modern office centre, for once successfully incorporating the strongest features of the original structure, notably the clock tower.

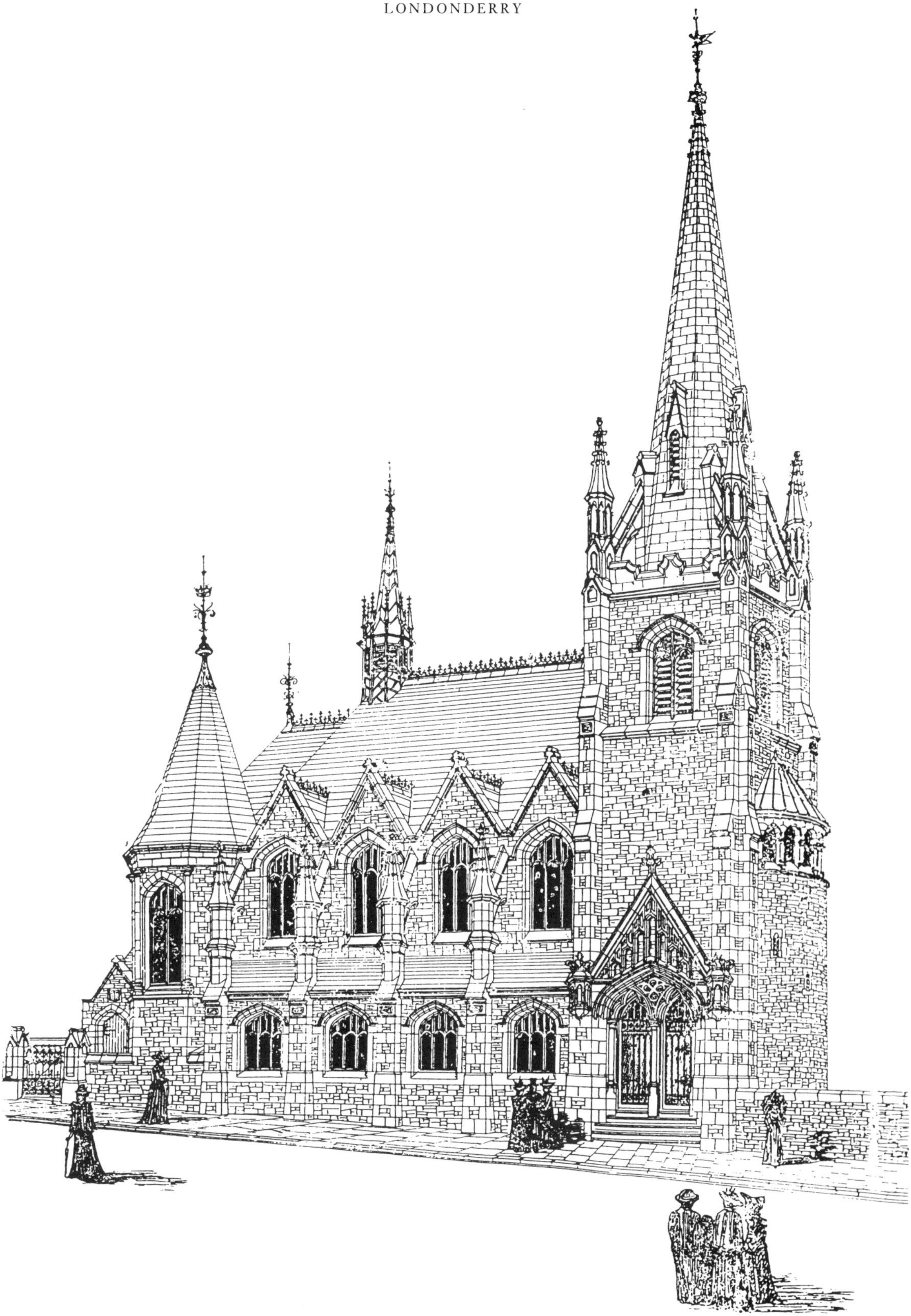

CARLISLE ROAD METHODIST CHURCH

DERRY, Butcher Street: No. 2, Central Chambers

Cheerful half-timber structure with a corbelled domed octagonal lantern which the architects (Forman and Aston) borrowed from their masterpiece, Ballynafeigh Methodist Church in Belfast (q.v.). Date: 1899.

DERRY, Carlisle Road: Methodist Church

Lively Late Gothic Revival design by Alfred Forman, dating from 1901, adapted to the street pattern to maximum effect—four gabled bays between an apsidal baptistery and an entrance tower topped with a delicate spire. What redeems this from the mundane is his fun with flying buttresses—double-tiered to prop up the spire, single-tiered elsewhere, taking the rainwater off the roof. Timber-clad interior.

DERRY, Carlisle Square: Tillie and Henderson

One of the earliest and most prominent of the city's commercial buildings, designed by J.G. Ferguson in 1856. Heavy French-inspired composition with mansard-roofed corner pavilions.

DERRY: Catholic Cathedral

Yet another Irish Catholic cathedral that embodies the involuntary combination of J.J. McCarthy and George Ashlin: indeed, they alternated for over half a century. McCarthy replaced an incompetent unknown in 1851 and completed the nave and choir (there are no transepts) twenty years later, apart from the furnishings. These were supplied by Earley and Powell during the 1870s. Ashlin was commissioned to complete the western tower in 1900 and add a spire in his more decorative Gothic, a companion to the central spire he was adding during the same period to Killarney Cathedral (q.v.). Here he was assisted by E.J. Toye, who further embellished the interior illuminated by the stained glass of Mayer. This was restructured in 1975 by Liam McCormack. His intervention, while disastrous in Armagh, here must be accounted a success. There was less destruction of the original fittings and what has replaced them is both avant-garde and discreet, and thoughtfully lit.

Adjoining bishop's palace by J.J. McCarthy (1873) with gatelodge by Toye (1905), who built the schools in 1895.

DERRY: Church of Ireland Cathedral

The cathedral, dating from 1633, despite its relative venerability was altered three times in the space of fifty years to conform to Victorian solemnity. Firstly by Joseph Welland who removed the side galleries, replaced the box pews and designed the eagle lectern and filigree spire intended for the pulpit but now above the bishop's throne. He also was responsible for the east window with its naive stained glass, but this was repositioned by the next architect, J.G. Ferguson, who extended the chancel in 1885 and replaced the Gothick vaults with open timber roofs in the Perpendicular style. However, the new fittings were left to a third architect, Thomas Drew, who took over in 1889. He had designed already the delicate Flamboyant Gothic pulpit in 1879. The rich mosaic, marble and alabaster reredos is his, and finally the vestry and the chapter house in 1910. The stained glass by Heaton, Butler and Bayne, though prominent, never achieves aesthetic distinction: the best window is by Charles Gibbs dated 1874 in the south aisle. Three windows by Powell and Son, commemorating Cecil Alexander, William Alexander and the famous siege. The only Victorian memorial to rise to the level of the earlier examples is the monument by Thomas Farrell (1861) depicting Capt. McNeill Boyd (below a life-sized angel) directing his sailors in their fight against the fatal storm.

DERRY, Clarendon Street: Reformed Presbyterian Church

Attributed to J.J. Stevenson and Campbell Douglas, since it is recorded that they built a church here between 1860 and 1868. By far the most original Gothic Revival in the city, despite its minor scale and its recent conversion into offices. Cruciform with wedge-shaped belfry attached to the transept. The tower is echoed in the enchanting hip-roofed porches with banded quatrefoil glazing on battered walls. The nave and transept gable elevations are subtly differentiated, a quatrefoil rose in the nave, a trefoil rose in the transept. The fenestration slyly reveals the staircase to the gallery. Apart from the blocking-up of the louvered trefoils of the belfry, the exterior has survived and its conversion has been commendably discreet. It is tempting to attribute to Stevenson and Campbell the pair of adjoining houses in Clarendon Street, since they are equally original. Three floors with square bays tapering into semi-octagons on the first floor. Marble colonettes between doors and windows sprouting Ruskinian plant sculpture.

DERRY, Clooney Terrace: Waterside Presbyterian Church

Won in competition by William Hague at the start of his career and built in 1868. Competent yet less radical than the Catholic churches he was building at the same time, but carefully adjusted to the different level of the site, its spire competing for attention with Lynn's on the slope above.

DERRY, Culmore Road: Thornhill

Large but uninspired Baronial house designed by Thomas Turner and Babington Hume. Built for A.A. Watt in 1848. The entrance front suffers from never having received an intended tower and *porte-cochère*. The garden front is symmetrical with a central bay to overlook the river, but it is equally morose. The staircase hall is double-height and arcaded, now top-lit through a dome of Art Nouveau glass. Well maintained as a convent.

DERRY, Great James Street: Third Presbyterian Church

The most elegant neo-Classical church in the city, designed by Stewart Gordon, built in 1835-7; remodelled internally in 1863 by Bowd and Batt. The tetrastyle Ionic portico with windows on either side plays down its scale, so that on entering one experiences an unexpected spaciousness. While the church is only four bays long, the slim cast-iron columns that subdivide the name and aisles are positioned at intervals half the width of each bay. They perforate the three-sided balcony to form segmental arcades that support an even shallower barrel vault. The well-polished mahogany box pews and galleries provide a weighty ballast to all the lightness of the structure.

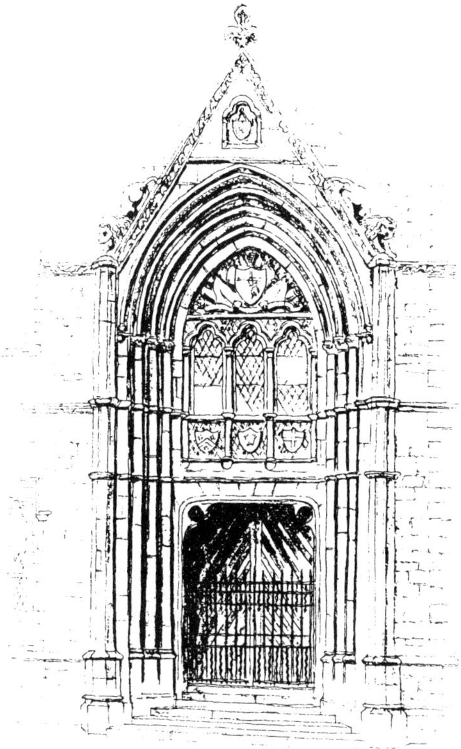

DERRY: The Guildhall

The Guildhall is unique in Ireland even if it was started in 1887 six hundred years after its counterparts on the European mainland and has been burnt out twice since (firstly in 1908 by accident, secondly in 1972 by design). The original architect was J.G. Ferguson and, while

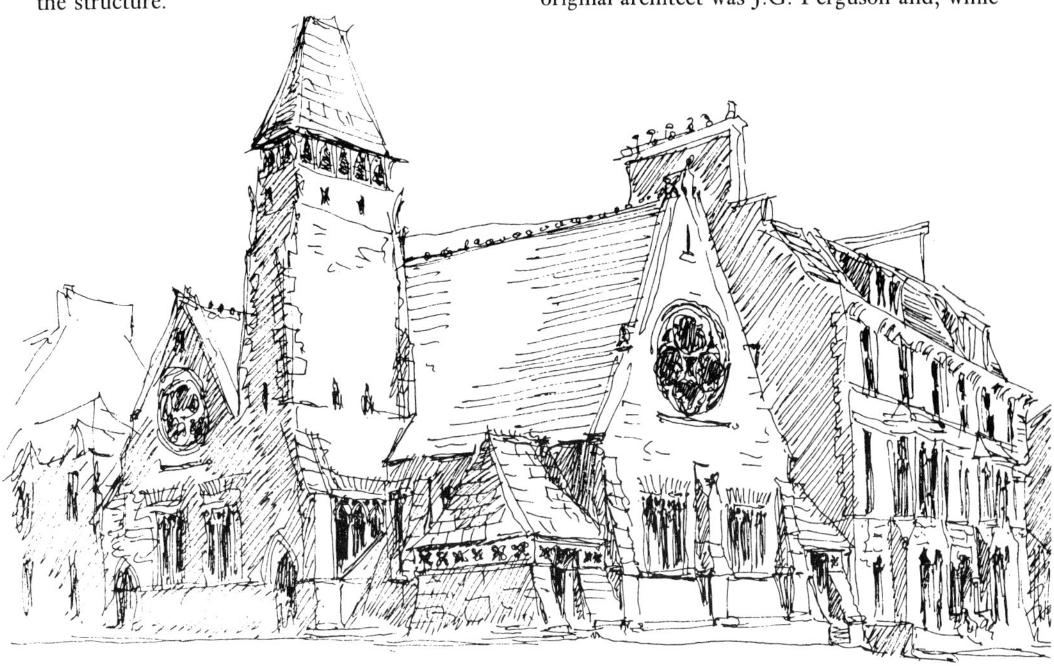

the basic composition survives, the Flamboyant Gothic fenestration on the south façade is due to M.A. Robinson (who completed the reconstruction in 1912). The interiors date from then. These were faithfully reinstated by the Building Design Partnership after the attack in 1972. The most impressive is the upstairs assembly hall, galleried at both ends, one gallery thronged with the pipework of a thundrous organ beneath an open hammer-beam roof. A separately roofed hall adjoins to take smaller crowds. A central passage on both floors is linked to a richly balustered stairs rising from a statue of an impressive Queen Victoria by F.T. Williamson. The most remarkable decoration is found in the stained and painted glass by Campbell and Co. of Belfast once called Caldermac (1911-13) presented by the Worshipful Glaziers of London, who also presented a Germanic depiction of the coronation of George V and Queen Mary by Mayer of Munich.

DERRY, Guildhall Street: Northern Bank

Freestanding palazzo with bevelled corners, three stories high and built out of Scottish sandstone. The interior hall has lost all its original features. Designed by Thomas Turner in 1866.

DERRY, Harbour Square: Harbour Commissioners' Office

A precise and sober structure in the shadow of the Guildhall, its effusive neighbour. Its only assertive note an Italianate tower. Staircase and boardroom with its Donegal carpets to be retained intact when transformed into a museum. Designed in 1882 by John Kennedy.

DERRY: Horace Street Factory

Designed in 1872 by J.G. Ferguson, who was as enterprising in his commercial buildings as he was the reverse in his churches. This factory is his finest work, three stories high above an arcaded basement carefully adapted to the gradient of the site. Polychromatically treated façades, red-brick walls, sandstone, voussoirs and green schist string coursing. The horizontality of the design is emphasized by corbelled cornices marking each floor level.

DERRY, Letterkenny Road: Government House

An Italianate villa with bay windows and verandah designed by Sir William Tite (1848) to view a more remote imperial vista rather than the River Foyle. Well-maintained by its present owners, the Christian Brothers.

DERRY, Letterkenny Road: Milton Lodge

Lombardesque farm buildings attached to the Georgian house overlooking the Foyle. Wide eaves overhanging brick arcades, at one point double-tiered. Similar to the farm at Anketell, Co. Monaghan (q.v.). Dated in Pevsner as *c.* 1840.

DERRY, Long Tower: St Columb's Catholic Church

E.J. Toye was commissioned to extend this church in 1903 after he had already built the neo-Gothic primary schools with their sculptural roundels (one portraying the parish priest). Toye added a second transept beyond the existing one which had been the original church. This meant repositioning the reredos with its antique Corinthian capitals. He also added Corinthian pilasters of his own and paired Corinthian columns between the old transepts and the new. These stand clear of the existing galleries which he extended across to the new chancel wall, thereby creating a theatrical space made even more so by its subsequent embellishments—woodwork by the local firm of Miller and Beatty, marble carving of the altars by Edmund Sharpe, opus sectile by Kyall of Leeds and Belfast, brass gates by William Earley. Earley was also responsible for the lavish stained glass, apart from the windows in the vestibule and in the upper stage of the transepts. These are by Mayer, and while Earley has shamelessly imitated their style he has surpassed them, giving an added Celticism to their borders. This serves as a corrective to the paintings, weak copies of old masters by a Dublin firm called McEvoy. The most architectural decoration is in the tiny baptistry, whose dome is lit by segments of stained glass; now used to enshrine a replica of the Book of Kells.

DERRY, Magazine Street: First Derry Presbyterian Church

Impressive tetrastyle Corinthian portico tacked on to the original Georgian church in 1863 by W.E. Pinkerton and built out of reddish sandstone to face the sun setting in the Celtic west.

DERRY: Mullenan House

Earlier house rebuilt in the 1850s and extended at the rear by a long block with a swaggering staircase in the middle and large rooms at either end; these form symmetrical side pavilions with smoking-rooms and billiard-room, once the most up to date, but now mellowed by time. Set in grounds of ornamental conifers.

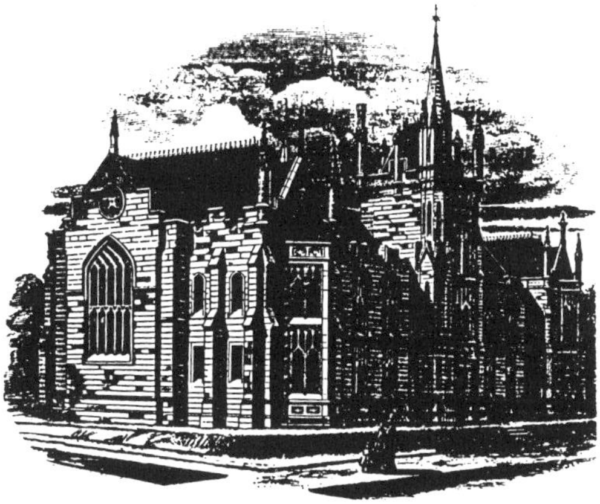

DERRY, Northland Road: Magee College
The masterpiece of its obscure Dublin architect, E.P. Gribbon, whose elegant working drawings survive in the college library, dated 1856. The building was completed by Stewart Gordon in 1865 and has not fared well since, though it is quite understandable that the assembly hall has had a mezzanine floor inserted to give extra classrooms below, while a raised stage seals off the most important windows. Sadder still has been the loss of the original staircase. The charming rear façade is now largely obscured by additions, but the liveliness of the front façade is happily maintained. Gribbon's façade is asymmetrical in the treatment of the central tower with its corner spiral staircase turret, and in the end pavilions (a double-storied triangular bay window projecting from one, a triangular oriel projecting from the other). Both treatments are naively reconciled by the double-storied oriel above the central door, but a subtler further asymmetry is achieved by staggering the intervening ranges. The skyline is enlivened by an array of spirelets, pinnacles and barley-sugar chimney-pots to distract the apprentice divines from the gravity of their studies.

DERRY, Queen Street: City Factory
Designed in 1863 by Young and Makenzie in red and yellow brickwork. Two long street frontages, arcaded with carved keystones to Patrick Street, three floors on semi-basement articulated by two entrance archways seven bays apart.

DERRY, Richmond Street: St Columb's Hall
Designed as a temperance hall in 1888 by Croom and Toye and still in use as a theatre, a simple galleried hall slipped in behind an imposing façade that recalls the opulence of Napoleon III, with steps rising to the main entrance sheltered by a serpentine columned porch. Above statutes of Erin, Temperance and Vulcan.

DERRY: Second Presbyterian Church
Stewart Gordon was responsible for this stiff Gothick church of 1863. Yet its symmetrical façade with octagonal pinnacled tower set back from the street between twin corner houses has an appealing gawkiness.

DERRY, Shipquay Street: Bank of Ireland
Designed in 1869 by Sandham Symes, a four-bay arcaded palazzo, treated as integral to the street.

DERRY, Shipquay Street: Former Belfast Bank
Unlike the Bank of Ireland across the street this is a free-standing palazzo in its own right. An emphatically symmetrical design by Charles Lanyon dating from 1853: entrance door set into central rusticated arch surmounted by an arched window. This is flanked with columns supporting a pediment that breaks into the fenestration of the attic. Sold off and currently disused.

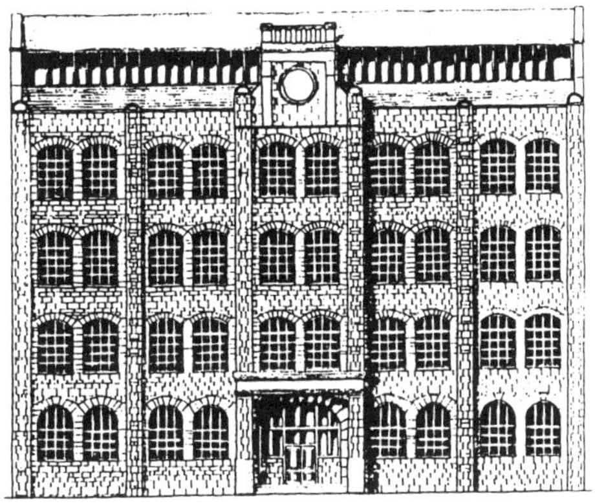

DERRY: Star Factory
Designed by Daniel Conroy, stone-fronted, four stories and ten bays wide on the scale of palazzo dominated by a central clock tower. Built in 1899. Currently derelict.

DERRY, Waterside: All Saints Church of Ireland
Designed by Lanyon, Lynn and Lanyon and built in 1864-7 as a case of W.H. Lynn's ability to exploit an awkward site. Compact nave, short transepts, raised polygonal chancel. The off-centre Germanic steeple dominates unexpected vistas. Stained glass by Heaton, Butler and Bayne.

DERRY, Waterside: St Columb's Catholic Church
Earliest recorded commission of J.J. McCarthy who built this church in 1838 as a single cell

with a steeple symmetrically placed. McCarthy had not yet discovered his idiom, so this could be Board of First Fruits. Transepts added in 1887.

DRAPERSTOWN: **County Library**
Built as the market house by W.J. Booth in 1839 as the pivotal building of his master plan for the village, prepared for his client, the Draper's Company. Neo-Classical but with the generous eaves of vernacular Italianate.

DUNGIVEN: **Catholic Church**
Designed in 1877 by O'Neill and Byrne in a hard French Gothic. Aisled nave of six bays lit by coupled quatrefoils terminating in apsidal chancel. Interior modernized.

DUNGIVEN: **Dungiven Castle**
Within the bawn of the Plantation castle, Robert Ogilby started to build a new castle in 1839, orientating the main rooms away from the village to overlook the valley of the Rowe and the mountains beyond. A long façade punctuated by three towers, all with stepped Irish battlements, the central tower an octagon, the outer ones both circular. The idiom is identical to the old gaol of Londonderry (now demolished) by Stewart Gordon. So he was probably responsible for the castle that was fated to be never completed.

DUNGIVEN: **Ogilby Memorial, Church of Ireland**
Gothic memorial *c.*1875 to R.L. Ogilby, who employed Fitzgibbon Louch in 1868. So he is the most likely candidate for this open shrine with heraldic lions at four corners.

KILREA: **Church of Ireland**
Prominently sited at the end of the main street and built in 1840-3 by George Smith, surveyor to the Mercers Company, assisted by William Barnes. The style chosen, if intended to be Irish Romanesque, is a London Wren church thinly cloaked with English Norman; a lofty aisleless hall with a central entry tower rising to an octagonal spire. At the other end a projecting chancel with a triple light window.

KILREA: **First Presbyterian Church**
Cubistic Gothic Revival church with symmetrical façade topped by octagonal spirelet. Illogical Norman door. Designed in 1837 by William Barnes. Interior with gallery on cast-iron columns.

KILREA: **Second Presbyterian Church**
Deceptively vernacular Gothic Revival, since this church has also been designed for the Mercers Company by William Barnes and built in 1837. To be responsible for building churches for three denominations at the same time in one town and give satisfaction is a unique achievement.

LIMAVADY: **Church of Ireland**
There is little external hint of the elaborate Gothic used to recast the interior by Babington and Turner in 1881. Enriched even further by R.E. Buchanan in 1913 with an embossed chancel arch. The war memorial is an arcade that extends along the north aisle framing the stained-glass windows. Arts and Crafts furnishings to the chancel.

LIMAVADY: **Drenagh**
The first major country-house commission given by Charles Lanyon by Marcus Mc-

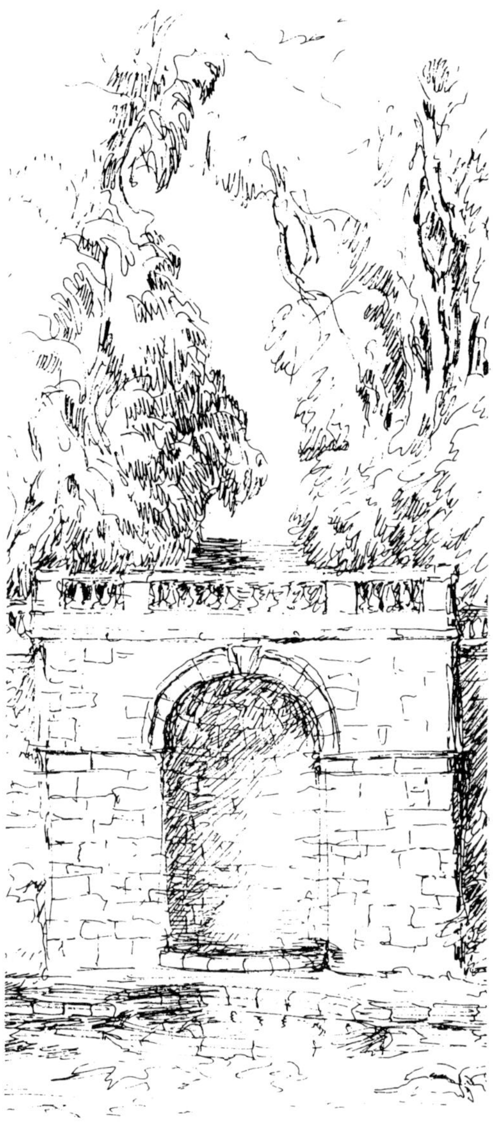

Causland in 1839. Its style looks back to Regency Greek and forward to Victorian Italianate, that momentary equilibrium between the primitive and the decadent. Carefully constructed out of ashlar sandstone, the house is freestanding apart from a service courtyard to the north. This allows Lanyon to modulate three complementary façades. His use of classical orders is sparing. He reserves a delicate Ionic for the entrance porch. The side elevation is treated more grandly with double-height pilasters, but these are subtly devalued by articulating a pedimented centrepiece with two bays rather than the expected three. At the rear he relies on canted bays that gives additional space to the principal rooms while still maintaining the overall symmetry of the structure. This is centred around a domed Corinthian-columned inner hall, that counterbalances claustrophobia by leading into an imperial staircase lit from windows at a higher level. Spacious interiors, some with their original wallpapers. Member of Hidden Ireland.

Lanyon also designed the two gatelodges in contrasting styles—Gothick and neo-Classical—as well as the Belvedere in the Italianate garden, a semi-domed recess overlooking a fountain; above a balustraded viewing platform reached down flights of steps between cypresses. The 'Moon' garden beyond was made *c.* 1960 by Frances Rhodes in an old pidgeon yard, partly Chinese, partly latterday Lutyens, overlooking the Victorian arboretum in the valley through a circle in the wall.

LIMAVADY: Myroes Church of Ireland

Chapel of ease built of polygonal basalt by Welland and Gillespie *c.* 1865.

LIMAVADY: Roe Valley Hospital

Built by George Wilkinson in 1841 as the Union Workhouse and converted with the minimum of alterations into the district hospital, so that the ensemble has been preserved remarkably intact. The governor's house, as always, is sited in front of the main block which has both ends accented by double gables and staircase towers at the rear.

LIMAVADY: The Townhall

Impressive, two-storied, pedimented façade with a curved balcony over the central doorway. The insecurity of the proportions has made uncertain its attribution to Thomas Turner. First proposed in 1858, but not built until 1872.

MAGHERAFELT: Catholic Church

Built in 1878-82 out of Dungannon stone to the designs of H. O'Neill. Off-centre tower and spire. Nave divided from aisles by columns of Aberdeen granite; capitals carved by Earley. The polygonal apse houses the original high altar although the memorial pulpit and the rails have vanished. Modern transept attached in defiance of the laws of gravity. Stained glass by Mayer, 1898-1904. A memorial pulpit by J.J. Mc- Donnell has been removed.

MAGHERAFELT: The Courthouse

The most forceful of Ulster's provincial courthouses by Turner and Williamson (1871), conceived to strike the guilty with terror rather than to reassure the innocent. The central pitch-roofed courthouse is guarded by four corner towers with pyramidal spires of varying height, linked by open loggias on two adjoining fronts.

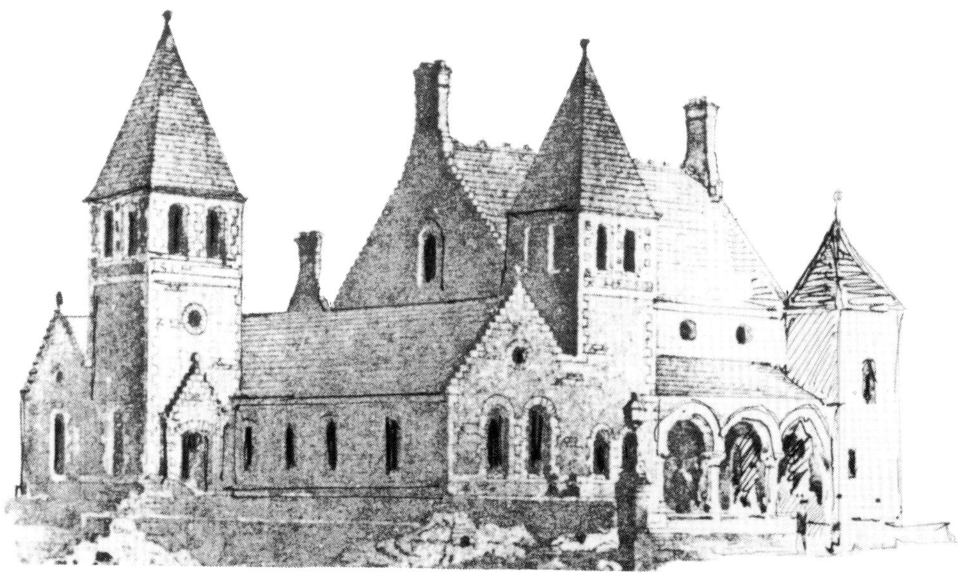

A minor hall and a constabulary extend the composition. Lit at night by search lights, rising up above the darkness of its outer defences, a formidable Valhalla awaiting its extinction.

MAGHERAFELT: **Church of Ireland**
One of Joseph Welland's most impressive churches, concealing from outward view proof that even he could be original: it appears externally that the separate roofs of aisles and nave are of equal height. On entering one sees that the roof of the nave rests on a frieze of trefoil windows now filled with stained glass to compensate for the lack of clerestory. Nobly proportioned interior with baptistry beneath the tower and opening through a splayed arch into the nave. Much timber bracing, especially at the crossing of the transept. Six-light window above the altar. Fine broached spire. Completed in 1858 with half the money coming from the London Salters.

MAGHERAFELT: **Presbyterian Church**
Humbler version of Corry's Elmwood Presbyterian Church (q.v.) in Belfast since here it is rendered with stucco and there is no tower. The architects were Boyd and Batt, who came up with this Lombardesque design in 1866. Entered through a five-bay enclosed loggia sporting bulbous capitals.

MONEYMORE: **New Market House**
Palladian composition with central triumphal arch flanked symmetrically by three-storied housing. The eaves line is carried above the archway to form the base of a pediment that projects almost as strongly as St Paul's, Covent Garden. This inference was not lost on the client, the Company of Drapers. Their architect was W.J. Booth (*c.*1795-1856), whom they had employed since 1827, and he completed this showpiece in 1839.

PARK: **Learmount Forest**
The neo-Elizabethan seat of the Beresfords descended from John Beresford, who commissioned the Dublin Custom House from Gandon. Now a holiday centre, whose owners have pulled down an earlier turreted wing, but have retained the adjoining later and grander range. This has five finialled gables across the façade and central battlemented porch. Inside, the hall leads to a bifurcating stairs. Elaborate plasterwork.

PORTSTEWART: **Catholic Church**
Lombardesque design by W.J. Moore of Belfast; built in 1916 out of brown basalt with sandstone trimmings. Nave with open roof, lean-to aisles and campanile attached alongside.

PORTSTEWART: **Church of Ireland**
Built originally in 1839 as a five-bay hall entered through a tower alongside the middle bay. Norman style chancel added by Thomas Drew in 1879. Martial memorial by the Fitzpatrick brothers of Belfast.

PORTSTEWART: **Methodist Church**
It is difficult to realize that this is the same church of local basalt and sandstone trimmings as depicted by W.J. Barre in one of his most exciting perspectives when he received the commission in 1861—a central fortified tower as in an Irish medieval abbey were it not for flying buttresses that proved insufficient since this tower was blown down in 1884 and was eventually replaced by the present gabled embrionic transept in 1914.

PORTSTEWART: **Presbyterian Church**
Now that Portstewart's Methodist church originality has been emasculated the town's most inventive architecture is to be found here—designed by Vincent Craig in 1905. Perpendicular Gothic but redefined in the consciousness of contemporary trends. Hence the

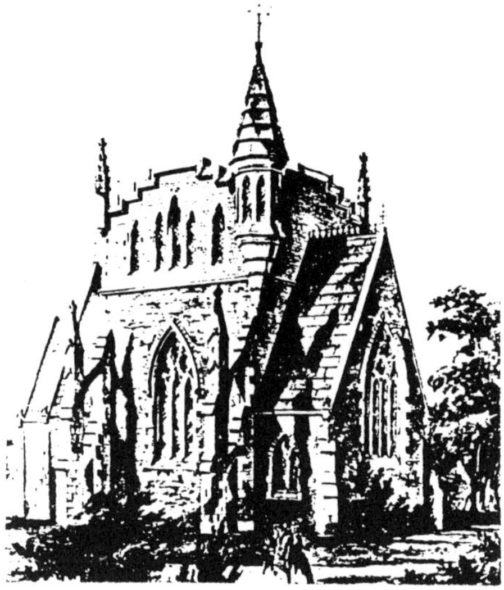

tracery in another context would be seen as Art Nouveau. However, the squashed-down tower and the buttress placed like a battering ram against the western window is a clearer indication that this is not international avant-garde but the continuation of the radical Gothic Revival of Street and Webb although softened by 'Sweetness and Light'.

PORTSTEWART: **Rock Castle**
Georgian house extended and castellated as a long rambling and in substantial fortress *c.*1875. The architect was S.P. Close. Now a convent.

LONGFORD

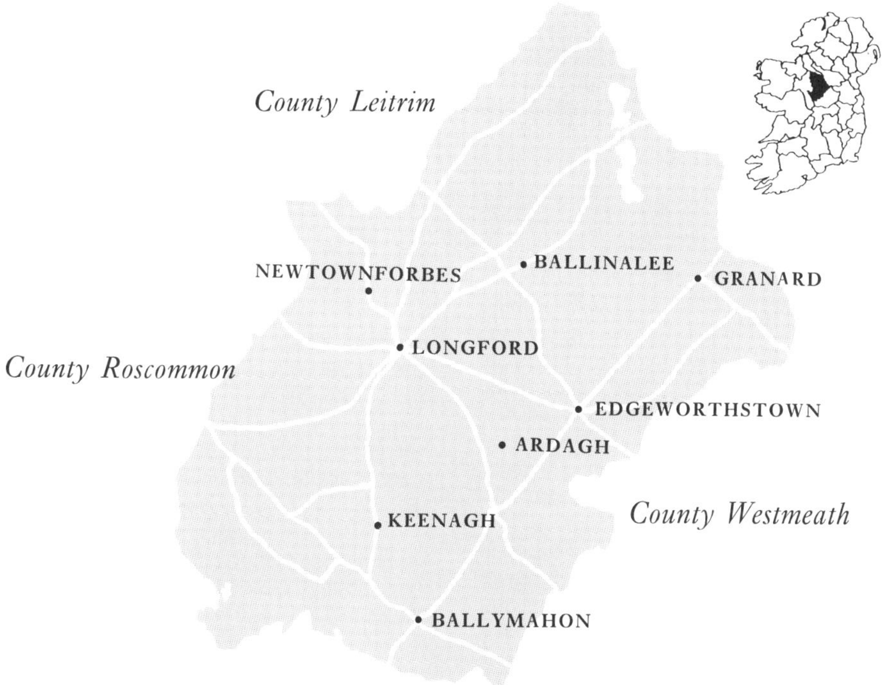

ARDAGH: **Catholic Church**
Tactfully sited at a distance from the village centre to avoid confrontation with the Church of Ireland, its lofty spire dominates all distant views. Once also the immediate surroundings must have been green fields, instead of asphalt car parks. The architect was William Hague, and this is one of his best churches. Started in 1881, its founder was Canon Reynolds. The matrix of the design is the belfry (completed in 1903 by T.F. McNamara) sited between transept and chancel, balanced by the gable of the sacristy topped by a formidable chimney. A semi-circular staircase turret built up against the side of the tower leads to an organ gallery in the north transept. Within, the arcades of the nave are carried across the transept in a modified form to link with a final variation in the chancel. There is much stone carving inside and out, climaxing with the high altar that still commemorates the architect, undisturbed by post-Vatican II mayhem. Glass varying in quality from modest Watson of Youghal to a spectacular Mayer over the high altar. Communion rails removed *c.*1976 but reinstated for the centenary (1981).

ARDAGH: **Featherstone Memorial**
The octagonal stone clock tower upholding a cruciform shrine encircled by a corona of pinnacles still dominates the model village of Ardagh. The memorial of Sir Ralph Featherstone was designed in 1861 by Rawson Carroll for his widow, Elizabeth; a symbol of mortality also meant to be intensely practical.

ARDAGH: **Model Village**
Having married into the family whose home a century earlier Goldsmith had mistaken for an inn, Lady Elizabeth Featherstone set up a brisk programme for reform. Rich but childless, she spent little money on her house; instead she

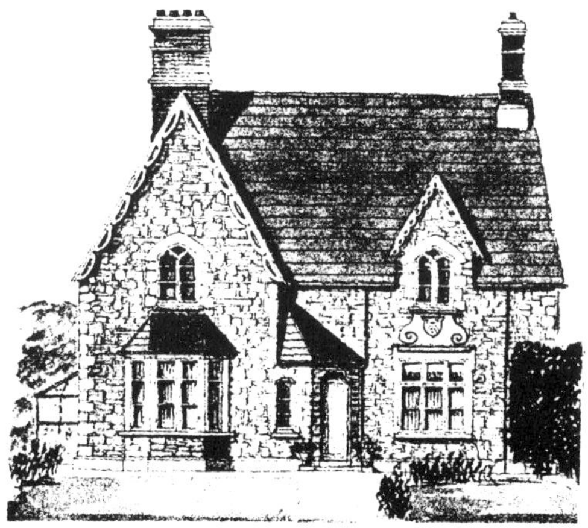

concentrated on her tenants, building for them spacious dwellings clustered round a village green in full view of her front door. Her

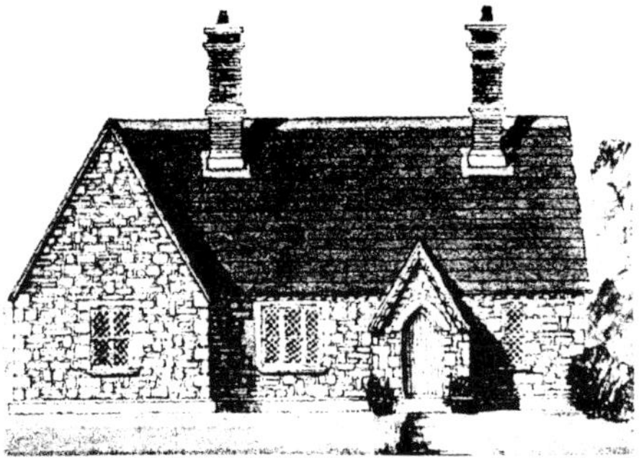

inspiration came from the idyllic English villages of her childhood but without their pubs.

Rawson Carroll, who designed everything was the ideal landlord's architect: he knew about Gothic, he knew about drains, and his surviving drawings show that he left nothing to chance. If he failed as a planner to achieve intimacy, it was because no cottage could be sited with its back towards the formidable patroness. His roofs, their low eaves broken by many gables, are well secured by diagonally positioned chimneys. His stone and brick have never needed rendering. The results are sensible and snug. The same idiom is discernable in her stableyard. The house, rebuilt this century, after a fire, is now a domestic science college. Ardagh is a perennial winner of Bord Fáilte's tidy towns competition. The influence of Lady Elizabeth lingers on.

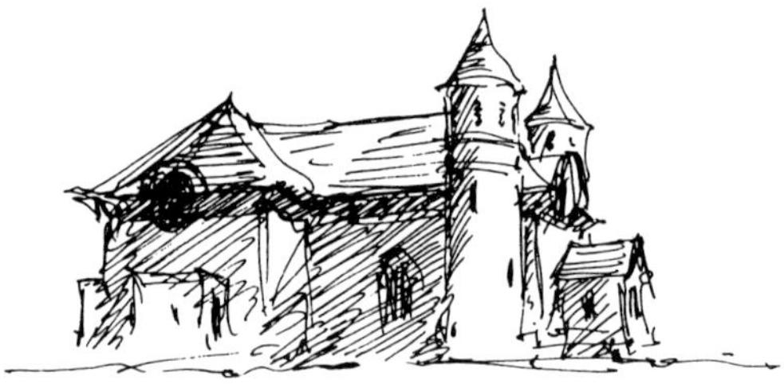

BALLINALEE: **Clonbroney Catholic Church**

Earlier vernacular chapel remodelled in 1912 by R.M. Butler to evoke the Moorish architecture of Spain (his client had been a seminarian in the Irish College of Salamanca). Squat round towers with conical roofs now flank the façade; the original pitched roofs have been replaced with hips. All this reveals unintentionally Butler's Germanic origins.

BALLYMAHON: **Pallas Memorial**

A railed-off grotto houses Foley's plaster model for the bronze of Goldsmith that stands at the entrance to Trinity College in Dublin. Acquired by Dublin Corporation with the contents of his studio after Foley's death; mutilated during the mass destruction of the collection by Republicans in the City Hall in 1922; retrieved from the cellars of the Mansion House, repaired by a voluntary local committee and erected on the site of his birthplace.

EDGEWORTHSTOWN: **Catholic Church**

Gothic Revival church, cruciform with later off-centre steeple (by Ashlin) attached to the façade. Designed in 1872 by William Caldbeck.

EDGEWORTHSTOWN: **Edgeworthstown House Gatelodge**

Edgeworthstown House, the home of Maria Edgeworth, has not been demolished (unlike Coole of Lady Gregory and Bowenscourt of Elizabeth Bowen). Were it not serving a useful purpose as a home for the elderly cared for by nuns, literary pilgrims should be forgiven for wishing that it had been pulled down, so ruthless its adaptation. But what has survived is a pretty gatelodge with a cast-iron porch redolent of India.

GRANARD: **Catholic Church**

Built by John Bourke in 1861 while engaged on Longford Cathedral (q.v.); the exterior typical of his Gothic manner, dominated by commanding tower and spire. Open timber roof within, braced horizontally by intersecting scissor arches, with results that were too disturbing to be repeated by other architects. Frescoes and mosaics were painted out when interior was made to conform to liturgical trends of the early 1960s.

KEENAGH: **Clock Tower**

Memorial raised by the grateful tenantry in 1878 to their late landlord and MP, Edward King-Harman, who had inherited most of the King family estates including Newcastle and Rockingham. Characterful tower with strongly tapered base and shaft. Corbelled and castellated clock stage topped by pyramidal spire. Inset white marble portrait. Possibly designed by Rawson Carroll.

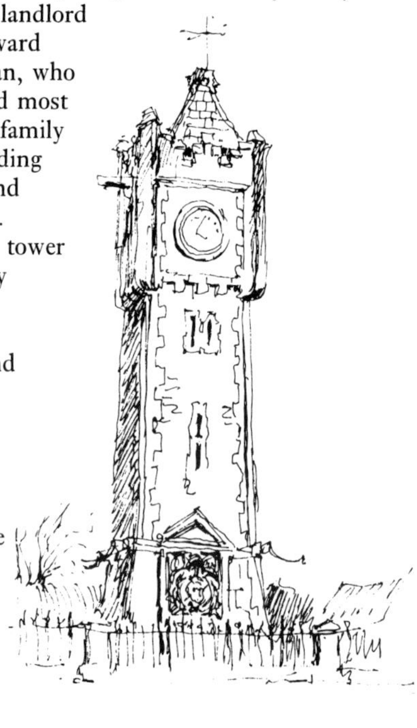

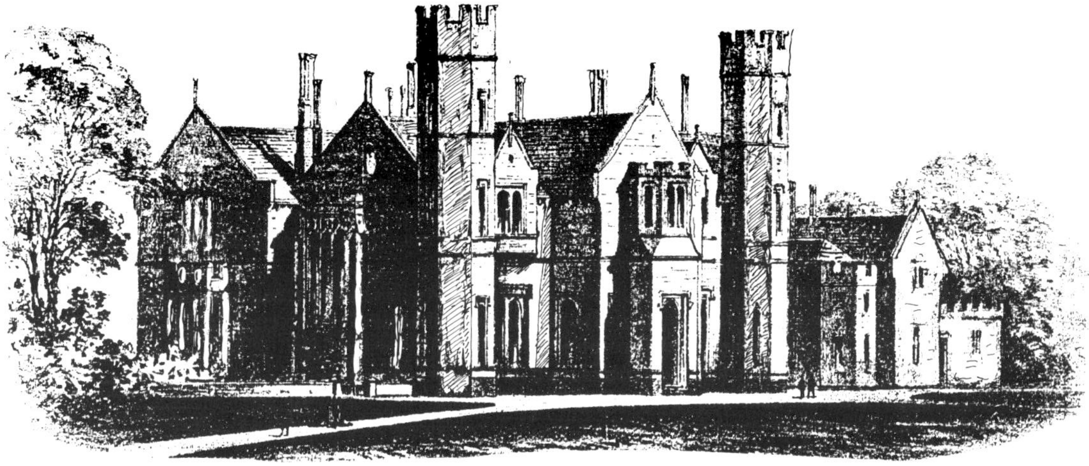

LONGFORD: **Carriglass Manor**
The only Daniel Robertson country house (apart from Ballinkeele: q.v.) still lived in by the family who commissioned him. Curiously, his client, Thomas Lefroy, the prototype of Jane Austen's Mr Darcy, did not ask for a Classical house to match the superb triumphal arch and stable block (already built by Gandon for the Newcomens, to serve a villa that never got beyond the drawing board due to the collapse of their family bank).

Robertson's designs, dated 1837, are still preserved in the house—a double-ranged structure, joined by a lower link to the earlier house (transformed into a service wing), all in his Tudor idiom. There are two contrasting fronts, forbidding to the north, with a projecting porch guarded by corner turrets, gracious to the south, where the main reception rooms overlook the gardens and the park beyond; to the east many rare conifers were planted by Robertson, one of his pioneering American gardens. In 1844, four years after the completion of the house, the garden front was extended by a Gothic curvilinear upheld by arcades of stone.

Since then the house has remained unaltered. One can see why. If as an architect, Robertson lacks the intensity of Woodward and the younger Morrison, both celibate consumptives, he is more companionable. He has the ability to be both playful and robust. In the staircase hall, despite the stained glass dimly illuminating an apse at the further end that once framed an organ, there is not a twinge of religiosity. This levity, still fashionable only in the remote countryside of Ireland, caused a more serious generation who experienced the horrors of the Famine, to consign him to oblivion. His death is unrecorded.

The sequence of his interiors is enlivened by alternating the axis of each room: thus the alignment of the drawingroom to the diningroom across the intervening library with its counter orientation to the formal gardens. All three rooms have ceilings with geometric designs framed by coves of frothy plasterwork, modelled by Italian stuccodores. Also from Italy the Cararra marble for the drawingroom chimneypiece, the gift of a cousin who had married the quarry owner. The library is surrounded by elaborately carved bookcases, and carved even more lavishly is the buffet at the end of the diningroom, framed within its arch, the focus of the enfilade. We know that Robertson liked his drink; we can surmise he also liked his food.

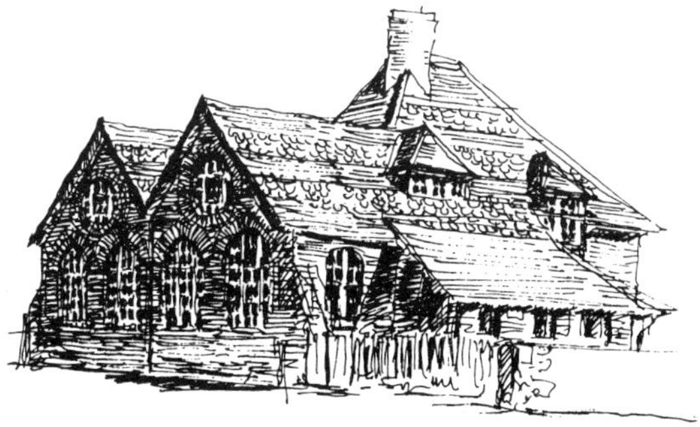

LONGFORD: **National School**
Snug little schoolhouse with overhanging eaves on the road out to Newtown Forbes. Master's house and parallel classrooms gathered under one roof and all sharing a diagonally sited chimney. Dated 1886; in the manner of Rawson Carroll.

LONGFORD: **Orange Hall**
Sedate round arched façade in local limestone. Designed by James Bell in 1863. Internal fittings by Swinburne.

LONGFORD: **St Mel's Cathedral**
The finest of Ireland's neo-Classical cathedrals, started in 1840. The original architect was J.B. Keane. Work was held up by the famine and doubtless also by Keane's chaotic private life that ended miserably in a debtor's prison. But of this no hint is given by the serenity of his external walling with vertical pilasters coolly deployed as foils to long horizontal bands of

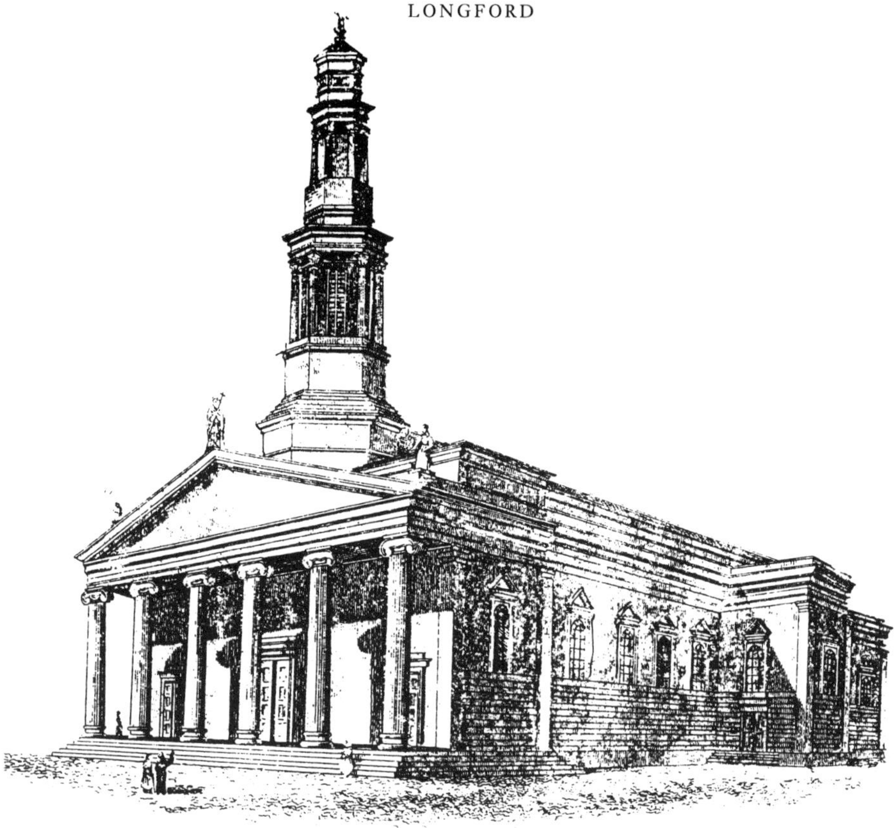

KEANE'S ORIGINAL SCHEME FOR ST MEL'S

ashlar. The plan is cruciform, with Ionic colonnades inspired by St Paul's Without the Walls between nave and aisles. Boldly projecting transepts are internally screened by double Ionic colonnades, and the chancel ends in a majestic apse. This is concealed from the irreverence of the outside world, as in many Roman temples, and also in the austere mausoleum that Keane was engaged on for Henry Bruen of Oak Park (q.v.), which he was also unable to complete. But here, instead of taking up space between the curved apse and the square east end with massive masonry or a colonnade, he contrives five floors of an episcopal palace, directly expressed in his external fenestration. Today this houses the local museum in rooms made extraordinary by the curvature of the apse. The west front is much more conventional, despite being the work of three different architects over half a century. The least satisfying contribution is the self-conscious companile (1860) by John Bourke, who took over from Keane and tried to christianise his improvisation on the Tower of the Winds. Bourke's finest improvement was to carry Keane's columns across the end of the nave and confine the organ into an arched lunette. The impeccably proportioned portico 1889-1913, with Christ blessing the faithful crowding into the pediment, is proof of George Ashlin's ability to adapt, even if St Mel's had been denounced by Pugin, his father-in-law, as 'a bad copy of that wretched compound of pagan and Protestant architecture, St Pancras New Church in London'. Pediment carved by George Smith.

The internal plasterwork is said to be by the Italians sent over to work on nearby Carriglas (q.v.). The altar of the inner south aisle is also Italian, having been rescued from the 'sacrilegious' troops of Garibaldi. The initial austerity of the interior has returned with the replacement by Wilfrid Cantwell and Ray Carroll of Bourke's lavish high altar and choir fittings—a simple slab in front of a bishop's throne set into an amphitheatre of seats—the only Irish cathedral to be improved by the Second Vatican Council. Unfortunately they stopped short of applying the same ruthlessness to the west end by removing the later organ gallery.

LONGFORD: The Seminary

Austere Italianate institution sited to view the cathedral across a formal park. Commissioned originally by the Christian Brothers from John Bourke, who was engaged on its construction in 1863 while he was working on the cathedral. Characteristically arcaded corridors as in his Dublin Mater Hospital (q.v.) but here the ambience has never been disrupted.

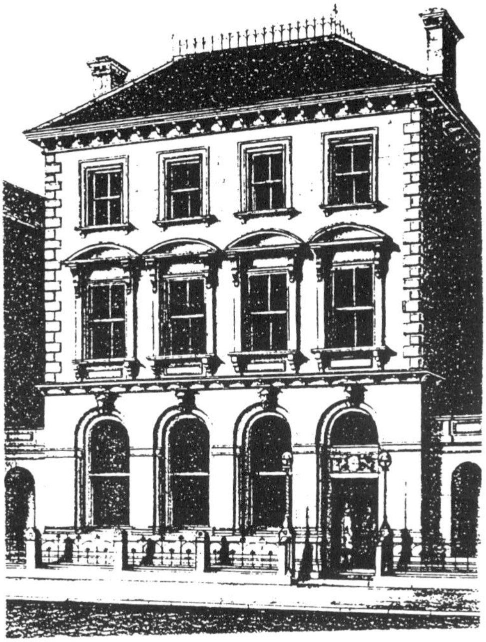

LONGFORD: **Ulster Bank**
Designed by James Bell in 1863. Four bays with segmented pediments framing the windows of the *piano nobile*. Riverine heads carved as keystones to the ground-floor arcade.

NEWTOWNFORBES: **Castle Forbes**
The present castle was rebuilt in 1826 by John Hargrave modelled on Castle Forbes in Scotland but retaining two wings of the 17th-century house that Francis Sandys had incorporated in an unexecuted scheme. The 7th earl of Granard, after his marriage to the heiress of Johnstown Castle, Co. Wexford (q.v.), and his conversion to Catholicism, commissioned J.J. McCarthy to remodel the stable block in Irish Baronial. This is reached through a gatehouse range resembling a miniature French chateau (1858). McCarthy altered the staircase of the entry vestibule and designed several fireplaces, of which the most monumental were removed along with his balconies when the castle was again remodelled, this time by Beatrice, the American wife of the 8th earl, from 1909 onwards. The Frenchman Fernand Allard and London interior decorators Lenyon and Morant recreated the era of Inigo Jones. The architects (mere executants of her ideas) were Frederick Foster in London and Kaye Parry of Dublin. Her most triumphant interior was the library made from two floors of the 17th-century west wing with its painted ceiling transplanted from an Italian palazzo. This is reached by Sandys' gallery altered by McCarthy who lit it by a series of hexagonal stained glass lanterns. An adjoining lightwell was glazed over to protect glass-roofed bathrooms. Outside, beyond the formal grounds, a secret Edwardian water garden was added, guarded by a floating metallic swan.

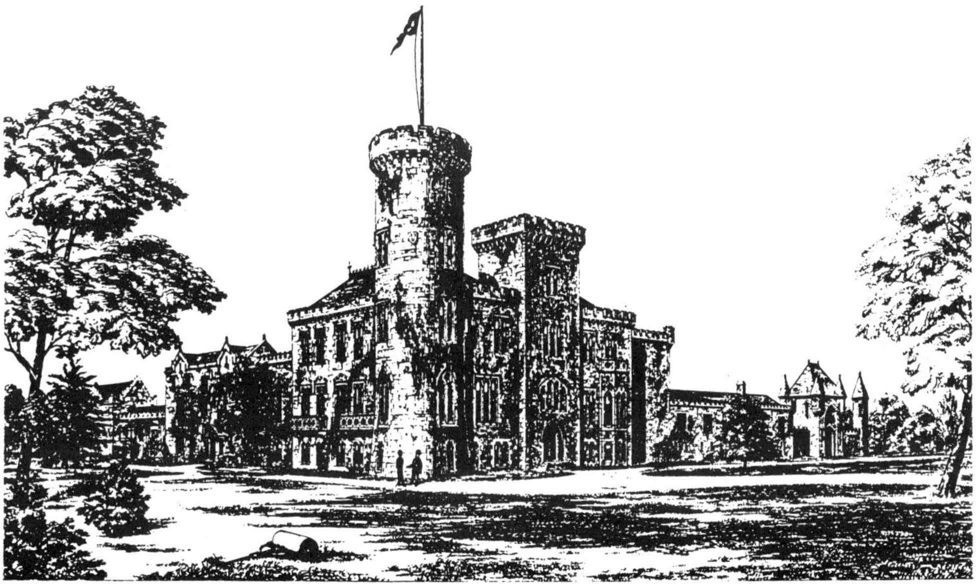

LOUTH

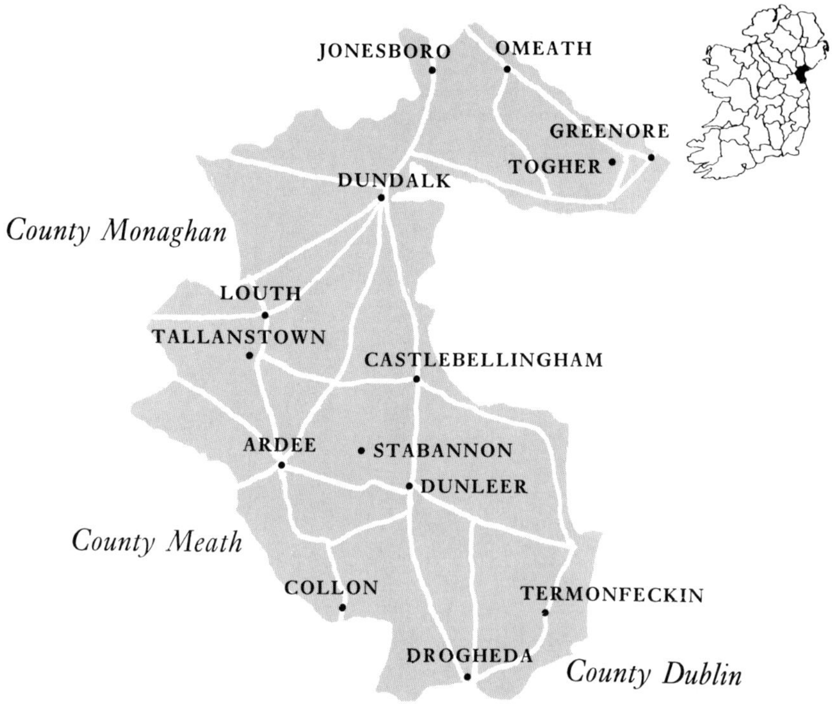

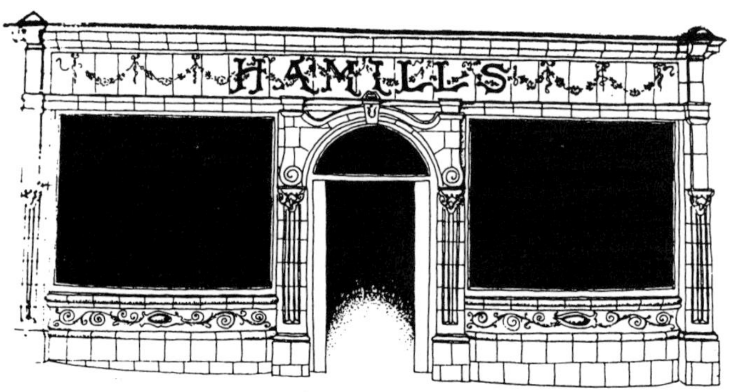

ARDEE: Convent of Mercy
Interesting attempt by the Louth surveyor, John Neville, to abandon the elegant of Regency Gothic and adopt the authenticity of Pugin. Built in 1855-8. Picturesquely composed façade with two three-storied gabled returns linked by a fragile ground-floor arcade, the belfry flush with the gable of the classroom block to the north, and chapel on the south. The exterior might have been acceptable to Pugin, but he would have been appalled if he had gone inside. The interior is hopelessly obsolete with its frivolous Gothic stucco work; but it has great charm—countless corbelled heads of saints and angels. Woodwork by a local firm, Moonan from Blakestown, who later worked in Maynooth.

ARDEE: Hamill's
Terracotta shopfront with twin-bay-window *c.*1900, enlivened by jolly swags of flowers and fruit, now a pub increasingly threatened by a bridge-widening scheme.

ARDEE: Cardistown
Sedate Italianate villa designed by John Neville *c.*1860.

ARDEE: Catholic Church
Gothick galleried church built *c.*1830 and remodelled in 1860 by J.J. McCarthy, who inserted a series of wedding-cake altars beneath stained glass at the eastern end. Abandoned

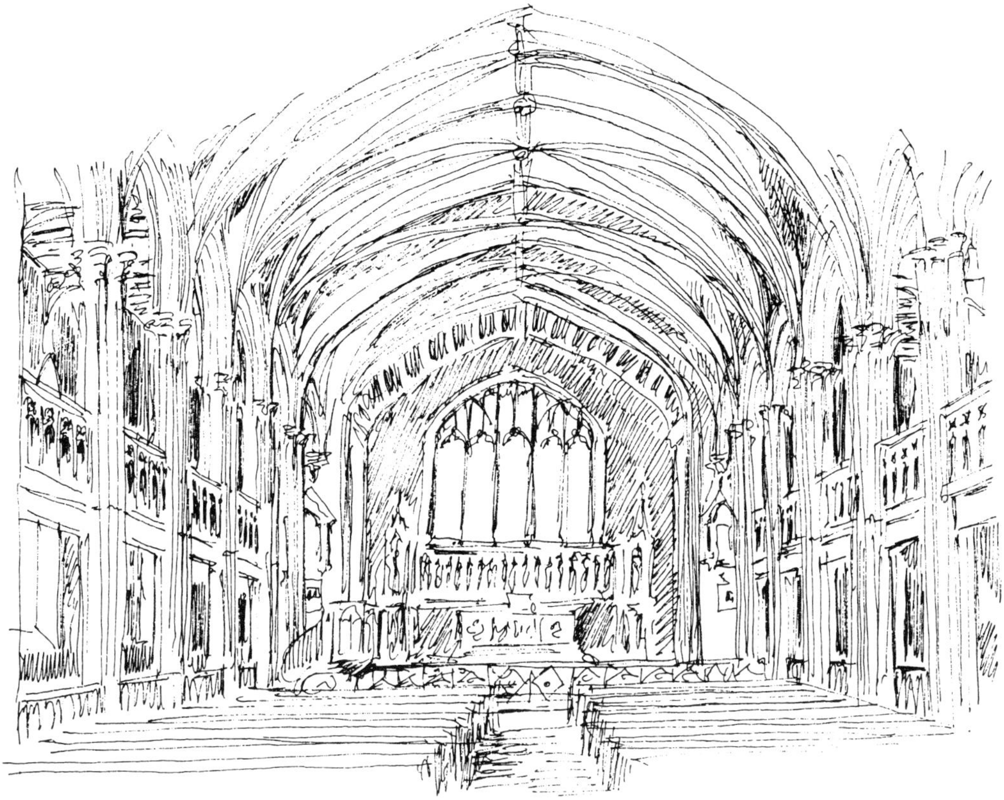

c. 1965 and replaced by a new church on the other side of the road that looks like an elegant community centre. Impractical plans to turn the original church into a community centre remain stillborn. Now serves as only a memorial to one parish priest's architectural misjudgment.

CASTLEBELLINGHAM: **Braganstown**
Georgian house, remodelled and extended as an Elizabethan manor, *c.* 1846, symmetrically on the entrance front, asymmetrically at the rear. The original Wyatt windows were disguised by hooded mouldings, and the doorcase concealed by a turreted porch. Additions at each end of the façade have bartizans and gables to frame two double-height castellated bays with loftier reception rooms. A polygonal bay window disguises the original house on the garden front. The architect was Thomas Smith, his client the Revd Anthony Garstin, who lived till he was almost eighty but never married, so the unusual castellated bannisters to the principal staircase, presumably had never to facilitate sliding children.

CASTLEBELLINGHAM: **Drumcar Church of Ireland**
Gothic Revival church with its furnishings complete and unaltered; nave of 1840; choir added by Slater and Carpenter. Commemorative stained glass. Set in a yew-planted graveyard approached through a red-tiled lych gate presumably by Thomas Drew. Hexagonal Gothic Revival mausoleum by Slater and Carpenter erected to commemorate the McClintock family.

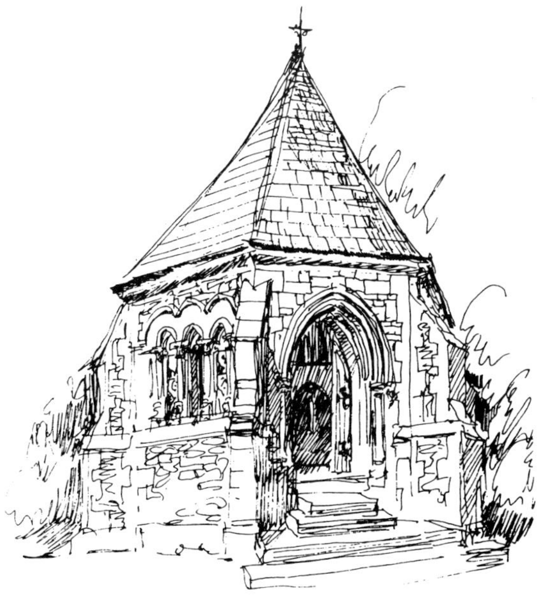

CASTLEBELLINGHAM: **Tenure Catholic Church**

Ambitious Gothic Revival village church by P.J. Dodd designed in 1894. Cruciform with a slender tower tucked into the angle of the nave and transept. Polygonal apse perforated by gabled eastern window. Unconventional tracery inserted in the rose windows. Well-preserved interior culminating in the chancel with mosaics and frescoes fused together and illuminated by Mayer's stained glass to create a foretaste of paradise.

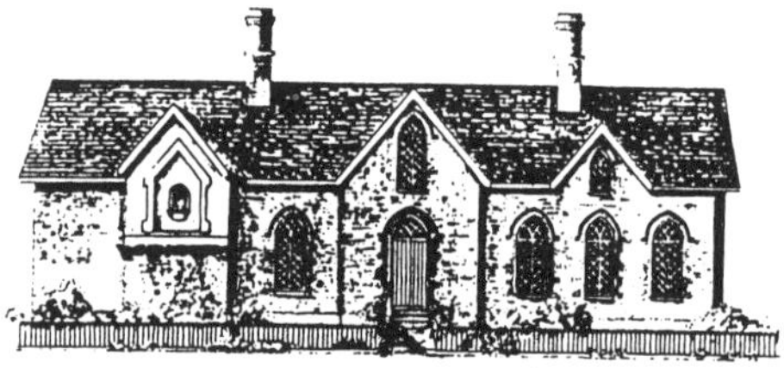

CASTLEBELLINGHAM: **Widows' Cottages**

Group of neo-Tudor almshouses built carefully to resemble individual suburban villas when they were commissioned *c.*1830 as a charitable donation by Sir Henry Bellingham at the gates of Castle Bellingham. His architect is not known, but their similarities to W.V. Morrison's Carpenham has been noted in the Morrison catalogue of 1989.

CASTLEBELLINGHAM: **Williamstown House**

Built by Finlay Chester JP in 1856-60 at a cost of £12,000 to the designs of William Caldbeck. An Italianate palazzo set on a rusticated basement. Steps rise to an Ionic porch, a balcony to a Wyatt window on the first floor set beneath a floating pediment, bracketed like the adjoining roof eaves. The front is made up of five bays, the side of four. In front, twin spacious reception rooms; at the rear, smaller rooms divided by partitions of peat. Interior intact (through inheritance) up to 1970.

COLLON: **Catholic Church**

Gothic Revival church containing an effigy of Dorcas (d.1876), daughter of Lord Massarene and Ferrard, by her husband, a sculptor called Percy Fitzgerald. Glass by Earley and Mayer.

DROGHEDA: **Augustinian Church**

The medieval foundation was rebuilt by an obscure architect called M.B. Moran, presumably the same Moran responsible for their church in Galway (q.v.). Of all the Victorian churches in the town, this is the only one that makes a serious attempt to build in an Irish style (1865). Porch rising steeply to a Celtic cross adjoins incomplete tower, walls rising to parapets. Seven-light western window illuminates the nave that leads through an archway to the chancel. The other illumination comes from reduced windows in the aisles now filled with glass by the Harry Clarke Studios. Refitted by William Scott.

DROGHEDA: **Beltichbourne**

A sanctuary for discarded conservatories due to the enthusiasm of the current owner. The curvilinear from Balyna (q.v.), and that from Knapton (now part of the Abbeyleix demesne) have been welded together and linked to the existing house.

DROGHEDA: **Boyne Viaduct**

One of the great achievements of early Irish railway construction, it carries the Dublin Belfast line over the port of Drogheda spanning the river with an immense bow spring girder, 81m long. Originally in wrought-iron with double tracks, it was repaced with steel supporting a single track designed by G.B. Howden in the 1920s. Otherwise the bridge remains as completed by Sir John McNeill and James Barton.

DROGHEDA: **Dominican Church**

The original medieval church has vanished, and its replacement by George Ashlin is a competent but chilly exercise in French Gothic built in 1878. A slender traceried west window is recessed in a cavernous arch and contrasted to an adjoining tower that terminates abruptly in a saddle-back roof. This is linked to the conventual buildings added by Ashlin in 1881. Barn-like interior.

DROGHEDA: **Allied Irish Bank**

Former Provincial Bank. A three-storied Lombardesque Gothic elevation, four bays wide; designed in 1865 by W.G. Murray.

DROGHEDA: **Newfoundwell Viaduct**

Massive stone viaduct built in 1855 to carry the Dublin-Belfast railway. Designed by Alexander Shaw, who was able in the best High Victorian tradition to blend the utilitarian with the fantastic. His architectural inspiration was the nearby medieval barbican St Lawrence's Gate through which the road to Termonfeckin passed. There are five archways with castellated parapets articulated by semi-circular towers.

DROGHEDA: **Obelisk Bridge**

Wrought-iron bridge across the Boyne, upstream, with a single span between tapering limestone abutments. Constructed by Thomas

Grendon and Co. of Drogheda in 1869. The obelisk that was once beside it marking the battle of the Boyne was blown up in 1921.

DROGHEDA: St Mary's Catholic Church

The last to be built of Drogheda's Victorian churches designed by the local architect P.J. Dodd and built from 1884 to 1892. The site is cramped between the street and rising ground but chosen so that the spire would dominate the Dublin approach to the town. Only one aisle has fenestration, but the other compensates with murals. Mosaics in the chancel and much stencilling counteract its internal grimness. Wall memorials in the Gothic manner to the Matthews family. Glass by Lobin and Mayer.

DROGHEDA: St Peter's Catholic Church

A lavish prizewinner of a competition held in 1876 for a church to house the head of Blessed (as he then was) Oliver Plunkett. The successful architects were O'Neill and Byrne, against contestants whose only recourse was to publicize their unsuccessful entries. An imposing flight of steps leads up to a French Gothic façade with sculptural relief above the doors dominated by an off-centre tower and spire. A nave of five widely spaced arches resting on coupled granite columns leads directly into a chancel with a polygonal apse. Screened transepts, one reserved for the head of the saint. Stained glass by Mayer. O'Neill died before the completion in 1900.

DROGHEDA: Whitworth Hall

William Barre's most important public building outside Ulster. Designed in 1865 in his eclectic manner, seeking to unite medieval vigour with classical repose. Double-storied façade with superimposed arcades in muted polychromy. The three central arches are grouped beneath a Renaissance pediment framing a Gothic rose window, and this is crowned by a French chateau roof. The internal layout is simple and effective. Twin flights of curving stairs lead to a first-floor conference room that extends the full length of the façade. At the rear is the great hall, now taken up with snooker and juke boxes. Note the unconventional rear elevation.

DUNDALK: Ballymascanlon House Hotel

Neo-Elizabethan manor house, rebuilt for R.G. Foster by P.J. Byrne in 1863, as an extension to an earlier Georgian house. Now the kernel of an hotel and leisure complex. Neo-Classical interiors show influence of Mulvany. Neo-Adamesque interiors in later extension *c.*1890 possibly by Sibthorpes. Home of the botanical artist Katherine Plunket, a contemporary of Queen Victoria, who died in 1932 aged 111.

DUNDALK, Bridge Street: St Nicholas' Catholic Church

Built also to the designs of John Murray and consecrated in 1860 on a prominent site which the church fails to live up to, although it must have made more impact with its original spire. However, this became unsafe in 1904 and was replaced by the present tower. Hidden single transept added by Ralph Byrne in 1913 to double its capacity. Stained-glass east window by J. and D. Casey.

DUNDALK: Catholic Church

Designed by Thomas Duff in 1860 on the model of King's College Chapel, Cambridge. Nave and choir continuous, nine bays in all. A drawing by Duff for the church is thought to have been once in possession of Thomas Turner, who was commissioned to design the entry screen, also in Perpendicular Gothic, but in sandstone, now much weathered, satisfyingly low and horizontal. The tower was added in 1903 by George Ashlin, modelled on Gloucester Cathedral. In 1860, J.J. McCarthy was commissioned to design the high altar, reredos, sedilia and a monument to the Revd Coyne carved by T. Kirk.

Ashlin added the decoration of the chancel with Italian mosaics. The earliest side altar was carved by Sir Thomas Farrell. The glass above the high altar comes from Hardman of Birmingham. Further glass by Mayer and Earley. Unlike the east end of Duff's Newry Cathedral

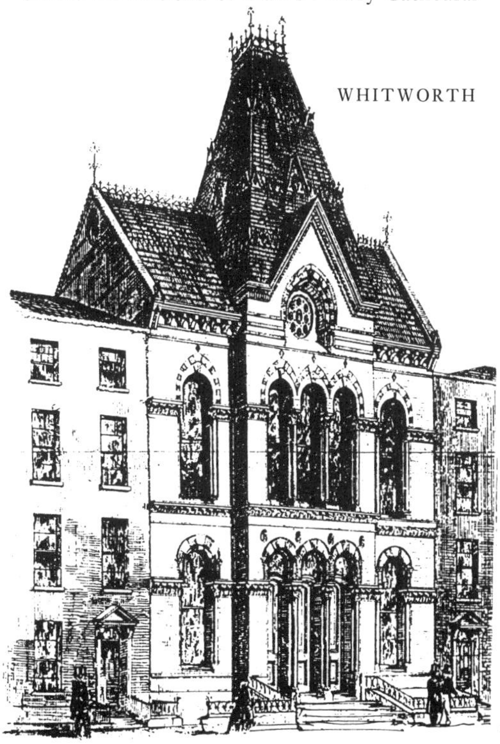

WHITWORTH

(which Ashlin totally transformed), here he restricted himself to embellishments—the stained glass and the pulpit—so that this church today is the least altered of Duff's churches.

DUNDALK, **Chapel Street: Christian Brothers**
Gothic institution built from 1853 to 1869 and ascribed to J.J. McCarthy.

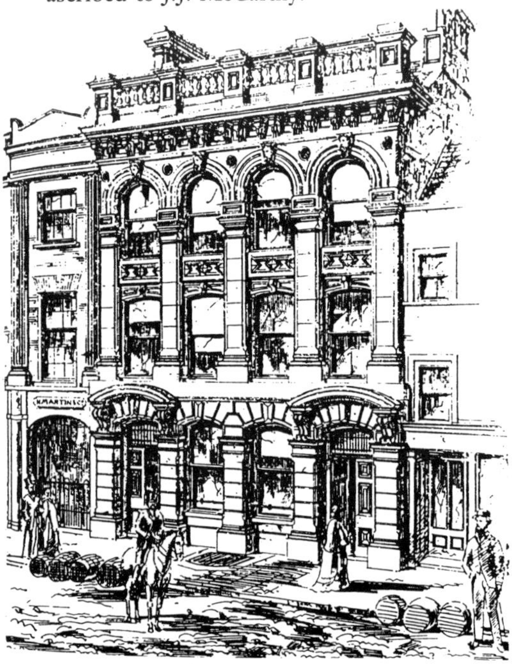

DUNDALK, **Clanbrassil Street: No. 70, Duffy's**
The most spectacular of the commercial premises that still give vitality to the main shopping street of the town. Built as a wine store for Nicholas Martin in 1868 to the designs of John Neville. A six-bayed palazzo, with its ground floor upholding a double-storied arcade. The parapet rests on coupled consoles that alternate with the carved riverine heads which form the keystones of each arch.

DUNDALK: **Convent of Mercy**
Georgian house acquired and extended in 1853 by John Neville, who lived in nearby Roden Place and whose two daughters became nuns. In 1857 a chapel was donated by Thomas Regan, a local businessman, and this was built to Neville's designs. Carved stalls by Charles Allpress. Later school extension (1879).

DUNDALK: **County Buildings**
Built as the Louth Hospital in a restrained neo-Tudor in brick with stone trimmings, with a symmetrical façade of three projecting gables separated by recessed ranges of four bays with ground-floor arcades built flush to the gables. Designed by the English architect, Thomas Smith, who came from Hertfordshire to become the architect of the County Louth establishment. The local rector, the Revd Thackeray, a cousin of the writer, is portrayed with the plans unrolled on a table beside him. Date: 1884.

DUNDALK: **Dominican Church**
Gothic Revival and adjoining priory by local architect, John Murray. Church completed in 1866, priory a year later; but the intended spire that was to dominate the two façades together has remained unexecuted. Large-boned nave entered through the columned gallery supporting organ, eight bays long, articulated by exposed braced trusses and culminating in compressed polygonal apse. The altars are turn-of-the-century, inlaid with mosaic, by Ashlin. The glass is late Harry Clarke studios. Central window in apse by Michael Healy. Other glass by Mayer. Horribly enjoyable side chapel made out of a grotto transplanted from Lourdes.

DUNDALK: **Dundalk House**
The 17th-century seat of the earls of Roden was acquired by the Carroll family at the turn of the century, demolished and replaced by a terracotta villa with curvilinear gables. Architect: S. Stevenson. Now offices.

DUNDALK: **Garda Barracks**
Designed as the county gaol by John Neville, a Limerick engineer who was county surveyor for Louth from 1840 to 1886. This is his most important, even over-important, classical design (1845-53). Into a façade of modest dimensions, he compresses a four-storied belvedere floating above a triple-arched arcade. This conceals rusticated doors and links twin double-storied pavilions. Further pavilions and massive chimneys visible behind, all in smooth ashlar contrasting to the rubble walls of the cell blocks and the yards on either side for the condemned. These remain intact, whereas the interior of the barracks has been trivialized beyond recognition.

DUNDALK, **Jocelyn Street: Presbyterian Church**
Compact Perpendicular Gothic, with triple-bayed façade articulated by buttresses with pinnacles. Designed by Thomas Duff and built in 1839.

DUNDALK: **Mount Pleasant, Ballymascanlon**
The writer of the guide to Carlingford Lough in 1846 found Sir John McNeill, the railway pioneer and the first Professor of Engineering

at Trinity College, engaged in enlarging his family home and embellishing the grounds. Although it is always said that he was his own architect, there are so many similarities to his collaborator, J.S. Mulvany, that it is tempting to assume a joint venture. However, the portico with its widely spaced columns based on the Tower of the Winds has no precedence in Mulvany's oeuvre and is most probably McNeill. Delightful side elevation with double-height library as a pedimented centrepiece between single-storied curved bows. A wing beside it has an Italianate belvedere tower. Double-height galleried hall with bifurcating staircase. All this must have been regretted by McNeill when he was dying in acute poverty in London making matchboxes for his subsistence.

DUNDALK: Redemptorist Church and Monastery

Monastery completed in 1881 and adjoining church consecrated in 1892, both designed by George Ashlin as an austere citadel of the Faith in rock-faced ashlar, built to shelter the faithful from the fires of Hell. Rich interior in Ashlin's Romanesque that is inspired by Italy, not Ireland, despite Ashlin's new-found nationalism. The softly hued and gilded colour scheme has so far survived 'improvement'. Altar carved by Thomas Earley.

DUNDALK, Roden Place: Century Bar

A rare but accomplished Art Nouveau corner pub built in 1898-1902 to celebrate the new century, and since then carefully maintained. Arcaded ground floor with etched glass ensuring privacy. Wide windows above and generous half-dormers ensure 'Sweetness and Light' to the landlord and his family. High up over the corner door a corbelled turret gives momentary respite from the inclement weather to the lingering revellers below, illuminated by overhanging lamps with lively ironwork. Simpler scrolls uphold the gutters. Comfortable interior warmed by Art Nouveau fireplace and the elusive sunlight. Designed by a Belfast firm called May, but built by Terence McDonald, whose carved initials form the centrepiece of the bar display. How easy to sit here and drink to a new dawn the morning after, rather than sleep off yesterday's hangover.

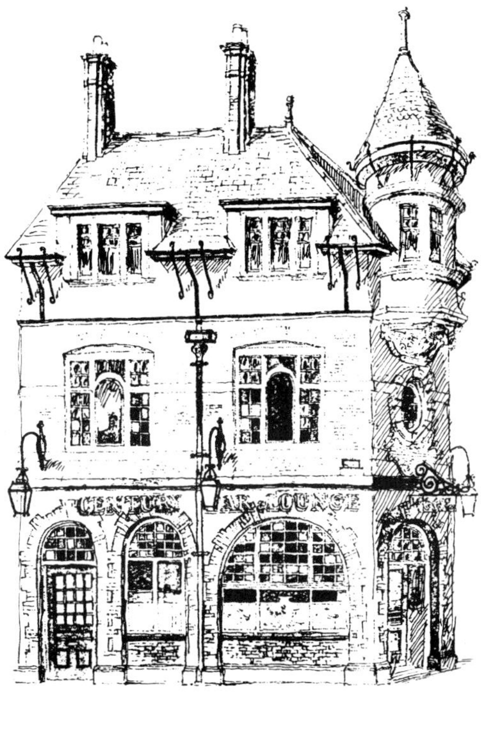

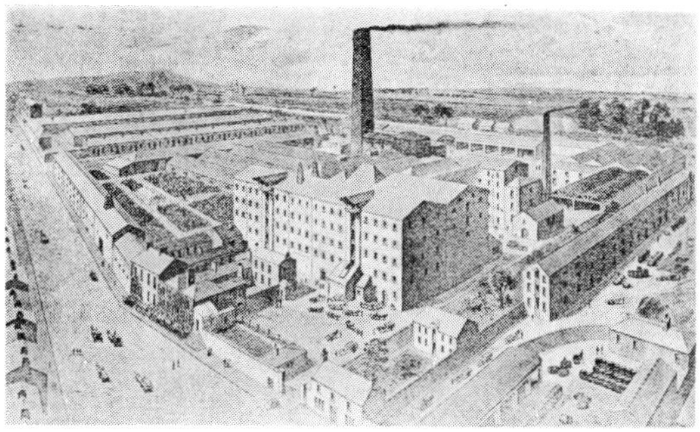

DUNDALK, Roden Place: The Distillery

Built for Malcolm Brown *c.*1870. Although its massive chimney had been dismantled, the distillery still looked impressive—a central range of eight bays, with projecting gables and a further four bays at either end. All windows set in three floors of arches, while the double-height access doors are set into the gables, sheltered by generously projecting platforms. All exposed timber was painted its original red against the dark black of the calpstone walls. A scheme by National Building Agency to demolish the two upper floors (allegedly to safeguard the remainder) has just been carried out.

DUNDALK, Roden Place: Kelly Memorial

Conventionally designed Gothic memorial erected in 1879 by Thomas Pettigrue, a builder from Navan, to commemorate a shipping disaster of twenty years before.

DUNDALK: The Station

Built *c.*1850 by Sir John McNeill but now much altered. Large industrial complex, since all Irish railway carriages were constructed here. Impressive neglected engine sheds.

DUNDALK: The Townhall

Built in 1859 for the Corn Exchange Company to the designs of John Murray after a competition that he failed to win. The cost of construction sent the company into liquidation and the Town Commissioners acquired it for £4,000. A double-storied palazzo, rendered coursing and rustication below, exposed brick above, crude but effective, its centrepiece, an Ionic-columned porch below, then a Wyatt window above surmounted by a weighty aedicule; yet all this top-heaviness is held in place by articulated piers on either side. Much altered assembly hall.

DUNLEER: Barmeath Castle

Seat of the Bellews. Earlier castle georgianized and then gothicized in 1839 to the designs of Thomas Smith. He extended it by adding a many-towered wing to the rear terminating in a chapel: the Bellews had retained their Catholic faith since medieval times. Isolated folly tower in the demesne.

DUNLEER: Rokeby Hall

One of the last of the curvilinear conservatories added *c.*1880 as an rectangular pavilion to the neo-Classical house of the 1st Lord Rokeby and archbishop of Armagh. This was designed by Thomas Cooley and executed by Francis Johnston. In its own way the conservatory is as serene and precise as the house itself. Curvilinear inner structure anticipates Art Nouveau. Possibly by William Turner.

GREENORE: Boherboy Catholic Church

Austere Gothic Revival church set on an windswept hillside above Carlingford Lough, and visible for miles around. Designed in 1863 by John Murray and built out of local sandstone and limestone trimmings. Tower with broached spire flanking west façade. Aisles with steeply rising roofs permitting only a narrow band of quatrefoils. Nave of six bays entered through arcaded tribune beneath the organ.

GREENORE: The Bush Church of Ireland

A tiny Gothic Revival church of four bays, monumentally articulated by buttresses capped with spires. Adjoining schoolhouse acts as a simpler foil. Erected in 1846, possibly by Frederick Darley, since he specialized in building churches that could be mistaken for those of his erstwhile rival, John Semple, were they not more polite.

GREENORE: The Bungalows

A hundred years ago, the hotel company discovered two devices to increase their custom, a golf course and chalets. Now that the hotel has closed down, these flourish in their own right. The chalets are known as the Bungalows, two blocks of doubled-storied, semi-detached villas. They are built out of Canadian timber clad with shingled tiles, with overhanging timber windows and tiled roofs. The horizontality of each is emphasized by continuous verandahs interrupted by brick chimney-stacks shored up by stone-capped buttressing, to give corner fire-

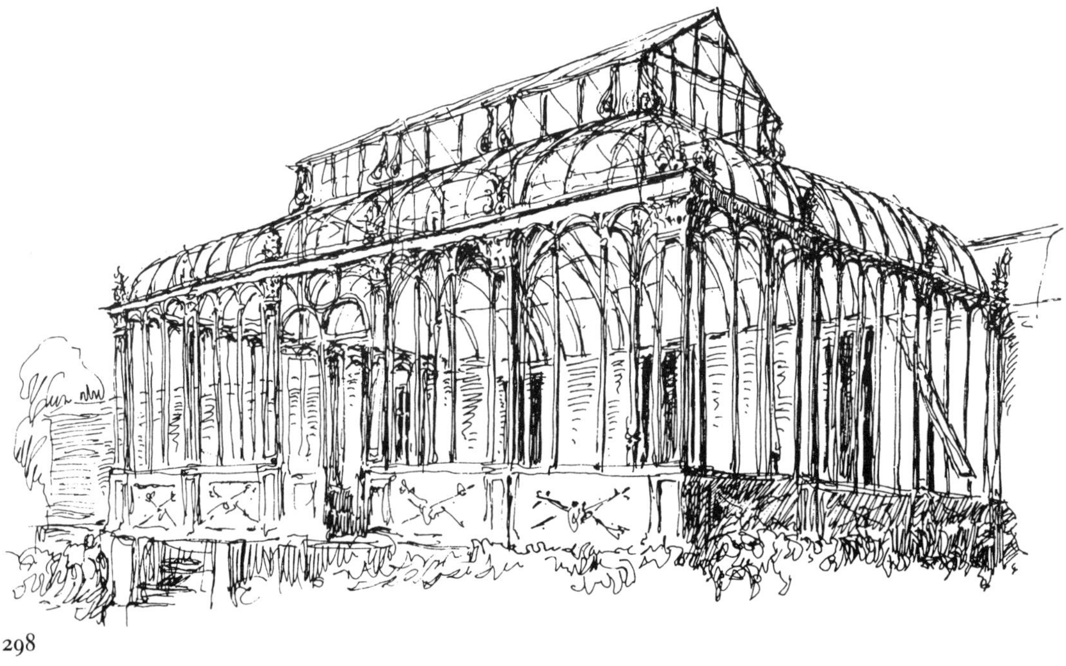

places to the principal rooms. The architect is unrecorded but is said to be an American. Was he Frank Lloyd-Wright?

GREENORE: **Coastguard Station**
Designed by James Owen *c.*1880, in a reduced Scottish Baronial, following his standard design to be found from Greystones to Rathmullen.

GREENORE: **Greenore Hotel**
Built as the terminus hotel of the Newry-Greenore railway line of 1873 in Queen Anne Revival by the Great Northern Railway as a companion to their hotel at Holyhead, since demolished by British Rail. Here, the Irish counterpart survives as offices, but only just.

GREENORE: **The Village**
Densely planned village built by N.A. Mills for the North British Railway Company (with the central school dated 1873) as a small-scale industrial Utopia unique in Southern Ireland—but then Greenore was chosen because Holyhead was nearer in journey time than anywhere else on the east coast. Its concentrated development is explicable not by shortage of land on this once treeless foreland, but by the need for shelter from the continuous wind. The materials used throughout are a forceful combination of brick and stone, especially in the central co-operative stores that still survive as such and the adjoining schoolhouse now a comfortable pub, with segregation no longer between boys and girls, but between the lounge and the public bar. Showing unquestioning belief in social order, the accommodation for the managers was provided alongside as semi-detached villas in their own grounds. All churches, by contrast, are kept at a tactful distance of several miles away, out of earshot of their rival chimes.

JONESBORO: **Church of Ireland**
Single-cell Gothic Revival church designed by W.H. Lynn while in partnership with the Lanyons; built in 1867. Now disused due to its exposed siting on the border.

LOUTH: **Catholic Church**
Substantial Gothic Revival church by W.H. Byrne (1890-1904).

OMEATH: **The Rectory**
Late Georgian rectory reorientated and extended *c.*1860 in simplified Gothic, after the Revd Peyton consulted Benjamin Woodward.

STABANNON: **Catholic Church**
A simple Gothic Revival nave of five bays attached to a chancel of one bay with trimmed lancets set into rock-faced ashlar. Adjoining belfry with broached spire. Designed by the prolific W.H. Byrne and completed in 1899.

TALLANSTOWN: **Glyde Court**
Georgian house with an extended façade made even longer in 1868 when the house was re-roofed and Jacobeanized by an unrecorded architect, who built out curved bays and crowned them with curvilinear gables. Home of the Utopian social reformer Vere Foster. Later inherited by the Vere-Foster family portrayed by Orpens grandest portrait, immortalized as the Hapsburgs were by Velázquez at the moment of their decline. House sold after the recent death of their youngest daughter.

TERMONFECKIN: **Sandpit Catholic Church**
Early Gothic Revival hall church with nave and aisles subdivided by clustered colonnettes upholding continuous tunnel valuting. The side altars no longer form the climax of the side aisles, having fallen victim to liturgical reformers (who have spared the original high altar). Original glazing replaced by later stained glass, apart from one window.

TOGHER: **Catholic Church**
Gothic Revival parish church built in 1866 to the designs of John Murray.

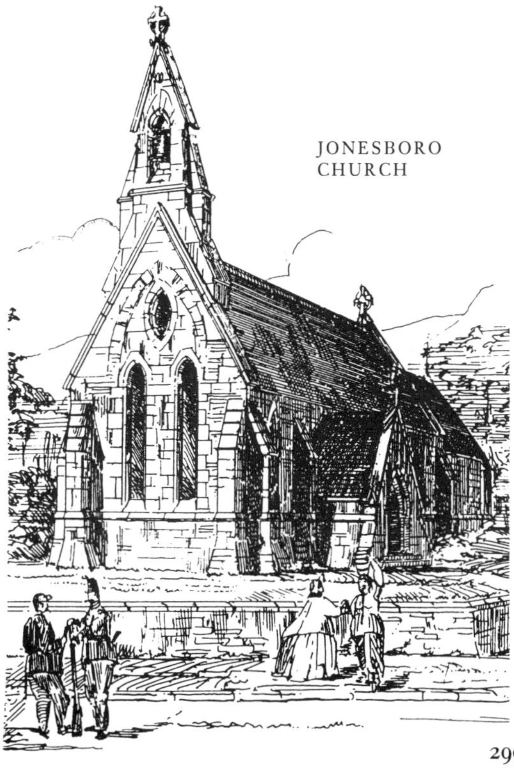

JONESBORO CHURCH

MAYO

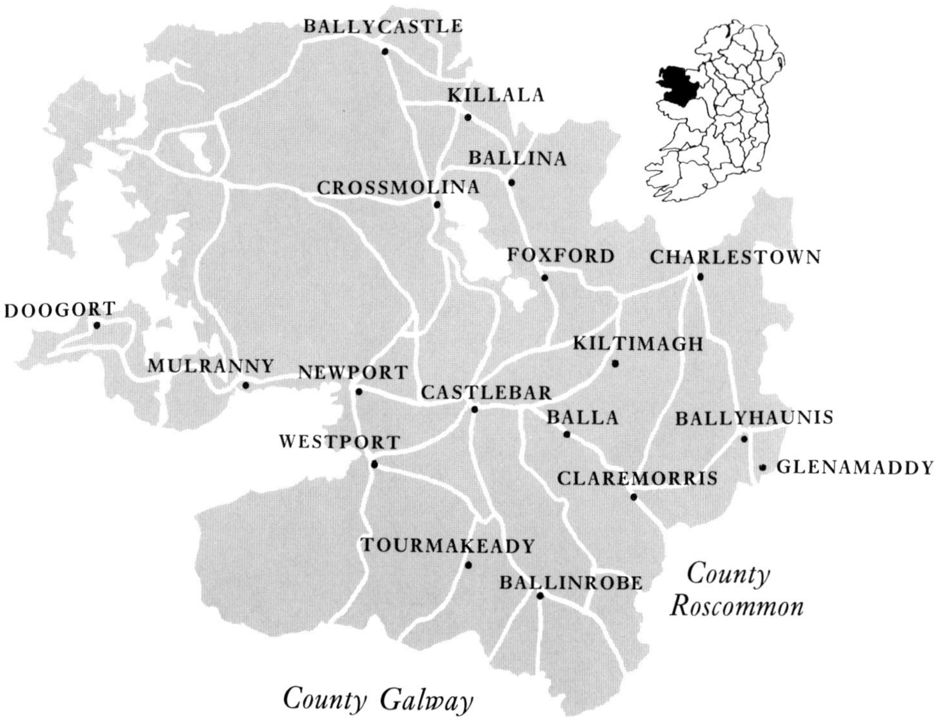

BALLA: **Catholic Church**
The best of R.M. Butler's Gothic churches, commissioned at the same time as Newport, which it resembles except in choice of style. Both are hall churches, the central aisle tunnel-vaulted, the side aisles flat-ceilinged as in the churches of Temple Moore. In Balla, the aisles roofs are flat, concealed by impressive Irish battlements. The southern porch paraphrases the medieval doorway to the abbey of Cong. The altar of the lady chapel is a cast of the sedilia in Holy Cross. But this careful historicism is absorbed into a space of such simplified Gothic that it could only date from this century. Multi-polychromatic marble high altar (1918). Good stained glass of the same period (windows by Harry Clarke and the Clarke Studios).

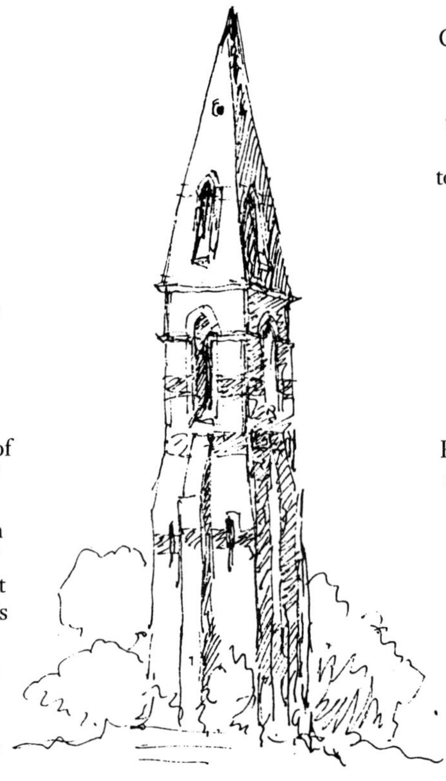

BALLA: **Church of Ireland**
Designed by Welland and Gillespie with their incisive missionary Gothic; built (*c.*1865) to last far longer than the century permitted by the Church authorities; today only the spire banded with polychromatic stone has been spared by exhausted demolitioners.

BALLINA: **Belleek**
Built by Francis Knox-Gore, afterwards first baronet, in Tudor Revival from 1825 onwards and known then as Belleek Manor. Today known as Belleek Castle. A 'friendly castle', this luxury hotel has roomfuls of old masters, tapestries, chandeliers, medieval carvings. In the dungeons beneath are collections of armour and fossils. One of few Gothic Revival castles where

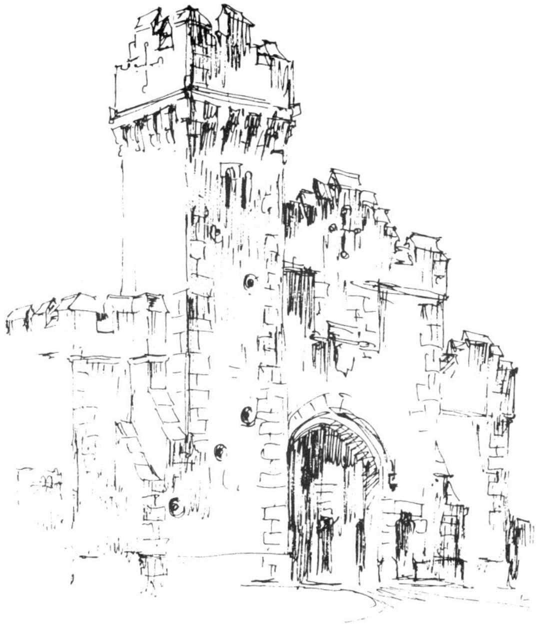

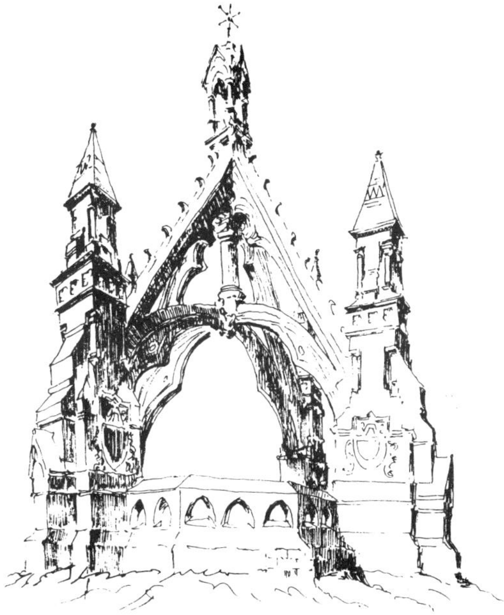

its original builder would feel at home (which could not be said about the more celebrated Ashford or Dromoland). But to enter the shrine of an Irish Grail, one must traverse many an ordeal like the knights of old. First a forbidding machicolated entrance arch, framing an unnerving vista of suburban bungalows. After a vicarious rear view of an industrial estate, then we plunge into the darkness of a state forest of monotonous conifers ultimately to confront a vision of a grimly symmetrical façade built of dark grey limestone, its severity relieved by an eccentric double oriel over the doorway.

That double oriel is the only outside clue to the elegant and festive interiors with their ribbed and embossed plaster vaulting, spacious bay windows, Georgian Gothic fireplaces, castellated doorcases. Scattered through the reception rooms are carvings reputably salvaged from a galleon of the Spanish Armada wrecked off the coast of Mayo. If so, the bow window in the bar is plundered wholesale from the galleon's poop. The adjoining banqueting hall contains fittings salvaged from Gibbstown, Navan (q.v.) and unidentified columns, possibly carved by Charles Harrison. How fortunate that the next generation of the family did not disturb the Gothic frivolity of the house attributed to J.B. Keane but concentrated on the grounds instead.

The second baronet called in J.F. Fuller. The entrance arch is attributed to the agent, Edmund Perry, but is a twin to the Fuller's gates to Ashford Castle. Formidable garden terraces descend from the house towards the sea and a pathway leads to a landing stage where every year the family, now the Saunders-Knox-Gore, would embark on their yacht and sail off to their estates in the Bahamas. Such an extravagant lifestyle led to the inevitable disintegration of their Irish property and the sale of their home to a convent, but not before they left one last abiding memorial—Fuller's mausoleum of 1872 for the 2nd baronet, now hidden deep in the state forest, to be found only by the most intrepid. Fuller's monument is a pinnacled central shrine held aloft by four flying buttresses rising from an octagonal base that surmounts with scant respect a prehistoric tumulus. One is reminded of the steeple of St Giles in Edinburgh but without the cross. The 2nd baronet insisted on being buried with his horse even if that meant scandalized relatives and an unconsecrated grave.

BALLINA: Catholic Cathedral

Cruciform structure in Decorated Gothic begun in 1828 to the designs of Dominic Madden. Interior lacks the individuality of his Tuam Cathedral or Ennis parish church (q.v.), but relies instead on being entirely illuminated by Victorian stained glass to give it a dim, religious air. Overscaled spire added in 1858 by John Benson. Ceiling executed by Arthur Canning with vanished painted decoration based on St Maria Minerva, Rome; altar commissioned in Rome by Sir Kenelm Digby, but only the table survives.

BALLINA: Convent of Sisters of Mercy

Gothic Revival convent of 1863-7 built round three sides of a cloister with chapel confined to the ground floor and externally articulated by polygonal apse perforated with rose windows set into dormers. Interior of chapel equally in-

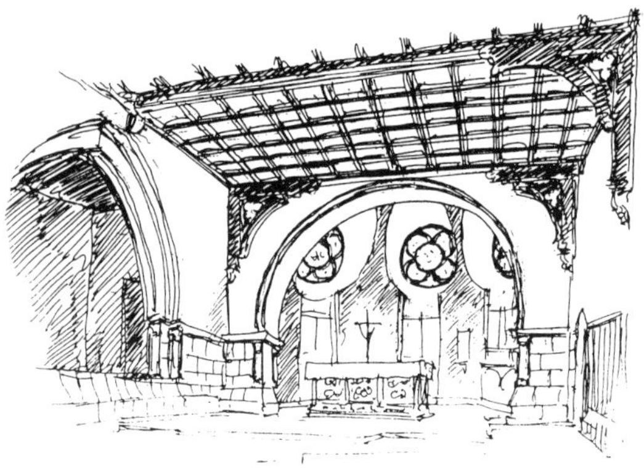

ventive, with rose windows cutting through apsidal semi-dome framed by semi-circular stone arches rising from tiny coupled columns. Most probably by George Goldie, who designed the sister convent of Sligo. Additions by W.H. Byrne, 1889.

BALLINA: **Clendining Memorial**
Polished granite fountain dating *c.*1895.

BALLINA: **1798 Memorial**
Statue of moping angel guarding draped flags. Sculpted by T. Denning; unveiled in 1898 by Maude Gonne McBride.

BALLINA: **Mount Falcon**
The earliest of J.F. Fuller's Scottish Baronial houses built in 1870 for Utred Knox (and saved from demolition in the 1960s by the late Major

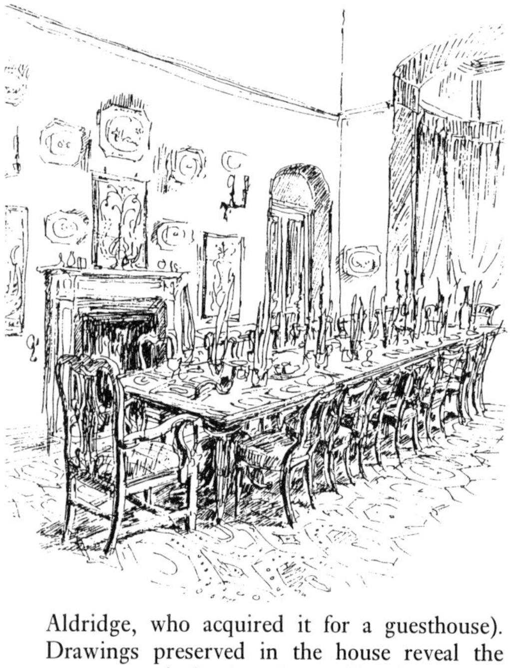

Aldridge, who acquired it for a guesthouse). Drawings preserved in the house reveal the tower was an afterthought to relieve its external grimness. Unexpectedly spacious interior with principal reception rooms opening off an impressive tiled and top-lit staircase hall. Back passages crammed with rods and wellingtons. Long table in the diningroom perennially presided over by Mrs Aldridge with the inaugural command to her French guests, 'Frogs at the end!'

BALLINDINE: **Catholic Church**
Rural Early Gothic Revival church with inventive plan—cruciform in shape with a rectangular chancel projecting from the central bay of a triple-sided apse. Interior retains its three galleries. The canted windows each side of the chancel arch have glass by Joshua Clarke. Lively memorial to Father Rhatigan (1911) carved by McHugh of Tuam.

BALLINROBE: **Catholic Church**
Built by Richard Pierce, the younger, of Wexford in 1863 (tower, spire and transepts) to replace its Regency Gothic predecessor; now an elegant ruin dominated by a tower-like medieval friary. The interior of its successor has been made memorable by Dean D'Alton's patronage of Harry Clarke during the 1920s.

BALLINROBE: **Creagh House**
Large, coarsely-detailed Italianate house, made asymmetrical and more picturesque by partial demolition that has spared its once central companile. Earlier house rebuilt in the mid-19th-century for Mr Knox by Samuel Ussher Roberts, who was appointed surveyor of Galway (grandson of 'honest' John Roberts). Now an agricultural institute.

BALLYCASTLE: **Castle Lackin**
Castellated outbuildings prolong a Georgian ruin once seat of the Knoxes. A castellated gate frames an eyecatcher on the hill inspired by the steeple of St Giles in Edinburgh.

BALLYHAUNIS: **Catholic Church**
Like Claremorris (q.v.), also designed by Doolin and Butler in 1904, yet another late weighty neo-Gothic church redeemed by good glass, and in this case a short-tempered redecoration.

CASTLEBAR: **Breaghy House**
Scottish Baronial, by an English architect, William Fawcett, for Dominic Browne (1881). The Brownes had lost much of their lands through their allegiance to the house of Stuart, and their home mirrors their unsuccessful sacrifice to a Scottish cause. Institutional entrance front (Fawcett extended unmemorably several colleges in Cambridge) in rough hewn limestone with sandstone window surrounds. Livelier

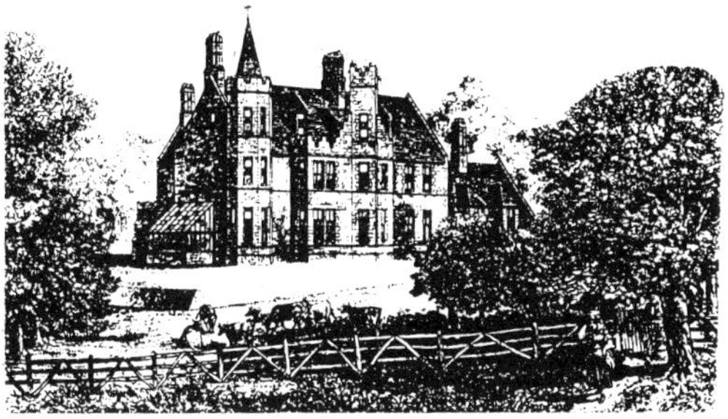

garden front with diagonal tower offset by polygonal turret. Now extended as an hotel.

CASTLEBAR: **Catholic Church**
The largest church built by Doolin designed in his characteristic Gothic (1892-1902). Unfinished façade flanked by monumental gateways. Double transepts externally expressed, internally concealed by the arcading of the nave. The choir equally heavyweight, well able to shrug off puerile alterations by liturgical reformers after the Second Vatican Council. Reredos by James Pearce. High altar carved in Italy. Polychromatic pulpit (1908). Glass by Mayer of Munich, especially notable over the altar.

CASTLEBAR: **Imperial Hotel**
A Georgian coaching inn conceals a late Victorian top-lit timber-panelled diningroom that retains the ambiance of a Somerville and Ross world destined to be swept away by the National Land League founded here in 1880 by Michael Davitt.

CASTLEBAR: **Post Office**
The liveliest architecture in the town, stylistically close to the Westport P.O. (q.v.) and therefore evidently designed by J.H. Pentland for the Board of Works in 1907, here working too far from his head office to be questioned over the extraordinary wrought-iron scrolls that uphold the gutters: no doubt all that rain in the west of Ireland called for extra precautions. Façades treated with a forceful horizontal combination of brick and stone, but oblivious of the sloping site.

CASTLEBAR: **St Mary's Hospital**
Designed by George Wilkinson (*c.*1860), who had just extended the courthouse here with its cast-iron fluted Doric portico. The Lunatic Asylum is also in a severe neo-Classical idiom, but reflects the disintegration of Georgian conventions. The long façade is punctuated by a series of pavilions treated like a series of town-houses that link an unexpectedly Italianate centre block to over-dominant corner blocks of unrelieved austerity, so that the overall composition subverts conventional formality. Built out of local limestone pared to the minimum. Latter-day descendants would be the mental hospitals in Downpatrick and Ennis (q.v.). Here, however, all later additions and alterations have been made uncomprehendingly from the sedate late Gothic Revival chapel by Dixon onward to the present day.

CASTLEBAR: **Turlough**
The best country house of Deane without Woodward, built for C.L. Fitzgerald in 1866 by T.N. Deane five years after his partner's death. The Fitzgeralds abandoned their original Georgian house, either due to it being low-lying, or else irredeemably associated with their ancestor Fighting George Fitzgerald, who was first imprisoned for setting his pet bear on his father, and was finally executed for murdering a servant. The plan of the new house is traditional, apart from the principal staircase ingeniously contrived to pass over the front door so that its half-landing is a glazed Venetian loggia. The façade is symmetrical, with a high-pitched roof and dormers, conventionally extended to a service wing and a lower stable block. The tension that Woodward would have transmitted to the

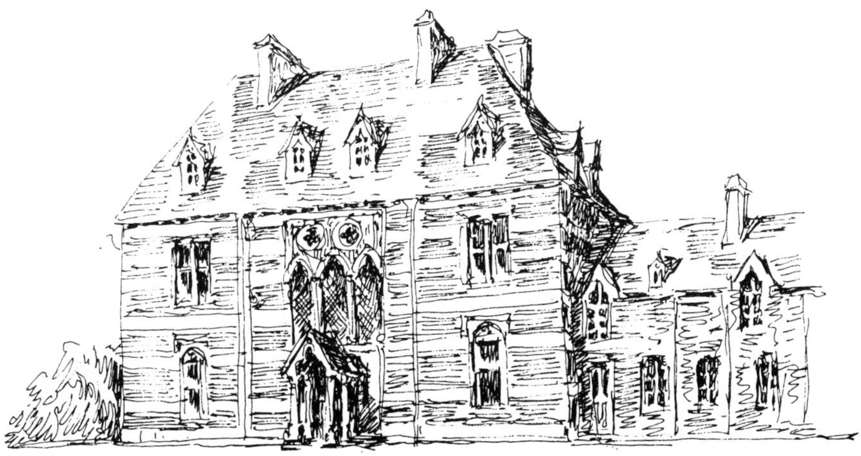

design is missing; instead the complacency of Deane and the aspirations of his clients towards respectability result in a house that would at first sight pass for a townhall. Now appropriately acquired by Mayo County Council.

CHARLESTOWN: **Catholic Church**
A simple nave with chamfered piers and lean-to aisles, southern porch and western bellcote, an early work of George Goldie obediently realizing the ideals of A.W.N. Pugin in the context of an Irish village. If the stained glass of the eastern window is contemporary with its consecration, this would date that to 1857, but the church was finally completed in 1860. Stained glass by Joshua Clarke and by the Clarke Studios in the 1930s.

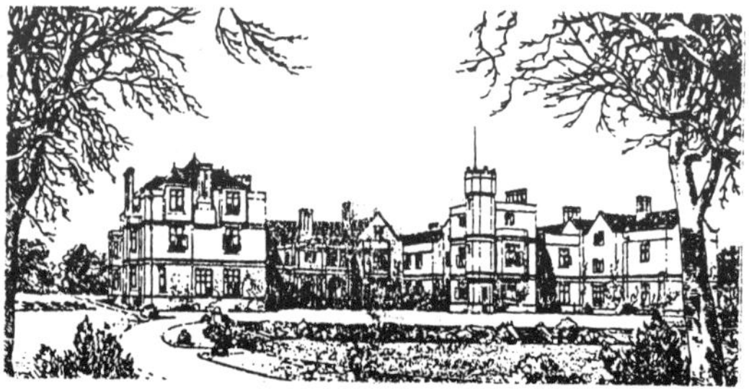

CLAREMORRIS: **Castlemacgarret**
Although not as gifted an artist as his younger brother, William, Richard Caulfield Orpen was a draughtsman of diverse ability, and nothing that he built for the 3rd Lord Oranmore and Browne at Castlemacgarret in 1906 exceeds the charm of his sketch of the house as it was, converted from a stable block into the family home a hundred years before. Orpen tried to extend its informal vernacular by his own rambling wings, which he further enlivened with scraps of medieval stonework, but in the end he was defeated by the grimness of his grey cement made ever greyer by the dampness of Connaught. Now cruelly exposed to public view across a denuded park. Internally the double-height staircase hall has a certain swagger but the neo-Adamesque reception rooms, with some ceilings copied from Leinster House despite impeccable craftmanship are casually strung together relying greatly on corridors to link them.

CLAREMORRIS: **Catholic Church**
Late neo-Gothic basilica by Doolin and Butler (1904-8) confronting a deconsecrated spiky church of Ireland across the street. Interior redeemed by stained glass, neo-Byzantine pulpit (1904-8), and altar sculpted by Patrick Tomlin (1914).

CROSSMOLINA: **Errew Grange**
Scottish Baronial built by J.F. Fuller for Major Arthur Knox modelled on his brother's house, Mount Falcon (q.v.), sited on a peninsular jutting out into Lough Conn. Converted into an hotel and destroyed by fire *c.*1930. Recently partially rebuilt, but not yet reopened.

DOOGORT: **Church of Ireland**
Built in a striking setting by Joseph Welland at his most conventional, *c.*1860, its capaciousness is the only indication of delusion. Its construction was the culmination of a lifetime of unrewarded endeavour by the Revd and Mrs Nangle to turn the starving Achill islanders away from Rome. Today he is commemorated by the name of the holiday resort, 'the missionary settlement'.

GLENAMADDY: **Catholic Church**
The best churches of R.M. Butler are often where he is restricted to the essentials by a tight budget, and here at Glenamaddy he has designed a simple Gothic Revival church built out of rubble with brick dressings both inside and out. Continuous nave and chancel buttressed by steeply sloping aisles (1904). Interior made memorable by the Clarke's Studios' triple window above the altar.

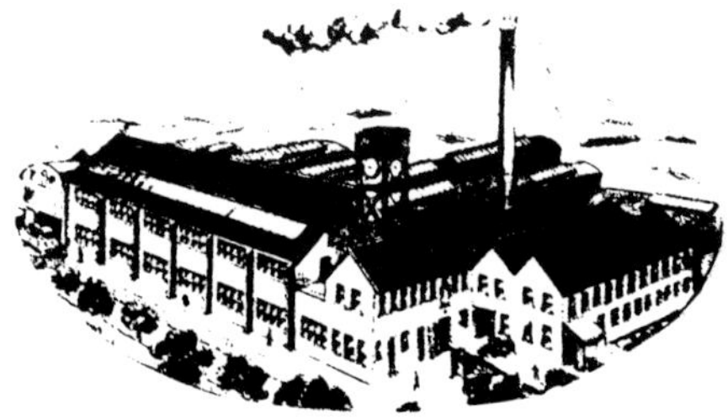

FOXFORD: **Woollen Mills**
Built from 1892 onwards due to the exertions of the formidable Mother Morrogh-Bernard of the Sisters of Charity, assisted by Mr Smith from Caledon, who as a Protestant and freemason was at first appalled by her request for advice, but who then devoted the next twenty years to helping her in the aptly named Providence Mills, as recalled in Lady Fingal's memoirs. Elegant timber-clad industrial structures with light segmental roofs built out across the river Moy. Carefully adapted reception centre. Open to the public.

KILLALA: **Cillalailthe**
Built in 1880 for the recently widowed Mrs Saunders-Knox-Gore from Rappa Castle, who took the fireplace with her for the entrance hall. A very feminine house, and therefore not

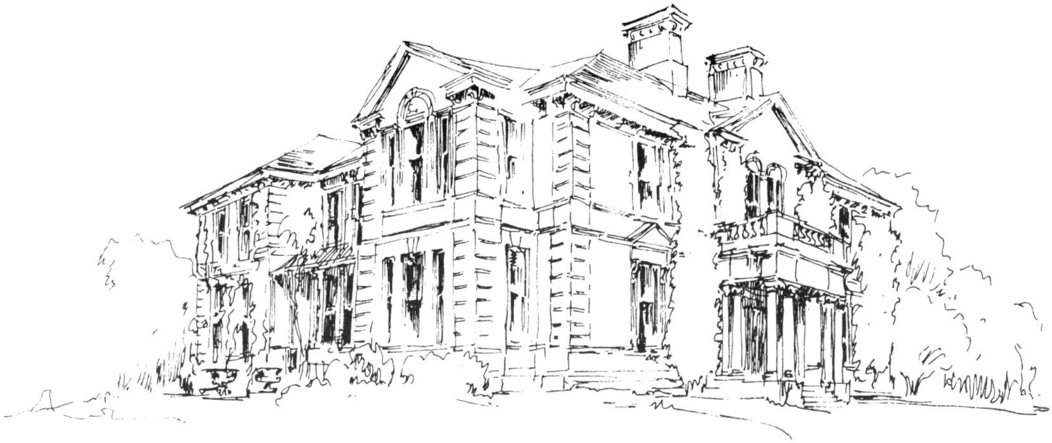

characteristic of J.F. Fuller, if indeed he was her architect. Rose marble-columned portico. Adjoining garden front centred on a verandah, where the wives of Japanese executives from the nearby Asahi plant used to take their tea. Now a youth hostel due to the generosity of that firm.

KILLALA: **Molloy Memorial, Meelick**
Powerful life-sized stone effigy carved in 1880.

KILTIMAGH: **Catholic Church**
Designed in his standardized Gothic Revival by W.H. Byrne and built from 1888 onwards. Façade extended in 1914, when apsidal chancel was decorated with sculptures and mosaics by Earley and Co. Roof overhead painted by the McHugh brothers. Albert Power's later pulpit has been consumed and regurgitated to serve as a lectern and celebrant's chair.

MULRANNY: **Catholic Church**
Built in understated Romanesque by R.M. Butler in 1904.

MULRANNY: **Great Southern Hotel**
Built by T.M. Deane for the Great Southern Railway Company in the late 1890s. Only the billiard room survives the banality of a 1960s updating.

MULRANNY: **Rossturk Castle**
Westernmost castle in Ireland that is still habitable, built above Clew Bay like a toy fortress in two phases—the earliest c.1860 by Col. Vaughan, father of Cardinal Vaughan, who commissioned Westminster Cathedral. Acquired and extended fifteen years later by another amateur architect, James Butler Stoney, who had designed railways in India and who added the principal reception rooms to the west. Entry tower inscribed 'for R.V.S. from his mother and sister'.

NEWPORT: **Catholic Church**
The most celebrated of R.M. Butler's churches, started in 1910, the same year as Balla (q.v.), freely adapting a blend of Irish and German Romanesque to the requirements of his time. Three aisles with only the central one barrell-vaulted and upheld by slender columns. Elevations vary from the unbroken austerity of the north, to the more picturesque south where additional porch, sacristy and minor belfry act as foils to the great roof behind that abuts against a massive western tower. Ponderously impressive approaches, as if to a Bismark memorial. Our premonitions of grandeur are resolved instead by Harry Clarke's Last Judgment.

NEWPORT: **The Viaduct**
Impressive railway viaduct built in 1895 by T. Barrington.

TOURMAKEADY: **Church of Ireland**
Shell of characteristic Joseph Welland church *c.*1850 now (apart from its asymmetrical belfry) engulfed in a jungle of conifers and rhododendrons.

WESTPORT: **Church of Ireland**
The finest of T.N. Deane's churches, his client being the marquis of Sligo, who gave the site at the entrance of his demesne (its wooded setting has since been infiltrated by housing). Consecrated in 1872, the church consists of a single cell that terminates in a polygonal apse enriched by gables breaking into the principal roof. Deane stresses the sculptural quality of the church by his treatment of the belfry, also polygonal and almost freestanding.

The church has one of the most decorated interiors of its time within the Church of Ireland, comparable to Clane and Timoleague (q.v.). Timber-sheeted vaulting. Beneath the stained-glass windows there is a continuous

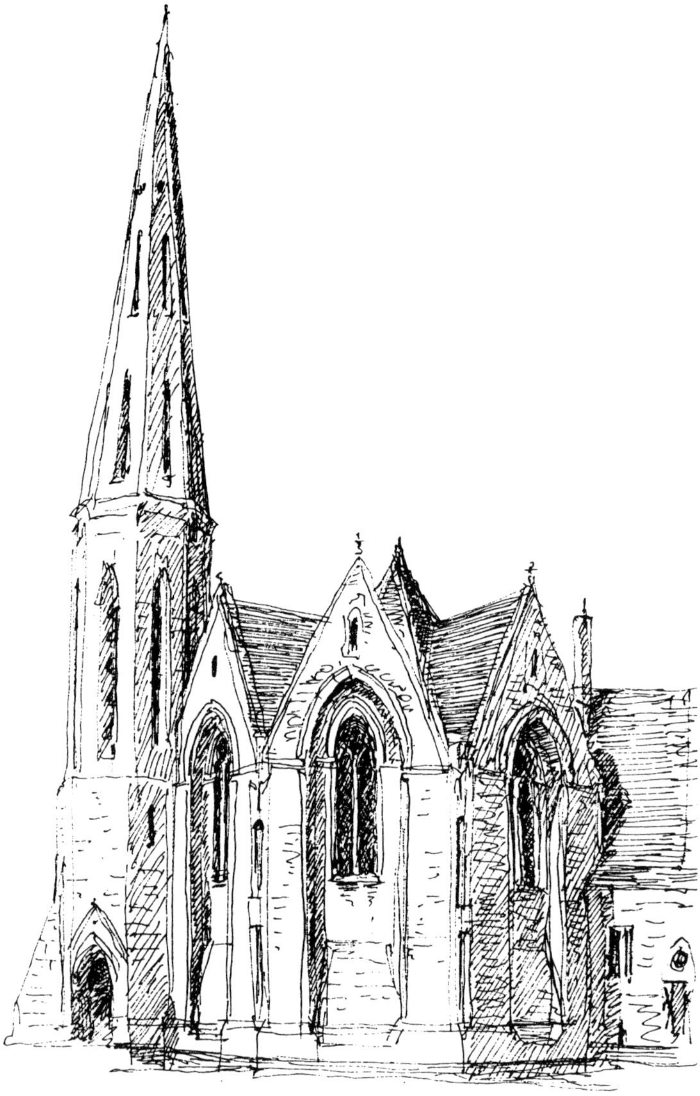

series of mosaic immortalizing the beneficence of the Brownes.

WESTPORT: **Post Office**
Built by J.H. Pentland in 1899 with a well-proportioned arcade revealing its architect's grasp of Classicism.

WESTPORT: **Westport House**
Although Westport House survives as one of the great Georgian houses of Ireland, the focus of its interior, the central imperial staircase of Sicilian marble, is Victorian. That this is so, is revealed less by its architecture than by its sculpture: a larger-than-life marble angel broods over the first flight from a niche on the half-landing. The designer of this 'I dreamed I dwelt among marble halls' interior was George Wilkinson, who must have found this commission for the 3rd marquis of Sligo in 1857 a welcome relief from his innumerable workhouses. The metal balustrading is by Skidmore, likewise the voyeuristic grille that screens the upper landing from the entrance hall, which is set into the lunette formed by the curve of the barrell vault. Wilkinson may also have designed the Classical stable block (*c.*1865).

If a Victorian staircase dominates the interior, an equally operatic Edwardian staircase presides over the gardens—the water staircase that descends from the house into the lake, answered by another staircase on the further shore. The architect for the 6th marquis was Romaine Walker, who completed his work in 1913, in time to allow a few months punting before the outbreak of the First World War.

MEATH

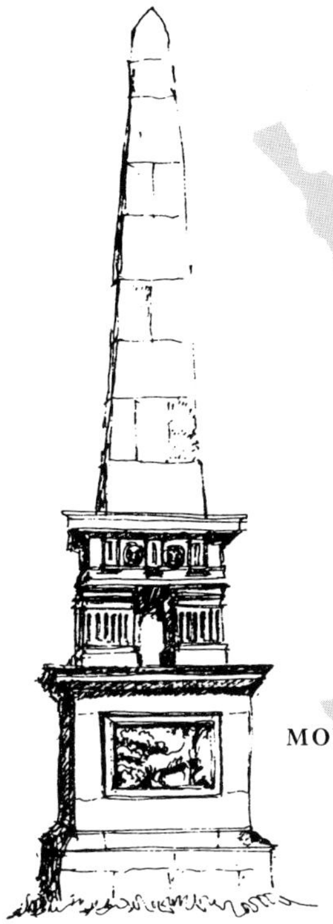

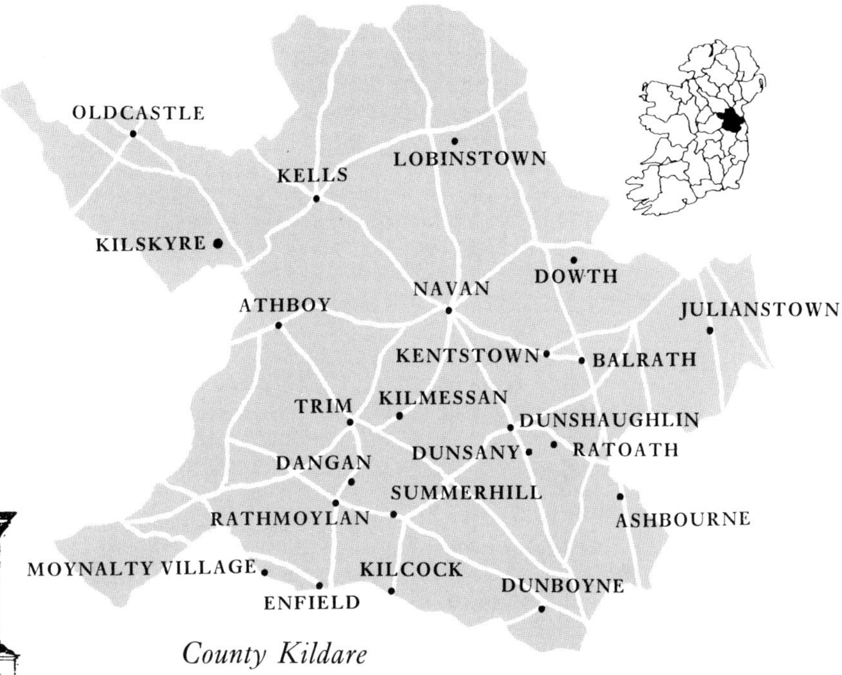

ASHBOURNE: **Brindley Memorial**
Here an unknown sculptor has broken classical precedent by raising a commemorative obelisk on four stunted fluted piers and embellishing the frieze with portraits of the dead man's hounds. The plinth is inset with delicate reliefs depicting the Ward Hunt, including a stag at bay against a forest background (1880).

ATHBOY: **Catholic Church**
Handsome Gothic revival church, a single cell on a large scale, showing the influence of W.D. Butler. Built in 1844.

ATHBOY: **Caucestown House**
Revival style *c.*1840 with a symmetrical façade; entered beneath a central first-floor oriel. A modest design but still too ambitious, since the family had to sell it through the Encumbered Estates on its completion.

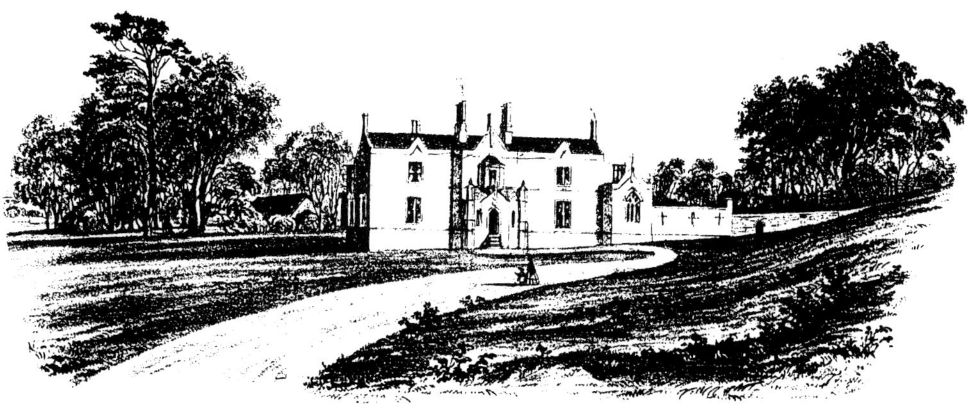

BALRATH: Post Office
Tudor Revival post office, *c.* 1840.

DANGAN: Catholic Church
Showy Late Gothic Revival Catholic church beside the abandoned demesne of the duke of Wellington. Built in rock-faced ashlar with off-centre western steeple. Interior decoration verging on the Celtic Revival. By W.H. Byrne (1901).

DOWTH: Netterville Almshouses
Built in 1877 as a charitable bequest by the last Viscount Netterville (apparently to atone for an ill-spent life), the last of a recusant family who had built Dowth Hall with its elegant Rococo interiors. The almshouses are abrasively Gothic Revival by George Ashlin, doubtlessly selected for his Catholicism by the executor, Lord Fingal. Built out of harsh red brick and stone trim, which added poignancy to its unloved decay. Saved at the eleventh hour by an American purchaser and converted into a private house.

DUNBOYNE: Church of Ireland
Typically assertive single cell in harshly detailed Gothic built in 1868; designed by S. Rollinson of Chesterfield. Steeply pitched roof rising to western bellcote. Apsidal east end that terminates the church without a break.

DUNBOYNE: Court Hill
While no architect is recorded for this villa, only J.S. Mulvany could have achieved such an

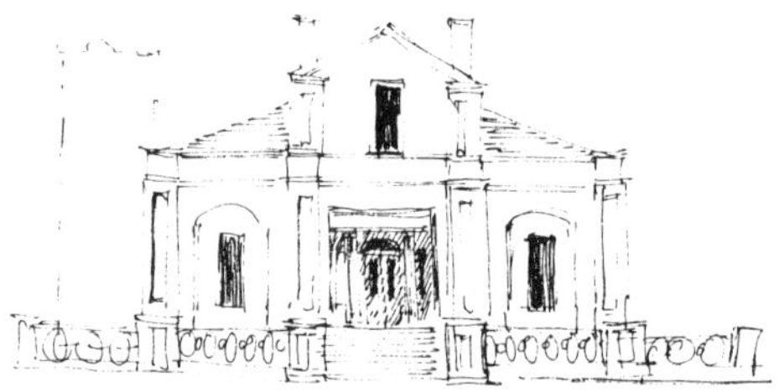

equilibrium between Classicism and convenience. The original external austerity was too extreme for the Edwardians, who consequently prettified it, but its monumentality on a miniature scale is still discernable. Approached by an imposing flight of steps with Mulvany's characteristic railings, it is entered through an apsidal recess screened by Doric columns. On either side articulated by panelled pilasters are windows in arched recesses. The central bay is carried up to form a pedimented dormer above the entrance. Jutting out from one of the sides is a three-storey service tower off the stairs.

DUNBOYNE: Herbertstown House
Large country house tightly strapped by an unknown architect into Classical apparel like an overweight roué. Built for the Whitworth family in 1916, trimly neo-Georgian but with bulging mansard attics and a double-height bay window almost the width of the drawingroom. Neo-Elizabethan staircase and diningroom for the port and cigars while the ladies retired to the neo-Adamesque of the drawingroom. Stables now an equestrian centre.

DUNSHAUGHLIN: Dunsany Castle
The last feudal castle handed down in the male line to survive in Ireland intact (though continuously altered). The 14th Lord Dunsany is thought to have commissioned James Sheil *c.* 1830 to extend the castle eastwards in a carefully scaled-down Gothic that does not deflect attention from the original fortress. Two of the principal rooms were remodelled—the downstairs diningroom and, on the first floor, the library with its magical compromise between delicate Gothick and the chunky Classicism of William IV. The battlemented Dunshaughlin gates appear to be also Sheil's. He is so successful in all his alterations that an attempt to bring over Sir Giles Gilbert Scott later in the century came to nothing. The final architect of Dunsany was an obscure but tactful Arts-and-Crafts-trained George Jack, who added the billiard room at the rear for the 18th Lord Dunsany, and most probably the stableyard with its similar crow stepped parapets. The billiard room interior reveals that among his many gifts Lord Dunsany was a big game hunter and a discriminating collector of the Arts and Crafts. These aspects were lost on a visitor, Evelyn Waugh, who became incensed by his host's attempts to downplay the castle's Georgian Gothic; he also found the grotesque heads Lord Dunsany modelled particularly odious.

DUNSHAUGHLIN: Killeen Castle
The medieval fortress of the earls of Fingal, made habitable by a bewildering succession of architects in the 18th century, ending with Francis Johnston, and then doubled in size in the 1830s by the mysterious James Sheil. Redecorated by Sir Hugh Lane for the wife of the 11th earl, as recounted in her memoirs *Seventy Years Young*. Almost burned down in the Troubles. Sold by the 12th and the last earl to Wildenstein, who bought it for its stud. Mostly destroyed by arson at the moment the next owner was about to restore it; now due to be a country-house hotel with attendant golf courses and bungalows.

In its present shattered state, it is the architecture of James Sheil that comes into its own,

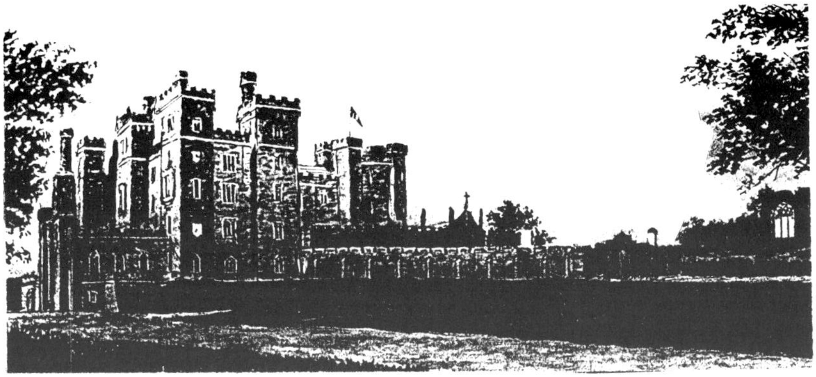

concealing the medieval core and making the Johnston's contribution particularly papery and insubstantial. Sheil's new entry front recreates a fairy-tale world of chivalry of tapering towers and sprouting turrets, emblazoned with heraldic devices, including a self-consciously modest Adam surprised beneath a tree, presumably an ancestor. The lower entrance hall, with its parapeted roof ready for the womenfolk of the castle to watch their admirers jousting beneath them, encloses a galleried staircase below a pendant fan vault. This miraculously survives, as does the subdivided diningroom in the western wing; Lady Fingal set the final pages of her memoirs in this room, waiting for the IRA beside her husband, who, as was his wont on state occasions, had fallen asleep exhausted by his continuing hunting.

DUNSHAUGHLIN: **Old Workhouse**
Characteristic Tudor Revival complex designed by George Wilkinson *c.*1845. For a long time abandoned; it has been partially renovated as an enterprise centre.

ENFIELD: **Rahinstown**
Georgian seat of the Bomford family rebuilt (after a fire *c.*1860) by John McCurdy in his Italianate manner. Columned porch, pedimented windows. Drawingroom opens into a bay window with curved glass.

JULIANSTOWN: **Ballygarth Castle**
Tower house extended in the 18th-century and then half-heartedly remodelled with pointed fenestration by John Louch in 1867 for the Pepper family.

JULIANSTOWN: **Church of Ireland**
Hard Gothic Revival cell by Welland and Gillespie, *c.*1865. Stained glass by Michael Healy and Heaton, Butler and Bayne.

KELLS: **Balrath Burry**
Gatelodge built in his pretentiously picturesque manner by the other William Chambers *c.* 1880. He also made elaborate designs to remodel the interiors of the house for the Nicholson family. Whatever was executed has not survived the rebuilding of 1942.

KELLS: **Donapatrick, Church of Ireland**
Medieval tower attached to church rebuilt by J.F. Fuller after the Disestablishment. Fuller added in 1866 a lean-to porch against the tower and a polygonal apse to the vestry, and re-roofed the nave. The arcaded cylindrical pulpit with matching lectern was added in 1890. Stained glass by Heaton, Butler and Baynes. Redbrick-and-stone sexton's cottage dated 1888.

KELLS: **Drumbarrow**
The family home of the Woodward family with a neo-Elizabethan gatelodge, according to family tradition the first commission of Benjamin Woodward and built shortly after 1838. The house itself, a severe neo-Classical cube, was sold by the Woodwards and subsequently enriched with Italianate trimmings by John McCurdy, who had been Woodward's arch-rival in the Trinity Museum Building.

KELLS: **Headford Mausoleum**
Lost deep in forest guarded from the outside world, this is one of J.F. Fuller's first commissions dating from 1869 and still strongly influenced by his apprenticeship to Waterhouse. The idiom is Gothic Revival at its most brutal—a free-standing octagon with central double-height rotunda surrounded by a lean-to ambulatory—but any suggestion of repose is countermanded: the entrance door is crowned by an acutely angled gable that penetrates the ambulatory lean-to roof, which is further indented by the buttresses of the upper lantern. On each face of the octagon these buttresses rise to a string-course that appears to dissect the coupled lancets above it. Only a probing master or an impulsive pupil could take such liberties with the conventional, and Fuller almost succeeds in

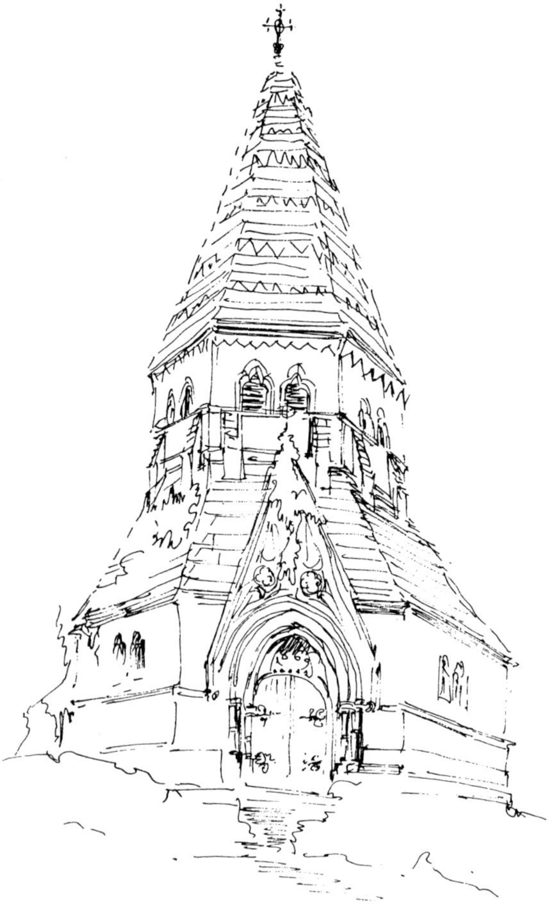

convincing us that he is the former. In this he is assisted by the incisive stone carving of Henry Sharp. Farm building complex also by Fuller (1874). Much Victorian planting in the arboretum.

KENTSTOWN: **Catholic Church**
Elegantly detailed Gothic Revival Catholic church, five bays long, dating from 1844.

KILCOCK: **Catholic Church**
Designed by J.J. McCarthy and built in 1868 in his Puginian manner; quatrefoil clerestory with steeply raked roofs over the aisles. The vertical uplift of the façade is abruptly cut short by the failure to build the intended spire.

KILCOCK: **Church of Ireland**
Designed in the Hiberno-Romanesque by J.E. Rogers and completed in 1870 with a belfry based on an Irish round tower, complemented by an un-Irish chancel apse. Recently sold off as a private house so the stained glass, contemporary with the church and possibly designed by Rogers himself, has been removed.

KILCOCK: **St Joseph's Hall**
Small Gothic Revival village hall with a symmetrical façade but with subtly asymmetrical fenestration. Built in 1860-8 and attributed to J.J. McCarthy.

KILMESSAN: **Catholic Church**
Tiny but delightful Late Gothic Revival façade tacked on to earlier barn church with prominent inscription beneath the adjoining bellcote recording the priest, the date of 1894, but not the architect (William Hague).

KILSKYRE: **Catholic Church**
One of the earliest and finest of J.J. McCarthy's rural churches, designed when he was most under the spell of Pugin's Gothic. Started in 1849, completed in 1854, spire added in 1887.

MOYNALTY VILLAGE
Estate village with one street linking Catholic and Protestant churches on the edge of a walled-in demesne. The houses are variants of a simple theme: the upper floors lit by gabled dormers. Described by Arthur Magan in *The Road to Ummera*.

MOYNALTY CATHOLIC CHURCH

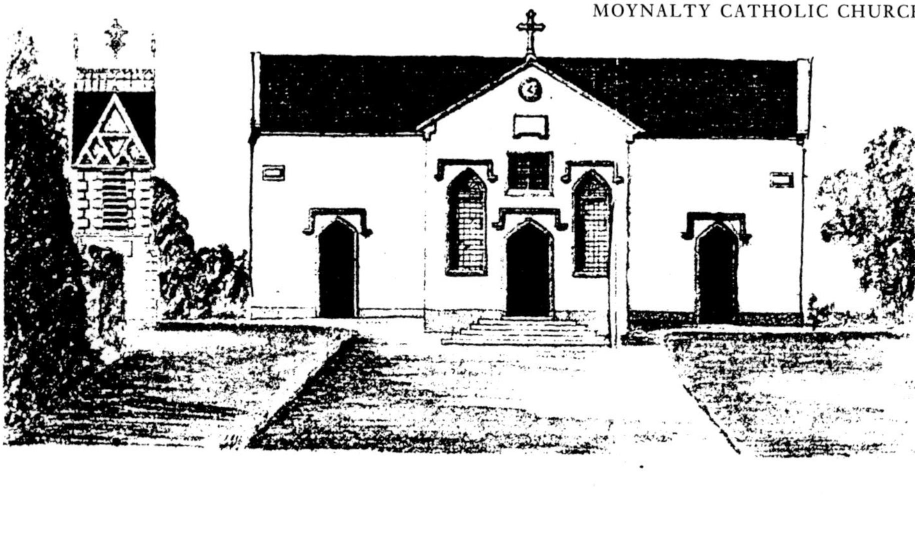

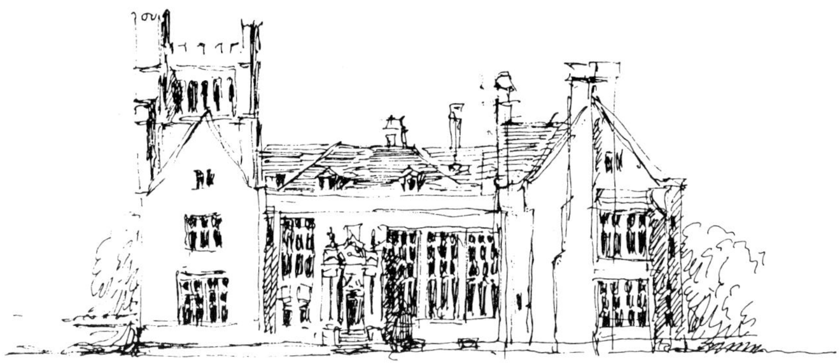

NAVAN: **Ardmulchan**
One of the few Edwardian country houses to be built in Ireland; dating from 1904. The architects were an Edinburgh firm, Sidney Mitchell and Wilson. Their client was a Glasgow tycoon who built it for his wife who loved to hunt in Ireland. Set in the wooded valley of the Boyne beside the ruins of the original keep, its red brick and limestone trim have refused to mellow. The profusely columned porch (guarded by heraldic beasts), the mullioned bays and the castellated tower remain as crisp as when first built. Double-height entrance hall boldly expressed by the fenestration of the façade along with its staircase. The entrance is overlooked by a sumptuously carved minstrels' gallery. Much neo-Caroline fibrous plaster. The architectural equivalent of an Edwardian 'swagger' portrait.

NAVAN: **Ardsallagh**
Tudor Revival manor house built beside the Boyne for the duke of Bedford in 1844. His architect is not recorded. Enlivened by diagonal chimneys and panels set over a central bay of tripartite windows. Two-storied façade, three-storied garden front. Rebuilt after a fire in 1903 by Sir Thomas Drew.

NAVAN: **Catholic Church**
Originally an austere neo-Classical church dating from 1838. Altar positioned in the centre of the longer side, galleries round the remaining sides. Demure exterior of round-arched windows still survives facing east. Italianate tower added by John Bourke, who in 1870 transformed the north and south elevations into rival façades, that on the south by inserting a wheel window taking its inspiration from the Lombardesque on the verge of Gothic. Extended and remodelled by T.F. McNamara. The interior suffered from banal stained glass and tawdry embellishments. Through all this the Christ Crucified sculpted by Edward Smyth in 1792 has presided, although enriched for the first half of this century with a plaster beard.

NAVAN: **Dowdstown House**
Grimly Baronial house by W.H. Lynn *c.*1870 and like many of his country houses far more appropriate as a religious institution which it has now become. Entrance front with strapwork porch set alongside frowning tower and almost windowless service wing. Adjoining garden front enlivened only by the curved glass inset into the side lights of the bow windows. Impressive Classical gates.

NAVAN: **Gibbstown**
The immense Italianate palazzo designed by W.H. Lynn for the Gerrards with domed music room and internal plasterwork sculpted by Lynn's brother, S.F. Lynn (who also carved the pediment), was gutted by fire in 1912; rebuilt by J.F. Fuller only to be later demolished. No trace remains apart from some outbuildings, most of which belong to an earlier house. The cut stone has been removed by the monks of New Mellifont for a church that was never built. The fountain has been sold. Only the cast-iron gates (now closed), piers and screens testify to one family's departed splendour.

NAVAN: **Loreto Convent**
First-floor chapel survives with Gothic fenestration framed by neo-Classical ornamentation.

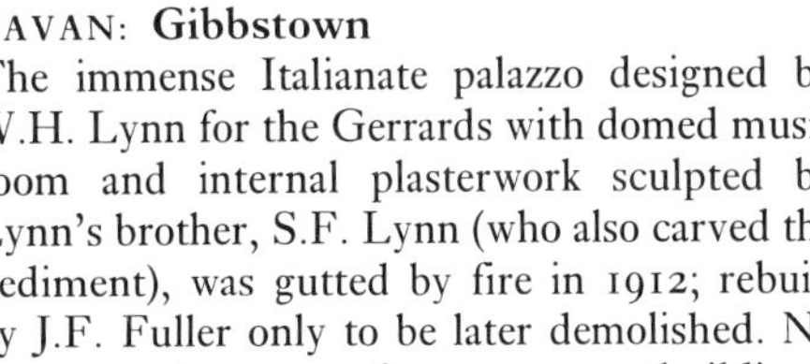

OLDCASTLE: **Ballinlough Catholic Church**
Delightful ensemble of Catholic church and schoolhouse, with an adjoining pub kept at a respectful distance. The twin gables of the

classrooms, linked by the double-porch, are counterpointed by the western gable of the church that links twin towers. The unconsciously sophisticated architect is not recorded; the date is *c.* 1840, but the interior of the church has been unhappily twice restored, *c.* 1950 and then thirty years later.

OLDCASTLE: **Catholic Church**
Elaborate Late Gothic Revival church still retains its marble altars and its chancel enriched with frescoes, mosaics and stained glass. Off-centre western tower and spire. Architect, W.H. Byrne (1899-1904).

RATHMOYLAN: **Church of Ireland**
Welland and Gillespie rebuilt in the 1860s an earlier church and added to the façade the off-centre geometrically-treated tower and spire.

RATOATH: **Hartlands**
Asymmetrical neo-Italianate villa with attached belvedere tower. Built in ashlar granite by Sandham Symes in the late 1840s for Capt. Donaldson, who went bankrupt during the building. Hence the interiors never received their intended decoration.

SUMMERHILL: **Agher Church of Ireland**
Romanesque Revival Church of Ireland built by Welland and Gillespie *c.* 1860.

SYDDAN: **Church of Ireland**
One of the most elaborate churches by J.F. Fuller, won by him in competition that took place in 1878 and built in 1881, his most prolific year. Sited in a remote rural valley, its existence is due the patronage of a Miss Ball. The west end is similar to Clane, though the idiom here is Gothic, not Romanesque. A central baptistery projects beneath a rose window into a polygonal apse lit by tiny quatrefoils. The church is entered through a porch beneath a massive tower and spire. The nave of five bays roofed with king post trusses leads to a chancel of two bays flanked by an organ compartment on one side and a vestry on the other. Painted decoration of choir still intact. Graveyard threatened by adjoining slurry pit.

TRIM: **Bank of Ireland**
A careful blend of red brick and limestone trim, L. McDonnell working in his most restrained neo-Tudor idiom. Symmetrical twin-gabled façade strikes a note of unassuming prosperity so rare in Ireland. Completed in 1909.

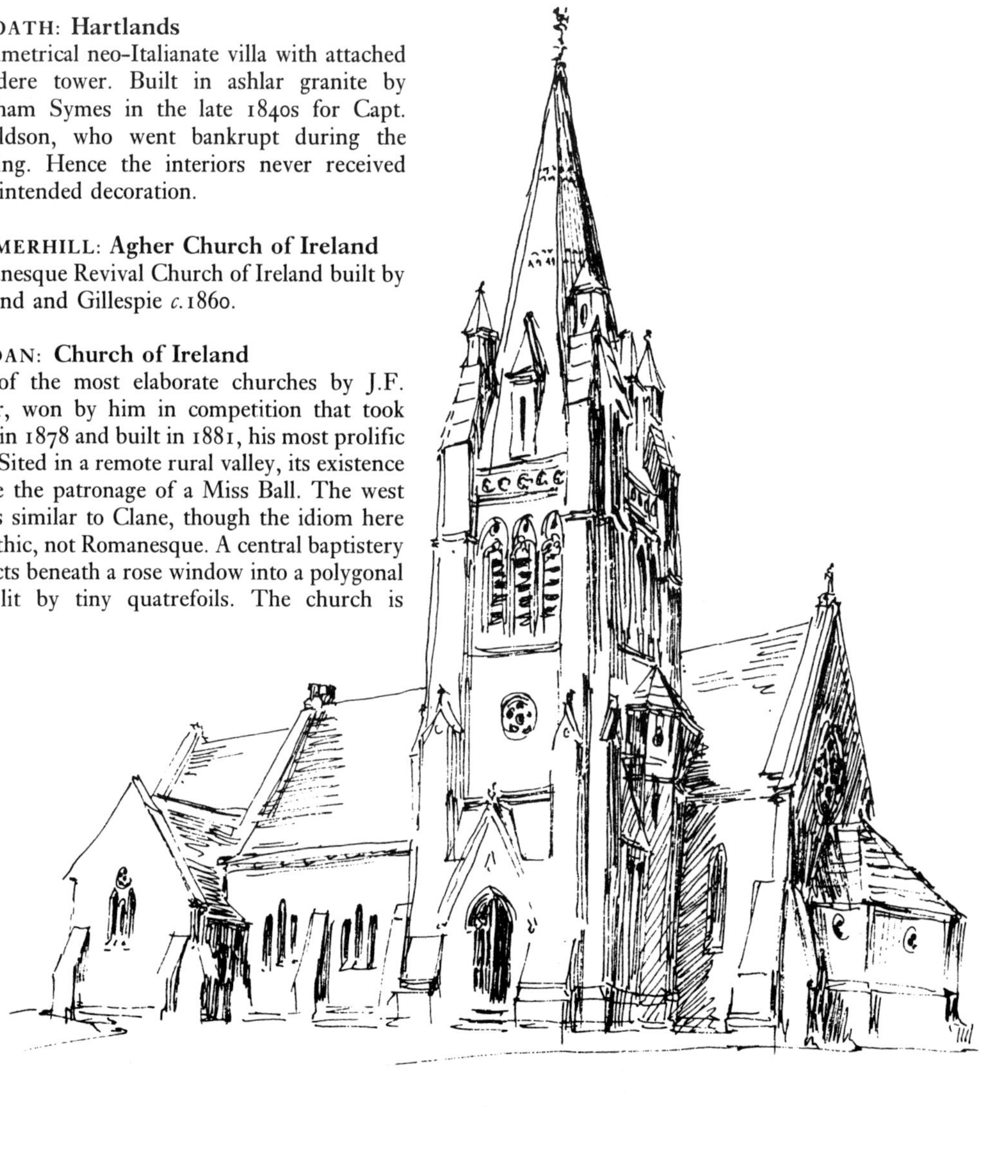

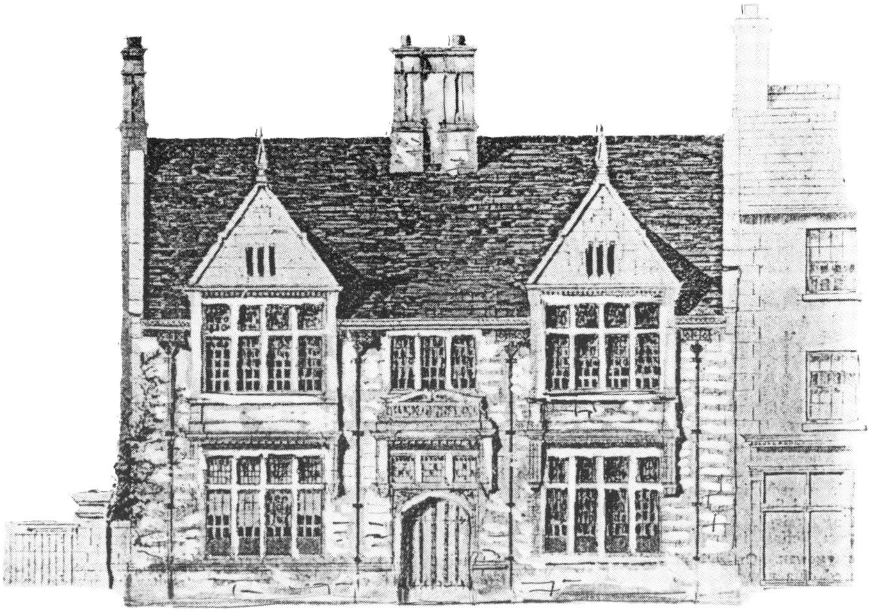

TRIM: **Catholic Church**
Expensive church by William Hague, designed in 1891 and characteristic of his later manner. Symmetrical façade with central tower and spire, nave of five bays; short aisleless transepts are defined by fragile corbelled columns of red marble. Rock-faced ashlar gives an external grimness, counterbalanced here as intended by the internal polychromy that culminates in the chancel, with its profusion of stained glass, frescoes and mosaics. In the interval between the design and the decoration, Hague had discovered the Celtic Revival, and Trim rivals his Letterkenny Cathedral (q.v.) in its orgy of self-biting beasts encircling unconcerned saints painted in the spandrels of the vault. Even the stained glass, predictably Mayer and Earley in the remainder of the church is affected by the same frenzy. Altar by James Pearse.

TRIM: **Church of Ireland Cathedral**
The medieval church dedicated to St Patrick was re-roofed in 1802 and restored in 1869 by J.E. Rogers, who added the chancel. East window, the Last Supper, by Heaton, Butler and Bayne. The most interesting stained glass, however, is in the organ gallery, a Burne-Jones window of 1857, the year he did a stained glass window in Christchurch Cathedral, Oxford for Benjamin Woodward. By coincidence, two late cartoons by Burne-Jones (designs for the stained glass of Brighouse, Yorks.) hang beneath the gallery, their sadness in poignant contrast to his youthful high spirits in the window above them.

TRIM: **Convent of Mercy**
William Caldbeck is occasionally remembered today for his competent banks, so this Puginesque convent of 1858 comes as a surprise with its asymmetrical façades and extrovert planning. Attached chapel and octagonal spirelet inscribed with the names of Lord Fingal and other donors.

TRIM: **Model Schools**
Built by Frederick Darley in 1850 as a replica of his model schools at Athy, in the same forthright asymmetrical Tudor.

TRIM: **Trimlestown House**
Comfortable neo-Tudor stud farm with residence, stables and gatelodges. Unadventurous architecture for Blackwood and Jury; built from 1915 onwards.

MONAGHAN

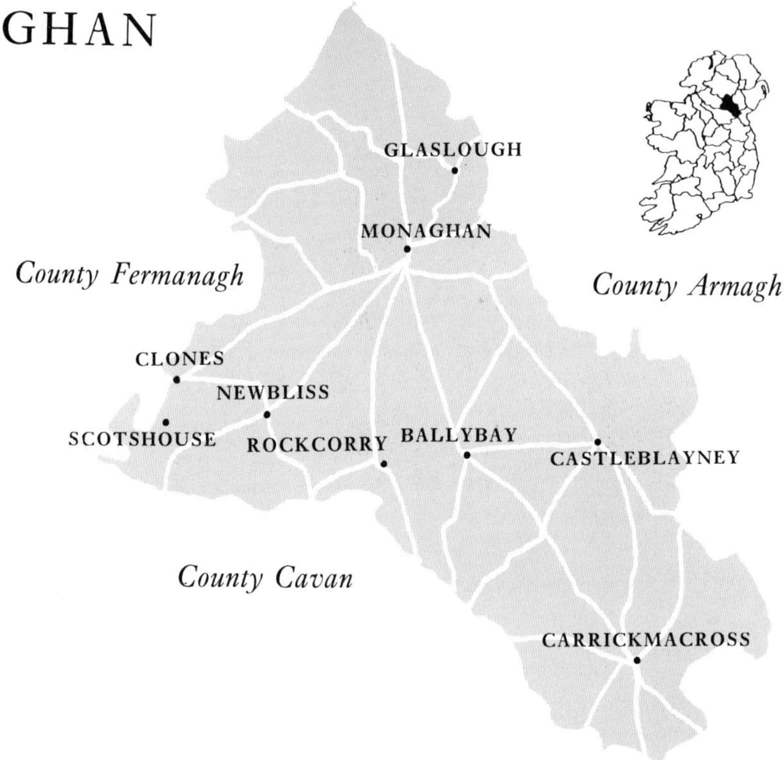

BALLYBAY: **Catholic Church**
An early design of William Hague. Built in 1859–62 in a manner that prefigures his later more conventional Gothic Revival. Entered beneath well-sited western tower and spire. Glass by Mayer.

BALLYBAY: **Market House**
Stately, four-bay, arcaded loggia, two bays projecting slightly forward to allow a pediment above the central windows. The outer corners are wittily emphasized by corner piers resting on the impost of the arches. Date inscribed 1848. Architect unknown.

CARRICKMACROSS: **Adragh Church of Ireland**
Commissioned from William Slater by the Shirley family in 1874. Hidden in the grove of trees just off the road from Carrickmacross to Shercock, this is a modest masterpiece, a church reduced to its essentials. A stone-roofed porch beneath a plate traceried rose window are both framed by a relieving arch, to be opened up if a new nave is required to accommodate an expanded congregation. The same missionary zeal is expressed by Street's church at Ardamine (q.v.). Above, a symmetrical bellcote is challenged by an asymmetrical cylindrical chimney. The nave of four bays leads to a stone-vaulted apse raised above a hidden crypt. Exquisite, geometrically patterned polychromatic marble baptismal font and stone-carved pulpit patterned with shamrocks (the church is dedicated to St Patrick). Stained glass of matching quality.

CARRICKMACROSS: **Catholic Church**
One of the later churches of J.J. McCarthy in his characteristic French Gothic, polished and impersonal. Exterior most remarkable for its astonishingly slender spire in limestone (recleaned so it glitters from afar). Interior remarkable for the glass of Harry Clarke in the aisles. Reredos designed by C.J. McCarthy, carved by P.J. O'Neill. East window by Earley and Powell.

CARRICKMACROSS: **Church of Ireland School**
Tudor Revival schoolhouse *c.*1840 on two floors, the upper floor reached by flanking external staircases from the main street, one side of which was owned by the marquises of Bath who gave lavish banquets and were absentees. The Shirleys of Lough Fea, who owned this side of the street, were resident and reclusive.

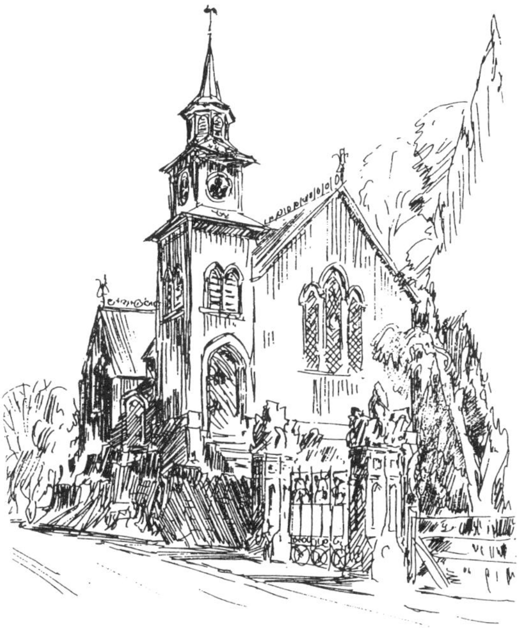

CARRICKMACROSS: **Laragh Church of Ireland,**

It is said that the owner of the local mill brought his wife to Switzerland for their honeymoon, and that they returned with this cast-iron church in light-hearted Gothic. They set it in a wooded ravine approached by winding steps cut into the rock. Although intended to be temporary, the church has outlasted their house and their mills, victims of nature's revenge against this remote outpost of the Industrial Revolution.

CARRICKMACROSS: **Lough Fea**

The first view of Lough Fea is of a medieval college transplanted from Oxford or Cambridge into a hidden forest protected from the outside world. The architect of E.J. Shirley was the historian Thomas Rickman, and this is his only Irish commission. Entered by an impressive forecourt with the main house framed between a chapel and a great hall. The elevations are asymmetrical, but the horizontality of the fenestration is underlined by string courses and parapets. As a foil to this are an off-centre central keep and a series of delicate balustraded towers crowned by sprocketted spires which have recently been removed. The garden front is more freely modelled with a service wing extending to an outlying tower on the crest of a hill. Beyond, a vista descends to a Gothic shrine-like fountain in the valley and then rises to a Celtic cross erected by grateful tenantry on the opposite hill and silhouetted against the sky.

The interior is as unconventional as the exterior. An arcaded hall leads to a series of low rambling rooms with (now faded) Puginian wallpapers. One marble overmantle frames a display of oval portraits. The wings contain the double-height hall and chapel. The hall approached by a magical room, half-conservatory, half-chantry, its glazed walls emblazoned by heraldic glass. These windows are repeated in the great hall, forming a central bay opposite the twin fireplaces which are set beneath an arcaded minstrel's gallery of seven bays resting on the door-height dado. Open hammerbeam trusses span the hall (designed to entertain the tenantry who never behaved well enough to be invited; they once stripped the agent F.S. Trench and tried to crucify him). Inherited by the reclusive E.P. Shirley, who rewrote the British peerage striking out all dukes with illegitimate descent. He also wrote a history of Monaghan. The County Library has the dedication of its copy to the 'Gentle Men of Monaghan' annotated with 'O Shirley, Thou should have been living at this hour'.

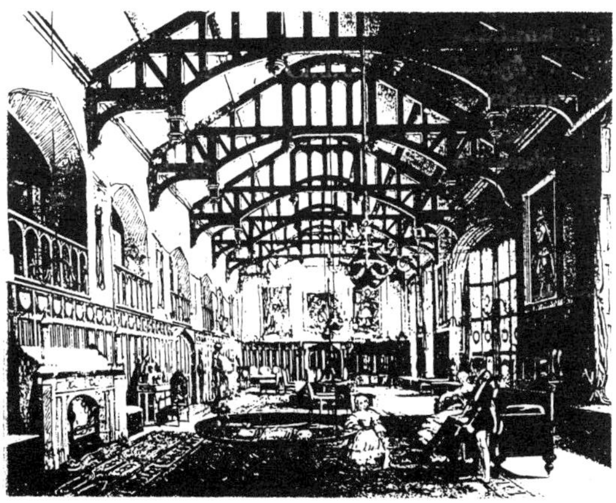

CASTLEBLAYNEY: **Anyalla Catholic Church**

One of the churches of William Scott, in a Gothic style which (unlike his Romanesque) he was never able to evolve beyond the limitations of his father. Adjoining uptight presbytery, so different from his houses, *c.*1920.

CASTLEBLAYNEY: **Blayney Castle**

Disappointing house even before its recent restoration that gutted the original interior destroying the most interesting feature, a Soanesque upper landing. Sold by the 12th and last Lord Blayney to the son of Thomas Hope of Deepdeene, the neo-Classicist furniture designer. Inherited (along with the famous diamond) by the dukes of Newcastle. All that remains of architectural interest are the Italianate entrance gates, with richly scrolled ironwork. Large gatelodges (one almost a country house in its own right) and adjoining stableyard.

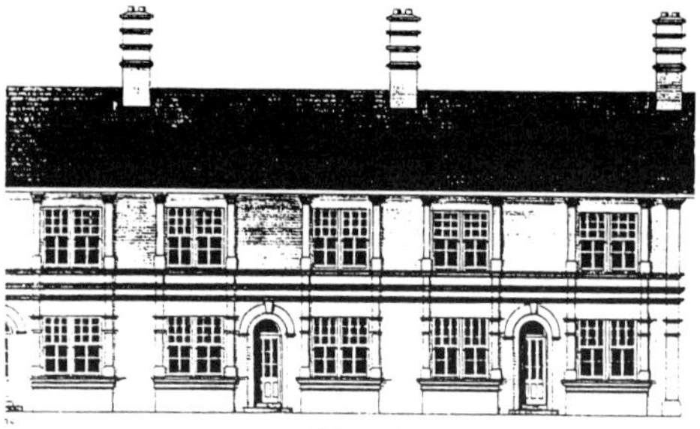

CASTLEBLAYNEY: **Almshouses**
Unusually urban row of red-brick housing in Flemish renaissance. Built *c.*1880 to comply with a bequest in the will of the last Lord Blayney.

CLONES: **Catholic Church**
Late example of the local architect, William Hague, with arcades of his favourite Aberdeen granite screening transepts in the Irish manner. Started in 1891; the tower and spire a few years later. Interior deserves special mention, as no one has tampered with it. Glass by Mayer.

CLONES: **Fortview National School**
Boys' and girls' school along with master's house, all treated as a picturesque Gothic villa, pivotting off a corner tower. Architect unknown.

CLONES: **Hilton Park**
The most important country-house commission of William Hague (1874), despite its being a remodelling of an earlier house possibly recast by Francis Johnston. Hague as a Catholic church architect was a surprising choice for his patron, John Madden, but then Madden was exceptional in his own right, spending much of his life exploring remote regions of the globe in order to write his magnum opus, *The Wilderness and its Tenants*. However, for his own house he sought his inspiration in the palaces of Italy, and he achieved this by excavating round the basement, so that the principal rooms become a *piano nobile*. They retain their existing internal decoration, Gothick in the diningroom. To reach them, Hague devised a grandiose Ionic portico to serve as *porte-cochère*, its columns coupled in the centre, upholding balustrades and urns. The arched vestibule, gleaming with brass and enamelled tiles, leads to an arcaded stairs that rises to the foot of its Georgian counterpart illuminated by stained glass. The exterior was re-cased with stone, pediments added to the first floor windows and balustrading to the roof.

The garden front relies on Hague's rusticated stonework to relieve Johnston's austerity. But what we see here is happily incomplete: Hague's intended central pavilion with an octagonal drawingroom and matching wing fails to reach the grandeur of the entrance front and would have given the house the semblance of a vast hotel to overwhelm the lake below. Hague's designs to enrich the plaster ceilings of the existing reception rooms, were, on the other hand, largely executed. Adjoining stableyard with cast-iron colonnade and multi-tiered watchtower more appropriate to an Arab fort. Gardens by Niven. Now a member of Hidden Ireland with four-poster beds and immense cast-iron baths filled with scalding water from taps that splutter like enraged field marshals.

CLONES: **Public Library**
Originally built as a market house designed by William Deane Butler in 1844, in a cool sophisticated Classicism, so much more urban than Connolly Street Station, which he designed the same year for Dublin. Arcades below and pedimented *piano nobile* above. Its symmetry is impaired by Symes building his Bank of Ireland as a subsidiary wing.

GLASLOUGH: **Castle Leslie**
Grimly earnest Scottish Baronial castle guarding a secret series of lakes reflecting primeval forests; part dream-chateau, part Belfast city bank. Sir John Leslie, who had commissioned the castle and then went off to gather treasures in Italy, exclaimed on his return in 1878 that it was not what he meant at all.

What he was disclaiming was the double reality of his own existence, as artist and land magnate. He had studied art in Rome and had made friends among the pre-Raphaelites, and at twenty-four painted his masterpiece, still in Castle Leslie. Then he had unexpectedly inherited thirty thousand acres from his brother and a venerable 17th-century mansion, which he decided to pull down and surpass by engaging the leading Irish architect of the day, W.H. Lynn. The original drawings (inspired by Chambord) exist. What was built takes the more modest Glamis as its point of departure. Once one comes to terms with its general dourness, there is much to admire in the way Lynn deploys the castle to conceal the gardens from outsiders. Note his masterly exploitation of the complex vistas set up by the diagonal orientation of the porch. The lake, first glimpsed through a screen of columns across the garden hall, is then savoured through the canted bays of the major rooms. These have retained their original decoration, now mellowed with time apart from the colouring of the terracotta fireplace of the drawingroom attributed to Della Robbia. Sir John Leslie is said himself to have designed the cloisters based on those by Michelangelo at Santa Maria degli Angeli. They frame two sides

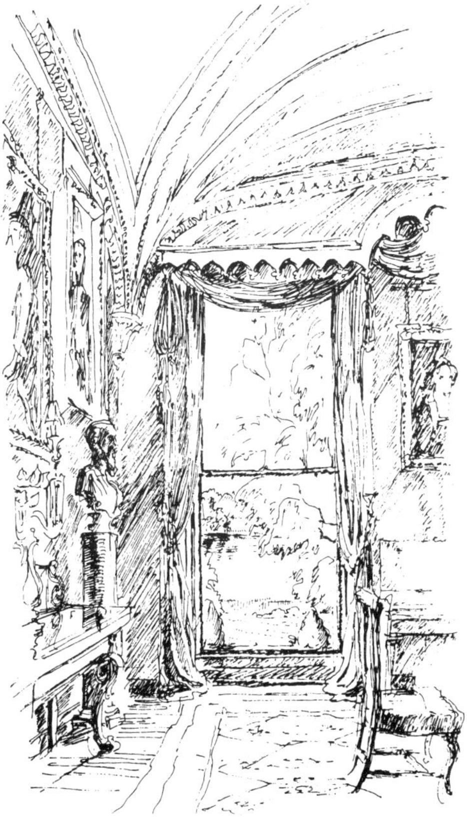

HILTON

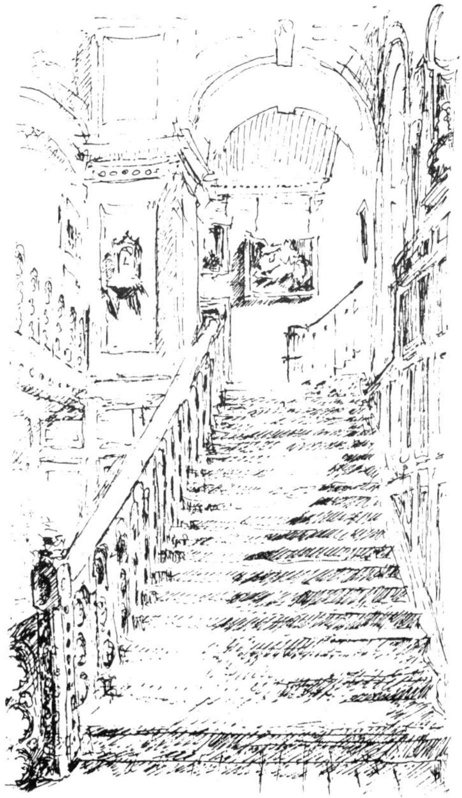

HILTON

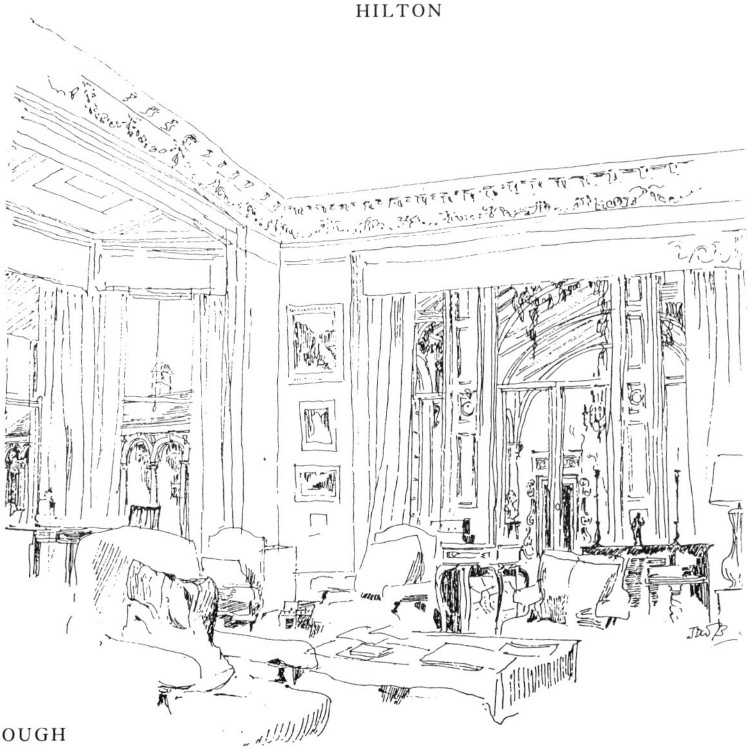

GLASLOUGH

of the formal gardens and screen first a conservatory and then a top-lit gallery frescoed by Sir John with *trompe-l'oeil* family portraits, some of which his great-grandson has brought up to date. This leads to a library and billiard room in a double pavilion once attached to the 17th-century house. There Jonathan Swift stayed and wrote of 'Glaslough with rows of books upon its shelves, written by Leslies all about themselves'. The late Sir Shane Leslie wrote twenty books here; his son Desmond ten novels and studies of Jesus and flying saucers. A basement laboratory has been set aside to record the music of the Martians.

However, it is not enthusiasm for a new planet that predominates, but nostalgia for the Ancient World. A line of latitude joins Castle Leslie to its Russian counterparts, mirrored in other misty lakes, linked by the same longing to an equidistant Italian Arcadia.

GLASLOUGH: Church of Ireland

Typical Board of First Fruits rebuilding of an earlier church sited overlooking the lake within the demesne of Castle Leslie. Stone vaulted apse added *c.*1880 to the designs of Sir John Leslie himself, who then designed the stained-glass windows. These had to be modified in execution after the local congragation had objected to the nudity depicted in the cartoons.

GLASLOUGH: The Memorial

Wall fountain designed *c.*1870 by Sir John Leslie in memory of his brother Charles, from whom he had inherited the estate. Bronze bust framed in arch benevolently surveys his model village.

GLASLOUGH: The Schoolhouse

Intensely serious neo-Gothic Orange Hall now abandoned. Heavily decorated bargeboards; eccentric glazing. Access from a private avenue linked with yews. Possibly by A.G. Jones, who was commissioned in 1850 to design gates (never executed) for Castle Leslie in the same restless idiom.

MONAGHAN: Bank of Ireland

Formerly the Hibernian Bank. A distinguished example of the campaign to attract new Catholic wealth by churchifying the appearance of their banks. The principal architect employed was Timothy Hevey, who was more assertive; O'Neill and Byrne, the architects here, were creamier and more accommodating in an even vaguer version of the Hiberno-Romanesque. Adapted with great care to the corner site, so that the main entrance beneath a corbelled balcony is on the curve itself.

BANK OF IRELAND, MONAGHAN

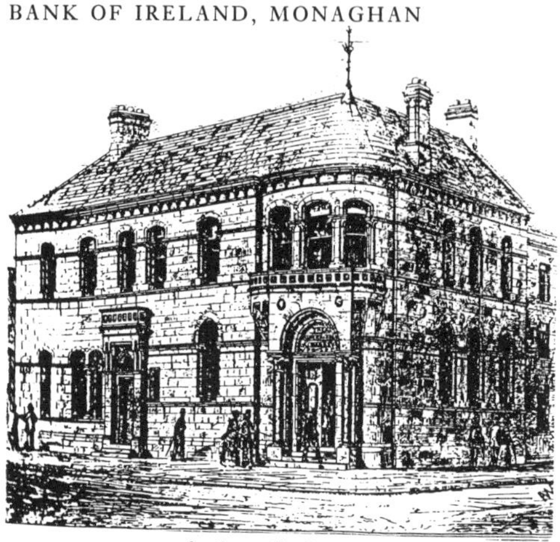

MONAGHAN: Anketell Grove

Lombardesque stable block *c.*1860 complements the architectural complexity of the adjoining house, early 18th-century, but the wings rebuilt in Gothick, the central tower remodelled to match the Victorian stables.

MONAGHAN: Bessmount

Classic case history of a symmetrical conventional Georgian house transformed into a dream chateau without planning permission. The architect is unknown, but might well be William Barre, who would have been involved at that time in the transformation of Roxborough for the Charlemonts. The client was William Henderson, immortalized along with his wife in stone medallions each side of the door (dated 1869). Apart from building a separate music room, and raising the house a floor, no extra accommodation was involved, but every known device was used to mask the low ceilings of the existing house, including adding a vertiginous oriel turret to the corner of the principal bedroom and building up a massive water tower in

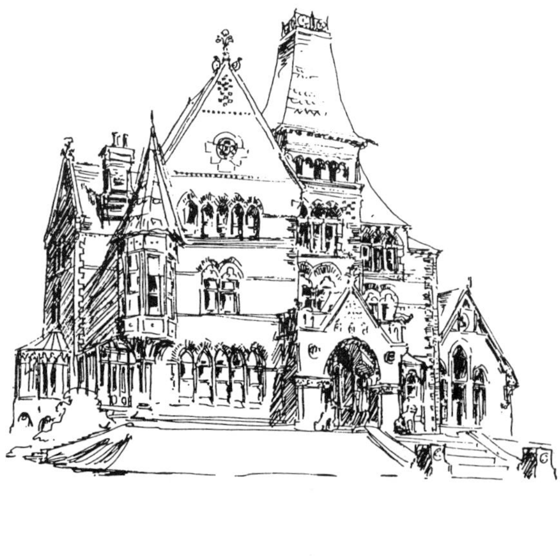

front of the original entrance hall, preceded by a boldly projecting porch. This porch is lavishly carved with a bestiary of stone—bats, snails, squirrels, owls, mice, hares, monkeys, pelicans, dogs, parrots, fish, lizards, eels, pike, eagles, thrushes, frogs and toads. This would appear to be carved by the Fitzpatrick brothers of Belfast.

What makes Bessmount so memorable is the concentration of its fantasy, so often diluted by sheer size in the case of many of its more ambitious and now vanished rival castles. The house is still the centrepiece of a prosperous farm, personally cared for by its present owner, who fortunately has a head for heights when he replaces the slates.

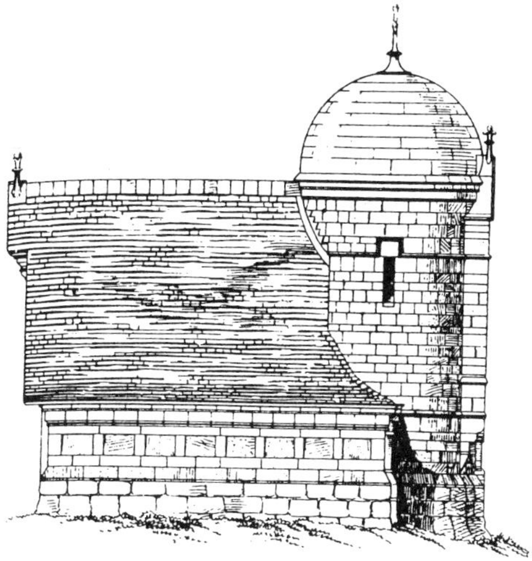

MONAGHAN: Castle Rossmore Mausoleum

With the eastern entrance gates and lodge, the only surviving structure on the Rossmore estate,

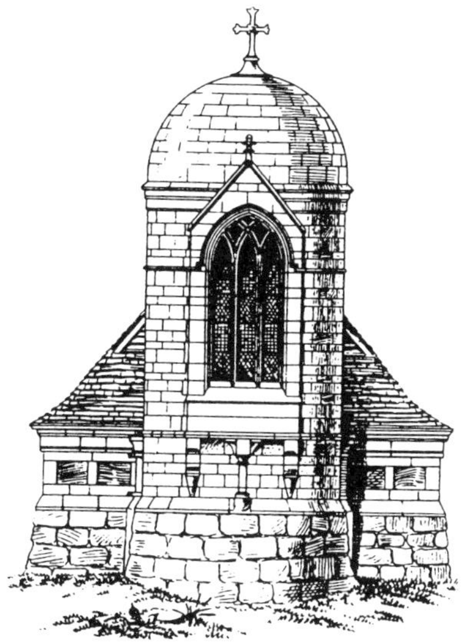

once the most spectacular demesne in Monaghan, now the most devastated. Dry rot that finished off first the castle and then the dower house was said to have been transplanted with the mould of the wine cellar. Then nearly all the trees in the demesne were felled by the Forestry Department, apart from those marked with whitewash by officials, and a lot more also marked with whitewash by the late Lady Rossmore under the cover of darkness the night before. The principal entrance was removed to make the Rossmore Industrial Estate. The final disaster was the meaningless destruction of her own cottage by the IRA. All its contents were lost (including letters from Jane Austen), and the original front door of the castle. The ruins of this had already been demolished as a danger to sightseekers, after Marianne Faithful, interviewed about her possible engagement to Lord Rossmore, had called Castle Rossmore a pile of ancestral rubble.

Even in its heyday Castle Rossmore looked better from a distance—a compilation of earlier houses, extended at various times by W.V. Morrison and W.H. Lynn to contrive the longest drawingroom in the county, all sprouting a medley of towers. The mausoleum is therefore comparatively modest, built by Derry, Lord Rossmore (author of *Things I Can Tell*) for his elder brother, 1876. The architect was from London, E.J. Tarver, who appears to have been inspired by Eastern Europe with its red-tiled roof, part dome, part spire. There is a feeling of Mayerling in this remote valley. But the 4th Lord Rossmore was killed simply by a fall from his horse.

MONAGHAN: Castle Shane

Seat of the Lucas-Scudamores, said to be medieval, later Georgianized, but its transformation *c.*1840 into a chubby stucco neo-Elizabethan castle thoughtlessly obliterated all evidence of antiquity. Burnt out in the Troubles, then demolished but not totally. Part of a three-storied bay window and a gable end survive to complement a few Wellingtonians spared from the devastation of the demesne. Also spared is a pretty gatelodge and a curiously elongated stuccoed bellcote that transforms a corner of the walled garden into a remote Californian mission.

MONAGHAN: Catholic Cathedral

The most impressive of J.J. McCarthy's new-built cathedrals, at least until its internal remodelling began ten years ago. Started in 1861, the shell was completed by 1868, but continued for another twenty years, with William Hague taking over. He built the tower and spire in 1881-3 and then embellished the interior; the cathedral was not consecrated until 1892.

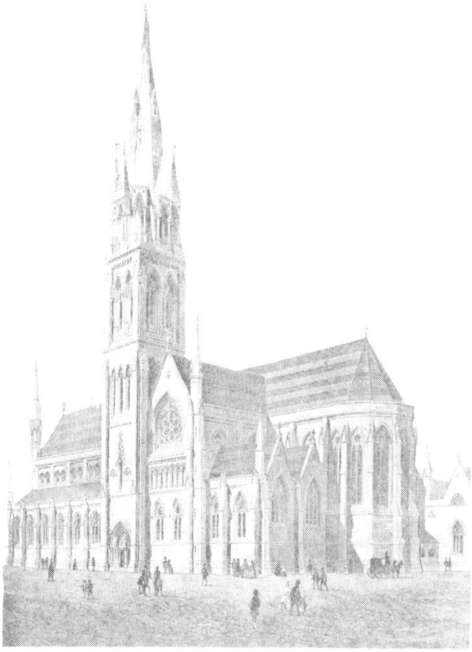

Despite its long gestation, the result is unified by Hague's fidelity to McCarthy's vision, which predated the start of the cathedral by many years. McCarthy, writing in 1865 to the exiled Charles Gavan Duffy (born in Monaghan) suggested that 'If you say that I have not fulfilled my friend's promise of twenty golden years ago, I will hang myself.' The cathedral was also due to two formidable bishops: the first, Bishop Kavanagh, was succeeded in 1865 by Bishop Donnelly. He feuded with his landlord, Lord Rossmore, who had been charmed by Bishop Kavanagh into donating the stone and the site.

The cathedral is set on a hill at the edge of the town and is approached by steps: an aisled nave of eight bays with projecting apsidal baptistry leads to the transept, projecting two bays on either side. That this is without aisles is masked to the south by the positioning of the tower. A short chancel, flanked by double chapels two bays long leading within to impressive diagonal vistas, terminates in a seven-sided buttressed apse. To the north extend sacristies and chapter house. Beyond, Hague built a bishop's house, forbidding due to the local sandstone used throughout. This contains two pairs of Irish saints in stained glass by Michael Healy. In the cathedral, grimness is offset by the judicious use of sculpture (some in marble, by Pietro Lazzarini), and the slender pinnacles that dramatize the silhouette, and are echoed by the eight spirelets that wreath the spire. The nave is nobly roofed with hammerbeam trusses resting on angels upheld on corbelled colonettes. Stained glass (1884-92) mainly by Mayer but also by Earley and Powell, and Cox and Buckley. Elaborate Telford organ remains on its intact western gallery. Not so the furnishings at the eastern end. Hague's altar, baldachino, unconventional throne and pulpit have been replaced by fittings devised by Michael Biggs to conform with liturgical trends of the 1960s following a formula already deployed in Longford Cathedral. But what has been successful in a neo-Classical setting here dispels all sense of the celestial.

MONAGHAN: **Church of Ireland**

Early Gothic Revival church built in the 1830s by William Farrell, a Classicist by temperament. But Farrell's church is Georgian in medieval dress, symmetrical and galleried. The exterior is harsh and spiky. The interior, entered through the western tower crowned with a spiky tower, is frothy and intimate, following the example set by Francis Johnston in his Chapel Royal of Dublin Castle. The decoration owes much to the Rossmore family. Their heraldic glass by Barff fills the east window. Most of the idiosyncratic wall memorials are to their family —Augusta Rossmore commemorated by her empty chair, sculpted by Lewis of Cheltenham; Mary Anne Rossmore commemmorated by Thomas Kirke's 'The Parting Glance'. Kirke's son John was the sculptor of the memorial to a Lloyd killed by Zulus a generation later; instead of mournful Grecian elegies, a battle hymn to the Empire.

MONAGHAN, **Church Square: Dawson Memorial**

Designed by William Barre in a moment of restraint as an austere ashlar obelisk dating from 1857.

MONAGHAN, **Emyvale Road: St Macartan's Seminary**

Formal complex built along the crest of a hill, by Thomas Duff. Georgian in every characteristic except the date—1840-8. Later chapel recently restored.

MONAGHAN, **Mill Street: Savings Bank**

Precise design with an intriguing amalgamation of the neo-Tudor and neo-Classicism. Entered through attached Grecian porch. Banking hall lit by glazed triple-arcade.

MONAGHAN, **Park Street: St Joseph's Catholic Church**

Late Gothic Revival church rebuilt in 1900 after the death of the architect, William Hague. His furnishing survives here better than in the cathedral. Whimsical belfry.

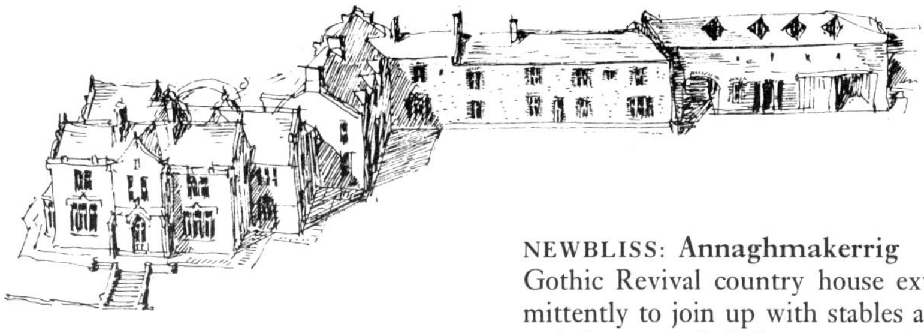

MONAGHAN: **Presbyterian Church**
A clever rebuilding by Roome and Loag, *c.*1900, who retained an earlier church as a ground floor assembly hall. This means that the new church is approached up a flight of steps. Austere interior with gallery on cast-iron columns.

MONAGHAN: **St Louis Convent**
Extended complex centred on the original Georgian house. The style of the additions in increasingly institutional Gothic, at its most formidable in the wing added by J.J. McDonnell in 1909 with adjoining chapel. Permanent exhibition on the order of St Louis and the history of the convent.

MONAGHAN: **St Davnet's Hospital**
Built in 1869-71 with a principal range said to be sixty bays long; of rubblestone with brick trimmings. Detached Catholic church of simple design. Additions by T. McNamara.

MONAGHAN, **The Diamond: Rossmore Memorial**
Octagonal Gothic shrine vaulted by a dome crowned with a spire, erected to the memory of the 4th Lord Rossmore, killed while steeplechasing. The architect, while unrecorded, is most likely to be E.J. Tarver, since he designed Lord Rossmore's mausoleum, built also in 1876 with the same Germanic combination of dome and spire.

MONAGHAN: **The Station**
Single-storied arcade, five larger central bays flanked by nine bays at either side built out of red and yellow brick; attributed to William Murray, *c.*1850. The polychromy has faded and the railway line has been made redundant.

NEWBLISS: **Aghabogue Church of Ireland**
Modest, single cell, Gothic Revival. Architect G.C. Henderson, 1875. The burial-ground of the Powers and Guthries, commemorating the first Tyrone Power, the most celebrated Irish actor of his time, who died at sea, and his daughter, Dame Alice Power, who died while playing in Cincinnati. The late Sir Tyrone Guthrie was born into this tradition. Here too he is buried.

NEWBLISS: **Annaghmakerrig**
Gothic Revival country house extended intermittently to join up with stables and farmyard, and then remodelled, a process that fortunately ceased after altering the main house. The remodelling, while replacing the diamond panes with plate glass and larger bays, opened up the main interiors to the lake below, ringed by woods and rhododendrons that seal it off from the drumlins of the countryside—a world apart. Built by the Moreheads, a family of hard-headed planters who intermarried with the theatrical Powers, who themselves intermarried with the philantropical Guthries. Ultimately inherited by the late Sir Tyrone Guthrie, who willed the house as a home for artists and writers with his capital to subsidise it, but not the farm: he had lost too much money himself making jam.

Such has been the success of the foundation through the efforts of both Irish Art Councils, that the farmyard has been acquired—as studios and rehearsal rooms. The portrait of the first Tyrone Power in three roles has been returned by the National Gallery to its place above the drawingroom fireplace. More miraculous has been the survival of Sir Tyrone's library, that was to have been removed to Monaghan Museum, where it would be burnt by the IRA.

Courageous conversion by Fergus Flynn-Rogers has placed the bathrooms and fire exits approached from each bedroom by individual 'Jacob's ladders' that ensure constant sobriety. Kitchen transformed to accommodate an evening meal inspired by French farmhouses rather than Oxford colleges as more conducive to good writing. Open to patrons on an annual fund-raising weekend.

NEWBLISS: **Killeevan Church of Ireland**
A grim design by Welland *c.*1850 with a slightly later tower and spire.

ROCKCORRY: **Church of Ireland**
The village with its elegant Georgian almshouses is dominated by this forceful church of William Barre, where nave and asymmetrically sited steeple, welded together, strive against each other for dominance. The steeple marks the entry porch, square on ground level but tapering upwards into an octagonal spire. The chancel is short and wide—five windows ranged behind the altar. The interior is devoid of Barre's distinctive detailing, no doubt due to his

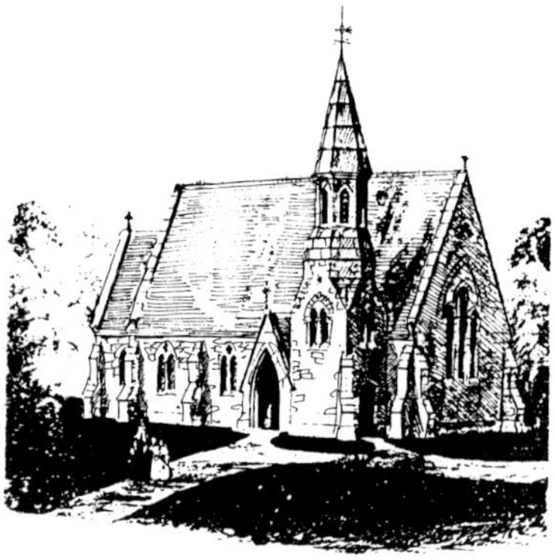

early death, but the open roofs of nave and chancel are strongly braced, and a formidable stone baptismal font confronts whoever enters.

ROCKCORRY: **Dartrey Church of Ireland**
Set in a quiet graveyard, with views across the lake to the primeval forest that alone was spared the devastation of the demesne of Dartrey; one feels that at least the Victorian Dawsons can rest in peace; but their Georgian mausoleum, designed by James Wyatt, though lost in now impenetrable forestry, has been vandalized almost beyond repair. Built as a cruciform structure by the Board of First Fruits; Welland and Gillespie reinforced the nave with brick buttresses and replaced the shallow chancel with a boldly projecting apse—brick buttressing contrasting with the delicate stonework of the cusped windows.

ROCKCORRY: **Dartrey Demesne**
The vast Elizabethan mansion built by William Burn for the Dawsons, earls of Dartrey, was demolished after the house, empty for many years, had been lent to the RSPCA for a ball, since the daughter of the last earl, Lady Edith Windham, was devoted to the welfare of donkeys. The morning after, the County Council demanded rates, and the fate of the house was sealed. What survives are four gatelodges; houses for the agent, the head gardener, and the farm manager; two derelict stableyards, a vandalized mausoleum and a triumphal column. What gives unity to all the architecture of the demesne is the use of local stone with rose brick fired on the estate. The most remarkable remaining structure is the impeccably detailed neo-Georgian stable block by William Burn *c.*1850, built round five sides of an octagon. Arcaded carriage rooms—with rounded quoins in case of injury to horses—alternate with stables below. Accommodation for visiting coachmen above.

SCOTSHOUSE: **Catholic Church**
Simplified Celtic Revival church with asymmetrical bellcote counterbalanced by the subtly expressed organ gallery staircase. Neo-Byzantine altar set below an exotic triple-light Clarke Studios window. Architect: R.M. Butler. Date, *c.*1920.

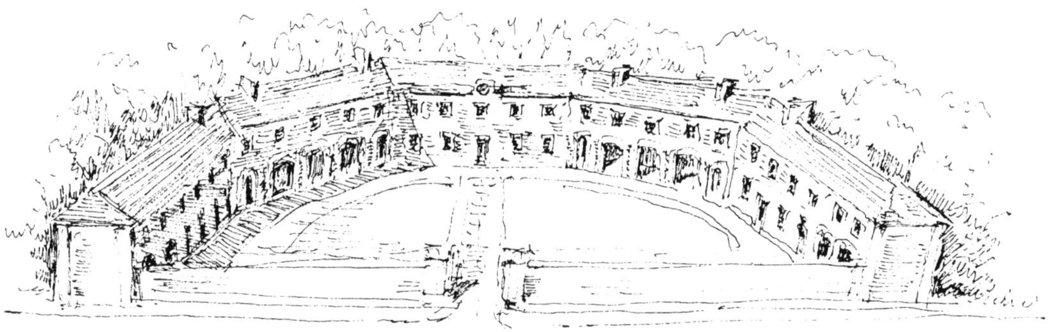

OFFALY

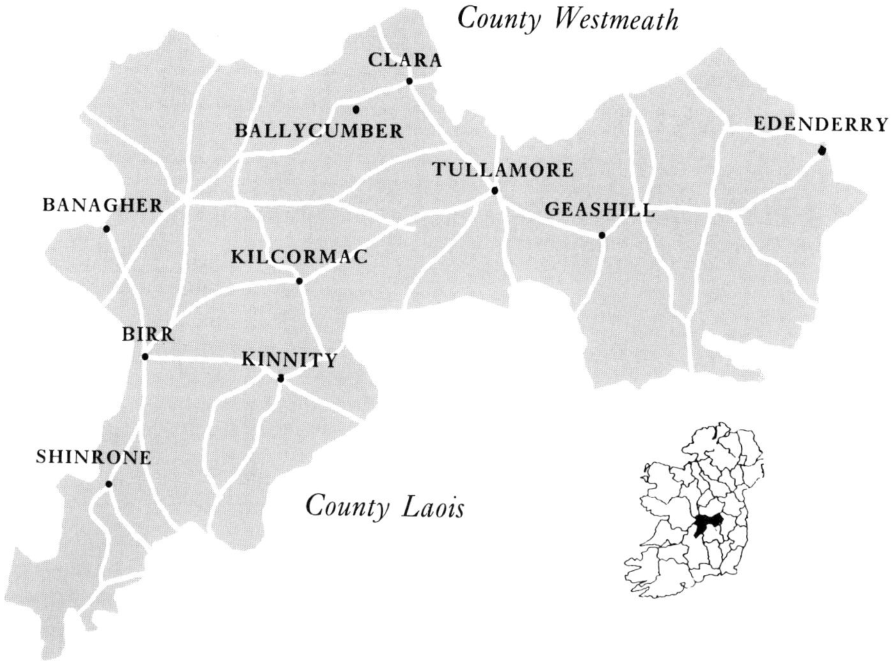

BALLYCUMBER: **Bellair House**
Neo-Classical villa by Sir Richard Morrison, extended in 1889 by Sir Reginald Bloomfield with a single-storied pilastered diningroom, a rare appearance in Ireland of the Queen Anne Revival. Commissioned by W.G. Mulock, whose unpublished memoirs survive. Inherited by the poetess Sheelagh Wingfield, Viscountess Powerscourt, who later sold it.

BANAGHER: **Church of Ireland**
This over-restored Board of First Fruits church contains memorials of the Bell family—a marble tomb to a doctor who died in India, meticulously detailing his surgical equipment; and a brilliantly coloured pre-Raphaelite stained-glass window above the altar, inserted a generation later, made by Revd A.L. Moore of London, whose best work can be seen in Ely Cathedral.

BANAGHER: **Waller's Maltings**
Large distilling complex sited dramatically on the edge of the river Shannon. Part demolished, the remainder derelict.

BIRR: **Birr Castle**
No other Irish castle can compete with Birr in the architectural complexity of its architectural evolution, from medieval gatehouse of a Celtic prince to a Plantation fortress repeatedly besieged and stormed in the Cromwellian and Williamite wars, and then into its ultimate transformation, a Regency Gothick fantasy as perceived by an improving earl. At the dawn of the Victorian era, the castle was so complete, and so attuned to the historical sensibility of the time, that there was no need for major work, only decorative embellishments. Most of these

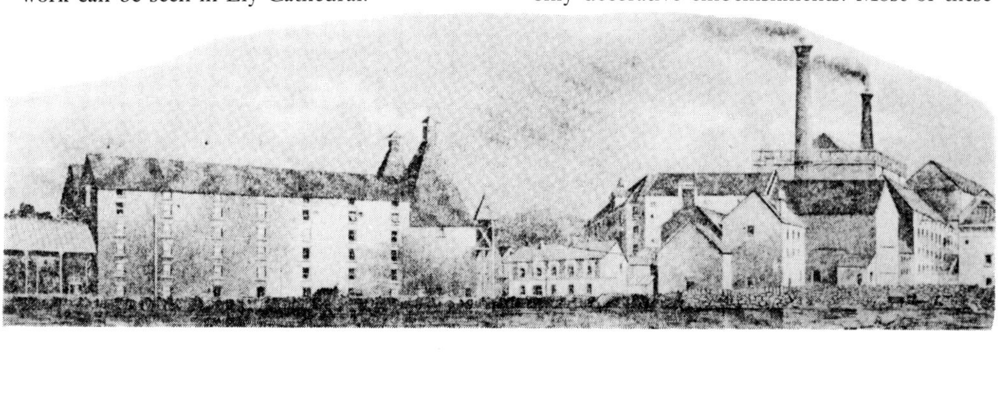

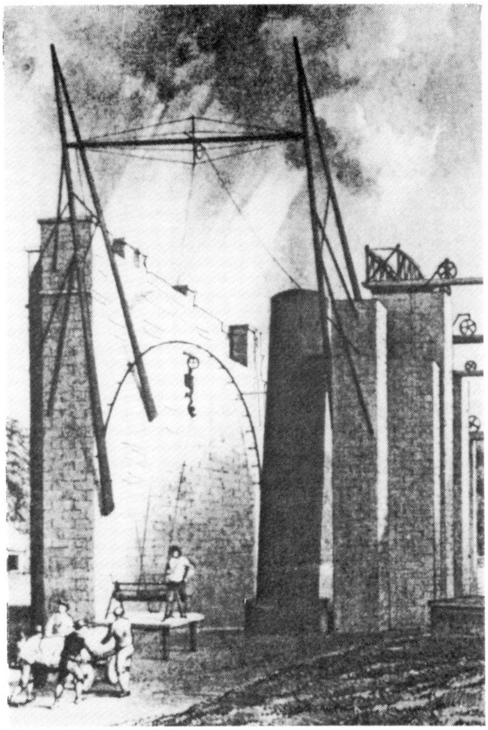

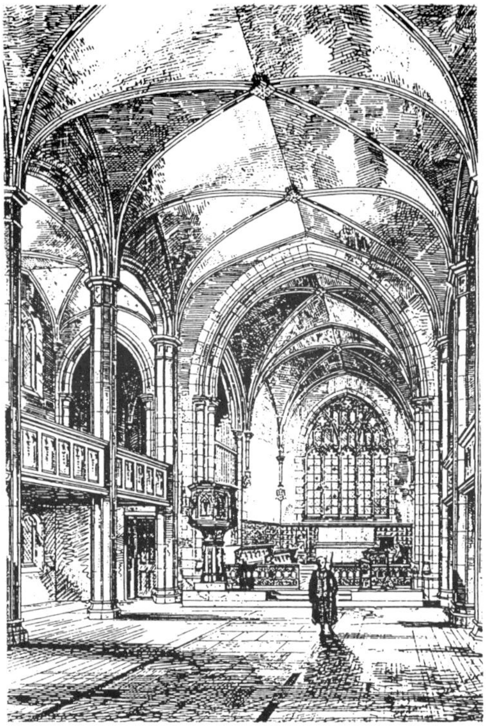

appear to have been designed by the astronomer 3rd earl, who succeeded in 1841, or else by his immediate family. His wife's uncle, Col. Richard Wharton Myddleton, designed the star-shaped ramparts that separate the castle from its park, looking as if they were dug in order to repel the armies of the Jacobites, rather than to give employment during the Famine. Access is through a gatehouse designed by the wife of the 3rd earl, with elaborate cast-iron Gothic gates here, and another pair before the front door, both cast on the estate; their design matches the plasterwork of the bedroom. Lady Rosse is also credited with the design of the stables, which today house her pioneering photographic experiments, and the incredible Gothic Revival furniture of her bedroom.

The most important architectural achievement of the 3rd earl himself was the Gothick folly in the park (1842-5), the most functional folly ever built, since its purpose was to support his telescope, the largest telescope in the world for three quarters of a century, which made Birr a pilgrimage centre not only for scientists, but also for the ordinary public, who were allowed view with their own eyes the outer confines of the Universe. The 3rd earl used his telescope to discover spiral nebulae and record them. He trained his two sons to assist him. The elder, who inherited, improved the workings of the telescope; the younger, Sir Charles Parsons, invented the turbine. During the Troubles the six-foot diameter reflector was deposited in the Kensington Science Museum, where it is now purely an exhibit. The tube was dismantled to its present state like a crashed leviathan. It is the ambition of the 7th earl to retrieve the reflector and resurrect the telescope to view again the stars. Stableyard due to be converted into Irish science museum by the OPW.

BIRR: Church of Ireland

Regency Gothick galleried church by John Johnston, extended in 1876 by Thomas Drew with a new chancel. He designed a reredos including the emblems of the four Evangelists which caused such uproar that they were deleted along with a few cherubs, but even this did not prevent the censored result being anonymously vandalized in the middle of the night. The original design, by Heaton, Butler and Bayne, commissioned from Charles Kempe by the 4th earl of Rosse for the great east window above the altar was also rejected and was finally accepted in 1891, provided that the Crucifixion was excluded. This condition seems to have been forgotten by the glassmakers. Marble memorials to the 3rd and 4th earls, the latter by Burke and Co. of London.

BIRR: Convent of Mercy

The Catholic church by Mullins of 1817 predates our period, but on the adjoining site A.W.N. Pugin designed in 1845 one of his least-known commissions for an English nun called Sister Beckett, a personal friend. Only two sides of the cloister were completed on Pugin's death, the north entry façade and the range to the west. The south range with its circular corner staircase tower, and the eastern range terminating in a projecting chapel were completed seven years later not in the original design. The orphanage and chancel were added (by George Ashlin himself). However, from the garden front the controlled freedom of E.W. Pugin can be savoured in stark contrast to the grim monotony of Ashlin's adjoining orphanage —the long restful roofs counterbalanced by the corner tower and a single powerful buttress, against which nestles a lean-to porch. Unassuming interiors with Gothic fireplaces. Small museum displaying a few architectural drawings. The chapel still contains a repositioned eastern window by Hardman of 1858, but its elaborate decoration on the walls and roofs have been painted over. Inevitably the rood screen has also vanished.

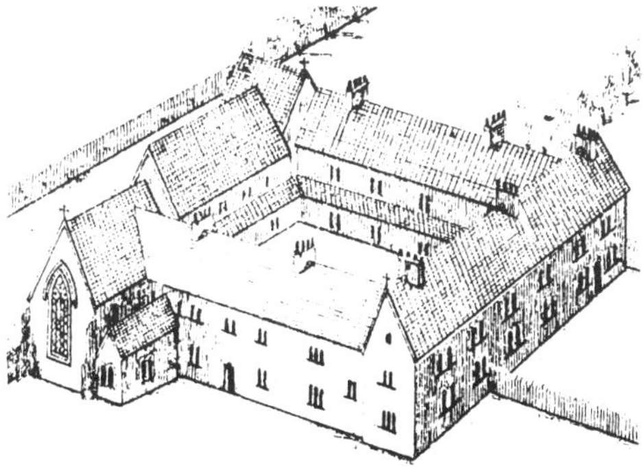

BIRR: **Model Schools**
Charming round-arched composition, not quite symmetrical due to the incorporation of the schoolmaster's residence. Designed by Jacob Owen and dating from 1860.

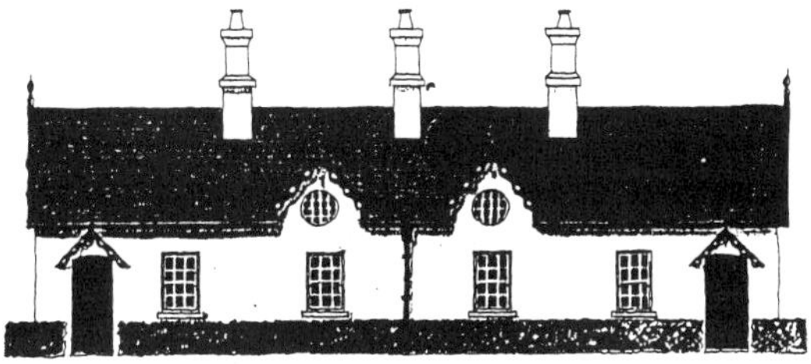

BIRR: **Model Cottages**
Designed as partly double-storied with their gables facing the road linked informally by single-storied ranges. Drawings in Birr Castle collection, signed R.E.B. (probably R.E. Buchanan). 1874.

BIRR: **Rosse Memorial**
The memorial statue of the 3rd earl of Rosse, the astronomer, who died in 1867. Carved by John Henry Foley.

BIRR, **The Mall: Church Hall**
Designed in neo-Tudor by J.F. Fuller in 1890. Gable end facing the road with entrance beneath a richly carved corbelled balcony. Sold off in the 1930s by the Church of Ireland and now disused.

CLARA, **Ballycumber Road: Experimental Housing**
Most of the housing in Clara was built over a period of a hundred years by the Goodbodys, a Quaker family who built up the largest jute-spinning business in Ireland. The housing they built for their workforce tends to be traditional, with pitched roofs, except for this terrace which has shallow segmental roofs covered with an experimental felt.

CLARA: **Charlestown House**
One of the several houses designed by J.S. Mulvany for the Goodbody family. Almost symmetrical with curved bows at each end of the façade. Interlaced parapet concealing the roof.

CLARA: **Franciscan Monastery**
The most domestic religious institution in Ireland, built like a small country house and adjoining farmyard. Its construction represented official recognition for its founder, Matthew Delahunty, who had set up small community of Franciscan brothers to make their living off the land and teach the children of their neighbours in 1820. The symmetrical façade of five bays flanked by double-height Gothic windows lighting chapel and refectory, would appear to date from that time, but in reality was not built until 1854. Elegant ribbed vault in the chapel and early painted glass.

CLARA: **Inchmore**
One of the houses built by J.S. Mulvany for the Goodbody family. Two-storied front with columned porch and bay windows characteristic of Mulvany's abbreviated Classicism. Built out of grey limestone set off against white rendered walls. Despite a three-storied tower, the house rambles off at the rear. Now owned by a religious institution; a startling version of the grotto of Lourdes, sliced off in the shape of a human heart, has just been dismantled.

CLARA: **Catholic Church**
J.J. O'Callaghan was the youngest pupil of Benjamin Woodward, and throughout his long life he never abandoned his faith in Gothic, whether for churches or for pubs. Here the predominant influence is Augustus Pugin, and the church stylistically dates from the 1840s. It was designed in 1876 and completed in 1881, a

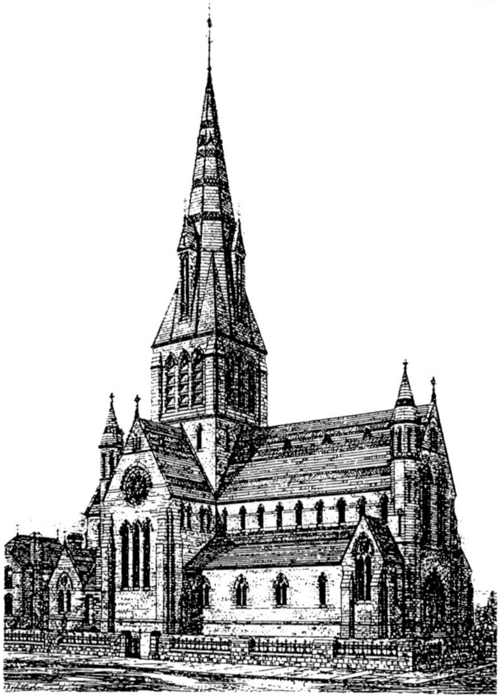

miniature version of Killarney Cathedral, cruciform with central tower and spire. The façade is made boldly asymmetrical by the staircase tower to the organ gallery. Interior of equal assurance with the timber roof underplayed to stress the stone-ribbed vaulting beneath the tower. The comparative narrowness of the nave, choir and transepts are emphasized by their end walls two windows wide. This duality is resolved in the nave and transepts by rose windows at a higher level. In the chancel the duality was once resolved by the high altar, but this was destroyed after the Second Vatican Council, when parts of it were relegated to a side chapel. Remarkably consistent stained glass by Mayer taking up the windows of both transepts, an admirable foil to the robustness of the architecture.

The Early Gothic Revival predecessor has been preserved nearby as the parochial hall.

CLARA: Meeting House

Quaker meeting house treated as Italianate garden pavilion surrounded by yews. Attributable to J.S. Mulvany.

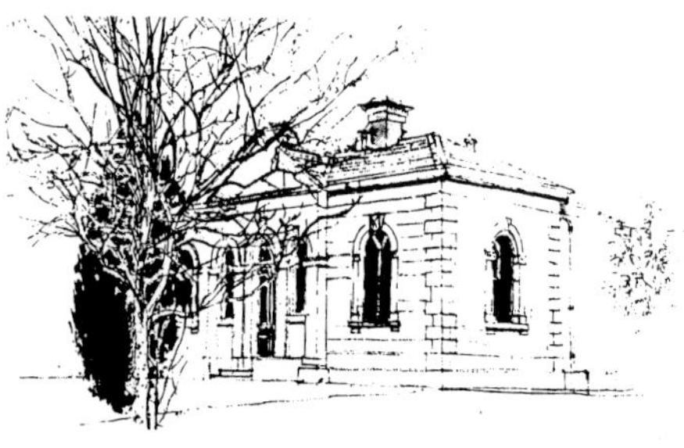

EDENDERRY: Catholic Church

Started in 1913 and completed three years later by Anthony and William Scott, this is a competent essay in Hiberno-Romanesque. But it should have been much more than that. Judged as successor to Spiddal, the interior is profoundly disappointing. The façade has a certain bombastic formality, contemporary with St Mary's College in Galway (q.v.), and there is the occasional detail like the staircases to the organ gallery, where William Scott reveals his finesse as the leading Irish Arts and Crafts designer of his day. Otherwise, no risks are taken with the traditional—continous nave and chancel, screened transepts, terminating apse. Good mosaic floor in the sanctuary. Lavish altars, communion rails and pulpit that would appear to predate William Scott but are dated 1929, eight years after his death.

EDENDERRY: Rahan Church of Ireland

J.F. Fuller at his most unassuming. A simple cell neo-Hiberno-Romanesque with projecting porch, vestry and organ chamber. Sited above the remnants of an entrance into the vanished demesne of the Dudley Palmers, who are buried alongside the chancel. Stylized carving on the arch of the porch, repeated on the arch of the chancel. Date: 1914.

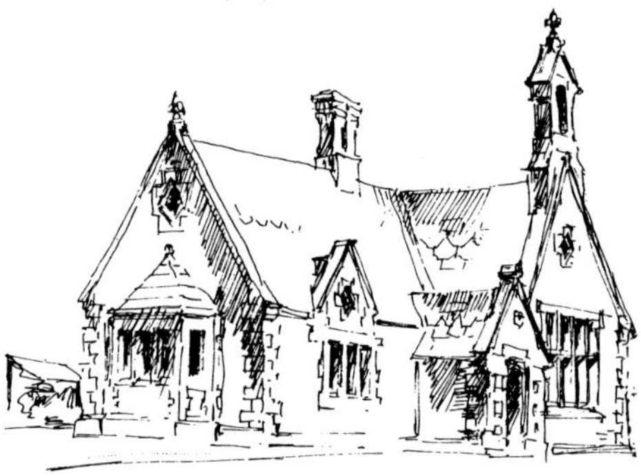

GEASHILL: The Schoolhouse

Picturesque, cut-stone, Gothic Revival schoolhouse with gabled porch, dormer and return, the latter topped by a dominant bellcote. Designed in 1864 by the architect of Glenveagh Castle (q.v.), John Townshend (Townie) Trench.

KILCORMAC: Rathrobin

The seat of the Biddulph family, rebuilt for them *c.*1880 by Sir Thomas Drew as an irregular and neo-Elizabethan pile with mullioned windows; gables and dormers topped by finials. Now an ivy-clad ruin but revealing unexpected experiments by Drew in ferro-concrete. Its destruction during the Troubles was recalled by

Arthur Magan in *The Magans of Ummera*, as it was his mother's home.

KINNITY: **Castle Bernard**

Gothic Revival castle by the brothers Pain, incorporating remnants of an earlier fortress set below the wooded foothills of the Slieve Bloom; dating from 1833. Three-storied façade with borrowings from Mitchelstown Castle (which

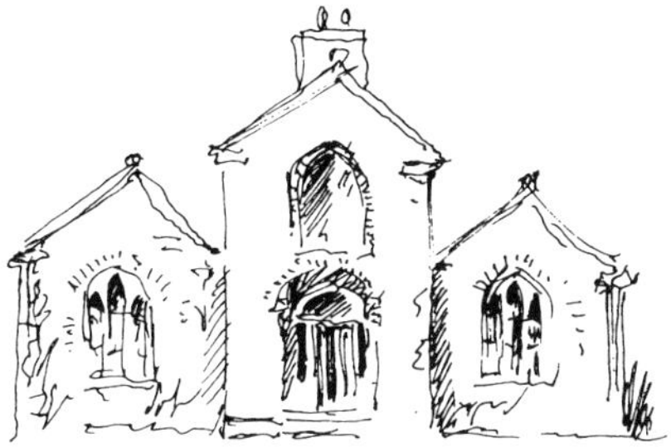

they designed fourteen years before)—an oriel inserted over a projecting porch to light an inner hall, and a corner octagonal tower crowned with crockets, all in limestone ashlar. Acquired by the department of forestry for use as a school. A recent bid to turn it into an open prison led to widespread opposition from the locals; now for sale.

KINNITY: **The Schoolhouse**

Delightful triple-gabled façade *c.*1840 survives but in a state of dereliction.

SHINRONE: **Mount St Joseph's**

The earliest building is a country house called Mount Heaton, bought by Count Arthur Moore and donated to the Cistercians on condition that his posterity had the right to be married there. His donation was certainly a more effective means of reviving Irish Catholicism than his other dream—to rebuild a replica of Cormac's chapel for his private worship.

Mount Heaton was one of those delightfully unpredictable styllistic hybrids, here Gothick to the front (now much mutilated) and Classical to the rear (reasonably intact). The first abbot was Dom Camillus Beardwood, a brother of W.H. Beardwood, an architect who spent his entire life building in Dublin churches designed by others. Here in the Irish midlands it would appear that he was merely implementing the ideas of his formidable brother, who had trained his monks to be builders as they would have been in the middle ages. The abbot left the Gothick front of Mount Heaton intact (a policy not followed by his successors) and built an adjoining cloister with the nearest range taken up by the abbey church which is imbued with the Cistercian tradition but also influenced by W.D. Butler's Roscrea church (q.v.) nearby. The church took only three years (1878-81) to build, apart from the later tower and spire, built unaccountably in smooth ashlar compared to the bush-hammered masonry of the remainder. The interior has a long nave and aisles, austere columnless arcades, generously porportioned clerestory and open roof leading to a tower-like crossing. Unfortunately the stained glass, banned by the early Cistercians, here trivializes its setting.

On the other side of the church, the abbot built his most remarkable range; its fenestration identifies the different functions of the rooms—the refectory, the dormitory and the sacristy treated as an outer chapel of the church. The austere internal cloister reflects the values of a life devoted to silence. Since the death of Abbot Camillus, the building programme has continued but with lessening motivation. The principal school complex from 1905 is crude if jolly. Finally Mount Heaton itself was transformed into a guesthouse with the loss of its Gothickry; it is ironic at the same time that the Gothic Revival should be deployed in 1941 to build the school chapel, to prove how long the movement lasted in rural Ireland.

TULLAMORE: **Catholic Church**

Designed by William Hague in a tired conventional Gothic—unbroken nave and chancel, polygonal apse, off-centre western steeple. Hague died a year after the foundations were laid in 1898. Work was restarted in 1902 under T.F. McNamara, who was responsible for fitting up the interior. Accidentally burnt out by intruders in 1983. Church rebuilt, retaining only the tower walls, the steeple, and the west façade, now the end wall of the reorientated chancel. Clarke Studios windows brought from Rathfarnham Castle, Dublin.

TULLAMORE: **Charleville Forest**

Francis Johnston's most impressive castle was unexpectedly inherited by the younger aunt of the 5th and last earl of Charleville after he had a row with her elder sister. Her husband was a Howard of Castle Howard, patrons at that time of Philip Webb and the later pre-Raphaelites. Hence the only commission of William Morris in Ireland—to redecorate the interiors, in 1875. By then he was so affected by Socialism that he was far more absorbed by the living conditions of the poor in rural Ireland and he never referred to his redecoration in his correspondence. Hence his contribution slipped into oblivion. His furnishings were dispersed in the great sale, *c.*1950. His wallpapers were removed during its recent restoration. Some painted decoration and a frieze survive in the diningroom. Open to the public.

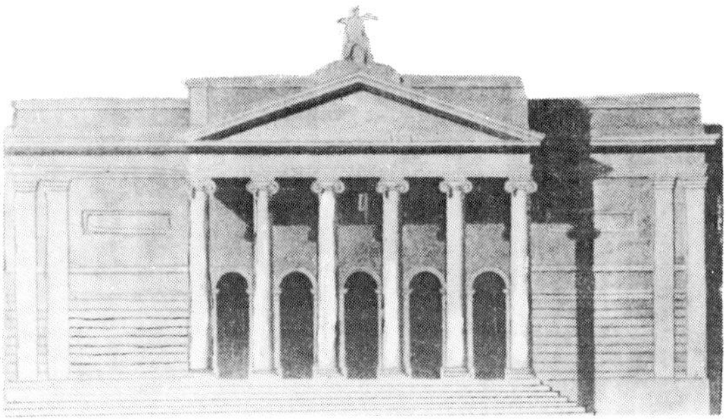

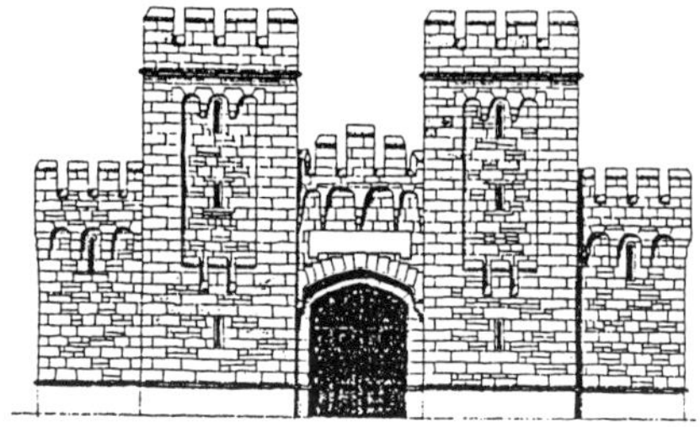

TULLAMORE: Courthouse and Gaol

An impressive neo-Classical design by J.B. Keane (built in 1833-5) which has survived its destruction by fire in 1922. In the rebuilding unfortunate changes were made to the internal planning; extra windows were inserted at the expense of its monumentality; and the statue of Justice seated with her scales above the six-columned portico was removed. Keane's drawings survive, with his horizontally channelled masonry carefully foiled by superimposed corner pilasters—an idea he was to reuse throughout his career (Longford Cathedral, Waterford Courthouse: q.v.). Two D-shaped courtrooms approached by columned halls.

Next to the serene courthouse is sited a formidable neo-Medieval gaol entered by a massive machiolated gatehouse, now converted into a factory. Attributed to John Killay.

TULLAMORE, Charleville Road: The Bungalow

Red-brick and tiled Anglo-Dutch cottage ornée set in matching garden designed by F.G. Hicks in 1906 for the author's great-grandfather.

TULLAMORE, Columcille Street: Gleeson's

Formerly Scally's; grandiose provincial emporium of three floors, the two lower devoted to shopping; designed by T.F. McNamara, the architect of the Catholic Church. It dates from 1911. The fenestration that had revealed the magic of Art Nouveau to the Irish midlands has long since been conventionalized, and its curvilinear oriel has been replaced—as has the telegraph system connecting each assistant to the central cash desk.

TULLAMORE: Durrow Abbey

Designs survive in the collection of William Murray dated 1837 for Lord Glandine, later 2nd earl of Norbury, transforming his Georgian house into a large, dull, Italianate palazzo. No drawings survive of the incomplete Tudor Revival scheme that was actually built, and where the 2nd earl was murdered just after he had just moved in. His descendants, the Otway-Tolers, were burnt out in 1922 but decided to rebuild in 1924, choosing Ralph Byrne, who improved Murray's proportions by lowering the front range to two floors. Within the shell he constructed a simplified Arts and Crafts interior full of space and light round a galleried tunnel-vaulted living hall. A rare example of a house improved as a result of its destruction in the Troubles.

TULLAMORE: Durrow Church of Ireland

Built by the Otway-Tolers to replace the still-extant Georgian church on the historic site, but embarrassingly close to their own house. Designed by J.F. Fuller in his characteristic Gothic. Corbelled spirelet on the western gable.

TULLAMORE: Lynalley Church of Ireland

Neo-Romanesque church built alongside the demesne wall of Charleville by Lady Emily Howard-Bury in 1887 to the designs of J.F. Fuller. A single cell ending with an apse. Open roof with arched trusses resting on corbelled brackets. Arcarded organ recess. Celtic Revival altar, pulpit and lectern. Painted decoration in vault of the apse. Now sold off to be a private house.

TULLAMORE, O'Connor Square: Goodbody's

Three-storied warehouse in Ruskinian Gothic built by an unknown architect, *c.*1870. Gabled roofs with decorative bargeboarding. Taken over and restored by adjoining Bank of Ireland.

ROSCOMMON

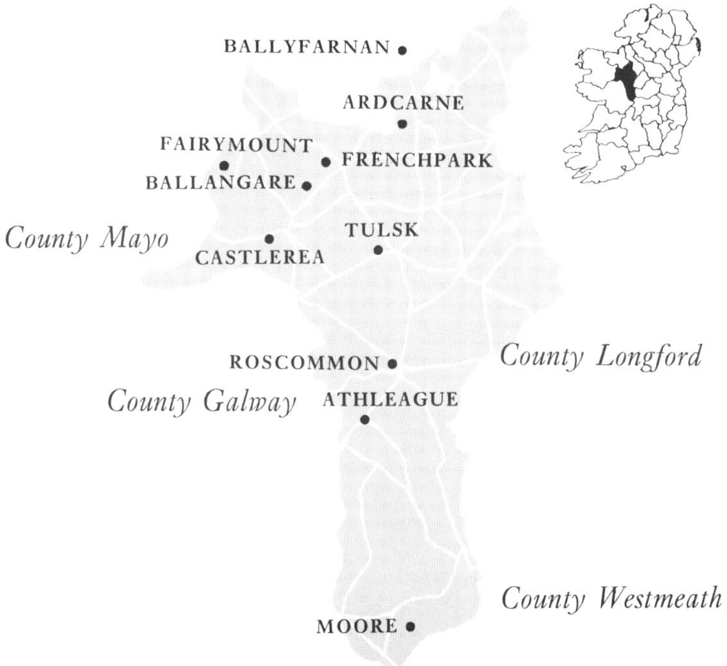

ATHLEAGUE: **Mount Talbot**
Two triumphal arches, one Gothic, the other Palladian, are the outward expression of the schizophrenic architecture of this house, now a ruin engulfed in ivy apart from its topmost flag tower and protruding Georgian stable wings joined by dissimilar arcades. A mantle of Gothic windows, pinnacles and towers, possibly by Richard Richards, made the central block into an insubstantial feudal fortress that failed, according to a jealous Mr Talbot Crosbie to repulse the incursions of his groom into his wife's bedroom. Left alone with a drunken butler, she was raped, lost her reason and was put away; the case against her was never fully resolved.

ARDCARNE: **Church of Ireland**
Georgian Gothic church overlooking Rockingham, extended by a single transept orientated on a pulpit repositioned in accordance to Non-Conformist ritual—an ingenious solution to accommodate the toffs in the nave, the *hoi polloi* in the new transepts. Highly coloured unsigned Evangelist window above the altar. Three adjoining windows by Child, including a Resurrection of 1911 and an Evie Hone in the transept of 1935.

ATHLEAGUE: **Catholic Church**
Late Gothic Revival church with chancel remodelled in an Arts and Crafts idiom, enlivened by dismantled portico; architect unknown.

BALLAGHADEREEN: **Catholic Cathedral**
George Goldie was an unexpected choice of architect and equally unexpected was the conventional result: the nave and aisles, reduced choir and side chapels are well proportioned but unmemorable (1860). Western tower and spire by W.H. Byrne. High altar carved by H. Lane. Fittings reasonably intact. Baptismal font (1865) in memory of Viscount Dillon reveals clearly Goldie's ability. Stained glass by Earley and Meyer apart from east window in the style of Wailes.

BALLAGHADEREEN: **Convent of the Sisters of Charity**
Earlier complex extended in his characteristic Gothic Revival idiom by J.J. O'Callaghan; built in 1876 with chapel, belfry and nun's accommodation interconnecting. The chapel is saved from the mundane by its forcefully carved stone capitals. The first Irish home of Mother Morrogh-Bernard, great-aunt of the President, Mary Robinson.

BALLAGHADEREEN: **Edmondstown**
Such is the sense of propriety conveyed by High Victorian Gothic, that the fantasy of a local

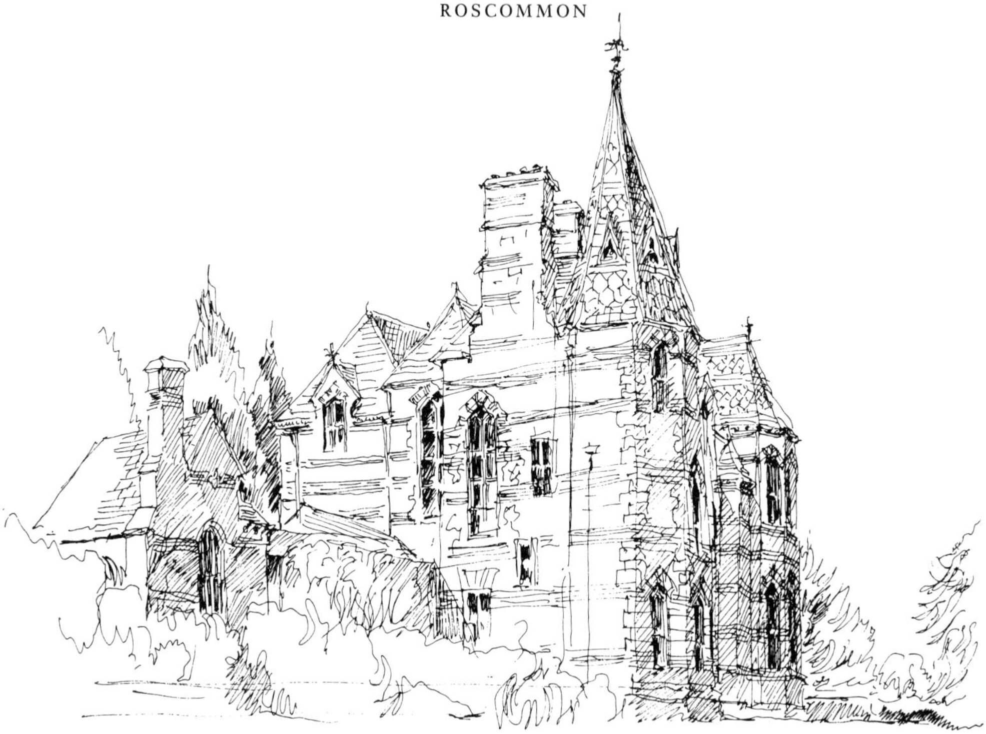

chancer should today make such an appropriate residence for an Irish bishop. The chancer was Robert Costelloe, a minor Irish squireen. He had married a rich English wife, whom he told that one had to have a grand house on one's own estate to acquire a title. Their architect was John McCurdy (soon to design Dublin's most fashionable hotel, the Shelbourne: q.v.). McCurdy ten years before had claimed the credit for Benjamin Woodward's Museum Building in Trinity. Now that Woodward was dead, McCurdy must have felt it safe in remote Roscommon to assume his identity. All Woodward motifs are used but without complete mastery. The pin-wheel plan is not stabilized by the octagonal corner tower, that besides has to hold its own against an adjoining crush of dormers. The expression of the split-level plan in the treatment of the elevations is dissonant, used without subtlety; the bands of brick and stone alternate monotonously. Where McCurdy is at his least affected, in the coachhouse, he rises closest to the level of his rival.

Work started in in 1864, but stopped when Mrs Costelloe (still Mrs) got fed up and returned to England. To complete the house, her husband had to borrow from the O'Conors, and tried in the end to sell it on to the McDermots, Princes of Coolavin. Eventually the house and avenue were sold off to the Catholic Church as a residence for the bishops of Achonry. Joshua Clarke was called in to decorate the entrance hall and screen off a more sumptuously decorated staircase hall. The entrance hall had an appropriate Celtic Revival ceiling, but those permitted beyond look up to frescoes of the four evangelists, a foretaste of an audience in the Vatican. Drawings exhibited in the RHA now lost.

BALLANGARE
Small castellated farmyard—all that has escaped destruction from the Irish Land Commission after they confiscated the estate owned by the O'Conors since the times of their high-kingship.

BALLYFARNAN: **Kilronan Castle**
There are today three ruined castles here—the farmyard transformed by corner towers to be an eye-catcher in the demesne, the Early Gothic Revival castle overlooking Lough Meelagh, and the Late Gothic Revival castle built across the front of it half a century later. Each castle is associated with a different family—the farmyard with the original owners, the MacDermot Roes, the patrons of Carolan, who lost most of their estates to the Tenisons; the Tenisons then rebuilt their Georgian house as a castle *c.*1820; and inherited through marriage by the earls of Kingston, the 8th earl built the bombastic addition to compensate for the loss of his inheritance after his family had refused to accept his legitimacy.

Even as a ruin, there is a telling contrast between the Early Gothic Revival and the Late. The earlier, by an unknown architect, is cool and formal, relying for its effects on subtle interplay of levels and controlled vistas. The entry was through a domed rotunda ingeniously contrived beneath the half-landing of an im-

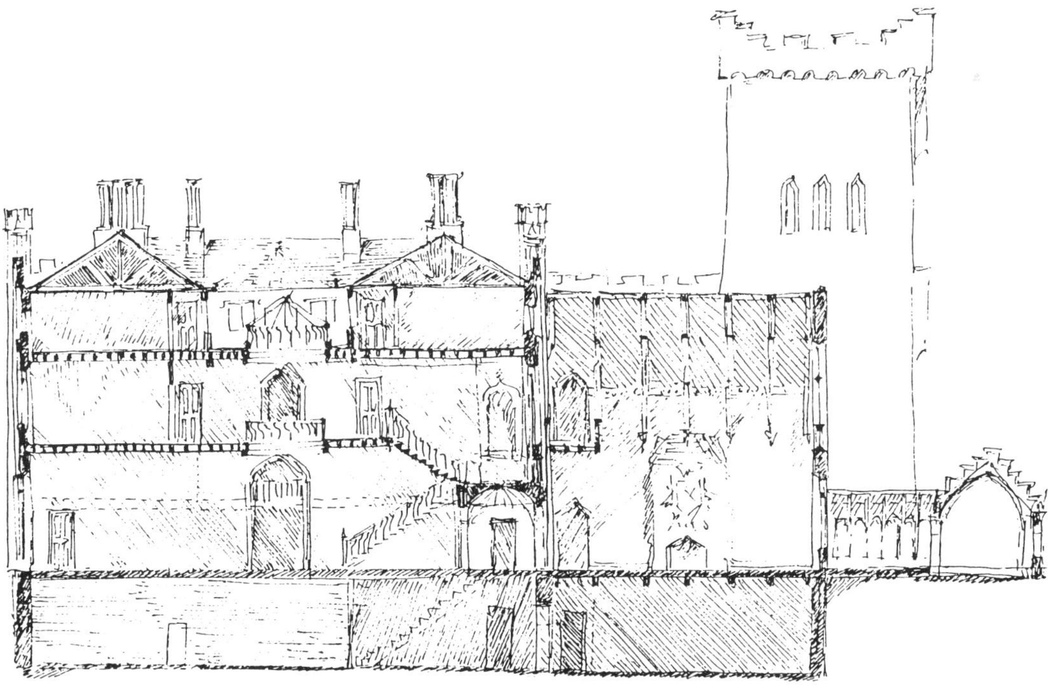

perial staircase that starts with twin flights relegated to the walls to keep clear the axial view; three floors high on one side, four floors on the other. Were it not an abruptly projecting kitchen wing, this would have been a pure Palladian villa set into the Irish countryside, but clad in a Gothic mantle.

Then Thomas Newenham Deane was called in *c.*1873 after Florence Tenison had married her penniless cousin, the 8th earl of Kingston. Deane's brief was to add very little accommodation (a great hall and drawingroom), but to make the most striking impact on every visitor. The new entry range is dominated by an immense flag tower so as to show off the earl's standard for miles around. Then one is greeted by a long, low, curved *porte-cochère* to dry one out before entering the galleried great hall and being confronted with a double-height chimneypiece holding up the Kingston coat of arms in all its splendour.

Unlike Mitchelstown Castle, which this great hall was built to rival, Kilronan survived the troubles but, after being occupied by the Irish Army, was acquired by the state forestry and ultimately abandoned to the elements. Designs for fireplace in hall by T.N. Deane in NGI.

BALLYFARNAN: Keadue Catholic Church

Gothic Revival church by J.J. McCarthy during the 1860s. The satisfying proportions of the interior survive but not the original fittings; they have been replaced by Druidic furnishings in a sugary setting of pink and white.

CASTLEREA: Bank of Ireland

On the corner of Market Square, in accomplished Hiberno-Romanesque. Symmetrical façade. Rose window on side elevation. Possibly by William Caldbeck.

CASTLEREA: Catholic Church

Norman revival with a quirky open roof, entirely illuminated by ugly but early stained glass. Designed by George Goldie. Elaborate high altar by unknown architect dates from 1899.

CASTLEREA: Clonalis

The ancestral seat of the O'Conor Don, the only Celtic chieftains to be recognized by the Anglo-Normans as kings in their own right. After the early death of his wife in 1872, Charles Owen O'Conor Don MP decided that the early Georgian house beside the River Suck was unhealthy and commissioned a replacement on higher ground set in formal gardens surrounded by conifers. His architect, F. Pepys Cockerell, had just built Bithan in Buckinghamshire for the Perrys, O'Conor's English cousins. Work started in 1878 and was stopped in 1880, two-thirds complete. The idiom is predominately Italianate, restlessly articulated in the High Victorian manner but with the minimal deployment of Classical orders. The result is that despite the curious amalgamations (such as the open-arcaded central chimney-stack recalling Vanbrugh alongside Swiss-chalet-type dormers), in this most *nouveau riche* of styles, there is no sense of *nouveau riche*. Nor is there any trace of nostalgia for the Celtic past. Instead,

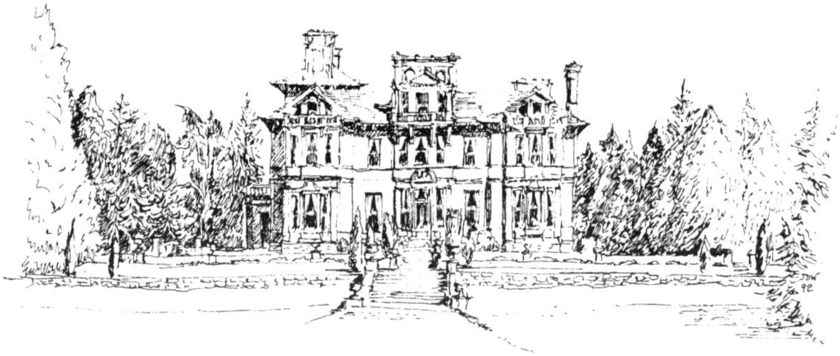

the values expressed are those of an efficient far-sighted Liberal MP, indistinguishable from his Home Counties counterparts. The latest technology is used in services and the structure—Clonalis—is the first major house in Ireland to be built in concrete. The shuttering is still stored in the yard.

The internal layout reflects the exterior with the three principal reception rooms along the garden front taking precedence over the parallel sequence of circulating spaces at the rear. There is a deceptive predictability until one realizes that every room is of a different size, and that only the diningroom is symmetrical. The main staircase is on the axis of the entrance door, but set at right angles to the porch and screened by arcades from direct approach; this allows the bolection fireplace framed between Ionic columns of Mallow marble to dominate the principal axis of the hall in the only instance of the monumental. The drawingroom re-uses Georgian fireplaces from the old house; those of the library and diningroom are flanked by recesses for turf and wood, as in Blessingbourne (q.v.).

That these spacious high-ceilinged rooms, occasionally illuminated by the elusive Connacht sunlight, still contain all their family treasures surveyed by ancestral portraits is entirely due to the determination of the present owners, the nephew of the previous O'Conor Don, Pyers O'Conor Nash, and his wife Marguerite, who have fought a long campaign against the new penal laws of spiralling death duties, smiting not rival tribesmen but faceless beaurocrats with unrecorded wounds. Open to the public in the summer and to Hidden Ireland, May to September.

FAIRYMOUNT: **Catholic Church**

Deceptively simple, rural, Late Gothic Revival church set high above the boglands. Nicely turned stone buttresses are rhythmically linked to stone-roofed lean-to confessionals. Twin entrances flank a bifurcating staircase to an organ gallery lit by two Michael Healy windows of 1911 (the only ones in the church to survive mutilation). Only the central figures survive of the 1908 Michael Healy window and the 1922 McGoldrick in the polygonal chancel.

FRENCHPARK: **Breedogue Catholic Church**

Forceful urban Gothic, somewhat perversely sited on Irish rural crossroads; saddlebacked

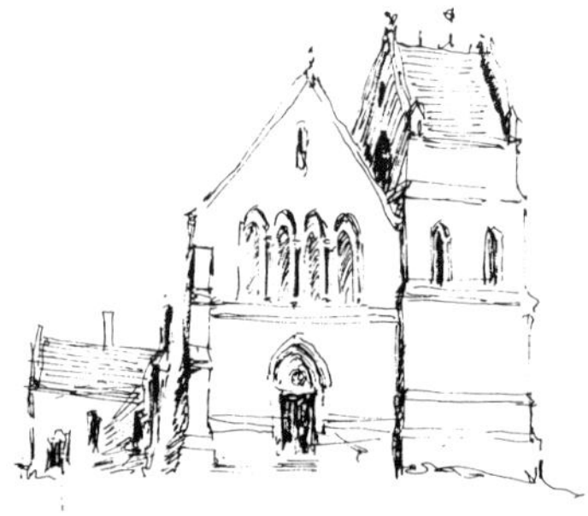

tower serving as porch, nave leading to apsidal chancel, between single lean-to aisle on one side, sacristy on the other, *c.*1860. Architect, possibly George Goldie.

MOORE: **Catholic Church**

Modest Romanesque village church, with detached round tower decorated with lively carvings in early concrete, dated 1910; architect, William Scott.

ROSCOMMON: **The Abbey**

Georgian home of the Gunning sisters remodelled as a neo-Classical villa and then as a miniature Gothic castle, a minor variant of Mount Talbot (q.v.). Garden likewise transformed with delicately battlemented towers to offset the ruins of the medieval abbey. Apsidally

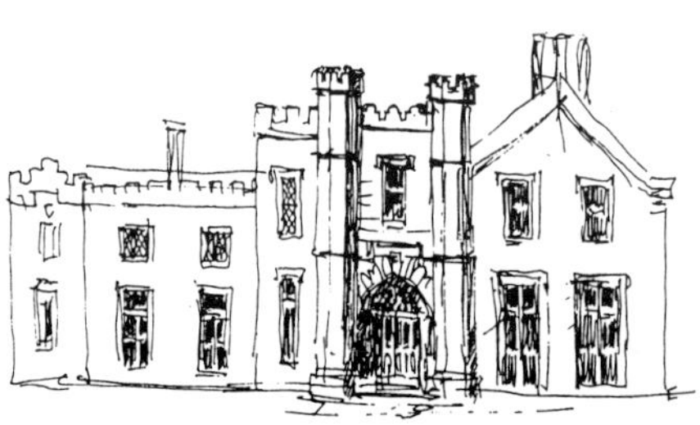

recessed doorway flanked by pinnacled niches. Imperial staircase lit by Gothic window with heraldic emblems of the Burkes. Possibly by the obscure local Gothic Revivalist, Richard Richards. Now extended as a nightclub and hotel.

ROSCOMMON: Convent of Mercy
This attractive Puginian complex has survived interminable additions, the loss of a belltower and the subdivision of the chapel; the lower part of this is now a series of common rooms, the upper part an attic revealing the original gilding and frescoed angels by William Brett (1924). The original building, with its distinctive triangular-headed windows, dates from 1854. The architect was John Neville of Dundalk. Alterations by Doolin (1899) happily remained largely unexecuted.

ROSCOMMON: Donamon Castle
There has been a fortress here since earliest times guarding a ford over the River Suck, held by the O'Finaghties; but they were supplanted by the MacDavid Burkes, who in 1400 built the present keep, remodelled in the 17th century by the Caulfields, who had been given the confiscated estates. St George Caulfield extended the castle in 1855. His architect is unknown, but may have been Richard Richards from Roscommon. His new wing carries on the cas-

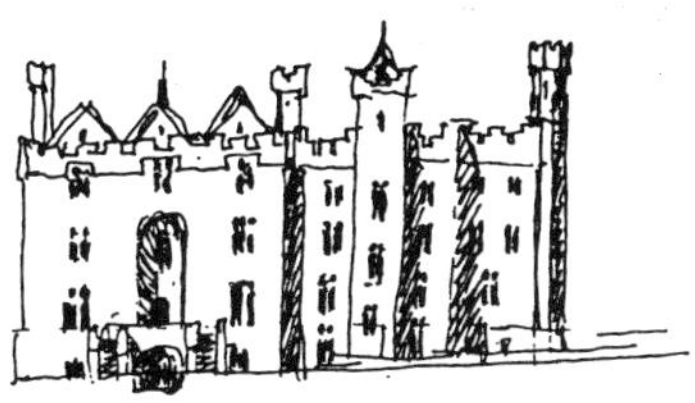

tellations of the original, interrupted by two higher staircase towers and a corner turret. This would have been even more successful, if he had been content to leave the original alone. But he abolished the *piano nobile*, removed the fake machicolations, and changed the windows. However, he retained the Early Gothic Revival interiors. Abandoned in 1920 by the last of the Caulfields, who died almost penniless in London. Saved from demolition in 1939 by the Divine Word Missionaries to serve as their western European outpost.

ROSCOMMON: Donamon Church of Ireland
Gothic Revival church, *c.*1850, designed by Joseph Welland for this remote wooded setting and following his most tried-out formula with chunky bellcote and spreading buttresses. The drawings held in the RCB date from 1852. Austere interior contains memorials to the Caulfield family of Donamon Castle.

ROSCOMMON: Gilhooly Memorial Catholic Church
One of the most important and best preserved commissions of Walter Doolin, started in 1899, and competed during the 1920s long after his death but in sympathy with his ideals. The grim rock-faced ashlar exterior dominates asphalt car parks. An over-elaborated posthumous spire by O'Callaghan and Webb (1914) ill accords with the Salviati mosaics above the principal doorway and the mosaic portraits of the parish priest, Monsignor Gilhooly, and chief donor. All this should not deter us from entering the interior, a resplendent synthesis of the arts, stained glass, sculpture, wought ironwork, mosaics and frescoes, still intact even to the multicoloured marbled pinnacled pulpit and a delicate wrought-iron rood screen (by McGloughlins). All this is firmly held in place by the architecture with its arcades screening in the Irish manner subtly varied transepts that include a rose window almost as large as the rose window of Maynooth Chapel (also donated by Monsignor Gilhooly).

ROSCOMMON: The Station
Elegant neo-Elizabethan with curvilinear gables and traceried cast-iron brackets.

TULSK: Catholic Church
Gothic Revival. Cruciform in shape with altar in columned recess. Stained glass by Earley. Also a four-light window by Child (1914) on the life of Christ.

TULSK: Taaffe Mausoleum
Brutalistic Gothic sepulchre (1874)—a truncated pyramid resting on a continuous frieze of quatrefoils broken by the gabled entrance door. It adjoins a more conventional Gothic stone vaulted funeral chapel built by the Graces in 1867.

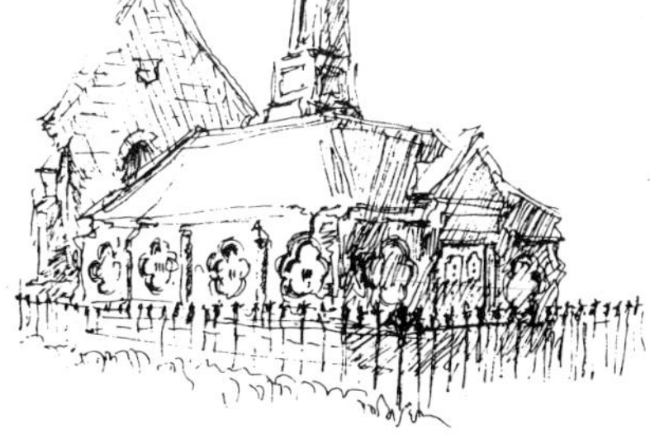

SLIGO

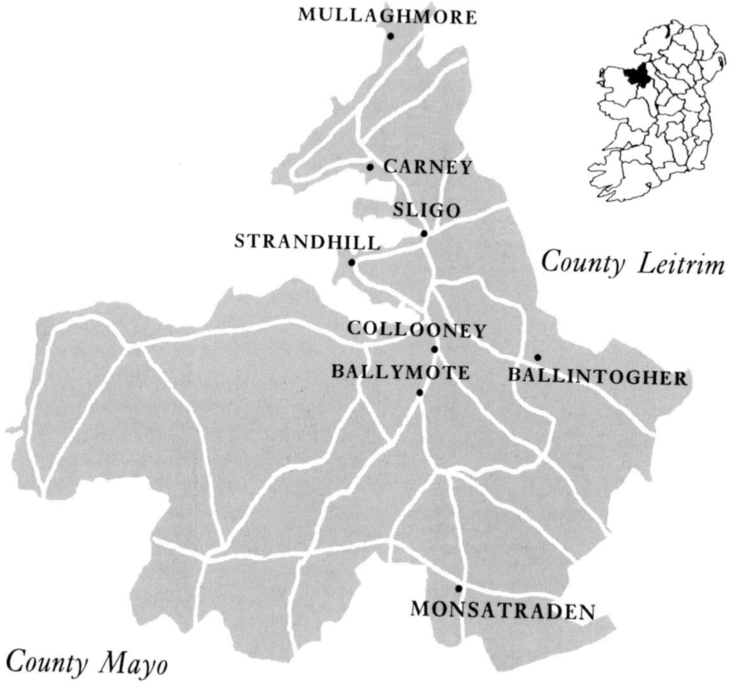

BALLYMOTE: **Catholic Church**
Handsome neo-Gothic church by George Goldie begun in 1857 and completed in 1861 (apart from the later spire).

BALLYMOTE: **Temple House**
An Italianate palazzo, as conceived by a self-made Hong Kong millionaire who was able to buy back the family estate in Ireland and commission a fashionable Bond Street firm. The firm were the decorators, Johnstone and Jeannes, and this their only important architectural commission recorded. Their drawings of 1863 (still in the house) were faithfully

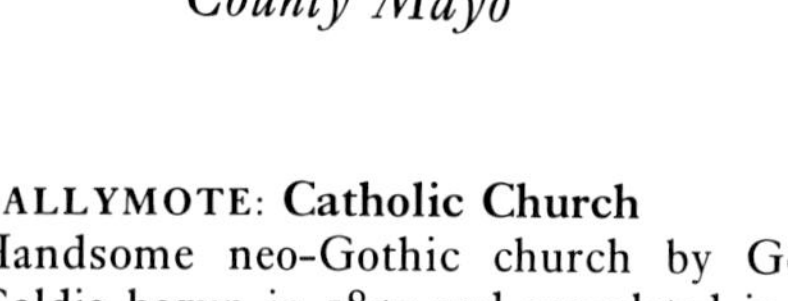

executed after their initial plans were rejected as not being large enough by the client, Alexander Perceval. Their problem was how to add to the earlier house built by the Percevals in the 1820s and therefore too large and too new to demolish. So the new range was built at right angles on a grander scale, centred on a *porte-cochère*. The entrance hall is linked asymmetrically with a magnificent arcaded staircase hall remodelled within the earlier house. The original front hall has been knocked into the drawingroom, and the original portico transformed into a bay window. The result is that grandeur is tempered by the unexpected sequence of interiors, and the passage of time. The damask green of the drawingroom is now an ivory that is more beautiful. The gilded pelmets blend better with the drapes, once yellow, now amber. The room also is now less cluttered, having been crammed with what a Sotheby's oriental expert called the largest collection of Chinese 19th-century fakes in the world. The diningroom furniture is reassuringly occidental with its massive sideboard upheld by well-fed *putti.* Here hangs the portrait of Alexander Perceval who died only two years after his return from China.

But the estate is still owned by his descendants. The present Alexander Perceval and his wife (a descendant of Herschel whose portrait by Julia Margaret Cameron is in a downstairs passage), have turned five of their ninety rooms into guest bedrooms for Hidden Ireland. One of their first decisions was to repair the *porte-cochère*, which had been propped up with fir trees. The trees were discovered to be dangerous, the *porte-cochère* to be perfectly sound.

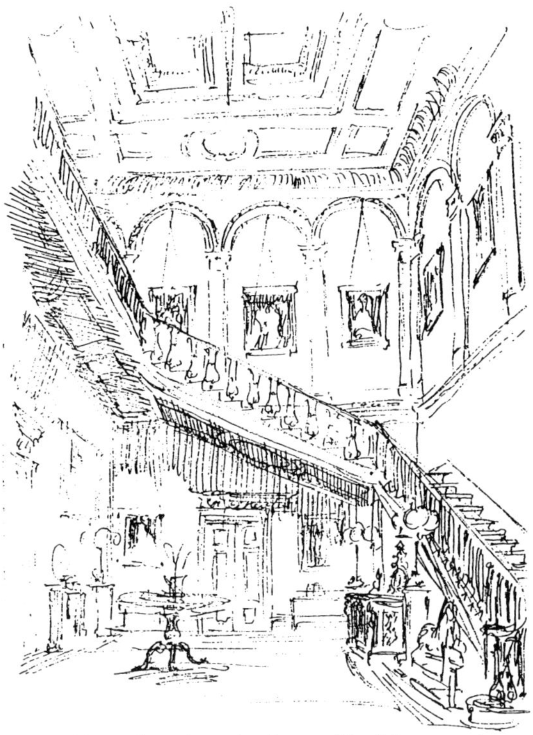

Formal gardens, landscaped by Niven to give vistas of the ruins of the Templars' castle and the lake.

BALLINTOGHER: Ballysumaghan Church of Ireland
Cruciform stone church built in the 1830s by the Neynoes at the gates of their elegant (but now derelict) Regency Gothic castle. Classed as redundant but reprieved after restoration by three local families, who at the cost of £16,000 have saved it from dereliction.

BALLINTOGHER: Church of Ireland
Typical Welland church, *c.*1850, carefully converted into a private house.

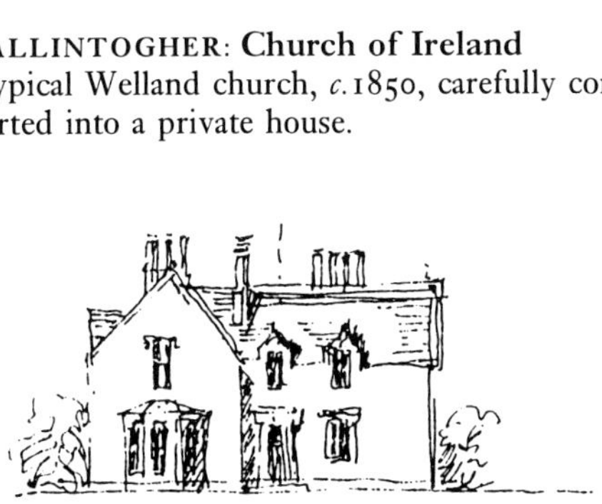

CARNEY, Lisadell: The Rectory
Asymmetrical Tudor-Revival villa dominated by elongated chimneystacks and entered through an unexpected Egyptian doorcase. This would suggest the involvement of Francis Goodwin, architect of the main house of Lisadell nearby.

COLLOONEY: Annaghmore
The commission to rebuild this Regency house, designed *c.*1820 by William Farrell, was, according to J.F. Fuller, the start of his independent career. His client was C.W. O'Hara, whose position as head of one of the longest recorded families in Europe must have appealed to Fuller, who devoted so much space in his autobiography *Ad Omniana* to genealogy and so little to architecture. Fuller's work was to prove characteristic of his career—a cavalier remodelling of the original house to harmonize with his own bluff self-confident Italianate, his new wing sporting a curved bay contrasting to a polygonal one at the other end. Twenty years ago, this wing was mainly demolished and today only Fuller's drawingroom remains intact with its gilded plasterwork. Earlier Tudor-style stable block by an unknown architect.

COLLOONEY: Camphill
Georgian home of the Lyons family but with drawingroom redecorated to welcome the Italian bride of the son of the house in 1880; dark, richly marbleized, and cluttered with ornaments.

COLLOONEY: Catholic Church
Sir John Benson, the architect of the 1852 Dublin exhibition, was born here and educated as an engineer by Edward Cooper of Markree Castle (q.v.). He returned to his native village to design the Catholic church in the 1850s, and after the destruction of his Dominican Church in Sligo and his countryhouse, Lisheen (q.v.), this is now his only commission still intact in his native country. Benson's Gothic is competent rather than inspired, but here he benefits from the influence of Pugin with the symmetrical composition of the east end. The chancel gable, flanked the smaller separate gables of the side chapels, contrasts with the asymmetry of the corner tower and spire that dominates the town—in the words of a contemporary, a sermon in stone uplifting us to heaven. Plaster vaulted interior made trivial by mosaics. Glass by Mayer.

COLLOONEY: Markree Castle Hotel
Georgian house remodelled and extended for Joshua Cooper by Francis Johnston in a cool geometic Gothick. This failed to live up to the romantic fantasies of the astronomer Edward Joshua Cooper, who on his inheritance transformed the castle into a formidable feudal pile dominated by a battered keep built to repel savage onslaughts over the centuries. Instead it has miraculously outlasted a divided inheritance, long periods of closure, civil unrest (when inherited by Bryan Cooper, the only Unionist

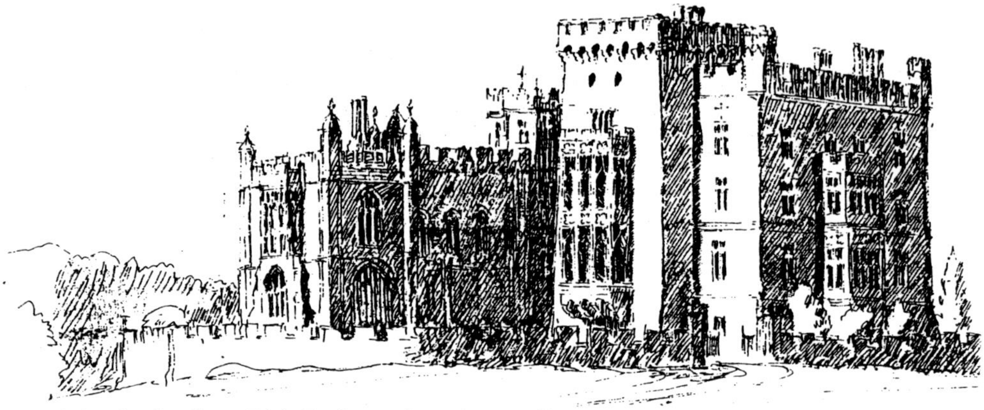

to sit in the Southern Irish Parliament), and a fake fire when filming J.G. Farrell's *Troubles*. Miraculously restored as the only castle hotel in Ireland still owned by the original family.

The *Dublin Builder* illustrated Markree in 1863, the year the astronomer died, complete apart from the billiard room above the *porte-cochère* and the adjoining chapel on a raised

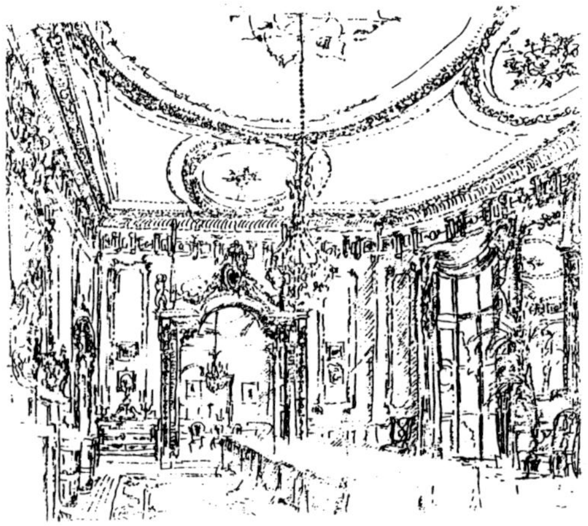

crypt. These were added by Col. E.H. Cooper to the designs of Wardrop of Edinburgh, who added the swaggering staircase that links the drawingroom to the garden. All these additions are correctly Gothic. But the architects who worked for Edward Joshua Cooper are more difficult to identify, apart from Francis Goodwin, who designed the Dublin gates of the estate. Goodwin died before he could proceed with the house, but may well have recommended Joseph Gwilt, remembered today only for his architectural encyclopedia but credited with Markree in his obituary.

The skill in which Johnston's symmetrical plan is turned into an asymmetrical sequence with a dramatic exploitation of the cross axis reveals many parallels with Goodwin's Lisadell. Both interiors are centred on a top-lit inner hall, but whereas Lisadell is austerely Greek, Markree reveals an astonishing diversity—neo-Classical in the library, famboyant Gothic in the circulation spaces, dominated by an imperial staircase sweeping up beneath a stained-glass window depicting early Coopers flanked by only the more significant Tudor monarchs. The neo-Baroque triple drawingrooms, with well-fed gilded putti upholding lapis lazuli cartouches, recall the Paris of Napoleon III. Cooper himself acquired Rococo stalls for his chapel, presented by his daughters to Tuam Cathedral. His protegé in the village was the architect and engineer Sir John Benson, also credited with Markree (in his obituary). It is tempting to see the input of Benson in the concrete vaulting of the bedrooms that held the castle together and preserved the opulence of the interiors below for posterity. However, the Church of England has expurgated the couplet written by Mrs Alexander, inspired by Markree: 'The rich man in his castle; the poor man at his gate.'

COLLOONEY: Teeling Memorial

The most effective of the centennial memorials commemorating 1798. Possibly by William Hague, who would have been engaged on Sligo

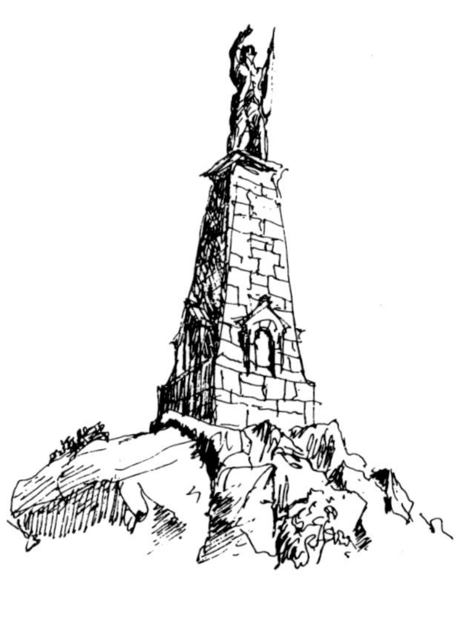

Townhall, where the truncated belfry resembles the pedestal for the statue of Teeling, portrayed at the moment of unfurling his standard.

MONASTRADEN: **Catholic Church**
Gothic Revival village church built in 1883 by O'Neill and Byrne, distinguished by its subtle external polychromy. Puginian interior with exposed trusses upholding steeply raked roof.

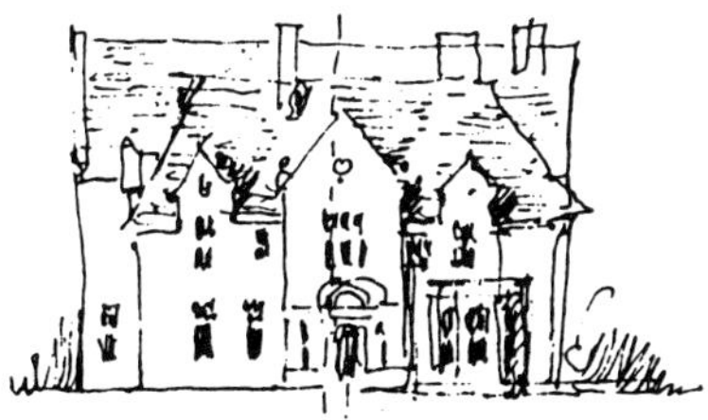

MONASTRADEN: **Coolavin**
The Prince McDermot of Coolavin commissioned (*c.*1898) J.F. Fuller to build him a dour Scottish Baronial retreat beside his ancestral Lough Gara. The two-storey entry block is almost completely taken up by a vestibule leading to a staircase hall framed by chubby columns. Behind a three-storey range connects to the service block beyond. Woodward achieved magical results with this formula at Browns Barn (q.v.). The house is of historical rather than architectural significance.

MULLAGHMORE: **Classiebawn Castle**
Formidable Baronial retreat commissioned by the Hon. Cowper Temple, son of the Victorian statesman Lord Palmerston, who hated Gothic. Built in 1875 on a windswept peninsular jutting out into the Atlantic with panoramic views of the South Donegal and North Sligo mountains. His architect, Rawson Carroll, designed a simple gabled range of local sandstone dominated by a square tower juxtaposed against a conical turret. Entry beneath carved coat of arms, and upstairs to the reception rooms over elevated basement. Close to where Lord Mountbatten and others were assasssinated by the IRA in the 1970s.

SLIGO: **Allied Irish Bank**
Formerly the Provincial Bank. A neo-Elizabethan cube four bays wide, of Mountcharles sandstone, elaborately carved; designed in 1877 by T.M. Deane. The bank of the county establishment in the Victorian era.

SLIGO: **Former National Bank, Grattan Street**
A vigorous neo-Palladian design dominating a street that has otherwise managed to retain its late 18th-century character. The banking hall is expressed by a spectacular semi-circular glazed arch. This carries two floors of offices above, subdivided by Ionic pilasters into four bays, so that the central pilaster rests on the keystones of the arch. The bays at each end serve as abutments, although they are pierced by twin entrances sheltered by corbelled segmental pediments. Carving equally powerful. Architect, Ralph Byrne (1918).

SLIGO: **Bank of Ireland, Stephen Street**
Uninspired palazzo by Millar in the manner of Symes, 1891.

SLIGO: **Catholic Cathedral**
Commissioned from George Goldie by the formidable Bishop Gilhooly in 1867, the cathedral was appropriately dedicated to the Immaculate Conception seven years later. The style chosen was a Germanic Romanesque; the exterior (of Ballisodare limestone that shows no sign of mellowing) is harsh and unlovable. Only the incisive articulation of its components, western tower clasped by staircase turrets, aisleless transepts linked to detached chapterhouse, apsidal chancel with projecting lady chapel, prepare one for the intelligence of the interior. Goldie solved the problem of vast crowds by introducing galleries and boldly carrying them across the transepts (two years before Pearson's St Augustine's, Kilburn). With seating for 4,000, no other Irish cathedral is as capacious and compact. But the nave galleries do not project into the body of the church following the Non-Conformist practice so disliked by the Ecclesiologists; instead they are housed in tribunes. These, with the sexpartite vaulting overhead, waft all who enter to beside the Rhine. The sixty-seven stained glass windows by Lobin of Tours are on the contrary aggressively French. The high altar, beneath a baldachino with its columns of Aberdeen granite, is designed by Goldie himself (an Englishman). The Lady chapel is dominated by an alabaster statue of the Virgin by an Italian, Benzoni. So that there is nothing of value here that is Irish, or suggests the impending Celtic Revival that would reverberate the name of Sligo across the world. That is why this cathedral, despite its qualities, has been relegated to obscurity.

SLIGO: **Convent of Mercy**
Large complex extending out from the original foundation of 1846. The best addition architecturally is that of Goldie in 1862. The chapel was rebuilt by an unknown architect in 1899.

SLIGO: **The Courthouse**
The finest Gothic Revival courthouse in Ireland, and the only one comparable to the neo-

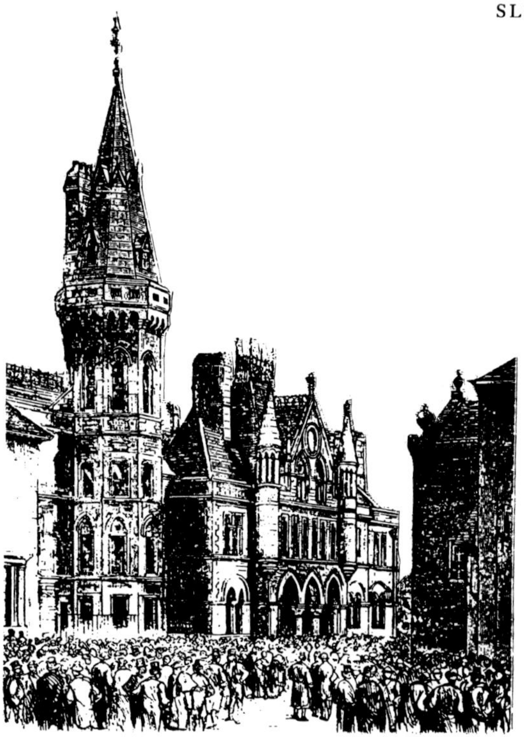

Classical masterpieces of the previous generation. Built in 1878 at the cost of £17,500. Its architect, Rawson Carroll, successfully related the design to the existing streetscape and sloping site—breaking the building up into separate components pivotting out from an asymmetrical octagonal tower, dramatized by a massive chimney-stack rising through its dormered spire. The entry block is symmetrical in itself, an imposing flight of steps mounting up to a triple arcade with a gabled superstructure above, flanked by a pair of jolly corner turrets. The grandest interior is the top-lit galleried central hall. The two courtrooms beyond are remarkably intact and retain all their fittings, whether through devotion or apathy is a question on which one can still speculate as long as one does not penetrate too far into the nether regions. Across the street, the sign of solicitors, Argue and Phibbs.

SLIGO: **Dominican Church**
Sir John Benson's church and monastery dates from 1845, but this was destroyed by fire *c.* 1970. Only the east end and its stained glass window by Michael Healy (1911) have been surrealistically preserved in the rebuilding.

SLIGO: **Douglas Hyde Bridge**
The main bridge in Sligo designed by Sir John Benson, built 1848-52 and dedicated originally to Queen Victoria.

SLIGO: **Gillooly Memorial Hall**
Built after his death in 1895 to commemorate Bishop Gillooly and his crusade against alcohol; architect, P.J. Kilgallen. Exterior memorable only for the statue of the bishop depicted in the act of denunciation: 'Ireland sober is Ireland free.' Interior with an assembly hall, billiard rooms and library, relies on polished mahogany and leaded glass, so that today it is indistinguishable from all those neo-Victorian pubs reborn to nurture the demon, drink.

SLIGO: **Library, Art Gallery and Museum**
Originally a Gothic Revival Congregationalist church, built for Andrew Mayburn by Lanyon, Lynn and Lanyon in 1851, this has been resourcefully converted in 1954. The church itself is now the library, the schoolrooms the art gallery, and the manse of 1867 the museum.

SLIGO: **Mental Hospital**
One of the last of the series of lunatic asylums commissioned from Irish architects after the Famine to revive the economy. The architect was W.D. Butler, who chose an Elizabethan idiom as more adaptable and more humane than the expected Gothic. In these aims Butler was hardly more successful than his gifted pupil, J.S. Mulvany, at Mullingar. Morevoer, he encountered so many difficulties that the job took twelve years and was handed over to Deane and Woodward, who appear to have made at first only minimal alterations to the design. In 1877 the Deanes added two further wings flanked by stunted towers to increase the accommodation. T.M. Deane built a new chapel *c.* 1905 in a robust Flemish Renaissance. All this results in a building far more lively and authentic than the arid symmetrical institution as revealed by Butler's drawings (recently come to light), and as such deserves retention. After closure and talk of demolition, the hospital is currently up for sale.

SLIGO: **Model School**
One of the best buildings by James Owen for the Board of Works *c.* 1855, well sited above a series of graded terraces to overlook the Mall. The master residence and ancillary accommodation on one side of two stories, and the single-storied schoolrooms on the other are tied together by continuous channelling, string courses, cornices and roofing. The style is Italianate but handled with an unexpected freedom—the arcaded loggia of the residence nicely balanced by the coupled arched windows of the classrooms. The material is a dark-grey limestone with Mountcharles sandstone dressings as a light relief. The school provided the best education in 18th-century Sligo to all denominations. Empty for a long time, but now an art gallery and exhibition centre.

SLIGO: St John's Church of Ireland
This Georgian cathedral by Castle, much modified, contains Victorian glass (by Mayer) and fittings (1890). Reredos by Percy Gethin (1912). Window by Child (1927).

SLIGO: St Mary's Presbytery
Commissioned by Bishop Gillooly and built in 1878-80 as a residence for both himself and his assistant clergy, this is an austere three-storied limestone cube, only slightly relieved by a projecting bay. One of the last works of the cathedral architect, George Goldie, assisted by P.J. Kilgallen.

SLIGO: Summerhill College
The final building venture of Bishop Gillooly, overlooking his residence and cathedral and completed in 1878-80, apparently to his own design, but realized by his engineer, P.J. Kilgallen. The result is an impressive but complacent Romanesque, that could have been built forty years before. Three floors over basement, with galleried tower adjoining bay-windowed oratory.

SLIGO: The Station
Built *c.*1850 and designed by J.S. Mulvany; the original roof was burned out during the civil war. The station offices were also rebuilt in the 1920s. The most spectacular architecture to survive is the massive windowless retaining walls, articulated by battered pilasters with a sense of the colossal.

SLIGO: Ulster Bank
The most palatial of Sligo's banks, prominently sited at Hyde Bridge, was inaugurated in 1970. One of the last works of the Glasgow/Belfast architect James Hamilton. Of two floors, the lower articulated by the Tuscan order, the upper by the Corinthian. Front elevation of five bays with coupled columns, side elevation of five bays also but with single columns between them. Balustrading above interrupted by a weighty clock surround to denote the entrance. Stone quarried in Glasgow. Receiving his Nobel Prize in Stockholm, W.B. Yeats was reminded by the Royal Palace there of this Sligo palazzo which had impressed him forty years before.

SLIGO: The Townhall
William Hague was the architect commissioned in 1865 to design this remote example of Victorian civic self-confidence; it was opened nine years later. Hague deployed the standard townhall formula—offices to the front, an upper floor assembly hall at the rear with a top-lit staircase between them that eventually leads to the council chamber above the entrance. But his

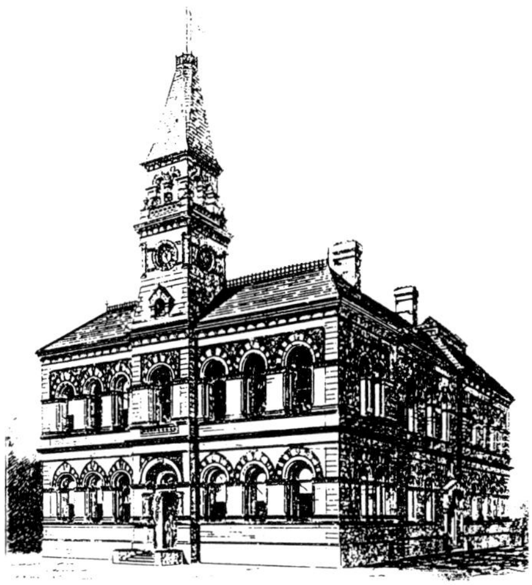

work is well-scaled and harmoniously proportioned (inspired by Benjamin Woodward although without his tension). The general style is Lombardic Romanesque with polychromatic voussoirs to the arched doors and windows. The symmetrical façade is dominated by a central clock tower roofed with a truncated spire. Staircase hall frescoed by Bernard McDonough *c.*1950. Assembly council room and assembly hall restored but without their original gravitas.

SLIGO: Ursuline Convent
Founded in 1850, the centre block was extended by austere round-arched wings by George Goldie; completed in 1862; the first of a series of commissions that terminated only with his death twenty years later.

SLIGO: Yeats Memorial Building
Designed as the Royal Bank *c.*1899 by the Belfast architect, Vincent Craig, brother of the first prime minister of Northern Ireland. An old English manor house rather than a bank, with tower and half-timbered gable. Donated by the Allied Irish Bank to the Yeats Society in 1973

STRANDHILL: Knockarea Church of Ireland
Small Gothic Revival church designed by Sir John Benson (1843). Neo-Elizabethan altar.

STRANDHILL: Lisheen
Imposing Italianate house designed in 1840 by Sir John Benson for William Phibbs. Adjoining symmetrical double-storey façades, the entrance centred on a recessed Ionic porch, the garden front centred on a trellised verandah. Top-lit gallery upstairs known as 'the museum' since it exhibited trophies from Egypt and Syria, said to be haunted, but this has been denied by the family half a century after the sale of the estate and the dismantling of the house. Now an ivy-clad ruin.

TIPPERARY

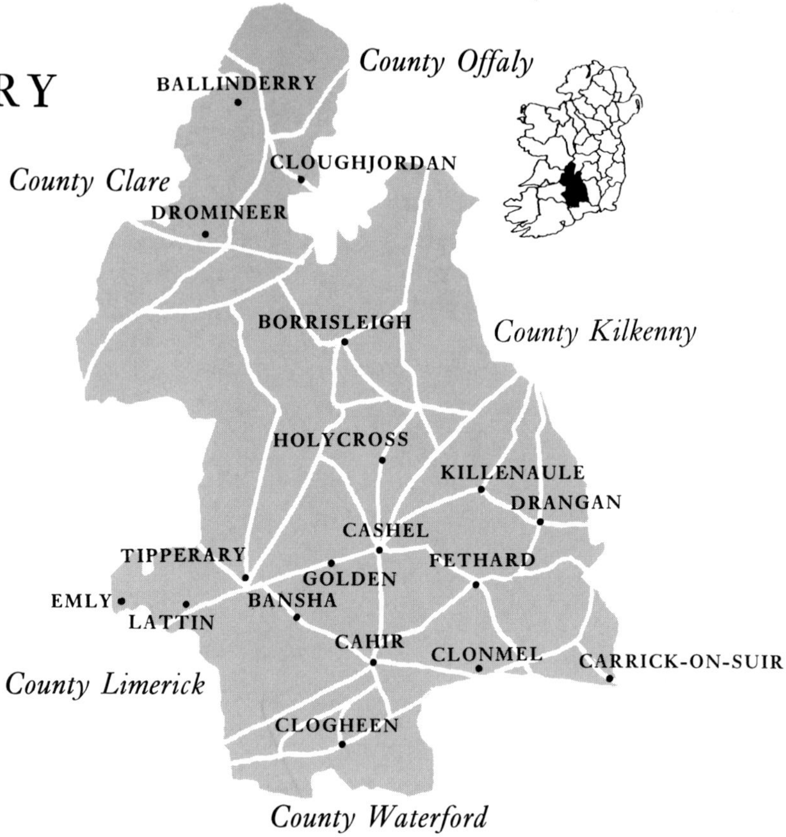

BALLINDERRY: **Gurtlougha House**
Victorian house built beside a wooded inlet of Lough Derg, more memorable for its setting than for its vaguely Italianate architecture; it has been transformed by the Wilkinsons into one of the most sought-after country-house hotel retreats. Member of Hidden Ireland. Originally symmetrical, a wing was added in the 1860s to contain the billiard room, which had to double up as a ballroom. An ingenious contraption hoisted the billiard table up above dancers, who then displayed a supreme gesture of confidence in Irish building construction. Now used as a playroom for children to recover from playing Swallows and Amazons along the shoreside.

BANSHA: **Bansha Castle**
Another Gothic folly fortress, fashioned out of an earlier Georgian House by the architect, Charles Anderson, *c.*1835 for the 'Lord Lieutenant of the County', drastically de-romanticized at the end of the last century, when it was stripped of turrets, battlements and rose windows leaving only a few blind arrow slits as evidence of its former fantasy. Demilitarization effected by the leading Victorian woman war artist, Lady Butler.

BANSHA: **Kilshane Church of Ireland**
Privately commissioned by the Lowes of Kilshane House, who are buried beneath an obelisk in the churchyard. They chose Joseph Welland, who in 1859 was just about to hand over his practice to his son Joseph. This is then more likely to be an early work of the son rather than a late work of the father. A simple cell enlivened by being entered through a corner tower with slated spire. Deconsecrated, and part of the rear wall removed to give access to combine harvesters.

BANSHA: **Kilshane House**
Neo-Classical country house, an early commission of C.F. Anderson, built from 1830 onwards for John Lowe, an austere design relieved only by a triple-bayed Ionic porch. Later Italianate interiors. Service courtyard masked by the most ambitious private conservatory to survive in Ireland, said to have been built for a consumptive daughter in accordance with the mistaken medical theories of the time. Triple-tiered lantern soars up above a central fountain, set in a decorative terrazzo flooring. A double-tiered off-shoot extends from one corner to screen the service courtyard from the approach. The only (two) exposed corners are quarter domes, which give a rippling effect when seen from the house itself. Due to the school of Richard Turner on the basis of its minimal wrought-iron curvilinear glazing bars. But there is a certain lack of clarity; the inner structure does not quite accord with the

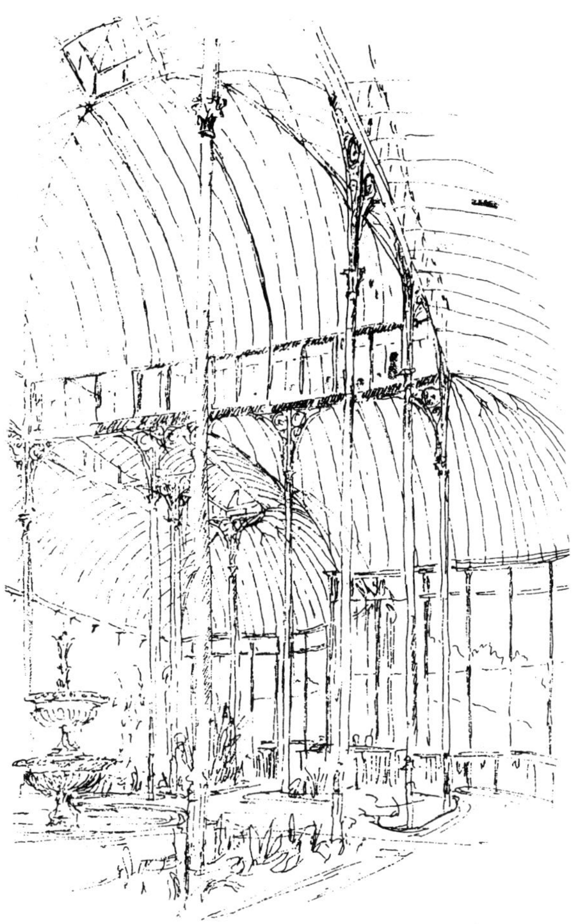

structure of the roof, and heavy timber vertical fenestration would suggest that this was a design of William Turner after his father had retired.

Now being restored by Mr and Mrs Ian Hurst, who have already dismantled accommodation for thirty staff (built last century) and a hundred missionaries (added this century) to return their house to its original dimensions.

BORRISOLEIGH: **Catholic Church**
Late Gothic Revival village church designed by W.G. Doolin in 1892. Cruciform with transepts screened by arcades and polygonal apse. A set of stained-glass windows by Joshua Clarke is eclipsed by the last of the series (dated 1922) showing the influence of Harry Clarke despite being partly blocked out by the organ gallery. Note also the four evangelists in the trefoils of the transepts.

BORRISOLEIGH: **Killoskehane Castle**
Medieval tower house extended by a Georgian range, and then recast by T.N. Deane in 1867, the keep in Scottish Baronial and the Georgian wing into something vaguely Flemish, since he retained the handsome rusticated Palladian doorcase, put stone mullions into the Georgian window openings and added dormers. The resulting mixture lacks the discipline of Woodward. Lodge by Deane at the gates.

CAHIR: **Cahir Park**
This dreary neo-Gothic pile built in 1861 by Lanyon, Lynn and Lanyon for Lady Margaret Charteris, was unlamented when it was destroyed by fire in 1961, a few weeks before it was to be opened as an hotel. Classical gates and Gothic lodge survive as evidence of Lynn's High Victorian schizophrenia.

CAHIR: **Duneske**
Country house by Sir Thomas Drew *c.*1890, or rather picturesque villa, built in yellow brick with stone dressings—asymmetrical façade terminating in a many-windowed octagon to overlook the River Suir.

CAHIR: **Rochestown**
Georgian house acquired and remodelled in 1867 by the Wise family, who commissioned T.N. Deane to add a third floor and an entrance porch that masks the earlier and more elegant Venetian doorcase. Destroyed by fire in the Civil War. Now a ruin.

CAHIR: **The Station**
Gothic Revival station designed by W.G. Murray in 1851 working for William Dargan, who was also responsible as engineer for the viaduct beside it carrying the Dublin-Cork line across the Suir.

CARRICK-ON-SUIR: **Catholic Church**
Designed in 1851 by George Ashlin as his earliest and purest essay in Italian Romanesque. Symmetrical façade with rose window set above the doorway. Detached campanile. Interior, a Roman basilica with coffered ceiling. Glass by Mayer. Organ by Telford (1883).

CASHEL: **Boherlannon Mausoleum**
Mausoleum with attached bell tower erected by Charles Bianconi in 1856 beside the family burial ground, within view of his home, Longfield. Attributed by his biographer to Bianconi himself inspired by memories of Italy. Effigy by Benzoni.

CASHEL: **Catholic Church**
Originally designed by John Roberts *c.*1790 with an austere neo-Classical galleried interior; remodelled insensitively by W.G. Doolin *c.*1890 when the highly coloured mosaic was inserted into the pediment of the façade and the chancel was likewise enlivened with a new altar and

decorations. Crude stained glass installed by Watson of Youghal. Modernized recently yet again, when a Gothick gatehouse was removed.

CASHEL: **Chez Hans**
Built as a Gothic Revival Methodist church but now a restaurant which serves food and wine with a gravity that is still religious if no longer non-alcoholic.

CASHEL: **Church of Ireland Cathedral**
The chancel of the Georgian cathedral was remodelled (1866) by William Atkins in an elaborate enamelled and gilded Italian Romanesque. However, this is the nearest that Atkins ever got to a cathedral commission, and his exquisite drawings survive, inviting comparison with those by Burges for the furnishings of Cork Cathedral, where Atkins had been an unsuccessful competitor. But here, unlike Cork, the reality does not live up to the drawings. The dimensions are too restricted; the contribution of Atkins is too deferential and lacks the dramatic impact of his rival, who would have unanswerably compensated for the loss of stylistic unity to the interior.

CASHEL: **Rockwell College**
The seat of the Roe family. Inherited by John Roe, the unwitting object of Dorothea Hebert's affections and the cause of her insanity. William Tinsley was commissioned to Gothicize the principal interiors in 1845. Acquired by Holy Ghost Fathers, who commissioned wings, a chapel and Italianate campanile from George Ashlin. Stained glass by Evie Hone.

CASHEL: **The Townhall**
Rebuilt (1866) in a diluted Romanesque by J.E. Rogers.

CLOGHEEN: **Catholic Church**
Gothic Revival church designed by J.J. McCarthy and built in 1862-4 in his austere manner. Powerful open-roof structure framing vista to reredos beneath triple lancet. Unusual Celtic Revival memorial cross at the gates.

CLONMEL: **Anner Castle**
A castle designed by C.F. Anderson *c.*1848 for the Revd Nicholas Mandeville, the nephew of the diarist Dorothea Herbert. He had married an heiress, who happened to be the daughter of John Roe, the unwitting cause of Dorothea's insanity due to unrequited love. Considering the Mandevilles (as Dorothea noted when her sister married into them) were far advanced into eccentricities and extravagance, the castle was sensible and even witty. It took twelve years to build; the executant architect was William Atkins. At the rear one part of the existing Georgian house was re-used, carefully disguised as a medieval keep; the other part became a half-octagon linked to twin octagonal towers, one of them the rector's study. Here he kept locked away the manuscript of the diary that was brought over to London during the Troubles. A few years later the castle was set on fire with the loss of all its contents by a mad gardener, who then committed suicide. Partially rebuilt by a younger brother who was his own architect and who also replanted the park before he was killed in the Second World War. His son is currently restoring the adjoining stable block, with its gateway between asymmetrical towers, one of them corbelled out in defiance of gravity.

CLONMEL: **Boer War Memorial in the Barracks**
One of the few Irish memorials to be termed Art Nouveau, erected in 1910 to the designs of R.C. Orpen in an unusual combination of stone (carved by C.W. Harrison Ltd) and bronze (modelled by Beatrice Elvery).

CLONMEL, **Carrick-on-Suir Road: Cemetery**
Gates and adjoining lodge austerely designed but rising to a snarling terracotta dragon perched on the topmost gable. Twin chapels behind it.

CLONMEL: **Church of Ireland**
Another medieval church but also much altered. Joseph Welland rebuilt the nave in 1857; his son added a north transept in 1864; pulpit (by M.J.C. Buckley, 1903) and lectern donated later. The medieval east window was filled (1903) with stained glass by Catherine O'Brien.

CLONMEL, **Fethard Road: Corporation Flats**
Grim but powerful multi-storied apartment block in brick and stone, dated 1878, with enclosed staircases and open-access balconies. Unexpectedly urban, a remodelling by a civic-minded corporation of a residential block built by the British army, since it appears to have once been within the confines of the barracks.

CLONMEL: **Franciscan Church**
The tower of the medieval friary survives and the original choir is now the north aisle. Unfortunate decisions were made to demolish the ruined nave *c.*1760 and then not to rebuild it in 1884; Walter Doolin was asked to build instead alongside the medieval choir. The result is that the new work overwhelms the old but lacks the vigour and self-confidence of the High Victorian in its own right.

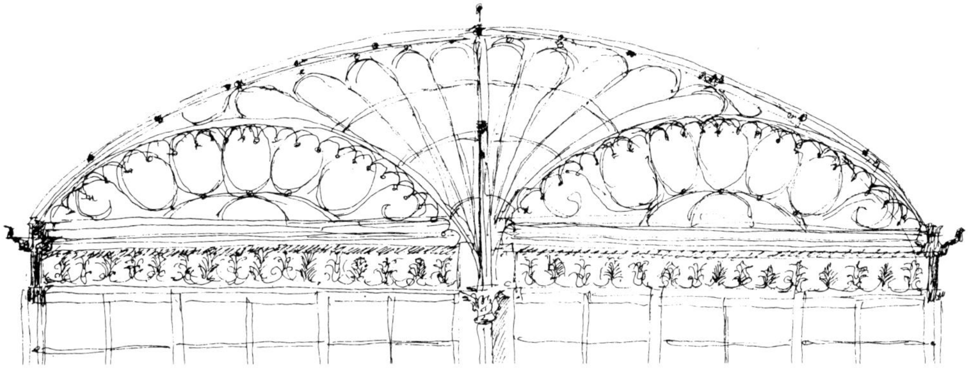

CLONMEL: **Marlfield**

The seat of the Bagwell family, now a country-house hotel. The centre block was rebuilt after have been burned out by the Republicans in the Civil War. The fire spared one of Richard Turner's most experimental curvilinear conservatories (inserted into one of the single-storied wings). The plan is conventionally rectilinear with glazed elevations impeccably supported by Ionic pilasters. But the interior is spanned by arches reinforced by pendant fringes that are gathered together in central palm-like columns. The exposed gable ends are braced by radiating fanlights. A reminder that it was as a fabricator of Dublin fanlights that Turner started his ironworks.

CLONMEL: **Loreto Convent**

An elegant Tudor Revival villa, suitably christened Roseville, built for the Murray family by William Tinsley *c.*1840. Verandah forming entry porch held between twin double-tiered bay windows, each roofed with a mini-gable. Convent since 1889.

CLONMEL: **Methodist Church**

Elegant Ionic temple designed and built by William Tinsley in 1843; the order is used *in antis* and the plain pediment is enlivened by acroteriae. No longer in religious use.

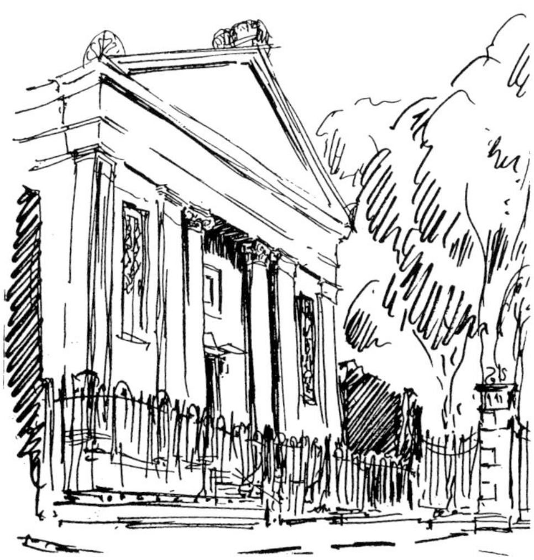

CLONMEL: **Minnella**

Neo-Classical villa built by J.S. Mulvany (*c.*1860) beside the River Suir for the Malcolmson family. Garden front of twin curved bows to view the river. Until the mid-1960s, its peeling stucco and overgrown grounds made it mysterious and remote, qualities that have not survived its transformation into an hotel and function suite.

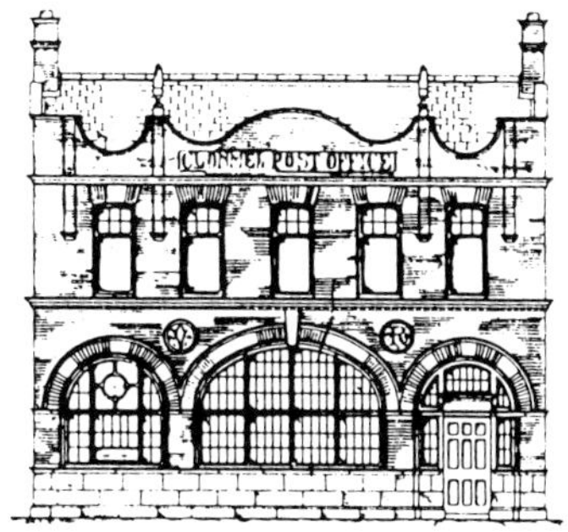

CLONMEL: **Post Office**

Accomplished example of the Flemish Revival in red brick and terracotta *c.*1905. Triple segmental arcades at ground-floor level. Upper floor of five arched windows crowned with curvilinear parapet. Architect: Edward Kavanagh.

CLONMEL: **Model Schools**

Characteristic complex in the Tudor idiom, as usual designed by Frederick Darley. The original design counterbalancing single-storied hall with double-storied classrooms is satisfying enough to warrant constant repetition. Dated 1849.

CLONMEL: **St Mary's Catholic Church**

Designed by J.B. Keane to enclose an earlier

thatched chapel that still continued in use—one reason why the church took twenty years to build. Completed after Keane's death by John Bourke, as happened in Longford Cathedral: begun four years earlier, with the same combination of portico, steeple and austere side elevations, St Mary's could be called the prototype. As at Longford, the steeple is much later (1880) and the portico later still (1890). Interior with elaborate plaster ceiling and high altar: this was completed in 1867 to the designs of George Goldie inspired by Michelangelo, and has survived 1974, the year that the rest of Catholic churches in Clonmel experienced the after-affects of the Second Vatican Council.

CLONMEL: St Peter's and Paul's Catholic Church

Designed in 1875 by J.J. O'Callaghan but not completed till 1934, by which time its second architect, George Ashlin, has long since died. The Romanesque style was an unusual choice for O'Callaghan, but not for Ashlin, whose Germanic square tower crowned with a curvilinear dome is instantly recognizable, since he deployed it elsewhere, such as Limerick and Newry. The mosaic decoration in the chancel is also characteristic of Ashlin, executed as always by Ludwig Oppenheimer of Manchester. Interior not improved during 1974, when the pulpit was dismantled and re-used to support the tabernacle. Ironically the austere and neo-Classical basilica of 1810 that O'Callaghan replaced was far closer to present-day religious sensibility.

CLONMEL: The Townhall

Georgian inn remodelled (1881) by an unknown architect in a jolly Flemish Renaissance style—central arched window breaking the eaves line and rising into pedimented gable, flanked by dormers. Statue in front (1881) commemorating the 1798 uprising executed by James Bracken of Templemore, uncle of Conservative statesman Brendan Bracken.

CLOUGHJORDAN: Catholic Church

Harsh late Gothic Revival church *c.*1890 remarkable only for the Harry Clarke Studios window behind the altar.

DRANGAN: Catholic Church

Imposing village church in Puginesque Gothic. Cruciform with splayed buttresses and inventive stone tracery in the windows. Inscription on the façade proclaims its completion by Revd Edward O'Shaughnessy in 1850. Interior has shallow Gothic vaulting resting on slender corbelled columns. Galleries across the transepts. Apart from new chancel fittings made out of a disassembled altar with its columns upside down, interior intact. Remarkable stencilled decoration on the walls and the vaulting.

DROMINEER: St David's

Delightful lakeside retreat built in the manner of Benjamin Woodward—ground floor with reception rooms opening on to the garden and bedrooms in the dormered roof.

EMLY: Catholic Church

The principal evidence of this Celtic monastic site is this ignored late Gothic Revival church by George Ashlin. Cruciform with nave of five bays. Unusual profusion of stone carving with the heads of the four evangelists upholding the crossing. Windows entirely taken up with stained glass, notably by Mayer, and by Watson of Youghal. Drawings for the church exibited in the RHA of 1880

FETHARD: Presentation Convent

Built in 1862 by Pugin and Ashlin with a thirteen-bay façade punctuated by massive chimney-stacks, terminated by more elaborate gable ends. The reflectory, with a meeting room above, both lit by triple lancets, lies to the south; and to the north the façade of the chapel steeply rising to a bellcote is barely able to contain a plate traceried rose window. Sparing polychromy in the voussoirs. The side elevation of the chapel shows how close the style of Pugin and Ashlin came to the Protestant churches of Welland and Gillespie. They were all radicals then.

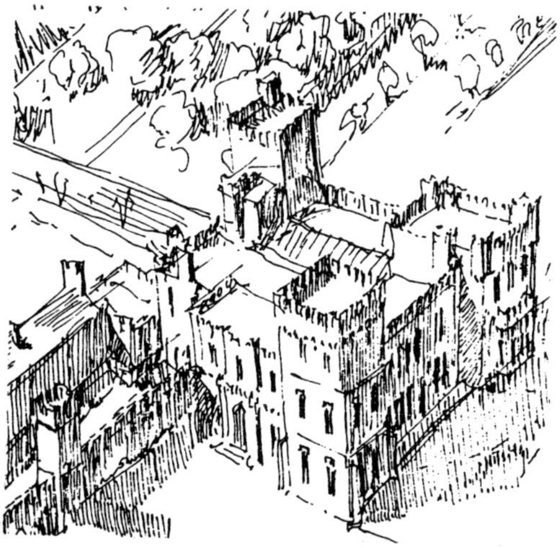

FETHARD: Tullamaine Castle

Earlier house of the Maher family, rebuilt as a castle for John Maher MP by William Tinsley in 1835-8. Four-storied battlemented corner keep with the adjoining ranges linked to further towers. Beyond, castellated stableyard and kitchen garden. Interior destroyed during the

LATTIN ALTAR

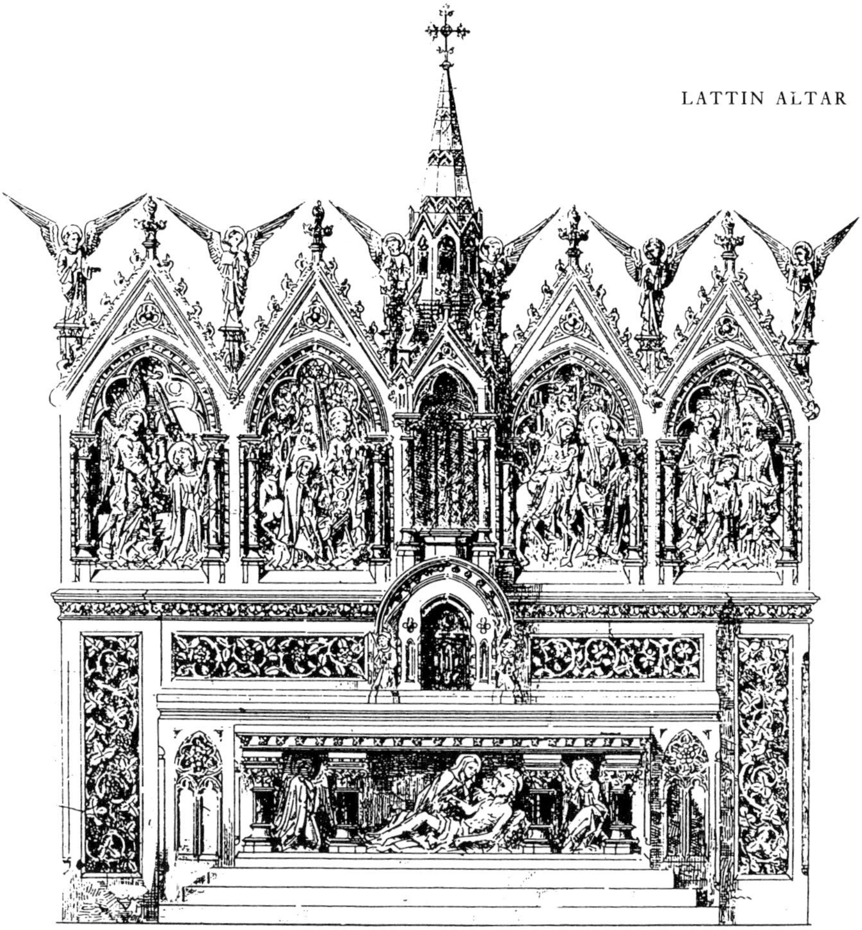

Troubles but subsequently rebuilt. The home of the eldest Mitford sister, Mrs Derek Jackson. Now part of Coolmore Stud.

GOLDEN: **Gortnakelly**
Small symmetrical castle with four-storied octagonal corner towers in the style of Charles Anderson, but not listed by him in his ouevre. More striking as a folly, now that it has fallen into ruin.

GOLDEN: **Thomastown Church**
Family tomb of the Mathew family, commissioned in 1842 by the brothers of the Apostle of Temperance within sight of the great castle of Thomastown, which they had expected to inherit from Lady Elizabeth Mathew, the sister of the last earl of Llandaff. At her death she left everything to her French cousin, the Comte de Chabot, whose terraced gardens, the only Victorian embellishment to the castle, have long since been swept away. The Mathew tomb (crocketted and pinnacled in the fragile Gothick introduced to Ireland by the Pains at least thirty years before) is now sadly damaged to match its ruined setting.

HOLYCROSS: **Catholic Church**
The parish church had a spectacular Gothick timber reredos, *c.* 1840, that took up the entire east wall but has not survived change of use from church to community hall.

KILLENAULE: **Catholic Church**
Designed in 1861 by J.J. McCarthy as one of his most impressive churches, especially when viewed up an immense flight of steps from the humble street below. Roof steeply pitched over the nave clasped by low lean-to aisles. The façade is articulated with such vertical force that the adjoining belfry designed by McCarthy was never attempted. Open braced roof inside with long lancets filled with stained glass.

LATTIN: **Catholic Church**
Gothic Revival church with elaborate altar designed by George Ashlin.

LATTIN: **Mooresfort**
Italianate remodelling of an earlier house by Charles Moore MP, who made the house two stories rather than three. Atmospheric interiors. Drawingroom with elaborate plaster ceiling and a dado wallpapered with delphiniums. Catholic

chapel upstairs with altar upheld by four archangels. There is no evidence of a far more ambitious scheme by George Ashlin to build for the family a replica of Cormac's chapel (recorded by the architect in one of his most striking internal perspectives, complete with his frock-coated client). Neo-Classical gatelodge presumably by Charles Anderson.

LIMERICK JUNCTION: Solohead Catholic Church

Late Gothic Revival church designed *c.*1835 by the Limerick partnership of O'Malley and O'Rourke with a larger budget than usual since they were able to include well-carved curvilinear tracery and an off-centre tower and spire. Cruciform interior with late windows by Harry Clarke and Co. and by Mayer.

LORRHA: Ballyquirke Castle

Elegant Regency Gothick fort, known after its builder as Kane's Folly, severely reduced in 1872 by the Ballinasloe architect, James Kempster, who removed three of the four corner towers, as well as the top floor and all its castellations. The interior resembles the Gothick interiors of Birr Castle.

MOYNE: Catholic Church

Unspoilt Catholic church designed by O'Malley and O'Rourke in 1910. Single cell with spirelet on western gable.

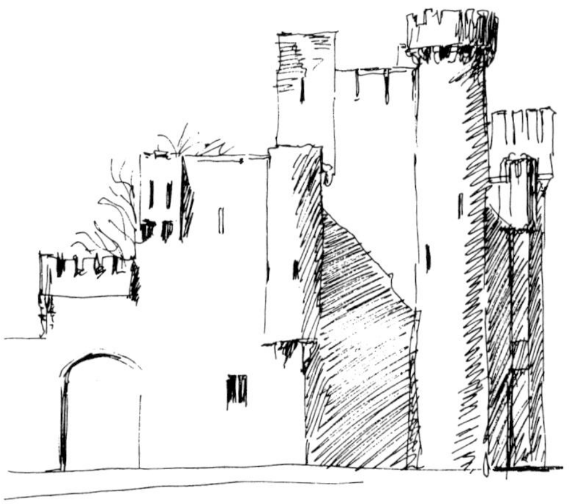

MOYNE: Lisheen Castle

An extraordinarily convincing reaction of a small medieval castle by an unknown architect recasing the adjoining typical Irish Palladian minor country house attached to the remnants of a keep. The floor was removed between the ground floor and the first and the new reception room were given pseudo-Norman vaulted ceilings and double-height Elizabethan windows. A central battlemented tower was added, recessed to give access to the front door. The high pitched roof was hidden by more battlements and corner turrets. All this ingenious, possibly witty, certainly odd. However, the adjoining keep and service wing are a different matter. The keep had been in such disrepair that it has not been recorded in the 1840 Ordnance map so what we see today is most probably a brilliant improvization. By keeping to the discipline of tiny windows and allowing the geometrical volumes to speak for themselves, the side elevation has no equal in Ireland as a feudal charade. It is a shock to enter and discover that there are just lean-tos behind the walls; but it would have been also a shock in medieval times.

The Lloyd family abandoned Lisheen after a fire in 1900 and disappeared in Australia, but they are still remembered by a neighbour as having built a castle in order 'to throw the house they lived in out the windows'.

NENAGH: Catholic Church

A new Catholic church was commissioned from Walter Doolin in 1894 after a hard-fought competition and completed ten years later. Doolin was one of the few young architects who succeeded in breaking into the world dominated by the dynasties of the Ashlins, Byrnes and McCarthys. He did this due partly to his connections (his father was a competent builder) but partly to his own ability, as shewn by winning this competition. He was Ashlin's choice. Why Ashlin was an assessor rather than competitor is another story.

All Doolin's churches are so grimly triumphalist built in random rock-faced ashlar, so depressing in the rain, that their interiors come as a welcome relief due to his determination to create a multi-coloured paradise out of the chancels, relying not only on frescoes, and stained glass, but also on mosaics, and wrought-iron grilles, painted and gilded. All this brilliance conceals the conservativeness of his architecture, derived from Ashlin himself (who got the job of its completion in 1910). The nave of the five bays is extended across the transepts into a chancel of the four bays. The arches into the transepts have open triforia above them. Frescoes on the vaulting; mosaics by Oppenheimer; glass by Mayer; altars by William Malone; wrought-iron by J. & C. McGloughlin, whose work removed from the chancel still survives as the external entrance gates. A plaque commemorates that Sisks built the church, and restored it in 1956.

NENAGH: The Courthouse

Built in 1843 to the designs of J.B. Keane, and the most Georgian, rather than neo-Classical, of his courthouses. This is due to the prominence of the roofs, a series of separately articulated

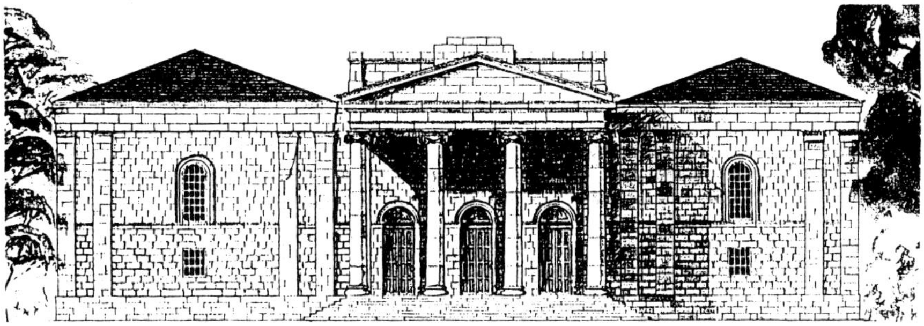

hips. Also, the natural light comes mainly from windows rather than skylights. The fenestration is large, arched and sashed, thereby competing uneasily with the central Ionic portico, so that it becomes the heaviest element of the façade rather than the lightest, as it had been in Waterford and Tullamore (q.v.).

PUCKAUN: Castle Lough

Early Georgian house retained by Lanyon, Lynn and Lanyon when they built a new block in front of it (1866). Comfortably Victorian with spacious reception rooms once shielded from the sun by a now-dismantled verandah. Entrance hall with elaborate multi-coloured tiled floor laid by Italian craftsmen. On one side the diningroom, and drawingroom on the other with a bay window to overlook Lough Derg, seen through wooded islets.

PUCKAUN: Kilteelagh

High Victorian house rebuilt in 1863 for the Gason family, overlooking Lough Derg. Polychromatic tiled roof, a combination of gables and hips.

RIVERSTON: Derrylahan

Only the gatelodge and the remnants of stables survive from the country house that the Heard family commissioned from Thomas Newenham Deane, who was working at that time on his major country-house commission nearby, Portumna Castle. In 1850, Deane was trying to don the stylistic manter of his partner Benjamin Woodward, who had died the year before, and Derrylahan was a heavy-handed version of Woodward's St Austin's Abbey, executed in a grim local limestone on the evidence of the surviving lodge.

ROSCREA: Allied Irish Bank

Formerly the Munster and Leinster Bank. Edwardian combination of pebbledash and smooth limestone deployed for slim columns and heavy console brackets. The architect is unrecorded.

ROSCREA: Catholic Church

One of the finest churches (1844) to be designed by W.D. Butler and praised as one of the best Catholic churches in Ireland by Bentley, architect of Westminster Cathedral. Sited so that the principal approach is through a ruined abbey and across a river with the church above framed by groves of tress—cruciform with the west front articulated by twin pinnacles. There is no belfry; instead, the tower of the ruined abbey fulfils this role. At the eastern end, a polygonal apse rises uncluttered by chapels. Butler died before the completion and his son J.S. Butler took over. However, he was replaced by J.J. McCarthy, who was working here in 1864. It is the contribution of McCarthy that has been the chief casualty of an attempt by Percy Leclerc to impose a liturgical solution acceptable to the Second Vatican Council in a scheme that gives a geometrical setting to a central altar. However, the destruction of most of the Victorian embellishments, apart from the stained glass by Mayer, has reinforced Butler's medieval aspirations, if we ignore the wall-to-wall carpeting.

ROSCREA: Methodist Church

One of G.F. Beckett's commissions for the Irish Methodist Church, dated from 1902. The façade articulated by tapering corner buttresses and a gabled door inserted into an apsidal porch suggest an unconventional interior inspired by Art Nouveau, instead of church and hall rigidly Late Gothic and underplayed.

TEMPLEMORE: Catholic Church

Designed by George Ashlin in 1877 in his more flowery Gothic manner. Cruciform with symmetrical western tower and spire. Intact interiors with mosaics, murals and stained glass by Mayer and Earley.

TEMPLETOUHY: Catholic Church

Late Gothic Revival single-cell polychromatic church with corbelled spirelet rising from the western gable. Built *c.* 1875 by George Ashlin. Similarities to nearby Moyne. Tombs in the graveyard to the Lalor Sheils, who are commemorated also by a fine east window above the altar.

TERRYGLASS: Catholic Church

Designed by Daniel O'Connell (+1919), the

architect grandson of the Liberator; completed in 1866. Gothic Revival with western tower and spire. Built by Lt. Col. J.F. Hickie for his Spanish wife. Family pew inserted in the chancel with a concealed central heating system—no doubt inserted for her to cope with the Irish climate.

TERRYGLASS: Slevyre
Built for Lt. Col. J.F. Hickie *c.*1870 by John McCurdy in an irregular Italianate; spectacularly sited to overlook Lough Derg. Its finest feature, the four-storied belvedere, is all that is visible from the present family home built after the main house had been sold to nuns; it looks like an exotic garden temple until one makes the mistake of climbing to the top of the hill and seeing the entire house. Denounced by Evelyn Waugh as an ugly villa when he had driven across Ireland to buy it after the last war.

THURLES: Brittas Castle
What should have been the most spectacular replica of a medieval castle in Ireland survives as a fragment rising from a placid moat that still demarcates the extent of the builder's ambition. He was not a duke but an obscure country squire called Henry Augustus Langley, who had acquired the estate from a first cousin. The existing ruined castle with three towers was absorbed by William Vitruvius Morrison into a tautly geometrical windowless barbican. In 1836, while directing operations, Langley was struck by a falling stone and died before he was halted by insolvency or madness.

THURLES: Catholic Cathedral
The only Romanesque cathedral designed by J.J. McCarthy, who started construction in 1865. Ten years later his patron Archbishop Leahy died, to be succeeded by Archbishop Croke, who replaced McCarthy with his most formidable rival, George Ashlin. By then there was little left to do, but it must have been galling all the same. Ashlin inserted the arch in front of the chancel arch and decorated the ceiling beyond, but McCarthy could console himself with the knowledge that Ashlin's ambitious baldachino remained unexecuted.

The exterior (entirely to McCarthy's design) achieves distinction if not originality by the directness of its borrowing from North Italian prototypes: the baptistery (a reduced version of Pisa) lines up with the campanile to deflect attention from an otherwise compressed and repetitive exterior; weaknesses are soon discernible within confined by the dimensions of the previous nave. However, the two formidable archbishops spared no effort on the decoration (sculpted by Pietro Lazzarini); Earley

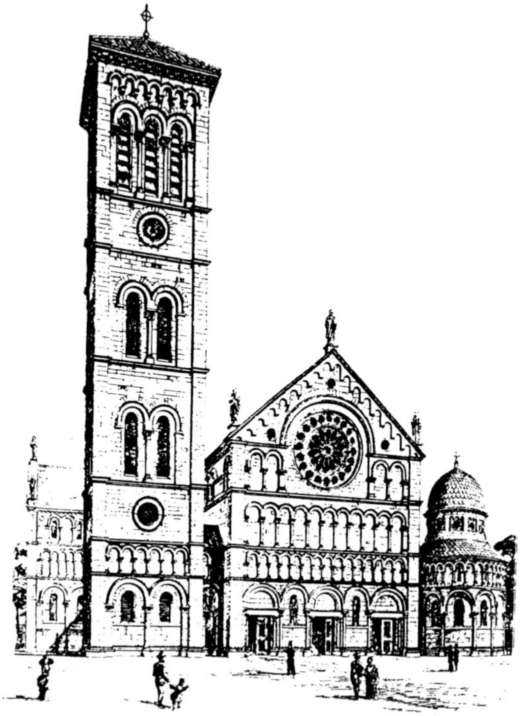

and Powell were responsible for Ashlin's ceiling and some of the sculpture and stained glass. Further statues by Benzoni on the transept altars; corbels carved by Joseph O'Reilly. The stained glass of the principal windows is by Mayer: most of the remainder is by Wailes of Newcastle. Totally unexpected is the Italian Baroque tabernacle designed by Giacomo della Porta for the Gesù in Rome, acquired and installed amid a bitter controversy that Irish altar carvers were being done out of the commission. Victorian stencilled decoration painted over in 1973.

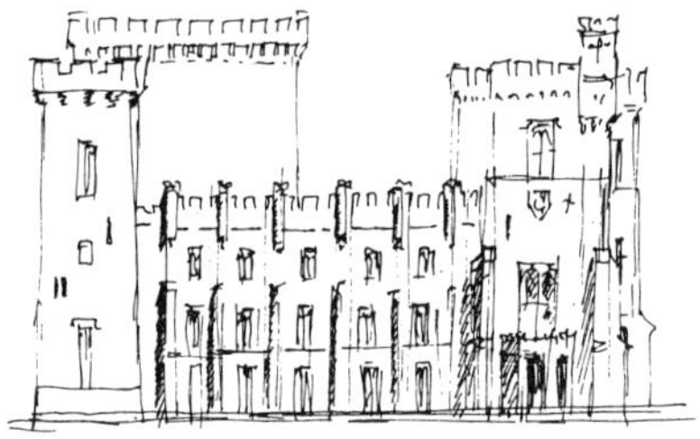

THURLES: Castle ffogarty
A castle that has passed by inheritance from one Gaelic family to another, from the Milesian ffogartys to the Lenigans to the Ryan-Lenigans to the Ryans, who still maintain the estate and the one habitable tower of the castle as rebuilt after the interior had been gutted by the Irregulars in 1922. The gradual ruination of the

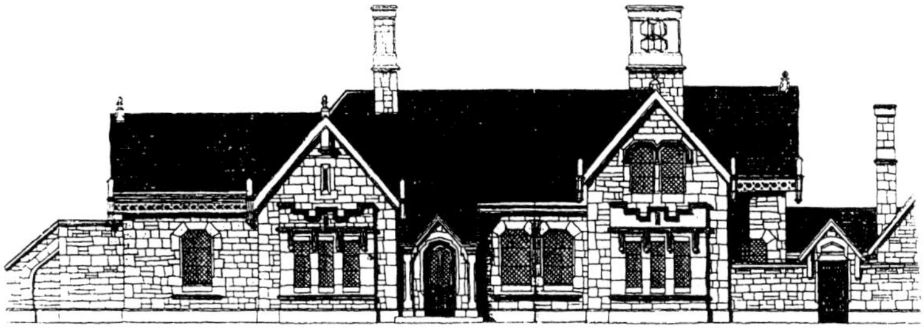

rest has exposed the different phases of its past; from medieval bawn to farmyard of Georgian squireen to the feudal delusions that clad the earlier structures with skin-deep Gothic. Who was responsible for the final transformation is not clear. When the castle was illustrated in the *Dublin Penny Journal* of 1836, James Lenigan was living abroad to avoid consumption and creditors. By then the Georgian house with its Regency windows has been crenellated, buttressed, and extended with corner towers, but the entrance range with its central polygonal tower had not yet been begun. No architect is recorded, but the style is characteristic of Charles Anderson.

THURLES: Stanwix Almhouses

Picturesque brick and half-timbered complex designed by Albert Murray in 1890. The cottages are enlivened by rustic gabled porches resting on chubby colonettes; their charm redeems the stiffness of the director's house and communal hall that they link together.

THURLES: The Station

One of the series of picturesque Gothic Revival stations designed by Sancton Wood for the Great Southern and Western Railway Company who had brought him over from England to design their terminus, now Heuston Station, Dublin (q.v.) in 1845.

THURLES: Turtulla House

Tudor Revival house asymmetrically composed to incorporate an earlier house. Built by William Tinsley for his client, Valentine Mayer, *c.*1835. Now used as a golf club.

TIPPERARY: Catholic Church

Said to have been started in 1820, and certainly completed in 1860, no architect was mentioned in the account of its consecration. In 1891, the *Skibbereen Eagle* attributed the church to its builder, Philip McAuliffe. However, there is no evidence of uncertainty or delay in the design. There can be no doubt that the dominant influence was A.W.N. Pugin—indeed this is one

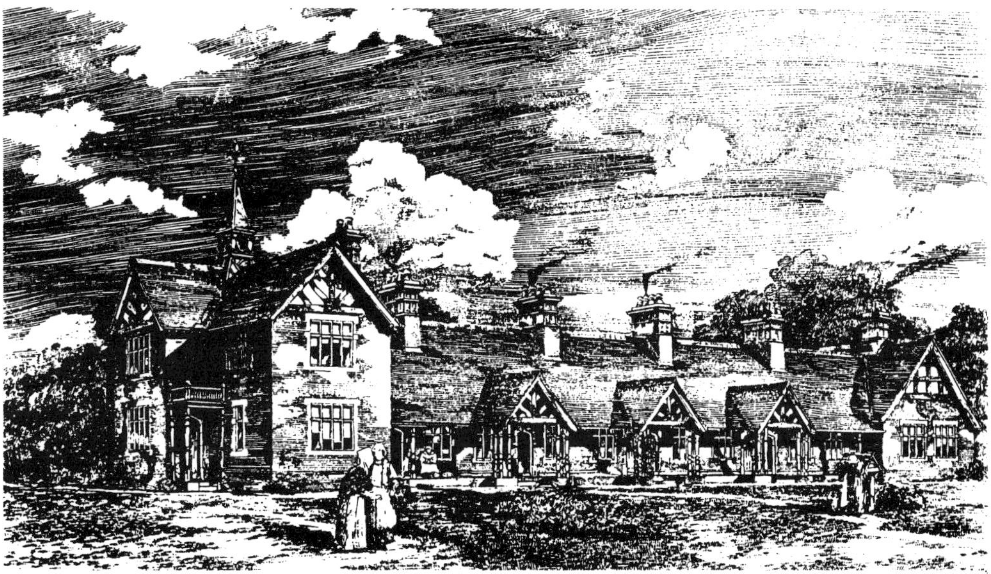

of the finest Puginian churches in Ireland. Simply, lofty nave leading to raised chancel; narrow steep-roofed lean-to aisles revealed through the cylindrical columns of widely spaced arcades, double the width of the clerestory bays above. Entrance through astonishingly low doorway, inspired by Cistercian prototypes such as Ballintubber but obscured by a later porch. Quintuplet of lancets above answered by quintuplet at the further end above the altar. Asymmetrical tower and spire fused to the façade by buttress enclosing staircase. The interior displays similar consistency and *élan*, effortlessly absorbing its furnishings, even the overbearing reredos by Hardman said, on its completion, to be the largest erected in the British Isles since the Reformation. Varied glass by Watson, Mayer and others—one portraying a cousin of the parish priest, a doomed officer in the First World War kneeling in the trenches to the Holy Family encouraging him from a covenient cloud.

TIPPERARY: Convent of Mercy
Chapel (*c.*1870) added by George Ashlin to earlier convent of 1844-6. Glass by Hardman, Earley and Clarke.

TIPPERARY: Kickham Statue
The first life-sized commission by John Hughes; unveiled in 1898, it commemorates the disabled novelist and Fenian, Charles Kickham (1828-82).

TIPPERARY: Presbyterian Church
Elegant Greek temple: order modelled on the Tower of the Winds. Built in the 1840s. Now serves as hall to the nearby Church of Ireland.

TIPPERARY: The Townhall
Accident-prone townhall, the only Irish work of the Oxford architect, Thomas Jackson, commissioned by the Smith-Barrys, the landlords of the town. Begun in 1876, in a Jacobean style but with an interesting premonition of the Queen Anne Revival. Tower with ogee lantern. All interiors destroyed in a fire in 1941. Semi-derelict after a further fire in 1970.

TWOMILEBORRIS: Kilcooley Abbey
Late 18th-century house inherited by the Ponsonby family and rebuilt by them (after a fire in the 1840s) round a galleried hall, partly lit by a glazed dome. Principal rooms overlook formal gardens and the ruined abbey.

TYRONE

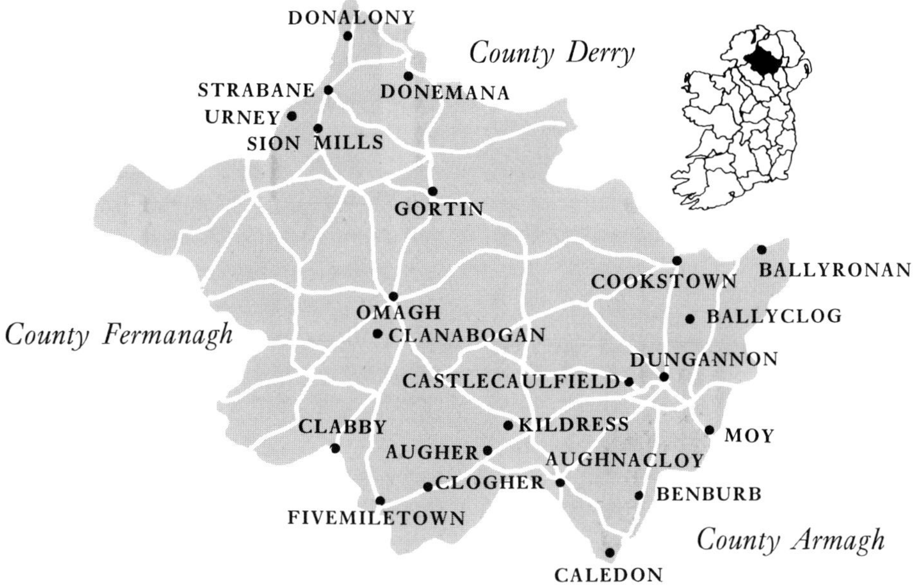

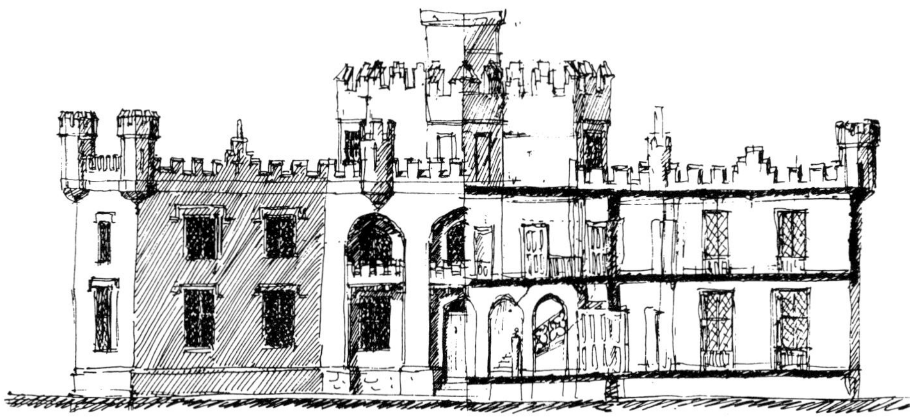

AUGHER: **The Castle, known as Spur Royal**

Elizabethan tower house formed from two overlapping cubes. Transformed *c.* 1830 by William Warren, an obscure architect from Sligo, to become the centrepiece of a delightful Gothick castle. Warren built a new range to the rear with canted wings that echoed the star shape of the original tower house. He reversed the entrance, so that his wings today screen the lake to give a sense of expectancy. The new work is kept as low as possible but enlivened with dummy bartizans, two of them positioned cheerfully above the outer arches of the double-height arcade accentuating the three central bays of the façade. This arcade encloses wittily castellated balconies. The interior reveals the same lightness of touch. The arcade behind the entrance hall appears to screen two staircases, when there is in reality only one, that twirls up into a hidden semi-spiral. The new drawingroom and diningroom are like lanterns with diamond-paned windows in three directions. How sad that Warren never built another house that we know of, because subsequent Irish castle builders never achieved his geometry and wit.

AUGHER: **Church of Ireland**

A modest chapel-of-ease by Welland and Gillespie, built of coursed rubble with steeply pitched roof and off-centre bellcote perched on the western gable. Built in 1861-4.

AUGHNACLOY: **Catholic Church**
Impressive Romanesque church by R.M. Butler with façade dominated by a forceful wheel window. Adjoining tower with cupola. Aisled barrel-vaulted nave terminating with apse. Designed in 1902.

AUGHNACLOY: **Jackson Almhouses**
Designed by Sandham Symes, nephew of William Warren, and built in 1851-4. A rare excursion by this architect into neo-Elizabethan with theatrical results: the verandahs are too cottagey, the chimney-stacks too overpowering, the triple-gabled composition too definitive for an organic housing settlement. Restored by 'Hearth'.

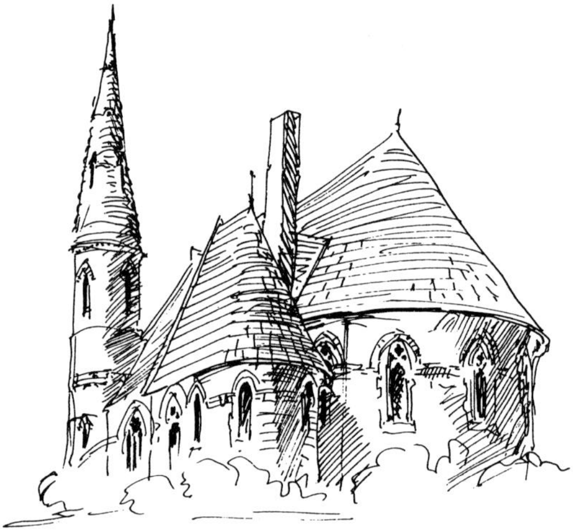

BALLYCLOG: **Church of Ireland**
Small church by Welland and Gillespie in 1865, experimenting with the Celtic Revival in rubble with polychromatic bands of stone and brick. Lean-to porch jammed up against the battered base of a round tower. Polychromatic interior with open roof. Both church and vestry end with apses that snuggle up against each other.

BALLYRONAN: **Woodchapel Church of Ireland**
The London Salters Company contributed almost half the cost of this church by Welland and Gillespie in 1866-8—which explains this ambitious urban church in a remote rural setting. The extraordinary saddle-roofed entry tower, which could be by Butterfield, is later, replacing an earlier tower that had collapsed bringing down half the uncompleted church. The bold design is perfectly realized by the materials—black basalt and sandstone trim. A rose window in the west gable illuminates the spacious nave with its single aisle. Airy transepts and polygonal apse beyond.

BENBURB: **Benburb Manor**
Designed in 1887 by W.H. Lynn for the new owner of the estate, James Bruce of Belfast, and as appropriate to the country as an umbrella and a city suit. Built in red brick with sandstone trim, two-storied with lofty gabled and dormered third floor above. Arched porch with adjoining staircase rising the full height of the interior. Despite elevations being asymmetrical, the formal gardens to the east are focused on a blank brick wall. Apart from a few lapses into charm, like the arched porch of the lodge doubling up as pedestrian access to the entrance gates, and the half-timbered stable range, this is far more appealing as an institution (which it is now) than as a private house. A Servite priory since 1947. The ballroom is now a chapel. Sculpture in the grounds commissioned from Gabriel Hayes and Seamus Murphy.

BENBURB: **Wilson Tomb, Church of Ireland Churchyard**
Elegant cenotaph of 1850 poised dramatically above the valley of the river Blackwater; erected by Lord Powerscourt to his agent; probably designed by John Louch.

CALEDON: **Church of Ireland**
Georgian church given a spire by Nash, and gothicized by Joseph Welland in 1848. Marble reredos sculpted by A.P. Sharp to the designs of Drew in 1890.

CALEDON: **Parish School**
Commissioned by the dowager countess of Caledon in 1852 in front of the church of Ireland, using a simplified Gothic made even harsher by unsympathetic plate-glass reglazing. Master's house attached.

CALEDON: **Public Weighbridge**
Curious if appropriate memorial to Lord Caledon's agent for over forty years, Henry Prentice. Designed by an unrecorded Gothic brutalist in 1873.

CASTLECAULFIELD: **Parkanaur**
A neo-Elizabethan manor house extended on an ever grander sacle, while retaining the original entrance hall and adjoining rooms. These date from 1802, but their symmetry was disrupted by a range added in 1820 at right angles to contain a library and staircase hall and a drawingroom in a wing beyond. Thomas Duff was called in by John Ynyr Burges, who inherited the estate from his father in 1839. He re-cased the façade and built at the rear a magnificent double drawingroom and a galleried minstrels' hall externally articulated by octagonal pinnacles; bay window on the ground floor and oriel

window above to overlook the gardens. Linked to stable court of 1870 where a plaque records that everything was built without incurring debt. Many fittings salvaged from Tudor houses in England. Now the Thomas Doran Home for handicapped children.

CLABBY: **Church of Ireland**
Designed by Welland and Gillespie and built 1864-70, their partnership as usual spurred to experiment by a rival commission. Nave and chancel interpenetrated by a series of gables with gabled porch set against a corner belfry. The lantern is lit by louvered Gothic arches with zig-zag voussoirs. This rises to a spire perforated with circular vents. These echo the patterns of the plate tracery in the fenestration. Unique internal roof structure with double trusses upholding a central plaster Gothic vault soaring above its tie-bars and the interpenetrating gables on either side.

CLANABOGAN: **Church of Ireland**
A conventional Gothic Revival church externally, by Welland and Gillespie; built in 1861-3, with off-centre octagonal tower and spire that serves as entrance and projecting vestry. All this is run-of-the-mill, but what makes the interior so memorable is the fitting-out by Thomas Drew commissioned in 1889 for the Galbraith family. The Galbraiths are commemorated by the heraldic glass in the east window and by the memorial sculpted in 1885 by Sir Thomas Brock from photographs depicting the last moments of James Galbraith, who was killed in action. Brock's studio carved the marble eagle lectern. This is to Drew's design but his finesse in combining different coloured marbles from France, Ireland and Italy is also to be found in the steps, the chancel rail and (at its most elaborate) the pulpit, inset with semi-precious stones and alabaster.

CLOGHER: **Ashfield Park**
Mid-Victorian Italianate villa with a *piano nobile* on an elevated basement. Built in smooth ashlar with round-arched windows. Front door approached by an impressive T-shaped staircase with scrolled ironwork. Attributed to William G. Murray on its similarities to Murray's banks. Central hall on the upper level lit by glass dome. Built by a prosperous Belfast merchant, called Breckenbridge, who was, despite or perhaps because of his patronage of the novelist William Carleton, ostracized by his county neighbours.

CLOGHER: **Breckenbridge's Monument**
Triple-tiered tower built above a mausoleum by the owner of Ashfield Park (q.v.). His neighbours, having despised him in life, have had to look up to him ever since. But the troops who desecrated the mausoleum in the 1940s have had the last laugh. He was buried upside down since he believed that the earth would reverse its axis on the Last Day and he alone would be standing upright before his Creator.

COOKSTOWN: **Catholic Church**
Simple but effective example of J.J. McCarthy's Gothic (1855-60), where nothing distracts from the soaring tower and spire, symmetrically sited at the west end, but not quite symmetrical in itself due to the outward expression of its spiral staircase. A nave of five bays leads to a reduced chancel with one of McCarthy's oversize altars, still reasonably intact. However, his pulpit and lectern have been dismantled and the organ sold out of the west gallery beneath the tower.

DONALONY: **New Buildings Church of Ireland**
Modest cell built of red-brick and rubble stone of four bays with plate tracery. Designed by Welland and Gillespie in 1866.

DONEMANA: **Altnachree Castle**
The architect responsible is unrecorded, but there are many parallels with the Londonderry Apprentice Boys' Hall of 1873 by J.G. Ferguson before bomb damage—the same segmental mul-

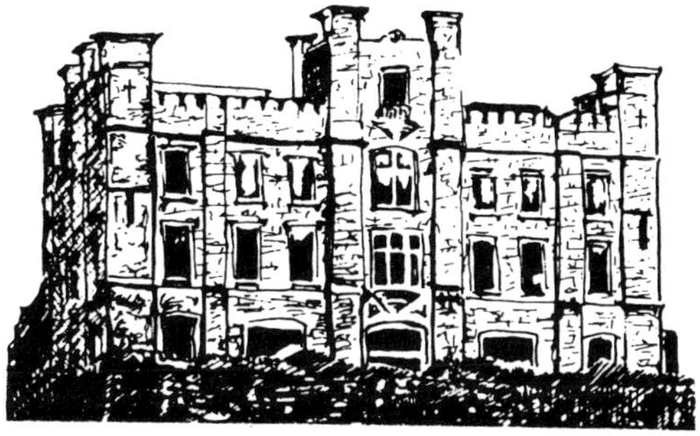

lioned windows and shallow oriels. Ferguson is more admired today for his industrial architecture, and, despite its appellation, Altnachree is more castellated mill than castle. It is referred to as a castle for the first time in 1872, a year before Claud William Ogilvy's inheritance at the age of twenty-three. Entered through a *porte-cochère* on the side along the axis of the central corridor, with the three main rooms strung out along the garden front. Main staircase set into triple-arched composition, but taking up the minimum of space, all like an office block. Four-storied towers in the centre of each front; three floors elsewhere.

Claude William Ogilvy is recorded in one edition of Burke's *Landed Gentry*, just after he had completed the vast castellated pile which he thronged with guests until they were displaced by creditors. His younger brother and heir escaped by giving a lift on his horse to a local girl walking to the mill that employed her. Their marriage was opposed. He vanished and returned seven years later to reclaim her. They eloped to Australia. Decades later he died, known only as a scientific expert on the fossils of the Great Reef. An island in Queensland is named after him. Unclaimed, his castle disintegrated. Today only a shell surveys a denuded park. Crisply observed in Pevsner to be better as a ruin.

DUNGANNON: **Catholic church**
Designed in 1867 by J.J. McCarthy. Completed by his son C.J. McCarthy in 1889, to whom is due the massive Caen stone pinnacled reredos that has so far survived liturgical agitation. The central shrine rises up between two windows surmounted by a rose. Exterior dominated by an off-centre belfry almost two hundred feet high.

DUNGANNON: **Church of Ireland**
The largest church commission of William Barre, dating from 1865, his most prolific year, and completed in 1869, after his death and Disestablishment. The exterior dominates all views of the town with its massive bell tower disengaging itself halfway up from both the clinging apsidal staircase turret and the massive bulk of the church itself, to culminate in a broached and pinnacled spire. Correct orientation and conventional symmetry are discarded so that the nave has only one lean-to aisle, tucked in behind the belfry, and this aisle turns a corner to serve one transept. It is also the entry space, of contrasting darkness to the luminosity of the remainder, which is lit by great windows carried down almost to the level of the pews. Two bays at the east end are given over to a steeply rising organ gallery (upheld by a pair of closely spaced columns) supporting a balustrade perforated by circles without any medieval precedent. Circles re-occur above, this time more correctly, in an immense rose window that leaves little space for the organ. The one-bay chancel, at the west end here, is comparatively conventional, partly due to the chancel fittings designed in 1869 by Purdy and Millard, but a vigorously designed pulpit corresponds to the font. The roof structure is exposed throughout, resting on colonnettes corbelled out at the upper level, soaring upwards to braced trusses, but segregated into separate compartments at the transepts, so there is a dramatic contrast between their height and the low arches of the crossing. Further tension is generated by the roof of the aisles, raked so steeply that there is only space left for a clerestory of equilateral triangles, each with a different tracery, giving Barre full scope for unfailing inventiveness. However, to make its full impact he was evidently relying on a consistent use of stained glass, which is still incomplete. Only in the south transept, in the richly coloured Ranfurley windows by Heaton, Butler and Bayne, can we gauge his full intentions. The later windows are too subtle—Stevenson memorial window by A.K. Nicholas, First World War window by Powell, glass in aisles by Clokey and A.E. Child.

DUNGANNON: **Howard Terrace**
Handsome range of nine houses, a continuation to an earlier Georgian range built along the east side of Northland Row. The uniformity of the earlier façades is broken up by canted bays, but the unknown designer has combined these with mullioned arcades given to every second house, so the scale is more impressive, and the rhythm of the fenestration unhurried and sedate.

DUNGANNON: **Northern Bank**
Built in 1855 for the Belfast Bank by W.H. Lynn when he was most strongly influenced by John Ruskin. A two-storey cube with a tripartite centrepiece of the ground floor, a quadruple arcade of the floor above. All arches are cusped ogees in accordance with Venetian convention. Likewise the corbelled cornice and the shallow pitch of the hipped roof, although the monumental stack has its precedence in Irish Regency vernacular.

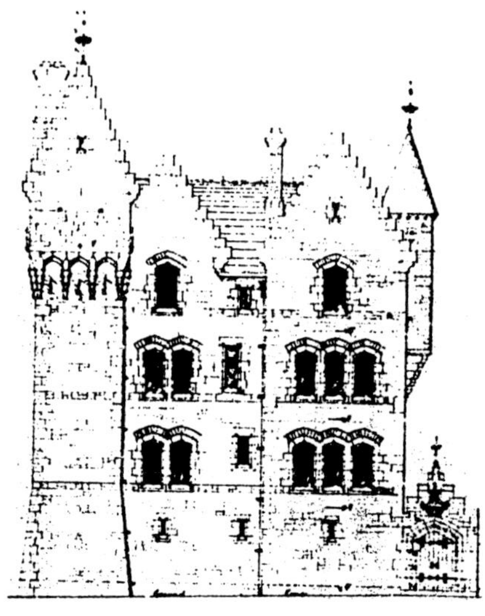

DUNGANNON: **Police Barracks**
Designed for the RUC by James H. Owen of the Board of Works, and built in 1871, in fortified Baronial, to form today a dramatic contrast with the composure of its neighbour, the Northern Bank (q.v.). The Fenian Rising

scare of 1867 had occurred in between the construction of both buildings and Owen's heavy machicolations overhang an exposed external staircase, the only entry. The crow-stepped battlements could shelter anxious look-outs. Ulster was reverting from the dynamism of entrepreneurial Venice to the introversion of an earlier age, racked by feud between Ghibeline and Guelph.

DUNGANNON: **Shiel Almshouses**
Designed by Lanyon, Lynn and Lanyon in 1867 for the Victorian philanthropist, Charles Sheil. They were his principal architects and while they used the same house-type combination on each scheme (of gabled upper floors linked by ranges of half dormers), they varied the overall composition. Dungannon has a rectangular symmetrical layout focussed on a central clock tower. The polychromatic architecture is of local sandstone rubble enlivened by bands of red sandstone alternating with green slate. Still maintained as a housing charity on nominal rents as decreed in Sheil's will.

DUNGANNON: **South Tyrone Hospital**
The core of this hospital is still a standard 1841 Union Workhouse as designed by George Wilkinson. Five-bay Tudor front with adjoining tower.

FIVEMILETOWN: **Blesssingbourne**
Neo-Jacobean house built by Hugh de Fellenberg Montgomery in 1870-4 and now carefully maintained by his descendants. His architect was Frederick Pepys Cockerill, the son of Charles Cockerill, better known as a painter but who also designed Clonalis (q.v.). Both houses are designed to have their principal façades to the garden and Blesssingbourne is entered from the rear. The *porte-cochère* so delightfully illustrated by Cockerill was never built since the rebuilding was financed from income, not capital. Despite such strictures Cockerill created a sequence of inventive and interlinked interiors that anticipate the era of 'Sweetness and Light'. The kernel of the house is the billiard room, entered from the staircase hall through a glazed screen, and transparent also to the garden terrace and the lake beyond. The drawingroom has a recessed fireplace with de Morgan tiles flanked by canted arches for wood and turf, echoed spatially by an adjoining arched oriel. The library and the diningroom both retain their original William Morris wallpapers. Member of Hidden Ireland.

FIVEMILETOWN: **Catholic Church**
Built on a well-manicured suburban site that makes its unrecorded architect's assault on the conventions of the 1870s even more astonishing. Attributed to Hugh de Fellenberg Montgomery of Blessingbourne by his descendants but possibly assisted by F.P. Cockerell. Here for once Catholic architecture rivals the radicalism of Welland and Gillespie. But whereas their work nestles into the Irish countryside, this façade stridently asserts itself with its red and

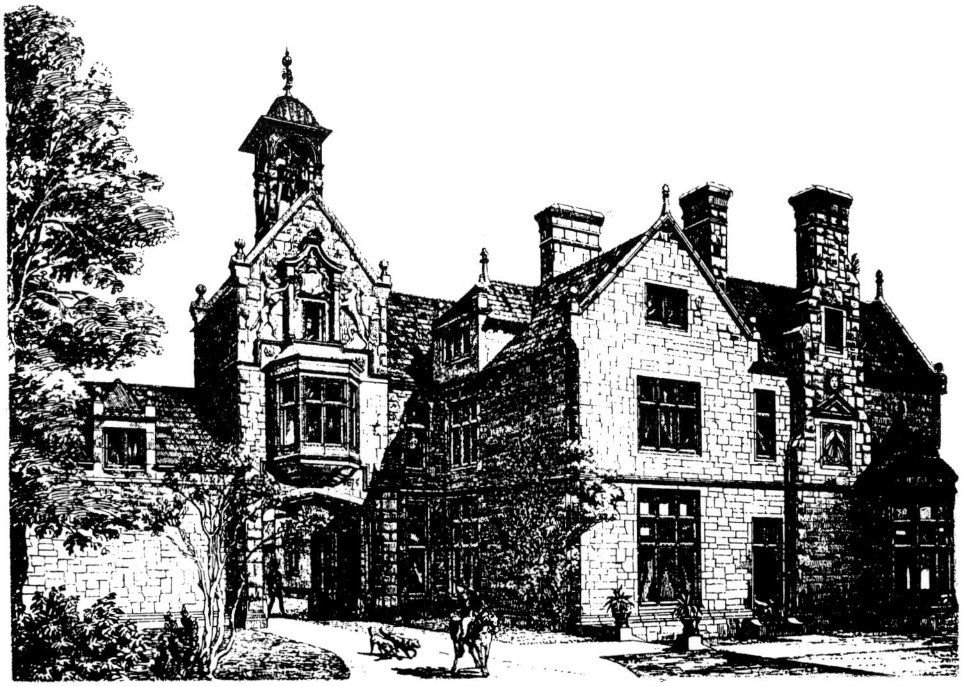

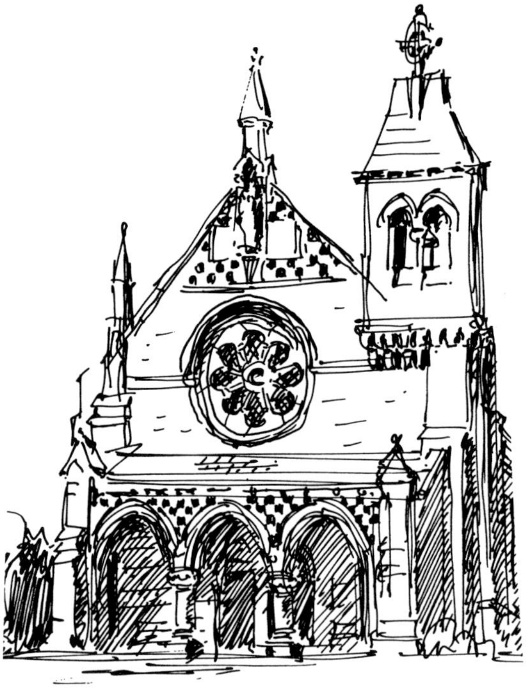

white chequeboard tiling and a white statute of the Virgin in the gable. A wheel window below is framed by projecting buttresses that advance to clamp a triple-arched loggia between them. These buttresses are not symmetrical: one spreads itself carefully inside the loggia since it has to take the extra stress of a corbelled double belfry which stands in for the expected tower; the Celtic cross that disrupts its wedge-shaped roof rises no higher than the Virgin on the gable. After all this bravado, the simplicity of the five-bayed interior offers reassurance and repose. The only tension is generated by a semi-octagonal organ gallery with the porch beneath; but this intrusion is counterbalanced at the far end by an all-embracing apse. Refitted by J. Brennan in 1910.

FIVEMILETOWN: **The Rectory**
Evidently the work of F.P. Cockerell, commissioned by Hugh de Fellenberg Montgomery in the 1870s. A small house but of great presence. Entered through an arched porch set into a projecting tower with stonework that extends just enough to give a rusticated surround to the adjoining staircase window. Forcefully modelled chimneys after Blessingbourne (q.v.).

GORTIN: **Catholic Church**
Late Gothic Revival church built in 1898-1902 by E.J. Toye with impressive façade, with arcaded gallery, rose window, arcading beneath, beside off-centre tower and spire. Apsidal chancel set between arcaded side chapels.

GORTIN: **Church of Ireland**
Standard single cell by Joseph Welland built in 1856. Stained glass (1872) by J.B. Capronnier of Brussels.

KILDRESS: **Drum Manor**
The castellated gatelodge happily survives, but the avenue that winds into the demesne maintained by the Forestry Commission leads now only to a sanitized ruin. A roofless courtyard preserves the lower parts of the outside walls that suggest more romanticism than once existed, for the Regency Gothic rebuilding by Richard Richardson Brady was rather staid, and one can understand the efforts of his heir, Viscount Stewart (in 1869), to introduce a livelier note. His architect was William Hastings, a Dublin architect who built mainly commercial work in Belfast. This was his only country house, and he was assisted by another novice in the genre, Timothy Hevey. Their interiors, around a new central hall, have vanished unrecorded, but the Gothic entrance porch of their new north front has been spared, guarded by their four-storied tower. This was retained as a belvedere to mount and view the ornamental shrubberies and the inevitable caravan park.

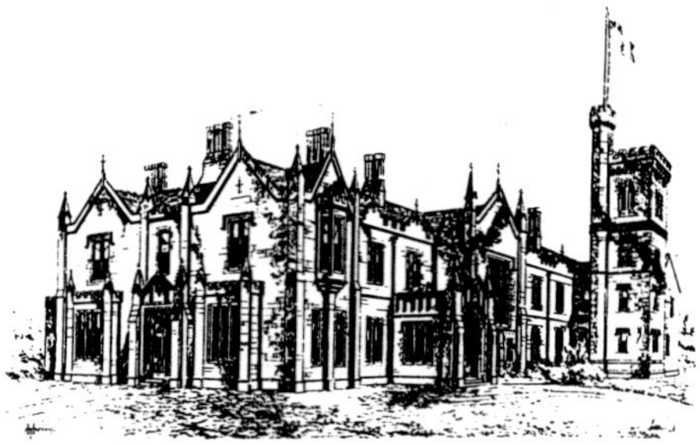

MOY: **Church of Ireland**
Board of First Fruits Gothic partially remodelled by William Barre in 1863. Barre's spire remained unbuilt. His apse was altered by Sherry and Hughes in 1868, who added the north transept. Prominent internal roof trusses and deeply champered arches.

MOY: **Gates and screen**
All that survives of the fantastic chateau of Roxborough William Barre created for the 3rd earl of Charlemont are the cast-iron entrance gates and screen. The house was destroyed by fire during the Troubles of 1922.

OMAGH: **Boer War Memorial**
Bronze memorial of a cloaked Victory brandishing a crown, by Sydney March dating from 1904.

OMAGH: **Catholic Church**
Although set on a lower level than the church of Ireland, its twin-towered façade rises far above it, dominating the landscape for miles around and transforming the principal street of Omagh into a wending processional way. But behind this façade the ground falls precipitously, leaving space only for a modest nave and lean-to aisles incorrectly orientated. Yet the conviction and exhilaration of the William Hague's architecture, furnishing and decoration have survived unchallenged since its completion in 1899, so that few Catholic churches today can rival it for consistency. Curiously, Hague's façade is twin-towered, but the spires are treated differently. The nave of seven bays is articulated by polished granite columns with richly carved capitals. Above, carved stone heads of prophets uphold colonettes at clerestory level to support the hammer trusses of the open roof. The two-bay choir is treated with a contrasting serenity. A wagon vault displaces the hammer trusses and floating angels and the prophets. The buttressed communion rail has been retained, the lavish pulpit and the confessionals designed to anticipate the reredos. This radiates out marble saints from its central vesicula. Above, Mayer's stained glass proclaims eternal verities.

OMAGH: **Church of Ireland**
A complex building since the choir was attached an earlier church which was then expanded laterally, replacing its side walls with arcades and adding spacious transepts which are screened from the main body of the church. What makes Omagh unusual is the great width of the transept giving an unexpected centralization. However, the architectural idiom fails to live up to the spatial individuality. The architect, J.E. Rogers, was Benjamin Woodward's most gifted pupil. The chancel he added here is one of his earliest, if we accept the date of 1862 for the remarkable stained glass of the east window by Michael O'Connor. Within a decade Rogers had abandoned architecture for water-colouring. The single off-centre steeple of his church here has since been upstaged by the twin towers of Hevey's Catholic church. Good Galbraith memorial *c.*1865; and other windows by Heaton, Butler and Bayne.

OMAGH, **Cookstown Road: Edenfels,**
Assertive Gothic Revival villa cluttered with many bargeboarded gables and lively chimneys. By Boyd and Batt for Mr Buchanan (1862).

OMAGH: **First Presbyterian Church**
Built *c.*1890, the design is attributed to Vincent Craig. Low, square tower with octagonal belfry; wide hall church behind.

OMAGH: **Knocknamoe Castle**
Neo-Jacobean pile built for the Stack family in 1875. Corner turret with ogee copper cupola characteristic of Thomas Turner. Converted into an hotel.

OMAGH: **Loreto Convent**
Built to the designs by Hadfield and Goldie with John Neville as an executive architect. Neville is the only name given by the *Irish Builder.* Five-bay façade with wing of two bays linked by a circular staircase. The addition is joined to the chapel with its fine interior. Glass by Mayer.

OMAGH: **AIB (Provincial Bank of Ireland)**
Full-blooded Lombardesque adapted to the rising street. Three storeys and four bays wide, each bay separately articulated on the ground floor, the fenestration of each floor above treated consistently. The simpler windows on the top floor are crowned by a medallioned freize and generous cornice. Architect: J.E. Rogers, 1864.

OMAGH: **The Courthouse**
A rare example of William Barre's architectural discretion, doubling in size the 1814 courthouse of John Hargrave without overbalancing what existed. Barre achieved this in 1863 by extending the horizontal fenestration of the earlier five bays into a further five, but thoughtfully omitted all the features that would compete with the grandeur of the original—the portico, pilasters, plinth and steps. This reticence allowed him to slip in an extra floor at ground level, taking advantage of the sloping site.

OMAGH: **The Hospital**
Far-flung complex still centred on the original block designed by William Farrell and built in 1847-53. Grimly symmetrical façade articulated by a series of staircase towers crowned with ogee cupolas. Extended by George Boyd in 1863. New county infirmary built in 1895-9 by C.A. Owen, who added the Catholic and Protestant chapels in 1901 and 1903 respectively.

SION MILLS: **Church of Ireland**
Designed in 1870 by the London architect, W.F. Unsworth, for his brother-in-law E.T. Herdman; a scholarly transcription of Tuscan Romanesque for Ulster Protestant worship, so all traces of overt Catholicism are thoughtfully eliminated. This is not the real Italy, but the English Italy that we find in the contemporary novels of E.M. Forster. A basilica of five bays lit by Diocletian windows. The projecting apsidal staircase framed by twin entrances is the focal point of the façade. At the eastern end,

three apses are separated by square towers. The central apse is lit by a series of rose windows that interpenetrate the semi-dome of the internal vault. Steps rise to the altar past lectern and pulpit in Connemara marble inspired by Santa Maria in Cosmedin, Rome.

SION MILLS: Sion House

As in the novels of Forster, the antipode to Tuscany is always Sussex, and so it is here in Sion Mills, where Unsworth remodelled his brother-in-law's house with much half-timbering, a red-tiled roof and decorative red-brick chimney-stacks, now partly dismantled. Timber verandahs are losing out in their struggle to support wysteria. The shingled stable block and the half-timbered gate house screen once-formal grounds from the outside world.

SION MILLS: The Mills

The Halls in their tour of Ireland in 1843 praise the full employment given to 700 workers, 500 of them women, living in sound and comfortable cottages and going to Sunday school that the Herdman family themselves attended, and all in the verdant countryside. The clean well-ventilated factory praised by the Halls was rebuilt ten years afterwards by W.H. Lynn—four floors of brick-vaulted construction, sixteen bays long, a further six added later. The chimney, a campanile to this industrial cathedral, was put up in 1877.

STRABANE: Catholic Church

Gothic Revival church designed in 1895 by William Hague. Symmetrically sited tower and spire above the western door between double-bay vestibules. Nave resting on pink granite columns with open-trussed roof leading to smaller chancel with a contrasting panelled wagon roof. Lavish marble altar. Celtic Revival mosaic floor. Stormy stained glass by Mayer.

STRABANE: Church of Ireland

The winning entry in a competition held in 1874 and won by a local architect John Kennedy. An early English Gothic Revival complex grouped satisfyingly alongside a tower with broached spire. Pointed barrel-vaulted nave. Glass by Heaton, Butler and Bayne.

URNEY: Church of Ireland

Rebuilt in 1866, by Welland and Gillespie. The façade is characteristic of their love of dissonance—porch half buried in the façade and partly masking a plate traceried rose window. Five-sided apse. Stained glass includes 'Suffer Little Children' by A.L. Moore (1894).

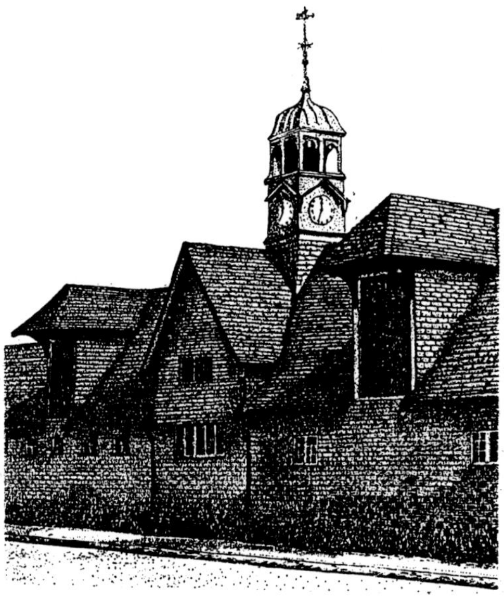

STABLES, SION HOUSE

WATERFORD

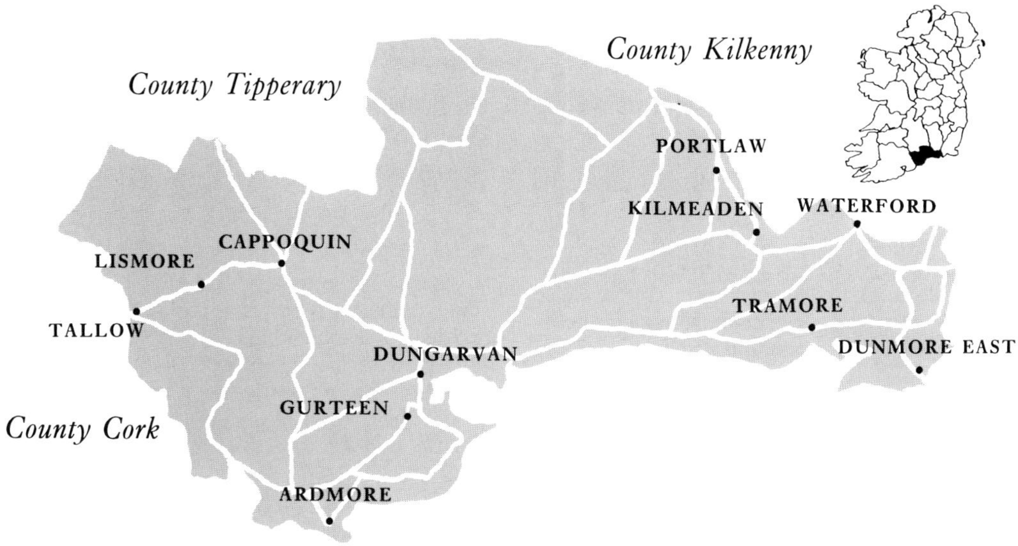

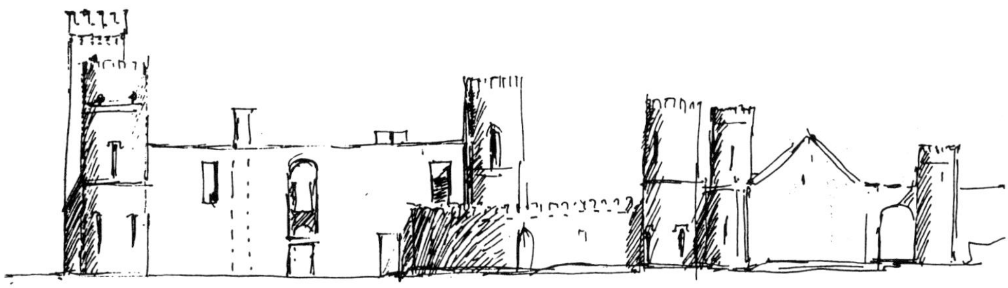

ARDMORE: **Ardo**
Only one of the strange ruined towers of Ardo is Victorian, since it was built as a granary during the Famine, possibly by the Revd Drew, the creator of Heathfield Towers (q.v.). So its humanitarian purpose was quite different from the earlier towers built by Mrs Jeremiah Coghlan (known as 'the Madam') to assist the smugglers landing in the secret harbour in the cliffs below and subsidizing the grandeur of her lifestyle. One daughter was sacrificed to the violent last earl of Barrymore, the other daughter married the elderly duc de Castries. Two sons were born congenital idiots, and became with their toys the responsibility of the eventual heir, the grandson of the duc de Castries, Marshal McMahon. When the marshal became President of the French Republic, he quietly sold his Irish seat to the London banker, Sir Stephen McKenna, who is buried with his wife and daughter in a mausoleum, now hidden in the undergrowth; this was discovered by Mark Bence-Jones guarded by a 'well-fed marble angel'. Castle abandoned in 1918.

CAPPOQUIN: **Mount Melleray**
Cistercian Monastery founded in 1834, and extended in 1910. The Gothic Revival church by Alfred Jones dating from the 1920s re-uses the cut stone of Mitchelstown Castle. Well restored by Patrick Rooney.

CAPPOQUIN: **Salterbridge**
Original Georgian house extended in 1849 with a new front block and wings that now contain the principal rooms looking south across the Blackwater.

CAPPOQUIN: **Strancally Castle**
Castle built by the Pains *c.*1830 for John Keily, elder brother of Arthur, the folly builder of Ballysaggartmore. Strancally is a sensible castle,

with spacious well-illuminated interiors and views through elegant mullioned windows of the wooded Blackwater valley. Gothic ornament confined to the chimneypieces. Still well-maintained despite being turned down (after inspecting photographs) by Evelyn Waugh, where he was offered it in a Dublin hotel after the last war by an elderly couple, 'wistful and resigned'. Folly tower at the end of the garden.

CAPPOQUIN: **Tourin**
Crisp and formal Italianate villa *c.*1850 beside a medieval keep on the river Blackwater.

CLONLEA: **Catholic Church**
Village church by George Ashlin, distinguished by the height of its serene interior and the verticality of its fenestration. Stained glass by Harry Clarke Studios, Joshua Clarke and Watson of Youghal.

DUNGARVAN: **Cappagh House**
Seat of the Usshers. The family fortune was spent by the grandfather of the writer and aphorist Arland Ussher. The Georgian house was pulled down and two architects were employed to build a new residence, on the strength of their skill in designing railways. They were called James Otway and Robert Watt. Their only other country-house commission was a seaside villa in Dunmore East. Work started in 1877 and the result was visited without architectural comment by Evelyn Waugh, while on a pilgrimage with Alastair Graham to the nearby monastery of Mount Melleray, celebrated for curing alcoholism. Evelyn Waugh regarded his host, Arland, as a good man for a pint. When this was published in Waugh's diaries, Arland Ussher remembered that the only fault of his guest was to take too much drink and 'do everything that one does with it'. Sold by Arland Ussher in the 1940s so he could devote his life to literature.

DUNGARVAN: **Carriglea**
Symmetrical Tudor-style manor house by an unknown architect, constructed out of honey-coloured local stone (also used eighty years later for the adjoining chapel by W.H. Byrne, who carefully adjusted his idiom to the house with a thoughtfulness not reflected in subsequent extensions). Principal interiors preserved with their lacy Gothick cornices. Staircase with elegant brass balusters rising over a cast-iron stove stamped with the heraldic device of the family who commissioned it—the Odells. Arcaded conservatory supporting two more recent floors for further nuns.

DUNMORE EAST: **Corballymore**
The grimly Baronial retreat of Hon. Dudley Fortescue, the friend of Edward Lear, built out of dark random ashlar only slightly relieved by bands of lighter stone. Entrance front enlivened by semicircular half-landing of the staircase projecting forward beside the porch; but the garden front is terminably dull. Designed in 1870 by Otway and Watt of Waterford and Belfast. Now an hotel.

DUNMORE EAST: **Ocean Hotel**
Maritime villa designed by J.S. Mulvany for the Malcolmson family roofed with convex 'Chinese' style roof like 'Glencar' Blackrock, Co. Dublin (q.v.) and built in 1864. Symmetrical garden front flanked by single-storey pavilions. Mulvany's interiors with his characteristic fireplaces are still discernible. Adjoining stable block of great charm, again with convex roofs railed off by decorative ironwork. Now an hotel. The setting of a film made from a Maeve Binchy novel, *Echoes.*

GURTEEN: **Gurteen Castle**
Designed by Samuel Ussher Roberts for the 16th Lord de la Poer and built in 1863-6 in a style reminiscent of Daniel Robertson. The de la Poers had started to build a castle beside the river forty years earlier to the designs of Thomas Cobden. This was abandoned, probably due to flooding, and all that survives of Cobden today is the Gothic entrance gates. The two other entrances are neo-Classical, with lodges like temples, one of them signed 'Anderson Architect'. These were built by Charles Frederick Anderson, whose lavish designs for them *c.*1843

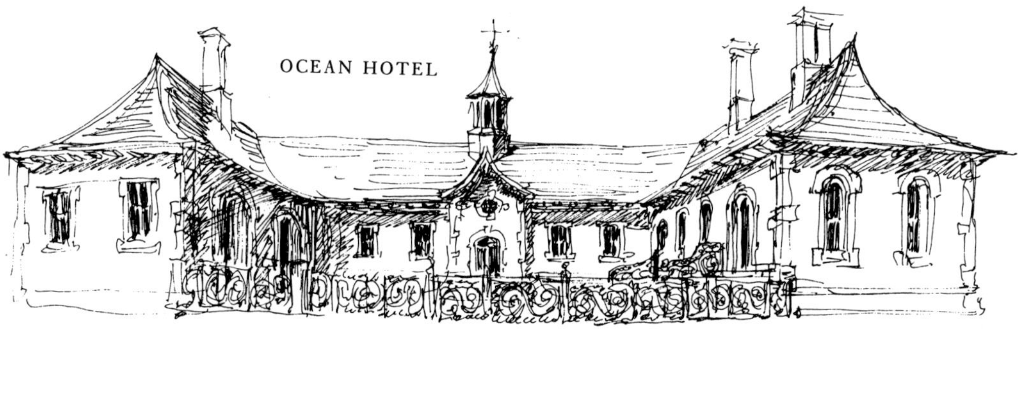
OCEAN HOTEL

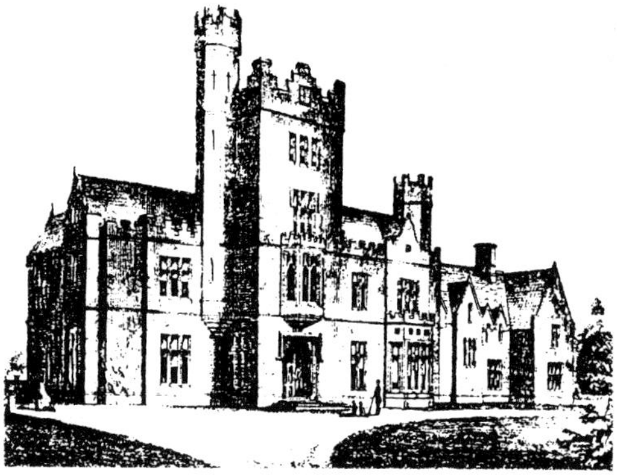

are still in Gurteen. But by the time the de la Poers were ready to start Anderson had emigrated to the United States.

Samuel Ussher Roberts was born in Waterford, the grandson of the architect 'Honest' John Roberts, but he made his career in Galway, where he built Kylemore (q.v.) with the help of J.F. Fuller. At Gurteen he was on his own. Castellated forecourt; entrance marked by massive flag tower. 'Poeraig Aboo' carved over the main door, translatable as 'Up the Powers'. Contrastingly symmetrical garden front, flanked by twin bay windows overlooking formal parterre. Long low-gabled service wing leading to a service court defined by chateau-like corner towers; further diminishing towers, terminate the 'bicycle tower', where the aunts of the present Count de la Poer kept their bicycles, and the 'Jamsy Murphy Tower' named after its builder *c.*1925.

Interior centred on top-lit arcaded and galleried hall rising three stories. Diningroom with oriel to the north, drawingrooms to the south, interconnecting along the garden front. An attached nursery wing ends with an oratory rebuilt by the present count.

KILL: Gardenmorris

Georgian seat of the O'Shees, remodelled by them as a French chateau *c.*1850 and rebuilt by them in 1923 after the house had been destroyed in the Troubles, to be sold up sixty years later. Its most distinctive characteristic is a double-storied octagonal tower with a pyramidal roof overlooking a formal garden and a lake sealed off by woods from the outside world.

KILMEADEN: Ballyduff, or Whitfield Court

The finest house designed by Abraham Denny, a Dublin architect with Waterford connections; Italianate without and, as defined by Girouard, neo-Greek within. Designed *c.*1841 for William Christmas to replace an earlier house on a different site. Asymmetrical façades with twin arcaded belvedere towers each side of the entrance protected by a single-storied portico. Adjoining garden front focused on a single-storied drawingroom bay window ringed by an Ionic colonnade. All the reception rooms open off the central staircase hall, with a central imperial staircase approached between Corinthian columns. This rises to a continuous landing with views down into the staircase well through openings framed with Corinthian pilasters. Double drawingroom with coffered ceilings. Run appropriately by its present owners, Mr and Mrs Hugh Dawnay, as a centre for polo tuition.

LISMORE: Ballysaggartmore Gates and Bridge

The most extraordinary example in Ireland of a prelude to a castle that was never built due to agrarian disputes culminating in the attempted murder of the builder of these follies on his own avenue. There followed a long-drawn-out collapse of the family finances and a retreat from creditors. The instigator of this disastrous extravagance was the grand-aunt of the writer Violet Martin, Elizabeth Martin, who married Arthur Kiely. His elder brother had rebuilt Strancally Castle—hence the rivalry. The young couple began with the entrance gates flanked by twin diagonally-positioned gatelodges, in the style of the Pains but designed by J. Smith, their gardener. Then, where their avenue crossed a

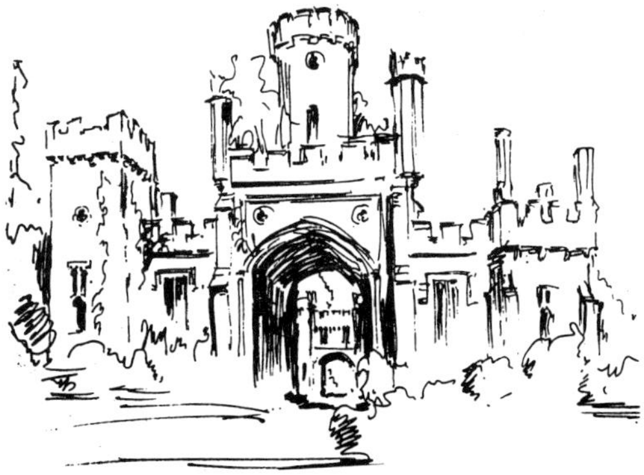

waterfall cascading through a wooded glen, they built a bridge guarded by two miniature castles. Smith had by then developed a personal language, giving his reddish stone a vermiculite finish and developing the form of each castle by a geometrical interplay of cubes, cylinders and triangles. Each castle is contrasted, that on the approach asymmetrical and picturesque while the one across the bridge is symmetrical and thereby more monumental. Regarded with wonder on its completion in 1834, these follies were forgotten in the undergrowth for more than a century. Now they are tidied up with a forest trail between them.

LISMORE: **Carnegie Library**
Constructed in cheerful red-brick and decorative terracotta (1900). Architect, G.P. Sheridan.

LISMORE: **Cathedral of St Carthage**
Built on medieval foundations by William Robinson, rebuilt *c.*1810 by Richard Morrison; tower and spire added 1827 by Pains. Internal entrance door of exaggerated Gothick; a memorial to Dean Scott by Henry Hill; tomb by Rickman. The stained glass window in the transept designed by Burne-Jones and made by William Morris.

LISMORE: **Catholic Church**
This comes early (1881) in the prolific church-building career of Walter Doolin, and is designed in an Italianate Romanesque he never repeated. The façade is a posthumous tribute to Burges, under whom he had studied. The rose window framed by the evangelists is modelled on St Finbarre's Cathedral (q.v.), carved by J.A. O'Connell against a ground of richly coloured mosaic. Asymmetrical tower, nave, aisles, screened transepts. Celtic Revival glass, *c.*1904; earlier window by Cox and Buckley, *c.*1890. At the gates, a tomb to the Revd Edward Wall by P. McGrath (1838)—an obelisk at the top of a table upheld by four Ionic columns.

LISMORE: **Lismore Castle**
The 6th duke (known as the 'Bachelor Duke') of Devonshire rebuilt Lismore Castle twice in his lifetime—at the start of his reign and at the end. His first restoration in 1812 under the direction of his architect William Atkinson was in a light-hearted and precocious Gothic Revival. The second restoration directed by Sir Joseph Paxton assisted by a young nephew, G.H. Stokes (1836-74), from 1849 onwards, appears serious and heavy-handed in its rebuilding of three sides of the great courtyard with a panoply of towers, faced with cut stone shipped over from Derbyshire. But we are not able to appreciate today that the second phase is as humorous as the first, from the viewpoint of the Bachelor Duke. It was the minds of his architects that had changed from frivolity to deadly seriousness. A.N.W. Pugin was enlisted by the decorator J.G. Crace to restore the ruined chapel, not back to its original use (as no doubt would have been Pugin's choice) but to transform it instead into an interior for banqueting and dancing. To house these entertainments Pugin created a minor version of his House of Lords in Westminster, with continuous seating like a choir stalls beneath richly stencilled walls rising to an open roof with gilded stars. The windows at each end of the hall are filled with stained glass by Hardman. At night the illumination comes from an hexagonal Gothic chandelier. The fireplace was intended by Pugin for Horstead and exhibited under Paxton's direction in the Medieval Court of the Great Exhibition adding the inscription of Céad Míle Fáilte'.

If Pugin's insanity had not cut short his career, such was his client's enthusiasm, and wealth, that Lismore Castle might well have rivalled Cardiff. Instead, no other interior is comparable to the banqueting hall. There is a fine fireplace in the billiard room and some furniture. After his death the fitting up of the varied towers lost momentum. The highest tower never received its upper floor and its interior is an empty shell. It is said today that the entire castle called by the Bachelor Duke 'my quasi-feudal and ultra-regal fortress' can accommodate only twelve guests.

PORTLAW
Industrial village laid out by the Malcolmson family, who opened their first cotton mill here in 1825. Most of the housing today is still inhabited by descendants of the original work-force and is still roofed with the mineralized felt

SCHEME FOR LISMORE BY PAXTON AND STOKES

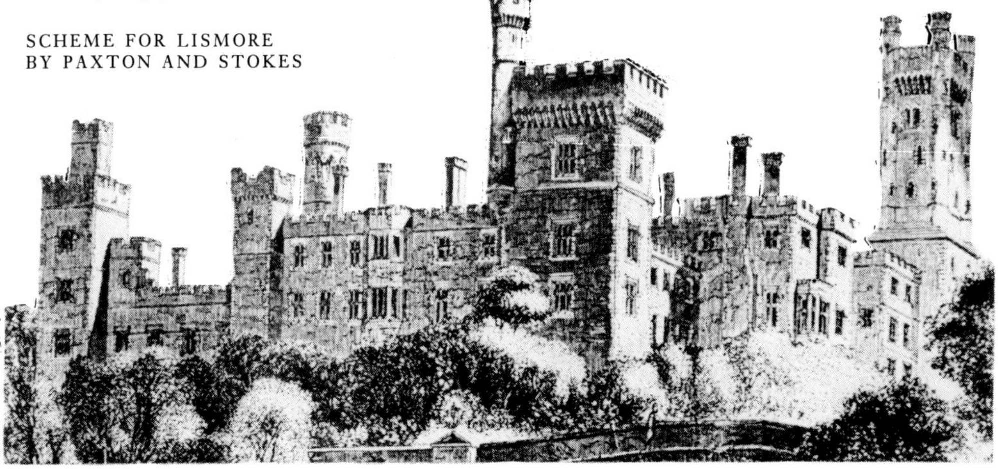

invented by the Malcolmsons and used by them to cover the arched roofs of Dublins' first Great Exhibition. The formality of the street pattern, the wide vistas and the horizontal parapets recall Italy rather than the Ruhr, where the Malcolmsons were among the first to discover coal.

PORTLAW: **Clonagam Church of Ireland**
Burial church of the Beresford family, containing several fine Victorian memorials including Marchioness of Waterford by Sir Richard Boehm.

PORTLAW: **Church of Ireland**
Designed by William Tinsley just before his emigration to the United States (1851). Gothic Revival with good internal stone carving. Stained glass memorials to the Beresfords.

PORTLAW: **Cuilcagh Church of Ireland and School**
Rural church in wooded valley, its gates guarded by a gabled diamond-paned schoolhouse nestling among further trees, dated 1849. Said to be among the last buildings to be designed by Wm. Tinsley in Ireland.

PORTLAW: **Curraghmore**
One of the earliest Irish commissions of Daniel Robertson in 1833 was to transform Curraghmore into a Gothic castle. Fortunately his proposals were not carried out. Instead the energies of Louisa marchioness of Waterford were channelled into the formal gardens, presumably with Robertson's assistance, to link the house to the lake. Its centrepiece was at one time an immense cast-iron fountain purchased at the Paris Exhibition of 1856 by the 4th marquis but sold off for scrap for his son. The designer of the parterres was James Fraser, who then created the formal vistas across the demesne to the north, and the American gardens along the river to the south. Samuel Ussher Roberts was called in to re-case the house in 1876 and insert plate-glass windows. At the same time Boehm sculpted the dragon on the pediment of the garden front and the stag on the tower. These are only lively touches since the enthusiasm of Roberts was limited to the Gothic Revival, and the boredom of his compulsory Classicism here is palpable.

PORTLAW: **Mayfield**
The principal seat of the entrepreneurial Malcolmson family—a rebuilding of an earlier house; three floors, projecting central campanile. The architect was William Tinsley. Ingenious entrance gates by Richard Turner, one leading to the adjoining mills. House now serves as offices.

PORTLAW: **Woodlock**
Built in 1864 for John Malcolmson by J.S. Mulvany in his simplified Italianate: central block of two stories and single-storey wings, one of them an apsidal conservatory now transformed into a chapel. Now a convent.

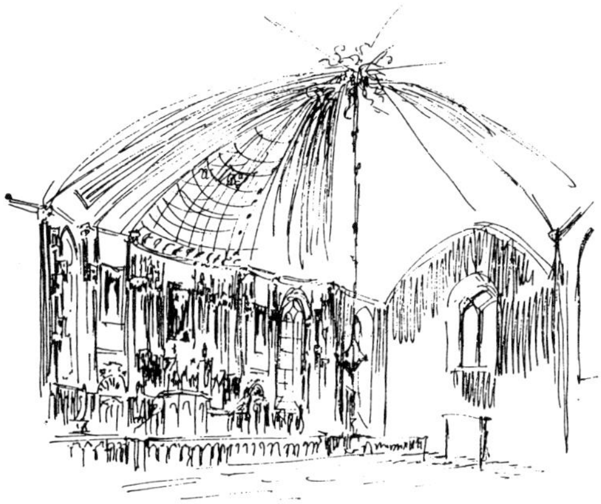

TALLOW: **Catholic Church**
Strawberry Hill Gothick interior with altar in shallow pinnacled apse *c.*1830-40.

TRAMORE: **Catholic Church**
Characteristic Gothic church by J.J. McCarthy dominated by asymmetrical tower and spire (1856-71). Interior stripped of its fittings and painted a pink that clashes with Mayer's glass.

TRAMORE: **Rockfield**
Handsome Italianate house built *c.*1840 with pillared porch, principal rooms on the garden front overlooking the sea, billiard room in an added wing.

WATERFORD: **Allied Irish Bank**
An urbane neo-Classical bank, impeccably proportioned, the severity of its idiom tempered by a gently curving bow. Designed in 1911 by Batchelor and Hicks on corner of Barronstrand Street and the Quay.

WATERFORD: **Ardkeen**
Crisp neo-Classical villa built for the Malcolmson family by J.S. Mulvany, now the administration block of the surrounding hospital.

WATERFORD: **Ballinamona Park**
The Georgian centre block was extended in 1866 by twin single-storied wings, one screening a conservatory. This was the only room to survive the fire of 1894. The architect of the rebuilding was R. St G. Moore, who kept the original layout. Parkland and lake romanticized at the end of the last century.

WATERFORD: The Courthouse

There was no preservation society to protest at the demolition of Gandon's courthouse in the 1840s when it was replaced by what we see today. J.B. Keane, the architect, was the most gifted Irish neo-Classicist of his generation, but here he simply repeated the façade he had designed for Tullamore (q.v.), with a five-bay Ionic portico played off against almost windowless walls articulated by shallow plasters. Executant architect, Terence O'Reilly. Restored ten years ago after a judge had refused to sit in it in case he was injured by collapsing plaster.

WATERFORD: Customs House & Post Office

Handsome palazzo in restrained Venetian Gothic, obsolete elsewhere but here expressing the prosperity of 19th-century Waterford. Designed in 1876 by an obscure architect called James Ryan, who appears to have spent some time in the Board of Works, with the Owen dynasty, on the stylistic evidence of this, his only important commission.

WATERFORD: Dominican Church

George Goldie as an architect was so committed to the Gothic Revival that a strong-minded client must have been responsible for the Classicism of this church; although like so many churches of the early Renaissance, the underlying feeling is medieval, especially in the bracing of its open roof. Twenty years ago was condemned as dangerous due to dry rot and scheduled for demolition, but it has survived after a last minute reprieve and a change of thought by the experts.

WATERFORD: Faithlegg

Georgian house re-cased and extended with rusticated portico, two-storied wings and an orangery *c.*1870 for the Power family. Now a school of the De La Salle Brothers.

WATERFORD: Ferrybank Catholic Church

The church was built in two phases. The first was a tower and spire built in front of an existing church in 1867 by Pugin and Ashlin above the family vault of the Barron family. The donor was Pierce Marcus Barron, who intended to rebuild the rest of the church. This did not happen until 1903 with legacy of Sir H.T.P. Barron, a cousin. The architect was George Ashlin working to a well-tried formula apart from the stone vaulted chapel alongside the chancel with its floor of restrained abstract mosaic and delicately stained glass, a miniature version of Myshall (q.v.). Here Gerald Fitzgerald Purcell preserved the body of his first wife in a glass coffin.

WATERFOOD: Grace Dieu

A neo-Classical villa *c.*1840 remodelled and extended in a coarse Italianate by Albert Murray in 1894, retaining the original cube and overlapping it with another block while masking the difference between the two by adding a pilastered porch, a glazed loggia and a pedimented timber conservatory; irregular arcaded hall leading to Murray's characteristic neo-Adamesque reception rooms. Conservatory and twin curvilinears in the walled garden have not survived the transformation of the house into a religious institution.

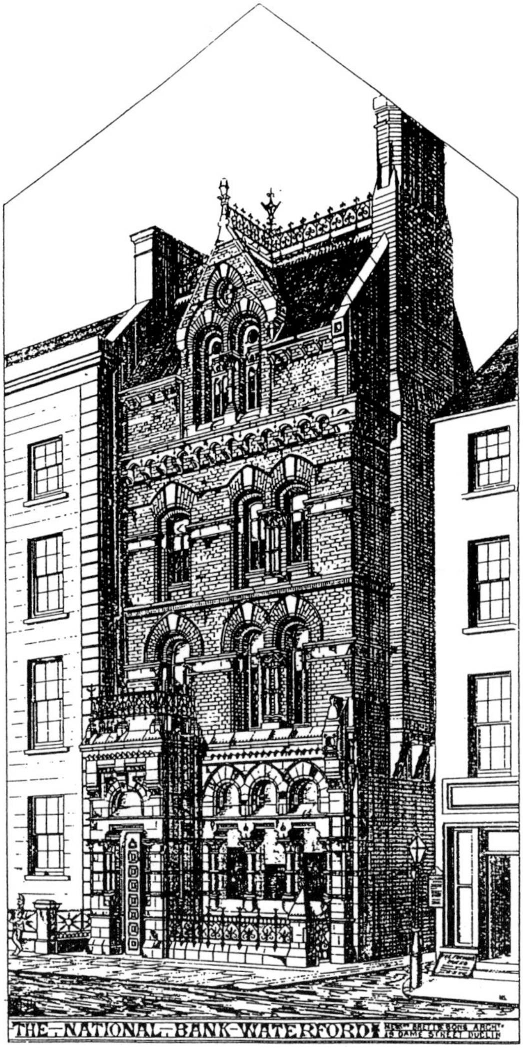

WATERFORD, Great George's Street: Hibernian Insurance

Lively if disrespectful neighbour to the Georgian townhouse of the Morres family, designed in 1877 in Ruskinian Gothic (by then disowned by its inspirer). Three stories topped by an immense iron-crested dormer; the polychromatic brickstone accented by stone voussoirs, corbelling and banding, disguises the underlying conventionality of its fenestration. Designed by J.H. Brett, who carried on an architectural practice with his father in Dublin where they are remembered only for their Mercer's Hospital extension, so inhibited compared to this.

WATERFORD: Holy Ghost Hospital
Large symmetrical and institutional, designed by J.J. O'Callaghan in his harsh characteristic Gothic (1880) that has survived redundancy and sale a century later, as has the livelier gatelodge.

WATERFORD: Presentation Convent
The most satisfying of the Irish monastic commissions given to A.N.W. Pugin, due to the site supervision that he was able to give to the job, and the respect accorded to his intentions ever since; witness the retention of his rood screen in the chapel. Well-sited to take advantage of the view southwards across what was once a rural valley. Enlivened by a circular staircase turret and built out of local stone, it must once have been as integrated into the landscaping as its medieval counterparts, but now it serenely presides over surrounding council housing. Gently asymmetrical elevations of four ranges wrapped round a central court. The circulation is by an internal cloister given its special character by exposing the steeply raked lean-to roofs that spring from head height, permitting only tiny windows that are reflected in the polished enamelled tilework of the floor.

A modest door gives access to the chapel, a simple rectangle with an open roof braced by Gothic arches, but given spatial complexity by the rood screen between the nave and choir, the framework of its central opening carried upwards to support the Virgin and Saint John each side of the resplendent Crucifixion.

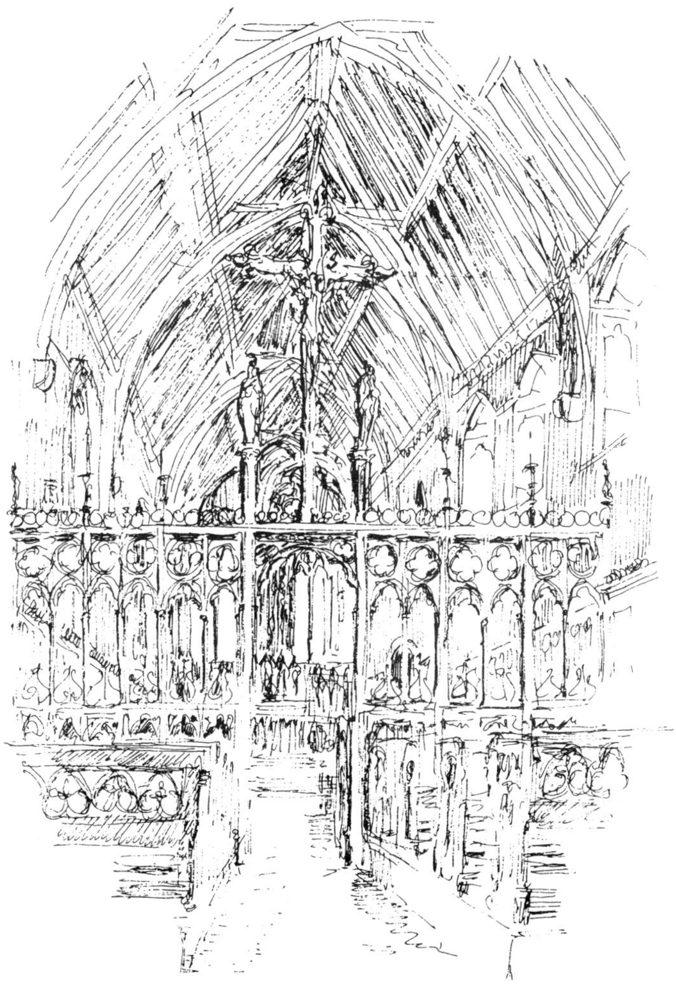

WATERFORD: St Catherine's Hall
Designed as the Protestant hall *c.*1850 by A. Denny at the same time as his best country house, Ballyduff (q.v.)—both characterized by Italianate corner towers. In the hall, they are deployed symmetrically flanking an arcade, revealing Denny to be one of the last of the provincial Palladians.

WATERFORD: St John's Catholic Church
Unassuming early Gothic Revival entered through symmetrical tower. Architect, J.B. Keane, *c.*1845.

WATERFORD: St John's College
Catholic seminary designed in 1867 by George Goldie, in his own full-blooded version of the Gothic Revival, but one of his least-known buildings due to its secluded setting. Slightly symmetrical façade with massive chimneys, two integrated into massive corner towers. Chapel in centre of range at rear approached through imposing cloisters.

WATERFORD: St John's Manor
Traditionally ascribed to A.W.N. Pugin but by those standards disappointing even before being surrounded by housing estates, so that it now appears to have been erected for its present use as a community centre. Built out of red brick

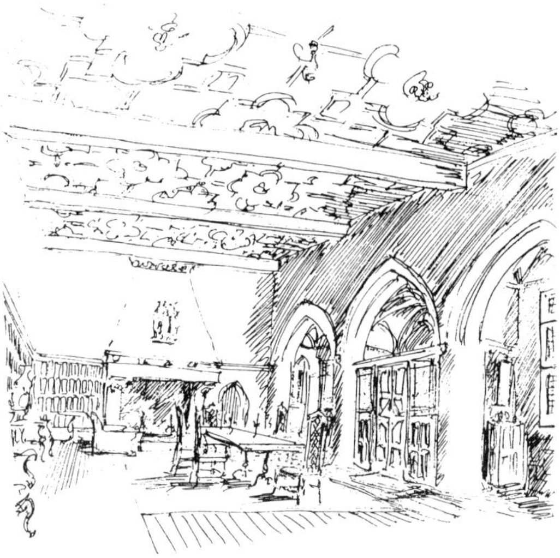

with starved stone trimmings *c.*1842. The client was Sir Thomas Wyse MP, the long-suffering husband of Laetitia, daughter of Lucien Bonaparte. She travelled through Europe giving birth to children by different fathers after she had escaped from the convent where she had been immured by her husband and father. Recounted in *The Spurious Brood*, by Olga Bonaparte-Wise.

WATERFORD: Waterford Castle, or The Island
The core of the castle is medieval, having been built by a branch of the Fitzgeralds who owned large estates in Suffolk, where the poet and translator of Omar Khayyam, Edward Fitz-Gerald, spent most of his life. The poet's great-nephew, Gerard Purcell-FitzGerald, embarked on a massive reconstruction *c.*1900s. He flanks the original towerhouse with wings of equal height which frankly express two and three storeys respectively of consistently mullioned windows, all crowned with Irish battlements, so as to be at first sight totally convincing. As so often happens when Irish medieval castles were recreated, the architect was an Englishman who had never worked in Ireland—Romayne Walker (here assisted by Albert Murray). His most impressive interior is the great hall walled in Portland stone and screened from the entrance lobby by an arcade of impeccable Gothic. At one end is a chateau-like heraldic fireplace reminiscent of Burges. The rest of the interiors fail to live up to the standards set by the exterior and the hall. Their proportions are too low and the decoration too perfunctory, no doubt to meet a deadline. But the client insisted on the latest technology—lift, internal telephone and luxurious bathrooms for his house parties, so that its recent transformation into an hotel has been extraordinarily painless. Indeed an hotel had been the original intention of his daughter and heiress, Princess Ferdinando d'Ardia Carraciola, if she had been permitted by her husband.

WATERFORD: Trustee Savings Bank
The finest of the city's banks despite the loss of its cupola thirty years ago. Pedimented and pilastered façade, of two storeys; banking hall on ground floor, impressive boardroom taking up the centre of the *piano nobile*. Designed by Thomas Jackson of Belfast after he had won a competition in 1841. In Mark Girouard's words: 'a gigantic and opulent boardroom which suggests a certain *folie de grandeur* in the original directors for it would not disgrace the Bank of England'.

WESTMEATH

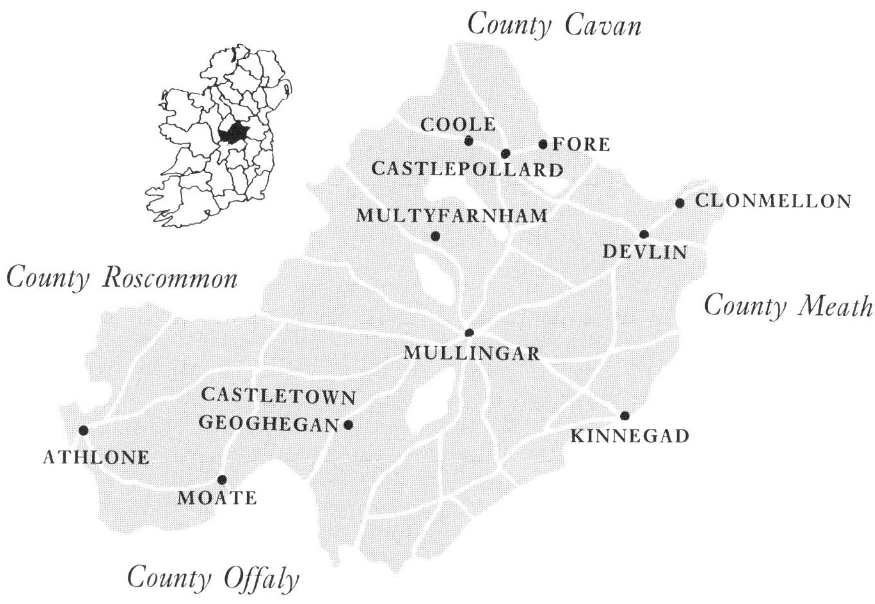

ATHLONE: **Custume Barracks**
One of the largest military barracks in Ireland. During the Victorian era there were two principal building campaigns: the earlier (of 1851) built fortifications along the main road beside the Shannon with a triumphal pedimented arch, and a series of symmetrical single-storied lodges called the cookhouses. The

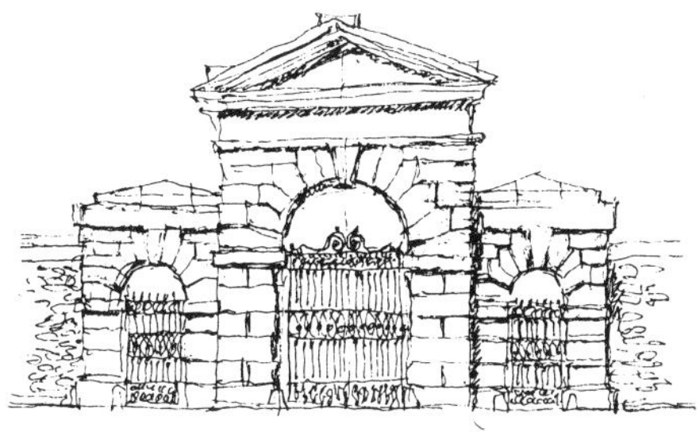

architect was an army engineer called Constable. He also may have been responsible for the geometrical waterworks and the Military Prison, with the elegant and sinister ironwork of its internal circulation remarkably intact, ready to immure recruits who had failed to fire on the Fenians. The later phase of building took place in the different climate of imperial optimism during the 1870s—the present canteen of 1873 and the gymnasium of 1875. The canteen is a remarkable example of the Classical Revival inspired by Georgian orangeries, lit by delicately paned, double-height, arched windows. The formality of the interior is still decipherable. The gymnasium shows the same progressive architectural leanings towards 'Sweetness and Light'. Its most remarkable feature is the central lantern astride the roof.

The Gothic Revival Garrison church was dismangled in 1931 and to make way for Ralph Byrne's SS. Peter and Paul, but was re-erected in Creagh, a suburb of Ballinasloe.

ATHLONE: **Glynnwood**
Just the stables survive with their enamelled tiled interiors and a few walls, fragments of the ostentatious re-casing of an earlier house commissioned by Henry Dames Longworth, lord lieutenant of the county, and a pillar of the Ancient Régime, complying with the eccentric will of a rich uncle. Burnt accidentally in 1917. A few well-built brick cottages for well-behaved tenants and a substantial agent's house also survive, and hidden in the undergrowth are rusty iron entrance gates with a double-storied octagonal lodge. The only countryhouse designed by Sir George Moyers, the Dublin builder, famed for his pomposity and known as the duke of Memel. Date: 1884.

ATHLONE: **Ladywell**
Neo-Classical villa overlooking Lough Ree, designed *c.*1850 by the Dublin architect Sandham Symes for Sir Ross Mahon. Symes was architect for the Bank of Ireland, and for his client, a banker, he used the Italianate formula that he would later employ for innumerable provincial branches. The entrance is, surprisingly, on the side elevation, sheltered by a minimalist cast-iron canopy that Symes had already used in Altidore, Glenageary (q.v.). This allows an unbroken sequence of reception rooms to face the lake, while an even more distant prospect extends from the arched half landing window. Castellated lodge beside the lake.

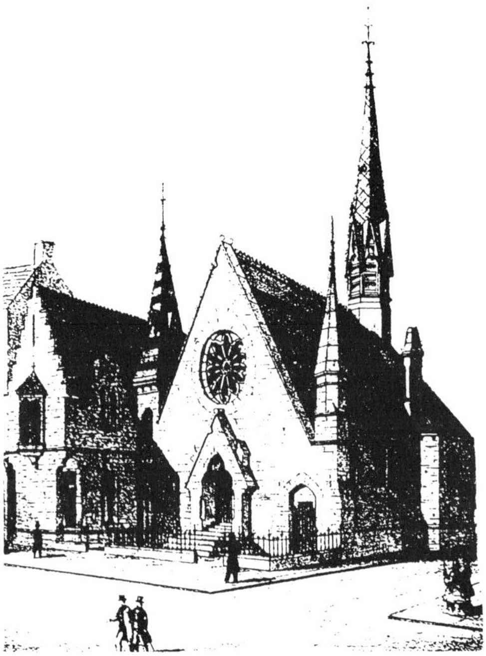

ATHLONE: **Methodist Church**
Quirky Gothic octagonal meeting hall by A.G. Jones, façade extended on each side by flying buttresses arching over side gates with access to the transepts. The centralized interior was clearly expressed by a spire-like lantern, but this became unsafe in 1950 and was then dismantled. Despite that disaster, the church remains Jones' most original.

ATHLONE: **The Moorings**
Italianate villa protected from intrusion by trim coniferous park and shrubberies. The family home of the Broderick family. Inherited by the novelist John Broderick, who sold up the house and contents to retire to Bath.

ATHLONE: **Moydrum Castle**
William Murray was called in by the Castlemaines to embellish their demesne with Baronial entrance gates (now vanished and replaced with RTE television masts), so it is possible that he designed their family church, *c.*1850. This is now a gutted shell overlooking the ivy clad ruins of the castle. The Castlemaines were unlucky: the first Lord Castlemaine, who had commissioned Richard Morrison to recast an earlier house in 1821, lost his life when he jumped out of a window to escape a minor blaze. In 1921, the last Lord Castlemaine lost all his possessions in the final blaze that his staff started, angered by his wife's refusing to acknowledge their existence.

ATHLONE: **Railway Bridge**
Heavy but competent design by G.W. Hemans (1850) bearing the Dublin-Galway line across the Shannon.

ATHLONE: **St Mary's Catholic Church**
One of John Bourke's finest churches, remarkable for its open roof structure, which was Bourke's personal contribution to the Gothic Revival, developing from the minimalism of the Catholic church of Baltinglass (q.v.) to the complexity of Granard's (q.v.). Athlone was designed a year before Granard and its open roof is more decorative and more conventional. The exterior is dominated by its symmetrically sited western tower and broached spire (which Bourke repeated when he built Dublin's St Lawrence O'Toole: q.v.). Lavishly carved high altar by Leonardi of Rome (1878) which no longer has to compete with the pulpit carved with biblical scenes by James Pearse to the designs of J.J. McCarthy, since this was dismantled after the Second Vatican Council and donated to the Padraig Pearse Museum in St Edna's Dublin, who have yet to resurrect it. The stained glass window depicting the Resurrection was made in Amiens and exhibited in the Paris Exhibition of 1878. The glass in the transepts is by Mayer of Munich.

At the entrance, elegant marble memorial to the founder, the Revd Kilroe, by John Hogan, junior (1878) depicting the priest holding a model of the church that he did not live to see completed (and now depleted).

ATHLONE: **Stations**
West: large station, double-storied since the railway was elevated to cross the Shannon. All the personal characteristics of J.S. Mulvany are deployed, his keystones and his pendant brackets. Exhibited in the RHA of 1851.

East: designed by George Wilkinson and built in 1858. Entrance recessed behind arcaded loggia.

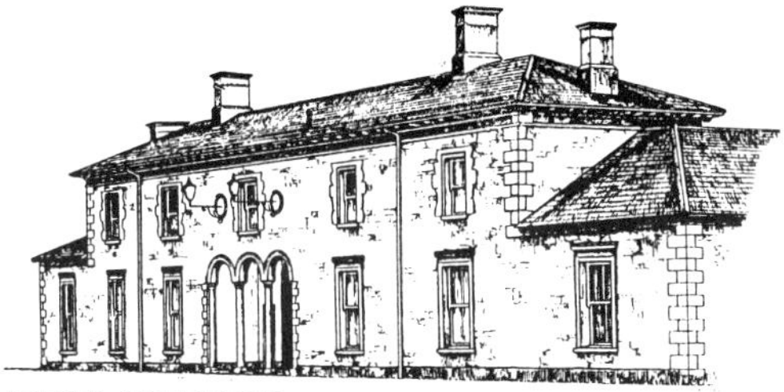

WEST STATION

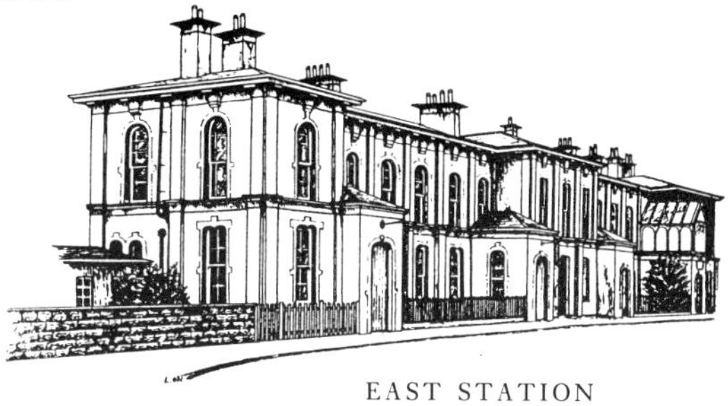

EAST STATION

CASTLEPOLLARD: **Tullynally Castle**
Originally a compact Georgian cube which has been retained at one end of what is, at least in ground area, Ireland's largest castle, presenting an array of varied towers round two service courts. Four architects were involved: Francis Johnston remodelled the original house in 1801-6 for the 2nd earl of Longford, who commissioned James Sheil to continue this work in the 1820s. Then came the turn of Sir Richard Morrison, commissioned by the trustees of the bachelor 3rd earl (1842-6). A final architect was Rawson Carroll (1860 onwards). Today Morrison's contribution is the most visible. He rebuilt the side ranges of the service courts. That facing the entrance front starts off with the tallest tower of all, linking the original cube to a turreted family wing, lowered and extended past an octagonal staircase tower to end in a battlemented gatehouse. Despite its variety, a certain weariness is revealed. This is one of Morrison's last commissions, and it could well have been the work of his rival, Francis Johnston, forty years before. His garden front is more inventive with a triple-arched window in a crow-stepped gable illuminating the kitchen, and a circular tower linking his wing to Sheil's remodelling of the original house. Rawson Carroll added a final tower, but was mainly responsible for the latest household improvements such as the laundry room. He installed one of the heating systems, the earliest having been installed by Richard Lovell Edgeworth, the father of Maria. Five boilers are ranged beside each other like stranded leviathans in a basement room. Rawson Carroll also designed Classiebawn (q.v.), inherited by Lord Mountbatten who thought that the Pakenhams would never have heard of his architect and was not entirely pleased to be told, 'Oh, yes, he did our drains.'

The present owner, the historian Thomas Pakenham, took his tractor from the farm to rescue the capitals of the staircase hall of Benjamin Woodward's Kildare Street club during its destruction in 1971 and they are in the stable yard. Diningroom papered by him with Pugin's designs for the House of Lords.

CASTLETOWN GEOGHEGAN: **Balnagore**
Milling village founded by a branch of the Perry family, who were entrepreneurial Quakers, and patrons of J.S. Mulvany. Two houses here can be attributed to him. The principal house is approached by an entrance gate designed in his personal neo-Classicism, which the dwelling itself is unable to live up to. There is too much complexity in its projections and recesses that leads to trouble at the level of his pedimented eaves, and although the principal rooms are well proportioned, there are too many abrupt changes of scale to minor rooms beside them. None of these criticisms could be levelled at the dower house, despite the incorporation of an earlier two-storied cottage, which Mulvany extends by two adjoining single-floor ranges to overlook the river. Here the style is a distilled Greek Revival. The windows are French casements set on plinths and framed by architraves that rest on ground level. The pediment overhanging the door rests not on columns but on geometrical latticing. In these unpretentious villas, Mulvany reveals himself as a precursor of Post-Modernism.

CASTLETOWN GEOGHEGAN: **Middleton Park**
Now that Kenure Park has been demolished,

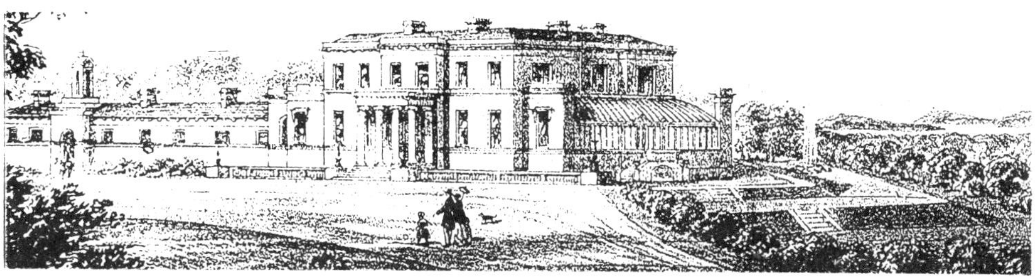

the staircase hall of this house remains George Papworth's most spectacular interior, with central stairs branching up to first-floor gallery. Balustrades of cast-iron foliage and cast-iron dome. Also cast-iron conservatory disguised as one of twin single-storied pavilions. Built *c.* 1846 by the Boyd-Rochforts and modelled on nearby Ballnegal by Francis Johnston. The birthplace of Sir Cecil Boyd-Rochfort, trainer to Queen Elizabeth II.

Castletown Geoghegan gatelodge, half-timber neo-Tudor (1895).

CASTLETOWN GEOGHEGAN: Catholic Church

Built *c.* 1880 in the harsh Gothic idiom of J.J.

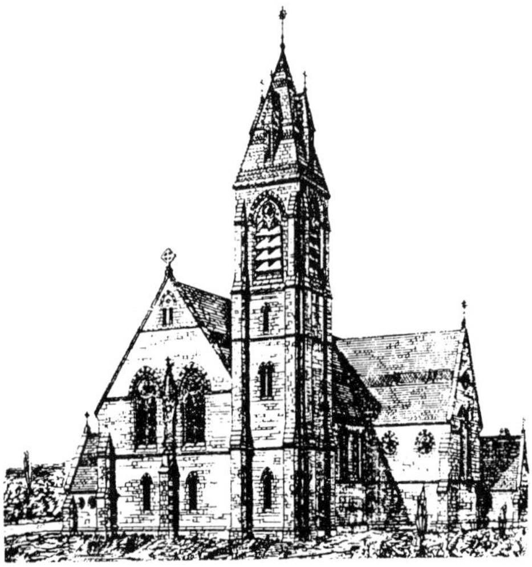

O'Callaghan to a conventional plan using the local limestone. Tower and spire at the corner of the façade rather than at the crossing as at Clara (q.v.; built by O'Callaghan at the same time nearby). Interior with arcades carried across the transepts. Mosaic enriching apsed chancel. *Sfumato* stained glass in the style of Earley. Completed by T.F. McNamara.

CLONMELLON: Killua Castle

Georgian house *c.* 1780 of three stories. Entry front with central polygonal bay containing entrance hall. Garden front with central curved bay containing elliptical drawingroom. Transformed *c.* 1830 into a feudal pile in a masterly manner relying on additional towers of a varied shape (square, circular and polygonal) with only minimal alterations to the existing house. The front door and drawingroom were gothicized and the parapet castellated. The idiom of the new towers is unusually horizontal, to harmonize with the earlier Georgian and emphasize the symmetry of the façade, but it is no less

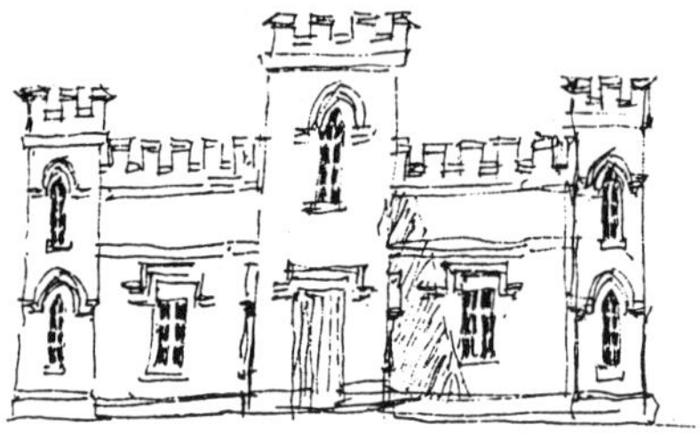

forceful and distinctive. Attributable on stylistic grounds to James Sheil. Killua should have been inherited by T.E. Lawrence if his father, Sir Robert Chapman Bt., who eloped with the family governess, had been ever able to marry her. Instead it was inherited by distant relations, who sold it to a firm of dismantlers after the Second World War. Now roofless in a denuded park. A toy Gothic triple-towered gatelodge at the gates to the village has been saved and sympathetically restored. Other follies crumbling, including an obelisk marking the spot where the first potato was planted in Ireland.

COOLE: The Hospital

The earliest buildings here were built as a convent, founded by the Deases, an old Catholic family who were in charge of the invitation list to the viceregal court, on which they refused to include George Moore. Extended subsequently by an early Arts and Crafts wing and then another more self-consciously Celtic Revival.

DELVIN: Catholic Church

Since the Nugents were Catholic, they gave the best site in their village to the Catholic church and engaged George Ashlin, who had already built for them their oratory at Fore (q.v.). There is a story (probably untrue) that Ashlin was so upset on the train travelling from Moate after the rejection of his designs for his church there, that a fellow-passenger, the parish priest of Devlin, on enquiring the reasons for such distress, fell in love with the plans.

Nave of six bays, transepts of two and a chancel of one bay terminating with a polygonal apse. Nave entered under corner tower with open octagonal lantern with slender spire. Elaborate altars have survived mutilation but not the alabaster pulpit. Work began in 1872 and was completed ten years later with the construction of a commodious parochial house for the contented parish priest, also by Ashlin.

DELVIN: Cooke Mausoleum, Reynella Graveyard

Built *c.* 1835 to his own design by the eccentric Adolphus Cooke of Cookesboro for his father, who died in 1835 and who, as Adolphus believed, had been reincarnated as a turkey-cock—hence the egg-shaped mausoleum. Here in 1850 he also interred a much-loved nanny, and here he lies himself. When he died in 1876, his heirs refused to bury him in a vaulted library where his embalmed corpse would await his own reincarnation within his own dwelling. House and his own mausoleum have now both been levelled.

DELVIN: Clonyn Castle

One of the last Gothic Revival castles to be built in Ireland, designed in 1874 by McCurdy and Mitchell for Lord Greville, who had married the heiress to the estate, Lady Rosa Nugent, the only surviving child of the last marquis of Westmeath. Utterly humourless, four identical circular corner towers rise up from a dry moat to guard a rectangular central block crowned with Irish battlements and machicolations throughout. But any semblance to antiquity is dispelled by serried ranks of humdrum, round-arched, plate-glass windows that contrive to give to this haughty pile a premonition of suburbia. Interiors later remodelled by Millar in 1890, apart from oratory by George Ashlin.

John McCurdy, the architect, throughout his life claimed that he had been the real designer of Woodward's Museum building in Trinity, and here we find the same formula of a top-lit double-height inner hall with an imposing staircase ascending to an arcaded tribune. But in Clonyn, despite its grandeur, it remains a formula and nothing more. Here the 1st Lord Greville slipped on the stairs in a fracas with three of his sons and fell to his death on the eve of his wife's burial. As his wife's coffin had been lost en route from England earlier that day, a curse issued against her father must have been remembered. An old woman whose son had been wrongfully executed for sheep-stealing had cursed the family for seven generations from the scaffold, with results that a daughter-in-law, writing many years later, felt that it would be too indiscreet to reveal. Her account of the banshees who followed the family from the old castle to the new is more explicit. They wailed in the dry moat before every death and terrified the dogs. Not surprisingly the family sold up in 1922; inevitably part of the demesne has become a golf course.

FORE: Greville Nugent Mausoleum and St Fechin's Hermitage

The earliest of the mausolea of George Ashlin, and the smallest (always for Ashlin the sign of quality), completed in 1867 and built by Sibthorpes.

A tiny stone-roofed cell ingeniously grafted on to a medieval tower house, which Ashlin opened up to serve as the chancel, overlooks the sacred valley of Fore, its ruined priory and its seven miracles. Were it not for its mechanical window tracery, we would be taken in and believe that it was built six centuries before the tower house, not six centuries after. Ashlin's prototype was the medieval church of Taghmon ten miles away, attached to a fortified tower which has ensured its survival. The living quarters of the priest were on the upper floor, an ancient Irish tradition that Ashlin's generation of church architects destroyed; and the tower in Fore had served in the 17th century as a refuge to a recluse who modelled his life on the early Irish saints and whose Latin epitaph, 'Therefore the traveller, whoever he may be, when he sees this vault let him request that the soul of the monk who dwells here will go to heaven', is now above the entrance door. Ashlin's attitude to the tower was ambiguous. He gave it new battlements but widened all the windows to match the fenestration of his addition, and deployed buttresses to mask the joint between the new and the old. So his treatment of the interior, where the differences between the old and new are underlined, comes as a shock. The smooth ashlar vaulting of the nave is contrasted to the original crude wickerwork vaulting of the chancel. What was once an external window in the room above has been carefully retained, even though it is off-centre, to look down into the nave and challenge the intruder. The tower also serves as a shelter for earlier heraldic tombs. Linking the new and the old church is the memorial slab that seals off the vault below, where lies Rose Greville, the last of the Devlin Nugents, and who, when vandals broke in a few years ago, had still retained her golden hair. Today, before we censure Ashlin for interfering with a listed ancient monument, we should consider what we have done in our own time to the prospect of the abbey in the valley—an immense asphalted car park with a wall-lined access across the bog, past tables (also of stone) set out like cenotaphs to outlast the ruins beyond for the benefit of picnickers.

KINNEGAD: Coralstown Catholic Church

J.P. Davis is remembered only for the churches built for other architects. An off-beat design for Bettystown illustrated in the *Irish Builder* remained unexecuted, but this small rural, parish church, with its polygonal apse, illustrated in 1870 was actually built (in a more simplified form and without the intended tower and spire). The steeple we see was transferred from the derelict Kinnegad church of Ireland by an enterprising parish priest in 1955.

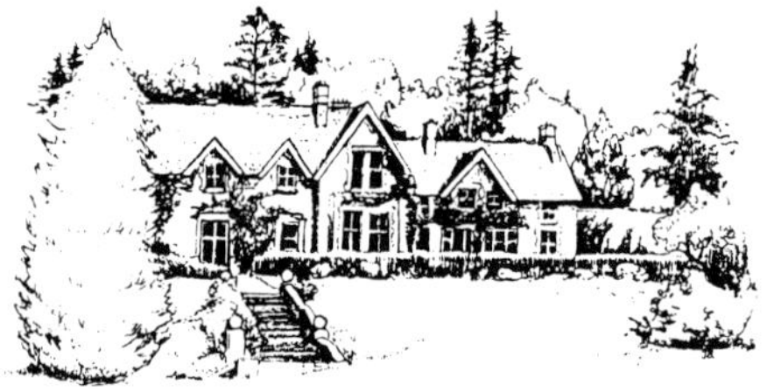

MOATE: **Coolatore**
An asymmetrically composed, simplified neo-Elizabethan country house. The exterior, grimly built out of local rubble with trimmings of yellow brick, belies the interior of great warmth and charm.

MULLINGAR: **Bishop's Palace**
Archetypal Gothic Revival bishop's residence with attached chapel grimly presiding over its own grounds; by William Hague (1873). The reason perhaps why a later incumbent should be so determined to build a Classical cathedral.

MULLINGAR: **Church of Ireland**
The church, which dates from 1733, was rebuilt in 1814. Remodelled in 1860 by Welland and in 1888 (when the adjoining church hall was built, most probably by J.F. Fuller). Romantic restoration of 1960, stripping the walls of plaster, and a policy of transferring Victorian stained glass here from outlying churches, have combined to dispel a dim religious light. These transplants include a window to commemorate the eccentric Adolphus Cooke. Original to the church are the Hopkins east window of 1864 and glass by Heaton, Butler and Bayne. The Swift window in the south transept (French glass of 1890) was acquired at the Paris Exhibition.

MULLINGAR: **County Buildings**
Elegant and restrained Italianate with a shallow, bow-fronted portico of contrasting delicacy. Architect, A.E. Joyce. Built in 1910-13.

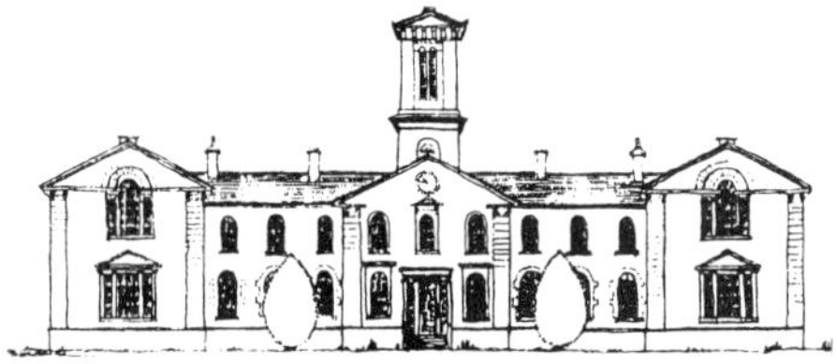

MULLINGAR: **The College**
In his best institutional buildings for the Catholic Church, John Bourke blends the ease of a Georgian country house with the picturesque of Italianate vernacular, thus expressing the new religious links between Ireland and Italy; the Hevey College, with its Palladian façade effectively screening later unsympathetic extensions, was designed in 1854.

MULLINGAR: **Dunboden Park**
Georgian house, remodelled by Sandham Symes, now a ruin. Classical mausoleum in the garden, attributable also to Symes, and also derelict.

MULLINGAR: **Presentation and Loreto Convents**
Twin convents built in the style of Trim convent, to which their foundation is connected. Trim was designed in 1858 by William Caldbeck, who also did a lot of work in Mullingar, but he died in 1872, possibly leaving the nuns some unexecuted plans. The chapel of the Presentation Convent was designed in 1873 by J.P. Davis.

MULLINGAR: **St Finian's College**
An immense symmetrical Italianate palazzo, set in open countryside to avoid the distraction of the town. Designed by Lucius O'Callaghan, evidently influenced by his father's All Hallows in Drumcondra and built in 1903-8. Entrance hall of glowering Hiberno-Romanesque (prophetic of the rise of nationalism), giving access to grimly institutional interiors. One feels that Lucius, as his name implies, was more relaxed when he came to design the swaggering entrance gates, far grander than any country house of the time, the last of a long tradition, presumably immortalizing an old boy's gratitude to his Alma Mater.

MULLINGAR: **The Station**
The quirkiest 19th century station in Ireland, designed to fit between two railway lines, one curving and the other straight, to meet in front of the main pavilion. This is approached through an eaved and columned entrance between two extended arms, one curved with the branch line, the other straight and linked to an arcaded railway shed. Designed by J.S. Mulvany *c.*1850.

MULLINGAR: **Knockdrin Castle**
The earliest masterpiece of James Sheil. An estate map commissioned by Sir Richard Levinge, the 6th baronet, in 1818 from Thomas Kearney shows the new castle intact—so it is Georgian rather than Victorian Gothic; therefore it is even more remarkable that Sheil, an unknown Irish provincial, should have evolved such a distinctive and even rumbustious castle style outclassing rival commissions by Sir Richard Morrison. The gatehouse at the end of the screen wall is omitted from Kearney's watercolour and lacks the simplicity of the castle

itself, resembling the Mullingar entrance gates added by the 7th baronet, an artist and explorer and star of amateur theatricals. The gates were designed by John McCurdy in 1863, and he was presumably the architect of the follies (mentioned in the *Dublin Builder* of 1862). These include 'the shooting tower' three stories high with corner battlements, built, no doubt, to facilitate the increasing portliness of the baronet (which his dramatic costumes could not entirely conceal from pioneer photographers). McCurdy also extended the gardens. The castle itself has been impeccably maintained by its present owners, Baron and Baroness von Prondzinski.

MULLINGAR: St Loman's Hospital

The lunatic asylum which forms the core of St Loman's was the largest commission of J.S. Mulvany and alas the dreariest. He was the most gifted neo-Classicist of his generation, but the only evidence here in this neo-Elizabethan structure is its unremitting symmetry and the monumental massing of the chimneys. The picturesque quality redeeming contemporary Gothic Revival asylums is lacking, even in the neo-medieval church, and of his personal experiments in Greek and Egyptian, there is not the slightest hint. Drawings exhibited in 1853 in the RHA.

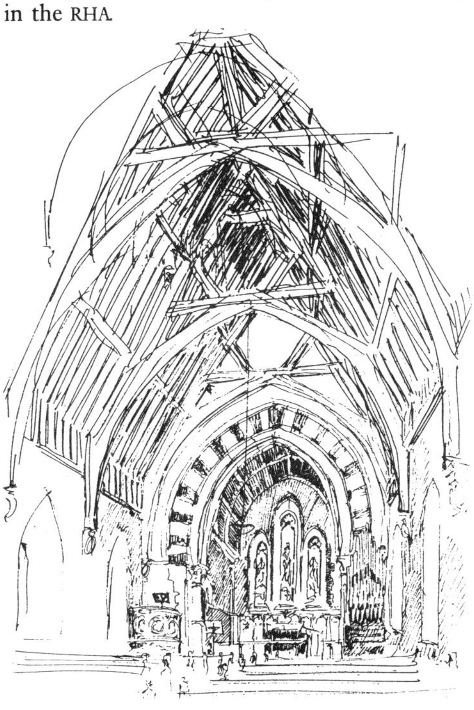

MULLINGAR: Moyaliskert Church of Ireland

Designed by Rawson Carroll (1895) in grim, uncompromising Gothic, made even grimmer by the local limestone. A spirelet corbelled from its western gable. Interior of contrasting brightness with polychromatic archway into chancel. Tough cylindrical pulpit inspired by Burges. Memorial window by Baillie (to Myles Cooker, killed in 1888 boarding a slave ship of Zanzibar) depicts a black child slave liberated by a white angel. Further glass by Heaton, Butler and Bayne

MULLINGAR: Tudenham Gatelodge

Handsome Italianate gatelodge dated 1865 beside heavy wrought-iron entrance gates, with an avenue that once led to Richard Castle's Tudenham Park, now a massive gutted shell. By John McCurdy, who worked here for Mrs Tottenham, the heiress to the Rochforts.

MULTYFARNHAM: Catholic Church

Earlier traditional T-shaped church re-cased in mid-Victorian Gothic, that still kept intact the early neo-Norman Revival interior of the style of James Sheil. Grisaille windows by the firm of Harry Clarke.

MULTYFARNHAM: Clonhugh

Earlier house rebuilt for Fulke Greville, later 1st Lord Greville, who was to die in mysterious circumstances at his other seat, Clonyn Castle, Devlin (q.v.). The architect was William Caldbeck, who worked here in 1864-7 and who modelled the façade on his own Williamstown in Co. Louth (q.v.)—five bays with a central Ionic porch below a triple window framed by an eaved pediment. But the scale of Clonhugh is comparatively modest, and the house is set into a stable-yard complex with farmyards beyond. From the drawingroom bay window extends a comfortable timber-framed conservatory. Its completeness and the beauty of its lakeside setting and not merely its convenience to Dublin, was the reason why William Trevor's *Fools of Fortune* was filmed here.

MULTYFARNHAM: Mornington House

Early Georgian house remodelled and extended *c.*1875 for the O'Hara family, who have retained the interiors unaltered ever since. Well preserved walled garden. Their architect was W.H. Byrne, a prolific church architect. Member of Hidden Ireland.

WEXFORD

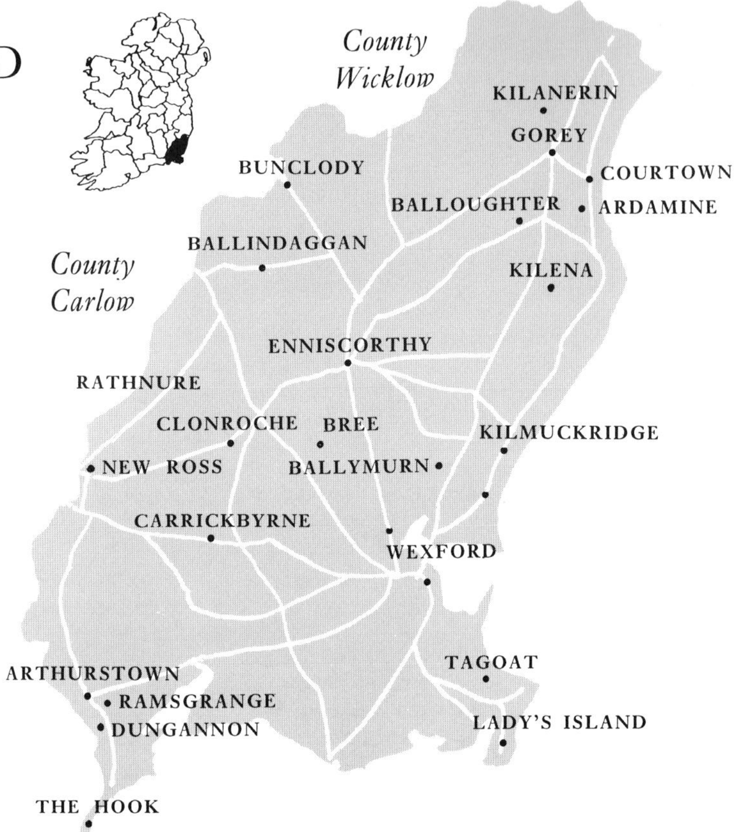

ARDAMINE: **Church of Ireland**
George Edmund Street built two churches in Ireland, and rebuilt two cathedrals. St John in Ardamine is the smallest commission, but the most forceful. Poised beside an ancient motte on a cliff above the Irish Sea, this little church expresses a sense of mission. As an English architect bringing the most advanced Gothic Revival architecture in Europe to a remote island, Street must have felt like St Patrick disembarking on an unknown shore in the dark ages.

His clients were Solomon Augustus and Sophia Richards, so appropriately named, who are commemorated in the western lancets—the only evidence of their existence since their house was burnt out in the Troubles; the site is now a caravan park. The design dates from 1860 and the church was consecrated in 1862. It is built out of irregular masonry, exposed within and without and bonded by bands of red brick. Single cell, apsidal choir, buttressed and corbelled western spirelet, surmounted by a copper cock, the weathervane; lean-to vestry to the north; open stone-roofed porch to the south; so one passes through a timeless world to enter. Interior only 66 feet long and 16.5 feet wide, dimensions that increase the monumentality of the cylindrical font and pulpit. Open timber roof contrastingly treated in nave and chancel with only one truss exposed; single timber-strutted column on a cross-bar above the altar. In the apse the lancets, with glass by Clayton and Bell, are set in deep embrasures framed by generous

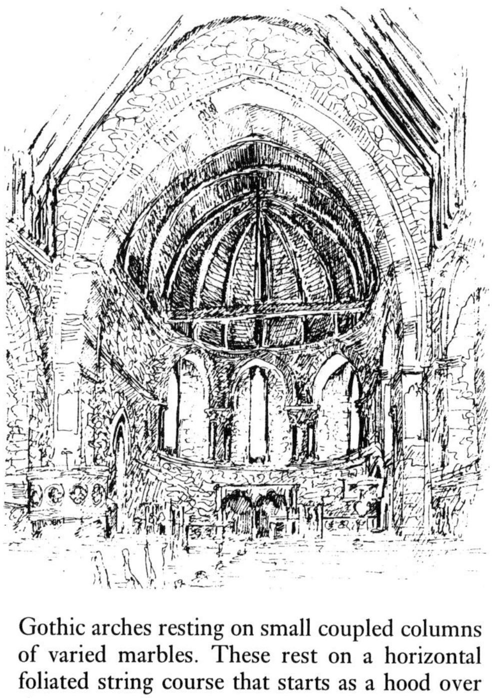

Gothic arches resting on small coupled columns of varied marbles. These rest on a horizontal foliated string course that starts as a hood over the vestry doorway, rises to encircle the apse, descends to arch over the sedilia, and ends by rising upwards defying gravity to blossom into flowers—the rod of Tannhauser. But Street is at his most challenging to the architecture of our time in. his treatment of the northern elevation of the nave. Provision is made for future expansion by building the arcade of brick and stone resting on short cylindrical columns. These arches are then filled in with masonry which is then pierced with lancets. Every phase of this process finds expression. Today architectural enthusiasts for the unconventional must feel relief that the congregation has not grown.

Such concentrated architecture proved unrepeatable, at least by Street when he was commissioned to rebuild the cathedrals of Christ Church and Kildare (q.v.). But if he was not able to surpass the cathedrals of Pugin and Burges, no church they built in Ireland can rival this.

ARTHURSTOWN: **Church of Ireland**
One of J.F. Fuller's best churches, designed *c.*1875 for the Chichester family of nearby Dunbrody Park. Low walls and steeply rising roofs. Effective liturgical sequence due to entering the church from a porch on the side so that the west end is reserved entirely for the baptismal font set into a low semicircular recess lit by three tiny trefoils. An outer Gothic arch frames a resplendent rose window, where the trefoil reappears seven times. Exposed king-post roof in the nave. Forceful cylindrical pulpit built in to the archway leading to the smaller choir.

BALLINDAGGAN: **Catholic Church**
Small Puginian church *c.*1846, with granite front and chequered-board elevations of rubble alternating with blocks of granite. Unusual arched trussed structure within.

BALLOUGHTER: **Catholic Church**
Rural Gothic church, George Ashlin at his most predictable (1874).

BALLYMURN: **Ballinkeele**
Apart from Carriglass (q.v.), the only Daniel Robertson house to remain intact and still belonging to the family who built it. It is also the best intact example of Robertson's Italianate manner after the burning of Castleboro (q.v.) and the demolition of St Matthias in Dublin. Front of seven bays, the central three on the ground floor screened by a balustraded Tuscan portico, projecting forward boldly to act as *porte-cochère*. Long, low service wing also projecting forward. Manneristic devices stress rather than conceal the problems of linking this wing and the portico to the principal block. More assured garden front with central shallow

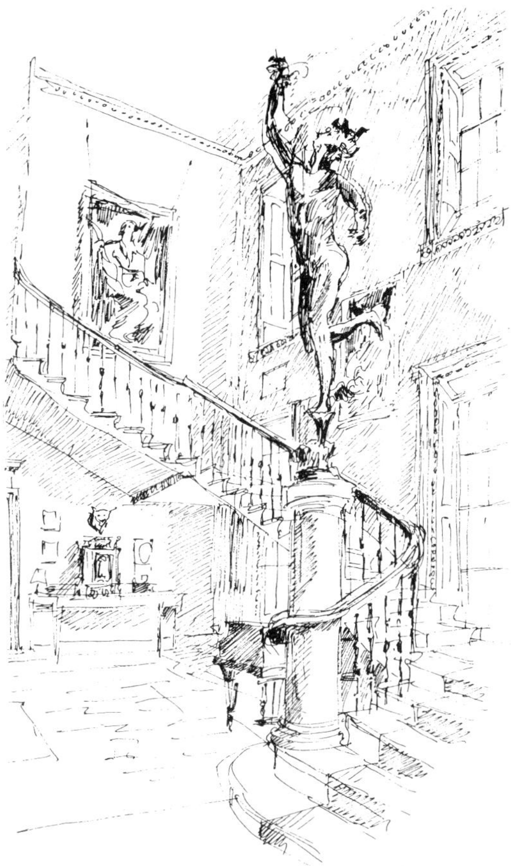

bow flanked by wide piers of rusticated granite, repeated at each corner of the main house, an unusual but effective substitute for conventional pilasters.

Drawings still in the house are dated 1840 for the exterior; for the interior, drawings continue until 1848, Robertson's last surviving work. They reveal his characteristic delicacy and robustness. Square entrance hall with side-lit recess screened by Corinthian scagliola columns. Separate staircase hall with cantilevered stair-rail—light decorative metal balusters descending to wrap around a column upholding Mercury. Three inter-connecting reception rooms along the garden front open on to a raised terrace above the parkland. Two avenues approach the house, one landscaped to glimpse a ruined keep reflected in an artificial lake. Both entrance gates to Robertson's designs. Member of Hidden Ireland.

BALLYMURN: **Catholic Church**
Church rebuilt in 1893 and badly restored ten years ago when the organ gallery was destroyed. Now of minor interest were it not for the altar, the collaboration of Daniel Robertson and John Hogan commissioned to commemorate Margaret Maher in 1838, the year before Robertson was asked by the Mahers to build a new house

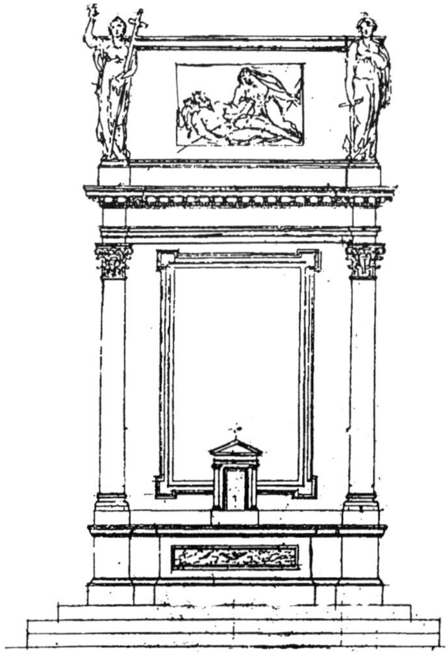

at Ballinkeele (q.v.). Hogan carved a marble *pietà* which Robertson proposed to raise up to the topmost level flanked by saints on a Corinthian baldachino. Another scheme shows the *pietà* more conventionally used as an altar frontal. This was carried out.

The tiny stone-roofed Gothic mausoleum, built in 1860 for the Mahers, is the earliest of Ashlin's funerary oratories, complete with stained glass and furnishing. Alas, its stonework has just been painted over with a cheerful white.

BLACKWATER: Catholic Church

Built in 1831 and remodelled *c.*1900 by James Shipley, who carved the Canadian ceiling with its elaborate centrepiece. Elegant Corinthian reredos dating from the building of the church.

BREE: Catholic Church

Pugin's earliest ecclesiastical commission in Ireland, for the uncle of Lady Shrewsbury (1837). Long simple nave joined to smaller polygonal chancel. Papery walls and gawky queen-post roof—an unusually early example of an open roof as noted by Douglas Richardson. Nave starved to gild the chancel, but money ran out before the gilders could be summoned.

BUNCLODY: Newtownbarry House

Large, harshly detailed, Italianate country house, built out of local granite. Asymmetrical composition with the principal rooms grouped around a double-height staircase hall. Designed by W.H. Lynn (1864).

BUNCLODY: Church of Ireland

Board of First Fruits Gothic, reorientated by Joseph Welland *c.*1860, who added chancel, nave and spire but retained the original entrance. This means that the entrance to the nave is never used, and the west façade by William Burges (1876) is rarely seen. Burges received this commission from the Hall-Dare family through Archbishop Gregg of Cork, the builder of Cork Cathedral. He added a further bay to the nave and treated the new façade as a memorial, a recessed door beneath an outsize cusped rose window set into the diapered stonework of the gable, with asymmetrical chimney all in local granite. Between window and door a frieze inscribed 'These stones shall be for a memorial'. The interior of Burges' addition depends solely on its stained glass by Lonsdale. Further Hall-Dare window by O'Brien (1927).

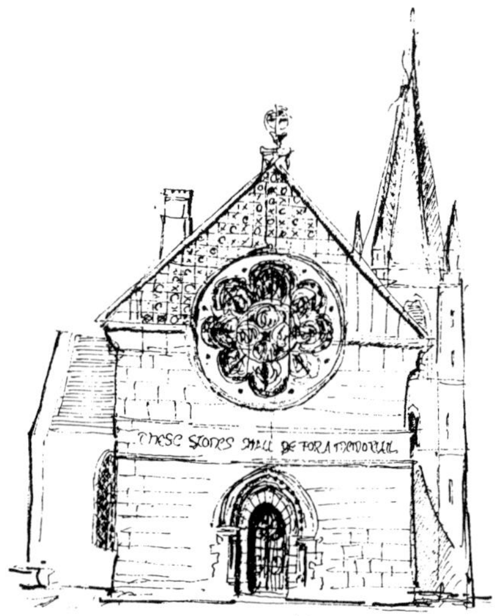

CARRICKBYRNE: Clayton Memorial

Triumphal Corinthian column to commemorate the conquest of Egypt, modelled on Pompey's column in Alexandria, sited on a bare rock with a few windswept trees. Winding stair to viewing platform above the capital. Designed for General Browne-Clayton by Thomas Cobden in 1839.

CLONROCHE: Castleboro

The most imposing of Daniel Robertson's Classical houses, even more so as a ruin revealing no evidence of domestic triviality—doors and window sashes and whatever else human beings (unlike gods or ghosts) require as protection against the elements. The grandeur of Robertson's conception survives, the faults of his realization have receded: the double-height portico is roofless and no longer deprives the first-floor windows of their daylight. The awkward upper windows of the links to the pavilions are now barely noticeable; the fissures caused by delapidations mask the unhappy junction of the main block and the wings.

Robertson's model was Wyatt's Castle Coole in Enniskillen, but with the top floor of the main block expressed, and a further floor added to each wing. The result lacks Wyatt's architectural serenity but at least must have been more pleasant for the staff. They were able to enjoy the view. The Corinthian double-height order is deployed throughout the main block, carried boldly forward assisted by hidden iron to make a superb portico spacious enough to shelter a carriage and four, but only three bays wide and without a pediment, so it does not overwhelm the house: Robertson follows the precedent of Sir Charles Barry in the London College of Surgeons. The Ionic order is used in the wings, recessed in the pavilions, projecting forward as single columns in the links, recalling the Clarendon Press in Oxford, the last building Robertson designed in England before he had to flee his creditors. The deceptively symmetrical garden front also contrasts the delicacy of the Ionic with the grandeur of the Corinthian, articulating with threequarter columns the central polygonal bay that holds the oval salon raised on a vaulted kitchen. A leisurely garden staircase swaggers down from terrace to terrace on to a balustraded landing stage that overwhelms a rather minor river, but once dammed to make a noble lake.

The reception rooms of Castleboro were restrained. Unlike Wyatt or the Morrisons, who reserved the Corinthian order for their grandest interiors, Robertson had already played that card. But there were three double-height spaces —the entrance hall, the staircase hall with an imperial stairs, and a galleried library. The detail, however, is perfunctory and lacks the refinement of Ballinkeele (q.v.), the explanation being that it is by Robertson's elderly collaborator, Martin Day, who had designed Dromana as early as 1822. Day may have been responsible here for the neo-Classical stable block dating back to the same era. When Castleboro was at last completed in 1858 at the staggering cost of £84,000 (this sum may have included the cost of bringing out Lord Carew's daughter in London, paid for by Day), all credit went to the executant. There was no mention of Robertson. Rendered drawings of the exterior survive in the possession of a Day descendant.

Two contrasting gatelodges remain, though ruined also like the house they guard. One is chastely Greek, the other decadently Roman. Even as a Classicist, Robertson was schizophrenic. A few miles away lies his dream castle of Wilton with nothing in common except its grandeur and its fate—destroyed the same night in 1923 by an Australian pyromaniac.

COURTOWN: Catholic Church

Designed by J.J. McCarthy, and posthumously executed in 1923 by his son, C.J. McCarthy. Influenced by the nearby Church of Ireland, Ardamine (q.v.), which was built by Street twenty years before. Is the single lean-to aisle of McCarthy's church a riposte to the walled-up arcade Street built in hopeful readiness for future expansion? Street uses local stone and local brick made by hand. McCarthy uses a harsh factory-made red brick with stone trimmings. He uses also a western bellcote, but asymmetrically positioned and braced by flying buttresses. Street's church looks as if it has been there for ever. McCarthy's, even after a century, looks brand new. Ingratiating stained glass by Earley.

COURTOWN: Courtown House

The seat of the Stopfords, earls of Courtown, much modified during the 19th century, was demolished in 1950. As William Burn was involved in remodelling the house (1865-7), so he is the most likely candidate for the delightful Tudor cottage ornée built at the gates to Gorey. Other gatelodges survive along with stables and farm buildings.

COURTOWN HARBOUR: Ounavarra

A long, low, Tudor Revival house with an asymmetrical façade expressing the half-landing of the staircase. Garden front overlooking the river Ounavarra.

DUNGANNON: Catholic Church

Church and presbytery linked by separately

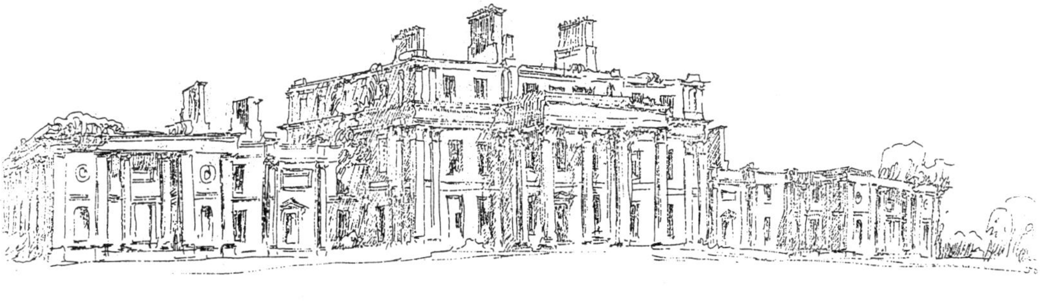

roofed sacristy in a formal Late Gothic Revival complex dated 1896, so late that the presbytery is no more than a surburban villa. Nave of seven bays leading to a polygonal apse. Spare, braced open-roof structure and organ gallery inspired by Pugin.

ENNISCORTHY: The Athenaeum

A grey cement Italianate rebuilding *c.*1880 of the earlier meeting house and theatre. Architect unknown.

ENNISCORTHY: Bloomfield

Scaled-down castellated manor house, in the style of Daniel Robertson. Certainly no one else had the ability to recreate the castle air on a manageable scale for the minor country gentry. Remains unaltered, to compensate for the lost glories of Wilton (q.v.) and Castleboro (q.v.).

ENNISCORTHY: Brownswood

The original Georgian house was the birthplace of the furniture designer Eileen Gray, who was appalled by her brother's decision to pull it down and replace it with a bumptious version of an old English manor house. Built out of bright-red brick and roofed with red tiles; terraced garden filled with much terracotta balustrading, so that the overall effect is suburban, despite its ostentation. The date (1894) is recorded also in terracotta. The architect was Thomas Drew, who crammed too much into his three-storied façade. Porch beneath projecting gabled centrepiece, entered from both sides by decorative cast-iron twin conservatories. Projecting gabled wings, their top rooms opening into arched loggias to glimpse the Slaney in its valley below. The architecturally more assured stable block is now semi-derelict. Charming gatelodges—Drew was at his best when at his least assuming.

One feels that Eileen Grey must have felt relief when Wexford County Council, having acquired the house as a sanitorium in 1930, screened it entirely from public view by constructing a new wing, one of the earliest examples of the International Style in Ireland. But the house is still there, its interiors intact, its baronial staircase hall lit by the Greys' heraldic glass, its inglenooks and verandahs making ideal retreats for the elderly, who lived there under residential care until 1992.

ENNISCORTHY: Catholic Cathedral

Designed by A.W.N. Pugin as his largest church in Ireland, modelled on the English Tintern Abbey whose monks had founded another Tintern Abbey in southern Wexford. Cruciform, nave of six bays, choir of three, transepts of two; central tower and spire dominate the town. From the river valley, the asymmetrical staircase turret attached to the southern transept is played off against the central spire. However, from nearby the site the building reveals limitations and its entrance is cramped and surburban, so that the impressiveness of the façade with its hinted polychromy rarely receives its due. The design dates from 1843; choir and transepts were completed by 1846. The nave was built in medieval manner over the existing chapel, which was pulled down in 1848. The central spire was finished in 1850. Entry portal under stone roofed porch slipped in between projecting buttresses. After the natural stonework of the exterior, the white-walled elevations and sparsely trussed roof show up only too clearly Pugin's attempt to build a cathedral on a budget appropriate for a parish church.

Whatever impression of immensity that Pugin may have achieved has vanished. There is no rood screen as intended and the reredos added by Pearse and Sharp to the design of J.J. McCarthy in 1857 under the eastern window is too assertive and overscaled. This window has the neo-medieval glass that Pugin would have intended (possibly to his design and by Hardman), characterized by heraldic and now much damaged tiny figures. The later more realistic stained glass (by Lobin of Tours and then inevitably by Mayer of Munich) has reduced the scale of the cathedral still further. The only Irish glass is the western window by Earley, lighting the organ gallery. McCarthy also added the screens between choir and side aisles. He had to dismantle the central tower and rebuild it without its lower stage; but unlike Ashlin at Killarney, he preserved the profile of Pugin's spire. As long ago as 1850, a temporary high altar was placed under the central tower by the new bishop, Myles Murphy. In his correspondence, Pugin recorded this with double exclamation marks and added that the Hottentots would have treated his cathedral better than the Irish bishops. The present modern high altar in the crossing has only just been completed and reconsecrated in a ceremony that would doubtlessly have appalled the architect.

ENNISCORTHY: Church of Ireland

Built at the same time as Pugin's cathedral, coeval but not comparable. Instead, a sensible essay in simplified Gothic (1844-6) by Joseph Welland. Western tower and spire added in 1850. Wide nave spanned by arcaded trusses leading to smaller chancel lit by heraldic glass.

ENNISCORTHY: Coolbawn

Elizabethan Revival house built for Francis Bruen in the 1839s by Frederick Darley, employed at the time by the Church of Ireland and

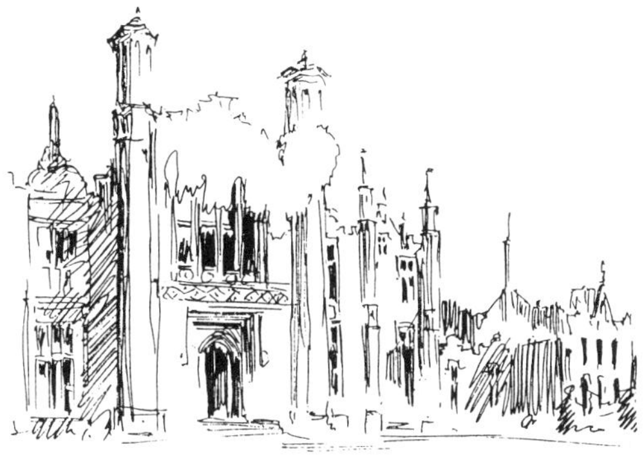

whose churches tempered the abrupt Gothic of his predecessor, John Semple. And in front of the ruined façade of Coolbawn it is Semple that one remembers. The chiselled mountain granite, the series of recessed planes that frame the main doorway, and the stark silhouette of gables and filials against the sky all reveal his influence, but without his crankiness and originality. The front range is built across the original house, which is incorporated into the asymmetrical rear façade above vanished overlooked a terraced garden. Burnt *c.*1920. Ruin sold recently to be shipped out to Japan, but still stands, as planning permission was withheld by the county council.

ENNISCORTHY: Edermine

Extraordinary architectural mélange—villa, chapel and conservatory all linked together to make a continuous if unpredictable structure, to overlook an elaborate but now partly vanished garden. Designed for the Power family, who divided their time, along with their workforce, between farming in Wexford and distilling in Dublin. The house itself is an interesting attempt by J.B. Keane to reduce his monumental neo-Classicism to a habitable scale. Carefully contrived sequence from hall with fluted Doric columns, up a staircase illuminated by an imposing Venetian window to an Ionic-columned landing. Simple and spacious reception rooms, all in a style vilified by A.W.N. Pugin, a family friend who went insane before he could design their chapel. This commission was then reserved for Pugin's son Edward Welby, and built *c.*1858. More remarkable today for its undisturbed interior than for the quality of its architecture. Even the wall decoration survives, though damp has dimmed its brilliance. There is no internal link between the chapel and the aviary in the Chinese style designed by Richard Turner and erected by James Pierce. The climax of this sequence, the extraordinary curvilinear conservatory with its central semi-dome flanked by plant houses, is designed by Pierce in Turner's manner, but even more delicate and fanciful with its frieze-like pilasters and its honeysuckle cresting seemingly so fragile but still holding out against the Irish climate. Within, the arcading and shelves are washed down, no longer by punctilious gardeners but by unpredictable rain showers pouring through the broken roof.

ENNISCORTHY: Macmine Castle

Early tower house rebuilt and extended as a neo-Tudor castle for the Richards family. Roman cement finish masks all differences between the old and new, even today fifty years after having been abandoned in the 1940s.

ENNISCORTHY: St Senan's Hospital

Picturesque Italianate composition—by Farrell and Bell; dominated by three towers; in brick and stone. Extended *c.*1899 by C.A. Owen.

ENNISCORTHY: Wilton Castle

A Georgian house of two periods belongs to the Alcock family and remodelled for them by Daniel Robertson just after 1841, when the estate was inherited by Col. Harry Alcock. By the skilful addition of varied towers, and by devising a new setting on a platform surrounded by a dry moat, parapets and turrets, Robertson achieved a total transformation with the minimum of disruption to the house itself, and the near symmetry of its three-storey façade. To the

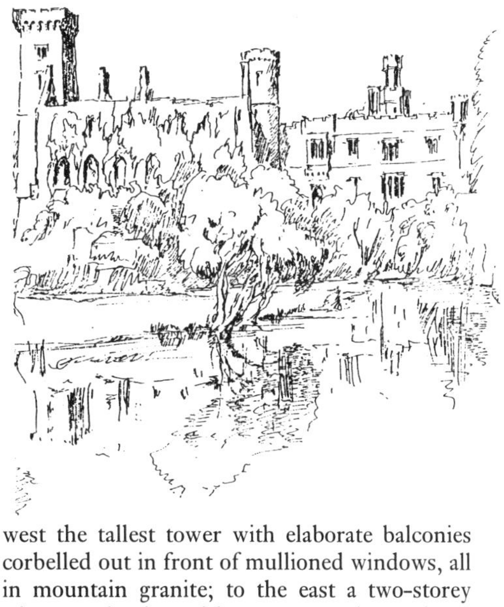

west the tallest tower with elaborate balconies corbelled out in front of mullioned windows, all in mountain granite; to the east a two-storey wing terminating with an octagonal two-tiered flag tower. At the rear a circular tower masks the link between the original house, which was left intact, and the addition, which was given a new Tudor front; all this dramatically sited above the River Boro. Destroyed, along with nearly all its contents in 1923, by, so it is said, an 'Australian pyromaniac' (cf. Castleboro': q.v.).

ENNISCORTHY: 1798 Memorial
Designed for the main square by Oliver Shepherd, following the success of his memorial in Wexford; erected in 1905-8.

FERRYCARRIG: Crimea Memorial
Fake round tower overlooking the estuary of the Slaney, built by local architect Thomas Willis in 1851.

GOREY: Brown's Pub
Arcaded corner pub with original sign painting still intact.

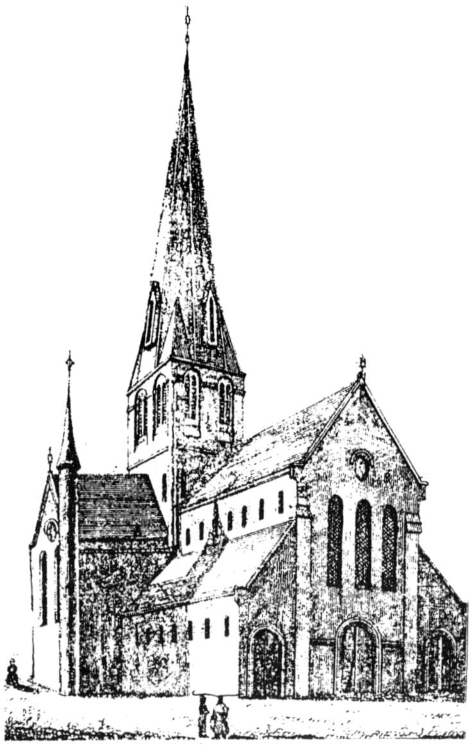

GOREY: Catholic Church
Exceptional among the churches of A.W.N. Pugin in that it is built in the Norman style, the only Norman church that he included in his aerial perspective of his most important churches. Built in 1839 and completed in 1842 along with the adjoining Loreto convent, it is therefore one of his earliest Irish commissions; its central tower, which has castellations and not the spire Pugin intended, is reached by a staircase turret attached to the transept but treated as if it were once a free-standing round tower, as he would have seen at Cashel, the prototype of his nearby Enniscorthy Cathedral. This combination of circular tower and a semi-circular apse is in defiance of Irish tradition but prefigure the architectural radicals of the 1860s. The interior is an effective contrast to the calp rubble of the external walling although the whitewashed walls were once brightly coloured. Further tension is generated by the contrast of the nave with its tautened web of roof trusses to the timeless simplicity of the crossing, illuminated by unseen windows in the tower. This would have thrown into relief the now vanished rood screen. Chancel altered to conform with the liturgical trends of the 1960s when the abstract mural decoration was painted over.

GOREY: Church of Ireland
As in Enniscorthy, Joseph Welland found himself building a church at the same time as Pugin, and not to be outdone in patriotism, he also built a round tower, attached in this case to a square belfry. Asymmetrical ground plan due to absence of northern aisle. Later altar (1895) carved by Charles Harrison. The stained glass windows, masterworks of Harry Clarke (1922), commemorating Capt. Lea-Wilson murdered in Gorey by the IRA, were commissioned by his widow, who acquired the Carravagio now in the National Gallery of Ireland. There is a west window by Warrington and one by M.J.C. Buckley above the altar. Further windows by Heaton, Butler and Bayne.

GOREY: Ramsfort
A modest Regency villa extended twice in contradictory styles, firstly by a severe *François Premier* wing attributed to T.H. Wyatt and then by a further range set back in a more lively Italianate Tudor with an arcade on the ground floor. This terminates in a circular turret with an open timber belvedere beneath a dormered spire. Built in 1871-2 by B.T. Patterson, who may have been standing in for another architect. Elaborate grounds with an Italianate chapel and a now vanished temple. House and garden are currently being restored after long neglect.

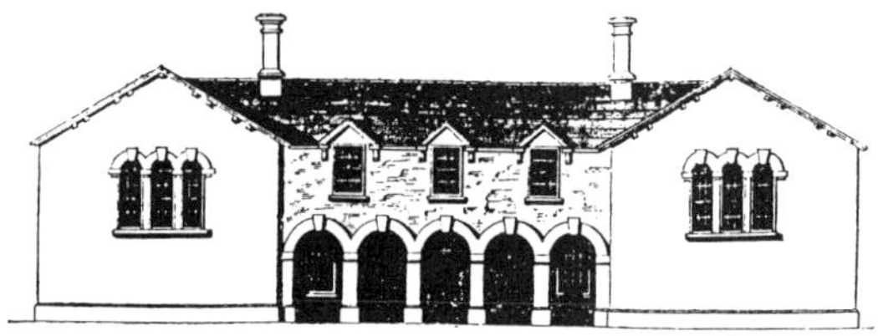

GOREY: National School
The usual formula of a central schoolmaster's house and classrooms on either side, but here executed in a delightful combination of brick and stone by an obscure local architect called John Kelly in 1840. The house is entered through a ground floor arcade; and triple-arched, high-level windows light the classrooms on either side. The composition is stabilized by two elegantly articulated chimney-stacks.

KILANERIN: **Catholic Church**
Built in 1865 by Pugin and Ashlin (working for the Esmonde family) out of local blue-green calp rubble and granite dressings, as in Enniscorthy Cathedral by A.W.N. Pugin. Elaborate spire with spirelets placed round the base rather than a simple broach as proposed. Nave lit by quatrefoils over lean-to aisles.

KILENA: **Parknashogue**
Modest residence with vernacular farm buildings built by Deane and Woodward for Arthur Guinness, a nephew of Sir Benjamin Lee Guinness, in 1858. Woodward's more forceful Gothic design remained unexecuted.

KILMUCKRIDGE: **Cahore**
Castellated Tudor *c.*1842 in the style of Daniel Robertson, with entrance front guarded by battlemented tower; garden front centred on two-storied bay window; all now grimly cemented against exposure from the sea. Now an hotel.

KILMUCKRIDGE: **Wells**
One of Daniel Robertson's country houses, erected *c.*1840 for the Doyne family in his favourite Elizabethan style, Wells is built of brick with stone trimmings, which is unusual for Robertson. Almost asymmetrical U-shaped façade with the half-landing of the staircase expressed by an oriel in one of the returns. The house was sold *c.*1960 to a German owner, who has carefully converted the mews and farm buildings into residential *gites*, retaining the architectural integrity of the complex. As always, Robertson was responsible for the landscaping, in this case also Elizabethan Revival: his long, straight front avenue looks as if it had been planted three centuries before.

LADY'S ISLAND: **Catholic Church**
The earliest of the Wexford parish churches by Pugin and Ashlin, started in 1863 and finished a year later. Furnishings completed in 1865. Built out of granite with red sandstone dressings. Entered through carefully placed belfry beneath an elegant organ gallery. The interior has shafts of polished Midleton marble between the nave and aisles, which are all rib-vaulted with decorative plaster giving a toy-like effect to the interior. Unaltered apsidal east end. Richard Pierce the younger was the executive architect until his death during construction.

NEWROSS: **Catholic Church**
The elegant neo-Classical church was evidently too discreet for the triumphalism that surged through the Irish Catholic Church during the last decade of the nineteenth century—hence its conversion into a theatre and the building of a new church higher up the hill, designed by Walter Doolin, who was the most successful of his generation in giving new vigour to an exhausted elderly Gothic Revival. An elaborate sacristy is linked by a porch to gabled double transepts. These interpenetrate a continuous choir and nave counterbalanced by the uplift of the off-central western tower, crowned by spire as forceful as a rocket. One can visualize the prize winning competition perspective, enhanced in materialization by a subtle polychromy and external sculpture by John A. O'Connell. Internally the suppression of the crossing lengthens the nave and gives a sense of discovery to the complex vistas through the transepts. However, this daring is not matched by the treatment of the clerestory when masked by the transepts—merely wall-up windows. Predictably overscaled reredos for main and side altars by Pearse, and stained glass by Mayer. Tabernacle by Smith; the pretty opus sectile pulpit has been permitted to remain.

NEWROSS: **Church of Ireland**
Rebuilt in 1830 presumably by Darley. Tower and spire by Welland and Gillespie in 1870.

RAMSGRANGE: **Church and Convent**
The church, built in 1835-48, has been attributed to A.W.N. Pugin; the convent, added by the Saint Louis nuns in 1871, has been attributed to his son, Edward Welby. It is difficult to distinguish today the work of either. The church was encased in concrete both outside and inside, when its original double-storied division into upper and lower church was abolished. Its open roof was masked by a plaster tunnel vault. Only the stained glass triple lancet remains unaltered. The tower was added in 1865. Much of the convent appears to pre-date 1871, built in a gauche Gothick that has parallels with the remodelling of Johnstown Castle (q.v.) by Martin Day. Arcaded dormered block an addition of 1912. Complex now abandoned after government education cuts in 1983.

RATHNURE: **Catholic Church**
Gothic church of minor interest—but not the entrance, a triple-tiered triumphal arch built out of local granite, a feature found only in Co. Wexford. This example is the most imposing.

TAGOAT: **Catholic Church**
One of the most impressive Irish churches of A.W.N. Pugin. He must have thought so himself, since he donated a pair of candlesticks made to his own design. The completion coincided with the death in 1846 of the parish priest, Walter Rower, who is commemorated with a

brass memorial bordered by Minton tiles. The design dates from 1843. What makes the church so unusual is the spatial treatment of the interior, with the progress from nave to chancel interrupted not by the expected crossing, but by an unbroken transept. This is filled with light from long lancets at either end and recalls the great Christian basilicas of Rome. The high altar is later, and heavier, than Pugin. The rood screen has predictably disappeared, so it is only in the side chapels that his screens survive. There is also an elegant font. A powerful sacristy links the church to an inadequate belfry. The recent restoration has been particularly successful in removing the later external cement, and revealing again the stone rubble walling. Good stained glass includes Hardman windows of the 1840s.

THE HOOK: Loftus Hall

Large three-storied palazzo built on a treeless spit jutting out into the Atlantic and buffeted by every wind. Designed in 1871 for the 8th marquis of Ely to ensemble a grand hotel with its repetitive, pedimented plate-glass window outstaring the sea. Some traces survive internally of the 17th-century house it replaced; all the front rooms are grouped round the top-lit staircase hall, where a heavy carved and inlaid Jacobean-style staircase rises laboriously to a surrounding gallery with columns of stunted Corinthian. Acquired as a convent but currently for sale.

WEXFORD: Barntown Catholic Church

Possibly the most serious casualty in the campaign to adapt Irish Catholic churches to the mistaken interpretation of the Second Vatican Council. Designed by A.W.N. Pugin and built in 1844-8 on a hillside west of Wexford, this village church was the most eloquent expression of his ideals in this country until the loss of its altar, pulpit, rood screen, font, floors and even a few stained-glass windows, all unrecorded and their loss unnoticed due to its continuous obscurity: there is only one brief, ambiguous reference to it in Pugin's own diaries.

The concept is of complete simplicity—a long, low nave lit only from both ends and flanked by two lean-to aisles. Western bellcote over relieving arch. Buttressed porch, diametrically counterbalanced by projecting sacristy. The exposed stonework of the exterior is deployed with a subtle polychromy—local reddish rubble, pink granite quoins, grey granite dressings, green limestone used to alternate the voussoirs of the arches. Within, the effect of a hall church but without height, similar to the Irish rural Gothick chapels that Pugin so despised, and like them giving a sense of shelter.

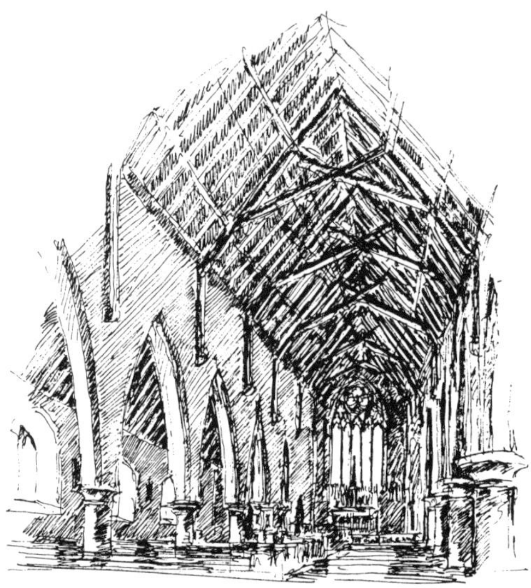

But if they are bright, this is dim and mysterious, and even more so before the alterations. There is no high-level windows to the nave and almost continuous chancel. So there are no distractions to the great arcades that rise from chubby columns, with their capitals only at head height, up to the scissor trusses of the open timber roof. These arches frame the steep lean-to roofs that span the aisles, their soffits stencilled with red, blue and gold, colouring restated with greater brilliance in the stained glass by Hardiman (to Pugin's own design), that culminate in the window above the altar, rising high up over the vanished rood screen to catch the first light of the dawn. The interior is now being changed yet again.

WEXFORD: Bellevue Catholic Church

Once attributed to A.W.N. Pugin, and now regarded as the earliest Irish commission of his son, Edward Welby, just before his partnership with George Ashlin. Commissioned by the Cliffe family, whose mass conversion to Catholicism (hence an upper gallery once linked to their house) did not prevent them from being burnt out in the Troubles. The church was completed by 1859. Forcefully detailed, triple lancets topped with trefoils behind the altar.

WEXFORD: Castlebridge House

The Pierces are remembered today for their less remarkable churches, but not for their exquisite conservatories that languish semi-derelict yet still intact due to their superb craftsmanship (superior even to Richard Turner's). James Pierce introduced a distinctive Gothicism into his work, especially here, where the free-standing rotunda is linked to the nondescript house by traceried Gothic arches. The rotunda still contains its circular, many-tiered jardiniere centred under a flower-like dome.

WEXFORD: Church of Our Lady's Assumption
One of the twin churches designed by A.N.W. Pugin's assistants, Richard and James Pierce, 1851-8. Without the subtlety of the master, but still simple and effective with its symmetrical western tower and spire rising as a foil to an unbroken nave and chancel. In the south aisle is the O'Keefe memorial window by Harry Clarke (1919), one of his early masterpieces, and the most imbued with Art Nouveau. Work supervised by J.J. McCarthy after Pierce's death.

WEXFORD: Church of Our Lady's Immaculate Conception
The almost identical church of the Pierce brothers with a slight variation in the tower and spire. The iron railings outside are a good example of the output of their ironworks. Glass by Mayer in the large seven-light eastern window. Work supervised by J.J. McCarthy after Pierce's death.

WEXFORD: Franciscan Church
The Italianate altar in his neo-Classical church is by Patrick Byrne, who presumably was also responsible for the Italianate campanile.

WEXFORD: Johnstown Castle
In 1810, John Knox Grogan regained the confiscated estates of his brother who as an involuntary participant in the Wexford uprising had been executed by the British Government in 1798. Most of the building work was done by his son Hamilton, completed by Hamilton's widow (who remarried Sir Thomas Esmonde). The castle was inherited by Hamilton's daughter, Lady Granard, then by her daughter, Lady Maurice Fitzgerald, and bequeathed to the Government by Lady Maurice's grandson, Captain M.V. Lakin, in 1942.

The Grogan family were enthusiastic but uncontrollable builders; for over three generations, they kept embellishing their home but it was only in 1835-50, during the meteoric career of Daniel Robertson, that they found an architect who could realize their fantasies and yet direct their exuberance. However, he arrived twenty years too late, when most of their castle was already built—a medieval tower house retained as the corner of a substantial Georgian house transformed into a castle, firstly in 1810 by an unknown architect working in a quaint neo-Norman, still visible in the central hall and the farmyard (an interesting agricultural mus-

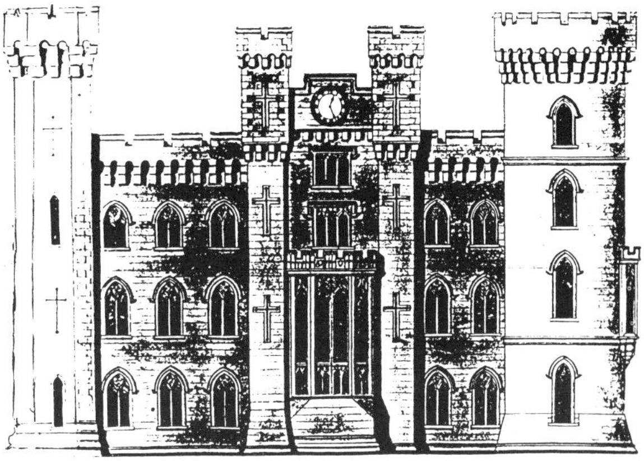

eum), now secondly in a more conventional Gothic style by Martin Day.

Day as a long-suffering collaborator may have called on Robertson for assistance, and regained his commission after Robertson's death, arbitrarily to extend the nursery wing to the west and glaze the arcade to the east adding an uninspired ballroom and chapel to the laboratory. So while Robertson's contribution to the landscaping, the interior and the furniture are immediately discernible, his architectural contribution remains problematical, confined to disrupting the symmetry of the south front, projecting a staircase out through the west front, and building to the east a separate laboratory for the chemical experiments of his client, Hamilton Knox Grogan-Morgan. This was approached by an open arcade that was designed to double up as a private *porte cochère*. Finally he added a further *porte cochère* (also carved in Carlow granite of almost Manueline complexity) when he changed the front entrance from the west front to the north, so that visitors would have to enter the castle itself to get their first view of the new lake. His new *porte cochère* is set beneath a massive tower linked to the entrance hall, the 'Apostles Hall', by a fragile, airy Gothic corridor. Beyond, the toplit neo-Norman central hall leads into the principal rooms along the garden front with fretted ceilings, elaborate panelling and fireplaces of ceaseless inventiveness. However, the drawing-room was on the first floor and, to reach it, Robertson replaced the original entrance hall with his most spectacular staircase, dismantled alas in 1950. It was an imperial in plan, dividing at the half-landing, the twin upper flights returning and rising to a Gothic triumphal arch, framing in its centre a life-size portrait of the young squire, his wife, his child, his hound, and an architectural drawing for his castle. The painting by Parris, now in the diningroom, predated Robertson's intervention since the drawing so proudly displayed is by Day for the west front that Robertson was to partly demolish to gain more space for his stairs. The mirrored drawingroom, the principal bedroom and an adjoining boudoir are the most elaborate of the first floor interiors, and contain furniture he designed in the 1840s. A hundred years later, no one would bid for it at the auction, so it has remained in the castle.

From the first floor one gains the best view of Robertson's most ambitious natural landscaping, the artificial lake (1842). This is bounded by a promenade that is partly Classical, past terraces and statues, then partly neo-Medieval along fortifications with a turret built out into the water. But we can no longer experience his most theatrical contrivance, a Gothic arch on the other bank framing a vista of a further lake: the arch has gone and trees now obscure the view. Also vanished the formal Italian garden to the north of the castle, designed evidently before the change of entrance and now sacrificed to car parking, sparing only the central fountain. Also vanished a fairy-tale Gothick conservatory. However, much of Robertson's rare tree planting survives. He was a pioneer of the American garden planted with rare conifers, and these have now come into their own. Today, with the gardens open to the public, this is his talent easiest to enjoy. But there are plans to open up the interior also to public, where his furniture is unparalleled in Ireland. His Irish rivals could equal him occasionally simply as an architect, but only he was the master of all the other arts that transform the experience of architecture into the enjoyment of life.

WEXFORD: Rathangan Catholic Church

Catholic church built in a hard, neo-Gothic manner (1871), possibly by George Ashlin.

WEXFORD: Rathaspick House

The timber gatelodge to this 17th-century house, now offering accommodation and golf, is of unparalled craziness, with bay windows and verandahs projecting from a central tower. One feels it must have been an Ethnic Eastern European pavilion transported back from the Paris International Exhibition (since 1900 is emblazoned over the main gable) or at the very least from a Wexford opera. Traces of a fauvist colour scheme of red, blue and yellow.

WEXFORD: St Peter's College

Architecturally the most important building in Wexford, not the college itself (which is anonymous) but the chapel, added by A.W.N. Pugin in 1838. The original Georgian house had already been extended by a range naively modelled on an Elizabethan Oxford college. Pugin's chapel projects forward to balance the Georgian house, its only external expression an immense rose window above the altar. The interior remained intact until 1958, when the authorities removed the chancel screen and rood (the earliest that Pugin designed and therefore the beginning of a lifelong obsession). Pugin's ideals differ from those of the liturgists of today, but not his fanaticism. What has survived is his reredos, a triptych balanced on the altar, with heraldic colouring taken up by Hardman's stained glass in the rose window.

WEXFORD: 1798 Memorial

The earliest of the two life-sized bronze memorials in Co. Wexford by Oliver Shepherd (the other being in Enniscorthy: q.v.). This dates from 1905.

WICKLOW

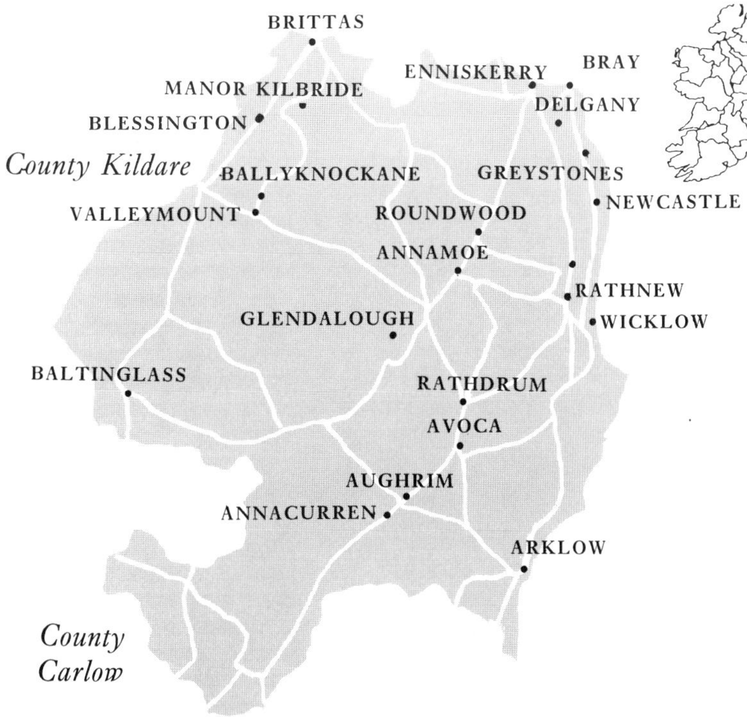

ANNACURREN: **Catholic Church**
Rural Gothic revival church with off-centre tower and spire. Designed by Richard Pierce and built in 1862. Eloquent interior with chamfered granite columns upholding spacious arches. Neo-medieval glass above the altars.

ANNAMOE: **Glendalough House**
The Tudor Revival house built for the Barton family was dismanted in the late 1970s, having

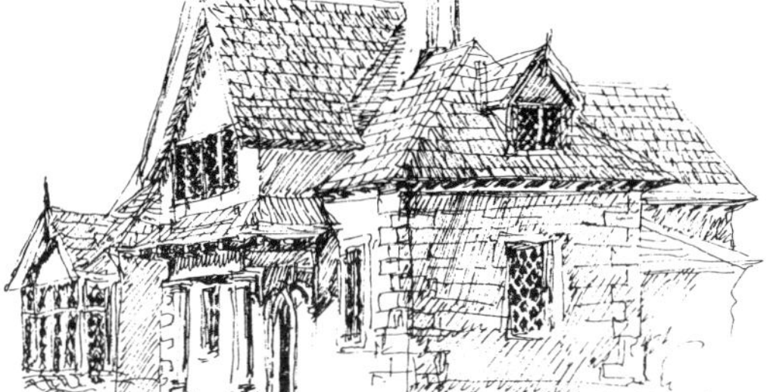

been uninhabited for a generation. The architect remains unknown but was strongly influenced by Daniel Robertson. The earlier rear portions that he remodelled survive, as does the delightful cottage ornée gatelodge at the gateway beside Lough Dan. Also of Ireland's most Impressionistic water gardens laid out at the end of 19th century.

ARKLOW: **Catholic Church**
Neo-Classical design due to Patrick Byrne *c.*1840; executed in granite. Symmetrical with western tower and cupola, pilastered façade, arched recesses relieve the austere and better proportioned side elevations. Cruciform interior centred on depressed dome with decorative stucco; heads of the four evangelists in the spandrels.

ARKLOW: **Church of Ireland**
One of the last privately built churches in Ireland, commissioned by the 5th earl of Carysfort in memory of his parents. Sir Arthur Blomfield, who died in 1899 before its completion, was the architect, and had to incorporate different features from the medieval churches close to Elton Hall, the Carysfort English home. The 5th earl was a conservative collector of contemporary English paintings, and Blomfield would have been their architectural counterpart. At first sight, symmetrical with massive western tower topped by a slender spire: The nave, aisles and chancel are roofed in lead to give a most unIrish appearance. At the west end of the nave is sited the font beneath a carved timber spire-like canopy. The vista down the nave is framed by an arch modelled on the Elton church. Columns of Irish marble support the richly bossed timber ceiling. The furnishing is consistently serious and scrup-

lously finished. The stained glass, all by Clayton and Bell, matches the gravity of the ensemble with a certain wintriness. The refusal to express human transience is the only evidence that this world which appears to be timeless was on the threshold of disintegration.

ARKLOW: **Church of Ireland, Kilbride**
The principal family church of the Howards, earls of Wicklow, who also contributed to the other church Kilbride by Barre in Bray (q.v.). Built by Cecilia Francis (*sic*) Howard in 1834, as recorded over the door. Three-light window by Harry Clarke above the altar; another over the door to the tower. Howard mausoleum nearby built as a Egyptian pyramid.

ARKLOW: **Glenart Castle**
Along with Coolbawn (q.v.) acquired by a theme park in Japan in a transaction that still requires planning permission for its migration across the globe. But a reprieve for the Canadian owner of Glenart may be at hand. The loss-making fertilizer factory that has polluted the wooded valley for the last thirty years in full view of the castle's front door, as the least satisfying of the memorials to the late President Childers, may have to close down, and allow tourists return to the vale of Avoca so that the formal terraced gardens, once as celebrated as Powerscourt, can revert to their former splendour. There will, however, always be architectural impediments, as Glenart was built in fits and starts, beginning with a modest Georgian hunting lodge, enlarged and castellated by the 1st earl of Carysfort in the early 19th century. Expensively extended from 1869 onwards in the random ashlar that has attracted the Japanese today. The architect of the Carysforts was John McCurdy, but theirs may have been the decision to revert to Regency Gothic to blend with the earlier house, especially a long, low, bay-windowed garden front contrasting with a square keep set back behind it. There is more High Victorian swagger in the clock tower at the topmost terrace flanked incongruously by immense conservatories, approached by flights of steps between parterres. The next generation, reacting against this formality, engaged William Sheppard to introduce serpentine paths and a more naturalistic planting. An artifical grotto was set into one of the conservatories beneath a glazed many-tiered dome. His naturalistic planting was extended to the farthest reaches of the demesne. The Woodenbridge avenue starts at a corbelled turreted gatelodge, and rises through a wooded glen interweaving with waterfalls.

Reality has since intruded into this world of makebelieve. First the garden front of the castle was burnt out in the Troubles. The Carysforts

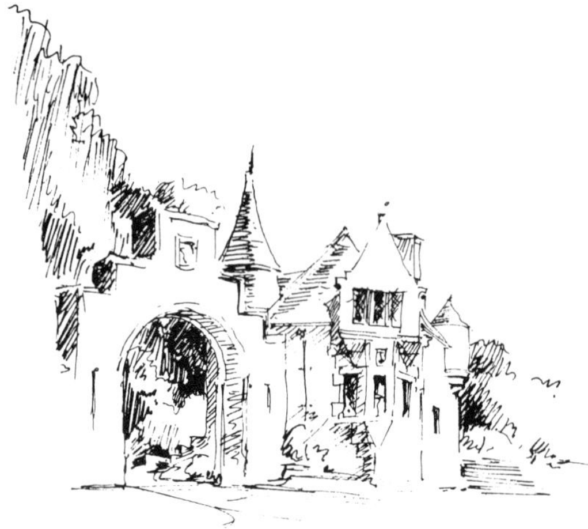

lived on in the other half, until they sold the estate during the Second World War to a religious order, who replaced the burnt-out wing with a grim dormitory block. This was partly financed by the sale of urns from the abandoned gardens from which the conservatories had vanished leaving just the rocks of the grotto.

ARKLOW: **Shelton Abbey**
A casualty to William Vitruvius Morrison's use of untreated timber and to death duties required by the government a century later. The house of 1770 was built by the 1st earl of Wicklow. Transformed into an abbey by Morrison for the 4th earl, with cloisters, chapterhouse-like study, and fan-vaulted double drawingrooms. The 4th earl had no sons but seven daughters, so he decided to house those that were not married in a new wing called the Nunnery, on a higher terrace, a long double-storied range with a central tower. Design attributed to Morrison but built posthumously *c.*1840. Surrounding Victorian parterres were extended by the wife of the 7th Lord Wicklow into shrubberies and sub-tropical glades along the river valley. But the maintenance of the gardens took precedence over the roof, and the house was riddled with dry rot in 1947 when inherited by the 8th and last earl. He opened an hotel, as remarked by Harold Acton, 'to save the family fortune, but lost instead the family silver'. In a farewell comment, Lord Wicklow expressed the hope that his home might be of service to Ireland. He did not foresee that the park would be the site of a fertilizer factory and the house would be drastically restored as an open prison (so open that the wrought iron entrance gates have been removed), whose inmates prove that it is possible to live beside pollution and survive. But it is difficult to visit unless one has a relation inside it.

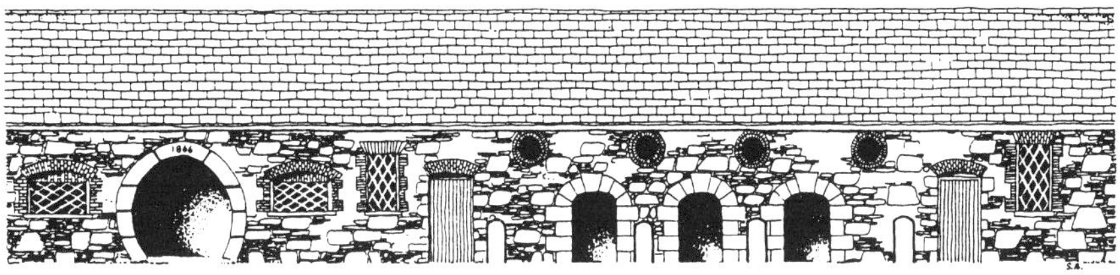

ASHFORD: **Tighlinn Farm**
Built in 1866 on what was then the Synge estate, an engaging use of brick arches, granite-dressed arches and local rubble. The horseshoe entrance to the forge is incorporated here into an overall composition. Now an adventure centre.

ASHFORD: **Bellair House Hotel**
Victorian villa with entry porch beneath a three-storied tower that terminates in a glazed loggia. Reasonably intact interior. Belonged to Julius Casement cousin of Sir Roger Casement who often stayed here. Architect unknown, but probably Thomas Drew (1890).

AUGHRIM: **Village Hall**
Compact design, built out of local granite in a blend of Tudor, Classical and unhappy modernization. But the pediment is still embellished with an elaborate coat of arms.

AVOCA: **Ballyarthur Gates**
Turreted entrance gates, controlled by gate-lodge designed as a miniature Gothick triumphal arch—an arcaded porch below, three lancets in the gable above, derelict but still light-hearted; modelled on Shelton Abbey gate-lodge by William Vitruvius Morrison (q.v.).

AVOCA: **Castlemacadam Church of Ireland**
J.F. Fuller, in his rambling autobiography *Ad Omniana*, which records a mere fraction of his output, absentmindedly credits himself with the design of this intensely serious church. However, the *Dublin Builder* of 1868 credits W.H. Lynn, and all surviving drawings are by the executant architects, Welland and Gillespie. The composition, in its grouping of saddle-roofed tower, square chancel and adjoining polygonally-ended chapel, display Lynn's contrived picturesqueness. The interior is equally serious and high-minded, but cannot compensate for the lost charm and intimacy of its Gothick predecessor, roofless and abandoned. Glass by Heaton, Butler and Bayne.

AVOCA: **Catholic Church**
High Victorian exterior: asymmetrical western tower with broached steeple balanced at the far end by a polygonal sacristy projecting beyond the transept. Interior harks back to the earlier Gothic of Patrick Byrne—medieval sedilia and arcading naively executed in plaster, with arches springing from the heads of saints more lively since they have lost their bodies. Four intact saints housed in canopied shrines cut into the corners of the crossing. High altar, 1901.

BALLYKNOCKANE: **The Village**
Rural village inhabited by the part-time workforce of the quarries in the hill above which supplied Wicklow granite to the public buildings of Dublin. The quarry owner's house remains, if in other hands. But the village with its winding lanes, its sculptural gate piers, its terraced outbuildings, and its panoramic vistas, not of the Mediterranean, but of a recent reservoir and the uplands of Kildare—all this, like its counterparts in Provence, except more

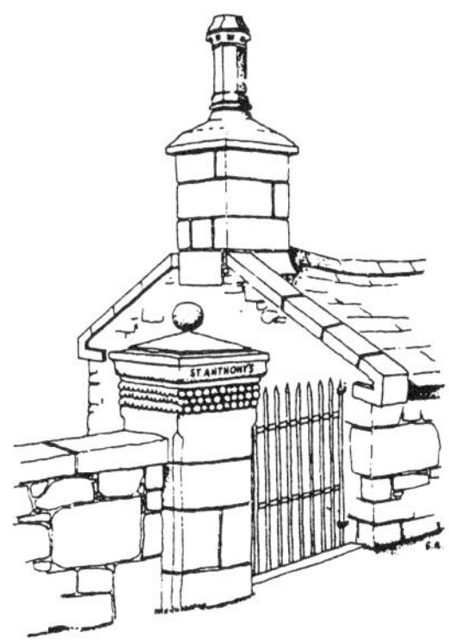

tastelessly—has been blighted by bungalow bliss. High above this lost Eden, the quarry remains, totally mechanized, but still a setting of biblical grandeur waiting for Moses to descend with the ten commandments.

BALTINGLASS: **Catholic Church**
Designed by John Bourke *c.*1860 in Early English Gothic, and his finest church. Exterior articulated into recessed panels to reduce the mass of masonry for economic reasons. Symmetrical façade with porch in projecting tower. Wide nave only three bays long, extended transepts, shallow choir. This results in a spacious interior without obstructing columns and with all attention focused on the altar. Open timber roof lost in darkness with widely spaced hammer-beams intersecting at the crossing.

High altar (unusually of timber, stained and gilded), added by J.S. Butler in 1873. Interior lit by Early English Gothic lancets, grouped in pairs or clusters, divided by colonettes and framing the resplendent stained glass throughout (mainly by Mayer). This culminates in the great window behind the high altar, where, flanked by frescoed angels, the Crucifixion is enacted with the dying Christ and Thieves silhouetted against the thunder and lightning of an approaching storm.

BLESSINGTON: Catholic Church

Characteristic Gothic of J.J. McCarthy, built in Wicklow granite in 1857-61. Consecrated by Archbishop Cullen to Mary, Mother of Mercy, the subject of its stained glass in the east window.

BLESSINGTON: Downshire Fountain

Italianate fountain to the marquis of Downshire, dated 1860. The inscription states that the water was 'supplied at the cost of a kind and generous landlord'.

BRAY: Ardmore

A large, uninspired, Italianate house, that fails to exploit the potential of its setting above the Dargle. Earlier villa extended for the Lefroy family by Lanyon, Lynn and Lanyon in 1861. Its garden front is redeemed from monotony by one bay window opening on to a pair of corbelled balconies (added by McCurdy and Mitchell in 1875). Now the Ardmore Film Studios, and its interiors transformed into spacious well lit offices without architectural loss.

BRAY: Catholic Church

Designed in 1852 and attributed to Patrick Byrne. Remodelled and extended by W.H. Byrne in 1898. Alterations this century have destroyed most of the original fittings which survive in night clubs and a private library. A new overpowering organ replaces W.H. Byrne's high altar in the apsidal chancel.

BRAY: Church of Ireland

A rare example of a parochial Church of Ireland on a grand scale, verging on triumphalism; designed by William Slater and built in 1860-5. Entered through an open porch beneath a tower and spire—a single vertical foil against the unbroken nave and choir. An external asperity is humanized within, and enriched by later generations: five-light, naive east window to the 10th earl of Meath, and a fine west window; windows to the 12th earl and his aunt—Celtic Revival, both by Child. Further glass by Heaton, Butler and Bayne. Arcaded chancel infilled with glass mosaics from Salviati in Venice. Elaborate walnut furnishings of unyielding Gothic, apart from a Celtic alms-box and a Renaissance bishop's choir copied from San Pietro in Perugia. The carving programme was started in 1887 as a choirboys' carving class directed by Mrs Faulkner which continued as the Bray Art Furniture Industry under Miss St John Whitty, who designed the stalls; it was completed under William Glover by the south aisle screen (1918) and the north screen of (1936). Tiled floor in choir *c.*1890 to the design of the dowager countess of Meath.

BRAY, Church Road: Glebe House

Sedate Gothic Revival rectory designed by Millar and Symes and built in 1878.

BRAY, Kilbride: Church of Ireland

An early masterpiece of William Barre, who was only twenty-four when he designed this church in 1857, and who died aged thirty-seven. His early death deprived the Church of Ireland of a High Victorian successor to Semple. For, like Semple he transformed the conventional Gothic idiom of his contemporaries into a personal language by distortion and simplification. This is no more apparent than in the way he cuts into the corners of the massive buttresses holding up the abruptly soaring spire and inserts delicate three-quarter-circle colonettes. These colonettes reappear, but this time corbelled, in the deep embrasure of the porch. In contrast to this complexity the interior is simple and devout. Open roof braced by open arches over the nave leading to raised chancel. Richly Victorian coloured glass apart from the memorial window put up by Lady Alice Howard, the diarist, to her brothers killed in the trenches of the First World War.

BRAY, King Edward Road: Ard Soluis

Partly dressed stone, partly tile-hung, partly half-timbered, rambling Arts and Crafts Tudor villa designed by T.M. Deane (1905). Recently the home of Gerard Sauter, the architect.

BRAY: Kilbride House

Spacious red-brick rectory overlooking the Dargle valley, now the Danish embassy. Matching gatelodge. The only southern Irish commission of W.J. Watson, *c.*1890.

BRAY: Kilcroney House

Extended neo-Tudor villa built for Humphrey Lloyd, a son of the provost of Trinity, on a picturesque site above the Dargle river. His architect was Sancton Wood, then working on various stations on the Dublin/Cork rail link during the early 1850s. Incisively detailed in Wicklow granite throughout, at its most delicate

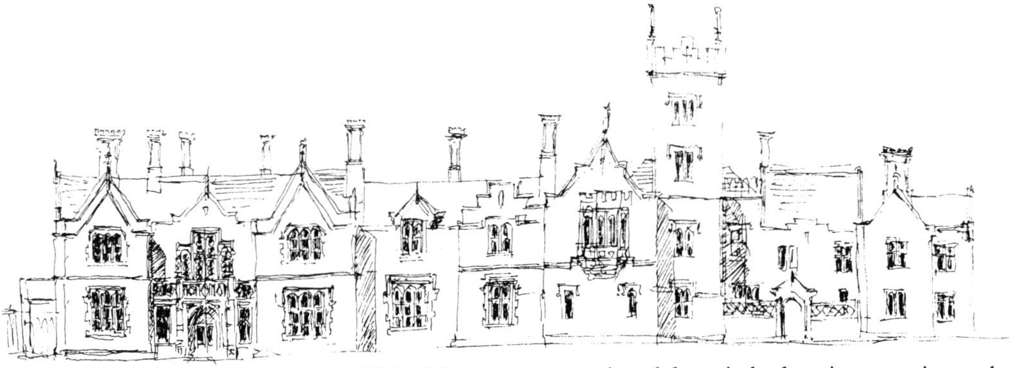

in the three-bay entrance block. This fails to dominate an irregular service wing that projects with orieled gable and recedes to a four-storied flag tower and then a screened service court. Later modifications by John McCurdy. Altered this century, first as a country-club hotel, then as a home for the elderly run by the St John of God. The fireplaces have vanished but not the superb tiled floor. The chapel is a converted conservatory revealing tantalizing glimpses of its Turneresque structure that is for once non-curvilinear. Currently for sale. Sold in 1993.

BRAY: Killarney Wood

Designed by E.H. Carson to overlook the Dargle valley, in his grimly Ruskinian Gothic manner. Carson has toned down the stylistic excesses of his suburban villas but with negative results. Commendably preserved as an avant-garde prep school, Brookhouse, in such marked contrast to St Gerard's across the river; but now closed.

BRAY: Kilruddery

Conservatory added (to 17th-century house remodelled as neo-Elizabethan by the Morrisons) by William Burn in 1852 with a dome at the intersection of four arched roofs, one prolonged to abut against the house. Designed not only to house plants but also Lord Meath's collection of statuary, so that the walls are masonry with arched windows rather than being in glass. But this heaviness is counterbalanced by a parapet of fretwork modelled on the diamond tiara sold by Lady Meath for charity during the Famine. Dome and pendentives replaced in a simpler form *c.*1960. Adjoining range of house given curvilinear gable and bay window by William Slater.

Daniel Robertson added the entrance to the forecourt and the gatehouse to the stableyard.

BRAY: Loreto Convent

A Georgian house gothicized with cast-iron battlements and turreted, arcaded porch in 1834 by an unknown ironmaster, Thomas Ring, who added an immense 22-sided conservatory (now detached) with its glazed pyramidal roof rising to an oriental dome in lead resting on an internal six-columned rotunda. Gothic windows articulated by pinnacled buttresses—continuous frieze of elephant's heads, the heraldic device of the Putlands, who sold the estate to the Loreto nuns in 1850. The convent extensions are institutional Gothic, built in random rock-faced ashlar; they include a chapel (designs exhibited in the RHA of 1866 by J.S. Butler; additions by J.L. Robinson, 1887, who is presumably responsible for the refined neo-Classical red brick oratory nestles which like a summer house in a wooded grove with views across the sea).

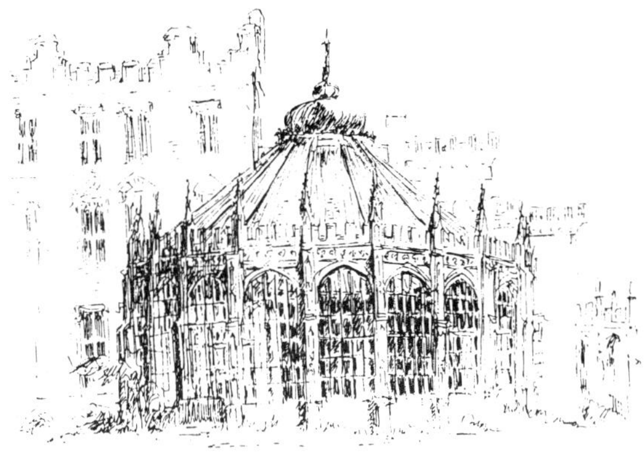

BRAY: Parish Hall

Gabled and buttressed parish hall enlivened by open porch in octagonal turret set into the angle of adjoining curator's lodge. Designed in 1886 by T. Phillips Figgis.

BRAY, Quinnsborough Road: Presbyterian Church

Designed in 1859 by William Barre in what is for him a conventional Gothic Revival. Façade with asymmetrical spire.

BRAY: St Paul's Church

First Fruits church remodelled by Joseph Welland *c.*1860 and then extended by Richard Orpen in 1911. Angels carved in the hammer-truss roof structure. Now deconsecrated but has found another role as the organ factory of Kenneth Jones.

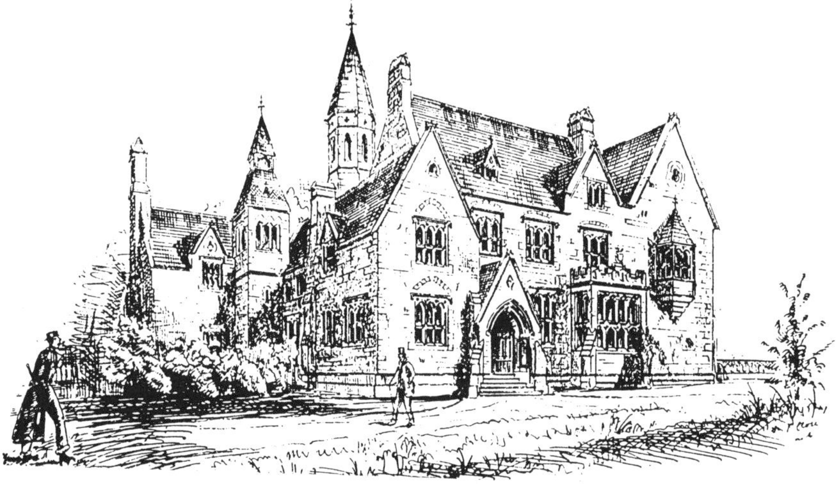

BRAY: **Old Conna**
A large and serious neo-Elizabethan country house, commissioned by Phineas Riall from W.H. Lynn (1861) on a prominent site with spectacular views from the garden front. Multi-gabled façades overwhelm lower tower and service wing. Competent internal layout but detailed with much mechanically cut panelling, stained glass and compartmented ceilings. Drawings preserved in the house. Redeemed (like so many residences of its kind) by an Edwardian garden that came into its own when the house was sold by the family to make a luxury hotel. Sold twice before finding its true vocation, a preparatory school.

BRAY: **Methodist Church**
Designed by Alfred Gresham Jones and built in 1864 in his characteristically attentuated Gothic.

BRAY: **The Townhall**
Commissioned in 1882 by the 11th earl of Meath to look down the town's principal street, this is one of T.M. Deane's successful essays in the Tudor Revival; due largely to his young assistant, Guy Dawber, who after his return to England was to set up his own country-house practice based in Oxfordshire and write on vernacular architecture. The Bray townhall, especially the market hall at the rear, evokes a prosperous agricultural community in the late middle ages with its lofty galleries and open timber roof lit by triangular dormers. The façade has oriels modelled on Sparrows House, Ipswich. The council chamber is imbued with a solemn, almost religious fervour, at odds with its often very acriminous proceedings. Woodwork carved by Reynolds Smith; stained glass by Heaton, Butler and Bayne.

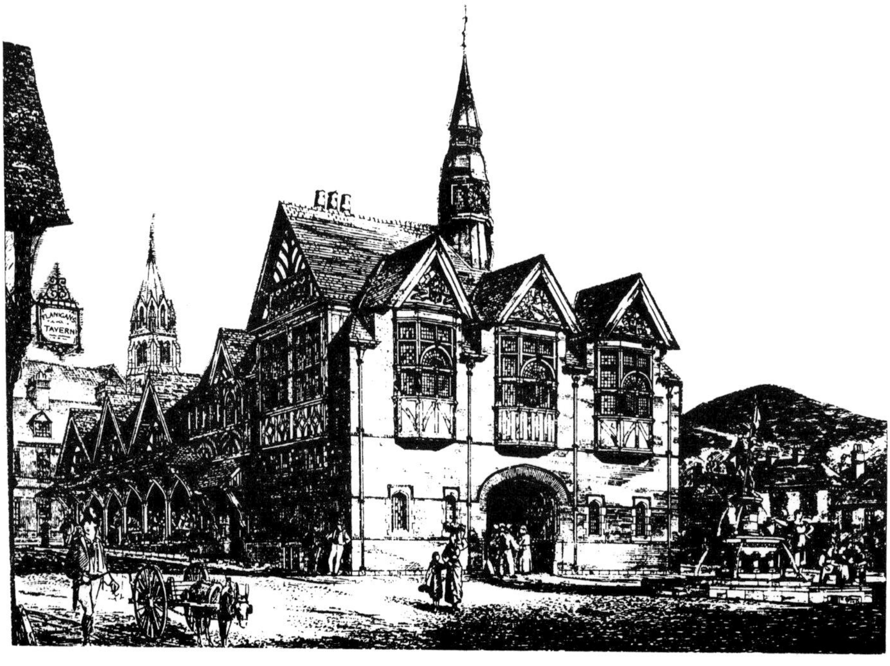

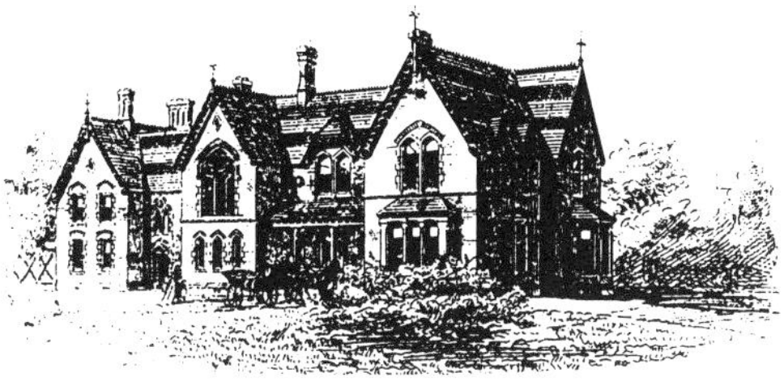

BRAY: **Violet Hill**

The most substantial Gothic Revival house designed by the Limerick architect William Fogerty (in 1862, for the Darley family). Asymmetrically composed with the entry verandah between the drawingroom and the staircase range; the staircase itself is forcefully expressed by a traceried Gothic window on the half-landing. Lower staff wing beyond. Similar graduation along the garden front except this terminates a billiard room pavilion. Gothic arcaded hall leads into well-proportioned double drawingroom, panelled library and diningroom wiht decorative neo-Tudor carving. Now subdivided into four residential units.

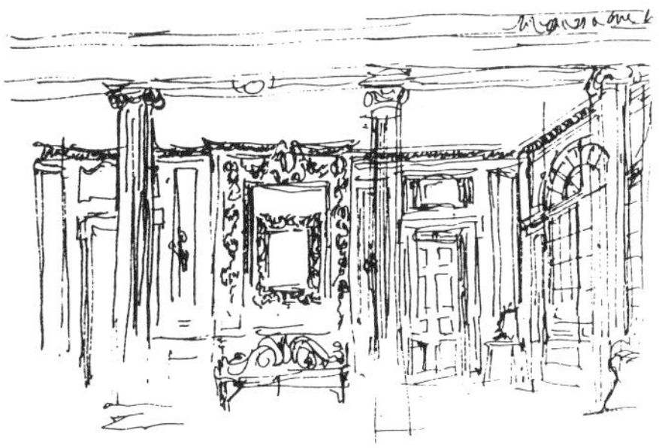

BRAY: **Woodbrook**

Georgian country house remodelled and extended for over a hundred years in a carefully controlled juxtaposition of styles, Elizabethan for the library, Caroline for the entrance hall, Regency for the reception rooms, Adamesque Revival for the ballroom that opens into a semi-Gothic octagonal conservatory. Architectural contributions from F.G. Hicks, George Beckett and more recently Desmond Fitzgerald. The timber carving is by a local dynasty of carvers called Glover. Further extensions reflect the twin passions of Sir Ernest Cochrane for cricket and opera. The cricket pavilion is now the core of the international golf club, screened from the main house by a 'Gloriette' originally the upper portion of W.G. Murray's College of Physicians in Dublin (q.v.). His opera house, which should have become the Irish Glyndebourne, has last been used as a roller-skating alley and is now a furniture salesroom.

BRITTAS: **Tinode**

Uninspired Gothic by William Caldbeck, built for the Cogan family in 1851 out of Wicklow granite; now, due to the beauty of its setting and material, a delightful ruin.

DELGANY: **Dromin**

Tudor Revival house designed by Frederick Batchelor for a retired judge called Moore. The date was 1900, so this is an early example of Batchelor's casual half-timbering that was to find so much favour in the stockbroker belt of north Wicklow.

ENNISKERRY: **Catholic Church**

Church designed in the late 1840s as an example of the conversion of its architect, Patrick Byrne, to the Gothic Revival due to his collaboration with A.N.W. Pugin at Rathfarnham Abbey. The asymmetrical belfry set flush with the façade dominates the Dargle valley. Plaster Gothic vaulting throughout.

ENNISKERRY: **Church of Ireland**

A Gothic Revival church nestling into its wooded site. The siting of its asymmetrical belfry at the entrance of its vestry attracted hostile criticism fueled by the decision of Lord Powerscourt in 1857 to import his architect (John Norton) from England. However, even if the rector was threatened by a swinging bell rope, first impressions are reassuring if unexciting for his congregation. But stained glass by O'Connor was smashed by vandals after its installation who wrote 'No surrender'. Windows repaired and reinstated by Lord Powerscourt.

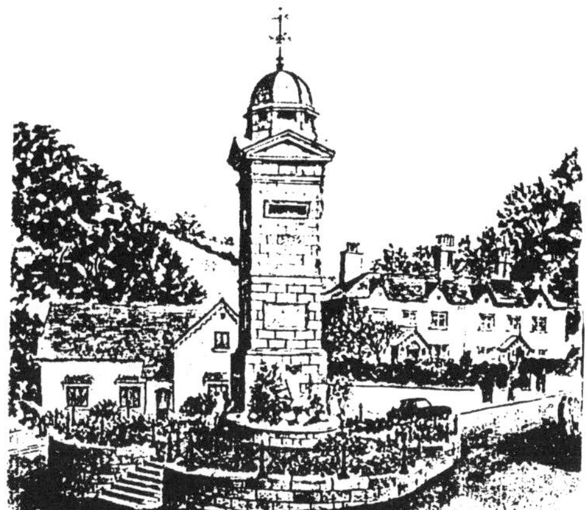

ENNISKERRY: **The Fountain**

Designed in 1843 and attributed by Jeanne Sheehy to John Louch. The dome was added in 1860 by Sir George Moyers (see Glynwood, Co. Meath).

ENNISKERRY: Powerscourt
The most ambitious formal gardens of the Victorian era in Ireland, uniting architecture, sculpture, pools, fountains and planting in spectacular confrontation to its setting of woods, mountains, river valley and the occasional bungalow. Today the house, rebuilt by Richard Castle on the ruins of a medieval castle and gutted accidentally by fire in 1974, screens the Arcadian 18th-century landscape to the north from the now formal gardens to the south as created by the 6th and 7th Viscounts Powerscourt from 1840 to 1895. Their starting point was the garden of the 1st Viscount in 1740, a flight of steps down a gentle slope to an artificial pond; but it took from 1840 to 1895 to remodel it into a terraced amphitheatre that one descends without ever losing sight of the lake below. Work started in the 19th century when the 6th viscount called in Daniel Robertson to construct the upper terrace, which he completed apart from the sculpture, while the half-landing of the central perron, the formalization of the pond and its enclosure by tiers of semi-elliptical terracing had to wait until the 1860s. They were implemented by the 7th viscount, whose childhood memories included Robertson escaping from creditors by hiding in the roof of the house and being pushed round in a wheelbarrow with a bottle of sherry (he had to drink to stop lapsing into a drunken stupor): all these revelations were published only after Queen Victoria's death.

The landscape gardeners consulted by the 7th viscount included James Howe, who died from alcohol (as also recounted in the memoirs), and Brodrick Thomas, the landscaper of Sandringham who was responsible for the parterres. The chief architect was Francis Penrose, the restorer of St Paul's, who designed the perron and integrated the 17th-century statuary; but all the important decisions were made by the 7th viscount, including the disparate gods, angels and urns of the upper terrace that come close to the 19th-century cemeteries of the Italians rather than to their 17th-century gardens. The Dargle lodge and possibly the so-called Golden Gates were designed by an amateur neighbour, Sir George Hodson. The last of the structures to be built in Powerscourt successfully poses as the earliest—a cylindrical tower (known as the Pepper Pot) set on a castellated outcrop to give a headstart over a circle of Italian cypresses that have long since outstripped it.

Of all the schemes for the south front, only Daniel Robertson's proposal measures up to castle's northern façade. This complements the splendour of his gardens. He added long colonnades terminating in airy belvederes, predating Sancton Wood's Kingsbridge Station. Now that the house is due to be rebuilt as an hotel, is there a chance of Robertson's dream becoming a reality?

GLENDALOUGH: Catholic Church
Gothic Revival church, an early example of the work of J.J. McCarthy; built in 1846-9. Convincing materialization of the Puginian village church. Belfry omitted in favour of western bellcote.

GREYSTONES: Burleigh
One of the principal houses of Greystones, built by Albert Murray in 1905.

GREYSTONES: Catholic Church
Modest exterior conceals a diluted Hiberno-Romanesque nave and chancel enriched by mosaics and stained glass—a real seafarer's place of worship. Architect, W.H. Byrne; date, 1904.

GREYSTONES: La Touche Hotel
Ambitious multi-storied hotel built *c.*1900 by McCurdy and Mitchell with formal terraces descending to the seashore. Much altered subsequently.

GREYSTONES: Nirvana
Residence of the Matheson family built before *c.*1910, to the design of Frank Batchelor. Picturesque composition due to welding a double-storied dormered roof resting on a single-storied light verandah and linking it to conventional double-storied wings.

GREYSTONES: Moorlands
Built *c.*1908 for the Jacob family by the architect of the Burnaby estate, Frank Batchelor. A characteristic example of his manner. Corner windows at ground level are echoed by unusual corner dormers in the roof.

GREYSTONES: The Shrubberies
Aptly named suburban villa built before 1910 by Frank Batchelor, who developed Greystones for the Barnaby family. Informal composition accented by verandahs and shingled gables.

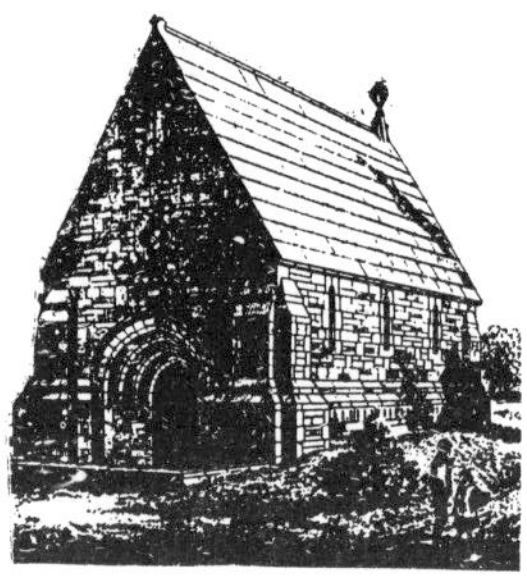

KILTEGAN: Church of Ireland
Board of First Fruits church, extended first by

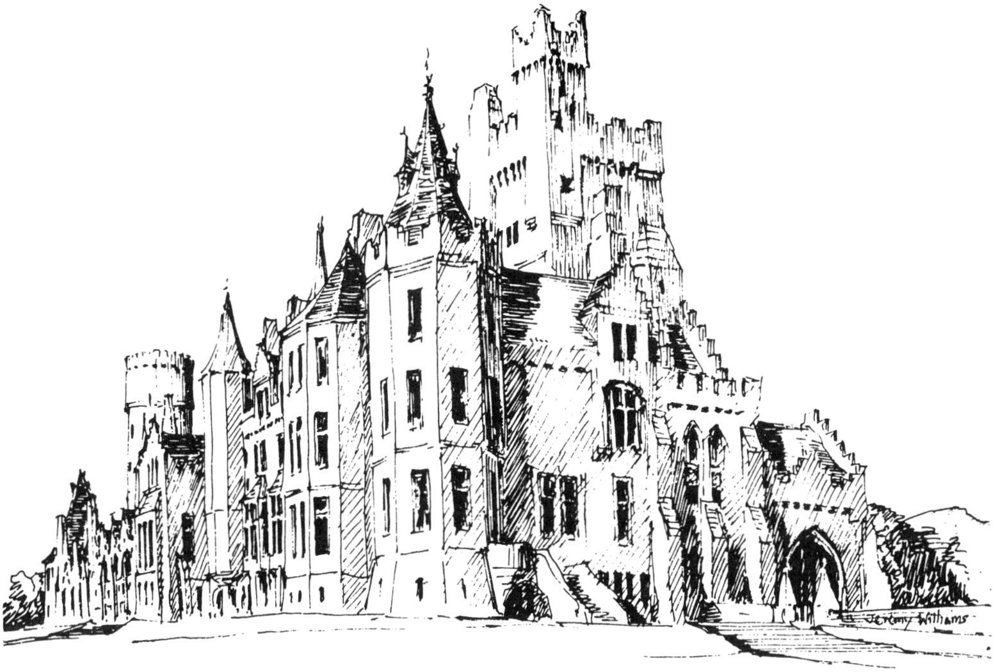

Welland and Gillespie and then by James Brooks at the same time as his completion of Humewood for William Hume Dick, who also commissioned the family mausoleum. Brooks' additions to the church consisted of a low lean-to southern aisle and the chancel. These are in his characteristically robust version of 13th-century French Gothic. For the mausoleum he took as his inspiration the oratory of Gallerus, and the result is one of the most bombproof of Ireland's mausolea with its exposed stone roof embedded in the earth to await the Last Judgment. The interior of the church contains marble memorials by the Kirks and anonymous stained-glass memorials to the Humes.

KILTEGAN: **Humewood Castle**

The most spectacular High Victorian castle to survive in Ireland, now that Godwin's Dromore (q.v.) and Christopher's Dunboy (q.v.) are reduced to gutted shells. Designed in 1866 by the English architect William White, inventor of the valveless water closet, a collapsible bed convertible to daytime mackintosh, and yodelling mountain horn to serenade himself as he scaled the Alps. There is a mountain-scaling quality to the composition of Humewood where the lower ranges dominated by crow-stepped gables and chimney-stacks made from cubes of local granite rise upwards through turrets and spires to the corner flag tower high up over main entrance. This is screened by a stone-vaulted *porte-cochère* which contains a built-in seat for the needy awaiting alms. The first person on the seat should have been the builder, Kimberly of Banbury, who had priced the job at £13,500, White having been given a budget of £15,000. When the builder presented a bill of £25,000, all parties went to law. White made himself ridiculous by claiming that he had merely provided adequate accommodation for an Irish country gentleman. After five years Kimberley won his demands and White never received a large country-house commission again.

But White's unbelievable defence had a point: the accommodation is limited. The raised basement is given over to defence against the Fenians, the towers to water storage and other services. The present diningroom had to be made *c.*1946 out of two bedrooms. Mr Hume Dick himself had to build on a ballroom and segregate the menservants within a new, cylindrical watertower.

These extensions, along with a new aisle to the village church and the Hume mausoleum, are the only Irish commissions of James Brooks. Humewood was the nearest he came to designing a country house, and reveals that his experience in building churches in the slums of London would have been an ideal training. Certainly the watertower of Humewood, by being such a total contrast to White's cubistic hulk, adds a further note of unattainability and mystery. It is equally effective when viewed from the park, where it responds to the tower of the corner oriel of the drawingroom at the fartherest end of the garden front. The intervening staircase turret is balanced by White on a single column. Brook's tower is equally dramatic when viewed from the stable court over lower ranges that retain the rusticated arches of the Georgian predecessor.

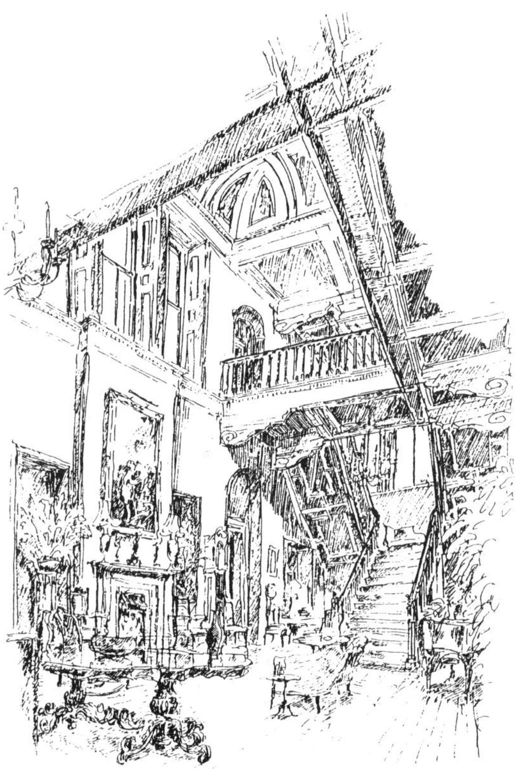

The low entrance hall leads into the triple-height staircase hall, where an initial sense of religiosity is dispelled by discovering that all the stained glass is heraldic, and that the stout black marble columns of the tribune frame a languid white marble nude with glimpses of further nudes beyond. The upper reaches of the stairs are of timber, treated like the *stave* churches of Norway. This complexity is at its most evident in the doors, made up of contrasting woods with polychromatic effects. A lighter note is introduced by the painted ceilings of the Italian artist Grispini, whose design book still survives, interspersed with sketches for a medieval tournament in the park.

Although the lands of Humewood were confined within the demesne in 1911, the castle still retains intact both the 18th-century park with its lake to the west and wooded mountain setting to the east. All is guarded by a consistent set of bay-windowed gatelodges and restrained gateways with piers flowering into thistles, the emblem of the Humes, immortalizing their tenure into granite. Sold after the death of the last of Humes, Madame Mimi Hume-Weygand, to a country-house hotel syndicate who never paid their deposit. Now being restored by the underbidder.

MANOR KILBRIDE: The Manor

Tudor Revival house built *c.*1835 by an unrecorded architect. Drawing room with painted landscapes by Edwin Hayes. Member of Hidden Ireland.

NEWCASTLE: The Hospital

Commisioned by the Government in 1892 from T.M. Deane, who exploited his half-timbered Tudor style to give large south-facing windows to the wards protected by continuous timber verandahs. These have been unsympathetically renewed in recent years. Once selected as the Victorian lunatic asylum in Sussex depicted in the film version of *Equus* if it had been shot in Ireland. Now this option is no longer possible.

RATHDRUM: Catholic Church

Designed by J.J. McCarthy in 1856 and dedicated in 1861, in his characteristic Gothic, built out of sturdy Wicklow granite. Nave, aisles and shallow chancel. Unexpected tributes to Pugin are the granite lychgate, and the asymmetrical painting of the ceilings of the aisle chapels, one predominantly red, the other predominantly blue. Stained glass by Mayer. Romantic restoration that has stripped off internal plaster. Favourite church of the late Archbishop John Charles McQuaid.

RATHNEW: Clermont

Georgian country house of the Somerville family, expensively extended in the Queen Anne Revival idiom *c.*1886. Heavy multi-paned bay windows encasing facetted glass. Attentuated panelling with acute pediments in the en suite reception rooms suggest Thomas Drew. Ingeniously top-lit billiard room at the rear, now converted into the library of a convent school.

RATHNEW: Tinakilly

Commissioned in 1870 by the Government to honour Captain Robert Halpin after he commanded the steamship, the *Great Eastern*, when she laid the first cable across the Atlantic. The architect was J.F. Fuller, whose drawings are still in the house. This is one of his best houses, in a style termed by Bence-Jones as vaguely Queen Anne. Symmetrical façade with pedimented porch comfortably flanked by two-storey bays. There is no external clue to the most dramatic interior, the double-height billiardroom-cum-living hall, with only the fireplace visible from the outer hall (through glass doors), but not the three windows that surmount it and deal the trick of the vanished flue. Natural light also pours down from the half-landing of an imperial staircase that leads to the open galleries of the bedroom floor. Coved and coffered ceiling that once held skylights to assist the billiard-players.

Lived in after the captain's death by his

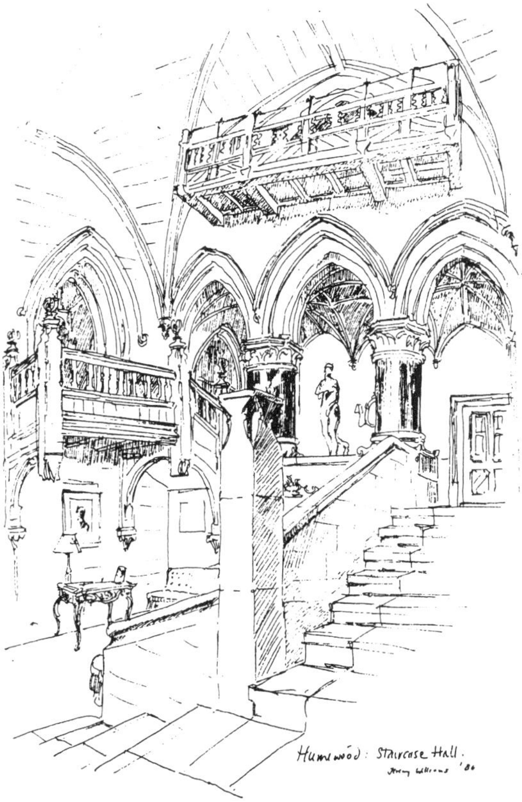

widow and then by his daughters in increasing penury. Saved from demolition by Mr and Mrs William Power, who, to recoup restoration costs, opened it as a country-house hotel. The *pièce de résistance* is the captain's bathroom, all mahogany and gleaming brass.

ROUNDWOOD: Vartry Reservoir

Architecturally this is Ireland's most impressive waterworks, a heady combination of utilitarian inventiveness and brooding fantasy. Smaller pumphouse on the lower lake. Larger isolated Gothic towerhouse rising from the water of the upper lake has not been built by an usurper to confine a princess who would otherwise be queen, but to serve as the pumphouse for Dublin's water supply. The great grotto in the woods below is part of a symmetrical terraced layout that rivals the Italian garden of a Renaissance cardinal. Lastly, the artificial river vanishing between its man-made cliffs is a fitting epilogue to this momentary take-over of nature's forces. But who is the puny individual entitled to the credit? Here contemporary accounts, while giving space to the two rival engineers, R. Hassard and C.E. Hawksley, who claimed the concept, are strangely silent on its architect. But it would appear that Parke Neville, the city's engineer, has the best claim, with Sir John McNeill in the wings.

TALBOTSTOWN: Catholic Church

Patrick Byrne, architect of Dublin's best Catholic churches after the Emancipation, came from nearby, and the design of this rural church has been attributed to him, though it was completed after his death in 1867. Triple-bay façade under wide pediment in the purest Palladian. Drastic restoration has removed all plaster from the internal walls, but has made the survival of the ceiling even more miraculous with its delicately coloured stucco tendrils of vine. Possibly painted by Grispini while he was working at Humewood (q.v.).

VALLEYMOUNT: Catholic Church

Said to be built to his own design by the parish priest, who had lived in Malta. High spirited, pinnacled façade built by the granite stone carvers of Ballyknockan in the hills above (now cut off from their place of worship by the reservoir). Harry Clarke Studios stained glass.

WICKLOW: Catholic Church

Built in 1844 by Patrick Byrne in an old-fashioned Regency Gothic, cruciform, wide-spanning, shallow-plaster Gothic vaulting and pillared narthex under western organ gallery. The client, Archdeacon Grant, is commemorated by the High Victorian Gothic altars, *c.*1864. Chancel further embellished by sparsely scattered saints in mosaic. The transepts received stained glass, most notably the south window by Harry Clarke Studios.

WICKLOW: Dominican Convent

The Dominicans in 1874 acquired a Georgian house, Bayview, to make a school; they had to extend the building in three directions, the northern and eastern wings ending up as two sides of an enclosed court. In 1903 the old house was pulled down, and replaced by reception rooms at ground level and a chapel above. The style throughout was an uncompromising Gothic in red brick and stone trimmings. This was due to the firm of O'Neill and Byrne, especially the architect, Ralph Byrne. The chapel is one of his earliest works, and the extra floor to the adjoining wing in 1939, one of his last. Byrne also designed the fragile Gothic altars, naughtily lit by tiny concealed glazed semi-domes. The stations are by Haugh (1951). The evolution of Irish stained glass from 1938 to 1969 can be followed in the stained glass, all windows being the work of one artist, Richard King. The convent, after the withdrawal of State educational grants, is now up for sale.

WICKLOW: **Memorials**
Two memorials—a good 1798 monument in the market square, carved by John(?) Smith; in Fitzwilliam Square, an obelisk memorial to Captain Robert Halpin (1936-94) of Tinakilly (q.v.).

WICKLOW: **Methodist Church**
By William Fogerty, 1866. Undersized aggressive Gothic Revival.

WICKLOW: **Sea Park, or Magherymore**
Designed by William G. Murray in a discontented Classicism for a rich, self-made lawyer, F. Ellis, in 1867. Asymmetrical façade partly two-storied, partly three. Impeccable granite-pillared portico, at variance with manneristic window surrounds, framed by strapwork and surmounted by shells giving a curious feeling of Russia. Parapet balustraded with tightly scrolled ironwork. Interior also uneasy—ponderous fireplaces, lacy pre-cast plasterwork. Much altered, first as an hotel, now as a convent.

ADDENDA

CO. ARMAGH: **Armagh: Umgola House**
Large suburban villa (*c.*1880) with attached curvilinear conservatory. Architect: J.H. Fullerton, who revelled in polychromatic brickwork.

CO. ARMAGH: **White's Cross: Ballymoyler Church of Ireland**
Board of First Fruits church revamped (1865) by Welland and Gillespie, who added gabled belfry, staircase tower and apsidal porch. They remodelled the interior, but the commemorative pulpit was commissioned from William Butterfield in 1874.

CO. CARLOW: **Rathvilly Church of Ireland**
Board of First Fruits church extended in 1847 by Daniel Robertson, who added transepts and chancel.

CO. CAVAN: **Kildorough Church of Ireland**
Small Gothic Revival church in the style of Welland and Gillespie; entered through the battered base of an octagonal belfry made of alternating trefoils and louvres.

CO. DOWN: **Clough Unitarian Church**
The Murland tomb. Pedimented miniature temple articulated by coupled scrolls (*c.*1860).

CO. DOWN: **Waringstown Church of Ireland**
Earlier church re-roofed with an elaborate truss structure by Sir Thomas Drew (*c.*1875); glass by Heaton, Butler and Bayne.

DUBLIN SOUTH SUBURBS: **Kilmainham Gaol**
The firm of Richard Turner was called in to create the flying staircases and galleries serving the new top-lit wing added in the 1860s.

CO. DUBLIN: **Shankill: Ardvarna**
Villa designed by Charles Harrison Townsend and built in 1894 for the Meredith family. Drawings now in the R.I.B.A.

CO. KERRY: **Listowel**
Pub with 'Erin go brá', on the main street; designed by Pat McAuliffe (*c.*1890), head of a flourishing school of folk art.

CO. KILDARE: **Straffan Lough Park**
Museum of Victorian technology recently set up in a Gothic Revival church transplanted (minus its belfry) from Inchicore. Architect: Percy Leclerc.

CO. LONDONDERRY: **Swatragh Church of Ireland**
Typical design by Joseph Welland with porch nestling against low tower topped by octagonal belfry; buttressed nave; reduced chancel with only one transept. Basalt and freestone dressings; dated 1852.

CO. OFFALY: **Clara: Kilcoursey**
Sister house to Lisnabrucka in Connemara (q.v.) presumably by the same architect, L.A. McDonnell (*c.*1910).

CO. SLIGO: **Sligo: Cloghereevagh House**
Gothic Revival villa overlooking Lough Gill. Built in 1843 by the Gore-Booths for a daughter who had married a Wynne of nearby Hazelwood. Remodelled and extended in 1899 for her daughter-in-law Maud, sister of the 2nd Lord Killanin, patron of William Scott. Scott is the most likely architect of the delicate Arts and Crafts interiors centred round a diametrically braced staircase hall. Well preserved as an Ursuline convent since 1950.

CO. TIPPERARY: **Borris-in-Ossory Church of Ireland**
Designed by J.E. Rogers, welding a Celtic round tower to a harshly detailed Gothic Revival cell. Set at the end of a village street to give a memorable silhouette against the setting sun.

INDEX OF BUILDINGS

This is principally an index of country houses and other buildings better known by name than by location.

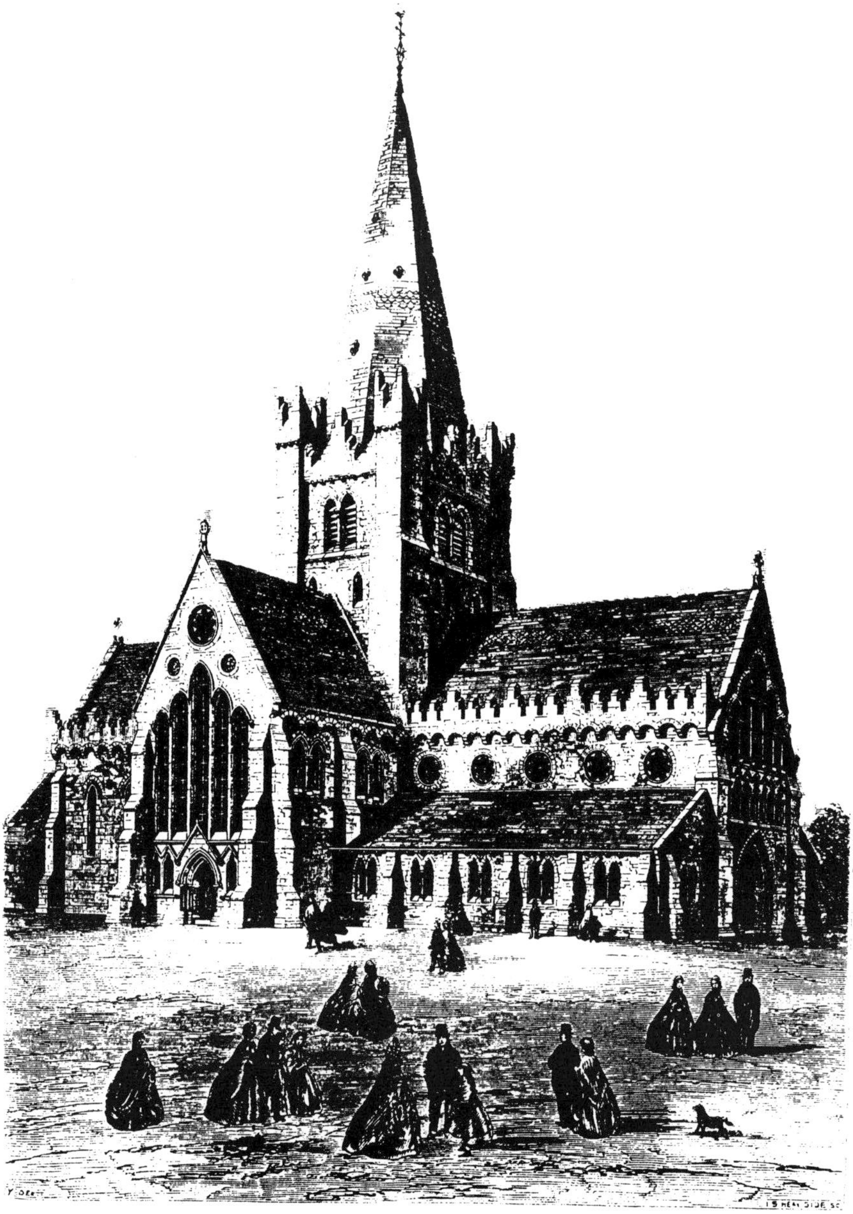

CHURCH OF IRELAND CATHEDRAL, TUAM, CO. GALWAY

GENERAL INDEX